BaseBall america®
PROSPECT
HANDBOOK

2005
Baseball America Inc.
Durham, N.C.

Baseball America
PROSPECT
HANDBOOK

EDITORS
Jim Callis, Will Lingo

ASSOCIATE EDITORS
John Manuel, Allan Simpson

CONTRIBUTING WRITERS
Bill Ballew, Mike Berardino, Pat Caputo, J.J. Cooper, Aaron Fitt, Kevin Goldstein, Tom Haudricourt, Will Kimmey, Chris Kline, Michael Levesque, Alan Matthews, John Perrotto, Tracy Ringolsby, Phil Rogers

PHOTO EDITORS
Gary Martin, Matthew Meyers

EDITORIAL ASSISTANTS
Mike Groopman, Gary Martin, Matthew Meyers, Jeffrey Simpson

DESIGN & PRODUCTION
Phillip Daquila, Matthew Eddy, Linwood Webb

COVER PHOTO
Delmon Young by Sports on Film

COVER DESIGN
Linwood Webb

BaseBall america

President/CEO: Catherine Silver
Vice President/Publisher: Lee Folger
Editor In Chief: Allan Simpson
Managing Editor: Will Lingo
Executive Editor: Jim Callis
Design & Production Director: Phillip Daquila

BaseballAmerica.com

TABLE OF **CONTENTS**

FOREWORD

Winning 13 consecutive division championships is an accomplishment unprecedented in professional sports. The primary constant throughout that amazing run of Braves' success has been the excellent work and remarkable productivity of our scouting and player development programs.

Building a championship team year after year demands more than simply knowing the talent you have. It's also accurately knowing and assessing the talent in each of the other 29 major league organizations.

Baseball America has demonstrated an abiding interest in prospects at all levels for many years. Their sincere interest in bringing their readers an inside look at our potential stars of the future has now grown into a comprehensive guide of 900 scouting reports on the top prospects in every organization, interesting projections for each organization's future, a comprehensive draft analysis and, the most interesting aspect for most of us, Baseball America's rankings of prospects and organizations.

From the major league general manager to the scouting director to the avid baseball fans around the globe, Baseball America's Prospect Handbook is an essential and informative guide.

With the continued excellent work of our scouting staff and the inside information provided in Baseball America's Prospect Handbook, we're well prepared to take on the challenges of the pursuit of another championship season.

John Schuerholz
Executive Vice President and General Manager
Atlanta Braves

INTRODUCTION

We really love prospects. Sometimes too much, I fear. As this year's edition of the Prospect Handbook wound to a close, I attempted to calculate how many hours go into each edition. I eventually gave up and figured I'd better think about something other than the Prospect Handbook for awhile.

Suffice to say that a lot of people work a lot of hours to make this book possible. Not that we're complaining; we are writing about baseball, after all. I just want to take a moment to emphasize how much labor goes into each of the 900 scouting reports you're about to read (You are going to read them all, aren't you?).

The writer who's compiling the prospect list for a particular organization starts off doing research to make sure he knows the population of players he's looking at. Then he talks to the farm director and scouting director from the organization, as well as at least a few other people, whether it's scouts or instructors or managers. He writes an overview for each organization, assembles charts, writes up the scouting reports for at least 30 players, then hopes no one gets traded from the top 30 list.

Once the writer is done, the work of the editors begins. Jim Callis spends hours massaging each top 30 list and meticulously editing the scouting reports, and we do even more editing when he's done. We massage the vitals and stats and marry them with the writeups, and our crack production department lays it all out on the pages and makes it look good. We cut it and proofread it, make last-minute changes, move around the guys who change organizations and continue tinkering until we just can't tinker any more.

And each year, just to keep things interesting, we try to add a feature or two. The additions this year are relatively minor, but one in particular we think is significant: signing scouts for all 900 players in the book. Traditionally we have listed the scouts who sign the Top 10 Prospects when those lists run in six issues of Baseball America during the year, but we dropped the information for the Prospect Handbook. We decided we needed to recognize the scouts in the book as well, and if we're going to do the top 10 we might as well go ahead and do all 30. That's how we end up working so many late nights. But it's worth it when you're doing something like getting scouts a little bit of recognition.

As always, it's important to recognize the work of all the people listed on the title page of this book. They give hours and hours of their time to make sure people across the country have prospect information to get them through another year. This year more than any other, the book would not have been completed without everyone pitching in.

Remember that for the purposes of this book, a prospect is anyone who is still rookie-eligible under Major League Baseball guidelines (no more than 50 innings pitched or 130 at-bats), without regard to service time. Players are listed with the organizations they were with on Feb. 1.

You'll also notice several grades in each team section. John Manuel graded each organization's impact potential—players who are potential all-stars or frontline players—and depth—the number of players who could become at least big league contributors. Those grades give you an idea of why organizations rank where they do in our minor league talent ratings. John also compiled a depth chart for each organization, in consultation with Allan Simpson, going at least 45 players deep for every team because 30 players just isn't enough.

Also, Jim graded each team's drafts from 1999–2002. The grades are based solely on the quality of the players signed, with no consideration given to whom they were traded for or how many first-round picks the club had or lost.

Will Lingo
Managing Editor
Baseball America

PROFILING PROSPECTS

Among all the scouting lingo you'll come across in this book, perhaps no terms are more telling and prevalent than "profile" and "projection."

When scouts evaluate a player, their main objective is to identify—or project—what the player's future role will be in the major leagues. Each organization has its own philosophy when it comes to grading players, so we talked to scouts from several teams to provide general guidelines.

The first thing to know is what scouts are looking for. In short, tools. These refer to the physical skills a player needs to be successful in the major leagues. For a position player, the five basic tools are hitting, hitting for power, fielding, arm strength and speed. For a pitcher, the tools are based on the pitches he throws. Each pitch is graded, as well as a pitcher's control, delivery and durability.

For most teams, the profiling system has gone through massive changes in recent years because of the offensive explosion in baseball. Where arm strength and defense used to be a must in the middle of the diamond, there has been an obvious swing toward finding players who can rake, regardless of their gloves. In the past, players like Jeff Kent and Alfonso Soriano wouldn't have been accepted as second basemen, but now they are the standard for offensive-minded second basemen.

While more emphasis is placed on hitting—which also covers getting on base—fielding and speed are still at a premium up the middle. As teams sacrifice defense at the corner outfield slots, they look for a speedy center fielder to make up ground in the alleys. Most scouts prefer at least a 55 runner (on the 20-80 scouting scale; see chart)

at short and center field, but as power increases at those two positions, running comes down (see Rich Aurilia, Jim Edmonds). Shortstops need range and at least average arm strength, and second basemen need to be quick on the pivot. Teams are more willing to put up with an immobile corner infielder if he can mash.

Arm strength is the one tool moving way down preference lists. For a catcher, it was always the No. 1 tool, but with fewer players stealing and the slide step helping to shut down running games, scouts are looking for more offensive production from the position. Receiving skills, including game-calling, blocking pitches and release times, can make up for the lack of a plus arm.

On the mound, it doesn't just come down to pure stuff. While a true No. 1 starter on a first-division team should have a couple of 70 or 80 pitches in his repertoire, like Josh Beckett and Mark Prior, they also need to produce 250-plus innings, 35 starts and 15-plus wins.

A player's overall future potential is also graded on the 20-80 scale, though some teams use a letter grade. This number is not just the sum of his tools, but rather a profiling system and a scout's ultimate opinion of the player.

70-80 (A): This category is reserved for the elite players in baseball. This player will be a perennial all-star, the best player at his position, one of the top five starters in the game or a frontline closer. Alex Rodriguez, Barry Bonds and Pedro Martinez reside here.

60-69 (B) You'll find all-star-caliber players here: No. 2 starters on a championship club and first-division players. See Mike Mussina, Miguel Tejada and Alfonso Soriano.

55-59 (C+) The majority of first-division starters are found in this range, including quality No. 2 and 3 starters, frontline set-up men and second-tier closers.

50-54 (C) Solid-average everyday major leaguers. Most are not first-division regulars. This group also includes No. 4 and 5 starters.

45-49 (D+) Fringe everyday players, backups, some No. 5 starters, middle relievers, pinch-hitters and one-tool players.

40-44 (D) Up-and-down roster fillers, situational relievers and 25th players.

38-39 (O) Organizational players who provide depth for the minor leagues but are not considered future major leaguers.

20-37 (NP) Not a prospect.

THE SCOUTING SCALE

When grading a player's tools, scouts use a standard 20-80 scale. When you read that a pitcher throws an above-average slider, it can be interpreted as a 60 pitch, or a plus pitch. Plus-plus is 70, or well-above-average, and so on. Scouts don't throw 80s around very freely. Here's what each grade means:

80	Outstanding
70	Well-above-average
60	Above-average
50	Major league average
40	Below-average
30	Well-below-average
20	Poor

MINOR LEAGUE DEPTH CHART

AN OVERVIEW

Another feature of the Prospect Handbook is a depth chart of every organization's minor league talent. This shows you at a glance where a system's strengths and weaknesses lie and provides even more prospects beyond an organization's top 30. Each depth chart is accompanied by analysis of the system's impact players and depth, as well as where it ranks in baseball (see facing page for the complete list). The rankings are based on our judgment of the quality and quantity of talent in each system, with higher marks to organizations that have more high-ceiling prospects or a deep system. The best systems have both.

To help you better understand why players are slotted at particular positions, we show you here what scouts look for in the ideal candidate at each spot, with individual tools ranked in descending order.

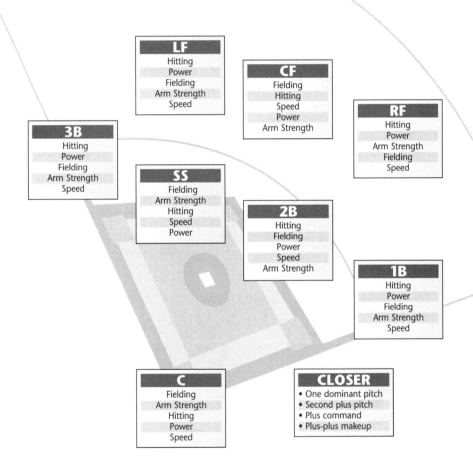

LF
Hitting
Power
Fielding
Arm Strength
Speed

CF
Fielding
Hitting
Speed
Power
Arm Strength

RF
Hitting
Power
Arm Strength
Fielding
Speed

3B
Hitting
Power
Fielding
Arm Strength
Speed

SS
Fielding
Arm Strength
Hitting
Speed
Power

2B
Hitting
Fielding
Power
Speed
Arm Strength

1B
Hitting
Power
Fielding
Arm Strength
Speed

C
Fielding
Arm Strength
Hitting
Power
Speed

CLOSER
• One dominant pitch
• Second plus pitch
• Plus command
• Plus-plus makeup

STARTING PITCHERS			
No. 1 starter	**No. 2 starter**	**No. 3 starter**	**No. 4-5 starters**
• Two plus pitches	• Two plus pitches	• One plus pitch	• Command of two major league pitches
• Average third pitch	• Average third pitch	• Two average pitches	• Average velocity
• Plus-plus command	• Average command	• Average command	• Consistent breaking ball
• Plus makeup	• Average makeup	• Average makeup	• Decent changeup

TALENT RANKINGS

	2004	2003	2002	2001	2000
1 Anahiem Angels	3	5	17	25	29
Polished, premium bats should allow Angels to supplement high-priced big league roster soon.					
2 Los Angeles Dodgers	2	14	25	28	23
Another prep-centered draft armed pitching-heavy Dodgers with more high-ceiling talent.					
3 Milwaukee Brewers	1	16	26	30	30
Despite setbacks on the mound, Brew Crew has as many impact hitters as any organization.					
4 Minnesota Twins	5	4	6	15	10
Organization of the Year uses many sources to obtain talent, then patiently develops it.					
5 Atlanta Braves	4	2	7	5	4
Even after dealing pitching prospects Jose Capellan and Dan Meyer, Atlanta's depth is impressive.					
6 Colorado Rockies	15	25	24	16	26
Rockies have so much talent that Minor League POY Jeff Francis ranks third on their list.					
7 Cleveland Indians	6	1	20	26	19
While Indians' depth has waned, righthander Adam Miller gives them an elite pitching prospect.					
8 Oakland Athletics	17	22	7	11	3
Nick Swisher, Joe Blanton and Dan Meyer are poised to earn big league jobs in 2005.					
9 Tampa Bay Devil Rays	9	10	15	6	13
Finally added elite arms in Scott Kazmir and Jeff Niemann to complement exciting hitters.					
10 Chicago Cubs	7	3	1	2	16
Attrition cost Cubs some depth, but Brian Dopirak emerged as one of the minors' top sluggers.					
11 Seattle Mariners	12	9	2	4	24
Depth at shortstop includes top draftees, international signings and trade acquisitions.					
12 Chicago White Sox	20	15	9	1	6
On the way back up thanks to outfielders such as Brian Anderson and Ryan Sweeney.					
13 Arizona Diamondbacks	13	21	23	29	12
Arizona remains stocked despite big league graduations, unsigned first-rounder Stephen Drew.					
14 Florida Marlins	14	8	10	9	2
Outfielder Jeremy Hermida, lefthander Scott Olsen give Marlins elite talent at two key spots.					
15 Toronto Blue Jays	8	6	13	17	8
Will expanded big league budget trickle down to player development?					
16 Texas Rangers	16	19	8	13	7
Departure of Grady Fuson means more emphasis on radar-gun readings than pitchability.					
17 San Francisco Giants	24	11	12	22	28
After years of almost singleminded focus on pitching, Giants go for bats in 2004 draft.					
18 Pittsburgh Pirates	11	18	22	19	14
Continued lack of impact players and decreased depth moves Pirates down the list.					
19 New York Mets	10	13	27	20	22
After steadily rebuilding farm system, Mets gave up much of their talent in big league trades.					
20 Philadelphia Phillies	21	7	11	12	17
Small group of elite prospects props up one of the minors' thinnest systems.					
21 Boston Red Sox	23	27	28	24	21
World Series championship wasn't built on farm system, and improving talent remains thin.					
22 Houston Astros	29	23	3	10	9
Former farm director Tim Purpura graduates to GM and needs to rebuild depth.					
23 Cincinnati Reds	26	24	14	3	20
Rampant injuries to pitching prospects have damaged chances to build rotation from within.					
24 New York Yankees	27	17	5	7	1
Plenty of emerging players, especially power arms, but none has played above Class A.					
25 Baltimore Orioles	19	30	29	27	18
Best use of system was to send prospects to Cubs for Sammy Sosa; cupboard remains bare.					
26 Washington Nationals	30	29	16	21	15
New location for former Expos should eventually mean more money for player development.					
27 San Diego Padres	25	20	4	8	11
Farm system is riddled with players who profile better as reserves than as regulars.					
28 Kansas City Royals	19	26	21	14	5
After graduating Zack Greinke to majors, Royals place hope in intriguing 2004 draft class.					
29 Detroit Tigers	22	12	18	18	25
High-risk, high-reward arms remain relative strength in system that has hit bottom.					
30 St. Louis Cardinals	28	28	30	23	27
Good thing big league team can rake, because Cardinals' only significant talent is on mound.					

TOP 50 PROSPECTS

E ven within the walls of Baseball America we don't have uniform opinions on who the best prospects in the game are. So we certainly don't expect you to agree with all of our rankings.

Joe Mauer returns to the top of these top 50 lists—unexpectedly, after an injury cut short what was supposed to be his rookie season in 2004. Three of the four lists here put Mauer at the top, but John Manuel rankings Mariners phenom Felix Hernandez No. 1. Hernandez is a clear winner as the best pitching prospect in the game, while Delmon Young is the unanimous choice for best hitting prospect (non-Mauer division). After that, our opinions range all over the map, as you might expect.

Delmon Young *Devil Rays*

These lists are snapshots after the end of winter ball and before spring training, and they would almost certainly change the next time we put them together. From lists like these (that actually extend through a top 150 assembled by each person), we assemble a consensus list, argue about it, run it by more people in the industry and argue about it more. That ends up as our annual Top 100 Prospects list, which we consider the best compilation of prospects in the game.

Allan Simpson

1. Joe Mauer, c, Twins
2. Delmon Young, of, Devil Rays
3. Felix Hernandez, rhp, Mariners
4. Joel Guzman, ss, Dodgers
5. Rickie Weeks, 2b, Brewers
6. Scott Kazmir, lhp, Devil Rays
7. Ian Stewart, 3b, Rockies
8. Lastings Milledge, of, Mets
9. Casey Kotchman, 1b, Angels
10. Jeff Francoeur, of, Braves
11. Matt Cain, rhp, Giants
12. Jose Capellan, rhp, Brewers
13. Dallas McPherson, 3b, Angels
14. Hanley Ramirez, ss, Red Sox
15. Jeff Niemann, rhp, Devil Rays
16. Jason Kubel, of, Twins
17. Adam Miller, rhp, Indians
18. Jeff Francis, lhp, Rockies
19. Andy Marte, 3b, Braves
20. Prince Fielder, 1b, Brewers
21. Carlos Quentin, of, Diamondbacks
22. Chad Billingsley, rhp, Dodgers
23. Brian Dopirak, of, Cubs
24. Franklin Gutierrez, of, Indians
25. J.J. Hardy, ss, Brewers
26. Ryan Howard, 1b, Phillies
27. Zach Duke, lhp, Pirates
28. Gavin Floyd, rhp, Phillies
29. Chris Nelson, ss, Rockies
30. Erick Aybar, ss, Angels
31. Brian Anderson, of, White Sox
32. Edwin Jackson, rhp, Dodgers
33. Felix Pie, of, Cubs
34. Ryan Sweeney, of, White Sox
35. Jeremy Hermida, of, Marlins
36. Nick Swisher, of, Athletics
37. Brandon McCarthy, rhp, White Sox
38. Mike Hinckley, lhp, Nationals
39. Michael Aubrey, 1b, Indians
40. Conor Jackson, of, Diamondbacks
41. Sergio Santos, ss, Diamondbacks
42. Brian McCann, c, Braves
43. Josh Barfield, 2b, Padres
44. Kyle Davies, rhp, Braves
45. Philip Humber, rhp, Mets
46. Homer Bailey, rhp, Reds
47. Daric Barton, c, Athletics
48. Jeremy Reed, of, Mariners
49. Eric Duncan, 3b, Yankees
50. Yusmeiro Petit, rhp, Mets

Will Lingo

1. Joe Mauer, c, Twins
2. Delmon Young, of, Devil Rays
3. Felix Hernandez, rhp, Mariners
4. Ian Stewart, 3b, Rockies
5. Dallas McPherson, 3b, Angels
6. Jeff Francoeur, of, Braves
7. Joel Guzman, ss/of, Dodgers
8. Andy Marte, 3b, Braves
9. Adam Miller, rhp, Indians
10. Casey Kotchman, 1b, Angels
11. Rickie Weeks, 2b, Brewers
12. Hanley Ramirez, ss, Red Sox
13. Scott Kazmir, lhp, Devil Rays
14. Nick Swisher, of, Athletics
15. Jeremy Hermida, of, Marlins
16. Ryan Howard, 1b, Phillies
17. Prince Fielder, 1b, Brewers
18. Jose Capellan, rhp, Brewers
19. Dan Meyer, lhp, Athletics
20. Chad Billingsley, rhp, Dodgers
21. Matt Cain, rhp, Giants
22. Jeff Niemann, rhp, Devil Rays
23. Jason Kubel, of, Twins
24. Carlos Quentin, of, Diamondbacks
25. Conor Jackson, of, Diamondbacks
26. Brian Dopirak, 1b, Cubs
27. Daric Barton, c/1b, Athletics
28. Lastings Milledge, of, Mets
29. Chris Nelson, ss, Rockies
30. Kyle Davies, rhp, Braves
31. Edwin Jackson, rhp, Dodgers
32. Jeff Francis, lhp, Rockies
33. Mike Hinckley, lhp, Nationals
34. Sergio Santos, ss, Diamondbacks
35. Brian Anderson, of, White Sox
36. Erick Aybar, ss, Angels
37. Gavin Floyd, rhp, Phillies
38. Jeremy Reed, of, Mariners
39. Edwin Encarnacion, 3b, Reds
40. Brian McCann, c, Braves
41. Homer Bailey, rhp, Reds
42. J.J. Hardy, ss, Brewers
43. Nick Markakis, of, Orioles
44. Josh Willingham, c/1b, Marlins
45. Chris Burke, 2b, Astros
46. Josh Barfield, 2b, Padres
47. Zach Duke, lhp, Pirates
48. Felix Pie, of, Cubs
49. Michael Aubrey, 1b, Indians
50. Ryan Sweeney, of, White Sox

Joe Mauer *Twins*

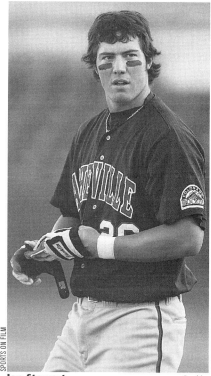

Ian Stewart *Rockies*

ANDREW WOOLLEY

Felix Hernandez *Mariners*

Jim Callis

1. Joe Mauer, c, Twins
2. Felix Hernandez, rhp, Mariners
3. Delmon Young, of, Devil Rays
4. Ian Stewart, 3b, Rockies
5. Andy Marte, 3b, Braves
6. Casey Kotchman, 1b, Angels
7. Scott Kazmir, lhp, Devil Rays
8. Joel Guzman, ss, Dodgers
9. Prince Fielder, 1b, Brewers
10. Rickie Weeks, 2b, Brewers
11. Dallas McPherson, 3b, Angels
12. Hanley Ramirez, ss, Red Sox
13. Jason Kubel, of, Twins
14. Adam Miller, rhp, Indians
15. Chad Billingsley, rhp, Dodgers
16. Lastings Milledge, of, Mets
17. Matt Cain, rhp, Giants
18. Jeremy Hermida, of, Marlins
19. Jeff Niemann, rhp, Devil Rays
20. Edwin Jackson, rhp, Dodgers
21. J.J. Hardy, ss, Brewers
22. Jeff Francoeur, of, Braves
23. Chris Nelson, ss, Rockies
24. Jeff Francis, lhp, Rockies
25. Nick Swisher, of, Athletics
26. Brian Dopirak, 1b, Cubs
27. Daric Barton, c/1b, Athletics
28. Dan Meyer, lhp, Athletics
29. Mike Hinckley, lhp, Nationals
30. Jose Capellan, rhp, Brewers
31. Jeremy Reed, of, Mariners
32. Carlos Quentin, of, Diamondbacks
33. Conor Jackson, of, Diamondbacks
34. Zach Duke, lhp, Pirates
35. Kyle Davies, rhp, Braves
36. Brian McCann, c, Braves
37. Scott Olsen, lhp, Marlins
38. Ryan Howard, 1b, Phillies
39. Gavin Floyd, rhp, Phillies
40. Cole Hamels, lhp, Phillies
41. Anthony Reyes, rhp, Cardinals
42. Yusmeiro Petit, rhp, Mets
43. Eric Duncan, 3b, Yankees
44. Merkin Valdez, rhp, Giants
45. Michael Aubrey, 1b, Indians
46. Felix Pie, of, Cubs
47. John Danks, lhp, Rangers
48. Mark Rogers, rhp, Brewers
49. Erick Aybar, ss, Angels
50. Chris Burke, 2b, Astros

John Manuel

1. Felix Hernandez, rhp, Mariners
2. Joe Mauer, c, Twins
3. Delmon Young, of, Devil Rays
4. Ian Stewart, 3b, Rockies
5. Scott Kazmir, lhp, Devil Rays
6. Casey Kotchman, 1b, Angels
7. Lastings Milledge, of, Mets
8. Joel Guzman, ss, Dodgers
9. Hanley Ramirez, ss, Red Sox
10. Matt Cain, rhp, Giants
11. Rickie Weeks, 2b, Brewers
12. Andy Marte, 3b, Braves
13. Jeremy Hermida, of, Marlins
14. Prince Fielder, 1b, Brewers
15. Adam Miller, rhp, Indians
16. Jeff Niemann, rhp, Devil Rays
17. Jeff Francis, lhp, Rockies
18. Dallas McPherson, 3b, Angels
19. Jeff Francoeur, of, Braves
20. Jason Kubel, of, Twins
21. Chad Billingsley, rhp, Dodgers
22. Ryan Howard, 1b, Phillies
23. Nick Swisher, of, A's
24. Scott Olsen, lhp, Marlins
25. Brian Dopirak, 1b, Cubs
26. Eric Duncan, 3b, Yankees
27. Mike Hinckley, lhp, Nationals
28. Jose Capellan, rhp, Brewers
29. Carlos Quentin, of, Diamondbacks
30. Chris Nelson, ss, Rockies
31. Edwin Jackson, rhp, Dodgers
32. Cole Hamels, lhp, Phillies
33. Erick Aybar, ss, Angels
34. J.J. Hardy, ss, Brewers
35. Felix Pie, of, Cubs
36. Brian Anderson, of, White Sox
37. Philip Humber, rhp, Mets
38. Brandon McCarthy, rhp, White Sox
39. Thomas Diamond, rhp, Rangers
40. Michael Aubrey, 1b, Indians
41. Daric Barton, c/1b, A's
42. John Danks, lhp, Rangers
43. Yusmeiro Petit, rhp, Mets
44. Curtis Granderson, of, Tigers
45. James Loney, 1b, Dodgers
46. Jeremy Reed, of, Mariners
47. Ryan Sweeney, of, White Sox
48. Shin-Soo Choo, of, Mariners
49. Brian McCann, c, Braves
50. Gavin Floyd, rhp, Phillies

BILL NICHOLS

Scott Kazmir

Devil Rays

ANAHEIM
ANGELS

BY **ALAN MATTHEWS**

While the Angels' season ended abruptly with a three-game Division Series sweep at the hand of the Red Sox, it was anything but disappointing. After dropping from a 2002 World Series championship to 77 wins in 2003, Anaheim rebounded in the first full year of **Arte Moreno's** ownership.

Moreno energized the fan base during the offseason, authorizing $145.75 million in contracts for free agents **Vladimir Guerrero**, Bartolo Colon, Kelvim Escobar and Jose Guillen. Those moves paid off, as the Angels edged the Athletics to clinch their first division title in 18 years.

The Angels' 92 wins were their third-most ever, and they set a franchise attendance record with 3,375,677 fans. For his efforts carrying the team down the stretch, Guerrero won the American League MVP award.

Anaheim appears poised to contend for several years. The Angels cleared $36 million from their 2004 payroll by electing not to bring back free agents Troy Glaus, Troy Percival and Ramon Ortiz and trading Guillen. The contracts of Kevin Appier and Aaron Sele finally expired. The Angels immediately put that savings to use, doling out another $53 million in free-agent contracts to Paul Byrd, Orlando Cabrera, Steve Finley and Esteban Yan.

Their AL West competition also appears to be softening, and the Angels' deep farm system is one of the best in the game. Corner infielders Casey Kotchman and Dallas McPherson both played their way onto the postseason roster, and McPherson's emer-

gence made Glaus expendable. Though Jeff Mathis struggled at Double-A Arkansas, he still has the minors' best all-around package of catching tools. All three of those players were products of Anaheim's vaunted 2001 draft, and new scouting director Eddie Bane may have assembled a similarly strong crop in 2004 with an aggressive approach.

Though righthander Jered Weaver's eight-figure contract demands scared off many clubs, the Angels jumped on the draft's top-rated prospect with the No. 12 overall pick and remained confident they would sign him. Anaheim took an 18th-round flier on Mark Trumbo, who had first-round potential as a righthanded pitcher, gave him a $1.475 million bonus—and announced he'd become a full-time hitter.

Anaheim's international department also has been aggressive and has signed plenty of talent, most notably Cuban defector Kendry Morales' major league deal in December. Since the hiring of supervisor Clay Daniel in 2000, the Angels have signed high-ceiling righthander Ervin Santana (Dominican Republic) and middle infielders Erick Aybar (Dominican) and Alberto Callaspo (Venezuela). First baseman Baltazar Lopez (Mexico) emerged in 2004.

The faces may change in the near future, but the farm system and Moreno's deep pockets should be able to add to the Angels' talent base for years to come.

TOP 30 PROSPECTS

1. Casey Kotchman, 1b	16. Maicer Izturis, ss/2b
2. Dallas McPherson, 3b	17. Rafael Rodriguez, rhp
3. Erick Aybar, ss	18. Jake Woods, lhp
4. Jeff Mathis, c	19. Kevin Jepsen, rhp
5. Kendry Morales, of/1b	20. Nick Adenhart, rhp
6. Brandon Wood, ss	21. Warner Madrigal, of
7. Ervin Santana, rhp	22. Anthony Whittington, lhp
8. Howie Kendrick, 2b	23. Nick Gorneault, of
9. Alberto Callaspo, 2b/ss	24. Reggie Willits, of
10. Steven Shell, rhp	25. Bob Zimmermann, rhp
11. Mark Trumbo, 3b/1b	26. Tim Bittner, lhp
12. Baltazar Lopez, 1b	27. Andrew Toussaint, 3b/of
13. Joe Saunders, lhp	28. Bobby Cassevah, rhp
14. Sean Rodriguez, 2b/ss	29. Mike Napoli, c/1b
15. Dustin Moseley, rhp	30. Mitchell Arnold, rhp

ORGANIZATION OVERVIEW

General manager: Bill Stoneman. **Farm director:** Tony Reagins. **Scouting Director:** Eddie Bane.

2004 PERFORMANCE

Class	Team	League	W	L	Pct.	Finish*	Manager
Majors	Anaheim	American	92	70	.568	t-3rd (14)	Mike Scioscia
Triple-A	Salt Lake Stingers	Pacific Coast	56	88	.389	16th (16)	Mike Brumley
Double-A	Arkansas Travelers	Texas	59	80	.424	7th (8)	Tyrone Boykin
High A	Rancho Cucamonga Quakes	California	69	71	.493	6th (10)	Bobby Meacham
Low A	Cedar Rapids Kernels	Midwest	75	64	.540	t-4th (14)	Bobby Magallanes
Rookie	†Provo Angels	Pioneer	44	32	.579	+1st (8)	Tom Kotchman
Rookie	AZL Angels	Arizona	12	43	.218	9th (9)	Brian Harper
OVERALL 2004 MINOR LEAGUE RECORD			315	378	.455	28th (30)	

*Finish in overall standings (No. of teams in league). +League champion. †Franchise will move to Orem, Utah, in 2005.

ORGANIZATION LEADERS

BATTING   *Minimum 250 At-Bats

*AVG	Casey Kotchman, Salt Lake/Arkansas	.371
R	Dallas McPherson, Salt Lake/Arkansas	107
H	Erick Aybar, Rancho Cucamonga	189
TB	Dallas McPherson, Salt Lake/Arkansas	349
2B	Dallas McPherson, Salt Lake/Arkansas	36
3B	Dallas McPherson, Salt Lake/Arkansas	14
HR	Dallas McPherson, Salt Lake/Arkansas	40
RBI	Dallas McPherson, Salt Lake/Arkansas	126
BB	Mike Napoli, Rancho Cucamonga	88
SO	Dallas McPherson, Salt Lake/Arkansas	169
SB	Erick Aybar, Rancho Cucamonga	51
*OBP	Casey Kotchman, Salt Lake/Arkansas	.429
*SLG	Dallas McPherson, Salt Lake/Arkansas	.670

PITCHING   #Minimum 75 Innings

W	Jake Woods, Salt Lake/Arkansas	15
L	Steve Green, Salt Lake	17
#ERA	Micah Posey, Rancho Cuca./Cedar Rapids	2.91
G	Dustin Griffith, Salt Lake/Ark./Rancho Cuca.	56
	Von Stertzbach, Rancho Cuca./Cedar Rapids	56
CG	Chris Bootcheck, Salt Lake	3
	Willie Collazo, Arkansas	3
SV	Von Stertzbach, Rancho Cuca./Cedar Rapids	26
IP	Jake Woods, Salt Lake/Arkansas	173
BB	Steve Green, Salt Lake	85
SO	Steven Shell, Rancho Cucamonga	190

BEST TOOLS

Best Hitter for Average	Casey Kotchman
Best Power Hitter	Dallas McPherson
Best Strike-Zone Discipline	Casey Kotchman
Fastest Baserunner	Quan Cosby
Best Athlete	D.T. McDowell
Best Fastball	Ervin Santana
Best Curveball	Bobby Jenks
Best Slider	Ervin Santana
Best Changeup	Abel Moreno
Best Control	Steven Shell
Best Defensive Catcher	Jeff Mathis
Best Defensive Infielder	Erick Aybar
Best Infield Arm	Erick Aybar
Best Defensive Outfielder	Reggie Willits
Best Outfield Arm	Warner Madrigal

PROJECTED 2008 LINEUP

Catcher	Jeff Mathis
First Base	Casey Kotchman
Second Base	Howie Kendrick
Third Base	Dallas McPherson
Shortstop	Orlando Cabrera
Left Field	Kendry Morales
Center Field	Darin Erstad

Right Field	Vladimir Guerrero
Designated Hitter	Garret Anderson
No. 1 Starter	Bartolo Colon
No. 2 Starter	Ervin Santana
No. 3 Starter	Kelvim Escobar
No. 4 Starter	John Lackey
No. 5 Starter	Steven Shell
Closer	Francisco Rodriguez

LAST YEAR'S TOP 20 PROSPECTS

1. Casey Kotchman, 1b
2. Jeff Mathis, c
3. Dallas McPherson, 3b
4. Ervin Santana, rhp
5. Bobby Jenks, rhp
6. Alberto Callaspo, 2b
7. Brandon Wood, ss
8. Erick Aybar, ss
9. Rafael Rodriguez, rhp
10. Steven Shell, rhp
11. Joe Saunders, lhp
12. Kevin Jepsen, rhp
13. Jake Woods, lhp
14. Howie Kendrick, 2b
15. Anthony Whittington, lhp
16. Warner Madrigal, of
17. Bobby Wilson, c
18. Nick Gorneault, of
19. Chris Bootcheck, rhp
20. Rich Fischer, rhp

TOP PROSPECTS OF THE DECADE

Year	Player, Pos.	Current Team
1995	Andrew Lorraine, lhp	Orioles
1996	Darin Erstad, of	Angels
1997	Jarrod Washburn, lhp	Angels
1998	Troy Glaus, 3b	Diamondbacks
1999	Ramon Ortiz, rhp	Reds
2000	Ramon Ortiz, rhp	Reds
2001	Joe Torres, lhp	Angels
2002	Casey Kotchman, 1b	Angels
2003	Francisco Rodriguez, rhp	Angels
2004	Casey Kotchman, 1b	Angels

TOP DRAFT PICKS OF THE DECADE

Year	Player, Pos.	Current Team
1995	Darin Erstad, of	Angels
1996	Chuck Abbott, ss (2)	Out of baseball
1997	Troy Glaus, 3b	Diamondbacks
1998	Seth Etherton, rhp	Reds
1999	John Lackey, rhp (2)	Angels
2000	Joe Torres, lhp	Angels
2001	Casey Kotchman, 1b	Angels
2002	Joe Saunders, lhp	Angels
2003	Brandon Wood, ss	Angels
2004	Jered Weaver, rhp	Has not signed

ALL-TIME LARGEST BONUSES

Kendry Morales, 2004	$3,000,000
Troy Glaus, 1997	$2,250,000
Joe Torres, 2000	$2,080,000
Casey Kotchman, 2001	$2,075,000
Joe Saunders, 2002	$1,825,000

MINOR LEAGUE DEPTH CHART

Anaheim ANGELS

Impact Talent: A
The Angels have impact bats around the infield at every position. They got their first extended looks at Casey Kotchman and Dallas McPherson in the big leagues last summer, and both should be above-average hitters at the team's infield corners for years. Erick Aybar and Alberto Callaspo could one day form a dynamic double-play duo, unless Brandon Wood and Howie Kendrick beat them to it.

Depth: A
Few clubs can match the Angels' stockpile of bats. Pitching depth is more the organization's strength than impact arms, and the health of top prospects such as righthanders Ervin Santana and Rafael Rodriguez and lefthander Joe Saunders will be key to keeping the Angels well stocked on the mound.

Depth charts prepared by John Manuel and Allan Simpson. Numbers in parentheses indicate prospect rankings.

LF
Andrew Toussaint (27)
Blake Balkcom

CF
Reggie Willits (24)
Stantrel Smith
Tommy Murphy
Quan Cosby
D.T. McDowell

3B
Dallas McPherson (2)
Mark Trumbo (11)
Freddy Sandoval
Greg Porter
Adam Pavkovich
Matt Brown

SS
Erick Aybar (3)
Brandon Wood (6)
Maicer Izturis (16)
Larry Infante
Hainley Statia

RF
Kendry Morales (5)
Warner Madrigal (21)
Nick Gorneault (23)
Jordan Renz

2B
Howie Kendrick (8)
Alberto Callaspo (9)
Sean Rodriguez (14)
Josh LeBlanc
Alexi Casilla
Brian Specht

1B
Casey Kotchman (1)
Baltazar Lopez (12)

SOURCE of TALENT

Homegrown		Acquired	
College	6	Trades	3
Junior College	2	Rule 5 draft	0
Draft-and-follow	1	Independent leagues	0
High school	11	Free agents/waivers	0
Nondrafted free agents	0		
Foreign	7		

C
Jeff Mathis (4)
Mike Napoli (29)
Bobby Wilson
Ryan Budde

LHP

Starters	Relievers
Joe Saunders (13)	Anthony Whittington (22)
Jake Woods (18)	Jon Rouwenhorst
Tim Bittner (26)	Dan Davidson
Kelly Shearer	
Nick Touchstone	

RHP

Starters	Relievers
Ervin Santana (7)	Bob Zimmermann (25)
Steven Shell (10)	Mitchell Arnold (30)
Dustin Moseley (15)	Scott Dunn
Rafael Rodriguez (17)	Matt Hensley
Kevin Jepsen (19)	Carlos Morban
Nick Adenhart (20)	Von Sterzbach
Bobby Cassevah (28)	Ryan Aldridge
Chris Bootcheck	Richard Thompson
Abel Moreno	
Felipe Arredondo	
Chris Hunter	
Gustavo Espinosa	
Bill Layman	

Best Pro Debut: 3B/DH Andrew Toussaint (13) made the Rookie-level Pioneer League all-star team by hitting .289-12-52. He still has to prove he can play the hot corner.

Best Athlete: After hitting .310 in the Rookie-level Arizona League, OF D.T. McDowell (20) surprised the Angels by leaving to play football at Troy, where he was the No. 2 quarterback as a true freshman. Anaheim expects he'll return to baseball. Physically gifted 3B Matt Moore (22) hasn't played competitive baseball since he was a high school junior in 2001, instead spending two years as a UCLA quarterback. By attending a junior college, he remained under Angels control. OF Tyler Johnson (12) turned down a Tulsa football scholarship.

Best Pure Hitter: Most teams saw him as a possible first-rounder as a pitcher, but the Angels liked 3B Mark Trumbo's (18) bat even more than his arm. They signed him for $1.425 million, a draft record for his round.

Best Raw Power: Trumbo drilled two balls off the rocks in left-center field at Angel Stadium during batting practice.

Fastest Runner: Johnson and McDowell have above-average speed.

Best Defensive Player: SS Hainley Statia (9), a Curacao native who had his pro debut delayed by visa issues.

Best Fastball: Trumbo threw 96 mph but won't take the mound again. RHP Jered Weaver (1), expected to sign in the spring, has excellent command of a fastball that sits at 91-92 mph and touches 95. RHP Bill Layman (7) also peaks at 95, as did RHP Nick Adenhart (14) before injuring his elbow in May.

Best Breaking Ball: Adenhart was a sure first-round pick before Tommy John surgery,

Weaver

and even that didn't deter the Angels from signing him for $710,000. When he was healthy, he showed one of the best curveballs in the draft.

Most Intriguing Background: Weaver's brother Jeff was a Tigers first-rounder in 1998 and pitches for the Dodgers. In addition to all the other football players, unsigned OF Patrick White (4) was a redshirt freshman quarterback at West Virginia in the fall. 3B Brooks Shankle's (32) father Jimmy is a former head baseball coach at Abilene Christián and Texas San-Antonio.

Closest To The Majors: Once he signs, Weaver should need little minor league time.

Best Late-Round Pick: Trumbo and Adenhart are the most obvious, but Johnson, McDowell and RHP Bobby Cassevah (34) also had early-round talent and signed after being considered unsignable.

The One Who Got Away: White, the highest-drafted high school player not to sign in 2004, told the Angels he would sign but changed his mind after the draft. RHP Erik Davis (47) could become a first-rounder after three years at Stanford.

Assessment: Eddie Bane wasn't afraid to gamble in his first draft as Angels scouting director. He took Weaver, the draft's top-rated prospect, with the No. 12 pick after other teams passed because of his reported desire for an eight-figure deal. He may get the equivalent of two extra first-rounders in Trumbo and Adenhart.

2003 SS Brandon Wood (1) is one of the game's best young middle-infield prospects, and INF/OF Sean Rodriguez (3) would rate an honorable mention on that list. Unsigned SS Jason Donald (20) is the top-rated middle infielder for the 2006 draft. **GRADE:** C+

2002 2B Howie Kendrick (10) won the low Class A Midwest League batting title in 2004. The Angels hope LHP Joe Saunders (1) is on the road back to his previous form after shoulder problems. **GRADE:** C+

2001 The best draft in this book started with 1B Casey Kotchman (1) and 3B Dallas McPherson (2) bookending C Jason Mathis (1). Less publicized RHP Steven Shell (3) and LHP Jake Woods (4) are solid as well. **GRADE:** A

2000 First-round pitchers Joe Torres and Chris Bootcheck have flamed out, as did RHP Bobby Jenks (5), lost on waivers to the White Sox. The Angels didn't sign the best player they picked, SS Aaron Hill (7), now on the verge of starting for Toronto. **GRADE:** F

Draft analysis prepared by Jim Callis. Numbers in parentheses indicate draft rounds.

Casey
KOTCHMAN

Born: Feb. 22, 1983.
Ht.: 6-3. **Wt.:** 210.
Bats: L. **Throws:** L.
School: Seminole (Fla.) HS.
Career Transactions: Selected by Angels in first round (13th overall) of 2001 draft; signed July 28, 2001.
Signed by: Tom Kotchman.

LARRY GOREN

Some club officials have known Kotchman, the son of longtime Angels scout and minor league manager Tom, since he was 7 years old. In 2004 they got a firsthand look at how he has developed into one the best pure batting prospects in baseball, as he made his major league debut after a red-hot month in Double-A. He was called up to Anaheim in May to replace injured first baseman Darin Erstad and recorded four multihit games in his first eight starts. He didn't strike out until his 48th plate appearance, and his first hit came off Mariano Rivera in a nine-pitch at-bat. Kotchman became Pedro Martinez' 2,500th career strikeout victim, but only after an epic 15-pitch at-bat. He was sent to Triple-A Salt Lake and continued to rake. He was back in Anaheim in September and received a spot on the postseason roster, thanks in part to injuries to other players.

Kotchman has more walks (116) than strikeouts (100) as a pro and manages the balance between selectivity and aggressiveness better than any hitter in the minors. He has a natural, fluid swing and keeps the barrel of his bat in the hitting zone a long time. He makes consistent, sharp contact to all fields. Kotchman is adept at quickly identifying the spin and break of pitches. He rarely chases pitches and frequently works deep into counts. When he gets his pitch, he's content to lash it to both alleys, though he displays more over-the-fence power potential in batting practice. He projects to hit at least 20-25 homers annually once he learns when to lift the ball. He is smooth around the bag at first and is a future Gold Glover. He has good hands and easily scoops up errant throws.

Kotchman never has been healthy for a complete season. He did play in a career-high 114 games in 2004 after totaling just 156 in his first three seasons, but he missed all but one game in July with a sprained right wrist and a bruised shoulder. In previous years, he missed time with wrist, back and hamstring injuries. After tearing his right hamstring running from first to third base in 2003, he was timid on the basepaths in 2004. His speed is below average, but he previously had shown good baserunning instincts. While his home run power is expected to develop, he has gone deep just 24 times in 985 pro at-bats and showed little pop in his big league debut.

Kotchman has hit .343 in the minors and has nothing left to prove at that level. Erstad profiles better as a center fielder, but the free-agent signing of Steve Finley means he won't move back there to open first base for Kotchman. As a result, he could return to Triple-A Salt Lake rather than sit on the bench in Anaheim at the start of 2005. If he gets a chance to play in the majors, Kotchman will be a leading contender for Rookie of the Year.

Year	Club (League)	Class	AVG	G	AB	R	H	2B	3B	HR	RBI	BB	SO	SB	OBP	SLG
2001	Angels (AZL)	R	.600	4	15	5	9	1	0	1	5	3	2	0	.632	.867
	Provo (Pio)	R	.500	7	22	6	11	3	0	0	7	2	0	0	.542	.636
2002	Cedar Rapids (Mid)	A	.281	81	288	42	81	30	1	5	50	48	37	2	.390	.444
2003	Rancho Cucamonga (Cal)	A	.350	57	206	42	72	2	0	8	28	30	16	2	.441	.524
	Angels (AZL)	R	.333	7	27	5	9	1	0	2	6	2	3	0	.379	.593
2004	Anaheim (AL)	MAJ	.224	38	116	7	26	6	0	0	15	7	11	3	.289	.276
	Salt Lake (PCL)	AAA	.372	49	199	32	74	22	0	5	38	14	25	0	.423	.558
	Arkansas (TL)	AA	.368	28	114	19	42	11	0	3	18	10	7	0	.438	.544
MAJOR LEAGUE TOTALS			.224	38	116	7	26	6	0	0	15	7	11	3	.289	.276
MINOR LEAGUE TOTALS			.342	233	871	151	298	80	1	24	152	109	90	4	.423	.519

Dallas McPherson, 3b

Born: July 23, 1980. **Ht.:** 6-4. **Wt.:** 230. **Bats:** L. **Throws:** R. **School:** The Citadel. **Career Transactions:** Selected by Angels in second round of 2001 draft; signed June 18, 2001. **Signed by:** Marc Russo.

After he led the minors in slugging (.670) and total bases (349) in 2004, injuries thrust McPherson into a starting role in Anaheim in the final two weeks of the regular season and he held his own. McPherson owns the organization's best raw power and translates it into game power. His swing is balanced and controlled, and he uses his lower half well. Because of his leverage and extension, he draws comparisons to Adam Dunn. McPherson's intense makeup is off the charts. He has an above-average arm. He must sharpen his ability to make contact and handle quality breaking balls. McPherson whiffed 169 times in the minors and 17 times in 40 big league at-bats. Defensively, he struggles to read balls off the bat and looks stiff at third base. With the Angels choosing not to keep Troy Glaus, McPherson faces the task of replacing him at third base and in the heart of the order. In time, he should match Glaus' production in the majors.

Year	Club (League)	Class	AVG	G	AB	R	H	2B	3B	HR	RBI	BB	SO	SB	OBP	SLG
2001	Provo (Pio)	R	.395	31	124	30	49	11	0	5	29	12	22	1	.449	.605
2002	Cedar Rapids (Mid)	A	.277	132	499	71	138	24	3	15	88	78	128	30	.381	.427
2003	Rancho Cucamonga (Cal)	A	.308	77	292	65	90	21	6	18	59	41	79	12	.404	.606
	Arkansas (TL)	AA	.314	28	102	22	32	9	1	5	27	19	25	4	.426	.569
2004	Arkansas (TL)	AA	.321	68	262	53	84	17	6	20	69	34	74	6	.404	.660
	Salt Lake (PCL)	AAA	.313	67	259	54	81	19	8	20	57	23	95	6	.370	.680
	Anaheim (AL)	MAJ	.225	16	40	5	9	1	0	3	6	3	17	1	.279	.475
MAJOR LEAGUE TOTALS			.225	16	40	5	9	1	0	3	6	3	17	1	.279	.475
MINOR LEAGUE TOTALS			.308	403	1538	295	474	101	24	83	329	207	423	59	.396	.567

Erick Aybar, ss

Born: Jan. 14, 1984. **Ht.:** 5-11. **Wt.:** 170. **Bats:** B. **Throws:** R. **Career Transactions:** Signed out of Dominican Republic by Angels, Feb. 4, 2002. **Signed by:** Leo Perez/Clay Daniel.

Aybar played alongside Alberto Callaspo during his first two pro seasons, and they were inseparable on and off the field. In 2004, the Angels decided to break them up so both could play shortstop. Aybar wasn't fazed and led the minors in hits. His older brother Willie is an infielder in the Dodgers system. Aybar possesses a rare blend of sound fundamentals, instincts and pure shortstop actions. He has excellent range, good hands and a plus arm. Offensively, he has a knack for making contact and enough power to hit 15 homers a year. He's adept from both sides of the plate. He has a tendency to force off-balance throws, which led to many of his system-high 34 errors in 2004. At the plate, Aybar gets pull-happy and needs to improve his pitch recognition. He'll chase pitches out of the strike zone, though he often manages to put them in play because he has quick wrists, thus limiting his walks. Aybar will be reunited with Callaspo, who's moving back to second base, at Double-A Arkansas in 2005. He should be ready for Anaheim the following season, but Orlando Cabrera's four-year, $32 million contract clouds Aybar's future with the club.

Year	Club (League)	Class	AVG	G	AB	R	H	2B	3B	HR	RBI	BB	SO	SB	OBP	SLG
2002	Provo (Pio)	R	.326	67	273	64	89	15	6	4	29	21	43	15	.395	.469
2003	Cedar Rapids (Mid)	A	.308	125	496	83	153	30	10	6	57	17	54	32	.346	.446
2004	Rancho Cucamonga (Cal)	A	.330	136	573	102	189	25	11	14	65	26	66	51	.370	.485
MINOR LEAGUE TOTALS			.321	328	1342	249	431	70	27	24	151	64	163	98	.366	.467

Jeff Mathis, c

Born: March 31, 1983. **Ht.:** 6-0. **Wt.:** 180. **Bats:** R. **Throws:** R. **School:** Marianna (Fla.) HS. **Career Transactions:** Selected by Angels in first round (33rd overall) of 2001 draft; signed June 5, 2001. **Signed by:** Tom Kotchman/Hank Sargent.

After Mathis got off to a strong start in 2004, he collapsed after Casey Kotchman and Dallas McPherson were promoted from Double-A. Mathis slumped to .165 the rest of the way and continued to struggle in instructional league. A premium athlete, Mathis has fast-twitch muscle movement and plenty of bat speed, enabling him to drive balls into the gaps. In instructional league, he worked on shortening his swing and closing his stance. He moves well behind the plate, blocks balls in the dirt and has slightly above-average arm strength. Mathis previously overcame his swing flaws with his athleticism, but he was exploited at Double-A. His plate discipline suffered as well. Like many intelligent players, Mathis can be too analytical and self-critical. Despite his defensive tools and acumen, he threw out just 21 percent of basestealers. Mathis' struggles may have stemmed from trying to carry a depleted Arkansas lineup. He'll try a revised approach at the plate in 2005, likely back in Double-A. He still could start for Anaheim in 2006 and develop into an all-star catcher.

Year	Club (League)	Class	AVG	G	AB	R	H	2B	3B	HR	RBI	BB	SO	SB	OBP	SLG
2001	Angels (AZL)	R	.304	7	23	1	7	1	0	0	3	2	4	0	.346	.348
	Provo (Pio)	R	.299	22	77	14	23	6	3	0	18	11	13	1	.387	.455
2002	Cedar Rapids (Mid)	A	.287	128	491	75	141	41	3	10	73	40	75	2	.346	.444
2003	Rancho Cucamonga (Cal)	A	.323	97	378	73	122	28	3	11	54	35	74	5	.384	.500
	Arkansas (TL)	AA	.284	24	95	19	27	11	0	2	14	12	16	1	.364	.463
2004	Arkansas (TL)	AA	.227	117	432	57	98	24	3	14	55	49	102	2	.310	.394
MINOR LEAGUE TOTALS			.279	395	1496	239	418	111	12	37	217	149	284	16	.348	.444

5 Kendry Morales, 1b/of

Born: June 20, 1983. **Ht.:** 6-1. **Wt.:** 225. **Bats:** B. **Throws:** R. **Career Transactions:** Signed out of Cuba by Angels, Dec. 1, 2004. **Signed by:** Clay Daniel/Tito Perez.

Morales signed a six-year major league contract in December, which included a $3 million bonus and could be worth as much as $10 million. In 2002, he became the first teenager to star for Cuba's national team since Omar Linares, but the government later banned him after repeated attempts to defect. He succeeded in June and established residency in the Dominican Republic, making him a free agent. Morales ranks with Linares as the best position player developed in post-revolution Cuba. He profiles as a middle-of-the-order run producer, with a level swing from both sides, power to all fields and an aggressive approach. Morales' speed is average at best, leading to questions about his defense. A first baseman on Cuba's national team in 2003, he has a plus arm and instincts to become a reliable corner outfielder. The Angels believe Morales is ready to contribute in the majors and will give him a chance to win a job this spring. He must overcome culture shock, obstacles that have waylaid several highly touted Cuban defectors in the past.

Year	Club (League)	Class	AVG	G	AB	R	H	2B	3B	HR	RBI	BB	SO	SB	OBP	SLG
2004	Did not play—Signed 2005 contract															

6 Brandon Wood, ss

Born: March 2, 1985. **Ht.:** 6-3. **Wt.:** 185. **Bats:** R. **Throws:** R. **School:** Horizon HS, Scottsdale, Ariz. **Career Transactions:** Selected by Angels in first round (23rd overall) of 2003 draft; signed June 6, 2003. **Signed by:** Jeff Scholzen.

Known as a skinny, defensive-minded shortstop before his high school senior season, Wood blossomed into a power hitter and signed for $1.3 million. He hit a wall in his first full pro season, batting .198 in August after an impressive start. Wood has strong, nimble wrists and quick hands. His swing has natural loft and he accelerates the bat head through the hitting zone well. He shows good instincts at the plate, in the field and on the bases. He has average range and arm strength. Wood struck out too often in 2004 and gets pull-conscious. He often fails to set his feet and hurries his throws. He may outgrow shortstop and could move to third base. Because of his athletic ability and aptitude, Wood has a high ceiling. He profiles as an everyday infielder who should hit for average with 15-20 homers annually. The Angels may give him another half-season at low Class A Cedar Rapids.

Year	Club (League)	Class	AVG	G	AB	R	H	2B	3B	HR	RBI	BB	SO	SB	OBP	SLG
2003	Angels (AZL)	R	.308	19	78	14	24	8	2	0	13	4	15	3	.349	.462
	Provo (Pio)	R	.278	42	162	25	45	13	2	5	31	16	48	1	.348	.475
2004	Cedar Rapids (Mid)	A	.251	125	478	65	120	30	5	11	64	46	117	21	.322	.404
MINOR LEAGUE TOTALS			.263	186	718	104	189	51	9	16	108	66	180	25	.331	.426

7 Ervin Santana, rhp

Born: Nov. 28, 1983. **Ht.:** 6-2. **Wt.:** 150. **Bats:** R. **Throws:** R. **Career Transactions:** Signed out of Dominican Republic by Angels, Sept. 2, 2000. **Signed by:** Clay Daniel/Donny Rowland.

Bothered by a sore shoulder, Santana began the 2004 season in extended spring training and didn't join Arkansas until mid-May. He broke down a month later with a sore elbow. Though an MRI showed no structural problems in his elbow, he didn't take the mound again until tossing three innings during the final week of instructional league. When healthy, Santana has the most electric stuff in the system. During his breakthrough 2003 season, he often opened games pitching at 90 mph before cranking his fastball up into the mid-90s. His heater has good, late life, especially down in the strike zone. When he follows through on his slider, it's a true put-away pitch that peaks at 87 mph. He also had a tender elbow in 2003, so health is the greatest concern with Santana. He's reluctant to change speeds, though his changeup has the makings of an average pitch. He still thinks more velocity is the solution to pitching out of jams. Despite his setbacks, Santana still could make his major league debut at some point in 2005. He'll begin his comeback back in Double-A.

Year	Club (League)	Class	W	L	ERA	G	GS	CG	SV	IP	H	R	ER	HR	BB	SO	AVG
2001	Angels (AZL)	R	3	2	3.22	10	9	1	0	59	40	27	21	0	35	69	.184
	Provo (Pio)	R	2	1	7.71	4	4	0	0	19	19	17	16	1	12	22	.247
2002	Rancho Cuca. (Cal)	A	10	2	2.53	20	20	1	0	125	98	44	35	9	36	130	.212
2003	Cedar Rapids (Mid)	A	14	8	4.16	27	27	0	0	147	133	75	68	10	48	146	.240
	Arkansas (TL)	AA	1	1	3.94	6	6	0	0	30	23	15	13	4	12	23	.211
2004	Arkansas (TL)	AA	2	1	3.30	8	8	0	0	44	41	19	16	3	18	48	.244
MINOR LEAGUE TOTALS			32	15	3.60	75	74	2	0	422	354	197	169	27	161	438	.223

Howie Kendrick, 2b

Born: July 12, 1983. **Ht.:** 5-10. **Wt.:** 180. **Bats:** R. **Throws:** R. **School:** St. John's River (Fla.) CC. **Career Transactions:** Selected by Angels in 10th round of 2002 draft; signed June 19, 2002. **Signed by:** Tom Kotchman.

Kendrick has improved exponentially since he was cut as a college freshman. After he found a home at little-known St. John's River (Fla.) CC, area scout Tom Kotchman loved his bat so much he urged the Angels to draft him in the 10th round in 2002. Though he missed two months with a groin injury in 2004, he won the low Class A Midwest League batting title and raised his career average to .357. Kendrick derives his hitting ability from extraordinary hand-eye coordination and a balanced, controlled swing. He has a clear plan for each at-bat and recalls pitchers' tendencies, allowing him to adjust from one pitch to the next. He has gap power and is an excellent situational hitter. Only Kendrick's bat grades as an above-average tool. He has improved defensively but remains a work in progress. His range and arm are average at best. Kendrick is a below-average runner but has good instincts on the basepaths. Kendrick has drawn comparisons to Orlando Hudson and fits the mold of a prototypical No. 2 hitter. He could do a lot of damage at high Class A Rancho Cucamonga, a hitter's haven, in 2005.

Year	Club (League)	Class	AVG	G	AB	R	H	2B	3B	HR	RBI	BB	SO	SB	OBP	SLG
2002	Angels (AZL)	R	.318	42	157	24	50	6	4	0	13	7	11	12	.368	.408
2003	Provo (Pio)	R	.368	63	234	65	86	20	3	3	36	24	28	8	.434	.517
2004	Cedar Rapids (Mid)	A	.367	75	313	66	115	24	6	10	49	12	41	15	.398	.578
MINOR LEAGUE TOTALS			.357	180	704	155	251	50	13	13	98	43	80	35	.404	.520

Albert Callaspo, 2b/ss

Born: April 19, 1983. **Ht.:** 5-11. **Wt.:** 173. **Bats:** B. **Throws:** R. **Career Transactions:** Signed out of Venezuela by Angels, Feb. 16, 2001. **Signed by:** Carlos Porte/Amador Arias.

The Angels usually are conservative with assignments, but chose to skip Callaspo over high Class A in 2004 so he could play shortstop. He didn't lead his league in hits for the third straight year, but did hold his own in the Texas League. Despite playing in Double-A at age 21, Callaspo was the toughest player to strike out in the minors. He lacks Erick Aybar's pop, but he's a pure-hitting singles machine. He proved he has the skills to play shortstop and he stands out more at second base. His arm and speed are average tools. Anaheim's player-development staff praises his work ethic. Though he drew a career-high 47 walks, Callaspo needs to improve his patience and pitch selection to become a quality leadoff hitter. He often puts pitches in play that he'd be better off taking. The Angels have decided to move Callaspo back to second base. That will allow him to team once again with Aybar, forming a dynamic double-play combination that should get to the majors in 2006. He'll return to Double-A to open 2005 but could force a promotion to Triple-A by mid-season.

Year	Club (League)	Class	AVG	G	AB	R	H	2B	3B	HR	RBI	BB	SO	SB	OBP	SLG
2001	Anges (DSL)	R	.356	66	275	55	98	11	4	2	39	22	16	14	.403	.447
2002	Provo (Pio)	R	.338	70	299	70	101	16	10	3	60	17	14	13	.374	.488
2003	Cedar Rapids (Mid)	A	.327	133	514	86	168	38	4	2	67	42	28	20	.377	.428
2004	Arkansas (TL)	AA	.284	136	550	76	156	29	2	6	48	47	25	15	.338	.376
MINOR LEAGUE TOTALS			.319	405	1638	287	523	94	20	13	214	128	83	62	.368	.425

10 Steven Shell, rhp

Born: March 10, 1983. **Ht.:** 6-5. **Wt.:** 190. **Bats:** R. **Throws:** R. **School:** El Reno (Okla.) HS. **Career Transactions:** Selected by Angels in third round of 2001 draft; signed June 17, 2001. **Signed by:** Kevin Ham.

Shell started the California-Carolina League all-star game in 2003, but faded in the second half after coming down with a tender elbow. The Angels decided to play it safe and sent him back to high Class A in 2004. He led the Cal League in strikeouts and walked more than two batters in just two of his 28 starts. Shell has the best command in the organization. He can work his 89-92 mph fastball in on righthanded hitters with cutting action, and it has natural sink as well. His 12-to-6 curveball grades out as slightly above average. He refined his splitter last year, and when it's on, he can be hard to beat. His changeup is a solid fourth pitch. Shell doesn't have a dominant pitch he can rely on to get outs. He has to mix his pitches and locations in order to succeed. He had a reputation for getting flustered easily, but he made strides with his poise in 2004. Shell projects as a middle-of-the-rotation starter. Ticketed for Double-A in 2005, he could compete for a big league job as early as 2006.

Year	Club (League)	Class	W	L	ERA	G	GS	CG	SV	IP	H	R	ER	HR	BB	SO	AVG
2001	Angels (AZL)	R	1	0	0.00	3	0	0	0	4	1	0	0	0	2	3	.077
	Provo (Pio)	R	0	3	7.17	14	4	0	1	38	52	31	30	3	15	33	.331
2002	Cedar Rapids (Mid)	A	11	4	3.72	22	21	1	0	121	119	59	50	12	26	86	.255
2003	Rancho Cucamonga (Cal)	A	6	8	4.24	22	21	1	0	127	123	66	60	13	26	100	.248
2004	Rancho Cucamonga (Cal)	A	12	7	3.59	28	28	2	0	165	151	76	66	19	40	190	.242
MINOR LEAGUE TOTALS			30	22	4.06	89	74	4	1	457	446	232	206	47	109	412	.254

11 Mark Trumbo, 3b/1b

Born: Jan. 16, 1986. **Ht.:** 6-5. **Wt.:** 210. **Bats:** R. **Throws:** R. **School:** Villa Park (Calif.) HS. **Career Transactions:** Selected by Angels in 18th round of 2004 draft; signed Aug. 14, 2004. **Signed by:** Tim Corcoran.

Most organizations targeted Trumbo as a hard-throwing righthander but were scared off by his bonus demands and commitment to Southern California. The Angels gambled an 18th-round pick on him and scouted him as a two-way player. After he deposited two balls into the rocks in left-center field at Angel Stadium during a workout, they signed him for $1.425 million, easily the highest bonus ever for his round. Trumbo's raw power rates a 70 on the 20-to-80 scouting scale. His swing has good leverage creating backspin and loft. During a soft-toss drill in instructional league, balls came off Trumbo's bat at 110 mph. He touched 96 mph off the mound in high school and has well above-average arm strength. Trumbo needs to improve on his pitch recognition and keep his weight back on offspeed pitches. His swing has some holes. Defensively, his hands and instincts need work. His foot speed is a hair below average. His value is greater at third base, but he spent instructional league at first base, where his hands and lack of range would be less of a factor. Because Trumbo faces a steep learning curve, the Angels will develop him slowly. He'll begin 2005 in extended spring training and should debut at short-season Orem in June.

Year	Club (League)	Class	AVG	G	AB	R	H	2B	3B	HR	RBI	BB	SO	SB	OBP	SLG
2004	Did not play—Signed 2005 contract															

12 Baltazar Lopez, 1b

Born: Nov. 22, 1983. **Ht.:** 6-1. **Wt.:** 180. **Bats:** L. **Throws:** L. **Career Transactions:** Signed out of Mexico by Angels, Jan. 27, 2003. **Signed by:** Clay Daniel.

International scouting supervisor Clay Daniel uncovered Lopez playing for Monterrey in the Mexican League, the same team on which the Diamondbacks found Erubiel Durazo and Oscar Villarreal. After a solid debut in the Rookie-level Arizona League, Lopez began 2004 in extended spring training. He hurt his right shoulder diving back into a base on a pickoff play, but was summoned to the Midwest League once he recovered. Shortly thereafter, Lopez officially emerged as a prospect. He has an effortless, fluid lefthanded stroke. His hands work free and easy, generating excellent bat speed through the hitting zone and line drives to all fields. His power is still developing, but Angels scouts believe he projects to have at least average pop once his wiry body fills out. Lopez needs to concentrate on hitting the top half of the baseball and improve his plate discipline, especially with offspeed stuff out of the zone. He's a below-average runner but isn't a baseclogger. He has soft hands and good actions at first base, though he needs to improve his range and at times rushes the exchange on his throws. Lopez should open the season in high Class A.

Year	Club (League)	Class	AVG	G	AB	R	H	2B	3B	HR	RBI	BB	SO	SB	OBP	SLG
2002	Monterrey (Mex)	AAA	.417	4	12	0	5	0	0	0	2	0	2	0	.417	.417
2003	Angels (AZL)	R	.301	44	173	26	52	12	3	2	23	16	46	3	.360	.439
2004	Cedar Rapids (Mid)	A	.314	64	236	34	74	14	3	9	35	19	65	6	.368	.513
MINOR LEAGUE TOTALS			.311	112	421	60	131	26	6	11	60	35	113	9	.365	.480

13 Joe Saunders, lhp

Born: June 16, 1981. **Ht.:** 6-2. **Wt.:** 200. **Bats:** L. **Throws:** L. **School:** Virginia Tech. **Career Transactions:** Selected by Angels in first round (12th overall) of 2002 draft; signed June 10, 2002. **Signed by:** Chris McAlpin.

After signing a predraft deal with a $1.825 million bonus in 2002, Saunders lasted through his first summer before joining a growing list of Angels pitching prospects on the disabled list. He had tears in his rotator cuff and labrum, though he managed to avoid surgery with an aggressive rehabilitation program. Last year, he showed he had regained the velocity as well as the movement on his pitches. His best pitch is a sinking fastball that sits at 89-90 mph, rising as high as 93 mph. He has slightly above-average control, working his fastball and cutter in and out and keeping them down in the zone. Saunders has a good feel for a plus changeup that he disguises well by maintaining his arm speed. He continued to struggle to craft a consistent breaking ball, however. He was hittable in his comeback, especially after a late-July promotion to Double-A. He'll likely begin this season back in Arkansas and will need another year and a half in the minors before he's ready to contribute in Anaheim.

Year	Club (League)	Class	W	L	ERA	G	GS	CG	SV	IP	H	R	ER	HR	BB	SO	AVG
2002	Provo (Pio)	R	2	1	3.62	8	8	0	0	32	40	19	13	1	11	21	.305
	Cedar Rapids (Mid)	A	3	1	1.88	5	5	0	0	29	16	7	6	2	9	27	.168
2003	Did not play—Injured																
2004	Rancho Cucamonga (Cal)	A	9	7	3.41	19	19	0	0	106	106	49	40	13	23	76	.261
	Arkansas (TL)	AA	4	3	5.77	8	8	0	0	39	51	26	25	5	14	25	.333
MINOR LEAGUE TOTALS			18	12	3.68	40	40	0	0	206	213	101	84	21	57	149	.271

14 Sean Rodriguez, 2b/ss

Born: April 26, 1985. **Ht.:** 6-0. **Wt.:** 180. **Bats:** R. **Throws:** R. **School:** Braddock HS, Miami. **Career Transactions:** Selected by Angels in third round of 2003 draft; signed June 4, 2003. **Signed by:** Mike Silvestri.

Playing in a system loaded with premium shortstop prospects, Rodriguez managed to improve his standing with a solid all-around 2004 season. He held his own for three months as a teenager in low Class A before scorching the Rookie-level Pioneer League for the rest of the summer. He was league MVP and led Provo to the championship with his bat, defensive versatility and makeup. Much like Casey Kotchman, Rodriguez shows a feel for the game you'd expect from someone who comes from a baseball family. His father Johnny is a minor league hitting coach for the Marlins, while his brother Robert catches in the Nationals organization. Rodriguez' tools play up because of his feel for the game. He has advanced plate discipline for his age, and his production should improve once he learns to use the entire field. He's aggressive and has a tendency to get pull-happy, especially after he hits home runs. Rodriguez is a fringe-average runner, which has led to questions about his future defensive home. His arm plays well and he gets to his share of balls at shortstop, though his range is better up the middle than to his right. Realistically, with Orlando Cabrera signed to a four-year contract in the majors and Erick Aybar and Brandon Wood ahead of him in the minors, Rodriguez will find another position. In deference to Wood when they were teammates at Cedar Rapids, Rodriguez saw time at second base, third base and the outfield. He'll likely return there to open 2005. The Angels will continue to develop his skills at shortstop for now, but a move to second base is likely in the near future.

Year	Club (League)	Class	AVG	G	AB	R	H	2B	3B	HR	RBI	BB	SO	SB	OBP	SLG
2003	Angels (AZL)	R	.269	54	216	30	58	8	5	2	25	14	37	11	.332	.380
2004	Provo (Pio)	R	.338	64	225	64	76	14	4	10	55	51	62	9	.486	.569
	Cedar Rapids (Mid)	A	.250	57	196	35	49	8	4	4	17	18	54	14	.333	.393
MINOR LEAGUE TOTALS			.287	175	637	129	183	30	13	16	97	83	153	34	.392	.451

15 Dustin Moseley, rhp

Born: Dec. 26, 1981. **Ht.:** 6-4. **Wt.:** 190. **Bats:** R. **Throws:** R. **School:** Arkansas HS, Texarkana, Ark. **Career Transactions:** Selected by Reds in first round (34th overall) of 2000 draft; signed Nov. 22, 2000 . . . Traded by Reds to Angels for RHP Ramon Ortiz, Dec. 14, 2004. **Signed by:** Jim Gonzales (Reds).

The Angels had no intention of picking up Ramon Ortiz' $5.5 million contract option for 2005 and considered nontendering him rather than go to arbitration with him. Instead, they were able to trade him to the Reds for Moseley in December. Moseley doesn't have a true out pitch, which limits his ceiling, but his pitching savvy has allowed him to rise quickly through the minors. He relies on his ability to locate his 88-92 mph fastball, cutter, curveball and changeup. Lower back problems cost him a few starts in 2004, but he otherwise has been durable throughout his pro career. Moseley is headed for Triple-A in 2005 but could get a callup if injuries create a hole in Anaheim's rotation.

Year	Club (League)	Class	W	L	ERA	G	GS	CG	SV	IP	H	R	ER	HR	BB	SO	AVG
2001	Dayton (Mid)	A	10	8	4.20	25	25	0	0	148	158	83	69	10	42	108	.271
2002	Stockton (Cal)	A	6	3	2.74	14	14	2	0	89	60	28	27	3	21	80	.188
	Chattanooga (SL)	AA	5	6	4.13	13	13	0	0	81	91	47	37	5	37	52	.293
2003	Chattanooga (SL)	AA	5	6	3.83	18	18	0	0	113	116	55	48	10	28	73	.264
	Louisville (IL)	AAA	2	3	2.70	8	8	0	0	50	46	19	15	5	14	27	.245
2004	Louisville (IL)	AAA	2	4	4.65	12	12	0	0	72	78	38	37	7	34	48	.286
	Chattanooga (SL)	AA	3	2	2.66	8	8	0	0	47	33	16	14	4	10	40	.196
MINOR LEAGUE TOTALS			33	32	3.71	98	98	2	0	599	582	286	247	44	186	428	.256

16 Maicer Izturis, ss/2b

Born: Sept. 12, 1980. **Ht.:** 5-8. **Wt.:** 150. **Bats:** B. **Throws:** R. **Career Transactions:** Signed out of Venezuela by Indians, April 1, 1998 . . . Traded by Indians with OF Ryan Church to Expos for LHP Scott Stewart, Jan. 5, 2004. **Signed by:** Luis Aponte (Indians).

Included by the Indians in a trade with the Expos for Scott Stewart in January 2004, Izturis responded with a breakthrough season. He led all minor league switch-hitters with a .338 average, and he ranked fifth among all batters in making contact (17.8 plate appearances per strikeout), earning his first major league callup. He seemed to be a candidate to start for the renamed Nationals in 2005, but new general manager Jim Bowden signed Cristian Guzman to a four-year, $16.8 million contract before dispatching Izturis and Juan Rivera to Anaheim for Jose Guillen. The younger brother of Dodgers shortstop Cesar Izturis, Maicer excels at putting the bat on the ball and is a good bunter. But he has little power and won't develop any, so he'll have to prove his 2004 average and on-base percentage were no fluke if he's to play regularly in the big leagues. Hitting a soft .206 for Montreal didn't dispel doubters. Izturis' speed is just average, so he's not much of a basestealing threat. He stands out most on defense—though he's not as good as his brother—with good range and an average arm. With all the shortstops in Anaheim, his best chance of finding regular work in the majors is as a utilityman.

Year	Club (League)	Class	AVG	G	AB	R	H	2B	3B	HR	RBI	BB	SO	SB	OBP	SLG
1998	Burlington (Appy)	R	.290	55	217	33	63	8	2	2	33	17	32	16	.342	.373
1999	Columbus (SAL)	A	.300	57	220	46	66	5	3	4	23	20	28	14	.357	.405
2000	Columbus (SAL)	A	.276	10	29	4	8	1	0	0	1	3	3	0	.344	.310
2001	Kinston (Car)	A	.240	114	433	47	104	16	6	1	39	31	81	32	.300	.312
2002	Kinston (Car)	A	.262	58	233	28	61	13	1	1	30	24	26	24	.332	.339
	Akron (EL)	AA	.277	67	253	34	70	12	7	0	32	17	28	8	.326	.379
2003	Akron (EL)	AA	.280	53	218	31	61	11	5	1	20	24	23	14	.351	.390
	Buffalo (IL)	AAA	.262	85	301	43	79	16	4	2	29	24	28	14	.317	.362
2004	Montreal (NL)	MAJ	.206	32	107	10	22	5	2	1	4	10	20	4	.286	.318
	Edmonton (PCL)	AAA	.338	99	376	65	127	19	2	3	36	57	30	14	.428	.423
MAJOR LEAGUE TOTALS			.206	32	107	10	22	5	2	1	4	10	20	4	.286	.318
MINOR LEAGUE TOTALS			.280	598	2280	321	639	101	30	14	243	217	279	136	.345	.369

17 Rafael Rodriguez, rhp

Born: Sept. 24, 1984. **Ht.:** 6-1. **Wt.:** 170. **Bats:** R. **Throws:** R. **Career Transactions:** Signed out of Dominican Republic by Angels, July 20, 2001. **Signed by:** Leo Perez.

After signing out of the Dominican for $780,000, Rodriguez has alternately dazzled the Angels with his potential and frustrated them with his inconsistency. He barely made any impression in 2004, making just seven starts while being shut down with a tender arm on two separate occasions. His physical problems resulted from his violent mechanics. He rushes through his delivery and struggles to stay online and balanced. He also tucks his head and bounces out of his motion, causing stress on his arm as well as poor control. If Rodriguez can refine his mechanics, he could harness his power stuff and regain his status as one of the organization's most promising pitching prospects. He has hit 97 mph in the past, though he pitched at 91 and topped out at 94 last year. He also has flashed a hard 87 mph slider with late bite. He doesn't have great feel for his breaking ball, which lapses into a slower slurve at times. Rodriguez made some progress with his changeup but it also remains inconsistent. If he can temper his delivery and realize the futility of trying to strike out each batter, Rodriguez will have a far greater chance of reaching his considerable ceiling. He's headed back to low Class A for the third straight year, but the good news is that he's still just 20.

Year	Club (League)	Class	W	L	ERA	G	GS	CG	SV	IP	H	R	ER	HR	BB	SO	AVG
2002	Angels (AZL)	R	2	1	3.99	8	8	0	0	38	37	19	17	4	20	50	.255
	Provo (Pio)	R	1	1	5.96	6	6	0	0	26	26	17	17	3	14	25	.268
2003	Cedar Rapids (Mid)	A	10	11	4.31	26	26	1	0	144	129	85	69	7	59	100	.236
2004	Cedar Rapids (Mid)	A	1	5	6.48	7	7	0	0	33	36	27	24	5	19	36	.267
MINOR LEAGUE TOTALS			14	18	4.74	47	47	1	0	241	228	148	127	19	112	211	.247

18 Jake Woods, lhp

Born: Sept. 3, 1981. **Ht.:** 6-1. **Wt.:** 190. **Bats:** L. **Throws:** L. **School:** Bakersfield (Calif.) JC. **Career Transactions:** Selected by Angels in third round of 2001 draft; signed June 13, 2001. **Signed by:** Bobby DeJardin.

Originally projected as a situational reliever, Woods continues to make a case for remaining in the rotation, leading Angels farmhands with 15 victories in 2004. He learned to pitch with less finesse and more confidence in Double-A, allowing two or fewer earned runs in 11 of his 14 starts at Arkansas. He doesn't have a plus pitch, but his fastball sits between 87-91 mph and gained more movement last year. He also improved his command of his heater, helping him set up a good change. When Anaheim drafted him in the third round out of Bakersfield (Calif.) JC in 2001, his hammer curveball had the makings of an out pitch. But he has lost some feel for his curve and will need to regain that to make it as a big league starter. When Woods doesn't control his fastball, he gets hit hard, as frequently was the case following his promotion to Triple-A. He'll return to Salt Lake and needs at least another full season in the minors before he's ready to contribute in Anaheim.

Year	Club (League)	Class	W	L	ERA	G	GS	CG	SV	IP	H	R	ER	HR	BB	SO	AVG
2001	Provo (Pio)	R	4	3	5.29	15	14	1	0	65	70	41	38	6	29	84	.275
2002	Cedar Rapids (Mid)	A	10	5	3.05	27	27	1	0	153	128	66	52	12	54	121	.228
2003	Rancho Cucamonga (Cal)	A	12	7	3.99	28	28	2	0	171	178	90	76	9	54	109	.270
2004	Salt Lake (PCL)	AAA	6	4	6.07	15	14	1	0	83	108	67	56	13	42	60	.312
	Arkansas (TL)	AA	9	2	2.70	14	14	1	0	90	86	29	27	5	19	60	.253
MINOR LEAGUE TOTALS			41	21	3.99	99	97	6	0	562	570	293	249	45	198	434	.264

19 Kevin Jepsen, rhp

Born: July 26, 1984. **Ht.:** 6-3. **Wt.:** 200. **Bats:** R. **Throws:** R. **School:** Bishop Manogue HS, Sparks, Nev. **Career Transactions:** Selected by Angels in second round of 2002 draft; signed July 10, 2002. **Signed by:** Todd Blyleven.

Jepsen has one of the best arms in the system, but injuries derailed him in each of his first two full seasons. He earned an assignment to low Class A as an 18-year-old with an impressive spring training in 2003, but a tender elbow ended his season after just 10 starts. He had surgery to remove bone chips and returned with a strong performance in low Class A, only to go down with a torn labrum at the end of the season. He had surgery to repair his right shoulder and could be ready to begin pitching again by spring training. When he comes back, the Angels will try to refine his laborious delivery. If he can develop an easier arm action, he'll be able to repeat his arm stroke more readily, which should help his command and his health. He led the Midwest League in walks last year. His stuff is undeniable. He owns a heavy 94-96 mph fastball that maxed out at 99 last slummer. His high-80s slider gives him a second power pitch, though it's inconsistent. His changeup is rudimentary at best. He'll open 2005 in extended spring training as he recovers from his latest setback.

Year	Club (League)	Class	W	L	ERA	G	GS	CG	SV	IP	H	R	ER	HR	BB	SO	AVG
2002	Angels (AZL)	R	1	3	6.84	8	5	0	0	26	29	22	20	3	12	19	.274
2003	Cedar Rapids (Mid)	A	6	3	2.65	10	10	0	0	51	32	24	15	2	28	42	.180
2004	Cedar Rapids (Mid)	A	8	10	3.43	27	27	1	0	144	122	68	55	6	77	136	.228
MINOR LEAGUE TOTALS			15	16	3.65	45	42	1	0	222	183	114	90	11	117	197	.223

20 Nick Adenhart, rhp

Born: Aug. 24, 1986. **Ht.:** 6-4. **Wt.:** 190. **Bats:** R. **Throws:** R. **School:** Williamsport (Md.) HS. **Career Transactions:** Selected by Angels in 14th round of 2004 draft; signed July 26, 2004. **Signed by:** Dan Radcliff.

Baseball America's 2003 Youth Player of the Year, Adenhart entered last spring as the consensus top prospect in the high school draft class. He opened his senior season with a seven-inning, 15-strikeout perfect game. His stock had started to slip ever so slightly by May, and then he blew out his elbow. After he had Tommy John surgery days before the draft, he seemed destined to attend college at North Carolina. But first-year area scout Dan Radcliff pushed first-year scouting director Eddie Bane to gamble on Adenhart, and Anaheim persuaded him to sign for a 14th-round-record $710,000 bonus. Prior to the injury, he showed dominant stuff and an advanced feel for pitching. He pitched at 90-93 mph and spun a tight,

12-to-6 curveball with excellent depth. He showed a good feel for his changeup and understood how to set up hitters. His cross-body delivery and rigid landing added stress to his elbow, though his arm works free and easy. A diligent worker, Adenhart has embraced his rehabilitation routine. He spent the offseason attending classes at Arizona State while working with Angels doctors and trainers at the club's base in Mesa, Ariz. Given the track record of Tommy John comebacks, Anaheim is confident he'll make a complete recovery. He might not make his pro debut until 2006, though he could see time in Rookie ball late this year.

Year	Club (League)	Class	W	L	ERA	G	GS	CG	SV	IP	H	R	ER	HR	BB	SO	AVG
2004	Did not play—Injured																

21 Warner Madrigal, of

Born: March 21, 1984. **Ht.:** 6-0. **Wt.:** 190. **Bats:** R. **Throws:** R. **Career Transactions:** Signed out of Dominican Republic by Angels, July 21, 2001. **Signed by:** Leo Perez.

After pummeling Pioneer League pitching in 2003, Madrigal was injured while taking a swing in the first game last season. He had surgery to remove the hook of the hamate bone below his left wrist and returned in time to play in August. Former scouting director Donny Rowland and international scouting supervisor Clay Daniel made several trips to the Angels' Dominican academy to scout Madrigal and signed him for $150,000. He has two plus tools in his arm and power, while his foot speed and defensive ability rank below average and his approach at the plate needs refinement. He draws physical comparisons to Albert Belle because of his thick body and swing mechanics. Madrigal has good plate coverage and drives balls out of the park to all fields. Though he's a good fastball hitter, he could struggle at the upper levels of the minors if he doesn't learn better pitch recognition and shorten his stroke. He makes routine plays in right field but doesn't have much range. Madrigal likely will open at low Class A in 2005, a pivotal year in his development.

Year	Club (League)	Class	AVG	G	AB	R	H	2B	3B	HR	RBI	BB	SO	SB	OBP	SLG
2001	Angels (DSL)	R	.181	22	72	5	13	5	0	0	8	0	30	0	.213	.250
2002	Angels (DSL)	R	.229	42	140	22	32	5	3	4	23	10	42	5	.312	.393
2003	Provo (Pio)	R	.369	70	279	75	103	28	2	9	51	12	58	2	.394	.581
2004	Cedar Rapids (Mid)	A	.275	26	91	10	25	3	1	2	10	7	24	1	.330	.396
MINOR LEAGUE TOTALS			.297	160	582	112	173	41	6	15	92	29	154	8	.342	.466

22 Anthony Whittington, lhp

Born: Oct. 9, 1984. **Ht.:** 6-5. **Wt.:** 220. **Bats:** L. **Throws:** L. **School:** Buffalo HS, Putnam, W. Va. **Career Transactions:** Selected by Angels in second round of 2003 draft; signed July 12, 2003. **Signed by:** Tom Burns.

Whittington threw four no-hitters as a high school senior and was the top prospect in West Virginia, but he's had little success as a pro. He was overworked in high school, and some scouts have compared him to Arthur Rhodes, another power lefthander who had a heavy prep workload without much formal instruction, which reinforces bad habits. Whittington remains a raw thrower who lacks much feel for pitching. He's still ironing out his mechanics and struggles to repeat his delivery and arm slot. He's too stiff and rigid through his windup, affecting his command. He has a live arm and a durable frame, though. He pitches between 88-92 mph and has flashed mid-90s heat. His inconsistent, slurvy breaking ball has good bite at times, but varies in break and effectiveness. His changeup still needs a lot of work. Whittington has considerable upside if he can learn to harness his stuff. He pitched well in instructional league but remains a project. He should finally make his full-season debut this year, his third pro season.

Year	Club (League)	Class	W	L	ERA	G	GS	CG	SV	IP	H	R	ER	HR	BB	SO	AVG
2003	Angels (AZL)	R	0	3	8.03	9	5	0	0	25	31	24	22	1	17	20	.320
2004	Angels (AZL)	R	1	1	0.64	3	3	0	0	14	14	3	1	0	6	15	.269
	Provo (Pio)	R	1	3	8.35	11	11	0	0	37	57	45	34	2	36	29	.373
MINOR LEAGUE TOTALS			2	7	6.81	23	19	0	0	75	102	72	57	3	59	64	.346

23 Nick Gorneault, of

Born: April 19, 1979. **Ht.:** 6-3. **Wt.:** 200. **Bats:** R. **Throws:** R. **School:** University of Massachusetts. **Career Transactions:** Selected by Angels in 19th round of 2001 draft; signed June 7, 2001. **Signed by:** Jon Bunnell.

Despite an impressive career at Massachusetts, Gorneault never wowed scouts with his tools. Former Angels scout Jon Bunnell (now with the Mets) first took notice when Gorneault homered at Fenway Park in the annual Beanpot Tournament as a sophomore. Gorneault's unorthodox swing is difficult to repeat and is the main reason scouts are slow to embrace him as a legitimate prospect, but Anaheim points to his tremendous bat speed that produces sharp line drives. Roving batting instructor Ty Van Burkleo has tweaked Gorneault's setup without affecting his power potential. He looks bad at the plate at times, as he chases pitches out of the zone and needs to be more efficient in his approach. The rest of his game is solid, as he has average speed, makes good reads in right field and has an accurate arm. While he has average arm strength, it's not a prototypical right-field arm strength. A bit of a tweener, he'll need to boost his power numbers if he's going to breakthrough as an everyday corner outfielder. When Gorneault hits balls well, they tend to have topspin and lack high trajectory, banging off walls instead of carrying over them. He plays with fervor and works hard. He homered in his first game at Triple-A Salt Lake after a September callup in 2004 and will open this season there.

Year	Club (League)	Class	AVG	G	AB	R	H	2B	3B	HR	RBI	BB	SO	SB	OBP	SLG
2001	Provo (Pio)	R	.315	54	168	38	53	12	4	6	30	11	65	5	.373	.542
2002	Cedar Rapids (Mid)	A	.289	103	346	60	100	17	7	10	53	30	106	12	.346	.465
2003	Rancho Cucamonga (Cal)	A	.321	97	374	67	120	36	2	14	72	20	82	11	.363	.540
	Arkansas (TL)	AA	.345	29	110	19	38	6	4	2	19	8	25	2	.395	.527
2004	Arkansas (TL)	AA	.281	130	495	91	139	28	4	21	81	45	128	7	.341	.481
	Salt Lake (PCL)	AAA	.316	6	19	4	6	1	0	1	5	1	7	0	.381	.526
MINOR LEAGUE TOTALS			.302	419	1512	279	456	100	21	54	260	115	413	37	.355	.503

24 Reggie Willits, of

Born: May 30, 1981. **Ht.:** 5-11. **Wt.:** 185. **Bats:** B. **Throws:** R. **School:** University of Oklahoma. **Career Transactions:** Selected by Angels in seventh round of 2003 draft; signed June 4, 2003. **Signed by:** Kevin Ham.

While the Angels boast one of baseball's deepest systems, they're surprisingly bereft of impact-potential outfielders. Former scouting director Donny Rowland planned to address that weakness in the 2003 draft, targeting outfielders Chris Lubanski, Lastings Milledge, Brian Anderson and Brad Snyder—but all were gone by the time Anaheim's first pick arrived at No. 23. Changing plans, Rowland spent mid-round picks on Blake Balkcom (fifth round), Willits (seventh) and Stantrel Smith (16th; he signed as a draft-and-follow in 2004). Willits is the best of that group, offering an intriguing combination of tools and skill. His sister Wendi played basketball in the WNBA and Willits is similarly gifted athletically. He's a solid-average runner with good instincts on the bases. He led the Big 12 Conference with 37 steals as a senior at Oklahoma in 2003 and handles the bat well from both sides of the plate. To utilize his wheels, he works walks and employs primarily a slap approach. His power is mainly shooting the ball into the gaps, though he tends to get around balls when batting lefthanded and needs to keep his hands in better. He also must make more consistent contact. Willits is a sound center fielder with good range and a slightly above-average arm, but he can improve his reads off the bat. He has good makeup, is consumed with the game and was one of the organization's most pleasant surprises in 2004. He'll hold down a spot in the Double-A outfield this year.

Year	Club (League)	Class	AVG	G	AB	R	H	2B	3B	HR	RBI	BB	SO	SB	OBP	SLG
2003	Provo (Pio)	R	.300	59	230	53	69	14	4	4	27	37	52	14	.410	.448
2004	Rancho Cucamonga (Cal)	A	.285	135	526	99	150	17	5	5	52	73	112	45	.374	.365
MINOR LEAGUE TOTALS			.290	194	756	152	219	31	9	9	79	110	164	59	.385	.390

25 Bob Zimmermann, rhp

Born: Nov. 17, 1981. **Ht.:** 6-5. **Wt.:** 225. **Bats:** R. **Throws:** R. **School:** Southwest Missouri State University. **Career Transactions:** Selected by Angels in fourth round of 2003 draft; signed June 26, 2003. **Signed by:** Brian Bridges.

Zimmermann established the career saves mark at Southwest Missouri State in his first two years with the Bears, then moved into the rotation and helped the program earn its first-ever College World Series berth in 2003. Though his inconsistency caused his draft stock to suffer somewhat, area scout Brian Bridges (now with the Marlins) remained high on Zimmermann and persuaded the Angels to take him in the fourth round. His two-pitch arsenal and varying arm angles gave low Class A batters fits last summer. Zimmermann's heater runs between 91-95 mph and features heavy, sinking action. His secondary stuff varies in quality, however, because he'll pitch at high three-quarters, true three-quarters and sidearm angles. What he gains in deception, he sacrifices in control. Zimmermann's slider is his No. 2 pitch, and he also worked on a changeup and splitter in instructional league. He's aggressive and is resilient enough to pitch on consecutive days, which should allow him to serve in a variety of relief roles in the future, perhaps even as a big league closer. Zimmermann likely will spend 2005 in high Class A, though the Angels would like to keep him and Mitch Arnold on different clubs so both could continue to close.

Year	Club (League)	Class	W	L	ERA	G	GS	CG	SV	IP	H	R	ER	HR	BB	SO	AVG
2003	Provo (Pio)	R	4	2	4.50	11	10	0	0	48	57	29	24	4	8	37	.285
2004	Cedar Rapids (Mid)	A	4	6	2.26	53	0	0	24	68	48	21	17	3	21	82	.202
MINOR LEAGUE TOTALS			8	8	3.19	64	10	0	24	116	105	50	41	7	29	119	.240

26 Tim Bittner, lhp

Born: June 9, 1980. **Ht.:** 6-2. **Wt.:** 200. **Bats:** L. **Throws:** L. **School:** Marist University. **Career Transactions:** Selected by White Sox in 10th round of 2001 draft; signed June 8, 2001 . . . Traded by White Sox with RHP Scott Dunn and RHP Gary Glover to Angels for RHP Doug Nickle and LHP Scott Schoeneweis, July 29, 2003. **Signed by:** Ken Stauffer/John Tumminia (White Sox).

The least-known player in the 2003 Scott Schoeneweis trade with the White Sox, Bittner made an immediate impression with his new organization, returning to the rotation and going 5-0, 0.26 in six high Class A starts. A two-way star at Marist and the highest-drafted player in school history, he took a regular turn in the Double-A rotation last year before being shut down with back pain in August. Bittner's fastball command is his greatest asset. He works to both sides of the plate and knows how to set up hitters. In terms of velocity, his fastball is slightly below average at 87-90 mph. He throws two breaking balls, a tight 80-83 mph slider that has the potential to be a plus pitch and a sweeping curveball that's effective against lefties. He's making progress with his changeup and needs to do a better job of throwing strikes with his secondary pitches. His back was healthy during the offseason, and the Angels plan on sending him back to Double-A. His ultimate role has yet to be defined.

Year	Club (League)	Class	W	L	ERA	G	GS	CG	SV	IP	H	R	ER	HR	BB	SO	AVG
2001	Bristol (Appy)	R	6	1	1.10	8	8	1	0	49	34	14	6	0	12	53	.190
2001	Kannapolis (SAL)	A	0	3	4.43	4	4	0	0	20	21	18	10	1	9	15	.269
2002	Kannapolis (SAL)	A	5	13	4.58	29	29	0	0	157	166	98	80	10	67	123	.274
2003	Kannapolis (SAL)	A	4	4	3.40	10	10	1	0	50	45	24	19	4	26	45	.242
	Winston-Salem (Car)	A	3	3	3.60	17	0	0	1	30	18	13	12	3	12	23	.176
	Rancho Cucamonga (Cal)	A	5	0	0.28	6	6	1	0	33	18	5	1	0	14	28	.161
2004	Arkansas (TL)	AA	8	6	4.46	22	22	0	0	119	113	65	59	10	57	82	.251
MINOR LEAGUE TOTALS			31	30	3.67	96	79	3	1	459	415	237	187	28	197	369	.242

27 Andrew Toussaint, 3b/of

Born: Oct. 24, 1982. **Ht.:** 6-2. **Wt.:** 175. **Bats:** R. **Throws:** R. **School:** Southern University. **Career Transactions:** Selected by Angels in 13th round of 2004 draft; signed June 8, 2004. **Signed by:** Chad MacDonald.

Toussaint was drafted by the Dodgers in the 10th round out of high school, but didn't sign and spent two years at Cal Poly before transferring to Southern in 2003. An all-Southwestern Athletic Conference pick in each of his two seasons with the Jaguars, he led the league with 14 homers last spring. The Angels drafted both Toussaint and Southern teammate Joshua LeBlanc, and they played key roles in Provo's Pioneer League championship run. Toussaint showed off his most impressive asset—his lightning-quick bat—in a showdown with Diamondbacks prospect Marion Duran last summer, turning around a 97 mph fastball and driving it for an opposite-field home run. His present power already grades as a plus, and he has slightly above-average arm strength and average speed. Toussaint spent most of his college career in the outfield, and he struggled at third base in the Cape Cod League in the summer of 2003 and at Southern last spring. Those difficulties continued as a pro, as he committed 13 errors in 27 games at the hot corner. He lacks soft hands, making a return to the outfield likely. Following the draft, he had two bouts with the flu and lost some weight. Anaheim can't wait to see him at full strength this year in low Class A.

Year	Club (League)	Class	AVG	G	AB	R	H	2B	3B	HR	RBI	BB	SO	SB	OBP	SLG
2004	Provo (Pio)	R	.289	55	194	39	56	12	2	12	52	34	68	6	.411	.557
MINOR LEAGUE TOTALS			.289	55	194	39	56	12	2	12	52	34	68	6	.411	.557

28 Bobby Cassevah, rhp

Born: Sept. 11, 1985. **Ht.:** 6-3. **Wt.:** 195. **Bats:** R. **Throws:** R. **School:** Pace (Fla.) HS. **Career Transactions:** Selected by Angels in 34th round of 2004 draft; signed Aug. 3, 2004. **Signed by:** Tom Kotchman.

Knowing first-round pick Jered Weaver would be a chore to sign, scouting director Eddie Bane took a number of calculated risks on highly regarded but highly unsignable players late in the 2004 draft. Corner infielder Mark Trumbo (18th round, $1.425 million) and right-hander Nick Adenhart (14th round, $710,000) were the most prominent members of that group, which also included Cassevah. He projected as a third-rounder before spraining his elbow as a quarterback during spring football practice in high school in 2003. He had Tommy John surgery in October 2003, and though he didn't pitch as a senior, Louisiana

State offered him a scholarship. Undeterred, the Angels took Cassevah in the 34th round and after Bane and area scout/minor league manager Tom Kotchman saw that he had regained enough velocity and feel, they signed him for $175,000. Cassevah continued his rehab in instructional league, where he struck out two of the first three batters he faced. Pitching at about 80 percent, he was up to 87 mph and showed a breaking ball with three-quarter tilt. He also threw a changeup. Most significant, his control and savvy were similar to what he showed prior to surgery. Cassevah was aggressive in his rehab, an indication of his competitive makeup and work ethic. He's slated to begin the season in extended spring training before making his pro debut at Provo.

Year	Club (League)	Class	W	L	ERA	G	GS	CG	SV	IP	H	R	ER	HR	BB	SO	AVG
2004	Did not play—Signed 2005 contract																

29 Mike Napoli, c/1b

Born: Oct. 31, 1981. **Ht.:** 6-0. **Wt.:** 200. **Bats:** R. **Throws:** R. **School:** Flanagan HS, Pembroke Pines, Fla. **Career Transactions:** Selected by Angels in 17th round of 2000 draft; signed June 21, 2000. **Signed by:** Todd Claus.

After a torn labrum ruined his 2003 season, Napoli returned to high Class A and enjoyed a breakthrough year. He led the California League with 29 homers and 118 RBIs after totaling just 20 homers and 101 RBIs over his first four seasons. He also topped the Cal League in walks. Napoli has a polished, professional hitting approach and obvious power. He has natural loft in his swing and drives the ball well from center to the opposite field. He gets in trouble when he tries to lift and pull the ball, and he needs to lay off high fastballs. He'll always produce more for power than for average. The biggest question surrounding Napoli is whether he'll be able to catch at higher levels. His catch-and-throw skills are adequate, but his flexibility and footwork are poor. He doesn't move well behind the plate—or on the bases, for that matter—and several Cal League observers didn't think he'd be able to serve as a backup catcher in the majors. Napoli also saw time at first base last year. He has arthritis in his nonthrowing shoulder that could plague his hitting if it worsens. He'll get his first taste of Double-A in 2005 and could fill a DH role if his catching doesn't improve.

Year	Club (League)	Class	AVG	G	AB	R	H	2B	3B	HR	RBI	BB	SO	SB	OBP	SLG
2000	Butte (Pio)	R	.231	10	26	3	6	2	0	0	3	8	8	1	.400	.308
2001	Rancho Cuca. (Cal)	A	.200	7	20	3	4	0	0	1	4	8	11	0	.429	.350
	Cedar Rapids (Mid)	A	.232	43	155	23	36	10	1	5	18	24	54	3	.341	.406
2002	Cedar Rapids (Mid)	A	.251	106	362	57	91	19	1	10	50	62	104	6	.362	.392
2003	Rancho Cucamonga (Cal)	A	.267	47	165	28	44	10	1	4	26	23	32	5	.364	.412
2004	Rancho Cucamonga (Cal)	A	.282	132	482	94	136	29	4	29	118	88	166	9	.394	.539
MINOR LEAGUE TOTALS			.262	345	1210	208	317	70	7	49	219	213	375	24	.374	.453

30 Mitchell Arnold, rhp

Born: Jan. 31, 1982. **Ht.:** 6-9. **Wt.:** 230. **Bats:** R. **Throws:** R. **School:** Modesto (Calif.) JC. **Career Transactions:** Selected by Angels in 23rd round of 2001 draft; signed May 14, 2002. **Signed by:** Jeff Scholzen/Todd Blyleven.

Growing up in Saratoga, Wyo., Arnold was more interested in rodeo than baseball, and he also was recruited to play football. The Angels tabbed him as a draft-and-follow out of New Mexico Junior College in 2001, and he transferred to Modesto before signing in May 2002. Following two uninspiring seasons in the Arizona League, Arnold blossomed last season. He made strides with his control and sharpened his stuff. He went to Triple-A in May as an emergency callup, and returned to extended spring training and committed himself to throwing strikes. Arnold joined Provo a month later and led the Pioneer League in saves. He learned to stay on top of his pitches, pitching downhill from his towering 6-foot-9 frame at 92-93 mph. His fastball peaks at 97 and he successfully kept it down in the zone. He improved the control of his out pitch, an 88-91 mph splitter. He also has a slider. Arnold has good mound presence, though he works too quickly at times, causing his mechanics to go awry. He can be effectively wild and make young hitters uncomfortable, but he'll have to add more polish at higher levels. Arnold profiles as a reliever and embraced his role as a closer, though he'll need to build off his breakout campaign. He'll pitch in Class A in 2005, possibly starting at Cedar Rapids if Bob Zimmermann goes to Rancho Cucamonga as expected.

Year	Club (League)	Class	W	L	ERA	G	GS	CG	SV	IP	H	R	ER	HR	BB	SO	AVG
2002	Angels (AZL)	R	0	1	7.54	15	2	0	0	23	29	34	19	1	29	19	.312
2003	Angels (AZL)	R	1	3	3.86	21	0	0	4	23	17	14	10	0	19	19	.205
2004	Salt Lake (PCL)	AAA	0	0	13.50	4	0	0	0	7	15	10	10	1	4	2	.455
	Provo (Pio)	R	2	0	2.48	25	0	0	13	33	12	10	9	1	14	41	.112
MINOR LEAGUE TOTALS			3	4	5.06	65	2	0	17	85	73	68	48	3	66	81	.231

ARIZONA
DIAMONDBACKS

BY **KEVIN GOLDSTEIN**

BILL MITCHELL

The Diamondbacks sent mixed messages this offseason after a miserable 2004 campaign. Just three years removed from a World Series title, they suffered through a rash of injuries and lost a major league-high 111 games. Fifty-two players suited up for Arizona and 13, including top prospect **Scott Hairston**, made their big league debut.

The Diamondbacks since have traded their lone superstar (Randy Johnson) and top run producer (Shea Hillenbrand). Their first choice for manager (Wally Backman) lasted just four days on the job before being fired and replaced by Bob Melvin. Then they made a splash in the free-agent market, though their two big signings were criticized for being excessive and optimistic. Troy Glaus received a four-year, $45 million deal despite playing just 149 games over the last two seasons because of injuries. Russ Ortiz, who has a career 4.00 ERA and slumped in the second half last season, got four years and $33 million. Royce Clayton, Craig Counsell and Shawn Estes also were added as stopgaps.

Though they have turned to veterans for immediate help, the Diamondbacks' future rests with their farm system, which has improved steadily over the past three years thanks to some astute drafts under scouting director Mike Rizzo. His biggest coup would be getting Florida State shortstop Stephen Drew, the top-rated position player in the 2004 draft, with the 15th overall pick—assuming Arizona can sign Drew. Once he does, he'll become the team's top prospect.

The Diamondbacks' high Class A Lancaster affiliate won Baseball America's Minor League Team of the Year award, going 43-27 in each half and reaching the California League finals despite never-ending roster turnover. Arizona's first three picks from 2003—Carlos Quentin, Conor Jackson and Jamie D'Antona—were quickly dubbed "The Three Amigos" and batted a combined .323-39-162 in 70 games before being promoted en masse to Double-A El Paso.

Seven of the top eight spots on this list are occupied by hitters, six of whom were selected in the top two rounds of the last three drafts. There's pitching on the way as well. After taking Drew and Zeringue, Arizona loaded up on college arms in the 2004 draft. Hard-throwing righthanders Garrett Mock (third round) and Ross Ohlendorf (fourth) both had a chance to go in the first round at one point.

Owning the worst record in baseball gives the Diamondbacks the first choice in the 2005 draft. While they've had a heavy focus on college players, they wouldn't shy away from a premium high school talent such as Virginia shortstop Justin Upton, whose older brother B.J. went No. 2 overall in 2002. He might be the ideal pick for a system lean on middle infielders. Lefthanded pitching is another priority, but entering the season no southpaw warranted going near the top of the draft.

TOP 30 PROSPECTS

1. Carlos Quentin, of
2. Conor Jackson, of
3. Sergio Santos, ss
4. Jon Zeringue, of
5. Greg Aquino, rhp
6. Chris Snyder, c
7. Josh Kroeger, of
8. Jamie D'Antona, 3b
9. Ramon Pena, rhp
10. Matt Chico, lhp
11. Garrett Mock, rhp
12. Koyie Hill, c
13. Brian Bruney, rhp
14. Dustin Nippert, rhp
15. Enrique Gonzalez, rhp
16. Mike Gosling, lhp
17. Jason Bulger, rhp
18. Bill Murphy, lhp
19. Carlos Gonzalez, of
20. Ross Ohlendorf, rhp
21. Marland Williams, of
22. Adam Peterson, rhp
23. Jarred Ball, of
24. Phil Avlas, c
25. A.J. Shappi, rhp
26. Chris Carter, of/1b
27. Jerome Milons, of
28. Brad Halsey, lhp
29. Lance Cormier, rhp
30. Reggie Abercrombie, of

ORGANIZATION OVERVIEW

General manager: Joe Garagiola Jr. **Farm Director:** Bob Miller. **Scouting director:** Mike Rizzo.

2004 PERFORMANCE

Class	Team	League	W	L	Pct.	Finish*	Manager(s)
Majors	Arizona	National	51	111	.315	16th (16)	Bob Brenley/Al Pedrique
Triple-A	Tucson Sidewinders	Pacific Coast	74	70	.514	7th (16)	Chip Hale
Double-A	#El Paso Diablos	Texas	48	89	.350	8th (8)	Scott Coolbaugh
High A	Lancaster JetHawks	California	86	54	.614	2nd (10)	Wally Backman
Low A	South Bend Silver Hawks	Midwest	77	63	.550	t-2nd (14)	Tony Perezchica
Short-season	Yakima Bears	Northwest	35	41	.461	7th (8)	Bill Plummer
Rookie	Missoula Osprey	Pioneer	27	46	.370	8th (8)	Jim Presley
OVERALL 2004 MINOR LEAGUE RECORD			347	363	.489	19th (30)	

*Finish in overall standings (No. of teams in league). #Affiliate will be in Tennessee (Southern) in 2005.

ORGANIZATION LEADERS

BATTING *Minimum 250 At-Bats
*AVG	Chris Carter, South Bend/Yakima	.339
R	Carlos Quentin, El Paso/Lancaster	103
H	Conor Jackson, El Paso/Lancaster	157
TB	Josh Kroeger, Tucson/El Paso	266
2B	Josh Kroeger, Tucson/El Paso	51
3B	Brian Barden, Tucson/El Paso	11
	Victor Hall, Tucson/El Paso	11
HR	Kyle Nichols, Tucson/El Paso	21
	Carlos Quentin, El Paso/Lancaster	21
RBI	Conor Jackson, El Paso/Lancaster	91
BB	Conor Jackson, El Paso/Lancaster	69
SO	Brian Barden, Tucson/El Paso	131
SB	Marland Williams, El Paso	49
*OBP	Carlos Quentin, El Paso/Lancaster	.435
*SLG	Chris Carter, South/Yakima	.590

PITCHING #Minimum 75 Innings
W	Clint Goocher, El Paso/Lancaster	15
L	Matt Chico, El Paso/South Bend	12
	Clint Goocher, El Paso/Lancaster	12
#ERA	Lance Cormier, Tucson/El Paso	2.46
G	Carlton Wells, Lancaster	71
CG	Sergio Lizarraga, Tucson/El Paso	3
SV	Jason Bulger, El Paso/Lancaster	19
IP	Clint Goocher, El Paso/Lancaster	177
BB	Chris Kinsey, South Bend	70
SO	Matt Chico, El Paso/South Bend	148

BEST TOOLS

Best Hitter for Average	Carlos Quentin
Best Power Hitter	Chris Carter
Best Strike-Zone Discipline	Conor Jackson
Fastest Baserunner	Marland Willaims
Best Athlete	Reggie Abercrombie
Best Fastball	Jason Bulger
Best Curveball	Dustin Nippert
Best Slider	Justin Wechsler
Best Changeup	Mike Gosling
Best Control	A.J. Shappi
Best Defensive Catcher	Orlando Mercado Jr.
Best Defensive Infielder	Jerry Gil
Best Infield Arm	Jerry Gil
Best Defensive Outfielder	Marland Williams
Best Outfield Arm	Carlos Gonzalez

PROJECTED 2008 LINEUP

Catcher	Chris Snyder
First Base	Conor Jackson
Second Base	Alex Cintron
Third Base	Troy Glaus
Shortstop	Sergio Santos
Left Field	Jon Zeringue
Center Field	Luis Terrero
Right Field	Carlos Quentin
No. 1 Starter	Brandon Webb
No. 2 Starter	Russ Ortiz
No. 3 Starter	Edgar Gonzalez
No. 4 Starter	Ramon Pena
No. 4 Starter	Matt Chico
Closer	Greg Aquino

LAST YEAR'S TOP 20 PROSPECTS

1. Scott Hairston, 2b	11. Luis Terrero, of
2. Sergio Santos, ss	12. Josh Kroeger, of
3. Dustin Nippert, rhp	13. Marland Williams, of
4. Chad Tracy, 3b	14. Jamie D'Antona, 3b
5. Adriano Rosario, rhp	15. Chris Snyder, c
6. Conor Jackson, of	16. Jared Doyle, lhp
7. Carlos Quentin, of	17. Brandon Medders, rhp
8. Brian Bruney, rhp	18. Matt Chico, lhp
9. Edgar Gonzalez, rhp	19. Jay Garthwaite, of
10. Mike Gosling, lhp	20. Phil Stockman, rhp

TOP PROSPECTS OF THE DECADE

Year	Player, Pos.	Current Team
1997	Travis Lee, 1b	Yankees
1998	Travis Lee, 1b	Yankees
1999	Brad Penny, rhp	Dodgers
2000	John Patterson, rhp	Nationals
2001	Alex Cintron, ss	Diamondbacks
2002	Luis Terrero, of	Diamondbacks
2003	Scott Hairston, 2b	Diamondbacks
2004	Scott Hairston, 2b	Diamondbacks

TOP DRAFT PICKS OF THE DECADE

Year	Player, Pos.	Current Team
1996	Nick Bierbrodt, lhp	Rangers
1997	Jack Cust, 1b	Orioles
1998	Darryl Conyer, of (3)	Out of baseball
1999	Corey Myers, ss	Diamondbacks
2000	Mike Schultz, rhp (2)	Diamondbacks
2001	Jason Bulger, rhp	Diamondbacks
2002	Sergio Santos, ss	Diamondbacks
2003	Conor Jackson, of	Diamondbacks
2004	*Stephen Drew, ss	Unsigned

*Unsigned as of Feb. 1.

ALL-TIME LARGEST BONUSES

Travis Lee, 1996	$10,000,000
John Patterson, 1996	$6,075,000
Byung-Hyun Kim, 1999	$2,000,000
Corey Myers, 1999	$2,000,000
Mike Gosling, 2001	$2,000,000

Arizona DIAMONDBACKS

RANK: **13**

Impact Potential: B
The Diamondbacks' future outfield should be homegrown, and the competition to get to Arizona should be fierce among the likes of mashers Carlos Quentin and Jon Zeringue, line-drive machine Josh Kroeger, speedster Marland Williams and athletic ex-Dodgers Jereme Milons and Reggie Abercrombie. More power bats are on the way with Conor Jackson and Sergio Santos, though their future positions are less certain.

Depth: C
During a tumultuous year that saw many players graduate to the big leagues, the Diamondbacks restocked to a degree through the draft and some player-for-prospect trades. There's not a future all-star in the group, but they have plenty of solid options behind the plate. The pitching depth improves measurably if Ramon Pena—the former Adriano Rosario—returns to form after missing most of a year due to visa trouble.

Depth charts prepared by John Manuel and Allan Simpson. Numbers in parentheses indicate prospect rankings.

LF
Josh Kroeger (7)
Alex Frazier
Brandon Burgess
Jay Garthwaite
Doug Devore
Noochie Varner
Jaen Centeno

CF
Marland Williams (21)
Jarred Ball (23)
Jereme Milons (27)
Reggie Abercrombie (30)

RF
Carlos Quentin (1)
Jon Zeringue (4)
Carlos Gonzalez (19)
Luis Lajara
Mike Goss
Marcus Townsend

3B
Brian Barden
Ricardo Sosa
Mark Reynolds

SS
Sergio Santos (3)
Jerry Gil
Danny Richar

2B
Emilio Bonafacio
Neb Brown
Steve Garrabrants

1B
Conor Jackson (2)
Jamie D'Antona (8)
Chris Carter (26)
Jesus Cota
Corey Myers
Javier Brito

SOURCE of TALENT

HOMEGROWN		ACQUIRED	
College	13	Trades	6
Junior College	1	Rule 5 draft	0
Draft-and-follow	1	Independent leagues	0
High School	5	Free agents/waivers	0
Nondrafted free agent	0		
Foreign	4		

C
Chris Snyder (6)
Koyie Hill (12)
Phil Avlas (24)
Orlando Mercado Jr.
Miguel Montero
Richard Mercado
Craig Ansman

LHP

Starters	Relievers
Matt Chico (10)	Jared Doyle
Mike Gosling (16)	Bill White
Bill Murphy (18)	Doug Slaten
Brad Halsey (28)	Hipolito Guerrero
Clint Goocher	

RHP

Starters	Relievers
Ramon Pena (9)	Greg Aquino (5)
Garrett Mock (11)	Brian Bruney (13)
Dustin Nippert (14)	Jason Bulger (17)
Enrique Gonzalez (15)	Adam Peterson (22)
Ross Ohlendorf (20)	Lance Cormier (29)
A.J. Shappi (25)	Justin Wechsler
Casey Daigle	Brandon Medders
Sergio Lizarraga	Billy Biggs
Adam Bass	Koley Kolberg
Chris Kinsey	Phil Stockman

2004

Best Pro Debut: OF Jon Zeringue (2) went straight to high Class A and hit .335-10-41 with nine steals in 56 games, then batted .447-0-12 in nine playoff games. OF/1B Chris Carter (17) led the short-season Northwest League in RBIs (63) and slugging (.576). RHP A.J. Shappi (9) joined Carter on the NWL all-star team after going 5-1, 1.85 with a 65-8 K-BB ratio in 67 innings.

Best Athlete: SS Stephen Drew (1), BA's top-rated position player in the draft, is a five-tool talent. He hasn't signed yet but is expected to before spring training. Zeringue's bat is his calling card, but his arm, speed and outfield play all grade out as average or better.

Best Pure Hitter: Drew, whom the Diamondbacks project to be every bit as good as his brother J.D. while playing a more premium position. They're also excited about the bats of Zeringue and OF Luis Lajara (22).

Best Raw Power: Highly touted out of high school, Carter never got untracked in three years at Stanford but showed off his massive power as a pro. During predraft workouts, switch-hitting OF Brandon Burgess (6) batted lefthanded against lefty Bill Bray (Montreal's first-rounder)—and deposited a slider in the pool at Bank One Ballpark.

Fastest Runner: OF Kevin Williams (30) has 6.4-second speed in the 60-yard dash. Drew is a solid plus runner.

Best Defensive Player: Though some clubs thought Drew might be better suited to play second base or center field, Arizona believes he'll be a big league shortstop. He's not flashy, but he has the arm, range and instincts to make all the plays.

Best Fastball: RHP Ross Ohlendorf (4)

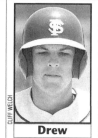

CLIFF WELCH

Drew

pitches at 94-96 mph and peaks at 98 coming out of the bullpen. RHP Garrett Mock (3), a starter, can touch the mid-90s and achieves a lot of sink with his fastball.

Best Breaking Ball: Shappi has very good command of three pitches, the best of which is his slider.

Most Intriguing Background: Drew followed his brothers J.D. and Tim as first-round picks, making his family the first to have three members drafted that high. Unsigned 2B Darryl Lawhorn's (11) twin brother Trevor went in the ninth round to the Reds. C Dan Pohlman (15) spent two years as a linebacker at Northwestern.

Closest To The Majors: Drew is so much better than Arizona's current cast of shortstops that he'll reach the big leagues very quickly once he signs. Zeringue also is on the fast track.

Best Late-Round Pick: Carter and C Frank Curreri (41). An offensive-minded catcher, Curreri parlayed a big summer in the Cape Cod League into a $200,000 bonus.

The One Who Got Away: RHP Jimmy Shull (8), a converted shortstop, took his low-90s fastball back to Cal Poly for his senior season.

Assessment: The Diamondbacks went into the draft looking for pitching but felt Drew and Zeringue were too good to pass up. They considered Mock and Ohlendorf in the second round, then got them with their next two picks.

2003 OFs Conor Jackson (1) and Carlos Quentin (1) are both poslished hitters who have wasted no time establishing themselves as Arizona's two best prospects. The club also has high hopes for 3B Jamie D'Antona (2) and LHP Matt Chico (3). *GRADE:* A

2002 Most teams didn't see SS Sergio Santos as a first-rounder, but he sure has looked like one as a pro. Chris Snyder (2) is the Diamondbacks' catcher of the future, and RHPs Lance Cormier (4) and Dustin Nippert (15) provide pitching depth. *GRADE:* B+

2001 2B Scott Hairston (3) and 3B Chad Tracy (7) were regulars for Arizona last season. RHP Jason Bulger (1) made progress in 2004 and could become a late-inning reliever. *GRADE:* B+

2000 With Randy Johnson gone to New York, RHP Brandon Webb (8) is the best pitcher on the big league staff. OF Josh Kroeger (4) continues to learn how to translate his athleticism into production. *GRADE:* B

Draft analysis prepared by Jim Callis. Numbers in parentheses indicate draft rounds.

LARRY GOREN

Carlos
QUENTIN

Born: Aug. 28, 1982.
Ht.: 6-2. **Wt.:** 220.
Bats: R. **Throws:** R.
School: Stanford University.
Career Transactions: Selected by Diamondbacks in first round (29th overall) of 2003 draft; signed July 2, 2003.
Signed by: Fred Costello.

Quentin had a storied amateur career. As a three-sport star at University of San Diego High—also Mark Prior's alma mater—he set school records for homers and RBIs; was his league's defensive player of the year in football; and was a member of a state champion basketball team. He hit a three-run homer in his first career at-bat at Stanford, where he was the Pacific-10 Conference freshman of the year in 2001 and an all-league selection in each of his three seasons. He led the Cardinal to a final four appearance at the College World Series each year. Though they knew impending Tommy John surgery would delay his pro debut until the following season, the Diamondbacks grabbed Quentin with the second of their two first-round picks in 2003 and signed him for $1.1 million. He was initially rusty when he returned to the diamond, hitting just .150 in his first 10 games at high Class A Lancaster. He hit .350 the rest of the year, which included a midseason promotion to Double-A El Paso. Quentin finished fifth in the minors with a .435 on-base percentage and set what is believed to be a minor league record by getting hit by 43 pitches.

Everything about Quentin's game screams prototypical right fielder, as his tools grade out average or above across the board. He's a strong yet graceful athlete with good bat speed and a smooth swing. He makes excellent contact with power to all fields, and projects as a .280-.300 hitter with 25-plus home run power. He has a mature approach at the plate and recognizes which pitches he can drive. An excellent defender, Quentin gets good jumps and has above-average range. His accurate arm already bounced back to a tick above average just 18 months removed from surgery. He displays tremendous baseball instincts, and Arizona loves his leadership and his bulldog mentality, which was made clear at Stanford when he played his entire junior season with the injured elbow.

Quentin's biggest strength is his lack of any glaring weakness. He sets up on top of the plate and his swing brings much of his torso over the plate, which is why he gets plunked so often. Some scouts think this will make him susceptible to getting busted inside with good fastballs, but he has yet to have that problem. He could become more patient at the plate, but his aggressive approach has done wonders so far. He hit lefthanders well in his pro debut, but rarely for power, and can be susceptible to outside breaking balls. Both of his minor league stops were hitter-friendly environments, so his 2004 numbers may be inflated.

The Diamondbacks believe Quentin could succeed in the majors right now, but they'll probably play it safe and start him at Triple-A Tucson in 2005. If Luis Gonzalez can't return from his own Tommy John surgery by Opening Day, Arizona fans might get an early preview of Quentin's skills. He's almost assured of making his major league debut in 2005 and assuming a starting job in 2006.

Year	Club (League)	Class	AVG	G	AB	R	H	2B	3B	HR	RBI	BB	SO	SB	OBP	SLG
2004	Lancaster (Cal)	A	.310	65	242	64	75	14	1	15	51	25	33	5	.428	.562
	El Paso (TL)	AA	.357	60	210	39	75	19	0	6	38	18	23	0	.443	.533
MINOR LEAGUE TOTALS			.332	125	452	103	150	33	1	21	89	43	56	5	.435	.549

Conor Jackson, of

Born: May 7, 1982. **Ht.:** 6-3. **Wt.:** 205. **Bats:** R. **Throws:** R. **School:** University of California. **Career Transactions:** Selected by Diamondbacks in first round (19th overall) of 2003 draft; signed June 16, 2003. **Signed by:** Fred Costello.

Jackson's power and patience made him one of the most desirable college hitters in the 2003 draft, and he has shown why so far in his brief pro career. He set a short-season Northwest League record with 35 doubles in just 68 games during his pro debut. He followed Carlos Quentin's path in 2004, splitting the season between high Class A and Double-A while producing every step of the way. Jackson is one of the best pure hitters in the minors. He has above-average bat speed and makes sharp contact to all fields. He rarely swings at bad pitches and rarely misses good ones. The Diamondbacks have worked on straightening his stance in order to produce more power, and he responded by tying for the Arizona Fall League lead with eight homers. Jackson's bat will be good enough for any position, good news considering his defensive skills. Primarily a third baseman in college, he has been disappointing as a pro left fielder. His below-average speed is only complicated by poor instincts and routes, and his arm is lacking. Like Quentin, Jackson will begin the season at Triple-A with the hope that he'll be ready for full-time duty in 2006. He eventually may have to move to first base.

Year	Club (League)	Class	AVG	G	AB	R	H	2B	3B	HR	RBI	BB	SO	SB	OBP	SLG
2003	Yakima (NWL)	A	.319	68	257	44	82	35	1	6	60	36	41	3	.410	.533
2004	Lancaster (Cal)	A	.345	67	258	64	89	19	2	11	54	45	36	4	.438	.562
	El Paso (TL)	AA	.301	60	226	33	68	13	2	6	37	24	36	3	.367	.456
MINOR LEAGUE TOTALS			.323	195	741	141	239	67	5	23	151	105	113	10	.407	.520

Sergio Santos, ss

Born: July 4, 1983. **Ht.:** 6-3. **Wt.:** 190. **Bats:** R. **Throws:** R. **School:** Mater Dei HS, Hacienda Heights, Calif. **Career Transactions:** Selected by Diamondbacks in first round (27th overall) of 2002 draft; signed June 26, 2002. **Signed by:** Mark Baca.

Santos first popped up on scouts' radar as a high school sophomore, but a disappointing senior season seemingly dropped him out of the first round. The Diamondbacks bucked the consensus by taking him 27th overall based on his track record, and they've looked smart for doing so. He reached Double-A at age 20 and was having a solid season until it was ended by surgery on his non-throwing shoulder. Santos' profile is that of the new breed of shortstop—big, strong and athletic. His pure bat speed is among the best in the system, and he has shown some aptitude for driving the ball. He makes the plays he gets to at shortstop and has one of the better infield arms among Arizona farmhands. He's an average runner. While Santos seems certain to hit, his long-term position remains in question. He may outgrow shortstop and his range probably fits better at third base anyway. His power and arm still profile well for the hot corner. An aggressive hitter, he needs to draw more walks. Santos' shoulder has bothered him throughout his pro career and the Diamondbacks believe it has held him back offensively and defensively. They believe he's on the verge of a breakout and have no intention of moving him off shortstop at this time. He could be their big league starter at short in 2006.

Year	Club (League)	Class	AVG	G	AB	R	H	2B	3B	HR	RBI	BB	SO	SB	OBP	SLG
2002	Missoula (Pio)	R	.272	54	202	38	55	19	2	9	37	29	49	6	.520	.367
2003	Lancaster (Cal)	A	.287	93	341	55	98	13	2	8	49	41	64	5	.408	.368
	El Paso (TL)	AA	.255	37	137	13	35	7	1	2	16	8	25	0	.365	.293
2004	El Paso (TL)	AA	.282	89	347	53	98	19	5	11	52	24	89	3	.332	.461
MINOR LEAGUE TOTALS			.278	273	1027	159	286	58	10	30	154	102	227	14	.346	.442

Jon Zeringue, of

Born: Aug. 29, 1983. **Ht.:** 6-2. **Wt.:** 205. **Bats:** R. **Throws:** R. **School:** Louisiana State University. **Career Transactions:** Selected by Diamondbacks in second round of 2004 draft; signed July 2, 2004. **Signed by:** Mike Valarezo.

The Diamondbacks targeted pitching for the second round of the 2004 draft, but with Zeringue still on the board they couldn't pass him up. After signing for $630,000, he obliterated high Class A pitching and kept mashing in the postseason, hitting .447 with 12 RBIs in nine games. Zeringue's quick, compact swing generates hard line drives and good power from gap to gap. Surprisingly athletic for his size, he has solid speed and baserunning aptitude. His arm is strong and accurate. Zeringue needs to become more disciplined at the plate. He's a mistake hitter and guesses on most pitches, leaving him behind fastballs or chasing breaking pitches. Despite his right-field arm, his routes and instincts may be better suited for left. His swing lacks loft, so his power upside is limited. Despite Arizona's depth on the outfield corners, Zeringue could move quickly. He'll begin his first full season at the organization's new Double-A Tennessee affiliate.

Year	Club (League)	Class	AVG	G	AB	R	H	2B	3B	HR	RBI	BB	SO	SB	OBP	SLG
2004	Lancaster (Cal)	A	.335	56	230	36	77	14	3	10	41	14	53	9	.374	.552
MINOR LEAGUE TOTALS			.335	56	230	36	77	14	3	10	41	14	53	9	.374	.552

5 Greg Aquino, rhp

Born: Jan. 11, 1978. **Ht.:** 6-1. **Wt.:** 188. **Bats:** R. **Throws:** R. **Career Transactions:** Signed out of Dominican Republic by Diamondbacks, Nov. 8, 1995. **Signed by:** Junior Noboa.

Originally signed as a shortstop, Aquino became a pitcher in 1999 after batting .156 in low Class A. His power arsenal led to a full-time move to the bullpen last year, and an emergency callup to Arizona despite struggling in Triple-A. He converted his first 10 save opportunities in the majors. When everything is clicking for Aquino, he's nearly unhittable. He throws a mid-90s fastball and has touched triple digits, but gets far better movement and location when he dials his heater down. His low-80s slider has gone from unreliable to a plus pitch featuring two-plane break. Aquino can still be inconsistent, particularly with his command. He needs to learn how to set hitters up, as opposed to simply trying to blow them away. The Diamondbacks were so bad last year that he has yet to close a meaningful big league game. Aquino's performance was one of Arizona's few pleasant developments in the majors last year. He enters 2005 as the team's closer.

Year	Club (League)	Class	AVG	G	AB	R	H	2B	3B	HR	RBI	BB	SO	SB	OBP	SLG
1996	Diamondbacks (DSL)	R	.200	58	160	21	32	3	0	0	9	22	11	7	.308	.219
1997	Diamondbacks (DSL)	R	.289	53	180	39	52	9	0	0	14	18	21	3	.355	.339
	South Bend (Mid)	A	.185	8	27	2	5	2	0	0	2	0	7	0	.185	.259
1998	Diamondbacks (AZL)	R	.282	45	163	20	46	11	1	0	11	7	34	2	.310	.362
1999	South Bend (Mid)	A	.156	53	186	18	29	4	2	0	10	9	46	1	.199	.199
MINOR LEAGUE TOTALS			.229	266	725	101	166	29	3	0	46	56	121	13	.268	.277

Year	Club (League)	Class	W	L	ERA	G	GS	CG	SV	IP	H	R	ER	HR	BB	SO	AVG
1999	Diamondbacks (AZL)	R	1	2	3.79	13	2	0	0	19	17	11	8	0	13	20	.246
2000	South Bend (Mid)	A	5	7	4.46	29	18	0	0	119	119	67	59	9	56	93	.260
2001	Lancaster (Cal)	A	2	5	8.14	25	4	0	0	42	59	40	38	7	24	39	.331
	Yakima (NWL)	A	4	2	3.30	8	8	0	0	46	39	18	17	2	14	39	.229
2002	Yakima (NWL)	A	1	1	2.06	6	6	0	0	35	26	9	8	0	17	34	.213
	Lancaster (Cal)	A	4	1	3.67	8	8	0	0	49	50	20	20	3	18	50	.267
2003	El Paso (TL)	AA	7	3	3.46	20	20	0	0	107	115	43	41	5	38	91	.278
2004	Arizona (NL)	MAJ	0	2	3.06	34	0	0	16	35	24	15	12	4	17	26	.194
	Tucson (PCL)	AAA	1	3	6.37	21	2	0	1	30	33	25	21	2	18	19	.270
MAJOR LEAGUE TOTALS			0	2	3.06	34	0	0	17	35	24	15	12	4	17	26	.194
MINOR LEAGUE TOTALS			25	24	4.27	130	68	0	1	447	458	233	212	28	198	385	.267

6 Chris Snyder, c

Born: Feb. 12, 1981. **Ht.:** 6-3. **Wt.:** 220. **Bats:** R. **Throws:** R. **School:** University of Houston. **Career Transactions:** Selected by Diamondbacks in second round of 2002 draft; signed June 16, 2002. **Signed by:** Trip Couch.

Snyder was already on the fast track entering 2004, when his timetable was moved up quite a bit. Following the trade of Brent Mayne and an injury to Koyie Hill, Snyder became Arizona's starting catcher for the final part of the season. He hit five homers in his first 14 big league games. Snyder has value both at the plate and behind it. He's a big, strong catcher with plus power and an advanced understanding of the strike zone. He's also a solid receiver with good actions and a strong arm. He has good instincts and natural leadership tendencies, with Randy Johnson praising him for his ability to call a game. Whether Snyder develops into a frontline catcher depends on his ability to hit for average. His long swing leads to plenty of strikeouts. He's a well below-average runner. The Diamondbacks don't want to enter 2005 with a pair of rookie backstops. Snyder will battle Hill for the starting job in spring training, with the loser heading to Triple-A.

Year	Club (League)	Class	AVG	G	AB	R	H	2B	3B	HR	RBI	BB	SO	SB	OBP	SLG
2002	Lancaster (Cal)	A	.258	60	217	31	56	16	0	9	44	25	54	0	.337	.456
2003	Lancaster (Cal)	A	.314	69	245	53	77	16	2	10	53	35	43	0	.414	.518
	El Paso (TL)	AA	.202	53	188	21	38	14	0	4	26	19	29	0	.286	.340

Year	Club (League)	Class	AVG	G	AB	R	H	2B	3B	HR	RBI	BB	SO	SB	OBP	SLG
2004	El Paso (TL)	AA	.301	99	346	66	104	31	0	15	57	46	57	3	.389	.520
	Arizona (NL)	MAJ	.240	29	96	10	23	6	0	5	15	13	25	0	.327	.458
MAJOR LEAGUE TOTALS			.240	29	96	10	23	6	0	5	15	13	25	0	.327	.458
MINOR LEAGUE TOTALS			.276	281	996	171	275	77	2	38	180	125	183	3	.365	.472

7 Josh Kroeger, of

Born: Aug. 31, 1982. **Ht.:** 6-2. **Wt.:** 200. **Bats:** L. **Throws:** L. **School:** Scripps Ranch HS, San Diego. **Career Transactions:** Selected by Diamondbacks in fourth round of 2000 draft; signed June 6, 2000. **Signed by:** James Keller.

Kroeger turned down a football scholarship from NCAA Division II Truman State (Mo.) as a wide receiver to sign with the Diamondbacks, and he was raw as a baseball player. He started to figure the game out in 2003 and took another step forward last year, when he tied for the minor league lead with 51 doubles. Kroeger is a natural hitter with a smooth, level swing and good power. He's adept at driving the ball in the gaps. He has the arm for right field and the slightly above-average speed to play center in a pinch. His overly aggressive approach was exploited in his big league debut, as he struck out 21 times and drew just one walk in 55 plate appearances. He already has lost a step from his high school days and may continue to slow down. His effort has come into question at times. Kroeger proved in September that he's not ready to hit big league pitching. Set to return to Triple-A, he could get buried by Arizona's outfield depth.

Year	Club (League)	Class	AVG	G	AB	R	H	2B	3B	HR	RBI	BB	SO	SB	OBP	SLG
2000	Diamondbacks (AZL)	R	.297	54	222	40	66	9	3	4	28	21	41	5	.359	.419
2001	South Bend (Mid)	A	.274	79	292	36	80	15	1	3	37	18	49	4	.324	.363
2002	Lancaster (Cal)	A	.235	133	497	63	117	20	7	7	58	23	136	2	.274	.346
2003	Lancaster (Cal)	A	.341	78	305	50	104	30	6	5	55	35	58	6	.409	.528
	El Paso (TL)	AA	.274	54	208	26	57	9	2	3	22	10	54	3	.315	.380
2004	Arizona (NL)	MAJ	.167	22	54	5	9	3	0	0	2	1	21	0	.182	.222
	El Paso (TL)	AA	.331	65	245	44	81	28	4	9	46	21	48	2	.393	.588
	Tucson (PCL)	AAA	.332	59	208	30	69	23	0	10	41	15	47	2	.376	.587
MAJOR LEAGUE TOTALS			.167	22	54	5	9	3	0	0	2	1	21	0	.182	.222
MINOR LEAGUE TOTALS			.290	522	1977	289	574	134	23	41	287	143	433	24	.343	.444

8 Jamie D'Antona, 3b

Born: May 12, 1982. **Ht.:** 6-2. **Wt.:** 215. **Bats:** R. **Throws:** R. **School:** Wake Forest University. **Career Transactions:** Selected by Diamondbacks in second round of 2003 draft; signed June 10, 2003. **Signed by:** Howard McCullough.

D'Antona broke Wake Forest's career home run record (58) and was the Atlantic Coast Conference player of the year in 2003. He teamed with Carlos Quentin and Conor Jackson at Lancaster, but unlike his cohorts he didn't thrive after a promotion to Double-A, mainly because of an ailing shoulder. D'Antona has massive power and doesn't need to perfectly center the ball to hit it out of the park. Scouts still talk about the home run he hit into the restaurant above the left-field bleachers at Bank One Ballpark in a pre-draft workout. He has a plus-plus arm at third base, but projects as a first baseman because he has limited range and sloppy footwork. He's pull-happy and has holes in his swing, which can get a bit long. He needs to learn how to work counts better. He's a below-average runner. D'Antona's injury has put him a step behind Jackson and Quentin for now. He'll be separated from them when he begins 2005 by returning to Double-A.

STEVE MOORE

Year	Club (League)	Class	AVG	G	AB	R	H	2B	3B	HR	RBI	BB	SO	SB	OBP	SLG
2003	Yakima (NWL)	A	.277	70	271	46	75	18	1	15	57	35	60	0	.356	.517
2004	Lancaster (Cal)	A	.315	68	273	45	86	18	1	13	57	16	36	2	.353	.531
	El Paso (TL)	AA	.211	19	71	2	15	3	1	0	7	2	16	0	.230	.282
MINOR LEAGUE TOTALS			.286	157	615	93	176	39	3	28	121	53	112	2	.341	.496

9 Ramon Pena, rhp

Born: May 16, 1985. **Ht.:** 6-2. **Wt.:** 190. **Bats:** R. **Throws:** R. **Career Transactions:** Signed out of Dominican Republic by Diamondbacks, June 13, 2002. **Signed by:** Junior Noboa.

He began last year as Adriano Rosario, 18-year-old phenom. He ended it as Ramon Pena, a 23-year-old who had falsified his visa information. The Diamondbacks weren't blamed, and they also were cleared of any wrongdoing when it came to light that independent talent developer Ivan Noboa (whose brother Junior coordinates Arizona's scouting in Latin America) double-dipped, collecting $100,000 from the team as well as $100,000 from Pena's $400,000 bonus. He may be much older than originally thought, but Pena still has the best pure stuff in the system. He effortlessly commands a 92-94 mph fastball that he can dial up to 97-98 to blow batters away or dial down to 88-91 to add movement. His slider has developed into a solid offering. The two-pitch combination is enough to make him a closer if he has to move to the bullpen. Pena needs to add deception to his changeup in order to remain a starter. He favors overpowering hitters as opposed to setting them up. With his true age revealed, he has gone from advanced to raw for his age. While he looked rusty in the Dominican League, his primary focus was on resolving his legal problems. Granted a visa in January, he'll begin the season by returning to Double-A.

Year	Club (League)	Class	W	L	ERA	G	GS	CG	SV	IP	H	R	ER	HR	BB	SO	AVG
2002	Diamondbacks (DSL)	R	3	1	2.05	10	10	1	0	57	41	16	13	0	7	57	.193
	Missoula (Pio)	R	1	2	6.30	4	4	0	0	20	26	15	14	0	3	14	.321
2003	South Bend (Mid)	A	9	5	2.86	27	27	0	0	160	149	46	51	3	30	119	.247
2004	El Paso (TL)	AA	3	3	5.44	7	7	0	0	43	47	27	26	4	5	36	.280
MINOR LEAGUE TOTALS			16	11	3.34	48	48	1	0	280	263	127	104	7	45	226	.247

10 Matt Chico, lhp

Born: June 10, 1983. **Ht.:** 5-11. **Wt.:** 190. **Bats:** L. **Throws:** L. **School:** Palomar (Calif.) JC. **Career Transactions:** Selected by Diamondbacks in third round of 2003 draft; signed June 12, 2003. **Signed by:** Mark Baca.

Chico's entry into pro baseball had more that its share of detours. Selected by the Red Sox in the second round out of high school, Chico turned down nearly $700,000. By his sophomore year, he had flunked out of Southern California and junior college, reducing him to pitching in a San Diego semipro league in 2003. The Diamondbacks signed him for $365,000 that June. Chico blew away low Class A hitters last year, using a low-90s fastball with good movement. His curveball features late, sharp, downward break and his changeup should become an average offering. Arizona praises his work ethic and bulldog mentality. Chico is a little short, so his pitches lack downward plane. While he spins his curveball well, he has problems throwing strikes with it. He has little confidence in his secondary pitches and sometimes tries to rely solely on his heater. Chico's shortcomings were more evident in Double-A, but he finished strong. He'll return there in 2005, working toward reaching his ceiling as a middle-of-the-rotation starter.

Year	Club (League)	Class	W	L	ERA	G	GS	CG	SV	IP	H	R	ER	HR	BB	SO	AVG
2003	Yakima (NWL)	A	7	4	3.53	17	13	0	0	71	75	28	28	4	25	71	.274
2004	El Paso (TL)	AA	3	7	5.78	14	12	0	0	62	82	53	40	7	36	59	.315
	South Bend (Mid)	A	8	5	2.57	14	14	2	0	88	59	26	25	9	27	89	.188
MINOR LEAGUE TOTALS			18	16	3.78	45	39	2	1	221	216	107	93	20	88	219	.255

11 Garrett Mock, rhp

Born: April 25, 1983. **Ht.:** 6-4. **Wt.:** 215. **Bats:** R. **Throws:** R. **School:** University of Houston. **Career Transactions:** Selected by Diamondbacks in third round of 2004 draft; signed June 12, 2004. **Signed by:** Trip Couch.

Mock was in line to be a first-round pick after a strong showing in the Cape Cod League before his junior year at Houston, but a broken ankle derailed him. He didn't allow a run in his first four professional outings, and more than held his own after a promotion to low Class A. Mock has a prototypical pitcher's body and unleashes a heavy 91-94 mph fastball with plenty of sink that can touch 97. He throws a big downward breaking ball and the Diamondbacks love his never say die attitude, as evidenced by the month he pitched at Houston with the broken ankle. Mock has trouble keeping his curveball in the strike zone, and his changeup is still well below his other offerings. Mock can be a bit of a perfectionist at times, trying too hard to make the perfect pitch as opposed to letting his stuff simply work for him. He'll begin the year on one of the two Arizona class A affiliates.

Year	Club (League)	Class	W	L	ERA	G	GS	CG	SV	IP	H	R	ER	HR	BB	SO	AVG
2004	Yakima (NWL)	A	2	0	1.54	5	5	0	0	23	18	8	4	1	4	14	.212
	South Bend (Mid)	A	3	2	3.00	8	8	1	0	54	49	21	18	2	12	37	.243
MINOR LEAGUE TOTALS			5	2	2.56	13	13	1	0	77	67	29	22	3	16	51	.233

12 Koyie Hill, c

Born: March 9, 1979. **Ht.:** 6-0. **Wt.:** 190. **Bats:** B. **Throws:** R. **School:** Wichita State University. **Career Transactions:** Selected by Dodgers in fourth round of 2000 draft; signed June 22, 2000 . . . Traded by Dodgers with OF Reggie Abercrombie and LHP Bill Murphy to Diamondbacks for OF Steve Finley and C Brent Mayne, July 30, 2004. **Signed by:** Mitch Webster (Dodgers).

Hill looked like the Dodgers' catcher of the future after they dealt Paul Lo Duca to the

Marlins, but that lasted less than 24 hours as he was shipped to Arizona in the deal that netted Steve Finley. Placed immediately into Arizona's starting lineup, Hill hit his first major league home run off Pittsburgh's Jose Mesa, but his stint lasted just 13 games when he broke his ankle in a home-plate collision. A switch-hitter with a contact-oriented approach, Hill's power took a major step forward in 2004, as he passed his previous career-high in home runs by mid-July. An infielder in high school and college, Hill was converted to catcher after being drafted and his defense still lags behind. He has a strong arm, but is easy to run on because it takes too long for him to get rid of the ball. He could use a more patient approach at the plate, especially as he begins to look for more pitches to drive. Hill's ankle is expected to be fine for spring training and he will battle Chris Snyder for the starting catcher's job.

Year	Club (League)	Class	AVG	G	AB	R	H	2B	3B	HR	RBI	BB	SO	SB	OBP	SLG
2000	Yakima (NWL)	A	.259	64	251	26	65	13	1	2	29	25	47	0	.324	.343
2001	Wilmington (SAL)	A	.301	134	498	65	150	20	2	8	79	49	82	21	.368	.398
2002	Jacksonville (SL)	AA	.271	130	468	67	127	25	1	11	64	76	88	5	.368	.400
2003	Jacksonville (SL)	AA	.228	25	101	9	23	7	0	0	7	6	19	2	.271	.297
	Las Vegas (PCL)	AAA	.314	85	312	48	98	18	0	3	36	15	39	5	.345	.401
	Los Angeles (NL)	MAJ	.333	3	3	0	1	1	0	0	0	0	2	0	.333	.667
2004	Las Vegas (PCL)	AAA	.286	91	350	57	100	26	0	13	54	28	69	0	.339	.471
	Arizona (NL)	MAJ	.250	13	36	3	9	1	0	1	6	2	6	1	.289	.361
MAJOR LEAGUE TOTALS			.231	16	39	3	9	2	0	1	6	2	8	1	.293	.359
MINOR LEAGUE TOTALS			.284	529	1980	272	563	109	4	37	269	199	344	33	.349	.400

13 Brian Bruney, rhp

Born: Feb. 17, 1982. **Ht.:** 6-3. **Wt.:** 225. **Bats:** R. **Throws:** R. **School:** Warrenton (Ore.) HS. **Career Transactions:** Selected by Diamondbacks in 12th round of 2000 draft; signed June 6, 2000. **Signed by:** Jason Goligoski.

Bruney had three stints with the Diamondback in 2004, with mixed results. While he was able to keep the ball off opposing hitters' bats, he also had trouble throwing strikes. He gained confidence as the season wore on, and allowed just four hits and one run in his final 10 appearances. Bruney is all about velocity. He gets a lot of leverage behind his 92-94 mph fastball, and can touch 96. An inability to find a second pitch has been Bruney's bugaboo throughout his career. At times he throws a curve, at times he throws a slider, and at times he throws a slurvy combination of the two. None of them have enough break to fool hitters, and he has problems commanding them as well. Bruney's motion is a little violent, and he tends to short-arm the ball. He has been passed by Greg Aquino for the major league closer job, but Bruney still projects as a major league set-up man, a role he'll ease into in 2005.

Year	Club (League)	Class	W	L	ERA	G	GS	CG	SV	IP	H	R	ER	HR	BB	SO	AVG
2000	Diamondbacks (AZL)	R	4	1	6.48	20	2	0	2	25	21	23	18	2	29	24	.221
2001	South Bend (Mid)	A	1	4	4.13	26	0	0	8	33	24	19	15	1	19	40	.205
	Yakima (NWL)	A	1	2	5.14	15	0	0	2	21	19	14	12	2	11	28	.226
2002	South Bend (Mid)	A	4	3	1.68	37	0	0	10	48	37	15	9	1	17	54	.210
	El Paso (TL)	AA	0	2	2.92	10	0	0	0	12	11	5	4	1	4	14	.268
2003	El Paso (TL)	AA	0	2	2.59	28	0	0	14	31	29	17	9	1	13	28	.234
	Tucson (PCL)	AAA	3	1	2.81	32	0	0	12	32	24	12	10	0	18	32	.207
2004	Tucson (PCL)	AAA	2	0	1.18	31	0	0	5	38	18	8	5	1	20	42	.141
	Arizona (NL)	MAJ	3	4	4.31	30	0	0	0	31	20	16	15	2	27	34	.189
MAJOR LEAGUE TOTALS			3	4	4.31	30	0	0	0	31	20	16	15	2	27	34	.189
MINOR LEAGUE TOTALS			15	15	3.07	199	2	0	53	241	183	113	82	9	131	262	.208

14 Dustin Nippert, rhp

Born: May 6, 1981. **Ht.:** 6-7. **Wt.:** 200. **Bats:** R. **Throws:** R. **School:** West Virginia University. **Career Transactions:** Selected by Diamondbacks in 15th round of 2002 draft; signed June 9, 2002. **Signed by:** Greg Lonigro.

Nippert entered the 2004 season as the No. 3 prospect in the system. He began the year in Double-A, but wasn't nearly as dominant as many expected, which was explained when he went down with an elbow injury in June and underwent Tommy John surgery. When healthy, Nippert offers two plus-plus pitches. His long physique allows him to throw his low 90s fastball with an incredible downward plane, and his curveball is a hard 12-to-6 breaker. He has very good command and surprisingly consistent mechanics, considering his size. His changeup has made great strides since signing and projects as an average pitch. Nippert needs to gain more confidence in his offspeed pitches, and not try to get by solely on his heater. The track record for Tommy John surgery survivors gets better with each season, so Arizona feels he can come back strong. His rehab is going as scheduled, and he'll look to return to the mound at some point in the second half of 2005.

Year	Club (League)	Class	W	L	ERA	G	GS	CG	SV	IP	H	R	ER	HR	BB	SO	AVG
2002	Missoula (Pio)	R	4	2	1.65	17	11	0	0	55	42	12	10	2	9	77	.208
2003	South Bend (Mid)	A	6	4	2.82	17	17	0	0	96	66	32	30	4	32	96	.191
2004	El Paso (TL)	AA	2	5	3.64	14	14	0	0	72	77	45	29	0	40	73	.267
MINOR LEAGUE TOTALS			12	11	2.80	48	42	0	0	222	153	89	69	6	81	246	.222

15 Enrique Gonzalez, rhp

Born: July 14, 1982. **Ht.:** 5-10. **Wt.:** 195. **Bats:** R. **Throws:** R. **Career Transactions:** Signed out of Venezuela by Diamondbacks, Oct. 30, 1998. **Signed by:** Carlos Porte.

Gonzalez lingered in the system for five years and was seen as little more than an extra arm entering the 2004 season, which he begin in the high Class A bullpen. Pressed into a starting role in June, Gonzalez exploded, going 10-2, 2.46 in 17 starts. Gonzalez lives off his fastball, but it's a dominant pitch. He's a strike thrower who delivers easy 92-95 mph gas, and has touched 98. His stamina was one of the biggest surprises in his sudden success, as he hit 96 mph on his 104th pitch in one outing. He's a good athlete who fields his position well. He throws both a curve and a slider, but most feel the slider is the pitch he could stick with by increasing its tilt and velocity. His changeup is an average pitch, but he knows how to use it in the right situation. Gonzalez' short stature is a concern, and many still think he'll end up as a swingman or long reliever despite his success in the rotation. He'll begin the year in Double-A, looking to prove that his second half in 2004 was for real.

Year	Club (League)	Class	W	L	ERA	G	GS	CG	SV	IP	H	R	ER	HR	BB	SO	AVG
1999	Diamondbacks (DSL)	R	7	3	1.64	12	11	1	0	71	41	21	13	0	24	82	.——
2000	Diamondbacks (AZL)	R	1	0	1.53	11	0	0	1	18	16	13	3	0	12	17	.239
	Tucson (PCL)	AAA	1	0	0.00	1	0	0	0	4	1	0	0	0	1	1	.091
2001	South Bend (Mid)	A	4	12	4.01	26	26	1	0	146	142	81	65	9	53	92	.257
2002	Lancaster (Cal)	A	1	4	2.27	5	5	0	0	18	34	27	25	3	14	11	.410
	Yakima (NWL)	A	5	2	2.45	11	11	0	0	66	53	27	18	2	23	57	.219
	South Bend (Mid)	A	1	2	3.74	4	4	0	0	22	23	16	9	1	9	20	.271
2003	South Bend (Mid)	A	4	3	2.13	55	0	0	3	72	58	22	17	5	29	63	.218
2004	Lancaster (Cal)	A	13	6	3.22	42	17	0	0	142	128	64	51	13	44	110	.242
MINOR LEAGUE TOTALS			37	32	3.24	167	74	2	4	559	496	271	201	33	209	453	.248

16 Mike Gosling, lhp

Born: Sept. 23, 1980. **Ht.:** 6-2. **Wt.:** 210. **Bats:** L. **Throws:** L. **School:** Stanford University. **Career Transactions:** Selected by Diamondbacks in second round of 2001 draft; signed Aug. 1, 2001. **Signed by:** Charles Scott.

After a strong pro debut in 2002 and a miserable 2003, Gosling had mixed results in 2004. He got of to a slow start in Triple-A as he returned from offseason arthroscopic shoulder surgery, but his velocity slowly returned and he earned his first big league promotion after going 5-1 in his final six starts. He got his first major league win with five-plus strong innings against St. Louis, but was otherwise ordinary. Gosling has solid stuff and throws strikes with a low 90s fastball, as well as a cutter and curve. His plus change is his most consistent out pitch. He's been described as a 'tweener, without enough command or break on his pitches to be a finesse pitcher, or enough pure velocity to be a power pitcher. His delivery is a bit clumsy, leading to concerns about future injury problems. He'll enter spring training as the favorite to win the fifth starter job over recently acquired lefty Brad Halsey.

Year	Club (League)	Class	W	L	ERA	G	GS	CG	SV	IP	H	R	ER	HR	BB	SO	AVG
2002	El Paso (TL)	AA	14	5	3.13	27	27	2	0	167	149	66	58	7	62	115	.238
2003	Tucson (PCL)	AAA	9	12	5.61	26	26	0	0	136	190	106	85	13	56	89	.330
2004	Arizona (NL)	MAJ	1	1	4.62	6	4	0	0	25	26	13	13	5	13	14	.274
	Tucson (PCL)	AAA	9	5	5.82	24	21	0	0	128	160	101	83	16	53	67	.305
MAJOR LEAGUE TOTALS			1	1	4.62	6	4	0	0	25	26	13	13	5	13	14	.274
MINOR LEAGUE TOTALS			32	22	4.72	77	74	2	0	431	499	273	226	36	171	271	.289

17 Jason Bulger, rhp

Born: Dec. 6, 1978. **Ht.:** 6-4. **Wt.:** 210. **Bats:** R. **Throws:** R. **School:** Valdosta State (Ga.) University. **Career Transactions:** Selected by Diamondbacks in first round (22th overall) of 2001 draft; signed Sept. 18, 2001. **Signed by:** Michael Valarezo.

Bulger was primarily an infielder at Division II Valdosta State, but he doubled as the team's closer in his senior year and opened scouts' eyes when he pumped mid-90s heat. He was a surprise first-round pick in 2001, and looked like a bust after ineffectiveness as a starter and 2003 Tommy John surgery. He returned to the bullpen in 2004 and took off. Bulger worked hard in his rehab and came back throwing harder than ever. His sinking fastball features great life and sits at 94-96 mph, and he can reach back and dial it up to 98. He throws a power curve for strikes, and the changeup he learned as a starter serves him well as a show-me pitch in the pen. Bulger is still raw despite being 26. He's inconsistent with his release point, which leads to command problems and a tendency to overthrow. Bulger was added to the 40-man roster, and the Diamondbacks believe he'll move quickly now. He'll begin the year as the closer in Triple-A, but should see the majors by September at the latest.

Year	Club (League)	Class	W	L	ERA	G	GS	CG	SV	IP	H	R	ER	HR	BB	SO	AVG
2002	South Bend (Mid)	A	4	9	4.94	20	20	1	0	95	111	65	52	5	39	84	.291
	Lancaster (Cal)	A	1	1	5.40	2	2	0	0	10	11	7	6	0	3	12	.289
2003	Lancaster (Cal)	A	2	1	6.75	4	4	0	0	17	23	13	13	3	5	20	.311
2004	Lancaster (Cal)	A	0	1	1.52	21	0	0	11	24	14	4	4	0	10	31	.171
	El Paso (TL)	AA	0	3	3.91	24	0	0	8	25	25	12	11	0	19	26	.255
MINOR LEAGUE TOTALS			7	15	4.53	71	26	1	19	171	184	101	86	8	76	173	.273

18 Bill Murphy, lhp

Born: May 9, 1981. **Ht.:** 6-0. **Wt.:** 190. **Bats:** L. **Throws:** L. **School:** Cal State Northridge. **Career Transactions:** Selected by Athletics in third round of 2002 draft; signed June 26, 2002 . . . Traded by Athletics to Marlins Dec. 23, 2003, to complete trade in which Marlins sent LHP Mark Redman to Athletics for RHP Mike Neu and a player to be named (Dec. 16, 2003) . . . Traded by Marlins with RHP Brad Penny and 1B Hee Seop Choi to Dodgers for C Paul Lo Duca, RHP Guillermo Mota, OF Juan Encarnacion, and cash, July 30, 2004 . . . Traded by Dodgers with C Koyie Hill and OF Reggie Abercrombie to Diamondbacks for OF Steve Finley and C Brent Mayne, July 31, 2004. **Signed by:** Rick Magnante (Athletics).

While Murphy has yet to reach the major leagues himself, he has already been involved in three trades for major leaguers. Originally drafted by Oakland, Murphy was seen as one of the top lefthanders in their system before being traded to the Marlins for Mark Redman. At the 2004 trade deadline, he was the only minor leaguer in a six-player deal between the Dodgers and Marlins, and the Dodgers sent him to Arizona a day later in the Steve Finley deal. His 88-91 mph fastball has good life and his curveball is a big breaker, but he has problems controlling them. His changeup is solid-average. Murphy's overall game took a step back in 2004, particularly his command. He needs to trust his pitches more, and spend less time trying to paint the corners. For the third straight year, Murphy ran out of gas toward the end of the year, raising more questions about his stamina. He'll begin the year in the rotation at Triple-A, where he will need to take a step forward to earn a big league call.

Year	Club (League)	Class	W	L	ERA	G	GS	CG	SV	IP	H	R	ER	HR	BB	SO	AVG
2002	Vancouver (NWL)	A	1	4	4.57	13	9	0	0	41	28	23	21	2	35	46	.192
2003	Kane County (Mid)	A	7	4	2.25	14	14	1	0	92	61	27	23	5	32	87	.188
	Midland (TL)	AA	3	3	4.09	11	11	0	0	55	44	25	25	4	26	34	.220
2004	Carolina (SL)	AA	6	4	4.08	20	20	0	0	104	80	48	47	17	59	113	.215
	El Paso (TL)	AA	3	3	6.68	6	6	0	0	31	41	28	23	6	17	24	.328
MINOR LEAGUE TOTALS			20	18	3.87	64	60	1	0	323	254	151	139	34	169	304	.218

19 Carlos Gonzalez, of

Born: Oct. 17, 1985. **Ht.:** 6-1. **Wt.:** 178. **Bats:** L. **Throws:** L. **Career Transactions:** Signed out of Venezuela by Diamondbacks, Aug. 3, 2002. **Signed by:** Miguel Nava.

The Diamondbacks felt Gonzalez was ready for a full-season league in 2004 despite being just 18, but he lasted just two weeks before a broken hand sidelined him for nearly two months. When he got healthy he reported to short-season Yakima, where he homered in five of his first 11 games. Gonzalez's raw package of tools gives plenty of reason for excitement. He's a good hitter with a natural uppercut who projects for power down the road. He's a solid runner with good range and easily has the best arm in the system. He threw 92 mph off the mound as an amateur and throws strikes from the outfield as well, having already amassed 20 outfield assists as a pro. Gonzalez, like most teenagers, is rough around the edges. He needs to develop patience at the plate, and refine his approach against lefthanded pitchers. The Diamondbacks believe Gonzalez has all-star potential, but he's far from reaching it. Arizona has no reason to rush him, and he'll get another shot at low Class A in 2005.

Year	Club (League)	Class	AVG	G	AB	R	H	2B	3B	HR	RBI	BB	SO	SB	OBP	SLG
2003	Missoula (Pio)	R	.258	72	275	45	71	14	4	6	25	16	61	12	.308	.404
2004	South Bend (Mid)	A	.262	12	42	3	11	4	0	1	6	1	11	0	.279	.429
	Yakima (NWL)	A	.277	73	300	44	83	15	2	9	44	22	69	2	.330	.430
MINOR LEAGUE TOTALS			.267	157	617	92	165	33	6	16	75	39	141	14	.317	.418

20 Ross Ohlendorf, rhp

Born: Aug. 8, 1982. **Ht.:** 6-4. **Wt.:** 235. **Bats:** R. **Throws:** R. **School:** Princeton University. **Career Transactions:** Selected by Diamondbacks in fourth round of 2004 draft; signed July 6, 2004. **Signed by:** Greg Lonigro.

Ohlendorf raised his status before the draft by pitching into the ninth inning against

Virginia in Princeton's first regional win since 2000. Huge and intimidating on the mound, Ohlendorf rears back and fires a 94-96 mph fastball that can touch 98 and features good sink and movement. He's aggressive in his approach and not afraid to pitch inside. Ohlendorf's secondary offerings are both well behind his heater. His slider lacks break and his change lacks deception, while his command is spotty. Highly intelligent, Ohlendorf can be his own worst enemy, analyzing everything he does on the mound and tinkering too often with his delivery, which is already violent. The Diamondbacks see Ohlendorf as a high risk/high reward pitcher who will take time to develop. His lack of a full arsenal leaves him most likely ending up as a power reliever, but he for the immediate future, he needs innings to develop. Ohlendorf will begin the year in the low Class A rotation.

Year	Club (League)	Class	W	L	ERA	G	GS	CG	SV	IP	H	R	ER	HR	BB	SO	AVG
2004	Yakima (NWL)	A	2	3	2.79	7	7	0	0	29	22	14	9	1	19	28	.200
MINOR LEAGUE TOTALS			2	3	2.79	7	7	0	0	29	22	14	9	1	19	28	.200

21 Marland Williams, of

Born: June 22, 1981. **Ht.:** 5-9. **Wt.:** 175. **Bats:** R. **Throws:** R. **School:** North Florida CC. **Career Transactions:** Selected by Diamondbacks in 36th round of 2001 draft; signed May 10, 2002. **Signed by:** Luke Wrenn.

Williams was better known for his exploits on the gridiron in high school, drawing attention from national powerhouses Florida and Florida State as a wide receiver. The Diamondbacks did their homework however, and signed him as a draft-and-follow in 2002. His game-breaking speed was once again on display in 2004 as he led the Double-A Texas League in triples while finishing second in stolen bases, but he made little progress in the other aspects of his game. Williams is not only the fastest player in the system, he's the fastest in the history of the organization, having run sub-6.3 60s in spring workouts. He knows how to use his speed in game situations, covering a remarkable amount of ground in centerfield while achieving at an 88 percent success rate as a base stealer. At the plate, Williams needs to learn how to be an effective leadoff man, including improving his patience at the plate. He has just enough power to make him dangerous, and needs to focus more on contact and putting the ball on the ground to beat out infield singles. Williams' 2005 assignment will depend on how much progress he makes in spring training playing the little man's game.

Year	Club (League)	Class	AVG	G	AB	R	H	2B	3B	HR	RBI	BB	SO	SB	OBP	SLG
2002	Yakima (NWL)	A	.246	70	280	46	69	4	8	3	17	27	86	51	.311	.350
2003	Lancaster (Cal)	A	.287	102	425	85	122	15	1	4	30	31	99	57	.340	.355
2004	El Paso (TL)	AA	.259	121	487	82	126	21	10	8	44	40	116	49	.317	.392
MINOR LEAGUE TOTALS			.266	293	1192	213	317	40	19	15	91	98	301	157	.324	.369

22 Adam Peterson, rhp

Born: May 18, 1979. **Ht.:** 6-3. **Wt.:** 220. **Bats:** R. **Throws:** R. **School:** Wichita State University. **Career Transactions:** Selected by Blue Jays in fourth round of 2002 draft; signed June 11, 2002 . . . Traded by Blue Jays to Diamondbacks for 3B Shea Hillenbrand, Jan. 12, 2005. **Signed by:** Ty Nichols (Blue Jays).

The signing of Troy Glaus and the move of Chad Tracy across the diamond to first base left arbitration-eligible Shea Hillenbrand the odd man out, and the Diamondbacks shipped him to Toronto for Peterson, the first draftee during the J.P. Ricciardi era to reach the big leagues. Peterson had a dominant first half for Double-A New Hampshire, but he got shelled in three games for Toronto and it seemed to sap Peterson's confidence, as he only regressed at Triple-A Syracuse when sent down. Peterson does have big-time stuff however. He uses a maximum-effort delivery, but he has a quick arm and generates upper-90s heat with good tailing action. He shows a nasty slider and a straight change with some sink. Improved command is his No. 1 priority for getting back on track. Peterson will compete for a job in a crowded Arizona bullpen, but an opening assignment to Triple-A Tuscon to find the stuff that got him to the big leagues in the first place is the most likely scenario.

Year	Club (League)	Class	W	L	ERA	G	GS	CG	SV	IP	H	R	ER	HR	BB	SO	AVG
2002	Auburn (NY-P)	A	2	0	2.30	18	0	0	5	31	29	10	8	2	9	19	.246
2003	Charleston, WV (SAL)	A	2	4	2.19	10	0	0	1	25	15	8	6	1	13	19	.190
	Dunedin (FSL)	A	1	0	0.71	9	0	0	1	13	5	1	1	1	0	13	.116
	New Haven (EL)	AA	2	2	4.88	24	0	0	9	24	24	13	13	1	7	24	.261
2004	New Hampshire (EL)	AA	2	2	2.54	27	0	0	15	28	20	8	8	1	10	38	.198
	Toronto (AL)	MAJ	0	0	16.88	3	0	0	0	3	7	5	5	1	3	2	.467
	Syracuse (IL)	AAA	2	2	12.86	19	0	0	0	21	38	30	30	6	16	19	.404
MAJOR LEAGUE TOTALS			0	0	16.87	3	0	0	0	3	7	5	5	1	3	2	.467
MINOR LEAGUE TOTALS			11	10	4.18	107	0	0	31	142	131	70	66	12	55	132	.249

23 Jarred Ball, of

Born: April 18, 1983. **Ht.:** 6-0. **Wt.:** 198. **Bats:** B. **Throws:** R. **School:** Tomball (Texas) HS. **Career Transactions:** Selected by Diamondbacks in ninth round of 2001 draft; signed July 29, 2001. **Signed by:** Ray Corbett.

Ball has made slow and steady progress through the system, and that continued in 2004 as he put up career-highs in numerous categories, with his 15 home runs more than tripling his previous best. Ball does many things well, hitting for a decent average with some power. An above average runner who can steal bases and play all three outfield positions, Ball is a gamer who consistently outplays his skills. Scouts have trouble warming up to Ball, as he lacks any single outstanding tool to project him as more that a fourth outfielder. He needs to be more selective at the plate and is prone to chasing breaking balls, which has led to lofty strikeout totals. His arm is average at best and his poor routes in the outfield leave some feeling he'll be relegated to a corner. The Diamondbacks have always seen Ball as a one-level-at-a-time player, and that will continue at Double-A in 2005.

Year	Club (League)	Class	AVG	G	AB	R	H	2B	3B	HR	RBI	BB	SO	SB	OBP	SLG
2001	Missoula (Pio)	R	.246	19	57	13	14	2	1	0	3	7	14	1	.348	.316
2002	South Bend (Mid)	A	.240	87	321	48	77	13	4	2	23	42	85	12	.338	.324
2003	South Bend (Mid)	A	.281	125	463	62	130	23	2	4	52	41	84	32	.342	.365
2004	Lancaster (Cal)	A	.297	125	472	82	140	26	6	15	66	45	123	17	.359	.472
MINOR LEAGUE TOTALS			.275	356	1313	205	361	64	13	21	144	135	306	62	.348	.391

24 Phil Avlas, c

Born: Dec. 17, 1982. **Ht.:** 5-11. **Wt.:** 175. **Bats:** R. **Throws:** R. **School:** John F. Kennedy HS, North Hills, Calif. **Career Transactions:** Selected by Diamondbacks in 24th round of 2001 draft; signed Aug. 28, 2001. **Signed by:** Hal Kurtzman.

When the Diamondbacks drafted Avlas in 2001, they intended to sign him as a draft-and-follow but he signed in late August and got a head start on his pro career. Seen as more of an organizational player entering the season, Avlas took a tremendous step forward with the bat in 2004 to establish him as a legitimate prospect. Avlas makes good contact and added power to his game in high Class A, slugging 13 home runs after entering the season with just one career home run as a pro. He's athletic behind the plate and while his arm has average strength, his remarkably quick release and accuracy make him effective against the running game. He has an excellent feel for the game and pitchers love throwing to him. Avlas doesn't offer much more in terms of power projection, and his slight build leaves doubts as to his ability to handle the every day grind of the position. He'll face a big test in Double-A in 2005.

Year	Club (League)	Class	AVG	G	AB	R	H	2B	3B	HR	RBI	BB	SO	SB	OBP	SLG
2002	Missoula (Pio)	R	.276	50	152	22	42	13	2	0	19	21	37	3	.371	.388
2003	South Bend (Mid)	A	.203	47	133	14	27	7	0	1	15	16	17	4	.283	.278
	Yakima (NWL)	A	.333	17	45	7	15	4	1	0	4	6	11	0	.412	.467
2004	Lancaster (Cal)	A	.315	109	384	64	121	22	8	13	68	29	54	5	.359	.516
MINOR LEAGUE TOTALS			.287	223	714	107	205	46	11	14	106	72	119	12	.350	.441

25 A.J. Shappi, rhp

Born: Oct. 16, 1982. **Ht.:** 6-2. **Wt.:** 195. **Bats:** R. **Throws:** R. **School:** UC Riverside. **Career Transactions:** Selected by Diamondbacks in the ninth round of 2004 draft; signed June 17, 2004. **Signed by:** Mark Baca.

Shappi was a true student-athlete at UC Riverside, serving as the team's ace while also being a Rhodes scholarship candidate as a chemistry major. His lack of velocity dropped him in the eyes of many scouts, but he was lights-out in his pro debut, finishing second in the Northwest League in ERA. Shappi's pitches are all evaluated at a full grade higher based on his exquisite control. His fastball sits at 86-89 mph and has plenty of sink. His best pitch is his slider, which features plenty of late break, and he's shown good aptitude with a circle changeup. Shappi's game offers little projection, and he needs to find an effective way to combat left-handed batters, who hit .309 against him. Shappi finally faced some adversity in the high Class A California League playoffs, where he gave up 12 runs in eight innings, including three home runs. He'll likely return there in 2005.

Year	Club (League)	Class	W	L	ERA	G	GS	CG	SV	IP	H	R	ER	HR	BB	SO	AVG
2004	Yakima (NWL)	A	4	1	1.75	12	11	0	0	67	64	17	13	4	8	65	.253
	Lancaster (Cal)	A	1	0	3.00	2	1	0	0	6	6	2	2	1	1	8	.261
MINOR LEAGUE TOTALS			5	1	1.85	14	12	0	0	73	70	19	15	5	9	73	.254

26 Chris Carter, of/1b

Born: Sept. 16, 1982. **Ht.:** 6-0. **Wt.:** 195. **Bats:** L. **Throws:** L. **School:** Stanford University. **Career Transactions:** Selected by Diamondbacks in 17th round of 2004 draft; signed June 16, 2004. **Signed by:** Fred Costello.

Carter was one of Stanford's top recruits in 2001 and was named the team's Most Valuable Freshman after hitting .375 in the NCAA postseason. A shoulder injury hampered him in 2002 and his poor sophomore showing and lack of defensive skills dropped him out of favor with the Cardinal, limiting him to DH duties as a junior. The Diamondbacks feel they got one of the best values of the draft in Carter, who led the Northwest League in slugging and RBIs in his pro debut. Carter has jaw-dropping power from the left side, eliciting gasps in batting practice while launching 500-plus foot shots when he turns on a ball. He has an advanced feel for the strike zone and draws a good number of walks. His bat will have to be his ticket to the majors as Carter has yet to show any aptitude defensively. He was a designated hitter in nearly half of his starts in his debut, an option unavailable to the Diamondbacks at Double-A and above. He has only one thought when he swings the bat— he's either going to hit the ball very hard, or miss it entirely. Carter has already proved completely incapable of playing left, and will move to first base in 2005, where he also has struggled. He could put up some big numbers in high Class A, where he'll begin the year.

Year	Club (League)	Class	AVG	G	AB	R	H	2B	3B	HR	RBI	BB	SO	SB	OBP	SLG
2004	Yakima (NWL)	A	.335	70	257	47	86	15	1	15	63	46	35	2	.436	.576
	South Bend (Mid)	A	.385	6	26	3	10	3	0	2	7	0	2	0	.385	.731
MINOR LEAGUE TOTALS			.339	76	283	50	96	18	1	17	70	46	37	2	.432	.590

27 Jereme Milons, of

Born: Feb. 5, 1983. **Ht.:** 6-2. **Wt.:** 205. **Bats:** R. **Throws:** R. **School:** Starkville (Miss.) HS. **Career Transactions:** Selected by Dodgers in 21st round of 2001 draft; signed May 21, 2002 . . . Traded by Dodgers to Diamondbacks for RHP Elmer Dessens and cash, Aug. 19, 2004. **Signed by:** Clarence Johns (Dodgers).

The Dodgers had two of the more athletic outfielders in the minors in Reggie Abercrombie and Milons, but both are Diamondbacks now, with Abercrombie coming over in the Steve Finley deal and Milons arriving in mid-August for righty Elmer Dessens. Milons comes from an athletic family, with all six siblings participating in college athletics, including older brother Freddie, who is Alabama football's all-time receptions leader. Milons is a wonderful athlete who would be the fastest runner in most organizations. He has a fluid swing with some power potential and made small strides in making more contact in 2004. He has good range in center and an average arm. Milons is still extremely raw offensively, and tries too hard to be a power hitter with some speed instead of his ideal slot as a leadoff man with some pop. His swing can get long when he gets pull conscious, and he needs to learn more patience at the plate. Milons still needs to learn the game, and the Diamondbacks will start him back in low A for 2005.

Year	Club (League)	Class	AVG	G	AB	R	H	2B	3B	HR	RBI	BB	SO	SB	OBP	SLG
2002	Dodgers (GCL)	R	.243	45	152	28	37	8	1	1	23	10	24	9	.297	.329
2003	Ogden (Pio)	R	.308	51	195	37	60	7	5	1	23	19	47	10	.369	.410
2004	Columbus (SAL)	A	.273	103	436	70	119	14	6	10	53	30	99	25	.321	.401
	Vero Beach (FSL)	A	.205	11	39	5	8	1	0	0	2	3	9	4	.256	.231
	South Bend (Mid)	A	.172	11	29	1	5	0	1	0	1	0	10	1	.200	.241
MINOR LEAGUE TOTALS			.269	221	851	141	229	30	13	12	102	62	189	49	.321	.377

28 Brad Halsey, lhp

Born: Feb. 14, 1981. **Ht.:** 6-1. **Wt.:** 180. **Bats:** L. **Throws:** L. **School:** University of Texas. **Career Transactions:** Selected by Yankees in eighth round of 2002 draft; signed July 1, 2002 . . . Traded by Yankees with C Dioner Navarro and RHP Javier Vazquez to Diamondbacks for LHP Randy Johnson, Jan. 3, 2005. **Signed by:** Steve Boros (Yankees).

Halsey reached the majors less than two years after signing his first pro contract, and went over to the Diamondbacks in the Randy Johnson deal. The No. 1 starter for Texas' 2002 College World Series championship team and one of four Longhorns drafted by New York in 2002, Halsey has proven the best of the bunch. He made seven big league starts last season, beating the Dodgers in his debut and turning in solid outings against the Red Sox and Blue Jays. He's a strike-thrower with an 87-90 mph fastball, a slider (his best pitch) and a changeup. However, none of them is a knockout pitch and Halsey usually is around the plate too much. He lacks the stuff to challenge good big league hitters on a consistent basis. He'll compete with Mike Gosling for the final rotation slot in spring training, but is most likely destined for Triple-A . His slider is good enough that he could help as a situational lefty out of the bullpen, filling an organizational weakness.

Year	Club (League)	Class	W	L	ERA	G	GS	CG	SV	IP	H	R	ER	HR	BB	SO	AVG
2002	Staten Island (NY-P)	A	6	1	1.93	11	10	0	0	56	39	15	12	0	17	53	.195
2003	Tampa (FSL)	A	10	4	3.43	14	13	1	0	84	96	36	32	3	14	56	.287
	Trenton (EL)	AA	7	5	4.93	15	15	0	0	91	123	51	50	4	22	78	.325
2004	New York (AL)	MAJ	1	3	6.47	8	7	0	0	32	41	26	23	4	14	25	.306
	Columbus (IL)	AAA	11	4	2.63	24	23	3	0	144	128	46	42	8	37	109	.237
MAJOR LEAGUE TOTALS			1	3	6.47	8	7	0	0	32	41	26	23	4	14	25	.306
MINOR LEAGUE TOTALS			34	14	3.26	64	61	4	0	375	386	148	136	15	90	296	.266

29 Lance Cormier, rhp

Born: Aug. 19, 1980. **Ht.:** 6-1. **Wt.:** 192. **Bats:** R. **Throws:** R. **School:** University of Alabama. **Career Transactions:** Selected by Diamondbacks in fourth round of 2002 draft; signed June 6, 2002. **Signed by:** Michael Valarezo.

Drafted as a senior after he declined to sign with the Astros following his junior season, Cormier was one of many emergency replacements who received a rough introduction to the majors in 2004. He earned his first big league win with six-plus solid innings against the Astros in late July, but was hammered for 12 runs in his next two starts and continued to get hit hard following a demotion to the bullpen. Cormier certainly doesn't project as a star, but he has enough stuff to be a serviceable major league pitcher. His fastball sits in the high 80s, but he has excellent command of it, as well as his curveball and plus changeup. He gave major league hitters too much credit when he reached Arizona, and lost his aggressiveness. Without a real out pitch, his future might be best as a swingman or long reliever. He'll begin 2005 looking to build back some confidence at Triple-A.

Year	Club (League)	Class	W	L	ERA	G	GS	CG	SV	IP	H	R	ER	HR	BB	SO	AVG
2002	Yakima (NWL)	A	0	0	7.00	1	0	0	0	1	4	4	3	0	0	3	.500
	South Bend (Mid)	A	3	0	2.93	11	3	0	1	28	29	9	9	1	2	17	.259
2003	Lancaster (Cal)	A	6	5	3.82	15	15	0	0	94	102	55	40	6	16	59	.280
	Tucson (PCL)	AAA	1	1	2.60	5	4	0	0	28	26	10	8	1	5	11	.260
	El Paso (TL)	AA	2	3	6.10	9	8	0	0	41	59	33	28	3	22	26	.337
2004	Tucson (PCL)	AAA	3	3	2.68	8	8	2	0	50	50	17	15	0	17	37	.260
	El Paso (TL)	AA	2	3	2.29	10	8	0	0	63	66	19	16	3	17	58	.277
	Arizona (NL)	MAJ	1	4	8.14	17	5	0	0	45	62	42	41	13	25	24	.333
MAJOR LEAGUE TOTALS			1	4	8.14	17	5	0	0	45	62	42	41	13	25	24	.333
MINOR LEAGUE TOTALS			17	15	3.51	59	46	2	1	305	336	147	119	14	79	211	.283

30 Reggie Abercrombie, of

Born: July 15, 1980. **Ht.:** 6-3. **Wt.:** 220. **Bats:** R. **Throws:** R. **School:** Lake City (Fla.) CC. **Career Transactions:** Selected by Dodgers in 23rd round of 1999 draft; signed May 24, 2000 . . . Traded by Dodgers with C Koyie Hill and LHP Bill Murphy to Diamondbacks for OF Steve Finley and C Brent Mayne, July 31, 2004. **Signed by:** Lon Joyce (Dodgers).

Abercrombie's tools have had scouts on him for years, but a lack of production and a 2003 knee injury have dimmed his star greatly. While he made an early return from ACL surgery in May, Abercrombie was completely lost against Double-A pitching and found himself back in the Florida State League before being shipped by the Dodgers to Arizona in the Steve Finley deal. The Diamondbacks shortened his swing in high Class A and elicited good results, but all of the other problems in his game remained. Abercrombie's athletic ability is without fault. He's a plus runner with an above-average arm and raw power. His approach at the plate is as unbridles as it gets, and it's actually gotten worse over the past two seasons, as he's struck out 287 times while drawing just 28 walks in 220 games. Abercrombie will turn 25 in June, and it's time for him to start turning his unquestioned potential into results. He'll get another shot at Double-A in what could be a make or break season.

Year	Club (League)	Class	AVG	G	AB	R	H	2B	3B	HR	RBI	BB	SO	SB	OBP	SLG
2000	Great Falls (Pio)	R	.273	54	220	40	60	7	1	2	29	22	66	32	.360	.341
2001	Wilmington (SAL)	A	.226	125	486	63	110	17	3	10	41	19	154	44	.272	.335
2002	Vero Beach (FSL)	A	.276	132	526	80	145	23	13	10	56	27	158	41	.321	.426
	Jacksonville (SL)	AA	.250	1	4	1	1	0	0	0	0	0	1	1	.250	.250
2003	Jacksonville (SL)	AA	.261	116	448	59	117	25	7	15	54	16	164	28	.298	.449
2004	Jacksonville (SL)	AA	.173	41	168	17	29	6	4	4	20	4	66	3	.193	.327
	Vero Beach (FSL)	A	.271	34	133	18	36	4	5	5	12	6	33	16	.305	.489
	Lancaster (Cal)	A	.342	29	120	24	41	10	2	3	19	2	24	8	.358	.533
MINOR LEAGUE TOTALS			.256	532	2105	302	539	92	35	49	231	96	666	173	.300	.403

ATLANTA
BRAVES

BY **BILL BALLEW**

N o team has used its farm system to a greater advantage over the past two decades than the Braves. Atlanta's current string of 13 straight division titles began in 1991 with the emergence of homegrown players such as Steve Avery, Ron Gant, Tom Glavine and David Justice. In 1993, the Braves were bolstered by a group tagged as "The Great Eight" at Triple-A Richmond, featuring Chipper Jones, Ryan Klesko and Javy Lopez.

The Braves have continued to add significant players from their system, including Rafael Furcal, Marcus Giles and two-time Minor League Player of the Year Andruw Jones. Last season included yet another infusion of youth, headed by **Adam LaRoche** and unexpected contributions from Nick Green and Charles Thomas.

Not only has Atlanta incorporated its minor leaguers into its big league club, but it also has used them in trades. Key performers such as Johnny Estrada, Mike Hampton and Chris Reitsma were acquired for minor leaguers, and general manager John Schuerholz was aggressive trading in the offseason, acquiring two 2004 all-stars for his pitching staff.

Schuerholz included the Braves' former top pitching prospect, righthander Jose Capellan, in a Winter Meetings deal that brought closer Dan Kolb from Milwaukee and allowed John Smoltz to return to the rotation. Five days later, Atlanta won the Tim Hudson sweepstakes with a package of Dan Meyer (one of the top lefties in the minors), Juan Cruz (acquired in March for

prospects) and Thomas. The previous offseason, Schuerholz sacrificed righty Adam Wainwright, then the best arm in the system, to get J.D. Drew from St. Louis.

Even after those deals, the Braves still have plenty of high-end talent. Pitching, as always, remains a strength from top to bottom, and the position players are as deep as they've been in years. The organization's depth is a testament to both exhaustive scouting and structured coaching and instruction that is taught in a consistent manner from the bottom of the farm system up to the major league level.

Atlanta continues to focus as much on makeup as tools. The returns are undeniable, as the Braves' run of success means they haven't drafted higher than 21st overall since 1992, yet scouting director Roy Clark and his staff continue to find talent.

More new faces are on the way in 2005. The big league roster should include infielder Wilson Betemit, righthander Roman Colon and outfielder Ryan Langerhans in reserve roles. By 2007, the lineup could feature four more homegrown players: outfielder Jeff Francoeur, shortstop Luis Hernandez, third baseman Andy Marte and catcher Brad McCann. Righty Kyle Davies is on track to crack the rotation by that point.

In other words, the more things change in Atlanta, the more they stay the same.

TOP 30 PROSPECTS

1. Jeff Francoeur, of	16. Macay McBride, lhp
2. Andy Marte, 3b	17. T.J. Pena, ss
3. Brian McCann, c	18. Charlie Morton, rhp
4. Kyle Davies, rhp	19. Gonzalo Lopez, rhp
5. Anthony Lerew, rhp	20. Chuck James, lhp
6. Jake Stevens, lhp	21. Billy McCarthy, of
7. Luis Hernandez, ss	22. Brandon Jones, of
8. Kelly Johnson, of	23. J.C. Holt, 2b
9. Jarrod Saltalamacchia, c	24. Gregor Blanco, of
10. Blaine Boyer, rhp	25. Josh Burrus, of
11. Jose Ascanio, rhp	26. Zach Miner, rhp
12. Scott Thorman, 1b	27. Luis Atilano, rhp
13. Roman Colon, rhp	28. Martin Prado, 2b
14. Ryan Langerhans, of	29. Diory Hernandez, ss
15. Wilson Betemit, 3b/ss	30. James Jurries, 1b

ORGANIZATION OVERVIEW

General manager: John Schuerholz. **Farm director:** Dayton Moore. **Scouting director:** Roy Clark.

2004 PERFORMANCE

Class	Team	League	W	L	Pct.	Finish*	Manager
Majors	Atlanta	National	96	66	.593	2nd (16)	Bobby Cox
Triple-A	Richmond Braves	International	79	62	.560	2nd (14)	Pat Kelly
Double-A	#Greenville Braves	Southern	63	76	.453	9th (10)	Brian Snitker
High A	Myrtle Beach Pelicans	Carolina	75	63	.543	3rd (8)	Randy Ingle
Low A	Rome Braves	South Atlantic	70	70	.500	t-7th (16)	Rocket Wheeler
Rookie	Danville Braves	Appalachian	41	25	.621	1st (10)	Jim Saul
Rookie	GCL Braves	Gulf Coast	23	36	.390	10th (12)	Ralph Henriquez
OVERALL 2004 MINOR LEAGUE RECORD			351	332	.514	9th (30)	

*Finish in overall standings (No. of teams in league). #Franchise will move to Pearl, Miss. (Southern) in 2005.

ORGANIZATION LEADERS

BATTING   *Minimum 250 At-Bats
*AVG	Napoleon Calzado, Richmond/Greenville	.353
R	Ryan Langerhans, Richmond	103
H	Napoleon Calzado, Richmond/Greenville	165
TB	Ryan Langerhans, Richmond	236
2B	Kelly Johnson, Greenville	35
	Brian McCann, Myrtle Beach	35
3B	Peter Orr, Richmond	10
HR	James Jurries, Richmond/Greenville	25
RBI	Scott Thorman, Greenville/Myrtle Beach	80
BB	Ryan Langerhans, Richmond	70
SO	Steve Doetsch, Rome	152
SB	Onil Joseph, Myrtle Beach	32
*OBP	Ryan Langerhans, Richmond	.397
*SLG	Mike Hessman, Richmond	.562

PITCHING   #Minimum 75 Innings
W	Jose Capellan, Richmond/Greenville/M.B.	14
L	Three tied at	10
#ERA	Chuck James, Rome	2.24
G	Matt Whiteside, Richmond	57
CG	Ten tied at	1
SV	Matt Whiteside, Richmond	38
IP	Blaine Boyer, Myrtle Beach	154
BB	Bryan Digby, Rome	71
SO	Kyle Davies, Richmond/Greenville/M.B.	173

BEST TOOLS

Best Hitter for Average	Jeff Francoeur
Best Power Hitter	Andy Marte
Best Strike-Zone Discipline	Wes Timmons
Fastest Baserunner	Gregor Blanco
Best Athlete	Jeff Francoeur
Best Fastball	Anthony Lerew
Best Curveball	Charlie Morton
Best Slider	Macay McBride
Best Changeup	Kyle Davies
Best Control	Jake Stevens
Best Defensive Catcher	Brian McCann
Best Defensive Infielder	Luis Hernandez
Best Infield Arm	Wilson Betemit
Best Defensive Outfielder	Ryan Langerhans
Best Outfield Arm	Jeff Francoeur

PROJECTED 2008 LINEUP

Catcher	Brian McCann
First Base	Adam LaRoche
Second Base	Marcus Giles
Third Base	Andy Marte
Shortstop	Rafael Furcal
Left Field	Chipper Jones
Center Field	Andruw Jones
Right Field	Jeff Francoeur

No. 1 Starter	Tim Hudson
No. 2 Starter	Kyle Davies
No. 3 Starter	Anthony Lerew
No. 4 Starter	Horacio Estrada
No. 5 Starter	Jake Stevens
Closer	Jose Ascanio

LAST YEAR'S TOP 20 PROSPECTS

1. Andy Marte, 3b
2. Jeff Francoeur, of
3. Bubba Nelson, rhp
4. Dan Meyer, lhp
5. Adam LaRoche, 1b
6. Macay McBride, lhp
7. Brian McCann, c
8. Kyle Davies, rhp
9. Anthony Lerew, rhp
10. Kelly Johnson, ss
11. Jose Capellan, rhp
12. Wilson Betemit, 3b
13. Gregor Blanco, of
14. Onil Joseph, of
15. Jake Stevens, lhp
16. Blaine Boyer, rhp
17. Matt Merricks, lhp
18. Scott Thorman, 1b
19. Jarrod Saltalamacchia, c
20. Carlos Duran, of

TOP PROSPECTS OF THE DECADE

Year	Player, Pos.	Current Team
1995	Chipper Jones, ss/3b	Braves
1996	Andruw Jones, of	Braves
1997	Andruw Jones, of	Braves
1998	Bruce Chen, lhp	Orioles
1999	Bruce Chen, lhp	Orioles
2000	Rafael Furcal, ss	Braves
2001	Wilson Betemit, ss	Braves
2002	Wilson Betemit, ss	Braves
2003	Adam Wainwright, rhp	Cardinals
2004	Andy Marte, 3b	Braves

TOP DRAFT PICKS OF THE DECADE

Year	Player, Pos.	Current Team
1995	*Chad Hutchinson, rhp	Out of baseball
1996	A.J. Zapp, 1b	Mariners
1997	Troy Cameron, ss	Out of baseball
1998	Matt Belisle, rhp (2)	Reds
1999	Matt Butler, rhp (2)	Out of baseball
2000	Adam Wainwright, rhp	Cardinals
2001	Macay McBride, lhp	Braves
2002	Jeff Francoeur, of	Braves
2003	Luis Atilano, rhp	Braves
2004	Eric Campbell, 3b (2)	Braves

*Did not sign.

ALL-TIME LARGEST BONUSES

Jeff Francoeur, 2002	$2,200,000
Matt Belisle, 1998	$1,750,000
Jung Bong, 1997	$1,700,000
Macay McBride, 2001	$1,340,000
Adam Wainwright, 2000	$1,250,000
Josh Burrus, 2001	$1,250,000

Atlanta BRAVES

RANK: **5**

Impact Potential: B

The Braves have two potential middle-of-the-lineup all-stars in Jeff Francoeur and Andy Marte, either of whom could rank as the No. 1 prospect in about half of the game's organizations. Brian McCann and Jarrod Saltalamacchia stand out in a minor league landscape bereft of catching prospects, giving the Braves a pair who can hit and stay behind the plate. Trading Jose Capellan and Dan Meyer in the offseason, however, cost Atlanta its top two minor league arms.

Depth: B

The Braves continue to churn out quality and quantity. Most organizations would be happy with Kyle Davies, Anthony Lerew and Jake Stevens as their top pitching prospects. The Braves have the depth to wait for the development of late bloomers such as Ryan Langerhans and to be patient with players like Wilson Betemit and Macay McBride. The Latin American program also continues to make a strong impact.

*Depth charts prepared by **John Manuel** and **Allan Simpson**. Numbers in parentheses indicate prospect rankings.*

LF
Kelly Johnson (8)
Billy McCarthy (21)
Brandon Jones (22)
Josh Burrus (25)
Onil Joseph
Carl Loadenthal

CF
Ryan Langerhans (14)
Gregor Blanco (24)
Matt Esquivel

RF
Jeff Francoeur (1)
Carlos Duran
Steve Doetsch

3B
Andy Marte (2)
Wilson Betemit (15)
Eric Campbell
Van Pope
Wes Timmons

SS
Luis Hernandez (7)
T.J. Pena (17)
Diory Hernandez (29)

2B
J.C. Holt (23)
Martin Prado (28)
Peter Orr
Aaron Herr

1B
Scott Thorman (12)
James Jurries (30)
Carlos Guzman
Keith Eichas

SOURCE of TALENT

HOMEGROWN		ACQUIRED	
College	3	Trades	0
Junior College	0	Rule 5 draft	0
Draft-and-follow	1	Independent leagues	0
High School	16	Free agents/waivers	0
Nondrafted free agent	0		
Foreign	10		

C
Brian McCann (3)
Jarrod Saltalamacchia (9)
Brayan Pena

LHP

Starters	Relievers
Jake Stevens (6)	Macay McBride (16)
Chuck James (20)	Matt Coenen
Jo Jo Reyes	Ray Aguilar
Matt Harrison	Brady Endl
	Jonny Venters

RHP

Starters	Relievers
Kyle Davies (4)	Jose Ascanio (11)
Anthony Lerew (5)	Roman Colon (13)
Blaine Boyer (10)	Zach Miner (26)
Charlie Morton (18)	Luis Atilano (27)
Gonzalo Lopez (19)	Ryan Basner
Matt Wright	Bryan Digby
Paul Bacot	Kevin Barry
Sean White	
James Parr	
Chris Vines	
Angelo Burrows	

DRAFT ANALYSIS

2004

Best Pro Debut: Primarily an outfielder at Louisiana State, J.C. Holt (3) moved to second base after signing, the first time he regularly played there since 2002. He had no trouble making the transition, or the Rookie-level Appalachian League all-star team after he hit .321 with 17 steals.

Best Athlete: RHP James Parr (4) was a two-way star on the La Cueva High (Albuquerque) team that won 58 straight games and consecutive New Mexico 5-A championships. On the day before the draft, he won the home-run derby at the All-American Baseball Game, a national event whose derby contestants included SS/3B Eric Campbell (2) and OF Jon Mark Owings (17), top sluggers and fellow Braves draftees.

Best Pure Hitter: Holt won the 2003 Cape Cod League batting title at .388, the highest average in the summer college league since 1990. He hit .350 in three seasons at Louisiana State, finishing second in the Southeastern Conference batting race at .393 during the spring.

Best Raw Power: Campbell, Owings and OF Adam Parliament (26) all can drive balls great distances. Campbell already has drawn comparisons to power-hitting infielders such as Jeff Kent and Matt Williams.

Fastest Runner: Holt, a high school track star, gets from home to first in 4.0 seconds.

Best Defensive Player: C Clint Sammons (6) earned raves for his ability to handle pitching staffs at Georgia, which made a surprise run to the College World Series, and at Danville, which finished second in the Appy League playoffs.

Best Fastball: Though he's just 6 feet tall and pitched at 85-87 mph at times during

Campbell

the spring, Parr usually pitches in the low 90s and tops out at 95 mph. LHP Trae Wiggins (7) also can reach 95.

Best Breaking Ball: Parr's curveball.

Most Intriguing Background: Owings' older brother Micah was considered a second- or third-round talent but slipped to the 19th round (Cubs) because of signability. LHP Brady Endl's (10) two-way skills earned him Division III player of the year and academic all-American of the year honors.

Closest To The Majors: Holt, though the Braves aren't exactly hurting at second base with Marcus Giles. Holt and Sammons were the only Division I college players Atlanta took in the first 10 rounds.

Best Late-Round Pick: The Braves signed LHP Tyler Wilson (21) and Parliament after watching them star in a summer tournament in suburban Atlanta. Wilson pitched at 90-91 mph and showed an intriguing curveball. Of Parliament, Braves scouting director Roy Clark says, "We call him Canseco."

The One Who Got Away: The Braves weren't able to steer SS Brad Emaus (18), their highest unsigned pick, away from attending Tulane. He has a solid bat and average tools across the board.

Assessment: The Braves' first pick didn't come until 71st overall. They compensated with a strong crop of 2003 draft-and-follows that included athletic OF Brandon Jones, hard-hitting OF Mark Jurich and hard-throwing LHP Jonny Venters.

2003 Atlanta had six picks in the first three rounds, and most of them have started slowly. The exceptions are C Jarrod Saltalamacchia (1) and LHP Jake Stevens (3). *GRADE:* C+

2002 The first three choices are all blue-chip prospects: OF Jeff Francoeur (1), LHP Dan Meyer (1) and C Brian McCann (2). Meyer was the key to the Tim Hudson trade with Oakland this offseason. Unsigned SS Tyler Greene (2) could be the first college position player drafted in 2005. *GRADE:* A

2001 Three first-rounders—LHP Macay McBride, SS Josh Burrus and 2B Richard Lewis—have had mixed success. Two later-round choices, RHPs Kyle Davies (4) and Anthony Lerew (11), are the cream of this crop. *GRADE:* B+

2000 1B Adam LaRoche (29) and OF Charles Thomas (19) reached the big leagues in 2004. Three first-rounders—RHP Adam Wainwright, 1B Scott Thorman and OF Kelly Johnson—are decent prospects, while a fourth, 2B Aaron Herr, has fallen by the wayside. *GRADE:* B+

Draft analysis prepared by Jim Callis. Numbers in parentheses indicate draft rounds.

Jeff
FRANCOEUR

Born: Jan. 8, 1984.
Ht.: 6-4. **Wt.:** 165.
Bats: B. **Throws:** R.
School: Parkview HS, Lilburn, Ga.
Career Transactions: Selected by Braves in first round (23rd overall) of 2002 draft; signed July 8, 2002.
Signed by: Al Goetz.

A two-sport standout in high school, Francoeur was a high school all-America defensive back who turned down the opportunity to play football and baseball at Clemson. Since signing for a club-record $2.2 million bonus, he twice has been named the top prospect in his minor league, first in the Rookie-level Appalachian League in 2002 and again in the high Class A Carolina League in 2004. Francoeur was on the verge of a promotion to Double-A Greenville last July when he squared around to bunt and the ball ricocheted off the bat up into his face, breaking his right cheekbone. Initially expected to miss the rest of the season after having surgery, Francoeur pushed himself and returned in five weeks. He finished the year in Double-A and made up for some lost time by batting .283 in the Arizona Fall League.

Francoeur is one of the purest five-tool players in the minor leagues. Scouts rave about the way he consistently gets the barrel of the bat on the ball. He uses his hands well in his swing and generates tremendous bat speed, which combined with his natural power should enable him to hit 30-plus home runs annually in the majors. Francoeur uses the entire field and used his season at pitcher-friendly Myrtle Beach to his advantage, becoming adept at driving outside pitches the opposite way. Defensively, he made a seamless move from center field to right last year. Managers rated his arm the best among Carolina League outfielders. He has outstanding range and gets good jumps on balls. His knack for being in the right position can be attributed to his speed as well as his baseball instincts and intelligence. As impressive as his tools may be, Francoeur's makeup may stand out even more. One of the most competitive players in the organization, he's a fiery team leader, which could be just what the big league team needs.

Francoeur's greatest need is to show more patience at the plate, and at this point it appears to be the only flaw in his game. While he doesn't strike out excessively, he also didn't draw a walk in 18 Double-A games and he worked just two in 25 AFL contests. The Braves don't want him to change his aggressive approach, but he understands that better strike-zone discipline will make him an even more dangerous hitter. After another year of making adjustments against advanced pitching, he should be ready for his major league debut soon thereafter.

Longtime Atlanta officials continue to compare Francoeur to Dale Murphy, and his swagger is more reminiscent of Chipper Jones. He's an exciting player who gives the game every ounce of his energy every time he takes the field. His natural ability and approach could make him a 30-30 man and an all-star for the Braves. Even if he's moved at a conservative pace, he should get his first taste of the big leagues by the end of 2006.

Year	Club (League)	Class	AVG	G	AB	R	H	2B	3B	HR	RBI	BB	SO	SB	OBP	SLG
2002	Danville (Appy)	R	.327	38	147	31	48	12	1	8	31	15	34	8	.395	.585
2003	Rome (SAL)	A	.281	134	524	78	147	26	9	14	68	30	68	14	.325	.445
2004	Myrtle Beach (Car)	A	.293	88	334	56	98	26	0	15	52	22	70	10	.346	.506
	Greenville (SL)	AA	.197	18	76	8	15	2	0	3	9	0	14	1	.208	.342
MINOR LEAGUE TOTALS			.285	278	1081	173	308	66	10	40	160	67	186	33	.334	.475

Andy Marte, 3b

Born: Oct. 21, 1983. **Ht.:** 6-1. **Wt.:** 180. **Bats:** R. **Throws:** R. **Career Transactions:** Signed out of Dominican Republic by Braves, Sept. 12, 2000. **Signed by:** Rene Francisco/Julian Perez.

Marte turned in another solid season in 2004, appearing in the Futures Game and being rated as the top prospect in the Double-A Southern League. Despite missing a month with sprains in both ankles, he finished second in homers among Braves farmhands. Marte's ability to drive the ball to all fields is outstanding and getting better. He already shows patience at the plate. His glovework is also above-average, as managers named him the best defensive third baseman and top infield arm in the Southern League. He shows impressive maturity for his age. Marte's swing has a slight uppercut and can get a little long when he tires, but the Braves consider those minor problems. Still, his strikeout rate jumped in 2004. His body has gotten a little thick over the past two years and might need monitoring. Marte is the Braves' long-term answer at third base. He needs another half-season in the minors and will begin 2005 at Triple-A Richmond, but he could take over full-time as soon as Opening Day 2006. His potential as an all-around impact player is unquestioned.

Year	Club (League)	Class	AVG	G	AB	R	H	2B	3B	HR	RBI	BB	SO	SB	OBP	SLG
2001	Danville (Appy)	R	.200	37	125	12	25	6	0	1	12	20	45	3	.306	.272
2002	Macon (SAL)	A	.281	126	488	69	137	32	4	21	105	41	114	2	.339	.492
2003	Myrtle Bch (Car)	A	.285	130	463	69	132	35	1	16	63	67	109	5	.372	.469
2004	Greenville (SL)	AA	.269	107	387	52	104	28	1	23	68	58	105	1	.364	.525
MINOR LEAGUE TOTALS			.272	400	1463	202	398	101	6	61	248	186	373	11	.354	.474

Brian McCann, c

Born: Feb. 20, 1984. **Ht.:** 6-3. **Wt.:** 210. **Bats:** L. **Throws:** R. **School:** Duluth (Ga.) HS. **Career Transactions:** Selected by Braves in second round of 2002 draft; signed July 11, 2002. **Signed by:** Al Goetz.

Despite playing at pitcher-friendly Myrtle Beach, McCann put together one of the best all-around seasons of any catcher in the minors. A Carolina League all-star, he tied for the organization lead in doubles and set a career high for homers. Older brother Brad, a third baseman, signed with the Marlins as a 2004 sixth-round pick, and his father Howard is the former head coach at Marshall. McCann has a sweet lefthanded swing and as much raw power as anyone in the organization. He employs a disciplined approach at the plate and makes solid contact. Drafted primarily for his bat, he has dedicated himself to improving behind the plate and was named the CL's best defensive catcher. He threw out 30 percent of basestealers with his strong, accurate arm and quick release. While pitchers like throwing to McCann, he needs to hone his skills behind the plate, particularly his footwork and agility. Offensively, he could draw more walks. He's a below-average runner. He has drawn comparisons to Eddie Taubensee, but the Braves say McCann has a higher ceiling. He'll spend 2005 at the new Double-A Mississippi affiliate and could reach Atlanta by late 2006.

Year	Club (League)	Class	AVG	G	AB	R	H	2B	3B	HR	RBI	BB	SO	SB	OBP	SLG
2002	Braves (GCL)	R	.220	29	100	9	22	5	0	2	11	10	22	0	.295	.330
2003	Rome (SAL)	A	.290	115	424	40	123	31	3	12	71	24	73	7	.329	.462
2004	Myrtle Beach (Car)	A	.278	111	385	45	107	35	0	16	66	31	54	2	.337	.494
MINOR LEAGUE TOTALS			.277	255	909	94	252	71	3	30	148	65	149	9	.329	.461

Kyle Davies, rhp

Born: Sept. 9, 1983. **Ht.:** 6-2. **Wt.:** 190. **Bats:** R. **Throws:** R. **School:** Stockbridge (Ga.) HS. **Career Transactions:** Selected by Braves in fourth round of 2001 draft; signed June 15, 2001. **Signed by:** Rob English.

Baseball America once rated Davies, a standout in the East Cobb program in suburban Atlanta, as the nation's top 14-year-old (1998) and 15-year-old (1999) player. After a breakthrough season in 2003 and reaching Triple-A in 2004, he's now the Braves' top pitching prospect following the trades of Jose Capellan and Dan Meyer. After revamping his mechanics in 2003, Davies showed consistency in 2004. His great command of his 89-93 mph fastball makes it a plus pitch. His changeup is the best in the system, and his curveball features nice bite. He also works both sides of the plate and alters the hitter's eye

level. With his delivery ironed out, Davies simply needs to compete against experienced hitters and prove he can make the necessary adjustments. His curveball could use a little more consistency. Some Braves instructors say Davies could win a job with the major league club this spring. He's more likely to open the season in Triple-A, but he'll make his big league debut soon enough.

Year	Club (League)	Class	W	L	ERA	G	GS	CG	SV	IP	H	R	ER	HR	BB	SO	AVG
2001	Braves (GCL)	R	4	2	2.25	12	9	1	0	56	47	17	14	2	8	53	.224
	Macon (SAL)	A	1	0	0.00	1	1	0	0	6	2	0	0	0	1	7	.105
2002	Macon (SAL)	A	0	1	6.00	2	1	0	0	6	6	4	4	1	4	4	.273
	Danville (Appy)	R	5	3	3.50	14	14	0	0	69	73	39	27	2	23	62	.263
2003	Rome (SAL)	A	8	8	2.89	27	27	1	0	146	128	52	47	9	53	148	.238
2004	Richmond (IL)	AAA	0	1	9.00	1	1	0	0	5	5	5	5	0	3	5	.263
	Greenville (SL)	AA	4	0	2.32	11	10	0	0	62	40	18	16	9	22	73	.183
	Myrtle Beach (Car)	A	9	2	2.63	14	14	0	0	75	55	24	22	3	32	95	.204
MINOR LEAGUE TOTALS			31	17	2.85	82	77	2	0	426	356	159	135	26	146	447	.226

5 Anthony Lerew, rhp

BILL MITCHELL

Born: Oct. 28, 1982. **Ht.:** 6-3. **Wt.:** 220. **Bats:** L. **Throws:** R. **School:** Northern Senior HS, Wellsville, Pa. **Career Transactions:** Selected by Braves in 11th round of 2001 draft; signed June 6, 200. **Signed by:** J.J. Picollo.

Lerew flew under the radar in high school because he also played football—he was an all-star punter in Pennsylvania—but area scout J.J. Picollo identified his talent and signability early on. The Braves stole him in the 11th round in 2001, and he has posted a 2.79 ERA in four pro seasons. Lerew's fastball suddenly jumped 4-5 mph in 2004. After touching 93 mph the year before, he started working at 91-94 and peaking at 97. The pitch also has nice movement, and he generates that velocity with an effortless delivery. He also has good overall control. At its best, his changeup can be a plus pitch and has the break of a splitter. The increase in velocity affected Lerew's command, as he still threw strikes but didn't locate his pitches as effectively in the zone. His secondary offerings also need refinement. He lost the feel for his changeup at times and must tighten his slider further. Provided he maintains his newfound velocity, Lerew has the makings of a power pitcher in the middle of a major league rotation. Added to the 40-man roster in November, he's expected to spend most of 2005 in Double-A.

Year	Club (League)	Class	W	L	ERA	G	GS	CG	SV	IP	H	R	ER	HR	BB	SO	AVG
2001	Braves (GCL)	R	1	2	2.92	12	7	0	0	49	43	25	16	3	14	40	.228
2002	Danville (Appy)	R	8	3	1.73	14	14	0	0	83	60	23	16	2	25	75	.205
2003	Rome (SAL)	A	7	6	2.38	25	25	0	0	144	112	45	38	7	43	127	.215
2004	Myrtle Beach (Car)	A	8	9	3.75	27	27	0	0	144	145	75	60	12	46	125	.266
MINOR LEAGUE TOTALS			24	20	2.79	78	73	0	0	420	360	168	130	24	128	367	.233

6 Jake Stevens, lhp

RODGER WOOD

Born: March 15, 1985. **Ht.:** 6-3. **Wt.:** 210. **Bats:** L. **Throws:** L. **School:** Cape Coral (Fla.) HS. **Career Transactions:** Selected by Braves in third round of 2003 draft; signed June 4, 2003. **Signed by:** Alex Morales.

Stevens had the best first full season of the five pitchers Atlanta selected in the first three rounds of the 2003 draft. He had a streak of 25 consecutive innings without an earned run in June and finished eighth in the minors in ERA. Scouts drool over Stevens' projectable body. He's a good athlete and shows excellent stamina. He has terrific command of three pitches, beginning with an 89-91 mph fastball that has registered as high as 94. He displays excellent feel for an overhand curveball that could become a plus power pitch. Stevens' changeup could give him a third above-average pitch. His competitiveness enhances his total package. Stevens showed his age at times in 2004, getting flustered on the rare occasions when he got hit hard. He needs to learn how to minimize the damage instead of throwing gas on the fire, as he did during two seven-run outings in July. His changeup needs more depth. Stevens is well ahead of the curve for a young lefthanded pitcher. A promotion to high Class A is in his immediate future. He has a ceiling as a No. 2 starter.

Year	Club (League)	Class	W	L	ERA	G	GS	CG	SV	IP	H	R	ER	HR	BB	SO	AVG
2003	Braves (GCL)	R	3	4	2.87	14	6	0	0	47	49	23	15	2	16	47	.262
2004	Rome (SAL)	A	9	5	2.27	27	19	0	2	135	100	41	34	7	39	140	.204
MINOR LEAGUE TOTALS			12	9	2.42	41	25	0	2	182	149	64	49	9	55	187	.220

Luis Hernandez, ss

Born: June 26, 1984. **Ht.:** 5-10. **Wt.:** 140. **Bats:** B. **Throws:** R. **Career Transactions:** Signed out of Venezuela by Braves, Sept. 16, 2000. **Signed by:** Rolando Petit/Julian Perez.

No one made greater strides in the Braves system in 2004 than Hernandez. The youngest player in the Carolina League, he boosted his batting average 41 points from the previous season while continuing to shine on defense. At least one opposing manager said he has as bright a future as teammates Jeff Francoeur and Brian McCann. Hernandez is a smooth fielder with soft, quick hands, drawing raves for the way he picks the ball at shortstop. His ability to transfer the ball from glove to hand enables him to make highlight plays, and he also completes the routine ones. An improving contact hitter, he has decent pop and should improve his ability to drive the ball as he gains strength and maturity. Hernandez needs more patience after drawing just 40 walks in 228 full-season games. His free-swinging approach will be challenged, and possibly exploited, at higher levels. His body is built more for quickness than speed, so he's not much of a threat to steal. The Braves say they're more convinced than ever that Hernandez will be a special player. He's slated for Double-A and will be one of the game's youngest players at that level.

Year	Club (League)	Class	AVG	G	AB	R	H	2B	3B	HR	RBI	BB	SO	SB	OBP	SLG
2001	Braves 2 (DSL)	R	.209	68	253	39	53	8	4	1	18	23	33	24	.287	.285
2002	Braves (GCL)	R	.254	53	201	34	51	8	4	0	20	19	29	11	.330	.333
2003	Rome (SAL)	A	.231	111	337	27	78	4	1	2	25	24	42	7	.287	.267
2004	Myrtle Beach (Car)	A	.272	117	401	49	109	23	4	6	45	16	70	8	.306	.394
MINOR LEAGUE TOTALS			.244	349	1192	149	291	43	13	9	108	82	174	50	.301	.325

Kelly Johnson, of

Born: Feb. 22, 1982. **Ht.:** 6-1. **Wt.:** 180. **Bats:** L. **Throws:** R. **School:** Westwood HS, Austin. **Career Transactions:** Selected by Braves in first round of 2000 draft; signed June 12, 2000. **Signed by:** Charlie Smith.

A supplemental first-round pick in 2000 who was initially a promising shortstop prospect, Johnson stalled in 2002-03 but got his career going again last season when he repeated Double-A. He also moved from shortstop to the outfield with relative ease, seeing time at all three spots and playing primarily in left field. Johnson has solid all-around tools and a hard-nosed, fearless approach. He spread his stance at the plate and regained the power he showed three years earlier in low Class A. As an outfielder, he showed a plus arm along with good speed and range. Johnson is still learning to trust himself. Once he reacts instead of thinking about every move, he'll have a better chance to blossom. He also has to make more consistent contact at the plate and work on the nuances of outfield play. It's easy to forget how young Johnson is. Another dash of maturity could allow him to move more quickly than he has to this point. The Braves have slated Johnson for Triple-A in 2005 and continue to count on him as an eventual contributor in the majors.

Year	Club (League)	Class	AVG	G	AB	R	H	2B	3B	HR	RBI	BB	SO	SB	OBP	SLG
2000	Braves (GCL)	R	.269	53	193	27	52	12	3	4	29	24	45	6	.349	.425
2001	Macon (SAL)	A	.289	124	415	75	120	22	1	23	66	71	111	25	.404	.513
2002	Myrtle Beach (Car)	A	.255	126	482	62	123	21	5	12	49	51	105	12	.323	.394
2003	Greenville (SL)	AA	.275	98	334	46	92	22	5	6	45	35	81	10	.340	.425
	Braves (GCL)	R	.385	6	26	10	10	1	1	1	3	3	4	1	.467	.615
2004	Greenville (SL)	AA	.282	135	479	70	135	35	3	16	50	49	102	9	.350	.468
MINOR LEAGUE TOTALS			.276	542	1929	290	532	113	18	62	242	233	448	63	.356	.449

Jarrod Saltalamacchia, c

Born: May 2, 1985. **Ht.:** 6-4. **Wt.:** 195. **Bats:** B. **Throws:** R. **School:** Royal Palm Beach (Fla.) HS. **Career Transactions:** Selected by Braves in first round (36th overall) of 2003 draft; signed June 3, 2003. **Signed by:** Alex Morrales.

The Braves thought they got the best catcher out of the draft in both 2002 (Brian McCann) and 2003 (Saltalamacchia), and nothing has happened to change that thought. Despite wrist and hamstring injuries, Saltalamacchia had a solid first full season. Saltalamacchia's calling card remains his bat. He possesses power from both sides of the plate, especially as a lefthander, where he has a sweet swing with natural loft. He has good physical skills behind the plate, with his arm strength and agility standing out the most. He's more athletic than most catchers. Though he made strides with his defense in

2004, Saltalamacchia's receiving and footwork need further improvement after he erased just 21 percent of basestealers. He's still learning the nuances of calling a game and working with pitchers. He could do a better job of loading his hands from the right side, where his swing looks somewhat mechanical. With his performance at low Class A Rome, Saltalamacchia quieted skeptics who wondered if he'd be able to stay behind the plate. He'll open 2005 in high Class A.

Year	Club (League)	Class	AVG	G	AB	R	H	2B	3B	HR	RBI	BB	SO	SB	OBP	SLG
2003	Braves (GCL)	R	.239	46	134	23	32	11	2	2	14	28	33	0	.382	.396
2004	Rome (SAL)	A	.272	91	323	42	88	19	2	10	51	34	83	1	.348	.437
MINOR LEAGUE TOTALS			.263	137	457	65	120	30	4	12	65	62	116	1	.358	.425

10 Blaine Boyer, rhp

Born: July 11, 1981. **Ht.:** 6-3. **Wt.:** 215. **Bats:** R. **Throws:** R. **School:** Walton HS, Marietta, Ga. **Career Transactions:** Selected by Braves in third round of 2000 draft; signed June 13, 2000. **Signed by:** Rob English.

Boyer is a product of the same Walton High (Marietta, Ga.) program that produced big leaguers Marc Pisciotta and Chris Stowers and recent Red Sox draft picks Scott White (third round, 2002) and Mickey Hall (second, 2003). Boyer has moved slowly, reaching high Class A in his fifth pro season, but he has made steady progress and led the system in innings pitched in 2004. Boyer operates with two plus pitches. His heavy sinker sits at 92-93 mph and generates plenty of groundball outs. His sharp curveball is a potential strikeout pitch. His command continues to get better each season. Boyer's change-up lags behind his other two pitches, and its development will determine whether he becomes a starter or reliever. He spent all of 2002 in the latter role before returning to the rotation. While he has matured in the last two seasons, he must remember to keep control of his emotions on the mound. In 2005, Boyer finally will get his first taste of Double-A. His long-term role is still undetermined, but if he puts everything together it's possible that he could be a big league closer in the future.

Year	Club (League)	Class	W	L	ERA	G	GS	CG	SV	IP	H	R	ER	HR	BB	SO	AVG
2000	Braves (GCL)	R	1	3	2.51	11	5	0	1	32	24	16	9	0	19	27	.200
2001	Danville (Appy)	R	4	5	4.32	13	12	0	0	50	48	35	24	4	19	57	.250
2002	Macon (SAL)	A	5	9	3.07	43	0	0	1	70	52	30	24	0	39	73	.207
2003	Rome (SAL)	A	12	8	3.69	30	26	1	0	137	146	70	56	5	58	115	.271
2004	Myrtle Beach (Car)	A	10	10	2.98	28	28	0	0	154	138	63	51	4	49	95	.241
MINOR LEAGUE TOTALS			32	35	3.33	125	71	1	2	443	408	214	164	13	184	367	.244

11 Jose Ascanio, rhp

Born: May 2, 1985. **Ht.:** 6-0. **Wt.:** 150. **Bats:** R. **Throws:** R. **Career Transactions:** Signed out of Venezuela by Braves, Oct. 10, 2001. **Signed by:** Rolando Petit.

After disciplinary issues limited him to eight games in the Rookie-level Gulf Coast League during his U.S. debut in 2003, Ascanio put in a full season in 2004 and showed the ability to dominate against more experienced hitters. The Braves assigned him to extended spring training at the outset of 2004, but summoned him to low Class A in mid-April when Ricardo Rodriguez came down with shoulder tendinitis. Ascanio had no problems adapting, quickly emerging as a reliable bullpen option and pitching well until running out of gas in August. Despite his relatively small frame, he has a big arm. He reached 97 mph on several occasions with his well above-average fastball, which also features good movement. He's still trying to gain a consistent feel of his changeup and breaking ball, and Atlanta believes that will happen if he stays healthy. He already does a good job of throwing strikes. He also has a strong desire to succeed. As with Odalis Perez in the late 1990s, the Braves are trying to protect Ascanio by limiting his appearances while his maturing body catches up with his arm strength. He'll be promoted to high Class A in 2005.

Year	Club (League)	Class	W	L	ERA	G	GS	CG	SV	IP	H	R	ER	HR	BB	SO	AVG
2002	Braves 2 (DSL)	R	1	4	3.38	12	9	0	0	43	38	21	16	1	21	35	.253
2003	Braves (GCL)	R	4	0	1.37	8	0	0	0	26	26	4	4	0	5	17	.271
2004	Rome (SAL)	A	3	3	3.84	34	0	0	9	66	58	39	28	6	15	64	.235
MINOR LEAGUE TOTALS			8	7	3.21	54	9	0	9	135	122	64	48	7	41	116	.247

12 Scott Thorman, 1b

Born: Jan. 6, 1982. **Ht.:** 6-3. **Wt.:** 200. **Bats:** L. **Throws:** R. **School:** Preston HS, Cambridge, Ontario. **Career Transactions:** Selected by Braves in first round (30th overall) of 2000 draft; signed June 19, 2000. **Signed by:** John Stewart.

A surprise first-round pick in 2000, when most teams rated him as a third-rounder, Thorman has been slow to develop. He missed all of 2001 after shoulder surgery, and after coming back with a promising season in low Class A, he has been inconsistent at the plate the last two years. But he gave the Braves hope late last season in Double-A, when he made some adjustments and batted .282 with seven homers in the final month. A 2003 Futures Game participant, Thorman is a hard-working student of the game with awesome natural strength that translates into big-time power potential. He makes consistent contact for a power hitter but tends to get pull-happy on occasion. The former third baseman/pitcher has made impressive strides with the leather at first base. Thorman has good hands and unlike a lot of first basemen, doesn't hesitate to take chances with his arm, which is strong for his position. He still has to improve his footwork around the bag. The Braves believe Thorman's greatest need centers on slowing down and not being so anxious at the plate. Those traits should come with additional experience, beginning with a possible return to Double-A to open 2005.

Year	Club (League)	Class	AVG	G	AB	R	H	2B	3B	HR	RBI	BB	SO	SB	OBP	SLG
2000	Braves (GCL)	R	.227	29	97	15	22	7	1	1	19	12	23	0	.330	.351
2001	Did not play—Injured															
2002	Macon (SAL)	A	.294	127	470	57	138	38	3	16	82	51	83	2	.367	.489
2003	Myrtle Beach (Car)	A	.243	124	445	44	108	26	2	12	56	42	79	0	.311	.391
2004	Myrtle Beach (Car)	A	.299	43	154	20	46	11	1	4	29	12	19	1	.358	.461
	Greenville (SL)	AA	.252	94	345	31	87	14	3	11	51	39	73	5	.326	.406
MINOR LEAGUE TOTALS			.265	417	1511	167	401	96	10	44	237	156	277	8	.338	.430

13 Roman Colon, rhp

Born: Aug. 13, 1979. **Ht.:** 6-3. **Wt.:** 170. **Bats:** R. **Throws:** R. **Career Transactions:** Signed out of Dominican Republic by Braves, Aug. 14, 1995. **Signed by:** Rene Francisco.

A move to the bullpen proved to be just what Colon needed to blossom into a major league prospect. A starter since signing out of the Dominican Republic in 1995, he didn't shift to relief until mid-June in 2003. Strictly a reliever in 2004, he improved his command in Triple-A and earned a chance to showcase his electric arm in the majors by August. By working shorter stints, Colon saw his velocity increase to the low 90s and peak at 95 mph. He also made considerable improvement with the consistency and movement on his slider ball and splitter. He became more of a pitcher than a thrower, and displayed the necessary demeanor required to pitch in relief. Big and strong, Colon remains a little raw and could use further refinement of his secondary pitches. His progress is undeniable, however, and could lead to a job in the Atlanta bullpen in 2005.

Year	Club (League)	Class	W	L	ERA	G	GS	CG	SV	IP	H	R	ER	HR	BB	SO	AVG
1996	Braves (DSL)	R	5	6	3.52	14	14	0	0	64	59	45	25	0	38	39	.229
1997	Braves (GCL)	R	3	4	4.29	14	12	0	0	63	68	47	30	2	28	44	.270
1998	Danville (Appy)	R	1	7	5.77	13	13	0	0	73	92	59	47	7	28	53	.302
1999	Jamestown (NY-P)	A	7	5	4.54	15	15	1	0	77	77	48	39	4	25	61	.258
2000	Did not play—Injured																
2001	Macon (SAL)	A	7	7	3.59	23	21	0	0	128	136	69	51	9	26	91	.271
2002	Myrtle Beach (Car)	A	9	8	3.53	26	26	1	0	163	170	81	64	8	38	94	.269
2003	Greenville (SL)	AA	11	3	3.36	39	12	1	2	107	104	48	40	9	33	58	.261
2004	Atlanta (NL)	MAJ	2	1	3.32	18	0	0	0	19	18	9	7	0	8	15	.254
	Richmond (IL)	AAA	4	1	3.65	51	0	0	0	74	72	33	30	4	22	64	.258
	Greenville (SL)	AA	1	0	0.00	3	0	0	0	3	1	1	0	0	0	5	.091
MAJOR LEAGUE TOTALS			2	1	3.32	18	0	0	0	19	18	9	7	0	8	15	.254
MINOR LEAGUE TOTALS			48	41	3.90	198	113	3	2	753	779	431	326	43	238	509	.265

14 Ryan Langerhans, of

Born: Feb. 20, 1980. **Ht.:** 6-3. **Wt.:** 195. **Bats:** L. **Throws:** L. **School:** Round Rock (Texas) HS. **Career Transactions:** Selected by Braves in third round of 1998 draft; signed June 28, 1998. **Signed by:** Charlie Smith.

Langerhans rewarded a faithful core of believers in the Atlanta front office by putting together the most consistent season of his career last year in Triple-A. He ranked among the International League leaders and topped Braves farmhands in runs and on-base percentage. Langerhans always has had a sweet swing from the left side of the plate, with above-average power and the ability to spray line drives to all fields. He also has good speed and is a plus baserunner. With his speed and baseball instincts, Langerhans is one of the best defensive outfielders in the organization as well as one of the most versatile. Add in his plus arm strength, and he should be able to play any of the three outfield positions in the major leagues. Langerhans enters spring training out of options, but the Braves are confident that his versatility and hard-nosed approach will enable him to make the 25-man roster. If he continues to hit, he could push for more than a reserve role. With J.D. Drew departing via free agency and Charles Thomas used in the Tim Hudson trade, Atlanta needs corner out-fielders. Declining veterans Brian Jordan and Raul Mondesi are all that stand behind Langerhans and regular playing time.

Year	Club (League)	Class	AVG	G	AB	R	H	2B	3B	HR	RBI	BB	SO	SB	OBP	SLG
1998	Braves (GCL)	R	.277	43	148	15	41	10	4	2	19	19	38	2	.357	.439
1999	Macon (SAL)	A	.268	121	448	66	120	30	1	9	49	52	99	19	.352	.400
2000	Myrtle Beach (Car)	A	.212	116	392	55	83	14	7	6	37	32	104	25	.286	.329
2001	Myrtle Beach (Car)	A	.287	125	450	66	129	30	3	7	48	55	104	22	.374	.413
2002	Greenville (SL)	AA	.251	109	391	57	98	23	2	9	62	68	83	10	.366	.389
	Atlanta (NL)	MAJ	.000	1	1	0	0	0	0	0	0	0	0	0	.000	.000
2003	Greenville (SL)	AA	.253	94	336	42	85	23	2	6	38	46	85	10	.348	.387
	Richmond (IL)	AAA	.280	38	132	13	37	10	2	4	11	11	29	2	.338	.477
	Atlanta (NL)	MAJ	.267	16	15	2	4	0	0	0	0	0	6	0	.267	.267
2004	Richmond (IL)	AAA	.298	135	456	103	136	34	3	20	72	70	113	5	.397	.518
MAJOR LEAGUE TOTALS			.250	17	16	2	4	0	0	0	0	0	6	0	.250	.250
MINOR LEAGUE TOTALS			.265	781	2753	417	729	174	24	63	336	353	655	95	.355	.414

15 Wilson Betemit, 3b/ss

Born: July 28, 1980. **Ht.:** 6-3. **Wt.:** 190. **Bats:** B. **Throws:** R. **Career Transactions:** Signed out of Dominican Republic by Braves, July 28, 1996. **Signed by:** Rene Francisco.

It wasn't that long ago when Betemit, No. 1 on this list in 2001 and 2002, was projected to be a fixture on the left side of Atlanta's infield. Of course, that was before Rafael Furcal took over at shortstop and Chipper Jones returned to third base to keep the hot corner warm for Andy Marte. Meanwhile, Betemit has gone backwards in his development, having only sporadic success with the bat in three years in Triple-A. He did have his best season at Richmond in 2004, but it was his third straight season there. While he set career highs in doubles and homers and improved his batting average, he still has holes in his swing and needs more patience at the plate. He has average speed. Betemit is an above-average defend-er at third base and at least average at shortstop, displaying good range, soft hands and the strongest infield arm in the system. Some club officials still believe Betemit is capable of blossoming into a regular, but he'll first need to prove himself as a backup infielder with Atlanta in 2005.

Year	Club (League)	Class	AVG	G	AB	R	H	2B	3B	HR	RBI	BB	SO	SB	OBP	SLG
1997	Braves (GCL)	R	.212	32	113	12	24	6	1	0	15	9	32	0	.270	.283
1998	Braves (GCL)	R	.220	51	173	23	38	8	4	5	16	20	49	6	.301	.399
1999	Danville (Appy)	R	.320	67	259	39	83	18	2	5	53	27	63	6	.383	.463
2000	Jamestown (NY-P)	A	.331	69	269	54	89	15	2	5	37	30	37	3	.393	.457
2001	Myrtle Beach (Car)	A	.277	84	318	38	88	20	1	7	43	23	71	8	.324	.412
	Greenville (SL)	AA	.355	47	183	22	65	14	0	5	19	12	36	6	.394	.514
	Atlanta (NL)	MAJ	.000	8	3	1	0	0	0	0	0	2	3	1	.400	.000
2002	Richmond (IL)	AAA	.245	93	343	43	84	17	1	8	34	34	82	8	.312	.370
	Braves (GCL)	R	.263	7	19	2	5	4	0	0	2	5	2	1	.417	.474
2003	Richmond (IL)	AAA	.262	127	478	55	125	23	13	8	65	38	115	8	.315	.414
2004	Atlanta (NL)	MAJ	.170	22	47	2	8	0	0	0	3	4	16	0	.231	.170
	Richmond (IL)	AAA	.278	105	356	48	99	24	2	13	59	32	99	3	.336	.466
MAJOR LEAGUE TOTALS			.160	30	50	3	8	0	0	0	3	6	19	1	.246	.160
MINOR LEAGUE TOTALS			.279	682	2511	336	700	149	26	56	343	230	586	49	.338	.426

16 Macay McBride, lhp

Born: Oct. 24, 1982. **Ht.:** 5-11. **Wt.:** 180. **Bats:** L. **Throws:** L. **School:** Screven County HS, Sylvania, Ga. **Career Transactions:** Selected by Braves in first round (24th overall) of 2001 draft; signed June 6, 2001. **Signed by:** Rob English.

McBride had progressed nicely after going 24th overall in the 2001 draft. He was the low Class A South Atlantic League pitcher of the year in 2002 and led the Carolina League in strikeouts in 2003. But after working out strenuously during the winter to prepare for the 2004 season, McBride lost the feel for his slider and changeup. He went 0-6, 5.61 in 10 Double-A starts before the Braves moved him to the bullpen to take some pressure off. With his secondary pitches at less than their best, McBride began working the outside corners with his low 90s fastball, which meant he was too often behind in the count. He regained the command of his best pitch, a sharp slider, and a solid changeup, and was back on the right track at season's end. After learning how to pitch on nights when he's not hitting his spots, McBride must continue to trust his stuff. He also needs to do a better job of altering the batter's eye level by working his pitches up and down in the strike zone, rather than just side to side. Atlanta still projects McBride as a starter, though he could fill a void as a quality lefty reliever in the majors. He'll return to Double-A to begin this season.

Year	Club (League)	Class	W	L	ERA	G	GS	CG	SV	IP	H	R	ER	HR	BB	SO	AVG
2001	Braves (GGL)	R	4	4	3.76	13	11	0	0	55	51	30	23	0	23	67	.248
2002	Macon (SAL)	A	12	8	2.12	25	25	2	0	157	119	49	37	6	48	138	.209
2003	Myrtle Beach (Car)	A	9	8	2.95	27	27	1	0	165	164	63	54	5	49	139	.262
2004	Greenville (SL)	AA	1	7	4.44	38	12	0	0	103	113	59	51	9	46	102	.279
MINOR LEAGUE TOTALS			26	27	3.09	103	75	3	0	480	447	201	165	20	166	446	.247

17 T.J. Pena, ss

Born: March 23, 1981. **Ht.:** 6-1. **Wt.:** 160. **Bats:** R. **Throws:** R. **Career Transactions:** Signed out of Dominican Republic by Braves, July 21, 1999. **Signed by:** Rene Francisco.

The 2004 campaign was a tale of two seasons for Pena, whose father Tony is a former all-star catcher and currently manages the Royals. T.J. received raves for his improved offensive contributions during the first half, hitting .298 with seven homers in Double-A. But he soon wore down and his already shaky plate discipline declined further. Pena batted just .183 with two homers after the all-star break, with 42 strikeouts and just five walks. While his bat always has been a question, Pena's defensive reputation took a hit as well as he made 26 errors. He has a strong arm, covers a lot of ground and does an excellent job of turning the double play. Consistency was a problem last year, with some scouts wondering if Pena was taking his offensive woes to the field late in the season. He must get stronger and adapt at the plate, especially with Luis Hernandez rising up the organization depth chart. After a strong showing in the Arizona Fall League, Pena is expected to start this season in Triple-A.

Year	Club (League)	Class	AVG	G	AB	R	H	2B	3B	HR	RBI	BB	SO	SB	OBP	SLG
2000	Danville (Appy)	R	.214	55	215	22	46	5	0	2	20	5	53	6	.230	.265
2001	Jamestown (NY-P)	A	.246	72	264	26	65	12	2	0	18	10	48	8	.278	.307
2002	Macon (SAL)	A	.249	118	405	42	101	9	5	2	36	14	68	11	.282	.311
2003	Myrtle Beach (Car)	A	.259	120	405	43	105	14	1	4	30	24	82	17	.304	.328
2004	Greenville (SL)	AA	.255	130	495	65	126	22	0	11	34	16	108	25	.280	.366
MINOR LEAGUE TOTALS			.248	495	1784	198	443	62	8	19	138	69	359	67	.280	.324

18 Charlie Morton, rhp

Born: Oct. 12, 1983. **Ht.:** 6-5. **Wt.:** 204. **Bats:** R. **Throws:** R. **School:** Joel Barlow HS, Redding, Conn. **Career Transactions:** Selected by Braves in third round of 2002 draft; signed June 19, 2002. **Signed by:** John Stewart.

Morton has yet to have a winning season or post an ERA less than 4.54, but he may be ready to take his game to the next level and surge up this list. The lanky hurler showed a lot of progress when the Braves made him a full-time starter last July after alternating him between the rotation and long relief in the first half of the season. Morton displayed improved command of all of his pitches and wound up limiting opponents to three earned runs or less in nine of his last 11 starts. His best offering is an overhand curveball that appears to fall out of the sky. His fastball features good movement while residing in the low 90s. He continues to work on getting a feel for his changeup, which could develop into a solid-average pitch. More innings to work on his command and feel for his pitches is Morton's greatest need. He'll move up to high Class A this year.

Year	Club (League)	Class	W	L	ERA	G	GS	CG	SV	IP	H	R	ER	HR	BB	SO	AVG
2002	Braves (GCL)	R	1	7	4.54	11	5	0	0	40	37	34	20	1	30	32	.243
2003	Danville (Appy)	R	2	5	4.67	14	13	0	0	54	65	32	28	3	25	46	.302
2004	Rome (SAL)	A	7	9	4.86	27	18	0	2	117	140	76	63	7	67	102	.295
MINOR LEAGUE TOTALS			10	21	4.75	52	36	0	2	210	242	142	111	11	122	180	.288

19 Gonzalo Lopez, rhp

Born: Oct. 6, 1983. **Ht.:** 6-2. **Wt.:** 175. **Bats:** R. **Throws:** R. **Career Transactions:** Signed out of Nicaragua by Braves, July 8, 2000. **Signed by:** Rene Francisco.

Few pitchers tease scouts as much as Lopez, who ranked No. 8 on this list in 2002 and No. 10 in 2003. He missed most of 2003 because of shoulder tendinitis and a team-imposed suspension, then turned in a solid season in low Class A last year—just as he had in 2002. The Braves believe Lopez has the ability to have a Jose Capellan-like breakthrough as soon as 2005, but several aspects of his game must come together in order for that to happen. He operates with three quality offerings, including a lively low-90s fastball, an ever-improving and already solid curveball and an effective changeup. He commands all of his pitches well and is capable of dominating when he keeps his stuff down in the strike zone. The moody righthander has been disciplined a couple of times by Atlanta for his attitude. If he can significantly improve his mindset and dedication, Lopez has the physical tools to move quickly. The Braves hope he starts doing that in high Class A this year.

Year	Club (League)	Class	W	L	ERA	G	GS	CG	SV	IP	H	R	ER	HR	BB	SO	AVG
2001	Braves (GCL)	R	5	4	2.45	12	11	0	0	59	44	17	16	2	10	69	.208
2002	Rome (SAL)	A	7	1	3.10	28	27	1	0	157	134	72	54	11	51	130	.233
2003	Myrtle Beach (Car)	A	0	2	9.00	3	2	0	0	10	12	10	10	4	4	10	.293
2004	Rome (SAL)	A	8	4	3.67	22	21	0	0	101	97	47	41	7	21	109	.249
MINOR LEAGUE TOTALS			20	11	3.34	65	61	1	0	326	287	146	121	24	86	318	.236

20 Chuck James, lhp

Born: Nov. 9, 1981. **Ht.:** 6-0. **Wt.:** 170. **Bats:** L. **Throws:** L. **School:** Chattahoochee Valley (Ala.) JC. **Career Transactions:** Selected by Braves in 20th round of 2002 draft; signed July 29, 2002. **Signed by:** Al Goetz.

The Braves were prepared to take James in the third round in 2002, but days before the draft he suffered serious injuries to both of his arms after attempting to jump off a roof into a pool. He hit the ground before the water, and it cost him 17 rounds and a large chunk of bonus money. In his first taste of full-season ball last year, he won the South Atlantic League's most valuable pitcher award. James displays great concentration and moxie on the mound. An aggressive pitcher who keeps hitters off balance, he challenges them with his 89-91 mph fastball. He also has a plus changeup that he'll use at any time in the count. He not only throws strikes, but he also locates his pitches well. Considered undersized by some scouts, James certainly doesn't have a projectable build. To continue to start at higher levels, he'll have to improve his slider. He also must upgrade his stamina, because his fastball dips into the mid-80s when he gets tired. A possible end-of-the-rotation starter in the majors, James will open the 2005 season in high Class A.

Year	Club (League)	Class	W	L	ERA	G	GS	CG	SV	IP	H	R	ER	HR	BB	SO	AVG
2003	Danville (Appy)	R	2	1	1.25	11	11	0	0	50	26	9	7	1	19	68	.151
2004	Rome (SAL)	A	10	5	2.24	26	22	1	0	133	92	41	33	6	48	156	.195
MINOR LEAGUE TOTALS			12	6	1.97	37	33	1	0	183	118	50	40	7	67	224	.184

21 Billy McCarthy, of

Born: Dec. 2, 1979. **Ht.:** 6-2. **Wt.:** 200. **Bats:** R. **Throws:** R. **School:** Rutgers University. **Career Transactions:** Selected by Braves in sixth round of 2001 draft; signed June 10, 2001. **Signed by:** J.J. Picollo.

Charles Thomas wasn't the only Richmond outfielder to have a breakthrough season in 2004. McCarthy did as well, and with Thomas sent to Oakland in the Tim Hudson trade, he has a chance to make the Braves. He advanced to Double-A to start his second full season, but a hand injury ended his 2003 in July. He bounced back last year, once again displaying good pop and the ability to drive the ball to all fields. He could develop into a 20-25 home run hitter. McCarthy is also a smart and aggressive baserunner with decent range in the outfield. His arm is strong enough for right field, but his future in the majors probably lies in left. Atlanta added McCarthy to its 40-man roster for the first time in November. He hit .379 against lefthanders in 2004, though his chances of serving the Braves in a platoon role took a hit when they signed veterans Brian Jordan and Raul Mondesi.

Year	Club (League)	Class	AVG	G	AB	R	H	2B	3B	HR	RBI	BB	SO	SB	OBP	SLG
2001	Jamestown (NY-P)	A	.295	74	285	38	84	17	2	2	39	20	47	7	.351	.389
2002	Myrtle Beach (Car)	A	.305	128	442	52	135	26	4	11	65	38	88	6	.386	.457
2003	Greenville (SL)	AA	.250	86	276	35	69	19	2	6	47	41	59	5	.355	.399
2004	Greenville (SL)	AA	.300	67	233	30	70	12	2	9	42	26	67	1	.375	.485
	Richmond (IL)	AAA	.354	54	178	26	63	13	1	6	23	14	32	0	.407	.539
MINOR LEAGUE TOTALS			.298	409	1414	181	421	87	11	34	216	139	293	19	.374	.447

22 Brandon Jones, of

Born: Dec. 10, 1983. **Ht.:** 6-1. **Wt.:** 190. **Bats:** L. **Throws:** R. **School:** Tallahassee (Fla.) CC. **Career Transactions:** Selected by Braves in 24th round of 2003; signed May 12, 2004. **Signed by:** Al Goetz.

Had Atlanta not signed Jones out of Tallahassee (Fla.) CC as a draft-and-follow last May, he could have gone in the first three rounds of the 2004 draft. The Royals drafted him in the sixth round out of high school, where he played quarterback, defensive back and punter for his high school football team and also served as a point guard in basketball. Compared to Garret Anderson, Jones has solid tools across the board. Speed is his greatest asset, though he didn't run wild on the bases in his pro debut. At the plate, he's a line-drive hitter who has shown flashes of budding power that will continue to blossom as his body matures. He has good defensive instincts with above-average arm strength, skills that could enable him to man center field at higher levels. Jones remains a raw product, but the polish he displayed after some initial coaching has the Braves believing he could develop rapidly. He'll spend his first full season in low Class A.

Year	Club (League)	Class	AVG	G	AB	R	H	2B	3B	HR	RBI	BB	SO	SB	OBP	SLG
2004	Danville (Appy)	R	.297	57	209	35	62	6	5	3	33	23	33	4	.366	.416
MINOR LEAGUE TOTALS			.297	57	209	35	62	6	5	3	33	23	33	4	.366	.416

23 J.C. Holt, 2b

Born: Dec. 8, 1982. **Ht.:** 5-10. **Wt.:** 172. **Bats:** L. **Throws:** R. **School:** Louisiana State University. **Career Transactions:** Selected by Braves in third round of 2004 draft; signed June 28, 2004. **Signed by:** Don Thomas.

A center fielder during his last two years at Louisiana State, Holt returned to second base after signing for $380,000 as a third-round pick last June. He played the position as a college freshman and displayed solid ability there as a pro. Holt made all the plays to his left and showed good overall range and a decent arm. Not surprisingly, he needs work on going up the middle as well as his double-play pivot. He also needs to make the adjustments to the speed of the game on defense. Offensively, Holt is a speed-oriented player who makes consistent contact with the ability to drive the ball from gap to gap. He's a proven hitter with wood bats, winning the 2003 Cape Cod League batting title at .388, so it was no surprise he hit .321 in his pro debut. His strike-zone judgment is decent and should get better with experience. A former Louisiana high school sprint champion, Holt has the quickness and savvy to steal 30 bases annually. He's a potential leadoff hitter who should reach high Class A at some point in 2005.

Year	Club (League)	Class	AVG	G	AB	R	H	2B	3B	HR	RBI	BB	SO	SB	OBP	SLG
2004	Danville (Appy)	R	.321	51	209	38	67	15	0	1	21	18	34	17	.377	.407
MINOR LEAGUE TOTALS			.321	51	209	38	67	15	0	1	21	18	34	17	.377	.407

24 Gregor Blanco, of

Born: Dec. 12, 1983. **Ht.:** 5-11. **Wt.:** 170. **Bats:** L. **Throws:** L. **Career Transactions:** Signed out of Venezuela by Braves, July 4, 2000. **Signed by:** Rolando Petit.

The Braves had Blanco repeat high Class A in 2004, when he posted numbers that mirrored those from his first season at Myrtle Beach. Nevertheless, he showed steady progress in all phases of his game. He put together a solid if unspectacular year at the plate while managers rated him the best defensive outfielder in the Carolina League. Blanco has outstanding athletic ability, which shows up best with his outstanding play in center field. He has plus speed and a strong arm. He has shortened his swing during the past two years in order to help him get on base and put his legs to work. He also continues to add strength and more pop at the plate. Blanco has a reputation as a slow starter, and didn't shake it by hitting just .228 last April. He needs to develop more overall consistency in his game, especially making more contact. Reversing his trend of declining walk totals also would let him use his speed more often. Blanco's next challenge will come in Double-A.

Year	Club (League)	Class	AVG	G	AB	R	H	2B	3B	HR	RBI	BB	SO	SB	OBP	SLG
2001	Braves 2 (DSL)	R	.330	58	215	45	71	6	10	0	18	31	31	21	.422	.451
2002	Macon (SAL)	A	.271	132	468	87	127	14	9	7	36	85	120	40	.392	.385
2003	Myrtle Beach (Car)	A	.271	126	461	66	125	19	7	5	36	54	114	34	.357	.375
2004	Myrtle Beach (Car)	A	.269	119	435	73	117	17	9	8	41	47	114	25	.342	.405
MINOR LEAGUE TOTALS			.279	435	1579	271	440	56	35	20	131	217	379	120	.373	.396

25 Josh Burrus, of

Born: Aug. 20, 1983. **Ht.:** 5-11. **Wt.:** 180. **Bats:** R. **Throws:** R. **School:** Wheeler HS, Marietta, Ga. **Career Transactions:** Selected by Braves in first round (29th overall) of 2001 draft; signed June 14, 2001. **Signed by:** Rob English.

A cousin of Jeffrey Hammonds, Burrus was considered one of the most advanced prep hitters in the 2001 draft. But after going 29th overall and signing for $1.25 million, he took three years to escape Rookie ball and entered last season with a .225 career average. However, his stock is on the rise again after he made some adjustments in low Class A and set career highs across the board. Burrus possesses strong, quick wrists and finally began driving the ball to all fields as it was anticipated he would do coming out of high school. Like many of Atlanta's position prospects, he must address his strike zone judgment and make more consistent contact. He also has above-average speed and shows the makings of becoming a plus baserunner. Defensively, the Braves tried Burrus at shortstop and third base before moving him to left field in 2003. He has good range but modest arm strength. He faces a pivotal season in high Class A this year, when he can prove if the gains he made in 2004 were for real.

Year	Club (League)	Class	AVG	G	AB	R	H	2B	3B	HR	RBI	BB	SO	SB	OBP	SLG
2001	Braves (GCL)	R	.193	52	197	24	38	8	2	3	19	14	40	10	.271	.299
2002	Danville (Appy)	R	.236	68	263	34	62	13	1	0	23	35	60	16	.338	.293
2003	Danville (Appy)	R	.254	53	189	25	48	11	1	1	16	15	48	10	.318	.339
	Rome (SAL)	A	.178	16	45	4	8	2	0	1	2	1	12	2	.245	.289
2004	Rome (SAL)	A	.272	126	503	82	137	30	3	11	46	33	123	30	.330	.410
MINOR LEAGUE TOTALS			.245	315	1197	169	293	64	7	16	106	98	283	68	.317	.350

26 Zach Miner, rhp

Born: March 12, 1982. **Ht.:** 6-3. **Wt.:** 190. **Bats:** R. **Throws:** R. **School:** Palm Beach Gardens (Fla.) HS. **Career Transactions:** Selected by Braves in fourth round of 2000 draft; signed Sept. 1, 2000. **Signed by:** Rene Francisco.

Miner has as much natural ability as any pitcher in the organization. He ranked as high as No. 7 on this list after the Braves bought him out of a commitment to the University of Miami with a $1.2 million bonus. But he has fared progressively worse as he has moved up the minor league ladder, and he won just one of his final 10 starts in Double-A last year. Miner needs to quit playing keep-away from hitters. He possesses a solid slider with sharp bite and good sinking movement on his low-90s fastball, but he's constantly behind in the count because he tries to be too fine with his offerings. That also leads to high pitch counts, the main reason he never went past seven innings in a start last season. More aggressiveness and more depth with his changeup would work wonders for him. He showed promise while pitching in the Arizona Fall League. Regardless of his future role, Miner must start challenging hitters this year when he returns to Double-A.

Year	Club (League)	Class	W	L	ERA	G	GS	CG	SV	IP	H	R	ER	HR	BB	SO	AVG
2001	Jamestown (NY-P)	A	3	4	1.89	15	15	0	0	91	76	26	19	6	16	68	.226
2002	Rome (SAL)	A	8	9	3.28	29	28	1	0	159	143	73	58	10	51	131	.243
2003	Myrtle Beach (Car)	A	6	10	3.69	27	27	2	0	154	150	74	63	10	61	88	.262
2004	Greenville (SL)	AA	6	10	5.22	27	22	1	0	129	132	87	75	14	55	111	.270
MINOR LEAGUE TOTALS			23	33	3.63	98	92	4	0	533	501	260	215	40	183	398	.252

27 Luis Atilano, rhp

Born: May 10, 1985. **Ht.:** 6-3. **Wt.:** 180. **Bats:** R. **Throws:** R. **School:** Gabriela Mistral HS, San Juan, P.R. **Career Transactions:** Selected by Braves in first round (35th overall) of 2003 draft; signed June 3, 2003. **Signed by:** Julian Perez.

Atlanta's top pick in 2003, Atilano signed for $950,000 as a supplemental first-rounder. The best thing he had going for him was his projectability, so it wasn't unexpected when he struggled initially after turning pro. He found more of a comfort zone last year at Rookie-level Danville. Atilano's fastball added velocity, moving from 88-91 to 92-93 mph. His changeup also showed flashes of becoming a solid-average pitch. He needs to work on the consistency of his curveball. Atilano has established himself as a strike-thrower, but his overall command and pitch quality need to show improvement before he's ready for the upper levels of the minors. He has a tendency to leave his pitches up in the zone, leaving him vulnerable to home runs. He'll move up to the full-season ranks in 2005, opening the season in low Class A.

Year	Club (League)	Class	W	L	ERA	G	GS	CG	SV	IP	H	R	ER	HR	BB	SO	AVG
2003	Braves (GGL)	R	3	2	3.83	12	12	1	0	54	61	25	23	5	7	24	.288
2004	Danville (Appy)	R	5	1	4.20	13	13	0	0	64	64	32	30	7	10	54	.255
MINOR LEAGUE TOTALS			8	3	4.03	25	25	1	0	118	125	57	53	12	17	78	.270

28 Martin Prado, 2b

Born: Oct. 27, 1983. **Ht.:** 6-1. **Wt.:** 170. **Bats:** R. **Throws:** R. **Career Transactions:** Signed out of Venezuela by Braves, Feb. 13, 2001. **Signed by:** Rolando Petit.

After spending three years in Rookie ball, Prado made a strong impression in his first shot at full-season ball last year. He ranked ninth in the South Atlantic League in batting and made the postseason all-star team. Managers also rated him the best defensive second baseman in the SAL, thanks to his soft hands, above-average range and ability to turn the double play. Prado has only minimal power, so his offensive game centers around making contact. He has good bat control but needs to show more patience so he can draw more walks. Prado has good speed, but he needs considerable work on his reads and jumps after getting caught on 10 of his 24 basestealing attempts in 2004. Though his body continues to mature,

Prado doesn't project off the charts. He'll try to keep his momentum going this year in high Class A.

Year	Club (League)	Class	AVG	G	AB	R	H	2B	3B	HR	RBI	BB	SO	SB	OBP	SLG
2001	Braves 2 (DSL)	R	.299	61	187	25	56	4	2	0	21	25	33	19	.388	.342
2002	Braves 2 (DSL)	R	.320	59	222	35	71	18	3	1	26	17	16	13	.373	.441
2003	Braves 2 (GCL)	R	.286	59	220	28	63	2	6	0	23	24	30	9	.358	.350
2004	Rome (SAL)	A	.315	107	429	68	135	25	6	3	38	30	47	14	.363	.422
MINOR LEAGUE TOTALS			.307	286	1058	156	325	49	17	4	108	96	126	55	.369	.397

29 Diory Hernandez, ss

Born: April 8, 1984. **Ht.:** 6-0. **Wt.:** 170. **Bats:** R. **Throws:** R. **Career Transactions:** Signed out of Dominican Republic by Braves, Aug. 20, 2002. **Signed by:** Roberto Aquino.

Few players in the organization receive more mixed reviews than Hernandez. His proponents love his offensive potential. He's much further along at the plate than Luis Hernandez (no relation) and T.J. Pena were at the same point of their careers. Twenty-four of Hernandez' 83 hits last year went for extra bases, and he finished with a flourish by batting .307 in the final month. Detractors point to Hernandez's free-swinging ways and his mediocre speed and question how he'll be able to produce against better pitching. Defensively, Hernandez is raw and his range might be better suited for third base than shortstop. The Braves wish he'd mature, because he gets moody and doesn't always deal with the daily grind of baseball. But like Gonzalo Lopez, he's considered to be worth the warts because of his potential. His next stop is high Class A.

Year	Club (League)	Class	AVG	G	AB	R	H	2B	3B	HR	RBI	BB	SO	SB	OBP	SLG
2003	Braves (GCL)	R	.221	54	190	26	42	9	2	1	12	14	24	2	.287	.305
2004	Rome (SAL)	A	.271	90	306	40	83	20	1	3	38	26	67	7	.325	.373
MINOR LEAGUE TOTALS			.252	144	496	66	125	29	3	4	50	40	91	9	.311	.347

30 James Jurries, 1b

Born: April 13, 1979. **Ht.:** 6-0. **Wt.:** 190. **Bats:** R. **Throws:** R. **School:** Tulane University. **Career Transactions:** Selected by Braves in sixth round of 2002 draft; signed June 6, 2002. **Signed by:** Don Thomas.

Jurries has been productive at the plate for as long as anyone can remember. He hit .500 in three of his four seasons in high school, beat out Mark Teixeira to win Baseball America's Freshman of the Year award in 1999 and earned all-Conference USA honors in each of his four seasons at Tulane. After totaling 15 homers in his first two pro seasons, Jurries drilled 25 to lead Braves farmhands in 2004. He uses the entire field at the plate, and can hit the ball out of any part of the park. His increased power came at a cost, as his plate discipline slipped last season. He's an offensive-only player, as he has below-average speed and is adequate at first base. He also has seen time at third base, and realistically projects as a corner-infield backup in the majors. Jurries probably will return to Triple-A to begin 2005.

Year	Club (League)	Class	AVG	G	AB	R	H	2B	3B	HR	RBI	BB	SO	SB	OBP	SLG
2002	Danville (Appy)	R	.333	4	15	4	5	1	0	1	4	2	2	0	.412	.600
	Myrtle Beach (Car)	A	.290	48	176	23	51	9	3	5	30	17	26	2	.352	.460
2003	Greenville (SL)	AA	.284	129	465	73	132	35	4	9	54	48	108	4	.354	.434
2004	Greenville (SL)	AA	.306	18	72	15	22	4	0	7	14	5	15	1	.359	.653
	Richmond (IL)	AAA	.267	102	318	46	85	16	0	18	56	32	96	0	.336	.487
MINOR LEAGUE TOTALS			.282	301	1046	161	295	65	7	40	158	104	247	7	.349	.472

BALTIMORE
ORIOLES

BY **WILL LINGO**

C an the Orioles ever be a consistent winner with Peter Angelos as owner? Angelos took over in August 1993, inheriting the respected Roland Hemond as general manager. Hemond had been on the job since 1987. By 1995 he was gone, and no GM since has lasted more than three years. The tandem of Jim Beattie and Mike Flanagan is the latest to try to right the ship.

What they have is an organization in disarray. The Orioles reached third place in the American League East in 2004 after six straight fourth-place finishes, but it was the seventh straight sub-.500 season. They got Sammy Sosa in the offseason, which provided a public-relations boost but didn't address the team's pitching problems and further thinned an already weak farm system.

The player-development operation continues to be in upheaval. Tony DeMacio, the scouting director hired during the brief Frank Wren administration, didn't have his contract renewed after the season. Nor did farm director Doc Rodgers, who in his two years brought discipline and planning to a system that previously had little of either. The Orioles hired Marlins crosschecker Joe Jordan to replace DeMacio, and promoted minor league hitting coordinator David Stockstill to replace Rodgers.

DeMacio's record wasn't outstanding, but scouts say almost all of his early selections involved compromise of some sort. It's illustrative that his best picks, such as pitchers **Erik Bedard** (sixth round, 1999) and John Maine (sixth round, 2002), came in later

rounds. With the eighth overall pick in 2004, DeMacio wanted high school shortstop Chris Nelson. After the draft started, Angelos insisted on a college pitcher who would sign for no more than $2.2 million. So Baltimore took Rice righthander Wade Townsend, offered him $1.85 million and lost his rights when he returned to school.

As many as one-third of the players DeMacio and his scouts ranked on their draft board after scouting them last spring were deemed undraftable by upper management. The reason? They didn't fit the psychological profiles the Orioles have relied more heavily on in the last two years. Flanagan brought in Dave Ritterpusch as the club's director of baseball information systems two years ago, and his influence has grown steadily. The problem extends beyond favoring one particular philosophy, however. The approach seems to change with the wind. The Orioles got righthander Denny Bautista in a trade with the Marlins, for example, but they traded him to the Royals last June for 37-year-old Jason Grimsley. The decision was apparently prompted by two bad outings in a late-May series against the Yankees.

If Stockstill and Jordan can get everyone working from the same blueprint, it would be a positive move. More likely, however, is that disarray and disappointing finishes will continue until there are changes at the top.

TOP 30 PROSPECTS

1. Nick Markakis, of	16. Eddy Rodriguez, rhp
2. Hayden Penn, rhp	17. Fredy Deza, rhp
3. Adam Loewen, lhp	18. James Johnson, rhp
4. Val Majewski, of	19. Aaron Rakers, rhp
5. Jeff Fiorentino, of	20. Brian Finch, rhp
6. John Maine, rhp	21. Scott Rice, lhp
7. Chris Ray, rhp	22. Jarod Rine, of
8. Tripper Johnson, 3b	23. Travis Brown, ss/2b
9. Eli Whiteside, c	24. Lorenzo Scott, of
10. Nate Spears, 2b/ss	25. Mike Huggins, 1b
11. Walter Young, dh/1b	26. Brian Forystek, lhp
12. Dave Haehnel, lhp	27. Richard Stahl, lhp
13. Bob McCrory, rhp	28. Ryan Finan, 1b
14. Jacobo Sequea, rhp	29. C.J. Smith, 1b
15. Dennis Robinson, rhp	30. Tony Neal, rhp

ORGANIZATION OVERVIEW

General Managers: Jim Beattie/Mike Flanagan. **Farm director:** David Stockstill. **Scouting director:** Joe Jordan.

2004 PERFORMANCE

Class	Team	League	W	L	Pct.	Finish*	Manager
Majors	Baltimore	American	78	84	.481	9th (14)	Lee Mazzilli
Triple-A	Ottawa Lynx	International	66	78	.458	t-11th (14)	Tim Leiper
Double-A	Bowie Baysox	Eastern	73	69	.514	5th (12)	Dave Trembley
High A	Frederick Keys	Carolina	52	87	.374	8th (8)	Tom Lawless
Low A	Delmarva Shorebirds	South Atlantic	69	69	.500	t-7th (16)	Bien Figueroa
Short-season	Aberdeen IronBirds	New York-Penn	35	40	.467	8th (14)	Don Buford
Rookie	Bluefield Orioles	Appalachian	28	39	.418	8th (10)	Gary Kendall
OVERALL 2004 MINOR LEAGUE RECORD			323	382	.458	26th(30)	

*Finish in overall standings (No. of teams in league)

ORGANIZATION LEADERS

BATTING
*Minimum 250 At-Bats
*AVG	Jose Leon, Ottawa	.322
R	Walter Young, Bowie	88
H	Mike Fontenot, Ottawa	146
TB	Walter Young, Bowie	261
2B	Ed Rogers, Bowie	33
3B	Nate Spears, Delmarva	11
HR	Walter Young, Bowie	33
RBI	Walter Young, Bowie	98
BB	Jack Cust, Ottawa	65
SO	Walter Young, Bowie	145
SB	Jarod Rine, Delmarva	31
*OBP	Jose Leon, Ottawa	.382
*SLG	Jose Leon, Ottawa	.583

PITCHING
#Minimum 75 Innings
W	Hayden Penn, Bowie/Frederick/Delmarva	13
L	Fredy Deza, Frederick/Delmarva	14
#ERA	Zach Dixon, Frederick/Delmarva	2.53
G	Ryan Keefer, Frederick	63
	Nick McCurdy, Frederick	63
CG	Three tied at	2
SV	Jacobo Sequea, Bowie	27
IP	John Maine, Ottawa/Bowie	148
BB	Brian Forystek, Ottawa/Bowie	73
SO	John Maine, Ottawa/Bowie	139

BEST TOOLS

Best Hitter for Average	Nick Markakis
Best Power Hitter	Walter Young
Best Strike-Zone Discipline	Val Majewski
Fastest Baserunner	Clifton Turner
Best Athlete	Lorenzo Scott
Best Fastball	Chris Ray
Best Curveball	Adam Loewen
Best Slider	Jacobo Sequea
Best Changeup	Hayden Penn
Best Control	John Maine
Best Defensive Catcher	Eli Whiteside
Best Defensive Infielder	Nate Spears
Best Infield Arm	Bryan Bass
Best Defensive Outfielder	Jarod Rine
Best Outfield Arm	Keith Reed

PROJECTED 2008 LINEUP

Catcher	Eli Whiteside
First Base	Walter Young
Second Base	Brian Roberts
Third Base	Tripper Johnson
Shortstop	Miguel Tejada
Left Field	Larry Bigbie
Center Field	Val Majewski
Right Field	Nick Markakis
Designated Hitter	Melvin Mora
No. 1 Starter	Sidney Ponson
No. 2 Starter	Hayden Penn
No. 3 Starter	Adam Loewen
No. 4 Starter	Erik Bedard
No. 5 Starter	Daniel Cabrera
Closer	B.J. Ryan

LAST YEAR'S TOP 20 PROSPECTS

1. Adam Loewen, lhp
2. John Maine, rhp
3. Nick Markakis, of
4. Val Majewski, of
5. Denny Bautista, rhp
6. Matt Riley, lhp
7. Erik Bedard, lhp
8. Rommie Lewis, lhp
9. Mike Fontenot, 2b
10. Dave Crouthers, rhp
11. Ryan Hannaman, lhp
12. Jose Bautista, 3b
13. Chris Ray, rhp
14. Brian Finch, rhp
15. Daniel Cabrera, rhp
16. Don Levinski, rhp
17. Eddy Rodriguez, rhp
18. Brian Forystek, lhp
19. Lorenzo Scott, of
20. Walter Young, 1b/dh

TOP PROSPECTS OF THE DECADE

Year	Player, Pos.	Current Team
1995	Armando Benitez, rhp	Giants
1996	Rocky Coppinger, rhp	Out of baseball
1997	Nerio Rodriguez, rhp	Out of baseball
1998	Ryan Minor, 3b	Out of baseball
1999	Matt Riley, lhp	Orioles
2000	Matt Riley, lhp	Orioles
2001	Keith Reed, of	Orioles
2002	Richard Stahl, lhp	Orioles
2003	Erik Bedard, lhp	Orioles
2004	Adam Loewen, lhp	Orioles

TOP DRAFT PICKS OF THE DECADE

Year	Player, Pos.	Current Team
1995	Alvie Shepherd, rhp	Out of baseball
1996	Brian Falkenborg, rhp (2)	Dodgers
1997	Jayson Werth, c	Dodgers
1998	Rick Elder, of	Out of baseball
1999	Mike Paradis, rhp	Orioles
2000	Beau Hale, rhp	Orioles
2001	Chris Smith, lhp	Orioles
2002	Adam Loewen, lhp	Orioles
2003	Nick Markakis, of	Orioles
2004	Wade Townsend, rhp	Did not sign

ALL-TIME LARGEST BONUSES

Adam Loewen, 2002	$3,200,000
Beau Hale, 2000	$2,250,000
Chris Smith, 2001	$2,175,000
Darnell McDonald, 1997	$1,900,000
Nick Markakis, 2003	$1,850,000

MINOR LEAGUE DEPTH CHART

Baltimore ORIOLES

Impact Potential: C

Nick Markakis, Val Majewski and Jeff Fiorentino all profile as starting corner outfielders in the big leagues, though none figures to dominate. Hayden Penn gives the Orioles a potential front-of-the-rotation starter, and Adam Loewen could as well, though he had a rough first full season that ended with a labrum injury.

Depth: F

The Orioles cleaned house after the season, changing scouting and farm directors. The lack of success of top-end draft picks can't be laid solely at the feet of former scouting director Tony DeMacio; owner Peter Angelos' meddling meant he rarely if ever drafted whom he wanted to take. But even when the Orioles came up with late-round finds or drafted raw players in need of polish, the player-development staff seldom did much to develop the modest talent.

*Depth charts prepared by **John Manuel** and **Allan Simpson**. Numbers in parentheses indicate prospect rankings.*

LF
Jeff Fiorentino (5)
Lorenzo Scott (24)
Woody Cliffords

CF
Jarod Rine (22)
Keith Reed

RF
Nick Markakis (1)
Val Majewski (4)

3B
Tripper Johnson (8)
Bryan Bass
Matt Pulley

SS
Travis Brown (23)
Ed Rogers

2B
Nate Spears (10)
Carlos Mendez

1B
Walter Young (11)
Mike Huggins (25)
Ryan Finan (28)
C.J. Smith (29)
Dustin Yount

SOURCE of TALENT

Homegrown		Acquired	
College	18	Trades	1
Junior College	1	Rule 5 draft	0
Draft-and-follow	1	Independent leagues	0
High school	6	Free agents/waivers	1
Nondrafted free agents	0		
Foreign	2		

C
Eli Whiteside (9)
Octavio Martinez

LHP

Starters	Relievers
Adam Loewen (3)	Dave Haehnel (12)
Richard Stahl (27)	Scott Rice (21)
Zach Dixon	Brian Forystek (26)
Ryan Hannaman	Trevor Caughey
Carlos Perez	Rommie Lewis
	Kurt Birkins

RHP

Starters	Relievers
Hayden Penn (2)	Jacobo Sequea (14)
John Maine (6)	Eddy Rodriguez (16)
Chris Ray (7)	Aaron Rakers (19)
Bob McCrory (13)	Tony Neal (30)
Dennis Robinson (15)	Kevin Hart
Fredy Deza (17)	Sendy Rleal
James Johnson (18)	Paul Henry
Brian Finch (20)	Ryan Keefer
Brad Bergeson	
Bryce Chamberlin	
Don Levinski	

DRAFT ANALYSIS

2004

Best Pro Debut: LHP Dave Haehnel (8) tied for the short-season New York-Penn League lead with 16 saves while posting a 1.69 ERA and 61-11 K-BB ratio in 37 innings. His 88-93 mph fastball features good life, and he gets righthanders out with his changeup. OF Jeff Fiorentino (3) hit .311 with 10 homers in 48 games in low Class A.

Best Athlete: OF Clifton Turner (49) is the best pure athlete in this draft crop, but he's extremely raw. Fiorentino may be able to play catcher (he saw some action there at Florida Atlantic) or third base.

Best Pure Hitter: Fiorentino.

Best Raw Power: OF/DH Drew Moffitt (10) led NCAA Division I with 26 homers in 2004 and won three Missouri Valley Conference home run titles at Wichita State. 1B C.J. Smith (5) also has good pop.

Fastest Runner: Turner is a flier who can cover 60 yards in 6.4 seconds.

Best Defensive Player: SS Denver Kitch's (13) good hands, arm and range helped him earn the Gold Glove award at the 2004 NAIA World Series. C Dan Puente (12) was hurt for much of the spring but got drafted on the basis of his catch-and-throw skills.

Best Fastball: RHP Brad Bergesen (4) not only has a 90-95 mph fastball, but he also maintains it deep into games.

Best Breaking Ball: RHP Bryce Chamberlin (6) has a hard slider. He never has had consistent success, however, with a 6.75 ERA at Washington State and a 6.29 ERA in his pro debut.

Most Intriguing Background: SS Drew Crisp (35) and OF Adam Crisp (38) are twins who led Riverside High to back-to-back South Carolina state 3-A titles and South

Townsend

Carolina to back-to-back Senior League World Series crowns. OF Will Venable's (15) father Max played 12 seasons in the majors. None of the three signed, with Venable returning to Princeton to play basketball.

Closest To The Majors: As a lefthanded pitcher, Haehnel should move faster than Fiorentino.

Best Late-Round Pick: RHP Kevin Hart (11) led Maryland with a .369 average during the spring, but the Orioles drafted him as a pitcher. He works with four pitches, most notably a heavy sinker and a tight slider. RHP Kyle Schmidt (14) projected as an early pick before an inconsistent junior season at South Florida, but at his best he has a plus curveball and average fastball.

The One Who Got Away: RHP Wade Townsend (1) gambled that he could return to classes at Rice and still negotiate with the Orioles via a perceived draft loophole, but Major League Baseball ruled against him. Had he signed, Townsend could have joined the big league rotation within two years.

Assessment: Scouting director Tony DeMacio wanted to draft shortstop Chris Nelson with the eighth overall pick, but owner Peter Angelos insisted he take a college pitcher who would sign for no more than MLB's recommended bonus, approximately $2.2 million. The Orioles infuriated Townsend by offering $1.85 million, then declined to renew DeMacio's contract when it expired in October.

2003 Most teams preferred him as a lefthanded pitcher, but Nick Markakis (1) has become the organization's top prospect as an outfielder. 2B/SS Nate Spears (5) is the next-best player in this group. **GRADE:** C

2002 Four of the system's six best prospects came from this draft: RHP Hayden Penn (5), LHP Adam Loewen (1), OF Val Majewski (3) and RHP John Maine (6). If Loewen and Majewski weren't recovering from torn labrums, the grade would be higher. **GRADE:** B

2001 Though 2B Mike Fontenot (1) and RHP Dave Crouthers (3) were used in the Sammy Sosa trade, they're not frontline prospects. But they're markedly better than the other two first-round picks, LHP Chris Smith and 3B Bryan Bass. **GRADE:** C

2000 3B Tripper Johnson (1) is making progress, but RHP Beau Hale (1) bombed quickly. Baltimore failed to sign RHPs Kyle Sleeth (18) and Tim Stauffer (36), who became the third and fourth overall choices in 2003. **GRADE:** D

---

*Draft analysis prepared by **Jim Callis**. Numbers in parentheses indicate draft rounds.*

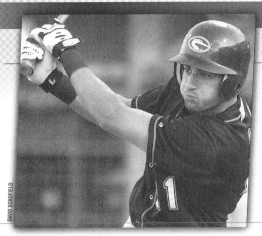

Nick
MARKAKIS

Born: Nov. 17, 1983
Ht.: 6-1. **Wt.:** 175.
Bats: L. **Throws:** L.
School: Young Harris (Ga.) JC.
Career Transactions: Selected by Orioles in first round (seventh overall) of 2003 draft; signed June 11, 2003.
Signed by: Lamar North.

DAVID SCHOFIELD

Markakis was drafted in the 23rd round by the Reds in 2002, then went seventh overall to the Orioles a year later after turning down a $1.5 million draft-and-follow offer from Cincinnati. He was Baseball America's Junior College Player of the Year in both seasons, and signed with Baltimore for $1.8 million. Markakis was an outstanding two-way player at Young Harris (Ga.) JC, and scouts within and outside the organization were divided about where he should play professionally. Hitting won out, and it has looked like the right decision so far. Markakis was batting just .239 through May at low Class A Delmarva, but his swing started coming together and he got red-hot. He batted .345 and hit 18 doubles in the next two months before departing for the Olympics to play for the Greek team assembled with help from Baltimore owner Peter Angelos. Most Orioles officials regarded the trip as a great opportunity, though they were chagrined when Markakis was also asked to pitch. He made two relief appearances—touching 94 mph, it should be noted—and he was one of the event's best hitters, going 9-for-26 (.346) with a home run. Because it was his first full pro season, Baltimore shut him down when he returned.

While his arm strength is undeniable, Markakis' hands and athletic body give him a higher ceiling as an outfielder. Never a full-time hitter before 2004, he made the adjustments that could make him an ideal No. 3 hitter. As one scout said, "He gets better every second." The speed and strength in his hands make him a pure hitter, and the natural snap in his bat gives him good power that should increase as he matures. Markakis established a solid foundation for his swing by getting his lower half more stable as the year went on, giving him better torque on his swing. He already shows good control of the strike zone. His strong, sinewy body earns him comparisons to Shawn Green and Johnny Damon. His athleticism allows him to play center field in a pinch, but his speed and arm make him perfectly suited for right field.

Markakis is inexperienced at the plate, so he's still trying to figure out his swing as well as understanding how to attack in hitter's counts. He came in with what the Orioles called "aluminum bat drift," meaning his body would get ahead of his hands. He's learning to keep his body back so it stays out of the way of his beautiful swing. He also needs to refine his outfield defense, improving his jumps and routes to balls.

As Markakis has slowly but surely put pitching behind him, he has started to emerge as a potential premium bat and standout defender. His lack of experience as a hitter and his Olympic sojourn have slowed down his progress a bit, but the way he came on in the second half of 2004 opened eyes. He'll begin 2005 at high Class A Frederick and could arrive in the big leagues by the second half of 2006.

Year	Club (League)	Class	AVG	G	AB	R	H	2B	3B	HR	RBI	BB	SO	SB	OBP	SLG
2003	Aberdeen (NYP)	A	.283	59	205	22	58	14	3	1	28	30	33	13	.372	.395
2004	Delmarva (SAL)	A	.299	96	355	57	106	22	3	11	64	42	66	12	.371	.470
MINOR LEAGUE TOTALS			.293	155	560	79	164	36	6	12	92	72	99	25	.371	.443

Hayden Penn, rhp

Born: Oct. 13, 1984. **Ht.:** 6-3. **Wt.:** 185. **Bats:** R. **Throws:** R. **School:** Santata HS, Santee, Calif. **Career Transactions:** Selected by Orioles in fifth round of 2002 draft; signed Aug. 1,2002. **Signed by:** Ray Krawczyk.

Penn's baseball experience and success were limited in high school because he spent a lot of time on the basketball court. He was the eastern San Diego player of the year after averaging 24 points and 11 rebounds a game as a senior. He broke out in 2004, jumping to Double-A and being named Baltimore's minor league pitcher of the year. Penn has the stuff to pitch at the front of a rotation. His plus changeup is his best pitch now, and he also has an 89-92 mph fastball that touches 94 and a curveball that's above-average when it's on. What the Orioles really like, though, is his savvy. He pitches above his experience, working inside, pitching to contact and showing a knack for reading hitters' weaknesses. Penn mainly needs innings. He pitched half a season in 2003, and opened 2004 in the Delmarva bullpen to reduce his workload. His curveball still requires work. It's early, but Penn's fast progress got the Orioles excited. He'll go back to Double-A Bowie to open 2005.

Year	Club (League)	Class	W	L	ERA	G	GS	CG	SV	IP	H	R	ER	HR	BB	SO	AVG
2003	Orioles (GCL)	R	0	0	2.70	1	1	0	0	3	3	1	1	0	1	4	.273
	Bluefield (Appy)	R	1	4	4.30	12	11	0	0	52	58	27	25	4	19	38	.283
2004	Frederick (Car)	A	6	5	3.80	13	13	0	0	73	59	33	31	7	20	61	.222
	Delmarva (SAL)	A	4	1	3.32	13	6	0	1	43	30	18	16	4	19	41	.195
	Bowie (EL)	AA	3	0	4.87	4	4	0	0	20	22	12	11	0	9	20	.282
MINOR LEAGUE TOTALS			14	10	3.92	43	35	0	1	193	172	91	84	15	68	164	.241

Adam Loewen, lhp

Born: April 9, 1984. **Ht.:** 6-6. **Wt.:** 230. **Bats:** L. **Throws:** L. **School:** Chipola (Fla.) JC. **Career Transactions:** Selected by Orioles in first round (fourth overall) of 2002 draft; signed May 26, 2003. **Signed by:** John Gillette/David Jennings.

The highest-drafted Canadian ever, Loewen went fourth overall in 2002 and signed for a $3.2 million bonus as part of a $4.02 million big league deal. But Loewen was too ineffective to be considered for Canada's 2004 Olympic team, and at the end of the year was diagnosed with a torn labrum. When he's healthy and on his game, Loewen has dominant stuff. He's effectively wild in the strike zone with a 90-92 mph fastball that reaches 95, and a curveball that's a knockout pitch. He's a good athlete with fluid mechanics that give him good deception. The major concern is Loewen's shoulder, though he didn't require surgery and completed a throwing program in October. His first full season was marred by inconsistent mechanics, a loss of command and the loss of faith in his stuff. The Orioles consider all of that correctable. His changeup lags behind his fastball and curve. Loewen's contract guaranteed him a spot in big league spring training in 2004, and he never seemed to recover after getting knocked around. He'll seek a fresh start in high Class A in 2005.

Year	Club (League)	Class	W	L	ERA	G	GS	CG	SV	IP	H	R	ER	HR	BB	SO	AVG
2003	Aberdeen (NY-P)	A	0	2	2.70	7	7	0	0	23	13	7	7	0	9	25	.167
2004	Frederick (Car)	A	0	2	6.75	2	2	1	0	8	7	6	6	2	9	3	.269
	Delmarva (SAL)	A	4	5	4.11	20	19	1	0	85	77	47	39	3	58	82	.249
MINOR LEAGUE TOTALS			4	9	4.01	29	28	2	0	117	97	60	52	5	76	110	.235

Val Majewski, of

Born: June 19, 1981. **Ht.:** 6-2. **Wt.:** 200. **Bats:** L. **Throws:** L. **School:** Rutgers University. **Career Transactions:** Selected by Orioles in third round of 2002 draft; signed July 22, 2002. **Signed by:** Jim Howard.

Majewski was Baltimore's minor league player of the year and a Double-A Eastern League all-star in 2004. He made his big league debut in August, but the year ended on a down note when doctors found a small labrum tear in his throwing shoulder. Majewski's makeup is off the charts, and he's intensely focused on the things he can control. He goes to the plate with a plan and shows good pitch selection. He makes hard contact and his home run power is starting to emerge. He has the tools for right field and also has seen time in center. Majewski's swing has more holes than Markakis', and left-handers still give him trouble at times. He also tries to be perfect with every swing, which sometimes makes him too rigid at the plate. He doesn't draw many walks. Assuming his shoulder is healthy—and the Orioles say it is—Majewski should be able to help in Baltimore soon. Scouts say he'll be a more physical version of Larry Bigbie. First, though, Majewski needs to get at-bats at Triple-A Ottawa.

Year	Club (League)	Class	AVG	G	AB	R	H	2B	3B	HR	RBI	BB	SO	SB	OBP	SLG
2002	Aberdeen (NY-P)	A	.300	31	110	22	33	7	4	1	15	13	14	8	.376	.464
	Delmarva (SAL)	A	.118	7	17	2	2	0	0	1	3	1	1	0	.158	.294
2003	Delmarva (SAL)	A	.303	56	208	38	63	15	8	7	48	28	20	10	.383	.553
	Orioles (GCL)	R	.333	1	3	0	1	0	0	0	0	1	0	0	.500	.333
	Aberdeen (NY-P)	A	.375	4	16	2	6	2	2	0	3	1	2	1	.412	.750
	Frederick (Car)	A	.289	41	159	15	46	18	1	5	20	7	23	0	.321	.509
2004	Bowie (EL)	AA	.307	112	433	71	133	24	5	15	80	33	68	14	.359	.490
	Baltimore (AL)	MAJ	.154	9	13	3	2	1	0	0	1	0	1	0	.154	.231
MAJOR LEAGUE TOTALS			.154	9	13	3	2	1	0	0	1	0	1	0	.154	.231
MINOR LEAGUE TOTALS			.300	252	946	150	284	66	20	29	169	84	128	33	.358	.504

5 Jeff Fiorentino, of

Born: April 14, 1983. **Ht.:** 6-1. **Wt.:** 185. **Bats:** L. **Throws:** R. **School:** Florida Atlantic University. **Career Transactions:** Selected by Orioles in third round of 2004 draft; signed June 24, 2004. **Signed by:** Nick Presto.

The Orioles botched their first-round pick and lost their second-round pick for signing Miguel Tejada, so Fiorentino will have to carry the flag for their 2004 draft class. He looked up to the task in his pro debut, though the Orioles played him in the outfield after the scouting department viewed him as a potential catcher. Fiorentino is athletic enough to play anywhere on the field, which is why he was able to catch at Florida Atlantic and why some in the organization wanted to try him there. He also has the bat to play just about anywhere, with a smooth line-drive swing and the ability to drive inside pitches and center the ball on the bat. While Fiorentino is athletic and versatile, he doesn't have overwhelming defensive tools for any position. His build and arm worked against him as a catcher. He should be an average left fielder down the road. He needs to cut down on his strikeouts. Fiorentino moved quickly after signing, and the Orioles won't try to slow him down. He'll open 2005 in high Class A.

Year	Club (League)	Class	AVG	G	AB	R	H	2B	3B	HR	RBI	BB	SO	SB	OBP	SLG
2004	Aberdeen (NY-P)	A	.348	14	46	9	16	7	1	2	12	9	4	3	.474	.674
	Delmarva (SAL)	A	.296	49	179	40	53	15	2	10	36	20	50	2	.374	.570
MINOR LEAGUE TOTALS			.307	63	225	49	69	22	3	12	48	29	54	5	.396	.591

6 John Maine, rhp

Born: May 8, 1981. **Ht.:** 6-4. **Wt.:** 190. **Bats:** R. **Throws:** R. **School:** UNC Charlotte. **Career Transactions:** Selected by Orioles in sixth round of 2002 draft; signed July 5, 2002. **Signed by:** Marc Tramuta.

The Orioles moved Maine aggressively in 2004, jumping him to Triple-A after just five Double-A starts. He struggled in his first two months at Ottawa (4.99 ERA) but started to come around afterward (2.89 ERA). The Twins shelled him when he made his major league debut in an emergency start in July. Maine succeeds more with command than pure stuff. He added a slider to give him four pitches, along with his fastball, curveball and changeup. He throws 90-91 mph with natural deception, and adds and subtracts from his fastball nicely. He's not afraid to work inside. None of Maine's pitches is overwhelming, which explains why he struggles when he moves up to a new level. He also needs to refine his command and throw quality strikes after learning that advanced hitters lay off balls out of the zone. Maine has a ceiling of a No. 3 starter, and probably a No. 4 or 5 guy on a first-division club. But he's a pitcher's pitcher and should get the most out of his ability.

Year	Club (League)	Class	W	L	ERA	G	GS	CG	SV	IP	H	R	ER	HR	BB	SO	AVG
2002	Aberdeen (NY-P)	A	1	1	1.74	4	2	0	0	10	6	2	2	0	3	21	.154
	Delmarva (SAL)	A	1	1	1.36	6	5	0	0	33	21	8	5	0	4	39	.178
2003	Delmarva (SAL)	A	7	3	1.53	14	14	1	0	76	43	16	13	1	18	108	.165
	Frederick (Car)	A	6	1	3.07	12	12	1	0	70	48	27	24	5	20	77	.190
2004	Baltimore (AL)	MAJ	0	1	9.82	1	1	0	0	4	7	4	4	1	3	1	.438
	Ottawa (IL)	AAA	5	7	3.91	22	22	0	0	120	123	59	52	12	52	105	.266
	Bowie (EL)	AA	4	0	2.25	5	5	0	0	28	16	8	7	1	7	34	.160
MAJOR LEAGUE TOTALS			0	1	9.82	1	1	0	0	4	7	4	4	1	3	1	.438
MINOR LEAGUE TOTALS			24	13	2.75	63	60	2	0	338	257	120	103	19	104	384	.208

Chris Ray, rhp

Born: Jan. 12, 1982. **Ht.:** 6-3. **Wt.:** 200. **Bats:** R. **Throws:** R. **School:** College of William & Mary. **Career Transactions:** Selected by Orioles in third round of 2003 draft; signed July 10, 2003. **Signed by:** Marc Tramuta.

Ray starred as a closer in the Cape Cod League in 2002 before moving to the rotation at William & Mary and struggling in 2003. He still went in the third round and has shown more success in that role as a pro, though he'll probably go back to the bullpen eventually. Ray's fastball sits at 93-95 mph, peaks at 97 and has heavy life. He has enough power to get hitters out with heat up in the zone. He complements his fastball with a hard slider and a good splitter, allowing him to work all four quadrants of the strike zone. Ray has a maximum-effort delivery and hasn't developed his changeup much, so he probably faces an eventual return to the bullpen. He throw strikes but needs better command within the zone because he gets hit more than he should with his stuff. One scout compared Ray to Goose Gossage both in his build and the life on his high fastball. He has not only the arsenal but also the mentality to close out games. When he moves to that role will be up to the next farm director.

Year	Club (League)	Class	W	L	ERA	G	GS	CG	SV	IP	H	R	ER	HR	BB	SO	AVG
2003	Aberdeen (NY-P)	A	2	0	2.82	9	8	0	0	38	32	15	12	0	10	44	.225
2004	Delmarva (SAL)	A	2	3	3.42	10	9	0	0	50	43	21	19	3	17	46	.230
	Frederick (Car)	A	6	3	3.80	14	14	1	0	73	82	31	31	6	20	74	.287
MINOR LEAGUE TOTALS			10	6	3.45	33	31	1	0	162	157	67	62	9	47	164	.255

Tripper Johnson, 3b

Born: April 28, 1982. **Ht.:** 6-1. **Wt.:** 200. **Bats:** R. **Throws:** R. **School:** Newport HS, Bellevue, Wash. **Career Transactions:** Selected by Orioles in first round (32nd overall) of 2000 draft; signed June 26, 2000. **Signed by:** John Gillette.

After a steady progression through the organization, Johnson had a disappointing 2003 season that earned him a return to high Class A. He regrouped and was the Carolina League's all-star third baseman after hitting more homers (21) than he had in 1,247 career at-bats coming into the year (20). Johnson finally figured out he could produce power to all fields by taking balls where they're pitched rather than trying to pull everything. He handles the bat well and showed a good two-strike approach. His defense at third base also has improved significantly. He has an average arm and moves well laterally. Johnson answered the Orioles' two main concerns in 2004 by hitting to the opposite field with authority and improving his focus on defense. His swing can get a little long, and he still hasn't proven himself above Class A. While some teams tend to rush players, the Orioles may have moved Johnson too slowly, having him repeat Rookie ball as well as high Class A. If he can put up numbers in Double-A, he could reach Baltimore in short order.

Year	Club (League)	Class	AVG	G	AB	R	H	2B	3B	HR	RBI	BB	SO	SB	OBP	SLG
2000	Orioles (GCL)	R	.306	48	180	22	55	5	3	2	33	13	38	7	.355	.400
2001	Bluefield (Appy)	R	.261	43	157	24	41	6	1	2	26	11	37	4	.312	.350
2002	Delmarva (SAL)	A	.260	136	493	73	128	32	6	11	71	62	88	19	.349	.416
2003	Frederick (Car)	A	.273	123	417	43	114	25	3	5	50	46	92	7	.359	.384
2004	Frederick (Car)	A	.269	129	465	62	125	19	2	21	74	51	93	14	.343	.454
MINOR LEAGUE TOTALS			.270	479	1712	224	463	87	15	41	254	183	348	51	.347	.411

Eli Whiteside, c

Born: Oct. 22, 1979. **Ht.:** 6-2. **Wt.:** 213. **Bats:** R. **Throws:** R. **School:** Delta State (Miss.) University. **Career Transactions:** Selected by Orioles in sixth round of 2001 draft; signed June 7, 2001. **Signed by:** Mike Tullier.

The Orioles drafted Whiteside as a defense-first catcher, but he showed enough offense in his first season and a half in the organization to make them think he could be more. Unfortunately, he tried to bulk up to generate more power at the plate. It not only didn't help his offense, but it also resulted in injuries and a stiff body. He missed nearly half the 2003 season, and one scout said when he did play it looked like he was walking around on stilts. He trimmed down and improved his flexibility in the offseason, then opened 2004 in extended spring training as he got healthy and worked on his batting stance. The Orioles put Whiteside in a deeper crouch and opened him up, and they were pleased with the results. He was more selective at the plate and showed more power, and fully healthy in the Arizona Fall League he had a .355 on-base percentage and .615 slugging percentage in 70 at-bats. If he puts up the offensive numbers he did in 2004 at higher levels, he will be an everyday big league catcher because he's so solid defensively. He's got the size and strength for the position, and he's got an above-average arm with a quick release. Even if he doesn't hit, his defense should allow him to be a backup. Whiteside was added to the 40-man roster and will battle for a Triple-A job in spring training. It's conceivable he could win the backup job in the big leagues, but he really needs a full season of at-bats to help his development.

Year	Club (League)	Class	AVG	G	AB	R	H	2B	3B	HR	RBI	BB	SO	SB	OBP	SLG
2001	Delmarva (SAL)	A	.250	61	212	30	53	11	0	7	28	9	45	1	.300	.401
2002	Frederick (Car)	A	.259	80	313	34	81	19	0	8	42	14	57	0	.296	.396
	Bowie (EL)	AA	.263	27	99	11	26	5	0	2	11	4	18	0	.311	.374
2003	Bowie (EL)	AA	.204	81	265	21	54	13	1	1	23	5	44	0	.230	.272
	Orioles (GCL)	R	.333	1	3	0	1	1	0	0	0	1	1	0	.500	.667
	Aberdeen (NY-P)	A	.700	2	10	0	7	3	0	0	4	0	1	1	.700	1.000
2004	Bowie (EL)	AA	.253	90	297	41	75	18	0	18	60	25	65	2	.310	.495
MINOR LEAGUE TOTALS			.248	342	1199	137	297	70	1	36	168	58	231	4	.291	.398

10 Nate Spears, 2b/ss

Born: May 3, 1985. **Ht.:** 5-11. **Wt.:** 165. **Bats:** L. **Throws:** R. **School:** Charlotte HS, Port Charlotte, Fla. **Career Transactions:** Selected by Orioles in fifth round of 2003 draft; signed June 10, 2003. **Signed by:** Nick Presto.

The Orioles penciled Spears in for the shortstop job at Rookie-level Bluefield in 2004 after he made his debut in the Gulf Coast League, but he played his way onto the low Class A roster in spring training. He spent most of the year at second base, but the organization says he could play shortstop down the road. He earned comparisons to David Eckstein from several scouts, all of whom said he has better tools and could be much  better with the bat. He centers the ball on the bat well and stays inside the ball even when pitchers pound him inside. He handles situational hitting like bunting and moves runners over well. He profiles as a No. 2 hitter and could steal 15-20 bases a year. He may not have enough arm for shortstop, but could play there occasionally even if he settles at second because he has average range and excellent hands. Like Eckstein, he earns praise for his determination and feel for the game. He should open the 2005 season in high Class A.

Year	Club (League)	Class	AVG	G	AB	R	H	2B	3B	HR	RBI	BB	SO	SB	OBP	SLG
2003	Orioles (GCL)	R	.289	56	180	38	52	7	5	1	19	40	32	18	.427	.400
2004	Delmarva (SAL)	A	.275	97	371	50	102	12	11	5	38	47	63	7	.358	.407
MINOR LEAGUE TOTALS			.279	153	551	88	154	19	16	6	57	87	95	25	.382	.405

11 Walter Young, dh/1b

Born: Feb. 18, 1980. **Ht.:** 6-5. **Wt.:** 298. **Bats:** L. **Throws:** R. **School:** Purvis (Miss.) HS. **Career Transactions:** Selected by Pirates in 31st round of 1999 draft; signed June 3, 1999 . . . Claimed on waivers by Orioles from Pirates, Nov. 20, 2003. **Signed by:** Russell Bowen (Pirates).

In an organization that needs players with premium tools, Young offers top-of-the-scale power. They grabbed him after the 2003 season when the Pirates tried to take him off their 40-man roster at the suggestion of Mickey White, who was the Pirates' scouting director who drafted Young. He showed his stuff in his first season in the organization, breaking the Bowie franchise home run record previously held by Calvin Pickering. Young earns obvious comparisons to Pickering, another giant human with plus power. While Pickering's big body proved to be his undoing, Orioles officials say Young is a better athlete and hitter who has worked hard to improve his conditioning. Aside from his power, he's a run producer who works counts and is willing to take a walk, though he has holes on the inner half. They say a better comparison might be to David Ortiz. Young also moves well around first base and has good hands, but his limited range probably will relegate him to DH. Young had a good winter in Venezuela, hitting six home runs, and if he comes to spring training in good shape he could contribute in the big leagues in 2005.

Year	Club (League)	Class	AVG	G	AB	R	H	2B	3B	HR	RBI	BB	SO	SB	OBP	SLG
1999	Pirates (GCL)	R	.231	37	130	9	30	6	2	0	15	4	34	2	.270	.308
2000	Pirates (GCL)	R	.296	45	162	32	48	11	1	10	34	8	29	3	.357	.562
	Williamsport (NY-P)	A	.185	24	92	5	17	4	0	2	12	1	26	0	.200	.293
2001	Williamsport (NY-P)	A	.289	66	232	40	67	10	1	13	47	19	43	1	.353	.509
2002	Hickory (SAL)	A	.333	132	492	84	164	34	2	25	103	36	102	2	.390	.563
2003	Lynchburg (Car)	A	.278	117	431	76	120	15	2	20	87	35	88	2	.348	.462
2004	Bowie (EL)	AA	.272	133	486	88	132	28	1	33	98	47	145	2	.341	.537
MINOR LEAGUE TOTALS			.285	554	2025	334	578	108	9	103	396	150	467	12	.347	.500

Dave Haehnel, lhp

Born: July 21, 1982. **Ht.:** 6-4. **Wt.:** 185. **Bats:** L. **Throws:** L. **School:** University of Illinois-Chicago. **Career Transactions:** Selected by Orioles in eighth round of 2004 draft; signed June 16, 2004. **Signed by:** Troy Hoerner.

Haehnel worked out of the bullpen in his first two seasons at Illinois-Chicago and ranked as the top prospect in the Jayhawk League in the summer of 2003, then moved into the rotation as a junior and finished third in the Horizon League in ERA. The Orioles sent him back to the bullpen in his first pro experience, as much because he threw 90 innings in the spring as any decision being made about his long-term role. Haehnel's best pitch is his sinker, which he throws from 89-93 mph with beautiful arm action and good deception. He uses his height to get a good downward plane on the pitch, and it has good life. His changeup also has the potential to be a plus pitch, with good depth and fade. He's still working on his breaking pitch, which most closely resembles a slider and is merely adequate at this point. Haehnel needs to refine his offspeed stuff but has tremendous makeup and challenges hitters. He'll need innings to develop, but has one of the most promising arms in the organization. He'll start the 2005 season in low Class A, and the progress of his third pitch will determine whether he ends up starting or relieving.

Year	Club (League)	Class	W	L	ERA	G	GS	CG	SV	IP	H	R	ER	HR	BB	SO	AVG
2004	Aberdeen (NY-P)	A	3	1	1.24	28	0	0	16	36	23	8	5	1	11	58	.178
MINOR LEAGUE TOTALS			3	1	1.24	28	0	0	16	36	23	8	5	1	11	58	.178

Bob McCrory, rhp

Born: May 3, 1982. **Ht.:** 6-1. **Wt.:** 205. **Bats:** R. **Throws:** R. **School:** University of Southern Mississippi. **Career Transactions:** Selected by Orioles in fourth round of 2003 draft; signed June 6, 2003. **Signed by:** Mike Tullier.

McCrory signed for $310,000 as a fourth-rounder in 2003, but he didn't pitch because of elbow tendinitis. The Orioles took a cautious approach with him in 2004, having him start the season in extended spring and giving him just 63 innings overall. They're being so careful because McCrory's arm has the potential to deliver power stuff. He can throw his fastball 95-96 mph and goes to the mound with domination in mind. He also throws a power slider, and he has no changeup to speak of now. His arm draws comparisons to Dave Crouthers', and the effort in his delivery is compared to that of Chris Ray, though it's not to the same degree. McCrory struggled with his command as he worked his arm into shape, and he needs mechanical work. His mechanics are not consistent and he sometimes rushes his delivery, and he just has a thrower's approach at this point. If he can get his mechanics under control, he could be a starter, but if not he should be a good power arm out of the bullpen. He will open the 2005 season in the low Class A rotation.

Year	Club (League)	Class	W	L	ERA	G	GS	CG	SV	IP	H	R	ER	HR	BB	SO	AVG
2003	Did not play—Injured																
2004	Delmarva (SAL)	A	0	1	7.59	8	0	0	0	11	13	16	9	3	15	11	.277
	Aberdeen (NY-P)	A	0	1	27.00	1	1	0	0	1	3	3	3	1	2	1	.600
	Bluefield (Appy)	R	4	3	1.92	11	11	0	0	52	42	21	11	3	32	51	.221
MINOR LEAGUE TOTALS			4	5	3.27	20	12	0	0	63	58	40	23	7	49	63	.240

Jacobo Sequea, rhp

Born: Aug. 31, 1981. **Ht.:** 6-1 **Wt.:** 194 **Bats:** R. **Throws:** R. **Career Transactions:** Signed out of Venezuela by Reds, Nov. 10, 1997 . . . Traded by Reds with LHP B.J. Ryan to Orioles for RHP Juan Guzman, July 31, 1999. **Signed by:** Johnny Almaraz (Reds).

Most of former general manager Syd Thrift's deals didn't amount to much for the Orioles, but the 1999 trade of Juan Guzman to the Reds has already paid dividends with B.J. Ryan, and could pay more if Sequea continues the progress he has made in the last season and a half. The progress has come after he moved to the bullpen, where his two-pitch mix has been much more effective. Sequea's best pitch is his slider, and he complements it with a fastball that has average velocity (90-92 mph) but good life. He doesn't have a power arm but he misses bats, works both sides of the plate consistently and has command of all his stuff. As a closer he has been aggressive and consistent from outing to outing. The only things he has left to work on are refinements such as holding runners better and getting quicker outs. He probably doesn't have the pure stuff to project as a major league closer, but he should develop into an effective middle reliever. He was added to the 40-man roster and will compete for a big league job in the spring, but it will be a surprise if he doesn't open the season in Triple-A.

Year	Club (League)	Class	W	L	ERA	G	GS	CG	SV	IP	H	R	ER	HR	BB	SO	AVG
1998	Charleston, WV (SAL)	A	3	5	6.02	13	11	0	0	55	68	42	37	3	33	33	.316
1999	Rockford (Mid)	A	4	6	4.92	16	16	2	0	90	88	52	49	6	44	67	.263
	Reds (GCL)	R	0	0	4.50	1	1	0	0	2	2	1	1	0	0	3	.286
	Delmarva (SAL)	A	0	2	3.90	6	6	0	0	30	35	19	13	4	16	25	.304
2000	Frederick (Car)	A	9	11	5.09	23	22	2	0	124	121	80	70	11	58	94	.260
2001	Frederick (Car)	A	6	9	3.97	18	18	0	0	102	85	54	45	16	37	80	.225
2002	Bowie (EL)	AA	1	6	5.40	15	14	0	0	73	69	53	44	11	35	37	.252
	Rochester (IL)	AAA	1	4	5.27	5	5	0	0	27	26	16	16	7	11	16	.245
2003	Bowie (EL)	AA	1	3	5.40	12	8	0	0	40	43	26	24	5	28	24	.279
	Frederick (Car)	A	1	0	2.87	32	0	0	20	31	27	11	10	2	11	26	.229
2004	Bowie (EL)	AA	3	5	2.62	59	0	0	27	65	51	25	19	5	25	53	.213
MINOR LEAGUE TOTALS			29	51	4.61	200	101	4	47	640	615	379	328	70	298	458	.255

15 Dennis Robinson, rhp

Born: July 29, 1982. **Ht.:** 6-4. **Wt.:** 195. **Bats:** R. **Throws:** R. **School:** Jacksonville University. **Career Transactions:** Signed by Orioles as nondrafted free agent, Aug. 4, 2004. **Signed by:** Ty Brown/Jeff Taylor.

Robinson was a 45th-round pick of the Blue Jays in 2000, after playing for his father Dennis Sr. at Lakeland High in Putnam Valley, N.Y., but he decided to attend North Carolina instead. He transferred to Jacksonville in 2003 for his junior season, sat out the year, and ranked second in NCAA Division I with 13 wins while posting a 2.85 ERA in 2004, but he wasn't drafted because scouts said he lacked a plus pitch. So Robinson went to the Cape Cod League to pitch instead, and he impressed scouts in compiling a 2.31 ERA for Orleans while showing better stuff than he did in the spring. The Orioles signed him in August and put him right to work, and he was impressive in two minor league stops as well. Robinson usually pitches at 88-90 mph, but he touched 94 on the Cape. Regardless, he succeeds with command over velocity and has a great feel for pitching. He's always around the plate, doesn't waste pitches and consistently keeps his pitches down. His curveball should be at least an average pitch, and he needs to work on his changeup. Robinson should open the season back in low Class A, where the Orioles will see if his stuff matches what he showed last summer.

Year	Club (League)	Class	W	L	ERA	G	GS	CG	SV	IP	H	R	ER	HR	BB	SO	AVG
2004	Aberdeen (NY-P)	A	0	0	2.00	2	1	0	0	9	9	3	2	1	3	9	.257
	Delmarva (SAL)	A	3	0	0.50	3	3	0	0	18	11	2	1	1	4	7	.177
MINOR LEAGUE TOTALS			3	0	1.00	5	4	0	0	27	20	5	3	2	7	16	.213

16 Eddy Rodriguez, rhp

Born: Aug. 8, 1981. **Ht.:** 6-1. **Wt.:** 195. **Bats:** R. **Throws:** R. **Career Transactions:** Signed out of Dominican Republic by Orioles, March 11, 1999. **Signed by:** Salvador Ramirez.

After Rodriguez had a breakout season in 2003, he made his major league debut in 2004 and spent a good part of the year in Baltimore, making his first appearance against the Red Sox at the end of May. He remained in the Orioles' bullpen until the end of August, when he was sent back down while the Orioles gave Bruce Chen an audition. Rodriguez has a 91-93 mph fastball that's made more effective because of its movement and his deceptive delivery, and solid-average slider. He doesn't have the stuff to close but has both the pitches and the mentality for big league middle relief. He still needs to improve his command to stick in the big leagues for good because big league hitters tended to wait him out. He had one five-walk, four-strikeout performance against the Phillies, throwing 63 pitches in three innings, though he gave up just one hit and no runs and picked up his first big league win. He'll have to be sharper than that to succeed long term, and will compete for a big league job this spring.

Year	Club (League)	Class	W	L	ERA	G	GS	CG	SV	IP	H	R	ER	HR	BB	SO	AVG
1999	Orioles (DSL)	R	2	2	4.78	25	0	0	8	49	51	35	26	5	21	47	.266
2000	Orioles (GCL)	R	2	1	2.00	18	0	0	6	27	17	8	6	0	19	31	.185
	Delmarva (SAL)	A	0	0	1.80	4	0	0	0	5	5	1	1	1	2	3	.263
2001	Delmarva (SAL)	A	5	3	3.39	41	0	0	1	61	58	27	23	4	23	64	.247
	Bowie (EL)	AA	1	1	2.08	5	0	0	2	9	7	2	2	0	6	10	.241
2002	Frederick (Car)	A	0	3	2.23	38	0	0	11	48	28	14	12	3	20	58	.169
	Bowie (EL)	AA	0	0	5.63	6	0	0	1	8	6	6	5	1	7	7	.200
2003	Bowie (EL)	AA	3	4	2.34	56	0	0	13	73	49	26	19	3	35	66	.188
2004	Ottawa (IL)	AAA	1	0	5.12	28	0	0	3	32	34	19	18	4	18	31	.266
	Baltimore (AL)	MAJ	1	0	4.78	29	0	0	0	43	36	23	23	5	30	37	.231
MAJOR LEAGUE TOTALS			1	0	4.78	29	0	0	0	43	36	23	23	5	30	37	.231
MINOR LEAGUE TOTALS			14	14	3.23	221	0	0	45	312	255	138	112	21	151	317	.221

17 Fredy Deza, rhp

Born: Dec. 11, 1982. **Ht.:** 6-2. **Wt.** 167. **Bats:** R. **Throws:** R. **Career Transactions:** Signed out of Dominican Republic by Orioles, Sept. 20, 1999. **Signed by:** Carlos Bernhardt.

Deza has made a slow progression through the organization, but there are some who expect him to have a breakout season in 2005, calling him the organization's next Daniel Cabrera. Last season was really his first full year. He pitched just 49 innings in 2002 because of elbow tendinitis and was brought back slowly in 2003, opening the season in extended spring. But he started in low Class A last year and showed occasionally dominant stuff, holding batters to a .226 average even though he had a losing record. He's a sinker/slider pitcher and opinions vary about which of those pitches is better. His fastball is 92-94 mph, but some say his quick slider is his best pitch. He's still developing his changeup. Deza is a strikethrower with a loose arm and compact delivery. He's thin and wiry now and could add velocity as he fills out. As it is, his arm is plenty strong and he goes right after hitters. He does have to work to keep the ball down. Deza is very much a work in progress, but the raw material is there for a quality pitcher. He'll begin the season in high Class A.

Year	Club (League)	Class	W	L	ERA	G	GS	CG	SV	IP	H	R	ER	HR	BB	SO	AVG
2000	Orioles (DSL)	R	7	2	1.73	13	13	1	0	78	59	25	15	0	14	71	.201
2001	Orioles (GCL)	R	1	4	3.14	9	7	1	0	49	49	26	17	3	15	42	.262
	Delmarva (SAL)	A	0	2	3.00	3	2	0	0	15	10	6	5	3	0	12	.179
2002	Delmarva (SAL)	A	0	5	4.38	12	12	0	0	49	50	26	24	4	15	38	.260
2003	Frederick (Car)	A	0	0	27.00	1	0	0	0	1	4	5	4	0	3	2	.444
	Aberdeen (NY-P)	A	3	5	3.25	15	14	1	0	75	75	32	27	1	20	69	.257
2004	Frederick (Car)	A	1	3	5.61	5	5	0	0	26	33	22	16	4	2	20	.306
	Delmarva (SAL)	A	8	11	3.31	22	21	2	0	120	102	52	44	7	21	93	.226
MINOR LEAGUE TOTALS			20	32	3.31	80	74	5	0	413	382	194	152	22	90	347	.240

18 James Johnson, rhp

Born: June 27, 1983. **Ht.:** 6-5. **Wt.:** 213. **Bats:** R. **Throws:** R. **School:** Endicott (N.Y.) HS. **Career Transactions:** Selected by Orioles in fifth round of 2001 draft; signed June 14, 2001. **Signed by:** Jim Howard.

Johnson has been a project who has been brought along exceedingly slowly by the Orioles, and he was held back in extended spring to open 2004 because he had mononucleosis. He eventually joined a Delmarva staff that was home to many of the organization's most promising arms at one point or another during the season, but team officials said he had the best arm on the staff by the end of the year. He won three of his last four starts, going at least six innings in each outing and allowing a total of four earned runs in 26 innings. He throws his fastball at 90-91 mph now and could add velocity as he fills out his big frame and continues to get experience. His curveball might be his best pitch, and he's a strike-thrower who likes to go right after hitters. His changeup is a work in progress. Johnson will be a long-range project because of his size and lack of amateur experience, but he started showing flashes of brilliance last year. He'll open the season in the high Class A rotation.

Year	Club (League)	Class	W	L	ERA	G	GS	CG	SV	IP	H	R	ER	HR	BB	SO	AVG
2001	Orioles (GCL)	R	0	1	3.86	7	4	0	0	19	17	10	8	3	7	19	.239
2002	Bluefield (Appy)	R	4	2	4.37	11	9	0	0	56	52	36	27	5	16	36	.250
2003	Bluefield (Appy)	R	3	2	3.68	11	11	0	0	51	62	24	21	2	18	46	.291
2004	Delmarva (SAL)	A	8	7	3.29	20	17	0	0	107	97	44	39	9	30	93	.243
	Frederick (Car)	A	0	0	9.00	1	1	0	0	3	6	4	3	0	1	6	.429
MINOR LEAGUE TOTALS			15	12	3.75	50	42	0	0	235	234	118	98	19	72	200	.259

19 Aaron Rakers, rhp

Born: Jan. 22, 1977. **Ht.:** 6-3. **Wt.:** 205. **Bats:** R. **Throws:** R. **School:** Southern Illinois University-Edwardsville. **Career Transactions:** Selected by Orioles in 23rd round of 1999 draft; signed June 7, 1999. **Signed by:** Earl Winn.

Rakers (pronounced "rockers") finally earned his first big league callup in September, getting promoted after leading Ottawa in appearances in 2004. It continued a slow but steady progression he has made through the organization, though it seems he might have reached the big leagues sooner based on his performance. As a 23rd-round pick out of Southern Illinois-Edwardsville (where he was a teammate of former Orioles pitcher Dave Crouthers), however, Rakers has had to prove himself every step of the way. He has done that in spite of a fastball that's average at best, usually coming in around 90 mph. His out pitch is his split-finger, however, which has made him effective against both lefthanders (.245) and righthanders (.220). Rakers has proven all he's going to prove in the minor leagues, so he'll compete for a big league bullpen spot in spring training.

Year	Club (League)	Class	W	L	ERA	G	GS	CG	SV	IP	H	R	ER	HR	BB	SO	AVG
1999	Bluefield (Appy)	R	0	0	2.57	3	0	0	0	7	5	2	2	1	3	12	.200
	Delmarva (SAL)	A	4	1	1.42	18	0	0	8	25	9	6	4	0	13	38	.108
2000	Frederick (Car)	A	1	1	1.55	26	0	0	8	41	23	8	7	2	12	57	.163
	Bowie (EL)	AA	3	2	2.79	24	0	0	8	29	20	11	9	5	10	21	.194
2001	Bowie (EL)	AA	4	4	2.39	51	0	0	14	60	53	21	16	8	20	74	.227
2002	Bowie (EL)	AA	5	1	2.06	36	0	0	10	48	39	12	11	3	12	45	.232
2003	Bowie (EL)	AA	5	0	2.75	31	0	0	8	39	27	12	12	7	19	42	.196
	Ottawa (IL)	AAA	2	4	5.13	21	0	0	1	26	19	18	15	1	11	26	.202
2004	Ottawa (IL)	AAA	4	5	2.75	54	1	0	1	79	65	27	24	8	25	80	.229
	Baltimore (AL)	MAJ	0	0	4.15	3	0	0	0	4	5	2	2	0	1	3	.278
MAJOR LEAGUE TOTALS			0	0	4.15	3	0	0	0	4	5	2	2	0	1	3	.278
MINOR LEAGUE TOTALS			28	18	2.54	264	1	0	58	355	260	117	100	35	125	395	.205

20 Brian Finch, rhp

Born: Sept. 27, 1981. **Ht.:** 6-4. **Wt.:** 195. **Bats:** R. **Throws:** R. **School:** Texas A&M University.
Career Transactions: Selected by Orioles in second round of 2003 draft; signed June 13, 2003. **Signed by:** Joe Almaraz.

Finch had a promising start to his professional career in 2003, after the Orioles made him a surprise second-round pick, and the outlook was even brighter after he got off to a dominant start in low Class A in 2004. A promotion to high Class A made sense, but the organization's psychological testing indicated he could handle a jump to Double-A, so he went to Bowie. He got his head handed to him there, finally getting sent back to Frederick after 48 rough innings. By then, his confidence was shattered and his arm was tired, so he put up bad numbers there as well. When he's right, Finch is a power pitcher who throws from 91-96 mph with good sink, with a power curveball and an average changeup that he doesn't use enough. His stuff is not a concern, however; his state of mind is after his difficult 2004 season. He could go back to high Class A in an effort to rebuild his confidence, and the organization will hope he can regain his previous form as a potential middle-of-the-rotation starter.

Year	Club (League)	Class	W	L	ERA	G	GS	CG	SV	IP	H	R	ER	HR	BB	SO	AVG
2003	Aberdeen (NY-P)	A	1	3	1.93	8	5	0	0	28	19	9	6	0	5	29	.183
2004	Delmarva (SAL)	A	2	2	1.44	5	5	0	0	25	23	11	4	0	2	14	.225
	Bowie (EL)	AA	2	6	8.69	11	10	0	0	48	73	46	46	5	16	32	.354
	Frederick (Car)	A	1	4	7.96	9	9	0	0	37	59	35	33	5	15	22	.358
MINOR LEAGUE TOTALS			6	15	5.80	33	29	0	0	138	174	101	89	10	38	97	.302

21 Scott Rice, lhp

Born: Sept. 21, 1981. **Ht.:** 6-6. **Wt.:** 217. **Bats:** L. **Throws:** L. **School:** Royal HS, Simi Valley, Calif. **Career Transactions:** Selected by Orioles in first round (44th overall) of 1999 draft; signed June 30, 1999. **Signed by:** Gil Kubski.

The Orioles made Rice a supplemental first-rounder in 1999 with a pick they received as compensation for the Rangers signing Rafael Palmeiro, and in his first three and a half seasons in the organization he didn't show them much. Even though he grew up in California, Rice spent more time playing basketball as a youngster and was relatively inexperienced on the mound. The Orioles considered him a projectable lefty and he finally started fulfilling those projections after they moved him to the bullpen in 2003. He had to start 10 games for Bowie in the middle of the 2004 season, so he was tired in August and in the Arizona Fall League, and got hit hard. Rice is a sinker/slider pitcher who pitches at 88-90 mph from a low three-quarters delivery. He has a nice changeup that still isn't consistent. None of his offerings is a true out pitch, so he relies more on deception and location. His command still needs refinement, however, as Double-A hitters showed a willingness to lay off his pitches out of the zone. Rice's body suggests he should still be able to add velocity. He'll compete for a bullpen job in Triple-A during spring training and will have to get hitters out there before getting consideration for a big league job.

Year	Club (League)	Class	W	L	ERA	G	GS	CG	SV	IP	H	R	ER	HR	BB	SO	AVG
1999	Orioles (GCL)	R	1	4	0.38	9	6	0	0	17	26	34	20	2	20	14	.338
2000	Orioles (GCL)	R	1	6	5.21	13	13	0	0	57	61	46	33	0	48	34	.288
2001	Bluefield (Appy)	R	4	3	4.12	12	12	0	0	63	58	44	29	4	28	53	.240
2002	Delmarva (SAL)	A	0	6	5.40	18	3	0	3	40	45	26	24	2	21	22	.288
	Aberdeen (NY-P)	A	1	7	4.47	11	10	0	1	56	66	40	28	2	24	41	.297
2003	Delmarva (SAL)	A	4	1	0.94	32	0	0	5	48	21	7	5	0	12	53	.130
	Frederick (Car)	A	1	3	3.19	25	0	0	0	31	34	12	11	1	14	27	.286
2004	Bowie (EL)	AA	6	5	3.66	41	10	0	1	96	94	48	39	3	40	61	.259
MINOR LEAGUE TOTALS			18	35	4.16	161	54	0	10	409	405	257	189	14	207	305	.261

22 Jarod Rine, of

Born: Nov. 14, 1981. **Ht.:** 6-1. **Wt.:** 190. **Bats:** L. **Throws:** R. **School:** West Virginia University. **Career Transactions:** Selected by Orioles in ninth round of 2003 draft; signed June 16, 2003. **Signed by:** Marc Tramuta.

The Orioles drafted Rine out of West Virginia and signed him for $70,000 on the recommendation of scout Marc Tramuta, who now works as an area scout for the Blue Jays. He shared Big East Conference player of the year honors with Notre Dame righthander Chris Niesel in 2003 after a breakout year when he batted .418. His only above-average tool is his speed, but scouts say he's the kind of player who grows on them after extended viewing. He's a lefthanded hitter with strength, but he'll have to refine his swing to become a better offensive threat with a wood bat. That would also allow him to add power. He has shown good plate discipline but could actually stand to be more aggressive. His speed not only allows him to steal bases, but also allows him to cover a lot of ground in the outfield. He also has a good arm and can definitely handle center field. He'll move up to high Class A in 2004, and his bat will determine if he's a potential starter or an extra outfielder.

Year	Club (League)	Class	AVG	G	AB	R	H	2B	3B	HR	RBI	BB	SO	SB	OBP	SLG
2003	Aberdeen (NY-P)	A	.252	67	230	36	58	8	5	2	14	15	44	20	.313	.357
2004	Delmarva (SAL)	A	.257	122	460	79	118	16	8	7	57	60	89	31	.345	.372
MINOR LEAGUE TOTALS			.255	189	690	115	176	24	13	9	71	75	133	51	.335	.367

23 Travis Brown, ss/2b

Born: Aug. 1, 1980. **Ht.:** 5-11. **Wt.:** 180. **Bats:** R. **Throws:** R. **School:** Western Kentucky University. **Career Transactions:** Selected by Orioles in 27th round of 2003 draft; signed June 11, 2003. **Signed by:** Marc Ziegler.

The Orioles have had more than their share of disappointments with their premium draft picks in recent years, but they've also had unheralded, later-round picks emerge as surprise contributors. Brown, who was a senior sign out of Western Kentucky, is another to keep an eye on after he built on his strong 2003 debut with a solid season in low Class A. He had a 13-game hitting streak in 2003, then put together an eight-game and 10-game streak in 2004. Brown isn't outstanding in any particular area, but he can run and throw and he's athletic in addition to being able to swing the bat. He has played mostly at shortstop in his first two stops but also saw brief action at second and third base in 2004 and probably profiles as a utility player down the road. But he has already exceeded expectations, so he could continue to boost his stock in 2005 in high Class A.

Year	Club (League)	Class	AVG	G	AB	R	H	2B	3B	HR	RBI	BB	SO	SB	OBP	SLG
2003	Bluefield (Appy)	R	.315	48	165	27	52	11	0	1	15	15	27	15	.383	.400
2004	Delmarva (SAL)	A	.286	115	420	69	120	19	2	1	36	35	76	4	.353	.348
MINOR LEAGUE TOTALS			.294	163	585	96	172	30	2	2	51	50	103	19	.361	.362

24 Lorenzo Scott, of

Born: March 1, 1982. **Ht.:** 6-3. **Wt.:** 210. **Bats:** L. **Throws:** L. **School:** Ball State University. **Career Transactions:** Selected by Orioles in 17th round of 2003 draft; signed June 9, 2003. **Signed by:** Marc Ziegler.

Whether Scott becomes a major league baseball player remains to be seen, but there's no doubt he's an outstanding athlete. He was an outstanding linebacker at Ball State, leading the team in tackles in his first three seasons. He returned for his senior season after playing a summer in the Orioles organization, finishing second on the team in tackles and winning all-Mid-American Conference honors. The 2004 season was his first concentrating solely on baseball, and he made progress in his transition from football but still has a ways to go. He looked great on some nights, and like he just walked off the football field on others. He has a strong body, good quickness and excellent bat speed, and perhaps more important he has strong makeup and plays with passion and energy. He'll need a lot of at-bats to develop his hitting, however, and he needs to improve his angles and reads in the outfield. The Orioles should disregard Scott's age and just put him in a situation where he can be successful and get lots of at-bats. That likely will come in low Class A in 2005.

Year	Club (League)	Class	AVG	G	AB	R	H	2B	3B	HR	RBI	BB	SO	SB	OBP	SLG
2003	Orioles (GCL)	R	.319	33	116	30	37	8	4	0	24	25	28	11	.441	.457
2004	Delmarva (SAL)	A	.184	16	38	5	7	1	1	0	2	11	25	4	.392	.263
	Bluefield (Appy)	R	.237	62	219	36	52	6	1	3	16	27	75	12	.320	.315
MINOR LEAGUE TOTALS			.257	111	373	71	96	15	6	3	42	63	128	27	.367	.354

25 Mike Huggins, 1b

Born: Aug. 29, 1980. **Ht.:** 6-3. **Wt.:** 212. **Bats:** R. **Throws:** R. **School:** Baylor University. **Career Transactions:** Selected by Orioles in 13th round of 2002 draft; signed June 7, 2002. **Signed by:** Ralph Garr Jr.

Huggins has won more recognition for his off-field achievements, which have included community service work at every minor league stop he has made, than for his accomplishments with the bat. After an encouraging year in 2003, Huggins took a step back in 2004, due mainly to an appendectomy that knocked him out of action for almost two months. He went to the Arizona Fall League to make up at-bats and overcame a slow start to hit .273 in 77 at-bats. Huggins is a blue-collar player who plays above his tools, which are not going to wow anyone. He has a solid approach at the plate and a good idea of the strike zone, and he's a good defender who makes all the routine plays. The main knock against Huggins is that he has average power at best, which won't be enough to make him a full-time player on a first-division club. But with no glaring weaknesses and strong makeup, he could be a useful reserve. He likely will return to Double-A to open the season.

Year	Club (League)	Class	AVG	G	AB	R	H	2B	3B	HR	RBI	BB	SO	SB	OBP	SLG
2002	Aberdeen (NY-P)	A	.262	76	271	32	71	15	2	1	27	31	55	9	.340	.343
2003	Frederick (Car)	A	.293	126	454	66	133	32	0	13	74	55	93	3	.367	.449
2004	Bowie (EL)	AA	.237	76	249	22	59	16	0	4	30	33	53	2	.334	.349
MINOR LEAGUE TOTALS			.270	278	974	120	263	63	2	18	131	119	201	14	.351	.394

26 Brian Forystek, lhp

Born: Oct. 30, 1978. **Ht.:** 6-1. **Wt.:** 182. **Bats:** L. **Throws:** L. **School:** Illinois State University. **Career Transactions:** Selected by Orioles in 14th round of 2000 draft; signed June 26, 2000. **Signed by:** Troy Hoerner.

After Forystek had a season that was disappointing from beginning to end (including a 9.49 ERA in the Arizona Fall League), there was speculation that he would be dropped from the 40-man roster. He opened the 2004 season in Triple-A but went back to Bowie at midseason, where he emerged in 2003 after spending most of his career in the bullpen. His breakout was predicated on pinpoint command, and he got away from that in 2004. He depends on his command because he lacks a plus pitch. His fastball is 88-89 mph, with good sink, and he complements it with a slider and changeup. Forystek had used his changeup effectively against righthanded hitters in 2003, but he could not find a way to get righthanded hitters out last season. They batted .322 against him, while lefthanders batted just .225. So it wouldn't be a surprise to see Forystek go back into a bullpen role in 2005 because as a starter he needs to be perfect every outing because his raw stuff isn't overwhelming. He'll open the season in Triple-A, with his role likely determined in spring training.

Year	Club (League)	Class	W	L	ERA	G	GS	CG	SV	IP	H	R	ER	HR	BB	SO	AVG
2000	Orioles (GCL)	R	4	0	3.72	11	0	0	1	19	18	10	8	1	8	28	.240
	Frederick (Car)	A	1	0	1.35	3	0	0	0	7	5	1	1	0	1	7	.185
2001	Frederick (Car)	A	1	3	2.88	41	1	0	0	59	61	27	19	3	30	68	.269
2002	Frederick (Car)	A	1	4	4.50	43	1	0	3	70	71	47	35	4	36	79	.258
2003	Bowie (EL)	AA	9	9	3.39	29	21	1	0	125	116	57	47	8	42	103	.251
2004	Bowie (EL)	AA	5	5	5.74	15	15	0	0	85	94	57	54	16	41	75	.284
	Ottawa (IL)	AAA	3	5	5.58	12	11	0	0	61	71	46	38	6	32	43	.302
MINOR LEAGUE TOTALS			24	26	4.27	154	49	1	1	426	436	245	202	38	190	403	.267

27 Richard Stahl, lhp

Born: April 11, 1981. **Ht.:** 6-7. **Wt.:** 222. **Bats:** R. **Throws:** L. **School:** Newton HS, Covington, Ga. **Career Transactions:** Selected by Orioles in first round (18th overall) of 1999 draft; signed Aug. 31, 1999. **Signed by:** Lamar North.

Back and arm injuries have sapped much of the promise that once made Stahl the organization's top prospect, but the Orioles are encouraged that he has stayed relatively healthy the last two seasons—though he has been used very carefully and has still battled nagging injuries like a bad groin—and anxious to see what he can show in 2005. Stahl was said to be disconsolate at one point during the season as he struggled at high Class A, a level he dominated in six starts three years earlier. But he has persevered and his fastball is back into the 89-92 mph range, occasionally touching 93 or 94. He also throws a power slider, as opposed to a curveball that he used to throw, and changeup. It's not likely he'll get back to the easy mid-90s velocity he used to show, and his arm is not as free and loose as it was several years ago. That he has made it this far back is a tribute to his work ethic. Stahl will try to win a Double-A rotation spot and prove his stuff is continuing to approach its previous form.

Year	Club (League)	Class	W	L	ERA	G	GS	CG	SV	IP	H	R	ER	HR	BB	SO	AVG
2000	Delmarva (SAL)	A	5	6	3.34	20	20	0	0	89	97	47	33	3	51	83	.280

Year	Club (League)	Class	W	L	ERA	G	GS	CG	SV	IP	H	R	ER	HR	BB	SO	AVG
2001	Delmarva (SAL)	A	2	3	2.67	6	6	0	0	34	24	15	10	3	15	31	.205
	Frederick (Car)	A	1	1	1.95	6	6	1	0	32	26	13	7	1	15	24	.232
	Orioles (GCL)	R	0	0	0.00	1	1	0	0	2	1	0	0	0	1	1	.167
2002	Delmarva (SAL)	A	1	1	5.59	2	2	0	0	10	10	8	6	3	5	9	.278
2003	Delmarva (SAL)	A	1	3	5.48	28	1	0	1	48	47	41	29	4	50	46	.261
2004	Aberdeen (NY-P)	A	0	0	0.00	1	1	0	0	3	1	0	0	0	0	1	.111
	Frederick (Car)	A	7	8	4.96	19	19	0	0	82	80	52	45	6	50	56	.259
MINOR LEAGUE TOTALS			17	22	3.91	83	56	1	1	299	286	176	130	20	187	251	.257

28 Ryan Finan, 1b

Born: Jan. 5, 1982. **Ht.:** 6-5. **Wt.:** 220. **Bats:** L. **Throws:** R. **School:** Lamar University. **Career Transactions:** Selected in 21st round of 2004 draft by Orioles; signed June 16, 2004. **Signed by:** Joe Almaraz.

Finan was an unheralded draft pick who showed Orioles officials something with the bat and his approach to the game in his professional debut. He was all-academic and third team all-Southland Conference player at Lamar in 2004, when he batted .289-8-43 and drew 52 walks, then was the all-star first baseman in the Rookie-level Appalachian League in spite of missing a good portion of the season with an infection in his knee. Finan showed the same plate discipline at Bluefield that he did in college, and he showed a smooth swing with power potential as well. He also proved to be good defender at first base. Finan's baseball IQ made the biggest impression on the organization, however. Officials noted several times when he, rather than a coach or the catcher, would go to the mound to settle pitchers down in tight situations. He will have to prove himself at higher levels after succeeding as a 22-year-old in Rookie ball, and he could jump to high Class A to get his chance.

Year	Club (League)	Class	AVG	G	AB	R	H	2B	3B	HR	RBI	BB	SO	SB	OBP	SLG
2004	Bluefield (Appy)	R	.333	36	123	27	41	12	0	5	21	18	16	0	.429	.553
MINOR LEAGUE TOTALS			.333	36	123	27	41	12	0	5	21	18	16	0	.429	.553

29 C.J. Smith, 1b

Born: Feb. 22, 1982. **Ht.:** 6-3. **Wt.:** 210. **Bats:** R. **Throws:** R. **School:** University of Florida. **Career Transactions:** Selected in fifth round of 2004 draft by Orioles; signed June 16, 2004. **Signed by:** Harry Shelton.

Smith was a sixth-round pick by the Pirates as a draft-eligible sophomore, and he boosted his stock a bit with a good summer in the Cape Cod League in 2003, when he tied for the league lead with 17 extra-base hits. Tall and wiry, Smith generates good bat speed and shows some power now, with the potential to hit for more in the future if he makes adjustments to his swing. He has added at least 15 pounds of muscle to his frame in the last couple of years, and scouts compare his build to that of Paul O'Neill. He plays with enthusiasm and is a good athlete. He played both first base and in the outfield in college, though he spent all of his time in Aberdeen at first. He has poor actions around the bag at first, and his arm would limit him to left if he moves to the outfield. He showed poor plate discipline in his first pro experience, but he could jump to Frederick to start his first full season.

Year	Club (League)	Class	AVG	G	AB	R	H	2B	3B	HR	RBI	BB	SO	SB	OBP	SLG
2004	Aberdeen (NY-P)	A	.242	61	207	28	50	14	3	3	19	24	50	3	.318	.382
MINOR LEAGUE TOTALS			.242	61	207	28	50	14	3	3	19	24	50	3	.318	.382

30 Tony Neal, rhp

Born: Sept. 12, 1980. **Ht.:** 6-2. **Wt.:** 210. **Bats:** R. **Throws:** R. **School:** University of South Alabama. **Career Transactions:** Selected in 20th round of 2003 draft by Orioles; signed June 9, 2003. **Signed by:** Dave Jennings.

Neal missed a year at South Alabama after having Tommy John surgery in February 2002, but by March 2003 he struck out 15 Jacksonville State batters in eight innings. The Orioles took him as a senior bargain pick and have been pleasantly surprised with his progress. He opened 2004 in the Delmarva bullpen but moved into the Frederick bullpen in May out of necessity. He struggled at first but became the Keys' closer by the end of June, getting hitters out with a 90-93 mph power sinker and a plus slider. He gets even higher marks for his feel for pitching and makeup. He doesn't have anything beyond his sinker/slider combo, but that has been enough to make him an effective reliever so far. Neal will have to work to keep his body in shape. He's already 24, so the Orioles will push him to Bowie to open the season. He'll likely close there but projects as a middle reliever in the big leagues.

Year	Club (League)	Class	W	L	ERA	G	GS	CG	SV	IP	H	R	ER	HR	BB	SO	AVG
2003	Aberdeen (NY-P)	A	2	1	1.94	19	0	0	1	42	30	15	9	1	19	43	.213
2004	Delmarva (SAL)	A	1	0	2.57	7	0	0	2	14	8	5	4	0	10	20	.163
	Frederick (Car)	A	2	6	4.33	50	0	0	18	62	48	30	30	8	25	64	.212
MINOR LEAGUE TOTALS			5	7	3.28	76	0	0	21	118	86	50	43	9	54	127	.207

BOSTON
RED SOX

BY **JIM CALLIS**

As you may have heard, the Red Sox won the World Series. Making that championship even sweeter, they pulled off an unprecedented comeback against the team they and their fans love to hate, the Yankees.

More than they may like to admit, the Red Sox were similar to the franchise team president Larry Lucchino dubbed the Evil Empire. New York had the highest payroll in the game at $188 million, but Boston came in second at $130 million. Both clubs had to rely on their wallets and not their farm systems to build winners. The Red Sox signed and fully developed only one player who was on their postseason roster for all three series: right fielder **Trot Nixon**, a 1993 first-round pick.

While former general manager Dan Duquette got Johnny Damon, Pedro Martinez and Manny Ramirez, he didn't make good on his pledge to build through the farm system. Boston selected Nomar Garciaparra and Carl Pavano in 1994, Duquette's first year, but had little draft success afterward. The Red Sox also spent heavily on the international market with little to show for it.

As a result, John Henry and Tom Werner inherited a barren farm system when they bought the team in December 2001. GM Theo Epstein spoke of assembling a "$100 million player-development machine" when he was hired in November 2002, but the Red Sox were so bereft of talent that he protected just 28 players on his initial 40-man roster.

LARRY GOREN

Boston's system still isn't among the game's best, but it has improved. While shortstop Hanley Ramirez remains the lone elite prospect, other farmhands are showing promise. Outfielder Brandon Moss was the low Class A South Atlantic League MVP and hit .422 in the high Class A Florida State League during August. Righthander Jon Papelbon and lefty Jon Lester emerged as two of the better power pitchers in the FSL. Dominican shortstop Luis Soto ranked as the top prospect in the Rookie-level Gulf Coast League, and righthander Anibal Sanchez was the best pitching prospect in the short-season New York-Penn League.

The Red Sox also invested heavily in the draft again. They gave 12th-round lefty Mike Rozier a $1.575 million bonus, the biggest ever for a player selected after the third round. Boston broke another mark in the eighth round by signing righty Kyle Bono for $432,000.

Following Boston's World Series triumph, scouting director David Chadd left to take the same job with the Tigers. The Red Sox promoted director of scouting administration Jason McLeod to replace Chadd, and McLeod will have plenty of picks to work with in his first draft. As compensation for the loss of free agents Orlando Cabrera, Derek Lowe and Pedro Martinez, Boston will make six selections before the middle of the second round.

TOP 30 PROSPECTS

1. Hanley Ramirez, ss
2. Brandon Moss, of
3. Jon Papelbon, rhp
4. Jon Lester, lhp
5. Anibal Sanchez, rhp
6. Dustin Pedroia, ss
7. Luis Soto, ss
8. Kelly Shoppach, c
9. Ian Bladergroen, 1b
10. Abe Alvarez, lhp
11. Manny Delcarmen, rhp
12. Christian Lara, ss
13. Mike Rozier, lhp
14. Mickey Hall, of
15. David Murphy, of
16. Chad Spann, 3b
17. Juan Cedeno, lhp
18. Tommy Hottovy, lhp
19. Andrew Dobies, lhp
20. Jimmy James, rhp
21. Cla Meredith, rhp
22. Kyle Bono, rhp
23. Adam Stern, of
24. Jeremy West, 1b
25. Beau Vaughan, rhp
26. David Pauley, rhp
27. Kenny Perez, ss/2b
28. Jose Vaquedano, rhp
29. Gary Galvez, rhp
30. Willy Mota, of

ORGANIZATION OVERVIEW

General manager: Theo Epstein. **Farm director:** Ben Cherington. **Scouting director:** Jason McLeod.

2004 PERFORMANCE

Class	Team	League	W	L	Pct.	Finish*	Manager
Majors	Boston	American	98	64	.605	2nd (14)	Terry Francona
Triple-A	Pawtucket Red Sox	International	73	71	.507	t-5th (14)	Buddy Bailey
Double-A	Portland Sea Dogs	Eastern	69	73	.486	t-7th (12)	Ron Johnson
High A	#Sarasota Red Sox	Florida State	76	61	.555	4th (12)	Todd Claus
Low A	@Augusta GreenJackets	South Atlantic	66	73	.475	12th (16)	Chad Epperson
Short-season	Lowell Spinners	New York-Penn	32	44	.421	11th (14)	Luis Alicea
Rookie	GCL Red Sox	Gulf Coast	34	24	.586	4th (12)	Ralph Treuel
OVERALL 2004 MINOR LEAGUE RECORD			350	346	.503	14th (30)	

*Finish in overall standings (No. of teams in league).
#Affiliate will be in Wilmington (Carolina) in 2005. @Affiliate will be in Capital City (South Atlantic) in 2005.

ORGANIZATION LEADERS

BATTING   *Minimum 250 At-Bats
*AVG   Brandon Moss, Sarasota/Augusta .... .353
   R   Adam Hyzdu, Pawtucket 92
   H   Brandon Moss, Sarasota/Augusta 182
  TB   Earl Snyder, Pawtucket 300
  2B   Earl Snyder, Pawtucket 43
  3B   Sheldon Fulse, Portland 7
       Brandon Moss, Sarasota/Augusta 7
  HR   Earl Snyder, Pawtucket 36
 RBI   Brandon Moss, Sarasota/Augusta 111
  BB   Adam Hyzdu, Pawtucket 84
  SO   Jeremy Owens, Pawtucket 140
  SB   Sheldon Fulse, Portland 29
*OBP   Adam Hyzdu, Pawtucket .... .412
*SLG   Stefan Bailie, Portland/Sarasota .... .576

PITCHING   #Minimum 75 Innings
   W   Jarrett Gardner, Portland/Augusta 14
   L   Kyle Jackson, Augusta 13
#ERA   Anibal Sanchez, Lowell 1.77
   G   Matt Duff, Pawtucket 53
  CG   Jamie Brown, Pawtucket 2
       Jon Papelbon, Sarasota 2
  SV   Cla Meredith, Sarasota/Augusta 18
  IP   Frank Castillo, Pawtucket 168
  BB   Charlie Zink, Portland/Sarasota 81
  SO   Jon Papelbon, Sarasota 153

BEST TOOLS

Best Hitter for Average .... Brandon Moss
Best Power Hitter .... Luis Soto
Best Strike-Zone Discipline .... Dustin Pedroia
Fastest Baserunner .... Hanley Ramirez
Best Athlete.. Hanley Ramirez
Best Fastball .... Jon Papelbon
Best Curveball .... Manny Delcarmen
Best Slider .... Jon Papelbon
Best Changeup .... Abe Alvarez
Best Control .... Abe Alvarez
Best Defensive Catcher .... Kelly Shoppach
Best Defensive Infielder .... Hanley Ramirez
Best Infield Arm...................................... Hanley Ramirez
Best Defensive Outfielder......................... Chris Durbin
Best Outfield Arm..................................... Willy Mota

PROJECTED 2008 LINEUP

Catcher .... Jason Varitek
First Base .... Ian Bladergroen
Second Base .... Dustin Pedroia
Third Base .... Kevin Youkilis
Shortstop .... Edgar Renteria
Left Field .... Manny Ramirez
Center Field.. Hanley Ramirez

Right Field.. Brandon Moss
Designated Hitter .... David Ortiz
No. 1 Starter .... Matt Clement
No. 2 Starter.. Bronson Arroyo
No. 3 Starter... Wade Miller
No. 4 Starter... Jon Papelbon
No. 5 Starter .... Jon Lester
Closer.. Keith Foulke

LAST YEAR'S TOP 20 PROSPECTS

1. Hanley Ramirez, ss   11. Luis Mendoza, rhp
2. Kelly Shoppach, c   12. Anastacio Martinez, rhp
3. David Murphy, of   13. Mickey Hall, of
4. Kevin Youkilis, 3b   14. Jon Papelbon, rhp
5. Matt Murton, of   15. Beau Vaughan, rhp
6. Chad Spann, 3b   16. Jerome Gamble, rhp
7. Abe Alvarez, lhp   17. Charlie Zink, rhp
8. Jon Lester, lhp   18. Dustin Brown, c
9. Juan Cedeno, lhp   19. Aneudis Mateo, rhp
10. Manny Delcarmen, rhp   20. Tim Hamulack, lhp

TOP PROSPECTS OF THE DECADE

Year	Player, Pos.	Current Team
1995	Nomar Garciaparra, ss	Cubs
1996	Donnie Sadler, ss.......................	Diamondbacks
1997	Nomar Garciaparra, ss	Cubs
1998	Brian Rose, rhp	Reds
1999	Dernell Stenson, of	Deceased
2000	Steve Lomasney, c	Reds
2001	Dernell Stenson, of/1b	Deceased
2002	Seung Song, rhp...	Expos
2003	Hanley Ramirez, ss..................................	Red Sox
2004	Hanley Ramirez, ss..................................	Red Sox

TOP DRAFT PICKS OF THE DECADE

Year	Player, Pos.	Current Team
1995	Andy Yount, rhp...........................	Out of baseball
1996	John Garrett, rhp	Out of baseball
1997	John Curtice, rhp	Out of baseball
1998	Adam Everett, ss...................................	Astros
1999	Rick Asadoorian, ss	Reds
2000	Phil Dumatrait, lhp	Reds
2001	Kelly Shoppach, c (2)	Red Sox
2002	Jon Lester, lhp (2)	Red Sox
2003	David Murphy, of	Red Sox
2004	Dustin Pedroia (2).................................	Red Sox

ALL-TIME LARGEST BONUSES

Rick Asadoorian, 1999................................ $1,725,500
Adam Everett, 1998 .... $1,725,000
Mike Rozier, 2004 .... $1,575,000
David Murphy, 2003..................................... $1,525,000
Phil Dumatrait, 2000..................................... $1,250,000

MINOR LEAGUE DEPTH CHART

Boston RED SOX

Impact Potential: C

In Hanley Ramirez, the Red Sox have a five-tool talent in the middle of the diamond who has had success at Double-A. The rest of Theo Epstein's player-development machine, however, shows less upside. Brandon Moss and Jon Papelbon burst onto the scene in 2004 and have to prove their seasons were not a fluke.

Depth: C

Boston has added some heft to its once-barren system, relying heavily (but not exclusively) on college players. The Sox have several promising shortstops—including some with plus power potential in Ramirez and Luis Soto—as well as quality lefthanded bats in Moss and Ian Bladergroen. Boston's corps of lefthanders also looks promising.

*Depth charts prepared by **John Manuel** and **Allan Simpson**. Numbers in parentheses indicate prospect rankings.*

LF
Justin Sherrod

CF
David Murphy (15)
Adam Stern (23)
Willy Mota (30)
Chris Turner
Matt Van Der Bosch

RF
Brandon Moss (2)
Mickey Hall (14)

3B
Chad Spann (16)
Scott White

SS
Hanley Ramirez (1)
Dustin Pedroia (6)
Luis Soto (7)
Christian Lara (12)

2B
Kenny Perez (27)

1B
Ian Bladergroen (9)
Jeremy West (24)
Stefan Bailie
Carlos Torres
Logan Sorensen

SOURCE of TALENT

Homegrown		Acquired	
College	11	Trades	2
Junior College	0	Rule 5 draft	1
Draft-and-follow	0	Independent leagues	0
High School	7	Free agents/waivers	0
Nondrafted free agent	0		
Foreign	9		

C
Kelly Shoppach (8)
Dusty Brown
Jesus Garcia

LHP

Starters	Relievers
Jon Lester (4)	Juan Cedeno (17)
Abe Alvarez (10)	Lenny DiNardo
Mike Rozier (13)	Mark Malaska
Tommy Hottovy (18)	Juan Perez
Andrew Dobies (19)	Brian Marshall
Adam Blackley	Justin Sturge
Kason Gabbard	Randy Beam
Mario Pena	
Jose Capellan	

RHP

Starters	Relievers
Jon Papelbon (3)	Manny Delcarmen (11)
Anibal Sanchez (5)	Cla Meredith (21)
Jimmy James (20)	Anastacio Martinez
Kyle Bono (22)	Tim Bausher
Beau Vaughan (25)	Victor Prieto
David Pauley (26)	Luis Mendoza
Jose Vaquedano (28)	Jessie Corn
Gary Galvez (29)	Ryan Schroyer
Kyle Jackson	
Chris Smith	
Charlie Zink	
Olivo Astacio	
Jesus Delgado	
Harvey Garcia	

DRAFT ANALYSIS

2004

Best Pro Debut: SS Dustin Pedroia (2) hit .357/.435/.535 in 42 games between low and high Class A, and he didn't commit a single error. A number of lefthanders had gaudy numbers, led by Tommy Hottovy (4) and Randy Beam (18). RHP Cla Meredith (6), a crossfiring sinkerballer, combined for an organization-high 18 saves and a 1.14 ERA between two full-season Class A stops.

Best Athlete: LHP Mike Rozier (12) turned down a scholarship to play quarterback at North Carolina. Hottovy also had Division I football offers as a quarterback coming out of high school in 2000.

Best Pure Hitter: Pedroia hit .384 in three years at Arizona State, including .393 to finish second in the Pacific-10 Conference batting race as a junior. The Red Sox see some Adam LaRoche in 1B Logan Sorensen (19), whose pro debut was cut short by wrist problems that required surgery.

Best Raw Power: OF Austin Easley (47) won the home run derby at the Cape Cod League all-star game last summer before signing in August.

Fastest Runner: OF Matt VanDerBosch (9) is a 5-foot-8 grinder out of the Darren Bragg mold. He runs better than Bragg, as his speed rates a 60 on the 20-80 scale.

Best Defensive Player: Other clubs have questioned whether Pedroia has enough range and arm to remain at shortstop, but the Red Sox believe he can stay there.

Best Fastball: After pitching at 88-92 mph and topping out at 94 during the spring, Rozier touched 95 during instructional league. There's more velocity in his projectable 6-foot-5, 210-pound frame.

Best Breaking Ball: Hottovy's curveball

RICH ABEL

Dobies

is slightly better than similar LHP Andrew Dobies' (3) slider.

Most Intriguing Background: The Red Sox drafted but didn't sign LHP Nick Francona (40), whose father Terry is their manager, and 3B Beau Mills (44), whose father Brad is the club's bench coach. Both played in the majors, as did Nick's grandfather Tito. VanDerBosch is the nephew of 1979 American League rookie of the year John Castino. SS Dustin Kelly's (15) uncle Pat had a brief big league career and managed Triple-A Richmond in the Braves system.

Closest To The Majors: Pedroia, Hottovy and Dobies all are on the fast track. Pedroia may start 2005 in Double-A.

Best Late-Round Pick: The Red Sox gave up their first-round pick as compensation for Keith Foulke, but they believe they landed the equivalent of a first-rounder in Rozier. He cost them $1.575 million, a record for a non-draft-and-follow selected after the third round.

The One Who Got Away: 1B Steve Pearce (10) has power and may be able to play catcher, third base or the outfield. He elected to return for his senior season at South Carolina.

Assessment: Signing Rozier was an aggressive move to make up for not having a first-rounder. He's a noticeable standout in an otherwise conservative draft class of advanced players who should move quickly but don't have huge ceilings.

2003 RHP Jon Papelbon (4) quickly emerged as Boston's best pitching prospect, and LHP Abe Alvarez (2) is a step closer to the majors. OFs David Murphy (1), Matt Murton (1/traded to the Cubs in the Nomar Garciaparra deal) and Mickey Hall (2) all show promise. *GRADE:* B

2002 The Red Sox lacked a first-rounder, but LHP Jon Lester (2) has a strong arm and is asked for in trade talks. LHP Tyler Pelland (2) is one of the Reds' better prospects after being used in a trade for Scott Williamson. *GRADE:* C+

2001 Again without a first-round pick, Boston found a legit prospect with its top choice, C Kelly Shoppach (2). Even better was the discovery of the favorte of the "Moneyball" set, 3B Kevin Youkilis (8). Signing LHP Matt Chico (2) would have been nice. *GRADE:* C+

2000 All of the best finds have had injury problems: 2B/SS Freddy Sanchez (11), RHP Manny Delcarmen (2) and LHP Phil Dumatrait (1). Sanchez and Dumatrait also have departed in 2003 pennant-drive trades. *GRADE:* C

Draft analysis prepared by Jim Callis. Numbers in parentheses indicate draft rounds.

Hanley
RAMIREZ

Born: Dec. 23, 1983.
Ht.: 6-3. **Wt.:** 195.
Bats: B. **Throws:** R.
Career Transactions: Signed out of Dominican Republic by Red Sox, July 2, 2000.
Signed by: Levy Ochoa.

Ramirez fell and injured his left wrist while running the bases on May 1. After sitting out a game with what initially was diagnosed as a sprain, Ramirez tried to play through the pain. He had six hits in four games before sliding into a 2-for-23 slump. Another examination revealed a hairline fracture that sidelined him for seven weeks. Once he was fully healthy, he took off. Ramirez batted .354 the rest of the way at high Class A Sarasota, where Florida State League managers rated him the circuit's best defensive shortstop and best infield arm. Following a promotion to Double-A Portland, he hit .310 with power and made just three errors in 32 games. The Red Sox named him their FSL player of the year, the third time in four pro seasons that Ramirez has won a team MVP award.

Shortstop has become a position of strength in the organization, yet Ramirez' five-tool package easily stands out among a crop that also includes Dustin Pedroia, Luis Soto, Christian Lara and Kenny Perez. He's the best athlete in the system with the potential to excel in all aspects of the game. A career .313 hitter, he has quick hands and a short stroke, allowing him to catch up to any fastball. He also excels at pitch recognition, so breaking pitches don't fool him. Ramirez signed as a switch-hitter but was so advanced from the right side that the Red Sox told him not to bother batting lefthanded. He also has plus raw power that started to show up in games after he reached Double-A. He can drive the ball out to all fields, and his home run totals would be higher if he didn't focus so much on hitting the ball up the middle, an approach Boston preaches at the lower levels of the minors. In addition to his offensive skills, Ramirez also has the most speed, best infield skills and strongest infield arm among Red Sox farmhands. After making 36 errors in 2003, he played more under control and cut his miscues to 20.

Coming into the 2004 season, Ramirez hadn't done a good job of handling the hype he started receiving after he was rated the No. 1 prospect in the Rookie-level Gulf Coast and short-season New-York Penn leagues in 2002. He was sent home from instructional league that fall for cursing at a trainer, and suspended in 2003 for making an obscene gesture to fans. But Ramirez matured and didn't have any behavioral problems in 2004. He's a hard worker, but his biggest need at this point is to improve his day-to-day preparation. When he's fully focused, he's usually the best player on the diamond. Ramirez doesn't draw as many walks as the Red Sox would hope, in part because he makes consistent hard contact so easily.

Ramirez showed enough at Portland that he may begin 2005 at Triple-A Pawtucket. Though he could be ready to play regularly in Boston by 2006, the Red Sox signed free agent Edgar Renteria to a four-year contract through 2008. That deal could make Ramirez a prime piece of trade bait.

Year	Club (League)	Class	AVG	G	AB	R	H	2B	3B	HR	RBI	BB	SO	SB	OBP	SLG
2001	Red Sox (DSL)	R	.345	54	197	32	68	18	2	5	34	15	22	13	.397	.533
2002	Red Sox (GCL)	R	.341	45	164	29	56	11	3	6	26	16	15	8	.402	.555
	Lowell (NY-P)	A	.371	22	97	17	36	9	2	1	19	4	14	4	.400	.536
2003	Augusta (SAL)	A	.275	111	422	69	116	24	3	8	50	32	73	36	.327	.403
2004	Sarasota (FSL)	A	.310	62	239	33	74	8	4	1	24	17	39	12	.364	.389
	Portland (EL)	AA	.310	32	129	26	40	7	2	5	15	10	26	12	.360	.512
MINOR LEAGUE TOTALS			.313	326	1248	206	390	77	16	26	168	94	189	85	.364	.462

Brandon Moss, of

Born: Sept. 16, 1983. **Ht.:** 6-0. **Wt.:** 181. **Bats:** L. **Throws:** R. **School:** Loganville HS, Monroe, Ga. **Career Transactions:** Selected by Red Sox in eighth round of 2002 draft; signed June 8, 2002. **Signed by:** Rob English.

Though Moss hit just .226 in his first two years as a pro, the Red Sox believed he was on the verge of a breakout. He proved them correct by winning the batting title and MVP award in the low Class A South Atlantic League, then batting .422 in high Class A during August. Moss has worked very hard to make himself the best hitter in the system. He has a good swing path and a sound approach, and line drives jump off his bat to all fields. Boston likes his raw power and thinks he'll mature into an annual 25-homer threat. Intense and dedicated, he runs OK, plays a solid right field and has a slightly above-average arm. Some SAL observers questioned Moss' pop. But he did have 49 extra-base hits as a 20-year-old, and he's learning how to work counts to get pitches he can drive. With Trot Nixon under contract through 2006 and Manny Ramirez tied up through 2008, the Red Sox can be patient with Moss. He'll probably open 2005 with Boston's new high Class A Wilmington affiliate.

Year	Club (League)	Class	AVG	G	AB	R	H	2B	3B	HR	RBI	BB	SO	SB	OBP	SLG
2002	Red Sox (GCL)	R	.204	42	113	10	23	6	2	0	6	13	40	1	.295	.292
2003	Lowell (NY-P)	A	.237	65	228	29	54	15	4	7	34	15	53	7	.290	.430
2004	Augusta (SAL)	A	.339	109	433	66	147	25	6	13	101	46	75	19	.402	.515
	Sarasota (FSL)	A	.422	23	83	16	35	2	1	2	10	7	15	2	.462	.542
MINOR LEAGUE TOTALS			.302	239	857	121	259	48	13	22	151	81	183	29	.364	.466

Jon Papelbon, rhp

Born: Nov. 23, 1980. **Ht.:** 6-4. **Wt.:** 230. **Bats:** R. **Throws:** R. **School:** Mississippi State University. **Career Transactions:** Selected by Red Sox in fourth round of 2003 draft; signed June 12, 2003. **Signed by:** Joe Mason.

Papelbon worked exclusively in relief during three years at Mississippi State, but the Red Sox drafted him with the idea of making him a starter. After keeping him on tight pitch counts in his pro debut, they turned him loose in 2004. He responded by finishing second in the Florida State League in ERA and strikeouts. Papelbon's fastball, which sits in the 92-94 mph range and touches 98, isn't the hardest in the system, but it's the best in terms of the combination of velocity, movement and command. He relied almost solely on his fastball early in the year, but learned to trust his slider and changeup as the year went on. All three are plus pitches at times, and he also has a curveball he can throw for strikes. He has a durable frame and did a great job with his offseason conditioning. Papelbon's slider and changeup need more consistency. The better they become, the better he'll do against lefthanders. When it's on, he can bury his slider down and in on them. Ticketed for Double-A in 2005, Papelbon has the stuff to become a frontline starter. At worst, he should be an innings-eater.

Year	Club (League)	Class	W	L	ERA	G	GS	CG	SV	IP	H	R	ER	HR	BB	SO	AVG
2003	Lowell (NY-P)	A	1	2	6.34	13	6	0	0	33	43	23	23	2	9	36	.312
2004	Sarasota (FSL)	A	12	7	2.64	24	24	2	0	130	97	43	38	6	43	153	.206
MINOR LEAGUE TOTALS			13	9	3.382	37	30	2	0	162	140	66	61	8	52	189	.230

Jon Lester, lhp

Born: Jan. 7, 1984. **Ht.:** 6-3. **Wt.:** 200. **Bats:** L. **Throws:** L. **School:** Bellarmine Prep, Puyallup, Wash. **Career Transactions:** Selected by Red Sox in second round of 2002 draft; signed Aug. 13, 2002. **Signed by:** Gary Rajsich.

Lester gets asked about in trade talks more than any Red Sox prospect, and he would have gone to the Rangers had Boston been able to finalize a deal for Alex Rodriguez last offseason. The top pick in the Red Sox' last draft before they adopted a strong college emphasis, he signed for $1 million as a second-rounder. Lester has a stronger arm than most left-handers, as he pitches at 92-93 mph and hits 96. He's very athletic and has a smooth delivery, which bodes well for his long-term control. He does an excellent job of keeping the ball down in the zone, yielding just nine homers in 197 pro innings. He picked up an effective cut fastball at midseason. He's far from a finished product. Lester's curveball and changeup have the potential to be average or better pitches, but they're not there yet. He missed most of June with shoulder tightness, but it's not a long-term concern.

How well Lester refines his secondary pitches will determine when he reaches Boston and where he'll slot into the rotation. He'll open 2005 in Double-A and could surface in the majors as early as mid-2006.

Year	Club (League)	Class	W	L	ERA	G	GS	CG	SV	IP	H	R	ER	HR	BB	SO	AVG
2002	Red Sox (GCL)	R	0	1	3.50	1	1	0	0	1	5	6	1	0	1	1	.714
2003	Augusta (SAL)	A	6	9	3.65	24	21	0	0	106	102	54	43	7	44	71	.262
2004	Sarasota (FSL)	A	7	6	4.28	21	20	0	0	90	82	46	43	2	37	97	.244
MINOR LEAGUE TOTALS			13	16	3.98	46	42	0	0	197	189	106	87	9	82	169	.258

5 Anibal Sanchez, rhp

RICH ABEL

Born: Feb. 27, 1984. **Ht.:** 6-0. **Wt.:** 180. **Bats:** R. **Throws:** R. **Career Transactions:** Signed out of Venezuela by Red Sox, Jan. 3, 2001. **Signed by:** Carlos Ramirez.

Sanchez pitched well for two seasons in the Rookie-level Venezuelan Summer League, then needed elbow surgery to transpose a nerve. After missing all of 2003, he came back in a huge way, leading the New York-Penn League in ERA and strikeouts and ranking as the circuit's top pitching prospect. Sanchez succeeded in Venezuela when he worked at 88-90 mph, and he dominated in 2004 when his velocity jumped to the mid-90s. His fastball is also notable for its movement and his ability to command it to both sides of the plate. Sanchez has one of the system's better curveballs. His changeup shows flashes of becoming a plus pitch. With an electric arm and pitching savvy, Sanchez just needs more innings and continued good health. His curveball and changeup aren't totally reliable yet, but should improve as he gains more experience. He's not physically dominating, but he generates velocity with arm speed rather than extra effort. Sanchez will move to full-season ball for the first time in 2005, pitching at Boston's new low Class A Capital City affiliate. He might not need much more than two more seasons in the minors.

Year	Club (League)	Class	W	L	ERA	G	GS	CG	SV	IP	H	R	ER	HR	BB	SO	AVG
2001	San Joaquin (VSL)	R	4	3	3.19	24	1	0	3	54	40	23	19	0	23	64	.000
2002	Ciudad Alianza (VSL)	R	5	3	3.50	11	11	1	0	62	50	31	24	3	11	73	.222
2003	Did not play—Injured																
2004	Lowell (NY-P)	A	4	4	1.77	15	15	0	0	76	43	24	15	3	29	101	.157
MINOR LEAGUE TOTALS			13	10	2.72	50	27	1	3	192	133	78	58	6	63	238	.267

6 Dustin Pedroia, ss

RODGER WOOD

Born: Aug. 17, 1983. **Ht.:** 5-8. **Wt.:** 180. **Bats:** R. **Throws:** R. **School:** Arizona State University. **Career Transactions:** Selected by Red Sox in second round of 2004 draft; signed July 13, 2004. **Signed by:** Dan Madsen.

Pedroia represents one extreme of the tools vs. performance debate. He's not physically gifted, but he wins. A two-time All-American at Arizona State, he had no problem adjusting to Class A in his pro debut. He batted a combined .357 and didn't commit an error in 42 games. Pedroia has tremendous ability to handle the bat and control the strike zone, making him a candidate to bat second in a big league lineup. His hands and fundamentals are excellent at shortstop, and the Red Sox believe he'll be able to stay at that position. He enhances his average speed with uncanny instincts. Several scouts have questioned whether Pedroia has enough arm and range to play shortstop. The presence of Hanley Ramirez in the system may make that question moot. Pedroia never will be a home run threat, though he'll have some gap power. Pedroia may start his first full season in Double-A. He could be Boston's next Jody Reed, who began his big league career at short-stop before moving to second base.

Year	Club (League)	Class	AVG	G	AB	R	H	2B	3B	HR	RBI	BB	SO	SB	OBP	SLG
2004	Augusta (SAL)	A	.400	12	50	11	20	5	0	1	5	6	3	2	.474	.560
	Sarasota (FSL)	A	.336	30	107	23	36	8	3	2	14	13	4	0	.417	.523
MINOR LEAGUE TOTALS			.357	42	157	34	56	13	3	3	19	19	7	2	.435	.535

Luis Soto, ss

Born: Dec. 7, 1985. **Ht.:** 6-1. **Wt.:** 179. **Bats:** B. **Throws:** R. **Career Transactions:** Signed out of Dominican Republic by Red Sox, Nov. 25, 2003. **Signed by:** Louie Eljaua.

International scouting director Louie Eljaua left to become a Pirates special assistant in January 2004, but he left Soto as a going-away present. Signed for $500,000 just before Eljaua departed, Soto rated as the Gulf Coast League's top prospect in his pro debut. Boston's minor league instructors have been told not to touch Soto's swing. He has great hand-eye coordination, quick hands and a fluid stroke from both sides of the plate. He has more power potential than any hitter in the system, with the chance to become a 30-homer hitter. His strong arm is his best defensive tool, and he also has good speed. He adapted well and picked up English quickly in his first year in the United States. While Soto has natural actions at shortstop, his instincts and fundamentals lag behind because he has limited game experience. He makes contact so easily that he won't draw many walks unless he becomes much more patient. Soto likely will begin 2005 in extended spring training before heading to short-season Lowell. With Edgar Renteria and Hanley Ramirez ahead of him, Soto could move to third base.

Year	Club (League)	Class	AVG	G	AB	R	H	2B	3B	HR	RBI	BB	SO	SB	OBP	SLG
2004	Red Sox (GCL)	R	.261	36	134	22	35	9	2	5	16	5	22	0	.288	.470
MINOR LEAGUE TOTALS			.261	36	134	22	35	9	2	5	16	5	22	0	.288	.470

Kelly Shoppach, c

Born: April 29, 1980. **Ht.:** 5-11. **Wt.:** 210. **Bats:** R. **Throws:** R. **School:** Baylor University. **Career Transactions:** Selected by Red Sox in second round of 2001 draft; signed Aug. 17, 2001. **Signed by:** Jim Robinson.

Shoppach has made steady progress through the minors since the Red Sox made him the first college catcher drafted in 2001. After winning team MVP honors in his first two seasons, he was the Triple-A International League's all-star catcher in 2004. Shoppach's 22 homers matched his previous career total. IL managers rated him the league's top defensive catcher. He has a strong arm and a quick release, and he's also a capable receiver. An outstanding leader, he won the trust of a veteran Pawtucket pitching staff and improved his game-calling skills. With 333 strikeouts in 321 minor league games, Shoppach may never make enough contact to hit for a high average. While he hit a career-low .233 in 2004, Boston still thinks he can put up .265/.340/.500 numbers in the majors. Like most catchers, Shoppach doesn't have much speed. Somewhat similar to Jason Varitek, Shoppach wouldn't have been ready to replace Varitek had he departed as a free agent. By re-signing back Varitek and backup Doug Mirabelli, Boston bought another year of much-needed development time for Shoppach.

Year	Club (League)	Class	AVG	G	AB	R	H	2B	3B	HR	RBI	BB	SO	SB	OBP	SLG
2002	Sarasota (FSL)	A	.271	116	414	54	112	35	1	10	66	59	112	2	.369	.432
2003	Portland (EL)	AA	.282	92	340	45	96	30	2	12	60	35	83	0	.353	.488
2004	Pawtucket (IL)	AAA	.233	113	399	62	93	25	0	22	64	46	138	0	.320	.461
MINOR LEAGUE TOTALS			.261	321	1153	161	301	90	3	44	190	140	333	2	.347	.459

Ian Bladergroen, 1b

Born: Feb. 23, 1983. **Ht.:** 6-5. **Wt.:** 210. **Bats:** L. **Throws:** L. **School:** Lamar (Colo.) CC. **Career Transactions:** Selected by Mets in 44th round of 2002 draft; signed May 22, 2003 . . . Traded by Mets to Red Sox for 1B Doug Mientkiewicz, Jan. 26, 2005. **Signed by:** Marlon Jones (Mets).

Bladergroen was a junior college all-American in both his seasons at Lamar (Colo.) Community College and led national juco players with 32 homers in 2003. A 44th-round pick the year before, he signed with the Mets as a draft-and-follow for ninth-round money (about $65,000). He continued to mash as a pro, chasing the South Atlantic League triple crown last year before tearing a ligament in his left wrist right after the league's all-star break. Bladergroen had season-ending surgery but is expected to be 100 percent for 2005, when he'll make his Red Sox organization debut after being acquired for surplus first base-man Doug Mientkiewicz, New York's consolation prize after failing to sign Carlos Delgado. Bladergroen's most obvious tool is his plus power, and because his bat stays in the zone for a long time, he also can hit for average. He uses the whole field and works counts well.

Though he has produced for average and power, he doesn't have exceptional bat speed and scouts wonder if he might have problems at higher levels. At 21 last year, he wasn't young for low Class A either. He's a below-average runner, but he's agile at first base and uses his big wingspan to nab high throws. Bladergroen now is the best first-base prospect in the system, surpassing Jeremy West, and could quickly push West after starting one level behind him in high Class A this year.

Year	Club (League)	Class	AVG	G	AB	R	H	2B	3B	HR	RBI	BB	SO	SB	OBP	SLG
2003	Brooklyn (NY-P)	A	.285	74	274	33	78	12	3	6	36	21	51	0	.416	.354
2004	Capital City (SAL)	A	.342	72	269	39	92	23	3	13	74	25	55	1	.397	.595
MINOR LEAGUE TOTALS			.313	146	543	72	170	35	6	19	110	46	106	1	.376	.505

10 Abe Alvarez, lhp

Born: Oct. 17, 1982. **Ht.:** 6-2. **Wt.:** 190. **Bats:** L. **Throws:** L. **School:** Long Beach State University. **Career Transactions:** Selected by Red Sox in second round of 2003 draft; signed June 27, 2003. **Signed by:** Jim Woodward.

The Red Sox believed Alvarez' exceptional feel for pitching would allow him to move rapidly, and he made his big league debut in an emergency start against the Orioles just 13 months after they drafted him. A childhood infection left him legally blind in his left eye, and he wears his cap askew to shield his right eye from too much light. Alvarez' command and his changeup, his main weapons, are the best in the system. Though his fastball registers a pedestrian 85-88 mph on radar guns, he gets outs by locating it with precision. His curveball can be a solid average pitch. Alvarez works with little margin for error. When he fell behind hitters in his big league start, he couldn't recover. Righthanders batted .271 off him in Double-A, and he needs to pitch inside to keep them honest. While he throws his curve for strikes, he needs to learn how to throw it out of the zone while still getting hitters to chase it. The most advanced pitching prospect in the organization, Alvarez will open the season in Triple-A. He projects as a No. 3-5 starter.

Year	Club (League)	Class	W	L	ERA	G	GS	CG	SV	IP	H	R	ER	HR	BB	SO	AVG
2003	Lowell (NYP)	A	0	0	0.00	9	9	0	0	19	9	2	0	0	2	19	.138
2004	Portland (EL)	AA	10	9	3.59	26	26	0	0	135	132	65	54	13	32	108	.252
	Boston (AL)	MAJ	0	1	9.00	1	1	0	0	5	8	5	5	2	5	2	.400
MAJOR LEAGUE TOTALS			0	1	9.00	1	1	0	0	5	8	5	5	2	5	2	.400
MINOR LEAGUE TOTALS			10	9	3.15	35	35	0	0	154	141	67	54	13	34	127	.239

11 Manny Delcarmen, rhp

Born: Feb. 16, 1982. **Ht.:** 6-2. **Wt.:** 190. **Bats:** R. **Throws:** R. **School:** West Roxbury (Mass.) HS. **Career Transactions:** Selected by Red Sox in second round of 2000 draft; signed Aug. 22, 2000. **Signed by:** Ray Fagnant.

Delcarmen was headed for a breakthrough 2003 until he blew out his elbow throwing a changeup in his fourth outing of the season. He had Tommy John surgery that May and returned to the mound 12 months later. His arm strength already has come back, as Delcarmen threw 92-94 mph during the season and topped out at 97 in the Arizona Fall League. There's no consensus on who owns the best curveball among Boston farmhands, but Delcarmen gets the most support. His changeup improved after he switched grips in 2003. He throws a lot of strikes for a power pitcher. Delcarmen can make a claim to having the best pure stuff in the system, but he's still learning how to pitch. His curveball can be very good but it's also inconsistent. His fastball has more velocity than life and isn't always difficult to hit. Relearning his delivery after his surgery will take some more time. Delcarmen should be at full strength in 2005, and the Red Sox would like to push him to Double-A. He can be unhittable in short stints, so his future may lie in the bullpen.

Year	Club (League)	Class	W	L	ERA	G	GS	CG	SV	IP	H	R	ER	HR	BB	SO	AVG
2001	Red Sox (GCL)	R	4	2	2.54	11	8	0	1	46	35	16	13	0	19	62	.211
2002	Augusta (SAL)	A	7	8	4.10	26	24	0	0	136	124	77	62	15	56	136	.242
2003	Sarasota (FSL)	A	1	1	3.13	4	3	0	0	23	16	9	8	1	7	16	.200
2004	Sarasota (FSL)	A	3	6	4.68	19	18	0	0	73	84	43	38	10	20	76	.291
MINOR LEAGUE TOTALS			15	17	3.91	60	53	0	1	278	259	145	121	26	102	290	.247

12 Christian Lara, ss

Born: April 11, 1985. **Ht.:** 5-11. **Wt.:** 150. **Bats:** B. **Throws:** R. **Career Transactions:** Signed out of Venezuela by Red Sox, July 2, 2002. **Signed by:** Miguel Garcia.

After Lara won the organization's Rookie-level Dominican Summer League player-of-the-year award in his 2003 pro debut, the Red Sox' scouting report was that he had classic shortstop tools and his bat would determine how far he would go. If his first year in the United States is any indication, it could take him all the way to Fenway Park. Lara made BA's Top 10 Prospects lists in both the Gulf Coast League, where he hit .433 in a brief stay, and the New York-Penn League. A switch-hitter, he showed promising bat-handling ability and patience at the plate. He needs to get stronger and perhaps more aggressive at the plate, though he'll never be a power hitter. His speed and arm both earn 55 grades on the 20-80 scouting scale, and his instincts help him play above those tools in the field and on the bases. Counting big leaguer Edgar Renteria, Lara ranks just fifth on Boston's depth chart at shortstop despite his promise. He'll try to improve his standing this year in low Class A.

Year	Club (League)	Class	AVG	G	AB	R	H	2B	3B	HR	RBI	BB	SO	SB	OBP	SLG
2003	Red Sox East (DSL)	R	.273	65	256	52	70	7	1	0	22	35	53	24	.365	.309
2004	Red Sox (GCL)	R	.433	15	60	14	26	8	2	0	9	7	10	8	.493	.633
	Lowell (NY-P)	A	.277	32	119	21	33	3	2	0	10	24	23	10	.404	.336
MINOR LEAGUE TOTALS				112	435	87	129	18	5	0	41	66	86	42	.389	.361

13 Mike Rozier, lhp

Born: July 4, 1985. **Ht.:** 6-5. **Wt.:** 210. **Bats:** L. **Throws:** L. **School:** Henry County HS, Stockbridge, Ga. **Career Transactions:** Selected by Red Sox in 12th round of 2004 draft; signed Aug. 24, 2004. **Signed by:** Rob English.

Since Theo Epstein became general manager in November 2002, the Red Sox have almost exclusively targeted college players in the draft. Though they have spent 30 of their 32 picks in the first 15 rounds on collegians, that didn't stop them from making a record investment in Rozier, a high school lefty. A consensus third-round talent whom Boston viewed as the equivalent of a first-rounder—a luxury it didn't have in the 2004 draft after giving up its choice to sign Keith Foulke—Rozier dropped to the 12th round last June because of signability questions. A three-sport star in high school, Rozier's football prowess (he had a scholarship to play quarterback at North Carolina) and agent (Scott Boras) scared off clubs. The Red Sox signed him for $1.575 million, the third-highest bonus in club history and a baseball record for a player taken after the third round. Rozier is a physical, projectable lefty who reminds Boston of Jon Lester, the top southpaw in the system. He has similar size, athleticism and projection, and he has a plus fastball. He pitched at 88-92 mph and topped out at 94 during the spring, then hit 95 in instructional league, where he reminded special assistant Bill Lajoie of Mark Mulder. Rozier's curveball may be better than Lester's, though his changeup has a ways to go. He could take off quickly now that he's committing full-time to baseball, but might even begin the season in extended spring training before making his pro debut in June.

Year	Club (League)	Class	W	L	ERA	G	GS	CG	SV	IP	H	R	ER	HR	BB	SO	AVG
2004	Did not play—Signed 2005 contract																

14 Mickey Hall, of

Born: May 20, 1985. **Ht.:** 6-1. **Wt.:** 195. **Bats:** L. **Throws:** L. **School:** Walton HS, Marietta, Ga. **Career Transactions:** Selected by Red Sox in second round of 2003 draft; signed July 11, 2003. **Signed by:** Rob English.

Brandon Moss made a huge breakthrough in 2004, and Hall, another Georgia high school product, may be on the verge of doing the same in 2005. Boston's only prep pick in the first 16 rounds in 2003, Hall went in the second round and signed for $800,000. His advanced approach at the plate appealed to the Red Sox, but it wasn't apparent when he hit .227 during his pro debut, then .190 in his first two months last year. The second-youngest everyday player in the South Atlantic League, Hall suddenly turned his game around and batted .274/.354/.489 for the remainder of the season. Boston loves his desire, as he worked hard to make it to low Class A out of spring training and then worked harder to make the adjustments he needed there. He has a sound, quick swing, and the ball should jump off his bat more frequently as he gets stronger. Hall has slightly above-average speed and arm strength, though he needs to settle down defensively after committing 14 outfield errors last year, worst in the Sally League. He played all three outfield positions in 2004 but should spend most of his time in right field this season while in high Class A.

Year	Club (League)	Class	AVG	G	AB	R	H	2B	3B	HR	RBI	BB	SO	SB	OBP	SLG
2003	Red Sox (GCL)	R	.227	21	66	7	15	6	0	0	9	19	24	1	.400	.318
2004	Augusta (SAL)	A	.246	118	403	67	99	24	5	13	63	58	134	13	.342	.427
MINOR LEAGUE TOTALS			.243	139	469	74	114	30	5	13	72	77	158	14	.351	.412

15 David Murphy, of

Born: Oct. 18, 1981. **Ht.:** 6-4. **Wt.:** 192. **Bats:** R. **Throws:** R. **School:** Baylor University. **Career Transactions:** Selected by Red Sox in first round (17th overall) of 2003 draft; signed June 12, 2003. **Signed by:** Jim Robinson.

Murphy was rarely at his best in his first full pro season. He was in the midst of a month-long .170 slump in May when he caught his spike in the batter's box and sustained a freak injury, pulling the muscle off the bone in his left foot. He missed a week, came back for five games, then spent the next two months on the sidelines. After he returned in August, he began to hit the ball with authority for the first time as a pro. As with many of the hitters they've drafted in recent years, the Red Sox really like Murphy's approach. The question is how much pop he'll have once he grows into his frame. He's more of a line-drive, gap-to-gap hitter right now and needs more loft in his swing, though he can show plus raw power in batting practice. Boston took him with the hopes he could play center field, and Murphy is adjusting well to that position after playing mostly right field at Baylor. His speed and arm are average, but his instincts and athleticism help him get the job done in center. He'll return to high Class A in 2005 so he can build confidence before he gets promoted.

Year	Club (League)	Class	AVG	G	AB	R	H	2B	3B	HR	RBI	BB	SO	SB	OBP	SLG
2003	Lowell (NY-P)	A	.346	21	78	13	27	4	0	0	13	16	9	4	.453	.397
	Sarasota (FSL)	A	.242	45	153	18	37	5	1	1	18	20	33	6	.329	.307
2004	Sarasota (FSL)	A	.261	73	272	35	71	11	0	4	38	25	46	3	.323	.346
MINOR LEAGUE TOTALS			.268	139	503	66	135	20	1	5	69	61	88	13	.347	.342

16 Chad Spann, 3b

Born: Oct. 25, 1983. **Ht.:** 6-1. **Wt.:** 190. **Bats:** R. **Throws:** R. **School:** Southland Academy, Americus, Ga. **Career Transactions:** Selected by Red Sox in fifth round of 2002 draft; signed June 10, 2002. **Signed by:** Rob English.

Georgia area scout Rob English signed four of the top 15 prospects on this list: Brandon Moss, Mike Rozier, Mickey Hall and Spann. Overmatched in his 2002 pro debut, Spann worked hard to improve his strength and discipline and took a huge step forward in 2003. An injury to his left knee wrecked his 2004 season, however, as he missed 2½ months following surgery to repair a torn meniscus. Spann sustained the injury sometime in the past, but it remained undetected until he strained a ligament and had an MRI. Even after he returned in late July, the knee curtailed Spann's effectiveness because it hindered his mobility and balance. Spann focuses on making contact and using the center of the field, but he'll need to get stronger and pull more pitches to develop suitable power for third base. He didn't command the strike zone nearly as well in 2004 as he did the previous season. He has enough arm and range to play third base, but he'll need to continue to work hard to become a sound defender. His hands are his biggest weakness and contributed to his 15 errors in 54 games at the hot corner last year. As with David Murphy, the Red Sox will have Spann repeat high Class A to get him back on track.

Year	Club (League)	Class	AVG	G	AB	R	H	2B	3B	HR	RBI	BB	SO	SB	OBP	SLG
2002	Red Sox (GCL)	R	.222	57	203	20	45	8	3	6	28	12	37	1	.271	.379
2003	Augusta (SAL)	A	.312	116	414	55	129	21	3	5	63	40	64	9	.379	.413
2004	Sarasota (FSL)	A	.252	61	214	26	54	9	0	4	22	9	53	6	.291	.350
MINOR LEAGUE TOTALS			.274	234	831	101	228	38	6	15	113	61	154	16	.331	.389

17 Juan Cedeno, lhp

Born: Aug. 19, 1983. **Ht.:** 6-1. **Wt.:** 160. **Bats:** L. **Throws:** L. **Career Transactions:** Signed out of Dominican Republic by Red Sox, Jan. 5, 2001. **Signed by:** Robinson Garcia.

Cedeno's signature moment remains blowing away Joe Mauer in two instructional league at-bats in 2002, but he was rarely that dominant last season. He still has one of the best fastballs in the system, sitting at 92-93 mph and pushing 95-96. He's not big but generates plenty of arm speed and could have even more velocity left in his tank. He also has developed a two-seam version of his fastball that has nice life. For a lefty with that kind of heat, Cedeno is far too hittable. He can't put batters away because he doesn't have reliable secondary pitches, and when he gets in jams he just throws as hard as he can. His curveball and changeup show signs of coming around, but he needs to trust them more. Cedeno had a groin pull early last year but never has had any arm problems. He can be frustrating, but few southpaws can match his sheer arm strength. The Red Sox hope he'll figure out how to pitch this year, when he'll probably return to high Class A to open the season. Because his tools currently outstrip his skills, he's also a candidate to get traded, and other teams have shown interest.

Year	Club (League)	Class	W	L	ERA	G	GS	CG	SV	IP	H	R	ER	HR	BB	SO	AVG
2001	Red Sox (DSL)	R	3	3	3.38	14	14	0	0	64	45	30	24	0	37	77	.198
2002	Red Sox (GCL)	R	2	5	4.19	11	7	0	0	43	55	31	20	1	12	32	.297
2003	Augusta (SAL)	A	7	9	3.02	23	21	0	0	101	87	38	34	8	44	87	.235
2004	Sarasota (FSL)	A	7	6	4.64	25	22	1	0	120	145	70	62	8	40	78	.300
MINOR LEAGUE TOTALS			19	23	3.83	73	64	1	0	329	332	169	140	17	133	274	.262

18 Tommy Hottovy, lhp

Born: July 9, 1981. **Ht.:** 6-1. **Wt.:** 190. **Bats:** L. **Throws:** L. **School:** Wichita State University. **Career Transactions:** Selected by Red Sox in fourth round of 2004 draft; signed June 10, 2004. **Signed by:** Ernie Jacobs.

Though Dustin Pedroia finished last year two levels ahead of him and may begin this year in Double-A, Hottovy still could beat him as Boston's first 2004 draftee to reach the majors. The Red Sox have taken a more performance-oriented and college approach to the last two drafts, and Hottovy's 92-10 strikeout-walk ratio (fifth-best in NCAA Division I) last spring appealed to them. A fourth-round senior sign who landed a $110,000 bonus, he showed the same exceptional command in his pro debut. Several teams projected him as a reliever, but Boston believes Hottovy has enough stuff and savvy to start. His best pitch is his plus curveball. His 86-89 mph fastball won't scare anyone, but he keeps it down and locates it with precision. His athleticism—Hottovy had scholarship offers as a quarterback coming out of high school—allows him to repeat his delivery with ease. His changeup gives him a third effective pitch. Because he signed as a college senior, Hottovy already is 23. He has a chance to open 2005 in Double-A, but most likely he won't get there until the second half of the season.

Year	Club (League)	Class	W	L	ERA	G	GS	CG	SV	IP	H	R	ER	HR	BB	SO	AVG
2004	Lowell (NY-P)	A	0	1	0.89	14	14	0	0	30	24	5	3	0	4	39	.214
MINOR LEAGUE TOTALS			0	1	0.89	14	14	0	0	30	24	5	3	0	4	39	.214

19 Andrew Dobies, lhp

Born: April 20, 1983. **Ht.:** 6-1. **Wt.:** 190. **Bats:** L. **Throws:** L. **School:** University of Virginia. **Career Transactions:** Selected by Red Sox in third round of 2004 draft; signed June 14, 2004. **Signed by:** Jeff Zona.

Dobies and Tommy Hottovy will be compared to each other as they rise through the Red Sox system together. Boston took Dobies in the third round last June, just ahead of Hottovy, and signed him for $400,000. Both were unhittable while being kept on tight pitch counts at short-season Lowell in their pro debuts, and they figure to be teammates again in 2005. Their styles on the mound are similar as well. Dobies throws a tick harder than Hottovy at 87-89 mph, getting good cutting movement on his fastball, and his changeup is slightly more consistent. While Hottovy's curveball is better than Dobies' slider, the slider is effective, as is Dobies' curve. His delivery and arm action are so consistent that he can throw strikes at will. As with Hottovy, many clubs projected Dobies as a reliever but Boston has no plans to move him out of the rotation.

Year	Club (League)	Class	W	L	ERA	G	GS	CG	SV	IP	H	R	ER	HR	BB	SO	AVG
2004	Lowell (NY-P)	A	0	2	2.03	14	14	0	0	27	17	9	6	0	8	36	.181
MINOR LEAGUE TOTALS			0	2	2.03	14	14	0	0	27	17	9	6	0	8	36	.181

20 Jimmy James, rhp

Born: Oct. 16, 1984. **Ht.:** 6-2. **Wt.:** 170. **Bats:** R. **Throws:** R. **Career Transactions:** Signed out of Venezuela by Red Sox, July 23, 2002. **Signed by:** Miguel Garcia/Jesus Laya.

Boston's 2004 Gulf Coast League entry had two righthanders, Jesus Delgado and Olivo Astacio, who can throw in the mid-90s. James doesn't have that kind of velocity, but he's a much more advanced pitcher and a better prospect, not to mention the GCL club's pitcher of the year. He also won a one-game playoff against the Mets with 5⅔ strong innings, putting the Red Sox into the GCL finals. A cousin of Kelvim Escobar, James already shows the ability to repeat his delivery, allowing him to find the strike zone consistently. He's still young and needs to fill out his skinny frame, but once he matures physically he should have three average to plus pitches. He has solid velocity on his fastball, which ranges from 89-93 mph, and throws a curveball and changeup. He's probably headed to Lowell in 2004, though James is precocious enough to make a push for low Class A.

Year	Club (League)	Class	W	L	ERA	G	GS	CG	SV	IP	H	R	ER	HR	BB	SO	AVG
2003	Red Sox East (DSL)	R	3	2	2.84	15	12	0	1	67	51	30	21	2	24	41	.207
2004	Red Sox (GCL)	R	5	1	2.33	11	9	0	0	46	51	19	12	3	15	35	.271
MINOR LEAGUE TOTALS			8	3	2.63	26	21	0	1	113	102	49	33	5	39	76	.233

21 Cla Meredith, rhp

Born: June 4, 1983. **Ht.:** 6-1. **Wt.:** 185. **Bats:** R. **Throws:** R. **School:** Virginia Commonwealth University. **Career Transactions:** Selected by Red Sox in sixth round of 2004 draft; signed June 13, 2004. **Signed by:** Jeff Zona.

The Red Sox loaded up on polished college pitchers in the 2004 draft. Meredith, who finished sixth (right behind Tommy Hottovy) in NCAA Division I with an 84-12 strikeout-walk ratio, signed as a sixth-round pick for $135,000. He pitched a Virginia Commonwealth with such top pitching prospects as Sean Marshall (Cubs) and Justin Orenduff (Dodgers), setting the Rams' career ERA record at 2.52 Though he didn't join the organization until June, Meredith led all Boston farmhands with 18 saves while splitting time between two full-season Class A teams. He used a crossfire, low three-quarters delivery that generates a lot of life and deception. The Red Sox compare the sink on his fastball to postseason hero Derek Lowe's, grading it as a 70 on the 20-80 scouting scale. Meredith's sinker arrives at 87-90 mph and is nearly impossible to lift, as evidenced by his 47-8 groundball-flyball ratio as a pro. His slider is a borderline average pitch that needs more consistency. After following up his scintillating debut with a strong performance in instructional league, Meredith could open 2005 in Double-A.

Year	Club (League)	Class	W	L	ERA	G	GS	CG	SV	IP	H	R	ER	HR	BB	SO	AVG
2004	Augusta (SAL)	A	1	0	0.00	13	0	0	6	15	8	0	0	0	3	18	.154
	Sarasota (FSL)	A	0	2	2.20	16	0	0	12	16	15	4	4	0	3	16	.254
MINOR LEAGUE TOTALS			1	2	1.14	29	0	0	18	32	23	4	4	0	6	34	.207

22 Kyle Bono, rhp

Born: June 29, 1983. **Ht.:** 6-2. **Wt.:** 200. **Bats:** R. **Throws:** R. **School:** University of Central Florida. **Career Transactions:** Selected by Red Sox in eighth round of 2004 draft; signed July 20, 2004. **Signed by:** James Orr.

Mike Rozier wasn't the only 2004 Red Sox draftee who landed a record bonus. A draft-eligible sophomore who could have returned to Central Florida without losing any bargaining power, Bono opened the summer in the Cape Cod League, where he didn't surrender a run in 12 appearances. That was enough to persuade Boston to sign him for $432,000, the most ever for an eighth-round pick. A late bloomer on the mound, Bono was primarily a third baseman and pitched sporadically as a high school senior. In two years of college, he set a Golden Knights record with a 1.66 career ERA and led NCAA Division I with five shutouts last spring. Bono's top two pitches are his heavy 88-91 mph sinker and his changeup. Whether he remains a starter in the long term depends primarily on how much improvement he can make with his ordinary slider. He likes to go right after hitters, and he locates all three of his pitches well in the strike zone. Because he's so polished—like many of Boston's 2004 pitching draft picks—Bono could handle starting his first full season in high Class A.

Year	Club (League)	Class	W	L	ERA	G	GS	CG	SV	IP	H	R	ER	HR	BB	SO	AVG
2004	Lowell (NY-P)	A	0	1	3.00	6	5	0	0	12	4	4	4	1	5	17	.108
MINOR LEAGUE TOTALS			0	1	3.00	6	5	0	0	12	4	4	4	1	5	17	.108

23 Adam Stern, of

Born: Feb. 12, 1980. **Ht.:** 5-11. **Wt.:** 180. **Bats:** L. **Throws:** R. **School:** University of Nebraska. **Career Transactions:** Selected by Braves in third round of 2001 draft; signed June 12, 2001 . . . Selected by Red Sox from Braves in major league Rule 5 draft, Dec. 13, 2004. **Signed by:** Tyrone Brooks (Braves).

Boston took Stern from the Braves in the major league Rule 5 draft in December and will give him the opportunity to make the big league club as a reserve outfielder. If he doesn't stick, he'll have to go through waivers and be offered back to Atlanta for half the $50,000 draft price before he could be sent to the minors. Stern hadn't done much as a pro before last year, missing most of 2003 with a hamstring injury. He earned Double-A Southern League all-star honors after finishing third in the batting race at .322, then helped Richmond win an International League playoff series by leading all players with a .357 average in the postseason. In between, he played center field for Canada at the Olympics. Stern's breakthrough came when he stopped worrying about power, shortened his swing and focused on putting the ball in play. He made much better contact than he had in the past, though he could make more use of his plus speed if he'd walk more often. After Johnny Damon, Stern is the best defensive center fielder on the roster, enhancing his chances of making the team. His arm strength is another asset.

Year	Club (League)	Class	AVG	G	AB	R	H	2B	3B	HR	RBI	BB	SO	SB	OBP	SLG
2001	Jamestown (NY-P)	A	.307	21	75	20	23	4	2	0	11	15	11	9	.413	.413
2002	Myrtle Beach (Car)	A	.253	119	462	65	117	22	10	3	47	27	89	40	.298	.364
2003	Braves (GCL)	R	.345	7	29	6	10	1	0	1	6	6	3	2	.457	.483
	Myrtle Beach (Car)	A	.194	28	103	11	20	2	0	0	6	13	21	7	.282	.214
2004	Greenville (SL)	AA	.322	102	394	64	127	26	6	8	47	35	58	27	.378	.480
MINOR LEAGUE TOTALS			.279	277	1063	166	297	55	18	12	117	96	182	85	.340	.399

24 Jeremy West, 1b

Born: Nov. 8, 1981. **Ht.:** 6-0. **Wt.:** 200. **Bats:** R. **Throws:** R. **School:** Arizona State University. **Career Transactions:** Selected by Red Sox in seventh round of 2003 draft; signed June 13, 2003. **Signed by:** Rob English.

The Red Sox don't have a blue-chip first-base prospect, but they do have several interesting possibilities at the position. Those include Stefan Bailie, who had a breakthrough .308/.376/.576 year in 2004; Carlos Torres, who tied for the Gulf Coast League lead with eight homers; and line drive-hitting, sweet-fielding Logan Sorensen, a 19th-round pick last June. The best of the group is West, who's similar to Kevin Millar. His power is his lone plus tool, and though he has an uppercut swing he's also a solid hitter for average. He controls the strike zone better than his walk total would indicate because he doesn't chase balls off the plate and drives his pitch when he gets it. A DH and third-string catcher at Arizona State, he didn't become a full-time first baseman until he turned pro. He works hard but has a long way to go with the glove, both with his actions and instincts. After earning all-star recognition in the Florida State League, he's ready for Double-A.

Year	Club (League)	Class	AVG	G	AB	R	H	2B	3B	HR	RBI	BB	SO	SB	OBP	SLG
2003	Lowell (NY-P)	A	.280	72	264	32	74	17	1	4	43	31	52	1	.369	.398
2004	Sarasota (FSL)	A	.293	124	461	60	135	28	4	18	68	37	83	0	.347	.488
MINOR LEAGUE TOTALS			.288	196	725	92	209	45	5	22	111	68	135	1	.355	.455

25 Beau Vaughan, rhp

Born: June 4, 1981. **Ht.:** 6-4. **Wt.:** 230. **Bats:** B. **Throws:** R. **School:** Arizona State University. **Career Transactions:** Selected by Red Sox in third round of 2003 draft; signed June 23, 2003. **Signed by:** Dan Madsen.

Though Vaughan is similar physically to Jon Papelbon and went one round ahead of him in the 2003 draft, their paths diverged last year. While Papelbon became the organization's top pitching prospect, Vaughan took a step backward, starting with arriving in spring training in less than optimal shape. He came down with a tired arm, so he opened the season in extended spring and didn't make his first start until late May. More arm fatigue meant his season also ended three weeks early. Not only does Vaughan need to improve his conditioning, but he also needs to change his approach on the mound. Though he has an 89-93 mph fastball and an 82-84 mph slider, he likes to nibble with offspeed stuff early in the count. He does have a true curveball and flashes a nice changeup, but Vaughan must realize he'll have more success if he gets ahead by establishing his fastball. The Red Sox hope Vaughan will be motivated to prove his disappointing 2004 was an aberration. He may have to go back to low Class A and start over.

Year	Club (League)	Class	W	L	ERA	G	GS	CG	SV	IP	H	R	ER	HR	BB	SO	AVG
2003	Lowell (NY-P)	A	1	0	2.32	11	6	0	0	31	27	8	8	1	15	30	.235
2004	Augusta (SAL)	A	7	3	3.30	14	13	0	0	71	58	30	26	8	27	73	.218
	Portland (EL)	AA	0	0	12.27	1	1	0	0	4	5	5	5	2	5	4	.313
MINOR LEAGUE TOTALS			8	3	3.32	26	20	0	0	106	90	43	39	11	47	107	.227

26 David Pauley, rhp

Born: June 17, 1983. **Ht.:** 6-2. **Wt.:** 170. **Bats:** R. **Throws:** R. **School:** Longmont (Colo.) HS. **Career Transactions:** Selected by Padres in eighth round of 2001 draft; signed June 7, 2001 . . . Traded by Padres with OF Jay Payton and IF Ramon Vazquez to Red Sox for OF Dave Roberts, Dec. 20, 2004. **Signed by:** Darryl Milne (Padres).

The Padres needed a center fielder who could cover enough ground at Petco Park, so Boston was able to trade them Dave Roberts for three players and $2.65 million in December. Jay Payton and Ramon Vazquez will help the major league bench in 2005, and the Red Sox were also able to add a pitching prospect in Pauley. Darryl Milne, now an area scout for the Sox, signed him out of high school when he worked for the Padres organization. Pauley progressed slowly but surely through the Padres system and has a ceiling as a back-of-the-rotation starter. His best pitch is his curveball—which can rate anywhere from 50 to 70 on the 20-80 scouting scale—but he sometimes throws it too much. His fastball runs from 87-91 mph with decent movement, and his changeup lacks deception. The next step in Pauley's development will take him to Double-A.

Year	Club (League)	Class	W	L	ERA	G	GS	CG	SV	IP	H	R	ER	HR	BB	SO	AVG
2001	Idaho Falls (Pio)	R	4	9	6.03	15	15	0	0	69	88	57	46	8	24	53	.308
2002	Eugene (NWL)	A	6	1	2.81	15	15	0	0	80	81	32	25	6	18	62	.266
2003	Fort Wayne (Mid)	A	7	7	3.29	22	21	0	1	118	109	51	43	9	38	117	.245
2004	Lake Elsinore (Cal)	A	7	12	4.17	27	26	0	0	153	155	89	71	8	60	128	.262
MINOR LEAGUE TOTALS			24	29	3.97	79	77	0	1	420	433	229	185	31	140	360	.266

27 Kenny Perez, ss/2b

Born: Sept. 28, 1981. **Ht.:** 6-2. **Wt.:** 190. **Bats:** B. **Throws:** R. **School:** South Miami HS, Miami. **Career Transactions:** Selected by Red Sox in sixth round of 2000 draft; signed June 27, 2000. **Signed by:** John DiPuglia.

Perez was considered the fourth-best high school shortstop in Miami in 2000, after first-rounders Luis Montanez (Cubs) and David Espinosa (Reds) and fourth-rounder Raul Tablado (Blue Jays). But it's Perez, a sixth-rounder, who's the lone member of that group to reach Double-A as a shortstop. His days at the position are numbered, however, more because of the organization's strength at shortstop than any deficiencies on his part. Perez doesn't have tremendous range at short, but he has sure hands and a strong, accurate arm. He'll probably see time at second and third base as well this year in Triple-A to groom him for a possible utility role. Offensively, Perez is a switch-hitter with good hand-eye coordination and plate discipline. He makes contact easily, though sometimes that works against him because it's not always a hitter's pitch that he puts into play. He has more raw power than the typical middle infielder, and he started to translate it into game production last season. He's an average runner with fine instincts on the bases. Perez enjoyed the best season of his career in 2004, though he missed time with a sore hamstring in August and most of the Arizona Fall League with a wrenched back.

Year	Club (League)	Class	AVG	G	AB	R	H	2B	3B	HR	RBI	BB	SO	SB	OBP	SLG
2000	Red Sox (GCL)	R	.285	43	158	28	45	7	0	1	23	12	12	3	.337	.348
2001	Augusta (SAL)	A	.248	120	407	44	101	21	2	6	37	48	62	11	.330	.354
2002	Sarasota (FSL)	A	.251	121	447	53	112	12	4	2	28	51	58	16	.329	.309
2003	Sarasota (FSL)	A	.278	65	230	32	64	17	4	2	39	15	24	11	.319	.413
	Red Sox (GCL)	R	.273	7	22	4	6	1	1	0	2	1	3	0	.304	.409
2004	Portland (EL)	AA	.280	109	400	47	112	31	5	5	61	23	59	12	.323	.420
MINOR LEAGUE TOTALS			.264	465	1664	208	440	89	16	16	190	150	218	53	.327	.366

28 Jose Vaquedano, rhp

Born: July 9, 1981. **Ht.:** 6-4. **Wt.:** 170. **Bats:** R. **Throws:** R. **School:** Vernon (Texas) JC. **Career Transactions:** Selected by Red Sox in 35th round of 2002 draft; signed June 8, 2002. **Signed by:** Jim Robinson.

Trying to become the first Honduras-born player to reach the big leagues, Vaquedano gained on his main competition (Cleveland's Mariano Gomez) in 2004. While Gomez was slowed with a finger injury, Vaquedano advanced two levels while getting his first exposure to full-season ball. He dominated low Class A, then pitched just as well after getting by a rocky first month in high Class A. His changeup currently is his best pitch, as he sells it well by using the same arm speed he does with his fastball. Vaquedano's fastball stands out more for its sink than its velocity (88-90 mph), but he could throw harder because he has a quick arm and a thin, projectable build. His slider is a usable third pitch. Though Vaquedano throws strikes, he'll need to locate his fastball better to set up more advanced hitters for his changeup. He should pitch in Double-A this year.

Year	Club (League)	Class	W	L	ERA	G	GS	CG	SV	IP	H	R	ER	HR	BB	SO	AVG
2002	Lowell (NY-P)	A	1	3	4.35	22	0	0	0	39	46	33	19	4	18	35	.293
2003	Lowell (NY-P)	A	7	4	3.30	14	10	0	0	74	67	30	27	4	15	70	.241
2004	Augusta (SAL)	A	4	2	1.88	11	11	0	0	67	59	22	14	5	12	66	.236
	Sarasota (FSL)	A	5	1	3.95	14	8	0	0	68	65	34	30	4	21	60	.253
MINOR LEAGUE TOTALS			17	10	3.262	61	29	0	0	248	237	119	90	17	66	231	.252

29 Gary Galvez, rhp

Born: March 24, 1984. **Ht.:** 6-3. **Wt.:** 210. **Bats:** R. **Throws:** R. **Career Transactions:** Signed out of Dominican Republic by Red Sox, Feb. 2003. **Signed by:** Louie Eljaua.

Galvez made three attempts to defect from Cuba before succeeding on his fourth in August 2002. The Red Sox beat out the Dodgers, Mariners, Phillies and Yankees to sign him for $450,000. Though one of the other clubs offered him $500,000, he chose the Sox because he developed a relationship with Louie Elajua, then Boston's director of international scouting. Visa problems restricted him to the Dominican Summer League in 2003, delaying his U.S. debut until last season. Galvez showed very good control for his age—

which, unlike with many Cubans, isn't in dispute—but must come up with a way to miss more bats. He can locate his fastball with precision, but it has below-average velocity (86-90 mph) and movement. His curveball and slider are effective, and he shows a feel for his changeup. But Galvez likes to toy with hitters and show all his pitches rather than finish them off. He could begin 2005 back in low Class A with an opportunity to move up later in the season.

Year	Club (League)	Class	W	L	ERA	G	GS	CG	SV	IP	H	R	ER	HR	BB	SO	AVG
2003	Red Sox East (DSL)	R	6	3	1.64	14	11	0	2	71	66	26	13	0	10	65	.234
2004	Augusta (SAL)	A	7	10	5.14	30	22	1	0	140	153	86	80	16	36	102	.279
MINOR LEAGUE TOTALS			13	13	3.96	44	33	1	2	211	219	112	93	16	46	167	.264

30 Willy Mota, of

Born: Oct. 25, 1985. **Ht.:** 6-1. **Wt.:** 160. **Bats:** R. **Throws:** R. **Career Transactions:** Signed out of Dominican Republic by Red Sox, July 2, 2002. **Signed by:** Louie Eljaua/Elvio Jimenez/Pablo Lantigua.

Mota has one of the most exciting packages of tools in the organization. He has the best outfield arm among Boston farmhands, and his raw power, speed and center-field ability are also plus tools. He will require a ton of refinement, but if everything comes together he could be a dynamite center fielder. "He's out of control at times," one club official says, "but he also makes you go, 'Wow!' at times too." Mota is wiry strong and should have considerable game power once he fills out physically. His biggest issue is pitch and strike-zone recognition, as he's too aggressive and struggles with breaking balls. The Red Sox acknowledge that Mota will need a lot of time in the minors to smooth out his rough edges, and they're willing to give it to him. Still just 19, he's not ready for full-season ball and could repeat the Gulf Coast League.

Year	Club (League)	Class	AVG	G	AB	R	H	2B	3B	HR	RBI	BB	SO	SB	OBP	SLG
2003	Red Sox East (DSL)	R	.237	62	236	23	56	5	1	2	25	22	72	9	.312	.292
2004	Red Sox (GCL)	R	.295	35	129	19	38	9	3	2	18	6	41	6	.328	.457
MINOR LEAGUE TOTALS			.258	97	365	42	94	14	4	4	43	28	113	15	.318	.351

CHICAGO
CUBS

BY **JIM CALLIS**

After the Cubs' 2003 ended with heartbreak in the National League Championship Series, their 2004 finish was more miserable. With nine games remaining in the regular season, they owned a 1½-game edge in the NL wild-card race. Chicago was one out away from beating the Mets when LaTroy Hawkins served

up a three-run homer to Mets rookie Victor Diaz in a game New York would win in 11 innings. The Cubs never recovered. They lost six of their next seven games to lose the wild card to the Astros, a team they held a seven-game lead over in late August.

On the final day of the season Sammy Sosa sparked furor when he left Wrigley Field without permission before the first inning was completed. That was a perfect feel-bad ending for a club that had Moises Alou alleging umpires had it in for Chicago, and several players and manager Dusty Baker complaining about broadcasters Chip Caray and Steve Stone. Sosa's behavior was also the last straw for Cubs management, which dumped him on the Orioles in a February trade that did nothing to improve Chicago.

While the Cubs shed the "lovable" part of their lovable losers tag, they're also doing a pretty good job of dropping the "losers" too. Their 89 wins may not have been enough to put them in the postseason, but they did post their first consecutive winning seasons since a six-year run from 1967-72. With their financial resources and farm system, they're in a better position than any other club to annually contend in the NL Central.

Chicago's farm system isn't as strong as it was when it ranked among the game's top three after the 2000-02 seasons, but it's still one of baseball's better collections of talent. The Cubs recently have produced two all-star starters (Mark Prior, Carlos Zambrano), their lineup's most dynamic player (Corey Patterson) and trade fodder that netted three-quarters of their infield (Derrek Lee, **Nomar Garciaparra**, Aramis Ramirez).

Chicago's affiliates combined for a .538 winning percentage in 2004 as second baseman Richard Lewis (Double-A Southern League) and first basemen Brandon Sing (Florida State League) and Brian Dopirak (Midwest League) all earned MVP awards.

Baker isn't noted for his willingness to break in young players, but Jason Dubois will get a look in left field and Lewis could push for the second-base job in 2006. The real gems are Dopirak and outfielders Felix Pie and Ryan Harvey, though they're at least a couple of years away.

The Cubs have produced more pitching recently, and they still have several promising arms—though the faces have changed. Lefthanders Justin Jones (Garciaparra trade), Andy Sisco and Luke Hagerty (both major league Rule 5 draft picks) went to other organizations in 2004, and righthanders Angel Guzman, Chadd Blasko and Jae-Kuk Ryu have suffered physical setbacks. Chicago still envisions Guzman becoming a frontline starter.

TOP 30 PROSPECTS

1. Brian Dopirak, 1b	16. Ronny Cedeno, ss
2. Felix Pie, of	17. Will Ohman, lhp
3. Ryan Harvey, of	18. Mike Wuertz, rhp
4. Angel Guzman, rhp	19. Ricky Nolasco, rhp
5. Billy Petrick, rhp	20. Carlos Marmol, rhp
6. Renyel Pinto, lhp	21. Mike Fontenot, 2b
7. Sean Marshall, lhp	22. Mark Reed, c
8. Jon Leicester, rhp	23. Eric Patterson, 2b
9. Grant Johnson, rhp	24. Rich Hill, lhp
10. Jason Dubois, of/1b	25. Jermaine Van Buren, rhp
11. Matt Murton, of	26. Matt Craig, 3b/1b
12. Richard Lewis, 2b	27. Raul Valdez, lhp
13. Bobby Brownlie, rhp	28. Jae-Kuk Ryu, rhp
14. Geovany Soto, c	29. Chadd Blasko, rhp
15. Brandon Sing, 1b	30. David Kelton, of

ORGANIZATION OVERVIEW

General manger: Jim Hendry. **Farm director:** Oneri Fleita. **Scouting director:** John Stockstill.

2004 PERFORMANCE

Class	Team	League	W	L	Pct.	Finish*	Manager
Majors	Chicago	National	89	73	.549	6th (16)	Dusty Baker
Triple-A	Iowa Cubs	Pacific Coast	79	64	.552	4th (16)	Mike Quade
Double-A	West Tenn Diamond Jaxx	Southern	70	68	.507	5th (10)	Bobby Dickerson
High A	Daytona Cubs	Florida State	70	56	.556	+5th (12)	Steve McFarland
Low A	#Lansing Lugnuts	Midwest	77	63	.550	t-2nd (14)	Julio Garcia
Short-season	Boise Hawks	Northwest	42	34	.553	+t-1st (8)	Tom Beyers
Rookie	AZL Cubs	Arizona	27	29	.482	6th (9)	Trey Forkerway
OVERALL 2004 MINOR LEAGUE RECORD			365	314	.538	6th (30)	

*Finish in overall standings (No. of teams in league) +League champion. #Affiliate will be in Peoria (Midwest) in 2005.

ORGANIZATION LEADERS

BATTING
*Minimum 250 At-Bats
*AVG	Trenidad Hubbard, Iowa	.330
R	Trenidad Hubbard, Iowa	101
H	Brian Dopirak, Lansing	166
TB	Brian Dopirak, Lansing	321
2B	Brian Dopirak, Lansing	38
	Russ Johnson, Iowa	38
3B	Adam Greenberg, Iowa/West Tenn/Daytona	14
HR	Brian Dopirak, Lansing	39
RBI	Brian Dopirak, Lansing	120
BB	Brandon Sing, Daytona	84
SO	Dwaine Bacon, West Tenn	139
SB	Dwaine Bacon, West Tenn	60
	Chris Walker, Lansing	60
*OBP	Trenidad Hubbard, Iowa	.407
*SLG	Jason Dubois, Iowa	.629

PITCHING
#Minimum 75 Innings
W	Carlos Marmol, Lansing	14
L	Rocky Cherry, Daytona	10
	Andy Sisco, Daytona	10
#ERA	Clay Rapada, Lansing	2.33
G	Russ Rohlicek, West Tenn	60
CG	Jon Connolly, West Tenn/Daytona	3
SV	Jermaine Van Buren, Iowa/West Tenn/Lansing	22
IP	Ronald Bay, Lansing	168
BB	Renyel Pinto, Iowa/West Tenn	80
SO	Renyel Pinto, Iowa/West Tenn	188

BEST TOOLS

Best Hitter for Average	Matt Murton
Best Power Hitter	Brian Dopirak
Best Strike-Zone Discipline	Matt Murton
Fastest Baserunner	Dwaine Bacon
Best Athlete	Felix Pie
Best Fastball	Angel Guzman
Best Curveball	Rich Hill
Best Slider	Will Ohman
Best Changeup	Jon Connolly
Best Control	Bobby Brownlie
Best Defensive Catcher	Geovany Soto
Best Defensive Infielder	Carlos Rojas
Best Infield Arm	Ronny Cedeno
Best Defensive Outfielder	Felix Pie
Best Outfield Arm	Felix Pie

PROJECTED 2008 LINEUP

Catcher	Michael Barrett
First Base	Brian Dopirak
Second Base	Richie Lewis
Third Base	Aramis Ramirez
Shortstop	Nomar Garciaparra
Left Field	Ryan Harvey
Center Field	Felix Pie
Right Field	Corey Patterson
No. 1 Starter	Mark Prior
No. 2 Starter	Kerry Wood
No. 3 Starter	Carlos Zambrano
No. 4 Starter	Angel Guzman
No. 5 Starter	Billy Petrick
Closer	John Leicester

LAST YEAR'S TOP 20 PROSPECTS

1. Angel Guzman, rhp
2. Justin Jones, lhp
3. Ryan Harvey, of
4. Andy Sisco, lhp
5. Felix Pie, of
6. Bobby Brownlie, rhp
7. Chadd Blasko, rhp
8. Brendan Harris, 3b/2b
9. David Kelton, of
10. Jae-Kuk Ryu, rhp
11. Luke Hagerty, lhp
12. Jason Dubois, of/1b
13. Todd Wellemeyer, rhp
14. Nic Jackson, of
15. Sergio Mitre, rhp
16. Francis Beltran, rhp
17. Brian Dopirak, 1b
18. Billy Petrick, rhp
19. Jason Wylie, rhp
20. Ricky Nolasco, rhp

TOP PROSPECTS OF THE DECADE

Year	Player, Pos.	Current Team
1995	Brooks Kieschnick, of	Brewers
1996	Brooks Kieschnick, of	Brewers
1997	Kerry Wood, rhp	Cubs
1998	Kerry Wood, rhp	Cubs
1999	Corey Patterson, of	Cubs
2000	Corey Patterson, of	Cubs
2001	Corey Patterson, of	Cubs
2002	Mark Prior, rhp	Cubs
2003	Hee Seop Choi, 1b	Dodgers
2004	Angel Guzman, rhp	Cubs

TOP DRAFT PICKS OF THE DECADE

Year	Player, Pos.	Current Team
1995	Kerry Wood, rhp	Cubs
1996	Todd Noel, rhp	Out of baseball
1997	Jon Garland, rhp	White Sox
1998	Corey Patterson, of	Cubs
1999	Ben Christensen, rhp	Out of baseball
2000	Luis Montanez, ss	Cubs
2001	Mark Prior, rhp	Cubs
2002	Bobby Brownlie, rhp	Cubs
2003	Ryan Harvey, of	Cubs
2004	Grant Johnson, rhp (2nd round)	Cubs

ALL-TIME LARGEST BONUSES

Mark Prior, 2001	$4,000,000
Corey Patterson, 1998	$3,700,000
Luis Montanez, 2000	$2,750,000
Bobby Brownlie, 2002	$2,500,000
Ryan Harvey, 2003	$2,400,000

MINOR LEAGUE DEPTH CHART

Chicago CUBS

RANK: **10**

Impact Potential: B
Dunedin (Fla.) High's 2002 team could have earned a similarly high grade. That spring, Brian Dopirak and Ryan Harvey were teammates, and now they bring 40-homer potential to the Cubs farm system. Young Dominican outfielder Felix Pie has five-tool potential but makes his biggest impact in the standings, as every team he has played for in pro ball has won a league championship.

Depth: B
Trades to help the big league club have thinned the organization, yet the system remains one of the game's deepest. The Cubs added a prospect (Matt Murton) while trading for Nomar Garciaparra. Chicago's depth is most pronounced on the mound, in both lefthanders and righthanders. For comparison's sake, the Orioles' No. 10 prospect before the Sammy Sosa trade, righthander Dave Crouthers, isn't good enough to make the Cubs' top 30 list.

*Depth charts prepared by **John Manuel** and **Allan Simpson**. Numbers in parentheses indicate prospect rankings.*

LF
Jason Dubois (10)
Matt Murton (11)
David Kelton (30)
Luis Montanez

CF
Felix Pie (2)
Adam Greenberg
Dwaine Bacon
Chris Walker
Nic Jackson

RF
Ryan Harvey (3)
Rene Reyes
Aron Weston
Carlos Quinones
Kyle Boyer

3B
Elvin Puello
Casey McGehee

SS
Ronny Cedeno (16)
Buck Coats
Carlos Rojas
Jonathan Mota

2B
Richard Lewis (12)
Mike Fontenot (21)
Eric Patterson (23)

1B
Brian Dopirak (1)
Brandon Sing (15)
Matt Craig (26)
Micah Hoffpauir
Kevin Collins
Ryan Norwood

SOURCE of TALENT

HOMEGROWN		ACQUIRED	
College	11	Trades	3
Junior College	0	Rule 5 draft	0
Draft-and-follow	0	Independent leagues	1
High School	8	Free agents/waivers	0
Nondrafted free agent	0		
Foreign	7		

C
Geovany Soto (14)
Mark Reed (22)
Jake Fox
Tony Richie

LHP

Starters	Relievers
Renyel Pinto (6)	Will Ohman (17)
Sean Marshall (7)	Rich Hill (24)
Jon Connolly	Raul Valdez (27)
Darin Downs	Russ Rohlicek
Andy Santana	John Koronka
Carmen Pignatiello	Clay Rapada
Carlos Vasquez	Jerry Blevins

RHP

Starters	Relievers
Angel Guzman (4)	Jon Leicester (8)
Billy Petrick (5)	Mike Wuertz (18)
Grant Johnson (9)	Jermaine Van Buren (25)
Bobby Brownlie (13)	Jae-Kuk Ryu (28)
Ricky Nolasco (19)	Jared Blasdell
Carlos Marmol (20)	Dave Crouthers
Chadd Blasko (29)	Jason Szuminski
Ronald Bay	
Sean Gallagher	

Best Pro Debut: LHP Jerry Blevins (17) made the short-season Northwest League all-star team after going 6-1, 1.62 with five saves and 42 strikeouts in 33 innings. He has an 89-91 mph fastball and fringy slider.

Best Athlete: 2B Eric Patterson (8) has a variety of tools, including 65 speed on the 20-80 scouting scale and some power. He signed for $300,000, the equivalent of mid-fourth-round money.

Best Pure Hitter: C Mark Reed's (3) batting skills are similar to those of his older brother Jeremy, who led the minors in hitting in 2003 and ended 2004 in the majors with the Mariners. If he can't stick behind the plate, he should hit enough to man a corner infield or outfield spot.

Best Raw Power: 1B Ryan Norwood (9) has the most present power, but OF Alfred Joseph (15) could surpass him in time.

Fastest Runner: OF Gerald Miller (50) is slightly faster than Patterson. OF Adrian Ortiz (5), who didn't sign, may have been the fastest player in the entire draft.

Best Defensive Player: OF Sam Fuld (10) runs well and possesses tremendous instincts. A shoulder injury kept him from making his pro debut last summer.

Best Fastball: The Cubs saw RHP Grant Johnson (2) work at 92-97 mph in his next-to-last outing for Notre Dame. Before that, they saw him throw 92-94 mph in five straight appearances, evidence he's making a full recovery from labrum surgery that sidelined him for all of 2003.

Best Breaking Ball: RHP Sean Gallagher (12) has a strong build, a good curveball and a fastball that tops out at 92 mph.

Most Intriguing Background: Reed isn't

Fuld

the only Cubs draftee with big league connections. Patterson's older brother Corey is Chicago's center fielder. RHP Casey Erickson's (25) uncle Roger pitched in the majors, while his brother Corey spent 2004 in the Cardinals system. Erickson didn't sign, though the Cubs control the rights to the top high school prospect in Illinois as a draft-and-follow.

Closest To The Majors: Johnson signed late for $1.26 million, the first-round money he was destined for before his shoulder injury. He could start his pro career in high Class A.

Best Late-Round Pick: Gallagher, who was considered a tough sign if he didn't go in the first three rounds. Also keep an eye on 3B Russ Canzler (30), who has some pop.

The One Who Got Away: The Cubs thought they could sign Ortiz fairly easily. They soon learned that he was set on going to Pepperdine. Owings, who transferred from Georgia Tech to Tulane, is one of college baseball's best two-way players. RHP Kenn Kasparek (41) had a chance to go in the first round thanks to his 6-foot-9 frame and a 92-93 mph fastball he showed in 2003. After a bad spring, he plummeted and is attending Texas.

Assessment: Chicago believes Johnson represents the first-rounder they forfeited as compensation for signing LaTroy Hawkins. Reed and Patterson add some position-player depth to a pitching-heavy system.

2003 OF Ryan Harvey (1) has a huge ceiling, and sleeper LHP Sean Marshall's (6) is considerable as well. Unsigned C Landon Powell (25) went in the first-round a year later. *GRADE:* B+

2002 1B Brian Dopirak has as much power as anyone in the minors. This would be an A if RHP Bobby Brownlie (1) hadn't lost velocity, and LHPs Luke Hagerty (1) and Justin Jones (2) and RHPs Chadd Blasko (1) and Matt Clanton (1) hadn't gotten hurt. RHP Billy Petrick (2) is developing rapidly. *GRADE:* B+

2001 Two words: Mark Prior (1). Biggest regret: Not signing SS Khalil Greene (14). Also promising: LHP Andy Sisco (2/lost in the Rule 5 draft), 2B/3B Brendan Harris (5/traded to the Expos), RHP Sergio Mitre (7), C Geovany Soto (11). *GRADE:* A

2000 OF Luis Montanez (1) has flopped, but the Cubs still had a good draft in one of the worst crops in recent memory. LHP Dontrelle Willis (8) is the biggest prize, but he was traded to Florida for Matt Clement. *GRADE:* B+

Draft analysis prepared by Jim Callis. Numbers in parentheses indicate draft rounds.

Brian
DOPIRAK

Born: Dec. 20, 1983.
Ht.: 6-4. **Wt.:** 230.
Bats: R. **Throws:** R.
School: Dunedin (Fla.) HS.
Career Transactions: Selected by Cubs in second round of 2002 draft; signed Aug. 4, 2002.
Signed by: Tom Shafer.

There must be something in the water at Dunedin (Fla.) High, because two of the minors' most dangerous power hitters came out of that program just a year apart. The Cubs drafted Dopirak in the second round in 2002, then took former teammate Ryan Harvey with the sixth overall pick in 2003. Dopirak, who had committed to St. Petersburg (Fla.) Junior College, turned pro for a $740,000 bonus. Though he was considered to have the most raw power in the 2002 draft—even more than Prince Fielder—the consensus among scouts was that Dopirak was a hit-or-miss player who could just as easily flame out in Double-A as succeed in the majors. The latter looks like the more realistic possibility now. He earned short-season Northwest League all-star honors in 2003, setting the stage for last season, when he destroyed the low Class A Midwest League. Dopirak tied for third in the minors in homers, finishing three shy of the MWL record, and led the league in hits, doubles, total bases and extra-base hits. He was named Midwest League MVP and Cubs minor league player of the year.

With quick hands, Dopirak generates tremendous bat speed and can hit the ball out to any part of any ballpark. If pitchers let him get his hands extended, they're dead. "When the ball comes off his bat," Kane County manager Dave Joppie said, "it's like hitting a golf ball with an aluminum bat." For a big guy, Dopirak has a short swing, and while he's not the most disciplined of hitters, he already has a sound approach and has shown improvement at working counts. He showed he could adjust against better pitching when Chicago decided to push him after the regular season with an assignment to the Arizona Fall League, where at 20 he was one of the youngest players. He responded to that challenge by hitting .274 with seven homers (one off the AFL lead) in 95 at-bats. In addition to hitting 35-plus homers on an annual basis, Dopirak may be able to hit for average as well. Unlike some young sluggers, he also appreciates the value of defense and has worked hard on that aspect of his game.

For all his effort, Dopirak never will be more than an adequate first baseman. He doesn't cover much ground and his hands are somewhat shaky, which is why he led MWL first basemen with 15 errors in 2004. He's also limited as a baserunner. Dopirak is going to produce a lot of strikeouts to go with his homers, a tradeoff the Cubs will accept. He'll be more valuable, however, if he can continue to increase his walk rate. Already a big man, he'll have to watch his weight as he gets older.

If Dopirak moves up one level to high Class A Daytona, he should make a run at the Florida State League home run record of 33. But given how he handled the AFL, he could make a push for Double-A West Tenn in spring training. With Derrek Lee signed through 2006, there's no immediate need to rush Dopirak. When his bat is ready, the Cubs will gladly find a spot for him.

Year	Club (League)	Class	AVG	G	AB	R	H	2B	3B	HR	RBI	BB	SO	SB	OBP	SLG
2002	Cubs (AZL)	R	.253	21	79	10	20	4	0	0	6	6	23	0	.306	.304
2003	Boise (NWL)	A	.240	52	192	25	46	4	0	13	37	24	58	0	.330	.464
	Lansing (Mid)	A	.269	19	78	8	21	3	0	2	10	2	22	0	.305	.385
2004	Lansing (Mid)	A	.307	137	541	94	166	38	0	39	120	48	123	4	.363	.593
MINOR LEAGUE TOTALS			.284	229	890	137	253	49	0	54	173	80	226	4	.346	.521

2 Felix Pie, of

BILL MITCHELL

Born: Feb. 8, 1985. **Ht.:** 6-2. **Wt.:** 170. **Bats:** L. **Throws:** L. **Career Transactions:** Signed out of Dominican Republic by Cubs, July 3, 2001. **Signed by:** Jose Serra.

Pie has won championships with each of the four teams he has played for as a pro. He also played in his second straight Futures Game in 2004. Florida State League managers recognized Pie's varied tools, voting him the circuit's best batting prospect, fastest baserunner, best defensive outfielder and most exciting player. From the Cubs' perspective, he's their best athlete, top defensive outfielder and strongest outfield arm. His speed stands out the most, and he consistently has hit for average despite being young for his leagues. While Pie has more than held his own, his skills remain raw. His plate discipline slipped in 2004, and he won't show much power until he adds strength and lift to his swing. He's still honing his basestealing, getting caught 16 times in 47 tries last year. He plays a shallow center field because he's not smooth coming in on balls, and needs to improve his routes. Pie has a lot of work to do, but he's just 20 and has plenty of time to do it. He'll move up to Double-A and is on course to arrive in Chicago in 2007.

Year	Club (League)	Class	AVG	G	AB	R	H	2B	3B	HR	RBI	BB	SO	SB	OBP	SLG
2002	Cubs (AZL)	R	.321	55	218	42	70	16	13	4	37	21	47	17	.385	.569
	Boise (NWL)	A	.125	2	8	1	1	1	0	0	1	1	1	0	.222	.250
2003	Lansing (Mid)	A	.285	124	505	72	144	22	9	4	47	41	98	19	.346	.388
2004	Daytona (FSL)	A	.299	105	412	79	123	17	9	8	47	38	113	31	.361	.442
MINOR LEAGUE TOTALS			.296	286	1143	194	338	56	31	16	132	101	259	67	.358	.441

3 Ryan Harvey, of

JOHN SPEAR

Born: Aug. 30, 1984. **Ht.:** 6-5. **Wt.:** 220. **Bats:** R. **Throws:** R. **School:** Dunedin (Fla.) HS. **Career Transactions:** Selected by Cubs in first round (sixth overall) of 2003 draft; signed June 21, 2003. **Signed by:** Rolando Pino.

Because he was recovering from blowing out his right knee at a high school showcase, Harvey barely played after signing for $2.4 million in 2003. His first real exposure to pro ball came last season, which he capped by homering four times in three games to lead short-season Boise to a Northwest League playoff sweep. Harvey's power is comparable to Brian Dopirak's, and Harvey is unquestionably a more well-rounded player. He has solid-average speed, and his strong arm delivered 90-93 mph fastballs when he pitched in high school. His size and physical gifts have prompted comparisons to Dale Murphy. As with Dopirak, the Cubs realize strikeouts will accompany Harvey's homers. But he needs to do a better job working counts, and his naturally long swing can get exploited by quality pitching. After getting injured in a collision, he's still tentative in right field. Harvey could be on the verge of a low Class A breakout like Dopirak had last year. At least three years away from the majors, he'll be Sammy Sosa's long-term successor in right field.

Year	Club (League)	Class	AVG	G	AB	R	H	2B	3B	HR	RBI	BB	SO	SB	OBP	SLG
2003	Cubs (AZL)	R	.235	14	51	9	12	3	2	1	7	6	21	0	.339	.431
2004	Boise (NWL)	A	.268	58	231	42	62	8	0	14	43	20	77	2	.331	.485
MINOR LEAGUE TOTALS			.262	72	282	51	74	11	2	15	50	26	98	2	.332	.475

4 Angel Guzman, rhp

Born: Dec. 14, 1981. **Ht.:** 6-3. **Wt.:** 180. **Bats:** R. **Throws:** R. **Career Transactions:** Signed out of Venezuela by Royals, March 4, 1999; contract voided, June 24, 1999 . . . Signed by Cubs, Nov. 12, 1999. **Signed by:** Hector Ortega.

Guzman was pushing for his first big league promotion in June 2003 before his shoulder acted up. Following his arthroscopic surgery to repair a slight labrum tear, the Cubs handled him cautiously in 2004, shutting him down in July because he was tired after working nonstop on his rehab. Before he got hurt, Guzman had an explosive 91-96 mph sinker, a sharp curveball and a deceptive changeup. All were plus-plus pitches at times. His velocity came back last summer, as did his above-average control. He throws strikes and keeps the ball down in the zone. Guzman's secondary pitches and location haven't gotten back to where they were, though that was expected. They should return in 2005. He still has to prove his health and durability, as he has worked more than 90 innings just once in five pro seasons. Assuming Guzman recaptures his previous stuff, he would give Chicago a fourth homegrown frontline starter alongside Mark Prior, Kerry Wood and Carlos Zambrano. The Cubs will continue to bring him back slowly, probably starting him in

Double-A this year.

Year	Club (League)	Class	W	L	ERA	G	GS	CG	SV	IP	H	R	ER	HR	BB	SO	AVG
2000	Cubs (VSL)	R	1	1	1.93	7	6	0	0	33	24	13	7	0	5	25	.197
2001	Boise (NWL)	A	9	1	2.23	14	14	0	0	77	68	27	19	2	19	63	.233
2002	Lansing (Mid)	A	5	2	1.89	9	9	1	0	62	42	18	13	3	16	49	.186
	Daytona (FSL)	A	6	2	2.39	16	15	1	0	94	99	34	25	2	33	74	.268
2003	West Tenn (SL)	AA	3	3	2.81	15	15	0	0	90	83	30	28	8	26	87	.249
2004	West Tenn (SL)	AA	0	3	5.60	4	4	0	0	18	20	11	11	2	4	13	.286
	Daytona (FSL)	A	3	1	4.20	7	7	0	0	30	27	15	14	2	0	40	.237
MINOR LEAGUE TOTALS			27	13	2.61	72	70	2	0	403	363	148	117	19	103	351	.238

5 Billy Petrick, rhp

BILL MITCHELL

Born: April 29, 1984. **Ht.:** 6-6. **Wt.:** 240. **Bats:** S. **Throws:** R. **School:** Morris (Ill.) HS. **Career Transactions:** Selected by Cubs in third round of 2002 draft; signed July 19, 2002. **Signed by:** Bob Hale.

Petrick was one of the nation's top long snapper recruits and was headed to Washington State to play football before the Cubs made him a third-round pick and signed him for $459,500. Moved one level at a time, he has made significant progress in three pro seasons. Petrick has a tall, thick frame with a lower half that resembles Mark Prior's, and he uses it to launch heavy 90-93 mph sinkers deep in the strike zone. He led the Midwest League in fewest homers per nine innings (0.2) last year and has allowed just seven longballs in three years. He has shown more aptitude for a slider than the loopy curveball he used to throw, and has improved his changeup. Chicago loves his makeup and his willingness to attack hitters inside. While Petrick throws strikes, he needs to improve the command of all three of his pitches so he won't be so hittable. He tends to telegraph his changeup by slowing his arm speed, one reason lefthanders batted .297 against him in 2004. With Petrick's strong build and stuff, he could grow into a dominant pitcher. He's ready for high Class A in 2005.

Year	Club (League)	Class	W	L	ERA	G	GS	CG	SV	IP	H	R	ER	HR	BB	SO	AVG
2002	Cubs (AZL)	R	2	1	1.71	6	6	0	0	32	21	8	6	0	6	35	.189
2003	Boise (NWL)	A	2	5	4.76	14	14	0	0	64	60	49	34	4	27	64	.241
2004	Lansing (Mid)	A	13	7	3.50	26	24	0	0	147	149	66	57	3	43	113	.267
MINOR LEAGUE TOTALS			17	13	3.60	46	44	0	0	243	230	123	97	7	76	212	.251

6 Renyel Pinto, lhp

Born: July 8, 1982. **Ht.:** 6-4. **Wt.:** 195. **Bats:** L. **Throws:** L. **Career Transactions:** Signed out of Venezuela by Cubs, Jan. 31, 1999. **Signed by:** Alberto Rondon.

Pinto went 21-31, 4.22 over his first five pro seasons and spent 2001-03 in Class A before he broke out last season. He led the Double-A Southern League in ERA and strikeouts, and was the Cubs' minor league pitcher of the year. Pinto's best pitch is a plus changeup with good deception, sink and fade. His lively 92-94 mph fastball darts in and out of the strike zone. He may throw harder as he fills out his lanky frame, and even if he doesn't, hitters have trouble picking up his pitches from his low three-quarters delivery. His slider shows flashes of becoming a third above-average pitch. Pinto's biggest need is to keep his fastball in the zone, because when hitters don't chase it he gives up too many walks. He needs added consistency with his slider. Some scouts think his stuff grades better than he pitches and question whether he can win in the majors without better command. Pinto will return to the Triple-A Pacific Coast League after pitching well there in the play-offs. Chicago has several lefty relief options, so he'll probably stay in the Iowa rotation all year.

Year	Club (League)	Class	W	L	ERA	G	GS	CG	SV	IP	H	R	ER	HR	BB	SO	AVG
1999	Cubs (DSL)	R	4	5	4.38	13	13	1	0	64	70	35	31	5	22	62	.289
2000	Cubs (AZL)	R	0	2	6.30	9	4	0	0	30	42	29	21	3	16	23	.326
2001	Lansing (Mid)	A	4	8	5.22	20	20	1	0	88	94	64	51	9	44	69	.278
2002	Daytona (FSL)	A	3	3	5.51	7	7	0	0	33	45	23	20	5	11	24	.338
	Lansing (Mid)	A	7	5	3.31	17	16	0	0	98	79	39	36	9	28	92	.221
2003	Daytona (FSL)	A	3	8	3.22	20	19	0	0	115	91	47	41	4	45	104	.221
2004	Iowa (PCL)	AAA	1	1	7.71	2	2	0	0	9	9	9	8	2	8	9	.250
	West Tenn (SL)	AA	11	8	2.92	25	25	0	0	142	107	50	46	10	72	179	.213
MINOR LEAGUE TOTALS			33	40	3.95	113	106	2	0	578	537	296	254	47	246	562	.250

7 Sean Marshall, lhp

Born: Aug. 30, 1982. **Ht.:** 6-5. **Wt.:** 185. **Bats:** L. **Throws:** L. **School:** Virginia Commonwealth University. **Career Transactions:** Selected by Cubs in sixth round of 2003 draft; signed June 7, 2003. **Signed by:** Billy Swoope.

Marshall and his twin brother Brian helped Virginia Commonwealth top NCAA Division I with a 2.54 ERA in 2003, when Boston drafted Brian in the fifth round and Chicago grabbed Sean in the sixth. He excelled in his first two pro stops before partially rupturing a tendon in his left middle finger while throwing a breaking pitch in mid June, and the problem recurred in the Arizona Fall League. Marshall's 88-92 mph sinker tops out at 95 and generates a lot of groundballs and strikeouts. His No. 2 pitch is a sharp downer curveball that he can change speeds with. His command and stuff allowed him to reach Double-A after 22 pro starts. Marshall also throws a slider and changeup, and improving the latter pitch is the key to him remaining a starter. His finger injury has perplexed the Cubs, but he saw a specialist in January and is expected to be ready for spring training. He got knocked around in Double-A before he got hurt, so Marshall will return there in 2005. He and Renyel Pinto are close to giving the Cubs a much-needed quality lefthanded starter.

Year	Club (League)	Class	W	L	ERA	G	GS	CG	SV	IP	H	R	ER	HR	BB	SO	AVG
2003	Boise (NWL)	A	5	6	2.57	14	14	0	0	74	66	31	21	1	23	88	.237
	Lansing (Mid)	A	1	0	0.00	1	1	0	0	7	5	1	0	0	0	11	.192
2004	Lansing (Mid)	A	2	0	1.11	7	7	1	0	49	29	7	6	1	4	51	.171
	West Tenn (SL)	AA	2	2	5.90	6	6	0	0	29	36	20	19	2	12	23	.310
MINOR LEAGUE TOTALS			10	8	2.61	28	28	1	0	158	136	59	46	4	39	173	.230

8 Jon Leicester, rhp

Born: Feb. 7, 1979. **Ht.:** 6-2. **Wt.:** 220. **Bats:** R. **Throws:** R. **School:** University of Memphis. **Career Transactions:** Selected by Cubs in 11th round of 2000 draft; signed June 19, 2000. **Signed by:** Mark Adair.

Area scout Mark Adair did a tremendous job seeing the potential in Leicester, who was better as a shortstop in college and went 0-11, 6.72 during his draft year. He never posted a winning record until 2004, when he made the transition from the Triple-A rotation to the big league bullpen and was one of the Cubs' most effective relievers in the second half. When Leicester pitches in short stints, his fastball sits at 95-96 mph and reaches 98. He can overmatch righthanders with his slider, and lefties with a splitter that serves as his changeup. He finally has gained the confidence he needs to win. Strong and durable, he can handle any role. Leicester's control wavers and he's hittable when he leaves his pitches up in the zone. His secondary pitches aren't always reliable, sometimes leaving him with nothing but his fastball. Surprisingly, those problems occurred less in the majors. Though he has earned manager Dusty Baker's trust, Leicester isn't guaranteed a bullpen spot in 2005. He could get a chance to start in the majors down the road.

Year	Club (League)	Class	W	L	ERA	G	GS	CG	SV	IP	H	R	ER	HR	BB	SO	AVG
2000	Eugene (NWL)	A	1	5	5.44	17	7	0	0	50	47	36	30	4	22	31	.247
2001	Lansing (Mid)	A	9	10	5.29	28	27	1	0	153	182	117	90	16	58	109	.297
2002	Daytona (FSL)	A	2	3	3.97	20	14	0	0	82	77	43	36	2	48	57	.248
	West Tenn (SL)	AA	2	2	4.61	5	4	0	0	27	24	16	14	1	13	18	.231
2003	West Tenn (SL)	AA	6	7	3.89	45	9	1	6	106	89	54	46	7	53	106	.227
	Iowa (PCL)	AAA	0	0	7.20	1	1	0	0	5	6	4	4	0	2	4	.316
2004	Chicago (NL)	MAJ	5	1	3.89	32	0	0	0	42	40	20	18	7	15	35	.256
	Iowa (PCL)	AAA	6	2	3.70	12	12	0	0	66	61	31	27	3	36	60	.244
MAJOR LEAGUE TOTALS			5	1	3.89	32	0	0	0	42	40	20	18	7	15	35	.256
MINOR LEAGUE TOTALS			26	29	4.55	128	74	2	6	489	486	301	247	33	232	385	.259

9 Grant Johnson, rhp

Born: May 26, 1983. **Ht.:** 6-6. **Wt.:** 215. **Bats:** R. **Throws:** R. **School:** University of Notre Dame. **Career Transactions:** Selected by Cubs in second round of 2004 draft; signed Aug. 14, 2004. **Signed by:** Stan Zielinski.

The Cubs scouted Johnson heavily as an Illinois high schooler, but backed off because of his commitment to Notre Dame. He established himself as a potential first-rounder with the Irish before tearing his labrum and missing all of 2003. After he returned to lead the Big East Conference with a 1.87 ERA in 2004, Chicago made him its top pick and signed him for $1.26 million, easily the highest bonus in the second round. Johnson consistently threw 92-94 mph last spring, showing he's fully healthy. His slider was better than his fastball before he got hurt. The Cubs rave about his mound presence as much as his stuff. Johnson pitched just 58 innings in college the last two years, then signed late and skipped instructional league to work toward his marketing degree. He needs mound time to get his old slider back and improve his changeup. Chicago won't take any chances with Johnson, so he may avoid the cold April climate in the Midwest League and start his pro career in the Florida State League. He has the makeup to handle high Class A.

Year	Club (League)	Class	W	L	ERA	G	GS	CG	SV	IP	H	R	ER	HR	BB	SO	AVG
2004	Did not play—Signed 2005 contract																

10 Jason Dubois, of/1b

Born: March 26, 1979. **Ht.:** 6-5. **Wt.:** 220. **Bats:** R. **Throws:** R. **School:** Virginia Commonwealth University. **Career Transactions:** Selected by Cubs in 14th round of 2000 draft; signed June 11, 2000 . . . Selected by Blue Jays from Cubs in major league Rule 5 draft, Dec. 16, 2002; returned to Cubs, March 15, 2003. **Signed by:** Billy Swoope.

The Cubs didn't protect Dubois after he led the Florida State League with a .562 slugging percentage in 2002, and they temporarily lost him to the Blue Jays in the major league Rule 5 draft. After returning to Chicago, he won the Arizona Fall League MVP award in 2003 and led the system in slugging last year. Managers rated Dubois the best power hitter in the Pacific Coast League. Though some scouts think he doesn't pull enough pitches, he's strong enough to drive the ball out to the opposite field with ease. He has a strong arm, no surprise considering he won 19 games as a pitcher at Virginia Commonwealth, and decent defensive instincts. Though Dubois draws a fair amount of walks, he can get impatient and needs to do a better job of waiting for pitches he can punish. He has below-average speed and range, making him just adequate at an outfield corner or first base. After the Cubs declined to pick up Moises Alou's $11.5 million option, Dubois figured to get a chance at playing time in left field. Then the Sammy Sosa trade with the Orioles included Jerry Hairston, who could get a long look in left field, as will Todd Hollandsworth. Dubois offers more offensive upside than either.

Year	Club (League)	Class	AVG	G	AB	R	H	2B	3B	HR	RBI	BB	SO	SB	OBP	SLG
2000	Did not play—Injured															
2001	Lansing (Mid)	A	.296	118	443	76	131	28	9	24	92	46	120	1	.377	.562
2002	Daytona (FSL)	A	.321	99	361	64	116	25	1	20	85	57	95	6	.422	.562
2003	West Tenn (SL)	AA	.269	130	443	57	119	31	4	15	73	57	118	2	.367	.458
2004	Chicago (NL)	MAJ	.217	20	23	2	5	0	1	1	5	1	7	0	.240	.435
	Iowa (PCL)	AAA	.314	109	385	75	121	26	1	31	99	41	97	2	.388	.629
MAJOR LEAGUE TOTALS			.217	20	23	2	5	0	1	1	5	1	7	0	.240	.435
MINOR LEAGUE TOTALS			.298	456	1632	272	487	110	15	90	349	201	430	11	.387	.550

11 Matt Murton, of

Born: Oct. 3, 1981. **Ht.:** 6-1. **Wt.:** 215. **Bats:** R. **Throws:** R. **School:** Georgia Tech. **Career Transactions:** Selected by Red Sox in first round (32nd overall) of 2003 draft; signed July 8, 2003 . . . Traded by Red Sox with SS Nomar Garciaparra to Cubs as part of four-way trade in which Red Sox received SS Orlando Cabrera from Expos and 1B Doug Mientkiewicz from Twins, Expos received 2B/3B Brendan Harris, RHP Francis Beltran and SS Alex Gonzalez from Cubs, and Twins received LHP Justin Jones from Cubs; July 31, 2004. **Signed by:** Rob English (Red Sox).

Not only did general manager Jim Hendry pull off a four-team deal trade at the deadline last July that netted Nomar Garciaparra and Alex Gonzalez, but he also picked up Murton as well. Murton has the best pure hitting skills and strike-zone judgment in the system. The Expos weren't interested in getting Murton from the Red Sox in the trade, so Hendry offered to give up Harris and take Murton at the last moment. He always hit well with wood bats in the Cape Cod League as an amateur, and Murton has had little trouble adapting to pro ball. Scouts don't project him to have quite as much power as they did when he was at Georgia Tech, but he should be at least a 20-homer guy. He needs to add loft to his swing to become more of a longball threat. He can put on a show in batting practice, having won home run derbies at the Connie Mack World Series (1998), Cape Cod League all-star game (2002) and Florida State League all-star game (2004). Murton is a good athlete for his size and has average speed. His biggest drawback is a weak arm that limits him to left field. He'll head to Double-A this year and could be ready for Wrigley Field at some point in 2006.

Year	Club (League)	Class	AVG	G	AB	R	H	2B	3B	HR	RBI	BB	SO	SB	OBP	SLG
2003	Lowell (NY-P)	A	.286	53	189	30	54	11	2	2	29	27	39	9	.374	.397
2004	Sarasota (FSL)	A	.301	102	376	60	113	16	4	11	55	42	61	5	.372	.452
	Daytona (FSL)	A	.253	24	79	13	20	1	1	2	8	8	10	2	.326	.367
MINOR LEAGUE TOTALS			.290	179	644	103	187	28	7	15	92	77	110	16	.367	.425

12 Richard Lewis, 2b

Born: June 29, 1980. **Ht.:** 6-1. **Wt.:** 190. **Bats:** R. **Throws:** R. **School:** Georgia Tech. **Career Transactions:** Selected by Braves in first round (40th overall) of 2001 draft; signed June 14, 2001 . . . Traded to Cubs with LHP Andy Pratt from Braves for RHP Juan Cruz and LHP Steve Smyth, March 25, 2004. **Signed by:** Rob English (Braves).

Another supplemental first-round pick out of Georgia Tech, Lewis hit just .255 in his first three seasons in the Atlanta system. He gave reason for optimism when he won the Arizona Fall League batting title with a .404 average in 2003, but when the Braves had a chance to acquire Juan Cruz from the Cubs last spring, they included Lewis in the trade. Chicago also received lefthander Andy Pratt, considered a better prospect at the time, but Pratt experienced control problems in 2004 while Lewis won the Southern League MVP. The only negative came when he was promoted to Triple-A and broke his right leg sliding into second base. Lewis doesn't have a standout tool, but he's a baseball rat with solid all-around skills. Though he still strikes out too much, he matured at the plate last season, hitting for average with more gap power than expected. With his plus speed, he can steal more than the 11 bases he swiped in 2004. Lewis has sure hands, committing just four errors in 129 games last year, and hangs in well on the double play. He was so aggressive rehabbing his leg this off-season that Chicago had to tell him to slow down. The initial expectation was that he'd miss the first month of the season, but he might be ready for Opening Day. If he can carry his success to Triple-A , Lewis will challenge Todd Walker for the Cubs' second-base job in 2006.

Year	Club (League)	Class	AVG	G	AB	R	H	2B	3B	HR	RBI	BB	SO	SB	OBP	SLG
2001	Jamestown (NY-P)	A	.242	71	285	37	69	7	1	4	27	20	50	16	.298	.316
2002	Myrtle Beach (Car)	A	.279	130	484	82	135	23	4	2	51	55	80	31	.359	.355
2003	Greenville (SL)	AA	.239	129	460	59	110	23	3	6	47	44	101	19	.305	.341
2004	West Tenn (SL)	AA	.329	99	380	68	125	27	10	10	59	37	94	7	.391	.532
	Iowa (PCL)	AAA	.246	32	118	14	29	8	1	3	11	4	21	4	.280	.407
MINOR LEAGUE TOTALS			.271	461	1727	260	468	88	19	25	195	160	346	77	.336	.387

13 Bobby Brownlie, rhp

Born: Oct. 5, 1980. **Ht.:** 6-0. **Wt.:** 210. **Bats:** R. **Throws:** R. **School:** Rutgers University. **Career Transactions:** Selected by Cubs in first round (21st overall) of 2002 draft; signed March 5, 2003. **Signed by:** Billy Blitzer.

After his first two years at Rutgers and strong summers in the Cape Cod League and with Team USA, Brownlie was the frontrunner to be the No. 1 overall pick in the 2002 draft. Biceps tendinitis as a junior and his selection of Scott Boras as an adviser caused him to slide, however. Following the third-longest holdout in draft history, Brownlie signed the following March for $2.5 million. Though he has had consistent success and reached Double-A, Chicago still hasn't seen the overpowering stuff he showed as a college sophomore. He had a 92-94 mph fastball that touched 97 then, but now he works at 88-90 mph. His curveball still is his signature pitch, but it's not the knee-buckler it once was. He has recovered from the tendinitis and shoulder soreness he had in 2003, so his health isn't the reason. Brownlie has compensated by becoming a more polished pitcher. He has developed an effective changeup, learned to locate his fastball to both sides of the plate and possesses the best overall command in the system. After some time in Triple-A, Brownlie will be able to help the Cubs in the back half of their rotation. If he regains the outstanding stuff he once had to go with his increased pitchability, he could be a frontline starter.

Year	Club (League)	Class	W	L	ERA	G	GS	CG	SV	IP	H	R	ER	HR	BB	SO	AVG
2003	Daytona (FSL)	A	5	4	3.00	13	13	1	0	66	48	26	22	2	24	59	.201
2004	West Tenn (SL)	AA	9	9	3.36	26	26	2	0	147	127	62	55	15	36	114	.236
MINOR LEAGUE TOTALS			14	13	3.25	39	39	3	0	213	175	88	77	17	60	173	.225

14 Geovany Soto, c

Born: Jan. 20, 1983. **Ht.:** 6-1. **Wt.:** 230. **Bats:** R. **Throws:** R. **School:** American Military Academy, Rio Piedras, P.R. **Career Transactions:** Selected by Cubs in 11th round of 2001 draft; signed June 26, 2001. **Signed by:** Jose Trujillo.

The Cubs have tried in vain to develop a catcher for more than decade, as prospects such as Pat Cline, Mike Hubbard, Brad Ramsey and Matt Walbeck teased them before dashing their hopes. Soto became the leading candidate to end that drought in Double-A at age 21. A cousin of former Cubs infielder Ramon Martinez, Soto was a corner infielder in high school and spent his first two years as a pro between catcher and first base. His body was soft when he first turned pro, but he lost 30 pounds to better deal with the rigors of catching. Soto offers potential both offensively and defensively. He shows bat-handling ability and has a little loft in his swing, and he could hit for a decent average with 10-15 homers annually. The best defensive catcher in the system, Soto has good receiving skills and handles pitchers well. At times he shows an above-average arm, though it's inconsistent. He doesn't run well but moves fine behind the plate. Soto has responded to being pushed aggressively, and Chicago will challenge him by sending him to Triple-A at age 22.

Year	Club (League)	Class	AVG	G	AB	R	H	2B	3B	HR	RBI	BB	SO	SB	OBP	SLG
2001	Cubs (AZL)	R	.260	41	150	18	39	16	0	1	20	15	33	1	.339	.387
2002	Cubs (AZL)	R	.269	44	156	24	42	10	2	3	24	13	35	0	.333	.417
	Boise (NWL)	A	.400	1	5	1	2	0	0	0	0	0	1	0	.400	.400
2003	Daytona (FSL)	A	.242	89	297	26	72	12	2	2	38	31	58	0	.313	.316
2004	West Tenn (SL)	AA	.271	104	332	47	90	16	0	9	48	40	71	1	.355	.401
MINOR LEAGUE TOTALS			.261	279	940	116	245	54	4	15	130	99	198	2	.336	.374

15 Brandon Sing, 1b

Born: March 13, 1981. **Ht.:** 6-5. **Wt.:** 210. **Bats:** R. **Throws:** R. **School:** Joliet (Ill.) West HS. **Career Transactions:** Selected by Cubs in 20th round of 1999 draft; signed July 31, 1999. **Signed by:** Scott May.

Sing's third stint in high Class A proved to be the charm. After washing out in a 2003 season marred by mononucleosis and hamstring problems, he destroyed the Florida State League last year. He made a run at the league's home run record, topped the FSL in hits, doubles, extra-base hits and homers, and won the MVP award. Sing worked hard during the offseason to get into the best shape of his career and retooled his swing under the tutelage of Daytona hitting coach Richie Zisk. Sing uses his patience to draw walks and get pitches he can hammer. His swing is a bit long and at 23 he was old for high Class A, so he still has much to prove at higher levels. Sing's position is a problem, and not because he's a below-average runner who's merely adequate at first base. With Derrek Lee ahead of him and top prospect Brian Dopirak behind him, his chances of playing regularly at first base for the Cubs are slim. He broke into pro ball as a third baseman and saw time in instructional league at second base, but his only other option is left field. Sing has a strong arm but not a lot of range. He should open the year as a first baseman in Double-A, moving to left if Dopirak receives a promotion.

Year	Club (League)	Class	AVG	G	AB	R	H	2B	3B	HR	RBI	BB	SO	SB	OBP	SLG
1999	Cubs (AZL)	R	.265	17	68	4	18	4	1	2	12	5	16	1	.311	.441
2000	Eugene (NWL)	A	.229	61	218	29	50	11	1	9	28	35	75	4	.339	.413
2001	Lansing (Mid)	A	.245	121	417	54	102	27	2	16	50	46	109	3	.328	.434
2002	Daytona (FSL)	A	.248	125	440	65	109	18	5	18	64	64	96	5	.348	.434
2003	West Tenn (SL)	AA	.209	42	139	15	29	7	0	5	23	10	39	2	.256	.367
	Daytona (FSL)	A	.235	39	136	20	32	6	0	4	23	17	29	0	.318	.368
2004	Daytona (FSL)	A	.270	122	408	86	110	27	0	32	94	84	101	1	.399	.571
MINOR LEAGUE TOTALS			.246	527	1826	273	450	100	9	86	294	261	465	16	.344	.452

16 Ronny Cedeno, ss

Born: Feb. 2, 1983. **Ht.:** 6-0. **Wt.:** 180. **Bats:** R. **Throws:** R. **Career Transactions:** Signed out of Venezuela by Cubs, Aug. 27, 1999. **Signed by:** Alberto Rondon.

After Cedeno won the Rookie-level Arizona League batting title with a .350 average in 2001, Chicago skipped him two levels and sent him to low Class A. His bat took a while to recover, as he hit a combined .212 the next two years. He finally caught his breath last season, when he started to spray line drives all over the field again. Cedeno still needs to improve his ability to make contact, work counts and get on base, but he's no longer an automatic out. He matured and stopped trying to break out of slumps by getting three hits in one trip to the plate. A plus runner, he's still feeling his way as a basestealer. The Cubs say anything Cedeno does with the bat is a bonus, and they proved it by protecting him on the 40-man roster after a 2003 season in which he batted .211. He has a cannon arm—the best among the system's infielders—good range and soft hands. He led Southern League infielders with a .963 fielding percentage last year. The only comparable glove man among Cubs farmhands is Carlos Rojas, whose offensive skills lag far behind Cedeno's. Assuming Cedeno continues to hold his own at the plate in Triple-A, he'd be an alternative for the Cubs in 2006 if they decide not to re-sign Nomar Garciaparra.

Year	Club (League)	Class	AVG	G	AB	R	H	2B	3B	HR	RBI	BB	SO	SB	OBP	SLG
2000	Cubs (VSL)	R	.287	51	167	35	48	8	3	3	14	19	37	13	.370	.425
2001	Lansing (Mid)	A	.196	17	56	9	11	4	1	1	2	2	18	0	.237	.357
	Cubs (AZL)	R	.350	52	206	36	72	13	4	1	17	13	32	17	.398	.466
2002	Lansing (Mid)	A	.213	98	376	44	80	17	4	2	31	22	74	14	.269	.295
	Boise (NWL)	A	.218	29	110	17	24	5	2	0	6	9	25	8	.275	.300
2003	Daytona (FSL)	A	.211	107	380	43	80	18	1	4	36	21	82	19	.257	.295
2004	West Tenn (SL)	AA	.279	116	384	39	107	19	5	6	48	24	74	10	.328	.401
MINOR LEAGUE TOTALS			.251	470	1679	223	422	84	20	17	154	110	342	81	.306	.356

17 Will Ohman, lhp

Born: Aug. 13, 1977. **Ht.:** 6-2. **Wt.:** 200. **Bats:** L. **Throws:** L. **School:** Pepperdine University. **Career Transactions:** Selected by Cubs in eighth round of 1998 draft; signed June 23, 1998 . . . Released by Cubs, Oct. 30, 2003 . . . Signed by Cubs, Feb. 26, 2004. **Signed by:** Steve Fuller.

Ohman broke into the majors in September 2000, but he blew out his elbow pitching winter ball in Mexico after the 2001 season, and missed the next two seasons following Tommy John surgery. He was released in October 2003, re-signed last February and, outside of a month on the disabled list with elbow soreness, blew away hitters all year. He finished second among Pacific Coast League relievers with 12.9 strikeouts per nine innings and was even tougher during the Mexican winter season, posting a 0.90 ERA with 30 whiffs in 20 innings. Like many Tommy John survivors, Ohman throws harder than he did before the operation, pitching at 91-95 mph after maxing out at 92 in the past. He also has a nasty slider with downward tilt. His biggest weakness is a propensity for pitching up in the zone, and he also could throw a few more strikes. Chicago is looking for a second bullpen lefty, and Ohman is an early favorite to win the job out of spring training.

Year	Club (League)	Class	W	L	ERA	G	GS	CG	SV	IP	H	R	ER	HR	BB	SO	AVG
1998	Williamsport (NY-P)	A	4	4	6.46	10	7	0	0	39	39	32	28	6	13	35	.260
	Rockford (Mid)	A	1	1	4.44	4	4	0	0	24	25	13	12	3	7	21	.269
1999	Daytona (FSL)	A	4	7	3.46	31	15	2	5	107	102	59	41	11	41	97	.254
2000	West Tenn (SL)	AA	6	4	1.89	59	0	0	3	71	53	20	15	3	36	85	.200
	Chicago (NL)	MAJ	1	0	8.10	6	0	0	0	3	4	3	3	0	4	2	.308
2001	Iowa (PCL)	AAA	5	2	4.06	40	1	0	4	51	51	24	23	9	18	66	.259
	Chicago (NL)	MAJ	0	1	7.71	11	0	0	0	12	14	10	10	2	6	12	.292
2002	Did not play—Injured																
2003	Did not play—Injured																
2004	Iowa (PCL)	AAA	3	3	4.30	45	1	0	0	52	53	28	25	6	29	75	.265
MAJOR LEAGUE TOTALS			1	1	7.80	17	0	0	0	15	18	13	13	2	10	14	.295
MINOR LEAGUE TOTALS			23	21	3.76	189	28	2	12	345	323	176	144	38	144	379	.247

18 Mike Wuertz, rhp

Born: Dec. 15, 1978. **Ht.:** 6-3. **Wt.:** 200. **Bats:** R. **Throws:** R. **School:** Austin (Minn.) HS. **Career Transactions:** Selected by Cubs in 11th round of 1997 draft; signed Aug. 18, 1997. **Signed by:** Mark Servais.

Will Ohman wasn't the only bullpen revelation for the Cubs last year. Wuertz had trouble coming up with a changeup to get lefthanders out as a starter, and he was quickly becoming an afterthought when he stalled in Triple-A. When he moved to relief in the middle of the 2003 season, his stuff surged; his fastball went from 87-88 mph to 91-93 with a peak of 95. His slider went from fringy to a plus pitch at times, though it's still inconsistent. He made such an impression in spring training that he won a spot on Chicago's Opening Day roster. Wuertz still has to spot his pitches well to succeed, but he has better command than Jon Leicester and Todd Wellemeyer, who also are trying to establish themselves in the big league bullpen. They'll be Wuertz' chief competition.

Year	Club (League)	Class	W	L	ERA	G	GS	CG	SV	IP	H	R	ER	HR	BB	SO	AVG
1998	Williamsport (NY-P)	A	7	5	3.44	14	14	1	0	86	79	36	33	4	19	59	.236
1999	Lansing (Mid)	A	11	12	4.80	28	28	1	0	161	191	104	86	11	44	127	.290
2000	Daytona (FSL)	A	12	7	3.78	28	28	3	0	171	166	79	72	15	64	142	.253
2001	West Tenn (SL)	AA	4	9	3.99	27	27	1	0	160	160	80	71	20	58	135	.260
2002	Iowa (PCL)	AAA	9	5	5.55	28	27	0	0	154	185	109	95	24	69	131	.295
2003	Iowa (PCL)	AAA	3	9	4.57	43	16	0	1	124	140	70	63	16	35	92	.288
2004	Iowa (PCL)	AAA	1	1	2.42	37	0	0	19	45	30	13	12	4	15	59	.186
	Chicago (NL)	MAJ	1	0	4.34	31	0	0	1	29	22	14	14	4	17	30	.218
MAJOR LEAGUE TOTALS			1	0	4.34	31	0	0	1	29	22	14	14	4	17	30	.218
MINOR LEAGUE TOTALS			47	48	4.31	205	140	6	20	902	951	491	432	94	304	745	.269

19 Ricky Nolasco, rhp

Born: Dec. 13, 1982. **Ht.:** 6-2. **Wt.:** 220. **Bats:** R. **Throws:** R. **School:** Rialto (Calif.) HS. **Career Transactions:** Selected by Cubs in fourth round of 2001 draft; signed July 31, 2001. **Signed by:** Spider Jorgensen.

If Rafael Palmeiro hadn't vetoed a 2003 deal, Chicago would have sent Nolasco and lefty Felix Sanchez (since traded to the Tigers) to Texas for Palmeiro. Instead, Nolasco reached Triple-A and passed his older brother David, a Brewers minor league righthander. Nolasco was too tentative in Triple-A but got back on track after returning to Double-A. He challenged hitters with his low-90s sinker and curveball. His curve is his best offering, but he relies on it too much. Conversely, he doesn't throw his changeup enough—and that's the pitch that can make the difference for him in Triple-A. Nolasco is a tough competitor, so Chicago doesn't expect him to be shellshocked when he gets his second chance in Iowa this year.

Year	Club (League)	Class	W	L	ERA	G	GS	CG	SV	IP	H	R	ER	HR	BB	SO	AVG
2001	Cubs (AZL)	R	1	0	1.50	5	4	0	0	18	11	3	3	0	5	23	.175
2002	Boise (NWL)	A	7	2	2.48	15	15	0	0	91	72	32	25	1	25	92	.214
2003	Daytona (FSL)	A	11	5	2.96	26	26	1	0	149	129	58	49	7	48	136	.232
2004	Iowa (PCL)	AAA	2	3	9.30	9	9	0	0	41	68	42	42	7	16	28	.384
	West Tenn (SL)	AA	6	4	3.70	19	19	0	0	107	104	50	44	13	37	115	.257
MINOR LEAGUE TOTALS			27	14	3.62	74	73	1	0	405	384	185	163	28	131	394	.250

20 Carlos Marmol, rhp

Born: Oct. 14, 1982. **Ht.:** 6-2. **Wt.:** 190. **Bats:** R. **Throws:** R. **Career Transactions:** Signed out of Dominican Republic by Cubs, July 3, 1999. **Signed by:** Jose Serra.

After signing him as a catcher/outfielder, the Cubs eventually decided to use Marmol's strong arm on the mound. He took to the conversion quickly, leading the Arizona League in strikeouts during his first summer as a pitcher. At times, Marmol flashed a plus-plus fastball and an above-average curveball, though he's still far from consistent. He usually pitched at 90-92 mph with nice life on his heater when he kept it down in the zone. Marmol is picking up a changeup quickly for a converted position player, and he throws a cut fastball that's too slurvy right now. There's a fair amount of effort in his delivery, so he struggles to command his pitches at times. If Marmol rounds out his repertoire, he could be a No. 3 starter. If not, he could be an effective set-up man. He'll continue to pitch out of the rotation this year in high Class A.

Year	Club (League)	Class	AVG	G	AB	R	H	2B	3B	HR	RBI	BB	SO	SB	OBP	SLG
2000	Cubs (DSL)	R	.314	41	140	32	44	7	2	0	22	11	27	3	.365	.393
2001	Cubs (AZL)	R	.295	40	129	15	38	11	0	0	12	9	30	4	.355	.380
2002	Lansing (Mid)	A	.149	15	47	2	7	0	1	0	4	1	7	0	.167	.191
	Cubs (AZL)	R	.258	47	186	22	48	6	3	1	16	3	35	10	.271	.339
MINOR LEAGUE TOTALS			.273	143	502	71	137	24	6	1	54	24	99	17	.311	.351

Year	Club (League)	Class	W	L	ERA	G	GS	CG	SV	IP	H	R	ER	HR	BB	SO	AVG
2002	Cubs (AZL)	R	0	0	0.00	1	0	0	0	1	1	0	0	0	1	1	.250
2003	Cubs (AZL)	R	3	5	4.19	14	9	0	0	62	54	38	29	5	37	74	.225
2004	Lansing (Mid)	A	14	8	3.20	26	24	0	0	155	131	64	55	15	53	154	.234
MINOR LEAGUE TOTALS			17	13	3.47	41	33	0	0	218	186	102	84	20	91	229	.231

21 Mike Fontenot, 2b

Born: June 9, 1980. **Ht.:** 5-8. **Wt.:** 160. **Bats:** L. **Throws:** R. **School:** Louisiana State University. **Career Transactions:** Selected by Orioles in first round (19th overall) of 2001 draft; signed Sept. 5, 2001 . . . Traded to Orioles with OF/2B Jerry Hairson and RHP Dave Crouthers to Cubs for OF Sammy Sosa, Feb. 2, 2005. **Signed by:** Mike Tullier (Orioles).

The Cubs vowed they wouldn't trade Sammy Sosa for the sake of trading him, but that's what they did when they sent him to the Orioles in February. With Chicago, Fontenot already takes a back seat to big leaguers Todd Walker and Jerry Hairston and prospect Richard Lewis, and 2004 draftee Eric Patterson soon could pass him as well. Fontenot has some useful offensive tools in his plus speed and surprising pop for his size. He sometimes gets caught up in trying to hit for power, leading to subpar plate discipline. He's limited defensively, as he's no more than adequate at second base. He doesn't cover as much ground as his speed might indicate, and his below-average arm makes it a stretch to try him at shortstop, reducing his value as a utilityman. Fontenot may serve the Cubs as trade bait because there's no spot for him on the big league roster, and Lewis needs to play every day in Triple-A.

Year	Club (League)	Class	AVG	G	AB	R	H	2B	3B	HR	RBI	BB	SO	SB	OBP	SLG
2002	Frederick (Car)	A	.264	122	481	61	127	16	4	8	53	42	117	13	.333	.364
2003	Bowie (EL)	AA	.325	126	449	63	146	24	5	12	66	50	89	16	.399	.481
2004	Ottawa (IL)	AAA	.279	136	524	73	146	30	10	8	49	48	111	14	.346	.420
MINOR LEAGUE TOTALS			.288	384	1454	197	419	70	19	28	168	140	317	43	.358	.420

22 Mark Reed, c

Born: April 13, 1986. **Ht.:** 5-11. **Wt.:** 175. **Bats:** L. **Throws:** R. **School:** Bonita HS, La Verne, Calif. **Career Transactions:** Selected by Cubs in second round of 2004 draft; signed July 8, 2004. **Signed by:** Jim Crawford.

Hitting apparently runs in the Reed family. Mark's older brother Jeremy won the minor league batting title with a .373 average in 2003 and hit .397 after the Mariners called him up last September. Mark hit .351 in his brief pro debut before he broke his thumb in a sliding mishap. The Cubs believe Mark will hit, as he has an advanced approach and a loose swing. He should have more power than his brother, who's more of a gap hitter. Reed lives for baseball and loves to hone his stroke in the batting cage. As a bonus, he swings from the left side. He'll have to prove he can handle the responsibilities of catching. Reed is athletic for a backstop, and he has the receiving skills and makeup to succeed, but his arm strength may be a little short. If he can't stay behind the plate, he profiles as a possible corner infielder or outfielder. Because the Cubs have signed a lot of catchers and have a backlog at the lower levels, Reed will probably open 2005 in extended spring before playing at Boise.

Year	Club (League)	Class	AVG	G	AB	R	H	2B	3B	HR	RBI	BB	SO	SB	OBP	SLG
2004	Cubs (AZL)	R	.351	10	37	5	13	5	1	1	7	4	8	0	.429	.622
MINOR LEAGUE TOTALS		R	.351	10	37	5	13	5	1	1	7	4	8	0	.429	.622

23 Eric Patterson, 2b

Born: April 8, 1983. **Ht.:** 5-11. **Wt.:** 173. **Bats:** L. **Throws:** R. **School:** Georgia Tech. **Career Transactions:** Selected by Cubs in eighth round of 2004 draft; signed Aug. 27, 2004. **Signed by:** Sam Hughes.

Reed wasn't the only Cubs 2004 draft pick with good bloodlines. If all goes well, Chicago one day could have two Patterson brothers batting atop its order. Eric earned all-Atlantic Coast Conference honors in each of his three years at Georgia Tech, where his older brother Corey committed before the Cubs took him third overall in the 1998 draft. Their father Don played defensive back for the Yellow Jackets and in the NFL. As with his brother, speed is Eric's best tool, though Eric's grades as a 65 on the 20-80 scouting scale, compared to Corey's 80. Eric, who has good instincts on the bases, led the ACC with 48 steals in 55 attempts last spring. The key to his game is his approach at the plate. He's not as strong as Corey but at times he gets too concerned with trying to match his power. Though Patterson made adjustments last spring to tone down his aggression, at times he'll get too patient and let hittable pitches go by. He just needs to focus on getting on base. His athleticism makes him a potential plus defender at second base. Patterson likely will make his pro debut in low Class A, with high Class A an outside possibility.

Year	Club (League)	Class	AVG	G	AB	R	H	2B	3B	HR	RBI	BB	SO	SB	OBP	SLG
2004	Did not play—Signed 2005 contract															

24 Rich Hill, lhp

Born: March 11, 1980. **Ht.:** 6-5. **Wt.:** 190. **Bats:** L. **Throws:** L. **School:** University of Michigan. **Career Transactions:** Selected by Cubs in fourth round of 2002 draft; signed July 10, 2002. **Signed by:** Scott May.

As good as Renyel Pinto and Sean Marshall are, they can't match Hill's stuff. In fact, one Cubs official says Hill may have the best stuff in the organization. The problem is that he has little command of it. He has averaged 12.1 strikeouts but also 6.3 walks per nine innings as pro. The Cubs tried lowering his arm angle in 2004, from a high three-quarters to a true three-quarters, and put him in the bullpen for a while, with only minimal results. He led the Florida State League in walks, hit batters (19) and balks (five). With his 88-93 mph fastball and power 12-to-6 curveball, Hill can be untouchable when he finds the plate. Chicago thinks his control issues are more mental than physical, and the only solution is to keep putting him on the mound. He also has a promising changeup, but the Cubs have to force him to throw it. Hill will be 25 this season, and perhaps it's too much to expect him to command three pitches well enough to be a starter in the majors. His fastball/curveball combo would allow him to be a dynamic reliever if he could be trusted to throw strikes.

Year	Club (League)	Class	W	L	ERA	G	GS	CG	SV	IP	H	R	ER	HR	BB	SO	AVG
2002	Boise (NWL)	A	0	2	8.36	6	5	0	0	14	15	19	13	0	14	12	.260
2003	Lansing (Mid)	A	0	1	2.76	15	4	0	0	29	14	12	9	0	36	50	.141
	Boise (NWL)	A	1	6	4.35	14	14	0	0	68	57	40	33	5	32	99	.233
2004	Daytona (FSL)	A	7	6	4.03	28	19	0	0	109	88	64	49	9	72	136	.215
MINOR LEAGUE TOTALS			8	15	4.23	63	42	0	0	221	174	135	104	14	154	297	.215

25 Jermaine Van Buren, rhp

Born: July 2, 1980. **Ht.:** 6-1. **Wt.:** 220. **Bats:** R. **Throws:** R. **School:** Hattiesburg (Miss.) HS. **Career Transactions:** Selected by Rockies in second round of 1998 draft; signed June 15, 1998 . . . Released by Rockies, March 23, 2003 . . . Signed by Fort Worth (Central), May, 2003 . . . Signed by Cubs, Jan. 24, 2004. **Signed by:** Damon Iannelli (Rockies).

A Rockies second-round pick in 1998, Van Buren led the Arizona League in ERA and strikeouts during his pro debut. But he couldn't get past low Class A, earning him his release in March 2003. He spent a year in the independent Central League, after which Cubs special assistant Gary Hughes (who worked for Colorado in 1999) recommended signing him. He rewarded the Cubs with a system-best 22 saves last year—his first full season in the bullpen—and finished second among minor league relievers in opponent average (.154). Before he got tired late in the season, Van Buren showed explosive stuff at times. Both his 91-93 mph fastball and his slider can be plus pitches, though he needs to improve his consistency when working on back-to-back nights. He also has to throw more strikes, and the effort in his delivery sometimes affects his control. Though he was running on fumes at the end of the year, Van Buren continued to compete well in Triple-A. He'll return there this year and could make his major league debut in the second half.

Year	Club (League)	Class	W	L	ERA	G	GS	CG	SV	IP	H	R	ER	HR	BB	SO	AVG
1998	Rockies (AZL)	R	7	2	2.22	12	11	1	0	65	42	20	16	2	22	92	.182
	Portland (NWL)	A	0	0	3.60	2	2	0	0	10	7	4	4	0	7	9	.212
1999	Asheville (SAL)	A	7	10	4.91	28	28	0	0	143	143	87	78	16	70	133	.266
2000	Portland (NWL)	A	4	5	2.61	13	13	0	0	69	54	27	20	1	30	41	.214
2001	Casper (Pio)	R	3	0	5.32	6	3	1	0	24	25	15	14	2	10	25	.275
	Tri-City (NWL)	A	1	0	7.20	1	1	0	0	5	7	4	4	0	3	2	.304
2002	Asheville (SAL)	A	6	9	4.96	30	17	0	0	107	115	71	59	13	44	88	.276
2003	Fort Worth (Cen)	IND	9	4	3.07	18	18	1	0	111	107	45	38	4	37	113	.255
2004	Iowa (PCL)	AAA	0	0	2.08	3	0	0	1	4	3	1	1	1	0	5	.188
	West Tenn (SL)	AA	3	2	1.87	51	0	0	21	53	23	11	11	2	24	64	.134
	Lansing (Mid)	A	0	1	1.80	3	0	0	0	5	6	1	1	0	5	7	.300
MINOR LEAGUE TOTALS			31	29	3.86	149	75	2	22	485	425	241	208	37	215	466	.237

26 Matt Craig, 3b/1b

Born: April 16, 1981. **Ht.:** 6-3. **Wt.:** 200. **Bats:** S. **Throws:** R. **School:** University of Richmond. **Career Transactions:** Selected by Cubs in third round of 2002 draft; signed June 17, 2002. **Signed by:** Billy Swoope.

The emergence of Richard Lewis at second base and Craig at third base allowed the Cubs to close the Nomar Garciaparra trade last July by including Brendan Harris, who played both positions and had been the best pure hitter in the system. Area scout Billy Swoope signed both Craig and Harris out of Virginia colleges, and they're similar at the plate. A switch-hitter, Craig doesn't always look pretty but has a gift for hitting. Even when he gets jammed, he usually seems to find a way to fist the ball into the outfield for a single. With natural loft in his swing, he has more pop than Harris. Craig's strikeout rate spiked in 2004, though he continued to draw his share of walks. His defensive liabilities may preclude him from playing regularly in the majors. Craig has worked hard at third base, but his hands, arm and agility are below-average. He doesn't run well enough to play the outfield, so first base may be his only option. Craig may have to settle for being a potent bat off the major league bench. Next on his agenda is proving himself in Triple-A.

Year	Club (League)	Class	AVG	G	AB	R	H	2B	3B	HR	RBI	BB	SO	SB	OBP	SLG
2002	Boise (NWL)	A	.193	37	140	19	27	2	0	5	20	12	28	0	.252	.314
2003	Daytona (FSL)	A	.285	119	442	56	126	25	2	11	66	46	87	4	.357	.425
2004	West Tenn (SL)	AA	.275	112	375	63	103	20	4	20	63	49	101	3	.363	.509
MINOR LEAGUE TOTALS			.268	268	957	138	256	47	6	36	149	107	216	7	.344	.442

27 Raul Valdez, lhp

Born: Nov. 27, 1977. **Ht.:** 5-11. **Wt.:** 190. **Bats:** L. **Throws:** L. **Career Transactions:** Signed out of Cuba by Cubs, March 31, 2004. **Signed by:** Jose Serra.

If you like statistics, you love Valdez. He led the DSL in ERA and strikeouts, fanning 20 in one seven-inning stint. However, as a 26-year-old, Valdez should have been in Double-A. Visa restrictions didn't afford the Cuban defector that opportunity. To his credit, he has proven himself against much stiffer competition in the Dominican League. He led the league in strikeouts (46 in 51 innings) in 2003 and in ERA (0.79) in 2004, when he was the league's pitcher of the year. Looking for lefthanded relievers, the Cubs have invited Valdez to big league camp as a nonroster player. There's no consensus on his best pitch. His fastball has fringy velocity at 83-88 mph, but it also has a lot of movement. Both his curveball and changeup grade out as plus pitches on the right day. His ability to locate all three offerings makes them even better. If Valdez doesn't make the major league team, Chicago will try to find a rotation spot for him in the upper minors.

Year	Club (League)	Class	W	L	ERA	G	GS	CG	SV	IP	H	R	ER	HR	BB	SO	AVG
2004	Cubs (DSL)	R	7	2	0.51	16	9	0	0	88	38	8	5	0	8	152	.127
MINOR LEAGUE TOTALS		R	7	2	0.51	16	9	0	0	88	38	8	5	0	8	152	.127

28 Jae-Kuk Ryu, rhp

Born: May 30, 1983. **Ht.:** 6-3. **Wt.:** 210. **Bats:** R. **Throws:** R. **Career Transactions:** Signed out of Korea by Cubs, June 1, 2001. **Signed by:** Leon Lee.

Ryu may be the most frustrating player in the system, especially considering he signed for $1.6 million. He has made his biggest headlines for killing an osprey in April 2003, throwing a baseball that knocked it from its perch at Daytona's Jackie Robinson Ballpark. He also has had run-ins with teammates, leading to questions about his makeup. Ryu opened 2004 on the disabled list with elbow tendinitis and worked just 26 innings. Also plagued by weakness in his lower back, he got hammered in an Arizona Fall League assignment. Ryu has shown the ability to throw three good pitches for strikes. He has a 92-93 mph fastball, a curveball and a changeup that has some run to it. But he needs to get healthy and grow up. Though he'll probably pitch out of the rotation this year in high Class A or Double-A, he may not be more than a reliever in the majors.

Year	Club (League)	Class	W	L	ERA	G	GS	CG	SV	IP	H	R	ER	HR	BB	SO	AVG
2001	Cubs (AZL)	R	1	0	0.61	4	3	0	0	15	11	2	1	0	5	20	.196
2002	Boise (NWL)	A	6	1	3.57	10	10	0	0	53	45	28	21	1	25	56	.223
	Lansing (Mid)	A	1	2	7.11	5	4	0	0	19	26	16	15	1	8	21	.333
2003	Daytona (FSL)	A	0	1	3.05	4	4	0	0	21	14	14	7	1	11	22	.187
	Lansing (Mid)	A	6	1	1.75	11	11	0	0	72	59	19	14	2	19	57	.225
	West Tenn (SL)	AA	2	5	5.43	11	11	1	0	58	63	37	35	3	25	45	.280
2004	West Tenn (SL)	AA	1	0	2.95	14	0	0	0	18	22	8	6	0	10	19	.289
	Iowa (PCL)	AAA	0	0	40.50	1	0	0	0	1	2	4	3	1	1	0	.500
	Boise (NWL)	A	0	2	2.57	5	0	0	0	7	7	3	2	0	5	7	.259
MINOR LEAGUE TOTALS			17	12	3.55	65	43	1	0	263	249	131	104	9	109	247	.248

29 Chadd Blasko, rhp

Born: March 9, 1981. **Ht.:** 6-7. **Wt.:** 220. **Bats:** R. **Throws:** R. **School:** Purdue University. **Career Transactions:** Selected by Cubs in first round (36th overall) of 2002 draft; signed Aug. 31, 2002. **Signed by:** Scott May.

The Cubs had high hopes for the three pitchers they took in 2002's supplemental first round (Blasko, Matt Clanton and Luke Hagerty), but injuries have struck them all. Blasko's rapid emergence was one of the system's most pleasant developments in 2003. His torn labrum was one of its most bitter disappointments last season. He led the Florida State League in ERA during his first full year and seemed poised to push for a big league spot in 2005, but after shoulder surgery he won't be ready for the start of the season. Before he got hurt, Blasko had a lot to offer. He's 6-foot-7 and has a deceptive delivery, which made his low- to mid-90s fastball that much tougher to hit. He used a big curveball as his second pitch and also employed a changeup and slider. Chicago will handle Blasko carefully this year and won't get a true indication as to whether he can regain his stuff until 2006.

Year	Club (League)	Class	W	L	ERA	G	GS	CG	SV	IP	H	R	ER	HR	BB	SO	AVG
2003	Lansing (Mid)	A	0	1	1.64	2	2	0	0	11	10	3	2	0	5	6	.256
	Daytona (FSL)	A	10	5	1.98	24	24	1	0	136	100	33	30	3	43	131	.205
2004	West Tenn (SL)	AA	5	4	5.67	13	13	0	0	67	77	45	42	12	24	65	.292
MINOR LEAGUE TOTALS			15	10	3.11	39	39	1	0	214	187	81	74	15	72	202	.236

30 David Kelton, of

Born: Dec. 17, 1979. **Ht.:** 6-3. **Wt.:** 195. **Bats:** R. **Throws:** R. **School:** Troup County HS, La Grange, Ga. **Career Transactions:** Selected by Cubs in second round of 1998 draft; signed June 3, 1998. **Signed by:** Oneri Fleita.

Signed as a third baseman, Kelton had mental and physical problems making throws from the hot corner, prompting his move to first base in 2002 and the outfield in 2003. Chicago thought fewer defensive responsibilities would help him develop an already promising bat, but Kelton has regressed. He has good bat speed and raw power, but he undermined himself last year by trying to hit homers. He developed an uppercut and got under too many pitches. Controlling the strike zone never has been Kelton's strong suit and he regressed last year. He has average speed and has made progress in the outfield, where he can handle either corner and serve as a fill-in in center field. Kelton is coming off a productive winter in Venezuela, where he finished fourth in homers (12) and RBIs (44), but he's still a longshot in the Cubs' left-field derby. He's also out of options, so if he can't stick on the major league roster he may find himself with a different organization.

Year	Club (League)	Class	AVG	G	AB	R	H	2B	3B	HR	RBI	BB	SO	SB	OBP	SLG
1998	Cubs (AZL)	R	.265	50	181	39	48	7	5	6	29	23	58	16	.353	.459
1999	Lansing (Mid)	A	.269	124	509	75	137	17	4	13	68	39	121	22	.322	.395
2000	Daytona (FSL)	A	.268	132	523	75	140	30	7	18	84	38	120	7	.317	.455
2001	West Tenn (SL)	AA	.313	58	224	33	70	9	4	12	45	24	55	1	.378	.549
2002	West Tenn (SL)	AA	.261	129	498	68	130	28	6	20	79	52	129	12	.332	.462
2003	Iowa (PCL)	AAA	.269	121	442	62	119	24	3	16	67	46	115	8	.338	.446
	Chicago (NL)	MAJ	.167	10	12	1	2	1	0	0	1	0	5	0	.167	.250
2004	Chicago (NL)	MAJ	.100	8	10	1	1	1	0	0	0	0	3	0	.100	.200
	Iowa (PCL)	AAA	.248	121	420	57	104	26	1	19	68	33	92	7	.305	.450
MAJOR LEAGUE TOTALS			.136	18	22	2	3	2	0	0	1	0	8	0	.136	.227
MINOR LEAGUE TOTALS			.267	735	2797	409	748	141	30	104	440	255	690	73	.329	.451

CHICAGO
WHITE SOX

BY **PHIL ROGERS**

Winning now is the goal for the White Sox. That's why general manager Ken Williams traded for veterans Carl Everett and Roberto Alomar in midseason deals in both 2003 and 2004.

That's right, two years in a row Williams has added Everett and Alomar. To acquire Everett twice, the White Sox gave up five prospects to the Rangers and Expos. Williams didn't stop there. He made one of baseball's biggest deals in 2004, acquiring Freddy Garcia from the Mariners for catcher Miguel Olivo and two of Chicago's top prospects, outfielder Jeremy Reed and shortstop Michael Morse.

Williams has traded 17 players who have ranked among the team's top 30 prospects in the last three years. And he's not about to apologize for it. "Two words: nineteen seventeen," Williams said, referring to the last year the White Sox won the World Series. "How many more generations of fans are going to have to wait? I don't want to wait."

It's a risky course for an organization that operates on a tight budget. Yet Williams feels he has little choice because he hasn't been successful in signing free agents.

The White Sox have moved Joe Crede, Willie Harris and **Aaron Rowand** from the farm system to their lineup, while Jon Adkins and Neal Cotts have claimed bullpen roles. But Chicago expected a bigger harvest, only to see outfielder Joe Borchard and pitchers Kris Honel, Corwin Malone and Jon Rauch hampered by injuries and inconsistency. Borchard, who signed for a record $5.3 million in 2000, had another disap-

pointing year in 2004. He started the season at Triple-A Charlotte and batted .174 in 63 big league games after replacing the injured Magglio Ordonez. His strikeout woes extended into the offseason, when his Mexican Pacific League club released him because of his lack of production. Honel made just two starts because of a sore shoulder, while Malone had Tommy John surgery before the season started. Rauch angered Williams by leaving U.S. Cellular Field early after getting hit hard in a May start, then was exiled to Montreal two months later.

There were some positive developments in 2004, however. Righthanders Brandon McCarthy and Sean Tracey took huge steps forward. McCarthy led the minors with 202 strikeouts in 172 innings, while Tracey started to harness the best fastball in the system.

Chicago's last two drafts have provided an infusion of talent. Outfielders Brian Anderson and Ryan Sweeney, the club's first two picks in 2003, played well in big league camp and then had solid 2004 seasons. Anderson advanced to Double-A and may not be that far away from contributing in the majors.

Third baseman Josh Fields, the No. 18 overall pick in 2004, contributed immediately in high Class A. The White Sox had six picks in the first two rounds and used four of them on lefthanders. Gio Gonzalez made the top 10, while Tyler Lumsden, Wes Whisler and Ray Liotta weren't far behind.

TOP 30 PROSPECTS

1. Brian Anderson, of	16. Arnie Munoz, lhp
2. Ryan Sweeney, of	17. Wes Whisler, lhp
3. Brandon McCarthy, rhp	18. Antoin Gray, 2b/3b
4. Josh Fields, 3b	19. Daniel Haigwood, lhp
5. Tadahito Iguchi, 2b	20. Micah Schnurstein, 3b
6. Sean Tracey, rhp	21. Bobby Jenks, rhp
7. Chris Young, of	22. Salvador Sanchez, of
8. Gio Gonzalez, lhp	23. Felix Diaz, rhp
9. Francisco Hernandez, c	24. Jeff Bajenaru, rhp
10. Pedro Lopez, ss	25. Mike Spidale, of
11. Kris Honel, rhp	26. Dwayne Pollok, rhp
12. Ray Liotta, lhp	27. Fabio Castro, lhp
13. Tyler Lumsden, lhp	28. Ryan Rodriguez, lhp
14. Robert Valido, ss	29. Wilson Valdez, ss
15. Casey Rogowski, 1b/of	30. Tom Collaro, of/1b

ORGANIZATION OVERVIEW

General manager: Ken Williams. **Farm director:** David Wilder. **Scouting director:** Duane Shaffer.

2004 PERFORMANCE

Class	Team	League	W	L	Pct.	Finish*	Manager(s)
Majors	Chicago	American	83	79	.512	7th (14)	Ozzie Guillen
Triple-A	Charlotte Knights	International	68	74	.479	9th (14)	Nick Capra
Double-A	Birmingham Barons	Southern	73	66	.525	t-2nd (10)	Razor Shines
High A	Winston-Salem Warthogs	Carolina	74	66	.529	4th (8)	Ken Dominguez/Nick Leyva
Low A	Kannapolis Intimidators	South Atlantic	69	70	.496	10th (16)	Chris Cron
Rookie	Bristol White Sox	Appalachian	27	38	.415	9th (10)	Jerry Hairston
Rookie	Great Falls White Sox	Pioneer	42	33	.560	2nd (8)	John Orton
OVERALL 2004 MINOR LEAGUE RECORD			353	347	.504	13th (30)	

*Finish in overall standings (No. of teams in league).

ORGANIZATION LEADERS

BATTING   *Minimum 250 At-Bats
*AVG	Boomer Berry, Great Falls	.307
R	Casey Rogowski, Winston-Salem	88
H	Bryant Nelson, Charlotte	161
TB	Bryant Nelson, Charlotte	272
2B	Brian Becker, Birmingham/Winston-Salem	38
3B	Ruddy Yan, Birmingham	10
HR	Darren Blakely, Birmingham/Winston-Salem	29
RBI	Brian Becker, Birmingham/Winston-Salem	93
BB	Casey Rogowski, Winston-Salem	91
SO	Chris Young, Kannapolis	146
SB	Ruddy Yan, Birmingham	35
*OBP	Casey Rogowski, Winston-Salem	.401
*SLG	Darren Blakely, Birmingham/Winston-Salem	.573

PITCHING   #Minimum 75 Innings
W	Brandon McCarthy, Birm./Win.-Salem/Kann.	17
L	Rafael Flores, Kannapolis	11
#ERA	Matt Smith, Birmingham	1.83
G	Matt Smith, Birmingham	70
CG	Brandon McCarthy, Birm./Win.-Salem/Kann.	3
SV	Dwayne Pollok, Winston-Salem	38
IP	Brandon McCarthy, Birm./Win.-Salem/Kann.	172
BB	Brian Miller, Winston-Salem/Kannapolis	70
SO	Brandon McCarthy, Birm./Win.-Salem/Kann.	202

BEST TOOLS

Best Hitter for Average	Ryan Sweeney
Best Power Hitter	Josh Fields
Best Strike-Zone Discipline	Casey Rogowski
Fastest Baserunner	Chris Young
Best Athlete	Chris Young
Best Fastball	Sean Tracey
Best Curveball	Gio Gonzalez
Best Slider	Dwayne Pollok
Best Changeup	Brian Miller
Best Control	Brandon McCarthy
Best Defensive Catcher	Chris Stewart
Best Defensive Infielder	Pedro Lopez
Best Infield Arm	Andy Gonzalez
Best Defensive Outfielder	Brian Anderson
Best Outfield Arm	Ryan Sweeney

PROJECTED 2008 LINEUP

Catcher	Francisco Hernandez
First Base	Casey Rogowski
Second Base	Tadahito Iguchi
Third Base	Josh Fields
Shortstop	Juan Uribe
Left Field	Aaron Rowand
Center Field	Brian Anderson
Right Field	Ryan Sweeney

Designated Hitter	Paul Konerko
No. 1 Starter	Freddy Garcia
No. 2 Starter	Mark Buehrle
No. 3 Starter	Brandon McCarthy
No. 4 Starter	Jon Garland
No. 5 Starter	Sean Tracey
Closer	Felix Diaz

LAST YEAR'S TOP 20 PROSPECTS

1. Jeremy Reed, of	11. Brandon McCarthy, rhp
2. Kris Honel, rhp	12. Brian Miller, rhp
3. Neal Cotts, lhp	13. Robert Valido, ss
4. Ryan Sweeney, of	14. Jon Rauch, rhp
5. Joe Borchard, of	15. Enemencio Pacheco, rhp
6. Ryan Wing, lhp	16. Fabio Castro, lhp
7. Brian Anderson, of	17. Mike Morse, ss
8. Shingo Takatsu, rhp	18. Felix Diaz, rhp
9. Chris Young, of	19. Ryan Meaux, lhp
10. Arnie Munoz, lhp	20. Pedro Lopez, 2b/ss

TOP PROSPECTS OF THE DECADE

Year	Player, Pos.	Current Team
1995	Scott Ruffcorn, rhp	Out of baseball
1996	Chris Snopek, ss/3b	Out of baseball
1997	Mike Cameron, of	Mets
1998	Mike Caruso, ss	Long Island (Atlantic)
1999	Carlos Lee, 3b	White Sox
2000	Kip Wells, rhp	Pirates
2001	Jon Rauch, rhp	Expos
2002	Joe Borchard, of	White Sox
2003	Joe Borchard, of	White Sox
2004	Jeremy Reed, of	Mariners

TOP DRAFT PICKS OF THE DECADE

Year	Player, Pos.	Current Team
1995	Jeff Liefer, 3b	Brewers
1996	*Bobby Seay, lhp	Devil Rays
1997	Jason Dellaero, ss	Out of baseball
1998	Kip Wells, rhp	Pirates
1999	Jason Stumm, rhp	White Sox
2000	Joe Borchard, of	White Sox
2001	Kris Honel, rhp	White Sox
2002	Royce Ring, lhp	Mets
2003	Brian Anderson, of	White Sox
2004	Josh Fields, 3b	White Sox

*Did not sign

ALL-TIME LARGEST BONUSES

Joe Borchard, 2000	$5,300,000
Jason Stumm, 1999	$1,750,000
Royce Ring, 2002	$1,600,000
Brian Anderson, 2003	$1,600,000
Josh Fields, 2004	$1,550,000

Chicago WHITE SOX

RANK: **12**

Impact Talent: B

The Sox' big league outfield went through a major makeover this offseason, perhaps in part because top prospects Brian Anderson and Ryan Sweeney both appear close to being everyday regulars. Brandon McCarthy led the minors in strikeouts, still is filling out his 6-foot-7 frame and has such good command that he was more effective the higher the level of competition. Dominican catcher Francisco Hernandez could emerge as one of the minors' top backstops in 2005.

Depth: B

A lack of righthanded starters forced the White Sox to hit that need hard in the 2004 draft. But Chicago's crew of southpaws compares favorably with division rivals such as Cleveland and Minnesota, who also count lefthanders as a strength. First-round pick Josh Fields shores up the organization's greatest need—power bats—and Japanese import Tadahito Iguchi adds depth up the middle.

*Depth charts prepared by **John Manuel** and **Allan Simpson**. Numbers in parentheses indicate prospect rankings.*

LF
Salvador Sanchez (22)
Thomas Collaro (30)
Ricardo Nanita
Brandon Allen
Evan Tartaglia

CF
Brian Anderson (1)
Chris Young (7)
Mike Spidale (25)

RF
Ryan Sweeney (2)
Thomas Brice

3B
Josh Fields (4)
Micah Schnurstein (20)

SS
Pedro Lopez (10)
Robert Valido (14)
Wilson Valdez (29)
Javier Castillo
Andy Gonzalez

2B
Tadahito Iguchi (5)
Antoin Gray (18)
Boomer Berry

1B
Casey Rogowski (15)
Travis Hinton
Chris Kelly

SOURCE of TALENT

Homegrown		Acquired	
College	8	Trades	2
Junior College	2	Rule 5 draft	0
Draft-and-follow	1	Independent leagues	0
High school	10	Free agents/waivers	1
Nondrafted free agents	0		
Foreign	6		

C
Francisco Hernandez (9)
Donny Lucy
Chris Stewart
Adam Ricks

RHP

Starters	Relievers
Brandon McCarthy (3)	Felix Diaz (23)
Sean Tracey (6)	Jeff Bajenaru (24)
Kris Honel (11)	Dwayne Pollok (26)
Bobby Jenks (21)	Matt Smith
Brian Miller	Ehren Wasserman
Eduardo Villacis	Wyatt Allen
Garry Bakker	Josh L. Fields
Grant Hansen	Orionny Lopez
Rafael Flores	Jason Stumm
Lucas Harrell	B.J. LaMura
Adam Russell	

LHP

Starters	Relievers
Gio Gonzalez (8)	Arnie Munoz (16)
Ray Liotta (12)	Fabio Castro (27)
Tyler Lumsden (13)	Ryan Meaux
Dan Haigwood (19)	Dennis Ulacia
Wes Whisler (17)	Jim Bullard
Ryan Rodriguez (28)	
Paulino Reynoso	
Corwin Malone	
Heath Phillips	
Josh Stewart	
Eric Everly	
Tim Murphey	

DRAFT ANALYSIS

2004

Best Pro Debut: LHP Ray Liotta (2) was the top pitching prospect and the ERA leader (2.54) in the Rookie-level Pioneer League. The White Sox had no reservations about sending 3B Josh Fields (1) directly to high Class A, and he justified their confidence by batting .285-7-39 in 66 games.

Best Athlete: A star quarterback at Oklahoma State, Fields set a school record for passing touchdowns (55) and a Cotton Bowl mark for passing yardage (307). LHP Wes Whisler (2) is an intriguing two-way talent. He was the Cape Cod League's top prospect in 2002—as a hitter.

Best Pure Hitter: The White Sox liken Fields to 2003 first-rounder Brian Anderson, describing both as tools guys who know how to play.

Best Raw Power: No Chicago draftee could put on a batting-practice show like Whisler, though his future appears to be on the mound. OF Brandon Allen (5) is very raw but can blast balls a long way.

Fastest Runner: OF Evan Tartaglia blazes from the left side of the plate to first base in 3.95 seconds.

Best Defensive Player: The White Sox thought C Donny Lucy (2) was the best defensive backstop in the draft.

Best Fastball: RHP Nick Lemon (8) doesn't always know where his heater is headed, but he hit 98 mph during the spring and 96 after signing. LHP Tyler Lumsden (1) pitches anywhere from 91-96 mph, while LHP Gio Gonzalez (1) has uncanny command of his fastball (87-90 to 94) for an 18-year-old.

Best Breaking Ball: Gonzalez has an electric curveball that's unhittable when he throws it for strikes. Liotta's out pitch is also

SPORTS ON FILM

Lumsden

his curve.

Most Intriguing Background: OF Kenny Williams Jr.'s (36) father is general manager of the White Sox. OF Daron Roberts' (12) dad Dave was the No. 1 overall pick in the 1972 draft and is a regional crosschecker for the Devil Rays. Both RHP Frank Viola Jr. (29) and C Pete Vuckovich Jr. (48) are the sons of former Cy Young Award winners.

Closest To The Majors: With Joe Crede faltering in the majors, the White Sox won't hesitate to promote Fields when he's ready. He could make his first big league appearance by the end of 2005. Gonzalez is so advanced that he'll make it much sooner than most high schoolers.

Best Late-Round Pick: Line drive-hitting INF Adam Ricks (10) hit .305 with a .411 on-base percentage in the Pioneer League, then shifted to catcher in instructional league. Ricks, who played sparingly behind the plate in college, made good progress.

The One Who Got Away: Chicago signed its first 20 draft choices and lost the rights to just two. As expected, the athletic Williams opted to attend Arizona.

Assessment: The White Sox thought the strength of the draft was lefthanded pitching, and after getting a quality position player with their top pick they wanted to load up on southpaws. Mission accomplished. They began with Fields, then grabbed Lumsden, Gonzalez, Whisler and Liotta before the third round.

2003 OFs Brian Anderson (1) and Ryan Sweeney (2) are Chicago's top two prospects. SS Robert Valido (4) could emerge as the shortstop of the future. **GRADE:** B

2002 The White Sox already have traded their top three picks: LHP Royce Ring (1), OF Jeremy Reed (2) and RHP Josh Rupe (3). They'll miss Reed, but got Freddy Garcia in that deal, and RHPs Brandon McCarthy (17) and Sean Tracey (8) are their two best mound prospects. **GRADE:** B+

2001 While RHP Kris Honel (1) is getting sidetracked by injuries, OF Chris Young (16) is blossoming into an intriguing multitooled player. The other first-rounder, RHP Wyatt Allen (1), isn't going to make it. **GRADE:** C+

2000 The best professional athlete has turned out to be Eagles wide receiver Freddie Mitchell (50) because OF Joe Borchard (1) is looking more and more like a $5.3 million bust. SS Mike Morse (3) had a career year in 2004 and was included in the Garcia trade. **GRADE:** D

Draft analysis prepared by Jim Callis. Numbers in parentheses indicate draft rounds.

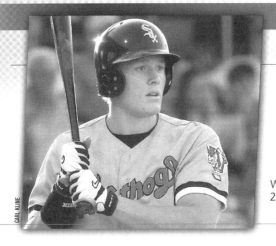

CARL KLINE

Brian
ANDERSON

Born: March 11, 1982.
Ht.: 6-2. **Wt.:** 205.
Bats: R. **Throws:** R.
School: University of Arizona.
Career Transactions: Selected by White Sox in first round (15th overall) of 2003 draft; signed June 19, 2003.
Signed by: John Kazanas.

Anderson had a roller-coaster career at Arizona, where he earned Freshman All-America honors as a two-way star in 2001. But he tailed off as a sophomore, in part because of knee and wrist injuries. When he gave up pitching and was fully healthy in 2003, his stock soared and the White Sox made him the 15th overall pick in the draft. After signing for $1.6 million, he launched his pro career by hitting .388 at Rookie-level Great Falls, only to have his pro debut end after 13 games when a recurrence of the wrist injury required minor surgery. He bounced back so strongly in 2004 that the White Sox had enough confidence to include outfielder Jeremy Reed—who preceded Anderson as the No. 1 prospect in the organization a year ago—in a midseason trade for Freddy Garcia. Anderson played a strong center field at high Class A Winston-Salem and Double-A Birmingham, hitting well at the lower level and holding his own while making adjustments following his promotion. He missed the last two weeks of the season with a groin strain.

Anderson is a good athlete who knows how to use his tools. He uses the entire field, showing both the ability to launch balls to left field and the willingness to go to right. He came out of college with solid plate discipline and has had no difficulty making consistent contact as a pro. If he has to move to an outfield corner, he projects to hit with enough power to be an asset at that position. Anderson runs well and has enough speed to play center field. He has enough arm to play anywhere in the outfield, as he threw in the low-90s as a reliever at Arizona. He thrives on competition and was not intimidated by the stiffer competition when he moved up to Double-A.

Minor injuries have continually bothered Anderson, who was limited at the end of the regular season and in the AFL by a groin strain. He appears to have a high-maintenance body. He needs to get more at-bats so he can continue to lock in the swing changes he started to incorporate as a junior under the guidance of Wildcats coach Andy Lopez. Anderson may not be more than adequate in center field, a position where adequate usually isn't good enough. Some scouts actually rate him as a below-average runner, and he needs to improve routes to balls.

Anderson could get to the big leagues in the second half of 2005 if the White Sox have an outfield opening. But they'd prefer for him to spend a full season at Triple-A Charlotte and prepare to become a regular at U.S. Cellular Field in 2006. Having seen $5.3 million man Joe Borchard struggle to establish himself, Chicago might take it a little slower with Anderson in hopes that he can stick around when he gets his first taste of the big leagues. Whether he plays in center or right field likely will depend on whether Aaron Rowand can maintain the offensive and defensive productivity he showed in 2004.

Year	Club (League)	Class	AVG	G	AB	R	H	2B	3B	HR	RBI	BB	SO	SB	OBP	SLG
2003	Great Falls (Pio)	R	.388	13	49	6	19	2	1	2	13	9	10	3	.492	.592
2004	Winston-Salem (Car)	A	.319	69	254	43	81	22	4	8	46	29	44	10	.394	.531
	Birmingham (SL)	AA	.270	48	185	26	50	9	3	4	27	19	30	3	.346	.416
MINOR LEAGUE TOTALS			.307	130	488	75	150	33	8	14	86	57	84	16	.386	.494

Ryan Sweeney, of

Born: Feb. 20, 1985. **Ht.:** 6-3. **Wt.:** 200. **Bats:** L. **Throws:** L. **School:** Xavier HS, Cedar Rapids, Iowa. **Career Transactions:** Selected by White Sox in second round of 2003 draft; signed July 12, 2003. **Signed by:** Nathan Durst.

The White Sox stole Sweeney in 2003's second round after a lackluster showcase performance on the eve of the draft hurt his stock. When injuries created a need for an outfielder in big league camp last spring, they summoned Sweeney—who responded by batting .367. Sox executive adviser Roland Hemond says he gets the same goosebumps watching Sweeney that he once did watching a young Harold Baines. Sweeney is athletic as well as a natural hitter with a textbook swing. He has few holes and uses the entire field. He has gap power and should add pop as he climbs toward Chicago. He also has a plus right-field arm. Some scouts in the high Class A Carolina League questioned Sweeney's bat speed. He opened the season slowly and made matters worse by pressing, causing concerns about his patience. He's still improving as a right fielder. Sweeney should advance to Double-A after holding his own as one of the youngest players in the Carolina League. He could get to Chicago quickly because manager Ozzie Guillen and hitting coach Greg Walker are absolutely in love with his potential.

Year	Club (League)	Class	AVG	G	AB	R	H	2B	3B	HR	RBI	BB	SO	SB	OBP	SLG
2003	Bristol (Appy)	R	.313	19	67	11	21	3	0	2	5	7	10	3	.387	.448
	Great Falls (Pio)	R	.353	10	34	0	12	2	0	0	4	2	3	0	.389	.412
2004	Winston-Salem (Car)	A	.283	134	515	71	146	22	3	7	66	40	65	8	.342	.379
MINOR LEAGUE TOTALS			.291	163	616	82	179	27	3	9	75	49	78	11	.350	.388

Brandon McCarthy, rhp

Born: July 7, 1983. **Ht.:** 6-7. **Wt.:** 180. **Bats:** R. **Throws:** R. **School:** Lamar (Colo.) CC. **Career Transactions:** Selected by White Sox in 17th round of 2002 draft; signed June 7, 2002. **Signed by:** Joe Butler/John Kazanas.

Scouts John Kazanas and Joe Butler did an excellent job when they locked onto McCarthy after he had gone 12-0 and struck out 14 per nine innings in junior college in 2002. He led the Rookie-level Arizona and Pioneer leagues in strikeouts in his first two pro seasons, then topped the entire minors with 202 whiffs in 2004. McCarthy's best pitch is a two-seam fastball that generally parks around 90 mph, and he has a four-seamer that hits 92-93. He also has a plus curveball. His height allows him to deliver pitches on a steep downward plane, and he throws strikes at will with an easily repeatable delivery. McCarthy has sailed to Double-A without a hitch. He can get better with his changeup, and he has started to make progress and use it more often. Chicago couldn't find a fifth starter in 2004, and McCarthy could jump into consideration with a strong spring. He'll probably return to Double-A but won't stay long if he picks up where he left off.

Year	Club (League)	Class	W	L	ERA	G	GS	CG	SV	IP	H	R	ER	HR	BB	SO	AVG
2002	White Sox (AZL)	R	4	4	2.76	14	14	0	0	78	78	40	24	6	15	79	.255
2003	Great Falls (Pio)	R	9	4	3.65	16	15	1	0	101	105	49	41	7	15	125	.263
2004	Birmingham (SL)	AA	3	1	3.46	4	4	0	0	26	23	10	10	2	6	29	.235
	Winston-Salem (Car)	A	6	0	2.08	8	8	0	0	52	31	12	12	3	3	60	.168
	Kannapolis (SAL)	A	8	5	3.61	15	15	3	0	94	80	41	38	10	21	113	.232
MINOR LEAGUE TOTALS			30	14	3.20	57	56	4	0	351	317	152	125	28	60	406	.238

Josh Fields, 3b

Born: Dec. 14, 1982. **Ht.:** 6-2. **Wt.:** 210. **Bats:** R. **Throws:** R. **School:** Oklahoma State University. **Career Transactions:** Selected by White Sox in first round (18th overall) of 2004 draft; signed June 16, 2004. **Signed by:** Alex Slattery/Nathan Durst.

A two-sport star at Oklahoma State, Fields set a school record for career passing touchdowns (55) and a Cotton Bowl mark for passing yards (307). He comes from athletic stock as his mother Rhonda was the first female athlete to earn a full scholarship to Oklahoma State. He gave up football to sign for $1.55 million as the 18th overall pick in the 2004 draft. He made a smooth transition to pro ball, helping Winston-Salem recover from a poor first half to reach the Carolina League playoffs. Fields is a potentially dynamic hitter, combining strength and bat speed to generate power. He drives the ball to all fields and should hit for average as well as extra bases. He has a hard-nosed approach and strong work ethic. He has a plus arm at third base. Fields spent just two seasons as a third baseman in college and needs work on his fielding, especially his footwork and his release. He can get impatient at the plate and pile up strikeouts. He's a below-average runner. He likely will spend 2005 in Double-A. The White Sox are growing increasingly disappointed with Joe Crede and are looking to Fields to provide an alternative—the sooner the better.

Year	Club (League)	Class	AVG	G	AB	R	H	2B	3B	HR	RBI	BB	SO	SB	OBP	SLG
2004	Winston-Salem (Car)	A	.285	66	256	36	73	12	4	7	39	18	74	0	.333	.445
MINOR LEAGUE TOTALS			.285	66	256	36	73	12	4	7	39	18	74	0	.333	.445

5 Tadahito Iguchi, 2b

Born: Dec. 4, 1974. **Ht.:** 5-10. **Wt.:** 185. **Bats:** R. **Throws:** R. **Career Transactions:** Selected by Fukuoka Daiei Hawks in first round of 1997 Japan draft . . . Signed by White Sox, Jan. 27, 2005. **Signed by:** Ken Williams.

While serving as the cornerstone of manager Sadaharu Oh's Fukuoka powerhouse in Japan, Iguchi eyed the challenge of playing in America, coming close to deals as a posted free agent before saying sayonora as a true free agent this winter. He signed a two-year, $4.95 million deal that includes a $2.3 million salary for 2005 and a $3.25 million club option for 2007. A four-time all-star in eight Pacific League seasons, Iguchi won three Japanese Gold Gloves and two stolen-base titles. He consistently has hit for power and took a huge jump as a hitter in the last two seasons. Few second baseman are as athletic or as complete. He uses his power to drive in runs and his speed to score them. He killed left-handers in Japan and became dangerous against righties as well. Iguchi is a surehanded fielder with average range. He totaled 22 errors in three seasons after moving from shortstop to second base. Iguchi's only liability is his arm, which hasn't been the same since a shoulder injury in 2002. That forced his move from shortstop and leaves him below-average turning the double play. Countryman Shingo Takatsu took over as their closer last season, and the White Sox think Iguchi could make a greater impact. He could be a rare 20-20 second baseman and a Rookie of the Year contender. Unlike Hideki Matsui and Kaz Matsui, he played in a pitcher's park in Japan and moves to a hitter's paradise. Willie Harris could take at-bats away against tough righthanders, but Iguchi should claim the bulk of Chicago's playing time at second base.

Year	Club (League)	Class	AVG	G	AB	R	H	2B	3B	HR	RBI	BB	SO	SB	OBP	SLG
1997	Fukuoka (PL)	JAP	.203	76	217	31	44	6	3	8	23	24	67	3	.304	.369
1998	Fukuoka (PL)	JAP	.221	135	421	58	93	18	4	21	66	28	121	12	.280	.432
1999	Fukuoka (PL)	JAP	.224	116	370	38	83	15	1	14	47	38	113	14	.310	.384
2000	Fukuoka (PL)	JAP	.247	54	162	21	40	9	2	7	23	15	29	5	.317	.457
2001	Fukuoka (PL)	JAP	.261	140	552	104	144	26	1	30	97	61	117	44	.346	.475
2002	Fukuoka (PL)	JAP	.259	114	428	64	111	14	1	18	53	27	84	21	.317	.423
2003	Fukuoka (PL)	JAP	.340	135	515	112	175	37	1	27	109	81	81	42	.438	.573
2004	Fukuoka (PL)	JAP	.333	124	510	96	170	34	2	24	89	47	90	18	.394	.549

6 Sean Tracey, rhp

Born: Nov. 14, 1980. **Ht.:** 6-3. **Wt.:** 205. **Bats:** L. **Throws:** R. **School:** UC Irvine. **Career Transactions:** Selected by White Sox in eighth round of 2002 draft; signed June 12, 2002. **Signed by:** Joe Butler/Matt Hattabaugh.

No one in the system has a better arm than Tracey, considered something of a project coming out of UC Irvine. He flashed his potential in his first two seasons but also had control problems. He turned a corner in 2004, thanks largely to his work with Winston-Salem pitching coach J.R. Perdew. Though Tracey can run his 93-94 mph fastball up to 97, his biggest asset may be his competitiveness. Winston-Salem manager Nick Leyva called him an animal, saying he'd pitch "every night if I let him." He has the basic Kevin Brown package: a hard sinker that gets grounders and a four-seam fastball that gets strikeouts up in the zone. He also uses a hard slider. Tracey smoothed out his mechanics and gained confidence as the 2004 season went on. Tracey led the Carolina League in walks and hit batters (23) but showed improvement over 2003. His mechanics require attention and make it difficult for him to throw a consistent slider or changeup. A better changeup would complement his power stuff. A full season at Double-A is the next step for Tracey. He has the arm strength to become an impact starter or power closer.

Year	Club (League)	Class	W	L	ERA	G	GS	CG	SV	IP	H	R	ER	HR	BB	SO	AVG
2002	Bristol (Appyy)	R	5	2	3.02	13	12	0	0	66	57	27	22	4	19	50	.241
2003	Kannapolis (SAL)	A	2	7	9.50	14	9	0	0	42	51	54	44	4	46	28	.305
	Great Falls (Pio)	R	8	5	3.69	16	12	1	0	93	90	45	38	5	22	74	.259

Year	Club (League)	Class																
2004	Winston-Salem (Car)	A	9	8	2.73	27	27	0	0	148	109	60	45	5	69	130	.210
MINOR LEAGUE TOTALS			24	22	3.85	70	60	1	0	348	307	186	149	18	156	282	.242

Chris Young, of

Born: Sept. 5, 1983. **Ht.:** 6-2. **Wt.:** 170. **Bats:** R. **Throws:** R. **School:** Bellaire (Texas) HS. **Career Transactions:** Selected by White Sox in 16th round of 2001 draft; signed Aug. 19, 2001. **Signed by:** Joe Butler/Paul Provas.

A star at national high school power Bellaire, Young lasted until the 16th round of the 2001 draft because he was rail-thin. He signed late that summer and spent two years in Rookie ball before making his full-season debut in 2004. He was inconsistent but his final numbers were proof he's worth the effort that will be required to smooth out his rough edges. While Young still hasn't bulked up, he's strong and has nearly as much raw power as anyone in the system. He uses his top-of-the-line speed to turn singles into doubles and to put pressure on pitchers. Some White Sox officials already consider him a major league-caliber center fielder. Young often gets overly aggressive at the plate, exacerbating his difficulties at making contact. He has struck out in 27 percent of his pro at-bats and must reduce that number to make better use of his speed and power. His arm strength is below average. Ticketed for high Class A in 2005, Young is somewhat reminiscent of former White Sox farmhand Mike Cameron. Chicago would love to see him reach the majors in 2007.

Year	Club (League)	Class	AVG	G	AB	R	H	2B	3B	HR	RBI	BB	SO	SB	OBP	SLG
2002	White Sox (AZL)	R	.217	55	184	26	40	13	1	5	17	19	54	7	.308	.380
2003	Bristol (Appy)	R	.290	64	238	47	69	18	3	7	28	23	40	21	.357	.479
	Great Falls (Pio)	R	.176	10	34	5	6	3	0	0	0	1	10	0	.200	.265
2004	Kannapolis (SAL)	A	.261	136	467	83	122	31	5	24	56	67	146	31	.365	.503
MINOR LEAGUE TOTALS			.257	265	923	161	237	65	9	36	101	110	250	59	.346	.464

Gio Gonzalez, lhp

Born: Sept. 19, 1985. **Ht.:** 5-11. **Wt.:** 180. **Bats:** R. **Throws:** L. **School:** Monsignor Pace HS, Miami. **Career Transactions:** Drafted by White Sox in first round (38th overall) of 2004 draft; signed June 9, 2004. **Signed by:** Jose Ortega.

A top pitching prospect since he won Florida 6-A state title games at Miami's Hialeah High as a freshman and sophomore, Gonzalez transferred to private Monsignor Pace High for his senior season. The White Sox might not have been able to grab him with the No. 38 pick had he not been dismissed from the team following a dispute between his mother and the coach over his brother's lack of playing time. He signed for $850,000. Gonzalez has an advanced feel for pitching for someone so young, with good command of a nice collection of pitches. His 87-90 mph fastball peaks at 94, but his out pitch is a tight curveball he throws in any count. He also has a decent changeup. Because he does not have a powerful build, some scouts wonder about Gonzalez' durability. He carries himself with an air of cockiness that could get tiresome, especially if he struggles. Gonzalez handled low Class A in his pro debut but probably will begin 2005 back in Kannapolis. He should move faster than most high school pitchers.

Year	Club (League)	Class	W	I	FRA	G	GS	CG	SV	IP	H	R	ER	HR	BB	SO	AVG
2004	Kannapolis (SAL)	A	1	2	3.76	8	8	0	0	41	39	20	17	1	20	34	.244
	Bristol (Appy)	R	1	2	2.25	7	6	0	0	24	17	8	6	0	8	36	.198
MINOR LEAGUE TOTALS			2	4	3.20	15	14	0	0	65	56	28	23	1	28	70	.228

Francisco Hernandez, c

Born: Feb. 4, 1986. **Ht.:** 5-9. **Wt.:** 160. **Bats:** S. **Throws:** R. **Career Transactions:** Signed out of Dominican Republic by White Sox, July 30, 2002. **Signed by:** Denny Gonzalez/Miguel Ibarra.

After Hernandez batted .296 with six homers in his pro debut in the Rookie-level Dominican Summer League in 2003, he was rewarded with a visa. He flashed tremendous potential in his first season in the United States, ranking second in the Rookie-level Appalachian League in batting and throwing out basestealers (33 percent). Though he's slightly built, Hernandez is a skilled switch-hitter with a strong arm. He's solid from both sides of the plate and has surprising power for his size. He has the ability to make adjustments, which should keep him out of slumps. His receiving, blocking and game-calling also earn praise. Hernandez needs polish behind the plate. Chicago is trying to get him to quicken his release. He sometimes chases bad pitches, something more advanced pitchers can exploit more easily. The White Sox believe Hernandez can be an all-star catcher, something they haven't had since 1991 (Carlton Fisk) and something they've never developed on their own. He's ready for a full season in low Class A.

Year	Club (League)	Class	AVG	G	AB	R	H	2B	3B	HR	RBI	BB	SO	SB	OBP	SLG
2003	White Sox (DSL)	R	.296	66	216	34	64	14	0	6	29	39	23	9	.412	.444
2004	Bristol (Appy)	R	.326	53	181	32	59	13	1	5	30	13	32	0	.372	.492
	Kannapolis (SAL)	A	.267	4	15	0	4	1	0	0	0	1	3	0	.313	.333
MINOR LEAGUE TOTALS			.308	123	412	66	127	28	1	11	59	53	58	9	.393	.465

10 Pedro Lopez, ss

Born: April 28, 1984. **Ht.:** 6-1. **Wt.:** 160. **Bats:** R. **Throws:** R. **Career Transactions:** Signed out of Dominican Republic by White Sox, Sept. 14, 2000. **Signed by:** Denny Gonzalez.

Because he always played alongside Andy Gonzalez, Lopez spent much of his first three pro seasons as a second baseman. Farm director Dave Wilder decided it was time to separate the two in 2004, allowing them both to play shortstop. Lopez made the most of that chance, flashing plus fielding skills while continuing to show promise as a hitter. Lopez' advanced bat control had been his calling card, but now his fielding skills draw him more attention. He has plus range and reliable hands. He has shown the ability to hit for average, make contact and use the whole field, and he started to drive more pitches during instructional league. He won't impress anyone with his arm strength, but Lopez' quick release allows him to make plays. While he has decent speed, he doesn't have much basestealing aptitude. He rarely swings and misses, but his walks and extra-base hits are infrequent as well. Birmingham's leading hitter (.357) during the Southern League playoffs, Lopez will return to Double-A. He should get lots of big league attention in spring training, and possibly in September.

Year	Club (League)	Class	AVG	G	AB	R	H	2B	3B	HR	RBI	BB	SO	SB	OBP	SLG
2001	White Sox (AZL)	R	.312	50	199	26	62	11	3	1	19	16	24	12	.359	.412
2002	Bristol (Appy)	R	.319	63	260	42	83	11	0	0	35	20	27	22	.370	.362
2003	Kannapolis (SAL)	A	.264	109	390	40	103	23	0	0	33	26	43	24	.314	.323
	Winston-Salem (Car)	A	.231	4	13	1	3	0	0	0	0	1	0	0	.286	.231
2004	Winston-Salem (Car)	A	.292	112	432	62	126	13	0	4	35	23	35	12	.331	.350
	Birmingham (SL)	AA	.217	7	23	3	5	0	1	0	0	5	2	2	.379	.304
MINOR LEAGUE TOTALS			.290	345	1317	174	382	58	4	5	122	91	131	72	.338	.352

11 Kris Honel, rhp

Born: Nov. 7, 1982. **Ht.:** 6-5. **Wt.:** 190. **Bats:** R. **Throws:** R. **School:** Providence Catholic HS, New Lenox, Ill. **Career Transactions:** Selected by White Sox in first round (16th overall) of 2001 draft; signed June 14, 2001. **Signed by:** Ken Stauffer/Nathan Durst.

The organization's top pitching prospect a year ago, Honel took the mound just three more times after an Opening Day 2004 start in Double-A. Initially expected to miss about a week, he struggled with shoulder tendinitis all season. Honel's knuckle-curve made him the 16th overall pick in 2001, the earliest an Illinois high school pitcher was drafted since Bob Kipper went eighth 19 years earlier. It has a sharp break and he generally can throw it for strikes in any count. He has good command and challenges hitters. Velocity seems to be a constant struggle for Honel. He pitched in the high 80s in 2002 before climbing to the low 90s in 2003. Chicago thinks his shoulder problems stemmed from bulking up and over-throwing. He developed bad habits that put stress on his shoulder. His changeup is a clear third pitch. The White Sox are crossing their fingers that Honel comes to spring training healthy and ready to pitch in Double-A. They've lowered their expectations for him, counting on him being no more than an end-of-the-rotation starter, no earlier than mid-2006.

Year	Club (League)	Class	W	L	ERA	G	GS	CG	SV	IP	H	R	ER	HR	BB	SO	AVG
2001	White Sox (AZL)	R	2	0	1.80	3	1	0	0	10	9	3	2	0	3	8	.257
	Bristol (Appy)	R	2	3	3.13	8	8	0	0	46	41	19	16	4	9	45	.240
2002	Kannapolis (SAL)	A	9	8	2.82	26	26	0	0	153	128	57	48	12	52	152	.228
	Winston-Salem (Car)	A	0	0	1.69	1	1	0	0	5	3	2	1	0	3	8	.150
2003	Winston-Salem (Car)	A	9	7	3.11	24	24	3	0	133	122	51	46	7	42	122	.248
	Birmingham (SL)	AA	1	0	3.75	2	2	0	0	12	9	6	5	2	6	13	.205
2004	Birmingham (SL)	AA	0	1	9.00	3	1	0	0	6	4	6	6	1	5	7	.200
	Bristol (Appy)	R	0	0	108.00	1	1	0	0	0	1	4	4	0	3	0	.500
MINOR LEAGUE TOTALS			23	19	3.15	68	64	3	0	366	317	148	128	26	123	355	.236

12 Ray Liotta, lhp

Born: April 3, 1983. **Ht.:** 6-3. **Wt.:** 220. **Bats:** L. **Throws:** L. **School:** Gulf Coast (Fla.) CC. **Career Transactions:** Selected by White Sox in second round of 2004 draft; signed June 11, 2004. **Signed by:** Warren Hughes.

Unwilling to wait for the 2005 draft, Liotta transferred from Tulane to Gulf Coast (Fla.) CC for his sophomore season. The decision paid off when the White Sox selected him in the second round and signed him for $499,000. He responded with a strong debut, leading the Pioneer League in ERA and turning in more solid work in instructional league. Liotta has a strong body and has improved his conditioning, helping him to deliver low-90s fastballs. His curveball is his out pitch, and he showed more command of his breeder—which has drawn comparisons to Barry Zito's—as a pro than he did in college. He has sound mechanics, though his motion lacks deception and his fastball sometimes straightens out. He spent the fall working to improve his changeup. He probably will move into the low Class A rotation in 2005, but he could get consideration for high Class A.

Year	Club (League)	Class	W	L	ERA	G	GS	CG	SV	IP	H	R	ER	HR	BB	SO	AVG
2004	Great Falls (Pio)	R	5	1	2.54	14	11	0	0	64	59	27	18	1	28	65	.248
MINOR LEAGUE TOTALS			5	1	2.54	14	11	0	0	64	59	27	18	1	28	65	.248

13 Tyler Lumsden, lhp

Born: May 9, 1983. **Ht.:** 6-4. **Wt.:** 205. **Bats:** R. **Throws:** L. **School:** Clemson University. **Career Transactions:** Selected by White Sox in first round (34th overall) of 2004 draft; signed June 11, 2004. **Signed by:** Nick Hostetler.

The White Sox can't wait to see what they can get from a rested Lumsden. A fifth-round pick by the Marlins out of high school, he went four rounds higher after three years at Clemson. Signed for $975,000, he spent most his first pro summer in the bullpen to give his arm a break. He draws comparisons to Andy Pettitte with his size and aggressiveness. Lumsden usually throw his fastball at 91-92 mph but can get up to 95-96. He even has been clocked at 80 mph throwing righthanded. Lumsden throws a sharp-breaking curveball, though it usually moves out of the strike zone and he has to rely on hitters to chase it. He also has a cut fastball with slider action that makes lefthanders look silly, as well as a decent changeup. Lumsden could move quickly if he throws strikes. He'll move back to the rotation this year, which he may begin by returning to high Class A.

Year	Club (League)	Class	W	L	ERA	G	GS	CG	SV	IP	H	R	ER	HR	BB	SO	AVG
2004	Winston-Salem (Car)	A	3	1	4.12	15	3	0	0	39	45	25	18	2	20	31	.283
MINOR LEAGUE TOTALS			3	1	4.12	15	3	0	0	39	45	25	18	2	20	31	.283

14 Robert Valido, ss

Born: May 16, 1985. **Ht.:** 6-2. **Wt.:** 180. **Bats:** R. **Throws:** R. **School:** Coral Park HS, Miami. **Career Transactions:** Selected by White Sox in fourth round of 2003 draft; signed June 4, 2003. **Signed by:** Jose Ortega.

Not many 18-year-old shortstops get a chance to play in a full-season league. Valido was assigned to the low Class A South Atlantic League in his first full year as a pro and held his own against college players and more experienced pros. He stood out in instructional league with his graceful fielding. Valido has a strong arm and soft hands but sometimes tries to force the action, resulting in errors. He makes good contact at the plate and is a skilled bunter. The challenge for him will be to get on base often enough to use his speed as a weapon. He's good enough in the field to project as a future big leaguer but his progress at the plate will determine if he can play every day. He won't ever hit for much power. The White Sox haven't had a homegrown regular as their primary shortstop since they traded Bucky Dent to the Yankees after 1976. Along with Pedro Lopez, Valido has a chance to end the drought. He'll spend this year in high Class A.

Year	Club (League)	Class	AVG	G	AB	R	H	2B	3B	HR	RBI	BB	SO	SB	OBP	SLG
2003	Bristol (Appy)	R	.307	58	215	39	66	15	2	6	31	17	28	17	.364	.479
2004	Kannapolis (SAL)	A	.251	123	458	66	115	25	0	4	44	36	59	28	.313	.332
MINOR LEAGUE TOTALS			.269	181	673	105	181	40	2	10	75	53	87	45	.329	.379

15 Casey Rogowski, 1b/of

Born: May 1, 1981. **Ht.:** 6-4. **Wt.:** 250. **Bats:** L. **Throws:** L. **School:** Catholic Central HS, Redford, Mich. **Career Transactions:** Selected by White Sox in 13th round of 1999 draft; signed June 22, 1999. **Signed by:** Nathan Durst.

Rogowski was a top all-around athlete as a high school athlete in Michigan. He won the state's Mr. Baseball award, played on two football state championship teams and captured

Michigan's heavyweight wrestling title. He has paid his dues in a slow climb up the ladder, showing promise at low Class A in 2001 before being slowed by a shoulder injury in 2002 and spending most of three years in high Class A. He finally put up big numbers again in 2004, showing both power and strong strike-zone judgment. Rogowski moves better than most players his size and has reached double figures in steals for five straight seasons. The White Sox have given him some time in left field, and he also played there in the Arizona Fall League. He never has hit for much of an average, and Rogowski will have to prove he can handle more advanced pitching and start to move more quickly toward Chicago. He'll get the chance to do that this season in Dobule-A. The White Sox haven't developed a quality lefthanded hitter since Robin Ventura, which increases the attention being paid Rogowski.

Year	Club (League)	Class	AVG	G	AB	R	H	2B	3B	HR	RBI	BB	SO	SB	OBP	SLG
1999	White Sox (AZL)	R	.288	52	160	23	46	7	2	0	27	26	34	2	.384	.356
2000	Burlington (Mid)	A	.231	122	412	62	95	19	1	6	41	47	89	11	.315	.325
2001	Kannapolis (SAL)	A	.287	130	439	66	126	18	3	14	69	62	95	16	.382	.437
2002	White Sox (AZL)	R	.484	8	31	4	15	6	0	2	8	1	5	2	.485	.871
	Winston-Salem (Car)	A	.255	55	184	27	47	5	0	3	23	28	46	16	.358	.332
2003	Winston-Salem (Car)	A	.246	116	357	46	88	20	1	7	38	53	73	18	.354	.367
2004	Winston-Salem (Car)	A	.286	136	465	88	133	28	2	18	90	91	94	16	.401	.471
MINOR LEAGUE TOTALS			.269	619	2048	316	550	103	9	50	296	308	436	81	.368	.401

16 Arnie Munoz, lhp

Born: June 21, 1982. **Ht.:** 5-9. **Wt.:** 170. **Bats:** L. **Throws:** L. **Career Transactions:** Signed out of Dominican Republic by White Sox, Dec. 20, 1998. **Signed by:** Denny Gonzalez.

When Munoz struggled in 2003, the White Sox wrote it off because he had pitched too much while starring in the Dominican Winter League during the offseason. But they don't know what to think about his 2004 season, which turned into a major bust after a promising start. He returned to Double-A to get a trial as a starter and was lights out, earning a big league start on June 19. Munoz gave up 11 runs in three innings in his big league debut against the Expos and never recovered, combining for a 6.43 ERA between the big leagues and Triple-A. Munoz' dynamite curveball lacked its usual sharpness and he lost track of the strike zone at the upper levels. Scouts say he needs to regain confidence in his 90-mph fastball, and his slider and changeup still have plenty of room for improvement. Munoz still is just 22 but is at a crossroads. His long-term future figures to be in the bullpen.

Year	Club (League)	Class	W	L	ERA	G	GS	CG	SV	IP	H	R	ER	HR	BB	SO	AVG
1999	White Sox (AZL)	R	0	2	5.25	14	0	0	1	12	13	10	7	1	8	12	.255
2000	Burlington (Mid)	A	2	3	6.81	22	0	0	0	38	45	34	29	2	25	44	.294
2001	Kannapolis (SAL)	A	6	3	2.49	60	0	0	12	80	41	24	22	2	42	115	.161
2002	Birmingham (SL)	AA	6	0	2.61	51	0	0	6	72	62	29	21	6	29	78	.231
2003	Charlotte (IL)	AAA	4	3	4.75	49	0	0	6	55	52	35	29	7	27	63	.254
2004	Charlotte (IL)	AAA	2	6	5.68	13	13	0	0	70	81	48	44	11	29	60	.288
	Birmingham (SL)	AA	7	2	2.05	13	13	0	0	75	52	24	17	1	22	68	.195
	Chicago (AL)	MAJ	0	1	10.05	11	1	0	0	14	20	16	16	4	12	11	.339
MAJOR LEAGUE TOTALS			0	1	10.05	11	1	0	0	14	20	16	16	4	12	11	.339
MINOR LEAGUE TOTALS			27	19	3.79	222	26	0	25	402	346	204	169	30	182	440	.234

17 Wes Whisler, lhp/dh

Born: April. 7, 1983. **Ht.:** 6-5. **Wt.:** 235. **Bats:** L. **Throws:** L. **School:** UCLA. **Career Transactions:** Selected by White Sox in 2nd round of 2004 draft; signed June 22, 2004. **Signed by:** Matt Hattabugh.

A natural hitter with power, Whisler ranked as the top prospect in the Cape Cod League after his freshman season but regressed at the plate the next two seasons at UCLA. He pitched out of the Bruins rotation but never dominated. Despite his underwhelming college career, he still went in the second round of the 2004 draft because of the collection of tools that allowed him to play both ways. The White Sox were sold on his great build and durability, not to mention his low-90s fastball. During his pro debut, he threw four pitches for strikes, including a hard slider, and had no problem fitting in after a promotion to high Class A. He touched the mid-90s with his fastball and showed a willingness to work the inside half of the plate. Chicago allowed Whisler to get at-bats as a DH at Kannapolis, and the organization remains split on where his future lies. His light-tower power is so intriguing that he could remain a two-way player for a bit longer as the White Sox decide whether his ceiling is higher on the mound or at the plate. He could reach Double-A during his first full pro season.

Year	Club (League)	Class	AVG	G	AB	R	H	2B	3B	HR	RBI	BB	SO	SB	OBP	SLG
2004	Kannapolis (SAL)	A	.289	11	38	2	11	2	0	1	5	1	7	0	.308	.421
MINOR LEAGUE TOTALS			.289	11	38	2	11	2	0	1	5	1	7	0	.308	.421

Year	Club (League)	Class	W	L	ERA	G	GS	CG	SV	IP	H	R	ER	HR	BB	SO	AVG
2004	Kannapolis (SAL)	A	4	1	3.38	10	7	0	0	45	52	29	16	2	11	28	.281
	Winston-Salem (Car)	A	2	1	3.38	5	5	0	0	27	17	10	10	3	7	13	.185
MINOR LEAGUE TOTALS			6	2	3.38	15	12	0	0	72	69	39	26	5	18	41	.249

18 Antoin Gray, 2b/3b

Born: May 19, 1981. **Ht.:** 5-9. **Wt.:** 195. **Bats:** R. **Throws:** R. **School:** Southern University. **Career Transactions:** Selected by White Sox in 25th round of 2003 draft; signed June 6, 2003. **Signed by:** Warren Hughes.

Gray hit .449 at Southern in 2002, finishing fourth in the NCAA Division I race behind teammate Rickie Weeks, Khalil Greene and Curtis Granderson. Greene became BA's Rookie of the Year in 2004, while Weeks (Brewers) and Granderson (Tigers) are their organization's top prospects. Gray isn't nearly as polished as they are, but his upside is intriguing. He led Kannapolis in hitting last year, handling lefthanders and righthanders alike while showing surprising power for his size. He can get too obsessed with trying to drive pitches, rather than focusing on working counts and drawing walks. Gray's bat will have to carry him because he doesn't have another above-average tool. He's a decent runner and shows just ordinary range at second base. He has a below-average arm and makes too many mistakes. Gray will try to show more patience and more reliable defense in high Class A this year.

Year	Club (League)	Class	AVG	G	AB	R	H	2B	3B	HR	RBI	BB	SO	SB	OBP	SLG
2003	Great Falls (Pio)	R	.292	69	277	63	81	20	0	8	43	49	62	4	.406	.451
2004	Kannapolis (SAL)	A	.294	123	480	82	141	32	4	13	49	39	97	10	.356	.458
MINOR LEAGUE TOTALS			.293	192	757	145	222	52	4	21	92	88	159	14	.375	.456

19 Daniel Haigwood, lhp

Born: Nov. 19, 1983. **Ht.:** 6-2. **Wt.:** 200. **Bats:** S. **Throws:** L. **School:** Midland HS, Batesville, Ark. **Career Transactions:** Selected by White Sox in 16th round of 2002 draft; signed June 4, 2002. **Signed by:** Alex Slattery.

Some pitchers just know how to win, and Haigwood fits into that category. He didn't lose until his final game as an Arkansas high schooler, going 43-1, and has won 18 of his 26 decisions as a pro. He tied for the staff lead in victories at Kannapolis last year after missing 2003 following surgery to repair a torn anterior cruciate ligament in his left knee. Because Haigwood was rusty, his trademark command was absent at first but got sharper as the 2004 season went along. Haigwood's best pitch is his curveball, which breaks sharply and makes him especially tough on lefthanders. His fastball is fringe average, topping out at 90 mph, but he has worked to develop a two-seamer with some sink. He's still refining his changeup but does a good job of throwing it for strikes. Following an impressive instructional league, Haigwood will pitch in the high Class A Winston-Salem rotation in 2005.

Year	Club (League)	Class	W	L	ERA	G	GS	CG	SV	IP	H	R	ER	HR	BB	SO	AVG
2002	White Sox (AZL)	R	8	4	2.28	14	14	0	0	75	69	31	19	2	26	74	.244
2003	Did not play—Injured																
2004	Kannapolis (SAL)	A	10	4	4.87	22	22	0	0	116	102	68	63	10	59	101	.238
MINOR LEAGUE TOTALS			18	8	3.86	36	36	0	0	191	171	99	82	12	85	175	.240

20 Micah Schnurstein, 3b

Born: July 18, 1984. **Ht.:** 6-1. **Wt.:** 200. **Bats:** R. **Throws:** R. **School:** Basic HS, Henderson, Nev. **Career Transactions:** Selected by White Sox in seventh round of 2002 draft; signed June 7, 2002. **Signed by:** George Kachigian.

The White Sox remain intrigued by Schnurstein's bat, though his last two seasons haven't been nearly as productive as his 2002 debut, when he set an Arizona League record with 26 doubles. He still has the ability to drive the ball to both gaps, but he doesn't show it as often because he doesn't work himself into favorable counts enough. He should be able to hit .300 but gets himself out too often by chasing pitcher's pitches. Schnurstein has a solid work ethic and has made strides in many facets of his game, but his impatience will only become more of a handicap as he faces smarter pitches. Though his speed is slightly below average, he stole 14 bases in 18 attempts in 2004. He has good reactions at third base and should be at least an average defender. At this point, it's a stretch to call Schnurstein a serious threat to Joe Crede and Josh Fields. He has moved one level at a time, a pace that would take him to high Class A this season.

Year	Club (League)	Class	AVG	G	AB	R	H	2B	3B	HR	RBI	BB	SO	SB	OBP	SLG
2002	White Sox (AZL)	R	.332	50	205	28	68	26	1	3	48	12	34	1	.373	.512
2003	Great Falls (Pio)	R	.264	50	193	35	51	9	1	1	16	11	39	0	.313	.337
2004	Kannapolis (SAL)	A	.278	132	493	53	137	33	0	6	59	27	104	15	.322	.381
MINOR LEAGUE TOTALS			.287	232	891	116	256	68	2	10	123	50	177	16	.332	.402

21 Bobby Jenks, rhp

Born: March 14, 1981. **Ht.:** 6-3. **Wt.:** 240. **Bats:** R. **Throws:** R. **School:** Inglemoor HS, Bothell, Wash. **Career Transactions:** Selected by Angels in fifth round of 2000 draft; signed June 13, 2000 . . . Claimed on waivers by White Sox from Angels, Dec. 17, 2004. **Signed by:** Jack Uhey (Angels).

Jenks has become as famous for his personal trials and tribulations as for his 100 mph fastball, and he didn't escape controversy in 2004. He was shut down for the third time in two seasons because of a stress reaction in his right elbow and eventually had surgery in August. While he was rehabbing at the Angels' base in Mesa, Ariz., he was involved in an altercation with a teammate, suspended and sent home. When Anaheim needed to find room on its 40-man roster for Cuban defector Kendry Morales in December, it designated Jenks for assignment and lost him on waivers to the White Sox. He's expected to miss the start of the season while he completes his rehab. Jenks seems to take a step in the wrong direction every time he makes progress on the diamond, where he has shown one of the most tantalizing arms in baseball. When healthy, he regularly generated mid-90s heat and has a two-plane hammer curveball. In his four appearances at the beginning of last season, his velocity was down and his curve lacked its usual sharp break. Jenks' changeup, command and maturity still have a long ways to go. The Angels suspended him for violating team rules in 2002, and an ESPN The Magazine article in 2003 exposed several troubling incidents from his past. Jenks still has time to salvage his career and make an impact in the majors, but he can't continue to hinder his progress with his behavior. Unless he makes major strides throwing strikes and coming up with a third pitch, his future probably will be in the bullpen.

Year	Club (League)	Class	W	L	ERA	G	GS	CG	SV	IP	H	R	ER	HR	BB	SO	AVG
2000	Butte (Pio)	R	1	7	7.86	14	12	0	0	53	61	57	46	2	44	42	.290
2001	Cedar Rapids (Mid)	A	3	7	5.27	21	21	0	0	99	90	74	58	10	64	98	.245
	Arkansas (TL)	AA	1	0	3.60	2	2	0	0	10	8	5	4	0	5	10	.200
2002	Arkansas (TL)	AA	3	6	4.66	10	10	1	0	58	49	34	30	2	44	58	.234
	Rancho Cucamonga (Cal)	A	3	5	4.82	11	10	1	0	65	50	42	35	4	46	64	.212
2003	Arkansas (TL)	AA	7	2	2.17	16	16	0	0	83	56	23	20	2	51	103	.191
	Angels (AZL)	R	0	0	.00	1	1	0	0	4	2	0	0	0	0	5	.154
2004	Salt Lake (PCL)	AAA	0	1	8.03	3	3	0	0	12	19	15	11	1	6	13	.358
	Rancho Cucamonga (Cal)	A	0	1	19.64	1	1	0	0	4	5	8	8	0	7	3	.357
MINOR LEAGUE TOTALS			18	29	4.92	79	76	2	0	388	340	258	212	21	267	396	.237

22 Salvador Sanchez, of

Born: Sept. 13, 1985. **Ht.:** 6-6. **Wt.:** 195. **Bats:** R. **Throws:** R. **Career Transactions:** Signed out of Dominican Republic by White Sox, Feb. 4, 2004. **Signed by:** Denny Gonzalez.

Francisco Hernandez made a strong transition from the Dominican Summer League in 2003 to the United States in 2004, and the White Sox say Sanchez can follow the same path this year. Given his size, some scouts say he resembles the second coming on Juan Gonzalez, though Chicago hasn't begun to tout his power potential that highly. Sanchez has terrific bat speed and makes good contact, finishing 10th in the DSL batting race last season. He's still raw on the bases and in the outfield, and while he can improve it's his offense that will be his ticket to the majors. He figures to spend the first half of 2005 in extended spring training and adapting to the United States before being turned loose at Rookie-level Bristol.

Year	Club (League)	Class	AVG	G	AB	R	H	2B	3B	HR	RBI	BB	SO	SB	OBP	SLG
2004	White Sox (DSL)	R	.326	56	215	35	70	14	2	4	37	8	21	4	.363	.465
MINOR LEAGUE TOTALS			.326	56	215	35	70	14	2	4	37	8	21	4	.363	.465

23 Felix Diaz, rhp

Born: July 27, 1980. **Ht.:** 6-1. **Wt.:** 180. **Bats:** R. **Throws:** R. **Career Transactions:** Signed out of Dominican Republic by Giants, March 20, 1998 . . . Traded by Giants with LHP Ryan Meaux to White Sox for OF Kenny Lofton, July 28, 2002. **Signed by:** John Dipuglia (Giants).

Acquired in a 2002 deadline deal from the Giants for Kenny Lofton, Diaz was a major disappointment for the White Sox last season. He dominated in Triple-A but failed to fill a need for a fifth starter in the big leagues. He went 2-4, 8.27 ERA in seven starts for Chicago, surrendering 10 homers (including four against the Orioles in his debut) in just 33 innings. The White Sox used him out of the bullpen for most of September, and he showed promise in that role. Diaz can reach 92-mph with his fastball but he doesn't get much movement on it. Though his slider and changeup were good pitches in the minors, he struggled to get them called for strikes in the majors. He went to winter ball looking to regain his confidence and will get a chance to win a spot in the bullpen in spring training.

Year	Club (League)	Class	W	L	ERA	G	GS	CG	SV	IP	H	R	ER	HR	BB	SO	AVG
1998	Giants (DSL)	R	0	4	7.55	14	5	0	0	39	52	44	33	4	26	34	.306
1999	Giants (DSL)	R	0	0	0.75	3	3	0	0	12	6	2	1	0	7	19	.150
2000	Giants (AZL)	R	3	4	4.16	11	11	0	0	63	56	35	29	0	16	58	.232
	Salem-Keizer (NWL)	A	0	1	8.10	3	0	0	0	3	6	6	3	2	1	2	.400
2001	Hagerstown (SAL)	A	1	4	3.66	15	12	0	0	52	49	27	21	4	16	56	.245
2002	Shreveport (TL)	AA	3	5	2.70	12	12	1	0	60	54	22	18	1	23	48	.240
	Birmingham (SL)	AA	4	0	3.48	7	6	0	0	31	25	14	12	4	8	30	.207
2003	Charlotte (IL)	AAA	5	7	3.97	27	18	1	0	116	122	59	51	12	33	83	.270
2004	Charlotte (IL)	AAA	10	2	2.97	19	17	0	0	115	95	41	38	14	24	96	.226
	Chicago (AL)	MAJ	2	5	6.75	18	7	0	0	49	62	38	37	13	16	33	.310
MAJOR LEAGUE TOTALS			2	5	6.75	18	7	0	0	49	62	38	37	13	16	33	.310
MINOR LEAGUE TOTALS			26	27	3.78	111	84	2	0	491	465	250	206	41	154	426	.247

24 Jeff Bajenaru, rhp

Born: March 21, 1978. **Ht.:** 6-1. **Wt.:** 190. **Bats:** R. **Throws:** R. **School:** University of Oklahoma. **Career Transactions:** Signed as nondrafted free agent by White Sox, June 6, 2000. **Signed by:** John Kazanas.

Give Bajenaru credit for his persistence. A two-way star at Oklahoma who signed as a fifth-year senior draft-and-follow in 2000, he cracked this Top 30 list after his first pro season. But he missed all of 2002 following Tommy John surgery, and the White Sox didn't protect him on their 40-man roster following the 2003 season. Bajenaru pitched himself back into their good graces last year, saving 22 games with a 1.51 ERA in the minors and making his major league debut in September. He got hit hard with Chicago because he was too tentative with his pitches and also may have been tired. Bajenaru operates with two pitches, a low-90s sinker and a splitter. He keeps the ball down in the strike zone and didn't beat himself with walks or homers—until he got to the majors. He may need to develop an offspeed pitch to keep hitters off his sinker/splitter combination. The signing of free agent Dustin Hermanson probably means that Bajenaru will open 2005 in Triple-A.

Year	Club (League)	Class	W	L	ERA	G	GS	CG	SV	IP	H	R	ER	HR	BB	SO	AVG
2000	Bristol (Appy)	R	1	1	3.77	12	0	0	5	14	10	6	6	2	5	31	.179
	Winston-Salem (Car)	A	2	0	4.38	10	0	0	2	12	7	6	6	1	5	15	.167
2001	Winston-Salem (Car)	A	2	4	3.35	35	0	0	10	40	32	16	15	3	21	51	.216
	Birmingham (SL)	AA	0	0	0.00	2	0	0	0	4	4	0	0	0	3	5	.222
2003	Birmingham (SL)	AA	4	2	3.20	50	0	0	14	65	53	29	23	2	28	62	.225
2004	Birmingham (SL)	AA	2	0	1.34	32	0	0	12	34	19	9	5	3	11	51	.158
	Charlotte (IL)	AAA	1	2	1.80	16	0	0	10	20	12	6	4	2	3	16	.171
	Chicago (AL)	MAJ	0	1	10.80	9	0	0	0	8	15	10	10	0	6	8	.405
MAJOR LEAGUE TOTALS			0	1	10.80	9	0	0	0	8	15	10	10	0	6	8	.405
MINOR LEAGUE TOTALS			12	9	2.80	157	0	0	53	190	137	72	59	13	76	231	.199

25 Mike Spidale, of

Born: March 12, 1982. **Ht.:** 6-2. **Wt.:** 190. **Bats:** R. **Throws:** R. **School:** Nazareth Academy, La Grange Park, Ill. **Career Transactions:** Selected by White Sox in 12th round of 2000 draft; signed June 14, 2000. **Signed by:** Nathan Durst.

If he can get to the big leagues, Spidale should be popular with White Sox fans. That's because he is one himself, having grown up in suburban Chicago as his father Mike has served as the club's manager of purchasing. Spidale is more baseball rat than tools guy, but he has logged some time in center field for playoff teams in high Class A and Double-A the last two years. He does have plus speed, averaging 31 stolen bases the past four seasons, and is a skilled defender. He did play more in left field than center at Birmingham, in deference to Brian Anderson. Spidale has very good strike-zone judgment and uses the whole field. He has made adjustments in his swing to drive the ball better, but he can get overpowered by good fastballs and doesn't have nearly as much pop as Anderson or Chris Young. While Spidale projects as more of an extra outfielder, he knows how to get on base and could benefit from big league manager Ozzie Guillen's emphasis on speed and defense. Spidale should spend this year in Triple-A.

Year	Club (League)	Class	AVG	G	AB	R	H	2B	3B	HR	RBI	BB	SO	SB	OBP	SLG
2000	White Sox (AZL)	R	.318	21	66	21	21	2	1	0	7	18	10	16	.477	.379
2001	Kannapolis (SAL)	A	.232	126	431	51	100	8	0	0	32	52	65	35	.331	.251
2002	Kannapolis (SAL)	A	.291	93	357	57	104	11	1	0	30	34	50	37	.372	.328
2003	Winston-Sal (Car)	A	.262	120	393	61	103	21	5	1	42	57	76	25	.362	.349
2004	Birmingham (SL)	AA	.306	126	484	87	148	27	7	7	47	61	72	26	.393	.434
MINOR LEAGUE TOTALS			.275	486	1731	277	476	69	14	8	158	222	273	139	.370	.345

26 Dwayne Pollok, rhp

Born: Nov. 12, 1980. **Ht.:** 6-4. **Wt.:** 200. **Bats:** R. **Throws:** R. **School:** Texas A&M University. **Career Transactions:** Selected by White Sox in 27th round of 2003 draft; signed June 5, 2003. **Signed by:** Keith Staab.

After pitching sparingly in four seasons at Texas A&M, Pollok has been a huge surprise. Area scout Keith Staab had his work cut out for him in selling Pollok to his scouting superiors, but he kept pushing until they listened to him and took him in the 27th round of the 2003 draft. In his first full season, Pollok saved 38 games to tie for the minor league lead. Working with White Sox coaches, he has improved his slider to where it's the best in the system. He also has gained velocity on his sinker, which now reaches 90 on occasion. He forces hitters to beat him by throwing strikes. He's not overpowering, so he doesn't project as a closer at higher levels, but he could have a career as a set-up man. Chicago will test him in Double-A this year and could move him fast.

Year	Club (League)	Class	W	L	ERA	G	GS	CG	SV	IP	H	R	ER	HR	BB	SO	AVG
2003	Bristol (Appy)	R	0	0	3.12	11	0	0	3	9	8	3	3	0	4	8	.267
	Winston-Salem (Car)	A	0	1	3.92	14	0	0	0	21	25	12	9	1	2	14	.298
2004	Winston-Salem (Car)	A	2	4	3.28	58	0	0	38	60	59	23	22	4	8	49	.260
MINOR LEAGUE TOTALS			2	5	3.41	83	0	0	41	90	92	38	34	5	14	71	.270

27 Fabio Castro, lhp

Born: Jan. 20, 1985. **Ht.:** 5-8. **Wt.:** 157. **Bats:** L. **Throws:** L. **Career Transactions:** Signed out of Dominican Republic by White Sox, Dec. 26, 2001. **Signed by:** Denny Gonzalez.

Few teenagers get regular work in the Dominican League, but Castro did during the off-season with the Cibao Giants. It was another step in a smooth progression that has seen him go 21-7 as a pro. He has worked mostly out of the bullpen, and continued to be tough to hit and show impressive poise after a late-August promotion to high Class A last year. Castro doesn't overpower hitters but knows how to maximize the effectiveness of his three pitches: a fastball that parks around 89-90 mph, a tight curveball and a changeup that shows signs of becoming an excellent pitch. The White Sox have been protective of Castro, worrying that his small frame couldn't handle a heavy workload, at least not while he's so young. He might not be far behind Gio Gonzalez if he does get a chance to start. Castro will start 2005 back in high Class A.

Year	Club (League)	Class	W	L	ERA	G	GS	CG	SV	IP	H	R	ER	HR	BB	SO	AVG
2002	White Sox (DSL)	R	10	2	1.95	25	2	0	8	65	37	17	14	3	23	89	.159
2003	Bristol (Appy)	R	6	2	1.72	19	0	0	2	47	29	14	9	1	19	59	.173
	Kannapolis (SAL)	A	0	2	3.27	2	2	0	0	11	8	5	4	0	5	16	.200
2004	Kannapolis (SAL)	A	4	0	3.00	37	0	0	3	51	44	20	17	2	23	44	.227
	Winston-Salem (Car)	A	1	1	2.08	7	0	0	0	9	3	2	2	0	2	9	.107
MINOR LEAGUE TOTALS			21	7	2.27	90	4	0	13	182	121	58	46	6	72	217	.183

28 Ryan Rodriguez, lhp

Born: July 10, 1984. **Ht.:** 6-4. **Wt.:** 215. **Bats:** L. **Throws:** L. **School:** Keller (Texas) HS. **Career Transactions:** Selected by White Sox in fourth round of 2002 draft; signed June 6, 2002. **Signed by:** Keith Staab.

Another member of Chicago's deep stable of lefthanders, Rodriguez led Kannapolis in starts and innings last year after missing the entire 2003 season with inflammation in his elbow. Though he's young, he already exhibits a good feel for pitching and has command of three pitches, including a low-90s fastball. His curveball makes him especially tough against lefthanders, who batted .207 with one homer in 111 at-bats against him in 2004. His size allows him to drive the ball down in the strike zone, making it difficult for hitters to lift the ball in the air against him. He's still working on his changeup and his composure. Rodriguez will move to high Class A in 2005 and could earn a spot on the 40-man roster with a strong showing.

Year	Club (League)	Class	W	L	ERA	G	GS	CG	SV	IP	H	R	ER	HR	BB	SO	AVG
2002	White Sox (AZL)	R	5	2	3.76	14	12	0	0	69	69	36	29	1	16	47	.260
2003	Did not play—Injured																
2004	Charlotte (IL)	AAA	0	1	6.00	1	1	0	0	6	8	4	4	1	3	6	.348
	Kannapolis (SAL)	A	10	9	4.04	26	26	0	0	147	150	83	66	10	59	100	.265
MINOR LEAGUE TOTALS			15	12	4.01	41	39	0	0	222	227	123	99	12	78	153	.266

29 Wilson Valdez, ss

Born: May 20, 1978. **Ht.:** 5-11. **Wt.:** 160. **Bats:** R. **Throws:** R. **Career Transactions:** Signed out of Dominican Republic by Expos, Feb. 4, 1997 . . . Claimed on waivers by Marlins from Expos, March 29, 2002 . . . Traded by Marlins to White Sox for RHP Billy Koch, June 17, 2004. **Signed by:** Fred Ferreira/Arturo DeFreites (Expos).

It never hurts a player's upward mobility to be acquired on the recommendation of the major league manager. That's the case with Valdez, who had stalled in the Marlins system before coming to the White Sox for Billy Koch last June. He became a pet project for Chicago skipper Ozzie Guillen in spring training two years ago, when Guillen was Florida's third-base coach. Valdez had been a good-field, no-hit shortstop known for his moodiness but came out of his shell after Guillen showered him with praise. Valdez' best tools are his range in the field and speed on the bases. His arm is average. He has become a better hitter by gaining some strength without losing the ability to use his speed to get on base. He's a good bunter and a decent hit-and-run man. His .311 average in Triple-A last season shows he's growing as a hitter but he doesn't collect enough extra-base hits or walks to be considered as a regular. Valdez does appear ready to be an extra infielder in the big leagues, especially for a White Sox team emphasizing speed and defense, and could be a pleasant surprise if he gets extended playing time.

Year	Club (League)	Class	AVG	G	AB	R	H	2B	3B	HR	RBI	BB	SO	SB	OBP	SLG
1997	Expos (DSL)	R	.303	62	244	39	74	13	1	2	29	25	19	19	.389	.370
1998	Expos (DSL)	R	.300	64	247	42	74	9	0	3	30	19	12	15	.372	.352
1999	Expos (GCL)	R	.293	22	82	12	24	2	0	0	7	5	7	10	.317	.330
	Vermont (NY-P)	A	.246	36	130	19	32	7	0	1	10	7	21	4	.323	.283
2000	Cape Fear (SAL)	A	.245	15	49	6	12	2	0	0	3	2	9	3	.286	.275
	Vermont (NY-P)	A	.266	65	248	32	66	8	1	1	30	17	32	16	.319	.312
2001	Clinton (Mid)	A	.252	59	214	31	54	8	1	0	11	9	22	6	.299	.286
	Jupiter (FSL)	A	.249	64	233	34	58	13	2	2	19	10	33	7	.348	.286
2002	Portland (EL)	AA	.261	114	375	51	98	19	5	1	30	15	47	18	.347	.294
2003	Carolina (SL)	AA	.313	37	144	28	45	6	2	0	14	15	17	16	.382	.373
	Albuquerque (PCL)	AAA	.287	90	338	45	97	12	4	0	18	19	37	33	.346	.326
2004	Albuquerque (PCL)	AAA	.319	66	285	36	91	11	3	2	25	16	35	19	.357	.400
	Charlotte (IL)	AAA	.302	70	281	37	85	7	2	2	15	12	41	13	.338	.363
	Chicago (AL)	MAJ	.233	19	43	8	10	1	0	1	4	2	0	5	.267	.326
MAJOR LEAGUE TOTALS			.233	19	43	8	10	1	0	1	4	2	0	5	.267	.326
MINOR LEAGUE TOTALS			.282	764	2870	412	810	117	21	14	241	171	332	179	.325	.352

30 Tom Collaro, of/1b

Born: April 4, 1983. **Ht.:** 6-4. **Wt.:** 210. **Bats:** R. **Throws:** R. **School:** Piper HS, Sunrise, Fla. **Career Transactions:** Selected by White Sox in 27th round of 2001 draft; signed May 23, 2002. **Signed by:** Jose Ortega.

Few minor leaguers put on better batting-practice displays than Collaro. One Pioneer League manager said last year that Collaro hits the ball as far as anyone he'd ever seen in the minors. He made tremendous strides at the plate overall in his third pro season, hitting a career-best .287 while finishing second in the league in homers, but it was his third straight year in Rookie ball. Collaro still has major holes in swing and poor plate discipline, chasing too many pitches out of the zone while taking too many strikes. He'll have to slug his way to the big leagues and the only way to do that is to strike out less often. He's no more than adequate on the bases and in the field, where he has played both outfield corners and first base. After a strong instructional league, Collaro could get consideration for high Class A, but he most likely will begin 2005 in low Class A.

Year	Club (League)	Class	AVG	G	AB	R	H	2B	3B	HR	RBI	BB	SO	SB	OBP	SLG
2002	White Sox (AZL)	R	.213	39	127	22	27	4	3	7	29	14	45	3	.292	.457
2003	Bristol (Appy)	R	.226	45	146	17	33	9	1	8	28	4	46	1	.252	.466
2004	Great Falls (Pio)	R	.287	66	268	48	77	7	6	18	67	13	82	4	.331	.560
MINOR LEAGUE TOTALS			.253	150	541	87	137	20	10	33	124	31	173	8	.301	.510

CINCINNATI
REDS

BY **JOHN MANUEL**

MORRIS FOSTOFF

T he last link to the Reds' past—a past when they contended for World Series championships—has left the building. Cincinnati native Barry Larkin, who played for the Reds for the last 19 seasons and helped them win the 1990 World Series, became a free agent. His departure continues a recent rash of changes, as the club also has opened a new ballpark and overhauled its front office and farm system.

Replacing Larkin on the field and as the face of the franchise hasn't proven easy. The Reds' options at short appear to be Felipe Lopez, whose glove seems better suited for second base or third, and declining veteran Rich Aurilia. Ken Griffey Jr., who was supposed to supplant Larkin as the face of the franchise, had another injury-riddled year in 2004.

Griffey started strong and hit his 500th career home run, and the team was 47-41 at the all-star break due in part to his resurgence. But three days after the break, he tore his right hamstring. The Reds went 4-13 to start the second half, Griffey had surgery in August and the club stumbled to its fourth straight losing season.

General manager Dan O'Brien acted boldly to remake the franchise in the offseason. He overhauled the minor league staff, replacing field coordinator Ron Oester with Bob Miscik and pitching coordinator Sammy Ellis with Vern Ruhle. Oester blasted the organization on the way out for lacking direction and talent. However, the Reds made progress on both fronts in 2004.

O'Brien implemented significant changes at the field level, encouraging plate discipline and adopting a tandem-starter system (pitchers alternate between starting and relieving) at Class A and below. The Reds also had a productive draft, snaring outfielder B.J. Szymanski, considered a first-round talent, with the 39th overall pick after drafting righthander Homer Bailey seventh overall.

While they didn't find a replacement for Larkin in the offseason, the Reds became an aggressive player in every other phase, adding $19 million to their 2005 payroll. They attempted to fortify a pitching staff that posted a franchise-worst 5.19 ERA last season by re-signing Paul Wilson, adding free agent Eric Milton and trading for Ramon Ortiz. The Reds should have competition for the last two spots in the rotation, with righties Josh Hancock, Aaron Harang and Luke Hudson and lefty Brandon Claussen in the mix.

The Reds also signed third baseman Joe Randa, after experimenting in instructional league with moving Austin Kearns to the hot corner. Manager Dave Miley will have to find another way to get four talented outfielders—Griffey, Kearns, Adam Dunn and **Wily Mo Pena**—on the field at the same time. Outfield talent has become the organization's new identity with Larkin gone. O'Brien hopes the moves he has made will help the Reds be identified as winners once again as well.

TOP 30 PROSPECTS

1. Homer Bailey, rhp	16. Miguel Perez, c
2. Edwin Encarnacion, 3b	17. Javon Moran, of
3. Richie Gardner, rhp	18. Steve Kelly, rhp
4. Joey Votto, 1b	19. Dane Sardinha, c
5. B.J. Szymanski, of	20. Rafael Gonzalez, rhp
6. Thomas Pauly, rhp	21. Daylan Childress, rhp
7. Todd Coffey, rhp	22. Chris Denorfia, of
8. William Bergolla, 2b/ss	23. Anderson Machado, ss
9. Tyler Pelland, lhp	24. Jesse Gutierrez, 1b
10. Paul Janish, ss	25. Chris Gruler, rhp
11. Elizardo Ramirez, rhp	26. Calvin Medlock, rhp
12. Chris Dickerson, of	27. Carlos Guevara, rhp
13. David Shafer, rhp	28. Matt Belisle, rhp
14. Kevin Howard, 2b	29. Stephen Smitherman, of/1b
15. Ben Kozlowski, lhp	30. Craig Tatum, c

ORGANIZATION OVERVIEW

General manager: Dan O'Brien. **Farm director:** Tim Naehring. **Scouting director:** Terry Reynolds.

2004 PERFORMANCE

Class	Team	League	W	L	Pct.	Finish*	Manager
Majors	Cincinnati	National	76	86	.469	10th (16)	Dave Miley
Triple-A	Louisville RiverBats	International	67	77	.465	10th (14)	Rick Burleson
Double-A	Chattanooga Lookouts	Southern	87	53	.621	1st (10)	Jayhawk Owens
High A	#Potomac Cannons	Carolina	67	72	.482	5th (8)	Edgar Caceres
Low A	Dayton Dragons	Midwest	48	92	.343	14th (14)	Alonzo Powell
Rookie	Billings Mustangs	Pioneer	37	37	.500	5th (8)	Donnie Scott
Rookie	GCL Reds	Gulf Coast	20	37	.351	12th (12)	Freddie Benavides
OVERALL 2004 MINOR LEAGUE RECOARD			326	368	.470	23rd (30)	

*Finish in overall standings (No. of teams in league). #Affiliate will be in Sarasota (Florida State) in 2005.

ORGANIZATION LEADERS

BATTING   *Minimum 250 At-Bats
*AVG Joey Votto, Potomac/Dayton .... .301
   R Chris Denorfia, Chattanooga/Potomac 82
   H Joey Votto, Potomac/Dayton 143
  TB Joey Votto, Potomac/Dayton 237
  2B Edwin Encarnacion, Chattanooga 35
     Stephen Smitherman, Louisville 35
  3B Kenny Kelly, Louisville/Chattanooga 7
     Ray Olmedo, Louisville 7
  HR Tony Blanco, Chattanooga/Potomac 29
 RBI Joey Votto, Potomac/Dayton 93
  BB Joey Votto, Potomac/Dayton 90
  SO Walter Olmstead, Dayton 132
  SB William Bergolla, Chattanooga 36
*OBP Joey Votto, Potomac/Dayton .... .413
*SLG Robert Mosby, Billings .... .522

PITCHING   #Minimum 75 Innings
   W Richie Gardner, Chattanooga/Potomac 13
     Brian Rose, Louisville/Chattanooga 13
   L Alexander Farfan, Dayton/Billings 12
     Bubba Nelson, Louisville/Chattanooga 12
#ERA Richie Gardner, Chattanooga/Potomac 2.53
   G Brian Shackelford, Louisville 59
  CG Seth Etherton, Louisville/Chattanooga 3
  SV Todd Coffey, Louisville/Chattanooga 24
  IP Matt Belisle, Louisville 163
  BB Jeffrey Bruksch, Potomac 63
  SO Calvin Medlock, Potomac/Dayton 157

BEST TOOLS

Best Hitter for Average .... Joey Votto
Best Power Hitter... Joey Votto
Best Strike-Zone Discipline .... Joey Votto
Fastest Baserunner...................................... Javon Moran
Best Athlete.. B.J. Szymanski
Best Fastball .... Homer Bailey
Best Curveball.. Homer Bailey
Best Slider .... Richie Gardner
Best Changeup... Steve Kelly
Best Control .... Richie Gardner
Best Defensive Catcher .... Miguel Perez
Best Defensive Infielder................................. Paul Janish
Best Infield Arm .... Paul Janish
Best Defensive Outfielder .... Chris Dickerson
Best Outfield Arm .... Chris Donorfia

PROJECTED 2008 LINEUP

Catcher.. Jason LaRue
First Base .... Sean Casey
Second Base .... D'Angelo Jimenez
Third Base .... Edwin Encarnacion
Shortstop.. Felipe Lopez
Left Field .... Adam Dunn

Center Field .... Wily Mo Pena
Right Field .... Austin Kearns
No. 1 Starter .... Eric Milton
No. 2 Starter .... Homer Bailey
No. 3 Starter .... Richie Gardner
No. 4 Starter .... Paul Wilson
No. 5 Starter .... Thomas Pauly
Closer .... Ryan Wagner

LAST YEAR'S TOP 20 PROSPECTS

1. Ryan Wagner, rhp   11. Miguel Perez, c
2. Edwin Encarnacion, 3b   12. William Bergolla, 2b
3. Brandon Claussen, lhp   13. Josh Hall, rhp
4. Dustin Moseley, rhp   14. Richie Gardner, rhp
5. Joey Votto, 1b   15. Rainer Feliz, rhp
6. Phil Dumatrait, lhp   16. Joe Valentine, rhp
7. Stephen Smitherman, of   17. Bobby Basham, rhp
8. Tyler Pelland, lhp   18. Thomas Pauly, rhp
9. Chris Gruler, rhp   19. David Mattox, rhp
10. Ty Howington, lhp   20. Habelito Hernandez, 3b/2b

TOP PROSPECTS OF THE DECADE

Year	Player, Pos.	Current Team
1995	Pokey Reese, ss	Mariners
1996	Pokey Reese, ss	Mariners
1997	Aaron Boone, 3b	Indians
1998	Damian Jackson, ss/2b	Padres
1999	Rob Bell, rhp	Devil Rays
2000	Gookie Dawkins, ss	Cubs
2001	Austin Kearns, of	Reds
2002	Austin Kearns, of	Reds
2003	Chris Gruler, rhp	Reds
2004	Ryan Wagner, rhp	Reds

TOP DRAFT PICKS OF THE DECADE

Year	Player, Pos.	Current Team
1995	Brett Tomko, rhp (2)	Giants
1996	John Oliver, of	Out of baseball
1997	Brandon Larson, ss/3b	Devil Rays
1998	Austin Kearns, of	Reds
1999	Ty Howington, lhp	Reds
2000	David Espinosa, ss	Tigers
2001	*Jeremy Sowers, lhp	Indians
2002	Chris Gruler, rhp	Reds
2003	Ryan Wagner, rhp	Reds
2004	Homer Bailey, rhp	Reds

*Did not sign.

ALL-TIME LARGEST BONUSES

Chris Gruler, 2002....................................... $2,500,000
Homer Bailey, 2004..................................... $2,300,000
Austin Kearns, 1998 .... $1,950,000
Ty Howington, 1999 .... $1,750,000
Ryan Wagner, 2003...................................... $1,400,000

Cincinnati REDS

Impact Potential: C

Few high school pitchers have the polish, stuff and swagger of Homer Bailey, but the Reds' first-round pick has pitched in only 12 innings at the Rookie-league level. Second-rounder B.J. Szymanski has five tools but will be a full-time baseball player for the first time in 2005. Edwin Encarnacion gets a year in Triple-A, and at his current pace should replace stopgap Joe Randa in 2006.

Depth: D

A pair of trades with the Phillies helped bring in more talent, and the '04 draft yielded a new crop of much-needed power arms. Yet the Reds remain short of power hitters who can also make consistent contact, as well as middle infielders with offensive upside. Injuries have decimated the organization's pitching in recent years, but healthy returns by the likes of Bobby Basham, Phil Dumatrait, Chris Gruler and Ty Howington would change the outlook immensely.

*Depth charts prepared by **John Manuel** and **Allan Simpson**. Numbers in parentheses indicate prospect rankings.*

LF
Stephen Smitherman (29)
Drew Anderson
Jason Vavao

CF
B.J. Szymanski (5)
Chris Dickerson (12)
Javon Moran (17)
Kenny Lewis

RF
Chris Donorfia (22)
Cody Strait

3B
Edwin Encarnacion (2)
Mark Schramek
Brad Key

SS
Paul Janish (10)
Anderson Machado (23)
Hector Tiburcio
Luis Bolivar

2B
William Bergolla (8)
Kevin Howard (14)
Willy Jo Ronda
Trevor Lawhorn
Mayker Sandoval

1B
Joey Votto (4)
Jesse Gutierrez (24)
Tonys Gutierrez
Robert Mosby

SOURCE of TALENT

HOMEGROWN		ACQUIRED	
College	13	Trades	6
Junior College	1	Rule 5 draft	0
Draft-and-follow	2	Independent leagues	0
High School	5	Free agents/waivers	1
Nondrafted free agent	0		
Foreign	2		

C
Miguel Perez (16)
Dane Sardinha (19)
Craig Tatum (30)
Brian Peterson
Lonny Roa

LHP

Starters	Relievers
Tyler Pelland (9)	Brian Shackelford
Ben Kozlowski (15)	Joe Wilson
Phil Dumatrait	Greg Goetz
Ty Howington	
Camilo Vazquez	
Philippe Valiquette	

RHP

Starters	Relievers
Homer Bailey (1)	Todd Coffey (6)
Richie Gardner (3)	David Shafer (13)
Thomas Pauly (7)	Rafael Gonzalez (20)
Elizardo Ramirez (11)	Daylan Childress (21)
Steve Kelly (18)	Calvin Medlock (26)
Chris Gruler (25)	Carlos Guevara (27)
Matt Belisle (28)	Joe Valentine
Bobby Basham	Jeff Bruksch
Bubba Nelson	Zach Stott
Alexander Farfan	Jared Sanders
Ranier Feliz	
Jon George	
Terrell Young	

2004

Best Pro Debut: C Craig Tatum (3) was a Rookie-level Pioneer League all-star, but he batted just .221-2-21. He stood out more on defense, leading the league by throwing out 36 percent of basestealers. The best numbers belonged to RHP Jared Sanders (14), who went 4-1, 2.00 with five saves as Tatum's batterymate.

Best Athlete: OF B.J. Szymanski (1) was the best athlete and five-tool talent among college players in the draft. He's a 6-foot-5, 215-pound switch-hitter with plus tools across the board. Also a wide receiver, he ranks ninth on Princeton's all-time receiving list.

Best Pure Hitter: Szymanski's swing looks almost identical from both sides of the plate.

Best Raw Power: Szymanski can take the best fastballs out of the park. He blasted the first pitch he saw in 2004—a 94-mph heater from No. 2 overall pick Justin Verlander—for a long home run.

Fastest Runner: Szymanski, OF Cody Strait (12) and OF/INF Drew Anderson (13) all can cover 60 yards in about 6.5 seconds. Szymanski wasn't at full speed in his pro debut because he had a quadriceps injury.

Best Defensive Player: Paul Janish (5) makes playing shortstop look easy. He made just four errors in 57 games at Rice, then only eight in 66 games in the Pioneer League. He's not speedy, but his instincts and quick first step give him plenty of range. His strong arm has been clocked as high as 93 mph, and the Owls would have given him a chance to pitch had he returned to school.

Best Fastball: RHP Homer Bailey (1), BA's High School Player of the Year, consistently

Bailey

throws 92-97 mph. That's a tick ahead of fellow high school RHP Rafael Gonzalez (4), who can hit 93-96 at his best. Two more high school arms, LHP Phillippe Valiquette (7) and RHP Terrell Young (10), both peaked at 94 mph during the spring.

Best Breaking Ball: Bailey has a nasty curveball to go with his wicked fastball.

Most Intriguing Background: Unsigned RHP Dylan Moseley's (33) older brother Dustin was a Reds supplemental first-round pick in 2000 and was traded to the Angels in the offseason. 1B Brandon Roberts' (45) father Leon played 11 seasons in the majors and is a roving hitting instructor for Cincinnati.

Closest To The Majors: Bailey and Gonzalez could advance rapidly, but if Janish continues to make progress with the bat he should beat them to the big leagues.

Best Late-Round Pick: When he throws strikes, Young's fastball-curveball combination is very difficult to hit. 3B Brad Key (48) is a sleeper with some pop in his bat.

The One Who Got Away: RHP Jason Urquidez (11) is the only player whom the Reds made a run at and failed to land. Urquidez, who likes to mix his pitches and arm slots, returned to Arizona State.

Assessment: A few weeks before the draft, the Reds couldn't have expected to get Bailey with the seventh overall pick and Szymanski with the 48th. Those two may have more upside than any other prospects in the system.

2003 RHP Ryan Wagner (1) went almost directly to the majors and should be the closer in the near future. RHPs Richie Gardner (6) and Thomas Pauly (2) are two more good arms. **GRADE:** C+

2002 Two years later, RHP Chris Gruler (1) and 3B Mark Schramek (1) were reduced to mere afterthoughts, though injuries can be blamed for Gruler's decline. 1B Joey Votto (2) is this draft's lone saving grace. Unsigned OF/LHP Nick Markakis (23) would have been a big help in either role. **GRADE:** C

2001 Looking to save money, the Reds didn't try to sign LHP Jeremy Sowers (1), who went sixth overall in 2004. They drafted Markakis (35) and Schramek (45) and didn't sign them either. RHP Steve Kelly (4) and 1B Jesse Gutierrez (20) are fringe prospects. **GRADE:** D

2000 Cincinnati has traded both its first-rounders, OF David Espinosa and RHP Dustin Moseley. The best players still on hand are C Dane Sardinha (2) and OF/1B Stephen Smitherman (23), and they won't help much. **GRADE:** D

Draft analysis prepared by Jim Callis. Numbers in parentheses indicate draft rounds.

rhp

Homer
BAILEY

Born: May 3, 1986.
Ht.: 6-4. **Wt.:** 185.
Bats: R. **Throws:** R.
School: La Grange (Texas) HS.
Career Transactions: Selected by Reds in first round (7th overall) of 2004 draft; signed July 19, 2004.
Signed by: Mike Powers.

A boot-wearing, drawling cowboy, Bailey plays the role of fireballing Texas righthander well. He grew up on an egg farm, and is an avid hunter who keeps a collection of the tusks of wild boar he has killed in his room. He also maintains that image on the mound. He established himself as a winner as a high school freshman, beating Forney High and current Reds reliever Ryan Wagner to win the state 3-A championship for La Grange High. Entering 2004, Bailey already was considered a certain top-10 draft pick, and scouts respected how he rose to that challenge as well as being the pitcher others teams gunned for during his entire prep career. He capped a tremendous senior season by leading La Grange to another state title, striking out 14 (including 10 of the last 12 outs). He was Baseball America's High School Player of the Year, though that in itself is far from a guarantee of future success. Three other righthanders have won it: Matt White in 1996, Matt Harrington in 2000 and Jeff Allison in 2003—none of whom won a game in Organized Baseball in 2004. The Reds believe Bailey's maturity and track record of dealing with success will set him apart from that disappointing trio. They gave him a $2.3 million bonus, the second-largest in organization history.

Bailey has the frame and arm speed to throw hard, and he does so consistently. His fastball sits at 92-97 mph when he's at his best, and it has good life as well. Scouts considered it the best fastball in the draft among high school pitchers, not just because of its velocity but also because he consistently throws it for strikes. Bailey's command also rated as best among prep pitchers. He's more polished than the average high school pitcher, though he won't be confused with Kansas City's Zack Greinke, either. The fastball is his best pitch, but he gets plenty of strikeouts with his plus downer curveball as well, the best bender available in the prep ranks in 2004. Athletic and projectable, Bailey should be able to throw harder and maintain his delivery as he fills out.

Bailey was used conservatively in his first pro season, and Cincinnati didn't get a long look at him in instructional league. He injured his right knee during the 2003 Area Code Games, leaving a game after just four pitches, and he tweaked the knee again in instructs. The Reds and Bailey decided it would be best if he had arthroscopic surgery to head off any long-term problems. He was back to full speed in December, beginning his offseason workouts. Now he needs to show he can pitch a full season. His changeup needs work to become a legitimate third pitch.

Bailey's combination of power and polish should allow him to move quickly. The Reds have had little success with taking high school pitchers in the first round as of late—Ty Howington (1999) and Chris Gruler (2002) have had repeated injury problems—so they'll be careful with Bailey. He'll be in their tandem-starter system, most likely at low Class A Dayton, which should keep him fresh. He could start to take off toward Cincinnati in 2006.

Year	Club (League)	Class	W	L	ERA	G	GS	CG	SV	IP	H	R	ER	HR	BB	SO	AVG
2004	Reds (GCL)	R	0	1	4.38	6	3	0	0	12	14	7	6	0	3	9	.274
MINOR LEAGUE TOTALS			0	1	4.38	6	3	0	0	12	14	7	6	0	3	9	.274

Edwin Encarnacion, 3b

Born: Jan. 7, 1983. **Ht.:** 6-1. **Wt.:** 195. **Bats:** R. **Throws:** R. **School:** Manuela Toro HS, Caguas, P.R. **Career Transactions:** Selected by Rangers in ninth round of 2000 draft; signed June 12, 2000 . . . Traded by Rangers with OF Ruben Mateo to Reds for RHP Rob Bell, June 15, 2001. **Signed by:** Sammy Melendez (Rangers).

Encarnacion enhanced his standing as the Reds' top position-player prospect with a solid 2004. Acquired in 2001 from the Rangers in a trade with Ruben Mateo for Rob Bell, Encarnacion impressed the Reds with his maturity, returning to Double-A Chattanooga after a failed stint there in 2003 and showing a more consistent work ethic and attitude. Encarnacion has excellent hitting tools, including developing patience (career-high 53 walks in 2004) and power (he tied for the Southern League doubles lead). His improved willingness to go the other way and good bat speed have scouts projecting him to hit .280-.300 with 20-25 homers annually. Defensively he has a plus arm, quick hands and middle-infield actions. While his 25 errors marked his first season with less than 30, Encarnacion still topped the SL. Many of his errors have come on poor throws related to his footwork. Offensively, his swing tends to get long when he tries too hard to hit for power. Cincinnati signed free agent Joe Randa to a one-year deal, giving Encarnacion another year to develop. He'll head to Triple-A Louisville this year with an eye on replacing Randa in 2006.

Year	Club (League)	Class	AVG	G	AB	R	H	2B	3B	HR	RBI	BB	SO	SB	OBP	SLG
2000	Rangers (GCL)	R	.311	51	177	31	55	6	3	0	36	21	27	3	.381	.379
2001	Savannah (SAL)	A	.306	45	170	23	52	9	2	4	25	12	34	3	.355	.453
	Dayton (Mid)	A	.162	9	37	2	6	2	0	1	6	1	5	0	.184	.297
	Billings (Pio)	R	.261	52	211	27	55	8	2	5	26	15	29	8	.307	.389
2002	Dayton (Mid)	A	.282	136	518	80	146	32	4	17	73	40	108	25	.338	.458
2003	Chattanooga (SL)	AA	.272	67	254	40	69	13	1	5	36	22	44	8	.331	.390
	Potomac (Car)	A	.321	58	215	40	69	15	1	6	29	24	32	7	.387	.484
2004	Chattanooga (SL)	AA	.281	120	469	73	132	35	1	13	76	53	79	17	.352	.443
MINOR LEAGUE TOTALS			.285	538	2051	316	584	120	14	51	307	188	358	71	.345	.431

Richie Gardner, rhp

Born: Feb. 1, 1982. **Ht.:** 6-3. **Wt.:** 185. **Bats:** R. **Throws:** R. **School:** University of Arizona. **Career Transactions:** Selected by Reds in sixth round of 2003 draft; signed Aug. 23, 2003. **Signed by:** Jeff Barton.

Gardner has overcome long odds. As a sophomore at Santa Rosa (Calif.) Junior College, his progress was stunted by mononucleosis and then by a concussion after he was hit in the head by a throw during infield drills. He has recovered nicely and was the best pitcher in the Reds system in 2004. Gardner has the best command in the organization, throwing three pitches for strikes. He keeps his plus sinker down while throwing it at 90-94 mph. His slider kept improving over the course of the season and now rates as the best in the system. His changeup mimics his fastball with late sink and helps him attack lefthanders. At times Gardner's slider gets slurvy, though he has improved the consistency of its power and bite. While he admits to lingering affects from the concussion, it hasn't showed up in his pitching. He just needs to stay healthy and get innings. The Reds like Gardner's no-fear attitude as much as his three-pitch mix. It will be hard to keep him out of Cincinnati if he repeats his pro debut in 2005, which should start in Double-A.

Year	Club (League)	Class	W	L	ERA	G	GS	CG	SV	IP	H	R	ER	HR	BB	SO	AVG
2004	Chattanooga (SL)	AA	5	2	2.56	11	11	0	0	70	68	24	20	7	13	59	.248
	Potomac (Car)	A	8	3	2.50	18	12	0	1	86	77	31	24	3	13	80	.229
MINOR LEAGUE TOTALS			13	5	2.53	29	23	0	1	157	145	55	44	10	26	139	.238

Joey Votto, 1b

Born: Sept. 10, 1983. **Ht.:** 6-3. **Wt.:** 200. **Bats:** L. **Throws:** R. **School:** Richview Collegiate Institute, Toronto. **Career Transactions:** Selected by Reds in second round of 2002 draft; signed June 5, 2002. **Signed by:** John Castleberry.

The Yankees had Votto fly in from Canada to work out before the 2002 draft. When the Reds found out, they asked him to work out for them first, and they picked him 44th overall after he put on an impressive display. Votto has excellent strength, discipline and savvy at the plate, a combination that makes him the best hitter in the system and gives him above-average power potential. He works hitter's counts and has a short, compact swing that he repeats well. His 90 walks ranked fifth in the minors in 2004. Votto's average bat speed prompted one scout to compare him to Brian Daubach. He can be patient to a fault, passing on pitches he can drive. He's still raw as a baserunner and defender. While Votto's upside is debatable, scouts agree he's a polished hitter who could rush through the minors. Sean Casey's contract has a club option for 2006, so Votto is a rare Reds prospect who could be pushed. He'll start this year back at high Class A, where he ended 2004.

Year	Club (League)	Class	AVG	G	AB	R	H	2B	3B	HR	RBI	BB	SO	SB	OBP	SLG
2002	Reds (GCL)	R	.269	50	175	29	47	13	3	9	33	21	45	7	.342	.531
2003	Dayton (Mid)	A	.231	60	195	19	45	8	0	1	20	34	64	2	.348	.287
	Billings (Pio)	R	.317	70	240	47	76	17	3	6	38	56	80	4	.452	.488
2004	Dayton (Mid)	A	.302	111	391	60	118	26	2	14	73	79	110	9	.419	.486
	Potomac (Car)	A	.298	24	84	11	25	7	0	5	20	11	21	1	.385	.560
MINOR LEAGUE TOTALS			.287	315	1085	166	311	71	8	35	184	201	320	23	.399	.464

5 B.J. Szymanski, of

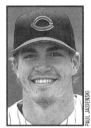

Born: Oct. 1, 1982. **Ht.:** 6-5. **Wt.:** 215. **Bats:** B. **Throws:** R. **School:** Princeton University. **Career Transactions:** Selected by Reds in second round of 2004 draft; signed July 2, 2004. **Signed by:** Mike Misuraca.

Szymanski broke out as a junior in two sports at Princeton. In football, he had more catches (44) and yards receiving (823) than in his first two years combined. He then led the Tigers to the Ivy League baseball title as their top hitter (.362). The Reds were surprised he fell to the 48th overall pick and signed him to a $750,000 bonus. Szymanski instantly became the top athlete in the organization and shows five-tool potential. He can cover 60 yards in 6.5 seconds, has plus arm strength and has shown above-average power potential. A switch-hitter, he shows a similar swing from either side. A quad injury short-circuited Szymanski's first pro season, and the Reds already had agreed to let him return to Princeton to complete his psychology degree. He may need to shorten his swing and develop more patience. His ability to make consistent, hard contact will determine his success. If he has a strong year in low Class A, he could zoom to the top of this list.

Year	Club (League)	Class	AVG	G	AB	R	H	2B	3B	HR	RBI	BB	SO	SB	OBP	SLG
2004	Billings (Pio)	R	.259	22	81	13	21	4	2	3	17	9	26	2	.330	.469
MINOR LEAGUE TOTALS			.259	22	81	13	21	4	2	3	17	9	26	2	.330	.469

6 Thomas Pauly, rhp

Born: July 28, 1981. **Ht.:** 6-1. **Wt.:** 195. **Bats:** R. **Throws:** R. **School:** Princeton University. **Career Transactions:** Selected by Reds in second round of 2003 draft; signed June 13, 2003. **Signed by:** Steve Mondile.

Pauly drew scouts' attention when he started reaching the low 90s as a sophomore reliever at Princeton, where he was B.J. Szymanski's teammate. He returned to Princeton each of the last two falls to complete his thesis and finish his chemical-engineering degree. He led the high Class A Carolina League in strikeouts in 2004. Pauly's fastball got him drafted and remains his best pitch. It touches 95 mph, sits in the low 90s and has good life down in the zone. Pauly has picked up a nifty, sweeping slider since signing, and it has become an above-average pitch at times. His changeup has shown flashes of brilliance. Pauly still is learning the nuances of starting, from throwing a changeup to using his offspeed stuff to set up his fastball. He's shown aptitude in all areas. The tandem-starter system worked well for Pauly, who gained innings and got acclimated to the rotation. His changeup will determine if he's effective as a starter at higher levels. His next test will come in Double-A.

Year	Club (League)	Class	W	L	ERA	G	GS	CG	SV	IP	H	R	ER	HR	BB	SO	AVG
2003	Dayton (Mid)	A	2	5	4.02	12	12	0	0	47	45	26	21	5	10	36	.247
2004	Potomac (Car)	A	8	7	2.97	28	19	0	0	121	96	47	40	12	26	135	.215
MINOR LEAGUE TOTALS			10	12	3.26	40	31	0	0	168	141	73	61	17	36	171	.224

7 Todd Coffey, rhp

Born: Sept. 9, 1980. **Ht.:** 6-5. **Wt.:** 230. **Bats:** R. **Throws:** R. **School:** Chase City HS, Forest City, NC. **Career Transactions:** Selected by Reds in 41st round of 1998 draft; signed June 6, 1998. **Signed by:** Steve Kring.

Coffey had a rough career before blossoming in 2004, reaching Triple-A and earning a 40-man roster spot after a strong Arizona Fall League. He battled weight problems early in his career, ballooning to as much as 280 pounds, and missed 2000 with Tommy John surgery. While the Reds nearly released him several times, he rewarded their patience with an organization-best 24 saves last year. Coffey has an intriguing combination of power and control. His fastball sits anywhere from 90-96 mph. His improved mechanics help him maintain a good downhill plane with the pitch. He plays off the heater with a good splitter, his strikeout pitch. He has impressive control of the strike zone. Coffey will need to keep an eye on his weight. He wore down as the 2004 season went on, causing his velocity in the AFL to fluctuate. His lack of a third pitch limits him to one turn through the order. Coffey's stuff profiles as a set-up man, but his command could make him a closer as he gains more experience. His perseverance should be rewarded with big league time in 2005.

Year	Club (League)	Class	W	L	ERA	G	GS	CG	SV	IP	H	R	ER	HR	BB	SO	AVG
1998	Billings (Pio)	R	0	0	3.00	3	2	0	0	12	13	4	4	1	1	8	.302
1999	Reds (GCL)	R	1	1	3.38	5	2	0	0	16	9	12	6	1	14	14	.145
2000	Did not play—Injured																
2001	Reds (GCL)	R	0	1	4.26	3	2	0	0	13	11	11	6	1	5	15	.234
	Billings (Pio)	R	2	2	3.51	14	2	0	1	33	34	21	13	2	15	33	.258
2002	Dayton (Mid)	A	6	4	3.59	38	5	0	2	80	78	34	32	8	25	62	.260
2003	Dayton (Mid)	A	3	3	2.25	39	0	0	9	56	61	20	14	1	14	53	.289
	Potomac (Car)	A	0	2	1.96	11	0	0	2	23	16	6	5	0	3	21	.208
2004	Chattanooga (SL)	AA	4	1	2.38	40	0	0	20	45	36	13	12	3	4	53	.216
	Louisville (IL)	AAA	1	0	5.27	15	0	0	4	14	15	8	8	1	2	11	.273
MINOR LEAGUE TOTALS			17	14	3.08	168	13	0	38	292	273	129	100	18	83	270	.250

8 William Bergolla, 2b/ss

Born: Feb. 4, 1983. **Ht.:** 6-0. **Wt.:** 175. **Bats:** R. **Throws:** R. **Career Transactions:** Signed out of Venezuela by Reds, Nov. 15, 1999. **Signed by:** Johnny Almaraz.

Shaking off the effects of a broken left hamate bone from the previous winter, Bergolla continued to win fans in the organization with his hustle, defense and line-drive bat in 2004. He missed the last three weeks when he aggravated the hamate injury. He returned in time to play winter ball again in his native Venezuela. Bergolla has good bat control, using the whole field with a compact, line-drive swing. He's also a good bunter and is learning the value of a walk. He's an above-average runner who led the organization in steals for the second straight year, and he has improved his baserunning savvy. He has the range and infield actions to play shortstop, as well as solid-average arm strength. Even if he fills out his skinny frame, Bergolla never will be a power threat. The Reds would like to use him at shortstop more often, but his arm comes up sore after extended playing time there. If Bergolla can keep his arm healthy, he'll be a shortstop candidate for Cincinnati this year, or his versatility and speed could earn him a spot as a major league utilityman soon.

Year	Club (League)	Class	AVG	G	AB	R	H	2B	3B	HR	RBI	BB	SO	SB	OBP	SLG
2000	Cagua (VSL)	R	.372	13	43	6	16	3	2	0	5	8	3	1	.481	.535
	Reds (GCL)	R	.182	8	22	2	4	0	0	0	0	4	2	3	.308	.182
2001	Billings (Pio)	R	.323	57	232	47	75	5	3	4	24	24	21	22	.387	.422
2002	Dayton (Mid)	A	.248	68	274	38	68	13	1	3	23	16	36	13	.291	.336
	Billings (Pio)	R	.352	53	210	35	74	9	1	3	29	24	26	16	.408	.448
2003	Potomac (Car)	A	.272	128	523	77	142	25	3	2	31	29	59	52	.309	.342
2004	Chattanooga (SL)	AA	.283	116	466	79	132	26	1	4	38	40	63	36	.342	.369
MINOR LEAGUE TOTALS			.289	443	1770	284	511	81	11	16	150	145	210	143	.342	.374

9 Tyler Pelland, lhp

Born: Oct. 9, 1983. **Ht.:** 6-0. **Wt.:** 200. **Bats:** R. **Throws:** L. **School:** Mount Abraham HS, Bristol, Vt. **Career Transactions:** Selected by Red Sox in ninth round of 2002 draft; signed Aug. 17, 2002 . . . Traded with LHP Phil Dumatrait by Red Sox to Reds for RHP Scott Williamson, July 29, 2003. **Signed by:** Ray Fagnant (Red Sox).

The Reds got Pelland, a Vermont prep phenom who led the state in strikeouts and ERA as a senior, from the Red Sox in the Scott Williamson trade in 2003. Pelland righted himself after a disastrous stint in low Class A with a strong second half at Rookie-level Billings. Pelland has power stuff. His four-seam fastball sits at 92-94 mph and reaches 95. He added an 89-90 mph two-seamer with good life last year. His circle changeup has the makings of a plus pitch, as it arrives in the low 80s with late tumble. He's athletic and has a durable frame. Midwest League hitters hammered Pelland because he threw across his body and couldn't spin his curveball for strikes. Billings pitching coach Vern Ruhle, now the Reds' minor league pitching coordinator, helped him pitch more directly to the plate, improving his curve and his command. Ruhle's adjustments and Pelland's aptitude turned a nightmare season into a learning experience. He'll get another shot at low Class A in 2005. The progress of his curve will determine whether he reaches his ceiling as a middle-of-the-rotation starter.

Year	Club (League)	Class	W	L	ERA	G	GS	CG	SV	IP	H	R	ER	HR	BB	SO	AVG
2003	Red Sox (GCL)	R	3	4	1.62	11	8	0	0	39	26	12	7	0	18	34	.186
	Reds (GCL)	R	0	0	.00	1	1	0	0	3	3	0	0	0	0	1	.273
2004	Dayton (Mid)	A	1	7	8.66	14	10	0	0	45	66	49	43	6	20	38	.340
	Billings (Pio)	R	9	3	3.44	18	12	0	0	73	67	36	28	3	39	81	.245
MINOR LEAGUE TOTALS			13	14	4.40	44	31	0	0	160	162	97	78	9	77	154	.262

10 Paul Janish, ss

Born: Oct. 12, 1982. **Ht.:** 6-2. **Wt.:** 180. **Bats:** R. **Throws:** R. **School:** Rice University. **Career Transactions:** Selected by Reds in fifth round of 2004 draft; signed June 11, 2004. **Signed by:** Mike Powers.

The shortstop on Rice's College World Series championship team in 2003, Janish would have gotten a chance to pitch in 2005 had he not turned pro for $210,000. He has hit 93 mph off the mound, but his defensive prowess will keep him at shortstop. He was the Reds' MVP in instructional league. Janish is a fluid athlete and a polished defender. He has tremendous hands, and his arm combines above-average strength with accuracy. One club official compared him to Adam Everett. Janish made major offensive strides in 2004, shortening his swing and showing a willingness to go the other way. He has the patience to draw walks and is an average runner. While he held his own in his pro debut, Janish's bat will never be his best tool. He lacks strength and has a sweepy swing that can get long, resulting in below-average power and too many strikeouts. If Janish continues to get on base, he should move quickly in an organization lacking shortstop depth. A jump to Cincinnati's new high Class A Sarasota affililate is possible for 2005.

Year	Club (League)	Class	AVG	G	AB	R	H	2B	3B	HR	RBI	BB	SO	SB	OBP	SLG
2004	Billings (Pio)	R	.263	66	205	39	54	11	0	2	22	45	45	7	.406	.346
MINOR LEAGUE TOTALS			.263	66	205	39	54	11	0	2	22	45	45	7	.406	.346

11 Elizardo Ramirez, rhp

Born: Jan. 28, 1983. **Ht.:** 6-0. **Wt.:** 180. **Bats:** R. **Throws:** R. **Career Transactions:** Signed out of Dominican Republic by Phillies, July 2, 1999 . . . Traded by Phillies with OF Javon Moran and LHP Joe Wilson to Reds Aug. 11, 2004, completing trade in which Phillies received RHP Cory Lidle from Reds, Aug. 9, 2004. **Signed by:** Wil Tejada (Phillies).

Ramirez spent a month last season in Philadelphia as an emergency fill-in reliever. He finished the year in a new organization. The Reds acquired him from the Phillies in a deal for righthander Cory Lidle. The other players in the trade, outfielder Javon Moran and lefthander Joe Wilson, have flashier tools, but Ramirez is much more polished. He emerged as a prospect with a 73-2 strikeout-walk ratio and 1.10 ERA in the Gulf Coast League in 2002. While he hasn't posted numbers quite that gaudy at higher levels, he's still pounding the strike zone with three average pitches. Ramirez has an effortless, easily repeatable delivery and a loose arm, which account for his excellent command. He has maintained his mechanics while going from 140 pounds when he signed to his current 180. He throws his fastball anywhere from 86-92 mph, complementing it with an average curveball and changeup. The Reds want him to be more aggressive early in the count because he lacks a true out pitch that misses bats. In past years, he'd stand a good chance of making the Cincinnati rotation, but the club's improved depth will allow it to give Ramirez his first taste of Triple-A in 2005.

Year	Club (League)	Class	W	L	ERA	G	GS	CG	SV	IP	H	R	ER	HR	BB	SO	AVG
2000	Phillies (DSL)	R	5	2	1.88	11	9	0	1	57	47	19	12	1	5	67	.216
2001	Phillies (DSL)	R	10	1	1.26	14	14	1	0	93	71	26	13	0	9	81	.208
2002	Phillies (GCL)	R	7	1	1.10	11	11	2	0	73	44	18	9	3	2	73	.165
2003	Clearwater (FSL)	A	13	9	3.78	27	25	1	0	157	181	85	66	4	33	101	.290
2004	Clearwater (FSL)	A	5	1	2.44	9	9	1	0	59	55	17	16	3	8	33	.249
	Reading (EL)	AA	2	5	6.68	8	8	1	0	34	51	34	25	4	14	20	.345
	Philadelphia (NL)	MAJ	0	0	4.80	7	0	0	0	15	17	8	8	3	5	9	.283
	Chattanooga (SL)	AA	1	0	3.19	5	5	1	0	31	35	11	11	6	4	23	.282
MAJOR LEAGUE TOTALS			0	0	4.80	7	0	0	0	15	17	8	8	3	5	9	.283
MINOR LEAGUE TOTALS			43	19	2.71	85	81	7	1	504	484	210	152	21	75	398	.249

12 Chris Dickerson, of

Born: April 10, 1982. **Ht.:** 6-4. **Wt.:** 212. **Bats:** L. **Throws:** L. **School:** University of Nevada. **Career Transactions:** Selected by Reds in 16th round of 2003 draft; signed June 9, 2003. **Signed by:** Keith Chapman.

Until B.J. Szymanski's arrival, Dickerson was the best athlete in the system. He has just started scratching the surface of his considerable potential as a power-speed players. So far as a pro, only the speed has shown up. Dickerson has taken to the organization's emphasis on patience and was effective as a leadoff man in low Class A. He's an above-average runner with good range in center field. In fact, with his combination of speed, route-running and an average, accurate arm, the Reds rate Dickerson as a 70 defender in center on the 20-80 scouting scale. Aggressive in the outfield, he hurt his left elbow diving for a fly ball last year. The injury was one reason that Dickerson has yet to translate his raw power into homers. The other reason, scouts say, is that he cuts himself off in his swing and settles for a little man's approach instead of taking advantage of his natural strength with a healthier cut. Dickerson will return to high Class A, where he finished last season, to begin 2005.

Year	Club (League)	Class	AVG	G	AB	R	H	2B	3B	HR	RBI	BB	SO	SB	OBP	SLG
2003	Billings (Pio)	R	.244	58	201	36	49	6	4	6	38	39	66	9	.376	.403
2004	Dayton (Mid)	A	.303	84	314	50	95	15	3	4	34	51	92	27	.410	.408
	Potomac (Car)	A	.200	15	45	5	9	2	0	0	5	7	14	3	.321	.244
MINOR LEAGUE TOTALS			.273	157	560	91	153	23	7	10	77	97	172	39	.390	.393

13 David Shafer, rhp

Born: March 7, 1982. **Ht.:** 6-2. **Wt.:** 180. **Bats:** R. **Throws:** R. **School:** Central Arizona JC. **Career Transactions:** Selected by Reds in 32nd round of 2001 draft; signed June 1, 2002. **Signed by:** Mark Corey.

The Reds' tandem-starter system obscured Shafer's 2004 performance, precluding him from putting up big numbers on a bad Dayton team. It couldn't obscure his development as one of the system's higher-ceiling arms. Shafer played at Junior College World Series champion Central Arizona Junior College in 2002, alongside Scott Hairston, Rich Harden and Rangers shortstop prospect Ian Kinsler, going 16-5 in two years as a starter. Cincinnati liked his loose arm, signed him as a draft-and-follow in 2002 and moved him to the bullpen. He worked as both a reliever and starter in 2004, finishing the year as high Class A Potomac's closer. The wiry-strong Shafer has some projection left on a fastball that sits at 88-92 mph and reaches 94. It has good life down in the zone, is always around the plate and works well with his slider, which he commands well but needs to tighten. His advanced command of both pitches could help him move quickly. Shafer has worked on a changeup that he would need as a starter, but his durability and live arm profile well for relief. The Reds say his makeup could make him a closer, and with a good spring he could open 2005 in that role in Double-A.

Year	Club (League)	Class	W	L	ERA	G	GS	CG	SV	IP	H	R	ER	HR	BB	SO	AVG
2002	Reds (GCL)	R	1	0	1.29	3	0	0	1	7	3	2	1	0	2	7	.125
	Billings (Pio)	R	5	2	1.72	19	0	0	4	31	30	14	6	0	11	30	.242
2003	Billings (Pio)	R	0	3	3.04	25	0	0	13	24	25	13	8	1	3	32	.253
2004	Potomac (Car)	A	0	0	0.00	3	0	0	3	4	5	0	0	0	0	5	.294
	Dayton (Mid)	A	5	3	2.92	31	7	0	5	77	60	32	25	8	16	84	.214
MINOR LEAGUE TOTALS			11	8	2.51	81	7	0	26	143	123	61	40	9	32	158	.226

14 Kevin Howard, 2b

Born: June 25, 1981. **Ht.:** 6-2. **Wt.:** 180. **Bats:** L. **Throws:** R. **School:** University of Miami. **Career Transactions:** Selected by Reds in fifth round of 2002 draft; signed Nov. 15, 2002. **Signed by:** Greg Zunino.

Howard has an impressive track record and keeps succeeding despite average tools and an unorthodox style. He was on the Long Beach team, led by Sean Burroughs, that won the 1993 Little League World Series, and he won a College World Series championship at Miami in 2001, a year after he was Baseball America's Freshman of the Year. He hit .413 as a freshman, played for Team USA as a sophomore and had a strong junior season, yet lasted until the fifth round in 2002 because he didn't have a clear position and lacked an outstanding tool. Howard is a good athlete whose best attribute is his bat. He's a patient, line-drive hitter who knows and exploits situations, and he has shown improved power. He hangs in well against lefthanders, and his overall game reminds the Reds of Adam Kennedy's. Howard played shortstop and third base in college, but Cincinnati moved him to second base because his arm strength, short-circuited by a funky delivery, is below average. Howard is taller and rangier than the usual second baseman and has average range, but he's still learning his way around the right side of the infield. He needs to improve his footwork around the bag on the double-play pivot. His winning makeup, athleticism and solid bat make him a good bet to reach the majors as at least a utilityman. After a solid Arizona Fall League performance, he's headed for Double-A.

Year	Club (League)	Class	AVG	G	AB	R	H	2B	3B	HR	RBI	BB	SO	SB	OBP	SLG
2003	Dayton (Mid)	A	.285	134	509	80	145	26	3	9	75	50	67	12	.355	.401
2004	Potomac (Car)	A	.284	124	468	68	133	24	0	11	79	58	70	8	.364	.406
MINOR LEAGUE TOTALS			.285	258	977	148	278	50	3	20	154	108	137	20	.359	.403

15 Ben Kozlowski, lhp

Born: Aug. 16, 1980. **Ht.:** 6-6. **Wt.:** 220. **Bats:** L. **Throws:** L. **School:** Santa Fe (Fla.) CC. **Career Transactions:** Selected by Braves in 12th round of 1999 draft; signed June 12, 1999 . . . Traded by Braves to Rangers for LHP Andy Pratt, April 9, 2002 . . . Claimed on waivers by Reds from Rangers, Oct. 8, 2004. **Signed by:** Marco Paddy (Braves).

In 2002, Kozlowski looked like one of the game's emerging prospects. After the Braves traded him to the Rangers, he reached the big leagues and entered 2003 as Texas' No. 2 prospect. He had Tommy John surgery that June, however. He got back on a mound in spring training last year and was pitching in games by June at high Class A. While the Rangers were pleased with his work ethic in his rehabilitation, as well as his leadership role on a prospect-laden Stockton staff, Kozlowski had the requisite post-Tommy John struggles with command and a feel for pitching. His fastball velocity was solid, though more in the high 80s than the low 90s he used to flash. The biggest difference last year was that his once-plus curveball wasn't biting as it had in the past, leaving Kozlowski without a strikeout pitch. The Rangers tried to move him off their 40-man roster in October, and the Reds claimed him on waivers. Cincinnati won't know exactly what it has in Kozlowski until spring training. He never has pitched in Triple-A, and 2005 seems like the perfect time.

Year	Club (League)	Class	W	L	ERA	G	GS	CG	SV	IP	H	R	ER	HR	BB	SO	AVG
1999	Braves (GCL)	R	1	1	1.87	15	0	0	3	34	28	9	7	0	6	29	.222
2000	Macon (SAL)	A	3	8	4.21	15	14	0	0	77	76	53	36	6	39	67	.252
2001	Myrtle Beach (Car)	A	0	2	3.77	2	2	0	0	14	15	7	6	1	3	13	.283
	Macon (SAL)	A	10	7	2.48	26	23	1	0	145	134	60	40	8	27	147	.248
2002	Myrtle Beach (Car)	A	0	1	4.50	1	1	0	0	4	4	5	2	0	3	3	.235
	Charlotte (FSL)	A	4	4	2.05	21	12	0	0	79	63	31	18	2	25	76	.219
	Tulsa (TL)	AA	4	2	1.90	8	8	0	0	52	28	12	11	3	22	41	.155
	Texas (AL)	MAJ	0	0	6.30	2	2	0	0	10	11	7	7	3	11	6	.289
2003	Frisco (TL)	AA	3	2	5.43	11	10	0	0	55	71	38	33	4	27	29	.313
2004	Frisco (TL)	AA	3	2	4.89	8	7	0	1	39	38	25	21	5	20	23	.270
	Stockton (CAL)	A	4	2	3.83	10	8	0	0	47	40	23	20	1	19	32	.234
MAJOR LEAGUE TOTALS			0	0	6.30	2	2	0	0	10	11	7	7	3	11	6	.289
MINOR LEAGUE TOTALS			32	31	3.20	117	85	1	4	546	497	263	194	30	191	460	.243

16 Miguel Perez, c

Born: Sept. 25, 1983. **Ht.:** 6-3. **Wt.:** 190. **Bats:** R. **Throws:** R. **Career Transactions:** Signed out of Venezuela by Reds, Nov. 15, 2000. **Signed by:** Jorge Oquendo.

The Reds have three catchers—Miguel Perez, Brian Peterson and Dane Sardinha—with advanced defensive skills who can catch and throw in the majors right now, but all three have serious questions about their offense. Perez is the youngest and has the most upside offensively. Some in the organization consider Perez its best position-player prospect after Edwin Encarnacion, based almost solely on his defense. Perez produces 1.8- to 1.9-second pop times to second base, and Cincinnati rates his arm and defense as 70 on the 20-80 scouting scale. He's agile, athletic and intelligent, all traits of an elite defender, though he threw out just 28 percent of basestealers last year. Perez has a long way to go for his offense to be in the same ballpark as his defense. His ceiling is .260 with 10-15 homers. He has average power potential and is filling out his solid frame. But he lacks the approach to make consistent contact to take advantage of his power. Perez is overly aggressive and lacks patience. He needs to start hitting at the Reds' new high Class A Sarasota affiliate this year if he's going to have a reasonable chance of fulfilling the organization's high hopes.

Year	Club (League)	Class	AVG	G	AB	R	H	2B	3B	HR	RBI	BB	SO	SB	OBP	SLG
2001	Cagua (VSL)	R	.331	48	163	20	54	3	1	0	19	12	33	6	.377	.362
2002	Cagua (VSL)	R	.213	34	108	14	23	4	0	2	18	9	23	1	.320	.306
	Reds (GCL)	R	.360	26	86	12	31	1	0	0	11	2	9	3	.396	.372
2003	Dayton (Mid)	A	.172	20	58	3	10	0	0	0	3	4	19	1	.273	.172
	Billings (Pio)	R	.339	60	227	46	77	11	2	1	25	18	27	1	.410	.419
2004	Dayton (Mid)	A	.237	74	249	22	59	7	0	1	22	16	62	2	.309	.277
	Potomac (Car)	A	.232	18	69	7	16	2	0	0	5	1	12	1	.239	.261
MINOR LEAGUE TOTALS			.281	280	960	124	270	28	3	4	103	62	185	15	.346	.329

17 Javon Moran, of

Born: Sept. 30, 1982. **Ht.:** 5-11. **Wt.:** 175. **Bats:** R. **Throws:** R. **School:** Auburn University. **Career Transactions:** Selected by Phillies in fifth round of 2003 draft; signed June 24, 2003 . . . Traded by Phillies with RHP Elizardo Ramirez and LHP Joe Wilson to Reds for RHP Cory Lidle, Aug. 9, 2004. **Signed by:** Mike Stauffer (Phillies).

Part of the Cory Lidle trade last August, Moran was particularly impressive after switching organizations, recording 11 multihit efforts in 25 games. He has good speed and instincts, and will profile as a center fielder/leadoff man if his bat plays. A plus runner, he had 52 steals last year, more than any Reds farmhand. He does need to boost his 72 percent success rate. Moran has enough range for center field, where he's a solid-average defender with a below-average arm. His slashing swing produces line drives from foul pole to foul pole, and his wiry strong frame keeps him from being overpowered by good fastballs. Plate discipline will dictate Moran's success. He drew 20 walks during his last two years of college combined, and that impatience continued with the Phillies. The Reds forced him to take a strike before swinging (as they do for all their minor league hitters), and Moran's patience and performance at the plate improved. Now the Reds want to see him do it again in high Class A.

Year	Club (League)	Class	AVG	G	AB	R	H	2B	3B	HR	RBI	BB	SO	SB	OBP	SLG
2003	Batavia (NY-P)	A	.284	60	250	33	71	9	3	1	12	16	32	27	.326	.356
2004	Lakewood (SAL)	A	.285	101	421	73	120	18	9	2	38	24	78	41	.340	.385
	Dayton (Mid)	A	.383	25	94	11	36	2	0	0	7	10	15	11	.448	.404
MINOR LEAGUE TOTALS			.297	186	765	117	227	29	12	3	57	50	125	79	.349	.378

18 Steve Kelly, rhp

Born: Sept. 30, 1979. **Ht.:** 6-1. **Wt.:** 195. **Bats:** R. **Throws:** R. **School:** Georgia Tech. **Career Transactions:** Selected by Reds in fourth round of 2001 draft; signed June 19, 2001. **Signed by:** Steve Kring.

When Kelly was a high school senior in 1998, a sudden leap in fastball velocity to the 90-92 mph range made his draft stock soar. Many scouts considered his curveball one of the best in the draft, and the White Sox selected him in the fifth round. He didn't sign, though, instead heading to Georgia Tech. After an injury-plagued freshman year, Kelly went 15-7, 4.63 his last two seasons. He has had his greatest success since moving up to Double-A, tying for the Southern League lead in wins, innings and starts last year. Kelly's curveball is no longer considered a plus pitch, but it's solid-average, as are his changeup and a slider he has added since turning pro. He commands his fastball well, but it usually has below-average velocity at 86-88 mph. He does the little things well, such as holding runners and fielding his position. His overall package resembles that of Jeff Suppan, though Kelly's fastball and curve are a notch below Suppan's. Kelly will head to Triple-A for the first time in 2005.

Year	Club (League)	Class	W	L	ERA	G	GS	CG	SV	IP	H	R	ER	HR	BB	SO	AVG
2001	Billings (Pio)	R	4	2	2.30	12	7	0	0	55	50	16	14	3	11	54	.236
2002	Stockton (CAL)	A	6	3	4.09	19	19	0	0	106	119	63	48	6	32	80	.280
	Dayton (Mid)	A	4	1	3.15	7	7	1	0	46	42	16	16	1	7	35	.243
2003	Potomac (Car)	A	7	5	3.87	17	17	0	0	95	105	52	41	3	28	69	.283
	Chattanooga (SL)	AA	4	2	2.09	6	6	0	0	39	34	11	9	0	12	30	.254
2004	Chattanooga (SL)	AA	12	7	2.96	28	28	0	0	161	156	69	53	12	48	116	.250
MINOR LEAGUE TOTALS			37	20	3.25	89	84	1	0	501	506	227	181	25	138	384	.261

19 Dane Sardinha, c

Born: April 8, 1979. **Ht.:** 6-0. **Wt.:** 215. **Bats:** R. **Throws:** R. **School:** Pepperdine University. **Career Transactions:** Selected by Reds in second round of 2000 draft; signed Sept. 1, 2000. **Signed by:** Craig Kornfeld.

The first round of the 2000 draft was one of the worst in baseball history, as clubs worried more about signability than ability in a lean year for talent. Complicating matters, Scott Boras was advising most of the top college players available. His stable included Sardinha, who signed a $1.75 million major league contract with no bonus as a second-rounder. But fears that he wouldn't hit have proven well-founded, and there were no takers when the Reds removed him from their 40-man roster in 2003. Sardinha, whose brothers Bronson (Yankees) and Duke (Rockies) were active in the minors last year, still has excellent catch-and-throw skills. He's as good a receiver as Miguel Perez is, but his arm isn't quite in the same league. It's better than his 24 percent rate of catching basestealers last year would indicate, however. Sardinha is more advanced offensively than Perez, but his ceiling with the bat is low. While he has improved at using the whole field and letting his natural strength produce average power, Sardinha is among the minors' least choosy hitters. He had his best year at the plate in 2004, though that's not saying much. Sardinha's bat is that of a backup at best, and the Reds will keep in Triple-A as big league insurance.

Year	Club (League)	Class	AVG	G	AB	R	H	2B	3B	HR	RBI	BB	SO	SB	OBP	SLG
2001	Mudville (Cal)	A	.235	109	422	45	99	24	2	9	55	12	97	0	.259	.365
2002	Chattanooga (SL)	AA	.206	106	394	34	81	20	0	4	40	14	114	0	.234	.287
2003	Chattanooga (SL)	AA	.256	72	246	21	63	15	0	3	32	22	61	5	.313	.354
	Cincinnati (NL)	MAJ	.000	1	2	0	0	0	0	0	0	0	1	0	.000	.000
2004	Louisville (IL)	AAA	.262	89	324	32	85	17	1	9	40	10	94	0	.294	.404
MAJOR LEAGUE TOTALS			.000	1	2	0	0	0	0	0	0	0	1	0	.000	.000
MINOR LEAGUE TOTALS			.237	376	1386	132	328	76	3	25	167	58	366	5	.270	.350

20 Rafael Gonzalez, rhp

Born: March 21, 1986. **Ht.:** 6-3. **Wt.:** 225. **Bats:** R. **Throws:** R. **School:** George Washington HS, New York, N.Y. **Career Transactions:** Selected by Reds in fourth round of 2004 draft; signed June 16, 2004. **Signed by:** Jason Baker.

Gonzalez drew scouts to George Washington High in the Bronx—Manny Ramirez' alma mater—before moving to the Dominican Republic, his parents' homeland, in 2003. The Yankees signed him for $200,000 after a tryout, but the commissioner's office voided the contract after discovering Gonzalez was an American citizen subject to the draft. He returned to New York but was ineligible for his senior season, pitching instead on a scout team once a week. His body, once long and lean, got out of shape, leaving his stuff and velocity in flux. The Reds took a chance on him and signed him for $315,000. As his conditioning improved, Gonzalez showed better velocity in the Gulf Coast League, touching 96 mph. He has a loose arm and is a power pitcher, throwing an inconsistent but at times nasty splitter. His knuckle-curve will have to improve for Gonzalez to remain a starter. His raw arm strength rates near the top in the organization, and the Reds are eager to see how it plays in low Class A this year.

Year	Club (League)	Class	W	L	ERA	G	GS	CG	SV	IP	H	R	ER	HR	BB	SO	AVG
2004	Reds (GCL)	R	1	6	4.20	12	8	0	0	41	38	25	19	3	18	32	.258
MINOR LEAGUE TOTALS			1	6	4.20	12	8	0	0	41	38	25	19	3	18	32	.258

21 Daylan Childress, rhp

Born: July 31, 1978. **Ht.:** 6-1. **Wt.:** 200. **Bats:** R. **Throws:** R. **School:** McLennan (Texas) CC. **Career Transactions:** Selected by Reds in fifth round of 2001 draft; signed June 6, 2001. **Signed by:** Jim Gonzales.

The Reds have several middle-relief prospects whose value would soar if they could cut it as starting pitchers, such as David Shafer, or if they had closer stuff and makeup, such as Todd Coffey. Childress sits in between. Cincinnati has decided its best role is in relief, and they think he has the resilience and makeup for a set-up role. His fastball velocity picks up in short stints, and he pitched at 90-93 mph in Double-A and the Arizona Fall League. His breaking ball is a slurvy hybrid. Sometimes it's more of a slider, but it works better when he stays on top of it and throws a true curve. After showing progress with a changeup earlier in his career, Childress never gained a feel for the pitch. His competitiveness and strong, compact frame should be assets in relief, though he needs to throw more strikes. Childress is a candidate for a big league job this spring but likely is headed for his first stint in Triple-A.

Year	Club (League)	Class	W	L	ERA	G	GS	CG	SV	IP	H	R	ER	HR	BB	SO	AVG
2001	Billings (Pio)	R	6	1	3.55	14	8	0	1	63	59	32	25	4	17	54	.246
2002	Dayton (Mid)	A	9	10	3.51	28	27	1	0	169	147	82	66	7	68	152	.233
2003	Potomac (Car)	A	5	9	3.00	17	16	2	0	96	78	44	32	3	45	89	.225
	Chattanooga (SL)	AA	2	4	6.75	9	9	0	0	48	53	41	36	4	26	35	.293
2004	Chattanooga (SL)	AA	3	5	3.42	29	9	0	7	82	73	37	31	9	31	77	.241
MINOR LEAGUE TOTALS			25	29	3.73	97	69	3	8	458	410	236	190	27	187	407	.241

22 Chris Denorfia, of

Born: July 15, 1980. **Ht.:** 6-1. **Wt.:** 185. **Bats:** R. **Throws:** R. **School:** Wheaton (Mass.) College. **Career Transactions:** Selected by Reds in 19th round of 2002 draft; signed June 8, 2002. **Signed by:** John Brickley.

Denorfia is the greatest player to come out of Wheaton College, which went from a women's college to a co-ed school in 1987, and the first player drafted from the school. They liken him to former Reds farmhand Brady Clark, though they admit Clark has the better bat due to his power. Denorfia relies on his savvy, patience and average strength, using the whole field and repeating his swing well. He's a good enough baserunner to steal 10-15 bases as well. His spike in home runs in 2004 owed mostly to his experience in the Carolina League, and his power is fringy. His defense will help him get to Cincinnati, as he's an average defender in center field with an above-average arm, the best of a weak lot in the organization and good enough for right field. On a championship team, Denorfia would be a solid fourth outfielder, like Clark. He'll likely be the center fielder in Double-A this year.

Year	Club (League)	Class	AVG	G	AB	R	H	2B	3B	HR	RBI	BB	SO	SB	OBP	SLG
2002	Reds (GCL)	R	.340	57	200	38	68	9	2	0	19	31	23	18	.425	.405
	Chattanooga (SL)	AA	.429	3	7	0	3	2	1	0	0	2	1	0	.556	1.000
	Dayton (Mid)	A	.000	3	10	2	0	0	0	0	0	0	3	0	.000	.000
2003	Potomac (Car)	A	.236	128	470	60	111	10	5	4	39	54	106	20	.317	.304
2004	Potomac (Car)	A	.312	75	269	52	84	18	4	11	51	48	66	10	.416	.532
	Chattanooga (SL)	AA	.249	61	221	30	55	10	2	6	27	30	42	5	.340	.394
MINOR LEAGUE TOTALS			.273	327	1177	182	321	49	14	21	136	165	241	53	.362	.392

23 Anderson Machado, ss

Born: Jan. 25, 1981. **Ht.:** 5-11. **Wt.:** 165. **Bats:** B. **Throws:** R. **Career Transactions:** Signed out of Venezuela by Phillies, Jan. 14, 1998 . . . Traded by Phillies with RHP Josh Hancock to Reds for RHP Todd Jones and OF Brad Correll, July 30, 2004. **Signed by:** Jesus Mendes (Phillies).

Machado came from Philadelphia in a trade-deadline deal for Todd Jones last July. He had been the Phillies' top middle-infield prospect, and they had been patient with him. He has been known for his glove, which got him to the big leagues in September with Cincinnati. He's a premium defender with soft hands, plus range and good arm strength. Offensively, Machado has tried different swings and approaches, to the same frustrating effect. His best offensive trait is he's patient and willing to take a walk, but he has dangerous power—just enough to think he can hit home runs. He's also an above-average runner. Machado was playing winter ball in his native Venezuela, tuning up for a shot at the Reds' shortstop job, when he injured his left knee. It took him a month to get a visa so he could come to the United States and have his knee examined. He didn't tear his anterior-cruciate ligament, as had been feared, but needed arthroscopic surgery and won't be ready for the start of the season.

Year	Club (League)	Class	AVG	G	AB	R	H	2B	3B	HR	RBI	BB	SO	SB	OBP	SLG
1998	Phillies (DSL)	R	.201	68	219	26	44	7	0	0	17	30	44	4	.313	.233
1999	Piedmont (SAL)	A	.233	20	60	7	14	4	2	0	7	7	20	2	.324	.367
	Phillies (GCL)	R	.259	43	143	26	37	6	3	2	12	15	38	6	.335	.385
	Clearwater (FSL)	A	.000	1	2	0	0	0	0	0	0	0	1	0	.000	.000
2000	Clearwater (FSL)	A	.245	117	417	55	102	19	7	1	35	54	103	32	.330	.331
	Reading (EL)	AA	.364	3	11	2	4	1	0	1	2	0	4	0	.364	.727
2001	Clearwater (FSL)	A	.261	82	272	49	71	5	8	5	36	31	66	23	.342	.393
	Reading (EL)	AA	.149	31	101	13	15	2	0	1	8	12	25	5	.237	.198
2002	Reading (EL)	AA	.251	126	450	71	113	24	3	12	77	72	118	40	.353	.398
2003	Reading (EL)	AA	.196	123	423	80	83	19	4	5	20	108	120	49	.360	.296
2004	Clearwater (FSL)	A	.227	7	22	0	5	0	0	0	1	4	2	0	.346	.227
	Scranton (IL)	AAA	.227	78	295	51	67	12	5	6	26	50	73	11	.337	.363
	Louisville (IL)	AAA	.229	31	109	14	25	5	2	0	12	10	26	3	.295	.312
	Cincinnati (NL)	MAJ	.268	17	56	6	15	5	1	0	4	10	26	3	.379	.393
MAJOR LEAGUE TOTALS			.268	17	56	6	15	5	1	0	4	10	26	3	.379	.393
MINOR LEAGUE TOTALS			.230	730	2524	394	580	104	34	33	253	393	640	175	.335	.337

24 Jesse Gutierrez, 1b

Born: June 16, 1978. **Ht.:** 6-2. **Wt.:** 195. **Bats:** R. **Throws:** R. **School:** St. Mary's (Texas) University. **Career Transactions:** Selected by Reds in 20th round of 2001 draft; signed June 6, 2001. **Signed by:** Jim Gonzales.

Gutierrez is one of the Reds' best hitters and stands out in the organization for his steady, solid track record with the bat. Gutierrez hit in college, leading NCAA Division I with an .855 slugging percentage at Texas-Pan American in 2000 and Division II with 28 homers for St. Mary's in 2001, leading the school to the D-II College World Series championship and winning tournament MVP honors. He's coming off his best full season as a pro, ranking third in the Southern League in RBIs and extra-base hits (53). Gutierrez is an above-average hitter who has excellent pull power, and he makes consistent contact for a power hitter. He stays on breaking balls and mashes against lefthanders (.312 average, .507 slugging in 2004). He's limited defensively at first base and profiles better as an American League player. He has played catcher in the minors and would enhance his value if he could stick there, but he didn't see time behind the plate last year. His defensive abilities lag far behind other Reds catching prospects. His most realistic role is as a righthanded bat who occasionally catches and plays first base. After a successful Arizona Fall League stint, he'll move up to Triple-A in 2005.

Year	Club (League)	Class	AVG	G	AB	R	H	2B	3B	HR	RBI	BB	SO	SB	OBP	SLG
2001	Billings (Pio)	R	.294	72	269	45	79	21	0	16	61	29	43	1	.369	.550
2002	Dayton (Mid)	A	.273	123	458	51	125	28	1	13	66	32	78	2	.324	.424
2003	Potomac (Car)	A	.278	108	400	52	111	26	0	16	76	22	52	1	.325	.463
	Chattanooga (SL)	AA	.215	27	107	12	23	8	1	4	20	9	16	0	.288	.421
2004	Chattanooga (SL)	AA	.292	127	487	74	142	32	4	17	82	36	64	0	.352	.478
MINOR LEAGUE TOTALS			.279	457	1721	234	480	115	6	66	305	128	253	4	.337	.468

25 Chris Gruler, rhp

Born: Sept. 11, 1983. **Ht.:** 6-3. **Wt.:** 200. **Bats:** R. **Throws:** R. **School:** Liberty Union HS, Brentwood, Calif. **Career Transactions:** Selected by Reds in first round (third overall) of 2002 draft; signed June 5, 2002. **Signed by:** Butch Baccala.

For Cincinnati fans who follow the draft, Gruler is a painful reminder of a missed opportunity. The Reds held the No. 3 pick in the 2002 draft, and Gruler's excellent workout and strong finish to the spring season swung the organization to pick him instead of Scott Kazmir.

Three years later Kazmir is the top lefthanded pitching prospect in the game, while Gruler is fighting his way back from shoulder surgery performed in April 2003. Gruler had both a torn labrum and rotator cuff, requiring a long year of rehab. He hasn't regained his pre-injury stuff, which included an 89-95 mph fastball and a plus curveball. His command hasn't come back either, but he was pain-free and pushing 90 mph in instructional league. His fall performance and relative youth (21) make him more likely to return from his injury than other top Reds pitching prospects who have gone down, including lefthanders Phil Dumatrait and Ty Howington and righty Bobby Basham. None of those three pitched in 2004. Cincinnati's immediate goal is for Gruler to turn in a full, healthy 2005 season in low Class A.

Year	Club (League)	Class	W	L	ERA	G	GS	CG	SV	IP	H	R	ER	HR	BB	SO	AVG
2002	Billings (Pio)	R	0	0	1.08	4	4	0	0	17	11	3	2	1	6	11	.183
	Dayton (Mid)	A	0	1	5.60	7	7	0	0	27	23	19	17	2	16	31	.228
2003	Dayton (Mid)	A	0	2	7.00	3	3	0	0	6	10	19	17	0	12	6	.370
2004	Billings (Pio)	R	0	0	19.29	1	1	0	0	2	4	5	5	0	2	2	.364
MINOR LEAGUE TOTALS			0	3	7.10	15	15	0	0	52	48	46	41	3	36	50	.241

26 Calvin Medlock, rhp

Born: Nov. 8, 1982. **Ht.:** 5-10. **Wt.:** 175. **Bats:** R. **Throws:** R. **School:** North Central Texas CC. **Career Transactions:** Selected by Reds in 39th round of 2002 draft; signed May 20, 2003. **Signed by:** Jimmy Gonzales.

A standout reliever in junior college and in his pro debut, Medlock got a chance to pitch in the rotation last year because Dayton needed arms for its tandem-starter system. He broke out in the first half before struggling after a promotion to high Class A. Medlock stands just 5-foot-10, which leaves his fastball on a relatively straight plane to home plate, and he commands just two pitches. His fastball can reach 93 mph on occasion and sit in the high 80s on others, and he's adept at using it inside. He also has a solid two-plane curveball that he uses as a strikeout pitch. He's poised with runners on base and is a tough competitor. The whole package screams middle reliever, slotting Medlock in behind Todd Coffey, David Shafer and Daylan Childress, all of whom either throw harder or have a better secondary pitch. Medlock will go back to high Class A as a reliever this year and could move quickly.

Year	Club (League)	Class	W	L	ERA	G	GS	CG	SV	IP	H	R	ER	HR	BB	SO	AVG
2003	Reds (GCL)	R	0	0	0.00	3	0	0	0	5	5	1	0	0	0	3	.263
	Billings (Pio)	R	1	0	1.88	19	0	0	1	29	25	7	6	1	9	31	.234
2004	Dayton (Mid)	A	8	3	2.57	22	15	0	0	95	74	33	27	5	21	111	.208
	Potomac (Car)	A	3	4	6.36	11	9	0	1	47	49	36	33	8	22	46	.265
MINOR LEAGUE TOTALS			12	7	3.39	55	24	0	2	175	153	77	66	14	52	191	.230

27 Carlos Guevara, rhp

Born: March 18, 1982. **Ht.:** 6-0. **Wt.:** 175. **Bats:** R. **Throws:** R. **School:** Saint Mary's (Texas) University. **Career Transactions:** Selected by Reds in seventh round of 2003 draft; signed June 7, 2003. **Signed by:** Jim Gonzales.

Guevara is a short righthander who went to St. Mary's, where he played with Jesse Gutierrez and helped the team win the 2001 NCAA Division II national championship. Guevara lacks a plus fastball, as his sits in the 87-89 mph range. His curveball is just a decent pitch, clearly his third-best. And he already has had elbow problems, as bone chips sidelined him for much of the 2003 season. But he's on this list because he has a plus screwball that he commands well. St. Mary's pitching coach John Maley was a disciple of Mike Marshall's pitching methods and taught Guevara the pitch, which he took to immediately. It makes hitters swing and miss, and it was the biggest reason that Guevara ranked third among minor league relievers last year with 14.3 strikeouts per nine innings. His build and elbow trouble, plus his reliance on a gimmick pitch, consign him to the bullpen. He probably will open this year as a closer in high Class A.

Year	Club (League)	Class	W	L	ERA	G	GS	CG	SV	IP	H	R	ER	HR	BB	SO	AVG
2003	Billings (Pio)	R	1	0	0.82	2	2	0	0	11	4	1	1	0	3	14	.108
	Dayton (Mid)	A	0	1	3.43	12	3	0	0	39	37	17	15	4	14	39	.247
2004	Dayton (Mid)	A	3	4	2.86	44	0	0	9	57	47	22	18	6	24	90	.221
MINOR LEAGUE TOTALS			3	4	2.86	44	0	0	9	57	47	22	18	6	24	90	.221

28 Matt Belisle, rhp

Born: June 6, 1980. **Ht.:** 6-3. **Wt.:** 190. **Bats:** B. **Throws:** R. **School:** McCallum HS, Austin. **Career Transactions:** Selected by Braves in second round of 1998 draft; signed Aug. 23, 1998 . . . Traded by Braves to Reds, Aug. 14, 2003, completing trade in which Reds sent LHP Kent Mercker to Braves for a player to be named (Aug. 12, 2003). **Signed by:** Charlie Smith (Braves).

The Reds system is dotted with former Braves pitching prospects, none of whom has helped Cincinnati in the big leagues yet. Scouts hold out more hope for Belisle than Bubba Nelson, who was pummeled in the majors last year. Nelson can show better stuff, but Belisle competes much harder. A former prep phenom, Belisle has relied more on guile and command than stuff since rupturing a disc in his back and missing the 2001 season. His fastball sits in the 86-89 mph range. When he's at his best, his heater scrapes the low 90s and gets lots of groundballs because he stays tall in his delivery and throws downhill. Belisle's curveball and changeup are fringe-average, and he needs to be fine to succeed. One Reds official called him the organization's hardest worker and champions Belisle as a future fourth or fifth starter as he gets stronger and gains consistency with his sinker. Both Belisle and Nelson were protected on the 40-man roster and should return to Triple-A this year.

Year	Club (League)	Class	W	L	ERA	G	GS	CG	SV	IP	H	R	ER	HR	BB	SO	AVG
1999	Danville (Appy)	R	2	5	4.67	14	14	0	0	71	86	50	37	3	23	60	.291
2000	Macon (SAL)	A	9	5	2.37	15	15	1	0	102	79	37	27	7	18	97	.216
	Myrtle Beach (Car)	A	3	4	3.43	12	12	0	0	79	72	32	30	5	11	71	.246
2001	Did not play—Injured																
2002	Greenville (SL)	AA	5	9	4.35	26	26	1	0	159	162	91	77	18	39	123	.261
2003	Greenville (SL)	AA	6	8	3.52	21	21	1	0	125	128	59	49	5	42	94	.272
	Richmond (IL)	AAA	1	1	2.25	3	3	0	0	20	17	6	5	1	0	10	.230
	Louisville (IL)	AAA	1	3	3.81	4	4	0	0	26	31	15	11	2	5	15	.304
	Cincinnati (NL)	MAJ	1	1	5.19	6	0	0	0	9	10	5	5	1	2	6	.303
2004	Louisville (IL)	AAA	9	11	5.26	28	28	2	0	163	192	104	95	16	51	106	.301
MAJOR LEAGUE TOTALS			1	1	5.19	6	0	0	0	9	10	5	5	1	2	6	.303
MINOR LEAGUE TOTALS			36	46	3.99	123	123	5	0	746	767	394	331	57	189	576	.268

29 Stephen Smitherman, of/1b

Born: Sept. 1, 1978. **Ht.:** 6-4. **Wt.:** 235. **Bats:** R. **Throws:** R. **School:** University of Arkansas-Little Rock. **Career Transactions:** Selected by Reds in 23rd round of 2000 draft; signed June 7, 2000. **Signed by:** Jim Gonzales.

No Reds farmhand had a bigger 2003 than Smitherman, who led the Southern League in on-base percentage, played in the Futures Game and finished the year in the big leagues. So his 2004 season was a major disappointment, as he regressed offensively and was left off the 40-man roster. Pitchers tied up Smitherman inside and he consistently expanded his strike zone when behind in the count. He salvaged his season by making adjustments in the second half, showing more patience and started going the other way, relying on his above-average natural raw power rather than trying to pull everything. Smitherman profiles best as a platoon corner outfielder against lefthanders, and he hit .337 against them in 2004. He'll return to Triple-A to see if he can recapture his prior form.

Year	Club (League)	Class	AVG	G	AB	R	H	2B	3B	HR	RBI	BB	SO	SB	OBP	SLG
2000	Billings (Pio)	R	.316	70	301	61	95	16	5	15	65	23	67	14	.373	.551
2001	Dayton (Mid)	A	.280	134	497	89	139	45	2	20	73	43	113	16	.348	.499
2002	Stockton (Cal)	A	.313	128	482	78	151	36	1	19	99	39	126	17	.362	.510
2003	Chattanooga (SL)	AA	.310	105	365	60	113	21	2	19	73	54	95	11	.402	.534
	Cincinnati (NL)	MAJ	.159	21	44	3	7	2	0	1	6	3	9	1	.213	.273
	Louisville (IL)	AAA	.127	17	63	1	8	0	0	0	5	4	19	0	.188	.127
2004	Louisville (IL)	AAA	.272	129	452	55	123	35	1	10	52	42	107	5	.340	.420
MAJOR LEAGUE TOTALS			.159	21	44	3	7	2	0	1	6	3	9	1	.213	.273
MINOR LEAGUE TOTALS			.291	583	2160	344	629	153	11	83	367	205	527	63	.358	.488

30 Craig Tatum, c

Born: March 18, 1983. **Ht.:** 6-1. **Wt.:** 215. **Bats:** R. **Throws:** R. **School:** Mississippi State University. **Career Transactions:** Selected by Reds in third round of 2004 draft; signed June 14, 2004. **Signed by:** Jerry Flowers.

The last thing the Reds would seem to need is a defense-first catcher, but they paid Tatum $450,000 as their third-round pick last June. He offers premium defensive skills, including an arm scouts rated as a 65 on the 20-80 scale. He used his plus arm and quick release to catch 36 percent of basestealers to lead the Rookie-level Pioneer League in his debut. His defense was good enough to earn him the nod on the league's postseason all-star team. Tatum will have to work hard to get stronger and keep his fundamentals sound over the course of a long season. He still has work to do offensively, though he has raw power and eventually could hit 15-20 homers a year. His plate discipline will have to improve for his power to show through, but he progressed after signing and had more walks with Billings than in either of his two seasons at Mississippi State. He should open 2005 in low Class A.

Year	Club (League)	Class	AVG	G	AB	R	H	2B	3B	HR	RBI	BB	SO	SB	OBP	SLG
2004	Billings (Pio)	R	.221	42	149	19	33	8	3	2	21	21	36	2	.322	.356
MINOR LEAGUE TOTALS			.221	42	149	19	33	8	3	2	21	21	36	2	.322	.356

CLEVELAND
INDIANS

BY **CHRIS KLINE**

When the Indians promoted Mark Shapiro to general manager in November 2001, he inherited a team coming off its sixth American League Central title in seven seasons. But beneath the surface, the major league roster was full of overpaid thirtysomethings and the farm system was in need of a major overhaul.

Shapiro said the organization needed to be rebuilt, and he started by trading Roberto Alomar to the Mets. Stars such as Bartolo Colon and Jim Thome followed Alomar out of town, and the club went into a spiral. It didn't mollify the fans, but Shapiro promised the Indians would contend again by 2005.

Thanks to trades, the draft and an ability to develop prospects, the Indians are on the brink of Shapiro's original timetable. They crept within a game of the eventual division champion Twins last Aug. 14, and even going 17-27 the rest of the way can't dim their bright future. Their 80-82 record was a 12-game improvement over 2003.

While Shapiro's blockbusters have drawn the most attention—he landed building blocks Grady Sizemore, Cliff Lee and Brandon Phillips from the Expos for Colon—he also has made several successful minor deals. He grabbed Ben Broussard from the Reds for Russell Branyan; added Coco Crisp from the Cardinals while shedding Chuck Finley's contract; got Francisco Cruceta from the Dodgers for Paul Shuey; stole Travis Hafner from the Rangers while dumping Einar Diaz (though Texas also got Ryan Drese); and picked up Josh Phelps

from the Blue Jays for former 41st-round pick Eric Crozier.

Cleveland also has integrated home-grown players into its roster. C.C. Sabathia has become one of the top lefthanders in baseball, while catcher **Victor Martinez** broke out with an all-star season in 2004.

There's more talent on the way. The Indians have been stockpiling arms as they attempt to complement an offense that ranked fifth in the majors in scoring in 2004. Their young pitching staff led by Sabathia and Jake Westbrook was hurt by injuries to Billy Traber and Brian Tallet, inconsistency from Lee and a disastrous season from Jason Davis.

No. 1 prospect Adam Miller is a couple of years away, but Fausto Carmona, Francisco Cabrera, Andrew Brown, Cruceta, Kyle Denney and Jeremy Guthrie should be able to contribute in 2005. More hitting is on the way as well, as Sizemore, Phillips and Jhonny Peralta are ready for full-time duty. While Cleveland hasn't quite returned to its winning ways in the majors, its minor league affiliates are getting the job done. The Indians became the first organization since the Dodgers in 1990 to win championships at four levels in the minors. They captured titles in the Triple-A International, high Class A Carolina, short-season New York-Penn and Rookie-level Dominican Summer leagues.

TOP 30 PROSPECTS

1. Adam Miller, rhp
2. Michael Aubrey, 1b
3. Franklin Gutierrez, of
4. Brad Snyder, of
5. Jeremy Sowers, lhp
6. Fausto Carmona, rhp
7. Fernando Cabrera, rhp
8. Ryan Garko, c/1b
9. Nick Pesco, rhp
10. Andrew Brown, rhp
11. Jake Dittler, rhp
12. Francisco Cruceta, rhp
13. Juan Valdes, of
14. Chuck Lofgren, lhp
15. Mike Butia, of
16. Justin Hoyman, rhp
17. Matt Whitney, 3b
18. Dan Cevette, lhp
19. Scott Lewis, lhp
20. Jason Cooper, of
21. J.D. Martin, rhp
22. Tony Sipp, lhp
23. Kyle Denney, rhp
24. Ryan Goleski, of
25. Jeremy Guthrie, rhp
26. Mariano Gomez, lhp
27. Brian Tallet, lhp
28. Kevin Kouzmanoff, 3b
29. Rafael Perez, lhp
30. Eider Torres, 2b

ORGANIZATION OVERVIEW

General manager: Mark Shapiro. **Farm director:** John Farrell. **Scouting director:** John Mirabelli.

2004 PERFORMANCE

Class	Team	League	W	L	Pct.	Finish*	Manager
Majors	Cleveland	American	80	82	.494	8th (14)	Eric Wedge
Triple-A	Buffalo Bisons	International	83	61	.576	+1st (14)	Marty Brown
Double-A	Akron Aeros	Eastern	63	78	.447	11th (12)	Brad Komminsk
High A	Kinston Indians	Carolina	88	50	.638	+1st (8)	Torey Lovullo
Low A	Lake County Captains	South Atlantic	73	66	.525	5th (16)	Luis Rivera
Short-season	Mahoning Valley Indians	New York-Penn	42	34	.553	+4th (14)	Mike Sarbaugh
Rookie	Burlington Indians	Appalachian	31	35	.470	7th (10)	Rouglas Odor
OVERALL 2004 MINOR LEAGUE RECORD			380	324	.540	5th (30)	

*Finish in overall standings (No. of teams in league). +League champion.

ORGANIZATION LEADERS

BATTING
*Minimum 250 At-Bats
*AVG	Pat Osborn, Kinston	.342
R	Jhonny Peralta, Buffalo	109
H	Jhonny Peralta, Buffalo	181
TB	Jhonny Peralta, Buffalo	274
2B	Jhonny Peralta, Buffalo	44
3B	Mike Conroy, Lake County	10
HR	Ryan Goleski, Lake County	28
RBI	Ryan Goleski, Lake County	104
BB	Corey Smith, Buffalo/Akron	64
SO	John Van Every, Kinston	129
SB	Eider Torres, Kinston	48
*OBP	Pat Osborn, Kinston	.424
*SLG	Russ Branyan, Buffalo	.591

PITCHING
#Minimum 75 Innings
W	Brian Slocum, Kinston	15
L	Francisco Cruceta, Buffalo/Akron	13
#ERA	Chris Cooper, Akron/Kinston	1.66
G	Lee Gronkiewicz, Buffalo/Akron	53
CG	Four tied at	2
SV	Lee Gronkiewicz, Buffalo/Akron	20
	Todd Pennington, Kinston/Mahoning Valley	20
IP	Francisco Cruceta, Buffalo/Akron	172
BB	Francisco Cruceta, Buffalo/Akron	69
SO	Adam Miller, Kinston/Lake County	152

BEST TOOLS

Best Hitter for Average	Michael Aubrey
Best Power Hitter	Brad Snyder
Best Strike-Zone Discipline	Michael Aubrey
Fastest Baserunner	Ricardo Rojas
Best Athlete	Ricardo Rojas
Best Fastball	Adam Miller
Best Curveball	J.D. Martin
Best Slider	Adam Miller
Best Changeup	Nick Pesco
Best Control	Fausto Carmona
Best Defensive Catcher	Javi Herrera
Best Defensive Infielder	Ivan Ochoa
Best Infield Arm	Ivan Ochoa
Best Defensive Outfielder	Franklin Gutierrez
Best Outfield Arm	Franklin Gutierrez

PROJECTED 2008 LINEUP

Catcher	Victor Martinez
First Base	Michael Aubrey
Second Base	Ronnie Belliard
Third Base	Aaron Boone
Shortstop	Jhonny Peralta
Left Field	Grady Sizemore
Center Field	Franklin Gutierrez

Right Field	Brad Snyder
Designated Hitter	Travis Hafner
No. 1 Starter	C.C. Sabathia
No. 2 Starter	Adam Miller
No. 3 Starter	Jake Westbrook
No. 4 Starter	Cliff Lee
No. 5 Starter	Jeremy Sowers
Closer	Fernando Cabrera

LAST YEAR'S TOP 20 PROSPECTS

1. Grady Sizemore, of
2. Jeremy Guthrie, rhp
3. Fausto Carmona, rhp
4. Jake Dittler, rhp
5. Fernando Cabrera, rhp
6. Michael Aubrey, 1b
7. Jason Cooper, of
8. Brad Snyder, of
9. Adam Miller, rhp
10. Matt Whitney, 3b
11. Nick Pesco, rhp
12. Kazuhito Tadano, rhp
13. Corey Smith, 3b
14. Francisco Cruceta, rhp
15. Rafael Perez, lhp
16. Jason Stanford, lhp
17. Mariano Gomez, lhp
18. Brian Tallet, lhp
19. Nathan Panther, of
20. Travis Foley, rhp

TOP PROSPECTS OF THE DECADE

Year	Player, Pos.	Current Team
1995	Jaret Wright, rhp	Braves
1996	Bartolo Colon, rhp	Angels
1997	Bartolo Colon, rhp	Angels
1998	Sean Casey, 1b	Reds
1999	Russell Branyan, 3b	Brewers
2000	C.C. Sabathia, lhp	Indians
2001	C.C. Sabathia, lhp	Indians
2002	Corey Smith, 3b	Padres
2003	Brandon Phillips, ss/2b	Indians
2004	Grady Sizemore, of	Indians

TOP DRAFT PICKS OF THE DECADE

Year	Player, Pos.	Current Team
1995	David Miller, 1b/of	Out of baseball
1996	Danny Peoples, 1b/of	Out of baseball
1997	Tim Drew, rhp	Rockies
1998	C.C. Sabathia, lhp	Indians
1999	Will Hartley, c (2)	Out of baseball
2000	Corey Smith, 3b	Padres
2001	Dan Denham, rhp	Indians
2002	Jeremy Guthrie, rhp	Indians
2003	Michael Aubrey, 1b	Indians
2004	Jeremy Sowers, lhp	Indians

ALL-TIME LARGEST BONUSES

Danys Baez, 1999	$4,500,000
Jeremy Guthrie, 2002	$3,000,000
Jeremy Sowers, 2004	$2,475,000
Michael Aubrey, 2003	$2,010,000
Dan Denham, 2001	$1,860,000

MINOR LEAGUE DEPTH CHART

Cleveland INDIANS

Impact Potential: C
The Indians have already graduated a lot of high-end talent to Cleveland, such as catcher Victor Martinez and outfielder Grady Sizemore. Right-hander Adam Miller has one of the best arms in the minors and should join C.C. Sabathia at the front of the Indians rotation. The last two first-round picks, Jeremy Sowers and Michael Aubrey, look more like solid big leaguers than impact talents. The system has several power bats, such as

Matt Whitney and Jason Cooper, who need to show they can make consistent contact.

Depth: B
The Tribe has variety in its system. What the organization has most are polished bats, from Aubrey and Ryan Garko to outfielders Brad Snyder, Mike Butia and Ryan Goleski. Cleveland's stable of lefthanders should provide at least a big leaguer or two. Perhaps its only weakness is a lack of premium athletes aside from outfielders Franklin Gutierrez and Juan Valdes.

*Depth charts prepared by **John Manuel** and **Allan Simpson**. Numbers in parentheses indicate prospect rankings.*

LF
Mike Butia (15)
Jason Cooper (20)
Cirillo Cumberbatch

CF
Franklin Gutierrez (3)
Juan Valdes (13)
Ben Francisco
Jon Van Every
Argenis Reyes

RF
Brad Snyder (4)
Ryan Goleski (24)
Nathan Panther

3B
Matt Whitney (17)
Kevin Kouzmanoff (28)
Jake Gautreau
Pat Osborn

SS
Ivan Ochoa
Chris De La Cruz
Bryan Finegan

2B
Eider Torres (30)
Brandon Pinckney
Joe Inglett
Micah Schilling

1B
Michael Aubrey (2)
Ryan Garko (8)
Chris Gimenez

SOURCE of TALENT

Homegrown		Acquired	
College	14	Trades	3
Junior College	0	Rule 5 draft	0
Draft-and-follow	1	Independent leagues	0
High school	8	Free agents/waivers	0
Nondrafted free agents	0		
Foreign	4		

C
Javi Herrera
David Wallace
Wyatt Toregas

LHP

Starters	Relievers
Jeremy Sowers (5)	Shea Douglas
Chuck Lofgren (14)	Cliff Bartosh
Dan Cevette (18)	Juan Lara
Scott Lewis (19)	Oscar Alvarez
Tony Sipp (22)	Michael Hernandez
Mariano Gomez (26)	
Brian Tallet (27)	
Rafael Perez (29)	
Aaron Laffey	
Reid Santos	
Keith Ramsey	

RHP

Starters	Relievers
Adam Miller (1)	Fernando Cabrera (7)
Fausto Carmona (6)	Jeremy Guthrie (25)
Nick Pesco (9)	Travis Foley
Andrew Brown (10)	Dan Eisentrager
Jake Dittler (11)	Nelson Hiraldo
Francisco Cruceta (12)	Brandon Rickert
Justin Hoyman (16)	Kyle Collins
J.D. Martin (21)	
Kyle Denney (23)	
Brian Slocum	
Dan Denham	
Sean Smith	
Tom Mastny	
Chris Neisel	

DRAFT ANALYSIS

2004

Best Pro Debut: After beginning the summer in the Cape Cod League, LHP Tony Sipp (45) went to the short-season New York-Penn League and fanned 74 in 43 innings while going 3-1, 3.16. OF Mike Butia (5) and INF/OF Chris Gimenez (19) were both NY-P all-stars.

Best Athlete: OF Alfred Ard (30) doubled as a wide receiver at Southern and led the Southwestern Athletic Conference with 11 touchdown receptions in 2003. RHP Cody Bunkelman (6) also played wide receiver at Itasca (Minn.) CC.

Best Pure Hitter: Butia should hit for average and power.

Best Raw Power: Butia over Gimenez and OF P.J. Hiser (29). Butia (18 at James Madison) and Hiser (21 at Pittsburgh) set school home run records during the spring.

Fastest Runner: Ard has been timed at 6.38 seconds in the 60-yard dash.

Best Defensive Player: SS Brian Finegan (15), despite his 22 errors in 68 NY-P games. His hands and arm are solid.

Best Fastball: Bunkelman, who threw in the mid-80s as a high school senior, hit 97 mph during a predraft workout for the Indians. LHP Chuck Lofgren (4) touched 96 last summer after entering the year more highly regarded as an outfielder.

Best Breaking Ball: LHP Scott Lewis (3) was on track to becoming a first-round pick before he succumbed to Tommy John surgery in 2003. He's nearly all the way back, showing a plus curveball and getting his fastball back up to 88-92 mph after signing.

Most Intriguing Background: LHP Jeremy Sowers (1), the 20th overall pick by the Reds in 2001, is the 12th two-time first-

Hoyman

RICH ABEL

round pick in draft history. OF Jason Denham's (13) brother Dan and RHP Carlton Smith's (21) brother Corey are former Cleveland first-round picks still in the system. RHP Jordan Chambless (12) is a quarterback at Texas A&M. The Indians drafted a third wideout—Minnesota-Duluth RHP Tim Battaglia (50), who had a tryout with the NFL's Dallas Cowboys. Smith, Chambless and Battaglia went unsigned, though Cleveland still hoped to land Battaglia and his 91-92 mph fastball.

Closest To The Majors: Sowers is a lefty with four pitches he can put wherever he wants, so he'll be one of the first 2004 draftees to get to the big leagues.

Best Late-Round Pick: Sipp has a low-90s fastball and a better slider than the Indians realized. He signed for $130,000, which is sixth- or seventh-round money. The Indians also are pleased with Gimenez and projectable LHP Michael Storey (23).

The One Who Got Away: Cleveland was very disappointed to lose out on Chambless and RHP Jeff Sues (14). The Indians thought they would sign both, but Chambless decided to attend college and Sues went back to Vanderbilt.

Assessment: Cleveland took eight pitchers with its first nine picks, getting a pair of advanced arms in Sowers and Justin Hoyman (2), then took some gambles on the upside of Lewis, Lofgren, Bunkelman and 6-foot-8 RHP Mark Jecmen (7).

2003 The Indians haven't done much with a wealth of first-round picks in recent years, but they scored big here with RHP Adam Miller, 1B Michael Aubrey and OF Brad Snyder. C/1B Ryan Garko's (3) bat also has been a revelation. **GRADE:** A

2002 Cleveland could go 0-for-3 with this group of first rounders because RHP Jeremy Guthrie has struggled above Double-A, 3B Matt Whitney has been hurt and 2B Micah Schilling hasn't hit. **GRADE:** C

2001 Among the four first-rounders, RHPs Dan Denham and OF Michael Conroy haven't progressed and Alan Horne didn't sign. RHP J.D. Martin, is a mild prospect but not a blue-chipper, as is RHP Jake Dittler (2). **GRADE:** C

2000 OF Ryan Church (14) emerged in 2004—after being traded to the Expos. The Indians finally gave up on 3B Corey Smith (1), dealing him to the Padres. The other first-rounder, LHP Derek Thompson, has had injury problems and is now with the Dodgers. **GRADE:** C

Draft analysis prepared by Jim Callis. Numbers in parentheses indicate draft rounds.

KEN BABBITT

Adam
MILLER

Born: Nov. 26, 1984.
Ht.: 6-4. **Wt.:** 175.
Bats: R. **Throws:** R.
School: McKinney (Texas) HS.
Career Transactions: Selected by Indians in first round (31st overall) of 2003 draft; signed June 10, 2003.
Signed by: Matt Ruebel.

Teams shied away from high school righthanders in the first round of the 2003 draft, with only Jeff Allison (Marlins, No. 16 overall) and Chad Billingsley (Dodgers, No. 24) getting picked. Miller went with the top pick of the supplemental first round, and he and Billingsley quickly have established themselves as two of the top pitching prospects in the game. A sore shoulder and strict pitch counts limited Miller in his pro debut, though he was still an easy choice as the No. 1 prospect in the Rookie-level Appalachian League. In 2004, his first full season, Miller elevated himself to the top of an organization strong in pitching prospects, particularly righthanders. After being promoted to high Class A Kinston, he dominated Carolina League hitters and won both his playoff starts, striking out 14 while not allowing an earned run in 12 innings. Miller didn't just seem to get stronger as the season wore on. His routine exit physical found that his rotator cuff actually had gotten stronger; something GM Mark Shapiro called "nothing short of freakish" and attributed to Miller's outstanding work ethic.

Miller has all the components to develop into a frontline starter in the big leagues. Cleveland brass believes he's ahead of former Indians phenoms Jaret Wright and Bartolo Colon at the same stage of development. Miller's arsenal begins with a heavy, boring fastball that sits anywhere from 92-97 mph and occasionally threatens triple digits. His late-breaking 87-88 mph slider has blossomed into a deadly out pitch. The power break on his slider eats up lefthanders, who batted at a .221 clip against him in 2004. Miller possesses a rare combination of power, intelligence and feel for a teenager. He has an almost photographic memory in terms of recalling pitch sequences, which has helped him make adjustments from inning to inning and start to start. Miller spent extra time with coaches to break down hitters on days before his turn in the rotation. His makeup and aptitude are off the charts.

Like many young power pitchers, Miller was able to overpower hitters with his two-pitch attack, but the Indians had to force him to throw his changeup more often to increase its depth and effectiveness as a third option. He made impressive strides with the changeup after working with Kinston pitching coach Greg Hibbard and continued to show improvement in instructional league. He needs to build more confidence in the pitch as he continues to move through the system.

Miller has earned comparisons to two-time Cy Young Award winner Bret Saberhagen for his explosive fastball-slider combination as well as his moxie. Miller is on the fast track and will begin 2005 at Double-A Akron. He could reach Cleveland the following year, and it might not be much longer before he's leading the big league rotation.

Year	Club (League)	Class	W	L	ERA	G	GS	CG	SV	IP	H	R	ER	HR	BB	SO	AVG
2003	Burlington (Appy)	R	0	4	4.96	10	10	0	0	33	30	20	18	2	9	23	.250
2004	Kinston (Car)	A	3	2	2.08	8	8	0	0	43	29	17	10	1	12	46	.192
	Lake County (SAL)	A	7	4	3.36	19	19	1	0	91	79	39	34	7	28	106	.238
MINOR LEAGUE TOTALS			10	10	3.34	37	37	1	0	167	138	76	62	10	49	175	.229

Michael Aubrey, 1b

RICH ABEL

Born: April 15, 1982. **Ht.:** 6-0. **Wt.:** 195. **Bats:** L. **Throws:** L. **School:** Tulane University. **Career Transactions:** Selected by Indians in first round (11th overall) of 2003 draft; signed June 14, 2003. **Signed by:** Scott Meaney.

Aubrey was Baseball America's Freshman of the Year in 2001, when he was a two-way star and led Tulane to its first-ever College World Series victory. A back injury ended his days on the mound, but his bat made him the 11th overall pick in 2003. A career .320 hitter as a pro, he has been held in check by only a nagging hamstring injury that sidelined him for five weeks in 2004. Aubrey's quick hands allow him to control the barrel of the bat and he has a knack for identifying pitches early, rarely swinging and missing. He projects as a top-notch defender with solid footwork around the bag and a strong throwing arm for a first baseman. There's some question as to how much power Aubrey will hit for in the majors. Most scouts see him as a gap hitter with occasional pop. He can get tied up by fastballs in on his hands, something he can rectify by incorporating his lower half more in his swing. Aubrey's on-base ability and gap power fit the mold of a No. 3 hitter. He'll return to Double-A and is in line for a midseason promotion to Triple-A Buffalo.

Year	Club (League)	Class	AVG	G	AB	R	H	2B	3B	HR	RBI	BB	SO	SB	OBP	SLG
2003	Lake County (SAL)	A	.348	38	138	22	48	13	0	5	19	14	22	0	.409	.551
2004	Kinston (Car)	A	.339	60	218	34	74	14	1	10	60	27	26	3	.438	.550
	Akron (EL)	AA	.261	38	134	13	35	7	0	5	22	15	18	0	.340	.425
MINOR LEAGUE TOTALS			.320	136	490	69	157	34	1	20	101	56	66	3	.403	.516

Franklin Gutierrez, of

RICH ABEL

Born: Feb. 21, 1983. **Ht.:** 6-2. **Wt.:** 175. **Bats:** R. **Throws:** R. **Career Transactions:** Signed out of Venezuela by Dodgers, Nov. 18, 2000 . . . Traded by Dodgers to Indians with a player to be named for OF Milton Bradley, April 4, 2004; Indians acquired RHP Andrew Brown, May 18, 2004, to complete trade. **Signed by:** Camilo Pascual (Dodgers).

While Milton Bradley's antics finally forced the Indians to trade him, they made the best of the situation by prying Gutierrez and Andrew Brown away from the Dodgers. Shortly after a promotion to Triple-A in 2004, he needed surgery to remove bone chips from his left elbow and missed two months. The most complete player in the system, Gutierrez has electrifying bat speed. He destroys pitches on the inner half of the plate. His strength and natural lift give him the potential to hit 30-plus homers in the majors, though his elbow injury muted his power in 2004. His speed and arm strength make him a standout defender in either center or right field. Hitting coordinator Derek Shelton worked overtime with Gutierrez in instructional league to address his pitch recognition and patience. He still has a tendency to expand the zone, chasing too many breaking balls in the dirt. Still somewhat raw, he needs a full season in Triple-A. He'll try to break into Cleveland's promising outfield corps in 2006.

Year	Club (League)	Class	AVG	G	AB	R	H	2B	3B	HR	RBI	BB	SO	SB	OBP	SLG
2001	Dodgers (GCL)	R	.269	56	234	38	63	16	0	4	30	16	39	9	.324	.389
2002	South Georgia (SAL)	A	.283	92	361	61	102	18	4	12	45	31	88	13	.344	.454
	Las Vegas (PCL)	AAA	.300	2	10	2	3	2	0	0	2	1	4	0	.364	.500
2003	Vero Beach (FSL)	A	.282	110	425	65	120	28	5	20	68	39	111	17	.345	.513
	Jacksonville (SL)	AA	.313	18	67	12	21	3	2	4	12	7	20	3	.387	.597
2004	Akron (EL)	AA	.302	70	262	38	79	24	2	5	35	23	77	6	.372	.466
	Buffalo (IL)	AAA	.148	7	27	4	4	1	0	1	3	1	11	0	.179	.296
MINOR LEAGUE TOTALS			.283	355	1386	220	392	92	13	46	195	118	350	48	.346	.468

Brad Snyder, of

RICH ABEL

Born: May 25, 1982. **Ht.:** 6-3. **Wt.:** 200. **Bats:** L. **Throws:** L. **School:** Ball State University. **Career Transactions:** Selected by Indians in first round (18th overall) of 2003 draft; signed June 15, 2003. **Signed by:** Bob Mayer/Chuck Ricci.

A car accident put Snyder's career in jeopardy following his freshman year at Ball State, but he made a full recovery and became the 2003 Mid-American Conference player of the year. He missed spring training and much of April in 2004 with an eye infection before contact lenses helped correct the problem. Snyder has drawn comparisons to the likes of Paul O'Neill and Grady Sizemore for his broad base of tools and advanced hitting approach. His sweet, compact stroke and his bat speed produce easy power to the opposite field. He runs well and displays good instincts on the bases. He also has a strong arm. While he plays an admirable center field, Snyder is better suited for a corner role and probably will settle into right field. He still needs to become more comfortable in turning on pitches on the inner half to fully tap into his power potential. Snyder fanned 82 times in 62 games in his pro debut, but after making better contact in 2004 he's on the verge of an offensive breakthrough. He'll begin his second full season in Double-A.

Year	Club (League)	Class	AVG	G	AB	R	H	2B	3B	HR	RBI	BB	SO	SB	OBP	SLG
2003	Mahoning Valley (NY-P)	A	.284	62	225	52	64	11	6	6	31	41	82	14	.393	.467
2004	Lake County (SAL)	A	.280	79	304	52	85	15	5	10	54	48	78	11	.382	.461
	Kinston (Car)	A	.355	29	110	20	39	7	1	6	21	13	28	4	.424	.600
MINOR LEAGUE TOTALS			.294	170	639	124	188	33	12	22	106	102	188	29	.393	.487

Jeremy Sowers, lhp

Born: May 17, 1983. **Ht.:** 6-1. **Wt.:** 165. **Bats:** L. **Throws:** L. **School:** Vanderbilt University. **Career Transactions:** Selected by Indians in first round (sixth overall) of 2004 draft; signed Aug. 27, 2004. **Signed by:** Scott Barnsby.

Sowers became the 12th player to be selected in the first round of two June drafts. The Reds took him 20th overall in 2001 with little or no intention of signing him, and he went sixth in 2004, making him the highest-drafted Vanderbilt player ever. He held out all summer before signing for $2.475 million. His twin brother Josh is a righthander/infielder at Yale. Sowers commands the zone with four pitches and goes right after hitters with an aggressive approach. He adds and subtracts from his fastball while mixing in a plus curveball, a cutter-type slider and a changeup. His fastball features good arm-side movement and sink from a deceptive three-quarters delivery. He can't overpower hitters with the 85-91 mph velocity on his fastball. He must further refine his changeup to put the finishing touches on his arsenal. While both of his breaking balls show tight, downward rotation, they can become more consistent. The most polished lefthander in the 2004 draft, Sowers should move swiftly up the ladder. He'll make his pro debut in high Class A and could make it to Cleveland as early as 2006.

Year	Club (League)	Class	W	L	ERA	G	GS	CG	SV	IP	H	R	ER	HR	BB	SO	AVG
2004	Did not play—Signed 2005 contract																

Fausto Carmona, rhp

Born: Dec. 7, 1983. **Ht.:** 6-4. **Wt.:** 185. **Bats:** R. **Throws:** R. **Career Transactions:** Signed out of Dominican Republic by Indians, Dec. 28, 2000. **Signed by:** Josue Herrera.

When the Indians signed Carmona out of the Dominican as a 16-year-old, he was a malnourished stringbean. As he has bulked up, his velocity has steadily increased. He tied for the minor league lead with 17 wins in 2003 and reached double figures again while advancing to Triple-A in 2004. Carmona pounds the ball down in the zone with good command of a heavy 90-95 mph sinker. He upgraded his deceptive changeup into a plus pitch with improved late action in 2004. His athletic, repeatable delivery allows him to consistently throw strikes. Despite his lively fastball, Carmona doesn't miss a lot of bats. While he induces a lot of ground balls, his strikeout totals won't increase until he tightens his slider. It's a slurvy breaking ball and hasn't been an effective third option for him. After coddling him earlier in his career, the Indians were more aggressive with Carmona in 2004. That won't stop in 2005, as they plan on assigning him to Triple-A.

Year	Club (League)	Class	W	L	ERA	G	GS	CG	SV	IP	H	R	ER	HR	BB	SO	AVG
2001	Indians (DSL)	R	4	2	3.11	14	13	0	0	75	69	36	26	0	12	47	.234
2002	Burlington (Appy)	R	2	4	3.30	13	11	0	1	76	89	36	28	4	10	42	.295
	Mahoning Valley (NY-P)	A	0	0	0.00	3	0	0	0	4	2	0	0	0	1	0	.182
2003	Lake County (SAL)	A	17	4	2.06	24	24	1	0	148	117	48	34	10	14	83	.214
	Akron (EL)	AA	0	0	4.50	1	1	0	0	6	8	3	3	1	0	3	.308
2004	Kinston (Car)	A	5	2	2.83	13	13	0	0	70	68	28	22	6	20	57	.249
	Buffalo (IL)	AAA	1	0	6.00	1	1	0	0	6	6	4	4	0	3	2	.261
	Akron (EL)	AA	4	8	4.76	15	15	0	0	87	114	52	46	3	21	63	.320
MINOR LEAGUE TOTALS			33	20	3.10	84	78	1	1	473	473	207	163	24	81	297	.258

Fernando Cabrera, rhp

Born: Nov. 16, 1981. **Ht.:** 6-4. **Wt.:** 170. **Bats:** R. **Throws:** R. **School:** Disciples of Christ Academy, Bayamon, P.R. **Career Transactions:** Selected by Indians in 10th round of 1999 draft; signed Aug. 23, 1999. **Signed by:** Henry Cruz.

Though Cabrera had a 7-2, 2.47 record as a 21-year-old starter in Double-A, the Indians moved him to the bullpen in mid-2003. He has continued to flourish and was impressive in a brief major league stint in August. Cabrera has all the makings of a power reliever with two plus pitches—a 92-96 mph fastball and a hard, diving splitter. He controls both sides of the plate with his fastball. His aggressive temperament benefits him late in games with the lead. Cabrera's slider and changeup aren't as useful as his fastball and splitter, though he doesn't need as diverse a repertoire coming out of the bullpen. He has improved his slider, but he tips off his changeup by reducing his arm speed. He's easy prey for basestealers. He'll get a long look in spring training, though he won't get thrown to the wolves immediately after Bob Wickman re-signed and will presumably open the season as Cleveland's closer. The Indians will bring him along slowly, but he showed he has the stuff to thrive with the game on the line.

Year	Club (League)	Class	W	L	ERA	G	GS	CG	SV	IP	H	R	ER	HR	BB	SO	AVG
2000	Burlington (Appy)	R	3	7	4.61	13	13	0	0	68	64	42	35	4	20	50	.252
2001	Columbus (SAL)	A	5	6	3.61	20	20	0	0	95	89	49	38	7	37	96	.242
2002	Kinston (Car)	A	6	8	3.52	21	21	0	0	110	83	48	43	7	40	107	.206
	Akron (EL)	AA	1	2	5.33	7	4	0	1	27	26	16	16	1	12	29	.252
2003	Akron (EL)	AA	9	4	2.97	36	15	0	5	109	96	41	36	8	40	115	.237
2004	Cleveland (AL)	MAJ	0	0	3.38	4	0	0	0	5	3	3	2	0	1	6	.167
	Buffalo (IL)	AAA	4	3	3.79	45	0	0	5	76	57	37	32	9	43	93	.208
MAJOR LEAGUE TOTALS			0	0	3.38	4	0	0	0	5	3	3	2	0	1	6	.167
MINOR LEAGUE TOTALS			28	30	3.71	142	73	0	11	485	415	233	200	36	192	490	.230

Ryan Garko, c/1b

Born: Jan. 2, 1981. **Ht.:** 6-2. **Wt.:** 225. **Bats:** R. **Throws:** R. **School:** Stanford University. **Career Transactions:** Selected by Indians in third round of 2003 draft; signed July 9, 2003. **Signed by:** Don Lyle.

Undrafted following his junior season at Stanford because of skepticism about his defensive ability, Garko turned in an All-America .402-18-92 performance as a senior. In his first full season as a pro, he was Cleveland's 2004 minor league player of the year. Garko climbed three levels and raked at every stop in 2004, hitting to all fields and showing above-average power. He's short to the ball with an efficient swing, helping him adjust to any type of pitch and location. His strong leadership skills are an asset behind the plate. While he is underrated defensively behind the plate, some scouts still question whether he can be an everyday catcher. He worked extensively with roving instructors Chris Bando and Ted Kubiak to improve on defense, both behind the plate and at first. He's a well below-average runner. The Indians believe Garko is ready to be a role player in the big leagues right now. However, he likely will start 2005 in Triple-A as he tries to find a full-time position.

Year	Club (League)	Class	AVG	G	AB	R	H	2B	3B	HR	RBI	BB	SO	SB	OBP	SLG
2003	Mahoning Valley (NY-P)	A	.273	45	165	23	45	8	1	4	16	12	19	1	.337	.406
2004	Kinston (Car)	A	.328	65	238	44	78	17	1	16	58	26	34	4	.425	.609
	Akron (EL)	AA	.331	43	172	29	57	15	0	6	38	14	28	1	.397	.523
	Buffalo (IL)	AAA	.350	5	20	2	7	1	0	0	4	2	3	0	.391	.400
MINOR LEAGUE TOTALS			.314	158	595	98	187	41	2	26	116	54	84	6	.392	.521

Nick Pesco, rhp

Born: Sept. 17, 1983. **Ht.:** 6-6. **Wt.:** 200. **Bats:** R. **Throws:** R. **School:** Cosumnes River (Calif.) JC. **Career Transactions:** Selected by Indians in 25th round of 2002; signed May 19, 2003. **Signed by:** Don Lyle.

In 2002, the Indians signed righthander Sean Smith for $1.1 million as a draft-and-follow out of Sacramento City College. A year later, they went back to the same northern California juco conference and spent the same amount on another draft-and-follow, Pesco. While Smith had elbow problems in 2004, Pesco had a strong first full season. He is armed with a four-pitch repertoire, including the most effective changeup in the organization. His extra-large frame and heavy, boring 90-94 mph fastball on a downhill plane elicit comparisons to Jason Davis. Pesco made strides with his slider and curveball last season, though both pitches have yet to reach their projections yet. He has the makings of a good, clean delivery, but he needs to continue working on staying over the rubber to create better overall balance. The Indians' pitching depth affords them the luxury of not needing to rush Pesco. His second trip to high Class A could be short-lived, with a quick promotion back to Double-A very possible.

Year	Club (League)	Class	W	L	ERA	G	GS	CG	SV	IP	H	R	ER	HR	BB	SO	AVG
2003	Burlington (Appy)	R	3	1	1.82	13	13	0	0	54	36	16	11	0	22	55	.188
2004	Kinston (Car)	A	1	2	3.21	3	3	0	0	14	15	9	5	0	4	12	.273
	Lake County (SAL)	A	6	7	3.91	21	21	0	0	106	96	49	46	10	30	97	.241
	Akron (EL)	AA	1	0	0.00	1	1	0	0	5	3	0	0	0	1	10	.176
MINOR LEAGUE TOTALS			11	10	3.11	38	38	0	0	179	150	74	62	10	57	174	.226

10 Andrew Brown, rhp

Born: Feb. 17, 1981. **Ht.:** 6-6. **Wt.:** 230. **Bats:** R. **Throws:** R. **School:** Trinity Christian Academy, Jacksonville. **Career Transactions:** Selected by Braves in sixth round of 1999 draft; signed June 3, 1999 . . . Traded by Braves with OF Brian Jordan and LHP Odalis Perez to Dodgers for OF Gary Sheffield, Jan. 15, 2002 . . . Traded by Dodgers to Indians May 26, 2004, completing trade in which Indians received OF Franklin Gutierrez and a player to be named for OF Milton Bradley, April 4, 2004. **Signed by:** Marco Paddy (Braves).

After sending Milton Bradley to Los Angeles for Gutierrez and a player to be named, Cleveland chose Brown from a group of prospects to complete the deal. Brown had made a strong first impression on the Dodgers in 2002 after coming from Atlanta in a trade for Gary Sheffield, but made only one start in 2003 because of elbow problems. Brown possesses an overpowering four-pitch mix, led by an effortless 92-96 mph fastball that he drives down in the zone. He also has two power breaking balls along with good touch on an average changeup. Health is the biggest question mark with Brown. He had Tommy John surgery in 2000 and bone chips removed from the same elbow in 2003. The Dodgers developed some concerns about his mental toughness, as have the Indians. Brown needs to show he's willing to accept criticism from coaches before he'll reach his potential. He'll start 2005 in Double-A and could make his major league debut later in the year.

Year	Club (League)	Class	W	L	ERA	G	GS	CG	SV	IP	H	R	ER	HR	BB	SO	AVG
1999	Braves (GCL)	R	1	1	2.34	11	11	0	0	42	40	15	11	4	16	57	.247
2000	Did not play—Injured																
2001	Jamestown (NY-P)	A	3	4	3.92	14	12	0	0	64	50	29	28	5	31	59	.215
2002	Vero Beach (FSL)	A	10	10	4.11	25	24	1	1	127	97	63	58	13	62	129	.215
2003	Jacksonville (SL)	AA	0	0	0.00	1	1	0	0	1	0	0	0	0	0	1	.000
2004	Jacksonville (SL)	AA	1	3	4.02	8	8	0	0	40	36	23	18	5	14	58	.232
	Akron (EL)	AA	3	6	4.66	17	17	0	0	77	66	44	40	7	36	67	.227
	Buffalo (IL)	AAA	1	0	0.00	1	1	0	0	5	4	0	0	0	3	4	.222
MINOR LEAGUE TOTALS			19	24	3.90	77	74	1	1	357	293	174	155	34	162	375	.223

11 Jake Dittler, rhp

Born: Nov. 24, 1982. **Ht.:** 6-4. **Wt.:** 220. **Bats:** R. **Throws:** R. **School:** Green Valley HS, Henderson, Nev. **Career Transactions:** Selected by Indians in second round of 2001 draft; signed July 21, 2001. **Signed by:** Doug Baker.

The Indians used three first-round picks on pitchers in 2001, but second-rounder Dittler has outperformed Dan Denham, unsigned Alan Horne and J.D. Martin. His stock soared high enough that he ranked No. 4 on this list a year ago, but nagging injuries contributed to inconsistent command during a disappointing 2004 season. Dittler posted a 2.20 ERA in his first five starts before stiffness in his upper back landed him on the disabled list for four weeks in May Upon his return, he had trouble locating his plus stuff. His two main pitches are a heavy, boring 90-95 mph fastball and an above-average curveball. His changeup came on as a viable third weapon in 2004. Though his fast-track development hit a snag, the Indians still believe he's on schedule to contribute in the majors by 2006. Dittler got back on course in the Arizona Fall League as he prepared for a return to Double-A in 2005.

Year	Club (League)	Class	W	L	ERA	G	GS	CG	SV	IP	H	R	ER	HR	BB	SO	AVG
2001	Burlington (Appy)	R	1	2	3.68	6	5	0	0	22	25	14	9	0	12	20	.287
2002	Columbus (SAL)	A	5	11	4.28	25	25	0	0	128	127	77	61	4	51	108	.257
2003	Lake County (SAL)	A	6	4	2.63	17	17	1	0	89	86	39	26	4	20	82	.244
	Kinston (Car)	A	5	1	2.40	8	8	1	0	49	47	17	13	2	11	32	.257
2004	Akron (EL)	AA	5	12	5.02	21	20	1	0	108	119	73	60	7	40	85	.275
MINOR LEAGUE TOTALS			22	30	3.84	77	75	3	0	396	404	220	169	17	134	327	.261

Francisco Cruceta, rhp

Born: July 4, 1981. **Ht.:** 6-2. **Wt.:** 180. **Bats:** R. **Throws:** R. **Career Transactions:** Signed out of Dominican Republic by Dodgers, May 20, 1999 . . . Traded by Dodgers with LHP Terry Mulholland and RHP Ricardo Rodriguez to Indians for RHP Paul Shuey, July 28, 2002. **Signed by:** Pablo Peguero (Dodgers).

Indians officials have regarded the Dodgers as one of baseball's deepest organizations in recent years, and they've done a good job of raiding that system in trades. Not only did Cleveland get Top 10 Prospects Franklin Gutierrez and Andy Brown for Milton Bradley last spring, but they also picked up a pair of quality arms when their primarily goal was just to dump Paul Shuey's contract in July 2002. In exchange, the Indians received Cruceta and Ricardo Rodriguez (since traded for Ryan Ludwick), along with veteran Terry Mulholland. Cruceta has proven to be one of the most durable starters in the system. He works with an 89-92 mph sinker that reaches 94, as well as a solid slider, splitter and changeup. His fastball has good life with late run and sink. When he added the splitter in 2004, it immediately became a go-to pitch and boosted the rest of his repertoire. While he has good command of all four pitches, Cruceta's tendency to pitch up in the strike zone gets him into trouble. Scouts differ in their opinions of his future role, with some seeing him as a setup man and others projecting him as a No. 4 starter. After getting a brief look in the big leagues last season, he'll have an opportunity to make a better second impression in spring training.

Year	Club (League)	Class	W	L	ERA	G	GS	CG	SV	IP	H	R	ER	HR	BB	SO	AVG
1999	Dodgers (DSL)	R	3	2	7.56	14	1	0	0	25	33	34	21	4	15	21	.308
2000	Dodgers (DSL)	R	4	2	3.31	21	6	0	3	49	33	29	18	1	36	49	.180
2001	Dodgers (DSL)	R	0	4	1.50	11	9	0	0	48	35	24	8	1	24	47	.200
2002	Columbus (SAL)	A	8	5	2.80	20	20	3	0	113	98	42	35	7	34	111	.231
	Kinston (CAR)	A	2	0	2.50	7	7	0	0	40	31	13	11	2	25	37	.217
2003	Akron (EL)	AA	13	9	3.09	27	25	6	0	163	141	70	56	7	66	134	.232
2004	Cleveland (AL)	MAJ	0	1	9.39	2	2	0	0	8	10	9	8	1	4	9	.303
	Buffalo (IL)	AAA	6	5	3.25	14	14	1	0	83	78	35	30	6	36	62	.252
	Akron (EL)	AA	4	8	5.28	15	15	1	0	89	89	58	52	11	33	45	.261
MAJOR LEAGUE TOTALS			0	1	9.39	2	2	0	0	8	10	9	8	1	4	9	.303
MINOR LEAGUE TOTALS			40	35	3.41	129	97	11	3	609	538	305	231	39	269	506	.235

Juan Valdes, of

Born: June 22, 1985. **Ht.:** 6-0. **Wt.:** 150. **Bats:** S. **Throws:** R. **School:** Fernando Callejo HS, Manati, P.R. **Career Transactions:** Selected by Indians in fifth round of 2003 draft; signed June 17, 2003. **Signed by:** Henry Cruz.

A cousin of Carlos Beltran, Valdes has similar potential. A switch-hitter since he was 14, he finishes his level swing with power and both hands on the bat all the way through the zone, a la Beltran. He has a more advanced approach from the left side, and he needs to show the ability to make more consistent hard contact from the right side. He recognized pitches well and shows a willingness to take walks. An adequate defender in center field, he has plus speed and arm strength. Valdes' quickness is more apparent than his power at this point, as he stole 41 bases in 47 attempts in just 63 games. He'll need to add more strength to his wiry frame to give himself a chance to continue to follow in Beltran's footsteps. He will begin his first full season at low Class A Lake County in 2005.

Year	Club (League)	Class	AVG	G	AB	R	H	2B	3B	HR	RBI	BB	SO	SB	OBP	SLG
2003	Burlington (Appy)	R	.223	39	130	14	29	3	1	1	14	10	33	5	.275	.285
2004	Burlington (Appy)	R	.267	38	135	24	36	4	4	1	5	17	27	21	.357	.378
	Lake County (SAL)	A	.237	25	97	18	23	0	0	1	10	15	23	20	.345	.268
MINOR LEAGUE TOTALS			.243	102	362	56	88	7	5	3	29	42	83	46	.325	.315

Chuck Lofgren, lhp

Born: Jan. 29, 1986. **Ht.:** 6-3. **Wt.:** 190. **Bats:** L. **Throws:** L. **School:** Serra HS, Burlingame, Calif. **Career Transactions:** Selected by Indians in fourth round of 2004 draft; signed June 29, 2004. **Signed by:** Don Lyle.

Lofgren was a standout for three seasons at Serra High, the same school that produced Barry Bonds and Greg Jefferies, as well as Patriots quarterback Tom Brady. He was under intense scrutiny his senior season as a two-way player and he may have suffered from a case of draftitis. Many clubs preferred Lofgren more for his bat than his arm, but by the midpoint of last spring, his average stood just above the Mendoza Line. He finished strong at the plate, but hit fewer snags on the mound and the Indians targeted him as a pitcher. Lofgren touched 96 mph in his first pro start and his fastball sat consistently at 92-93 mph all summer. His curveball has the makings of being a plus pitch, but can get a little loopy at times and needs tighter spin. He also has to refine his changeup. Lofgren is aggressive and has impressed Cleveland with his savvy and makeup. Rookie-level Burlington pitching coach Ruben Niebla worked extensively on Lofgren's delivery to help his leverage and plane to the plate. He lands violently on his front leg, which affects his command. Though the Tribe drafted him as a pitcher, Lofgren's contract included a clause allowing him to swing the bat as a DH once a week. His days as a two-way player should be short-lived, however, as he opens this year in low Class A.

Year	Club (League)	Class	W	L	ERA	G	GS	CG	SV	IP	H	R	ER	HR	BB	SO	AVG
2004	Burlington (Appy)	R	0	0	6.04	9	9	0	0	22	25	16	15	4	13	23	.287
MINOR LEAGUE TOTALS			0	0	6.04	9	9	0	0	22	25	16	15	4	13	23	.287

15 Mike Butia, of

Born: Nov. 29, 1982. **Ht.:** 6-2. **Wt.:** 215. **Bats:** L. **Throws:** R. **School:** James Madison University. **Career Transactions:** Selected by Indians in fifth round of 2004 draft; signed June 15, 2004. **Signed by:** Bob Mayer.

With crosscheckers blanketing the talent-laden Colonial Athletic Association to scout the likes of Justin Verlander, Bill Bray and Justin Orenduff—all of whom became first-round picks in 2004—Butia received plenty of exposure last spring. He set a James Madison record with 18 homers and finished third in NCAA Division I with a .782 slugging percentage, but hurt his cause with a miserable series against William & Mary in front of dozens of high-ranking scouting officials. Cleveland scouting director John Mirabelli watched him scuffle, but saw correctable flaws and trusted veteran area scout Bobby Mayer, who liked Butia. He showed above-average pull power as an amateur, but didn't load his hands well at the plate and was exposed by better pitching. The Indians saw immediate results after revamping his approach to create a better trigger, opening his stance and widening his base. He began to drive pitches to the opposite field more often. Butia has good bat speed and natural loft in his swing, though he'll need to cut down on his strikeouts. A slightly below-average runner, he's limited to left field by his subpar arm strength and defensive ability. He has a mild thyroid condition and put on a lot of weight during his college career. Butia will begin his first full season in low Class A.

Year	Club (League)	Class	AVG	G	AB	R	H	2B	3B	HR	RBI	BB	SO	SB	OBP	SLG
2004	Mahoning Valley (NY-P)	A	.315	62	232	32	73	17	1	5	44	24	54	0	.396	.461
MINOR LEAGUE TOTALS			.315	62	232	32	73	17	1	5	44	24	54	0	.396	.461

16 Justin Hoyman, rhp

Born: April 17, 1982. **Ht.:** 6-3. **Wt.:** 195. **Bats:** R. **Throws:** R. **School:** University of Florida. **Career Transactions:** Selected by Indians in second round of 2004 draft; signed July 24, 2004. **Signed by:** Chris Jefts.

A 43rd-round pick by the Rockies out of Brevard (Fla.) Community College in 2002, Hoyman declined to sign as a draft-and-follow and instead went to Florida, where he became the Gators' highest pick since the Expos took Brad Wilkerson in 1998's first round. A former soccer standout in high school, Hoyman oozes athleticism. He commands the ball down in the zone with a sinking 89-92 mph fastball that topped out at 95 last spring. While he primarily throws his hard sinker, Hoyman also operates with a slurvy breaking ball and a deceptive changeup. He needs to improve his secondary stuff, especially his changeup. Hoyman has excellent lower body strength after adding 20 pounds last year, and has put 50 pounds on his frame since graduating from high school as a wiry 6-foot-3, 145-pounder. He does an effective job of controlling the running game because he's quick to the plate and has a good pickoff move. Tribe officials have likened Hoyman to Aaron Sele and Charles Nagy, and they think he could develop just as rapidly. They'll skip him a level and start him in high Class A this year.

Year	Club (League)	Class	W	L	ERA	G	GS	CG	SV	IP	H	R	ER	HR	BB	SO	AVG
2004	Mahoning Valley (NY-P)	A	0	0	2.08	5	5	0	0	13	9	3	3	1	4	8	.200
MINOR LEAGUE TOTALS			0	0	2.08	5	5	0	0	13	9	3	3	1	4	8	.200

17 Matt Whitney, 3b

Born: Feb. 13, 1984. **Ht.:** 6-4. **Wt.:** 190. **Bats:** R. **Throws:** R. **School:** Palm Beach Gardens (Fla.) HS. **Career Transactions:** Selected by Indians in first round (33rd overall) of 2002 draft; signed June 14, 2002. **Signed by:** Jim Gabella.

The Indians were delighted when Whitney unexpectedly fell to them as the No. 33 pick in the 2002 draft, and his strong debut in the Appalachian League encouraged them even more. But then he broke his left leg while playing basketball at spring training the following year, costing him all of 2003 and limiting him to DH last year. The break required two surgeries and he has recovered slower than expected. Compensating for the lack of strength in his left leg, he developed tendinitis in his right knee in 2004. Scar tissue also accumulated in his left foot, which affected his balance and led to more surgery at season's end. Nevertheless, Whitney is the best third-base prospect in the system. He has a solid righthanded stroke that produces power to all fields. Balls jump off his bat and have a lot of carry. He also has arm strength at third base, though his speed and agility are below average. Whitney obviously needs to prove he's completely healthy, and he'll have to improve his quickness and mobility. The Indians like his work ethic and think he'll be able to do so this year in high Class A.

Year	Club (League)	Class	AVG	G	AB	R	H	2B	3B	HR	RBI	BB	SO	SB	OBP	SLG
2002	Burlington (Appy)	R	.286	45	175	33	50	12	1	10	33	18	49	5	.359	.537
	Columbus (SAL)	A	.111	6	18	0	2	0	0	0	0	3	4	0	.238	.111
2003	Did not play—Injured															
2004	Lake County (SAL)	A	.256	55	195	21	50	11	0	5	31	23	81	0	.347	.390
MINOR LEAGUE TOTALS			.263	106	388	54	102	23	1	15	64	44	134	5	.347	.443

18 Dan Cevette, lhp

Born: Oct. 19, 1983. **Ht.:** 6-3. **Wt.:** 180. **Bats:** L. **Throws:** L. **School:** Elkland (Pa.) HS. **Career Transactions:** Selected by Indians in third round of 2002 draft; signed June 7, 2002. **Signed by:** Bob Mayer.

Cevette was Pennsylvania's high school player of the year as a senior in 2002, when he signed for $400,000 as a third-round pick. The Indians have brought him along slowly, not promoting him to full-season ball until late July last year. He appeared to turn a corner after spending the previous offseason working out for six weeks with Shawn Estes and other veteran big league pitchers. Cevette has a big, athletic body with a loose arm and clean delivery. He consistently works down and away with good command of a 90-92 mph fastball. His out pitch is a plus changeup in which he has enough confidence to throw in any count. He has the makings of a solid curveball, but it gets slurvy at times and he needs to throw it more often to improve its effectiveness. He's still a bit of a project, and the Indians will challenge him with his first taste of high Class A this spring.

Year	Club (League)	Class	W	L	ERA	G	GS	CG	SV	IP	H	R	ER	HR	BB	SO	AVG
2002	Burlington (Appy)	R	2	4	4.67	13	13	0	0	52	52	32	27	3	31	36	.271
2003	Burlington (Appy)	R	2	5	3.45	13	13	0	0	57	58	27	22	3	29	48	.261
	Mahoning Valley (NY-P)	A	0	2	8.22	2	2	0	0	8	14	11	7	1	5	3	.368
2004	Lake County (SAL)	A	2	0	2.47	9	9	0	0	44	43	13	12	4	14	41	.254
	Mahoning Valley (NY-P)	A	3	0	1.25	7	6	0	0	36	24	5	5	2	6	39	.182
MINOR LEAGUE TOTALS			9	11	3.34	44	43	0	0	197	191	88	73	13	85	167	.254

19 Scott Lewis, lhp

Born: Sept. 26, 1983. **Ht.:** 6-0. **Wt.:** 185. **Bats:** B. **Throws:** L. **School:** Ohio State University. **Career Transactions:** Selected by Indians in third round of 2004 draft; signed June 16, 2004. **Signed by:** Bob Mayer.

Lewis struck out 16 and 20 in consecutive outings for Ohio State in the spring of 2003 and looked liked a certain 2004 first-rounder. But he injured his elbow late in his sophomore season and had Tommy John surgery. Lewis made a rapid recovery and got back on the mound last April, just 11 months after having his elbow reconstructed. He pitched well at times, but lacked the usual velocity on his fastball and snap on his curveball. The Indians banked on Lewis regaining his previous form when they took him in the third round in June, and initial indications are that his $460,000 bonus may have been a bargain. His velocity climbed back toward its familiar 90-92 mph range during his brief stint at short-season Mahoning Valley. His curveball was a plus pitch again, and his changeup also looked strong. The Indians kept Lewis on a strict pitch count last summer and will continue to monitor him closely. But they believe he'll be fully equipped to open 2005 in low Class A.

Year	Club (League)	Class	W	L	ERA	G	GS	CG	SV	IP	H	R	ER	HR	BB	SO	AVG
2004	Mahoning Valley (NY-P)	A	0	1	5.40	2	2	0	0	3	2	2	2	0	1	9	.167
MINOR LEAGUE TOTALS			0	1	5.40	2	2	0	0	3	2	2	2	0	1	9	.167

20 Jason Cooper, of

Born: Dec. 6, 1980. **Ht.:** 6-2. **Wt.:** 220. **Bats:** L. **Throws:** L. **School:** Stanford University. **Career Transactions:** Selected by Indians in third round of 2002 draft; signed July 23, 2002. **Signed by:** Don Lyle.

Cooper never got fully untracked during his injury-plagued career at Stanford, but he looked like he was headed in the right direction after hitting 21 homers and leading the system with a .542 slugging percentage in 2003, his first full season. That may have been just a tease, however as his production fell off when he moved to the upper levels of the system last year. The former Stanford backup punter struggled to make consistent contact, a problem that also plagued him in college. He has a slight uppercut stroke that produces good carry when he connects, but he doesn't make adjustments well. Cooper does use the whole field and has above-average pull power to the left side. He's one of the most intense players in the organization, which worked against him in Double-A because he started pressing too much. He has average speed and fits best in left field because he has had below-average arm strength since hurting his shoulder at Stanford. Cooper needs to relax more and better adapt to Double-A when he returns there this season.

Year	Club (League)	Class	AVG	G	AB	R	H	2B	3B	HR	RBI	BB	SO	SB	OBP	SLG
2002	Columbus (SAL)	A	.255	17	55	9	14	5	0	4	17	6	17	0	.339	.564
2003	Lake County (SAL)	A	.297	69	263	50	78	17	7	12	36	32	52	3	.385	.551
	Kinston (Car)	A	.307	61	218	36	67	17	2	9	36	25	46	3	.380	.528
2004	Akron (EL)	AA	.239	111	422	54	101	24	6	14	69	47	106	2	.321	.424
	Buffalo (IL)	AAA	.176	16	51	6	9	1	0	3	7	9	15	1	.300	.373
MINOR LEAGUE TOTALS			.267	274	1009	155	269	64	15	42	165	119	236	9	.350	.485

21 J.D. Martin, rhp

Born: Jan. 2, 1983. **Ht.:** 6-4. **Wt.:** 170. **Bats:** R. **Throws:** R. **School:** Burroughs HS, Ridgecrest, Calif. **Career Transactions:** Selected by Indians in first round (35th overall) of 2001 draft; signed June 20, 2001. **Signed by:** Jason Smith.

Though Martin got off to the fastest start of any pitcher in Cleveland's arm-rich 2001 draft, since then he only has flashed the potential he showed in his debut. He strained an elbow ligament in 2003 but was able to avoid surgery. Getting an emergency start last July at Triple-A Buffalo boosted his confidence, as he went 3-2, 2.98 in his final seven regular-season starts at Kinston afterward. He ended his season by locking up the Carolina League championship with a dominant 10-strikeout performance against Wilmington. Martin improved his arsenal last year, working off two- and four-seam fastballs with good movement in the 89-91 mph range, but he's still more projectable than overpowering. His best pitch is a curveball that ranks as the best in the system. He has developed a cutter and also throws a decent changeup. Martin will spend 2005 in Double-A.

Year	Club (League)	Class	W	L	ERA	G	GS	CG	SV	IP	H	R	ER	HR	BB	SO	AVG
2001	Burlington (Appy)	R	5	1	1.38	10	10	0	0	46	26	9	7	3	11	72	.164
2002	Columbus (SAL)	A	14	5	3.90	27	26	0	0	138	141	76	60	12	46	131	.266
2003	Kinston (Car)	A	5	3	4.27	16	16	0	0	86	95	50	41	7	30	57	.281
2004	Kinston (Car)	A	11	10	4.39	25	24	2	0	148	139	75	72	15	41	98	.255
	Buffalo (IL)	AAA	0	0	10.80	1	1	0	0	5	9	6	6	1	2	2	.375
MINOR LEAGUE TOTALS			35	19	3.96	79	77	2	0	423	410	216	186	38	130	360	.257

22 Tony Sipp, lhp

Born: July 12, 1983. **Ht.:** 6-0. **Wt.:** 185. **Bats:** L. **Throws:** L. **School:** Clemson University. **Career Transactions:** Selected by Indians in 45th round of 2004 draft; signed July 1, 2004. **Signed by:** Tim Moore.

Sipp transferred from Mississippi Gulf Coast CC to Clemson for his junior year in 2004, and expected to go on the first day of the draft after seeing double duty as a left fielder and pitcher. But his agent's demands scared teams away and he lasted until the 45th round, when area scout Tim Moore convinced the Indians to take Sipp as a summer draft-and-follow. He headed to the Cape Cod League and pitched well, earning a $130,000 bonus, and continued to overmatch hitters in the short-season New York-Penn League. Sipp comes right after hitters with a deceptive, high-effort delivery and quick arm that produces an 89-93 mph fastball with late tailing action. His solid slider is better than Cleveland expected, and he has made strides with his changeup. Sipp profiles as a short reliever and has two pitches he can put hitters away with. He'll remain in the bullpen and move to low Class A this season. He won't stay there long if he continues to ring up hitters at the same pace.

Year	Club (League)	Class	W	L	ERA	G	GS	CG	SV	IP	H	R	ER	HR	BB	SO	AVG
2004	Mahoning Valley (NY-P)	A	3	1	3.16	10	10	0	0	43	33	23	15	5	13	74	.202
MINOR LEAGUE TOTALS			3	1	3.16	10	10	0	0	43	33	23	15	5	13	74	.202

23 Kyle Denney, rhp

Born: July 27, 1977. **Ht.:** 6-2. **Wt.:** 190. **Bats:** R. **Throws:** R. **School:** University of Oklahoma. **Career Transactions:** Selected by Indians in 26th round of 1999 draft; signed June 14, 1999. **Signed by:** Chad MacDonald.

After coming back from Tommy John surgery in 2001 and completing a six-year climb from 26th-round draft pick to Cleveland, Denney made national news two weeks into his big league debut. While he was riding the team bus to the airport in Kansas City, a stray bullet grazed his right calf. He escaped serious injury, thanks in part to the cheerleader boots he was wearing as part of rookie hazing. The random shooting incident ended a solid break-through year for Denney. His changeup and sharp curveball are the keys to his success. His fastball is an average 88-92 mph, but he has a sound delivery and his arm works well, allowing him to consistently find the strike zone. At 27 he has no projection left, but his combination of pitchability and three solid pitches should allow him to help the Indians, either at the back of the rotation or in middle relief.

Year	Club (League)	Class	W	L	ERA	G	GS	CG	SV	IP	H	R	ER	HR	BB	SO	AVG
1999	Burlington (Appy)	R	3	4	3.44	12	3	0	1	34	26	17	13	7	15	37	.215
	Mahoning Valley (NY-P)	A	1	0	1.80	1	1	0	0	5	5	1	1	1	0	5	.313
2000	Columbus (SAL)	A	8	6	3.05	28	24	0	0	139	135	55	47	12	46	131	.255
2001	Kinston (Car)	A	5	3	2.05	11	10	0	0	57	32	14	13	2	13	80	.159
2002	Kinston (Car)	A	7	6	3.60	15	14	0	0	85	76	37	34	5	41	68	.242
	Akron (EL)	AA	3	1	1.56	6	5	0	0	35	23	7	6	2	5	32	.183
2003	Akron (EL)	AA	7	3	2.42	18	18	1	0	104	97	34	28	7	24	87	.244
	Buffalo (IL)	AAA	2	1	5.28	6	6	0	0	31	35	18	18	4	10	26	.276
2004	Buffalo (IL)	AAA	10	5	4.41	24	24	1	0	135	134	74	66	17	39	113	.251
	Cleveland (AL)	MAJ	1	2	9.56	4	4	0	0	16	32	17	17	3	8	13	.421
MAJOR LEAGUE TOTALS			1	2	9.56	4	4	0	0	16	32	17	17	3	8	13	.421
MINOR LEAGUE TOTALS			46	29	3.26	121	105	2	1	624	563	257	226	57	193	579	.238

24 Ryan Goleski, of

Born: March 19, 1982. **Ht.:** 6-3. **Wt.:** 225. **Bats:** R. **Throws:** R. **School:** Eastern Michigan University. **Career Transactions:** Selected by Indians in sixth round of 2003 draft; signed June 8, 2003. **Signed by:** Bill Schudlich.

Despite setting Eastern Michigan and Mid-American Conference records with 51 homers, Goleski lasted until the 24th round of the 2003 draft. The Indians knew they were buying a ton of raw power potential when they selected him, and he has exceeded their expectations since signing. With the exception of outfielder Jonathan Van Every, Goleski was the most improved player in the organization in 2004. He's a dead-pull hitter and is primarily a two-tool player, featuring a power bat and a cannon arm from right field. Goleski needs to use the whole field more often, and some scouts wonder if his power will decrease when he shortens his swing to make better contact. There also are questions about his ability to hit quality breaking stuff. He'll be challenged in high Class A this year.

Year	Club (League)	Class	AVG	G	AB	R	H	2B	3B	HR	RBI	BB	SO	SB	OBP	SLG
2003	Mahoning Valley (NY-P)	A	.296	64	243	39	72	15	2	8	37	21	66	3	.358	.473
2004	Lake County (SAL)	A	.297	130	505	83	150	22	5	28	104	55	100	6	.372	.527
MINOR LEAGUE TOTALS			.297	194	748	122	222	37	7	36	141	76	166	9	.367	.509

25 Jeremy Guthrie, rhp

Born: April 8, 1979. **Ht.:** 6-1. **Wt.:** 200. **Bats:** B. **Throws:** R. **School:** Stanford University. **Career Transactions:** Selected by Indians in first round (22nd overall) of 2002 draft; signed Oct. 3, 2002. **Signed by:** Don Lyle.

Guthrie has been a huge disappointment since signing a big league contract worth $4 million as a first-round pick in 2002. He dominated in Double-A during his pro debut the following spring, but got hammered after a promotion to Triple-A and didn't fare any better last year. He made the Eastern League all-star team after he was demoted to Double-A, but was relegated to the bullpen by the end of the season and no longer projects as a major league starter. When he shifted to relief, his fastball sat at 92-94 mph and topped out at 95-96. The rest of Guthrie's stuff—slider, changeup, curveball—is more notable for his ability to throw strikes with it rather than its quality. His delivery and arm action aren't as clean as they once were. His cerebral nature works against him at times, as he'll try to outthink hitters rather than challenge them. Because he went on a two-year Mormon mission while he was in college, he'll be 26 shortly after he begins his third full season. He's running out of time to justify Cleveland's huge investment.

Year	Club (League)	Class	W	L	ERA	G	GS	CG	SV	IP	H	R	ER	HR	BB	SO	AVG
2003	Akron (EL)	AA	6	2	1.44	10	9	2	0	63	44	11	10	0	14	35	.196
	Buffalo (IL)	AAA	4	9	6.52	18	18	1	0	97	129	75	70	15	30	62	.321
2004	Buffalo (IL)	AAA	1	2	7.91	4	4	0	0	19	23	19	17	0	18	10	.303
	Akron (EL)	AA	8	8	4.21	23	21	1	0	130	145	76	61	16	42	94	.277
	Cleveland (AL)	MAJ	0	0	4.63	6	0	0	0	12	9	6	6	1	6	7	.214
MAJOR LEAGUE TOTALS			0	0	4.63	6	0	0	0	12	9	6	6	1	6	7	.214
MINOR LEAGUE TOTALS			19	21	4.60	55	52	4	0	309	341	181	158	31	104	201	.278

26 Mariano Gomez, lhp

Born: Sept. 12, 1982. **Ht.:** 6-5. **Wt.:** 170. **Bats:** L. **Throws:** L. **Career Transactions:** Signed out of Honduras by Indians, July 1, 1999. **Signed by:** Les Pajari.

Bidding to become the first big leaguer from Honduras, Gomez was on the fast track until mid-2003. He was shut down in July that season with a strained ligament in his left middle finger, then made just eight appearances last season because of the same problem. The Indians hired a specialist to help him with his rehabilitation, as the injury is rare and more regularly seen in rock climbers. When he's healthy, Gomez has impressive stuff. He works with a 91-93 mph fastball, a plus changeup and a slurvy breaking ball and plus changeup. He'll have to do a better job of consistently repeating his pitches. Overly demonstrative on the mound, he also could use some maturity. But his biggest need is to get back on the mound and make up for missed time. Cleveland hopes he'll be ready to go in 2005 and plans on sending him back to Double-A.

Year	Club (League)	Class	W	L	ERA	G	GS	CG	SV	IP	H	R	ER	HR	BB	SO	AVG
2000	Burlington (Appy)	R	0	5	4.31	13	11	0	0	54	77	44	26	7	16	30	.341
2001	Burlington (Appy)	R	2	8	6.07	13	12	0	0	59	69	47	40	4	21	57	.289
	Mahoning Valley (NY-P)	A	1	0	5.40	1	1	0	0	5	5	3	3	1	2	6	.263
2002	Columbus (SAL)	A	8	2	2.75	34	13	0	1	111	106	44	34	3	40	98	.247
2003	Kinston (Car)	A	6	4	3.67	18	18	1	0	101	91	49	41	11	38	69	.243
2004	Akron (EL)	AA	0	1	5.31	7	3	0	0	20	27	14	12	2	8	15	.321
	Mahoning Valley (NY-P)	A	0	0	0.00	1	1	0	0	2	2	0	0	0	0	3	.250
MINOR LEAGUE TOTALS			17	20	3.98	87	59	1	1	353	377	201	156	28	125	278	.273

27 Brian Tallet, lhp

Born: Sept. 21, 1977. **Ht.:** 6-7. **Wt.:** 210. **Bats:** L. **Throws:** L. **School:** Louisiana State University. **Career Transactions:** Selected by Indians in second round of 2000 draft; signed Aug. 1, 2000. **Signed by:** Rene Gayo.

Tallet won 15 games and started the title game for Louisiana State's 2000 College World Series championship team. Two years later, he was pitching in Cleveland and figured to be a key part of the Indians' future. But he blew out his elbow midway through the 2003 season and needed Tommy John surgery. (Fellow lefty Billy Traber, who no longer qualifies for the Top 30, suffered the same fate.) Tallet was expected to miss all of 2004, but his rehab progressed so rapidly that he returned at the end of June. He finished the year by pitching a perfect ninth inning in the clinching game of the Triple-A International League playoffs. Tallet's velocity was back to normal, as he pitched at 89-92 mph in the postseason. His slider and changeup also were solid, another indication that he's fully recovered. While he had trouble repeating his delivery in the past, the extended rehab gave him ample time to improve his mechanics. He'll compete for a big league bullpen role in spring training.

Year	Club (League)	Class	W	L	ERA	G	GS	CG	SV	IP	H	R	ER	HR	BB	SO	AVG
2000	Mahoning Valley (NY-P)	A	0	0	1.15	6	6	0	0	16	10	2	2	0	3	20	.172
2001	Kinston (Car)	A	9	7	3.04	27	27	2	0	160	134	62	54	12	38	164	.224
2002	Akron (EL)	AA	10	1	3.08	18	16	1	0	102	93	41	35	9	32	73	.243
	Buffalo (IL)	AAA	2	3	3.07	8	7	0	0	44	47	17	15	1	16	25	.281
	Cleveland (AL)	MAJ	1	0	1.50	2	2	0	0	12	9	3	2	0	4	5	.214
2003	Buffalo (IL)	AAA	4	4	5.14	15	15	0	0	84	89	50	48	10	34	67	.270
	Cleveland (AL)	MAJ	0	2	4.74	5	3	0	0	19	23	14	10	2	8	9	.303
2004	Mahoning Valley (NY-P)	A	0	0	0.00	2	1	0	0	3	3	3	0	0	0	2	.273
	Lake County (SAL)	A	0	0	0.00	2	1	0	0	2	1	0	0	0	0	1	.143
	Akron (EL)	AA	1	1	5.56	14	0	0	1	23	26	15	14	0	13	23	.292
	Buffalo (IL)	AAA	0	0	4.15	5	0	0	0	9	7	4	4	0	3	7	.226
MAJOR LEAGUE TOTALS			1	2	3.48	7	5	0	0	31	32	17	12	2	12	14	.271
MINOR LEAGUE TOTALS			26	16	3.50	97	73	3	1	442	410	194	172	32	139	382	.245

28 Kevin Kouzmanoff, 3b

Born: July 25, 1981. **Ht.:** 6-1. **Wt.:** 200. **Bats:** R. **Throws:** R. **School:** University of Nevada. **Career Transactions:** Selected by Indians in sixth round of 2003 draft; signed June 3, 2003. **Signed by:** Don Lyle.

The Indians drafted Kouzmanoff in the sixth round out of Nevada, the same school that produced former Tribe prospect Ryan Church (now a big league outfielder with the Nationals) and current farmhands Joe Inglett and Chris Gimenez (who led the New York-Penn League with 36 extra-base hits and a .527 slugging percentage in his 2004 pro debut). Kouzmanoff doesn't wow scouts with his tools, but he's one of the hardest workers in the system and tore up the low Class A South Atlantic League in his first full season debut. He's obsessed with breaking down video of each of his at-bats, and while his swing is unorthodox, he makes consistently hard contact. The Indians worked with him to stand up straighter in the box to maximize his lower half in his swing, allowing him to drive more balls to the opposite field. Defensively, he makes all the routine plays at third base. Kouzmanoff was a bit old for low Class A last year, and at 23 he'll be ahead of most of his competition in high Class A in 2005.

Year	Club (League)	Class	AVG	G	AB	R	H	2B	3B	HR	RBI	BB	SO	SB	OBP	SLG
2003	Mahoning Valley (NY-P)	A	.272	54	206	31	56	8	1	8	33	21	36	2	.342	.437
2004	Lake County (SAL)	A	.330	123	473	74	156	35	5	16	87	44	75	5	.394	.526
	Akron (EL)	AA	.208	7	24	3	5	1	1	1	6	2	5	0	.259	.458
MINOR LEAGUE TOTALS			.309	184	703	108	217	44	7	25	126	67	116	7	.374	.498

29 Rafael Perez, lhp

Born: May 15, 1982. **Ht.:** 6-3. **Wt.:** 170. **Bats:** L. **Throws:** L. **Career Transactions:** Signed out of Dominican Republic by Indians, Jan. 25, 2002. **Signed by:** Rene Gayo.

Known as Hanlet Ramirez when he first signed, Perez helped pitch the Indians to the Rookie-level Dominican Summer League championship in 2002 and earned Appalachian League pitcher-of-the-year honors in 2003. He was greeted a bit roughly when he made his full-season debut last year. His fastball did climb from 89-91 to 91-94 mph, continuing to show late running action. He projects to add more velocity because he has a lanky frame and his arm works free and easy. In addition to his plus fastball, Perez throws a nasty slider that emerged as a true out pitch last season. His changeup lags far behind his first two pitches, and was the main cause of his struggles. The consensus is that Perez will move to the bullpen down the road, and that certainly will be the case if he can't improve his changeup. He'll pitch in high Class A this year.

Year	Club (League)	Class	W	L	ERA	G	GS	CG	SV	IP	H	R	ER	HR	BB	SO	AVG
2002	Indians (DSL)	R	7	1	0.96	13	13	1	0	75	58	14	8	3	16	81	.208
2003	Burlington (Appy)	R	9	3	1.70	13	12	0	0	69	56	23	13	1	16	63	.220
2004	Lake County (SAL)	A	7	6	4.85	23	22	0	0	115	121	75	62	9	47	99	.273
	Kinston (Car)	A	0	0	11.57	1	1	0	0	5	10	6	6	1	2	3	.435
MINOR LEAGUE TOTALS			23	10	3.03	50	48	1	0	264	245	118	89	14	81	246	.245

30 Eider Torres, 2b

Born: Jan. 16, 1983. **Ht.:** 5-8. **Wt.:** 160. **Bats:** S. **Throws:** R. **Career Transactions:** Signed out of Venezuela by Indians, May 3, 2000. **Signed by:** Luis Aponte.

Torres was a pint-sized 5-foot-7 and 140 pounds when the Indians signed him as a 17-year-old. While he hasn't grown much in stature since then, several aspects of his game certainly have. Many scouts in the organization tab him as a sleeper, and he even has garnered some early comparisons to Roberto Alomar. Torres likely won't reach Alomar's status, but he's a career .303 hitter in the minors. A switch-hitter, he makes consistent contact from both sides of the plate with a compact stroke. He's aggressive at the plate, so he doesn't draw many walks, and he'll never be counted on to provide much power. He has plus speed and is a basestealing threat. Defensively, Torres has made just 14 errors in 196 games at second base over the last two years. His footwork and actions around the bag are solid, and his range is better than average. He wore down late in 2003, but worked hard on conditioning his body and finished strong last season. Torres will be Cleveland's everyday second baseman in Double-A this year.

Year	Club (League)	Class	AVG	G	AB	R	H	2B	3B	HR	RBI	BB	SO	SB	OBP	SLG
2000	Indians (VSL)	R	.310	41	155	40	48	6	1	0	19	14	18	19	.389	.361
2001	Indians (VSL)	R	.398	55	216	67	86	17	4	2	37	38	11	41	.488	.542
2002	Burlington (Appy)	R	.320	45	194	26	62	6	1	0	13	15	22	28	.371	.361
	Mahoning Valley (NY-P)	A	.307	19	75	9	23	5	0	0	8	3	9	9	.342	.373
2003	Kinston (Car)	A	.248	124	447	63	111	13	0	1	39	39	73	43	.314	.284
2004	Kinston (Car)	A	.302	113	440	68	133	24	3	3	46	22	46	48	.337	.391
MINOR LEAGUE TOTALS			.303	397	1527	273	463	71	9	6	162	131	179	188	.363	.373

COLORADO
ROCKIES

BY **TRACY RINGOLSBY**

I n the franchise's early years, the Rockies annually loaded up on pitching in the draft. Not any longer.

Colorado kicked off its 2004 draft by taking Georgia high school shortstop Chris Nelson ninth overall, the first of five position players it drafted in the first six rounds. The Rockies also spent $925,000 to sign another Georgia prep product, outfielder Dexter Fowler, in the 14th round. The year before, they chose California prep third baseman Ian Stewart 10th overall, and four of their top six selections were position players. Before Stewart and Nelson, Colorado had taken just one hitter in the first round of its first 11 drafts: Todd Helton, the best player in franchise history.

Rockies scouting director Bill Schmidt says the club hasn't made a conscious effort to stock up on hitters. Like most teams, Colorado sorts through the talent and takes the best player available. What the Rockies have tried to do is create better balance in their farm system, which they're now counting on to feed the big league roster. After disastrous results with Mike Hampton and Denny Neagle, they're no longer pursuing free agents. They'll try to build their own nucleus from within.

Colorado's projected 2005 lineup includes four homegrown players: Helton, second-year left fielder **Matt Holliday** and a pair of rookies, third baseman Garrett Atkins and shortstop Clint Barmes. Rookie catcher J.D. Closser spent three years developing in the Rockies system after being acquired from

DAVID SEELIG

Arizona for Mike Myers. Another rookie, right fielder Brad Hawpe, figures to platoon with Dustan Mohr in right field.

The Rockies are growing their own pitching as well. Of the six candidates for their rotation, five originally signed with Colorado: Shawn Chacon, Aaron Cook, Baseball America Minor League Player of the Year Jeff Francis, Jason Jennings and Jamey Wright. Their bullpen could feature homegrown Scott Dohmann, Ryan Speier and Chin-Hui Tsao. After coming up short in last year's attempt to convert Chacon into a closer, the Rockies may try it with Tsao this season.

Colorado also has brought in a slew of young players from other organizations, such as Closser. Key lefty reliever Brian Fuentes arrived when the Rockies dumped Jeff Cirillo's contract on the Mariners. Second baseman Aaron Miles, who finished fourth in National League rookie of the year voting in 2004, came from the White Sox for Juan Uribe. Utilityman Luis Gonzalez and lefty Javier Lopez were Rule 5 draft-related acquisitions.

The Rockies made similar moves to supplement their bullpen this offseason. They plucked righty Marcos Carvajal and lefty Matt Merricks from the Dodgers in the major league Rule 5 draft, and traded for righty Aaron Taylor when the Mariners ran out of 40-man roster space. Colorado also claimed reserve infielder Alfredo Amezaga off waivers from the Angels.

TOP 30 PROSPECTS

1. Ian Stewart, 3b	16. Jim Miller, rhp
2. Chris Nelson, ss	17. Matt Macri, 3b/2b
3. Jeff Francis, lhp	18. Brad Hawpe, of
4. Ubaldo Jimenez, rhp	19. Scott Dohmann, rhp
5. Juan Morillo, rhp	20. Chris Iannetta, c
6. Jeff Baker, 3b	21. Ryan Speier, rhp
7. Seth Smith, of	22. Samuel Deduno, rhp
8. Jeff Salazar, of	23. Aaron Taylor, rhp
9. Jayson Nix, 2b	24. Allan Simpson, rhp
10. Clint Barmes, ss	25. Choo Freeman, of
11. Dexter Fowler, of	26. Ching-Lung Lo, rhp
12. Garrett Atkins, 3b	27. Marcos Carvajal, rhp
13. J.D. Closser, c	28. Cory Sullivan, of
14. Ryan Shealy, 1b	29. Matt Merricks, lhp
15. Chris Narveson, lhp	30. Mike Esposito, rhp

ORGANIZATION OVERVIEW

General manager: Dan O'Dowd. **Farm director:** Bill Geivett. **Scouting director:** Bill Schmidt.

2004 PERFORMANCE

Class	Team	League	W	L	Pct.	Finish*	Manager
Majors	Colorado	National	68	94	.420	12th (16)	Clint Hurdle
Triple-A	Colorado Springs Sky Sox	Pacific Coast	78	65	.545	6th (16)	Marv Foley
Double-A	Tulsa Drillers	Texas	71	68	.511	5th (8)	Tom Runnells
High A	#Visalia Oaks	California	56	84	.400	9th (10)	Stu Cole
Low A	Asheville Tourists	South Atlantic	64	75	.460	13th (16)	Joe Mikulik
Short-season	Tri-City Dust Devils	Northwest	40	36	.526	5th (8)	Ron Gideon
Rookie	Casper Rockies	Pioneer	33	40	.452	7th (8)	P.J. Carey
OVERALL 2004 MINOR LEAGUE RECORD			342	368	.482	20th (30)	

*Finish in overall standings (No. of teams in league). #Affiliate will be in Modesto (California) in 2005.

ORGANIZATION LEADERS

BATTING
*Minimum 250 at-bats
*AVG	Garrett Atkins, Colorado Springs	.366
R	Jeff Salazar, Tulsa/Visalia	118
H	Clint Barmes, Colorado Springs	175
TB	Ian Stewart, Asheville	300
2B	Garrett Atkins, Colorado Springs	43
3B	Jeff Salazar, Tulsa/Visalia	11
HR	Andy Tracy, Colorado Springs	33
RBI	Andy Tracy, Colorado Springs	120
BB	K.J. Hendricks, Visalia	85
SO	Shawn Garrett, Colorado Springs/Tulsa	132
SB	Christian Colonel, Asheville	35
*OBP	Garrett Atkins, Colorado Springs	.434
*SLG	Brad Hawpe, Colorado Springs	.652

PITCHING
#Minimum 75 Innings
W	Jeff Francis, Colorado Springs/Tulsa	16
L	Brian Tollberg, Colorado Springs	13
#ERA	Jeff Francis, Colorado Springs/Tulsa	2.21
G	Ryan Speier, Tulsa	61
CG	Alberto Arias, Asheville	4
SV	Ryan Speier, Tulsa	37
IP	Marc Kaiser, Asheville	181
BB	Justin Hampson, Tulsa	63
SO	Jeff Francis, Colorado Springs/Tulsa	196

BEST TOOLS

Best Hitter for Average	Ian Stewart
Best Power Hitter	Ian Stewart
Best Strike-Zone Discipline	Garrett Atkins
Fastest Baserunner	K.J. Hendricks
Best Athlete	Chris Nelson
Best Fastball	Juan Morillo
Best Curveball	Ubaldo Jimenez
Best Slider	Jim Miller
Best Changeup	Jeff Francis
Best Control	Jeff Francis
Best Defensive Catcher	Chris Iannetta
Best Defensive Infielder	Matt Macri
Best Infield Arm	Chris Nelson
Best Defensive Outfielder	Jeff Salazar
Best Outfield Arm	Brad Hawpe

PROJECTED 2008 LINEUP

Catcher	J.D. Closser
First Base	Todd Helton
Second Base	Matt Macri
Third Base	Ian Stewart
Shortstop	Chris Nelson
Left Field	Seth Smith
Center Field	Jeff Salazar
Right Field	Matt Holliday

No. 1 Starter	Jason Jennings
No. 2 Starter	Joe Kennedy
No. 3 Starter	Jeff Francis
No. 4 Starter	Aaron Cook
No. 5 Starter	Ubaldo Jimenez
Closer	Chin-Hui Tsao

LAST YEAR'S TOP 20 PROSPECTS

1. Chin-Hui Tsao, rhp	11. Brad Hawpe, of/1b
2. Ian Stewart, 3b	12. Jeff Baker, 3b
3. Jeff Francis, lhp	13. Garrett Atkins, 3b
4. Ubaldo Jimenez, rhp	14. Scott Dohmann, rhp
5. Jayson Nix, 2b	15. Oscar Materano, ss
6. Rene Reyes, of	16. Neil Wilson, c
7. Jason Young, rhp	17. Choo Freeman, of
8. Zach Parker, lhp	18. Juan Morillo, rhp
9. Matt Holliday, of	19. J.D. Closser, c
10. Ching-Lung Lo, rhp	20. Jeff Salazar, of

TOP PROSPECTS OF THE DECADE

Year	Player, Pos.	Current Team
1995	Doug Million, lhp	Deceased
1996	Derrick Gibson, of	Angels
1997	Todd Helton, 1b	Rockies
1998	Todd Helton, 1b	Rockies
1999	Choo Freeman, of	Rockies
2000	Choo Freeman, of	Rockies
2001	Chin-Hui Tsao, rhp	Rockies
2002	Chin-Hui Tsao, rhp	Rockies
2003	Aaron Cook, rhp	Rockies
2004	Chin-Hui Tsao, rhp	Rockies

TOP DRAFT PICKS OF THE DECADE

Year	Player, Pos.	Current Team
1995	Todd Helton, 1b	Rockies
1996	Jake Westbrook, rhp	Indians
1997	Mark Mangum, rhp	Out of baseball
1998	Choo Freeman, of	Rockies
1999	Jason Jennings, rhp	Rockies
2000	*Matt Harrington, rhp	Fort Worth (Central)
2001	Jayson Nix, ss	Rockies
2002	Jeff Francis, lhp	Rockies
2003	Ian Stewart, 3b	Rockies
2004	Chris Nelson, ss	Rockies

*Did not sign.

ALL-TIME LARGEST BONUSES

Jason Young, 2000	$2,750,000
Chin-Hui Tsao, 1999	$2,200,000
Chris Nelson, 2004	$2,150,000
Ian Stewart, 2003	$1,950,000
Jeff Francis, 2002	$1,850,000

Colorado ROCKIES

RANK: **6**

Impact Potential: B

Ian Stewart is one of the best young hitters in the minor leagues, holds his own at a key defensive position and has off-the-charts makeup. Shortstop Chris Nelson could soon join him on the fast track to form a dynamic left side of the Rockies' infield. With the exception of Minor League Player of the Year Jeff Francis, the Rockies' top pitchers all feature high-90s cheddar.

Depth: B

The Rockies have several waves of prospects approaching Denver. Garrett Atkins, Clint Barmes and J.D. Closser should see plenty of big league time in 2005. Next in line are outfielders Brad Hawpe and Jeff Salazar, then Stewart, then the possible fruits of an intriguing group of hitters drafted in 2004. If the Rockies had more young arms, their farm system would rank even higher.

Depth charts prepared by **John Manuel** *and* **Allan Simpson**. *Numbers in parentheses indicate prospect rankings.*

LF
Seth Smith (7)
Sean Barker
Brian Barre
Jud Thipgen

CF
Jeff Salazar (8)
Dexter Fowler (11)
Choo Freeman (25)
Cory Sullivan (28)
Tony Miller

RF
Brad Hawpe (18)
Jorge Piedra
Sean Barker
Jordan Czarniecki

3B
Ian Stewart (1)
Jeff Baker (6)
Garrett Atkins (12)
Matt Macri (17)
Dustin Hahn

SS
Chris Nelson (2)
Clint Barmes (10)
Jonathan Herrera
Omar Materano

2B
Jayson Nix (9)
Randy Blood
K.J. Hendricks
Eric Young

1B
Ryan Shealy (14)
Joe Koshansky

SOURCE of TALENT

HOMEGROWN		ACQUIRED	
College	14	Trades	4
Junior College	0	Rule 5 draft	2
Draft-and-follow	0	Independent leagues	0
High School	5	Free agents/waivers	0
Nondrafted free agent	1		
Foreign	4		

C
J.D. Closser (13)
Chris Iannetta (12)
Neil Wilson
Garet Gentry
Rick Guarno

LHP

Starters	Relievers
Jeff Francis (3)	Matt Merricks (29)
Chris Narveson (15)	Jake Postlewait
Justin Hampson	Adam Bright
Franklin Morales	
Zack Parker	
Aaron Marsden	

RHP

Starters	Relievers
Ubaldo Jimenez (4)	Jim Miller (16)
Juan Morillo (5)	Scott Dohmann (19)
Samuel Deduno (22)	Ryan Speier (21)
Ching-Lung Lo (26)	Aaron Taylor (23)
Mike Esposito (30)	Allan Simpson (24)
Tomas Santiago	Marcos Carvajal (27)
Ryan Mattheus	Manuel Corpas
Steven Register	Scott Beerer
Jason Young	Jentry Beckstead
Mark Kaiser	Chris Young

DRAFT ANALYSIS

2004

Best Pro Debut: RHP Jim Miller (8) led the short-season Northwest League with 17 saves and 34 appearances, whiffing 65 in 37 innings en route to a 0.97 ERA. SS Chris Nelson (1) ranked as the top prospect in the Rookie-level Pioneer League after hitting .347-4-20. OF Seth Smith (2) batted .369-9-61 to earn Pioneer League all-star honors, while 3B Matt Macri (5) hit .333-7-43 to garner similar recognition in the NWL.

Best Athlete: OF Dexter Fowler's (14) five-tool skills have prompted comparisons to Andre Dawson and Andruw Jones. Nelson and Macri were two-way stars who threw in the low 90s before Tommy John surgery. Smith was the backup quarterback behind No. 1 overall NFL draft pick Eli Manning at Mississippi.

Best Pure Hitter: Nelson and Smith, two of the draft's most gifted hitters, will call Coors Field home.

Best Raw Power: Macri and Smith. 1B Joe Koshansky (6), who hit 12 homers in the NWL, isn't far behind.

Fastest Runner: Fowler flies from the right side of the plate to first base in 4.06 seconds. Nelson is a tick behind him, as is draft-and-follow 2B Eric Young Jr. (30 in 2003)—whose father holds the franchise record for stolen bases.

Best Defensive Player: Fowler is a quality center fielder. C Chris Iannetta (4) is solid behind the plate and held his own with the bat in low Class A, hitting .314.

Best Fastball: Miller worked consistently at 93-95 mph all summer. RHP Chris Buechner (11) and David Patton (12) touched 95 at times.

Best Breaking Ball: RHP Steven

TONY FARLOW

Iannetta

Register's (3) out pitch is a slider, and he used it to record 25 saves at Auburn. Draft-and-follow RHP Ryan Mattheus' (19 in 2003) power slider can be more devastating than Register's.

Most Intriguing Background: The Rockies love quarterbacks, and their latest is OF Brian Brohm (49). The younger brother of former NFL quarterback and Indians minor leaguer Jeff Brohm, Brian made a big impact as a Louisville freshman. OF Todd Frazier (37) was the most outstanding player at the 1998 Little League World Series, where he led Toms River (N.J.) to the championship. His brother Jeff went in the third round to the Tigers, while another brother, Charles, already was in the Marlins system.

Closest To The Majors: Miller could develop rapidly as a reliever. So could Register if he returns to that role.

Best Late-Round Pick: The Rockies didn't have the money to sign Fowler until they traded Larry Walker. Fowler, who had a chance to go in the first round, received $925,000, a record for the 14th round.

The One Who Got Away: Colorado lost the rights to just five players, none before the 37th round. Frazier would have gone in the first five rounds had teams believed they could sign him away from Rutgers.

Assessment: Nelson was destined for Baltimore until Orioles owner Peter Angelos insisted his club draft a cost-effective college pitcher. Landing him and Smith was a coup.

2003 Colorado coveted 3B Ian Stewart (1) with the 10th overall pick and got its man, and he has become the club's top prospect. RHP Ryan Mattheus (19) became one of the top draft-and-follow signings last spring. **GRADE:** B+

2002 The Rockies wanted to take OF Denard Span at No. 9, but when he balked at a predraft deal they wound up with LHP Jeff Francis (1). They made their own luck later in the draft, finding 3B Jeff Baker (4), OF Jeff Salazar (8) and 1B Ryan Shealy (11). **GRADE:** B+

2001 2B Jayson Nix (1) is this group's only real hope, and he took a step back last season. **GRADE:** C

2000 Colorado got embroiled in the nastiest draft negotiations ever and failed to sign RHP Matt Harrington (1), and appears to have wasted a club-record $2.75 million bonus on RHP Jason Young (2). But the Rockies salvaged the draft with four players who should contribute in the majors this year: SS Clint Barmes (10), 3B Garrett Atkins (5), OF Brad Hawpe (11) and RHP Scott Dohmann (6). **GRADE:** B

Draft analysis prepared by Jim Callis. Numbers in parentheses indicate draft rounds.

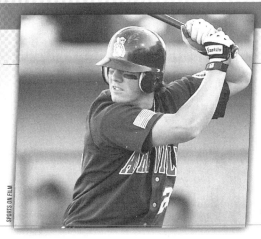

Ian
STEWART

Born: April 5, 1985.
Ht.: 6-3. **Wt.:** 205.
Bats: L. **Throws:** R.
School: La Quinta HS, Garden Grove, Calif.
Career Transactions: Selected by Rockies in first round (10th overall) of 2003 draft; signed June 11, 2003.
Signed by: Todd Blyleven.

S tewart had a decorated amateur career. On the U.S. team that won the bronze medal at the 2002 World Junior Championship, he hit in the middle of a powerful lineup behind fellow 2003 first-round picks Delmon Young and Lastings Milledge. The next spring he teamed with righthander Ian Kennedy, now the ace at Southern California, to make La Quinta High the preseason No. 1 team in the country. Stewart earned All-America honors with a .462-16-61 senior season as La Quinta finished third in the nation. The Rockies drafted him 10th overall in 2003, the first time they took a position player in the first round since franchise cornerstone Todd Helton in 1995. Since signing for $1.95 million, Stewart has ranked as the No. 1 prospect in the Rookie-level Pioneer League in 2003 and the No. 2 prospect (behind Young) in the low Class A South Atlantic League last season. He led the SAL in extra-base hits (70) and slugging percentage.

Colorado hasn't had a hitter like Stewart in its system since Helton. Stewart punishes good fastballs and has the strength and hand speed to wait back and drive offspeed stuff. He has good plate coverage and learned to use the whole field during the season. He adjusted when SAL pitchers began throwing him junk, and did damage at both Asheville's cozy McCormick Field (.621 slugging percentage) and on the road (.568). Stewart has average speed, and he's a savvy and aggressive baserunner. While he fell short of his goal of a 30-30 season, he did steal 19 bases in 28 attempts. Defensively, he has an above-average arm. Along with his tools, Stewart has strong desire. He wants to be an all-star and a Gold Glove third baseman, and he's willing to do what it takes to get there. The Rockies rave about his work ethic and focus on team goals.

The biggest question facing Stewart in high school was whether he would be able to stay at third base as a pro. Colorado sent adviser Walt Weiss, a former all-star shortstop, to watch his workouts before the draft. Weiss not only gave Stewart his stamp of approval, but he also has brought him to his home in Denver for offseason training. Stewart has worked hard to improve his lateral mobility and quickened his first step. He gets himself in trouble by dropping down on throws, but that can be easily overcome with coaching and experience.

Even when a spot opened up in high Class A, the Rockies kept Stewart at Asheville for all of last season. Farm director Bill Geivett wanted Stewart to finish 2004 where he began, just as Vladimir Guerrero spent all of 1995 in the SAL when Geivett was his farm director with the Expos. Geivett likens Stewart's hitting ability to that of Guerrero, who finished his next season in the majors. He says a similar quick path could be in store for Stewart, who probably will start 2005 at Colorado's new high Class A Modesto affiliate. He already has forced the move of 2004 fifth-round pick Matt Macri to second base and will push Jeff Baker to an outfield corner.

Year	Club (League)	Class	AVG	G	AB	R	H	2B	3B	HR	RBI	BB	SO	SB	OBP	SLG
2003	Casper (Pio)	R	.317	57	224	40	71	14	5	10	43	29	54	4	.401	.558
2004	Asheville (SAL)	A	.319	131	505	92	161	31	9	30	101	66	112	19	.398	.594
MINOR LEAGUE TOTALS			.318	188	729	132	232	45	14	40	144	95	166	23	.399	.583

2 Chris Nelson, ss

Born: Sept. 3, 1985. **Ht.:** 5-11. **Wt.:** 175. **Bats:** R. **Throws:** R. **School:** Redan HS, Decatur, Ga. **Career Transactions:** Selected by Rockies in first round (ninth overall) of 2004 draft; signed July 1, 2004. **Signed by:** Damon Iannelli.

Despite having Tommy John surgery prior to his senior season, Nelson hit .552-8-44 to earn BA High School All-America honors. The Orioles were poised to take him eighth overall last June before owner Peter Angelos insisted on a college pitcher. The Rockies gladly pounced on Nelson with the next pick, signed him for $2.15 million and watched him rank as the top prospect in the Pioneer League. Nelson already has a feel for using the entire field, and he has the power to drive the ball the opposite way. His quick hands and strong wrists will allow him to catch up to inside fastballs. He's an above-average runner. Nelson needs to learn to play under control in the field. He tends to spin when he throws, and must set his feet to improve his accuracy. He struck out more than once a game in his debut and will have to make better contact at higher levels. Nelson is a rare shortstop with the potential to bat in the middle of the order. Ticketed for low Class A in 2005, he and Ian Stewart should lock down the left side of Colorado's infield for years to come.

Year	Club (League)	Class	AVG	G	AB	R	H	2B	3B	HR	RBI	BB	SO	SB	OBP	SLG
2004	Casper (Pio)	R	.347	38	147	36	51	6	3	4	20	20	42	6	.432	.510
MINOR LEAGUE TOTALS			.347	38	147	36	51	6	3	4	20	20	42	6	.432	.510

3 Jeff Francis, lhp

Born: Jan. 8, 1981. **Ht.:** 6-5. **Wt.:** 200. **Bats:** L. **Throws:** L. **School:** University of British Columbia. **Career Transactions:** Selected by Rockies in first round (ninth overall) of 2002 draft; signed June 19, 2002. **Signed by:** Greg Hopkins.

After finishing 2003 with a 10-1, 1.06 flourish, Francis won BA's Minor League Player of the Year award last season. He led the Double-A Texas League in ERA, adjusted to thin air at Triple-A Colorado Springs, and after a rocky start in the majors, won his last three decisions with Colorado. Francis is a power pitcher without power, along the lines of Sid Fernandez. He possesses pinpoint command of his 86-91 mph fastball and creates a deceptive look for hitters, in part because of the extension he gets in his delivery. He also has the best changeup in the system, and his slider is a solid third pitch. As good as his changeup and slider are, Francis has to be careful to not use them too much. He must remember that his success stems from pitching off his fastball. Francis heads into spring training with a spot all but locked up in the big league rotation. He's a classic example of a pitcher who's much better than his radar-gun readings.

Year	Club (League)	Class	W	L	ERA	G	GS	CG	SV	IP	H	R	ER	HR	BB	SO	AVG
2002	Tri-City (NWL)	A	0	0	0.00	4	3	0	0	11	5	0	0	0	4	16	.143
	Asheville (SAL)	A	0	0	1.80	4	4	0	0	20	16	6	4	2	4	23	.232
2003	Visalia (Cal)	A	12	9	3.47	27	27	2	0	161	135	66	62	8	45	153	.229
2004	Tulsa (TL)	AA	13	1	1.98	17	17	1	0	114	73	26	25	9	22	147	.180
	Colorado Springs (PCL)	AAA	3	2	2.85	7	7	0	0	41	35	16	13	3	7	49	.230
	Colorado (NL)	MAJ	3	2	5.15	7	7	0	0	37	42	22	21	8	13	32	.286
MAJOR LEAGUE TOTALS			3	2	5.15	7	7	0	0	37	42	22	21	8	13	32	.286
MINOR LEAGUE TOTALS			28	12	2.70	59	58	3	0	346	264	114	104	22	82	388	.211

4 Ubaldo Jimenez, rhp

Born: Jan. 22, 1984. **Ht.:** 6-2. **Wt.:** 165. **Bats:** R. **Throws:** R. **Career Transactions:** Signed out of Dominican Republic by Rockies, April 25, 2001. **Signed by:** Rolando Fernandez.

Jimenez dominated the high Class A California League at age 20, striking out 12 in his first outing and never allowing more than three earned runs in a start. Then the Rockies discovered the beginnings of a stress fracture, and his season ended in mid-May. He returned to the mound last fall in instructional league. Jimenez has a raw power fastball regularly clocked from 94-97 mph. He also has a big league curveball and the confidence to throw his changeup in any situation. Once he got comfortable with his English in mid-2003, he became much more confident and has been on a roll ever since. Jimenez still is learning how to mix his pitches. He wraps his wrist a little bit in the back of his delivery, and Colorado plans on ironing out that flaw to avoid more arm problems. Though he figures to open at high Class A, Jimenez should force a quick promotion to Double-A Tulsa if he's healthy. He could be pitching in the majors as early as 2006.

Year	Club (League)	Class	W	L	ERA	G	GS	CG	SV	IP	H	R	ER	HR	BB	SO	AVG
2001	Rockies (DSL)	R	2	5	4.88	13	13	0	0	48	41	36	26	1	44	36	.225
2002	Rockies (DSL)	R	2	0	0.00	3	3	0	0	18	10	1	0	0	6	25	.152
	Casper (Pio)	R	3	5	6.53	14	14	0	0	62	72	46	45	6	29	65	.288
2003	Asheville (SAL)	A	10	6	3.46	27	27	0	0	154	129	67	59	11	67	138	.230
	Visalia (Cal)	A	1	0	0.00	1	0	0	0	5	3	0	0	0	1	7	.176
2004	Visalia (Cal)	A	4	1	2.23	9	9	1	0	44	29	15	11	1	12	61	.186
MINOR LEAGUE TOTALS			22	17	3.83	67	66	1	0	331	284	165	141	19	159	332	.230

5 Juan Morillo, rhp

Born: Nov. 5, 1983. **Ht.:** 6-1. **Wt.:** 160. **Bats:** R. **Throws:** R. **Career Transactions:** Signed out of Dominican Republic by Rockies, April 26, 2001. **Signed by:** Rolando Fernandez.

Though Morillo has yet to reach full-season ball, his pure arm strength caught the attention of enough scouts that the Rockies felt compelled to protect him on their 40-man roster. The White Sox reportedly clocked him at 104 mph. Morillo has an electric fastball and consistently hits 96 mph without exerting himself. He has dumped his curveball and come up with a hard slider. Overhauling his mechanics allowed him to repeat his delivery more consistently and led to his breakthrough success last year. At the big league level, Morillo's philosophy of hard, hard and harder isn't going to work. His change-up is rudimentary and he doesn't throw it because he doesn't trust it. His control also is sporadic, and even when he throws strikes he doesn't always locate his pitches well. With his fastball and slider, Morillo has a chance to ascend quickly once he makes that transition from thrower to pitcher. He could skip a level and start 2005 in high Class A.

Year	Club (League)	Class	W	L	ERA	G	GS	CG	SV	IP	H	R	ER	HR	BB	SO	AVG
2001	Rockies (DSL)	R	2	4	6.81	14	7	0	0	36	35	31	27	1	38	20	.248
2002	Rockies (DSL)	R	1	5	4.75	14	11	0	0	55	49	44	29	1	33	43	.230
2003	Casper (Pio)	R	1	6	5.91	15	15	0	0	64	85	73	42	6	40	44	.318
2004	Tri-City (NWL)	A	3	2	2.98	14	14	0	0	66	56	34	22	0	41	73	.225
MINOR LEAGUE TOTALS			7	17	4.89	57	47	0	0	221	225	182	120	8	152	180	.259

6 Jeff Baker, 3b/of

Born: June 21, 1981. **Ht.:** 6-2. **Wt.:** 210. **Bats:** R. **Throws:** R. **School:** Clemson University. **Career Transactions:** Selected by Rockies in fourth round of 2002 draft; signed Sept. 27, 2002. **Signed by:** Jay Matthews.

Baker set a Clemson career record with 59 homers, but a lackluster junior season and a poor history with wood bats caused him to drop to the fourth round in 2002. He has been held back by wrist problems since signing a $2 million big league contract with a $50,000 bonus, but he has hit 26 homers and 128 RBIs in 166 pro games. Baker has the tools to make an impact both at the plate and in the field. He has plus power to all fields and has improved his selectivity at the plate. He handles inside pitches well and stays back on breaking stuff. Defensively, he has soft hands and a solid arm. Both of Baker's two pro seasons have been marred by injuries to his left wrist. He had three surgeries, and then sprained it in a different area last August. He'll always strike out a lot, but has enough power to make his whiffs acceptable. He'll open 2005 in Double-A. Given Ian Stewart's rapid development, Baker will have to move to the outfield or perhaps second base in the future.

Year	Club (League)	Class	AVG	G	AB	R	H	2B	3B	HR	RBI	BB	SO	SB	OBP	SLG
2003	Asheville (SAL)	A	.289	70	263	44	76	17	0	11	44	30	79	4	.377	.479
2004	Visalia (Cal)	A	.330	72	267	60	88	23	1	11	64	47	70	1	.439	.547
	Tulsa (TL)	AA	.297	24	91	10	27	5	1	4	20	7	22	1	.343	.505
MINOR LEAGUE TOTALS			.308	166	621	114	191	45	2	26	128	84	171	6	.400	.512

7 Seth Smith, of

Born: Sept. 30, 1982. **Ht.:** 6-3. **Wt.:** 215. **Bats:** L. **Throws:** L. **School:** University of Mississippi. **Career Transactions:** Selected by Rockies in second round of 2004 draft; signed June 16, 2004. **Signed by:** Damon Iannelli.

Smith was Eli Manning's backup quarterback at Mississippi, but he didn't take a snap in three years. He projected as a first-round pick after finishing second on Team USA with a .332 average and four homers in 2003, but a slow start last spring dropped him to the 50th overall pick. After signing for $690,000, he made the Pioneer League all-star team in his debut. Smith should hit for average and plus power. He exhibits excellent hand-eye coordination and makes consistent, hard contact with natural loft in his swing. He has above-average speed and solid average arm strength. The Rockies also like his mental toughness. His athleticism is impressive, but it's not enough. Smith has to get more aggressive on the diamond. A center fielder in college, he likely will have to play on a corner as a pro. He needs to improve his throwing, which should happen as his upper body loosens up now that he's not playing football. Colorado may skip Smith a level to high Class A to begin his first full season. He's the Rockies' right fielder of the future.

Year	Club (League)	Class	AVG	G	AB	R	H	2B	3B	HR	RBI	BB	SO	SB	OBP	SLG
2004	Casper (Pio)	R	.369	56	233	46	86	21	3	9	61	25	47	9	.427	.601
	Tri City (NWL)	A	.259	9	27	6	7	1	1	2	5	1	3	0	.276	.593
MINOR LEAGUE TOTALS			.358	65	260	52	93	22	4	11	66	26	50	9	.412	.600

Jeff Salazar, of

Born: Nov. 24, 1980. **Ht.:** 6-0. **Wt.:** 180. **Bats:** L. **Throws:** L. **School:** Oklahoma State University. **Career Transactions:** Selected by Rockies in eighth round of 2002 draft; signed June 11, 2002. **Signed by:** Dar Cox.

A senior sign out of Oklahoma State, Salazar quickly established himself as a legitimate prospect, leading the South Atlantic League with 29 homers and 98 RBIs and just missing a 30-30 season in his first full year. He hit the wall after a promotion to Double-A last year. Salazar is a plus defensive center fielder with offensive potential. He has above-average arm strength and tremendous natural instincts in center. He's a potential top-of-the-lineup threat with gap power. He works deep counts, bunts well and can steal bases. Salazar has to redefine himself at the plate. Though he hit 29 homers two years ago, power is not his game. He'll hit a few naturally, but his strength is getting on base and using his speed. Given his second-half struggles, Salazar needs to return to Double-A. Preston Wilson's contract expires following the 2005 season, and the Rockies hope to turn the position over to Salazar at that point.

Year	Club (League)	Class	AVG	G	AB	R	H	2B	3B	HR	RBI	BB	SO	SB	OBP	SLG
2002	Tri-City (NWL)	A	.235	72	268	38	63	5	4	4	21	47	43	10	.351	.328
2003	Asheville (SAL)	A	.284	129	486	109	138	23	4	29	98	77	74	28	.387	.527
	Visalia (Cal)	A	.000	1	5	1	0	0	0	0	0	0	0	0	.000	.000
2004	Visalia (Cal)	A	.347	75	314	79	109	18	9	13	44	38	33	17	.419	.586
	Tulsa (TL)	AA	.223	58	224	39	50	13	2	1	17	35	31	10	.331	.313
MINOR LEAGUE TOTALS			.278	335	1297	266	360	59	19	47	180	197	181	65	.376	.461

Jayson Nix, 2b

Born: Aug. 26, 1982. **Ht.:** 5-11. **Wt.:** 180. **Bats:** R. **Throws:** R. **School:** Midland (Texas) HS. **Career Transactions:** Selected by Rockies in first round (44th overall) of 2001 draft; signed July 14, 2001. **Signed by:** Dar Cox.

The younger brother of Rangers outfielder Laynce Nix, Jayson led the minors with 46 doubles in 2003 but suffered a season-long slump in 2004. His struggles carried over into the Arizona Fall League, where he hit .191. Nix was a shortstop/pitcher in high school and the Rockies have discussed making him a catcher, but he has cemented himself as a second baseman. Nix entered last year with a rap as being an offensive minded second baseman, but he has developed into a plus defender. He shows good range and arm strength, and he turns the double play well. He has the speed to be a factor on the bases, and good pop for a middle infielder. He displays a natural feel for the game, and his work ethic is excellent. Nix may have too much power for his own good because he gets overly pull-conscious trying to hit homers. He needs to use the opposite field more often, show more selectivity and worry about attacking the gaps. Last year, he seemed to lose his ability to adjust to pitches. He still figures into the Rockies' future, but he's in line for a refresher course in Double-A. If Nix gets back on track, Aaron Miles won't pose an obstacle at second base.

Year	Club (League)	Class	AVG	G	AB	R	H	2B	3B	HR	RBI	BB	SO	SB	OBP	SLG
2001	Casper (Pio)	R	.294	42	153	28	45	10	1	5	24	21	43	1	.385	.471
2002	Asheville (SAL)	A	.246	132	487	73	120	29	2	14	79	62	105	14	.340	.400
2003	Visalia (Cal)	A	.281	137	562	7	158	46	0	21	86	54	131	24	.351	.475
2004	Tulsa (TL)	AA	.213	123	456	58	97	17	1	14	58	40	101	14	.292	.346
MINOR LEAGUE TOTALS			.253	434	1658	166	420	102	4	54	247	177	380	53	.335	.417

10 Clint Barmes, ss

Born: March 6, 1979. **Ht.:** 6-0. **Wt.:** 175. **Bats:** R. **Throws:** R. **School:** Indiana State University. **Career Transactions:** Selected by Rockies in 10th round of 2000 draft; signed June 9, 2000. **Signed by:** Ty Coslow.

Barmes will have the opportunity to claim Colorado's everyday short-stop job this spring. Viewed as a utilityman entering 2004, he had the best year of his career and capped it by hitting his first big league homer off Carl Pavano in August. Barmes doesn't make an outstanding first impression because he doesn't have an overwhelming tool, but his solid all-around game grows on you. His competitiveness is obvious at the plate. He makes contact and uses the whole field in the mold of a traditional No. 2 hitter. He'll need to draw more walks to bat near the top of the order, however. Barmes is strong enough that he can drive balls on the outer half if he stays on them. He has good speed and even better instincts on the bases. He's not flashy in the field, but his hands and footwork allow him to make troutine plays consistently. A center fielder at Indiana State, he possesses a strong arm, positions himself well and takes charge of situations. If he hits as expected, Barmes will give the Rockies more offense than they've ever gotten from a shortstop.

Year	Club (League)	Class	AVG	G	AB	R	H	2B	3B	HR	RBI	BB	SO	SB	OBP	SLG
2000	Portland (NWL)	A	.282	45	181	37	51	6	4	2	16	18	28	12	.361	.392
	Asheville (SAL)	A	.173	19	81	11	14	4	0	0	4	10	13	4	.269	.222
2001	Asheville (SAL)	A	.260	74	285	40	74	14	1	5	24	17	37	21	.314	.368
	Salem (Car)	A	.248	38	121	17	30	3	3	0	9	15	20	4	.350	.322
2002	Carolina (SL)	AA	.272	103	438	62	119	23	2	15	60	31	72	15	.329	.436
2003	Colorado Sprngs (PCL)	AAA	.276	136	493	63	136	35	1	7	54	22	63	12	.316	.394
	Colorado (NL)	MAJ	.320	12	25	2	8	2	0	0	2	0	10	0	.357	.400
2004	Colorado (NL)	MAJ	.282	20	71	14	20	3	1	2	10	3	10	0	.320	.437
	Colorado Springs (PCL)	AAA	.328	125	533	104	175	42	2	16	51	28	61	20	.376	.505
MAJOR LEAGUE TOTALS			.292	32	96	16	28	5	1	2	12	3	20	0	.330	.427
MINOR LEAGUE TOTALS			.281	540	2132	334	599	127	13	45	218	141	294	88	.337	.416

11 Dexter Fowler, of

Born: March 22, 1986. **Ht.:** 6-4. **Wt.:** 173. **Bats:** R. **Throws:** R. **School:** Milton HS, Alpharetta, Ga. **Career Transactions:** Selected by Rockies in 14th round of 2004 draft; signed Aug. 17, 2004. **Signed by:** Damon Iannelli.

Fowler, who played with Chris Nelson in the prestigious East Cobb amateur program, emerged as one of the top high school prospects for the 2004 draft. While he elicited comparisons to the likes of Andre Dawson and Andruw Jones, concerns about his commitment to the University of Miami caused him to plummet on draft day. The Rockies didn't have the money in their budget to sign him until they cleared $9.25 million by trading Larry Walker in August, after which they gave Fowler a $925,000 bonus. He signed too late to make his debut, though he did make a positive first impression with his workouts late in the season when he traveled with the Rookie-level Casper club and again in instructional league. Fowler, who also had the opportunity to play basketball at Harvard, is an impressive athlete with raw skills. He creates outstanding bat speed and his projectable frame gives the promise of a middle-of-the-order center fielder. His swing tends to get long and he moves too much at the plate in an attempt to generate bat speed. Until he refines his approach, his raw power will remain just a show in batting practice. He's smooth in center field, where his plus-plus speed affords him tremendous range. He also has good arm strength and should be a basestealing threat. Fowler could be reunited with Nelson this year in low Class A.

Year	Club (League)	Class	AVG	G	AB	R	H	2B	3B	HR	RBI	BB	SO	SB	OBP	SLG
2004	Did not play—Signed 2005 contract															

12 Garrett Atkins, 3b

Born: Dec. 12, 1979. **Ht.:** 6-3. **Wt.:** 210. **Bats:** R. **Throws:** R. **School:** UCLA. **Career Transactions:** Selected by Rockies in fifth round of 2000 draft; signed June 22, 2000. **Signed by:** Bo Hughes.

The Rockies could have an all-rookie left side to their infield if Atkins and Clint Barmes win jobs as expected. Atkins came out of UCLA as a first baseman, but with Todd Helton established at Coors Field, he shifted across the diamond to third base. The position change hasn't gone smoothly. Two years ago there were serious questions about whether Atkins could be adequate defensively because of his poor range and footwork. He made strides last season in Triple-A and spent the winter in stretching and agility classes to help his glove-work. Atkins' defense will be the determining factor as to whether he's in the Opening Day lineup. He has hit for average at every level throughout his career, leading the minors in batting and the Pacific Coast League in doubles and on-base percentage in 2004. He closed a hole he had on the inner half of the plate, and took his already fine plate discipline up a notch. Though Atkins is a gifted line-drive hitter, his power (or lack thereof) doesn't profile well for the hot corner. He rarely tries to drive the ball and never has hit more than 15 homers in a minor league season.

Year	Club (League)	Class	AVG	G	AB	R	H	2B	3B	HR	RBI	BB	SO	SB	OBP	SLG
2000	Portland (NWL)	A	.303	69	251	34	76	12	0	7	47	45	48	2	.411	.434
2001	Salem (Car)	A	.325	135	465	70	151	43	5	5	67	74	98	6	.421	.471
2002	Carolina (SL)	AA	.271	128	510	71	138	27	3	12	61	59	77	6	.345	.406
2003	Colorado Sprngs (PCL)	AAA	.319	118	439	68	140	30	1	13	67	45	52	2	.382	.481
	Colorado (NL)	MAJ	.159	25	69	6	11	2	0	0	4	3	14	0	.205	.188
2004	Colorado Springs (PCL)	AAA	.366	122	445	88	163	43	3	15	94	57	45	0	.434	.578
	Colorado (NL)	MAJ	.357	15	28	3	10	2	0	1	8	4	3	0	.424	.536
MAJOR LEAGUE TOTALS			.216	40	97	9	21	4	0	1	12	7	17	0	.274	.289
MINOR LEAGUE TOTALS			.317	572	2110	343	668	155	12	52	336	280	320	16	.397	.475

13 J.D. Closser, c

Born: Jan. 15, 1980. **Ht.:** 5-10. **Wt.:** 175. **Bats:** B. **Throws:** R. **School:** Monroe HS, Alexandria, Ind. **Career Transactions:** Selected by Diamondbacks in fifth round of 1998 draft; signed June 28, 1998 . . . Traded by Diamondbacks with OF Jack Cust to Rockies for LHP Mike Myers, Jan. 7, 2002. **Signed by:** Scott Jaster (Diamondbacks).

When the Rockies traded Mike Myers to the Diamondbacks in January 2002, minor league slugger Jack Cust appeared to be the key to the deal for Colorado. While Cust has washed out, the second player the Rockies received is poised to become their starting catcher. Closser is a switch-hitter with decent power from both sides. He should hit for a solid average as long as he doesn't become too pull-conscious. He's an average runner, good for a catcher, but his lower half is becoming stockier as he puts in more time behind the plate. Closser has solid arm strength but gets erratic with his throwing when he starts to rush his footwork and exchange. He threw out just 22 percent of basestealers in Triple-A and 21 percent in the majors, so he's going to have to work at staying under control mechanically. Closser has become a better signal caller, thanks to the help of former big league catcher Marv Foley, his minor league manager the last two years, and Colorado Springs pitching coach Bob McClure in 2004. Closser never has received much attention as a prospect, but he has turned himself into an offensive threat after a slow start to his career.

Year	Club (League)	Class	AVG	G	AB	R	H	2B	3B	HR	RBI	BB	SO	SB	OBP	SLG
1998	Diamondbacks (AZL)	R	.313	45	150	26	47	13	2	4	21	37	36	3	.453	.507
	South Bend (Mid)	A	.214	4	14	3	3	1	0	0	2	2	7	0	.313	.286
1999	South Bend (Mid)	A	.241	52	174	29	42	8	0	3	27	34	37	0	.363	.339
	Missoula (Pio)	R	.324	76	275	73	89	22	0	10	54	71	57	9	.458	.513
2000	South Bend (Mid)	A	.224	101	331	54	74	19	1	8	37	60	61	6	.347	.360
2001	Lancaster (Cal)	A	.291	128	468	85	136	26	6	21	87	65	106	6	.377	.506
2002	Carolina (SL)	AA	.283	95	315	43	89	27	1	13	62	44	69	9	.369	.498
2003	Tulsa (TL)	AA	.283	118	410	62	116	28	5	13	54	47	79	3	.359	.471
2004	Colorado (NL)	MAJ	.319	36	113	5	36	6	0	1	10	6	22	0	.364	.398
	Colorado Springs (PCL)	AAA	.299	83	298	58	89	19	1	7	54	41	47	0	.384	.440
MAJOR LEAGUE TOTALS			.319	36	113	5	36	6	0	1	10	6	22	0	.364	.398
MINOR LEAGUE TOTALS			.281	702	2435	428	685	163	16	79	398	401	499	36	.383	.459

14 Ryan Shealy, 1b

Born: Aug. 29, 1979. **Ht.:** 6-5. **Wt.:** 240. **Bats:** R. **Throws:** R. **School:** University of Florida. **Career Transactions:** Selected by Rockies in 11th round of 2002 draft; signed June 10, 2002. **Signed by:** Mike Day.

The Rockies drafted Shealy in the fifth round out of a Fort Lauderdale high school in 1998, ahead of Matt Holliday (seventh round) and Juan Pierre (13th). They made an aggressive attempt to sign him, but Shealy opted to attend Florida, though he failed to improve his draft stock and went in the 11th round after his senior season. He has won two minor league home run titles in three pro seasons, including 2004 in the Texas League. His strength gives him 30-plus homer potential in any park, and it's scary to think of what he might do at Coors Field. He's also a quality hitter capable of making adjustments quickly, which is why he's a career .323 hitter in the minors. Shealy is purely an offensive player, and knee problems that hampered him in college and during 2003 limit him to first base. Though he doesn't cover a lot of ground, he has soft hands and smooth actions around the bag. But with Todd Helton in Colorado, Shealy has no chance of playing there for the Rockies. His production could skyrocket this year in the thin air of Colorado Springs, where he'll serve as insurance for Helton and possible trade bait.

Year	Club (League)	Class	AVG	G	AB	R	H	2B	3B	HR	RBI	BB	SO	SB	OBP	SLG
2002	Casper (Pio)	R	.368	69	231	55	85	21	1	19	70	50	52	0	.497	.714
2003	Visalia (Cal)	A	.299	93	341	70	102	31	1	14	73	42	72	0	.391	.519
2004	Tulsa (TL)	AA	.318	132	469	88	149	32	3	29	99	61	123	1	.411	.584
MINOR LEAGUE TOTALS			.323	294	1041	213	336	84	5	62	242	153	247	1	.426	.592

15 Chris Narveson, lhp

Born: Dec. 20, 1981. **Ht.:** 6-3. **Wt.:** 180. **Bats:** L. **Throws:** L. **School:** T.C. Roberson HS, Skyland, N.C. **Career Transactions:** Selected by Cardinals in second round of 2000 draft; signed June 27, 2000 . . . Traded by Cardinals with LHP Luis Martinez to Rockies for OF Larry Walker, Aug. 11, 2004. **Signed by:** Randy Benson (Cardinals).

Narveson was the key to the Larry Walker trade for the Rockies last August. He broke out as a prospect in 2001, only to need Tommy John surgery, but his last two seasons have reaffirmed that his arm is healthy. He has flashed above-average stuff since bouncing back from his injury and was the top lefty in the Cardinals system. Narveson's fastball hits 92-93 mph and usually sits at 88-90. He also has a plus curveball and an average changeup. His delivery is both smooth and deceptive. Narveson usually shuts down lefthanders, who didn't take him deep in 2004, and holds his own against righties. His primary needs are to improve his command and build his stamina. He has the assortment of pitches to start and enough fastball to be a factor out of the bullpen. He'll pitch in the Triple-A rotation this year.

Year	Club (League)	Class	W	L	ERA	G	GS	CG	SV	IP	H	R	ER	HR	BB	SO	AVG
2000	Johnson City (Appy)	R	2	4	3.27	12	12	0	0	55	57	33	20	7	25	63	.263
2001	Peoria (Mid)	A	3	3	1.98	8	8	0	0	50	32	14	11	3	11	53	.185
	Potomac (Car)	A	4	3	2.57	11	11	1	0	67	52	22	19	4	13	53	.212
2002	Johnson City (Appy)	R	0	2	4.91	6	6	0	0	18	23	12	10	2	6	16	.307
	Peoria (Mid)	A	2	1	4.46	9	9	0	0	42	49	24	21	5	8	36	.283
2003	Palm Beach (FSL)	A	7	7	2.86	15	14	1	0	91	83	34	29	4	19	65	.242
	Tennessee (SL)	AA	4	3	3.00	10	10	0	0	57	56	21	19	6	26	34	.262
2004	Tulsa (TL)	AA	0	3	3.15	4	4	0	0	20	16	14	7	1	13	14	.222
	Tennessee (SL)	AA	5	10	4.16	23	23	0	0	128	114	64	59	11	51	121	.240
MINOR LEAGUE TOTALS			27	36	3.32	98	97	2	0	528	482	238	195	43	172	455	.243

16 Jim Miller, rhp

Born: April 28, 1982. **Ht.:** 6-1. **Wt.:** 200. **Bats:** R. **Throws:** R. **School:** University of Louisiana-Monroe. **Career Transactions:** Selected by Rockies in eighth round of 2004; signed June 9, 2004. **Signed by:** Damon Iannelli.

Undrafted as a junior, Miller turned down offers to sign out of the National Baseball Congress World Series in August 2003 so he could finish his degree in mathematics. That worked out fine for the Rockies, who signed him for $12,000 last summer. After working just 33 innings last spring for Louisiana-Monroe, Miller led short-season Northwest League relievers with 17 saves and 15.8 strikeouts per nine innings. He works off a 93-95 mph fastball he can locate on both sides of the plate. His heater is fairly straight, but he complements it nicely with a darting slider. He'll also mix in an occasional changeup. With his aggressive approach and the way he has taken to the closer's role, Miller could move quickly through the system. He should be able to handle a jump to high Class A in 2005.

Year	Club (League)	Class	W	L	ERA	G	GS	CG	SV	IP	H	R	ER	HR	BB	SO	AVG
2004	Tri-City (NWL)	A	1	1	0.97	34	0	0	17	37	21	6	4	1	11	65	.162
MINOR LEAGUE TOTALS			1	1	0.97	34	0	0	17	37	21	6	4	1	11	65	.162

17 Matt Macri, 3b/2b

Born: May 29, 1982. **Ht.:** 6-2. **Wt.:** 200. **Bats:** R. **Throws:** R. **School:** University of Notre Dame. **Career Transactions:** Selected by Rockies in fifth round of 2004; signed June 11, 2004. **Signed by:** Scott Corman.

If Macri had been willing to give up his scholarship from Notre Dame, he would have been Iowa's first-ever high school first-rounder in 2001. A two-way star armed with a low-90s fastball, his pitching aspirations came to an end when he had Tommy John surgery as a freshman. Some clubs soured on him when he hit .172 with wood bats in the Cape Cod League in 2003, though others were intrigued by the power he showed. Macri helped allay concerns about his bat with an all-star performance in the Northwest League. The lone negative was plantar fasciitis in his foot, which ended his debut in mid-August. His power is his best tool, and he shows it to all fields. After having trouble with wood bats on the Cape, he figured out to how get his hands inside the ball quicker. He did strike out a lot, something he'll have to watch at higher levels. Macri is a first-class defensive player with soft hands and arm strength. Because Ian Stewart looks like the Rockies' third baseman of the future, Macri spent time at second base in instructional league. He also could get time at shortstop this year, which he'll probably open in low Class A.

Year	Club (League)	Class	AVG	G	AB	R	H	2B	3B	HR	RBI	BB	SO	SB	OBP	SLG
2004	Tri City (NWL)	A	.333	52	195	33	65	17	4	7	43	23	52	4	.410	.569
MINOR LEAGUE TOTALS			.333	52	195	33	65	17	4	7	43	23	52	4	.410	.569

18 Brad Hawpe, of

Born: June 22, 1979. **Ht.:** 6-3. **Wt.:** 200. **Bats:** L. **Throws:** L. **School:** Louisiana State University. **Career Transactions:** Selected by Rockies in 11th round of 2000 draft; signed June 21, 2000. **Signed by:** Damon Iannelli.

Todd Helton's presence hasn't deterred the Rockies from drafting more college first basemen such as Hawpe. He tied an NCAA Division I record when he hit 36 doubles in 2000 and helped Louisiana State win the national championship, and earned high Class A Carolina League MVP honors in 2002. After that, Colorado asked him to become a full-time outfielder. He took the change seriously enough to decide on his own to spend that offseason in Venezuela to focus on his defense. He's still a work in progress, but he has plenty of arm strength and moves well for his size. Hawpe's bat is going to decide how much he plays in the majors anyway. He flashes legitimate middle-of-the-order power and can drive the ball out of any part of the ballpark. Though he's lefthanded, he reminds veteran scouts of a young Gorman Thomas. The key for Hawpe is trusting his strength and hand-eye coordination. He gets in a hurry trying to speed up his bat, and winds up late on fastballs because he ties his arms up. He didn't make enough contact to make good use of his power with the Rockies. He always has struggled against lefthanders, so he looks like more of a platoon player. Colorado expects him to serve in that role in 2005, sharing right field with Dustan Mohr.

Year	Club (League)	Class	AVG	G	AB	R	H	2B	3B	HR	RBI	BB	SO	SB	OBP	SLG
2000	Portland (NWL)	A	.288	62	205	38	59	19	2	7	29	40	51	2	.398	.502
2001	Asheville (SAL)	A	.267	111	393	78	105	22	3	22	72	59	113	7	.363	.506
2002	Salem (Car)	A	.347	122	450	87	156	38	2	22	97	81	84	1	.447	.587
2003	Tulsa (TL)	AA	.277	93	346	52	96	27	0	17	68	31	84	1	.338	.503
2004	Colorado Springs (PCL)	AAA	.322	92	345	62	111	19	1	31	86	36	91	3	.384	.652
	Colorado (NL)	MAJ	.248	42	105	12	26	3	2	3	9	11	24	1	.322	.400
MAJOR LEAGUE TOTALS			.248	42	105	12	26	3	2	3	9	11	24	1	.322	.400
MINOR LEAGUE TOTALS			.303	480	1739	317	527	125	8	99	352	247	423	14	.389	.555

19 Scott Dohmann, rhp

Born: Feb. 13, 1978. **Ht.:** 6-1. **Wt.:** 180. **Bats:** R. **Throws:** R. **School:** University of Louisiana-Lafayette. **Career Transactions:** Selected by Rockies in sixth round of 2000 draft; signed June 23, 2000. **Signed by:** Damon Iannelli.

Dohmann led Louisiana-Lafayette's College World Series team in victories and earned Sun Belt Conference pitcher of the year honors in 2000. His development accelerated rapidly when the Rockies made him a reliever in Double-A in May 2003. Little more than a year later, Colorado summoned him to the major leagues. When he moved to the bullpen, Dohmann's fastball jumped from 88-90 mph to 92-94. He also uses a hard slider that he runs in on lefthanders. He has a history of throwing strikes but seemed a little too cautious in the majors. Even when he wasn't having trouble finding the zone, he would leave pitches up, making him vulnerable to homers. Now that he has gotten his first season in the majors under his belt, the Rockies hope Dohmann will be as aggressive going after hitters as he was in the minors. He's the type of strikeout pitcher they need in their bullpen and should make the Opening Day roster this year.

Year	Club (League)	Class	W	L	ERA	G	GS	CG	SV	IP	H	R	ER	HR	BB	SO	AVG
2000	Portland (NWL)	A	2	1	0.78	5	4	0	0	23	14	3	2	0	5	23	.177
	Asheville (SAL)	A	1	5	6.06	7	7	0	0	33	43	24	22	3	8	36	.319
2001	Asheville (SAL)	A	11	13	4.32	28	28	3	0	173	165	88	83	27	33	154	.251
2002	Salem (Car)	A	13	5	4.23	28	28	0	0	170	149	85	80	22	53	131	.233
2003	Tulsa (TL)	AA	9	4	4.13	50	4	0	4	94	94	47	43	11	29	102	.259
2004	Colorado Springs (PCL)	AAA	1	0	1.64	18	0	0	2	22	22	5	4	1	7	31	.250
	Colorado (NL)	MAJ	0	3	4.11	41	0	0	0	46	41	22	21	8	19	49	.236
MAJOR LEAGUE TOTALS			0	3	4.11	41	0	0	0	46	41	22	21	8	19	49	.236
MINOR LEAGUE TOTALS			37	28	4.09	136	71	3	6	515	487	252	234	64	135	477	.248

20 Chris Iannetta, c

Born: April 8, 1983. **Ht.:** 5-11. **Wt.:** 195. **Bats:** R. **Throws:** R. **School:** University of North Carolina. **Career Transactions:** Selected by Rockies in fourth round of 2004 draft; signed July 5, 2004. **Signed by:** Jay Matthews.

The latest in a long line of catchers from North Carolina that includes Dwight Lowry, Scott Bradley, B.J. Surhoff and Jesse Levis, Iannetta has the talent to reach the major leagues as they did. He has a compact stroke and makes hard, line-drive contact to the gaps. Sent straight to low Class A after signing for $305,000 last summer, he had little trouble adapting and showed an aptitude for drawing walks. He had more difficulty in instructional league, a sign he'll need to make adjustments to handle wood bats against more experienced pitching. He started to get his hands back in his stance, allowing him more time to load them into hitting position. Iannetta has average catch-and-throw skills and a quick release. He threw out 29 percent of basestealers in his pro debut. He quickly gained a feel for the Asheville pitching staff and has good game-calling skills. He'll head to high Class A in 2005.

Year	Club (League)	Class	AVG	G	AB	R	H	2B	3B	HR	RBI	BB	SO	SB	OBP	SLG
2004	Asheville (SAL)	A	.314	36	121	23	38	5	1	5	17	27	29	0	.454	.496
MINOR LEAGUE TOTALS			.314	36	121	23	38	5	1	5	17	27	29	0	.454	.496

21 Ryan Speier, rhp

Born: July 24, 1979. **Ht.:** 6-7. **Wt.:** 200. **Bats:** R. **Throws:** R. **School:** Radford University. **Career Transactions:** Signed as nondrafted free agent by Rockies, July 23, 2001. **Signed by:** Jay Matthews.

Undrafted out of Radford in 2001, Speier starred in the Cape Cod League that summer and got scouts' attention. After he set a Cape saves record with 16 and didn't allow an earned run in 20 innings, he signed with the Rockies as a nondrafted free agent for $10,000. He set a Tulsa franchise mark with 37 saves last year, one off the minor league lead, and led all minor league relievers by holding batters to a .154 average. The 6-foot-7 Speier creates deception with his long arms, and further baffles hitters by throwing from an assortment of angles ranging from submarine to three-quarters. None of his pitches is exceptional, but he locates them well and batters have trouble picking them up. His fastball works around 89-90 mph, with its movement improving as its velocity drops. Speier also uses a slider, as well as a changeup he'll throw in any count. He's durable and coming off two strong seasons in a row, so the Rockies will move him up to Triple-A to see if he can befuddle more advanced hitters. He could make the big league club if he has an impressive spring.

Year	Club (League)	Class	W	L	ERA	G	GS	CG	SV	IP	H	R	ER	HR	BB	SO	AVG
2001	Casper (Pio)	R	1	2	3.16	17	0	0	1	26	19	12	9	2	9	24	.196
2002	Asheville (SAL)	A	3	1	3.93	28	0	0	1	37	32	21	16	3	13	39	.235
	Salem (Car)	A	2	2	3.94	24	0	0	4	32	35	21	14	0	11	33	.285
2003	Visalia (Cal)	A	4	2	1.53	56	0	0	18	59	50	14	10	2	17	73	.226
2004	Tulsa (TL)	AA	3	1	2.04	61	0	0	37	62	33	14	14	3	25	70	.154
MINOR LEAGUE TOTALS			13	8	2.64	186	0	0	61	215	169	82	63	10	75	239	.213

22 Samuel Deduno, rhp

Born: July 2, 1983. **Ht.:** 6-1. **Wt.:** 150. **Bats:** R. **Throws:** R. **Career Transactions:** Signed out of Dominican Republic by Rockies, March 5, 2003. **Signed by:** Felix Feliz.

In his first year in the United States, Deduno was named Pioneer League pitcher of the year after leading the league in strikeouts and strikeouts per nine innings (13.9). His best pitch is a fastball that has natural cutting action and regularly registers at 90-91 mph, topping out at 93. He also throws a hard curveball that overmatched Pioneer Leaguers. His changeup isn't nearly as advanced as the rest of his repertoire, but it does show potential. Deduno struggled early in the summer, but responded when Casper manager P.J. Carey challenged him. Besides improving his changeup, he needs to do a better job of throwing strikes, maintaining his focus and showing mound presence. Deduno was a bit old for Rookie ball and will get a sterner test in low Class A this year.

Year	Club (League)	Class	W	L	ERA	G	GS	CG	SV	IP	H	R	ER	HR	BB	SO	AVG
2003	Rockies (DSL)	R	3	4	2.47	12	12	0	0	69	53	26	19	1	26	61	.202
2004	Casper (Pio)	R	6	4	3.18	15	15	0	0	76	62	40	27	3	32	118	.216
MINOR LEAGUE TOTALS			9	8	2.84	27	27	0	0	146	115	66	46	4	58	179	.209

23 Aaron Taylor, rhp

Born: Aug. 20, 1977. **Ht.:** 6-8. **Wt.:** 240. **Bats:** R. **Throws:** R. **School:** Lowndes HS, Valdosta, Ga. **Career Transactions:** Selected by Braves in 11th round of 1996 draft; signed June 5, 1996 . . . Selected by Mariners from Braves in minor league Rule 5 draft, Dec. 13, 1999 . . . Traded by Mariners to Rockies for RHP Sean Green, Dec. 20, 2004. **Signed by:** Rob English (Braves).

In each of the last two offseasons, Colorado has picked up a relief prospect from Seattle when the Mariners needed to make room on their 40-man roster. In 2003, they got Allan Simpson in exchange for Chris Buglovsky. This winter, they received Taylor for Sean Green. Seattle did a nice job of resurrecting Taylor's career after acquiring him in the Double-A phase of the 1999 Rule 5 draft. He quit baseball briefly in 2001 and blossomed after returning. With his 6-foot-8, 240-pound build and a heavy mid-90s fastball, Taylor can intimidate hitters. He pitched mostly at 92-93 mph last year while building his arm back up after surgery to repair a small tear in his rotator cuff, but should be at full strength in 2005. He's still trying to develop consistency with his slider and splitter, which show flashes of being plus pitches. If those pitches come around, he could be a late-innings weapon in a big league bullpen. If Taylor doesn't make the Rockies out of spring training, he'll open 2005 in Triple-A.

Year	Club (League)	Class	W	L	ERA	G	GS	CG	SV	IP	H	R	ER	HR	BB	SO	AVG
1996	Braves (GCL)	R	0	9	7.74	13	9	0	0	52	68	54	45	0	28	33	.315
1997	Danville (Appy)	R	1	8	5.53	15	7	0	0	55	65	49	34	4	31	38	.288
1998	Danville (Appy)	R	3	6	6.25	14	14	1	0	72	87	60	50	9	36	55	.300
1999	Macon (SAL)	A	6	7	4.88	27	8	0	1	79	86	56	43	9	27	78	.270
2000	Everett (NWL)	A	1	4	7.43	15	14	0	0	63	76	54	52	5	37	57	.304
2001	Wisconsin (Mid)	A	3	1	2.45	28	0	0	9	29	19	9	8	1	11	50	.184
2002	San Antonio (TL)	AA	4	3	2.34	61	0	0	24	77	51	28	20	5	34	93	.184
	Seattle (AL)	MAJ	0	0	9.00	5	0	0	0	5	8	5	5	2	0	6	.348
2003	Tacoma (PCL)	AAA	1	3	2.45	33	0	0	16	40	30	11	11	3	13	34	.208
	Seattle (AL)	MAJ	0	0	8.53	10	0	0	0	13	17	12	12	0	6	9	.315
2004	San Antonio (TL)	AA	3	1	2.89	30	0	0	0	37	27	13	12	2	14	37	.200
	Inland Empire (Cal)	A	0	1	13.50	1	1	0	0	1	2	3	2	0	1	2	.400
	Seattle (AL)	MAJ	0	0	9.82	5	0	0	0	4	5	4	4	2	3	4	.313
MAJOR LEAGUE TOTALS			0	0	8.86	20	0	0	0	21	30	21	21	4	9	19	.323
MINOR LEAGUE TOTALS			22	43	4.91	237	53	1	50	507	511	337	277	38	232	477	.260

24 Allan Simpson, rhp

Born: Aug. 26, 1977. **Ht.:** 6-4. **Wt.:** 180. **Bats:** R. **Throws:** R. **School:** Taft (Calif.) JC. **Career Transactions:** Selected by Mariners in eighth round of 1997 draft; signed June 3, 1997 . . . Traded by Mariners to Rockies for RHP Chris Buglovsky, Dec. 15, 2003. **Signed by:** Steve Jongewaard (Mariners).

Simpson received a scare after the 2002 season when he was diagnosed with lupus, a chronic inflammatory disease that can be fatal. Further tests revealed he only has a circulatory problem in his right index finger, the result of throwing too many splitters. Healthy again, he finally reached the majors in 2004, his eighth pro season, and could win a job in the Colorado bullpen during spring training. Simpson consistently dials his fastball up to 95 mph and has peaked at 99 in the past. He creates an uncomfortable feeling for hitters from a low three-quarters arm angle. He complements his fastball with a decent slider, and only rarely uses the splitter. Simpson's command never has been consistent, in part because his arm slot tends to wander. Maintaining his mechanics is vital to his success.

Year	Club (League)	Class	W	L	ERA	G	GS	CG	SV	IP	H	R	ER	HR	BB	SO	AVG
1997	Everett (NWL)	A	0	3	6.84	16	0	0	0	26	26	23	20	1	24	26	.263
1998	Wisconsin (Mid)	A	3	5	4.44	19	19	0	0	93	89	52	46	5	61	86	.257
	Mariners (AZL)	R	1	0	0.96	3	0	0	1	9	8	2	1	1	3	12	.235
1999	Wisconsin (Mid)	A	2	9	4.38	24	13	1	0	90	83	56	44	4	48	88	.245
	Lancaster (Cal)	A	0	0	6.33	9	0	0	1	21	17	16	15	4	14	25	.218
2000	Lancaster (Cal)	A	3	2	2.08	46	0	0	6	52	34	17	12	1	27	67	.184
2001	San Bernardino (Cal)	A	1	0	1.80	16	0	0	1	30	19	7	6	1	12	40	.178
	San Antonio (TL)	AA	2	1	1.86	22	0	0	9	39	25	8	8	1	15	37	.184
2002	San Antonio (TL)	AA	10	5	3.06	56	0	0	7	82	53	33	28	4	50	99	.189
2003	Tacoma (PCL)	AAA	2	5	4.16	43	0	0	1	63	60	30	29	7	42	69	.251
2004	Colorado Springs (PCL)	AAA	2	1	2.80	27	0	0	4	35	30	14	11	1	10	43	.236
	Colorado (NL)	MAJ	2	1	5.08	32	0	0	0	39	44	26	22	4	20	46	.289
MAJOR LEAGUE TOTALS			2	1	5.08	32	0	0	0	39	44	26	22	4	20	46	.289
MINOR LEAGUE TOTALS			26	31	3.65	281	32	1	29	542	444	258	220	30	306	592	.225

25 Choo Freeman, of

Born: Oct. 20, 1979. **Ht.:** 6-2. **Wt.:** 200. **Bats:** R. **Throws:** R. **School:** Dallas Christian HS, Mesquite, Texas. **Career Transactions:** Selected by Rockies in first round (36th overall) of 1998 draft; signed July 13, 1998. **Signed by:** Dar Cox.

The Rockies keep hoping Freeman will break through as a late-blooming athlete, as did his cousin Torii Hunter. But where Hunter was playing regularly in the majors by his seventh year as a pro, Freeman has just 90 big league at-bats. There never has been a question about his athleticism or work ethic, but Freeman never has had consistent success. His 2004 numbers look solid, but they were inflated by the altitude at Colorado Springs. Freeman was more of a football player in high school, when he set a Texas state record with 50 touchdown catches and was Texas A&M's top wide receiver recruit in 1998. He has tried to make adjustments, but Freeman is still mechanical in his hitting approach. He never has put up power numbers and should just focus on getting on base to make some use of his plus speed. He lacks basestealing instincts, however. Freeman has grown into a quality center fielder, albeit with a below-average arm. He still has one minor league option remaining, so he faces a third year in Triple-A unless he takes a huge step forward in spring training.

Year	Club (League)	Class	AVG	G	AB	R	H	2B	3B	HR	RBI	BB	SO	SB	OBP	SLG
1998	Rockies (AZL)	R	.320	40	147	35	47	3	6	1	24	15	25	14	.391	.442
1999	Asheville (SAL)	A	.274	131	485	82	133	22	4	14	66	39	132	16	.336	.423
2000	Salem (Car)	A	.266	127	429	73	114	18	7	5	54	37	104	16	.326	.375
2001	Salem (Car)	A	.240	132	517	63	124	16	5	8	42	31	108	19	.292	.337
2002	Carolina (SL)	AA	.291	124	430	81	125	18	6	12	64	64	101	15	.400	.444
2003	Colorado Sprngs (PCL)	AAA	.254	103	327	44	83	9	4	7	36	23	71	2	.315	.370
2004	Colorado (NL)	MAJ	.189	45	90	15	17	3	2	1	11	14	21	1	.298	.300
	Colorado Springs (PCL)	AAA	.297	103	360	58	107	21	7	10	50	26	84	7	.350	.478
MAJOR LEAGUE TOTALS			.189	45	90	15	17	3	2	1	11	14	21	1	.298	.300
MINOR LEAGUE TOTALS			.272	760	2695	436	733	107	39	57	336	235	625	89	.339	.404

26 Ching-Lung Lo, rhp

Born: Aug. 20, 1985. **Ht.:** 6-6. **Wt.:** 190. **Bats:** R. **Throws:** R. **Career Transactions:** Signed out of Taiwan by Rockies, Oct. 20, 2001. **Signed by:** Kent Blasingame.

The Rockies have brought Lo along slowly since signing him for $1.4 million out of Taiwan's Koio Yuan High, which is also the alma mater of Chin-Hui Tsao. Lo made his pro debut as a 16-year-old, and Colorado wants to make sure he's physically ready for each challenge he faces. He opened the 2004 season in extended spring training, then split time between the rotation and bullpen in low Class A in order to restrict his workload. Lo has started to fill out his tall, rangy frame and still has more room for physical projection. His fastball velocity was down at Asheville, but he was consistently popping 92-93 mph by the end of the fall in instructional league. Roving pitching instructor Jim Wright helped Lo get his mind off his mechanics by simply playing catch in the outfield, which helped him get back to his natural delivery. He'll start throwing his splitter again in 2005 after putting it on the shelf the last three years to avoid strain on his elbow. His slider needs to be more consistent and he has to develop an offspeed pitch he can use to get out of jams. His control slipped a bit last year, but he's still a teenager and has plenty of time to make refinements. Lo will open 2005 in high Class A.

Year	Club (League)	Class	W	L	ERA	G	GS	CG	SV	IP	H	R	ER	HR	BB	SO	AVG
2002	Casper (Pio)	R	2	4	3.20	14	9	0	0	45	44	22	16	3	22	21	.246
2003	Tri-City (NWL)	A	3	7	2.85	14	14	0	0	76	66	27	24	1	27	48	.237
2004	Asheville (SAL)	A	4	3	5.05	17	9	0	1	62	70	49	35	9	30	49	.288
MINOR LEAGUE TOTALS			9	14	3.69	45	32	0	1	183	180	98	75	13	79	118	.257

27 Marcos Carvajal, rhp

Born: April 19, 1984. **Ht.:** 6-4. **Wt.:** 175. **Bats:** R. **Throws:** R. **Career Transactions:** Signed out of Venezuela by Dodgers, Sept. 26, 2000 . . . Selected by Brewers from Dodgers in major league Rule 5 draft, Dec. 13, 2004 . . . Sold by Brewers to Rockies, Dec. 13, 2004. **Signed by:** Camilo Pascual.

The Rockies wanted power bullpen arms in December's major league Rule 5 draft and came away with a pair from the Dodgers: Carvajal and Matt Merricks. The Brewers selected Carvajal from the Dodgers, then sold him to Colorado for $75,000. The Rockies believe Carvajal, who has a 2.10 ERA as a pro, can make the jump from low Class A to the majors. If he can't, he'll have to clear waivers and be offered back to Los Angeles for $25,000. Carvajal has the live, athletic pitcher's body that scouts like, with an explosive but easy arm action. He relies heavily on his fastball, which can reach the upper 90s with hard run and sink. Some scouts and player-development personnel have questioned Carvajal's intensity, because his velocity will dip along with his focus. He settles into the low 90s too often. He began to develop a slurve in 2004, and by season's end was able to put hitters away with it. Carvajal almost certainly will struggle in the majors this season, as his pitches and command still need a lot of refinement.

Year	Club (League)	Class	W	L	ERA	G	GS	CG	SV	IP	H	R	ER	HR	BB	SO	AVG
2001	La Pradera (VSL)	R	1	2	2.12	9	6	0	1	30	24	11	7	0	11	26	—
2002	Dodgers (GCL)	R	3	2	1.71	13	5	0	0	42	30	12	8	0	15	35	.201
2003	Ogden (Pio)	R	2	1	3.08	23	0	0	2	38	32	16	13	1	22	50	.224
2004	Columbus (SAL)	A	4	2	1.88	36	0	0	1	72	50	19	15	2	35	72	.199
	Jacksonville (SL)	AA	0	0	0.00	1	0	0	0	3	2	0	0	0	2	2	.182
MINOR LEAGUE TOTALS			10	7	2.10	82	11	0	4	185	138	58	43	3	85	185	.206

28 Cory Sullivan, of

Born: Aug. 20, 1979. **Ht.:** 6-0. **Wt.:** 180. **Bats:** L. **Throws:** L. **School:** Wake Forest University. **Career Transactions:** Selected by Rockies in seventh round of 2001 draft; signed June 7, 2001. **Signed by:** Jay Matthews.

After leading the South Atlantic League in runs and doubles in 2002, and the Texas League in hits after skipping a level in 2003, Sullivan appeared to be on the fast track to the big leagues. He had an outside chance to make the big league roster last year before doctors discovered he had torn his left labrum, ending his season in spring training. He made his comeback in the Arizona Fall League, where he showed the expected signs of rust. Sullivan could force his way into Colorado's uncertain outfield situation this year, but he would benefit from opening the year in Triple-A to make up for lost at-bats. While he doesn't have an off-the-chart tool, he's fundamentally sound player. He has leadoff-hitter speed, true center-field defensive ability and a plus arm. Sullivan has a line-drive approach and gap power, but he needs to draw more walks and improve his basestealing efficiency. He doesn't make mental mistakes, another reason the Rockies envision him fitting into their future plans.

Year	Club (League)	Class	AVG	G	AB	R	H	2B	3B	HR	RBI	BB	SO	SB	OBP	SLG
2001	Asheville (SAL)	A	.275	67	258	36	71	12	1	5	22	25	56	13	.344	.388
2002	Salem (Car)	A	.288	138	560	90	161	42	6	12	67	36	70	26	.340	.448
2003	Tulsa (TL)	AA	.300	135	557	81	167	34	8	5	61	39	83	17	.347	.417
2004	Did not play—Injured															
MINOR LEAGUE TOTALS			.290	340	1375	207	399	88	15	22	150	100	209	56	.344	.424

29 Matt Merricks, lhp

Born: Aug. 6, 1982. **Ht.:** 5-11. **Wt.:** 180. **Bats:** L. **Throws:** L. **School:** Oxnard (Calif.) HS. **Career Transactions:** Selected by Braves in sixth round of 2000 draft; signed June 26, 2000 . . . Traded by Braves to Dodgers for LHP Tom Martin, July 31, 2004 . . . Selected by Rockies from Dodgers in major league Rule 5 draft, Dec. 13, 2004. **Signed by:** Mike Baker (Braves).

The Rockies think enough of Merricks that, after taking him in the major league Rule 5 draft from the Dodgers, they were willing to listen to offers for incumbent lefty specialist Javier Lopez. Acquired by Los Angeles last July in exchange for Tom Martin, Merricks never has had a winning season as a pro and tied for the minor league lead with 15 losses in 2003. His brother Charles pitched three years in the Colorado system, and another sibling, Alex, pitches in the Twins organization. Used primarily as a starter in the minors, Merricks will try relieving for the Rockies this spring. He has a live arm with a low-90s fastball that reaches 95 mph, and he has shown the makings of a decent changeup. His curveball has been inconsistent, but a third pitch won't be as necessary out of the bullpen. He tends to be overly aggressive and has to keep himself under control so he can throw strikes. He was bothered by a bone chip in his left elbow, which required surgery after the 2004 season, but should be 100 percent for spring training. Like Marcos Carvajal, Merrick will have to clear waivers and be offered back to the Dodgers for half his $50,000 draft price before he can be sent to the minors this year.

Year	Club (League)	Class	W	L	ERA	G	GS	CG	SV	IP	H	R	ER	HR	BB	SO	AVG
2000	Braves (GCL)	R	1	0	2.53	9	0	0	0	21	21	15	6	0	11	28	.250
2001	Danville (Appy)	R	4	5	2.79	12	11	0	0	58	42	19	18	5	18	78	.209
2002	Macon (SAL)	A	5	5	5.12	19	14	0	0	83	82	54	47	6	51	60	.256
2003	Rome (SAL)	A	5	7	2.82	14	10	0	0	67	58	27	21	1	19	60	.232
	Myrtle Beach (Car)	A	1	8	3.23	11	8	0	0	47	45	29	17	5	23	37	.251
2004	Greenville (SL)	AA	1	3	4.91	6	5	0	0	22	26	21	12	4	11	27	.292
	Myrtle Beach (Car)	A	5	3	3.31	13	12	1	0	73	61	32	27	4	24	67	.228
	Vero Beach (FSL)	A	2	2	3.12	6	5	0	0	26	30	9	9	2	10	16	.294
MINOR LEAGUE TOTALS			24	33	3.55	90	65	1	0	398	365	206	157	27	167	373	.245

30 Mike Esposito, rhp

Born: Aug. 27, 1981. **Ht.:** 6-0. **Wt.:** 190. **Bats:** R. **Throws:** R. **School:** Arizona State University. **Career Transactions:** Selected by Rockies in 12th round of 2002 draft; signed Aug. 9, 2002. **Signed by:** Mike Ericson.

Injuries slowed Esposito throughout his amateur career. He had Tommy John surgery in his freshman year at Arizona State, and developed forearm stiffness during the spring of his junior year. The Rockies, however, saw enough when he was healthy to sign him for $750,000 as a 12th-rounder in 2002. In two full pro seasons he has made solid progress and stayed away from the trainer's room. He is not overpowering but throws quality strikes and mixes four effective pitches. His fastball generally sits at 89 mph, and he showed improvement with both his curveball and slider last year. The changeup is his fourth pitch, but he needs to use it earlier in counts to keep hitters off his fastball. He will get quick in his delivery and it costs him control, but that can be smoothed out quickly. Esposito will open 2005 at Colorado Springs if he has a good spring, but he could wind up back at Tulsa.

Year	Club (League)	Class	W	L	ERA	G	GS	CG	SV	IP	H	R	ER	HR	BB	SO	AVG
2003	Visalia (Cal)	A	12	6	3.75	27	27	1	0	161	173	83	67	14	55	116	.277
2004	Tulsa (TL)	AA	10	6	3.33	24	24	0	0	143	138	57	53	12	35	90	.256
MINOR LEAGUE TOTALS			22	12	3.55	51	51	1	0	304	311	140	120	26	90	206	.267

DETROIT
TIGERS

BY **PAT CAPUTO**

MICHAEL WALBY

While the Tigers made a comeback to moderate respectability at the major league level in 2004, improving from 43-119 to 72-90, the farm system may have hit a new low. Given the organization's dismal track record in player development over the past quarter century, that's quite a statement.

Detroit won Baseball America's Organization of the Year award in 1997, but only one time since has BA rated the Tigers system in the top half of baseball. They entered 2004 ranked No. 22, then saw the bottom fall out.

Instead of their best prospects stepping forward, most of them headed in the other direction. Righthander Kyle Sleeth, the No. 3 overall pick in the 2003 draft, did well early in his pro debut, only to get tattooed for a 6.30 ERA after a midseason promotion to Double-A. Righthander Joel Zumaya had one of the better years, but his ERA was 4.63. Oft-injured lefty Rob Henkel had shoulder surgery and missed all of 2004. Righty Jay Sborz showed his control still has a long way to go. Oft-injured 2001 first-round pick Kenny Baugh pitched a career-high 143 innings but ended the season in the trainer's room.

There were plenty of setbacks among the hitters as well. While outfielder Curtis Granderson and shortstop Tony Giarratano enhanced their standing, the other position players on last year's top 10 took a nosedive. Outfielder Brent Clevlen hit .223 in high Class A. Third basemen Kody Kirkland and Scott Moore also floundered, combining for 274 strikeouts in 247 games.

Making all the failures more difficult to stomach is that the Tigers have been picking near the top of the draft each year. Their first selection has come no lower than No. 14 each year since 1995, and they've chosen eighth or earlier seven times. To this point, only Jeff Weaver has panned out among that group of top picks—and he has yet to have a winning season and was traded in mid-2002. One member of the group played in Detroit in 2004: **Eric Munson**, who got a club-record $3.5 million bonus as part of a $6.75 million big league contract when he signed as the No. 3 pick in 1999. Munson hit .212 in 2004, then was not offered a contract after the season and signed with the Twins.

The perennial draft disappointments led to the hiring of former Red Sox scouting director David Chadd in November. Detroit reassigned Greg Smith, scouting director since August 1996, to a special-assignment scout. In Smith's defense, he doubled as farm director from 2000-02 and had his hands tied at times during former general manager Randy Smith's tenure.

The Tigers also have a new farm director after Ricky Bennett left to become an assistant general manager in charge of the farm system for the Astros. Detroit replaced Bennett with Dan Lunetta, who had been a special assistant to the GM for the Expos. Lunetta worked under Tigers GM David Dombrowski with the Marlins.

TOP 30 PROSPECTS

1. Curtis Granderson, of
2. Kyle Sleeth, rhp
3. Justin Verlander, rhp
4. Joel Zumaya, rhp
5. Humberto Sanchez, rhp
6. Tony Giarratano, ss
7. Jeff Frazier, of
8. Ryan Raburn, 2b
9. Eulogio de la Cruz, rhp
10. Chris Shelton, 1b/c
11. Wilkin Ramirez, 3b
12. Roberto Novoa, rhp
13. Dallas Trahern, rhp
14. Brent Clevlen, of
15. Juan Tejeda, 1b
16. Bo Flowers, of
17. Eric Beattie, rhp
18. Collin Mahoney, rhp
19. Kody Kirkland, 3b
20. Scott Moore, 3b
21. Andrew Kown, rhp
22. Jair Jurrjens, rhp
23. Byron Gettis, of
24. Kenny Baugh, rhp
25. David Espinosa, of
26. Mark Woodyard, rhp
27. Jay Sborz, rhp
28. Matt Vasquez, rhp
29. Juan Francia, ss
30. Brent Dlugach, ss

ORGANIZATION OVERVIEW

General manager: Dave Dombrowski. **Farm director:** Dan Lunetta. **Scouting director:** David Chadd.

2004 PERFORMANCE

Class	Team	League	W	L	Pct.	Finish*	Manager
Majors	Detroit	American	72	90	.444	10th (14)	Alan Trammell
Triple-A	Toledo Mud Hens	International	65	78	.455	14th (14)	Larry Parrish
Double-A	Erie Sea Wolves	Eastern	80	62	.563	3rd (12)	Rick Sweet
High A	Lakeland Tigers	Florida State	51	81	.386	12th (12)	Gary Green
Low A	West Michigan Whitecaps	Midwest	69	70	.496	11th (14)	Matt Walbeck
Short-season	Oneonta Tigers	New York-Penn	33	41	.446	10th (14)	Mike Rojas
Rookie	GCL Tigers	Gulf Coast	24	36	.400	9th (12)	Kevin Bradshaw
OVERALL 2004 MINOR LEAGUE RECORD			322	368	.467	t-24th (30)	

*Finish in overall standings (No. of teams in league).

ORGANIZATION LEADERS

BATTING
*Minimum 250 At-Bats
*AVG	Tony Giarratano, Lakeland/West Michigan	.335
R	David Espinosa, Erie	89
	Curtis Granderson, Erie	89
H	Kelly Hunt, West Michigan	150
TB	Kelly Hunt, West Michigan	241
2B	Chris Maples, Lakeland	33
3B	Kody Kirkland, West Michigan	11
HR	Kurt Airoso, Erie	34
RBI	Kelly Hunt, West Michigan	102
BB	Kurt Airoso, Erie	82
SO	Garth McKinney, West Michigan	175
SB	Nook Logan, Toledo	38
*OBP	Curtis Granderson, Erie	.405
*SLG	Kurt Airoso, Erie	.548

PITCHING
#Minimum 75 Innings
W	Matt Vasquez, West Michigan	14
L	Pat Ahearne, Toledo	12
#ERA	Daniel Zell, West Michigan	2.27
G	Jason Karnuth, Toledo/Erie	56
CG	Five tied at	3
SV	Franklyn German, Toledo	27
IP	Pat Ahearne, Toledo	179
BB	Jordan Tata, West Michigan	68
SO	Humberto Sanchez, Erie/Lakeland	130

BEST TOOLS

Best Hitter for Average	Curtis Granderson
Best Power Hitter	Scott Moore
Best Strike-Zone Discipline	Curtis Granderson
Fastest Baserunner	Juan Francia
Best Athlete	Bo Flowers
Best Fastball	Eulogio de la Cruz
Best Curveball	Justin Verlander
Best Slider	Kyle Sleeth
Best Changeup	Kyle Sleeth
Best Control	Matt Vasquez
Best Defensive Catcher	Maxim St. Pierre
Best Defensive Infielder	Tony Giarratano
Best Infield Arm	Tony Giarratano
Best Defensive Outfielder	Vincent Blue
Best Outfield Arm	Jeff Frazier

PROJECTED 2008 LINEUP

Catcher	Brandon Inge
First Base	Carlos Pena
Second Base	Ryan Raburn
Third Base	Carlos Guillen
Shortstop	Tony Giarratano
Left Field	Craig Monroe
Center Field	Curtis Granderson
Right Field	Jeff Frazier
Designated Hitter	Dmitri Young
No. 1 Starter	Jeremy Bonderman
No. 2 Starter	Kyle Sleeth
No. 3 Starter	Mike Maroth
No. 4 Starter	Nate Robertson
No. 5 Starter	Justin Verlander
Closer	Joel Zumaya

LAST YEAR'S TOP 20 PROSPECTS

1. Kyle Sleeth, rhp
2. Brent Clevlen, of
3. Joel Zumaya, rhp
4. Rob Henkel, lhp
5. Tony Giarratano, ss
6. Kody Kirkland, 3b
7. Scott Moore, 3b
8. Curtis Granderson, of
9. Jay Sborz, rhp
10. Kenny Baugh, rhp
11. Ryan Raburn, 3b/2b
12. Wilkin Ramirez, 3b
13. Chris Shelton, 1b/c
14. Cody Ross, of
15. Humberto Sanchez, rhp
16. Fernando Rodney, rhp
17. Preston Larrison, rhp
18. Jon Connolly, lhp
19. Donald Kelly, ss/3b
20. Nook Logan, of

TOP PROSPECTS OF THE DECADE

Year	Player, Pos.	Current Team
1995	Tony Clark, 1b	Diamondbacks
1996	Mike Drumright, rhp	Out of baseball
1997	Mike Drumright, rhp	Out of baseball
1998	Juan Encarnacion, of	Marlins
1999	Gabe Kapler, of	Japan
2000	Eric Munson, 1b/c	Twins
2001	Brandon Inge, c	Tigers
2002	Nate Cornejo, rhp	Tigers
2003	Jeremy Bonderman, rhp	Tigers
2004	Kyle Sleeth, rhp	Tigers

TOP DRAFT PICKS OF THE DECADE

Year	Player, Pos.	Current Team
1995	Mike Drumright, rhp	Out of baseball
1996	Seth Greisinger, rhp	Twins
1997	Matt Anderson, rhp	Tigers
1998	Jeff Weaver, rhp	Dodgers
1999	Eric Munson, c/1b	Twins
2000	Matt Wheatland, rhp	Astros
2001	Kenny Baugh, rhp	Tigers
2002	Scott Moore, ss	Tigers
2003	Kyle Sleeth, rhp	Tigers
2004	Justin Verlander, rhp	Tigers

ALL-TIME LARGEST BONUSES

Eric Munson, 1999	$3,500,000
Kyle Sleeth, 2003	$3,350,000
Justin Verlander, 2004	$3,120,000
Matt Anderson, 1997	$2,505,000
Scott Moore, 2002	$2,300,000

MINOR LEAGUE DEPTH CHART

Detroit TIGERS

Impact Potential: D

The Tigers have some of the hardest throwers in the minor leagues under one roof. Justin Verlander, Joel Zumaya and Collin Mahoney all either touch 100 mph or get darn close. The bullpen is full of power arms, and Kyle Sleeth was the consensus pick as the top college pitcher in the 2003 draft. But no position player is a blue-chip talent, and the adjective most often used to describe top prospect Curtis Granderson is "overachiever."

Depth: F

Poor seasons by prospects such as Brent Clevlen, Kody Kirkland and Scott Moore thinned an already poor crop of hitters in the system, leaving Granderson and Tony Giarratano as the only hitters at premium positions who have held their own against better competition. The organization's greatest weaknesses show up in a lack of power bats and lefthanded pitching. The combination led to the reassignment of scouting director Greg Smith.

*Depth charts prepared by **John Manuel** and **Allan Simpson**. Numbers in parentheses indicate prospect rankings.*

LF
Byron Gettis (23)
David Espinosa (25)

CF
Curtis Granderson (1)
Victor Mendez
Vincent Blue
Alexis Gomez

RF
Jeff Frazier (7)
Brent Clevlen (14)
Bo Flowers (16)
Brandon Timm

3B
Wilkin Ramirez (11)
Kody Kirkland (19)
Scott Moore (20)
Cory Middleton
Jack Hannahan

SS
Tony Giarratano (6)
Juan Francia (29)
Brent Dlugach (30)
Donald Kelly

2B
Ryan Raburn (8)
Eric Rodland
Michael Woods
Chris Maples

1B
Chris Shelton (10)
Juan Tejeda (15)
Kelly Hunt
Rafael Mendez

SOURCE of TALENT

Homegrown		Acquired	
College	12	Trades	3
Junior College	1	Rule 5 draft	1
Draft-and-follow	1	Independent leagues	0
High school	6	Free agents/waivers	1
Nondrafted free agents	0		
Foreign	5		

C
Cole Miller
Maxim St. Pierre
Mike Rabelo
Danilo Sanchez

LHP

Starters	Relievers
Luke French	Danny Zell
Chris Steinborn	Kevin McDowell
Rob Henkel	Ed Clelland
	Damien Myers
	Tony Peralta

RHP

Starters	Relievers
Kyle Sleeth (2)	Eulogio de la Cruz (9)
Justin Verlander (3)	Roberto Novoa (12)
Joel Zumaya (4)	Collin Mahoney (18)
Humberto Sanchez (5)	Mark Woodyard (26)
Dallas Trahern (13)	Fernando Rodney
Eric Beattie (17)	Randor Bierd
Andrew Kown (21)	
Jair Jurrgens (22)	
Kenny Baugh (24)	
Jay Sborz (27)	
Matt Vasquez (28)	
Preston Larrison	
Matt Roney	
Nate Bumstead	
Matt Pender	

DRAFT ANALYSIS
2004

Best Pro Debut: RHP Nate Bumstead (32) went 3-1, 2.03 at short-season Oneonta, including a 75-15 K-BB ratio in 58 innings. He relies on command, deception and moxie to succeed. RHP Dallas Trahern (34) had a 0.59 ERA in 31 innings in the Rookie-level Gulf Coast League.

Best Athlete: OF Jeff Frazier (3) knows how to translate his physical tools into production. He hit .304 in 20 games at Oneonta before his pro debut ended when an errant pitch broke a bone in his left forearm. OF Brandon Timm (9) threw 90-91 mph in high school.

Best Pure Hitter: Frazier shows the ability to both turn on pitches and drive them the other way.

Best Raw Power: Frazier, who holds the Rutgers career home run record with 34.

Fastest Runner: OF Leonardo Grullon (31) didn't play at South Florida last spring, but he displayed his above-average speed in a tryout camp in Lakeland, Fla.

Best Defensive Player: Though he's 6-foot-5 and made 18 errors at Oneonta, SS Brent Dlugach (6) is more fluid than those numbers would indicate.

Best Fastball: RHP Justin Verlander, who didn't sign until after the 2004 season was over, runs his fastball up to 99 mph. RHP Collin Mahoney (4) spent two years as a backup catcher at Clemson before his strong arm earned him some mound time in 2004. Though he's still figuring things out, he hit 100 mph several times during the spring.

Best Breaking Ball: Verlander's power curveball is a true hammer. Bumstead's slider is his best pitch.

Most Intriguing Background: Frazier's

RICH ABEL

Dlugach

older brother Charles plays in the Marlins system, while younger brother Todd went in the 37th round to the Rockies. Mahoney's brother Ryan is a backup catcher at South Carolina, Clemson's arch-rival. 3B/SS Cory Middleton's (10) older brother Kyle pitches in the Royals system.

Closest To The Majors: RHP Eric Beattie (2) was the Cape Cod League pitcher of the year in 2003, when he posted the second-lowest ERA in league history (0.39). His sinker, slider and control should allow him to help Detroit in short order.

Best Late-Round Pick: Trahern is athletic and poised, and he owns a 90-92 mph fastball and a good curve. He was headed to Oklahoma as a two-way player before the Sooners unexpectedly fired pitching coach Ray Hayward, a former Tigers scout.

The One Who Got Away: Verlander nearly did, until Detroit offered him a major league contract worth more than the $3.35 million bonus they gave No. 3 choice Kyle Sleeth in 2003. With negotiations going nowhere, the Tigers pulled the offer in mid-October. A week later, however, Verlander's father called then-scouting director Greg Smith personally and a deal was done quickly. Verlander had arguably the best pure stuff of any pitcher in the 2004 draft.

Assessment: The draft would have been a disaster if they hadn't signed Verlander, though not everyone was sold that he was the best college talent in the draft.

2003 RHP Kyle Sleeth (1) is Detroit's best pitching prospect, but he didn't live up to No. 3 overall pick status in his pro debut. SS Tony Giarratano (3) has exceeded expectations so far. **GRADE:** C+

2002 OF Curtis Granderson (3) had a breakthrough year in 2004 and is the Tigers' top prospect, providing a counterbalance to 3B Scott Moore (1), who has never hit, and OF Brent Clevlen (2), whose bat disappeared last year. RHP Joel Zumaya (11) has an electric arm but needs to learn how to pitch. **GRADE:** C+

2001 Both first-rounders, RHP Kenny Baugh and 2B Michael Woods, have been ravaged by injuries. RHP Humberto Sanchez (31, draft-and-follow) and 2B Ryan Raburn (5) are two of the Tigers' better prospects. **GRADE:** C

2000 RHP Matt Wheatland (1) had even worse injury problems than Baugh or Woods and was released last year and picked up by the Astros. That makes either RHP Mark Woodyard (4) or OF Nook Logan (3) the best this draft can offer. Ouch. **GRADE:** F

Draft analysis prepared by Jim Callis. Numbers in parentheses indicate draft rounds.

KEVIN PATAKY

Curtis
GRANDERSON

Born: March 16, 1981.
Ht.: 6-1. **Wt.:** 185.
Bats: L. **Throws:** R.
School: University of Illinois-Chicago.
Career Transactions: Selected by Tigers in third round of 2002 draft, signed June 28, 2002.
Signed by: Jerome Cochran.

G randerson proved he could hit in 2002. He finished second in the NCAA Division I batting race with a .483 average, trailing only Rickie Weeks (.495)—who would become the No. 2 overall pick the following year. After signing for $469,000 as a third-round pick, Granderson again finished runner-up for a hitting crown, this time with a .344 average in the short-season New York-Penn League. But for all his hitting ability, scouts weren't impressed by the rest of his game. Though he skipped a level and had a solid if unspectacular performance at high Class A Lakeland in 2003, he still didn't win scouts over. Even some Tigers officials began to lose faith in him. But Granderson quickly gained believers with his breakout year at Double-A Erie in 2004. He ranked fourth in RBIs and eighth in batting in the Eastern League, and his other tools all seemed to climb a notch. His September callup made him the first Illinois-Chicago player to reach the majors.

Granderson is a classic line-drive, gap-to-gap hitter. He has a quick and compact batting stroke, a good grasp of the strike zone and identifies pitches early. He made an adjustment to become more selective upon reaching Double-A, as reflected in his career-best 80 walks. His gap-hitting approach seems tailor-made for Detroit's spacious Comerica Park. Once labeled as a corner outfielder who wouldn't have enough power to play every day in the majors, Granderson nearly doubled his previous career high in homers and made defensive strides in center field. He gets good jumps and takes correct routes to the ball. His range is average for center and above average on the corners. Granderson's arm is accurate, and he's a smart player who throws to the right base. His makeup and work habits are outstanding, as evidenced by his decision to complete his college degree after signing as a junior. He shows the potential to be a clubhouse leader if he continues to perform on the field.

Granderson isn't going to produce big-time power. He benefited from playing his home games at Erie's cozy Jerry Uht Park, though 13 of his 21 homers and 27 of his 48 extra-base hits came on the road. Another rap on Granderson was that many scouts considered him a fringe-average runner who lacked the speed of a true center fielder. Now there are just as many scouts who say that knock is overstated, however, and that his speed may actually rate a tick above average.

If the Tigers had decided to nontender Alex Sanchez, Granderson would have been the frontrunner to take over in center field. But Detroit re-signed Sanchez for one year, allowing Granderson to begin 2005 at Triple-A Toledo. He still could push for Sanchez' job by midseason.

Year	Club (League)	Class	AVG	G	AB	R	H	2B	3B	HR	RBI	BB	SO	SB	OBP	SLG
2002	Oneonta (NY-P)	A	.344	52	212	45	73	15	4	3	34	20	35	9	.417	.495
2003	Lakeland (FSL)	A	.286	127	476	71	136	29	10	11	51	49	91	10	.365	.458
2004	Erie (EL)	AA	.301	123	462	89	139	19	8	21	94	80	95	14	.405	.513
	Detroit (AL)	MAJ	.240	9	25	2	6	1	1	0	0	3	8	0	.321	.360
MAJOR LEAGUE TOTALS			.240	9	25	2	6	1	1	0	0	3	8	0	.321	.360
MINOR LEAGUE TOTALS			.303	302	1150	205	348	63	22	35	179	149	221	33	.392	.487

2 Kyle Sleeth, rhp

RICH ABEL

Born: Dec. 20, 1981. **Ht.:** 6-5. **Wt.:** 205. **Bats:** R. **Throws:** R. **School:** Wake Forest University. **Career Transactions:** Selected by Tigers in first round (third overall) of 2003 draft; signed Aug. 8, 2003. **Signed by:** Bill Buck.

The winner of an NCAA-record-tying 26 straight decisions at Wake Forest and the second overall pick in the 2003 draft, Sleeth ranked as the organization's top prospect before throwing his first pro pitch. He didn't sign until August 2003, when he received a $3.35 million bonus. He was very inconsistent after a promotion to Double-A, with seven quality starts but he had a 9.50 ERA in his other six outings. Sleeth has the makings of an electric arsenal with above-average major league pitches. He runs his fastball between 92-94 mph and tops out at 96. His sharp, mid-80s slider is an out pitch, and his curveball has put-away potential. Sleeth needs to improve his changeup to complement his power pitches. He's still working on smoothing out his mechanics so he can consistently repeat them. He throws slightly across his body and elevates too many fastballs, one of the factors affecting his command. Despite his problems in Double-A, scouts still project Sleeth to have a high ceiling and become at least a No. 3 starter. He'll try to rebound when he returns to Erie to begin 2005.

Year	Club (League)	Class	W	L	ERA	G	GS	CG	SV	IP	H	R	ER	HR	BB	SO	AVG
2004	Lakeland (FSL)	A	3	4	3.67	9	9	1	0	54	47	26	22	3	15	55	.230
	Erie (EL)	AA	4	4	6.30	13	13	0	0	80	93	58	56	14	34	57	.297
MINOR LEAGUE TOTALS			7	8	5.24	22	22	1	0	134	140	84	78	17	49	112	.271

3 Justin Verlander, rhp

Born: Feb. 20, 1983. **Ht.:** 6-5. **Wt.:** 200. **Bats:** R. **Throws:** R. **School:** Old Dominion University. **Career Transactions:** Selected by Tigers in first round (second overall) of 2004 draft; signed Oct. 23, 2004. **Signed by:** Greg Smith.

Verlander had as electric an arm as anyone in the 2004 draft, though he went just 21-18 in three college seasons. The Tigers drafted him second overall, then broke off negotiations with him and his agent in October. Verlander's father jumpstarted the talks the following week, and Verlander signed a five-year big league contract with a $3.12 million bonus and $4.5 million guaranteed. Equipped with a lightning-quick arm, Verlander regularly pitches in the mid-90s and touched 99 mph several times during the spring of his junior year. His curveball is a knee-buckling hammer with vicious downward bite, and his changeup could give him a third plus pitch. The Tigers will have to make up for lost time and start reshaping Verlander's delivery when he reports to spring training. His command is affected by his upright finish and short stride, which causes him to leave too many pitches up in the zone. He doesn't use his changeup as much as he should. Verlander has the stuff to front a rotation, but scouts are divided on whether he profiles better as a closer. Detroit hopes he'll remain a starter and will begin his career in high Class A.

Year	Club (League)	Class	W	L	ERA	G	GS	CG	SV	IP	H	R	ER	HR	BB	SO	AVG
2004	Did not play—Signed 2005 contract																

4 Joel Zumaya, rhp

RICH ABEL

Born: Nov. 9, 1984. **Ht.:** 6-3. **Wt.:** 210. **Bats:** R. **Throws:** R. **School:** Bonita Vista HS, Chula Vista, Calif. **Career Transactions:** Selected by Tigers in 11th round of 2002 draft; signed June 20, 2002. **Signed by:** Rob Wilfong.

Zumaya wasn't an unknown in the talent-rich San Diego area, but he lasted until the 11th round out of high school because few scouts projected his velocity would spike so quickly. His fastball jumped from the low to mid-90s right after he signed. Filling a void created by injuries, he reached Double-A at age 19. Zumaya has pure power arm strength and has shown the ability to overpower more experienced hitters at each stop in his three-year career. His fastball tops out at 98 mph, and his hard slurve has late depth. His intensity would serve him well in a late-inning relief role. Zumaya's shortcomings also may lead him to the bullpen. His maximum-effort delivery makes it difficult for him to command his fastball and breaking ball and also leads to questions about his durability. He barely has averaged five innings per start as a pro. He lacks a changeup. For now, the Tigers plan on leaving Zumaya in the rotation and seeing whether he can improve his secondary pitches and control. He's heading back to Double-A in 2005.

Year	Club (League)	Class	W	L	ERA	G	GS	CG	SV	IP	H	R	ER	HR	BB	SO	AVG
2002	Tigers (GCL)	R	2	1	1.93	9	8	0	0	37	21	9	8	2	11	46	.163
2003	West Michigan (Mid)	A	7	5	2.79	19	19	0	0	90	69	35	28	3	38	126	.209
2004	Erie (EL)	AA	2	2	6.30	4	4	0	0	20	19	20	14	6	10	29	.238
	Lakeland (FSL)	A	6	4	3.54	16	16	1	0	94	65	41	37	8	43	92	.198
MINOR LEAGUE TOTALS			17	12	3.24	48	47	1	0	242	174	105	87	19	102	293	.200

Humberto Sanchez, rhp

Born: May 28, 1983. **Ht.:** 6-6. **Wt.:** 230. **Bats:** R. **Throws:** R. **School:** Connors State (Okla.) JC. **Career Transactions:** Selected by Tigers in 31st round of 2001 draft; signed May 27, 2002. **Signed by:** Rob Guzik.

Sanchez moved from the Dominican Republic to the Bronx when he was 10. Taken as a 31st-round draft-and-follow out of Rockland (N.Y.) CC in 2001, he garnered some first-round interest the following spring after transferring to Connors State (Okla.) JC. He signed before the 2002 draft for $1 million. Sanchez presents an imposing figure on the mound and has drawn comparisons to Roberto Hernandez. His fastball can overpower hitters at 92-95 mph with hard sink. His curveball shows flashes of already being an above-average strikeout pitch. Sanchez has spotty control and finds himself behind in the count too often. He needs to build confidence in his changeup. He spent last offseason working his way into shape at the Tigers' spring training complex. They were pleased with his progress, but he needs to keep an eye on his body and maintain his focus. After handling his first taste of Double-A well, he'll return to Erie. Sanchez has middle-of-the-rotation potential, but needs to show better feel to avoid going to the bullpen.

Year	Club (League)	Class	W	L	ERA	G	GS	CG	SV	IP	H	R	ER	HR	BB	SO	AVG
2002	Oneonta (NY-P)	A	2	2	3.62	9	9	0	0	32	29	18	13	1	21	26	.244
2003	West Michigan (Mid)	A	7	7	4.42	23	23	0	0	116	107	71	57	3	78	96	.249
2004	Lakeland (FSL)	A	7	11	5.21	19	19	3	0	105	103	67	61	9	51	115	.258
	Erie (EL)	AA	1	0	2.13	2	2	0	0	13	10	5	3	1	6	15	.213
MINOR LEAGUE TOTALS			17	20	4.53	53	53	3	0	266	249	161	134	14	156	252	.250

Tony Giarratano, ss

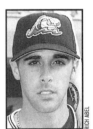

Born: Nov. 29, 1982. **Ht.:** 6-0. **Wt.:** 180. **Bats:** B. **Throws:** R. **School:** Tulane University. **Career Transactions:** Selected by Tigers in third round of 2003 draft; signed June 30, 2003. **Signed by:** Steve Taylor.

Giarratano lasted until the third round of the 2003 draft in part because of lingering doubts from his sophomore season, when he hit .238 at Tulane and .187 in the Cape Cod League. He has had no problems as a pro, with a career .333 average. He injured his left shoulder in August, ending his season and requiring surgery. Giarratano has pure shortstop actions with outstanding glovework and soft, quick hands. He has answered questions about his ability to hit with wood, employing a contact approach and producing consistent line drives to all fields from both sides of the plate. He runs well and has the instincts to reach double digits in steals annually. The lone hole in Giarratano's game is his power. His other tools are solid, and he showed improved patience after walking infrequently in his pro debut. Middle infield is one of Detroit's few areas of depth. Giarratano is poised for a jump to Double-A, and if he keeps producing the Tigers will find a spot for him.

Year	Club (League)	Class	AVG	G	AB	R	H	2B	3B	HR	RBI	BB	SO	SB	OBP	SLG
2003	Oneonta (NY-P)	A	.328	47	189	31	62	11	4	3	27	12	22	9	.369	.476
2004	West Michigan (Mid)	A	.285	43	165	20	47	6	1	1	13	25	22	11	.383	.352
	Lakeland (FSL)	A	.376	53	202	30	76	11	0	5	25	16	38	14	.423	.505
MINOR LEAGUE TOTALS			.333	143	556	81	185	28	5	9	65	53	82	34	.393	.450

Jeff Frazier, of

Born: Aug. 10, 1982. **Ht.:** 6-4. **Wt.:** 215. **Bats:** R. **Throws:** R. **School:** Rutgers University. **Career Transactions:** Selected by Tigers in third round of 2004 draft; signed June 20, 2004. **Signed by:** Derrick Ross.

Frazier batted .382-13-59 as a junior and set Rutgers' career home run mark with 34 before signing for $500,000. His pro debut ended after 20 games when an errant pitch broke his left forearm. His older brother Charlie is an outfielder in the Marlins organization and his younger brother Todd (the MVP of the 1998 Little League World Series) is a freshman third baseman at Rutgers. A good all-around hitter who uses the entire field, Frazier has the strength and leverage to turn on pitches and drive them out to any part of the park. His makeup is outstanding. He has a chance to be an above-average outfielder with a strong, accurate arm. Frazier had to tone down a deep hand hitch in his swing to avoid getting under too many balls. He's a solid athlete, but he doesn't get down the line very well. Though his instincts help him on the bases and in the outfield corner spots, his speed and range are somewhat limited. Frazier likely will start 2005 at low Class A West Michigan. He's advanced enough to get pushed to high Class A after a strong first half.

Year	Club (League)	Class	W	L	ERA	G	GS	CG	SV	IP	H	R	ER	HR	BB	SO	AVG
2004	Oneonta (NY-P)	A	.304	20	79	15	24	5	1	1	13	9	11	2	.387	.430
MINOR LEAGUE TOTALS			.304	20	79	15	24	5	1	1	13	9	11	2	.387	.430

8 Ryan Raburn, 2b

Born: April.17, 1981. **Ht.:** 6-0. **Wt.:** 180. **Bats:** R. **Throws:** R. **School:** South Florida CC. **Career Transactions:** Selected by Tigers in fifth round of 2001 draft; signed June 20, 2001. **Signed by:** Steve Nichols.

Raburn's career was sidetracked in 2002 when he dislocated his hip falling off an all-terrain vehicle. He moved from third base to second in instructional league after 2003, then missed the first six weeks of the 2004 season after dislocating his left pinky in spring training. He recovered from the injury and a slow start to hit .381 in July and August and join the Tigers in September. Raburn hits the ball to all fields with authority and has elicited comparisons to Jeff Kent as an offensive-minded second baseman since he shifted from the hot corner. He was a poor defensive third baseman, but his hands are good and he has an average arm. Raburn is making progress at second base but must get more consistent on routine plays. He strikes out in bunches, and pitchers at higher levels may be able to exploit him. He has below-average speed and his maturity has been questioned at times. The Tigers have a greater need at third base, but Raburn will stay put at second. He'll begin 2005 in Triple-A.

Year	Club (League)	Class	AVG	G	AB	R	H	2B	3B	HR	RBI	BB	SO	SB	OBP	SLG
2001	Tigers (GCL)	R	.155	19	58	4	9	2	0	1	5	9	19	2	.300	.241
	Oneonta (NY-P)	A	.363	44	171	25	62	17	8	8	42	17	42	1	.418	.696
2002	Tigers (GCL)	R	.300	8	30	4	9	3	1	1	5	3	7	0	.364	.567
	West Michigan (Mid)	A	.220	40	150	27	33	10	1	6	28	16	46	0	.306	.420
2003	West Michigan (Mid)	A	.351	16	57	14	20	7	0	3	12	6	14	1	.431	.632
	Lakeland (FSL)	A	.222	95	325	52	72	14	3	12	56	45	89	2	.332	.394
2004	Lakeland (FSL)	A	.273	3	11	1	3	1	0	1	3	1	6	0	.333	.636
	Erie (EL)	AA	.301	98	366	66	110	29	4	16	63	47	96	3	.390	.533
	Detroit (AL)	MAJ	.138	12	29	4	4	1	0	0	1	2	15	1	.194	.172
MAJOR LEAGUE TOTALS			.138	12	29	4	4	1	0	0	1	2	15	1	.194	.172
MINOR LEAGUE TOTALS			.272	323	1168	193	318	83	17	48	214	144	319	9	.363	.496

9 Eulogio de la Cruz, rhp

Born: March 12, 1984. **Ht.:** 5-11. **Wt.:** 170. **Bats:** R. **Throws:** R. **Career Transactions:** Signed out of Dominican Republic by Tigers, Sept. 6, 2001. **Signed by:** Ramon Pena.

West Michigan won the low Class A Midwest League championship without a can't-miss prospect on the playoff roster. De la Cruz has the best future among the Whitecaps and emerged as their closer in June. He faded in August, however, and served as a set-up man in the postseason. De la Cruz routinely blows his heater in the high 90s and occasionally touches triple digits on the radar gun. In one outing, he hit or topped 100 mph with four straight pitches. His control is good for someone this young who throws this hard. His strikeout totals aren't high because de la Cruz essentially operates with one pitch. He lacks deception in his delivery, in part because he has a small build and his pitches arrive on a flat plane. His fastball is straight and his curveball hasn't progressed as quickly as expected. The Tigers desperately need bullpen help, and de la Cruz made a positive first impression on big league manager Alan Trammell in instructional league. They could rush him, but he needs to develop a second pitch and will work on that in high Class A in 2005.

Year	Club (League)	Class	W	L	ERA	G	GS	CG	SV	IP	H	R	ER	HR	BB	SO	AVG
2002	Tigers (GCL)	R	1	1	2.63	20	0	0	1	38	40	24	11	0	21	46	.260
	Oneonta (NY-P)	A	0	0	23.14	2	0	0	0	2	7	8	6	0	4	4	.500
2003	Tigers (GCL)	R	2	2	2.59	22	0	0	7	24	18	10	7	0	15	30	.205
	Oneonta (NY-P)	A	0	0	10.80	2	0	0	0	3	6	4	4	0	1	4	.400
2004	West Michigan (Mid)	A	2	4	3.83	54	0	0	17	54	51	30	23	2	33	44	.244
MINOR LEAGUE TOTALS			5	7	3.77	100	0	0	25	122	122	76	51	2	74	128	.254

10 Chris Shelton, 1b/c

MIKE JANES

Born: June 26, 1980. **Ht.:** 6-0. **Wt.:** 220. **Bats:** R. **Throws:** R. **School:** University of Utah. **Career Transactions:** Selected by Pirates in 33rd round of 2001 draft; signed June 10, 2001 . . . Selected by Tigers from Pirates in major league Rule 5 draft, Dec. 15, 2003. **Signed by:** Ted Williams (Pirates).

The first pick in the 2003 major league Rule 5 draft, Shelton spent all of last season on the Tigers' 25-man roster but saw little playing time. He wasn't protected by the Pirates despite being named their minor league player of the year and the high Class A Carolina League MVP. He has a career .332 batting average in the minors, and continued his torrid hitting in the Arizona Fall League, where he led the circuit in hitting (.404), on-base percentage (.470), slugging percentage (.667) and RBIs (33) and won another MVP award. In the minors, he hit all types of pitching, used the entire field and did an excellent job of working counts and drawing walks. He rarely stung the ball with Detroit, though he did grow rusty sitting on the bench. If Shelton is going to have an impact in the major leagues, his bat will have to continue to carry him. He's a below-average catcher in every way and likely will be used in that role only in an emergency. He also is limited at first base because he's stiff and lacks athleticism. He has had unsuccessful trials in the outfield and at third base, and likely profiles as a DH or righthanded bat off the bench when he returns to the majors. Shelton needs some time in Triple-A after getting just 108 at-bats last season.

Year	Club (League)	Class	AVG	G	AB	R	H	2B	3B	HR	RBI	BB	SO	SB	OBP	SLG
2001	Williamsport (NY-P)	A	.305	50	174	22	53	11	0	2	33	33	31	4	.415	.402
2002	Hickory (SAL)	A	.340	93	332	72	113	27	2	17	65	47	74	0	.425	.587
2003	Lynchburg (Car)	A	.359	95	315	71	113	24	1	21	69	68	67	1	.478	.641
	Altoona (EL)	AA	.279	35	122	17	34	10	1	0	14	8	23	0	.331	.377
2004	Toledo (IL)	AAA	.339	18	62	5	21	2	0	0	7	10	13	0	.425	.371
	Detroit (AL)	MAJ	.196	27	46	6	9	1	0	1	3	9	14	0	.321	.283
MAJOR LEAGUE TOTALS			.196	27	46	6	9	1	0	1	3	9	14	0	.321	.283
MINOR LEAGUE TOTALS			.332	291	1005	187	334	74	4	40	188	166	208	5	.430	.533

11 Wilkin Ramirez, 3b

Born: Oct. 25, 1985. **Ht.:** 6-2. **Wt.:** 190. **Bats:** R. **Throws:** R. **Career Transactions:** Signed out of Dominican Republic by Tigers, Feb. 5, 2003. **Signed by:** Ramon Pena.

After signing for $300,000 out of the Dominican Republic prior to the 2003 season, Ramirez had a promising pro debut in the Rookie-level Gulf Coast League. But he wasn't able to build on it last year because he tore the labrum in his right shoulder, sidelining him for the entire season. He returned for instructional league, though he still wasn't able to throw. He was impressive at the plate, hitting a couple of tape-measure blasts. Ramirez has one of the highest offensive ceilings in the system. For his age, he's exceptionally strong, has good knowledge of the strike zone, recognizes pitches well and handles breaking stuff. He has average speed and had arm strength to match before his injury, which has put his chances of sticking at third base at risk. If he can't make the throws from the hot corner, he'll move to first base, where he should still have enough power to project as a regular. Even before the injury, he wasn't a sure thing at third base, making 21 errors in 42 games in 2003. He's advanced enough at the plate to go to low Class A despite missing a full season.

Year	Club (League)	Class	AVG	G	AB	R	H	2B	3B	HR	RBI	BB	SO	SB	OBP	SLG
2003	Tigers (GCL)	R	.275	54	200	34	55	6	7	5	35	13	51	6	,321	.450
2004	Did not play—Injured															
MINOR LEAGUE TOTALS			.275	54	200	34	55	6	7	5	35	13	51	6	.321	.450

12 Roberto Novoa, rhp

Born: Aug.15, 1979. **Ht.:** 6-5. **Wt.:** 200. **Bats:** R. **Throws:** R. **Career Transactions:** Signed out of Dominican Republic by Pirates, July 3, 1999 . . . Traded by Pirates to Tigers, Dec. 17, 2002, as part of trade in which Tigers sent 1B Randall Simon to Pirates for LHP Adrian Burnside and a player to be named (Nov. 25, 2002); Tigers acquired 3B Kody Kirkland to complete trade (May 24, 2003). **Signed by:** Pablo Cruz (Pirates).

When the Tigers had no desire to go to arbitration with Randall Simon following the 2002 season, they were able to trade him to the Pirates for three minor leaguers. First lefthander Adrian Burnside and then third baseman Kody Kirkland appeared to be the prize of that deal for Detroit, but now it's Novoa who looks like the biggest keeper. He became the first of the trio to reach the majors, doing so last July. A starter throughout his career before last season, Novoa moved to the bullpen and took a step forward. He gradually grew into the closer role in Double-A, but his future is as a long reliever or setup man. Tall and gangly, Novoa consistently throws in the low 90s and up to 95 mph with sinking action on his fastball. He has solid command of his hard, slurvy breaking ball. When Novoa keeps his fastball down in the strike zone, he's effective. When he gets the ball up, which he did too often with the Tigers, he gets hit hard. Pitching out of the bullpen, he didn't worry about his changeup or splitter as much as he did while in the rotation. Detroit needs relievers, so Novoa could begin 2005 in the majors if he has a good spring. If not, he'll bide his time in Triple-A.

Year	Club (League)	Class	W	L	ERA	G	GS	CG	SV	IP	H	R	ER	HR	BB	SO	AVG
2000	Pirates (DSL)	R	4	6	4.15	13	13	1	0	82	99	65	38	5	29	44	.289
2001	Williamsport (NY-P)	A	5	5	3.39	14	13	1	0	80	76	40	30	4	20	55	.255
2002	Hickory (SAL)	A	1	5	5.48	10	10	0	0	43	61	30	26	2	15	29	.335
	Williamsport (NY-P)	A	8	3	3.65	12	12	0	0	67	62	32	27	4	8	56	.240
2003	Lakeland (FSL)	A	4	5	3.73	19	15	2	0	99	93	45	41	8	25	71	.243
2004	Detroit (AL)	MAJ	1	1	5.57	16	0	0	0	21	25	15	13	4	6	15	.309
	Erie (EL)	AA	7	0	2.96	41	0	0	4	79	63	32	26	7	18	59	.216
MAJOR LEAGUE TOTALS			1	1	5.57	16	0	0	0	21	25	15	13	4	6	15	.309
MINOR LEAGUE TOTALS			29	24	3.76	109	63	4	4	449	454	244	188	30	115	314	.259

13 Dallas Trahern, rhp

Born: Nov. 29, 1985. **Ht.:** 6-3. **Wt.:** 190. **Bats:** R. **Throws:** R. **School:** Owasso (Okla.) HS. **Career Transactions:** Selected by Tigers in 34th round of 2004 draft; signed July 10, 2004. **Signed by:** Steve Taylor.

Trahern starred as a two-way player while leading Owasso High to the Oklahoma 6-A state title, the school's fifth in seven years. A second-team High School All-American, Trahern batted .450-13-50 as a shortstop and went 11-0, 1.37 on the mound. Scouts preferred him on the mound but believed he was set on attending Oklahoma, so he dropped all the way to the 34th round. But when the Sooners fired pitching coach/recruiting coordinator Ray Hayward, a former Tigers scout, Trahern did an about-face. He signed with Detroit and had an excellent pro debut. Trahern has good command of three pitches: a lively 90-92 mph fastball, a curveball and a changeup. His considerable athleticism—Oklahoma planned on playing him both ways—allows him to throw more strikes than the typical teenager, and he's also poised beyond his years. The Tigers believe he could handle a jump to low Class A in his first full season.

Year	Club (League)	Class	W	L	ERA	G	GS	CG	SV	IP	H	R	ER	HR	BB	SO	AVG
2004	Tigers (GCL)	R	1	2	0.59	7	6	0	0	31	22	8	2	1	7	24	.198
MINOR LEAGUE TOTALS			1	2	0.59	7	6	0	0	31	22	8	2	1	7	24	.198

14 Brent Clevlen, of

Born: Oct. 27, 1983. **Ht.:** 6-2. **Wt.:** 190. **Bats:** R. **Throws:** R. **School:** Westwood HS, Cedar Park, Texas. **Career Transactions:** Selected by Tigers in second round of 2002 draft; signed July 23, 2002. **Signed by:** Tim Grieve.

The top position player and the No. 2 prospect on this list a year ago, Clevlen's star dropped as he struggled mightily in high Class A. He had far more strikeouts than hits, didn't show his anticipated power and topped Florida State League outfielders with 15 errors. Coming off two solid seasons as a pro, he hit .283 in the first two months last season but just .187 the rest of the way. Pitchers repeatedly got him out by working him on the outer half of the plate. A solid all-around athlete who had college potential as a quarterback, Clevlen still endeared himself to scouts by playing hard throughout his slump and showing aptitude in other areas of the game. His speed and arm are above-average tools, and he should hit for at least average power. He controlled the strike zone well in 2003, so there's hope he can recover. Clevlen will return to Lakeland to start the 2005 season.

Year	Club (League)	Class	AVG	G	AB	R	H	2B	3B	HR	RBI	BB	SO	SB	OBP	SLG
2002	Tigers (GCL)	R	.330	28	103	14	34	2	3	21	8	24	2	.372	.495
2003	West Michigan (Mid)	A	.260	138	481	67	125	22	7	12	63	72	111	6	.359	.410
2004	Lakeland (FSL)	A	.223	117	421	49	94	23	6	6	50	44	127	2	.300	.349
MINOR LEAGUE TOTALS			.252	283	1005	130	253	47	16	21	134	124	262	10	.336	.393

15 Juan Tejeda, 1b

Born: Jan. 26, 1982. **Ht.:** 6-2. **Wt.:** 190. **Bats:** R. **Throws:** R. **Career Transactions:** Signed out of Dominican Republic by Tigers, July 7, 1999. **Signed by:** Ramon Pena.

Tejeda always had hit for average and produced runs, but last season was the first time in his career that he showed home run power. Whether or not that was just a mirage caused by a favorable hitter's park at Erie (15 of his 23 longballs came at home) remains to be seen, however. Questions still abound as to how good a prospect Tejeda is because he's not athletic and doesn't have a particularly quick bat. Despite his success, scouts question whether he'll continue to rake at the upper levels against better pitching. Tejeda is a smart hitter with good knowledge of the strike zone, though his strikeout totals rose last season. He has poor speed and is limited defensively to playing first base, where he's adequate at best. If it turns out that he doesn't have more than gap power, he won't be a big league regular. Tejeda will begin 2005 in Triple-A as he tries to keep hitting his way into a big league role.

Year	Club (League)	Class	AVG	G	AB	R	H	2B	3B	HR	RBI	BB	SO	SB	OBP	SLG
1999	Detroit (DSL)	R	.276	42	152	26	42	9	2	5	26	14	33	1	.360	.461
2000	Detroit (DSL)	R	.312	66	260	52	81	20	3	10	46	16	45	2	.374	.527
2001	Tigers (GCL)	R	.295	50	173	17	51	8	1	4	37	8	32	0	.344	.422
2002	West Michigan (Mid)	A	.300	137	524	68	157	34	6	11	106	60	89	5	.372	.450
2003	Lakeland (FSL)	A	.280	125	461	63	129	28	4	10	76	56	68	6	.360	.423
2004	Erie (EL)	AA	.289	125	457	71	132	29	3	23	92	51	102	0	.362	.516
MINOR LEAGUE TOTALS			.292	545	2027	297	592	128	19	63	383	205	369	14	.364	.467

16 Bo Flowers, of

Born: Nov. 12, 1983. **Ht.:** 6-0. **Wt.:** 190. **Bats:** R. **Throws:** R. **School:** Walther Lutheran HS, Maywood, Ill. **Career Transactions:** Selected by Tigers in fifth round of 2002 draft; signed July 23, 2002. **Signed by:** Jerome Cochran.

As a high school senior in 2002, Flowers was one of the top quarterback prospects in the nation and verbally committed to play football and baseball at Arizona State. The Tigers changed those plans, however, when they drafted him in the fifth round and signed him for $215,000. The best athlete in the system, Flower has a live body with an interesting combination of power and speed, but his baseball skills were very slow to develop before last year. He earned his first promotion to a full-season league in August, serving in a reserve role as West Michigan won the Midwest League title. Flowers has a quick bat, though he still chases too many pitches and will need to tighten his strike zone. His whole game needs refinement, as he's still learning how to use his speed on the bases and in right field. He led New York-Penn League outfielders with 10 errors and takes erratic routes to fly balls. Flowers' game is anything but refined, though he works hard and is receptive to coaching. He'll try to make more strides this year in low Class A.

Year	Club (League)	Class	AVG	G	AB	R	H	2B	3B	HR	RBI	BB	SO	SB	OBP	SLG
2002	Tigers (GCL)	R	.278	26	97	18	27	4	1	0	7	3	24	8	.320	.340
2003	Oneonta (NY-P)	A	.177	37	124	17	22	1	2	0	9	9	42	5	.244	.218
	Tigers (GCL)	R	.182	15	44	3	8	3	1	0	2	2	12	2	.234	.295
2004	West Michigan (Mid)	A	.273	6	22	4	6	1	0	1	1	0	6	0	.360	.455
	Oneonta (NY-P)	A	.280	66	246	38	69	7	6	4	26	19	65	16	.341	.407
MINOR LEAGUE TOTALS			.267	150	533	80	132	16	10	5	45	33	149	31	.307	.343

17 Eric Beattie, rhp

Born: April 2, 1983. **Ht.:** 6-3. **Wt.:** 190. **Bats:** R. **Throws:** R. **School:** University of Tampa. **Career Transactions:** Selected by Tigers in second round of 2004 draft; signed Aug. 15, 2004. **Signed by:** Steve Nichols.

Beattie topped NCAA Division II with 15 victories in 2003, but he really caught scouts' attention by dominating the Cape Cod League that summer. He led the Cape with a 0.39 ERA, the second-lowest in league history, and won pitcher-of-the-year honors. After a strong junior year at Tampa, he went in the second round and signed late in the summer for $800,000. He didn't see any game action for the Tigers, instead joining them for instructional league. While Detroit expected Beattie to be rusty, his control was so poor that it was scary. As an amateur, Beattie had shown excellent command of an 88-92 mph sinker, locating it at will and keeping it down in the zone. He backed it up with an effective slider that he also threw for strikes. He had shown much more feel than 2004 first-rounder Justin Verlander, and the Tigers are waiting anxiously to see if Beattie can regain it. Once he does, his main points of emphasis will be to improve his changeup and not overthrow when he gets into jams. Detroit originally thought Beattie could make his pro debut in high Class A, but where he starts will depend on how he looks in spring training.

Year	Club (League)	Class	W	L	ERA	G	GS	CG	SV	IP	H	R	ER	HR	BB	SO	AVG
2004	Did not play—Signed 2005 contract																

18 Collin Mahoney, rhp

Born: Dec. 26, 1982. **Ht.:** 6-4. **Wt.:** 200. **Bats:** R. **Throws:** R. **School:** Clemson University. **Career Transactions:** Selected by Tigers in fourth round of 2004 draft; signed June 29, 2004. **Signed by:** Bill Buck.

Mahoney spent two years as a backup catcher at Clemson until he and a teammate were fooling around with a radar gun toward the end of the 2003 season. Trying to see how hard he could throw, Mahoney hit 94, which began his conversion to the mound. Mahoney pitched just five innings between his four years of high school and his first two seasons of college, and his inexperience shows. Though he attracted droves of scouts by repeatedly hitting 100 mph as a junior, he went just 1-3, 6.63 in 19 innings. The Tigers couldn't resist his raw arm strength, taking him in the fourth round and signing him for $375,000. They were pleased with his first pro summer, as they took a recoil out of his delivery and lengthened his follow-through. Mahoney showed better control, and though his fastball dropped to 90-94 mph, Detroit expects his mid- to upper-90s velocity will return as he gets used to his mechanics. He reminds scouts of Troy Percival, a catcher-turned-closer who signed with the Tigers this offseason. To follow Percival's path, Mahoney will have to continue to improve his command, learn how to pitch and come up with something to back up his fastball. He uses a slider, but it's little more than a change-of-speed pitch at this point. Mahoney had a strong instructional league and will pitch in Class A in 2005.

Year	Club (League)	Class	W	L	ERA	G	GS	CG	SV	IP	H	R	ER	HR	BB	SO	AVG
2004	Oneonta (NY-P)	A	1	0	4.94	21	0	0	2	31	38	24	17	2	23	31	.297
MINOR LEAGUE TOTALS			1	0	4.94	21	0	0	2	31	38	24	17	2	23	31	.297

19 Kody Kirkland, 3b

Born: June 9, 1983. **Ht.:** 6-4. **Wt.:** 200. **Bats:** R. **Throws:** R. **School:** JC of Southern Idaho. **Career Transactions:** Selected by Pirates in 30th round of 2001 draft; signed May 24, 2002 . . . Traded by Pirates to Tigers, May 24, 2003, completing trade in which Tigers sent 1B Randall Simon to Pirates for LHP Adrian Burnside and two players to be named (Nov. 25, 2002); Tigers acquired RHP Roberto Novoa (Dec. 16, 2002) to complete trade. **Signed by:** Kevin Clouser (Pirates).

The Tigers thought Kirkland was ready for low Class A in 2003, but with 2002 first-rounder Scott Moore ahead of him, he had to settle for tearing up the New York-Penn League. But even with another year under his belt, Kirkland proved overmatched in full-season ball in 2004. He struggled to make contact and lost all semblance of his strike zone, whiffing nearly 10 times for every walk. Kirkland has a compact stroke and had shown an ability to drive the ball to all parts of the field, but his approach needs a serious overhaul. Detroit also has become concerned about what his 2004 performance might have done to Kirkland's confidence because he gets down on himself too easily. An underrated athlete, he moves well at third base and has a strong arm. He still needs to improve the accuracy of his throws after topping Midwest League third basemen with 29 errors. Despite his struggles, he'll move up to high Class A this year.

Year	Club (League)	Class	AVG	G	AB	R	H	2B	3B	HR	RBI	BB	SO	SB	OBP	SLG
2002	Pirates (GCL)	R	.306	46	157	22	48	10	2	0	18	14	39	2	.373	.395
2003	Oneonta (NY-P)	A	.303	67	254	46	77	15	11	4	49	25	60	14	.390	.496
2004	West Michigan (Mid)	A	.236	129	496	50	117	30	11	10	61	15	149	6	.276	.401
MINOR LEAGUE TOTALS			.267	242	907	118	242	55	24	14	128	54	248	22	.327	.427

20 Scott Moore, 3b

Born: Nov. 17, 1983. **Ht.:** 6-2. **Wt.:** 180. **Bats:** L. **Throws:** R. **School:** Cypress HS, Long Beach, Calif. **Career Transactions:** Selected by Tigers in first round (eighth overall) of 2002 draft; signed June 4, 2002. **Signed by:** Rob Wilfong.

Moore is fighting the notion it was a mistake for Detroit to select him eighth overall and hand him a $2.3 million bonus in 2002. His tools have played below average across the board, but he manages to keep the Tigers and scouts intrigued with his raw power potential, which is the best in the system. Despite a career-high 14 homers in 2004, Moore continued to be a disappointment. Though his batting stroke is sound, he hit a career-low .223 and struck out more than once a game. He has had problems making contact. He was compared to Eric Chavez as a high schooler, but Moore hit just .329 as a senior—and, in retrospect, that should have been a tipoff. Drafted as a shortstop, Moore shifted to third base after his first pro season. He continues to struggle with throws across the diamond because of inconsistent fundamentals—he led Florida State League third basemen with 28 errors last year—though his arm strength is good. He doesn't run very well and lacks the lively actions found in most players taken in the upper half of the first round. If Moore moves up to Double-A this season, he'll face a major challenge in refining his approach against more advanced pitching. He may repeat high Class A in an attempt to build his confidence.

Year	Club (League)	Class	AVG	G	AB	R	H	2B	3B	HR	RBI	BB	SO	SB	OBP	SLG
2002	Tigers (GGL)	R	.293	40	133	18	39	6	2	4	25	10	31	1	.349	.459
2003	West Michigan (Mid)	A	.239	107	372	40	89	16	6	6	45	41	110	2	.325	.363
2004	Lakeland (FSL)	A	.223	118	391	52	87	13	4	14	56	49	125	2	.322	.384
MINOR LEAGUE TOTALS			.240	265	896	110	215	35	12	24	126	100	266	5	.327	.386

21 Andrew Kown, rhp

Born: Oct. 7, 1982. **Ht.:** 6-7. **Wt.:** 210. **Bats:** L. **Throws:** R. **School:** Georgia Tech. **Career Transactions:** Selected by Tigers in fifth round of 2004 draft; signed June 22, 2004. **Signed by:** Steve Nichols.

Though Kown was 6-foot-7 and won MVP awards at the 2000 Dizzy Dean World Series and the 2001 Continental Amateur Baseball Association World Series, he went undrafted out of high school. After blossoming as a junior at Georgia Tech in 2004, when he tied for the Atlantic Coast Conference lead with 10 victories, he signed for $224,500 as a fifth-round pick. Kown got stronger each year with the Yellow Jackets, throwing a low-90s fastball from a high three-quarters arm slot last spring. He tired in his introduction to pro ball, pitching mostly in the high 80s during the summer and working only sparingly in instructional league. Even without his usual velocity, Kown had little difficulty in short-season ball. He needs to refine all his pitches, achieving more sink and command with his fastball and more consistency with his slider and changeup. Kown has a lot of upside and could progress rapidly after beginning 2005 in low Class A.

Year	Club (League)	Class	W	L	ERA	G	GS	CG	SV	IP	H	R	ER	HR	BB	SO	AVG
2004	Oneonta (NY-P)	A	1	2	2.85	9	9	0	0	41	40	19	13	4	13	37	.253
MINOR LEAGUE TOTALS			1	2	2.85	9	9	0	0	41	40	19	13	4	13	37	.253

22 Jair Jurrjens, rhp

Born: Jan. 29, 1986. **Ht.:** 6-1. **Wt.:** 160. **Bats:** R. **Throws:** R. **Career Transactions:** Signed out of Curacao by Tigers, May 22, 2003. **Signed by:** Greg Smith.

Jurrjens has pleased the Tigers with his development since former scouting director Greg Smith signed him out of Curacao in May 2003. His best attribute is his ability to control three pitches as a teenager. Not only does he throw his fastball, breaking ball and changeup for strikes, but he also locates them well within the zone. Jurrjens moved from the bullpen to the rotation in 2004, and his fastball got stronger. It sat at 90-92 mph, up from 88-90 in his debut, and he projects to add more velocity as he fills out. His fastball is fairly straight, so it's his command that makes it effective. Jurrjens has so much feel and poise that he could move quickly. He may never have a dominant pitch, but he has enough savvy to project as a possible end-of-the-rotation starter in the major leagues. With a good spring, he could start this season in low Class A.

Year	Club (League)	Class	W	L	ERA	G	GS	CG	SV	IP	H	R	ER	HR	BB	SO	AVG
2003	Tigers (GCL)	R	2	1	3.21	7	2	0	0	28	33	16	10	3	3	20	.292
2004	Oneonta (NY-P)	A	1	5	5.31	7	7	0	0	39	50	25	23	0	10	31	.313
MINOR LEAGUE TOTALS			3	6	4.43	14	9	0	0	67	83	41	33	3	13	51	.304

23 Byron Gettis, of

Born: March 13, 1980. **Ht.:** 6-0. **Wt.:** 240. **Bats:** R. **Throws:** R. **School:** Cahokia (Ill.) HS. **Career Transactions:** Signed as nondrafted free agent by Royals, June 29, 1998 . . . Claimed on waivers by Tigers from Royals, Oct. 15, 2004. **Signed by:** Craig Struss (Royals).

The Royals named Gettis their minor league player of the year in 2003, then removed him from their 40-man roster after he disappointed in Triple-A and the majors last year. He made his big league debut and had his first multihit game against the Tigers, who claimed him off waivers to fortify their Triple-A roster. They may have gotten more than they bargained for, as he went on to become one of the top hitters in the Puerto Rican League. A former University of Minnesota quarterback recruit and the cousin of former NFL linebacker Dana Howard, Gettis is more athletic than his 6-foot, 240-pound frame might indicate. He can punish fastballs and his arm, speed and right-field range are all solid. He struggles with offspeed pitches, and there are concerns that he carries too much weight. If his winter was for real, Gettis could find himself breaking through a la Craig Monroe later in the year.

Year	Club (League)	Class	AVG	G	AB	R	H	2B	3B	HR	RBI	BB	SO	SB	OBP	SLG
1998	Royals (GCL)	R	.216	27	88	11	19	2	0	0	4	4	20	0	.247	.239
1999	Royals (GCL)	R	.316	28	95	20	30	6	2	5	21	17	21	3	.424	.579
	Charleston, WV (SAL)	A	.295	43	149	19	44	7	2	2	13	10	36	10	.361	.409
2000	Wilmington (Car)	A	.155	30	97	13	15	2	0	0	10	13	33	2	.265	.175
	Charleston, WV (SAL)	A	.215	94	344	43	74	18	3	5	50	31	95	11	.297	.328
2001	Burlington (Mid)	A	.314	37	140	26	44	9	2	5	26	14	25	4	.385	.514
	Wilmington (Car)	A	.251	82	303	34	76	21	2	6	51	20	70	4	.321	.393
2002	Wilmington (Car)	A	.283	120	449	76	127	33	2	8	70	48	103	10	.364	.419
2003	Wichita (TL)	AA	.302	140	510	80	154	31	4	16	103	55	110	15	.377	.473
2004	Omaha (PCL)	AAA	.257	51	179	23	46	7	0	4	19	33	61	4	.366	.363

Wichita (TL)	AA	.362	17	58	6	21	4	1	2	11	8	12	0	.448	.569
Kansas City (AL)	MAJ	.179	21	39	7	7	1	1	0	1	8	14	0	.327	.256
MAJOR LEAGUE TOTALS		.179	21	39	7	7	1	1	0	1	8	14	0	.327	.256
MINOR LEAGUE TOTALS		.269	669	2412	351	650	140	18	53	378	253	586	63	.350	.408

24 Kenny Baugh, rhp

Born: Feb. 5, 1979. **Ht.:** 6-4. **Wt.:** 190. **Bats:** R. **Throws:** R. **School:** Rice University. **Career Transactions:** Selected by Tigers in first round (11th overall) of 2001 draft; signed June 5, 2001. **Signed by:** Tim Grieve.

Baugh went 11th overall in the 2001 draft and handled Double-A so easily in his debut that he seemed almost ready to step into the big league rotation. But his progress was halted by injuries, starting with shoulder problems that first surfaced that summer. He had surgery to fix a torn labrum and missed all of 2002, and it has been a slow climb back. Baugh still hasn't made it past Double-A, and he closed 2004 on the disabled list with a biceps ailment. The Tigers remain optimistic enough to have kept him on the 40-man roster. Baugh's velocity got back to 88-91 mph last year, enough to get by because he commands an average curveball and changeup. The key for him is to stay on top of his pitches, because his fastball and curve flatten out when he drops down. If Baugh can stay healthy in Triple-A this year, he could get his first shot in the major leagues.

Year	Club (League)	Class	W	L	ERA	G	GS	CG	SV	IP	H	R	ER	HR	BB	SO	AVG
2001	West Michigan (Mid)	A	2	1	1.59	6	6	0	0	34	31	14	6	0	10	39	.238
	Erie (EL)	AA	1	3	2.97	5	5	1	0	30	23	16	10	5	6	30	.207
2002	Did not play—Injured																
2003	Lakeland (FSL)	A	3	0	3.86	4	4	0	0	21	21	14	9	2	11	12	.263
	Erie (EL)	AA	7	9	4.60	19	19	1	0	110	111	71	56	16	32	58	.262
2004	Erie (EL)	AA	8	8	3.72	24	24	1	0	143	154	70	59	13	41	107	.274
MINOR LEAGUE TOTALS			21	21	3.73	58	58	3	0	338	340	185	140	36	100	246	.260

25 David Espinosa, of

Born: Dec. 16, 1981. **Ht.:** 6-2. **Wt.:** 190. **Bats:** B. **Throws:** R. **School:** Gulliver Prep, Miami. **Career Transactions:** Selected by Reds in first round (23rd overall) of 2000 draft; signed, Sept. 1, 2000 . . . Traded by Reds with two players to be named to Tigers for RHP Brian Moehler, 3B Matt Boone and cash, July 23, 2002; Tigers acquired OF Noochie Varner (Aug. 30, 2002) and RHP Jorge Cordova (Sept. 24, 2002) to complete trade. **Signed by:** Greg Zunino (Reds).

The Marlins considered taking Espinosa with the No. 1 overall choice in 2000, but he lasted 23 picks because of signability worries. The Reds had spent most of their draft budget before the draft, so they gave him a unique eight-year big league contract with no bonus but a guaranteed worth of $2.75 million. Halfway through that deal, he's making only slow progress toward the majors. After repeating high Class A in 2003, he had the best year of his career in Double-A in 2004, but he tailed off in the second half of the season. Espinosa can drive balls a long way and also has slightly above-average speed. But he's indecisive at the plate and doesn't put the ball in play nearly enough. He'll take walks, but he strikes out too much and needs to develop a better plan at the plate. Drafted as a shortstop, he had severe throwing problems because of his footwork and moved to second base in 2002 and the outfield in 2003. He fits best in right field, though he has seen time in center. Shifting to the outfield helps him relax and improve both his offense and defense. His best chance for a big league role is as a utilityman. He likely will head to Triple A this year.

Year	Club (League)	Class	AVG	G	AB	R	H	2B	3B	HR	RBI	BB	SO	SB	OBP	SLG
2001	Dayton (Mid)	A	.262	122	493	88	129	29	8	7	37	55	120	15	.340	.396
2002	Stockton (Cal)	A	.245	95	367	71	90	13	7	7	44	62	104	26	.356	.376
2003	Lakeland (FSL)	A	.271	92	350	57	95	18	7	4	46	50	78	13	.359	.397
2004	Erie (EL)	AA	.264	134	511	89	135	23	5	19	52	80	134	20	.366	.440
MINOR LEAGUE TOTALS			.261	443	1721	305	449	83	27	37	179	247	436	74	.355	.405

26 Mark Woodyard, rhp

Born: Dec. 19, 1978. **Ht.:** 6-2. **Wt.:** 190. **Bats:** R. **Throws:** R. **School:** Bethune-Cookman College. **Career Transactions:** Selected by Tigers in fourth round of 2000 draft; signed June 29, 2000. **Signed by:** Steve Nichols.

The Rockies drafted Woodyard twice as a first baseman before the Tigers made him a surprise fourth-round choice in 2000. Because he was raw and inexperienced, Detroit knew it would take him a while to develop. After going 15-33, 5.09 in his first four seasons, he may have found his ticket to the majors when he moved full-time to the bullpen in 2004. Woodyard always has had a good arm, and he finally started to harness it last season. He sits consistently at 92 mph with his fastball, sometimes touching 95. He also has a solid power curveball and has developed a serviceable splitter. He still has work to do, as he struggles to put hitters away and his command is still inconsistent. He's also 26, so his stuff isn't likely to get much better. Woodyard's solid performance in the Arizona Fall League cemented the Tigers' decision to protect him on the 40-man roster for the first time. He'll begin 2005 in Triple-A, with a shot of reaching Comerica Park at some point.

Year	Club (League)	Class	W	L	ERA	G	GS	CG	SV	IP	H	R	ER	HR	BB	SO	AVG
2000	Oneonta (NY-P)	A	1	5	4.59	11	9	0	0	51	48	32	26	0	39	38	.244
2001	West Michigan (Mid)	A	7	12	4.51	25	25	2	0	144	147	81	72	5	69	84	.267
2002	Lakeland (FSL)	A	2	8	7.64	17	7	0	2	66	81	62	56	10	32	22	.302
2003	Lakeland (FSL)	A	4	8	4.53	23	23	1	0	117	133	69	59	7	53	84	.287
	Erie (EL)	AA	1	0	5.56	2	2	0	0	11	14	7	7	1	5	6	.326
2004	Erie (EL)	AA	6	4	3.52	43	9	0	5	102	102	53	40	5	37	55	.263
MINOR LEAGUE TOTALS			21	37	4.76	121	75	3	7	492	525	304	260	28	235	289	.275

27 Jay Sborz, rhp

Born: Jan. 24, 1985. **Ht.:** 6-4. **Wt.:** 210. **Bats:** R. **Throws:** R. **School:** Langley HS, Great Falls, Va. **Career Transactions:** Selected by Tigers in second round of 2003 draft; signed June 30, 2003. **Signed by:** Bill Buck.

Based solely on his arm strength and sturdy, projectable frame, Sborz projected as a possible first-round pick in 2003. The Tigers got him in the second round, because his high-effort delivery and immaturity caused clubs to back off. After signing for $865,000, Sborz has pitched erratically, with just one victory to show for 20 outings in Rookie ball. Sborz can light up a radar gun, pitching at 93-95 mph with room to throw even harder. He has an arm action conducive to a power breaking ball, and his slider shows flashes of being a plus pitch. But his throwing mechanics are flawed, affecting the quality and command of his stuff. His delivery often changes from pitch to pitch. In high school, Sborz got away with just rearing back and throwing. The Tigers are attempting to refine his mechanics, but he has struggled mightily to repeat a proper delivery. Also lacking an offspeed pitch, he may profile better as a reliever. Unless he makes a drastic and unexpected improvement in spring training, Sborz likely will begin 2005 in extended spring before going to Oneonta.

Year	Club (League)	Class	W	L	ERA	G	GS	CG	SV	IP	H	R	ER	HR	BB	SO	AVG
2003	Tigers (GCL)	R	0	2	4.85	8	7	0	0	26	20	18	14	2	14	35	.206
2004	Tigers (GCL)	R	1	4	4.48	12	12	0	0	60	52	32	30	9	44	62	.230
MINOR LEAGUE TOTALS			1	6	4.60	20	19	0	0	86	72	50	44	11	58	97	.223

28 Matt Vasquez, rhp

Born: June 7, 1982. **Ht.:** 6-3. **Wt.:** 205. **Bats:** R. **Throws:** R. **School:** UC Santa Barbara. **Career Transactions:** Selected by Tigers in seventh round of 2003 draft; signed June 17, 2003. **Signed by:** Tom Hinkle.

Drafted in the seventh round by the Rangers out of high school in 2000 and again by the Tigers after three years at UC Santa Barbara, Vasquez had never won consistently until 2004. He went 14-18 for the Gauchos and 3-4 in his pro debut before leading the Midwest League in victories and innings in his first full pro season. He also kicked off West Michigan's drive to the league title with eight innings of one-hit ball in the Whitecaps' playoff opener. Though he has a strong frame, Vasquez achieved his success with location—he has the best control in the system—rather than velocity. He doesn't throw hard, usually working in the upper 80s, and his curveball and changeup are ordinary as well. He pitches above his stuff because he mixes his offerings, moves them around the strike zone and challenges hitters. While Vasquez unquestionably has feel and poise, he also was a bit old for low Class A at age 22. He still has to prove himself against more advanced hitters. Vasquez probably will start 2005 in high Class A but could start to move quickly.

Year	Club (League)	Class	W	L	ERA	G	GS	CG	SV	IP	H	R	ER	HR	BB	SO	AVG
2003	Oneonta (NY-P)	A	3	4	6.92	11	11	0	0	53	76	43	41	5	10	35	.328
2004	West Michigan (Mid)	A	14	6	3.64	27	27	0	0	168	156	73	68	14	34	120	.245
MINOR LEAGUE TOTALS			17	10	4.43	38	38	0	0	222	232	116	109	19	44	155	.267

29 Juan Francia, ss

Born: Jan. 4, 1982. **Ht.:** 5-9. **Wt.:** 150. **Bats:** B. **Throws:** R. **Career Transactions:** Signed out of Venezuela by Tigers, Aug. 28, 1998. **Signed by:** Ramon Pena.

The third season in low Class A turned out to be the charm for Francia. He finished one hit shy of winning the Midwest League batting title and served as a catalyst for West Michigan's championship club. Francia is the fastest baserunner in the system, and some scouts think that tool is enough to carry him. He's still not a particularly effective basestealer, however, as he led the MWL by getting caught stealing 19 times (in 56 attempts).

Despite his performance in 2004, there are plenty of concerns about Francia's hitting ability. He makes consistent contact, but at the expense of drawing walks or hitting for power. If he doesn't hit over .300, he's not going to be worth playing on a regular basis. Francia spent most of last season at shortstop, but fits better at second base—where he spent his first five seasons—because he lacks arm strength. He's finally ready for high Class A.

Year	Club (League)	Class	AVG	G	AB	R	H	2B	3B	HR	RBI	BB	SO	SB	OBP	SLG
1999	San Felipe (VSL)	R	.321	37	84	20	27	6	0	0	15	15	29	9	.457	.393
2000	Tigers (GCL)	R	.268	53	194	34	52	5	3	0	14	19	43	23	.336	.325
	Lakeland (FSL)	A	.225	11	40	3	9	2	0	0	0	7	9	5	.340	.275
2001	Oneonta (NY-P)	A	.340	47	191	30	65	5	2	0	8	11	32	17	.380	.387
2002	West Michigan (Mid)	A	.270	128	503	94	136	13	5	2	41	53	94	53	.346	.328
2003	West Michigan (Mid)	A	.240	118	405	49	97	7	6	0	27	42	78	31	.316	.286
2004	West Michigan (Mid)	A	.320	111	413	73	132	11	3	0	32	34	44	37	.384	.361
MINOR LEAGUE TOTALS			.283	505	1830	303	518	49	19	2	137	181	329	175	.356	.334

30 Brent Dlugach, ss

Born: March 3, 1983. **Ht.:** 6-4. **Wt.:** 200. **Bats:** R. **Throws:** R. **School:** University of Memphis. **Career Transactions:** Selected by Tigers in sixth round of 2004 draft; signed July 1, 2004. **Signed by:** Harold Zonder.

Dlugach might be 6-foot-5 and have committed 18 errors in his first 47 games as a pro, but there's no position change in his future. Though he's lanky, he's very fluid in the field, throws well and has surprisingly good footwork considering his size. He's a pure shortstop, which works in his favor because he doesn't have enough bat to play regularly at third base. Dlugach's offense remains an issue, as he never reached .300 in three seasons at Memphis and batted just .213 in his debut. He has little power, doesn't recognize pitches well and showed little discipline during the summer. He's also a below-average runner for a middle infielder. Dlugach is headed for West Michigan, where Fifth Third Ballpark favors pitchers. He'll need to make significant offensive strides to climb the ladder to the majors. His father Mike fell just short, topping out in Triple-A as a catcher in the White Sox system.

Year	Club (League)	Class	AVG	G	AB	R	H	2B	3B	HR	RBI	BB	SO	SB	OBP	SLG
2004	Oneonta (NY-P)	A	.213	47	183	17	39	7	2	1	12	8	59	5	.256	.290
MINOR LEAGUE TOTALS			.213	47	183	17	39	7	2	1	12	8	59	5	.256	.290

FLORIDA
MARLINS

BY **MIKE BERARDINO**

En route to a World Series title and Baseball America's Organization of the Year award in 2003, the Marlins dipped liberally into their farm system. Both in lightning-bolt callups such as **Miguel Cabrera** and Dontrelle Willis, and trade pieces such as Denny Bautista and 2000 No. 1 overall draft pick Adrian Gonzalez, they found creative and essential uses for their prospects.

Opportunities weren't as plentiful in 2004 for those in the minors, and the falloff was such that South Florida baseball writers chose not to name a Marlins rookie of the year at the big league level. When a spate of doubleheaders and an injury to A.J. Burnett left Florida looking for a starter in the middle of September's wild-card push, the assignment fell by default to righthander Logan Kensing—who was promoted from high Class A. Though he has a solid future, Kensing went 0-3, 12.65 in three fill-in starts with the season on the line.

On the positive side, the Marlins didn't have to raid their system as much as they had the year before. They did ship off slick-fielding shortstop Wilson Valdez to get setup man Billy Koch from the White Sox in June, a deal they might like to have back. At the July trading deadline, they put left-hander Bill Murphy, their only Futures Game representative, in a six-player blockbuster with the Dodgers that brought Guillermo Mota, Paul Lo Duca and Juan Encarnacion back east. They also parted with low Class A swingman Travis Chick to

get Ismael Valdez from the Padres, and Chick promptly saw his velocity and effectiveness jump.

Florida's minor league teams finished a combined 63 games under .500, and only Double-A Carolina among the top five affiliates finished with a winning record. That's evidence the system isn't as strong as it was when BA rated it among the game's 10 best entering each year from 1999-2003. But the Marlins would willingly pay that price again if it meant another championship.

They did restock their system through the 2004 draft. Second-year scouting director Stan Meek took college lefthanders with his first two picks, and Taylor Tankersley and Jason Vargas immediately surged onto our Marlins Top 10 Prospects list. They could move quickly through the system.

Florida grabbed a pair of athletic high school outfielders in rounds three and four, and both Greg Burns and Jamar Walton showed considerable potential in Rookie ball. Fifth-rounder Brad Davis, who caught Vargas at Long Beach State, also showed fine all-around skills.

As the Marlins try to rejuvenate their system, they appointed Brian Chattin to oversee it. Chattin was promoted to farm director in December after serving as an assistant to his predecessor, Marc DelPiano. DelPiano now works with Fred Ferreira in the club's international operations department.

TOP 30 PROSPECTS

1. Jeremy Hermida, of
2. Scott Olsen, lhp
3. Yorman Bazardo, rhp
4. Jason Stokes, 1b
5. Josh Willingham, c/1b
6. Eric Reed, of
7. Taylor Tankersley, lhp
8. Jason Vargas, lhp
9. Robert Andino, ss
10. Trevor Hutchinson, rhp
11. Josh Johnson, rhp
12. Josh Wilson, ss
13. Luke Hagerty, lhp
14. Randy Messenger, rhp
15. Rick Vandenhurk, rhp
16. Jai Miller, of
17. Greg Burns, of
18. Logan Kensing, rhp
19. Jamar Walton, of
20. Chris Resop, rhp
21. Jon Fulton, 3b/ss
22. Rodrigo Rosario, rhp
23. Jose Campusano, ss
24. Franklyn Gracesqui, lhp
25. Ronald Belizario, rhp
26. Cole Seifrig, 2b
27. Allen Baxter, rhp
28. Chris Aguila, of
29. Lincoln Holdzkom, rhp
30. Jeff Allison, rhp

ORGANIZATION OVERVIEW

General manager: Larry Beinfest. **Farm director:** Brian Chattin. **Scouting director:** Stan Meek.

2004 PERFORMANCE

Class	Team	League	W	L	Pct.	Finish*	Manager
Majors	Florida	National	83	79	.512	9th (16)	Jack McKeon
Triple-A	Albuquerque Isotopes	Pacific Coast	67	77	.465	12th (16)	Tracy Woodson
Double-A	Carolina Mudcats	Southern	73	66	.525	t-2nd (10)	Ron Hassey
High A	Jupiter Hammerheads	Florida State	64	71	.474	8th (12)	Luis Dorante
Low A	Greensboro Bats	South Atlantic	50	89	.360	15th (16)	Steve Phillips
Short-season	Jamestown Jammers	New York-Penn	30	45	.400	12th (14)	Benny Castillo
Rookie	GCL Marlins	Gulf Coast	31	29	.517	t-6th (12)	Tim Cossins
OVERALL 2004 MINOR LEAGUE RECORD			315	377	.455	27th (30)	

*Finish in overall standings (No. of teams in league).

ORGANIZATION LEADERS

BATTING
*Minimum 250 At-Bats

*AVG	Larry Sutton, Albuquerque	.370
R	Joe Dillon, Albuquerque/Carolina	122
H	Joe Dillon, Albuquerque/Carolina	171
TB	Joe Dillon, Albuquerque/Carolina	348
2B	Joe Dillon, Albuquerque/Carolina	46
3B	Joe Dillon, Albuquerque/Carolina	7
HR	Joe Dillon, Albuquerque/Carolina	39
RBI	Joe Dillon, Albuquerque/Carolina	117
BB	Josh Willingham, Carolina	91
SO	Jai Miller, Greensboro	163
SB	Billy Hall, Albuquerque/Carolina	40
*OBP	Larry Sutton, Albuquerque	.472
*SLG	Larry Sutton, Albuquerque	.682

PITCHING
#Minimum 75 Innings

W	Nic Ungs, Carolina	11
	Ross Wolf, Jupiter	11
L	Jon Nickerson, Greensboro/Jamestown	13
#ERA	Ross Wolf, Jupiter	2.60
G	Randy Messenger, Carolina	58
CG	Yorman Bazardo, Jupiter	2
	Aaron Small, Albuquerque	2
SV	Randy Messenger, Carolina	21
IP	Peter Bauer, Albuquerque/Carolina	162
BB	Bill Murphy, Carolina	59
SO	Adam Bostick, Greensboro	163

BEST TOOLS

Best Hitter for Average	Jeremy Hermida
Best Power Hitter	Jason Stokes
Best Strike-Zone Discipline	Josh Willingham
Fastest Baserunner	Eric Reed
Best Athlete	Jai Miller
Best Fastball	Yorman Bazardo
Best Curveball	Allen Baxter
Best Slider	Scott Olsen
Best Changeup	Mike Neu
Best Control	Nic Ungs
Best Defensive Catcher	Ryan Jorgensen
Best Defensive Infielder	Robert Andino
Best Infield Arm	Robert Andino
Best Defensive Outfielder	Eric Reed
Best Outfield Arm	Angel Molina

PROJECTED 2008 LINEUP

Catcher	Josh Willingham
First Base	Carlos Delgado
Second Base	Luis Castillo
Third Base	Mike Lowell
Shortstop	Alex Gonzalez
Left Field	Miguel Cabrera
Center Field	Juan Pierre
Right Field	Jeremy Hermida
No. 1 Starter	Josh Beckett
No. 2 Starter	A.J. Burnett
No. 3 Starter	Dontrelle Willis
No. 4 Starter	Scott Olsen
No. 5 Starter	Yorman Bazardo
Closer	Guillermo Mota

LAST YEAR'S TOP 20 PROSPECTS

1. Jeremy Hermida, of	11. Lincoln Holdzkom, rhp
2. Jason Stokes, 1b	12. Cole Seifrig, 2b
3. Jeff Allison, rhp	13. Lee Mitchell, 3b/ss
4. Scott Olsen, lhp	14. Ronald Belizario, rhp
5. Yorman Bazardo, rhp	15. Robert Andino, ss
6. Josh Willingham, c	16. Kevin Cave, rhp
7. Bill Murphy, lhp	17. Wilson Valdez, ss/2b
8. Eric Reed, of	18. Chris Aguila, of
9. Jai Miller, of	19. Franklyn Gracesqui, lhp
10. Trevor Hutchinson, rhp	20. Jon-Michael Nickerson, lhp

TOP PROSPECTS OF THE DECADE

Year	Player, Pos.	Current Team
1995	Charles Johnson, c	Rockies
1996	Edgar Renteria, ss	Red Sox
1997	Felix Heredia, lhp	Yankees
1998	Mark Kotsay, of	Athletics
1999	A.J. Burnett, rhp	Marlins
2000	A.J. Burnett, rhp	Marlins
2001	Josh Beckett, rhp	Marlins
2002	Josh Beckett, rhp	Marlins
2003	Miguel Cabrera, 3b	Marlins
2004	Jeremy Hermida, of	Marlins

TOP DRAFT PICKS OF THE DECADE

Year	Player, Pos.	Current Team
1995	Jaime Jones, of	Royals
1996	Mark Kotsay, of	Athletics
1997	Aaron Akin, rhp	Out of baseball
1998	Chip Ambres, of	Marlins
1999	Josh Beckett, rhp	Marlins
2000	Adrian Gonzalez, 1b	Rangers
2001	Garrett Berger, rhp (2)	Brewers
2002	Jeremy Hermida, of	Marlins
2003	Jeff Allison, rhp	Marlins
2004	Taylor Tankersley, lhp	Marlins

ALL-TIME LARGEST BONUSES

Josh Beckett, 1999	$3,625,000
Adrian Gonzalez, 2000	$3,000,000
Livan Hernandez, 1996	$2,500,000
Jason Stokes, 2000	$2,027,000
Jeremy Hermida, 2002	$2,012,500

MINOR LEAGUE DEPTH CHART

Florida MARLINS

Impact Potential: B

In Jeremy Hermida and Scott Olsen, the Marlins have two premium prospects, a lefthanded hitter and a lefty pitcher, who rank among the top five at their positions in the minors. Josh Willingham is ready to hit in any lineup, but needs to find a defined position. The stable of power arms in high Class A Jupiter's 2004 rotation should provide at least one middle-of-the-rotation pitcher.

Depth: C

Olsen and 2004 draftees Taylor Tankersley and Jason Vargas give the Marlins an enviable group of lefthanders. Florida's pitching depth looks good on the other side, too, bolstered by international signees such as Yorman Bazardo (Venezuela) and Rick Vandenhurk (Netherlands). In the field, the Marlins are teeming with athletes, but hitters like Willingham—who can work counts and take every at-bat seriously—are too few and far between.

*Depth charts prepared by **John Manuel** and **Allan Simpson**. Numbers in parentheses indicate prospect rankings.*

LF
Pablo Sosa
Travis Ezi
Jose Aponte

CF
Eric Reed (6)
Jai Miller (16)
Greg Burns (17)
Xavier Arroyo

3B
Jonathan Fulton (21)
Brad McCann
Lee Mitchell
Joe Dillon

SS
Robert Andino (9)
Josh Wilson (12)
Jose Campusano (23)
Rex Rundgren

RF
Jeremy Hermida (1)
Jamar Walton (19)
Chris Aguila (28)
Angel Molina
Matt Padgett

2B
Cole Seifrig (26)
Dusty Wathan
Chris Bass
Matt DeMarco
Brian Cleveland

1B
Jason Stokes (4)
Eliezer Alfonzo
Ryan Bear
J.T. Restko

SOURCE of TALENT

HOMEGROWN		ACQUIRED	
College	6	Trades	0
Junior College	1	Rule 5 draft	3
Draft-and-follow	0	Independent leagues	0
High School	17	Free agents/waivers	0
Nondrafted free agent	0		
Foreign	3		

C
Josh Willingham (5)
Brad Davis
Matt Treanor
Ryan Jorgensen

LHP

Starters	Relievers
Scott Olsen (2)	Frank Gracesqui (24)
Taylor Tankersley (7)	Zach McCormack
Jason Vargas (8)	Matt Yourkin
Luke Hagerty (13)	Craig Lybarger
David Marchbanks	
Jon Nickerson	
Adam Bostick	
Jeff Gogal	

RHP

Starters	Relievers
Yorman Bazardo (3)	Randy Messenger (14)
Trevor Hutchinson (10)	Chris Resop (20)
Josh Johnson (11)	Rodrigo Rosario (22)
Rick Vandenhurk (15)	Ronald Belizario (25)
Logan Kensing (18)	Lincoln Holdzkom (29)
Allen Baxter (27)	Mike Neu
Jeff Allison (30)	Mike Flannery
Nic Ungs	Esequier Pie
Ryan Warpinski	Carlos Martinez
Jeff Fulchino	James Russ
	Ross Wolf

DRAFT ANALYSIS

2004

Best Pro Debut: No longer splitting time between pitching and DH as he did at Long Beach State, LHP Jason Vargas (2) excelled. He went 5-2, 2.09 in 11 starts and worked the first seven innings of a combined no-hitter in his second outing after a promotion to low Class A.

Best Athlete: OF Jamar Walton (4) was an all-Virginia performer in baseball, basketball and football. He has the best combination of power and speed among Marlins draftees.

Best Pure Hitter: 3B Brad McCann (6) has an advanced approach and a natural feel for hitting, as might be expected for someone whose father Howard is a former college coach (Marshall). 1B Nathan Messner (18) used a short stroke to hit .310 in the Rookie-level Gulf Coast League.

Best Raw Power: Playing high school ball in White Salmon, Wash. (pop. 1,861), OF Brandon Verley (15) was relatively unknown until he started unleashing tape-measure shots last spring. INF/OF Brett Carroll (10) hit six homers at short-season Jamestown, including a 420-foot blast.

Fastest Runner: OFs Greg Burns (3) and Joe Pietro (9) are both 80 runners on the 20-80 scouting scale. Burns does it a little easier, gliding 60 yards in 6.4 seconds and sprinting from the left side of the plate to first in 3.6 seconds on a drag bunt.

Best Defensive Player: C Brad Davis (5) played first base and right field at Long Beach State in 2003 because Todd Jennings, who became a second-round pick of the Giants, was behind the plate. Davis is very athletic and has solid catch-and-throw skills. He also has a chance to hit.

Best Fastball: Vargas usually pitches at

McCann

91-94 mph, slightly harder than LHP Taylor Tankersley (1), who works at 90-93.

Best Breaking Ball: The Marlins drafted Tankersley ahead of Vargas because he has a better breaking ball. Tankersley's hard slider is the best breaking pitch in this draft crop.

Most Intriguing Background: McCann's brother Brian also has a baseball connection, as he's a top catching prospect in the Braves system. Vargas is the nephew of former big leaguer Randy Velarde. C John Parker Wilson (19) was a Parade all-America quarterback who's playing football at Alabama. OF Ted Ledbetter (23) was the NAIA player of the year after hitting .504-20-90 at Oklahoma City. But after going 2-for-9 in three pro games, he abruptly retired. LHP Parrish Castor (31) had a 20-strikeout game for St. Anselm (N.H.) in May. RHP Aaron Easton (29) is 6-foot-10 and originally attended college on a partial Nordic skiing scholarship.

Closest To The Majors: Tankersley and Vargas rank neck and neck.

Best Late-Round Pick: Messner. Verley's power could be a steal in the 15th round.

The One Who Got Away: The Marlins signed their first 16 picks, but couldn't persuade Wilson to give up football.

Assessment: With Tankersley and Vargas joining Scott Olsen in the system, Florida's rotation could have a decidedly lefty look in a few years. The Marlins also maintained their usual focus on athleticism and speed.

2003 RHP Jeff Allison (1) looked like a steal with the 16th overall pick, but now it looks like drug addiction will ruin his career before it really got started. Several of the other choices had disappointing 2004 seasons, with RHP Logan Kensing (2) a rare exception. *GRADE:* D

2002 OF Jeremy Hermida (1) and LHP Scott Olsen (6) are easily the top two prospects in the system. OF Eric Reed (9), SS Robert Andino (2) and RHP Trevor Hutchinson (3) also rank among the best Florida has to offer. *GRADE:* B+

2001 The Marlins didn't have a first-round pick, and their top two choices, RHPs Garrett Berger (2) and Allen Baxter (3), have barely pitched because of arm problems. *GRADE:* F

2000 1Bs Adrian Gonzalez (1) and Jason Stokes (2) started off strong, but they've regressed. Florida did parlay Gonzalez, LHP Rob Henkel (3) and OF Will Smith (6) into deals for Ugueth Urbina and Mark Redman in the 2003 World Series drive. C/1B Josh Willingham (17) was a nice find. *GRADE:* B

Draft analysis prepared by Jim Callis. Numbers in parentheses indicate draft rounds.

Jeremy
HERMIDA

Born: Jan. 30, 1984.
Ht.: 6-4. **Wt.:** 200.
Bats: L. **Throws:** R.
School: Wheeler HS, Marietta, Ga.
Career Transactions: Selected by Marlins in first round (11th overall) of 2002 draft; signed July 5, 2002.
Signed by: Joel Smith.

A s a high school senior, Hermida went from a decent prospect seemingly destined for Clemson to a possible top-three selection. Baseball America rated him the top pure hitter on the prep level and the fourth-best position player overall in the 2002 draft, and the Marlins were pleased when he was still available for them with the No. 11 pick. The Marlins chose him over high school lefthander Scott Kazmir, then gave Hermida a $2.0125 million signing bonus. His father groomed his hitting ability, converting him from a righthanded hitter to a lefty at age 4, having him practice with wood bats starting when he was 13 and hiring former big leaguer Terry Harper as a private instructor. Though Hermida missed nearly five weeks early in 2004 with a pulled right hamstring, he still managed to set career highs in batting average, slugging percentage and homers. He ranks as the organization's top prospect for the second straight year, the first Marlin to accomplish that feat since Josh Beckett (2001-02).

Hermida has a polished hitting approach. He has a smooth, quick stroke, advanced plate discipline for his age, a strong work ethic and good makeup. He's comfortable working deep in counts and projects to have power to all fields. For now, he's mainly content to line singles and doubles to the opposite field. Hermida has drawn comparisons to a slew of all-stars. Some scouts called him the best high school hitter since Eric Chavez, others likened him to Paul O'Neill and Andy Van Slyke, and Hermida saw himself more along the lines of Shawn Green. The Marlins would be happy if he resembles any of those hitters and believe he will. He has slightly above-average speed and even better instincts on the bases. He has 38 steals in 43 tries over the last two seasons and projects to swipe 20 bases a year in the majors. He has average arm strength.

He has come a long way defensively, but Hermida still needs to improve his jumps, routes and the accuracy of his throws in right field. It would help if he showed as much interest in his defense as his hitting. He projects as at least a 25-homer threat in the big leagues, but he has adjustments to make first. He'll have to add lift to his swing, learn to pull inside pitches for power and add bulk on his frame. He showed developing power in the Arizona Fall League, hitting seven home runs. Durability is a minor concern, as injuries have bothered Hermida in each of his first three seasons. He dealt with an ankle problem in 2002 and a heel injury in 2003.

After his solid showing in the AFL, where he was one of the youngest players, Hermida should start 2005 at Double-A Carolina. If he shows he can handle that level, he could reach the majors by the end of the year. The Marlins have Juan Encarnacion under contract at $4.4 million through 2005, but they hope Hermida will be ready to take over as their everyday right fielder in 2006.

Year	Club (League)	Class	AVG	G	AB	R	H	2B	3B	HR	RBI	BB	SO	SB	OBP	SLG
2002	Marlins (GCL)	R	.224	38	134	15	30	7	3	0	14	15	25	5	.316	.321
	Jamestown (NY-P)	A	.319	13	47	8	15	2	1	0	7	7	10	1	.407	.404
2003	Greensboro (SAL)	A	.284	133	468	73	133	23	5	6	49	80	100	28	.387	.393
	Albuquerque (PCL)	AAA	.000	1	3	0	0	0	0	0	0	0	3	0	.000	.000
2004	Jupiter (FSL)	A	.297	91	340	53	101	17	1	10	50	42	73	10	.377	.441
MINOR LEAGUE TOTALS			.281	276	992	149	279	49	10	16	120	144	211	44	.374	.399

Scott Olsen, lhp

Born: Jan. 12, 1984. **Ht.:** 6-4. **Wt.:** 170. **Bats:** L. **Throws:** L. **School:** Crystal Lake (Ill.) South HS. **Career Transactions:** Selected by Marlins in sixth round of 2002 draft; signed June 9, 2002. **Signed by:** Scot Engler.

Olsen was relatively unknown and had mechanical problems in high school, so the Marlins got him in the sixth round and signed him for $160,000. Jeff Schwarz, his pitching coach in the Rookie-level Gulf Coast League, smoothed him out in his pro debut, and now he's one of the game's top lefty prospects. Olsen continues to increase his velocity, and he now pitches at 91-93 mph and tops out at 96. His fastball has late life and he has tightened his slider to give it more depth. He's learning to use his slider as an out pitch. He's confident and aggressive, with a bit of a mean streak. Olsen has a tendency to leave his fastball up in the zone and he needs to use his changeup much more than he's willing to now. His slight frame could use another 15-20 pounds of muscle. He needs to add maturity and learn to control his emotions better on the mound. For the second straight year, Olsen finished strong. He went 3-0, 0.78 in his final six starts at high Class A Jupiter, showing he's ready for Double-A. He could land in the majors as soon as he shows he's ready.

Year	Club (League)	Class	W	L	ERA	G	GS	CG	SV	IP	H	R	ER	HR	BB	SO	AVG
2002	Marlins (GCL)	R	2	3	2.96	13	11	0	0	52	39	18	17	0	17	50	.204
2003	Greensboro (SAL)	A	7	9	2.81	25	24	0	0	128	101	51	40	4	59	129	.220
2004	Jupiter (FSL)	A	7	6	2.97	25	25	1	0	136	127	57	45	8	54	158	.246
MINOR LEAGUE TOTALS			16	18	2.90	63	60	1	0	316	267	126	102	12	130	337	.229

Yorman Bazardo, rhp

Born: July 11, 1984. **Ht.:** 6-2. **Wt.:** 170. **Bats:** R. **Throws:** R. **Career Transactions:** Signed out of Venezuela by Marlins, July 19, 2000. **Signed by:** Miguel Garcia.

Signed for $85,000 out of Venezuela by former Marlins scout Miguel Garcia, Bazardo might have the best overall arm in the system. Part of a talented pitching staff at Jupiter in 2004, Bazardo distinguished himself in that company. The Marlins designated him one of four untouchables in their system at the July trade deadline. Bazardo's long limbs allow him to deliver a 92-94 mph fastball that has touched 98 as late as the eighth inning. He has good action on his sinker, and also throws a plus changeup and a developing slider. He junked his curveball early in the year to concentrate on his slider. He's aggressive, going right at hitters, and gets lots of quick outs. He has excellent makeup. Bazardo tired late in the season and was pitching closer to 90 mph, but the Marlins aren't concerned about that. His mechanics still go out of whack from time to time, and he sometimes tries to manipulate his changeup instead of letting it work naturally. He doesn't miss as many bats as he should with his stuff. The Marlins will be careful not to rush Bazardo, but he isn't that far away from the majors. He'll open 2005 in Double-A.

Year	Club (League)	Class	W	L	ERA	G	GS	CG	SV	IP	H	R	ER	HR	BB	SO	AVG
2001	Ciudad Alianza (VSL)	R	7	2	2.43	12	12	1	0	70	59	26	19	0	18	62	—
2002	Jamestown (NY-P)	A	5	0	2.72	25	0	0	6	36	39	11	11	0	6	26	.275
2003	Greensboro (SAL)	A	9	8	3.12	21	21	4	0	130	132	56	45	8	26	70	.261
2004	Jupiter (FSL)	A	5	9	3.27	25	25	2	0	154	161	78	56	3	30	95	.266
MINOR LEAGUE TOTALS			26	19	3.02	83	58	7	6	391	391	171	131	11	80	253	.265

Jason Stokes, 1b

Born: Jan. 23, 1982. **Ht.:** 6-4. **Wt.:** 225. **Bats:** R. **Throws:** R. **School:** Coppell (Texas) HS. **Career Transactions:** Selected by Marlins in second round of 2000 draft; signed Aug. 29, 2000. **Signed by:** Bob Laurie.

Stokes would have gone early in the first round as the top high school power hitter in the 2000 draft, but his commitment to the University of Texas dropped him to the first pick in the second round. After signing for $2.027 million, he eventually surpassed 2000's No. 1 overall pick, Adrian Gonzalez, in Florida's plans. That led to Gonzalez' inclusion in a 2003 trade for Ugueth Urbina. Stokes' greatest tool remains his powerful bat. He shows prodigious power to all fields. He runs well for a big man and has decent hands. His high strikeout totals have inspired some doubts, and Stokes never shortens his long swing, not even with two strikes. He has poor lateral movement, which means he'll never be more than average at best as a first baseman. His left wrist required a bone graft in 2002 and flared up again last season. He may require another operation. If the Marlins fully believed in Stokes, they wouldn't have signed Carlos Delgado to a four-year, $52 million contract in January. Stokes now looks like a prime piece of trade bait, if he can show he can stay healthy for a full season. He could return to Double-A to start 2005.

Year	Club (League)	Class	AVG	G	AB	R	H	2B	3B	HR	RBI	BB	SO	SB	OBP	SLG
2001	Utica (NY-P)	A	.231	35	130	12	30	2	1	6	19	11	48	0	.299	.400
2002	Kane County (Mid)	A	.341	97	349	73	119	25	0	27	75	47	96	1	.421	.645
2003	Jupiter (FSL)	A	.258	121	462	67	119	31	3	17	89	36	135	6	.312	.448
2004	Carolina (SL)	AA	.272	106	394	66	107	26	0	23	78	42	121	5	.345	.513
MINOR LEAGUE TOTALS			.281	359	1335	218	375	84	4	73	261	136	400	12	.350	.514

5 Josh Willingham, c/1b

Born: Feb. 17, 1979. **Ht.:** 6-1. **Wt.:** 200. **Bats:** R. **Throws:** R. **School:** University of North Alabama. **Career Transactions:** Selected by Marlins in 17th round of 2000 draft; signed June 8, 2000. **Signed by:** Larry Keller.

With Stokes and Miguel Cabrera blocking him at the corner-infield spots, Willingham tried catching in instructional league in 2002. He has made enough strides to handle a surprising jump from Double-A to the majors last July. He led the minor leagues in on-base percentage. Willingham has made himself into the best hitter in the system. He has a short swing, power to all fields and a willingness to work counts, a rarity for the tools-first Marlins. He's instinctive and has a great work ethic. He has solid-average arm strength and works hard at calling a game. Because he's a late-comer to catching, Willingham might run out of time to make the full transition. He could wind up like Craig Wilson, bouncing from first to the outfield and slugging all the way. Staying healthy has been a concern, as persistent knee problems undercut his 2003 season and have made him a below-average runner. When the Marlins signed Paul Lo Duca to a three-year contract, they probably closed the door on Willingham starting behind the plate for them. But he could help the big league club in a utility role.

Year	Club (League)	Class	AVG	G	AB	R	H	2B	3B	HR	RBI	BB	SO	SB	OBP	SLG
2000	Utica (NY-P)	A	.263	65	205	37	54	16	0	6	29	39	55	9	.400	.429
2001	Kane County (Mid)	A	.259	97	320	57	83	20	2	7	36	53	85	24	.382	.400
2002	Jupiter (FSL)	A	.274	107	376	72	103	21	4	17	69	63	88	18	.394	.487
2003	Jupiter (FSL)	A	.264	59	193	46	51	17	1	12	34	46	42	9	.422	.549
	Carolina (SL)	AA	.299	22	67	15	20	2	1	5	14	13	20	0	.434	.582
	Marlins (GCL)	R	.429	2	7	3	3	1	0	1	3	1	2	0	.500	1.000
2004	Florida (NL)	MAJ	.200	12	25	2	5	0	0	1	1	4	8	0	.310	.320
	Carolina (SL)	AA	.281	112	338	81	95	24	0	24	76	91	87	6	.449	.565
MAJOR LEAGUE TOTALS			.200	12	25	2	5	0	0	1	1	4	8	0	.310	.320
MINOR LEAGUE TOTALS			.272	464	1506	311	409	101	8	72	261	306	379	66	.412	.493

6 Eric Reed, of

Born: Dec. 2, 1980. **Ht.:** 5-11. **Wt.:** 170. **Bats:** L. **Throws:** L. **School:** Texas A&M University. **Career Transactions:** Selected by Marlins in ninth round of 2002 draft; signed June 6, 2002. **Signed by:** Dennis Cardoza.

Reed led the Cape Cod League in hitting in 2001 but fell in the 2002 draft after a poor junior season. Despite a wiry frame, he's a former high school powerlifting champion who squatted 450 pounds at Texas A&M. He missed the last three months in 2004 after breaking his wrist in a bar fight. Reed has 80 speed, regularly timed at 3.8 seconds to first base. Often compared to Marlins center fielder Juan Pierre, he may be faster and a better defender. He's a tremendous bunter with gap power. His arm is average. Reed still strikes out too much for his skill set. He must do a better job of sticking to his strike zone and not expanding with two strikes. Taking more pitches would help as well. He's in great shape and has just 3 percent body fat, but he still needs to add bulk to his upper body. To scrape off rust, Reed played in the Arizona Fall League after the 2004 season. He figures to return to Double-A, where he'll continue to prepare himself as Pierre's eventual replacement. Pierre could receive a huge bump through arbitration after 2005, which could add urgency to Reed's development.

Year	Club (League)	Class	AVG	G	AB	R	H	2B	3B	HR	RBI	BB	SO	SB	OBP	SLG
2002	Jamestown (NY-P)	A	.308	60	250	35	77	5	1	0	17	17	30	19	.348	.336
	Kane County (Mid)	A	.360	12	50	11	18	1	0	0	2	3	11	7	.396	.380
2003	Jupiter (FSL)	A	.300	134	514	86	154	15	8	0	25	52	83	53	.367	.360
2004	Carolina (SL)	AA	.306	55	222	32	68	9	6	3	14	14	55	24	.345	.441
MINOR LEAGUE TOTALS			.306	261	1036	164	317	30	15	3	58	86	179	103	.359	.373

Taylor Tankersley, lhp

Born: March 7, 1983. **Ht.:** 6-2. **Wt.:** 225. **Bats:** L. **Throws:** L. **School:** University of Alabama. **Career Transactions:** Selected by Marlins in first round (27th overall) of 2004 draft; signed July 9, 2004. **Signed by:** Dave Dangler.

The son of a nuclear physicist, Tankersley gets his sporting genes from his paternal grandfather, Earl Tankersley, who pitched briefly in the minors. He taught his grandson the importance of pitching inside at an early age. The lessons paid off, as Tankersley became the 27th pick in the 2004 draft. Tankersley's best pitch is a plus slider. His fastball usually ranges from 90-93 mph. He shows a bulldog mentality and throws from a low three-quarters arm slot, making him particularly tough on lefties. He throws strikes and has great versatility having started and relieved in college. Tankersley doesn't have an overpowering fastball and his velocity sometimes dips into the high 80s. Refining his changeup would make his heater more effective. His emotions sometimes get the best of him, and he must watch his weight. With his college background and maturity level, both physical and mental, Tankersley should move quickly through the system. Though he could get to the majors quicker as a reliever, the Marlins will leave him in the rotation at low Class A Greensboro so he can develop fully.

Year	Club (League)	Class	W	L	ERA	G	GS	CG	SV	IP	H	R	ER	HR	BB	SO	AVG
2004	Jamestown (NY-P)	A	1	1	3.38	6	6	0	0	27	21	14	10	2	8	32	.208
MINOR LEAGUE TOTALS			1	1	3.38	6	6	0	0	27	21	14	10	2	8	32	.208

Jason Vargas, lhp

Born: Feb. 2, 1983. **Ht.:** 6-0. **Wt.:** 215. **Bats:** L. **Throws:** L. **School:** Long Beach State University. **Career Transactions:** Selected by Marlins in second round of 2004 draft; signed July 6, 2004. **Signed by:** Robby Corsaro.

Vargas was a two-way player during a circuitous college career that saw him spend a year each at Louisiana State, Cypress (Calif.) JC and Long Beach State. He's the nephew of former major league infielder Randy Velarde. Vargas has good arm strength, working at 91-94 mph with his fastball. His tight slider is a putaway pitch against lefties. His changeup has good downward action at times and could become a plus pitch. He works quickly and goes right after hitters. He has sound mechanics and command. Some scouts wonder if Vargas may wind up as a reliever because he has just one plus pitch against righthanders. Though he has a good physique, there's some concern about potential weight gain in his lower half. He tired near the end of the year after a promotion to low Class A, but that's typical for first-year players. Vargas should stay with top draft pick Taylor Tankersley, beginning 2005 back at Greensboro. If he continues to show the progress he made in his pro debut, he'll reach high Class A by season's end.

Year	Club (League)	Class	W	L	ERA	G	GS	CG	SV	IP	H	R	ER	HR	BB	SO	AVG
2004	Jamestown (NY-P)	A	3	1	1.96	8	8	0	0	41	35	17	9	2	13	41	.224
	Greensboro (SAL)	A	2	1	2.37	3	3	0	0	19	9	5	5	1	2	17	.143
MINOR LEAGUE TOTALS			5	2	2.09	11	11	0	0	60	44	22	14	3	15	58	.201

Robert Andino, ss

Born: April 25, 1984. **Ht.:** 6-0. **Wt.:** 170. **Bats:** R. **Throws:** R. **School:** Southridge HS, Miami. **Career Transactions:** Selected by Marlins in second round of 2002 draft; signed Aug. 4, 2002. **Signed by:** John Martin.

After signing for $750,000, Andino hit just .188 in his full-season debut. He got off to another slow start in 2004, batting .141 through early May before he suddenly began producing at the plate. He hit .313 the rest of the way. Andino has tremendous range, a plus arm and a little flair at shortstop. His defense is his biggest asset and will get him to the big leagues. He does have plus bat speed, and he shored up some of the holes in his swing. He learned to stay back on offspeed pitches and trusted his hands more. He's figuring out how to put his good speed to use on the bases. Andino will have to prove his offensive resurgence was no fluke. He needs to get stronger after fading at the end of 2004. He takes plays off occasionally and sometimes flips throws to first base. While Josh Wilson has a head start in the race to eventually replace Alex Gonzalez, Andino could catch and pass Wilson by the time the change is made. He figures to begin the season back in high Class A.

Year	Club (League)	Class	AVG	G	AB	R	H	2B	3B	HR	RBI	BB	SO	SB	OBP	SLG
2002	Marlins (GCL)	R	.259	9	27	2	7	0	0	0	2	5	6	3	.364	.259
	Jamestown (NY-P)	A	.167	9	36	2	6	1	1	0	3	1	9	1	.189	.250
2003	Greensboro (SAL)	A	.188	119	416	45	78	17	2	2	27	46	128	6	.266	.252
2004	Greensboro (SAL)	A	.281	76	295	27	83	10	1	8	46	18	83	9	.321	.403
	Jupiter (FSL)	A	.281	48	196	18	55	7	2	0	15	7	43	6	.304	.337
MINOR LEAGUE TOTALS			.236	261	970	94	229	35	6	10	93	77	269	25	.290	.315

10 Trevor Hutchinson, rhp

Born: Oct. 8, 1979. **Ht.:** 6-5. **Wt.:** 220. **Bats:** R. **Throws:** R. **School:** University of California. **Career Transactions:** Selected by Marlins in third round of 2002 draft; signed Feb. 24, 2003. **Signed by:** John Hughes.

The younger brother of former Cardinals pitcher and current Chicago Bears quarterback Chad Hutchinson, Trevor has far better command this his sibling. Drafted as a college senior in 2002, he held out for almost nine months before signing for $375,000. When he's on, Hutchinson throws a heavy sinker at 89-91 mph. His slider and changeup are solid-average pitches. He has outstanding makeup and a good feel for pitching, changing speeds and eye levels on unsuspecting hitters. He's a strike-thrower who produces lots of groundballs. A minor elbow problem dropped Hutchinson's velocity into the mid-80s and sidelined him for six weeks in 2004. An MRI failed to turn up anything definitive, and the condition was written off as arm fatigue. Muscle spasms in his right shoulder ended his Arizona Fall League stint after two starts; another MRI came up negative. Hutchinson projects as a fourth starter and could emerge initially as a workhorse set-up man. He figures to return to Double-A for a third straight year, but could reach Florida by midseason.

Year	Club (League)	Class	W	L	ERA	G	GS	CG	SV	IP	H	R	ER	HR	BB	SO	AVG
2003	Jupiter (FSL)	A	9	2	2.77	14	13	2	0	84	77	30	26	3	16	58	.243
	Carolina (SL)	AA	3	3	3.86	8	6	0	0	35	32	21	15	1	13	18	.244
2004	Carolina (SL)	AA	10	7	4.23	24	24	0	0	123	133	70	58	11	38	86	.281
MINOR LEAGUE TOTALS			22	12	3.67	46	43	2	0	243	242	121	99	15	67	162	.263

11 Josh Johnson, rhp

Born: Jan. 31, 1984. **Ht.:** 6-7. **Wt.:** 220. **Bats:** L. **Throws:** R. **School:** Jenks HS, Tulsa, Okla. **Career Transactions:** Selected by Marlins in fourth round of 2002 draft; signed June 8, 2002. **Signed by:** Darrell Brown.

Johnson roared out of the gate in his first exposure to high Class A, but the wins were harder to come by after a strong first month. He still impressed club brass with his smooth mechanics and solid all-around effort. He has added velocity since signing for $300,000 out of high school, due in part to mechanical changes and to physical maturation. He pitches at 91-93 mph and tops out at 96 mph. His changeup and slider showed progress. Johnson was shut down shortly after signing with shoulder tendinitis and a pulled hip flexor. He has bounced back and avoided injury since. In fact, he got stronger as the year went along. He has excellent makeup and mound presence. He has the aggressiveness to match his large frame, but does a good job of keeping his emotions under control. Some see him as a future innings-eater in the Carl Pavano mode. Johnson figures to keep improving as he climbs the ladder. He will probably start 2005 at Double-A.

Year	Club (League)	Class	W	L	ERA	G	GS	CG	SV	IP	H	R	ER	HR	BB	SO	AVG
2002	Marlins (GGL)	R	2	0	0.60	4	3	0	0	15	8	3	1	0	3	11	.154
	Jamestown (NY-P)	A	0	2	2.38	2	2	0	0	8	15	15	11	0	7	5	.385
2003	Greensboro (SAL)	A	4	7	3.61	17	17	0	0	82	69	44	33	5	29	59	.223
2004	Jupiter (FSL)	A	5	12	3.38	23	22	1	0	114	124	63	43	4	47	103	.278
MINOR LEAGUE TOTALS			11	21	3.61	46	44	1	0	220	216	125	88	9	86	178	.255

12 Josh Wilson, ss

Born: March 26, 1981. **Ht.:** 6-1. **Wt.:** 160. **Bats:** R. **Throws:** R. **School:** Mount Lebanon HS, Pittsburgh. **Career Transactions:** Selected by Marlins in third round of 1999 draft; signed June 5, 1999. **Signed by:** Ty Brown.

No Marlins prospect did a better job of reestablishing himself in 2004 than Wilson. After falling to No. 21 on this list a year ago, Wilson came back focused and ready. He showed more patience at the plate, used the whole field and did a better job of staying on top of the ball. His reemergence allowed the Marlins to trade Triple-A shortstop Wilson Valdez to the White Sox for reliever Billy Koch. Wilson moved up to Albuquerque, and the Isotopes hardly missed a beat. Wilson improved his basestealing skills, and some think he could steal 25 bases a year. He projects as a solid No. 2 hitter in the mold of Pirates shortstop Jack Wilson (no relation), though Josh is more patient. Wilson is strong-willed and set in his ways at times, in part because he has been around the game so long. His father Mike is the baseball coach at Duquesne and remains a strong influence. Wilson was slated to play second base in the Arizona Fall League, but a pulled ribcage muscle caused him to miss the bulk of the season. The Marlins still feel he has enough arm and range to play shortstop in the big leagues.

Year	Club (League)	Class	AVG	G	AB	R	H	2B	3B	HR	RBI	BB	SO	SB	OBP	SLG
1999	Marlins (GCL)	R	.266	53	203	29	54	9	4	0	27	24	36	14	.352	.350
2000	Kane County (Mid)	A	.269	13	52	2	14	3	1	1	6	3	14	0	.316	.423
	Utica (NY-P)	A	.344	66	259	43	89	13	6	3	43	29	47	9	.418	.475
2001	Kane County (Mid)	A	.285	123	506	65	144	28	5	4	61	28	60	17	.325	.383
2002	Jupiter (FSL)	A	.256	111	398	51	102	17	1	11	50	28	67	7	.318	.387
	Portland (EL)	AA	.341	12	41	5	14	3	0	2	5	2	6	0	.372	.561
2003	Carolina (SL)	AA	.253	118	434	53	110	30	6	3	58	27	70	6	.294	.371
2004	Carolina (SL)	AA	.315	81	311	63	98	21	1	10	41	42	50	8	.396	.486
	Albuquerque (PCL)	AAA	.279	56	240	32	67	12	2	5	23	19	51	6	.337	.408
MINOR LEAGUE TOTALS			.283	633	2444	343	692	136	26	39	314	202	401	67	.342	.408

13 Luke Hagerty, lhp

Born: April 1, 1981. **Ht.:** 6-7. **Wt.:** 230. **Bats:** R. **Throws:** L. **School:** Ball State University. **Career Transactions:** Selected by Cubs in first round (32nd overall) of 2002 draft; signed June 27, 2002 . . . Selected by Orioles from Cubs in major league Rule 5 draft, Dec. 13, 2004 . . . Traded by Orioles to Marlins for a player to be named, Dec. 13, 2004. **Signed by:** Scott May (Cubs).

Several teams showed interest in Hagerty in the second half of the first round of 2002's draft, but he slipped to the Cubs in the supplemental round. That looked like a steal when he was throwing a mid-90s fastball with life and an improved slider the next spring. But before his final spring start in 2003, Hagerty felt a pop in his elbow, and he needed Tommy John surgery. He made it back to the mound in June 2004, but he worked just 23 innings and was shut down early because between rehabbing and pitching, he had worked nonstop for 14 months. Hagerty showed flashes of his old stuff, but like most pitchers recovering from Tommy John surgery, his control was off. Because he's so far from being ready for the majors, Chicago didn't protect him on its 40-man roster, only to see the Orioles take him in the major league Rule 5 draft and trade him to the Marlins. Florida will have to carry Hagerty on its major league roster all year or offer him back to the Cubs for half the $50,000 draft price. Hagerty needs more minor league seasoning, but the Marlins will try to nurse him back to full strength while giving him on-the-job training in middle relief. His mechanics are smooth, especially considering his size, which bodes well for his future health. Besides getting back to 100 percent, his biggest need is to improve a rudimentary changeup.

Year	Club (League)	Class	W	L	ERA	G	GS	CG	SV	IP	H	R	ER	HR	BB	SO	AVG
2002	Boise (NWL)	A	5	3	1.13	10	10	0	0	48	32	15	6	2	15	50	.189
2003	Did not play—Injured																
2004	Boise (NWL)	A	0	2	12.00	4	3	0	0	9	15	13	12	0	9	5	.385
	Cubs (AZL)	R	0	1	2.63	4	3	0	0	14	13	7	4	0	5	7	.260
MINOR LEAGUE TOTALS			5	6	2.79	18	16	0	0	71	60	35	22	2	29	62	.226

14 Randy Messenger, rhp

Born: Aug. 13, 1981. **Ht.:** 6-0. **Wt.:** 220. **Bats:** R. **Throws:** R. **School:** Sparks (Nev.) HS. **Career Transactions:** Selected by Marlins in 11th round of 1999 draft; signed June 6, 1999. **Signed by:** Wally Walker.

Through the first five years of Messenger's pro career, the book on him remained far more consistent than his pitching: impressive arm, disappointing makeup. Then he returned to Double-A last year and reinvented himself as a short reliever. No longer was he resisting instruction and challenging authority. At 23, he started blowing hitters away with a 93-96 mph fastball. His breaking ball still needs work. It remains an ineffective combination of a slider and a curve. But he showed the makeup and mentality of a closer after replacing Kevin Cave in the role two months into the season. He is durable and wants the ball. He earned an assignment to the Arizona Fall League, where he struggled mightily, but that could have been due to fatigue. The Marlins left Messenger off their 40-man roster the past two winters, exposing him to the Rule 5 draft. They didn't take the same risk again this offseason.

Year	Club (League)	Class	W	L	ERA	G	GS	CG	SV	IP	H	R	ER	HR	BB	SO	AVG
1999	Marlins (GCL)	R	0	3	7.52	13	2	0	2	26	28	25	22	1	19	23	.283
2000	Marlins (GCL)	R	2	2	4.83	12	12	0	0	60	66	37	32	6	22	29	.280
2001	Kane County (Mid)	A	2	1	3.93	14	0	0	0	18	22	13	8	0	5	14	.301
	Brevard County (FSL)	A	7	4	4.08	18	18	0	0	93	99	55	42	3	35	42	.277
2002	Jupiter (FSL)	A	11	8	4.37	28	27	1	0	157	178	94	76	4	58	96	.284
2003	Carolina (SL)	AA	5	7	5.46	29	23	0	0	114	137	83	69	7	51	78	.296
2004	Carolina (SL)	AA	6	3	2.58	58	0	0	21	70	67	21	20	4	29	71	.262
MINOR LEAGUE TOTALS			33	28	4.51	172	82	1	23	537	597	328	269	25	219	353	.283

15 Rick Vandenhurk, rhp

Born: May 22, 1985. **Ht.:** 6-5. **Wt.:** 190. **Bats:** R. **Bats:** R. **Career Transactions:** Signed out of Netherlands by Marlins, Nov. 14, 2002. **Signed by:** Fred Ferreira.

Signed at 17 out of the Marlins' Dutch academy, Vandenhurk has been far more successful than most of his fellow European imports in the system. A converted catcher, he has been pitching for only two years but shows far more polish than you would expect. Despite a big frame with a lot of moving parts he features a smooth, effortless delivery. One of the youngest pitchers in the high Class A Florida State League at age 19, he distinguished himself on a strong high Class A rotation that landed all five members on this Top 30 list. He is a hard worker with good mound presence who prides himself on his physical conditioning. His pitches at 90-92 mph, tops out at 94 mph and has late life on his fastball. He has a developing changeup and an average curveball with good spin that he simply needs to tighten up. A strike thrower, he was dominant for his first eight starts, for the most part beating hitters with just his fastball. His command suffered somewhat in his final six outings, and he missed a couple of late-season starts with biceps tendinitis. If he doesn't start the year at Double-A, it won't be long before he gets there.

Year	Club (League)	Class	W	L	ERA	G	GS	CG	SV	IP	H	R	ER	HR	BB	SO	AVG
2003	Marlins (GCL)	R	2	6	5.35	11	10	0	0	39	49	30	23	2	20	30	.308
2004	Jupiter (FSL)	A	2	3	3.26	14	14	0	0	58	54	22	21	2	31	43	.250
MINOR LEAGUE TOTALS			4	9	4.08	15	24	0	0	97	103	52	44	4	51	73	.275

16 Jai Miller, of

Born: Jan. 17, 1985. **Ht.:** 6-4. **Wt.:** 195. **Bats:** R. **Throws:** R. **School:** Selma (Ala.) HS. **Career Transactions:** Selected by Marlins in fourth round of 2003 draft; signed June 3, 2003. **Signed by:** Dave Dangler.

The first three-sport, all-state athlete in Alabama prep history, Miller was headed to Stanford as a wide receiver and basketball guard until the Marlins signed him for $250,000 on draft night. Miller's mother and grandmother were killed in a car crash when he was younger, but he overcame that tragedy. Wowed by his tools, the Marlins pushed him up the ladder in his first full professional season and he struggled against low Class A competition. He handled his share of fastballs but fared poorly against what became a steady diet of breaking balls. He made progress with his pitch recognition by season's end and will return to low Class A in 2005. He now understands the importance of maintaining strong work habits and the grind of a long season. He has a strong arm but has an unusual grip and release that causes his throws to fade off line at times. His routes need work and he has a tendency to drift on balls. He doesn't project as a high-average hitter but should develop gap power with the chance to hit 15-20 homers a year. He lacks the first-step quickness and instincts that could make him a basestealing threat but is a plus runner once he gets rolling. He has been timed at 4.1 seconds to first base from the right side. His makeup is sound, but there were times when he openly pined for football and basketball.

Year	Club (League)	Class	AVG	G	AB	R	H	2B	3B	HR	RBI	BB	SO	SB	OBP	SLG
2003	Marlins (GCL)	R	.199	46	146	17	29	4	1	1	15	15	45	9	.279	.260
	Jamestown (NY-P)	A	.233	11	43	5	10	3	0	0	6	3	15	1	.292	.302
2004	Greensboro (SAL)	A	.205	113	390	51	80	15	3	12	49	32	163	11	.273	.351
MINOR LEAGUE TOTALS			.206	170	579	73	119	22	4	13	70	50	223	21	.276	.325

17 Greg Burns, of

Born: Nov. 7, 1986. **Ht.:** 6-2, **Wt.:** 185. **Bats:** L. **Throws:** L. **School:** Walnut HS, West Covina, Calif. **Career Transactions:** Selected by Marlins in third round of 2004 draft; signed June 22, 2004. **Signed by:** Robby Corsaro.

Some scouts compare Burns to a young Kenny Lofton, only with more gap power. Marlins national crosschecker Joe Jordan, who since has become Baltimore's scouting director, saw him four times at a summer showcase in California and was wowed by his blazing speed on an inside-the-park homer. Burns signed quickly for $395,000. An 80 runner on the 20-80 scouting scale, Burns is regularly timed at 3.9 seconds or faster from the left side of the plate to first base. He is a plus defender because of his range and he has better arm strength than initially thought because of his funky arm action. His arm is accurate as well despite his form. He showed good plate judgment in the Gulf Coast League but must improve his basestealing instincts after getting caught in half his attempts. He has strong hands, and his swing mechanics were shockingly clean for such a young player. His upside is great as he didn't turn 18 until November. He has good makeup, a quiet demeanor, great confidence and wants to learn. His broad shoulders suggest he will add muscle as he matures.

Year	Club (League)	Class	AVG	G	AB	R	H	2B	3B	HR	RBI	BB	SO	SB	OBP	SLG
2004	Marlins (GCL)	R	.243	42	136	28	33	5	4	0	7	26	48	7	.372	.338
MINOR LEAGUE TOTALS			.243	42	136	28	33	5	4	0	7	26	48	7	.372	.338

18 Logan Kensing, rhp

Born: July 3, 1982. **Ht.:** 6-1. **Wt.:** 185. **Bats:** R. **Throws:** R. **School:** Texas A&M University. **Career Transactions:** Selected by Marlins in second round of 2003 draft; signed June 21, 2003. **Signed by:** David Crowson.

When the Marlins were hit with a spate of doubleheaders in September and needed an emergency starter, they reached all the way down to high Class A for a solution. That Kensing wound up going 0-3, 12.65 in three fill-in starts hardly hurts his standing in the organization. Rather, his strong makeup shined through as he made the best of a difficult situation. Kensing stuck around and built some confidence in a few mop-up relief outings. He figures to start this season at Double-A, where he will use a 91-94 mph fastball, solid-average slider and developing changeup to keep working toward a permanent spot in the Marlins rotation. He throws out of a three-quarters arm slot and has done a better job maintaining a consistent delivery. He struggled with his slider in the majors as it tends to flatten out. A minor groin injury caused Kensing to miss some time at midseason, but his arm has been sound throughout his pro career. Primarily a shortstop in high school and a part-time reliever at Texas A&M, Kensing signed for $675,000. A former college teammate of Marlins outfield prospect Eric Reed, Kensing has a calm mound presence and doesn't let bad calls or defensive miscues rattle him.

Year	Club (League)	Class	W	L	ERA	G	GS	CG	SV	IP	H	R	ER	HR	BB	SO	AVG
2003	Jamestown (NY-P)	A	2	4	5.73	8	6	0	0	33	48	23	21	1	6	20	.333
	Greensboro (SAL)	A	0	2	4.50	4	4	0	0	20	18	10	10	2	5	11	.243
2004	Jupiter (FSL)	A	6	7	2.96	23	23	1	0	128	120	53	42	5	35	100	.251
	Florida (NL)	MAJ	0	3	9.88	5	3	0	0	14	19	15	15	5	9	7	.345
MAJOR LEAGUE TOTALS			0	3	9.88	5	3	0	0	14	19	15	15	5	9	7	.345
MINOR LEAGUE TOTALS			8	13	3.64	35	33	1	0	181	186	86	73	8	46	131	.267

19 Jamar Walton, of

Born: Jan. 5, 1986. **Ht.:** 6-4. **Wt.:** 195. **Bats:** L. **Throws:** R. **School:** Greensville County HS, Emporia, Va. **Career Transactions:** Selected by Marlins in fourth round of 2004 draft; signed June 12, 2004. **Signed by:** Joel Matthews.

A three-sport all-state selection at a rural Virginia high school, Walton signed to play at Virginia Commonwealth. Area scout Joel Matthews established a trust with Walton and his family, however, and he signed quickly for $245,000. The Phillies and Cubs were among the other teams on Walton's tantalizing combination of power and speed, and the Marlins decided to take him a round or two earlier than they might otherwise have. He is tremendously raw and swings at everything but makes excellent contact because of his hand-eye coordination. His swing mechanics still need an overhaul as he has a tendency to drop his head when he swings. He reminds some scouts of a young Cliff Floyd, though he could fill out even more than that physically. He showed a solid work ethic and a plus attitude. His arm could be a plus weapon but he needs to take better routes. He projects as a corner outfielder but could have the arm to stay in right. He is a smart baserunner who could steal some bases once he learns that part of the game.

Year	Club (League)	Class	AVG	G	AB	R	H	2B	3B	HR	RBI	BB	SO	SB	OBP	SLG
2004	Marlins (GCL)	R	.238	42	143	17	34	3	1	1	13	13	32	6	.296	.294
MINOR LEAGUE TOTALS			.238	42	143	17	34	3	1	1	13	13	32	6	.296	.294

20 Chris Resop, rhp

Born: Nov. 4, 1982. **Ht.:** 6-3. **Wt.:** 200. **Bats:** R. **Throws:** R. **School:** Barron Collier HS, Naples, Fla. **Career Transactions:** Selected by Marlins in fourth round of 2001 draft; signed July 12, 2001. **Signed by:** Mike Tosar.

In his first full professional season on the mound, Resop kept opening eyes. Having made the conversion from outfield in July 2003 at the suggestion of former farm director Marc DelPiano, Resop overpowered low Class A South Atlantic League hitters with a 95-98 mph fastball. He posted a nearly 10-1 strikeout-walk ratio and maintained his mechanics and composure throughout the year. He has the makings of a plus curve but needs to trust it more. Resop has a changeup but hasn't used it much so far. He thrives on the pressure that comes with the closer's role and allowed just one home run all year. A strong two-way talent in high school who signed with the University of Miami, Resop is aggressive and wants the ball. He admits to some regrets at not returning to pitching sooner after hitting a combined .193 with just one homer in 269 at-bats over parts of three pro seasons. Now that he has his feet under him as a pitcher, he could move quickly through the system. He projects as a short reliever and could eventually close in the majors as he polishes his breaking ball. He was left off the 40-man roster last winter but the Marlins probably won't take that risk again.

Year	Club (League)	Class	AVG	G	AB	R	H	2B	3B	HR	RBI	BB	SO	SB	OBP	SLG
2001	Marlins (GCL)	R	.116	26	86	5	10	2	0	0	5	7	34	0	.189	.140
	Utica (NY-P)	A	.333	2	3	0	1	0	0	0	0	0	2	0	.333	.333
2002	Marlins (GCL)	R	.264	28	91	7	24	5	2	0	11	5	21	1	.323	.363
2003	Greensboro (SAL)	A	.191	37	89	6	17	4	1	1	8	1	29	0	.209	.292
MINOR LEAGUE TOTALS			.193	93	269	18	52	11	3	1	24	13	86	1	.243	.268

Year	Club (League)	Class	W	L	ERA	G	GS	CG	SV	IP	H	R	ER	HR	BB	SO	AVG
2003	Greensboro (SAL)	A	0	1	4.97	11	0	0	0	13	11	7	7	1	5	15	.224
2004	Greensboro (SAL)	A	3	1	2.11	42	0	0	13	43	28	12	10	1	8	71	.181
MINOR LEAGUE TOTALS			3	2	2.77	53	0	0	13	55	39	19	17	2	13	86	.191

21 Jon Fulton, 3b/ss

Born: Dec. 1, 1983. **Ht.:** 6-4. **Wt.:** 200. **Bats:** R. **Throws:** R. **School:** George Washington HS, Danville, Va. **Career Transactions:** Selected by Marlins in third round of 2003 draft; signed June 5, 2003. **Signed by:** Joel Matthews.

After letting him play shortstop for a season and a half, the Marlins moved Fulton to third during their prospect minicamp last fall. Some see him as a young Scott Rolen, with huge hands and big power potential. He has thrived ever since getting his vision corrected with contacts and prescription sunglasses midway through his first professional season. After hitting .150 in his first 133 pro at-bats, Fulton has put himself on the fast track. While he was a little short in terms of range at shortstop, third base seems to suit him better. He has a plus arm and quick feet. He needs to simplify his game, however, and stop brooding over bad at-bats. He also must improve his plate judgment and use the middle of the field more. In order to keep improving his vision, Fulton does 30 to 40 minutes of daily eye exercises on a computer program in his room. The same doctor who prescribed the program for Fulton gave the same thing to Barry Bonds. Fulton has a strong work ethic and should start the year in low Class A.

Year	Club (League)	Class	AVG	G	AB	R	H	2B	3B	HR	RBI	BB	SO	SB	OBP	SLG
2003	Marlins (GCL)	R	.196	47	168	9	33	9	0	1	13	9	51	0	.247	.268
2004	Jupiter (FSL)	A	.217	6	23	2	5	2	0	1	1	1	5	0	.250	.304
	Jamestown (NY-P)	A	.254	65	252	39	64	12	5	11	40	20	82	2	.312	.472
MINOR LEAGUE TOTALS			.230	118	443	50	102	23	5	12	54	30	138	2	.284	.386

22 Rodrigo Rosario, rhp

Born: March 14, 1978. **Ht.:** 6-2. **Wt.:** 165. **Bats:** R. **Throws:** R. **Career Transactions:** Signed by Astros out of Dominican Republic, July 6, 1996 . . . Selected by Marlins from Astros in minor league Rule 5 draft, Dec. 13, 2004. **Signed by:** Ricardo Aponte (Astros).

Luke Hagerty isn't the only former top pitching prospect the Marlins took a chance on in the Rule 5 draft. In the Triple-A phase of the draft, Florida grabbed Rosario, who beat the Rangers in his major league debut in June 2003, then went down with a major shoulder injury when he faced Texas again six days later. He hasn't pitched in a game since. Rosario had surgery to repair labrum and rotator-cuff tears and to shore up some instability in his shoulder, and also to fix a torn biceps tendon. Before he got hurt, he owned a lively 91-92 mph fastball, an average slider and a so-so changeup. The Marlins had reports that Rosario was throwing well this winter despite sitting out the winter season in his native Dominican Republic, so they figured he was worth the gamble. If he doesn't make a comeback, they'll only be out the $12,000 Triple-A Rule 5 draft price.

Year	Club (League)	Class	W	L	ERA	G	GS	CG	SV	IP	H	R	ER	HR	BB	SO	AVG
1997	Astros (DSL)	R	6	4	2.46	15	14	0	0	91	63	30	25	2	24	81	.195
1998	Astros (GCL)	R	2	2	4.12	13	12	0	0	68	61	36	31	6	30	65	.245
	Auburn (NY-P)	A	0	0	0.00	2	0	0	0	2	0	0	0	0	3	2	.000
1999	Martinsville (Appy)	R	5	5	4.69	14	14	0	0	79	78	46	41	9	32	86	.267
2000	Auburn (NY-P)	A	5	6	3.45	14	14	0	0	76	67	36	29	3	32	67	.221
2001	Lexington (SAL)	A	13	4	2.14	30	21	1	2	147	105	46	35	8	36	131	.198
2002	Round Rock (TL)	AA	11	6	3.11	26	23	0	0	130	106	56	45	5	59	94	.222
2003	New Orleans (PCL)	AAA	5	7	4.03	15	15	1	0	87	71	40	39	7	32	68	.222
	Houston (NL)	MAJ	1	0	1.13	2	2	0	0	8	5	2	1	0	3	6	.172
2004	Did not play—Injured																
MAJOR LEAGUE TOTALS			1	0	1.13	2	2	0	0	8	5	2	1	0	3	6	.172
MINOR LEAGUE TOTALS			47	34	3.24	129	113	2	2	680	551	290	245	40	248	594	.222

23 Jose Campusano, ss

Born: Dec. 19, 1983. **Ht.:** 5-11. **Wt.:** 160. **Bats:** B. **Throws:** R. **Career Transactions:** Signed out of Dominican Republic by Marlins April 29, 2003. **Signed by:** Jesus Campos.

Though he signed once the 2003 season had gotten under way, it hasn't taken the switch-hitting Campusano long to establish a reputation in the system. A natural righthanded hitter, he shows some pop from that side but is mostly a slap-and-dash type from the left side. Some believe he is every bit as fast as Double-A outfielder Eric Reed. In fact, some of the Gulf Coast League instructors had the two lined up for a match race in the outfield before a trainer called it off. Campusano has been timed at 3.35 seconds to first on a bunt from the left side. He made 28 errors but showed a 75 arm that could be even better than Class A shortstop Robert Andino's. His arm isn't just strong but accurate, too. He struggles at times with his footwork and balance on double plays. He has good makeup and is coachable. Some see him as another Tony Fernandez, while others think he'll wind up hitting more like an Alfredo Griffin. His father died in the middle of the year but he did not return home for the funeral. He fouled a ball off his foot late in the season but played through the pain.

Year	Club (League)	Class	AVG	G	AB	R	H	2B	3B	HR	RBI	BB	SO	SB	OBP	SLG
2003	Marlins (DSL)	R	.244	57	205	30	50	9	4	0	12	33	43	27	.366	.327
2004	Marlins (GCL)	R	.255	59	196	24	50	8	4	1	16	10	38	11	.319	.352
MINOR LEAGUE TOTALS			.249	116	401	54	100	17	8	1	28	43	81	38	.344	.339

24 Franklyn Gracesqui, lhp

Born: Aug. 20, 1979. **Ht.:** 6-5. **Wt.:** 210. **Bats:** B. **Throws:** L. **School:** George Washington HS, New York. **Career Transactions:** Selected by Blue Jays in 21st round of 1998 draft; signed June 7, 1998 . . . Selected by Marlins from Blue Jays in minor league Rule 5 draft, Dec. 16, 2002. **Signed by:** Charles Aliano (Blue Jays).

Plucked out of the Blue Jays system in the minor-league Rule 5 draft, Gracesqui reached the majors last year and immediately got thrown into the fire. He registered his first career save in San Francisco and seemingly appeared in or warmed up for every game he was with the big club in a 12-day early-season trial. He had too many command problems to stick around, however, and was sent back to Triple-A, where he missed significant time with shoulder tendinitis. He has a live fastball that tops out at 96 mph and complements that with a fair slider and the occasional change. He is just as tough on righthanded batters as lefties, which helps him project as something more than a situational lefty. His slider could morph into a cut fastball that would make him even more effective against righties. He has good mound presence, showing the occasional glower at opposing hitters, and shows no fear. Like Manny Ramirez, he is a native Dominican who came through the strong baseball program at New York's George Washington High.

Year	Club (League)	Class	W	L	ERA	G	GS	CG	SV	IP	H	R	ER	HR	BB	SO	AVG
1998	St. Catharines (NY-P)	A	1	0	6.61	11	0	0	0	16	16	12	12	2	12	19	.242
1999	St. Catharines (NY-P)	A	2	3	5.05	15	10	0	1	46	44	30	26	4	41	45	.253
2000	Medicine Hat (Pio)	R	0	1	2.63	8	4	0	0	24	15	11	7	1	21	20	.185
	Hagerstown (SAL)	A	0	1	4.91	3	1	0	0	7	4	4	4	1	9	6	.174
2001	Charleston, WV (SAL)	A	2	8	3.17	35	2	0	1	65	60	40	23	1	34	66	.245
	Dunedin (FSL)	A	1	0	0.00	4	0	0	0	6	2	0	0	0	8	6	.125
2002	Tennessee (SL)	AA	4	2	4.64	41	0	0	1	43	40	26	22	3	34	48	.258
	Dunedin (FSL)	A	2	1	2.49	10	0	0	1	22	15	8	6	1	11	25	.192
2003	Carolina (SL)	AA	3	3	2.48	44	0	0	5	58	44	19	16	0	43	75	.211
2004	Florida (NL)	MAJ	0	1	11.25	7	0	0	1	4	6	5	5	0	3	1	.333
	Albuquerque (PCL)	AAA	1	0	3.27	19	0	0	1	22	10	9	8	2	19	16	.139
MAJOR LEAGUE TOTALS			0	1	8.44	7	0	0	1	5	6	5	5	0	3	1	.333
MINOR LEAGUE TOTALS			16	19	3.61	190	17	0	10	309	250	159	124	15	232	326	.223

25 Ronald Belizario, rhp

Born: Dec. 31, 1982. **Ht.:** 6-2. **Wt.:** 150. **Bats:** R. **Throws:** R. **Career Transactions:** Signed out of Venezuela by Marlins, Aug. 2, 1999. **Signed by:** Miguel Garcia.

On pure arm strength alone, Belizario will get a longer leash than many of his fellow pitching prospects. He pitches at 93-95 mph and tops out at 98. He also shows a decent splitter and a slider that needs to be tightened up. He has shown a decent change but needs to throw it more. He spent the bulk of the year in the Double-A rotation, but struggled with his command. A minor back injury caused him to be sent back to high Class A, where he pitched out of the bullpen. The organization continues to be split on whether Belizario projects as a starter or a short reliever. Makeup has been a question throughout his career as he can be hard to coach. He missed the end of the 2003 season with a minor shoulder problem, and durability is an issue as well. Signed the same week as fellow Venezuelan Miguel

Cabrera, Belizario weighed just 148 pounds at the time. His bonus was less than $60,000. He should return to Double-A, though a promotion to Triple-A could come early if he succeeds.

Year	Club (League)	Class	W	L	ERA	G	GS	CG	SV	IP	H	R	ER	HR	BB	SO	AVG
2000	Universidad (VSL)	R	2	3	7.39	17	5	0	6	35	37	34	29	1	18	27	.253
2001	Marlins (GCL)	R	4	6	2.34	13	10	1	0	73	62	29	19	4	20	54	.229
2002	Kane County (Mid)	A	6	5	3.46	23	22	1	0	140	131	67	54	4	56	98	.247
2003	Greensboro (SAL)	A	5	1	3.00	10	8	1	0	48	41	23	16	3	18	45	.229
	Jupiter (FSL)	A	1	2	4.91	6	4	0	0	18	20	10	10	0	8	13	.278
2004	Jupiter (FSL)	A	1	1	0.00	6	0	0	1	9	2	1	0	0	4	7	.074
	Carolina (SL)	AA	3	5	5.55	15	15	0	0	73	75	52	45	10	43	58	.270
MINOR LEAGUE TOTALS			22	23	3.93	90	64	3	7	397	368	216	173	22	167	302	.245

26 Cole Seifrig, 2b

Born: Sept. 10, 1984. **Ht.:** 6-3. **Wt.:** 190. **Bats:** R. **Throws:** R. **School:** Heritage Hills HS, Lincoln City, Ind. **Career Transactions:** Selected by Marlins in fifth round of 2003 draft; signed June 11, 2003. **Signed by:** Scot Engler.

A Purdue football signee as a wide receiver, Seifrig accepted a $200,000 bonus to play baseball instead. He is serious, disciplined and a hard worker, but was overmatched in the low Class A South Atlantic League during his first full professional season. When a midyear demotion to short-season ball was discussed, though, Seifrig argued successfully to stick things out. A quiet kid, there was concern he pouted at times. He showed below-average arm strength and had problems with the pivot, leading to speculation he will wind up at third or in center field. He has average to below-average range and made just 11 errors, including a pair of three-error games. He did improve defensively on his angles as the year went on. At the plate, he showed below average bat speed and only rarely gave the glimpses of the short, quick swing that had Marlins scouts comparing him to Paul Molitor and Ryne Sandberg a year earlier. Breaking balls gave him particular trouble. He'll return to low Class A, where it's hoped he'll make the necessary adjustments to get back on the fast track.

Year	Club (League)	Class	AVG	G	AB	R	H	2B	3B	HR	RBI	BB	SO	SB	OBP	SLG
2003	Marlins (GCL)	R	.285	50	186	27	53	7	2	2	7	10	44	11	.335	.376
	Jamestown (NY-P)	A	.261	11	46	3	12	3	0	0	8	2	12	2	.286	.326
2004	Greensboro (SAL)	A	.196	121	443	55	87	20	3	4	30	13	128	6	.228	.282
MINOR LEAGUE TOTALS			.225	182	675	85	152	30	5	6	45	25	184	19	.262	.311

27 Allen Baxter, rhp

Born: July 6, 1983. **Ht.:** 6-4. **Wt.:** 215. **Bats:** R. **Throws:** R. **School:** Varina HS, Sandston, Va. **Career Transactions:** Selected by Marlins in third round of 2001 draft; signed June 14, 2001. **Signed by:** Ty Brown.

Baxter ranked fifth on this list after his first pro season then blew out his elbow four starts into his follow-up campaign. Tommy John surgery and a couple of minor setbacks left him back in the New York-Penn League last year. His numbers were ugly, but his fastball was reaching 98 mph, about three mph better than before surgery. He pitches at 93-94 mph with great natural movement on both his four- and two-seam fastballs. His hard-breaking curve remains a plus pitch and his changeup is advanced. Signed quickly for $450,000 out of a Virginia high school, he has a prototypical pitcher's frame that has drawn comparisons to Curt Schilling and Kerry Wood. He still needs to add mental maturity and show more outward desire but his work habits have improved greatly due to the strains of rehab. He had to fight through a mental funk during the year, especially with the results not where he would like them, but the Marlins are encouraged by his progress.

Year	Club (League)	Class	W	L	ERA	G	GS	CG	SV	IP	H	R	ER	HR	BB	SO	AVG
2001	Marlins (GCL)	R	2	3	2.38	9	7	0	0	34	25	13	9	0	8	40	.207
	Utica (NY-P)	A	0	0	3.60	1	1	0	0	5.0	3	2	2	0	3	5	.176
2002	Kane County (Mid)	A	0	2	3.06	4	4	0	0	18	19	9	6	0	8	15	.288
2003	Did not play—Injured																
2004	Jamestown (NY-P)	A	0	4	6.17	10	10	0	0	35	34	31	24	1	32	27	.262
MINOR LEAGUE TOTALS			2	9	4.03	24	22	0	0	92	81	55	41	1	51	87	.243

28 Chris Aguila, of

Born: Feb. 23, 1979. **Ht.:** 5-11. **Wt.:** 180. **Bats:** R. **Throws:** R. **School:** McQueen HS, Reno, Nev. **Career Transactions:** Selected by Marlins in third round of 1997 draft; signed June 18, 1997. **Signed by:** Wally Walker.

Seven years after tying the national single-season high school home run record with 29, Aguila finally made it to the big leagues. He could find a spot as a reserve outfielder with the Marlins in 2005. His steady progression included a Double-A Southern League batting title in 2003, even though he missed 41 games with a fractured right wrist. He has some of the best bat speed in the organization, ranking perhaps behind only Jai Miller, and continues to incorporate a power stroke into his game. He can handle even the best fastballs, especially those that are middle-in, though plus breaking balls give him trouble. He is considered unselfish, upbeat and a good teammate, traits that make him a solid candidate for big-league bench duty. He is a plus defender who can handle all three outfield spots, if necessary, though he's best suited for right field. He runs well, gets good jumps and has solid instincts. A modest-sized late bloomer, Aguila seems to get a little better each year.

Year	Club (League)	Class	AVG	G	AB	R	H	2B	3B	HR	RBI	BB	SO	SB	OBP	SLG
1997	Marlins (GCL)	R	.217	46	157	12	34	7	0	1	17	21	49	2	.309	.280
1998	Marlins (GCL)	R	.269	51	171	29	46	12	3	4	29	19	49	6	.349	.444
1999	Kane County (Mid)	A	.244	122	430	74	105	21	7	15	78	40	127	14	.320	.430
2000	Brevard County (FSL)	A	.241	136	518	68	125	27	3	9	56	37	105	8	.292	.357
2001	Brevard County (FSL)	A	.276	73	272	44	75	15	3	10	34	21	54	8	.328	.463
	Portland (EL)	AA	.257	64	241	25	62	16	1	4	29	18	50	5	.312	.382
2002	Portland (EL)	AA	.294	130	429	62	126	28	4	6	46	48	101	14	.369	.420
2003	Carolina (SL)	AA	.320	93	337	58	108	21	3	11	55	36	67	6	.384	.499
	Marlins (GCL)	R	.750	1	4	1	3	0	0	1	2	0	1	0	.750	1.500
2004	Albuquerque (PCL)	AAA	.312	97	330	61	103	23	2	11	56	37	82	8	.380	.494
	Florida (NL)	MAJ	.222	29	45	10	10	2	1	3	5	2	12	0	.255	.511
MAJOR LEAGUE TOTALS			.222	29	45	10	10	2	1	3	5	2	12	0	.255	.511
MINOR LEAGUE TOTALS			.272	813	2889	434	787	170	26	72	402	277	685	71	.339	.424

29 Lincoln Holdzkom, rhp

Born: March 23, 1982. **Ht.:** 6-4. **Wt.:** 240. **Bats:** R. **Throws:** R. **School:** Arizona Western CC. **Career Transactions:** Selected by Marlins in seventh round of 2001 draft; signed June 5, 2001. **Signed by:** David Finley.

Just when Holdzkom's career was on a roll, elbow problems put him on the sidelines. He couldn't perform the way he hoped in his first big-league spring camp and wound up having Tommy John surgery in June 2004. He is expected back by midseason and probably won't challenge for a big league spot until 2006. But the notion of his 97 mph fastball adding a few ticks is tantalizing. Some believe the setback was a blessing in disguise for Holdzkom, as it taught him a better work ethic. Drafted in the seventh round in 2001, he signed for $105,000 after getting kicked off the baseball team at Arizona Western. He believes he would have gone much higher that year if not for the problems with his college coach, John Stratton. Holdzkom is physically imposing and has a glowering mound presence. He complements his big fastball with a hard-breaking curve. He projects as a premium set-up man but might not have the makeup to close. While his nipple rings and tattoos sometimes give people the wrong impression, Holdzkom insists he is devoted to his craft.

Year	Club (League)	Class	W	L	ERA	G	GS	CG	SV	IP	H	R	ER	HR	BB	SO	AVG
2001	Marlins (GCL)	R	1	3	2.49	12	7	0	2	43	26	18	12	0	27	43	.176
2002	Kane County (Mid)	A	1	5	2.53	30	0	0	11	32	21	11	9	0	29	42	.181
2003	Greensboro (SAL)	A	1	4	2.84	43	0	0	4	57	36	24	18	0	27	74	.182
	Jupiter (FSL)	A	0	2	3.07	13	0	0	2	15	9	6	5	0	7	20	.167
2004	Did not pitch—Injured																
MINOR LEAGUE TOTALS			3	14	2.69	98	7	0	19	147	92	59	44	0	90	179	.178

30 Jeff Allison, rhp

Born: Nov. 7, 1984. **Ht.:** 6-2. **Wt.:** 195. **Bats:** R. **Throws:** R. **School:** Veterans Memorial HS, Peabody, Mass. **Career Transactions:** Selected by Marlins in first round (16th overall) of 2003 draft; July 22, 2003. **Signed by:** Steve Payne.

One of the saddest stories in the minors, Allison plummeted from No. 3 on last year's list after nearly dying from a heroin overdose last summer. Allison sought offseason outpatient treatment for a reliance on the painkiller Oxycontin and reported to spring training late. He stayed about a month then returned home to Massachusetts after reportedly failing multiple drug tests. The heroin episode came a couple of months later, and the Marlins have no idea if he will pitch for them again. When healthy, the talent is obvious. Baseball America's High School Player of the Year as a senior, he signed for $1.85 million. Often compared to Josh Beckett for his stuff, mound demeanor and cocky attitude, Allison had a 93-97 mph fastball and a big-breaking curve in the mid-80s. Should he make it back this year, the Marlins will take things slowly with Allison as they try to reestablish him as a viable professional. A minor bout of shoulder tendinitis cut short his first pro season in 2003.

Year	Club (League)	Class	W	L	ERA	G	GS	CG	SV	IP	H	R	ER	HR	BB	SO	AVG
2003	Marlins (GCL)	R	0	2	1.00	3	3	0	0	9	7	2	1	0	4	11	.206
2004	Did not play																
MINOR LEAGUE TOTALS			0	2	1.00	3	3	0	0	9	7	2	1	0	4	11	.206

HOUSTON
ASTROS

BY **JIM CALLIS**

After underachieving in 2002 and 2003, the Astros appeared to be doing more of the same last year. By late August, they had wasted the buzz from bringing Roger Clemens and Andy Pettitte back home and hosting their first All-Star Game at Minute Maid Park. When Houston dropped two of three home games to the Cubs, it fell to 61-62 and a distant sixth in the National League wild-card race.

Then the Astros suddenly reversed course, winning 31 of their final 39 games to surge into the playoffs. They beat the Braves in the Division Series and took a three-games-to-two lead in the NL Championship Series before the Cardinals rallied to deny them a trip to the World Series. That disappointment only took away slightly from the most successful season in the franchise's 44-year history, both on the field (Houston hadn't won a postseason series) and at the box office (a record 3,087,872 fans).

Shortly after the World Series ended, the architect of the Astros' success resigned. General manager Gerry Hunsicker tired of haggling with owner Drayton McLane over big league payroll and player-development costs. Hunsicker presided over five playoff teams in nine years. Though he never had the biggest budget or the deepest farm system, Hunsicker was able to make trades both large (Carlos Beltran) and small (Brandon Backe) to address the team's needs.

Fortunately for Houston, it had one of the game's top GM prospects on hand. Assistant GM/farm director **Tim Purpura** was pro-

moted and spent much of his first winter as GM waiting for Beltran to decide if he'd accept a club-record $105 million contract offer. Beltran ultimately declined, costing the Astros a dynamic talent.

Virtually every key management position has seen a change since the beginning of the 2004 season. Houston hired Tigers farm director Ricky Bennett to fill Purpura's old role. Hunsicker reassigned scouting director David Lakey in June and gave those duties to Paul Ricciarini, the club's coordinator of pro scouting. The farm system has gone through upheaval on the field as well, after sliding from third in Baseball America's talent ratings after 2001 to 29th after 2003. Five of Houston's 10 best prospects have joined the organization since the end of the 2003 season. Righthanders Ezequiel Astacio and Taylor Buchholz arrived in the Billy Wagner trade with the Phillies. Outfielder Willy Taveras was plucked from the Indians in the major league Rule 5 draft, and Hunsicker swung a deal with Cleveland to retain his rights. Outfielders Mitch Einerston and Hunter Pence and lefthander Troy Patton were products of Lakey's last draft, with early returns indicating it may have been one of his best. Those draft picks contributed to Astros affiliates winning a championship in the Rookie-level Appalachian League and finishing as runners-up in the New York-Penn League.

TOP 30 PROSPECTS

1. Chris Burke, 2b	16. Ben Zobrist, ss
2. Ezequiel Astacio, rhp	17. Luke Scott, of
3. Willy Taveras, of	18. Lou Santangelo, c
4. Mitch Einertson, of	19. Jordan Parraz, of
5. Troy Patton, lhp	20. Chad Reineke, rhp
6. Matt Albers, rhp	21. Jared Gothreaux, rhp
7. Taylor Buchholz, rhp	22. Mitch Talbot, rhp
8. Fernando Nieve, rhp	23. Brooks Conrad, 2b
9. Josh Anderson, of	24. Edwin Maysonet, 2b/ss
10. Hunter Pence, of	25. Mark McLemore, lhp
11. Chad Qualls, rhp	26. Jason Hirsh, rhp
12. Juan Gutierrez, rhp	27. Ervin Alcantara, of
13. Tommy Whiteman, ss	28. Todd Self, 1b
14. Hector Gimenez, c	29. Eric Bruntlett, ss/of
15. Jimmy Barthmaier, rhp	30. Wladimir Sutil, ss

ORGANIZATION OVERVIEW

General manager: Tim Purpura. **Farm director:** Ricky Bennett. **Scouting director:** Paul Ricciarini.

2004 PERFORMANCE

Class	Team	League	W	L	Pct.	Finish*	Manager(s)
Majors	Houston	National	92	70	.568	4th (16)	J. Williams/P. Garner
Triple-A	#New Orleans Zephyrs	Pacific Coast	66	78	.458	13th (16)	Chris Maloney
Double-A	@Round Rock Express	Texas	86	54	.614	1st (8)	Jackie Moore
High A	Salem Avalanche	Carolina	65	74	.468	6th (8)	Russ Nixon
Low A	Lexington Legends	South Atlantic	67	72	.482	11th (16)	Ivan DeJesus
Short-season	Tri-City ValleyCats	New York-Penn	50	25	.667	2nd (14)	Gregg Langbehn
Rookie	Greeneville Astros	Appalachian	41	26	.612	+2nd (10)	Tim Bogar
OVERALL 2004 MINOR LEAGUE RECORD			375	329	.529	7th (30)	

*Finish in overall standings (No. of teams in league). +League champion.
#Affiliate will be in Round Rock (Pacific Coast) in 2005. @Affiliate will be in Corpus Christi (Texas) in 2005.

ORGANIZATION LEADERS

BATTING
*Minimum 250 at-bats
*AVG	Ben Zobrist, Tri-City	.339
R	Josh Anderson, Salem/Lexington	114
H	Josh Anderson, Salem/Lexington	172
TB	Luke Scott, Round Rock/Salem	249
2B	Brooks Conrad, Round Rock	39
	Royce Huffman, New Orleans	39
3B	Edwin Maysonet, Lexington	10
HR	Mike Coolbaugh, New Orleans	30
	Phil Hiatt, New Orleans	30
RBI	Luke Scott, Round Rock/Salem	97
BB	Todd Self, Round Rock	89
SO	Charlton Jimerson, Round Rock	163
SB	Josh Anderson, Salem/Lexington	79
*OBP	Ben Zobrist, Tri-City	.438
*SLG	Mike Coolbaugh, New Orleans	.592

PITCHING
#Minimum 75 innings
W	Ezequiel Astacio, Round Rock	13
L	Four tied at	11
#ERA	Mike Burns, Round Rock	1.67
G	Monte Mansfield, Salem	59
	Aaron Williams, Lexington	59
CG	Jared Fernandez, New Orleans	3
	D.J. Houlton, Round Rock	3
SV	Santiago Ramirez, Round Rock	32
IP	Jared Fernandez, New Orleans	196
BB	Derick Grigsby, Lexington	92
SO	Ezequiel Astacio, Round Rock	185

BEST TOOLS

Best Hitter for Average	Chris Burke
Best Power Hitter	Mitch Einertson
Best Strike-Zone Discipline	Todd Self
Fastest Baserunner	Willy Taveras
Best Athlete	Charlton Jimerson
Best Fastball	Ezequiel Astacio
Best Curveball	Taylor Buchholz
Best Slider	Chad Qualls
Best Changeup	Mitch Talbot
Best Control	Ezequiel Astacio
Best Defensive Catcher	Hector Gimenez
Best Defensive Infielder	Wladimir Sutil
Best Infield Arm	Tommy Whiteman
Best Defensive Outfielder	Willy Taveras
Best Outfield Arm	Charlton Jimerson

PROJECTED 2008 LINEUP

Catcher	Hector Gimenez
First Base	Lance Berkman
Second Base	Chris Burke
Third Base	Morgan Ensberg
Shortstop	Adam Everett
Left Field	Jason Lane

Center Field	Willy Taveras
Right Field	Mitch Einertson
No. 1 Starter	Roy Oswalt
No. 2 Starter	Andy Pettitte
No. 3 Starter	Brandon Backe
No. 4 Starter	Ezequiel Astacio
No. 5 Starter	Troy Patton
Closer	Brad Lidge

LAST YEAR'S TOP 20 PROSPECTS

1. Taylor Buchholz, rhp
2. Jason Lane, of
3. John Buck, c
4. Chris Burke, 2b/ss
5. Fernando Nieve, rhp
6. Hector Gimenez, c
7. Chad Qualls, rhp
8. Jason Hirsh, rhp
9. Matt Albers, rhp
10. Jimmy Barthmaier, rhp
11. Willy Taveras, of
12. Mitch Talbot, rhp
13. Mike Gallo, lhp
14. Tommy Whiteman, ss/3b
15. Ezequiel Astacio, rhp
16. Jared Gothreaux, rhp
17. Cliff Davis, rhp
18. Josh Anderson, of
19. Raymar Diaz, rhp
20. Scott Robinson, 1b

TOP PROSPECTS OF THE DECADE

Year	Player, Pos.	Current Team
1995	Brian Hunter, of	Out of baseball
1996	Billy Wagner, lhp	Phillies
1997	Richard Hidalgo, of	Rangers
1998	Richard Hidalgo, of	Rangers
1999	Lance Berkman, of	Astros
2000	Wilfredo Rodriguez, lhp	Nationals
2001	Roy Oswalt, rhp	Astros
2002	Carlos Hernandez, lhp	Astros
2003	John Buck, c	Royals
2004	Taylor Buchholz, rhp	Astros

TOP DRAFT PICKS OF THE DECADE

Year	Player, Pos.	Current Team
1995	Tony McKnight, rhp	Out of baseball
1996	Mark Johnson, rhp	Dodgers
1997	Lance Berkman, 1b	Astros
1998	Brad Lidge, rhp	Astros
1999	Mike Rosamond, of	Pirates
2000	Robert Stiehl, rhp	Astros
2001	Chris Burke, ss	Astros
2002	Derick Grigsby, rhp	Astros
2003	Jason Hirsh, rhp (2)	Astros
2004	Hunter Pence, of (2)	Astros

ALL-TIME LARGEST BONUSES

Chris Burke, 2001	$2,125,000
Robert Stiehl, 2000	$1,250,000
Derick Grigsby, 2002	$1,125,000
Brad Lidge, 1998	$1,070,000
Lance Berkman, 1997	$1,000,000

Houston ASTROS

RANK: **22**

Impact Potential: D

No. 1 prospect Chris Burke should step in and contribute in Houston in 2005, but he's not going to replace Jeff Kent's production and profiles more as an average big league regular. Ezequiel Astacio's stuff got noticeably better last season, and outfielder Mitch Einertson put up bigger power numbers than anyone imagined the fifth-rounder was capable of. Now they need to prove they can do it again.

Depth: D

The Astros have graduated players such as Morgan Ensberg, Adam Everett and Jason Lane to Houston the last couple of years. Combined with low-risk drafts, it has steadily eroded the talent since Houston was BA's 2001 Organization of the Year. The organization has no viable future options at third base. Lefthanded starters are also noticeably lacking. Fernando Nieve, Hector Gimenez and Juan Gutierrez are the best recent products from the traditional Venezuelan pipeline.

*Depth charts prepared by **John Manuel** and **Allan Simpson**. Numbers in parentheses indicate prospect rankings.*

LF
Hunter Pence (10)
Luke Scott (17)
Beau Hearod

CF
Willy Taveras (3)
Josh Anderson (9)
Ervin Alcantara (27)
Charlton Jimerson

3B
None

SS
Tommy Whiteman (12)
Ben Zobrist (16)
Eric Bruntlett (29)
Wladimir Sutil (30)
Ronald Ramirez

RF
Mitch Einertson (4)
Jordan Parraz (19)

2B
Chris Burke (1)
Brooks Conrad (23)
Edwin Maysonet (24)

1B
Todd Self (28)
Scott Robinson
Mario Garza
Carlos Rivera
Mark Saccomanno
Royce Huffman

SOURCE of TALENT

HOMEGROWN		ACQUIRED	
College	16	Trades	3
Junior College	1	Rule 5 draft	1
Draft-and-follow	1	Independent leagues	0
High School	3	Free agents/waivers	0
Nondrafted free agent	0		
Foreign	5		

C
Hector Gimenez (14)
Lou Santangelo (18)
J.R. Towles

LHP

Starters	Relievers
Troy Patton (5)	Mark McLemore (25)
	Enyelbert Soto
	Wandy Rodriguez
	Josh Muecke

RHP

Starters	Relievers
Ezequiel Astacio (2)	Chad Qualls (11)
Matt Albers (6)	Chad Reineke (20)
Taylor Buchholz (7)	Jared Gothreaux (21)
Fernando Nieve (8)	Jason Hirsh (26)
Juan Gutierrez (12)	Mike Burns
Jimmy Barthmaier (15)	Levi Romero
Mitch Talbot (22)	Felipe Paulino
Ronnie Martinez	Monte Mansfield
Jimmy Barratt	Robert Stiehl
Cliff Davis	Jeremy Griffiths
Derick Grigsby	
Raymar Diaz	
Tony Pluta	
Celsan Polanco	

DRAFT ANALYSIS

2004

Best Pro Debut: OF Mitch Einertson (5) tied a 44-year-old Rookie-level Appalachian League home run record with 24. He was named MVP and topped the league in extra-base hits (39), RBIs (67) and slugging (.692) while hitting .308. He also homered twice in the playoffs and again in his first game after a promotion to the short-season New York-Penn League. SS Ben Zobrist (6) was old for the NY-P at 23, but he did lead the league in hitting (.339) and on-base percentage (.438).

Best Athlete: Zobrist is a switch-hitter with average tools across the board. OF Hunter Pence (2) is a gangly 6-foot-4 and 200 pounds, but he's a pretty good athlete and played a solid center field in his pro debut. OF Jordan Parraz (3) was the highest unsigned draft-and-follow from 2003, failing to sign with the Phillies as a sixth-rounder—after they took him as a pitcher.

Best Pure Hitter: Pence was a surprise second-round pick, but his hitting ability was obvious. He batted .395 at Texas-Arlington to win the Southland Conference batting title during the spring, then hit .296 with eight homers in the NY-P.

Best Raw Power: Despite Einertson's exploits, the Astros say he doesn't have the most pop in their draft class. That honor belongs to C Lou Santangelo (4). Parraz and Pence also possess a lot of power.

Fastest Runner: OF Luke Barganier (30) goes from the left side of the plate to first base in 4.05 seconds.

Best Defensive Player: C J.R. Towles' (20) catch-and-throw skills stand out in an organization that lost a big chunk of its catching depth when it included John Buck in the Carlos Beltran trade.

RICH ABEL

Santangelo

Best Fastball: RHP Chad Reineke's (13) fastball received a boost when he moved to the bullpen last spring at Miami (Ohio). He now throws 92-96 mph.

Best Breaking Ball: LHP Troy Patton (9) had one of the best curveballs in the draft, and hitters can't sit on it because he also has a low-90s fastball.

Most Intriguing Background: RHP Jared Brite (26) was a punter and placekicker at Kansas State. He signed with the Astros, but a pre-existing elbow injury led them to void his contract. RHP Garrett Murdy (16) was the NCAA Division II 2004 player of the year after leading that level in wins (14-1,1.88) and strikeouts (158 in 115 innings) for Texas A&M-Kingsville.

Closest To The Majors: Pence or Zobrist. Patton, who had a 1.93 ERA at Rookie-level Greeneville, is advanced for a high school lefty.

Best Late-Round Pick: Reineke or Towles. Towles also has some power to go with his defensive ability.

The One Who Got Away: The Astros signed their top 17 picks but couldn't get RHP Jared Clark (19) to turn pro rather than attending Cal State Fullerton.

Assessment: Houston reassigned scouting director David Lakey after this draft, but he did well for not having a first-round pick. The first five choices—Pence, Parraz, Santangelo, Einertson and Zobrist—addressed a need for position players.

2003 The Astros lacked a first-rounder and let the commissioner's office talk them out of signing the best player they chose, OF Drew Stubbs (3). OF Josh Anderson (4) and RHP Jimmy Barthmaier (13), as well as top pick RHP Jason Hirsh (2), all have nice ceilings but require a lot of polish. *GRADE:* C

2002 RHP Derick Grigsby (1) pitched his way off the top 30 list in just two years. RHPs Jared Gothreaux (16) and Mitch Talbot (2) stand out, and neither is a frontline guy. *GRADE:* D

2001 2B Chris Burke (1) should be a solid starter for years to come. Draft-and-follow RHP Matt Albers (23) has one of the best arms in the system, while since-traded RHP Kirk Saarloos (3) reached the majors quickly. *GRADE:* B

2000 RHPs Robert Stiehl (1) and Tony Pluta (3) have fallen to surgery. RHP Chad Qualls (2) was Houston's second-best reliever down the stretch, while Eric Bruntlett (9) filled a utility role. SS Tommy Whiteman (6) could start on the left side of the infield soon. *GRADE:* C+

Draft analysis prepared by Jim Callis. Numbers in parentheses indicate draft rounds.

BILL MITCHELL

Chris
BURKE

Born: March 11, 1980.
Ht.: 5-11. **Wt.:** 180.
Bats: R. **Throws:** R.
School: University of Tennessee.
Career Transactions: Selected by Astros in first round (10th overall) of 2001 draft; signed June 22, 2001.
Signed by: Danny Watkins.

The Astros have finished below .500 in just one of their last 13 seasons, so they usually have drafted toward the bottom of the first round. The lone exception came in 2001, when they owned the 10th pick, their highest since they took Phil Nevin No. 1 overall in 1992. Houston used that choice on Burke, who was coming off an All-America junior year at Tennessee. The Southeastern Conference player of the year, he led NCAA Division I in runs (105), hits (118) and total bases (221) and was the only player to rank in the top 10 in hitting (.435), homers (20) and steals (49). As a middle infielder who was a catalyst atop the lineup, Burke drew immediate comparisons to Craig Biggio after the Astros took him. He had a rocky first full season in 2002, when he was assigned to Double-A Round Rock because Houston lacked a high Class A affiliate, but has regrouped since. He returned there to win Texas League all-star honors in 2003 and earned similar acclaim in the Triple-A Pacific Coast League in 2004. He made his major league debut last year and also got to play in the Futures Game in Houston. Though the Astros initially believed Burke could play shortstop, last season marked the first time he played solely at second base. The lesser defensive responsibilities allowed him to relax, and he improved in all phases of the game.

Burke is Biggio's logical successor as Houston's leadoff hitter, though he'll probably bat No. 2 behind him this year. He does a fine job of getting on base, both via hitting for average and drawing walks, and he's a basestealing threat once he gets there. He handles the bat very well, making consistent contact and showing surprising gap power for his size and position. One scout describes him as Mark Loretta with better speed. Burke made better use of his wheels in 2004, improving his leads, jumps and ability to read pitches. Defensively, he has good range to both sides. He made significant strides turning the double play last season. Managers rated Burke the best defender at his position in the PCL, where he led second basemen in every positive fielding category. His work ethic and professionalism also earn high marks.

Burke has too much power for his own good at times. He'll occasionally have to be reminded that he's better off letting extra-base hits come naturally. His arm is his weakest tool, though at second base it's not the liability it was at shortstop. He has smoothed out most of the rough edges, but his second-base play needs a little more cleaning up.

If the Athletics had been willing to pick up Jeff Kent's salary for the final six weeks of 2004, he would have been traded and Burke would have started for the Astros last August. Now that Kent has signed with the Dodgers, Burke is ready to take over. Likening him to a possible Hall of Famer is unfair, but Burke does resemble a young Biggio.

Year	Club (League)	Class	AVG	G	AB	R	H	2B	3B	HR	RBI	BB	SO	SB	OBP	SLG
2001	West Michigan (Mid)	A	.300	56	233	47	70	11	6	3	17	26	31	21	.376	.438
2002	Round Rock (TL)	AA	.264	136	481	66	127	19	8	3	37	39	61	16	.330	.356
2003	Round Rock (TL)	AA	.301	137	549	88	165	23	8	3	41	57	57	34	.379	.388
2004	New Orleans (PCL)	AAA	.315	123	483	93	152	33	6	16	52	55	76	37	.396	.507
	Houston (NL)	MAJ	.059	17	17	2	1	0	0	0	0	3	3	0	.200	.059
MAJOR LEAGUE TOTALS			.059	17	17	2	1	0	0	0	0	3	3	0	.200	.059
MINOR LEAGUE TOTALS			.294	452	1746	294	514	86	28	25	147	177	225	108	.370	.419

Ezequiel Astacio, rhp

Born: Nov. 4, 1979. **Ht.:** 6-3. **Wt.:** 150. **Bats:** R. **Throws:** R. **Career Transactions:** Signed out of Dominican Republic by Phillies, Feb. 22, 1998 . . . Traded by Phillies with RHP Brandon Duckworth and RHP Taylor Buchholz to Astros for LHP Billy Wagner, Nov. 3, 2003. **Signed by:** Wil Tejada (Phillies).

When the Astros traded Billy Wagner last winter, Astacio ranked as the third-most important player they got from the Phillies, behind Taylor Buchholz and Brandon Duckworth. A year later, he looks like the best part of the deal. His stuff jumped dramatically as he led the Texas League in innings and strikeouts. Astacio now has the best fastball in the system. Its velocity has increased from 85-90 in 2002 to 88-93 in 2003 to 90-95 mph in 2004, and it has more sink now as well. His curveball is harder and has more bite, and he picked up a splitter that works well as a change of pace. He has three plus pitches at times and commands all of them. Because his curveball is a hard downer, Astacio ultimately may be better served by a true changeup than relying on his splitter. He sometimes loses his focus on the mound. Astacio rode his momentum through the offseason, when he was named rookie of the year in the Dominican Winter League. He'll probably begin 2005 back in Round Rock, now Houston's Triple-A affiliate, but could help Houston as a starter or reliever later in the season.

Year	Club (League)	Class	W	L	ERA	G	GS	CG	SV	IP	H	R	ER	HR	BB	SO	AVG
1998	Phillies (DSL)	R	0	3	7.71	15	4	0	0	21	26	29	18	3	22	16	.283
1999	Phillies (DSL)	R	5	2	2.67	12	12	0	0	64	50	24	19	4	27	42	.221
2000	Phillies (DSL)	R	7	5	2.20	15	15	0	0	90	70	40	22	1	20	97	.207
2001	Phillies (GCL)	R	4	2	2.30	9	9	0	0	47	48	16	12	2	10	42	.268
2002	Lakewood (SAL)	A	10	7	3.31	25	25	1	0	152	159	61	56	9	46	100	.275
2003	Clearwater (FSL)	A	15	5	3.29	25	22	2	1	148	140	60	54	9	29	83	.247
2004	Round Rock (TL)	AA	13	10	3.89	28	28	1	0	176	155	89	76	12	56	185	.238
MINOR LEAGUE TOTALS			54	34	3.31	129	115	4	1	698	648	319	257	40	210	565	.246

Willy Taveras, of

Born: Dec. 25, 1981. **Ht.:** 6-0. **Wt.:** 160. **Bats:** R. **Throws:** R. **Career Transactions:** Signed out of Dominican Republic by Indians, May 27, 1999 . . . Selected by Astros from Indians in major league Rule 5 draft, Dec. 15, 2003. **Signed by:** Winston Llenas (Indians).

In a quest to find a quality defensive center fielder, Houston took Taveras in the 2003 major league Rule 5 draft, then sent Jeriome Robertson to Cleveland for his rights and slugger Luke Scott. Taveras led the Texas League in hitting and steals, while managers rated him the circuit's best baserunner, top defensive outfielder and most exciting player. Taveras' speed makes him a prolific and high-percentage basestealer, and gives him the range to catch nearly anything hit in the gaps. His quickness also enhances his hitting ability, as he makes good contact and can beat out all but the most routine grounders. He has above-average arm strength and even better accuracy with his throws. To maximize his leadoff ability, Taveras has to develop more patience at the plate. He'll never hit for power, but he needs to add strength to at least deter pitchers from pounding him inside. If it all comes together for Taveras, he could be a superior version of Juan Pierre. After he spends a year in Triple-A, the Astros would love to make him their center fielder in 2006.

Year	Club (League)	Class	AVG	G	AB	R	H	2B	3B	HR	RBI	BB	SO	SB	OBP	SLG
1999	Indians (DSL)	R	.354	68	277	57	98	19	6	3	44	32	32	26	.435	.498
2000	Burlington (Appy)	R	.263	50	190	46	50	4	3	1	16	23	44	36	.356	.332
2001	Columbus (SAL)	A	.271	97	395	55	107	15	7	3	32	22	73	29	.317	.367
2002	Columbus (SAL)	A	.265	85	313	68	83	14	1	4	27	45	68	54	.385	.355
2003	Kinston (Car)	A	.282	113	397	64	112	9	6	2	35	52	68	57	.381	.350
2004	Round Rock (TL)	AA	.335	103	409	76	137	13	1	2	27	38	76	55	.402	.386
	Houston (NL)	MAJ	.000	10	1	2	0	0	0	0	0	0	1	1	.000	.000
MAJOR LEAGUE TOTALS			.000	10	1	2	0	0	0	0	0	0	1	1	.000	.000
MINOR LEAGUE TOTALS			.296	516	1981	366	587	74	24	15	181	212	361	257	.379	.381

4 Mitch Einertson, of

Born: April 4, 1986. **Ht.:** 5-11. **Wt.:** 185. **Bats:** R. **Throws:** R. **School:** Rancho Buena Vista HS, Oceanside, Calif. **Career Transactions:** Selected by Astros in fifth round of 2004 draft; signed June 30, 2004. **Signed by:** Mark Ross.

An unheralded fifth-round pick in June, Einertson tied a 44-year-old home run record in the Rookie-level Appalachian League. He went deep twice in the playoffs as Greeneville won the title, won the MVP award, and led the league in extra-base hits, RBIs, total bases and slugging. One scout said the last Astros prospect to have the ball jump off his bat like Einertson was Jeff Bagwell. He can turn around good fastballs and already has started to use the whole field. He's aggressive in the outfield, where his range, jumps and arm are all decent to solid. Einertson struck out in nearly one-third of his at-bats, so it remains to be seen if he'll be as explosive against higher quality pitching. While he played mostly center field in his pro debut, he doesn't cover enough ground to play there in the majors. Houston tried him at second base in instructional league, but he had problems with his footwork and the switch didn't take. Einertson projects best as a right fielder. He's headed to low Class A Lexington, where the franchise home run mark of 25 is within his reach.

Year	Club (League)	Class	AVG	G	AB	R	H	2B	3B	HR	RBI	BB	SO	SB	OBP	SLG
2004	Greeneville (Appy)	R	.308	63	227	53	70	15	0	24	67	32	70	4	.415	.692
	Tri-City (NY-P)	A	.143	2	7	1	1	0	0	1	1	0	2	0	.143	.571
MINOR LEAGUE TOTALS			.303	65	234	54	71	15	0	25	68	32	72	4	.408	.688

5 Troy Patton, lhp

Born: Sept. 3, 1985. **Ht.:** 6-1. **Wt.:** 185. **Bats:** B. **Throws:** L. **School:** Tomball HS, Magnolia, Texas. **Career Transactions:** Selected by Astros in ninth round of 2004 draft; signed July 26, 2004. **Signed by:** Rusty Pendergrass.

Patton was the ace of a Tomball High team that ranked No. 1 in the nation last spring before losing in the Texas 5-A playoffs. Pro clubs thought he was headed to the University of Texas but the Astros signed him for $550,000, by far the highest bonus in the ninth round. Patton's curveball was one of the best in the 2004 draft. He sets it up by throwing his 90-94 mph fastball to all four quadrants of the strike zone. He has an advanced feel for his changeup and for throwing strikes, which could allow him to develop quickly. He has an intellectual curiosity about pitching, trying to pick up a cutter on his own during instructional league. Patton's one obvious flaw is his inability to maintain a consistent arm slot. When he drops down, he loses velocity on his pitches and some crispness on his curve. Like most young pitchers, he needs additional work on his changeup. In addition to his stuff and pitchability, Patton stands out because the system lacks lefthanded pitching prospects. He'll start his first full season in low Class A and shouldn't need a full season at each level.

Year	Club (League)	Class	W	L	ERA	G	GS	CG	SV	IP	H	R	ER	HR	BB	SO	AVG
2004	Greeneville (Appy)	R	2	2	1.93	6	6	0	0	28	23	8	6	1	5	32	.215
MINOR LEAGUE TOTALS			2	2	1.93	6	6	0	0	28	23	8	6	1	5	32	.215

6 Matt Albers, rhp

Born: Jan. 20, 1983. **Ht.:** 6-0. **Wt.:** 205. **Bats:** L. **Throws:** R. **School:** San Jacinto (Texas) JC. **Career Transactions:** Selected by Astros in 23rd round of 2001 draft; signed May 31, 2002. **Signed by:** Rusty Pendergrass.

Drafted out of a suburban Houston high school and signed as a draft-and-follow out of local junior college power San Jacinto, Albers has had more strikeouts than innings in each of his three pro seasons. He was suspended for an alcohol-related incident at the low Class A South Atlantic League all-star game last June and spent a month in rehab. He didn't miss a beat when he returned. Albers achieves late, heavy sink with a fastball that sits at 92-93 mph and tops out at 96. He can overmatch hitters simply by pitching inside. He also throws a curveball, slider and changeup, all of which have their moments. He's durable and throws with little effort after improving his delivery. Albers' greatest need is for more consistency on the mound and off the field. His secondary pitches and command come and go, and he must take his career more seriously. His body isn't as soft as it was when he signed, but it's still a concern. Slated for high Class A Salem, Albers could force his way to Houston's new Double-A Corpus Christi affiliate by the end of 2005. He has a high ceiling but also a long distance to go to reach it.

Year	Club (League)	Class	W	L	ERA	G	GS	CG	SV	IP	H	R	ER	HR	BB	SO	AVG
2002	Greeneville (Appy)	R	2	3	5.13	13	13	0	0	60	61	38	34	2	38	72	.274
2003	Tri-City (NY-P)	A	5	4	2.92	15	14	0	0	86	69	37	28	1	25	94	.214
2004	Lexington (SAL)	A	8	3	3.31	22	21	0	0	111	95	51	41	3	57	140	.228
MINOR LEAGUE TOTALS			15	10	3.60	50	48	0	0	257	225	126	103	6	120	306	.234

7 Taylor Buchholz, rhp

Born: Oct. 13, 1981. **Ht.:** 6-4. **Wt.:** 220. **Bats:** R. **Throws:** R. **School:** Springfield (Pa.) HS. **Career Transactions:** Selected by Phillies in sixth round of 2000 draft; signed June 19, 2000 . . . Traded by Phillies with RHP Brandon Duckworth and RHP Ezequiel Astacio to Astros for LHP Billy Wagner, Nov. 3, 2003. **Signed by:** Ken Hultzapple (Phillies).

Buchholz topped this list a year ago after arriving in the Billy Wagner trade with the Phillies. He started poorly with the Astros, going 0-5, 7.92 in his first six outings at Triple-A New Orleans. He was pitching better when a shoulder strain shut him down in early July. He didn't need surgery, but made just three more relief appearances in mid-August. Buchholz has one of the best curveballs in the minors, a hard, sharp bender that he can change speeds with. He has plus velocity on his fastball at 91-95 mph. He has improved his changeup, which should become a solid average pitch, and come up with a two-seam fastball with more sink. After his shoulder problems and bone chips in his elbow in 2003, Buchholz needs to get stronger and more durable. He usually throws a four-seam fastball and works too high in the strike zone. He tries to be too perfect and out-thinks himself, and there are some worries that he may give in to adversity too easily. Buchholz should be fully healthy for spring training. He needs some extended success in Triple-A before he'll get his first big league callup.

Year	Club (League)	Class	W	L	ERA	G	GS	CG	SV	IP	H	R	ER	HR	BB	SO	AVG
2000	Phillies (GCL)	R	2	3	2.25	12	7	0	0	44	46	22	11	2	14	41	.269
2001	Lakewood (SAL)	A	9	14	3.36	28	26	5	0	177	165	83	66	8	57	136	.250
2002	Clearwater (FSL)	A	10	6	3.29	23	23	4	0	159	140	66	58	11	51	129	.233
	Reading (EL)	AA	0	2	7.43	4	4	0	0	23	29	19	19	5	6	17	.315
2003	Reading (EL)	AA	9	11	3.55	25	24	1	0	145	136	62	57	14	33	114	.249
2004	New Orleans (PCL)	AAA	6	7	5.23	20	17	1	0	98	107	60	57	16	29	74	.273
MINOR LEAGUE TOTALS			36	43	3.74	112	101	11	0	645	623	312	268	56	190	511	.253

8 Fernando Nieve, rhp

Born: July 15, 1982. **Ht.:** 6-0. **Wt.:** 195. **Bats:** R. **Throws:** R. **Career Transactions:** Signed out of Venezuela by Astros, May 11, 1999. **Signed by:** Andres Reiner.

Though Nieve has pitched just 17 innings above Class A in six pro seasons, his upside has led the Astros to carry him on their 40-man roster since the end of the 2003 season. He dominated the Venezuelan League last winter, but didn't enjoy the same success there this offseason. Nieve pitches off his electric 91-97 mph fastball. He gets heavy sink on his two-seamer, likes to challenge hitters up with a four-seamer and mixes in some cutters. He throws both a curveball and a slider, and they can be strikeout pitches at times. He has a strong body and resilient arm. Nieve lacks consistent feel for a changeup because he prefers to throw hard. For that same reason, he can fall in love with his straight four-seamer, and doesn't always locate it where he wants. He can get caught in between his two breaking balls, resulting in a slurve. If his secondary pitches don't improve, Nieve could become a power reliever in the mold of Guillermo Mota. He competed well in Double-A at the end of 2004 and will pitch in the rotation there this season.

Year	Club (League)	Class	W	L	ERA	G	GS	CG	SV	IP	H	R	ER	HR	BB	SO	AVG
1999	La Pradera (VSL)	R	0	6	4.50	11	7	0	0	32	31	22	16	0	16	41	—
2000	San Joaquin (VSL)	R	3	4	2.71	14	13	0	0	80	56	29	24	5	28	64	.199
2001	Greeneville (Appy)	R	4	2	3.79	12	8	1	0	38	27	20	16	2	21	49	.197
2002	Greeneville (Appy)	R	4	1	2.39	13	13	0	0	68	46	23	18	5	27	60	.185
	Lexington (SAL)	A	0	1	6.00	1	1	0	0	3	6	5	2	0	0	2	.353
2003	Lexington (SAL)	A	14	9	3.65	28	28	1	0	150	133	69	61	10	65	144	.238
2004	Round Rock (TL)	AA	2	0	1.56	3	3	0	0	17	12	4	3	0	8	17	.197
	Salem (Car)	A	10	6	2.96	24	24	2	0	149	136	52	49	9	40	117	.242
MINOR LEAGUE TOTALS			37	29	3.17	106	97	4	0	537	447	224	189	31	205	494	.239

9 Josh Anderson, of

Born: Aug. 10, 1982. **Ht.:** 6-2. **Wt.:** 195. **Bats:** L. **Throws:** R. **School:** Eastern Kentucky University. **Career Transactions:** Selected by Astros in fourth round of 2003 draft; signed June 13, 2003. **Signed by:** Nick Venuto.

Anderson led NCAA Division I in 2003 with 57 steals and finished third in hitting at .447 behind first-round picks Rickie Weeks and Mitch Maier. He has swiped 105 bases in 213 games and topped the minors with 79 last year. Anderson has plus-plus speed and knows how to use it. He has succeeded on 83 percent of his pro steal attempts, and he also covers a lot of ground in center field. He's similar to Willy Taveras, with Anderson owning significantly more gap power. He has solid average arm strength. Anderson's full-tilt style borders on recklessness. He's too aggressive in the outfield, often breaking wrong on balls and hoping his speed will help him recover. He tore up low Class A, but was far less effective when his plate discipline evaporated following a promotion to high Class A. Taveras is the frontrunner to be Houston's center fielder of the future, but Anderson can close the gap if he learns to play within himself and show more patience at the plate. He'll probably open 2005 in Double-A.

Year	Club (League)	Class	AVG	G	AB	R	H	2B	3B	HR	RBI	BB	SO	SB	OBP	SLG
2003	Tri-City (NY-P)	A	.286	74	297	44	85	11	4	3	30	16	53	26	.339	.380
2004	Lexington (SAL)	A	.326	73	298	69	97	12	3	4	31	33	47	48	.403	.426
	Salem (Car)	A	.268	66	280	45	75	13	6	2	21	13	53	31	.314	.379
MINOR LEAGUE TOTALS			.294	213	875	158	257	36	13	9	82	62	153	105	.354	.395

10 Hunter Pence, of

Born: April 13, 1983. **Ht.:** 6-4. **Wt.:** 210. **Bats:** R. **Throws:** R. **School:** University of Texas-Arlington. **Career Transactions:** Selected by Astros in second round of 2004 draft; signed July 3, 2004. **Signed by:** Rusty Pendergrass.

After Pence won the Southland Conference batting title (.395) and player-of-the-year award last spring, the Astros made him their top draft pick. Most teams didn't expect him to go as early as the second round, but he showed diverse tools during a strong pro debut. He doesn't have a classic swing and chokes up on the bat more than most players his size, but it works for Pence. He has quick hands, a feel for hitting and as much raw power as anyone in the system. He also controls the strike zone. Pence's gangly body is deceptive, because he's a good athlete with solid speed. He plays hard while keeping himself under control. Though Pence acquitted himself well playing center field at short-season Tri-City, his reads and arm are slightly below-average. He's going to have to move left field at higher levels, but the good news is that he should have enough bat for the position. Pence will begin his first full season with one of Houston's full-season Class A clubs, and he should be able to handle the jump to Salem if he skips a level. He quickly has become an organization favorite and could move more quickly than initially expected.

Year	Club (League)	Class	AVG	G	AB	R	H	2B	3B	HR	RBI	BB	SO	SB	OBP	SLG
2004	Tri-City (NY-P)	A	.296	51	199	36	59	18	1	8	37	23	30	3	.369	.518
MINOR LEAGUE TOTALS			.296	51	199	36	59	18	1	8	37	23	30	3	.369	.518

11 Chad Qualls, rhp

Born: Aug. 17, 1978. **Ht.:** 6-5. **Wt.:** 220. **Bats:** R. **Throws:** R. **School:** University of Nevada. **Career Transactions:** Selected by Astros in second round of 2000 draft; signed Aug. 16, 2000. **Signed by:** Gene Wellman.

If Qualls can shake off a couple of meltdowns in the playoffs—a three-run homer to Adam LaRoche to blow Game Four of the National League Division Series, and a five-run sixth-inning to take the loss in Game One of the NL Championship Series—he has the stuff to become Houston's top set-up man for Brad Lidge. Summoned by the Astros late last July, he posted the best ERA among their regular relievers after Lidge and Octavio Dotel. He showed the poise Houston hoped for. Groomed exclusively as a starter in the minors until the Astros traded Dotel last June, Qualls has well-above-average command of a plus slider. Since he has signed, Houston has worked to get him to keep his arm slot up, and that lesson finally seems to be sinking in. A true three-quarters angle adds more sink to his 87-94 mph fastball and gets groundballs. To better combat lefthanders, he's been working on a splitter, but didn't use it much in the majors last year. Qualls has enough pitches to start, but he's more valuable to Houston serving as a bridge to Lidge right now.

Year	Club (League)	Class	W	L	ERA	G	GS	CG	SV	IP	H	R	ER	HR	BB	SO	AVG
2001	Michigan (Mid)	A	15	6	3.72	26	26	3	0	162	149	77	67	2	31	125	.239
2002	Round Rock (TL)	AA	6	13	4.36	29	29	0	0	163	174	92	79	3	67	142	.273
2003	Round Rock (TL)	AA	8	11	3.85	28	28	3	0	175	174	85	75	12	61	132	.264
2004	Houston (NL)	MAJ	4	0	3.55	25	0	0	1	33	34	13	13	3	8	24	.266
	New Orleans (PCL)	AAA	3	6	5.57	32	14	1	1	107	134	69	66	8	30	72	.312
MAJOR LEAGUE TOTALS			4	0	3.55	25	0	0	1	33	34	13	13	3	8	24	.266
MINOR LEAGUE TOTALS			32	36	4.26	115	97	7	1	607	631	323	287	25	189	471	.269

12 Juan Gutierrez, rhp

Born: July 14, 1983. **Ht.:** 6-3. **Wt.:** 200. **Bats:** R. **Throws:** R. **Career Transactions:** Signed out of Venezuela by Astros, Dec. 14, 2000. **Signed by:** Andres Reiner/Pablo Torrealba/Rafael Lara.

Because Gutierrez has repeated both the Rookie-level Venezuelan Summer and Appalachian leagues, he had to be protected on the 40-man roster this offseason, before he even threw a pitch in full-season ball. While he remains raw, the Astros weren't going to risk losing him in the major league Rule 5 draft. He tied for the Appy League lead in victories with Greeneville teammate Levi Romero, and Gutierrez capped his season by pitching seven innings of one-run ball in the championship clincher. He already has two plus pitches in his 90-96 mph fastball and a big-breaking curveball. Houston also praises his makeup, pointing to his leadership as a key factor in Greeneville's championship. Guttierez' changeup should become at least average, but he needs to use it more. He had difficulty maintaining his mechanics early in the summer, so for a while he won with just his fastball. If he learns how to repeat his delivery, he'll also improve his control, which wavers at times. He has a sturdy frame but needs to make sure it doesn't go soft on him. Gutierrez was old for the Appy League at 21, and now that the clock on his options has started ticking, the Astros will accelerate his development. It's possible he could skip a level and open 2005 in high Class A.

Year	Club (League)	Class	W	L	ERA	G	GS	CG	SV	IP	H	R	ER	HR	BB	SO	AVG
2001	San Joaquin (VSL)	R	1	0	1.78	10	3	0	4	25	23	8	5	0	8	17	.000
2002	San Joaquin (VSL)	R	3	2	2.13	13	7	0	1	38	35	14	9	0	12	28	.252
2003	Greeneville (Appy)	R	1	2	4.76	16	3	0	2	34	42	22	18	2	13	30	.302
2004	Greeneville (Appy)	R	8	2	3.70	13	13	0	0	66	74	31	27	4	30	59	.290
MINOR LEAGUE TOTALS			13	6	3.26	52	26	0	7	163	174	75	59	6	63	134	.326

13 Tommy Whiteman, ss

Born: July 14, 1979. **Ht.:** 6-3. **Wt.:** 180. **Bats:** R. **Throws:** R. **School:** University of Oklahoma. **Career Transactions:** Selected by Astros in sixth round of 2000 draft; signed June 16, 2000. **Signed by:** David Henderson.

Whiteman got himself back in the Astros' good graces in 2004, a year after he turned them off with a mediocre performance and a poor attitude. Last season, he was more driven and focused and took a much better approach at the plate. The lone negative came in mid-July, when he broke the tip of his right thumb during a bunt attempt. He played just one more game before the Arizona Fall League, and had he not been hurt he would have received big league playing time in September. Whiteman continues to show five tools at shortstop. He hit a career-high .320 in 2004 and has good gap power for a middle infielder. An average runner, he moves well and has a strong arm and sure hands at shortstop. After getting too bulky in 2003, he got stronger without losing flexibility last season. Whiteman still needs more strength. His swing can get long, making it a struggle for him to catch up to quality fastballs, and he tends to chase high pitches. He'll play every day at Triple-A, but he may start to push big league incumbent Adam Everett because Whiteman has a superior bat. He would become the first member of the Crow Nation to reach the big leagues.

Year	Club (League)	Class	AVG	G	AB	R	H	2B	3B	HR	RBI	BB	SO	SB	OBP	SLG
2000	Auburn (NY-P)	A	.250	70	232	33	58	10	3	1	22	22	52	7	.318	.332
2001	Lexington (SAL)	A	.319	114	389	58	124	26	8	18	57	34	106	17	.380	.566
	Round Rock (TL)	AA	.250	4	16	1	4	0	0	1	1	0	5	0	.294	.438
2002	Round Rock (TL)	AA	.179	15	56	3	10	2	1	0	5	4	17	1	.246	.250
	Lexington (SAL)	A	.303	90	350	50	106	29	2	10	49	36	66	6	.374	.483
2003	Round Rock (TL)	AA	.261	133	532	65	139	18	2	13	70	35	102	3	.310	.376
2004	Round Rock (TL)	AA	.336	68	277	39	93	14	0	8	45	20	45	5	.381	.473
	New Orleans (PCL)	AAA	.276	25	98	11	27	6	0	0	9	8	21	2	.336	.337
MINOR LEAGUE TOTALS			.288	519	1950	260	561	105	16	51	258	159	414	41	.346	.436

14 Hector Gimenez, c

Born: Sept. 28, 1982. **Ht.:** 5-10. **Wt.:** 180. **Bats:** S. **Throws:** R. **Career Transactions:** Signed out of Venezuela by Astros, July 2, 1999. **Signed by:** Andres Reiner.

The inclusion of John Buck in the Carlos Beltran trade left Gimenez as Houston's best catching prospect by default. In order to hold off 2004 draftees Lou Santangelo and J.R. Towles, Gimenez will need to start showing more offensively. While he has some pop, he has little feel for the strike zone and his batting average has declined in each of his five pro seasons. His bat looked sluggish last year, and few Texas League observers had faith in his ability to hit. A switch-hitter, he consistently has performed better from his natural right side. Defensively, Gimenez has all the tools. He has a strong arm and a quick release, moves well behind the plate and has a durable frame. He's not afraid to try to pick off baserunners. As his English has improved, so has his ability to call a game, and he's doing a better job of not allowing bad at-bats to affect his work behind the plate. His speed, like that of most catchers, is below-average. Though Gimenez will have to repeat Double-A this year, the good news is that he's still just 22.

Year	Club (League)	Class	AVG	G	AB	R	H	2B	3B	HR	RBI	BB	SO	SB	OBP	SLG
2000	Venoco (VSL)	R	.297	34	91	9	27	8	0	1	13	12	21	0	.396	.418
2001	Venoco (VSL)	R	.278	42	144	27	40	12	3	5	34	26	30	4	.388	.507
2002	Lexington (SAL)	A	.263	85	297	41	78	16	1	11	42	25	78	2	.320	.434
2003	Salem (Car)	A	.247	109	381	41	94	17	1	7	54	29	75	2	.304	.352
2004	Round Rock (TL)	AA	.245	97	331	38	81	16	3	6	46	18	64	2	.284	.366
MINOR LEAGUE TOTALS			.257	367	1244	156	320	69	8	30	189	110	268	10	.320	.398

15 Jimmy Barthmaier, rhp

Born: Jan. 6, 1984. **Ht.:** 6-4. **Wt.:** 210. **Bats:** R. **Throws:** R. **School:** Roswell (Ga.) HS. **Career Transactions:** Selected by Astros in 13th round of 2003 draft; signed July 3, 2003. **Signed by:** Ellis Dungan.

Teams viewed Barthmaier as a possible supplemental first-round pick in 2003, but they couldn't gauge his signability. Several Atlantic Coast and Southeastern conference football programs recruited him as a quarterback, and though he never officially accepted a scholarship, clubs weren't sure he'd give up the gridiron. Barthmaier told Astros area scout Ellis Dungan he was willing to turn pro, however, so Houston was able to take him in the 11th round and sign him for $750,000, more money than they gave any other 2003 draft pick. He has spent both of his pro seasons in the Appalachian League, which he led in innings last summer. He won the championship clincher in the playoffs, working three scoreless innings in relief. As expected from a former quarterback, Barthmaier is tall, athletic and owns a strong arm. His fastball sits at 91-92 mph, already touches 93-94 and features late life. Houston changed his grip on his hard curveball, which now has more of a downward break. He's still in the early stages of developing his changeup. His mechanics have improved, but he still throws across his body too much and needs more refinement. His fastball command has gotten better, but he has to work on his control and consistency of his other pitches. He overthrows his curveball at times. Barthmaier will move up to low Class A this year.

Year	Club (League)	Class	W	L	ERA	G	GS	CG	SV	IP	H	R	ER	HR	BB	SO	AVG
2003	Greeneville (Appy)	R	1	1	2.49	8	3	0	0	22	19	9	6	0	7	18	.226
2004	Greeneville (Appy)	R	4	3	3.78	13	13	0	0	69	70	32	29	3	22	65	.258
MINOR LEAGUE TOTALS			5	4	3.47	21	16	0	0	91	89	41	35	3	29	83	.251

16 Ben Zobrist, ss

Born: May 26, 1981. **Ht.:** 6-3. **Wt.:** 200. **Bats:** S. **Throws:** R. **School:** Dallas Baptist University. **Career Transactions:** Selected by Astros in sixth round of 2004 draft; signed June 16, 2004. **Signed by:** Rusty Pendergrass.

The Astros aren't sure exactly what they have in Zobrist, who led Olivet Nazarene (Ill.) to the NAIA World Series in 2003 and Dallas Baptist to the Christian College Athletic Association World Series title last spring. After signing for $55,000 as a sixth-round pick, he topped the short-season New York-Penn League in batting and on-base percentage. But at 23, he was one of the oldest players in the league. Zobrist has average tools across the board, but his makeup and instincts stick out more than his physical attributes. He does everything well, from controlling the strike zone as a switch-hitter to running the bases to making the plays at shortstop. Zobrist's power lags behind his other skills, but he's 6-foot-3 and 200 pounds, and Houston expects him to develop more pop. Though the transition to pro ball didn't slow him down, he has a few adjustments to make. His swing can get a little long from the right side, and he can be a better bunter. Defensively, he needs to do a better job of setting his feet so he's in position to make throws on routine plays. Realistically, Zobrist's ceiling is probably as a utility player in the mold of former Astro Bill Spiers, yet it's too early to discount him as a possible everyday shortstop. He needs to be challenged with an assignment to high Class A, but that's also the likely destination of shortstop prospects Edwin Maysonet and Osvaldo Fernando.

Year	Club (League)	Class	AVG	G	AB	R	H	2B	3B	HR	RBI	BB	SO	SB	OBP	SLG
2004	Tri-City (NY-P)	A	.339	68	257	50	87	14	3	4	45	43	31	15	.438	.463
MINOR LEAGUE TOTALS			.339	68	257	50	87	14	3	4	45	43	31	15	.438	.463

17 Luke Scott, of

Born: June 25, 1978. **Ht.:** 6-0. **Wt.:** 210. **Bats:** L. **Throws:** R. **School:** Oklahoma State University. **Career Transactions:** Selected by Indians in ninth round of 2001 draft; signed June 9, 2001 . . . Traded by Indians with the rights to OF Willy Taveras to Astros for LHP Jeriome Robertson, March 31, 2004. **Signed by:** Chad MacDonald (Indians).

Every time Scott seems to make progress, his career takes a detour. He announced himself as a legitimate prospect when he led the Cape Cod League with 11 homers in 2000, but blew out his elbow and required Tommy John surgery in 2001, preventing him from making his pro debut after signing with the Indians as a ninth-round pick. He started to establish himself in the Cleveland system with a 20-homer season while reaching Double-A in 2003, only to get included in the Jeriome Robertson-Willy Taveras trade last March. Because he joined the Astros after they had their minor league rosters mostly set, Scott had to go back to high Class A at age 25. When Houston finally found a Double-A job for him in late June, he raked for the rest of the season. The Astros are short on lefthanded power, and that's Scott's best tool. They love his makeup but want to see him do a better job of using the whole field and dealing with breaking pitches. His speed and arm are below-average but not terrible, and he fits better in left field than in right. Scott will begin this year in Triple-A and could get his first big league callup later in the season.

Year	Club (League)	Class	AVG	G	AB	R	H	2B	3B	HR	RBI	BB	SO	SB	OBP	SLG
2001	Did not play—Injured															
2002	Columbus (SAL)	A	.257	49	171	28	44	15	4	7	32	21	58	9	.345	.515
	Kinston (Car)	A	.239	48	163	22	39	7	1	8	30	16	47	2	.326	.442
2003	Kinston (Car)	A	.278	67	241	37	67	12	1	13	44	27	62	6	.360	.498
	Akron (EL)	AA	.273	50	183	21	50	13	1	7	37	11	37	0	.317	.470
2004	Salem (Car)	A	.278	66	241	45	67	20	1	8	35	41	58	6	.376	.469
	Round Rock (TL)	AA	.298	63	208	45	62	17	0	19	62	33	43	0	.401	.654
MINOR LEAGUE TOTALS			.273	343	1207	198	329	84	8	62	240	149	305	23	.358	.510

18 Lou Santangelo, c

Born: March 16, 1983. **Ht.:** 6-1. **Wt.:** 200. **Bats:** R. **Throws:** R. **School:** Clemson University. **Career Transactions:** Selected by Astros in fourth round of 2004 draft; signed June 30, 2004. **Signed by:** Brian Keegan.

Pitchers grabbed 20 of the 30 spots on this list a year ago, and Houston addressed its need for position prospects in the 2004 draft, spending its first five picks on hitters who made the top 30: Hunter Pence, Jordan Parraz, Santangelo, Mitch Einertson and Ben Zobrist. While Einertson tied the Appalachian League record for homers, one Astros scout says Santangelo has more raw power. The difference between the two is that Santangelo does more of his damage against fastballs out over the plate or mistake breaking balls, while Einertson handles himself better against quality pitches. The key for Santangelo is making consistent contact. A hitch in his swing prevented him from topping .300 with aluminum bats at Seton Hall and Clemson. Though he shortened his stroke after turning pro, he was overmatched by breaking balls, in part because his pitch recognition is lacking. Santangelo won't need to hit for a high average to be a valuable catcher with his power and defense, but a .201 average in the New York-Penn League won't cut it. He's a below-average runner but runs well for a catcher. His defensive skills are nearly as good as those of Hector Gimenez. Santangelo has a strong and accurate arm, finishing second among NY-P regulars by throwing out 36 percent of basestealers. He'll begin his first full season in Class A, perhaps at Lexington in order to get his bat going.

Year	Club (League)	Class	AVG	G	AB	R	H	2B	3B	HR	RBI	BB	SO	SB	OBP	SLG
2004	Tri-City (NY-P)	A	.201	47	164	28	33	5	2	6	20	21	58	2	.299	.366
MINOR LEAGUE TOTALS			.201	47	164	28	33	5	2	6	20	21	58	2	.299	.366

19 Jordan Parraz, of

Born: Oct. 18, 1984. **Ht.:** 6-3. **Wt.:** 212. **Bats:** R. **Throws:** R. **School:** CC of Southern Nevada. **Career Transactions:** Selected by Astros in third round of 2004 draft; signed June 16, 2004. **Signed by:** Doug Deutsch.

Parraz went to the Community College of Southern Nevada after the Phillies took him in the sixth round in 2003, making him the highest pick among draft-and-follows from that draft. Philadelphia selected him as a pitcher, and Parraz touched 96 mph in junior college. But his control was so poor that he lost his job in the rotation, and when he re-entered the

2004 draft, the Astros made him a third-round choice as an outfielder. Signed for $400,000, Parraz offers a tantalizing array of tools and a frustrating lack of baseball acumen. Though he hit .359 with wood bats at Southern Nevada during the spring, he arrived in pro ball with an ugly swing. He batted just .198 through July before the Greeneville staff adjusted how he held his hands in his stance. Able to catch up to fastballs better after the change, he hit .295 the rest of the way. Parraz has average power and slightly above-average speed, but he'll have to make more contact to use them. He's probably not consistent enough to play center field, and he undermines his plus-plus arm strength by throwing to the wrong base. Parraz will need plenty of time to develop, and his next step is low Class A.

Year	Club (League)	Class	AVG	G	AB	R	H	2B	3B	HR	RBI	BB	SO	SB	OBP	SLG
2004	Greeneville (Appy)	R	.244	53	180	35	44	6	5	4	21	24	44	9	.349	.400
MINOR LEAGUE TOTALS			.244	53	180	35	44	6	5	4	21	24	44	9	.349	.400

20 Chad Reineke, rhp

Born: April 9, 1982. **Ht.:** 6-7. **Wt.:** 210. **Bats:** R. **Throws:** R. **School:** Miami (Ohio) University. **Career Transactions:** Selected by Astros in 13th round of 2004 draft; signed Jun 16, 2004. **Signed by:** Nick Venuto.

Reineke served as a midweek starter and long reliever in his first three years at Miami (Ohio), enjoying only sporadic success and drawing no interest in the 2003 draft. Moved to short relief as a senior, he saw his velocity and pro prospects improve. After signing as a 13th-round pick, Reineke showed a 92-96 mph fastball and mid-80s slider at times during his pro debut. He hides the ball well, and at 6-foot-7 he throws on a steep downhill plane, making him that much more difficult on hitters. He's also a tough competitor. Whether Reineke becomes a late-inning reliever in the majors depends on whether he can find consistency. He's not flexible, so he can't always finish his delivery. That makes it tough for him to repeat his stuff and to throw strikes. Reineke is a project, but he has a solid two-pitch foundation to build upon. He'll probably start 2005 in low Class A.

Year	Club (League)	Class	W	L	ERA	G	GS	CG	SV	IP	H	R	ER	HR	BB	SO	AVG
2004	Tri-City (NY-P)	A	0	2	2.45	23	0	0	3	37	27	13	10	0	23	52	.206
MINOR LEAGUE TOTALS			0	2	2.45	23	0	0	3	37	27	13	10	0	23	52	.206

21 Jared Gothreaux, rhp

Born: Jan. 27, 1980. **Ht.:** 6-0. **Wt.:** 200. **Bats:** R. **Throws:** R. **School:** McNeese State University. **Career Transactions:** Selected by Astros in 16th round of 2002 draft; signed June 6, 2002. **Signed by:** James Farrar.

Coming into 2004, Gothreaux and newly acquired Ezequiel Astacio had similar résumés. They had comparable stuff and nearly identical statistics in 2003, when they both led high Class A leagues in victories. But as Astacio took a huge step forward last year, surprisingly becoming the organization's best pitching prospect, Gothreaux leveled off in Double-A. Though he finished strong with a 1.57 ERA in his final eight starts, he now looks like he'd be best off going the Chad Qualls route and using his plus slider to become a set-up man. Moving to the bullpen likely would boost Gothreaux' 88-92 mph fastball a couple of notches, making him more effective. He also has developed a decent changeup. Gothreaux throws strikes but can work in the zone too often, becoming hittable because he doesn't have a true put-away pitch. Though he'll remain a starter in Triple-A for now, he could see the bullpen—and his first glimpse of the big leagues—in 2005.

Year	Club (League)	Class	W	L	ERA	G	GS	CG	SV	IP	H	R	ER	HR	BB	SO	AVG
2002	Tri-City (NY-P)	A	2	3	2.72	28	0	0	4	46	55	23	14	3	12	53	.288
2003	Salem (Car)	A	13	4	2.82	29	22	1	1	147	144	54	46	4	26	85	.259
2004	Round Rock (TL)	AA	9	7	3.96	27	24	2	0	157	172	82	69	16	35	110	.279
MINOR LEAGUE TOTALS			24	14	3.32	84	46	3	5	350	371	159	129	23	73	248	.272

22 Mitch Talbot, rhp

Born: Oct. 17, 1983. **Ht.:** 6-2. **Wt.:** 175. **Bats:** R. **Throws:** R. **School:** Canyon View HS, Cedar City, Utah. **Career Transactions:** Selected by Astros in second round of 2002 draft; signed Aug. 20, 2002. **Signed by:** Doug Deutsch.

The only Utah high schooler taken in the first 35 rounds in 2002, Talbot got caught in the Astros' temporary embargo on signing draft picks and didn't make his pro debut until the following summer. His polish served as a contrast to the rest of Lexington's 2004 rotation, which included more electric but less refined arms in Matt Albers, Derick Grigsby and Chance Douglass. Talbot already has the best changeup in the organization and a feel for pitching beyond his years. His athletic delivery and arm action, which have prompted comparisons to Ron Darling and Todd Stottlemyre, allow him to throws strikes with little diffi-culty. He runs his 90-91 mph fastball, which peaks at 93, in on hitters. What Talbot needs to reach his ceiling as a No. 3 or 4 starter is a better breaking ball. He has been working on a slider, but his arm action might be more conducive to throwing a curveball. Ticketed for high Class A in 2005, he could move quickly once he finds a reliable breaking pitch.

Year	Club (League)	Class	W	L	ERA	G	GS	CG	SV	IP	H	R	ER	HR	BB	SO	AVG
2003	Greeneville (Appy)	R	4	4	2.83	12	12	0	0	54	45	26	17	1	11	46	.224
2004	Lexington (SAL)	A	10	10	3.83	27	27	1	0	153	145	78	65	16	49	115	.247
MINOR LEAGUE TOTALS			14	14	3.57	39	39	1	0	207	190	104	82	17	60	161	.241

23 Brooks Conrad, 2b

Born: Jan. 16, 1980. **Ht.:** 5-11. **Wt.:** 190. **Bats:** S. **Throws:** R. **School:** Arizona State University. **Career Transactions:** Selected by Astros in eighth round of 2001 draft; signed June 18, 2001. **Signed by:** Andrew Cotner.

Though Conrad hasn't cracked the 40-man roster the last two years and drawn nary a nib-ble in the Rule 5 draft, he has two team MVP awards and two league all-star selections in four seasons of pro ball and seems destined to scrap his way to the majors. He's not pretty but finds a way to get the job done, and he has winning makeup. A switch-hitter, Conrad gets on base and has surprising pop for his size. At times he'll get too much loft in his swing or too much length in his righthanded stroke, but he made progress in both areas last year. More of a run producer than the typical middle infielder, he has averaged 83 RBIs per full season and tied for the minor league lead with 12 sacrifice flies in 2004. Conrad has aver-age speed and good instincts on the bases. Defensively, he won't always show the best reads or footwork, but he has sure hands and makes plays. With Chris Burke ahead of him, Conrad probably won't ever start for the Astros. But he has proven himself at every step of the way, with Triple-A the only hurdle remaining before he can help a big league club.

Year	Club (League)	Class	AVG	G	AB	R	H	2B	3B	HR	RBI	BB	SO	SB	OBP	SLG
2001	Pittsfield (NY-P)	A	.280	65	232	41	65	16	5	4	39	26	52	14	.375	.444
2002	West Michigan (Mid)	A	.287	133	499	94	143	25	14	14	94	62	102	18	.368	.477
2003	Lexington (SAL)	A	.186	38	140	20	26	5	2	3	11	17	25	7	.288	.314
	Salem (Car)	A	.284	99	345	50	98	24	3	11	61	42	60	4	.369	.467
2004	Round Rock (TL)	AA	.290	129	480	84	139	39	6	13	83	63	105	8	.365	.477
MINOR LEAGUE TOTALS			.278	464	1696	289	471	109	30	45	288	210	344	51	.362	.457

24 Edwin Maysonet, 2b/ss

Born: Oct. 17, 1981. **Ht.:** 6-1. **Wt.:** 180. **Bats:** R. **Throws:** R. **School:** Delta State (Miss.) University. **Career Transactions:** Selected by Astros in 19th round of 2003 draft; signed June 5, 2003. **Signed by:** Mike Rosamond.

Maysonet is a sleeper shortstop prospect, but his teammates have prevented him from logging much time at the position since he turned pro. Wade Robinson handled most of the shortstop duties at Tri-City in 2003, and Osvaldo Fernando was the primary shortstop at Lexington last year. Maysonet had to settle for playing short once or twice a week and spending the rest of his time at second base. His range and arm are average at shortstop, and his hands and instincts are assets. He's not as slick a fielder as Robinson or Fernando, but Maysonet is much more dangerous at the plate. He has a knack for drawing walks, can play the gaps and can steal bases with his average speed. With 2004 sixth-rounder Ben Zobrist also pushing for playing time at shortstop in Class A, Maysonet may never get to play regularly there. But he just might make a good utilityman, and he'll keep working toward the majors this year in high Class A.

Year	Club (League)	Class	AVG	G	AB	R	H	2B	3B	HR	RBI	BB	SO	SB	OBP	SLG
2003	Tri-City (NY-P)	A	.275	45	138	30	38	7	1	1	13	29	28	9	.411	.362
2004	Lexington (SAL)	A	.261	109	391	79	102	22	10	11	64	64	91	18	.372	.453
MINOR LEAGUE TOTALS			.265	154	529	109	140	29	11	12	77	93	119	27	.382	.429

25 Mark McLemore, lhp

Born: Oct. 9, 1980. **Ht.:** 6-2. **Wt.:** 220. **Bats:** L. **Throws:** L. **School:** Oregon State University. **Career Transactions:** Selected by Astros in fourth round of 2002 draft; signed June 15, 2002. **Signed by:** Dan Houston.

McLemore's arm always has been light years ahead of his confidence. He never had a win-ning record at Oregon State, where he went 3-9 in three seasons, and he dropped 17 of his 20 decisions in his first two years of pro ball. McLemore started to believe in himself when he opened 2004 with 12 consecutive scoreless outings out of the bullpen, and he finished the year by posting a 3.63 ERA in 14 starts after moving to the rotation. If he can believe in his stuff as the Astros do, he can reach the big leagues. He has good velocity for a lefty, as his fastball ranges from 88-93 mph. His breaking ball is deceptive and inconsistent. When it has true curveball break, it can be unhittable. Even when it's slurvy and has more sideways movement, he still keeps it down in the zone. He has good feel if not total command of his changeup, and took to throwing it more often as a starter. McLemore came down with shoulder tendinitis late last season—his 93 innings were a career high—but he's fine now. He just needs to avoid giving in to hitters. When he's reluctant to challenge them, he falls behind in the count, then too often lays a straight fastball over the heart of the plate. When he's aggressive and maintains his arm slot, he can flash a plus fastball and curve and an average change. The Astros hope he can build on his 2004 success this year in Double-A.

Year	Club (League)	Class	W	L	ERA	G	GS	CG	SV	IP	H	R	ER	HR	BB	SO	AVG
2002	Martinsville (Appy)	R	0	1	1.80	4	2	0	0	10	9	3	2	0	5	11	.237
	Tri-City (NY-P)	A	1	5	4.09	9	6	0	0	23	42	37	36	2	17	16	.393
2003	Lexington (SAL)	A	2	11	4.58	36	7	0	0	92	84	57	47	4	55	101	.243
2004	Salem (Car)	A	7	7	3.66	37	14	1	6	93	80	38	38	8	44	79	.228
MINOR LEAGUE TOTALS			10	24	5.06	86	29	1	6	219	215	135	123	14	121	207	.256

26 Jason Hirsh, rhp

Born: Feb. 20, 1982. **Ht.:** 6-8. **Wt.:** 250. **Bats:** R. **Throws:** R. **School:** California Lutheran University. **Career Transactions:** Selected by Astros in second round of 2003 draft; signed July 3, 2003. **Signed by:** Mel Nelson.

Hirsh spent his first full pro season in high Class A last year, and the challenge was a bit too much for him. After throwing just 86-88 mph in high school and flying under the radar of scouts and NCAA Division I programs, he blossomed at Division III Cal Lutheran. By 2003, he was flashing a mid-90s fastball and a mid-80s slider, which made him a second-round pick. With those pitches and a 6-foot-8 frame, Hirsh can be intimidating. But in 2004 he didn't scare hitters very often. While trying to improve his secondary pitches, he lost velocity on his fastball. It dipped to the low 90s and had inconsistent sink to begin with, so it no longer blew away hitters. The quality of his stuff varied wildly from start to start, and his changeup didn't make much progress. Some scouts projected Hirsh as a set-up man to begin with, and the bullpen will be his destination if he can't develop three usable pitches. He might benefit from starting 2005 back in high Class A.

Year	Club (League)	Class	W	L	ERA	G	GS	CG	SV	IP	H	R	ER	HR	BB	SO	AVG
2003	Tri-City (NY-P)	A	3	1	1.95	10	8	0	0	32	22	10	7	0	7	33	.190
2004	Salem (Car)	A	11	7	4.01	26	23	0	0	130	128	66	58	8	57	96	.262
MINOR LEAGUE TOTALS			14	8	3.60	36	31	0	0	163	150	76	65	8	64	129	.248

27 Ervin Alcantara, of

Born: Oct. 3, 1980. **Ht.:** 6-2. **Wt.:** 175. **Bats:** R. **Throws:** R. **Career Transactions:** Signed out of Dominican Republic by Astros, Aug. 6, 2001. **Signed by:** Julio Linares/Rafael Ramirez/A. Linares.

If Alcantara truly had been 16 when the Astros signed him out of the Dominican Republic in 2001, he'd rank much higher. But Houston discovered in 2003 that he was four years older than originally believed. That has been a kiss of death for many prospects, but Alcantara has been able to generate positive momentum with his performance and his tools. He earned Appalachian League all-star honors in 2003 and Lexington's team MVP award last year. Alcantara began to tap into his raw power in 2004. He also has average speed and runs better than that once he gets under way. He does strike out a fair amount, but tempers that by drawing his share of walks. Alcantara has seen time at all three outfield positions, showing enough range to handle center field and a slightly above-average arm. Now 24, he needs to get to Double-A this year and face competition closer to his age.

Year	Club (League)	Class	AVG	G	AB	R	H	2B	3B	HR	RBI	BB	SO	SB	OBP	SLG
2002	Houston (DSL)	R	.271	69	258	49	70	18	3	7	51	36	48	24	.373	.446
2003	Martinsvlle (Appy)	R	.344	54	195	25	67	18	0	2	33	19	39	1	.407	.467
2004	Lexington (SAL)	A	.277	131	477	66	132	25	2	16	83	59	111	28	.355	.438
MINOR LEAGUE TOTALS			.289	254	930	140	269	61	5	25	167	114	198	53	.371	.446

28 Todd Self, 1b

Born: Nov. 9, 1978. **Ht.:** 6-5. **Wt.:** 215. **Bats:** L. **Throws:** R. **School:** University of Louisiana-Monroe. **Career Transactions:** Selected by Astros in 15th round of 2000 draft; signed June 8, 2000. **Signed by:** James Farrar.

The Astros have come to accept that Self is what he is. He has a talent for getting on base, but has so little home run power that he's not going to make a case for playing every day in the majors. Managers rated his strike-zone discipline the best in the Texas League in 2004, no surprise considering he led the TL in on-base percentage and earned the same recognition in the high Class A Carolina League the year before. Using an extremely level swing, Self topped .300 for the fourth consecutive season. He has hit just 33 homers in five years as a pro, however, because he doesn't lift pitches and is usually content to line soft singles to the opposite field. Self broke into pro ball as an outfielder and has the arm strength to play right field. But his speed, range and routes are all below-average, limiting him to first base. Though Houston has declined to protect Self on its 40-man roster the last two seasons, he could carve out a big league role as a lefty bat off the bench. He'll move up to Triple-A in 2005.

Year	Club (League)	Class	AVG	G	AB	R	H	2B	3B	HR	RBI	BB	SO	SB	OBP	SLG
2000	Auburn (NY-P)	A	.194	52	160	13	31	3	1	1	19	28	42	10	.326	.244
2001	Pittsfield (NY-P)	A	.303	73	261	52	79	13	4	3	49	46	61	10	.403	.418
2002	Michigan (Mid)	A	.310	136	491	81	152	36	5	12	94	65	104	10	.394	.477
2003	Salem (Car)	A	.318	126	431	84	137	27	2	6	57	87	93	2	.433	.432
2004	Round Rock (TL)	AA	.315	131	476	86	150	34	1	11	81	89	95	8	.420	.460
MINOR LEAGUE TOTALS			.302	518	1819	316	549	113	13	33	300	315	395	40	.406	.433

29   Eric Bruntlett, ss/of

Born: March 29, 1978. **Ht.:** 6-0. **Wt.:** 190. **Bats:** R. **Throws:** R. **School:** Stanford University. **Career Transactions:** Selected by Astros in ninth round of 2000 draft; signed June 21, 2000. **Signed by:** Gene Wellman.

Bruntlett's mental toughness has enabled him to become a big league utilityman. The Astros jumped him from Rookie ball in his debut to Double-A in his first full season, and he survived. He had never played anywhere but shortstop and second base when he received his first callup in 2003, yet he was able to handle third base, left field and center field in the majors. Bruntlett never has hit for much of an average, but he's not an easy out and has solid pop for a middle infielder. He draws his share of walks and has average speed and savvy on the bases. Bruntlett doesn't have a plus defensive tool, but he gets by with athleticism and instincts. He's solid fundamentally and rarely makes mistakes. He'll probably never be a major league regular, but Bruntlett is a favorite of managers and could have a long career as a versatile reserve.

Year	Club (League)	Class	AVG	G	AB	R	H	2B	3B	HR	RBI	BB	SO	SB	OBP	SLG
2000	Martinsvlle (Appy)	R	.273	50	172	40	47	11	4	1	21	30	22	14	.413	.401
2001	Round Rock (TL)	AA	.266	123	503	84	134	23	3	3	40	50	76	23	.340	.342
	New Orleans (PCL)	AAA	.125	5	16	3	2	0	0	0	1	2	1	0	.222	.125
2002	New Orleans (PCL)	AAA	.206	18	68	9	14	3	0	0	1	10	10	1	.308	.250
	Round Rock (TL)	AA	.265	116	464	81	123	21	2	2	48	56	61	35	.351	.332
2003	New Orleans (PCL)	AAA	.259	84	324	48	84	10	0	2	27	35	51	9	.332	.309
	Houston (NL)	MAJ	.259	31	54	3	14	3	0	1	4	0	10	0	.255	.370
2004	New Orleans (PCL)	AAA	.250	86	332	50	83	12	4	6	37	35	72	14	.331	.364
	Houston (NL)	MAJ	.250	45	52	14	13	2	0	4	8	7	13	4	.328	.519
MAJOR LEAGUE TOTALS		.255		76	106	17	27	5	0	5	12	7	23	4	.293	.443
MINOR LEAGUE TOTALS			.259	482	1879	315	487	80	13	14	175	218	293	96	.345	.338

30   Wladimir Sutil, ss

Born: Oct. 31, 1984. **Ht.:** 5-10. **Wt.:** 140. **Bats:** R. **Throws:** R. **Career Transactions:** Signed out of Venezuela by Astros, May 16, 2003. **Signed by:** Andres Reiner.

In his U.S. debut last summer, Sutil made an impression with his speed and defense. A plus runner, he led the Appalachian League in steals (but also in times caught stealing, with eight). For a teenager, he displayed tremendous poise, body control, and footwork. He always seems to be in perfect position to make a throw, enhancing his slightly above-average arm. Wiry and undersized, Sutil knows he has to play the little man's game at the plate. He can reach the gaps on occasion but has focused on making contact and reaching base. His bat ultimately may hold him back, but he held his own last year. The Astros are interested in seeing what he can do in low Class A this year.

Year	Club (League)	Class	AVG	G	AB	R	H	2B	3B	HR	RBI	BB	SO	SB	OBP	SLG
2003	Venoco (VSL)	R	.266	45	154	35	41	11	1	1	21	22	21	11	.378	.370
2004	Greeneville (Appy)	R	.298	53	188	31	56	9	0	0	29	17	24	24	.372	.346
MINOR LEAGUE TOTALS			.278	98	342	66	97	20	1	1	50	39	45	35	.375	.357

KANSAS CITY
ROYALS

BY **WILL KIMMEY**

The Royals and their fans entered 2004 with guarded optimism. Kansas City was coming off its first winning season in nine years and supplemented a young roster with veteran free agents at reasonable prices.

The Royals won four of their first six games, but then dropped six straight and never climbed above .500 again. Injuries piled up (new acquisition Juan Gonzalez played just 33 games), the pitching staff crumbled and the team elected to trade free-agent-to-be Carlos Beltran in June. Shortstop Angel Berroa, the 2003 American League rookie of the year, struggled so much that he was sent down to Double-A Wichita. The cumulative result was a franchise-record 104 losses.

"Disappointment was an understatement," general manager Allard Baird said.

The rough year did provide a few bright spots. The club may have filled three organizational needs with the Beltran deal, acquiring John Buck to become the everyday catcher, Mark Teahen to take over at third base and Mike Wood to add depth to the pitching staff. Righthander **Zack Greinke** reached the majors before he turned 21 and emerged as the team's best pitcher. Fellow farmhands Andres Blanco, David DeJesus and Ruben Gotay also gained major league experience, and the club added prospects Denny Bautista and Justin Huber at little expense in astute trades.

"We never changed our rebuilding-mode approach," Baird said. "We didn't hold anybody back. If a young player is ready to

BILL NICHOLS

come to the big leagues, he does."

The Royals enter 2005 in the same development-first mindset. Baird made low-cost acquisitions such as Kevin Appier, Jose Lima, Eli Marrero and Luis Ugueto to use as roster filler until players such as Bautista, Huber and Teahen are ready for full-time duty. The Royals have seen the Twins succeed under similar small-market budget constraints and wish to build their team in the same mold.

Kansas City took steps toward that goal in 2004. Baird strengthened the player-development and scouting systems by hiring Donny Rowland, the former Angels scouting director who restocked that organization's prospect coffers, to oversee both departments. The initial returns on scouting director Deric Ladnier's draft were positive, as the Royals added a slugger in Billy Butler, polished college pitchers with their next three selections, then a few high-ceiling high schoolers and some budget-conscious picks that emerged as pleasant surprises. Signing 2003's top draft-and-follow, hard-throwing righthander Luis Cota, gave the organization another shot in the talent arm.

The Royals must continue to draft and develop players to aid a farm system that still lacks an abundance of star-caliber players. Those are the types needed to win at the major league level, and it's much cheaper for Kansas City to produce its own than to try to sign them on the open market.

TOP 30 PROSPECTS

1. Billy Butler, 3b
2. Denny Bautista, rhp
3. Mark Teahen, 3b
4. Chris Lubanski, of
5. Justin Huber, c
6. Ambiorix Burgos, rhp
7. Luis Cota, rhp
8. Shane Costa, of
9. Mitch Maier, 3b
10. Donald Murphy, 2b
11. J.P. Howell, lhp
12. Andy Sisco, lhp
13. Brian McFall, of
14. Leo Nunez, rhp
15. Billy Buckner, rhp
16. Matt Campbell, lhp
17. Santiago Ramirez, rhp
18. Andres Blanco, ss
19. Brian Bass, rhp
20. Miguel Vega, 1b/3b
21. Ryan Braun, rhp
22. Dusty Hughes, lhp
23. Erik Cordier, rhp
24. Devon Lowery, rhp
25. Mike Aviles, ss
26. Mario Lisson, ss/3b
27. Chad Blackwell, rhp
28. Colt Griffin, rhp
29. Chris McConnell, ss
30. Henry Barrera, rhp

ORGANIZATION OVERVIEW

General manager: Allard Baird. **Farm director:** Shaun McGinn. **Scouting director:** Deric Ladnier.

2004 PERFORMANCE

Class	Team	League	W	L	Pct.	Finish*	Manager
Majors	Kansas City	American	58	104	.358	14th (14)	Tony Pena
Triple-A	Omaha Royals	Pacific Coast	71	73	.493	9th (16)	Mike Jirschele
Double-A	Wichita Wranglers	Texas	73	66	.525	3rd (8)	Frank White
High A	#Wilmington Blue Rocks	Carolina	77	62	.554	2nd (8)	Billy Gardner
Low A	Burlington Bees	Midwest	56	84	.400	13th (14)	Jim Gabella
Rookie	Idaho Falls Chukars	Pioneer	42	35	.545	3rd (8)	Brian Rupp
Rookie	AZL Royals	Arizona	29	27	.518	5th (9)	Lloyd Simmons
OVERALL 2004 MINOR LEAGUE RECORD			348	347	.501	18th (30)	

*Finish in overall standings (No. of teams in league). #Affiliate will be in High Desert (California) in 2005.

ORGANIZATION LEADERS

BATTING
*Minimum 250 At-Bats

*AVG	Billy Butler, Idaho Falls	.373
R	Mel Stocker, Wichita/Wilmington	85
H	Mitch Maier, Wilmington/Burlington	141
TB	Jed Hansen, Omaha	234
2B	Mike Aviles, Wilmington	40
3B	Alexis Gomez, Omaha	8
HR	Calvin Pickering, Omaha	35
RBI	Brandon Berger, Omaha/Wichita	87
BB	Calvin Pickering, Omaha	70
SO	Chad Santos, Wichita	119
SB	Mel Stocker, Wichita/Wilmington	47
*OBP	Billy Butler, Idaho Falls	.486
*SLG	Calvin Pickering, Omaha	.712

PITCHING
#Minimum 75 Innings

W	Les Walrond, Omaha/Wichita	14
L	Greg Atencio, Burlington	14
#ERA	Trae McGill, Wilmington	2.08
G	J.J. Trujillo, Wichita	59
CG	Three tied at	2
SV	Ryan Braun, Wilmington	24
IP	Kris Wilson, Omaha	167
BB	Ambiorix Burgos, Burlington	75
SO	Ambiorix Burgos, Burlington	172

BEST TOOLS

Best Hitter for Average	Billy Butler
Best Power Hitter	Billy Butler
Best Strike-Zone Discipline	Billy Butler
Fastest Baserunner	Mel Stocker
Best Athlete	Chris Lubanski
Best Fastball	Denny Bautista
Best Curveball	Denny Bautista
Best Slider	Denny Bautista
Best Changeup	Danny Tamayo
Best Control	Dusty Hughes
Best Defensive Catcher	Matt Tupman
Best Defensive Infielder	Andres Blanco
Best Infield Arm	Andres Blanco
Best Defensive Outfielder	Mel Stocker
Best Outfield Arm	Brian McFall

PROJECTED 2008 LINEUP

Catcher	Justin Huber
First Base	Billy Butler
Second Base	Donald Murphy
Third Base	Mark Teahen
Shortstop	Angel Berroa
Left Field	Shane Costa
Center Field	David DeJesus
Right Field	Mitch Maier
Designated Hitter	Mike Sweeney

No. 1 Starter	Zack Greinke
No. 2 Starter	Denny Bautista
No. 3 Starter	Luis Cota
No. 4 Starter	J.P. Howell
No. 5 Starter	Mike Wood
Closer	Jeremy Affedt

LAST YEAR'S TOP 20 PROSPECTS

1. Zack Greinke, rhp
2. Chris Lubanski, of
3. Mitch Maier, of/3b
4. David DeJesus, of
5. Colt Griffin, rhp
6. Donald Murphy, 2b
7. Shane Costa, of
8. Brian Bass, rhp
9. Andres Blanco, ss
10. Byron Gettis, of
11. Ruben Gotay, 2b
12. Jonah Bayliss, rhp
13. Adam Donachie, c
14. Kyle Middleton, rhp
15. Carlos Rosa, rhp
16. Jorge Vasquez, rhp
17. Rich Thompson, of
18. Travis Chapman, 3b/1b
19. Alexis Gomez, of
20. Ryan Bukvich, rhp

TOP PROSPECTS OF THE DECADE

Year	Player, Pos.	Current Team
1995	Johnny Damon, of	Red Sox
1996	Jim Pittsley, rhp	Out of baseball
1997	Glendon Rusch, lhp	Cubs
1998	Dee Brown, of	Royals
1999	Carlos Beltran, of	Mets
2000	Dee Brown, of	Royals
2001	Chris George, lhp	Royals
2002	Angel Berroa, ss	Royals
2003	Zack Greinke, rhp	Royals
2004	Zack Greinke, rhp	Royals

TOP DRAFT PICKS OF THE DECADE

Year	Player, Pos.	Current Team
1995	Juan LeBron, of	Pennsylvania (Atlantic)
1996	Dee Brown, of	Royals
1997	Dan Reichert, rhp	Mariners
1998	Jeff Austin, rhp	Reds
1999	Kyle Snyder, rhp	Royals
2000	Mike Stodolka, lhp	Royals
2001	Colt Griffin, rhp	Royals
2002	Zack Greinke, rhp	Royals
2003	Chris Lubanski, of	Royals
2004	Billy Butler, 3b	Royals

ALL-TIME LARGEST BONUSES

Jeff Austin, 1998	$2,700,000
Mike Stodolka, 2000	$2,500,000
Zack Greinke, 2002	$2,475,000
Colt Griffin, 2001	$2,400,000
Kyle Snyder, 1999	$2,100,000
Chris Lubanski, 2003	$2,100,000

Kansas City ROYALS

Impact Potential: D

Billy Butler is the system's best hitting prospect, though most observers thought it was a stretch to take him 14th overall, especially if he can't play third base. That he jumps to the front of the organization's prospect rankings speaks volumes. Mark Teahen is ready for the majors but doesn't profile as a middle-of-the-order bat. Righthanded power arms Denny Bautista, Ambiorix Burgos and Luis Cota all have front-of-the-rotation stuff, but none has shown enough command of it.

Depth: D

Unfulfilled first-round potential dots the depth chart, from Mike Stodolka (2000) and Colt Griffin (2001) to 2004 pick Matt Campbell, whose velocity tumbled after a strenuous year at South Carolina. Campbell and fellow '04 draftee J.P. Howell are the best hopes to develop a lefthander among a thin crop. After graduating David DeJesus to Kansas City to replace Carlos Beltran, the outfielders left include three prospects and not much else.

*Depth charts prepared by **John Manuel** and **Allan Simpson**. Numbers in parentheses indicate prospect rankings.*

LF
Shane Costa (8)
Kennard Springer
Jared Ellis

CF
Chris Lubanski (4)
Geraldo Valentin

SS
Andres Blanco (18)
Mike Aviles (25)
Chris McConnell (29)
Josh Johnson
Angel Sanchez

RF
Brian McFall (13)

3B
Mark Teahen (3)
Mitch Maier (9)
Mario Lisson (26)

2B
Donald Murphy (10)
Irving Falu
Darren Fenster
Adam Keim
Brandon Powell

1B
Billy Butler (1)
Miguel Vega (20)
Kila Kaaihue
Chad Santos
Russell Brown
Brad Hayes

SOURCE of TALENT

HOMEGROWN		ACQUIRED	
College	9	Trades	4
Junior College	2	Rule 5 draft	1
Draft-and-follow	1	Independent leagues	0
High school	9	Free agents/waivers	1
Nondrafted free agents	0		
Foreign	3		

C
Justin Huber (5)
Adam Donachie
Paul Phillips
Matt Tupman
Damaso Espino
Mike Tonis
Scott Walter

LHP

Starters	Relievers
J.P. Howell (11)	Brian Nendza
Andy Sisco (12)	Nate Holster
Matt Campbell (16)	
Dusty Hughes (22)	
Mike Stodolka	

RHP

Starters	Relievers
Denny Bautista (2)	Leo Nunez (14)
Ambiorix Burgos (6)	Santiago Ramirez (17)
Luis Cota (7)	Ryan Braun (21)
Billy Buckner (15)	Chad Blackwell (27)
Brian Bass (19)	Colt Griffin (28)
Erik Cordier (23)	Nate Moore
Devon Lowery (24)	Barry Armitage
Henry Barrera (30)	Justin Huisman
Danny Tamayo	Stephen Bray
Jonah Bayliss	
Carlos Rosa	
Kyle Middleton	
Jason Kaanoi	

DRAFT ANALYSIS

2004

Best Pro Debut: Despite being young for the Rookie-level Pioneer League, 3B Billy Butler (1) dominated. He hit .376-10-68, leading the league in hitting and runs (74).

Best Athlete: SS Josh Johnson (3) and Chris McConnell (9). Johnson's speed sticks out the most among his tools, while McConnell has classic infield actions.

Best Pure Hitter: Most teams had Butler as a second-round pick, but the Royals loved his bat and signed him for $1.45 million, $250,000 below Major League Baseball's recommendation. If he can stay at third base—he worked on his flexibility in instructional league—he'll be even more valuable.

Best Raw Power: Butler's power is his best tool. He understands how to work counts to draw walks (57 in 72 games) as well as to get pitches he can punish.

Fastest Runner: The Royals drafted OF Ethien Santana (22) for his speed. He flies from the left side of home plate to first base in 4.0 seconds, and he stole 23 bases in 52 games in the Rookie-level Arizona League.

Best Defensive Player: Johnson is steadier than McConnell, who gets to a few more balls but is more erratic at this point.

Best Fastball: RHP Henry Barrera (5) can reach 96-98 mph and reminds Kansas City of RHP Luis Cota (10 in 2003), a draft-and-follow coup. Signed for $1.05 million, Cota has a similar build (6-foot-1, 180 pounds) and velocity. RHP Erik Cordier (2) already throws 90-94 mph and should throw harder as his frame fills out.

Best Breaking Ball: The Royals signed several pitchers with quality curveballs, none better than RHP Billy Buckner's (2). Polished LHP Matt Campbell (1) and J.P.

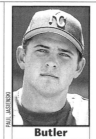

PAUL JASIENSKI

Butler

Howell (1) both have nice benders, and Howell can alter his arm angle and velocity with his. Cordier flashes a power curve at times.

Most Intriguing Background: Butler and Rangers RHP Eric Hurley made Wolfson High (Jacksonville, Fla.) the fifth high school to produce two first-rounders in the same draft. Johnson's father Larry Doby Johnson played in the majors.

Closest To The Majors: Though he's a college lefty, Howell has some similarities to high school righty Zach Greinke, who reached Kansas City two years after going sixth overall in the 2002 draft. Like Greinke, Howell can mess up hitters by adding and subtracting from all his pitches. Though he tops out at 89 mph, Howell pitches inside and gets hitters to swing and miss at his sinker, curveball and splitter.

Best Late-Round Pick: RHPs Zane Carlson (27) and Kyle Crist (34) both can touch 93 mph and have effective secondary pitches. Carlson also throws a splitter and slider, while Crist flashes a plus curveball.

The One Who Got Away: LHP Myles Ioane (24) has some polish and projection, but he opted to go to college at Hawaii. The Royals signed their first 16 picks.

Assessment: Butler looks like a cost-effective steal, and Buckner and Cordier looked like first-round picks at one point during the spring. Campbell and Howell are by far the best lefthanders in the system.

2003 OF Chris Lubanski (1), 3B Mitch Maier and RHP Luis Cota (10), a $1.05 million draft-and-follow, all have lost a little of their luster after turning pro. It's possible OF Shane Costa (2) could end up being better than any of them. **GRADE:** C+

2002 RHP Zack Greinke, already the ace of the big league staff, is the best first-round pick the Royals have made since Kevin Appier in 1987 and possibly their best ever. 2B Donald Murphy (5) also bears watching. **GRADE:** A

2001 Kansas City spent $4.15 million on RHP Colt Griffin (1) and OF Roscoe Crosby (2), with nothing to show for it. They would have been better off signing LHP Taylor Tankersley (39), who became a 2004 first-rounder. **GRADE:** F

2000 OF David DeJesus (4) is a rare homegrown bright spot on the Royals roster. Draft-and-follow 2B Ruben Gotay (31) also could become a regular. RHP Mike Stodolka (1) has won 16 games in five pro seasons, none above Class A. **GRADE:** C+

*Draft analysis prepared by **Jim Callis**. Numbers in parentheses indicate draft rounds.*

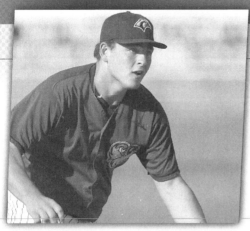

Billy
BUTLER

Born: April 18, 1986.
Ht.: 6-2. **Wt.:** 225.
Bats: R. **Throws:** R.
School: Wolfson HS, Jacksonville, Fla.
Career Transactions: Selected by Royals in first round (14th overall) of 2004 draft; signed June 7, 2004.
Signed by: Cliff Pastornicky.

Area scout Cliff Pastornicky helped the Royals decide to select Zack Greinke in 2002, selling them on his precocious feel for pitching. Greinke held the top spot on this list from that point until he made his major league debut on May 22, 2004. Two weeks later, Pastornicky and the Royals found Greinke's successor atop this list by cutting a predraft deal to sign Butler for $1.45 million—$250,000 below Major League Baseball's recommendation for the 14th overall pick. He would have attended Florida had he not turned pro. Like Greinke, Butler is a Florida high schooler who's very advanced for his age, and he too could move quickly through the system. Butler and righthander Eric Hurley (30th overall to the Rangers) made Jacksonville's Wolfson High the fifth high school to produce two first-rounders in the same draft.

Butler instantly became the best hitting and power prospect in the organization. Using a patient approach and line-drive mentality, he led the Rookie-level Pioneer League in batting and ranked second in extra-base hits. Butler's stance looks unorthodox—he stands very open and spread out, holding his hands high and tapping his toes before engaging the ball—but has quick hands and excellent hand-eye coordination that allow him to let the ball get deep in the zone and to make quick adjustments. He centers the ball well, uses the whole field and generates natural loft without slipping into the uppercut swing plane that befalls many power hitters. He has the best raw pop of any player in the 2004 draft. Pitchers weren't able to sneak fastballs or sliders by him in his pro debut. Some Pioneer League scouts questioned Butler's maturity, but the Royals love his makeup. He displays ample confidence and was well-liked by his Idaho Falls teammates. He also possesses a strong arm that propelled fastballs up to 93 mph when he pitched in high school.

If Butler rates as a certainty with the bat, his glove is the complete opposite. He must improve his flexibility to enhance his range at third base. He can catch the ball, but isn't fluid when doing so. Though he has plenty of arm strength, he must set his feet better to avoid throwing errors. At best, the Royals hope Butler can become an average defender who makes the routine plays. He eventually may have to move to first base, and has the hands and the bat to profile well at this position. Butler is a below-average runner but not a base-clogger, so left field also could be a possibility. Some scouts are so skeptical of his defensive ability that they think he'll be limited to DH.

Butler rates as one of the few players in the system with all-star potential. His offensive abilities outstrip his defensive deficiencies and should allow him to rise quickly up the ladder. He'll begin 2005 at low Class A Burlington and could be ready for Kansas City at some point in 2007. He's the Royals' No. 3 hitter of the future.

Year	Club (League)	Class	AVG	G	AB	R	H	2B	3B	HR	RBI	BB	SO	SB	OBP	SLG
2004	Idahol Falls (Pio)	R	.373	72	260	74	97	22	3	10	68	57	63	5	.486	.596
MINOR LEAGUE TOTALS			.373	72	260	74	97	22	3	10	68	57	63	5	.486	.596

2 Denny Bautista, rhp

Born: Oct. 23, 1982. **Ht.:** 6-5. **Wt.:** 170. **Bats:** R. **Throws:** R. **Career Transactions:** Signed out of Dominican Republic by Marlins, April 11, 2000 . . . Traded by Marlins with RHP Don Levinski to Orioles for 1B Jeff Conine, Aug. 31, 2003 . . . Traded by Orioles to Royals for LHP Jason Grimsley, June 21, 2004. **Signed by:** Pablo Lantigua/Louie Eljaua (Marlins).

Pedro and Ramon Martinez helped Bautista learn his craft in the Dominican Republic, and he pitched in the Futures Game in 2003. Bautista has been traded twice since then, and also had his age adjusted upward two years. Still, the Royals consider acquiring him from Baltimore for Jason Grimsley as a coup. Bautista's fastball, slider and curveball all can rate as average or better on any given day, while his changeup can be a solid pitch as well. His fastball sits in the mid-90s and has touched 99 mph with good boring life down in the zone. Like many tall and lanky pitchers, Bautista struggles to repeat his delivery and throws across his body. His lack of command often renders him a one-pitch guy. Bautista can be a No. 2 or 3 starter if he can locate his secondary pitches consistently. He'll get a chance to win a job in the Kansas City rotation in spring training. It's also possible he could return to Triple-A, or contribute as a late-inning reliever.

Year	Club (League)	Class	W	L	ERA	G	GS	CG	SV	IP	H	R	ER	HR	BB	SO	AVG
2000	Marlins (GCL)	R	6	2	2.43	11	11	2	0	63	49	24	17	1	17	58	.209
	Marlins (DSL)	R	0	1	2.57	3	3	0	0	14	11	6	4	2	9	17	.216
	Utica (NY-P)	A	0	0	3.60	1	1	0	0	5	4	3	2	0	2	5	.222
2001	Kane County (Mid)	A	3	1	4.35	8	7	0	0	39	43	21	19	2	14	20	.281
	Utica (NY-P)	A	3	1	2.08	7	7	0	0	39	25	16	9	0	6	31	.174
2002	Jupiter (FSL)	A	4	6	4.99	19	15	0	0	88	80	52	49	6	40	79	.242
2003	Jupiter (FSL)	A	8	4	3.21	14	14	0	0	84	68	32	30	2	35	77	.219
	Carolina (SL)	AA	4	5	3.71	11	11	0	0	53	45	33	22	5	35	61	.226
2004	Bowie (EL)	AA	3	5	4.74	14	13	0	0	63	58	37	33	5	33	72	.243
	Baltimore (AL)	MAJ	0	0	36.00	2	0	0	0	2	6	8	8	1	2	1	.545
	Wichita (TL)	AA	4	3	2.53	12	12	2	0	82	68	32	23	3	32	73	.227
	Kansas City (AL)	MAJ	0	4	5.61	5	5	0	0	28	38	20	20	2	11	18	.333
MAJOR LEAGUE TOTALS			0	4	8.49	7	5	0	0	30	44	28	28	3	13	19	.352
MINOR LEAGUE TOTALS			35	28	3.53	100	94	4	0	530	451	256	208	26	223	493	.228

3 Mark Teahen, 3b

Born: Sept. 6, 1981. **Ht.:** 6-3. **Wt.:** 210. **Bats:** L. **Throws:** R. **School:** St. Mary`s. **Career Transactions:** Selected by Athletics in first round (39th overall) of 2002 draft; signed June 9, 2002 . . . Traded by Athletics with RHP Mike Wood to Royals as part of three-way trade in which Athletics received RHP Octavio Dotel from Astros, Astros received OF Carlos Beltran from Royals, and Royals received C John Buck from Astros, June 24, 2004. **Signed by:** Will Schock (Athletics).

Part of the "Moneyball" draft class, Teahen helped the Athletics get Octavio Dotel in a three-way deal that sent Carlos Beltran to Houston and Teahen, John Buck and Mike Wood to Kansas City. Teahen has a good grasp of the strike zone, uses the whole field and makes consistent, hard contact. His instincts, range and accurate arm led managers to rate him the best defensive third baseman in the Triple-A Pacific Coast League. Teahen has yet to demonstrate the power desired from a corner infielder. While in the Arizona Fall League, he worked on incorporating his legs more into his swing and picking out pitches to pull, rather than simply serving balls into left field. Teahen is Kansas City's safest bet to become a solid major leaguer. He could open the season as the everyday third baseman, or free-agent signee Chris Truby could serve as a stopgap as Teahen gains more Triple-A seasoning during the first half.

Year	Club (League)	Class	AVG	G	AB	R	H	2B	3B	HR	RBI	BB	SO	SB	OBP	SLG
2002	Vancouver (NWL)	A	.404	13	57	10	23	5	1	0	6	5	9	4	.444	.526
	Modesto (Cal)	A	.239	59	234	25	56	9	1	1	26	21	53	1	.307	.299
2003	Modesto (Cal)	A	.283	121	453	68	128	27	4	3	71	66	113	4	.377	.380
2004	Midland (TL)	AA	.335	53	197	31	66	15	4	6	36	29	44	0	.419	.543
	Sacramento (PCL)	AAA	.275	20	69	9	19	8	0	0	10	11	22	0	.383	.391
	Omaha (PCL)	AAA	.280	66	246	33	69	15	1	8	31	21	69	0	.344	.447
MINOR LEAGUE TOTALS			.287	332	1256	176	361	79	11	18	180	153	310	9	.368	.411

JOHN SPEAR

4 Chris Lubanski, of

Born: March 24, 1985. **Ht.:** 6-3. **Wt.:** 185. **Bats:** L. **Throws:** L. **School:** Kennedy-Kenrick HS, Schwenksville, Pa. **Career Transactions:** Selected by Royals in first round (fifth overall) of 2003 draft; signed June 6, 2003. **Signed by:** Sean Rooney.

Lubanski was pegged as a mid-first rounder before settling for a slightly below-market $2.1 million bonus as the fifth overall pick in 2003. In his first full season, he hit just .224 through June before moving from first to third in Burlington's order and batting .315 with improved power the rest of the way. The Royals like the adjustments Lubanski made and believe he can be an above-average hitter with at least average power. He has slowed some since being drafted, but is still a plus runner. His work ethic and makeup are also positives. Lubanski needs to improve in all aspects of the game. He struggles against lefthanders, can be fooled by breaking pitches and needs more plate discipline. He got nailed 11 times in 27 steal attempts. As a center fielder, he needs to improve his reads and first-step quickness. He has a below-average arm and several scouts project him as a left fielder. Initially compared to Johnny Damon, Lubanski now seems more likely to make his mark with his strength rather than his speed. The Royals think he's on the verge of a breakout, possibly in 2005 at their new high Class A High Desert affiliate.

Year	Club (League)	Class	AVG	G	AB	R	H	2B	3B	HR	RBI	BB	SO	SB	OBP	SLG
2003	Royals 1 (AZL)	R	.326	53	221	41	72	4	6	4	27	18	50	9	.382	.452
2004	Burlington (Mid)	A	.275	127	483	64	133	26	7	9	56	43	104	16	.336	.414
MINOR LEAGUE TOTALS			.291	180	704	105	205	30	13	13	83	61	154	25	.351	.426

5 Justin Huber, c

Born: July 1, 1982. **Ht.:** 6-5. **Wt.:** 190. **Bats:** R. **Throws:** R. **Career Transactions:** Signed out of Australia by Mets, July 26, 2000 . . . Traded by Mets to Royals for 3B Jose Bautista July 30, 2004. **Signed by:** Omar Minaya (Mets).

The Royals acquired Huber from the Pirates for Jose Bautista as part of the three-team trade that sent Kris Benson to the Mets. In his last game in the New York system, he tore cartilage in his left knee in a home-plate collision. Arthroscopic surgery cost him the rest of the season and a chance to play for Australia in the Olympics. Huber has more offensive potential than most catchers. He should hit for a high average with 20-homer power, and he also draws plenty of walks. He has average arm strength. Huber has a better bat than fellow trade acquisition John Buck, but his defense lags behind Buck's and may push Huber to first base or left field. His footwork is his most glaring deficiency, the major reason why he never has thrown out more than 25 percent of basestealers at any level. After a brief stop at Triple-A Omaha, Huber should be ready for the majors. He's likely to see time in several roles for the Royals rather than become their everyday catcher.

Year	Club (League)	Class	AVG	G	AB	R	H	2B	3B	HR	RBI	BB	SO	SB	OBP	SLG
2001	St. Lucie (FSL)	A	.000	2	6	0	0	0	0	0	0	0	2	0	.000	.000
	Kingsport (Appy)	R	.314	47	159	24	50	11	1	7	31	17	42	4	.415	.528
	Brooklyn (NY-P)	A	.000	3	9	0	0	0	0	0	0	0	4	0	.000	.000
2002	Columbia (SAL)	A	.291	95	330	49	96	22	2	11	78	45	81	1	.408	.470
	St. Lucie (FSL)	A	.270	28	100	15	27	2	1	3	15	11	18	0	.370	.400
2003	St. Lucie (FSL)	A	.284	50	183	26	52	15	0	9	36	17	30	1	.370	.514
	Binghamton (EAS)	AA	.264	55	193	16	51	13	0	6	36	19	54	0	.350	.425
2004	St. Lucie (FSL)	A	.283	15	53	13	15	2	0	2	10	5	8	2	.356	.434
	Binghamton (EL)	AA	.271	70	236	44	64	16	1	11	33	46	57	2	.414	.487
	Norfolk (IL)	AAA	.313	5	16	3	5	2	0	0	3	3	3	0	.421	.438
MINOR LEAGUE TOTALS			.280	370	1285	190	360	83	5	49	242	163	299	10	.387	.467

6 Ambiorix Burgos, rhp

Born: April 19, 1984. **Ht.:** 6-3. **Wt.:** 230. **Bats:** R. **Throws:** R. **Career Transactions:** Signed out of Dominican Republic by Royals, Nov. 14, 2000. **Signed by:** Luis Silverio.

Burgos features the best fastball in the system. It tops out at 98 mph, 10 mph more than it did when he signed as a 16-year-old. His heater sits in the low to mid-90s and moves away from righthanders with some cutting action. He struggles to locate his changeup and slider consistently, but can dominate if either is working. More often than not, he can't command them—which led to his ranking second in the low Class A Midwest League in walks last year. Burgos may throw more strikes once he does a better job of maintaining his delivery, which could happen soon because he finally has stopped growing and begun to get used to his body. He showed an average splitter late in the year, and it could become a key pitch if Burgos ends up in the bullpen. That's a move he'd favor because of his strong ambition to become a closer. To succeed as a starter, he'll need to trust his stuff more and do more than simply trying to blaze fastballs by hitters. Burgos also needs to show more maturity and focus. He'll remain in the rotation in high Class A this year.

Year	Club (League)	Class	W	L	ERA	G	GS	CG	SV	IP	H	R	ER	HR	BB	SO	AVG
2001	Royals (DSL)	R	2	5	4.97	13	11	0	0	51	51	36	28	1	35	38	.262
2002	Royals (DSL)	R	0	9	5.47	13	12	0	0	51	47	42	31	1	28	33	.241
2003	Royals 1 (AZL)	R	3	2	4.00	9	7	0	0	36	37	22	16	1	16	43	.261
	Burlington (Mid)	A	0	1	5.40	2	2	0	0	5	3	3	3	1	6	4	.200
2004	Burlington (Mid)	A	7	11	4.38	27	26	0	0	134	109	70	65	13	75	172	.221
MINOR LEAGUE TOTALS			12	28	4.66	64	58	0	0	276	247	173	143	17	160	290	.238

Luis Cota, rhp

Born: Aug. 19, 1985. **Ht.:** 6-1. **Wt.:** 180. **Bats:** R. **Throws:** R. **School:** South Mountain (Ariz.) CC. **Career Transactions:** Selected by Royals in 10th round of 2003 draft; signed May 17, 2004. **Signed by:** Mike Brown.

A native Panamanian, Cota was a strong-armed shortstop who also pitched at Tucson's Sunnyside High. The Royals spent a 10th-round choice on him in 2003 and watched him blossom in junior college before signing him as a draft-and-follow for $1.05 million—a record for a 10th-rounder. Cota throws his four-seam fastball at 92-96 mph range, and it has so much boring action that scouts mistook it for a two-seamer. He scrapped his curveball after signing to focus on his slider, and it now clocks in at 86-88 mph, giving him a second plus pitch. He's very athletic, allowing him to repeat a sound delivery and field his position. Cota struggled with his command in his pro debut, which may have been a result of being tired after working 93 innings in junior college. He needs to work down in the zone more often. He didn't start using a changeup until instructional league, but made good initial progress. With his stuff, Cota can become a frontline starter, though he's quite a ways from the majors. He'll begin his first full season in low Class A.

Year	Club (League)	Class	W	L	ERA	G	GS	CG	SV	IP	H	R	ER	HR	BB	SO	AVG
2004	Idaho Falls (Pio)	R	2	1	5.81	13	12	0	0	48	61	37	31	5	21	40	.311
MINOR LEAGUE TOTALS			2	1	5.81	13	12	0	0	48	61	37	31	5	21	40	.311

Shane Costa, of

Born: Dec. 12, 1981. **Ht.:** 6-0. **Wt.:** 200. **Bats:** L. **Throws:** R. **School:** Cal State Fullerton. **Career Transactions:** Selected by Royals in second round of 2003 draft; signed July 17, 2003. **Signed by:** Gary Johnson.

Costa signed for $775,000 after earning the 2003 Big West Conference player of the year award. His father Leo is a former college football player and national bodybuilding champion who works as a personal trainer. That upbringing gives Costa an aggressive mentality. A polished hitter, Costa has quick hands that allow him to turn pitches into line drives. He easily makes adjustments and consistent contact. He's an average baserunner and defender. Costa's below-average arm relegates him to left field, where he'll need to produce for more power. The Royals want him to do a better job of loading his hands in his swing. If he does that and starts to turn on more pitches, he could translate his strength into 20-25 homers per year. One Royals scout compares Costa, physically and statistically, to Brian Giles. Giles always posted solid on-base percentages in the minors but never slugged better than .400 until he reached Double-A. Costa has followed a similar path, and needs to ratchet up his power production at Double-A Wichita in 2005. He should be in the majors by 2006.

Year	Club (League)	Class	AVG	G	AB	R	H	2B	3B	HR	RBI	BB	SO	SB	OBP	SLG
2003	Royals 2 (AZL)	R	.386	23	88	22	34	6	4	1	24	6	7	4	.444	.580
	Wilmington (Car)	A	.143	3	7	1	1	1	0	0	0	2	1	0	.400	.286
2004	Wilmington (Car)	A	.308	123	451	70	139	20	4	7	60	32	43	9	.364	.417
MINOR LEAGUE TOTALS			.319	149	546	93	174	27	8	8	84	40	51	13	.378	.441

Mitch Maier, 3b

Born: June. 30, 1982. **Ht.:** 6-2. **Wt.:** 200. **Bats:** L. **Throws:** R. **School:** University of Toledo. **Career Transactions:** Selected by Royals in first round (30th overall) of 2003 draft; signed June 4, 2003. **Signed by:** Jason Bryans.

Maier turned down an offer to walk on the Michigan football team as a defensive back, opting instead to play baseball at Toledo, where he led the Mid-American Conference in batting as a freshman and junior. The Rockets' all-time leading hitter at .414, he agreed to a $900,000 predraft deal in 2003. Maier's hand-eye coordination allows for patience and consistent contact, though his plate discipline slipped in 2004. The Royals have encouraged him to move his hands closer to his body, which should shorten his swing and help him improve against breaking balls. Maier runs well underway and displays good instincts along the basepaths. A college catcher, Maier moved to third base to address an organizational weakness. The results have been mixed, as he lacks first-step quickness and doesn't read balls well off the bat. His likely destination is an outfield corner. He needs to add a touch of leverage to his swing to develop more power. Maier could move quickly once he finds a position. If he has a good spring, he could open 2005 in Double-A.

Year	Club (League)	Class	AVG	G	AB	R	H	2B	3B	HR	RBI	BB	SO	SB	OBP	SLG
2003	Royals 1 (AZL)	R	.350	51	203	41	71	14	6	2	45	18	25	7	.403	.507
2004	Burlington (Mid)	A	.300	82	317	41	95	24	3	4	36	27	51	34	.354	.432
	Wilmington (Car)	A	.264	51	174	25	46	9	2	3	17	15	29	10	.326	.391
MINOR LEAGUE TOTALS			.305	184	694	107	212	47	11	9	98	60	105	51	.361	.444

Donald Murphy, 2b

Born: March 10, 1983. **Ht.:** 5-10. **Wt.:** 180. **Bats:** R. **Throws:** R. **School:** Orange Coast (Calif.) JC. **Career Transactions:** Selected by Royals in fifth round of 2002 draft; signed June 23, 2002. **Signed by:** Gary Johnson.

Scouts first took notice of Murphy at Orange Coast College in 2002 when they went to see teammate Matt Clanton, whom the Cubs took in the supplemental first round. Murphy has been a consistent run producer as a pro, with 201 RBIs in 322 minor league games. Murphy's offense is his strong suit. He has gap power and a solid approach at the plate. As a second baseman, he offers a strong arm and a good double-play pivot. Murphy hit .302 through June before falling into a .202 tailspin afterward. He needs to stop wiggling his hands before unloading on a pitch, because it makes his swing longer and forces him to commit sooner, leaving him vulnerable to pitchers who change speeds well. He can be a little pull-conscious. His below-average speed makes his range average at best. Murphy rates an edge over Ruben Gotay as the Royals' second baseman of the future because his athleticism makes him a better defender. He'll move up to Double-A in 2005. Murphy got a surprise September call up and should reach the majors to stay in 2006.

Year	Club (League)	Class	AVG	G	AB	R	H	2B	3B	HR	RBI	BB	SO	SB	OBP	SLG
2002	Spokane (NWL)	A	.303	28	109	20	33	10	2	0	15	6	17	0	.356	.431
	Burlington (Mid)	A	.225	33	120	12	27	6	3	0	15	11	31	0	.300	.325
2003	Burlington (Mid)	A	.313	132	504	77	158	29	6	5	98	65	78	15	.397	.425
2004	Wilmington (Car)	A	.254	129	485	67	123	32	4	10	73	52	96	1	.326	.398
	Kansas City (AL)	MAJ	.185	7	27	1	5	3	0	0	3	0	7	1	.185	.296
MAJOR LEAGUE TOTALS			.185	7	27	1	5	3	0	0	3	0	7	1	.185	.296
MINOR LEAGUE TOTALS			.280	322	1218	176	341	77	15	15	201	134	222	16	.356	.405

J.P. Howell, lhp

Born: April 25, 1983. **Ht.:** 6-0. **Wt.:** 180. **Bats:** L. **Throws:** L. **School:** University of Texas. **Career Transactions:** Selected by Royals in first round (31st overall) of 2004 draft; signed July 5, 2004. **Signed by:** Chet Sergo.

Howell led Texas to the College World Series finals in 2004, tying for the Division I lead in wins (15-2, 2.13) while ranking second in strikeouts (166 in 135 innings). He cut a predraft deal for a $1 million bonus as the first supplemental pick after the first round. Howell mirrors Zack Greinke's ability to add and subtract from four pitches that he'll throw in any count. His four-seam fastball tops out at 89 mph, but both it and his lively two-seamer play above-average because of his command. His plus curveball comes in two varieties, one he can bury in the dirt for a strikeout and another he throws for strikes. Howell's splitter elicits swings-and-misses because it closely resembles his two-seamer. He also uses a fosh changeup. He's not afraid to throw inside, but Howell needs to do so more often. He can rely too much on his curveball at times. His bulldog nature is often an asset, though he sometimes loses control of his emotions. Howell is refined and could begin 2005 in high Class A. Despite his lack of velocity, his feel for pitching and heart could make him a middle-of-the-rotation starter.

Year	Club (League)	Class	W	L	ERA	G	GS	CG	SV	IP	H	R	ER	HR	BB	SO	AVG
2004	Idaho Falls (Pio)	R	3	1	2.77	6	4	0	0	26	16	9	8	1	12	38	.176
MINOR LEAGUE TOTALS			3	1	2.77	6	4	0	0	26	16	9	8	1	12	38	.176

12 Andy Sisco, lhp

Born: Jan. 13, 1983. **Ht.:** 6-9. **Wt.:** 260. **Bats:** L. **Throws:** L. **School:** Eastlake HS, Sammamish, Wash. **Career Transactions:** Selected by Cubs in second round of 2001 draft; signed June 26, 2001 . . . Selected by Royals from Cubs in major league Rule 5 draft, Dec. 13, 2004. **Signed by:** Al Geddes (Cubs).

It would have seemed implausible heading into 2004, but the Cubs opted not to protect Sisco on their 40-man roster after the season and lost him to the Royals in the major league Rule 5 draft. The No. 4 prospect in the Cubs organization a year ago, Sisco had a lot going for him. A 6-foot-9 hulk of a pitcher who had been recruited as a defensive end by Pacific-10 Conference football programs, he threw a 92-94 mph fastball and an effective changeup, flashed a plus curveball and projected to add velocity. But he didn't follow his offseason conditioning properly and arrived in spring training too bulky and tight. That cost him arm speed and velocity, and he pitched at 87-89 mph and rarely topped 90 for much of the year. He also lost the feel for his breaking pitch. His control regressed significantly and he was much more hittable than he had been in the past. Sisco also has to answer questions about his maturity and off-field issues. While his ceiling is as huge as he is, it may be a stretch for Kansas City to keep him in the majors all season when he'd be best served by returning to high Class A. Before the Royals could send Sisco to the minors in 2005, however, Rule 5 guidelines stipulate that he'd have to be placed on waivers and offered back to Chicago for half the $50,000 draft price.

Year	Club (League)	Class	W	L	ERA	G	GS	CG	SV	IP	H	R	ER	HR	BB	SO	AVG
2001	Cubs (AZL)	R	1	0	5.24	10	7	0	0	34	36	28	20	1	10	31	.267
2002	Boise (NWL)	A	7	2	2.43	14	14	0	0	78	51	23	21	3	39	101	.188
2003	Lansing (Mid)	A	6	8	3.54	19	19	3	0	94	76	44	37	3	31	99	.220
2004	Daytona (FSL)	A	4	10	4.21	26	25	0	0	126	118	64	59	11	65	134	.253
MINOR LEAGUE TOTALS			18	20	3.71	69	65	3	0	332	281	159	137	18	145	365	.231

13 Brian McFall, of

Born: June 17, 1984. **Ht.:** 6-3. **Wt.:** 205. **Bats:** R. **Throws:** R. **School:** Chandler-Gilbert (Ariz.) CC. **Career Transactions:** Selected by Royals in third round of 2003 draft; signed June 3, 2003. **Signed by:** Mike Brown.

McFall was a surprise third-round pick in 2003, but the Royals didn't want to risk losing him. They liked his athleticism and power, and he threw 92 mph as a righthander. After signing for $385,000, he struggled with the transition from junior college to Rookie ball. He also was overmatched in low Class A at the beginning of 2004, though he fared well after a demotion, leading the Pioneer League in doubles, RBIs, slugging percentage and steals. McFall is an emotional player, and often carries one at-bat into the next. That's a big reason for his struggles in Burlington and for his success at Idaho Falls. His bat speed and strength give him raw power to rival that of any Kansas City farmhand, especially when he gets his arms extended. He strikes out too much because he struggles to recognize breaking balls and sometimes pull off pitches when he tries to muscle up. McFall has slightly above-average speed and moves well, enabling him to make a smooth adjustment from first base to right field last year. He also continues to show a plus arm, though he needs to make better reads on balls hit over his head. McFall could have five tools that all play average or better in the majors, though the Royals will handle him cautiously. They know jumping him past low Class A in 2005 could lead to more difficulties.

Year	Club (League)	Class	AVG	G	AB	R	H	2B	3B	HR	RBI	BB	SO	SB	OBP	SLG
2003	Royals 1 (AZL)	R	.220	51	191	34	42	9	4	6	36	17	50	1	.296	.403
2004	Burlington (Mid)	A	.172	53	151	16	26	7	0	0	14	13	48	7	.270	.219
	Idaho Falls (Pio)	R	.363	68	262	64	95	23	1	14	68	30	64	23	.438	.618
MINOR LEAGUE TOTALS			.270	172	604	114	163	39	5	20	118	60	162	31	.352	.450

14 Leo Nunez, rhp

Born: Aug. 14, 1980. **Ht.:** 6-1. **Wt.:** 150. **Bats:** R. **Throws:** R. **Career Transactions:** Signed out of Dominican Republic by Pirates, Feb. 16, 2000 . . . Traded by Pirates to Royals for C Benito Santiago, Dec. 16, 2004. **Signed by:** Jose Luna (Pirates).

After trading for John Buck and Justin Huber in 2004, the Royals had no need for Benito

Santiago, whom they signed to a two-year contract before the season. So they traded Santiago to the Pirates for Nunez, who has been called "Little Pedro" because of his physical resemblance to fellow Dominican Pedro Martinez. Scouts say he's a closer match for another Dominican, Julian Tavarez. Nunez has a live arm, throwing 92-94 mph and reaching 97. Strictly a fastball pitcher when he signed, he since has developed a curveball and slider. Though he's not very big, he generates his heat with very little effort. He could stand to add some weight, though his velocity and stamina haven't been problems to this point. He'll go through periods where he has trouble finding the strike zone, but for the most part Nunez has shown good command. Nunez is still quite raw but has shown consistent improvement. His ability to refine a usable changeup will determine whether he can stay in the rotation or will be better suited for the bullpen. He'll make his Royals debut in high Class A.

Year	Club (League)	Class	W	L	ERA	G	GS	CG	SV	IP	H	R	ER	HR	BB	SO	AVG
2000	Pirates (DSL)	R	5	3	2.19	14	14	1	0	86	69	26	21	0	27	82	—
2001	Pirates (GCL)	R	2	2	4.39	10	7	1	0	53	62	28	26	4	9	34	.284
2002	Pirates (GCL)	R	4	2	3.43	11	11	0	0	60	54	23	23	5	5	52	.238
	Hickory (SAL)	A	0	0	0.00	1	1	0	0	4	5	0	0	0	3	1	.333
2003	Hickory (SAL)	A	2	1	5.59	13	7	0	0	48	59	34	30	6	14	37	.304
	Williamsport (NY-P)	A	4	3	3.05	8	8	0	0	38	31	14	13	0	12	41	.211
2004	Hickory (SAL)	A	10	4	3.13	27	20	3	1	144	121	53	50	16	46	140	.229
MINOR LEAGUE TOTALS			27	15	3.38	84	68	5	1	434	401	178	163	31	116	387	.250

15 Billy Buckner, rhp

Born: Aug. 27, 1983. **Ht.:** 6-2. **Wt.:** 215. **Bats:** R. **Throws:** R. **School:** University of South Carolina. **Career Transactions:** Selected by Royals in second round of 2004 draft; signed July 12, 2004. **Signed by:** Spencer Graham.

Buckner, who will tell you quickly he isn't related to the former major leaguer of the same name, played alongside Orioles first-rounder Nick Markakis at Young-Harris (Ga.) Junior College in 1999, but chose to attend South Carolina instead of signing with the Devil Rays after they took him in the ninth round. Buckner found immediate success with the Gamecocks. His fastball velocity improved from 87-88 mph to the low 90s, serving as a perfect complement to an excellent knuckle-curve that drops off the table. He struck out 14 against Clemson in early March in front of several scouting directors, including Kansas City's Deric Ladnier, and appeared destined for the first round. But he came down with mononucleosis and never got back to full strength as the draft approached, so the Royals were able to get him in the second round—one round after South Carolina teammate Matt Campbell. Buckner also owns a changeup with plus potential but he needs to throw it more. Also on his to-do list are getting stronger and establishing his fastball more after relying heavily on his breaking ball in college. He has the polish and college pedigree to move quickly after starting 2005 in low Class A. He could end up as a No. 3 or 4 starter.

Year	Club (League)	Class	W	L	ERA	G	GS	CG	SV	IP	H	R	ER	HR	BB	SO	AVG
2004	Idaho Falls (Pio)	R	2	2	3.93	8	5	0	0	34	44	18	15	4	8	37	.317
MINOR LEAGUE TOTALS			2	2	3.93	8	5	0	0	34	44	18	15	4	8	37	.317

16 Matt Campbell, lhp

Born: Dec. 27, 1982. **Ht.:** 6-2. **Wt.:** 170. **Bats:** L. **Throws:** L. **School:** University of South Carolina. **Career Transactions:** Selected by Royals in first round (29th overall) of 2004 draft; signed July 5, 2004. **Signed by:** Spencer Graham.

The Royals grabbed a pair of similar college lefthanders with the 29th and 31st picks in last June's draft, taking Campbell ahead of J.P. Howell and signing him for $1.1 million. Campbell has slightly better pure stuff, as he throws his fastball with more velocity (87-91 mph) and generates a bigger break on his 2-to-7 curveball that hitters often swing through. Howell has better command and feel for pitching. Campbell was worn out after pitching South Carolina to the College World Series for the third time in three years, and wasn't at his best in his pro debut. Kansas City shut him down early and expects to see the true Campbell in 2005. As with his South Carolina teammate Billy Buckner, the Royals want Campbell to use his fastball more often than he did in college. They figure his heater, which features arm-side tail, could gain velocity as he throws it more and improves his conditioning work. Campbell can locate his fastball to both sides of the plate, and he shows promise with his changeup. He may begin 2005 in low Class A but could advance fast.

Year	Club (League)	Class	W	L	ERA	G	GS	CG	SV	IP	H	R	ER	HR	BB	SO	AVG
2004	Idaho Falls (Pio)	R	0	2	8.44	4	4	0	0	11	11	10	10	1	10	10	.275
MINOR LEAGUE TOTALS			0	2	8.44	4	4	0	0	11	11	10	10	1	10	10	.275

17 Santiago Ramirez, rhp

Born: Aug. 15, 1978. **Ht.:** 5-11. **Wt.:** 200. **Bats:** R. **Throws:** R. **Career Transactions:** Signed out of Dominican Republic by Astros, June 23, 1997 . . . Granted free agency, Oct. 15, 2004 . . . Signed by Royals, Nov. 12, 2004. **Signed by:** Luis Coronado (Astros).

Ramirez rebounded from a shoulder injury, which didn't require surgery but cost him most of 2003, to save 32 games and earn Texas League all-star honors in 2004. He signed with the Royals as a minor league free agent, and a strong winter performance in his native Dominican Republic had them worried they might lose him in the major league Rule 5 draft. Ramirez has good sinking life on his 90-93 mph fastball, and his curveball and changeup are also reliable pitches. He keeps the ball down in the zone, though he'll get himself into trouble at times with walks. Outside of his shoulder problems in 2003, he has been durable and resilient. He'll compete for a set-up job in the beleaguered big league bullpen as a nonroster invitee to big league camp.

Year	Club (League)	Class	W	L	ERA	G	GS	CG	SV	IP	H	R	ER	HR	BB	SO	AVG
1997	Astros (DSL)	R	4	1	2.65	15	2	0	0	34	26	13	10	1	6	24	.217
1998	Astros (DSL)	R	6	5	2.17	14	13	0	0	83	64	32	20	1	18	62	.203
1999	Martinsville (Appy)	R	2	1	1.45	25	0	0	17	31	26	9	5	1	14	35	.232
2000	Michigan (Mid)	A	3	3	6.07	23	0	0	5	30	27	28	20	6	32	22	.245
	Auburn (NY-P)	A	3	6	4.25	20	9	0	2	53	36	34	25	3	39	57	.197
2001	Lexington (SAL)	A	8	2	3.63	45	0	0	4	79	69	35	32	2	28	85	.237
2002	Round Rock (TL)	AA	5	2	2.56	33	0	0	4	63	45	19	18	3	26	73	.199
	New Orleans (PCL)	AAA	2	0	3.38	18	0	0	1	21	17	8	8	2	11	15	.221
2003	New Orleans (PCL)	AAA	4	0	4.26	10	0	0	0	13	7	7	6	1	9	9	.175
	Round Rock (TL)	AA	0	0	0.00	6	1	0	1	5	5	0	0	0	4	3	.278
2004	Round Rock (TL)	AA	6	4	2.63	55	0	0	32	79	71	24	23	2	38	83	.244
MINOR LEAGUE TOTALS			43	24	3.06	264	25	0	66	491	393	209	167	22	225	468	.220

18 Andres Blanco, ss

Born: April 11, 1984. **Ht.:** 5-10. **Wt.:** 155. **Bats:** S. **Throws:** R. **Career Transactions:** Signed out of Venezuela by Royals, Aug. 2, 2000. **Signed by:** Juan Indriago/Wilmer Castillo.

The Royals still rate Blanco's defensive abilities as better than Angel Berroa's. They underlined that point when they promoted Blanco to replace the former American League rookie of the year in the lineup twice in 2004, first when Berroa was hurt in April and again when he was demoted briefly in August. Blanco has exceptional hands, arm strength and range. While there's no question he can play shortstop in the majors, the jury is still out on his bat. He possesses what Kansas City calls offensive survival skills—he can bunt and make consistent contact from both sides of the plate. Blanco needs to get stronger because he can be overpowered at the plate. He also needs to play more of the small man's game. He often takes long swings to lift balls, though he's still looking for his first professional home run. He has above-average speed, but he hasn't shown the instincts to steal bases. Blanco has to start making these offensive adjustments at Triple-A in 2005 if he's to emerge as anything more than a defensive-minded utilityman. The Royals believe that can happen, pointing to the minor league career path of Omar Vizquel, and like Blanco enough to consider trading Berroa.

Year	Club (League)	Class	AVG	G	AB	R	H	2B	3B	HR	RBI	BB	SO	SB	OBP	SLG
2001	Royals (DSL)	R	.298	54	188	39	56	0	3	0	16	28	23	9	.411	.330
2002	Royals (GCL)	R	.249	52	193	27	48	8	0	0	14	15	29	16	.315	.290
	Wilmington (Car)	A	.308	5	13	2	4	1	0	0	0	1	4	0	.357	.385
2003	Wilmington (Car)	A	.244	113	394	61	96	11	3	0	26	44	50	13	.330	.287
2004	Wichita (TL)	AA	.247	93	324	34	80	10	2	0	21	18	44	7	.299	.290
	Kansas City (AL)	MAJ	.317	19	60	9	19	2	2	0	5	5	6	1	.379	.417
MAJOR LEAGUE TOTALS			.317	19	60	9	19	2	2	0	5	5	6	1	.379	.417
MINOR LEAGUE TOTALS			.255	317	1112	163	284	30	8	0	76	106	150	45	.334	.297

19 Brian Bass, rhp

Born: Jan. 6, 1982. **Ht.:** 6-0. **Wt.:** 190. **Bats:** R. **Throws:** R. **School:** Robert E. Lee HS, Montgomery, Ala. **Career Transactions:** Selected by Royals in sixth round of 2000 draft; signed June 9, 2000. **Signed by:** Dennis Woody.

After a breakout 2003 in high Class A, when his fastball jumped from 87-89 mph to the low 90s and his curveball improved from below- to above-average, Bass made Kansas City's 40-man roster and ranked seventh on this list. Shoulder problems ruined his 2004 season, however, as he didn't make his first start until May and took the mound just nine times all season. The Royals were encouraged by how he bounced back pitching in relief in the Arizona Fall League, as he regained the fastball and curveball he had shown the previous year. Bass' success comes from locating the ball to both sides of the plate and keeping it down, enticing loads of groundouts. He still needs to make progress with his changeup and slider. Assuming Bass remains healthy, he'll begin 2005 in Double-A with the chance for a swift promotion to Triple-A.

Year	Club (League)	Class	W	L	ERA	G	GS	CG	SV	IP	H	R	ER	HR	BB	SO	AVG
2000	Royals (GCL)	R	3	5	3.89	12	9	0	0	44	36	27	19	0	18	44	.211
	Charleston, WV (SAL)	A	0	0	6.75	1	1	0	0	4	6	3	3	0	0	1	.333
2001	Burlington (Mid)	A	3	10	4.65	26	26	1	0	139	138	82	72	16	53	75	.257
2002	Burlington (Mid)	A	5	7	3.83	20	20	1	0	110	103	57	47	8	31	60	.246
2003	Wilmington (Car)	A	9	8	2.84	26	26	2	0	152	129	59	48	7	43	119	.229
2004	Wichita (TL)	AA	0	4	7.96	9	9	0	0	32	48	28	28	4	20	16	.353
MINOR LEAGUE TOTALS			20	34	4.10	94	91	4	0	482	460	256	217	35	165	315	.249

20 Miguel Vega, 1b/3b

Born: July 31, 1985, in Guayama, P.R. **Ht.:** 6-3. **Wt.:** 205. **Bats:** R. **Throws:** R. **School:** Carmen B. Huyke HS, Arroyo, P.R. **Career Transactions:** Selected by Royals in fourth round of 2003 draft; signed July 18, 2003. **Signed by:** Johnny Ramos.

Vega first showed off his power potential in the 2002 Perfect Game/Baseball America World Wood Bat Association fall championship. There was talk the Royals or Reds might snag Vega in the first or supplemental first round in the 2003 draft, but Kansas City was able to pick him up in the fourth and sign him for $375,000. Vega looked raw struggling through his pro debut, but showed the benefits of instruction in a solid second trip through the Rookie-level Arizona League in 2004. Royals coaches helped Vega simplify his swing mechanics and eliminate a bad bat wrap that left him long and slow to the ball. He still struggles reacting to offspeed pitches and lets his swing get too long at times, but he showed improvements that allowed him to unleash his strength and loft power. He could develop into a special hitter if he can keep his stroke short and add the ability to hit for average to his plus power. Vega moved from third base to first last season. Though the new position makes little use of his above-average arm strength, he was a much better defender and was able to concentrate more on his hitting. He has good hands and body control, and his lack of range wasn't as much of an issue. Kansas City will continue to move Vega slowly, and it's possible he could open the season in extended spring training before heading to Idaho Falls in June.

Year	Club (League)	Class	AVG	G	AB	R	H	2B	3B	HR	RBI	BB	SO	SB	OBP	SLG
2003	Royals 1 (AZL)	R	.222	25	81	12	18	5	0	2	11	2	25	0	.238	.358
2004	Royals (AZL)	R	.275	56	229	36	63	15	5	10	44	16	74	6	.328	.515
MINOR LEAGUE TOTALS			.261	81	310	48	81	20	5	12	55	18	99	6	.302	.474

21 Ryan Braun, rhp

Born: July 29, 1980. **Ht.:** 6-2. **Wt.:** 205. **Bats:** R. **Throws:** R. **School:** University of Nevada-Las Vegas. **Career Transactions:** Selected by Royals in sixth round of 2003 draft; signed June 6, 2003. **Signed by:** Mike Brown.

Looking to save money, Kansas City drafted college seniors with their fifth- through ninth-round picks in 2003, then offered them all take-it-or-leave-it $1,000 bonuses. A two-way player plagued by injuries during his college career at Wake Forest and Nevada-Las Vegas, Braun is the best prospect of the group. In his first full pro season, he finished second in saves and seventh in appearances in the high Class A Carolina League. He overpowered hitters with a 93-96 mph fastball and two plus breaking pitches, a mid-80s slider and a curveball. He showed the give-me-the-ball mentality organizations want from a potential closer, and no signs of injury or fatigue. Braun's big, strong frame and clean arm action give the Royals hope that his injury problems are behind him. He's 24, so they're putting him on the fast track to the majors, with the next stop coming in Double-A.

Year	Club (League)	Class	W	L	ERA	G	GS	CG	SV	IP	H	R	ER	HR	BB	SO	AVG
2003	Royals 1 (AZL)	R	0	0	2.95	18	0	0	3	21	15	9	7	0	10	25	.185
2004	Wilmington (Car)	A	2	3	2.21	51	0	0	24	57	48	25	14	2	25	58	.227
MINOR LEAGUE TOTALS			2	3	2.41	69	0	0	27	78	63	34	21	2	35	83	.216

22 Dusty Hughes, lhp

Born: June 29, 1983. **Ht.:** 5-9. **Wt.:** 195. **Bats:** L. **Throws:** L. **School:** Delta State (Miss.) University. **Career Transactions:** Selected by Royals in 11th round of 2003 draft; signed June 20, 2003. **Signed by:** Mark Willoughby.

Hughes ranked third among NCAA Division II pitchers with 12.4 strikeouts per nine innings in 2003 and enjoyed a solid pro debut. But he never drew much attention until he opened the 2004 season with eight no-hit innings for Burlington. Hughes never looked back. He commands the strike zone with pinpoint accuracy and a fearless demeanor, never walking more than three batters in any of his 26 appearances last year. Hughes throws his fastball anywhere from 84-91 mph. It appears faster than radar readings indicate because he keeps the ball behind him during his delivery, and his deception forces hitters to pick up his pitches late. He likes to vary speeds with his fastball and isn't afraid to buzz hitters inside. His low-80s slider features a late break. It's the pitch he puts hitters away with. He throws his average changeup sparingly, but uses it effectively when needed. Hughes' sustained success at both Class A levels has led the Royals to project him as a back-of-the-rotation starter rather than a set-up man. He should start 2005 in Double-A.

Year	Club (League)	Class	W	L	ERA	G	GS	CG	SV	IP	H	R	ER	HR	BB	SO	AVG
2003	Royals 1 (AZL)	R	5	2	2.84	11	6	0	0	51	38	21	16	4	18	54	.207
2004	Burlington (Mid)	A	4	2	1.56	8	8	0	0	52	39	12	9	2	15	36	.209
	Wilmington (Car)	A	5	5	2.41	18	18	0	0	108	95	37	29	5	31	68	.235
MINOR LEAGUE TOTALS			14	9	2.30	37	32	0	0	211	172	70	54	11	64	158	.222

23 Erik Cordier, rhp

Born: Feb. 25, 1986. **Ht.:** 6-3. **Wt.:** 195. **Bats:** R. **Throws:** R. **School:** Southern Door HS, Sturgeon Bay, Wis. **Career Transactions:** Selected by Royals in second round of 2004 draft; signed June 25, 2003. **Signed by:** Phil Huttmann.

When the Royals took Cordier in the second round last June, he became the highest-drafted Wisconsin player since the Angels drafted Jarrod Washburn 31st overall in 1995. Cordier, who impressed scouts at multiple showcase events, signed for $575,000. He throws three pitches that have plus potential. His fastball regularly sits in the 90-92 mph range, he demonstrates a good feel for his changeup and gets good rotation on his curveball. Because he's athletic and he's a lanky 6-foot-3 and 197 pounds, he has plenty of projection remaining. Cordier's pro debut was lackluster, as he had trouble adjusting to the intense heat of Arizona as well as the rigors of pro ball. The Royals will bring him along slowly. He's a candidate for Idaho Falls in 2005, but he could emerge as a No. 2 or 3 starter once he masters the nuances of pitching professionally.

Year	Club (League)	Class	W	L	ERA	G	GS	CG	SV	IP	H	R	ER	HR	BB	SO	AVG
2004	Royals (AZL)	R	2	4	5.19	11	11	0	0	35	38	27	20	1	21	22	.279
MINOR LEAGUE TOTALS			2	4	5.19	11	11	0	0	35	38	27	20	1	21	22	.279

24 Devon Lowery, rhp

Born: March 24, 1983. **Ht.:** 6-1. **Wt.:** 190. **Bats:** L. **Throws:** R. **School:** South Point HS, Belmont, N.C. **Career Transactions:** Selected by Royals in 14th round of 2001 draft; signed June 9, 2001. **Signed by:** Junior Vizcaino.

Lowery's arm strength made him one of North Carolina's top high school quarterbacks in 2001, and he drew interest from several NCAA Division I-A football programs, including Wake Forest. He chose instead to sign with the Royals and is one of the organization's better athletes. His transition to a baseball-only life has been slow as his fastball dropped from 90-94 mph in high school to 86-88 as he became accustomed to professional throwing and conditioning regimens. Lowery's velocity returned midway through 2003, earning him a move to the rotation and a boost in the organizational hierarchy. He kept his heavy, lively fastball down in the zone and used his late-breaking slider as an out pitch in 2004, when he ranked sixth in the Carolina League in strikeouts and eighth in ERA. Lowery shows good arm speed on a changeup that fades away from lefthanders and displays an outstanding delivery overall. His velocity began to dip late in the season as he reached a career high in innings for the second straight year, so he skipped instructional league. Lowery will focus on keeping his strength and stamina over an entire season in the Double-A rotation in 2005. He profiles as an innings-eating No. 4 starter.

Year	Club (League)	Class	W	L	ERA	G	GS	CG	SV	IP	H	R	ER	HR	BB	SO	AVG
2001	Royals (GCL)	R	2	3	4.17	11	6	0	1	41	38	25	19	2	12	19	.238
2002	Royals (GCL)	R	0	3	3.86	15	0	0	4	26	25	13	11	1	11	26	.255
2003	Burlington (Mid)	A	6	4	3.36	26	10	0	5	96	78	39	36	9	34	74	.222
2004	Wilmington (Car)	A	9	9	3.66	28	28	1	0	145	139	74	59	16	52	115	.253
MINOR LEAGUE TOTALS			17	19	3.65	80	44	1	10	308	280	151	125	28	109	234	.242

25 Mike Aviles, ss

Born: March 13, 1981. **Ht.:** 5-11. **Wt.:** 193. **Bats:** R. **Throws:** R. **School:** Concordia (N.Y.) College. **Career Transactions:** Selected by Royals in seventh round of 2003 draft; signed June 12, 2003. **Signed by:** Steve Connelly.

Area scout Steve Connelly wanted to sign Aviles after his junior season at Concordia

College, but had to wait until he earned NCAA Division II player of the year honors as a senior in 2003. Aviles shortened his stroke and led D-II in batting (.500), slugging (1.016), homers (22) and runs (83) that spring, and the Royals made sure they got him by spending a seventh-round pick on him (albeit with only a $1,000 bonus). Aviles was the Arizona League MVP in 2003, then capped his banner season by holding his own in winter ball in Puerto Rico. He played for Carolina, where his uncle Ramon (a former big leaguer) was a coach. Aviles kept producing in 2004, thanks to a compact swing and solid strength for his size. He led the Carolina League in doubles and ranked third in hits after jumping three levels to high Class A. He makes good contact but could stand to draw more walks. Aviles' arm and hands rate as solid-average, though he's not as quick or rangy as most shortstops. Aviles is the sort of overachiever organizations love to uncover, but also one who must prove himself at each level. His bat will determine whether he becomes an everyday middle infielder or a utility player, and his next test will come in Double-A.

Year	Club (League)	Class	AVG	G	AB	R	H	2B	3B	HR	RBI	BB	SO	SB	OBP	SLG
2003	Royals 1 (AZL)	R	.363	52	212	51	77	19	5	6	39	13	28	11	.404	.585
2004	Wilmington (Car)	A	.300	126	463	66	139	40	4	6	68	39	57	2	.352	.443
MINOR LEAGUE TOTALS			.320	178	675	117	216	59	9	12	107	52	85	13	.368	.487

26 Mario Lisson, ss/3b

Born: May 31, 1984. **Ht.:** 6-2. **Wt.:** 170. **Bats:** R. **Throws:** R. **Career Transactions:** Signed out of Venezuela by Royals, April 1, 2002. **Signed by:** Juan Indriago.

Lisson is one of general manager Allard Baird's favorite sleepers. The Royals' Rookie-level Dominican Summer League player of the year in 2003, he made a successful U.S. debut last season. Lisson offers a live, athletic body but has also demonstrated the ability to play under control. He possesses the strength and bat speed to produce plus power, but he's also selective at the plate. He can be almost too patient at times, as he struck out 82 times in 70 games in 2004. Lanky and long-limbed, he should improve his coordination as he grows into his body. Lisson's strong arm and soft hands have allowed him to excel defensively all over the diamond. He spent time at catcher and first base after signing, but soon moved to shortstop and third base. His size could mean a permanent move to the hot corner, which fits well in an organization shallow at third base but deep up the middle. There's no reason to rush him with Mark Teahen well ahead of him, so Lisson will move one level at a time and go to low Class A in 2005.

Year	Club (League)	Class	AVG	G	AB	R	H	2B	3B	HR	RBI	BB	SO	SB	OBP	SLG
2002	Royals (GCL)	R	.200	6	10	0	2	0	0	0	0	4	4	0	.467	.200
	Kansas City (DSL)	R	.198	30	81	12	16	2	0	0	9	16	22	1	.330	.222
2003	Kansas City (DSL)	R	.290	62	210	26	61	11	1	3	28	35	36	9	.416	.395
2004	Idaho Falls (Pio)	R	.289	70	256	60	74	10	2	8	49	44	82	15	.398	.438
MINOR LEAGUE TOTALS			.275	168	557	98	153	23	3	11	86	99	144	25	.396	.386

27 Chad Blackwell, rhp

Born: Jan. 7, 1983. **Ht.:** 6-1. **Wt.:** 145. **Bats:** R. **Throws:** R. **School:** University of South Carolina. **Career Transactions:** Selected by Royals in sixth round of 2004 draft; signed June 28, 2004. **Signed by:** Spencer Graham.

Blackwell led NCAA Division I with 20 saves at South Carolina in 2004 after transferring from Pensacola (Fla.) Junior College. He's one of three Gamecocks pitchers taken early by Kansas City in last June's draft, following first-rounder Matt Campbell and second-rounder Billy Buckner. Though he has a wiry frame and a funky, low three-quarters delivery, Blackwell has proven resilient and durable as a closer. The Royals don't plan on tinkering with his motion because he never has experienced any arm problems, and his arm action is clean with good extension. His delivery also creates deception. Blackwell's fastball clocks in around 90 mph, and he commands it and his slider to both sides of the plate. He also elevates his fastball successfully. His changeup is an effective weapon against lefthanders. Blackwell's pitching style reminds the Royals of 2004 supplemental first-rounder J.P. Howell's because he competes hard and is adept at changing speeds to keep hitters off balance. He should end up as an effective set-up man, and his polish should make his route to the majors a quick one after he begins 2005 in low Class A.

Year	Club (League)	Class	W	L	ERA	G	GS	CG	SV	IP	H	R	ER	HR	BB	SO	AVG
2004	Idaho Falls (Pio)	R	1	1	3.27	21	0	0	7	33	32	15	12	2	16	46	.244
MINOR LEAGUE TOTALS			1	1	3.27	21	0	0	7	33	32	15	12	2	16	46	.244

28 Colt Griffin, rhp

Born: Sept. 29, 1982. **Ht.:** 6-4. **Wt.:** 200. **Bats:** R. **Throws:** R. **School:** Marshall (Texas) HS. **Career Transactions:** Selected by Royals in first round (ninth overall) of 2001 draft; signed Aug. 8, 2001. **Signed by:** Gerald Turner.

Griffin opens 2005 with plenty to prove if he's to remain in the organization's plans. The first documented high school pitcher to hit 100 mph, he parlayed his velocity into becoming the ninth overall pick in 2001 and signing for a $2.4 million bonus. Four years later, he's a middle reliever who has yet to have a winning season. Griffin still flashes that great fastball, as well as a plus slider that reaches 88 mph, but he never has found the strike zone consistently. Though he often dials down his fastball to 90-94 mph in hopes of improving his location, he still gives up too many walks and is too hittable. He has yet to show the ability to retain and apply instruction. The Royals are frustrated with his slow development, though they continue to praise his effort. He continued to search for a consistent release point in instructional league. He'll return to the Double-A bullpen this year, and his fastball-slider combination still could be lethal if he ever develops command.

Year	Club (League)	Class	W	L	ERA	G	GS	CG	SV	IP	H	R	ER	HR	BB	SO	AVG
2001	Spokane (NWL)	A	0	1	7.00	3	2	0	0	2	4	7	7	0	7	0	.364
2002	Burlington (Mid)	A	6	6	5.36	19	19	0	0	91	75	60	54	1	82	66	.233
	Wilmington (Car)	A	0	1	3.86	3	0	0	0	5	3	2	2	0	5	3	.214
2003	Burlington (Mid)	A	9	11	3.91	27	27	0	0	150	127	80	65	7	97	107	.233
	Wilmington (Car)	A	1	0	0.00	1	1	0	0	6	3	1	0	0	0	5	.143
2004	Wichita (TL)	AA	1	1	4.02	26	0	0	1	31	29	14	14	2	16	26	.246
	Wilmington (Car)	A	1	4	8.73	8	8	0	0	33	40	35	32	1	28	28	.313
MINOR LEAGUE TOTALS			18	24	4.93	87	57	0	1	318	281	199	174	11	235	235	.243

29 Chris McConnell, ss

Born: Dec. 18, 1985. **Ht.:** 5-11. **Wt.:** 170. **Bats:** R. **Throws:** R. **School:** Delsea HS, Franklinville, N.J. **Career Transactions:** Selected by Royals in ninth round of 2004 draft; signed June 10, 2004. **Signed by:** Sean Rooney.

After McConnell's pleasantly surprising offensive debut, the Royals compare him to Mike Aviles, another overachieving shortstop from the New York/New Jersey area. Kansas City drafted him in the ninth round and signed him for $40,000—primarily for his glove. A flashy defender, McConnell has plus-plus range, soft hands and an average arm. His bat was something of a concern, but he hit well in the Arizona League thanks to excellent hand-eye coordination and what scouting director Deric Ladnier calls "good hitting hands." Even when he starts his swing early, McConnell can keep his hands back long enough to make solid contact. His bat control and short, quick swing mean he puts a lot of balls in play. It's questionable how much pop he'll have down the road. McConnell can make spectacular plays at shortstop, but he'll have to cut down on his errors after making 16 errors in 29 games at shortstop. He'll likely move through the system with fellow 2004 draftee Josh Johnson (third round), and they could share shortstop duties at Idaho Falls this year.

Year	Club (League)	Class	AVG	G	AB	R	H	2B	3B	HR	RBI	BB	SO	SB	OBP	SLG
2004	Royals (AZL)	R	.339	37	124	22	42	5	0	3	11	17	19	8	.420	.452
MINOR LEAGUE TOTALS			.339	37	124	22	42	5	0	3	11	17	19	8	.420	.452

30 Henry Barrera, rhp

Born: Nov. 25, 1985. **Ht.:** 6-1. **Wt.:** 175. **Bats:** R. **Throws:** R. **School:** Rosemead (Calif.) HS. **Career Transactions:** Selected by Royals in fifth round of 2004 draft; signed July 8, 2004. **Signed by:** Bob Bishop.

Barrera is similar to 2003 draft-and-follow Luis Cota, as both are short righthanders with lightning arms. Barrera can reach 96-98 mph with his fastball and 84-87 with his slider. On the other hand, his mechanics and command are raw. He came to the Royals with a hop in his delivery that took his foot off the rubber and placed him off line from home plate. Barrera signed a 2005 contract, passing on a commitment to Rio Hondo (Calif.) Junior College, so Kansas City didn't begin extensive work with him until instructional league. He'll be able to find the strike zone more often once he establishes a more consistent release point. The Royals will take it slow with Barrera, likely assigning him to extended spring training before he makes his pro debut in the Rookie-level Gulf Coast League. His focus in his first year will be to locate his fastball (which sits mostly at 89-93 mph) and slider while developing a changeup.

Year	Club (League)	Class	W	L	ERA	G	GS	CG	SV	IP	H	R	ER	HR	BB	SO	AVG
2004	Did not play—Signed 2005 contract																

LOS ANGELES
DODGERS

BY **ALAN MATTHEWS**

LARRY GOREN

Despite rumors that Athletics general manager Billy Beane was bound to replace Dan Evans in that role for the Dodgers, new owner Frank McCourt opted for Beane's top assistant. **Paul DePodesta** became the ninth GM in franchise history last February, at 31 the third-youngest GM ever in baseball.

DePodesta put the finishing touches on a roster largely assembled by Evans, and the Dodgers won their first postseason game since they were World Series champions in 1988. He wasted little time shaking up the roster, packaging quality prospects Franklin Gutierrez and Andrew Brown to get Milton Bradley from the Indians in April.

That wasn't the only controversial move the rookie GM made. With Los Angeles leading the National League West in late July, he shipped Paul Lo Duca, Guillermo Mota and Juan Encarnacion to the Marlins for Brad Penny, Hee Seop Choi and Double-A lefty Bill Murphy. DePodesta planned on spinning those players into subsequent deals for Randy Johnson and Charles Johnson, but both fell through. While he did use Murphy to get Steve Finley from the Diamondbacks, Penny made just three starts before a nerve problem in his upper arm sidelined him, Choi hit .162 and the Dodgers were left with a huge hole behind the plate.

While St. Louis bounced Los Angeles in four games in the NL Division Series, there was a buzz around Chavez Ravine that had been absent in recent seasons. After the season, DePodesta continued to mold the ros-

ter more to his liking.

Contrary to what many expected, DePodesta did mesh well with scouting director Logan White. White had two of the game's best drafts in his first two years on the job, taking high-ceiling high school prospects. Four of Los Angeles' top six picks last June, including both first-rounders, came from the prep ranks. There was a hint of DePodesta's influence as the Dodgers spent early choices on Virginia Commonwealth righthander Justin Orenduff (supplemental first round), George Washington outfielder Anthony Raglani (third) and Rhode Island first baseman Daniel Batz (sixth).

The front office went through a number of changes during the offseason. Senior scouting adviser Don Welke, instrumental in constructing much of the current roster, was fired, coinciding with the departures of special assistant Jeff Schugel, senior baseball operations adviser John Boles and baseball operations assistant A.J. Preller. DePodesta will now rely on a reconstructed group consisting of vice president of player development Roy Smith, previously an assistant GM for Pittsburgh, and coordinator of baseball operations Dan Feinstein, another Beane disciple from Oakland. Field coordinator Terry Collins was promoted to farm director, a position that was in flux all of last season after previously being filled by current Mariners GM Bill Bavasi.

TOP 30 PROSPECTS

1. Joel Guzman, ss/of	16. Xavier Paul, of
2. Chad Billingsley, rhp	17. Joel Hanrahan, rhp
3. Edwin Jackson, rhp	18. Delwyn Young, 2b
4. James Loney, 1b	19. Cory Dunlap, 1b
5. Andy LaRoche, 3b	20. Mike Megrew, lhp
6. Russell Martin, c	21. Etanislao Abreu, 2b/ss
7. Greg Miller, lhp	22. Steve Schmoll, rhp
8. Blake DeWitt, 3b	23. Blake Johnson, rhp
9. Jonathan Broxton, rhp	24. Justin Orenduff, rhp
10. Chuck Tiffany, lhp	25. Willy Aybar, 2b
11. Scott Elbert, lhp	26. Javy Guerra, rhp
12. Julio Pimentel, rhp	27. Franquelis Osoria, rhp
13. Chin-Lung Hu, ss	28. Matt Kemp, of
14. Dioner Navarro, c	29. Juan Rivera, ss
15. Yhency Brazoban, rhp	30. Jason Repko, of

ORGANIZATION OVERVIEW

General manager: Paul DePodesta. **Farm director:** Terry Collins. **Scouting director:** Logan White.

2004 PERFORMANCE

Class	Farm Team	League	W	L	Pct.	Finish*	Manager
Majors	Los Angeles	National	93	69	.574	3rd (16)	Jim Tracy
Triple-A	Las Vegas 51s	Pacific Coast	67	76	.469	11th (16)	Terry Kennedy
Double-A	Jacksonville Suns	Southern	66	71	.482	7th (10)	Dino Ebel
High A	Vero Beach Dodgers	Florida State	77	57	.575	1st (12)	Scott Little
Low A	Columbus Catfish	South Atlantic	69	69	.500	t-7th (16)	Dann Bilardello
Rookie	Ogden Raptors	Pioneer	35	40	.467	6th (8)	Travis Barbary
Rookie	GCL Dodgers	Gulf Coast	31	29	.517	t-6th (12)	Luis Salazar
OVERALL 2004 MINOR LEAGUE RECORD			345	342	.502	15th (30)	

*Finish in overall standings (No. of teams in league).

ORGANIZATION LEADERS

BATTING
*Minimum 250 at-bats

*AVG	John Barnes, Las Vegas	.348
R	Shane Victorino, Las Vegas/Jacksonville	98
H	Luis Garcia, Las Vegas	156
TB	Luis Garcia, Las Vegas	290
2B	Jason Repko, Las Vegas/Jacksonville	37
3B	Joel Guzman, Jacksonville/Vero Beach	11
HR	Luis Garcia, Las Vegas	32
RBI	Luis Garcia, Las Vegas	95
BB	Russell Martin, Vero Beach	72
SO	Delwyn Young, Vero Beach	134
SB	Alex Requena, Vero Beach	50
*OBP	Jose Flores, Las Vegas	.407
*SLG	Chin-Feng Chen, Las Vegas	.584

PITCHING
#Minimum 75 innings

W	Chad Billingsley, Jacksonville/Vero Beach	11
	Jonathan Broxton, Vero Beach	11
L	Mark Johnson, Las Vegas	12
#ERA	Marcos Carvajal, Jacksonville/Columbus	1.80
G	Troy Brohawn, Las Vegas	72
CG	Julio Pimentel, Columbus	2
SV	Jose Diaz, Vero Beach/Columbus	20
IP	Heath Totten, Las Vegas	160
BB	Glenn Bott, Jacksonville	75
	Joel Hanrahan, Las Vegas	75
SO	Chad Billingsley, Jacksonville/Vero Beach	158

BEST TOOLS

Best Hitter for Average	Blake DeWitt
Best Power Hitter	Joel Guzman
Best Strike-Zone Discipline	Cory Dunlap
Fastest Baserunner	Jason Repko
Best Athlete	Matt Kemp
Best Fastball	Edwin Jackson
Best Curveball	Chuck Tiffany
Best Slider	Chad Billingsley
Best Changeup	Alfredo Gonzalez
Best Control	Steve Schmoll
Best Defensive Catcher	Russell Martin
Best Defensive Infielder	Ching-Lung Hu
Best Infield Arm	Andy LaRoche
Best Defensive Outfielder	Jason Repko
Best Outfield Arm	Xavier Paul

PROJECTED 2008 LINEUP

Catcher	Russell Martin
First Base	Hee Seop Choi
Second Base	Tony Abreu
Third Base	Andy LaRoche
Shortstop	Cesar Izturis
Left Field	J.D. Drew
Center Field	Milton Bradley

Right Field	Joel Guzman
No. 1 Starter	Chad Billingsley
No. 2 Starter	Edwin Jackson
No. 3 Starter	Brad Penny
No. 4 Starter	Odalis Perez
No. 5 Starter	Derek Lowe
Closer	Eric Gagne

LAST YEAR'S TOP 20 PROSPECTS

1. Edwin Jackson, rhp
2. Greg Miller, lhp
3. Franklin Gutierrez, of
4. James Loney, 1b
5. Joel Hanrahan, rhp
6. Chad Billingsley, rhp
7. Xavier Paul, of
8. Andy LaRoche, 2b/ss
9. Koyie Hill, c
10. Reggie Abercrombie, of
11. Joel Guzman, ss
12. Steve Colyer, lhp
13. Willy Aybar, 3b
14. Jonathan Broxton, rhp
15. Chuck Tiffany, lhp
16. Chin-Feng Chen, of/1b
17. Jonathan Figueroa, lhp
18. Russell Martin, c
19. Mike Megrew, lhp
20. Andrew Brown, rhp

TOP PROSPECTS OF THE DECADE

Year	Player, Pos.	Current Team
1995	Todd Hollandsworth, of	Cubs
1996	Karim Garcia, of	Orioles
1997	Paul Konerko, 3b	White Sox
1998	Paul Konerko, 1b	White Sox
1999	Angel Pena, c	Out of baseball
2000	Chin-Feng Chen, of	Dodgers
2001	Ben Diggins, rhp	Brewers
2002	Ricardo Rodriguez, rhp	Rangers
2003	James Loney, 1b	Dodgers
2004	Edwin Jackson, rhp	Dodgers

TOP DRAFT PICKS OF THE DECADE

Year	Player, Pos.	Current Team
1995	David Yocum, lhp	Out of baseball
1996	Damian Rolls, 3b	Devil Rays
1997	Glenn Davis, 1b	Sioux Falls (Northern)
1998	Bubba Crosby, of	Yankees
1999	Jason Repko, ss/of	Dodgers
2000	Ben Diggins, rhp	Brewers
2001	Brian Pilkington, rhp (2nd round)	Dodgers
2002	James Loney, 1b	Dodgers
2003	Chad Billingsley, rhp	Dodgers
2004	Scott Elbert, lhp	Dodgers

ALL-TIME LARGEST BONUSES

Joel Guzman, 2001	$2,250,000
Ben Diggins, 2000	$2,200,000
Hideo Nomo, 1995	$2,000,000
Scott Elbert, 2004	$1,575,000
Kazuhisha Ishii, 2002	$1,500,000
James Loney, 2002	$1,500,000

MINOR LEAGUE DEPTH CHART

Los Angeles DODGERS

Impact Potential: A

Joel Guzman probably will outgrow shortstop, but his bat has made significant progress, and his raw power is immense. A healthy James Loney should rank among the minors' top hitters, while third basemen Andy LaRoche and Scott DeWitt and catcher Russell Martin all profile as above-average bats at their positions. While several high-profile Dodgers pitchers faced setbacks in 2004, Chad Billingsley established himself as one of the game's top future pitchers.

Depth: A

These Dodgers do it the way the O'Malley-owned clubs did, with a farm system fashioned from top high school players as well as all parts of the globe. In his first year as general manager, Paul DePodesta didn't interfere as scouting director Logan White again loaded up on premium prep talent. The Dodgers had the outfield and pitching depth to make trades both at the July deadline and later at the Winter Meetings.

*Depth charts prepared by **John Manuel** and **Allan Simpson**. Numbers in parentheses indicate prospect rankings.*

LF
Delwyn Young (18)
Chin-Feng Chen
James McDonald

CF
Jason Repko (30)
Cody Ross
Alejandro de Aza

3B
Andy LaRoche (5)
Blake DeWitt (8)
Jamie Hoffmann
Luis Castillo
Russ Mitchell

SS
Chin-Lung Hu (13)
Juan Rivera (29)
Lucas May

RF
Joel Guzman (1)
Xavier Paul (16)
Matt Kemp (28)

2B
Tony Abreu (21)
Willy Aybar (25)
Joey Thurston
Travis Denker

SOURCE of TALENT

HOMEGROWN		ACQUIRED	
College	1	Trades	1
Junior College	3	Rule 5 draft	0
Draft-and-follow	1	Independent leagues	0
High School	15	Free agents/waivers	0
Nondrafted free agent	1		
Foreign	8		

1B
James Loney (4)
Cory Dunlap (19)
James Peterson
Daniel Batz

C
Russell Martin (6)
Dioner Navarro (14)
Mike Nixon
Chris Westervelt
Edwin Bellorin
Kengshill Pujols
Rosten Gil

RHP

Starters	Relievers
Chad Billingsley (2)	Yhency Brazoban (15)
Edwin Jackson (3)	Steve Schmoll (22)
Jonathan Broxton (9)	Franquelis Osoria (27)
Julio Pimentel (12)	Jumbo Diaz
Joel Hanrahan (17)	Beltran Perez
Blake Johnson (23)	William Juarez
Justin Orenduff (24)	Howard Zuleta
Javy Guerra (26)	Richard Bartlett
Jesus Castillo	Alfredo Gonzalez
D.J. Houlton	Alvis Ojeda
Heath Totten	Jose Rojas
T.J. Nall	Alvin Hayes
Zach Hammes	
Brandon Weeden	
Jordan Pratt	
Mario Alvarez	

LHP

Starters	Relievers
Greg Miller (7)	Eric Stults
Chuck Tiffany (10)	Beau Dannemiller
Scott Elbert (11)	Glenn Bott
Mike Megrew (20)	Jonathan Figueroa
Derek Thompson	Luis Gonzalez
Ryan Ketchner	Chad Bailey
David Pfeiffer	Orlando Rodriguez
	Hong-Chi Kuo

Best Pro Debut: 1B Cory Dunlap (3) hit .351-7-53 and led the Rookie-level Pioneer League in on-base percentage (.492). C/DH Chris Westervelt (11) batted .341-10-37 in the same league.

Best Athlete: LHP Scott Elbert (1) has the power and speed to make it as an outfielder, though the Dodgers have no intention of moving him off the mound. He was Missouri's top high school running back as a junior in 2002, rushing for 2,449 yards and scoring 36 touchdowns.

Best Pure Hitter: Dunlap. A high school teammate of Dontrelle Willis, he weighed 300 pounds as a prepster but since has dropped down to 230. He led California community colleges with a .523 average at Contra Costa during the spring.

Best Raw Power: 3B Blake DeWitt (1) has excellent hand-eye coordination and more pop than Dunlap. One of the best high school bats in the draft, DeWitt hit .284-12-47 in the Pioneer League.

Fastest Runner: SS/2B David Nicholson runs the 60-yard dash in 6.7 seconds.

Best Defensive Player: A high school shortstop, DeWitt immediately took to third base as a pro. He has the actions and arm to make all the plays there.

Best Fastball: RHP Javy Guerra (4) scared some scouts with his high school delivery, which featured a crow hop that catapulted him toward the plate. But Rookie-level Gulf Coast League pitching coach George Culver smoothed it out without costing him velocity, as Guerra was throwing 93-95 by the end of the summer. Elbert and RHP Blake Johnson (2) both touch 94.

Best Breaking Ball: All four pitchers that

Elbert

the Dodgers took in the first two rounds, including RHP Justin Orenduff (1), have good breaking pitches. Johnson's curveball is the best right now, while Elbert has the top slider.

Most Intriguing Background: 2B Matt Paul's (18) brother Xavier was Los Angeles' fourth-round pick in 2003 and is the organization's best outfield prospect. 2B Brandon Carter's (40) uncle Jerry Royster is Los Angeles' infield coordinator.

Closest To The Majors: Orenduff, whose 4.74 ERA in the Pioneer League masked his 57 strikeouts in 44 innings.

Best Late-Round Pick: Westervelt may not have enough arm to catch regularly in the majors, but the Dodgers like his pop and on-base ability.

The One Who Got Away: Los Angeles took fliers on several highly touted prospects. LHP/OF Joe Savery (15) could be a two-way star at Rice as a freshman. OF Jeff Larish (13) entered 2004 as the best hitting prospect in college baseball, but hurt his wrist and had a disappointing spring. He returned to Arizona State.

Assessment: After the Dodgers hired general manager Paul DePodesta from the Athletics, industry insiders wondered if the club would adopt a "Moneyball" draft approach. But scouting director Logan White and his staff continued to bring in a lot of talent without worrying about demographics.

2003 RHP Chad Billingsley (1) emerged as one of the game's top pitching prospects in 2004. 3B Andy LaRoche (39) and LHP Chuck Tiffany (2) also are quite gifted, and keep an eye on athletic OFs Xavier Paul (4) and Matt Kemp (6). *GRADE: A*

2002 If 1B James Loney (1) and LHP Greg Miller (1) could stay healthy, this would be an easy A. C Russell Martin (17), RHP Jonathan Broxton (2) and 2B Delwyn Young (4) are picking up the slack. *GRADE: B+*

2001 RHP Edwin Jackson (6) was the best pitching prospect in baseball before backsliding last season. His development made up for the lack of a first-rounder and injuries striking the top pick, RHP Brian Pilkington (2). *GRADE: B*

2000 Except for RHP Joel Hanrahan (2), the Dodgers have traded their best choices in this draft. C Koyie Hill (4) is with the Diamondbacks, and OF Victor Diaz (37) is with the Mets. RHP Ben Diggins (1) blew out his elbow after joining the Brewers. *GRADE: C*

Draft analysis prepared by Jim Callis. Numbers in parentheses indicate draft rounds.

DAVID STONER

Joel
GUZMAN

Born: Nov. 24, 1984.
Ht.: 6-5. **Wt.:** 225.
Bats: R. **Throws:** R.
Career Transactions: Signed out of Dominican Republic by Dodgers, July 2, 2001.
Signed by: Pablo Peguero.

G uzman's physical ability has been lauded since he signed for a club- and Dominican-record $2.25 million as a 16-year-old. Following two inconsistent seasons, he made significant progress last year turning his potential into performance. He was rated the No. 1 prospect in the high Class A Florida State League and ranked No. 2 in the Double-A Southern League. At the Futures Game in July, he turned heads with his power display during batting practice at Minute Maid Park. Guzman's maturity was questioned when he clashed with his low Class A manager Dann Bilardello early in 2003, but the Dodgers were pleased with his makeup and work ethic in 2004. Guzman's affluent background—his mother is a teacher and his father is a lawyer in the Dominican Republic—has aided his development as he communicates well with teammates and absorbs instruction.

Guzman might best be described as a manchild. He has as much offensive upside as almost any prospect in the minors, drawing tremendous raw power from his 6-foot-6, 225-pound frame. Last year he made adjustments at the plate to help translate his batting-practice blasts into similarly prodigious homers during games. He made strides with his pitch recognition, which hampered him during his first two seasons, and stayed back on offspeed stuff better. Guzman has remarkable plate coverage and is learning to drive the ball out of all parts of the park. He does a tremendous job of staying inside the ball and keeping his hands ahead of the barrel. He generates exceptional bat speed. His approach is similar to Vladimir Guerrero's in that Guzman is aggressive in all counts. Defensively, he features a plus-plus arm and soft, easy hands. He has good actions and makes smooth transitions around the bag. While he almost certainly will outgrow the middle infield, scouts grade his overall defensive package now as average to slightly above-average for a shortstop.

Guzman's future playing weight figures to be somewhere near 250 pounds, which will necessitate a position change. His range and speed project as below-average for a big league shortstop. His instincts, athleticism and arm strength will allow him to move to a corner infield or outfield spot. With prospects James Loney (first base) and Andy LaRoche (third base) working their way up the ladder, the Dodgers likely will put Guzman in right field. He swings and misses too frequently, though his power numbers help justify his lofty strikeout totals. Though he has improved his pitch recognition, he still has a tendency to allow situations to dictate his approach. For instance, he often chases pitches when he's trying to come through with runners in scoring position.

Despite being just 19, Guzman answered every challenge Los Angeles threw at him in 2004, including a promotion to Double-A. He likely will open the season back at Jacksonville and would benefit from at least another full season in the minors. With patience and another year of refinement, Guzman could be ready to contribute in Los Angeles by 2006.

Year	Club (League)	Class	AVG	G	AB	R	H	2B	3B	HR	RBI	BB	SO	SB	OBP	SLG
2002	Dodgers (GCL)	R	.212	10	33	4	7	2	0	0	2	5	8	1	.316	.273
	Great Falls (Pio)	R	.252	43	151	19	38	8	2	3	27	18	54	5	.331	.391
2003	South Georgia (SAL)	A	.235	58	217	33	51	13	0	8	29	9	62	4	.263	.406
	Vero Beach (FSL)	A	.246	62	240	30	59	13	1	5	24	11	60	0	.279	.371
2004	Vero Beach (FSL)	A	.307	87	329	52	101	22	8	14	51	21	78	8	.347	.550
	Jacksonville (SL)	AA	.280	46	182	25	51	11	3	9	35	13	44	1	.325	.522
MINOR LEAGUE TOTALS			.266	306	1152	163	307	69	14	39	168	77	306	19	.311	.452

Chad Billingsley, rhp

Born: July 29, 1984. **Ht.:** 6-2. **Wt.:** 215. **Bats:** R. **Throws:** R. **School:** Defiance (Ohio) HS. **Career Transactions:** Selected by Dodgers in first round (24th overall) of 2003 draft; signed June 9, 2003. **Signed by:** Marty Lamb.

Teams shied away from high school righthanders in the first round of the 2003 draft, with only two chosen, but the Dodgers don't regret spending their first-rounder and $1.375 million on Billingsley. His stock soared in his first full season, as he was rated the top pitching prospect in the Florida State League before earning a promotion to Double-A before his 20th birthday. Billingsley attacks hitters with plus power stuff. He shows good control of an explosive fastball that sits at 94 mph and tops out at 97. His slider has depth and late life, and he throws a hard curveball. Strong and durable with calves like Mark Prior's, he also has tremendous makeup. While Billingsley has a good idea on the mound, he has a tendency to try to overpower every hitter, which leads to too many walks. He needs to improve his offspeed stuff to keep hitters off balance, but he doesn't have a great feel for his changeup yet and hasn't been forced to use it much. The Dodgers might slow the pace of Billingsley's development after watching Edwin Jackson and Greg Miller get hurt when they were rushed. He'll probably go back to Double-A in 2005.

Year	Club (League)	Class	W	L	ERA	G	GS	CG	SV	IP	H	R	ER	HR	BB	SO	AVG
2003	Ogden (Pio)	R	5	4	2.83	11	11	0	0	54	49	24	17	0	15	62	.243
2004	Jacksonville (SL)	AA	4	0	2.98	8	8	0	0	42	32	16	14	1	22	47	.213
	Vero Beach (FSL)	A	7	4	2.35	18	18	0	0	92	68	32	24	6	49	111	.202
MINOR LEAGUE TOTALS			16	8	2.63	37	37	0	0	188	149	72	55	7	86	220	.216

Edwin Jackson, rhp

Born: Sept. 9, 1983. **Ht.:** 6-3. **Wt.:** 190. **Bats:** R. **Throws:** R. **School:** Shaw HS, Columbus, Ga. **Career Transactions:** Selected by Dodgers in sixth round of 2001 draft; signed June 18, 2001. **Signed by:** Lon Joyce.

Jackson was dominant at times in his September 2003 big league callup, beating Randy Johnson on his 20th birthday in his first outing. A prime Rookie of the Year candidate for 2004, he struggled in spring training and never got untracked. His confidence suffered and he missed a month with a strained forearm. Though his velocity fluctuated last year, Jackson's lively fastball sits at 93 mph and touches 97 when he's healthy and pitching downhill. His slider was also inconsistent, but at times showed the tight, late break that makes it a potential out pitch. He has outstanding makeup and work ethic. The Dodgers tweaked Jackson's delivery and he seldom repeated the same free and easy motion. He was primarily an outfielder until 2002 and still lacks an advanced feel for pitching despite his meteoric rise. He needs to hone his control and consistency, especially of his offspeed stuff. While Jackson regressed a year ago, he remains a premium prospect. The Dodgers had him rest during the offseason and hope he makes a better showing in spring training this year. Unless he's lights out, he'll open 2005 back at Triple-A Las Vegas.

Year	Club (League)	Class	W	L	ERA	G	GS	CG	SV	IP	H	R	ER	HR	BB	SO	AVG
2001	Dodgers (GCL)	R	2	1	2.45	12	2	0	0	22	14	12	6	1	19	23	.173
2002	South Georgia (SAL)	A	5	2	1.98	19	19	0	0	105	79	34	23	2	33	85	.206
2003	Jacksonville (SL)	AA	7	7	3.70	27	27	0	0	148	121	68	61	9	53	157	.220
	Los Angeles (NL)	MAJ	2	1	2.45	4	3	0	0	22	17	6	6	2	11	19	.221
2004	Los Angeles (NL)	MAJ	2	1	7.30	8	5	0	0	25	31	20	20	7	11	16	.307
	Las Vegas (PCL)	AAA	6	4	5.86	19	19	0	0	91	90	65	59	4	55	70	.265
MAJOR LEAGUE TOTALS			4	2	5.01	12	8	0	0	47	48	26	26	9	22	35	.270
MINOR LEAGUE TOTALS			20	14	3.67	77	67	0	0	366	304	179	149	16	160	335	.225

James Loney, 1b

Born: May 7, 1984. **Ht.:** 6-3. **Wt.:** 220. **Bats:** L. **Throws:** L. **School:** Elkins HS, Missouri City, Texas. **Career Transactions:** Selected by Dodgers in first round (19th overall) of 2002 draft; signed June 11, 2002. **Signed by:** Chris Smith.

After batting .343 with five doubles in 35 at-bats in big league camp last spring, Loney appeared ready to blast off. But he fractured the tip of the middle finger on his left hand and developed an infection in the finger, costing him three weeks and hampering his production afterward. Loney did bat .314 in the Arizona Fall League and remains one of the game's most promising first-base prospects. Loney makes hard, line-drive contact and projects to hit for a high average. He stays inside the ball well, and his swing path allows the bat head to stay in the zone for an extended time. His defense is major league quality already. He's smooth and fluid with exceptionally soft hands and a well-above-average arm. Scouts have wondered when Loney's power is going to come—he has a .407 slugging percentage as a pro—and some have suggested his swing path might not be conducive for big-time home run production. He has below-average speed, though he runs the bases well. Since Loney reached high Class A Vero Beach at age 18, hand-related injuries have kept him from peak performance. He needs another full year and a healthy one before contending for a job in Los Angeles in 2006. He'll probably start this year in Double-A.

Year	Club (League)	Class	AVG	G	AB	R	H	2B	3B	HR	RBI	BB	SO	SB	OBP	SLG
2002	Great Falls (Pio)	R	.371	47	170	33	63	22	3	5	30	25	18	5	.457	.624
	Vero Beach (FSL)	A	.299	17	67	6	20	6	0	0	5	6	10	0	.356	.388
2003	Vero Beach (FSL)	A	.276	125	468	64	129	31	3	7	46	43	80	9	.337	.400
2004	Jacksonville (SL)	AA	.238	104	395	39	94	19	2	4	35	42	75	6	.314	.327
MINOR LEAGUE TOTALS			.278	293	1100	142	306	78	8	16	116	116	183	20	.349	.407

5 Andy LaRoche, 3b

Born: Sept. 13, 1983. **Ht.:** 6-1. **Wt.:** 200. **Bats:** R. **Throws:** R. **School:** Grayson County (Texas) CC. **Career Transactions:** Selected by Dodgers in 39th round of 2003 draft; signed Aug. 14, 2003. **Signed by:** Mike Leuzinger.

The Dodgers had to fight the commissioner's office's bonus recommendations to sign LaRoche for $1 million in 2003. After establishing himself as the best hitter in the Cape Cod League that summer, they believed he would become a first-rounder if he went to Rice. His father Dave was an all-star pitcher and his brother Adam starts at first base for the Braves. LaRoche has big-time power potential. He has good strength, a quick bat and excellent load for his swing, helping him generate backspin and loft. He owns the organization's best arm and has above-average range and hands. He's an average runner. LaRoche is almost exclusively a pull hitter and can be too aggressive in his approach. He swings and misses too often, so he may never hit for a huge average. He battled arm soreness, which led to throwing errors, after moving to third base last year. He played shortstop before turning pro. If he reaches his ceiling, LaRoche could hit 35-40 homers annually. He may start 2005 back in high Class A but should reach Double-A by the end of the season.

Year	Club (League)	Class	AVG	G	AB	R	H	2B	3B	HR	RBI	BB	SO	SB	OBP	SLG
2003	Ogden (Pio)	R	.211	6	19	1	4	1	0	0	5	1	4	0	.238	.263
2004	Columbus (SAL)	A	.283	65	244	52	69	20	0	13	42	29	30	12	.375	.525
	Vero Beach (FSL)	A	.233	62	219	26	51	13	0	10	35	17	42	2	.290	.429
MINOR LEAGUE TOTALS			.257	133	482	79	124	34	0	23	82	47	76	14	.332	.471

6 Russell Martin, c

Born: Feb. 15, 1983. **Ht.:** 5-11. **Wt.:** 202. **Bats:** R. **Throws:** R. **School:** Chipola (Fla.) JC. **Career Transactions:** Selected by Dodgers in 17th round of 2002 draft; signed June 13, 2002. **Signed by:** Clarence Johns.

Outside of Joel Guzman, Martin made the most significant leap in the system last year. A 35th-round pick by the Expos out of Montreal ABC baseball academy in 2000, he played two years at Chipola Junior College before signing with the Dodgers for $40,000. He moved from third base to catcher in 2003. Martin made strides in his defensive game last year. He's quick, uses his excellent footwork to help him block balls in the dirt and has a well-above-average arm. Offensively, he has a line-drive stroke, good plate discipline and the potential to hit 15-20 homers annually. He's durable, works hard and has a strong makeup. Martin's swing can get long at times. He needs to maintain his focus throughout games on his receiving, but more than anything else he requires more experience behind the plate. He's a below-average runner, though not a baseclogger. After taking a step forward in the Arizona Fall League, Martin will open the season in Double-A. He has no challenger as the Dodgers' catcher of the future and may be ready for the majors by September 2006.

Year	Club (League)	Class	AVG	G	AB	R	H	2B	3B	HR	RBI	BB	SO	SB	OBP	SLG
2002	Dodgers (GCL)	R	.286	41	126	22	36	3	3	0	10	23	18	7	.412	.357
2003	South Georgia (SAL)	A	.286	25	98	15	28	4	1	3	14	9	11	5	.343	.439
	Ogden (Pio)	R	.271	52	188	25	51	13	0	6	36	26	26	3	.368	.436
2004	Vero Beach (FSL)	A	.250	122	416	74	104	24	1	15	64	72	54	9	.366	.421
MINOR LEAGUE TOTALS			.264	240	828	136	219	44	5	24	124	130	109	24	.371	.417

Greg Miller, lhp

Born: Nov. 3, 1984. **Ht.:** 6-5. **Wt.:** 190. **Bats:** L. **Throws:** L. **School:** Esperanza HS, Yorba Linda, Calif. **Career Transactions:** Selected by Dodgers in first round (31st overall) of 2002 draft; signed June 14, 2002. **Signed by:** Scott Groot.

After establishing himself as baseball's top lefthanded pitching prospect in 2003, Miller never took the mound last season. He had shoulder pain toward the end of the 2003 season and had the bursa sac removed from his shoulder last March. Doctors discovered a bone spur in January, and performed a second operation on his shoulder. Before he got hurt, Miller's velocity had steadily increased, from the mid-80s to low 90s in high school to regularly touching 95 in 2003. His hard slider has developed into a plus pitch, and he has a power curveball. A solid-average changeup completes his repertoire. What separates Miller, though, is his cerebral approach and deft command of all his pitches. Miller's health is a major question mark. Some Dodgers officials believe his shoulder troubles resulted from being rushed, and that the club reacted too slowly to treat the problem. Following changes in the player-development department, Los Angeles will take a more conservative approach with Miller. He was expected to begin throwing again by spring training and could join Class A Vero Beach by mid-June.

Year	Club (League)	Class	W	L	ERA	G	GS	CG	SV	IP	H	R	ER	HR	BB	SO	AVG
2002	Great Falls (Pio)	R	3	2	2.37	11	7	0	0	38	27	14	10	1	13	37	.199
2003	Vero Beach (FSL)	A	11	4	2.49	21	21	1	0	116	103	40	32	5	41	111	.240
	Jacksonville (SL)	AA	1	1	1.01	4	4	0	0	27	15	5	3	1	7	40	.156
2004	Did not play—Injured																
MINOR LEAGUE TOTALS			15	7	2.25	36	32	1	0	180	145	59	45	7	61	188	.219

Blake DeWitt, 3b

Born: Aug. 20, 1985. **Ht.:** 5-11. **Wt.:** 175. **Bats:** L. **Throws:** R. **School:** Sikeston (Mo.) HS. **Career Transactions:** Selected by Dodgers in first round (28th overall) of 2004 draft; signed June 11, 2004. **Signed by:** Mitch Webster.

Considered the best hitter in the 2004 high school draft class, DeWitt lived up to his reputation after signing for $1.2 million. He moved from shortstop to third base and strung together a 19-game hitting streak in his first month as a pro. He was rated the No. 2 prospect in the Rookie-level Pioneer League. DeWitt has a pretty lefthanded stroke. He generates good bat speed with a nice load that allows him to set his hands before unleashing. He has the potential to develop into a 30-35 home run threat. He made adjustments well and handled offspeed stuff better as the season went on. His arm is slightly above-average. DeWitt's speed and range are fringe-average, and his hands are just adequate. He led Pioneer League third basemen with 20 errors. The Dodgers say he can become at least an average third baseman because of his work ethic. He needs to stay back on breaking balls and use all fields, and he showed a feel for doing so last summer. DeWitt figures to begin his first full season at low Class A Columbus. As he gets acclimated to pro ball, he could move quickly.

Year	Club (League)	Class	AVG	G	AB	R	H	2B	3B	HR	RBI	BB	SO	SB	OBP	SLG
2004	Ogden (Pio)	R	.284	70	299	61	85	19	3	12	47	28	78	1	.350	.488
MINOR LEAGUE TOTALS			.284	70	299	61	85	19	3	12	47	28	78	1	.350	.488

Jonathan Broxton, rhp

Born: June 16, 1984. **Ht.:** 6-4. **Wt.:** 240. **Bats:** R. **Throws:** R. **School:** Burke County HS, Waynesboro, Ga. **Career Transactions:** Selected by Dodgers in second round of 2002 draft; signed June 30, 2002. **Signed by:** Lon Joyce.

After missing much of 2003 with wrist tendinitis and a biceps strain, Broxton reported to spring training healthy and in much better shape. Nicknamed "Bull," he's the most physically imposing pitching prospect in the system. Broxton pounds the strike zone with a heavy 92-93 mph sinker, which he complements with a sharp, mid-80s slider. He throws from a high three-quarters arm slot and repeats his delivery consistently despite his size. He has good makeup and pitches with tenacity. Broxton struggles with his changeup grip. He prefers to throw the pitch similar to a palmball and tends to raise his arm angle, tipping it off to astute hitters. Maintaining his body will be important after his weight soared as high as 277 pounds in 2003. If he develops the changeup, Broxton profiles as a potential No. 2 starter in the big leagues. He should open the season in the Double-A rotation, though he could move to late-inning relief down the road.

Year	Club (League)	Class	W	L	ERA	G	GS	CG	SV	IP	H	R	ER	HR	BB	SO	AVG
2002	Great Falls (Pio)	R	2	0	2.76	11	6	0	0	29	22	9	9	0	16	33	.212
2003	South Georgia (SAL)	A	4	2	3.13	9	8	0	0	37	27	15	13	1	22	30	.208
2004	Vero Beach (FSL)	A	11	6	3.23	23	23	1	1	128	110	49	46	7	43	144	.231
MINOR LEAGUE TOTALS			17	8	3.14	43	37	1	1	195	159	73	68	8	81	207	.224

10 Chuck Tiffany, lhp

Born: Jan. 25, 1985. **Ht.:** 6-1. **Wt.:** 195. **Bats:** L. **Throws:** L. **School:** Charter Oak HS, Covina, Calif. **Career Transactions:** Selected by Dodgers in second round of 2003 draft; signed Aug. 6, 2003. **Signed by:** Scott Groot.

Days before he was to attend class at Cal State Fullerton in the fall of 2003, Tiffany signed for $1.1 million, the second-highest bonus any second-rounder got that year. He started a combined no-hitter last May, then improved on that effort two weeks later with a seven-inning perfect game. He finished the season by reaching double-digit strikeouts in each of his last four starts. Tiffany shows an advanced feel for setting up hitters with three potential pitches. He pitches at 86-90 mph with his fastball, which features late life and tops out at 92. Both his 12-to-6 curveball and circle changeup already rate as plus pitches at times. Like most young pitchers, Tiffany lacks consistency with his secondary pitches. Because he's just 6-foot-1, it's hard for him to maintain a downhill plane for added deception. He tends to get under or around his pitches, causing his stuff to flatten out and sit high in the strike zone. His stocky body always has concerned scouts. Few left-handers have better all-around stuff than Greg Miller or Tiffany. The Dodgers see no need to rush Tiffany and will send him to high Class A this year.

Year	Club (League)	Class	W	L	ERA	G	GS	CG	SV	IP	H	R	ER	HR	BB	SO	AVG
2003	Ogden (Pio)	R	0	0	10.13	3	0	0	0	3	4	4	3	0	2	4	.364
2004	Columbus (SAL)	A	5	2	3.70	22	22	1	0	100	76	42	41	11	40	141	.208
MINOR LEAGUE TOTALS			5	2	3.87	25	22	1	0	102	80	46	44	11	42	145	.213

11 Scott Elbert, lhp

Born: May 13, 1985. **Ht.:** 6-2. **Wt.:** 190. **Bats:** L. **Throws:** L. **School:** Seneca (Mo.) HS. **Career Transactions:** Selected by Dodgers in first round (17th overall) of 2004 draft; signed June 9, 2004. **Signed by:** Mitch Webster.

Elbert, who grew up less than 10 miles from where Dodgers scouting director Logan White went to grade school, was considered the top prep lefthander in the 2004 high school draft class. Elbert was also an all-state running back as a junior, rushing for a Missouri-high 2,449 yards with 36 touchdowns in 2002 before giving up football. His athleticism translates well on the mound. His arm works loose and easy, creating effortless 90-94 mph velocity on his hard, sinking fastball. He scrapped his curveball in favor of a mid-80s slider that has plus potential, and his changeup also has late, diving action. He projects to have above-average control and command. Elbert didn't pitch as aggressively in his pro debut as he did as an amateur, leading to high pitch counts and too many walks. He needs to throw his changeup more frequently. With two developing plus power pitches, Elbert could profile as a closer down the line. The Dodgers will continue to develop him as a starter. He needs innings and will make his full-season debut in the low Class A rotation in 2005.

Year	Club (League)	Class	W	L	ERA	G	GS	CG	SV	IP	H	R	ER	HR	BB	SO	AVG
2004	Ogden (Pio)	R	2	3	5.26	12	12	0	0	50	47	33	29	5	30	45	.253
MINOR LEAGUE TOTALS			2	3	5.26	12	12	0	0	50	47	33	29	5	30	45	.253

12 Julio Pimentel, rhp

Born: Dec. 14, 1985. **Ht.:** 6-1. **Wt.:** 190. **Bats:** R. **Throws:** R. **Career Transactions:** Signed out of Dominican Republic by Dodgers, July 14, 2003. **Signed by:** Santana Peguero.

After he performed well as an outfielder at a tryout in the Dominican Republic, the Dodgers signed Pimentel for $70,000 and promptly moved him to the mound. Built similar to Yhency Brazoban, Pimentel has a live arm with premium athletic ability. He dominated at times when he got his breaking ball over for strikes, including a 16-strikeout, seven-inning performance in June. His fastball has been clocked as high as 94 mph and sits around 90 with boring action. Pimentel also has a hard, downer breaking ball, a changeup and a sinker. His frame is broad, and he's projectable because of his arm action and athleticism. At times it seemed as if Pimentel wasn't sure where his pitches were headed, and he needs to learn how to harness his stuff. He showed a grasp for setting up hitters, though his learning curve is considerable. Pimentel has good aptitude, raw but electric stuff and the durability to profile as a future middle-of-the-rotation starter. He's slated to open 2005 in high Class A.

Year	Club (League)	Class	W	L	ERA	G	GS	CG	SV	IP	H	R	ER	HR	BB	SO	AVG
2003	Dodgers (DSL)	R	1	1	4.09	8	3	0	0	22	17	12	10	1	13	24	.221
2004	Columbus (SAL)	A	10	8	3.48	23	23	2	0	111	106	56	43	14	47	102	.254
MINOR LEAGUE TOTALS			11	9	3.58	31	26	2	0	133	123	68	53	15	60	126	.248

13 Chin-Lung Hu, ss

Born: Feb. 2, 1984. **Ht.:** 5-9. **Wt.:** 150. **Bats:** R. **Throws:** R. **Career Transactions:** Signed out of Taiwan by Dodgers, Jan. 31, 2003. **Signed by:** Pat Kelly/Vincent Liao.

While the Dodgers' high-profile Pacific Rim signings of Hong-Chih Kuo and Chin-Feng Chen have not paid off, Hu has stepped forward as a potential impact Taiwanese prospect. Former special assistant to the GM Jeff Schugel scouted Hu during the 2002 World Junior Championship in Sherbrooke, Quebec and the Dodgers signed him five months later. He hit safely in 15 of 20 games following a late-season promotion to high Class A before going down with a right elbow injury. Hu's best tool is his glove. He was named the best defensive shortstop in the low Class A South Atlantic League and turns in acrobatic highlight plays up the middle with regularity. He makes good reads on grounders, has a smooth exchange from glove to throwing hand, plus range and an accurate, adequate arm. Hu is undersized and his frame doesn't lend to considerable growth potential, but his strength shouldn't be underestimated. Some scouts project Hu's power potential as average. He generates good bat speed and drives the ball to both alleys, with occasional home-run power. He handles the bat well, shows good instincts on the bases and is an above-average runner, though he's not a burner. Moreover, Hu has embraced American culture, is beginning to grasp the language and has adapted well. He likely will open the season in high Class A.

Year	Club (League)	Class	AVG	G	AB	R	H	2B	3B	HR	RBI	BB	SO	SB	OBP	SLG
2003	Ogden (Pio)	R	.305	53	220	34	67	9	5	3	23	14	33	5	.343	.432
2004	Columbus (SAL)	A	.298	84	332	58	99	15	4	6	25	20	50	17	.342	.422
	Vero Beach (FSL)	A	.307	20	75	12	23	4	1	0	10	5	6	3	.350	.387
MINOR LEAGUE TOTALS			.301	157	627	104	189	28	10	9	58	39	89	25	.343	.421

14 Dioner Navarro, c

Born: Feb. 9, 1984. **Ht.:** 5-10. **Wt.:** 190. **Bats:** B. **Throws:** R. **Career Transactions:** Signed out of Venezuela by Yankees, Aug. 21, 2000 . . . Traded by Yankees with LHP Brad Halsey and RHP Javier Vazquez to Diamondbacks for LHP Randy Johnson, Jan. 11, 2005 . . . Traded by Diamondbacks with RHP William Juarez, RHP Danny Muegge and RHP Beltran Perez to Dodgers for OF Shawn Green, Jan. 12, 2005. **Signed by:** Carlos Rios (Yankees).

After a breakout year in 2003, Navarro entered last year as the Yankees' top prospect. But he showed up in Double-A overconfident and his play suffered. An attempt to get stronger in the offseason backfired, as he came in overweight and lost bat speed. New York sent him to Arizona in January, and the Diamondbacks sent him and three minor league pitchers to the Dodgers for Shawn Green the next day. Navarro has a compact swing that helps him make consistent, hard contact from both sides of the plate. He's a gap-to-gap, line-drive hitter and isn't afraid to take a walk or work deep counts. A converted infielder, he has a strong throwing arm that helped him nab 33 percent of basestealers in 2004. His receiving skills are average. He never has hit for much power, however, and his lack of conditioning made matters worse. Like most catchers, he's not much of a runner. A strong finish helped Navarro salvage an otherwise uninspiring season. Though the Dodgers need catching help, Navarro clearly isn't ready yet. He needs to re-establish himself in Triple-A.

Year	Club (League)	Class	AVG	G	AB	R	H	2B	3B	HR	RBI	BB	SO	SB	OBP	SLG
2001	Yankees (GCL)	R	.280	43	143	27	40	10	1	2	22	17	23	6	.345	.406
2002	Greensboro (SAL)	A	.238	92	328	41	78	12	2	8	36	39	61	1	.326	.360
	Tampa (FSL)	A	.500	1	2	1	1	0	0	0	0	0	0	0	.500	.500
2003	Tampa (FSL)	A	.299	52	197	28	59	16	4	3	28	17	27	1	.364	.467
	Trenton (EL)	AA	.341	58	208	28	71	15	0	4	37	18	26	2	.388	.471
2004	Trenton (EL)	AA	.271	70	255	32	69	14	1	3	29	33	44	1	.354	.369
	Columbus (IL)	AAA	.250	40	136	18	34	8	2	1	16	14	17	1	.316	.360
	Yankees (AL)	MAJ	.429	5	7	2	3	0	0	0	1	0	0	0	.429	.429
MAJOR LEAGUE TOTALS			.429	5	7	2	3	0	0	0	1	0	0	0	.429	.429
MINOR LEAGUE TOTALS			.277	356	1269	175	352	75	10	21	168	138	198	12	.349	.402

15 Yhency Brazoban, rhp

Born: June 11, 1980. **Ht.:** 6-1. **Wt.:** 170. **Bats:** R. **Throws:** R. **Career Transactions:** Signed out of Dominican Republic by Yankees, July 10, 1997 . . . Traded by Yankees with RHP Jeff Weaver, RHP Brandon Weeden and cash to Dodgers for RHP Kevin Brown, Dec. 13, 2003. **Signed by:** Victor Mata (Yankees).

When the Dodgers included Guillermo Mota in a trade deadline deal with the Marlins last year, they were hoping to get a boost in the pen from Edwin Jackson and Duaner Sanchez.

But it was Brazoban who stepped up as the most reliable set-up man down the stretch. He was converted from an outfielder in 2002 by the Yankees, and the Dodgers acquired him in the Kevin Brown-Jeff Weaver swap in December 2003. His career took off after he switched organizations. He allowed just three earned runs in his first 26 big league appearances and was unflappable late in games. Brazoban works primarily with a two-pitch arsenal consisting of a 94-97 mph fastball that explodes out of his hand and an above-average, but inconsistent slider. He displays good command of both pitches. The Dodgers were working to improve his changeup, which he doesn't throw often. Brazoban is still learning the nuances of pitching. The Dodgers still haven't replaced the invaluable Mota, and Brazoban is the favorite to bridge the gap to Eric Gagne.

Year	Club (League)	Class	AVG	G	AB	R	H	2B	3B	HR	RBI	BB	SO	SB	OBP	SLG
1998	Yankees (DSL)	R	.319	68	251	51	80	19	2	9	46	31	75	10	.399	.518
1999	Yankees (GCL)	R	.320	56	200	33	64	14	5	1	26	12	47	7	.367	.455
2000	Greensboro (SAL)	A	.188	12	48	6	9	3	0	0	8	3	15	1	.231	.250
	Yankees (GCL)	R	.303	54	201	36	61	14	4	5	28	11	28	2	.349	.488
2001	Greensboro (SAL)	A	.273	124	469	51	128	23	3	6	52	19	98	6	.311	.373
	Columbus (IL)	AAA	.200	1	5	2	1	1	0	0	0	0	2	0	.200	.400
2002	Greensboro (SAL)	A	.242	69	252	33	61	11	2	3	28	15	74	0	.290	.337
MINOR LEAGUE TOTALS			.283	384	1426	212	404	85	16	24	188	91	339	26	.334	.416

Year	Club (League)	Class	W	L	ERA	G	GS	CG	SV	IP	H	R	ER	HR	BB	SO	AVG
2002	Yankees (GCL)	R	0	0	4.50	6	0	0	0	6	3	3	3	0	4	11	.136
2003	Tampa (FSL)	A	0	2	2.83	24	0	0	15	29	27	13	9	0	12	34	.245
	Trenton (EL)	AA	2	2	7.81	20	0	0	3	28	33	25	24	5	14	19	.314
	Yankees (GCL)	R	0	0	6.00	3	0	0	0	3	5	3	2	0	1	5	.385
2004	Jacksonville (SL)	AA	4	4	2.65	37	0	0	13	51	38	18	15	4	22	61	.210
	Las Vegas (PCL)	AAA	2	0	2.19	10	0	0	1	12	14	3	3	1	1	17	.286
	Los Angeles (NL)	MAJ	6	2	2.48	31	0	0	0	33	25	9	9	2	15	27	.219
MAJOR LEAGUE TOTALS			6	2	2.48	31	0	0	0	33	25	9	9	2	15	27	.219
MINOR LEAGUE TOTALS			8	8	3.92	100	0	0	32	129	120	65	56	10	54	147	.250

16 Xavier Paul, of

Born: Feb. 25, 1985. **Ht.:** 6-0. **Wt.:** 200. **Bats:** L. **Throws:** R. **School:** Slidell (La.) HS. **Career Transactions:** Selected by Dodgers in fourth round of 2003 draft; signed June 11, 2003. **Signed by:** Clarence Johns.

Most scouts expected Paul to honor his commitment to Tulane after joining Chad Billingsley as a Baseball America second-team High School All-American in 2003, but he signed with the Dodgers for $270,000 instead. The Dodgers drafted his brother Matthew in the 18th round last year out of Southern University. Paul earned a spot in the organization's top 10 after his encouraging debut, then came out of the gates with a .361-3-20 start last April before struggling the rest of the way. He tweaked his hitting mechanics during the year, reducing his stride, but seems most comfortable with a full stride at the plate. He generates good power from his strong, compact body and quick wrists. Paul is patient to a fault at the plate. He often found himself behind in counts as he waited for his pitch, but too frequently failed to make contact in two-strike counts. He is adequate at best in the outfield. He is an above-average runner with well-above-average arm strength, but doesn't make good reads and needs to improve his routes. He could repeat low Class A in 2005 depending on his showing this spring, but should see time at high Class A sometime during the season.

Year	Club (League)	Class	AVG	G	AB	R	H	2B	3B	HR	RBI	BB	SO	SB	OBP	SLG
2003	Ogden (Pio)	R	.307	69	264	60	81	15	6	7	47	34	58	11	.384	.489
2004	Columbus (SAL)	A	.265	126	460	69	122	26	6	9	72	54	124	10	.342	.407
MINOR LEAGUE TOTALS			.280	195	724	129	203	41	12	16	119	88	182	21	.357	.436

17 Joel Hanrahan, rhp

Born: Oct. 6, 1981. **Ht.:** 6-3. **Wt.:** 215. **Bats:** R. **Throws:** R. **School:** Norwalk (Iowa) Community HS. **Career Transactions:** Selected by Dodgers in second round of 2000 draft; signed June 22, 2000. **Signed by:** Mitch Webster.

Hanrahan has been on the cusp of the big leagues for the last couple of seasons but has struggled to get over the hump. He was roughed up in Triple-A during a late-season promotion in 2003, and followed that up with his worst season as a pro. He has three solid-average pitches, but doesn't repeat his arm slot, neutralizing his stuff and hurting his control. Hanrahan's sinker/slider combination, as well as a good straight changeup, is effective from his usual high three-quarters arm slot, but he often drops down and causes his pitches to flatten out. He gave up a lot of home runs last year after managing to keep the ball in the yard in his first three years in the organization. Hanrahan also had a tendency to spin off his front side toward first base, which contributed to his career-high walk total in just 119 innings, his low for a full season. He has good makeup, pitches with tenacity and pitched through a bout of shoulder stiffness last year. When his mechanics are in sync, His boring sinker sits at 91-92 mph and maxes out at 94. His mid-80s slider has good tilt and bite, and his changeup has nice sink as well. This season is pivotal for Hanrahan, who needs to improve his conditioning, make adjustments and show he can fulfill his potential as a middle-of-the-rotation starter in the big leagues. He'll start the season back in Triple-A.

Year	Club (League)	Class	W	L	ERA	G	GS	CG	SV	IP	H	R	ER	HR	BB	SO	AVG
2000	Great Falls (Pio)	R	3	1	4.75	12	11	0	0	55	49	32	29	4	23	40	.231
2001	Wilmington (SAL)	A	9	1	3.38	27	26	0	0	144	136	71	54	13	55	116	.250
2002	Vero Beach (FSL)	A	10	6	4.20	25	25	2	0	144	129	74	67	11	51	139	.242
	Jacksonville (SL)	AA	1	1	10.64	3	3	0	0	11	15	14	13	2	7	10	.326
2003	Jacksonville (SL)	AA	10	4	2.43	23	23	1	0	133	117	44	36	5	53	130	.239
	Las Vegas (PCL)	AAA	1	2	10.08	5	5	0	0	25	36	28	28	2	20	13	.343
2004	Las Vegas (PCL)	AAA	7	7	5.05	25	22	0	0	119	128	78	67	22	75	97	.276
MINOR LEAGUE TOTALS			41	22	4.19	120	115	3	0	631	610	341	294	59	284	545	.255

18 Delwyn Young, 2b/of

Born: June 30, 1982. **Ht.:** 5-10. **Wt.:** 180. **Bats:** S. **Throws:** R. **School:** Santa Barbara (Calif.) CC. **Career Transactions:** Selected by Dodgers in fourth round of 2002 draft; signed June 12, 2002. **Signed by:** James Merriweather.

Young validated his status as one of the organization's best hitting prospects with his third straight productive season, leading the Florida State League in extra-base hits (61) and finishing second in homers and third in RBIs and doubles. His 36 doubles broke Henry Rodriguez' Vero Beach club record, which had stood since 1989. Young's hit and power tools grade out as above-average. An aggressive, confident switch-hitter, he has good bat speed and rarely gets cheated at the plate. His swing gets long at times, leading to swings-and-misses, but when he centers the ball he generates loft and carry. Young has better bat control from the right side and more power from the left. He is a below-average runner. Scouts doubt he has the range to play second base in the big leagues, but he made strides defensively in 2004. He embraced the instruction of minor league infield coordinator Jerry Royster and assistant field coordinator John Shoemaker, which helped him improve his footwork around the bag. He still allows ground balls to get too deep, though he has a solid arm. Young will join Joel Guzman up the middle in Double-A this year and could end up at a corner outfield spot down the line.

Year	Club (League)	Class	AVG	G	AB	R	H	2B	3B	HR	RBI	BB	SO	SB	OBP	SLG
2002	Great Falls (Pio)	R	.300	59	240	42	72	18	1	10	41	27	60	4	.380	.508
2003	South Georgia (SAL)	A	.323	119	443	67	143	38	7	15	73	36	87	5	.381	.542
2004	Vero Beach (FSL)	A	.281	129	470	76	132	36	3	22	85	57	134	11	.364	.511
MINOR LEAGUE TOTALS			.301	307	1153	185	347	92	11	47	199	120	281	20	.374	.522

19 Cory Dunlap, 1b

Born: April 13, 1984. **Ht.:** 6-1. **Wt.:** 230. **Bats:** L. **Throws:** L. **School:** Contra Costa (Calif.) JC. **Career Transactions:** Selected by Dodgers in third round of 2004 draft; signed June 9, 2004. **Signed by:** Mark Sheehy.

Dunlap has dropped 70 pounds after ballooning to 300 in high school in Alameda, Calif., where he was a teammate of Dontrelle Willis. He maintained his conditioning at Contra Costa Junior College with the help of former major league all-star Willie McGee and climbed draft boards last spring. He led all California juco hitters with a .523 average. Described as a professional hitter, Dunlap had a strong debut and led the Pioneer League in walks and on-base percentage while ranking as the league's No. 7 prospect. Dunlap's spray approach has drawn comparisons to Tony Gwynn's. He has a simple, level stroke with good strike-zone judgment. His power is mostly to the gaps now, but he shows potential to hit 25-30 home runs a year, and will pull pitches deep to right field on occasion. Dunlap has good plate coverage but is susceptible to balls in on his hands. He is a 30 runner on the 20-80 scouting scale. Defensively, Dunlap shows good instincts and adequate hands at first, though his range could improve. He tends to rush throws, leading to inaccuracy, though his arm strength is at least average. Sustaining his conditioning and improving his strength will be integral to his development. Dunlap could move quickly and should open 2005 in low Class A.

Year	Club (League)	Class	AVG	G	AB	R	H	2B	3B	HR	RBI	BB	SO	SB	OBP	SLG
2004	Ogden (Pio)	R	.351	71	245	57	86	18	1	7	53	68	40	0	.492	.518
MINOR LEAGUE TOTALS			.351	71	245	57	86	18	1	7	53	68	40	0	.492	.518

Mike Megrew, lhp

20

Born: Jan. 29, 1984. **Ht.:** 6-6. **Wt.:** 210. **Bats:** L. **Throws:** L. **School:** Chariho Regional HS, Hope Valley, R.I. **Career Transactions:** Selected by Dodgers in fifth round of 2002 draft; signed June 5, 2002. **Signed by:** John Kosciak.

Megrew, who strained a ligament in his elbow late in his debut 2002 season, was making progress last summer before he tweaked his elbow in July, causing him to miss a start. Still, he finished the season by tossing seven no-hit innings in late August. Following the season, though, he had Tommy John surgery and probably won't get back on the mound in 2005. When healthy, Megrew relies on good command and a deceptive circle changeup, one of the best in the system. Megrew's changeup has good sink and fade, especially away from righthanded hitters. His fastball sits between 87-91 mph and he shows a feel for changing speeds and locating it. His 77-78 mph breaking ball is a hard slider with good life. The long, lanky Megrew had a clean arm stroke and repeatable mechanics, so if he returns to form injuries shouldn't be a long-term concern. Rehab will give him an opportunity to bulk up his frame, and the Dodgers hope he'll throw off a mound by instructional league in 2005.

Year	Club (League)	Class	W	L	ERA	G	GS	CG	SV	IP	H	R	ER	HR	BB	SO	AVG
2002	Dodgers (GCL)	R	1	1	2.03	5	4	0	0	13	8	4	3	0	3	12	.178
2003	Ogden (Pio)	R	5	3	3.40	14	14	0	0	77	64	40	29	6	24	99	.222
2004	Vero Beach (FSL)	A	7	6	3.41	22	22	0	0	106	84	45	40	7	43	125	.214
MINOR LEAGUE TOTALS			13	10	3.31	41	40	0	0	196	156	89	72	13	70	236	.215

Tony Abreu, 2b/ss

21

Born: Nov. 13, 1984. **Ht.:** 5-11. **Wt.:** 160. **Bats:** R. **Throws:** R. **Career Transactions:** Signed out of Dominican Republic by Dodgers, Oct. 17, 2002. **Signed by:** Pablo Peguero.

Without much fanfare, Abreu and Ching-Lung Hu provided one of the most dynamic middle-infield combinations in the minor leagues last year. Abreu, who has been compared to Jose Vizcaino, has the tools to play shortstop but played second base alongside Hu last season in low Class A before a late promotion to Vero Beach. When Hu went down with an arm injury in August, Abreu moved to shortstop, where his arm is fringe-average. His glove is ahead of his bat at this stage. He has good range, aided by good first-step quickness, and soft hands. One Dodgers staff member said of Abreu's approach, "He wants to hit so bad he's insulted to take a walk." He needs to be more selective, but makes consistent, solid contact and drives balls all over the field, especially when he finishes his stroke and gets extended. Abreu generates his bat speed from a good load and could be a run producer if he gets stronger and refines his approach. He has average speed. He and Hu will team up again up the middle at Vero Beach this year, and the Dodgers see him as a second baseman long-term.

Year	Club (League)	Class	AVG	G	AB	R	H	2B	3B	HR	RBI	BB	SO	SB	OBP	SLG
2003	Dodgers (GCL)	R	.294	45	163	30	48	7	5	0	20	11	24	9	.358	.399
	Vero Beach (FSL)	A	.000	3	10	0	0	0	0	0	0	1	2	0	.091	.000
2004	Columbus (SAL)	A	.302	104	358	50	108	21	8	8	54	8	59	16	.327	.472
	Vero Beach (FSL)	A	.419	11	43	8	18	3	1	0	3	1	8	4	.435	.535
MINOR LEAGUE TOTALS			.303	163	574	88	174	31	14	8	77	21	93	29	.340	.448

Steve Schmoll, rhp

22

Born: Feb. 4, 1980. **Ht.:** 6-2. **Wt.:** 200. **Bats:** R. **Throws:** R. **School:** University of Maryland. **Career Transactions:** Signed as nondrafted free agent by Dodgers, May 25, 2003. **Signed by:** Clair Rierson.

Veteran area scout Clair Rierson raved about Schmoll during the 2003 college season, as he tied for the Atlantic Coast Conference lead with 124 strikeouts in just 88 innings. As a fifth-year senior, Schmoll was eligible to sign before the draft, and the Dodgers outbid several teams with a $75,000 bonus. Schmoll was in Double-A by August last season and was impressive in 19 innings in the Arizona Fall League, posting a 1.42 ERA. Schmoll has always been a sidewinder, but former Dodgers minor league pitching instructor Mark Brewer dropped his arm slot to near submarine level and Schmoll flashed 93 mph velocity at times in the AFL. He sits regularly around 87-90 with nasty running movement. His slot isn't quite as low but is comparable to Kent Tekulve's and Dan Quisenberry's, creating outstanding late movement, while his cutter actually rises. Schmoll's slider will never have great break from that angle, so he needs to craft an effective offspeed offering either with a variant of his fastball or his changeup, which has potential. He attacks the zone and pitches ahead in the count. He profiles as a set-up man or long reliever, but could provide relief help as early as midseason. He'll likely open the season in Double-A.

Year	Club (League)	Class	W	L	ERA	G	GS	CG	SV	IP	H	R	ER	HR	BB	SO	AVG
2003	Ogden (Pio)	R	3	1	3.68	24	1	0	7	37	27	23	15	2	15	53	.200

2004	Jacksonville (SL)	AA	0	2	1.83	11	0	0	2	20	14	7	4	0	7	18	.206
	Vero Beach (FSL)	A	3	3	1.80	37	0	0	10	65	57	18	13	0	18	58	.237
MINOR LEAGUE TOTALS			6	6	2.37	72	1	0	19	121	98	48	32	2	40	129	.221

23 Blake Johnson, rhp

Born: June 14, 1985. **Ht.:** 6-5. **Wt.:** 195. **Bats:** R. **Throws:** R. **School:** Parkview Baptist HS, Baton Rouge, La. **Career Transactions:** Selected by Dodgers in second round of 2004 draft; signed June 9, 2004. **Signed by:** Clarence Johns.

Johnson ranked among the top prep righthanders in the country entering his senior season, but he injured his triceps muscle diving back into a bag early in the year and his velocity suffered all spring. He still managed to lead Parkview Baptist to a third consecutive Louisiana 3-A state championship. At the prestigious National Classic tournament in California last April, Tommy Lasorda was among the Dodgers staff members who saw Johnson ring up 12 strikeouts, 10 with his outstanding breaking ball. His curve is a two-plane out pitch that has true 12-to-6 break and changes the hitter's eye level. It already rates as one of the best curveballs in the organization. His fastball tops out at 94 mph and sits at 90. He also throws a changeup that needs work. Johnson has a projectable frame and his arm works well, fitting Dodgers scouting director Logan White's pitching profile to a tee. He made adjustments well in his first taste of pro ball, but still needs to learn the nuances of pitching. Johnson profiles as a starter, and has potential to pitch at the front end of a rotation if everything develops according to plan. His next step will be low Class A in 2005.

Year	Club (League)	Class	W	L	ERA	G	GS	CG	SV	IP	H	R	ER	HR	BB	SO	AVG
2004	Ogden (Pio)	R	3	3	6.47	13	12	0	0	57	73	46	41	5	19	57	.317
MINOR LEAGUE TOTALS			3	3	6.47	13	12	0	0	57	73	46	41	5	19	57	.317

24 Justin Orenduff, rhp

Born: May 27, 1983. **Ht.:** 6-4. **Wt.:** 205. **Bats:** R. **Throws:** R. **School:** Virginia Commonwealth University. **Career Transactions:** Selected by Dodgers in first round (33rd overall) of 2004 draft; signed June 17, 2004. **Signed by:** Clair Rierson.

Orenduff bolstered his draft stock in the summer of 2003 when he was part of a dominant Team USA pitching staff that won a silver medal in the Pan American Games, going 6-0, 1.31 with 40 strikeouts in 41 innings. He finished second in the Colonial Athletic Association with a 2.43 ERA for Virginia Commonwealth last spring, and signed quickly with the Dodgers for $1 million in June. He became the Dodgers' earliest college draft pick since Ben Diggins (17th overall) in 2000. After pitching 100 innings for VCU in the spring, Orenduff's professional debut was uninspiring. He has a compact delivery and loose, easy arm action from a three-quarters slot. He operates with a heavy, 87-93 mph sinker, a hard slider and a fringe-average changeup. He has shown a tendency to rely too heavily on his breaking ball, which was the case in Rookie ball. Orenduff also needs to quicken his delivery from the stretch and hold runners better. He has outstanding makeup and could move fast through the system. He projects as a No. 3 or 4 starter but could pitch in middle relief as soon as 2006 if the Dodgers chose to move him to the bullpen. He'll open 2005 in high Class A.

Year	Club (League)	Class	W	L	ERA	G	GS	CG	SV	IP	H	R	ER	HR	BB	SO	AVG
2004	Ogden (Pio)	R	2	3	4.74	13	10	0	0	44	46	26	23	4	25	57	.272
MINOR LEAGUE TOTALS			2	3	4.74	13	10	0	0	44	46	26	23	4	25	57	.272

25 Willy Aybar, 2b

Born: March 9, 1983. **Ht.:** 6-0. **Wt.:** 185. **Bats:** B. **Throws:** R. **Career Transactions:** Signed out of Dominican Republic by Dodgers, Jan. 31, 2000. **Signed by:** Felix Feliz.

With Aybar posting modest power numbers in four minor league seasons and third baseman Andy LaRoche entering the system, the Dodgers moved Aybar from third to second in 2004. He responded with a career-high 15 homers and a career-best RBI total. His brother Erick also enjoyed a strong season in the Angels system and is considered one of the minors' top middle-infield prospects. Willy doesn't have his brother's speed or athleticism, and some scouts doubt he can stick at second base. He has good hands and an above-average arm, but his range is average to slightly below and he has stiff actions around the bag. His best tool is his bat. Aybar has a fluid, natural swing from the left side, and shows more bat speed and a shorter stroke from the right. He makes good contact and began driving balls with more regularity last year. He uses the whole field early in counts but gets pull-conscious when he's behind and chases fastballs up in the zone. He is better defensively than Delwyn Young but doesn't have the same power potential of Young or Etanislao Abreu. Aybar could reach the majors in the next two years, but he has fallen behind other players on the Dodgers depth chart and could become trade bait. He will spend most of 2005 at Triple-A.

Year	Club (League)	Class	AVG	G	AB	R	H	2B	3B	HR	RBI	BB	SO	SB	OBP	SLG
2000	Great Falls (Pio)	R	.263	70	266	39	70	15	1	4	49	36	45	5	.349	.372
2001	Wilmington (SAL)	A	.237	120	431	45	102	25	2	4	48	43	64	7	.307	.332
	Vero Beach (FSL)	A	.286	2	7	0	2	0	0	0	0	1	2	0	.375	.286
2002	Vero Beach (FSL)	A	.215	108	372	56	80	18	2	11	65	69	54	15	.339	.363
2003	Vero Beach (FSL)	A	.274	119	445	47	122	29	3	11	74	41	70	9	.336	.427
2004	Jacksonville (SL)	AA	.276	126	482	56	133	27	0	15	77	50	77	8	.346	.425
MINOR LEAGUE TOTALS			.254	545	2003	243	509	114	8	45	313	240	312	44	.335	.386

26 Javy Guerra, rhp

Born: Oct. 31, 1985. **Ht.:** 6-1. **Wt.:** 185. **Bats:** R. **Throws:** R. **School:** Denton Ryan HS, Denton, Texas. **Career Transactions:** Selected by Dodgers in fourth round of 2004 draft; signed June 13, 2004. **Signed by:** Mike Leuzinger.

Teams were apprehensive when scouting Guerra because of an unorthodox delivery that was similar to that of a fast-pitch softball pitcher but from a traditional three-quarters arm angle. College coaches even sent video of Guerra's motion to the NCAA to determine if it was legal by college standards before recruiting him. He committed to Arizona but instead signed with the Dodgers for a $275,000 bonus. Gulf Coast League pitching coach George Culver ironed out Guerra's mechanics, eliminating his crow hop without sacrificing velocity. He pitched at 90-92 mph, touching 95 mph his fastball. Guerra allowed just five runs in his last seven starts. His arm works fast with a loose and easy motion and he pitches downhill, though he needs to improve his feel for pitching and control. Guerra features a curveball, slider and advanced changeup, an impressive repertoire considering he was 17 when the Dodgers drafted him. The curveball, which has tight rotation, is the better of his two breaking balls. He has a dogged demeanor on the mound and good makeup. Despite his age, the Dodgers are considering starting Guerra in low Class A this season.

Year	Club (League)	Class	W	L	ERA	G	GS	CG	SV	IP	H	R	ER	HR	BB	SO	AVG
2004	Dodgers (GCL)	R	4	1	3.38	11	9	0	0	40	31	18	15	3	19	36	.213
MINOR LEAGUE TOTALS			4	1	3.38	11	9	0	0	40	31	18	15	3	19	36	.213

27 Franquelis Osoria, rhp

Born: Sept. 12, 1981. **Ht.:** 6-0. **Wt.:** 165. **Bats:** R. **Throws:** R. **Career Transactions:** Signed out of Dominican Republic by Dodgers, Dec. 28, 1999. **Signed by:** Pablo Peguero/Ramon Perez.

The Dodgers added Osoria to their 40-man roster over a handful of other promising pitchers, including Marcos Carvajal, who was taken in the major league Rule 5 draft by the Brewers and sold to the Rockies. Osoria doesn't throw as hard as Carvajal but shows the ability to command a nasty sinker. Osoria has a sixth digit on his right hand but doesn't use it to grip the ball. He spent most of 2004 in Double-A, where he was used in middle relief and a set-up role, and he should occupy a similar role in the big leagues. Osoria throws from a low three-quarters arm slot to generate late movement on his 88-92 mph sinker. Hitters know it's coming yet struggle to square the ball, making it difficult to lift and drive because of its boring action. Righthanders managed a .212 average and one homer against him in Double-A last year. Like the sidewinding Steve Schmoll, Osoria's slot prevents him from getting on top of a breaking ball. He needs to improve a second offspeed offering. His low-80s slider starts at a righthander's front hip and runs across the plate, but it's inconsistent. Osoria hasn't mastered English yet, and the language barrier has become troublesome for coaches and the player-development staff. He's on the cusp of pitching out of the Dodgers bullpen and will be challenged in Triple-A this season.

Year	Club (League)	Class	W	L	ERA	G	GS	CG	SV	IP	H	R	ER	HR	BB	SO	AVG
2000	Dodgers (DSL)	R	3	4	2.52	13	12	0	0	64	58	33	18	1	23	46	.230
2001	Dodgers (DSL)	R	4	4	3.16	15	11	0	0	77	69	38	27	5	16	67	.237
2002	Vero Beach (FSL)	A	0	1	2.45	3	0	0	0	7	4	2	2	0	2	10	.154
	South Georgia (SAL)	A	2	2	3.32	21	1	0	1	43	40	22	16	1	13	30	.226
2003	Vero Beach (FSL)	A	3	6	3.00	33	3	0	6	75	69	34	25	4	19	53	.244
2004	Las Vegas (PCL)	AAA	0	0	6.48	4	0	0	0	8	13	6	6	0	1	3	.351
	Jacksonville (SL)	AA	8	5	3.56	51	0	0	5	81	71	36	32	2	18	73	.237
MINOR LEAGUE TOTALS			20	22	3.18	140	27	0	12	356	324	171	126	13	92	282	.237

28 Matt Kemp, of

Born: Sept. 23, 1984. **Ht.:** 6-4. **Wt.:** 215. **Bats:** R. **Throws:** R. **School:** Midwest City (Okla.) HS. **Career Transactions:** Selected by Dodgers in sixth round of 2003 draft; signed June 5, 2003. **Signed by:** Mike Leuzinger.

Dodgers scouting director Logan White drove a few blocks down the street after scouting high-profile Oklahoma prepster Michael Rogers—signed by the Twins for $300,000 after sliding to the 16th round in 2003—to get a look at Kemp, who was better known as a basketball prospect. Without the grades to secure a Division I college scholarship, Kemp signed in the sixth round. He was flanked in the Columbus outfield by two more polished prospects in Xavier Paul and Jereme Milons (since traded to the Diamondbacks for Elmer Dessens), but made a positive impression on scouts. Kemp's chiseled, 6-foot-4, 215-pound frame has that effect. He has four potential plus tools and made as much improvement in the last year as Joel Guzman, according to some in the organization. Like Guzman, Kemp has monstrous raw power. Balls jump off his bat and he showed a willingness to use all fields. He's a slightly below-average runner down the line and better under way. Kemp is still learning the nuances of playing the outfield, but has an average arm for right field. He can look bad on breaking pitches out of the zone, but also has the aptitude to make adjustments. The Dodgers will likely move him to high Class A this season. He is a bit of a work in progress but showed the potential for a breakthrough season in 2005.

Year	Club (League)	Class	AVG	G	AB	R	H	2B	3B	HR	RBI	BB	SO	SB	OBP	SLG
2003	Dodgers (GCL)	R	.270	43	159	11	43	5	2	1	17	7	25	2	.298	.346
2004	Columbus (SAL)	A	.288	112	423	67	122	22	8	17	66	24	100	8	.330	.499
	Vero Beach (FSL)	A	.351	11	37	5	13	5	0	1	9	4	12	2	.405	.568
MINOR LEAGUE TOTALS			.288	166	619	83	178	32	10	19	92	35	137	12	.327	.464

29 Juan Rivera, ss

Born: March 17, 1987. **Ht.:** 6-0. **Wt.:** 148. **Bats:** B. **Throws:** R. **Career Transactions:** Signed out of Dominican Republic by Dodgers, July 21, 2003. **Signed by:** Pablo Peguero/Angel Santana.

The Dodgers signed Rivera as a 16-year-old in 2003, but he didn't make his professional debut until last summer because of a broken hand. He hit safely in 11 of his first 27 at-bats and earned comparisons to former all-star shortstop Tony Fernandez because of his pure shortstop actions and live, athletic body. Rivera plays with flair and his makeup is off the charts. He has good range up the middle and to his right and plenty of arm to make plays deep in the hole. At times he allowed a poor at-bat to affect his defense, but the Dodgers expect those kinds of problems to go away as he matures. Rivera has a slap approach from both sides of the plate now but projects to have gap power eventually, thanks to good bat control, projectable strength and solid eye-hand coordination. He can be beaten on hard stuff up and in. An average runner, Rivera has narrow shoulders, leading some scouts to wonder how much he'll fill out, but he has the instincts and tools to become a solid shortstop. He will most likely start 2005 in extended spring training and join Ogden in June.

Year	Club (League)	Class	AVG	G	AB	R	H	2B	3B	HR	RBI	BB	SO	SB	OBP	SLG
2004	Dodgers (GCL)	R	.243	52	185	28	45	6	0	0	14	13	30	5	.296	.276
MINOR LEAGUE TOTALS			.243	52	185	28	45	6	0	0	14	13	30	5	.296	.276

30 Jason Repko, of

Born: Dec. 27, 1980. **Ht.:** 5-11. **Wt.:** 175. **Bats:** R. **Throws:** R. **School:** Hanford HS, Richland, Wash. **Career Transactions:** Selected by Dodgers in first round (37th overall) of 1999 draft; signed June 3, 1999. **Signed by:** Hank Jones.

Following five frustrating seasons marked by nagging back and hamstring injuries, a position change and inconsistent performance, Repko may have turned a corner in 2004. He posted career highs in homers, RBIs, doubles, average and at-bats between two advanced levels and was protected on the 40-man roster. Repko's hard work has helped him become the organization's best defensive outfielder. He moved to center field from shortstop in 2002 and now makes good reads on line drives, gets good jumps on balls, has above-average speed and plus arm strength. He probably profiles as an extra outfielder on a contending team, but still has a chance to play every day in the big leagues. In order to do that, he'll have to improve his on-base skills. He has an unorthodox, open stance at the plate and he carries his hands low. His swing can get long, though he has good hand-eye coordination and shows enough bat speed to drill the ball to all parts of the park. Repko is slated to start 2005 back in Triple-A but is an injury away from earning his first big league callup.

Year	Club (League)	Class	AVG	G	AB	R	H	2B	3B	HR	RBI	BB	SO	SB	OBP	SLG
1999	Great Falls (Pio)	R	.304	49	207	51	63	9	9	8	32	21	43	12	.375	.551
2000	Yakima (NWL)	A	.294	8	17	3	5	2	0	0	1	1	7	0	.333	.412
2001	Wilmington (SAL)	A	.220	88	337	36	74	17	4	4	32	15	68	17	.257	.329
2002	Vero Beach (FSL)	A	.272	120	470	73	128	29	5	9	53	25	92	29	.319	.413
2003	Jacksonville (SL)	AA	.240	119	416	62	100	14	5	10	23	42	89	21	.317	.370
2004	Jacksonville (SL)	AA	.291	46	189	26	55	11	2	6	19	13	43	10	.341	.466
	Las Vegas (PCL)	AAA	.311	75	302	55	94	26	4	7	41	18	57	13	.355	.493
MINOR LEAGUE TOTALS			.268	505	1938	306	519	108	29	44	201	135	399	102	.322	.422

MILWAUKEE
BREWERS

BY **TOM HAUDRICOURT**

Heading into the 2004 season, the Brewers' braintrust felt confident its plan to build around a farm system that Baseball America rated as the best in the game was proceeding at a promising pace. Then disaster struck, at both the big league and minor league levels. After making it to the all-star break with a 45-41 record, Milwaukee suffered baseball's worst-ever second-half collapse among teams with a winning first half. The Brewers lost 53 of their final 75 games to finish last in the National League for the third straight year. It also was their 12th consecutive losing season, tying the Pirates for the longest streak in baseball.

Meanwhile, injuries ravaged the farm system. The most devastating was a shoulder injury to shortstop J.J. Hardy, whose season ended in early May. He might have emerged as Milwaukee's shortstop during the summer had he not been hurt. The most discouraging involved righthander Mike Jones, a 2001 first-round pick. He was shut down after six Double-A starts and had shoulder surgery that will sideline him for the 2005 season. Jones already endured elbow problems that sidelined him for half of 2003.

Lefthander Manny Parra also came down with a balky shoulder, avoiding surgery but costing him an Arizona Fall League assignment. Lefty Jorge de la Rosa had arm and command problems. And righty Chris Saenz, who beat the Cardinals in an emergency start in April with six shutout innings, blew out his elbow in June and had Tommy John surgery.

None of the farm teams made the playoffs, a further indication things didn't go as expected. The Brewers hoped to foster a winning atmosphere by keeping prospects together in clusters at a couple of levels in 2003, but the tactic didn't pan out last year.

The Brewers tried to recover from their pitching setbacks with a bold trade, sending all-star closer Dan Kolb to Atlanta for righthanders Jose Capellan, the Braves' top pitching prospect, and Alec Zumwalt. Capellan will get a shot to make Milwaukee's rotation in spring training.

GM Doug Melvin made two other promising trades in December, acquiring slugger Carlos Lee from the White Sox for Scott Podsednik, Luis Vizcaino and fringe prospect Travis Hinton. Lee's righthanded bat will fit nicely between lefty hitters **Lyle Overbay** and Geoff Jenkins in the middle of the lineup. Melvin also dealt backup infielder Keith Ginter to the Athletics for promising outfielder Nelson Cruz and righty Justin Lehr, who could make the big league bullpen in 2005.

Other than Ben Hendrickson and Hardy, the Brewers aren't counting on much help from their farm system in 2005, putting them another year behind in their ongoing rebuilding project. Rickie Weeks and Prince Fielder struggled at times after jumping to Double-A, but both remain among the game's elite prospects and should reach the majors in 2006.

LARRY GOREN

TOP 30 PROSPECTS

1. Rickie Weeks, 2b
2. Prince Fielder, 1b
3. J.J. Hardy, ss
4. Jose Capellan, rhp
5. Mark Rogers, rhp
6. Corey Hart, of
7. Ben Hendrickson, rhp
8. Brad Nelson, of
9. Hernan Iribarren, 2b
10. David Krynzel, of
11. Manny Parra, lhp
12. Dana Eveland, lhp
13. Jorge de la Rosa, lhp
14. Nelson Cruz, of
15. Lou Palmisano, c
16. Yovanni Gallardo, rhp
17. Jeff Housman, lhp
18. Dennis Sarfate, rhp
19. Josh Baker, rhp
20. Josh Wahpepah, rhp
21. Justin Lehr, rhp
22. Mike Jones, rhp
23. Luis Pena, lhp
24. Anthony Gwynn, of
25. Alcides Escobar, ss
26. Angel Salome, c
27. Steve Moss, of
28. Adam Heether, 3b
29. Vinny Rottino, of/inf
30. Chris Saenz, rhp

ORGANIZATION OVERVIEW

General manager: Doug Melvin. **Farm director:** Reid Nichols. **Scouting director:** Jack Zduriencik.

2004 PERFORMANCE

Class	Team	League	W	L	Pct.	Finish*	Manager
Majors	Milwaukee	National	67	94	.416	14th (16)	Ned Yost
Triple-A	#Indianapolis Indians	International	66	78	.458	t-11th (14)	Cecil Cooper
Double-A	Huntsville Stars	Southern	65	75	.464	8th (10)	Frank Kremblas
High A	@High Desert Mavericks	California	49	91	.350	10th (10)	Mel Queen
Low A	†Beloit Snappers	Midwest	72	68	.514	t-7th (14)	Don Money
Rookie	Helena Brewers	Pioneer	40	37	.519	4th (8)	Johnny Narron
Rookie	AZL Brewers	Arizona	24	32	.429	8th (9)	Mike Guerrero
OVERALL 2004 MINOR LEAGUE RECORD			316	381	.453	29th (30)	

*Finish in overall standings (No. of teams in league). #Affiliate will be in Nashville (Pacific Coast) in 2005.
@Affiliate will be in Brevard County (Florida State) in 2005. †Affiliate will be in West Virginia (South Atlantic) in 2005.

ORGANIZATION LEADERS

BATTING
*Minimum 250 at-bats
*AVG	Steve Sollmann, Helena	.364
R	Callix Crabbe, High Desert	89
H	Travis Hinton, High Desert	163
TB	Travis Hinton, High Desert	273
2B	Travis Hinton, High Desert	36
3B	Callix Crabbe, High Desert	11
HR	Prince Fielder, Huntsville	23
RBI	Vinny Rottino, Beloit	124
BB	Prince Fielder, Huntsville	65
SO	Brad Nelson, Huntsville	146
SB	Terry Trofholz, Beloit	48
*OBP	Steve Sollmann, Helena	.487
*SLG	Grant Richardson, Beloit/Helena	.523

PITCHING
#Minimum 75 innings
W	Ben Hendrickson, Indianapolis	11
L	Khalid Ballouli, High Desert	14
#ERA	Ben Hendrickson, Indianapolis	2.02
G	Brian Adams, Huntsville	52
	Roberto Giron, Indianapolis/Huntsville	52
CG	Ben Hendrickson, Indianapolis	2
SV	John Novinsky, Indianapolis/Huntsville	17
IP	Ryan Costello, Huntsville/High Desert	141
BB	Dennis Sarfate, Huntsville	78
SO	Jeff Housman, Indianapolis/Huntsville	134

BEST TOOLS

Best Hitter for Average	Rickie Weeks
Best Power Hitter	Prince Fielder
Best Strike-Zone Discipline	Prince Fielder
Fastest Baserunner	David Krynzel
Best Athlete	David Krynzel
Best Fastball	Jose Capellan
Best Curveball	Ben Hendrickson
Best Slider	Jeff Housman
Best Changeup	Glenn Woolard
Best Control	Manny Parra
Best Defensive Catcher	Angel Salome
Best Defensive Infielder	J.J. Hardy
Best Infield Arm	J.J. Hardy
Best Defensive Outfielder	David Krynzel
Best Outfield Arm	David Krynzel

PROJECTED 2008 LINEUP

Catcher	Lou Palmisano
First Base	Prince Fielder
Second Base	Rickie Weeks
Third Base	Wes Helms
Shortstop	J.J. Hardy
Left Field	Carlos Lee
Center Field	Dave Krynzel

Right Field	Geoff Jenkins
No. 1 Starter	Ben Sheets
No. 2 Starter	Doug Davis
No. 3 Starter	Mark Rogers
No. 4 Starter	Ben Hendrickson
No. 5 Starter	Manny Parra
Closer	Jose Capellan

LAST YEAR'S TOP 20 PROSPECTS

1. Rickie Weeks, 2b
2. Prince Fielder, 1b
3. J.J. Hardy, ss
4. Manny Parra, lhp
5. Brad Nelson, of/1b
6. Mike Jones, rhp
7. Corey Hart, 3b/of
8. Ben Hendrickson, rhp
9. David Krynzel, of
10. Jorge de la Rosa, lhp
11. Lou Palmisano, c
12. Dennis Sarfate, rhp
13. Luis Martinez, lhp
14. Tom Wilhelmsen, rhp
15. Chris Capuano, lhp
16. Dana Eveland, lhp
17. Anthony Gwynn, of
18. Pedro Lirano, rhp
19. Tim Bausher, rhp
20. Jeff Housman, lhp

TOP PROSPECTS OF THE DECADE

Year	Player, Pos.	Current Team
1995	Antone Williamson, 3b	Out of baseball
1996	Jeff D'Amico, rhp	Indians
1997	Todd Dunn, of	Out of baseball
1998	Valerio de los Santos, lhp	Out of baseball
1999	Ron Belliard, 2b	Indians
2000	Nick Neugebauer, rhp	Out of baseball
2001	Ben Sheets, rhp	Brewers
2002	Nick Neugebauer, rhp	Out of baseball
2003	Brad Nelson, 1b	Brewers
2004	Rickie Weeks, 2b	Brewers

TOP DRAFT PICKS OF THE DECADE

Year	Player, Pos.	Current Team
1995	Geoff Jenkins, of	Brewers
1996	Chad Green, of	Out of baseball
1997	Kyle Peterson, rhp	Out of baseball
1998	J.M. Gold, rhp	Out of baseball
1999	Ben Sheets, rhp	Brewers
2000	David Krynzel, of	Brewers
2001	Mike Jones, rhp	Brewers
2002	Prince Fielder, 1b	Brewers
2003	Rickie Weeks, 2b	Brewers
2004	Mark Rogers, rhp	Brewers

ALL-TIME LARGEST BONUSES

Rickie Weeks, 2003	$3,600,000
Ben Sheets, 1999	$2,450,000
Prince Fielder, 2002	$2,400,000
Mark Rogers, 2004	$2,200,000
Mike Jones, 2001	$2,075,000

MINOR LEAGUE DEPTH CHART

Milwaukee BREWERS

Impact Potential: A
The Brewers pushed their prospects aggressively in 2004, and some of them buckled. Rickie Weeks and Prince Fielder held their own in Double-A—it was Weeks' first full pro season—and both could be future stars. A healthy J.J. Hardy should step in as the Brewers' big league shortstop in 2005 and be a Rookie of the Year candidate. Hard-throwing first-round pick Mark

Rogers has big stuff and some projection left.
Depth: B
Injuries thinned the Brewers' pitching depth, from Mike Jones' shoulder surgery to Manny Parra's shoulder fatigue to Tommy John surgery for righthander Chris Saenz. Other pitchers, though, such as lefty Dana Eveland and righty Yovani Gallardo, stepped forward. General manager Doug Melvin added high-ceiling talents through trades in flamethrowing Jose Capellan (from the Braves) and outfielder Nelson Cruz (Athletics).

Depth charts prepared by John Manuel and Allan Simpson. Numbers in parentheses indicate prospect rankings.

LF
Brad Nelson (8)
Vinny Rottino (29)
Drew Anderson
Kenard Bibbs
Josh Brady
Adam Mannon

CF
David Krynzel (10)
Anthony Gwynn (24)
Steve Moss (27)
Terry Trofholz
Stephen Chapman

RF
Corey Hart (6)
Nelson Cruz (14)
Charlie Fermaint
Freddy Parejo

3B
Adam Heether (28)
Enrique Cruz
Jeff Eure
Tony Festa
Freddy de la Cruz

SS
J.J. Hardy (3)
Alcides Escobar (25)
Ozzie Chavez
Gilberto Acosta
Josh Murray

2B
Rickie Weeks (1)
Hernan Iribarren (9)
Callix Crabbe
Steven Sollmann
Will Lewis
Guilder Rodriguez

1B
Prince Fielder (2)
Brandon Gemoll
Manny Ramirez
Carlos Corporan
Grant Richardson

SOURCE of TALENT

HOMEGROWN		ACQUIRED	
College	5	Trades	4
Junior College	4	Rule 5 draft	0
Draft-and-follow	2	Independent leagues	0
High School	9	Free agents/waivers	0
Nondrafted free agent	1		
Foreign	5		

C
Lou Palmisano (15)
Angel Salome (26)
Brian Opdyke
John Vanden Berg

LHP

Starters	Relievers
Manny Parra (11)	Mitch Stetter
Dana Eveland (12)	Brian Adams
Jorge de la Rosa (13)	Eric Henderson
Jeff Housman (17)	Edwin Walker
Luis Pena (23)	
Andy Pratt	
Sam Narron	
Matt Ford	
Ryan Costello	
Brandon Parillo	

RHP

Starters	Relievers
Jose Capellan (4)	Justin Lehr (21)
Mark Rogers (5)	Ben Diggins
Ben Hendrickson (7)	Alec Zumwalt
Yovani Gallardo (16)	John Novinsky
Dennis Sarfate (28)	Bo Hall
Josh Baker (19)	Dave Nolasco
Josh Wahpepah (20)	Nick Slack
Mike Jones (22)	Justin Barnes
Chris Saenz (30)	Robert Wooley
Glenn Woolard	
Tom Wilhelmsen	
Jesse Harper	
Khalid Ballouli	
Kenny Durost	
Tommy Hawk	

2004

Best Pro Debut: 2B Steve Sollmann (10) batted .364, stole 23 bases and led the Rookie-level Pioneer League with 99 hits. RHP Mark Rogers' (1) numbers weren't as gaudy—he went 0-3, 4.73 in 27 innings—but he rated as the top pitching prospect in the Rookie-level Arizona League.

Best Athlete: Rogers, Maine's first-ever high school first-rounder, had the talent to pursue a career in the NHL. He was all-state as a pitcher, a hockey forward and a soccer midfielder. RHP Yovani Gallardo (2) also was a soccer standout as a Texas high schooler. Among the position players, OF Stephen Chapman (6) is the best athlete.

Best Pure Hitter: Sollmann or OF Josh Brady (19). Sollmann has tremendous discipline (52 walks, 30 strikeouts in his debut), while Brady has a compact, efficient stroke.

Best Raw Power: 1B Grant Richardson (14) hit 11 homers in his pro debut, including six in 28 games at low Class A Beloit.

Fastest Runner: The quickest player the Brewers signed was draft-and-follow Hasan Rasheed (26 in 2003). Rasheed rates a 70 on the 20-80 scouting scale, while Chapman tops the 2004 draft class with 60 wheels.

Best Defensive Player: C Angel Salome (5) has well above-average arm strength. His receiving skills aren't as advanced, but with his hands and work ethic, he'll be fine.

Best Fastball: Rogers hit 98 mph as an amateur and after a long summer he still was pitching at 91-94 in instructional league. Gallardo, who had 25 strikeouts in an 11-inning high school game in March, tops out at 96. So does RHP Josh Wahpepah (3), who also features electric sink.

Best Breaking Ball: Rogers' curveball.

BILL MITCHELL

Salome

RHP Josh Baker (4) has the top slider.

Most Intriguing Background: It's all relative with Baker. His father Johnny was an NFL linebacker, his uncle Frank was a big league infielder, his brother Jacob was an outfielder in the Royals system and his brother-in-law is Lance Berkman.

Closest To The Majors: Baker was Milwaukee's only four-year college draftee in the first eight rounds.

Best Late-Round Pick: RHP Alexandre Periard (16), one of a draft-high seven Canadians selected by Milwaukee, projected as a top-five-rounds pick, but perhaps teams stayed away knowing that his pro debut would be delayed because of the visa crunch. Periard, who didn't turn 17 until a week after the draft, is athletic and shows a 90-91 mph sinker and a promising curveball.

The One Who Got Away: RHP Sean Morgan (25) had one of the better sliders in the draft. As a strong student with a scholarship from Tulane, he was next to impossible to sign.

Assessment: The Brewers system is loaded with impact position players, so they made a conscious decision to draft some arms for balance. Several teams coveted Rogers early in the first round, and LHP Brandon Parillo (8) was a nice addition to the righthanders Milwaukee took with its first four picks.

2003 2B Rickie Weeks (1) certainly has the potential to make this an A all by himself if he fulfills his promise. C Lou Palmisano (3) will also do his part. OF Anthony Gwynn (2) looks like a reach at this point. *GRADE:* B+

2002 This draft is very similar to Milwaukee's 2003 effort. There's a young hitter whose ceiling would earn the class an A if he reaches it (1B Prince Fielder, 1), and a solid second-tier prospect (draft-and-follow LHP Dana Eveland, 16). *GRADE:* B+

2001 RHP Mike Jones (1) has shoulder problems, but this group is strong enough to carry on without him. SS J.J. Hardy (2) soon should claim a big league job, and OF Brad Nelson (4) and draft-and-follow Manny Parra (26) could do the same soon thereafter. *GRADE:* B+

2000 OFs Corey Hart (11) and David Krynzel (1) also could soon play key roles in what should be a brighter future for the Brewers. But most everyone else from this class has already fallen by the wayside. *GRADE:* C+

*Draft analysis prepared by **Jim Callis**. Numbers in parentheses indicate draft rounds.*

DANNY PARKER

Rickie
WEEKS

Born: Sept. 13, 1982.
Ht.: 6-0. **Wt.:** 195.
Bats: R. **Throws:** R.
School: Southern University.
Career Transactions: Selected by Brewers in first round (second overall) of 2003 draft; signed Aug. 7, 2003.
Signed by: Ray Montgomery.

While he was undrafted and barely recruited out of a Florida high school, Weeks won consecutive NCAA Division I batting titles at Southern and set an NCAA record with a .473 career average. Baseball America's 2003 College Player of the Year, Weeks went second overall in the draft that June and signed for a club-record $3.6 million bonus, part of a five-year big league contract that guarantees him at least $4.8 million. The Brewers have been very aggressive with his development path. They jumped him to full-season ball at low Class A Beloit after one game in the Rookie-level Arizona League, and last year they sent him to Double-A Huntsville with all of 67 pro at-bats to his credit. As might be expected, he struggled at times, but the Brewers liked the way Weeks competed. He finished 2004 by hitting .382 with six homers in 76 at-bats in the Arizona Fall League, ranking as the league's No. 2 prospect behind Devil Rays outfielder Delmon Young—also the only player picked ahead of him in the 2003 draft.

Despite his periodic struggles at the plate in Double-A, Weeks continued to display the skills that made him a No. 2 overall pick. He has a compact swing, and his bat gets through the hitting zone in lightning-quick fashion, giving him surprising pop for his size. He's able to turn on inside heat, while his quick hands also allow him to cover the outer half of the plate. He also has plus speed to go with his power. Weeks has good patience at the plate, though he must continue to work on his strike-zone discipline. As a sign of his mental toughness, he played much of the season with a hamstring strain, refusing to come out of the lineup. Weeks worked hard to improve his defense, which was considered a weakness in college. The Brewers love his drive and determination. He determinedly stands on top of the plate, which is why he ranked third in the minors by getting hit with 28 pitches last year. His combination of athleticism and work ethic makes Weeks a special player.

Weeks faced predominantly weak competition at Southern, and given his lack of pro experience, he often was fooled by breaking pitches in Double-A. He sometimes gets impatient and swings at pitcher's pitches, but improved in that regard over the course of his first full season. Despite his plus speed, he still has a lot to learn on the basepaths after getting caught 12 times in 23 steal attempts last year. For all his effort, Weeks still has a lot of work to do with his glove. He led Southern League second basemen with 17 errors. He sometimes makes fundamental mistakes in the field and throws without getting his feet under him.

The Brewers knew they were putting a lot of pressure on Weeks by pushing him to Double-A in his first full season but were pleased with the way he handled himself. They feel he's ready to handle an assignment to their new Triple-A Nashville affiliate this year, with hopes of seeing him in a big league uniform for good in 2006, if not before.

Year	Club (League)	Class	AVG	G	AB	R	H	2B	3B	HR	RBI	BB	SO	SB	OBP	SLG
2003	Brewers (AZL)	R	.500	1	4	0	2	0	0	0	4	0	2	1	.600	.500
	Beloit (Mid)	A	.349	20	63	13	22	8	1	1	16	15	9	2	.494	.556
	Milwaukee (NL)	MAJ	.167	7	12	1	2	1	0	0	0	1	6	0	.286	.250
2004	Huntsville (SL)	AA	.259	133	479	67	124	35	6	8	42	55	107	11	.366	.407
MAJOR LEAGUE TOTALS			.167	7	12	1	2	1	0	0	0	1	6	0	.286	.250
MINOR LEAGUE TOTALS			.271	154	546	80	148	43	7	9	62	70	118	14	.385	.425

Prince Fielder, 1b

Born: May 9, 1984. **Ht.:** 6-0. **Wt.:** 260. **Bats:** L. **Throws:** R. **School:** Eau Gallie HS, Melbourne, Fla. **Career Transactions:** Selected by Brewers in first round (seventh overall) of 2002 draft; signed June 17, 2002. **Signed by:** Tom McNamara/Jack Zduriencik.

Fielder earned low Class A Midwest League MVP honors in 2003. But if there wasn't already enough pressure on the seventh overall pick in 2002 and the son of a former big league home run king, things got more difficult when reports of his father Cecil's seven-figure gambling debts surfaced in October. Fielder has outstanding power to all fields and enhances it by recognizing pitches early. He shows the patience to take a walk and rarely chases bad pitches out of his zone. He employs a compact stroke with tremendous bat speed, making him a constant threat. He has worked hard to control his weight, which was a concern in high school, and must remain diligent in that area. Fielder never will be more than adequate at first base, though he's no longer a liability. He may have limited range, but he has soft hands and good reactions. There is little doubt that he'll rake in the majors. The question is when. With Lyle Overbay busting out last year, there's no immediate need to rush Fielder to the big leagues, even if he'll play in Triple-A as a 21-year-old.

Year	Club (League)	Class	AVG	G	AB	R	H	2B	3B	HR	RBI	BB	SO	SB	OBP	SLG
2002	Ogden (Pio)	R	.390	41	146	35	57	12	0	10	40	37	27	3	.531	.678
	Beloit (Mid)	A	.241	32	112	15	27	7	0	3	11	10	27	0	.320	.384
2003	Beloit (Mid)	A	.313	137	502	81	157	22	2	27	112	71	80	2	.409	.526
2004	Huntsville (SL)	AA	.272	136	497	70	135	29	1	23	78	65	93	11	.366	.473
MINOR LEAGUE TOTALS			.299	346	1257	201	376	70	3	63	241	183	227	16	.401	.510

J.J. Hardy, ss

Born: Aug. 19, 1982. **Ht.:** 6-2. **Wt.:** 180. **Bats:** R. **Throws:** R. **School:** Sabino HS, Tucson. **Career Transactions:** Selected by Brewers in second round of 2001 draft; signed July 16, 2001. **Signed by:** Brian Johnson.

Following a 2003 campaign that put him in place to compete for major league playing time, Hardy's left shoulder popped out of its socket on a swing during spring training. He tore his labrum and tried to play through it before having season-ending surgery in May. Hardy doesn't have overwhelming tools, but his competitiveness and savvy have allowed him to make up for any shortcomings. He displays a natural feel for hitting, rarely striking out while spraying line drives to all fields. For a middle infielder, he has solid gap power. His instincts serve him well defensively, where he has a plus arm, good hands and range. Scouts have questioned Hardy's bat since his amateur days, and his swing sometimes gets out of whack. He's an average runner at best, though he plays above his speed on the bases and in the field. For most players, losing most of a season would be a significant setback, but the Brewers aren't concerned because of Hardy's makeup. He'll get a chance to win the big league shortstop job in spring training, where his main competition will be Bill Hall.

Year	Club (League)	Class	AVG	G	AB	R	H	2B	3B	HR	RBI	BB	SO	SB	OBP	SLG
2001	Brewers (AZL)	R	.250	5	20	6	5	2	1	0	1	1	2	0	.286	.450
	Ogden (Pio)	R	.248	35	125	20	31	5	0	2	15	15	12	1	.326	.336
2002	High Desert (Cal)	A	.293	84	335	53	98	19	1	6	18	19	30	9	.327	.409
	Huntsville (SL)	AA	.228	38	145	14	33	7	0	1	13	9	19	1	.269	.297
2003	Huntsville (SL)	AA	.279	114	416	67	116	26	0	12	62	58	54	6	.368	.428
2004	Indianapolis (IL)	AAA	.277	26	101	17	28	10	0	4	20	9	8	0	.330	.495
MINOR LEAGUE TOTALS			.272	302	1142	177	311	69	2	25	159	111	133	17	.335	.402

Jose Capellan, rhp

Born: Jan. 13, 1981. **Ht.:** 6-4. **Wt.:** 235. **Bats:** R. **Throws:** R. **Career Transactions:** Signed out of Dominican Republic by Braves, Aug. 6, 1998 . . . Traded by Braves with RHP Alec Zumwalt to Brewers for RHP Dan Kolb, Dec. 11, 2004. **Signed by:** Julian Perez/Rene Francisco (Braves).

The Brewers wouldn't have traded closer Dan Kolb to the Braves without getting Capellan. While Tommy John surgery limited him to just 80 innings from 2001-03, he dominated at three levels and made his big league debut last year. Capellan not only can hit triple digits with his fastball, but he can maintain his velocity over the course of a game. He's consistently clocked at 94-97 mph with an effortless delivery. He gave up only one home run last year because he keeps his pitches down in the zone. Capellan's spike curveball and changeup still need a lot of work. Despite urging from Atlanta's development staff, he rarely used his changeup. He has become soft around his midsection, so he'll have to watch his conditioning. Because Capellan sometimes has only one consistent pitch, some scouts suggest he's headed for the bullpen. But he'll get a shot at starting in Milwaukee this year.

Year	Club (League)	Class	W	L	ERA	G	GS	CG	SV	IP	H	R	ER	HR	BB	SO	AVG
1999	Braves (DSL)	R	3	3	3.58	14	10	0	2	60	54	31	24	1	28	46	.242
2000	Braves (DSL)	R	3	8	3.69	14	14	0	0	68	58	45	28	0	36	68	.221
2001	Danville (Appy)	R	0	0	1.72	3	3	0	0	16	12	7	3	1	4	25	.200
2002	Did not play																
2003	Rome (SAL)	A	1	2	3.80	14	12	1	0	47	43	23	20	2	19	32	.253
	Braves (GCL)	R	0	1	2.65	5	5	0	0	17	18	7	5	0	8	17	.277
2004	Atlanta (NL)	MAJ	0	1	11.25	3	2	0	0	8	14	10	10	2	5	4	.400
	Richmond (IL)	AAA	4	2	2.51	7	7	0	0	43	33	13	12	0	15	37	.214
	Myrtle Beach (Car)	A	5	1	1.94	8	8	1	0	46	27	11	10	0	11	62	.168
	Greenville (SL)	AA	5	1	2.50	9	8	0	0	50	53	15	14	1	19	53	.270
MAJOR LEAGUE TOTALS			0	1	11.25	3	2	0	0	8	14	10	10	2	5	4	.400
MINOR LEAGUE TOTALS			21	18	3.00	74	67	2	2	348	298	152	116	5	140	340	.231

5 Mark Rogers, rhp

Born: Jan. 30, 1986. **Ht.:** 6-2. **Wt.:** 205. **Bats:** R. **Throws:** R. **School:** Mount Ararat HS, Orr's Island, Maine. **Career Transactions:** Selected by Brewers in first round (fifth overall) of 2004 draft; signed June 16, 2004. **Signed by:** Tony Blengino.

Rogers surfaced as a prospect when he pumped 96-97 mph fastballs at the 2003 East Coast Showcase. The first Maine high schooler ever to go in the first round, he signed for $2.2 million. He was an all-state performer as a pitcher, a hockey forward with legitimate NHL potential and a soccer midfielder. Rogers has a pure power arm, reaching the mid-90s consistently. Even after pitching all spring and summer, he was throwing 91-94 in instructional league. He also has a knee-buckling hammer curveball and a decent changeup. Rogers also attracted scouts with his strong makeup. He scored higher than any draft prospect on his predraft psychological tests. Rogers has some effort to his delivery and throws slightly across his body, flaws Brewers instructors are trying to correct. He has trouble repeating his mechanics, affecting the quality of his command and pitches. An intense competitor, he'll revert to old habits at times to get outs. Rogers profiles as a frontline starter. He'll begin his first full season at Milwaukee's new low Class A West Virginia affiliate.

Year	Club (League)	Class	W	L	ERA	G	GS	CG	SV	IP	H	R	ER	HR	BB	SO	AVG
2004	Brewers (GCL)	R	0	3	4.73	9	6	0	0	27	30	21	14	0	14	35	.294
MINOR LEAGUE TOTALS			0	3	4.73	9	6	0	0	27	30	21	14	0	14	35	.294

6 Corey Hart, of

Born: March 24, 1982. **Ht.:** 6-6. **Wt.:** 200. **Bats:** R. **Throws:** R. **School:** Greenwood HS, Bowling Green, Ky. **Career Transactions:** Selected by Brewers in 11th round of 2000 draft; signed June 12, 2000. **Signed by:** Mike Gibbons.

After signing as a first baseman and winning the 2003 Southern League MVP award as a third baseman, Hart spent last season learning to play right field. A slight shoulder injury limited him to one at-bat in his first big league callup in September. With a long wingspan that generates leverage, Hart is capable of generating tremendous raw power and has drawn comparisons to Richie Sexson since his high school days. He drives the ball into the alleys and still hasn't tapped into his full home run potential. Hart displays solid average arm strength suitable for right field, and he also has above-average speed for his size. Hart has a tendency to get long with his swing and is prone to striking out. Because of his long frame and arms, he gets challenged inside regularly, and he needs a shorter stroke to cope. He's also susceptible to breaking stuff, and he could afford to be more patient. The move to the outfield was a good one for Hart. He will start 2005 back in Triple-A but isn't far off from forcing his way into Milwaukee's plans.

Year	Club (League)	Class	AVG	G	AB	R	H	2B	3B	HR	RBI	BB	SO	SB	OBP	SLG
2000	Ogden (Pio)	R	.287	57	216	32	62	9	1	2	30	13	27	6	.332	.366
2001	Ogden (Pio)	R	.340	69	262	53	89	18	1	11	62	26	47	14	.395	.542
2002	High Desert (Cal)	A	.288	100	393	76	113	26	10	22	84	37	101	24	.356	.573
	Huntsville (SL)	AA	.266	28	94	16	25	3	0	2	15	7	16	3	.340	.362
2003	Huntsville (SL)	AA	.302	130	493	70	149	40	1	13	94	28	101	25	.340	.467
2004	Indianapolis (IL)	AAA	.282	121	440	68	124	29	8	15	67	42	92	17	.344	.486
	Milwaukee (NL)	MAJ	.000	1	1	0	0	0	0	0	0	0	1	0	.000	.000
MAJOR LEAGUE TOTALS			.000	1	1	0	0	0	0	0	0	0	1	0	.000	.000
MINOR LEAGUE TOTALS			.296	505	1898	315	562	125	21	65	352	153	384	89	.351	.487

Ben Hendrickson, rhp

Born: Feb. 4, 1981. **Ht.:** 6-4. **Wt.:** 190. **Bats:** R. **Throws:** R. **School:** Jefferson HS, Bloomington, Minn. **Career Transactions:** Selected by Brewers in 10th round of 1999 draft; signed Sept. 1, 1999. **Signed by:** Harvey Kuenn Jr.

Despite bouncing back and forth between Triple-A Indianapolis and Milwaukee last season, Hendrickson was the International League pitcher of the year and topped the league in ERA. He lost his first six decisions in a rough major league debut before beating the Reds. Hendrickson relies on spotting his 88-91 mph fastball to set up a sharp 12-to-6 curveball. His changeup was much improved last year and helped him to keep hitters off balance. He has clean arm action and good command, though it wandered during his major league trial. He didn't show any signs of the elbow troubles that hindered him in 2003. Sometimes Hendrickson relies on his curveball too much, allowing hitters to sit on it. Because he doesn't blow the ball by hitters, he can't afford to work behind in the count, which he did too often in the majors. He'll need to continue to hone his changeup. Hendrickson looked more comfortable in his last few starts with the Brewers. It gave him an idea of the adjustments he needs to make in order to make the 2005 rotation in spring training.

Year	Club (League)	Class	W	L	ERA	G	GS	CG	SV	IP	H	R	ER	HR	BB	SO	AVG
2000	Ogden (Pio)	R	4	3	5.68	13	7	0	1	51	50	37	32	7	29	48	.245
2001	Beloit (Mid)	A	8	9	2.84	25	25	1	0	133	122	58	42	3	72	133	.246
2002	High Desert (Cal)	A	5	5	2.55	14	14	0	0	81	61	31	23	3	41	70	.209
	Huntsville (SL)	AA	4	2	2.97	13	13	0	0	70	57	31	23	2	35	50	.231
2003	Huntsville (SL)	AA	7	6	3.45	17	16	0	0	78	82	35	30	6	28	56	.278
2004	Indianapolis (IL)	AAA	11	3	2.02	21	21	2	0	125	114	32	28	6	26	93	.246
	Milwaukee (NL)	MAJ	1	8	6.22	10	9	0	0	46	58	33	32	6	20	29	.310
MAJOR LEAGUE TOTALS			1	8	6.22	10	9	0	0	46	58	33	32	6	20	29	.310
MINOR LEAGUE TOTALS			39	28	2.98	103	96	3	1	538	486	224	178	27	231	450	.243

Brad Nelson, of

Born: Dec. 23, 1982. **Ht.:** 6-2. **Wt.:** 220. **Bats:** L. **Throws:** R. **School:** Bishop Garrigan HS, Algona, Iowa. **Career Transactions:** Selected by Brewers in fourth round of 2001 draft; signed July 25, 2001. **Signed by:** Harvey Kuenn Jr./Larry Doughty.

Nelson was the organization's top prospect entering 2003 after leading the minors with 49 doubles and 116 RBIs as a 19-year-old. He was shelved for much of that season with a broken hamate bone in his right wrist, but he had a solid Double-A effort last year. A third baseman/pitcher in high school, he began his pro career at first base before moving to left field in 2003. Once he recovered from his wrist injury, Nelson got his smooth, powerful swing back and started driving the ball again. He uses the entire field and hits with power to both gaps. He shows good instincts and an average arm in left field. Everybody, including Nelson, knows what he must do to advance to the majors: improve his plate discipline and cut down on his strikeouts. Though he tries hard and is a smart defender, he has limited range. Nelson is progressing despite missing most of a year of development. He'll head to Triple-A and likely remain there for the entire season to get at-bats.

Year	Club (League)	Class	AVG	G	AB	R	H	2B	3B	HR	RBI	BB	SO	SB	OBP	SLG
2001	Brewers (AZL)	R	.302	17	63	10	19	6	1	0	13	8	18	0	.392	.429
	Ogden (Pio)	R	.262	13	42	5	11	4	0	0	10	3	9	0	.298	.357
2002	Beloit (Mid)	A	.297	106	417	70	124	38	2	17	99	34	86	4	.353	.520
	High Desert (Cal)	A	.255	26	102	24	26	11	0	3	17	12	28	0	.333	.451
2003	High Desert (Cal)	A	.311	41	167	23	52	9	1	1	18	12	22	2	.363	.395
	Huntsville (SL)	AA	.210	39	143	15	30	12	0	1	14	11	34	2	.274	.315
2004	Huntsville (SL)	AA	.254	137	500	61	127	31	1	19	77	47	146	11	.434	.321
MINOR LEAGUE TOTALS			.271	379	1434	208	389	111	5	41	248	127	343	19	.334	.441

Hernan Iribarren, 2b

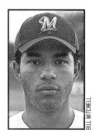

Born: June 29, 1984. **Ht.:** 6-1. **Wt.:** 160. **Bats:** L. **Throws:** R. **Career Transactions:** Signed out of Venezuela by Brewers, March 26, 2002. **Signed by:** Epy Guerrero.

Iribarren scorched Arizona League pitching in 2004, winning the batting race by 88 points and finishing with the second-highest average in league history. He also led the league in hits, on-base percentage and slugging en route to earning MVP honors. He's a hit machine who batted .329 in two years in the Rookie-level Dominican Summer League and .373 after a late-season promotion to low Class A. Iribarren puts the ball in play with consistent hard contact that belies his lean, wiry frame. He has very strong wrists and turns on inside pitches while taking offerings away to the opposite field. Iribarren projects to develop more power. He's an aggressive baserunner with decent range, good hands and arm strength in the field. Sometimes Iribarren takes bad at-bats into the field with him. He needs to continue to work on his defense, but should be able to make the necessary adjustments. Iribarren didn't miss a beat after his callup and will open 2005 back in low Class A. A natural hitter, he should move through the system quickly.

Year	Club (League)	Class	AVG	G	AB	R	H	2B	3B	HR	RBI	BB	SO	SB	OBP	SLG
2002	Brewers (DSL)	R	.314	66	223	35	70	13	2	2	34	19	43	7	.383	.417
2003	Brewers (DSL)	R	.344	64	227	43	78	12	7	2	27	24	36	17	.403	.485
2004	Beloit (Mid)	A	.373	15	67	12	25	6	5	1	10	5	16	1	.411	.657
MINOR LEAGUE TOTALS			.335	145	517	90	173	31	14	5	71	48	95	25	.395	.478

10 David Krynzel, of

Born: Nov. 7, 1981. **Ht.:** 6-1. **Wt.:** 180. **Bats:** L. **Throws:** L. **School:** Green Valley HS, Henderson, Nev. **Career Transactions:** Selected by Brewers in first round (11th overall) of 2000 draft; signed June 12, 2000. **Signed by:** Bruce Seid.

Krynzel fouled a ball off his right foot in late April last year, forcing him to miss two months. He recovered nicely and earned his first taste of big league action in September. Krynzel is a superb center fielder, combining range, athleticism and arm strength. His greatest asset is pure speed that can create havoc on the basepaths. He has a line-drive stroke, with more raw power than his numbers suggest. Krynzel needs to work counts better and reach base more consistently to hit atop the order. His swing can get long, leading to high strikeout totals. Despite his quickness, he has succeeded on just 66 percent of his pro steal attempts and must learn to read pitchers better. With Scott Podsednik gone to the White Sox in the Carlos Lee trade, Brady Clark is all that stands between Krynzel and the center-field job. He'll get a long look in spring training, but if he doesn't improve his plate discipline soon, he could get pigeon-holed into reserve-outfielder status.

Year	Club (League)	Class	AVG	G	AB	R	H	2B	3B	HR	RBI	BB	SO	SB	OBP	SLG
2000	Ogden (Pio)	R	.359	34	131	25	47	8	3	1	29	16	23	8	.442	.489
2001	Beloit (Mid)	A	.305	35	141	22	43	1	1	1	19	9	28	11	.364	.348
	High Desert (Cal)	A	.277	89	383	65	106	19	5	5	33	27	122	34	.329	.392
2002	High Desert (Cal)	A	.268	97	365	76	98	13	12	11	45	64	100	29	.391	.460
	Huntsville (SL)	AA	.240	31	129	13	31	2	3	2	13	4	30	13	.269	.349
2003	Huntsville (SL)	AA	.267	124	457	72	122	13	11	2	34	60	119	43	.357	.357
2004	Indianapolis (IL)	AAA	.271	69	258	36	70	10	4	6	26	20	63	10	.327	.411
	Milwaukee (NL)	MAJ	.220	16	41	6	9	1	0	0	3	3	15	0	.319	.244
MAJOR LEAGUE TOTALS			.220	16	41	6	9	1	0	0	3	3	15	0	.319	.244
MINOR LEAGUE TOTALS			.277	479	1864	309	517	66	39	28	199	200	485	148	.356	.400

11 Manny Parra, lhp

Born: Oct. 30, 1982. **Ht.:** 6-3. **Wt.:** 200. **Bats:** L. **Throws:** L. **School:** American River (Calif.) JC. **Career Transactions:** Selected by Brewers in 26th round of 2001 draft; signed May 27, 2002. **Signed by:** Justin McCray.

After signing for $1.55 million as a draft-and-follow in 2002, Parra blossomed in his first full season and was poised to move quickly in 2004. That didn't happen, because he experienced shoulder problems that cost him all of April, six months late in the season and an assignment to the Arizona Fall League. When healthy, Parra features an exciting combination of power pitching and control. His fastball sits in the low 90s and touches 95 with good movement, and his curveball can be devastating at times. He has improved his changeup. He aggressively attacks the strike zone, getting ahead of hitters and making them swing at his pitches. However, health has become an issue. Parra missed time in 2003 with a strained pectoral muscle before he began feeling weakness in his shoulder during last spring training. He must refine his mechanics to take stress off his arm and avoid future breakdowns. If Parra proves he's 100 percent in spring training, he'll be sent to Double-A. He can still move fast and has considerable upside as a starter—if he can stay healthy.

Year	Club (League)	Class	W	L	ERA	G	GS	CG	SV	IP	H	R	ER	HR	BB	SO	AVG
2002	Brewers (AZL)	R	0	0	4.50	1	1	0	0	2	1	1	1	1	0	4	.143
	Ogden (Pio)	R	3	1	3.21	11	10	0	0	48	59	30	17	3	10	51	.298
2003	Beloit (Mid)	A	11	2	2.73	23	23	1	0	139	127	50	42	9	24	117	.243
2004	Huntsville (SL)	AA	0	1	4.50	3	3	0	0	6	6	3	3	0	0	10	.240
	High Desert (Cal)	A	5	2	3.48	13	12	1	0	67	76	41	26	3	19	64	.284
MINOR LEAGUE TOTALS			19	6	3.06	51	49	2	0	262	269	125	89	16	53	246	.264

Dana Eveland, lhp

Born: Oct. 29, 1983. **Ht.:** 6-1. **Wt.:** 240. **Bats:** L. **Throws:** L. **School:** JC of the Canyons (Calif.). **Career Transactions:** Selected by Brewers in 16th round of 2002 draft; signed May 26, 2003. **Signed by:** Corey Rodriguez.

Like Manny Parra, a draft-and-follow originally taken in 2002, Eveland dominated as a closer in his pro debut before making a transition to the rotation last year. Though he's projected as a reliever in the long term, the Brewers wanted him to start so he could hone his entire four-pitch repertoire. Eveland throws an 89-92 mph fastball and runs it up to 94 mph. His curveball and slider are average at times but inconsistent, and he also has a changeup. He displays good poise on the mound and has some deception as well as a feel for setting hitters up. He pounds the strike zone and usually works ahead in the count. Only one thing about Eveland scares the Brewers: his stocky frame. He's built a bit too much like David Wells for their liking, though he hired a personal trainer and vowed to spend more time on conditioning. If he can keep his weight in control, he should move quickly. Milwaukee won't hesitate to keep him in Double-A, where he jumped after spending most of last season in low Class A, if he arrives in shape and performs well in spring training.

Year	Club (League)	Class	W	L	ERA	G	GS	CG	SV	IP	H	R	ER	HR	BB	SO	AVG
2003	Helena (Pio)	R	2	1	2.08	19	0	0	14	26	30	9	6	1	8	41	.286
2004	Huntsville (SL)	AA	0	2	2.28	4	4	0	0	24	23	9	6	0	4	14	.253
	Beloit (Mid)	A	9	6	2.84	22	16	1	2	117	108	48	37	8	24	119	.242
MINOR LEAGUE TOTALS			11	9	2.64	45	20	1	16	167	161	66	49	9	36	174	.250

Jorge de la Rosa, lhp

Born: April 5, 1981. **Ht.:** 6-1. **Wt.:** 190. **Bats:** L. **Throws:** L. **Career Transactions:** Signed out of Mexico by Diamondbacks, March 20, 1998 . . . Contract purchased by Monterrey (Mexican) from Diamondbacks, April 2, 2000 . . . Contract purchased by Red Sox from Monterrey, Feb. 22, 2001 . . . Traded by Red Sox with LHP Casey Fossum, RHP Brandon Lyon and OF Mike Goss to Diamondbacks for RHP Curt Schilling, Nov. 28, 2003 . . . Traded by Diamondbacks with 2B Junior Spivey, 1B Lyle Overbay, C Chad Moeller, INF Craig Counsell and LHP Chris Capuano to Brewers for 1B Richie Sexson, LHP Shane Nance and OF Noochie Varner, Dec. 1, 2003. **Signed by:** Oswaldo Alvarez (Diamondbacks).

The Brewers were pleased to acquire de la Rosa as one of six players from Arizona in the blockbuster Richie Sexson deal last offseason. Just days earlier, he had been traded by the Red Sox to the Diamondbacks in the Curt Schilling deal. Milwaukee thought de la Rosa was further along in his development than he turned out to be, however. He first fought command problems in Triple-A, then experienced elbow discomfort, which likely contributed to his difficulties finding the strike zone. He was shut down for a month before returning to the rotation and eventually making it to Milwaukee for a late-season cup of coffee. De la Rosa gets his fastball to the plate at 90-93 mph and has reached 95 in the past. He also shows a solid curveball with sweeping action and depth, along with a much-improved changeup. Control continues to be a major concern. When he throws strikes, he looks the part of a top pitching prospect. With a decent camp, he could start knocking at the door of the Brewers rotation. Some scouts say he could eventually evolve into a late-inning reliever.

Year	Club (League)	Class	W	L	ERA	G	GS	CG	SV	IP	H	R	ER	HR	BB	SO	AVG
1998	Diamondbacks (DSL)	R	1	0	4.50	13	0	0	1	14	8	7	7	3	8	21	.160
1999	Diamondbacks (AZL)	R	0	0	3.21	8	0	0	2	14	12	5	5	1	3	17	.226
	High Desert (Cal)	A	0	0	0.00	2	0	0	0	3	1	0	0	2	3	.100
	Missoula (Pio)	R	0	1	7.98	13	0	0	2	15	22	17	13	2	9	14	.333
2000	Monterrey (Mex)	AAA	3	2	6.28	37	0	0	1	39	38	27	27	2	32	50	.257
2001	Sarasota (FSL)	A	0	1	1.21	12	0	0	2	30	13	7	4	0	12	27	.127
	Trenton (EL)	AA	1	3	5.84	29	0	0	0	37	56	35	24	4	20	27	.348
2002	Sarasota (FSL)	A	7	7	3.65	23	23	1	0	121	105	53	49	10	52	95	.231
	Trenton (EL)	AA	1	2	5.50	4	4	0	0	18	17	12	11	0	9	15	.239
2003	Portland (EL)	AA	6	3	2.80	22	20	0	1	100	87	39	31	6	36	102	.236
	Pawtucket (IL)	AAA	1	2	3.75	5	5	0	0	24	27	14	10	0	12	17	.278
2004	Milwaukee (NL)	MAJ	0	3	6.35	5	5	0	0	23	29	20	16	1	14	5	.309
	Indianapolis (IL)	AAA	5	6	4.52	20	20	0	0	86	80	45	43	9	36	86	.249
MAJOR LEAGUE TOTALS			0	3	6.35	5	5	0	0	23	29	20	16	1	14	5	.309
MINOR LEAGUE TOTALS			25	27	4.04	188	72	1	9	499	466	261	224	37	231	474	.245

Nelson Cruz, of

Born: July 1, 1981. **Ht.:** 6-3. **Wt.:** 175. **Bats:** R. **Throws:** R. **Career Transactions:** Signed out of Dominican Republic by Mets, Feb. 17, 1998 . . . Traded by Mets to Athletics for SS Jorge Velandia, Aug. 30, 2000 . . . Traded by Athletics with RHP Justin Lehr to Brewers for 2B Keith Ginter, Dec. 16, 2004. **Signed by:** Eddy Toledo (Mets).

With the A's looking to improve their depth at second base, the Brewers were able to get

Cruz and reliever Justin Lehr for Keith Ginter in December. Cruz, whom Oakland stole from the Mets in a 2000 deal for Jorge Velandia, improved his stock significantly in 2004, when he was one of five hitters in the minors to reach 300 total bases. He's a legitimate five-tool talent. He has power to all fields and made tremendous strides in his pitch recognition last year, learning to lay off high fastballs and take pitches the other way. He has a plus arm, runs well and is an asset in right field. Despite the progress he made in his approach, Cruz still has a tendency to overswing. He tries to hit every ball farther than the last, leaving him slow out of the box. He'll open 2005 in Triple-A and should be ready for the majors by 2006, though Geoff Jenkins and newly acquired Carlos Lee have a firm hold on the corner-outfield spots in Milwaukee. Cruz also will have to contend with Corey Hart and Brad Nelson for playing time.

Year	Club (League)	Class	AVG	G	AB	R	H	2B	3B	HR	RBI	BB	SO	SB	OBP	SLG
1998	Mets (DSL)	R	.271	30	70	10	19	0	0	1	13	7	21	6	.363	.314
1999	Mets (DSL)	R	.200	35	90	7	18	4	1	0	11	6	21	6	.255	.267
	Mets 2 (DSL)	R	.278	36	115	20	32	4	1	1	21	16	27	14	.366	.357
2000	Mets East (DSL)	R	.351	69	259	60	91	14	4	15	80	33	56	17	.434	.610
2001	Athletics (AZL)	R	.250	23	88	11	22	3	1	3	16	4	29	6	.283	.409
2002	Vancouver (NWL)	A	.276	63	214	23	59	14	0	4	25	9	58	12	.316	.397
2003	Kane County (Mid)	A	.238	119	470	65	112	26	2	20	85	29	128	10	.292	.430
2004	High Desert (Cal)	A	.345	66	261	54	90	27	1	11	52	24	73	8	.407	.582
	Midland (TL)	AA	.313	67	262	51	82	14	2	14	46	26	69	8	.377	.542
	Sacramento (PCL)	AAA	.231	4	13	4	3	1	0	1	2	1	7	0	.286	.538
MINOR LEAGUE TOTALS			.287	512	1842	305	528	107	12	70	351	155	489	87	.349	.472

15 Lou Palmisano, c

Born: Sept. 16, 1982. **Ht.:** 6-1 **Wt.:** 205. **Bats:** R. **Throws:** R. **School:** Broward (Fla.) CC. **Career Transactions:** Selected by Brewers in third round of 2003 draft; signed June 3, 2003. **Signed by:** Larry Pardo.

Palmisano's reputation as a leader took something of a hit in low Class A last year, when he was involved in a curfew violation on a road trip. The Brewers believe that was an isolated incident, however, and still rank Palmisano as their top catching prospect. He won Rookie-level Pioneer League MVP honors in his 2003 pro debut after he led the league in hitting, on-base percentage and slugging. Palmisano has a quick bat and hits to all fields, and he could develop more power as he matures. He sometimes gets too aggressive at the plate and chases pitches out of the strike zone. He does draw walks, however, and he runs well for a catcher. Palmisano is athletic behind the plate and has soft hands, a quick release and a strong arm. His throwing mechanics got out of whack in low Class A, where he erased 30 percent of basestealers, prompting the club to bring him to Milwaukee for a refresher course on defense. He also worked with instructor Charlie Greene during instructional league. After those sessions, he seemed back on track. Short of catching at the top levels of the organization, the Brewers would like to keep pushing Palmisano. He could open the 2005 season in Double-A.

Year	Club (League)	Class	AVG	G	AB	R	H	2B	3B	HR	RBI	BB	SO	SB	OBP	SLG
2003	Helena (Pio)	R	.391	47	174	32	68	13	2	6	43	18	29	13	.458	.592
2004	Beloit (Mid)	A	.293	113	409	59	120	22	3	7	65	43	93	3	.371	.413
MINOR LEAGUE TOTALS			.322	160	583	91	188	35	5	13	108	61	122	16	.398	.467

16 Yovanni Gallardo, rhp

Born: Feb. 27, 1986. **Ht.:** 6-3. **Wt.:** 185. **Bats:** R. **Throws:** R. **School:** Trimble Tech HS, Fort Worth, Texas. **Career Transactions:** Selected by Brewers in second round of 2004 draft; signed June 30, 2004. **Signed by:** Jim Stevenson.

The Brewers were excited that Gallardo, who rang up 25 strikeouts in an 11-inning high school game in March, was still on the board in the second round last June. A talented athlete who was a terrific soccer player in high school, Gallardo attracted scouts with a live arm and athleticism. Signed for $725,000, he has a 91-94 mph fastball that already reaches 96, a power curveball and an improving change. Scouts also love his strong, projectable frame and the poise he shows on the mound. The Brewers were so impressed with his performance in his debut that they promoted him to low Class A as an 18-year-old. Gallardo was invited to instructional league to work on his mechanics and sharpen his delivery, but he couldn't stay for the duration because of an illness in his family. Though he'll still be a teenager, he should be able to earn a full-season assignment with a good spring training.

Year	Club (League)	Class	W	L	ERA	G	GS	CG	SV	IP	H	R	ER	HR	BB	SO	AVG
2004	Brewers (AZL)	R	0	0	0.47	6	6	0	0	19	14	3	1	0	4	23	.203
	Beloit (Mid)	A	0	1	12.27	2	2	0	0	7	12	10	10	2	4	8	.400
MINOR LEAGUE TOTALS			0	1	3.71	8	8	0	0	27	26	13	11	2	8	31	.263

17 Jeff Housman, lhp

Born: Aug. 4, 1981. **Ht.:** 6-3. **Wt.:** 180. **Bats:** L. **Throws:** L. **School:** Cal State Fullerton. **Career Transactions:** Selected by Brewers in 33rd round of 2002 draft; signed June 10, 2002. **Signed by:** Bruce Seid.

Housman didn't look like much when the Brewers signed him as a 33rd-round pick in 2002. He went 0-4, 4.89 at Cal State Fullerton, then 1-3, 8.07 in Rookie ball during his pro debut. His stuff still doesn't turn heads, as his fringy fastball tops out at 89-90 mph, his changeup is inconsistent and his pitch counts get out of hand on occasion. But Housman knows how to pitch, which qualifies him as a crafty lefty and got him to Double-A in his first full season. His slider is his best pitch, especially against lefthanders, who managed a .225 average against him in Double-A last year. Like many southpaws who rely on location, he's susceptible to giving up a lot of hits. However, he has also been able to pile up strikeouts without walking many hitters. Using deception and location rather than velocity, he makes batters fish for pitches they shouldn't go after. Housman has good size and a consistent delivery but he missed his spots and took a beating when promoted to Triple-A in the final weeks last season. He'll have to continue to be fine in the upper levels to survive, and he'll get another shot at confusing Triple-A hitters this year.

Year	Club (League)	Class	W	L	ERA	G	GS	CG	SV	IP	H	R	ER	HR	BB	SO	AVG
2002	Ogden (Pio)	R	1	3	8.07	16	5	0	0	32	55	38	29	5	12	23	.372
2003	Beloit (Mid)	A	2	7	1.81	20	15	0	0	89	79	40	18	5	26	50	.231
	Huntsville (SL)	AA	3	2	3.30	8	8	1	0	46	49	21	17	4	17	26	.274
2004	Huntsville (SL)	AA	5	8	3.13	23	20	0	1	112	108	55	39	10	38	121	.247
	Indianapolis (IL)	AAA	1	1	7.71	5	3	0	0	19	31	16	16	3	13	13	.383
MINOR LEAGUE TOTALS			12	21	3.59	72	51	1	1	299	322	170	119	27	106	233	.271

18 Dennis Sarfate, rhp

Born: April 9, 1981. **Ht.:** 6-4. **Wt.:** 215. **Bats:** R. **Throws:** R. **School:** Chandler-Gilbert (Ariz.) CC. **Career Transactions:** Selected by Brewers in ninth round of 2001 draft; signed June 18, 2001. **Signed by:** Brian Johnson.

After taking a big step forward in 2003, Sarfate took a big step back last year for one simple reason: He couldn't throw strikes. While his control wasn't sterling in low Class A, it declined in Double-A, and against better hitters he was far more vulnerable when he couldn't locate his pitches. With a heavy fastball in the 91-95 mph range, he became too consumed with radar-gun readings and overthrew, getting his mechanics out of whack. Sarfate finally settled in and pitched better in August. With his above-average fastball, a sharp slider and decent changeup, he has the pitches to succeed. But unlike 2003, when he clicked off 11 victories in a row to end the season, his confidence waned when he struggled. His command was absent again in the Arizona Fall League, where he walked 17 in 22 innings and hit 98 mph with his fastball. Considering Sarfate skipped high Class A, there's no reason to push him to Triple-A yet. If he can't find the strike zone more consistently, he may be converted to a late-inning reliever.

Year	Club (League)	Class	W	L	ERA	G	GS	CG	SV	IP	H	R	ER	HR	BB	SO	AVG
2001	Ogden (Pio)	R	1	2	4.63	9	4	0	1	23	20	13	12	4	10	32	.230
2002	Brewers (AZL)	R	0	0	2.57	5	5	0	0	14	6	4	4	0	7	22	.125
	Ogden (Pio)	R	0	0	9.00	1	0	0	0	1	2	1	1	0	1	2	.400
2003	Beloit (Mid)	A	12	2	2.84	26	26	0	0	140	114	50	44	11	66	140	.227
2004	Huntsville (SL)	AA	7	12	3.98	28	25	0	0	129	128	71	57	12	78	113	.266
MINOR LEAGUE TOTALS			20	16	3.46	69	60	0	1	307	270	139	118	27	162	309	.240

19 Josh Baker, rhp

Born: March 28, 1983. **Ht.:** 6-5. **Wt.:** 220. **Bats:** R. **Throws:** R. **School:** Rice University. **Career Transactions:** Selected by Brewers in fourth round of 2004 draft; signed June 8, 2004. **Signed by:** Ray Montgomery.

Baker got lost in the shuffle behind Philip Humber, Jeff Niemann and Wade Townsend at Rice—all three went in the top eight picks of the 2004 draft—but scouts were well aware of his arm. Drafted in the fourth round out of high school, he went in the same spot last June and signed for $320,000. If bloodlines count for anything, Baker is in great shape. His father Johnny was an NFL linebacker, his uncle Frank played in the majors and his brother Jacob played in the minors. He even has a big league brother-in-law in Lance Berkman. Baker's fastball resides in the 88-92 mph range, and he also throws a hard slider, a curveball and an improving changeup. He also used a splitter in college. He demonstrates solid command of each pitch. Convinced that he threw too many breaking balls at Rice, the Brewers got Baker to throw more fastballs and work on locating his heater. None of his pitches is exceptional, so Baker must hit his spots and learn to set up hitters. After pitching at an advanced college program, he could move through the system at a rapid pace, depending on his ability to work ahead of hitters and keep his pitch counts in check. At this point, he projects as a bottom-of-the-rotation pitcher in the majors and probably will start 2004 in low Class A.

Year	Club (League)	Class	W	L	ERA	G	GS	CG	SV	IP	H	R	ER	HR	BB	SO	AVG
2004	Helena (Pio)	R	1	1	3.66	15	8	0	2	52	37	22	21	5	20	44	.203
MINOR LEAGUE TOTALS			1	1	3.66	15	8	0	2	52	37	22	21	5	20	44	.203

20 Josh Wahpepah, rhp

Born: July 17, 1984. **Ht.:** 6-5. **Wt.:** 195. **Bats:** R. **Throws:** R. **School:** Cowley County (Kan.) CC. **Career Transactions:** Selected by Brewers in third round of 2004 draft; signed June 8, 2004. **Signed by:** Jim Stevenson.

The Tigers made Wahpepah a priority draft-and-follow after taking him in the 18th round in 2003, but they wouldn't meet his bonus demands after he repeated as a junior college all-American last spring. A full-blooded Native American, he signed with the Brewers for $400,000 as a third-round pick. Wahpepah's fastball has good velocity at 91-93 mph, but the pitch's hard downward sink is what makes him so effective in mowing down hitters. He also throws a slider and changeup, and he impressed Milwaukee by breaking out a nasty curveball in instructional league. In fact, no first-year pitcher was more impressive during the fall program. With a somewhat unorthodox delivery that hitters find deceptive, Wahpepah must stay on top of his mechanics to stay away from arm problems and continue to throw strikes. Some scouts questioned whether his motion would allow him to have consistent control of his secondary pitchers. He'll start 2005 in low Class A.

Year	Club (League)	Class	W	L	ERA	G	GS	CG	SV	IP	H	R	ER	HR	BB	SO	AVG
2004	Helena (Pio)	R	4	2	4.40	15	7	0	2	47	58	28	23	3	17	35	.307
MINOR LEAGUE TOTALS			4	2	4.40	15	7	0	2	47	58	28	23	3	17	35	.307

21 Justin Lehr, rhp

Born: Aug. 3, 1977. **Ht.:** 6-1. **Wt.:** 200. **Bats:** R. **Throws:** R. **School:** University of Southern California. **Career Transactions:** Selected by Athletics in eighth round of 1999 draft; signed June 29, 1999 . . . Traded by Athletics with OF Nelson Cruz to Brewers for 2B Keith Ginter, Dec. 15, 2004. **Signed by:** Rick Magnante (Athletics).

Lehr spent his first three years in college as a catcher at UC Santa Barbara before transferring to Southern California and becoming a two-way player, serving as the No. 2 starter behind Barry Zito. Acquired in the Keith Ginter trade with Oakland, Lehr had modest success in the minors as a starter, and began to develop more quickly after moving to the bullpen in 2002. Pitching in shorter stints helped his fastball, which has gone from 88-91 mph to 91-95 and features nice run. His main secondary pitch is a slider, and he occasionally will turn to the splitter and changeup he used in his rotation days. The key for Lehr is to throw strikes and stay ahead in the count. When he did that in Triple-A, he was able to put hitters away. He has good but not great stuff, so when his control wavered in the majors, he had trouble getting outs. Lehr also had trouble with lefthanders in the big leagues, so he may need to dust off his changeup more often. The Brewers traded their top two relievers from 2004, Dan Kolb and Luis Vizcaino, so Lehr will get every opportunity to fill a hole in the big league bullpen.

Year	Club (League)	Class	W	L	ERA	G	GS	CG	SV	IP	H	R	ER	HR	BB	SO	AVG
1999	So. Oregon (NWL)	A	2	6	5.95	14	4	0	0	42	62	36	28	3	17	40	.341
2000	Modesto (Cal)	A	13	6	3.19	29	25	0	0	175	161	71	62	10	46	138	.249
	Sacramento (PCL)	AAA	0	0	1.25	1	1	0	0	4	7	5	5	1	3	3	.389
2001	Midland (TL)	AA	11	1	5.45	29	27	0	0	155	206	107	94	20	43	103	.318
2002	Midland (TL)	AA	8	3	4.05	58	0	0	4	80	88	39	36	7	31	59	.290
2003	Sacramento (PCL)	AAA	3	2	3.72	53	0	0	4	75	74	34	31	3	27	64	.259
2004	Sacramento (PCL)	AAA	4	2	2.65	32	0	0	13	37	37	14	11	1	10	40	.250
	Oakland (AL)	MAJ	1	1	5.23	27	0	0	0	33	35	19	19	3	14	16	.280
MAJOR LEAGUE TOTALS			1	1	5.24	27	0	0	0	33	35	19	19	3	14	16	.280
MINOR LEAGUE TOTALS			41	20	4.22	216	57	0	21	569	635	306	267	45	177	447	.285

22 Mike Jones, rhp

Born: April 23, 1983. **Ht.:** 6-4. **Wt.:** 200. **Bats:** R. **Throws:** R. **School:** Thunderbird HS, Phoenix. **Career Transactions:** Selected by Brewers in first round (12th overall) of 2001 draft; signed June 27, 2001. **Signed by:** Brian Johnson.

Entering 2003, Jones was the top pitching prospect in the organization and ranked among the best in baseball. But following an outstanding beginning to his season in Double-A, he was shut down for the entire second half of '03 with an ailing elbow. Returning to action last year, Jones overcompensated for the elbow and developed a lesion on the labrum in his shoulder. After surgery, he'll miss all of the 2005 season. The 12th overall pick in 2001 and recipient of a $2.075 million bonus, Jones didn't look like a breakdown candidate coming out of high school. He operated with textbook mechanics, but they deteriorated after he turned pro. Whether Jones recovers his lively low- to mid-90s fastball and sharp-breaking curveball remains to be seen. He still needs to refine his changeup and control when he returns. His work ethic and maturity will be tested with a long rehabilitation program.

Year	Club (League)	Class	W	L	ERA	G	GS	CG	SV	IP	H	R	ER	HR	BB	SO	AVG
2001	Ogden (Pio)	R	4	1	3.74	9	7	0	0	34	29	17	14	1	10	32	.236
2002	Beloit (Mid)	A	7	7	3.12	27	27	0	0	139	135	63	48	3	62	132	.256
2003	Huntsville (SL)	AA	7	2	2.40	17	17	0	0	98	87	35	26	4	47	63	.238
2004	Huntsville (SL)	AA	1	4	4.18	6	6	0	0	24	22	14	11	0	13	16	.247
MINOR LEAGUE TOTALS			19	14	3.03	59	57	0	0	294	273	129	99	8	132	243	.247

23 Luis Pena, lhp

Born: Jan 10, 1983. **Ht.:** 6-5. **Wt.:** 160. **Bats:** R. **Throws:** R. **Career Transactions:** Signed out of Venezuela by Brewers, July 12, 1999. **Signed by:** Epy Guerrero.

After three years in Rookie ball and an unremarkable season in low Class A, Pena returned to Beloit last year and suddenly took off. The velocity on his fastball spiked, and he began to regularly dial it into the low to mid-90s. With a tall, lanky build and fluid arm action, he overpowered hitters at times. Pena also throws a curveball and changeup and is working on a splitter as well. He has good life on his fastball but must continue to develop his breaking stuff. Though some scouts say Pena could be a successful late-inning reliever, the Brewers want him to continue to start so he can develop all of his pitches. Still young at 22, he'll be given plenty of time to develop. A classic example of a pitcher who benefited from repeating levels, Pena probably will move up to Milwaukee's new high Class A Brevard County affiliate this year. The Brewers have been impressed with his intelligence and focused approach on the mound, which they think will allow him to contine to improve.

Year	Club (League)	Class	W	L	ERA	G	GS	CG	SV	IP	H	R	ER	HR	BB	SO	AVG
2000	San Joaquin (VSL)	R	2	3	4.02	20	7	0	2	54	35	31	24	7	30	41	.190
2001	Brewers (AZL)	R	3	4	4.63	11	2	0	0	35	42	23	18	2	13	20	.300
2002	Brewers (AZL)	R	4	1	3.49	11	7	0	0	49	45	28	19	1	24	52	.239
2003	Beloit (Mid)	A	2	6	3.90	23	18	1	0	90	92	51	39	6	46	53	.267
2004	Beloit (Mid)	A	9	3	3.92	21	16	0	0	99	101	50	43	7	35	76	.262
MINOR LEAGUE TOTALS			20	17	3.94	86	50	1	2	326	315	183	143	23	148	242	.254

24 Anthony Gwynn, of

Born: Oct. 4, 1982. **Ht.:** 6-0. **Wt.:** 185. **Bats:** L. **Throws:** R. **School:** San Diego State University. **Career Transactions:** Selected by Brewers in second round of 2003 draft; signed June 19, 2003. **Signed by:** Bruce Seid.

Though he's not as advanced, Gwynn has been hurried along at the same pace as fellow 2003 draftee Rickie Weeks. The wisdom of that approach is debatable. Unlike his father—future Hall of Famer Tony Gwynn, who coached him at San Diego State—Anthony might not hit enough to be a regular player. Slight of build, Gwynn also wore down at the end of the 2004 season and was overmatched in the Arizona Fall League, where he managed a .167 average and one extra-base hit in 72 at-bats. With little pop in his bat, he must get stronger and prove he can handle himself at the plate on a regular basis. He sometimes thinks too much at the plate and gets himself in trouble. His best offensive skill is his outstanding bunting. There are no doubts about Gwynn's defensive capabilities. A superb center fielder with good instincts and speed, he chases down drives in the gaps with the greatest of ease. He reads the ball well off the bat and gets good jumps. Because he can run, steal bases and play outstanding defense, Gwynn will continue to get chances to prove he should be an everyday player. The Brewers need to be more realistic about his development path and allow him to succeed before moving him to Triple-A.

Year	Club (League)	Class	AVG	G	AB	R	H	2B	3B	HR	RBI	BB	SO	SB	OBP	SLG
2003	Beloit (Mid)	A	.280	61	236	35	66	8	0	1	33	32	31	14	.364	.326
2004	Huntsville (SL)	AA	.243	138	534	74	130	20	5	2	37	53	95	35	.318	.311
MINOR LEAGUE TOTALS			.255	199	770	109	196	28	5	3	70	85	126	49	.333	.316

25 Alcides Escobar, ss

Born: Dec. 16, 1986. **Ht.:** 6-1. **Wt.:** 155. **Bats:** R. **Throws:** R. **Career Transactions:** Signed out of Venezuela by Brewers, July 9, 2003. **Signed by:** Epy Guerrero.

The more the Brewers saw Escobar in his first year of pro ball last year, the harder it was to believe he was only 17 years old. He looked even better in instructional league, where he showed an uncanny knack for putting the ball in play, striking out just two times. Milwaukee scouts liken Escobar to a young Tony Fernandez, with a lean and lanky build and knack for making the plays in the field. He displays good hands, quickness and range on defense. His arm is nothing spectacular but strong enough to keep him at shortstop for now. On the bases, he's a legitimate threat to steal with above-average speed. Primarily a contact hitter at present, the Brewers think Escobar will develop power as he fills out and matures. They plan on teaming him with second- base prospect Hernan Iribarren in low Class A this season, and they're excited about watching that double-play combination in action.

Year	Club (League)	Class	AVG	G	AB	R	H	2B	3B	HR	RBI	BB	SO	SB	OBP	SLG
2004	Helena (Pio)	R	.281	67	231	38	65	8	0	2	24	20	44	20	.345	.342
MINOR LEAGUE TOTALS			.281	67	231	38	65	8	0	2	24	20	44	20	.345	.342

26 Angel Salome, c

Born: June 8, 1986. **Ht.:** 5-7. **Wt.:** 190. **Bats:** R. **Throws:** R. **School:** George Washington HS, New York, N.Y. **Career Transactions:** Selected by Brewers in fifth round of 2004 draft; signed June 12, 2004. **Signed by:** Tony Blengino.

When the Brewers drafted Salome out of the same high school that produced Manny Ramirez—George Washington in the Bronx—they considered him primarily a defensive specialist, though he was able to match Ramirez' production last spring by hitting .720 with 14 homers during his high school season. Salome suffered a broken hamate bone after 20 games in Rookie ball. When he arrived in instructional league, he started whacking the ball all over the park, socking two homers and a double in one game. Should he continue to swing the bat as he did in instructional league, showing good pop and hitting to all fields, Milwaukee will have much more than it bargained for. Salome's throwing arm stands out the most, grading as a 70 on the 20-80 scouting scale. He gets the ball to second in a hurry, drawing comparisons to Pudge Rodriguez at the same age. Salome threw out 32 percent of basestealers in his pro debut. He also has good hands behind the plate, though he needs to work on his receiving. He handles pitchers well and has a great work ethic. With advanced defensive skills for a teenager and the desire to improve, Salome has a lot of upside at a position where the Brewers have struggled to develop prospects. He could make it to low Class A this year, though beginning the season in extended spring is also an option.

Year	Club (League)	Class	AVG	G	AB	R	H	2B	3B	HR	RBI	BB	SO	SB	OBP	SLG
2004	Brewers (AZL)	R	.235	20	81	7	19	7	0	0	8	4	14	2	.271	.321
MINOR LEAGUE TOTALS			.235	20	81	7	19	7	0	0	8	4	14	2	.271	.321

27 Steve Moss, of

Born: Jan. 12, 1984. **Ht.:** 6-2. **Wt.:** 180. **Bats:** R. **Throws:** R. **School:** Notre Dame HS, Sherman Oaks, Calif. **Career Transactions:** Selected by Brewers in 29th round of 2002 draft; signed July 13, 2002. **Signed by:** Corey Rodriguez.

Moss has struggled to stay on the field. He slid to the 29th round in 2002 when an ankle injury hampered him as a high school senior (scouts also believed he was intent on attending UCLA). Since signing, he dislocated his left shoulder diving for a ball in the outfield in 2003, then missed time last year with a broken bone in his foot. Moss' bad luck continued when he contracted mononucleosis during instructional league. During the few extended spells when he has been healthy, Moss has shown enough talent to keep the Brewers intrigued. He's an aggressive player with a nice, short stroke, yet he lacks patience at the plate and strikes out too much. He offers power potential as well as speed. He gets good breaks on balls in center field, and has a plus arm for the position. Moss' raw talent could all come together at once and allow him to make up for lost time. He'll jump to high Class A in 2005 and try to show what he's capable of over the course of a full, healthy season.

Year	Club (League)	Class	AVG	G	AB	R	H	2B	3B	HR	RBI	BB	SO	SB	OBP	SLG
2002	Brewers (AZL)	R	.292	30	106	20	31	8	2	1	20	22	32	3	.414	.434
	Ogden (Pio)	R	.500	5	8	3	4	2	1	0	3	1	1	0	.538	1.000
2003	Beloit (Mid)	A	.290	57	186	25	54	8	3	1	22	32	44	7	.398	.382
2004	Beloit (Mid)	A	.235	102	362	41	85	17	4	8	34	35	90	6	.318	.370
MINOR LEAGUE TOTALS			.263	194	662	89	174	35	10	10	79	90	167	16	.361	.391

28 Adam Heether, 3b

Born: Jan. 14, 1982. **Ht.:** 6-0. **Wt.:** 200. **Bats:** R. **Throws:** R. **School:** Long Beach State University. **Career Transactions:** Selected by Brewers in 11th round of 2003 draft; signed June 10, 2003. **Signed by:** Bruce Seid.

The Rockies drafted Heether in the 31st round out of high school and the 28th round out of Modesto (Calif.) Junior College, but he didn't sign until the Brewers took him in the 11th round after one season at Long Beach State. His first taste of pro ball wasn't kind to him, but he rebounded to tie for the club lead with 17 homers when he returned to Beloit last year. He was old for low Class A at age 22, but Milwaukee took note of his power potential, which he could unlock further as he develops more plate discipline. He continued to hit balls hard regularly in instructional league. Heether holds his own defensively at third base, with good hands and a strong arm. Before he signed, some scouts thought he projected better at second base and might be an interesting project as a catcher. The Brewers have been impressed with Heether's mature approach to the game and could jump him to Double-A to start 2005.

Year	Club (League)	Class	AVG	G	AB	R	H	2B	3B	HR	RBI	BB	SO	SB	OBP	SLG
2003	Brewers (AZL)	R	.000	3	11	1	0	0	0	0	0	2	1	0	.214	.000
	Beloit (Mid)	A	.228	47	171	28	39	12	1	2	22	18	28	4	.313	.345
2004	Beloit (Mid)	A	.252	128	476	65	120	35	4	17	72	37	93	2	.313	.450
MINOR LEAGUE TOTALS			.242	178	658	94	159	47	5	19	94	57	122	6	.311	.415

29 Vinny Rottino, util

Born: April 7, 1980. **Ht.:** 6-1. **Wt.:** 200. **Bats:** R. **Throws:** R. **School:** University of Wisconsin-La Crosse. **Career Transactions:** Signed by Brewers as nondrafted free agent, Feb. 3, 2003. **Signed by:** Brian Johnson.

Rottino hit .410 at Wisconsin-La Crosse to earn NCAA Division III all-america honors in 2002, but that wasn't enough to get him drafted. He enrolled in pharmacy school at Wisconsin and played in the semipro Land O' Lakes League. Signed as a nondrafted free agent before the 2003 season, Rottino was the Brewers' minor league player of the year in 2004. He broke Prince Fielder's Beloit record for RBIs, leading the Midwest League as well, and capped his season by playing all nine positions on the final day of the season. He even pitched a perfect ninth inning. Though at age 24 he was much older than the typical low Class A player, Rottino showed legitimate offensive tools. He has quick hands, good balance and a knack for putting the bat on the ball. He has good pop but is more of a gap hitter than a slugger, and he could stand to draw a few more walks. Rottino's biggest problem is that he hasn't found a position. He spent most of last year at DH, and even before the final day he saw playing time at left field, right field, third base, first base, second base and catcher. Milwaukee brought Rottino to instructional league to try to make a catcher out of him. He looked OK behind the plate, but the club ultimately decided to make him a super utility player. He'll be 25 this season, so he needs to show what he can do in Double-A.

Year	Club (League)	Class	AVG	G	AB	R	H	2B	3B	HR	RBI	BB	SO	SB	OBP	SLG
2003	Helena (Pio)	R	.311	64	222	42	69	10	0	1	20	28	25	5	.404	.369
2004	Beloit (Mid)	A	.304	139	529	78	161	25	9	17	124	40	71	5	.352	.482
MINOR LEAGUE TOTALS			..306	203	751	120	230	35	9	18	144	68	96	10	.368	.449

30 Chris Saenz, rhp

Born: Aug. 14, 1981. **Ht.:** 6-3. **Wt.:** 200. **Bats:** R. **Throws:** R. **School:** Pima (Ariz.) CC. **Career Transactions:** Selected by Brewers in 28th round of 2001 draft; signed June 6, 2001. **Signed by:** Brian Johnson.

Saenz was minding his own business in Double-A when Milwaukee summoned him for an emergency big league start last April 24. After depleting their bullpen in a 15-inning game and placing Chris Capuano on the disabled list, the Brewers decided Saenz was their best option. Against the Cardinals, the highest scoring team in the National League, he struck out seven over six shutout innings to earn the victory. Afterward, Saenz returned to Double-A and pitched well—until late June, when he blew out his elbow. Following Tommy John surgery, he'll miss the entire 2005 season. Before he got hurt, Saenz had an 88-94 mph fastball, an improving slider and a changeup. A reliever his first two years in pro ball, he initially struggled as a starter in 2003. Then former roving pitching coordinator Dwight Bernard fixed a glitch in his delivery, allowing Saenz to do a better job of staying on top of his pitches. That improved the sink on his fastball, the depth on his slider and his overall command.

Year	Club (League)	Class	W	L	ERA	G	GS	CG	SV	IP	H	R	ER	HR	BB	SO	AVG
2001	Ogden (Pio)	R	3	1	4.24	21	4	0	0	47	43	25	22	5	14	48	.251
2002	Beloit (Mid)	A	3	5	3.51	37	0	0	8	74	59	31	29	5	32	99	.217
2003	High Desert (Cal)	A	9	9	5.20	26	26	1	0	128	121	80	74	20	56	136	.251
	Huntsville (SL)	AA	0	0	1.50	1	0	0	0	6	4	2	1	0	3	6	.200
2004	Milwaukee (NL)	MAJ	1	0	0.00	1	1	0	0	6	2	0	0	0	3	7	.100
	Huntsville (SL)	AA	5	5	4.15	14	14	0	0	85	76	41	39	10	18	84	.238
MAJOR LEAGUE TOTALS			1	0	.000	1	1	0	0	6	2	0	0	0	3	7	.100
MINOR LEAGUE TOTALS			20	20	4.37	99	44	1	8	340	303	179	165	40	123	373	.240

MINNESOTA
TWINS
BY **MIKE BERARDINO**

I t was business as usual for the Twins in 2004. They won their third American League Central title in a row and second Baseball America Organization of the Year award in three years, integrating young talent into their major league club while continuing to bring in another wave at the lower levels of the system.

Losing top relievers Eddie Guardado and LaTroy Hawkins to free agency after 2003 wasn't the worst thing that could have happened to Minnesota. The Twins replaced them with trade acquisition Joe Nathan and, later in the year, homegrown set-up man Jesse Crain. What's more, the four draft picks received as compensation enabled scouting director Mike Radcliff to piece together the best draft in the game in June. With five picks in the top 39 slots and seven in the top 91, Radcliff stocked up on young pitching. High school shortstop Trevor Plouffe got things started at No. 20, but the Twins filled in behind him with a pair of college arms (Glen Perkins, Matt Fox) and four impressive prep pitchers (Kyle Waldrop, Jay Rainville, Anthony Swarzak, Eduardo Morlan). The combined outlay for the seven picks was $6.745 million.

The Twins managed to break in several key rookies in 2004, although Joe Mauer missed the bulk of the year following knee surgery. Mauer, rated Minnesota's top prospect for the fourth straight winter, is expected to reclaim the starting catching job in 2005. Other products of the farm system who contributed to a franchise-best third consecutive

LARRY GOREN

postseason appearance included first baseman **Justin Morneau**, outfielders Lew Ford and Jason Kubel, third baseman Terry Tiffee, and relievers Grant Balfour and Crain.

While the Twins experience roster turnover every year, front-office stability is a hallmark of the organization. Terry Ryan is entering his 11th season as general manager and has been in the organization since 1986. Jim Rantz has been with the franchise since it moved to Minnesota in 1961 and has overseen the farm system since 1986. Radcliff is entering his 18th year with the Twins and 12th as scouting director. Rantz and Radcliff are the longest-tenured farm and scouting directors in the game, while only Atlanta's John Schuerholz has longer continuous service as a GM than Ryan.

The system's greatest strength is its pitching depth, which dovetails with the big league club's greatest need. In August, 29 Twins farmhands averaged 90 mph or better with their fastballs. When their competitors were wearing down or landing on the shelf, most of Minnesota's pitchers were getting stronger. Not that velocity is emphasized. Twins scouts are more interested in finding well-rounded pitchers who can command multiple offerings.

Minnesota affiliates had a combined .502 winning percentage in 2004. The system has endured just one losing season (1999) in the past 13 years and just two losing campaigns since 1987.

TOP 30 PROSPECTS

1. Joe Mauer, c	16. Justin Jones, lhp
2. Jason Kubel, of	17. Matt Fox, rhp
3. Jesse Crain, rhp	18. Michael Restovich, of
4. J.D. Durbin, rhp	19. Terry Tiffee, 3b
5. Francisco Liriano, lhp	20. Alexander Smit, lhp
6. Kyle Waldrop, rhp	21. Scott Tyler, rhp
7. Anthony Swarzak, rhp	22. Johnny Woodard, 1b
8. Matt Moses, 3b	23. David Winfree, 3b/1b
9. Jason Bartlett, ss	24. Frank Mata, rhp
10. Scott Baker, rhp	25. Boof Bonser, rhp
11. Adam Harben, rhp	26. Alex Romero, of
12. Trevor Plouffe, ss	27. David Shinskie, rhp
13. Glen Perkins, lhp	28. Juan Portes, inf
14. Denard Span, of	29. Eduardo Morlan, rhp
15. Jay Rainville, rhp	30. Errol Simonitsch, lhp

ORGANIZATION OVERVIEW

General manager: Terry Ryan. **Farm director:** Jim Rantz. **Scouting director:** Mike Radcliff.

2004 PERFORMANCE

Class	Team	League	W	L	Pct.	Finish*	Manager
Majors	Minnesota	American	92	70	.568	t-3rd (14)	Ron Gardenhire
Triple-A	Rochester Red Wings	International	73	71	.507	t-5th (14)	Phil Roof
Double-A	New Britain Rock Cats	Eastern	70	70	.500	6th (12)	Stan Cliburn
High A	Fort Myers Miracle	Florida State	61	74	.452	9th (12)	Jose Marzan
Low A	#Swing of the Quad Cities	Midwest	68	68	.500	10th (14)	Kevin Boles
Rookie	Elizabethton Twins	Appalachian	38	29	.567	4th (10)	Ray Smith
Rookie	GCL Twins	Gulf Coast	31	26	.544	5th (12)	Riccardo Ingram
OVERALL 2004 MINOR LEAGUE RECORD			**341**	**338**	**.502**	**16th (30)**	

*Finish in overall standings (No. of teams in league). #Affiliate will be in Beloit (Midwest) in 2005.

ORGANIZATION LEADERS

BATTING
*Minimum 250 At-Bats

*AVG	Jason Kubel, Rochester/New Britain	.352
R	Jason Kubel, Rochester/New Britain	96
H	Jason Kubel, Rochester/New Britain	172
TB	Garrett Jones, New Britain/Fort Myers	291
2B	Kevin West, Rochester/New Britain	43
3B	Doug Deeds, Fort Myers	12
	Scott Whitrock, Quad Cities	12
HR	Garrett Jones, New Britain/Fort Myers	31
RBI	Kevin West, Rochester/New Britain	109
BB	Brock Peterson, Quad Cities	56
	J.R. Taylor, Quad Cities	56
SO	Scott Whitrock, Quad Cities	155
SB	Josh Rabe, Rochester	26
*OBP	Jason Bartlett, Rochester	.415
*SLG	Justin Morneau, Rochester	.615

PITCHING
#Minimum 75 Innings

W	Dave Gassner, Rochester	16
L	Henry Bonilla, Rochester/New Britain	12
	Jeff Randazzo, Fort Myers	12
#ERA	Travis Bowyer, New Britain/Fort Myers	1.29
G	Bobby Korecky, New Britain	55
CG	Scott Baker, Rochester/New Britain/Fort Myers	2
	Matt Yeatman, Fort Myers	2
SV	Bobby Korecky, New Britain	31
IP	Dave Gassner, Rochester	174
BB	Adam Harben, Quad Cities	68
SO	Francisco Liriano, New Britain/Fort Myers	174

BEST TOOLS

Best Hitter for Average	Joe Mauer
Best Power Hitter	Michael Restovich
Best Strike-Zone Discipline	Jason Kubel
Fastest Baserunner	Denard Span
Best Athlete	Denard Span
Best Fastball	J.D. Durbin
Best Curveball	J.D. Durbin
Best Slider	Jesse Crain
Best Changeup	Julio DePaula
Best Control	Kyle Waldrop
Best Defensive Catcher	Joe Mauer
Best Defensive Infielder	Trevor Plouffe
Best Infield Arm	Omar Burgos
Best Defensive Outfielder	Denard Span
Best Outfield Arm	Jason Kubel

PROJECTED 2008 LINEUP

Catcher	Joe Mauer
First Base	Justin Morneau
Second Base	Luis Rivas
Third Base	Michael Cuddyer
Shortstop	Jason Bartlett
Left Field	Jacque Jones
Center Field	Torii Hunter
Right Field	Jason Kubel
Designated Hitter	Matthew LeCroy
No. 1 Starter	Johan Santana
No. 2 Starter	Brad Radke
No. 3 Starter	J.D. Durbin
No. 4 Starter	Francisco Liriano
No. 5 Starter	Kyle Waldrop
Closer	Jesse Crain

LAST YEAR'S TOP 20 PROSPECTS

1. Joe Mauer, c
2. Justin Morneau, 1b
3. Matt Moses, 3b
4. J.D. Durbin, rhp
5. Jesse Crain, rhp
6. Jason Bartlett, ss
7. Denard Span, of
8. Jason Kubel, of
9. Grant Balfour, rhp
10. Michael Restovich, of
11. Adam Harben, rhp
12. Alexander Smit, lhp
13. Alex Romero, of
14. Evan Meek, rhp
15. Errol Simonitsch, lhp
16. Lew Ford, of
17. Boof Bonser, rhp
18. Francisco Liriano, lhp
19. Scott Baker, rhp
20. Dave Shinskie, rhp

TOP PROSPECTS OF THE DECADE

Year	Player, Pos.	Current Team
1995	LaTroy Hawkins, rhp	Cubs
1996	Todd Walker, 2b	Cubs
1997	Todd Walker, 2b	Cubs
1998	Luis Rivas, ss	Twins
1999	Michael Cuddyer, 3b	Twins
2000	Michael Cuddyer, 3b	Twins
2001	Adam Johnson, rhp	Twins
2002	Joe Mauer, c	Twins
2003	Joe Mauer, c	Twins
2004	Joe Mauer, c	Twins

TOP DRAFT PICKS OF THE DECADE

Year	Player, Pos.	Current Team
1995	Mark Redman, lhp	Athletics
1996	*Travis Lee, 1b	Yankees
1997	Michael Cuddyer, ss	Twins
1998	Ryan Mills, lhp	Twins
1999	B.J. Garbe, of	Mariners
2000	Adam Johnson, rhp	Twins
2001	Joe Mauer, c	Twins
2002	Denard Span, of	Twins
2003	Matt Moses, 3b	Twins
2004	Trevor Plouffe, ss	Twins

*Did not sign.

ALL-TIME LARGEST BONUSES

Joe Mauer, 2001	$5,150,000
B.J. Garbe, 1999	$2,750,000
Adam Johnson, 2000	$2,500,000
Ryan Mills, 1998	$2,000,000
Michael Cuddyer, 1997	$1,850,000

MINOR LEAGUE DEPTH CHART

Minnesota TWINS

Impact Potential: B

Joe Mauer will be an all-star whether he can hold up as a catcher or has to move to another position. He should hit .300 annually, and his power was starting to blossom despite his knee injury last season. J.D. Durbin and Francisco Liriano have front-of-the-rotation stuff but must prove they can stay healthy. Some club officials liked Matt Moses as their top pure hitter before his injury-riddled 2004 season; his balky back will be closely monitored.

Depth: A

This is as good as it gets in baseball. Despite graduating player after player to its penurious big league club, the Twins organization keeps bringing up reinforcements. Minnesota's pitching looks especially deep, particularly after it spent six of its first seven draft picks (all among the top 91 selections) in 2004 on pitchers.

*Depth charts prepared by **John Manuel** and **Allan Simpson**. Numbers in parentheses indicate prospect rankings.*

LF
Mike Restovich (18)
Trent Oeltjen
Mark Robinson
Scott Whitrock
Deacon Burns
Josh Rabe
Doug Deeds

CF
Denard Span (14)
Edward Ovalle
James Tomlin
Javier Lopez

RF
Jason Kubel (2)
Alex Romero (26)
Kevin West
Jeremy Pickrel

3B
Matt Moses (8)
Terry Tiffee (19)
David Winfree (23)
Omar Burgos

SS
Jason Bartlett (9)
Trevor Plouffe (12)
J.R. Taylor

2B
Juan Portes (28)
Luke Hughes
Luis Rodriguez
Luis Maza

1B
Johnny Woodard (22)
Garrett Jones
Brock Peterson
Danny Matienzo

SOURCE of TALENT

HOMEGROWN		ACQUIRED	
College	5	Trades	4
Junior College	3	Rule 5 draft	0
Draft-and-follow	0	Independent leagues	0
High school	15	Free agents/waivers	0
Nondrafted free agents	0		
Foreign	3		

C
Joe Mauer (1)
Jose Morales
Rob Bowen
Kyle Phillips

LHP

Starters	Relievers
Francisco Liriano (5)	Ryan Rowland-Smith
Glen Perkins (13)	Jay Sawatski
Justin Jones (16)	Jason Miller
Alexander Smit (20)	John Thomas
Errol Simonitsch (30)	John Williams
Mike Rogers	Jeff Schoenbachler
Chris Marini	
Dave Gassner	

RHP

Starters	Relievers
J.D. Durbin (4)	Jesse Crain (3)
Kyle Waldrop (6)	Frank Mata (24)
Anthony Swarzak (7)	Eduardo Morlan (29)
Scott Baker (10)	Travis Bowyer
Adam Harben (11)	Justin Olson
Jay Rainville (15)	Pat Neshek
Matt Fox (17)	Julio DePaula
Scott Tyler (21)	Evan Meek
Boof Bonser (25)	
David Shinskie (27)	
Oswaldo Sosa	
Chris Schutt	
Matt Yeatman	
Colby Miller	

DRAFT ANALYSIS

2004

Best Pro Debut: 3B/SS Juan Portes (15) hit .327 and tied for the Rookie-level Gulf Coast League lead with eight homers. LHPs Glen Perkins (1) and Jay Sawatski (8) both reached low Class A Quad Cities and posted sub-1.40 ERAs with more than a strikeout per inning. RHP Kyle Waldrop (1) went 5-2, 2.14 between two Rookie clubs and was rated as the top pitching prospect in the Appalachian League.

Best Athlete: OF Ricky Prady (29) combines speed and power, though he'll be a long-term project. SS Trevor Plouffe (1) entered 2004 more highly regarded as a pitcher, but his potential as an all-around shortstop was too much for Minnesota to ignore. RHP Jay Rainville (1) was an NHL prospect as a defenseman.

Best Pure Hitter: Plouffe, with Portes right on his heels.

Best Raw Power: OF Jeremy Pickrel (10). He's a 6-foot-4, 210-pounder who's a good athlete for his size.

Fastest Runner: Prady.

Best Defensive Player: The Twins see Plouffe as a shortstop in the mold of Greg Gagne. Few infielders have quicker hands than 2B Matt Tolbert (16), who also hit .308 in the Appy League.

Best Fastball: Rainville projects to throw the hardest, currently working at 93-94 mph with heavy sink. RHP Eduardo Morlan (3) has the best present velocity, hitting 95-96 during instructional league. RHP Anthony Swarzak (2) can touch 95, while RHP Matt Fox (1) can reach 94.

Best Breaking Ball: Swarzak's and Waldrop's curveballs, with Swarzak's more consistent at this point. Sawatski's slider is his

SPORTS ON FILM

Plouffe

out pitch.

Most Intriguing Background: Sawatski's grandfather Carl caught for 11 years in the majors and served as president of the Texas League. Four draftees have football connections. RHP Shane Boyd (12) was Kentucky's starting quarterback in the fall. The Twins thought they had him signed as a 13th-round pick out of high school in 2000, but his mom nixed the deal. RHP Tate Casey (19) is a tight end and OF Tony Joiner (44) is a defensive back at Florida.

Closest To The Majors: Perkins or Sawatski. Perkins has command of three average or better pitches, plus he's lefthanded. So is Sawatski, who pitches aggressively with his high-80s fastball and his slider.

Best Late-Round Pick: Portes slipped through the cracks of the draft after dropping out of his Massachusetts high school to play in Iowa's spring wood-bat league. He still needs to find a position, however.

The One Who Got Away: The Twins thought they could get Casey signed, but the pressure to play football was too much. He had a disappointing spring, but he does have a strong body and a low-90s fastball.

Assessment: Minnesota had baseball's best draft, replenishing the talent in the game's most consistently productive system. Though other clubs wondered about the Twins' budget, they didn't sacrifice talent for signability and signed their top 15 picks, including five first-rounders.

2003 RHP Scott Baker (2) reached Triple-A in his first pro season. 3B Matt Moses (1) could be a dynamic hitter, but heart and back ailments have limited his playing time. **GRADE:** C+

2002 If Joe Nathan falters, RHP Jesse Crain (2) could be next in line to close for the Twins. RHP Adam Harben (15) is a good example of the club's pitching depth and scouting wisdom. Speedy OF Denard Span (1) is off to a slow start. Unsigned C Jeff Clement (12) will be an early first-round choice in 2005. **GRADE:** B

2001 Despite knee problems as a rookie, C Joe Mauer (1) should be able to stay behind the plate and be a two-way force. He might be all Minnesota gets out of this draft—though RHP Angel Garcia (4) was the No. 1 pick in December's Rule 5 draft—but that's enough. **GRADE:** A

2000 The Twins blew the second overall choice on RHP Adam Johnson (1), then failed to sign RHP Aaron Heilman (1) and 1B Tagg Bozied (2). But they recovered with OF Jason Kubel (12) and RHP J.D. Durbin (2). **GRADE:** B

Draft analysis prepared by Jim Callis. Numbers in parentheses indicate draft rounds.

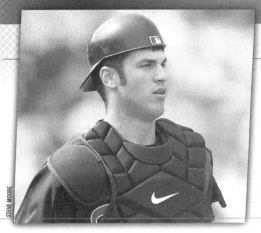

STEVE MOORE

Joe
MAUER

Born: April 19, 1983.
Ht.: 6-4. **Wt.:** 220.
Bats: L. **Throws:** R.
School: Cretin-Derham Hall, St. Paul.
Career Transactions: Selected by Twins in first round (first overall) of 2001 draft; signed July 17, 2001.
Signed by: Mark Wilson.

Seemingly out of central casting, Mauer grew up about 10 minutes from the Metrodome. He developed into one of the country's top quarterback recruits, signing with Florida State, where he would follow in the footsteps of fellow Cretin-Derham Hall product Chris Weinke. Like Weinke, Mauer signed to play baseball first. Unlike Weinke, Mauer never had to use football as a fallback. Twins scouts saw Mauer more than 100 times as an amateur and had no reservations in picking him No. 1 overall in 2001, even though they passed on Mark Prior in the process. After signing for a club-record $5.15 million, Mauer roared through the minor leagues and was Baseball America's Minor League Player of the Year in 2003. Two of his older brothers also play in the Twins system: Jake, a second baseman, was at Double-A New Britain in 2004; Bill, a righthander, pitched at low Class A Quad Cities. With the trade of A.J. Pierzynski to San Francisco after the 2003 season, Minnesota handed its catching job to Mauer. He had a strong spring but tore the meniscus in his left knee in the second game of the year. After surgery, he faced a four- to five-month rehabilitation. Mauer tried to rush back into a pennant race, suffering a setback that led to a second operation. He didn't play after July 15.

There's nothing not to like about Mauer. He has a smooth lefthanded stroke that promises a high career average, if not a batting title or two. He shows strong strike-zone judgment and sprays line drives up the middle and to left-center. Though he hit just nine homers in three minor league seasons, he showed much more power in Minnesota, building the Twins' confidence that he could hit as many as 35-40 homers on an annual basis. He's excellent defensively and worked hard last spring to learn the major league staff and call games to their liking. He blocks balls well, has soft hands and plus arm strength. Only veteran Sandy Alomar is taller among contemporary major league catchers, but Mauer is smooth and sound behind the plate. He has a quick release and is accurate with his throws, shown by the 52 percent of basestealers he nailed in 2003. He shows quiet leadership, simmering confidence and maintains a low profile that makes him popular with teammates.

Prior to surgery he ran better and was more athletic than most of his catching counterparts. There is some concern about that at this point. Inexperience is a factor, as Mauer skipped Triple-A and went straight to the majors before rehab sent him back to the minors.

Rumors have cropped up about a possible position change for Mauer. With Corey Koskie leaving as a free agent, there has been talk about Mauer moving to the hot corner to take pressure off his knees. The Twins insist he'll remain behind the plate and should have no further setbacks. They expect him to become an all-star in short order.

Year	Club (League)	Class	AVG	G	AB	R	H	2B	3B	HR	RBI	BB	SO	SB	OBP	SLG
2001	Elizabethtn (Appy)	R	.400	32	110	14	44	6	2	0	14	19	10	4	.492	.491
2002	Quad City (Mid)	A	.302	110	411	58	124	23	1	4	62	61	42	0	.393	.392
2003	Fort Myers (FSL)	A	.335	62	233	25	78	13	1	1	44	24	24	3	.395	.412
	New Britain (EL)	AA	.341	73	276	48	94	17	1	4	41	25	25	0	.400	.453
2004	Minnesota (AL)	MAJ	.308	35	107	18	33	8	1	6	17	11	14	1	.369	.570
	Fort Myers (FSL)	A	.667	2	6	0	4	0	0	0	2	2	2	0	.750	.667
	Rochester (IL)	AAA	.316	5	19	1	6	3	0	0	2	1	4	0	.333	.474
MAJOR LEAGUE TOTALS			.308	35	107	18	33	8	1	6	17	11	14	1	.369	.570
MINOR LEAGUE TOTALS			.332	284	1055	146	350	62	5	9	165	132	107	7	.407	.426

2 Jason Kubel, of

Born: May 25, 1982. **Ht.:** 5-11. **Wt.:** 190. **Bats:** L. **Throws:** R. **School:** Highland HS, Palmdale, Calif. **Career Transactions:** Selected by Twins in 12th round of 2000 draft; signed June 13, 2000. **Signed by:** Bill Mele.

Kubel landed in the majors by the end of 2004 and made the Twins' postseason roster. The organization's minor league player of the year, he tore the anterior cruciate ligament and sustained further damage to his left knee in an outfield collision in the Arizona Fall League. Called a poor man's Brian Giles, Kubel shows a professional approach at the plate. He has a strong grasp of the strike zone, features a quick, compact stroke and offers opposite-field power. He hits both lefties and righties with equal force. His best defensive tool is a legitimate right-field arm. Unlike Giles, Kubel isn't much of a basestealing threat. He has limited speed and range in the outfield, so the knee injury won't affect his game too much. He has a tendency to get pull-happy at times. Kubel could miss all or most of 2005, ending his chances of possibly claiming the right-field job. Because speed wasn't a big part of his game before the injury, the Twins hope he'll come back as the same player.

Year	Club (League)	Class	AVG	G	AB	R	H	2B	3B	HR	RBI	BB	SO	SB	OBP	SLG
2000	Twins (GCL)	R	.282	23	78	17	22	3	2	0	13	10	9	0	.367	.372
2001	Twins (GCL)	R	.331	37	124	14	41	10	4	1	30	19	14	3	.422	.500
2002	Quad City (Mid)	A	.321	115	424	60	136	26	4	17	69	41	48	3	.380	.521
2003	Fort Myers (FSL)	A	.298	116	420	56	125	20	4	5	82	48	54	4	.361	.400
2004	New Britain (EL)	AA	.377	37	138	25	52	14	4	6	29	19	19	0	.453	.667
	Rochester (IL)	AAA	.343	90	350	71	120	28	0	16	71	34	40	16	.398	.560
	Minnesota (AL)	MAJ	.300	23	60	10	18	2	0	2	7	6	9	1	.358	.433
MAJOR LEAGUE TOTALS			.300	23	60	10	18	2	0	2	7	6	9	1	.358	.433
MINOR LEAGUE TOTALS			.323	418	1534	243	496	101	18	45	294	171	184	26	.388	.501

3 Jesse Crain, rhp

Born: July 5, 1981. **Ht.:** 6-1. **Wt.:** 205. **Bats:** R. **Throws:** R. **School:** University of Houston. **Career Transactions:** Selected by Twins in second round of 2002 draft; signed July 13, 2002. **Signed by:** Marty Esposito.

Part of the pitching pipeline at the University of Houston, Crain preceded the Reds' Ryan Wagner as the Cougars' closer. Also a shortstop in college, Crain blew through the Twins system on his way to the majors. He worked just 162 innings before coming to the majors in August. Crain has two plus-plus pitches and uses them both to great effect. His fastball sits at 92-94 mph and tops out at 96. He also has a late-breaking slider that he uses to get strikeouts. He's able to repeat his delivery, throws strikes and generates good leverage despite his average size. Except for keeping the ball down in the zone more consistently, Crain has little to work on. He has a usable changeup but rarely needs to break it out because his first two pitches are so solid. With closer Joe Nathan not eligible for free agency until after 2007, Crain figures to settle in as his setup man. Should arbitration-fed raises push Nathan out of Minnesota's budget, however, Crain would be poised to take over.

Year	Club (League)	Class	W	L	ERA	G	GS	CG	SV	IP	H	R	ER	HR	BB	SO	AVG
2002	Elizabethton (Appy)	R	2	1	0.57	9	0	0	2	16	4	2	1	0	7	18	.082
	Quad Cities (Mid)	A	1	1	1.50	9	0	0	1	12	6	3	2	0	4	11	.154
2003	Fort Myers (FSL)	A	2	1	2.84	10	0	0	0	19	10	6	6	0	5	25	.154
	New Britain (EL)	AA	1	1	0.69	22	0	0	9	39	13	4	3	0	10	56	.099
	Rochester (IL)	AAA	3	1	3.12	23	0	0	10	26	24	10	9	0	10	33	.245
2004	Minnesota (AL)	MAJ	3	0	2.00	22	0	0	0	27	17	6	6	2	12	14	.179
	Rochester (IL)	AAA	3	2	2.49	41	0	0	19	51	38	20	14	5	17	64	.208
MAJOR LEAGUE TOTALS			3	0	2.00	22	0	0	0	27	17	6	6	2	12	14	.179
MINOR LEAGUE TOTALS			12	7	1.94	114	0	0	41	162	95	45	35	5	53	207	.168

4 J.D. Durbin, rhp

Born: Feb. 24, 1982. **Ht.:** 6-0. **Wt.:** 200. **Bats:** R. **Throws:** R. **School:** Coronado HS, Scottsdale, Ariz. **Career Transactions:** Selected by Twins in second round of 2000 draft; signed July 18, 2000. **Signed by:** Lee MacPhail.

Known for his confidence and brash personality, Durbin has dubbed himself "Real Deal." Stalled by minor shoulder surgery in May to shave his labrum and repair a partial tear, he came back strong. He touched 97 mph and allowed two earned runs or fewer in his first seven starts to earn a promotion to Triple-A and later a September callup. Durbin flashes a mid-90s fastball and maintains his velocity deep into games. He reached triple digits in the Arizona Fall League. He has a power curveball that's the system's best and a slider he can pump at 87 mph. He showed improved mound presence and did a better job of pitching to contact in 2004. Durbin needs more polish before he's ready to start in the majors. He still needs to improve his changeup and sharpen his location, though he made strides with the change last season. Some scouts think his size, stuff and mentality will fit better in the bullpen. Durbin could get a shot at Minnesota's rotation in 2005 but most likely will break in as a middle reliever.

Year	Club (League)	Class	W	L	ERA	G	GS	CG	SV	IP	H	R	ER	HR	BB	SO	AVG
2000	Twins (GCL)	R	0	0	.00	2	0	0	0	2	2	0	0	0	0	4	.222
2001	Elizabethton (Appy)	R	3	2	1.87	8	7	0	0	34	23	13	7	2	17	39	.190
2002	Quad Cities (Mid)	A	13	4	3.19	27	27	0	0	161	144	66	57	14	51	163	.239
2003	Fort Myers (FSL)	A	9	2	3.09	14	14	0	0	87	73	35	30	3	22	69	.224
	New Britain (EL)	AA	6	3	3.14	14	14	2	0	95	102	39	33	10	29	70	.278
2004	New Britain (EL)	AA	4	1	2.52	13	13	0	0	64	62	21	18	4	22	53	.251
	Rochester (IL)	AAA	3	2	4.54	7	7	0	0	36	49	27	18	4	16	38	.329
	Minnesota (AL)	MAJ	0	1	7.36	4	1	0	0	7	12	6	6	0	6	6	.387
MAJOR LEAGUE TOTALS			0	1	7.36	4	1	0	0	7	12	6	6	0	6	6	.387
MINOR LEAGUE TOTALS			38	14	3.07	85	82	2	0	479	455	201	163	37	157	436	.250

5 Francisco Liriano, lhp

Born: Oct. 26, 1983. **Ht.:** 6-2. **Wt.:** 185. **Bats:** L. **Throws:** L. **Career Transactions:** Signed out of Dominican Republic by Giants, Sept. 9, 2000 . . . Traded by Giants with RHP Boof Bonser and RHP Joe Nathan to Twins for C A.J. Pierzynski and a player to be named, Nov. 14, 2003. **Signed by:** Rick Ragazzo (Giants).

The least known of the three players Minnesota received in last winter's A.J. Pierzynski trade, Liriano could wind up as the jewel of the deal. Considering Joe Nathan was an all-star closer in 2004, that's saying something. Liriano missed most of 2003, but Twins scout Sean Johnson recommended him after seeing him in instructional league. After two years of shoulder woes, Liriano stayed healthy in 2004 and flashed a package that made the Twins daydream about having another Johan Santana. Liriano pitches at 93-95 mph and has hit 97. He has a plus changeup and a big-breaking curveball. His makeup and work ethic are excellent. A former outfielder who converted to the mound shortly after signing with the Giants, Liriano is still raw, both in terms of experience and his build. He still must prove he can stay healthy over the long haul. He has trouble at times commanding his fastball, his curve can be inconsistent and his slider is a work in progress. Added to the 40-man roster, Liriano should begin 2005 in Double-A and could help Minnesota by the end of the year.

Year	Club (League)	Class	W	L	ERA	G	GS	CG	SV	IP	H	R	ER	HR	BB	SO	AVG
2001	Giants (AZL)	R	5	4	3.63	13	12	0	0	62	51	26	25	3	24	67	.232
	Salem-Keizer (NWL)	A	0	0	5.00	2	2	0	0	9	7	5	5	2	1	12	.206
2002	Hagerstown (SAL)	A	3	6	3.49	16	16	0	0	80	61	45	31	6	31	85	.210
2003	San Jose (Cal)	A	0	1	4.00	1	1	0	0	1	5	4	4	0	2	0	.714
	Giants (AZL)	R	0	1	4.32	4	4	0	0	8	5	4	4	1	6	9	.192
2004	Fort Myers (FSL)	A	6	7	4.00	21	21	0	0	117	118	56	52	6	43	125	.263
	New Britain (EL)	AA	3	2	3.18	7	7	0	0	40	45	14	14	4	17	49	.276
MINOR LEAGUE TOTALS			17	21	3.84	64	63	0	0	317	292	154	135	22	124	347	.245

6 Kyle Waldrop, rhp

Born: Oct. 27, 1985. **Ht.:** 6-5. **Wt.:** 205. **Bats:** R. **Throws:** R. **School:** Farragut HS, Knoxville, Tenn. **Career Transactions:** Selected by Twins in first round (25th overall) of 2004 draft; signed June 8, 2004. **Signed by:** Tim O'Neil.

Kentucky-based Twins scout Tim O'Neil managed Waldrop in the East Coast Showcase in 2003, and familiarity played a big role in Minnesota drafting him 25th overall a year later. A Vanderbilt recruit, he signed for $1 million as the last of the club's three first-round picks. Though he went 22-0 in his last two prep seasons, some clubs liked him more as a power-hitting first baseman/outfielder. Waldrop has an advanced feel for pitching. He spots his 86-92 mph fastball and has one of the best changeups in recent memory for a pitcher just out of high school. His spike curveball has good bite. A strike-thrower, he maintains his velocity into the late innings. He also earns high marks for his poise, work ethic and professionalism. Waldrop's fastball doesn't light up radar guns, but it's more than enough to set up his other pitches. His main need is consistency with secondary pitches, which should come with experience. Rated the top pitching prospect in the Rookie-level Appalachian League, Waldrop could move quickly for a prep pitcher. He figures to start 2005 in a stacked rotation at low Class A Beloit.

Year	Club (League)	Class	W	L	ERA	G	GS	CG	SV	IP	H	R	ER	HR	BB	SO	AVG
2004	Twins (GCL)	R	3	2	1.42	7	7	0	0	38	32	9	6	1	4	30	.228
	Elizabethton (Appy)	R	2	0	3.24	4	4	0	0	25	21	10	9	1	3	25	.221
MINOR LEAGUE TOTALS			5	0	2.14	11	11	0	0	63	53	19	15	2	7	55	.225

7 Anthony Swarzak, rhp

Born: Sept. 10, 1985. **Ht.:** 6-3. **Wt.:** 195. **Bats:** R. **Throws:** R. **School:** Nova HS, Fort Lauderdale. **Career Transactions:** Selected by Twins in second round of 2004 draft; signed Ju15, 2004. **Signed by:** Brad Weitzel.

Swarzak was the ace of a Nova High team that won the Florida 5-A championship in 2004, the first state title for a Broward County public school in 57 years. Area scout Brad Weitzel started following him the summer before his senior year and stayed on him. Swarzak spurned Louisiana State to sign for $575,000 and quickly proved to be a bargain. The fifth of six pitchers Minnesota drafted in the first three rounds in 2004, Swarzak may have the highest ceiling of the group. He pitches at 90-92 mph and has touched 95. His curveball is a strikeout pitch, and his changeup also induces swings-and-misses. He's tall with a loose arm, lean body and impressive arm strength that should only increase. He also has a strong mound presence. Swarzak's slider is the least advanced of his pitches. He joined the Twins with a reputation for cockiness, but he has shown a willingness to learn and a receptiveness to coaching. Like many of Minnesota' promising young arms, Swarzak will begin his first full season in low Class A. He's nearly as polished as Kyle Waldrop and should move along with him.

Year	Club (League)	Class	W	L	ERA	G	GS	CG	SV	IP	H	R	ER	HR	BB	SO	AVG
2004	Twins (GCL)	R	5	3	2.63	11	9	0	1	48	46	20	14	1	6	42	.251
MINOR LEAGUE TOTALS			5	3	2.63	11	9	0	1	48	46	20	14	1	6	42	.251

8 Matt Moses, 3b

Born: Feb. 20, 1985. **Ht.:** 6-1. **Wt.:** 210. **Bats:** L. **Throws:** R. **School:** Mills Godwin HS, Richmond, Va. **Career Transactions:** Selected by Twins in first round (21st overall) of 2003 draft; signed July 9, 2003. **Signed by:** John Wilson.

A routine physical after the Twins drafted Moses in 2003 revealed a tiny hole in his heart. A 20-minute surgical procedure remedied the problem, and he signed for $1.45 million. A more serious setback came in 2004, when he missed nearly four months with a stress fracture in his lower back, a recurrence of an injury he sustained before high school. One of the best pure hitters in the 2003 draft, Moses has a smooth, compact swing. He has the frame to develop power as he matures. He shows advanced pitch recognition and plate discipline, and scouts compare his offensive package to Hank Blalock's. Moses' back didn't require surgery, but it will require monitioring. He has played just 47 pro games so far, and a sprained thumb limited him in instructional league. A high school shortstop, Moses needs time to adjust to third base, where his arm and range are average and his throws are erratic. He's a below-average runner. Moses worked out at second base in instructional league and could wind up at first or left field. His bat will be his ticket to the majors, and he could open 2005 at high Class A Fort Myers.

Year	Club (League)	Class	AVG	G	AB	R	H	2B	3B	HR	RBI	BB	SO	SB	OBP	SLG
2003	Twins (GCL)	R	.385	18	65	6	25	5	1	0	11	5	9	0	.417	.492
2004	Quad Cities (Mid)	A	.223	29	112	16	25	7	0	3	14	12	25	0	.304	.366
MINOR LEAGUE TOTALS			.282	47	177	22	50	12	1	3	25	17	34	0	.345	.412

9 Jason Bartlett, ss

Born: Oct. 30, 1979. **Ht.:** 6-0. **Wt.:** 180. **Bats:** R. **Throws:** R. **School:** University of Oklahoma. **Career Transactions:** Selected by Padres in 13rd round of 2001 draft; signed June 14, 2001 . . . Traded by Padres to Twins for OF Brian Buchanan, July 12, 2002. **Signed by:** Lane Decker (Padres).

Less than two weeks after signing Khalil Greene as a 2002 first-round pick, the Padres put another former college shortstop in a minor deal for Brian Buchanan. Twins scout John Leavitt had seen Bartlett in the minors and projected him as an everyday shortstop in the majors—a role he could assume in 2005. Despite missing two months with a broken right wrist, Bartlett made strides at the plate last season, putting balls in play and battling pitchers every time up. He understands his role as a contact hitter. He has the arm to make plays from the hole and range to both sides. None of Bartlett's tools is overwhelming. He has limited power and his barely above-average speed is below the standard for a middle infielder. He needs to improve his jumps and technique on the bases, as well as his concentration on defense. Minnesota opted not to pick up Cristian Guzman's $5.25 million contract option, making the starting shortstop job Bartlett's to lose. The hope is he can hold the job for several years, or at least until 2004 first-round pick Trevor Plouffe is ready.

Year	Club (League)	Class	AVG	G	AB	R	H	2B	3B	HR	RBI	BB	SO	SB	OBP	SLG
2001	Eugene (NWL)	A	.300	68	267	49	80	12	4	3	37	28	47	12	.371	.408
2002	Lake Elsinore (Cal)	A	.250	75	308	57	77	14	4	1	33	32	53	24	.329	.331
	Fort Myers (FSL)	A	.262	39	145	24	38	7	0	2	9	17	24	11	.341	.352
2003	New Britain (EL)	AA	.296	139	548	96	162	31	8	8	48	58	67	41	.380	.425
2004	Rochester (IL)	AAA	.331	67	269	54	89	15	7	3	29	33	37	7	.415	.472
	Minnesota (AL)	MAJ	.083	8	12	2	1	0	0	0	1	1	1	2	.154	.083
MAJOR LEAGUE TOTALS			.083	8	12	2	1	0	0	0	1	1	1	2	.154	.083
MINOR LEAGUE TOTALS			.290	388	1537	280	446	79	23	17	156	168	228	95	.371	.405

10 Scott Baker, rhp

RICH ABEL

Born: Sept. 19, 1981. **Ht.:** 6-4. **Wt.:** 215. **Bats:** R. **Throws:** R. **School:** Oklahoma State University. **Career Transactions:** Selected by Twins in second round of 2003 draft; signed June 20, 2003. **Signed by:** Gregg Miller.

Baker reached Triple-A 13 months after signing. In his first full season, he started the Hall of Fame game for the Twins, who named him their minor league pitcher of the year. He continued to build on his success with a strong Arizona Fall League performance. Baker pitches at 91-93 mph with sink and occasionally reaches 95. He has plus fastball command, an advanced changeup and a smooth delivery. He also throws a quick-breaking slider and a knuckle-curve. He has an outstanding work ethic and is one of the most focused, intense prospects in the system. Though he's polished, Baker doesn't have a true out pitch and already is close to his ceiling. He projects as a No. 3 or 4 starter. He struggled in Triple-A, so he needs to prove he can maintain his stuff over a full season and get more advanced hitters out. Baker could get a chance to make Minnesota's rotation in spring training. He may need a few more starts in Triple-A before he's ready.

Year	Club (League)	Class	W	L	ERA	G	GS	CG	SV	IP	H	R	ER	HR	BB	SO	AVG
2003	Quad City (Mid)	A	3	1	2.49	11	11	0	0	51	45	16	14	4	8	47	.234
2004	Fort Myers (FSL)	A	4	2	2.40	7	7	0	0	45	40	13	12	1	6	37	.233
	New Britain (EL)	AA	5	3	2.43	10	10	2	0	70	44	23	19	2	13	72	.173
	Rochester (IL)	AAA	1	3	4.97	9	9	0	0	54	65	31	30	3	15	36	.295
MINOR LEAGUE TOTALS			13	9	3.06	37	37	2	0	220	194	83	75	10	42	192	.231

11 Adam Harben, rhp

Born: Aug. 19, 1983. **Ht.:** 6-5. **Wt.:** 205. **Bats:** R. **Throws:** R. **School:** University of Arkansas-Fort Smith JC. **Career Transactions:** Selected by Twins in 15th round of 2002 draft; signed July 10, 2002. **Signed by:** Gregg Miller.

The Tigers weren't able to sign Harben as a 38th-round pick in 2001 out of Central Arkansas Christian (Little Rock), the same high school that produced A.J. Burnett. Harben instead attended Westark (Ark.) CC, where he roomed with Toby Gardenhire, whose father Ron manages the Twins. Based in part on Toby Gardenhire's recommendation, as well as area scout Gregg Miller's, Minnesota stole Harben in the 15th round in 2002. Harben made significant strides last season, proving to Twins brass that he has enough to profile as a big league starter. He showed a full mix of pitches, starting with a 91-95 mph fastball that touches 97 and a solid-average hard slider. His changeup came along nicely and his overall pitching presence was sound. Harben maintains his stuff through the late innings. He has improved his conditioning and mechanics since signing, now showing a smooth, effortless delivery. He has one of the more electric arms in a stacked system and acquitted himself well in a loaded Quad Cities rotation that also included Glen Perkins, Justin Jones, Scott Tyler and Errol Simonitsch. After two years in low Class A, Harben is ready to move up a level.

Year	Club (League)	Class	W	L	ERA	G	GS	CG	SV	IP	H	R	ER	HR	BB	SO	AVG
2002	Twins (GCL)	R	4	1	3.20	12	3	0	0	25	27	11	9	0	8	27	.270
2003	Quad City (Mid)	A	5	6	4.33	16	15	0	0	87	91	54	42	5	35	77	.259
2004	Quad Cities (Mid)	A	9	7	3.09	26	26	0	0	143	114	60	49	5	68	171	.218
MINOR LEAGUE TOTALS			18	14	3.53	54	44	0	0	255	232	125	100	10	111	275	.238

12 Trevor Plouffe, ss

Born: June 15, 1986. **Ht.:** 6-1. **Wt.:** 175. **Bats:** R. **Throws:** R. **School:** Crespi HS, Northridge, Calif. **Career Transactions:** Selected by Twins in first round (20th overall) of 2004 draft; signed June 11, 2004. **Signed by:** Bill Mele.

Plouffe was a two-way star in high school, and the Twins didn't make the call on whether they liked him more as a pitcher or a hitter until last March. On the mound he had a four-pitch mix and could hit 91 mph with great feel and command. He went 25-2 his final two seasons and reminded Minnesota of Brad Radke, but area scout Bill Mele saw enough of Plouffe to recommend he be drafted as a position player. Plouffe accepted a $1.5 million bonus as the first of five Twins picks before the second round. He has special hands both offensively and defensively and projects to hit 15-20 homers a year in the majors. As a position player, he draws comparisons to Greg Gagne from some Twins officials. Plouffe has a plus arm and his advanced makeup and work ethic should push him along quickly. However, none of his tools blows scouts away. He's an average runner and his smallish frame is somewhat of a concern. In the field, he doesn't go as strong to his right as to his left. His power for now is strictly to the pull side. But when Minnesota threw him into the Appalachian League against mostly older foes, Plouffe more than held his own. He should start 2005 in low Class A.

Year	Club (League)	Class	AVG	G	AB	R	H	2B	3B	HR	RBI	BB	SO	SB	OBP	SLG
2004	Elizabethton (Appy)	R	.283	60	237	29	67	7	2	4	28	19	34	3	.340	.380
MINOR LEAGUE TOTALS			.283	60	237	29	67	7	2	4	28	19	34	3	.340	.380

13 Glen Perkins, lhp

Born: March 2, 1983. **Ht.:** 6-0. **Wt.:** 190. **Bats:** L. **Throws:** L. **School:** University of Minnesota. **Career Transactions:** Selected by Twins in first round (22nd overall) of 2004 draft; signed June 27, 2004. **Signed by:** Mark Wilson.

The 25th and last signee out of the Twins' 2004 draft, Perkins accepted a $1.425 million bonus and promptly set about turning heads. He pitches at 88-90 mph and touches 92, but he's all about command and control. Area scout Mark Wilson and Midwest supervisor Joel Lepel liked his advanced changeup, average curveball and strong mound presence. Perkins knows how to attack hitters' weaknesses, use all four quadrants of the strike zone and work inside. At some point he'll incorporate a cut fastball into his repertoire. Perkins isn't much of an athlete and has flat feet, which keeps him from working out as aggressively as preferred. He also missed 2 1/2 weeks during instructional league with a lower back problem. There's some question about his stamina and whether he'll ultimately wind up in the bullpen. As a product of a solid college program, Perkins could move quickly through the system, especially one that lacks a multitude of upper-level lefties. He could start his first full season in Double-A as the Twins seek to ease a rotation logjam at the lower levels.

Year	Club (League)	Class	W	L	ERA	G	GS	CG	SV	IP	H	R	ER	HR	BB	SO	AVG
2004	Elizabethton (Appy)	R	1	0	2.25	3	3	0	0	12	8	3	3	0	4	22	.195
	Quad Cities (Mid)	A	2	1	1.30	9	9	0	0	48	33	9	7	2	12	49	.192
MINOR LEAGUE TOTALS			3	1	1.49	12	12	0	0	60	41	12	10	2	16	71	.192

14 Denard Span, of

Born: Feb. 27, 1984. **Ht.:** 6-1. **Wt.:** 180. **Bats:** L. **Throws:** L. **School:** Tampa Catholic HS. **Career Transactions:** Selected by Twins in first round (20th overall) of 2002 draft; signed Aug. 15, 2002. **Signed by:** Brad Weitzel.

Span began his high school career at famed baseball power Hillsborough High in Tampa—the alma mater of Carl Everett, Dwight Gooden and Gary Sheffield, among others—before transferring to Tampa Catholic and winning a Florida 3-A title as a junior. Also a star wide receiver, he drew interest from NCAA Division I-A football programs until it became clear his future was in baseball. The Rockies wanted to cut a predraft deal with Span and take him ninth overall in 2002, but he wouldn't accede and fell to the Twins at No. 20, where he signed for $1.7 million. He has played just 114 games as a pro because he signed a 2003 contract, spent that season in Rookie ball and then broke the hamate bone in his right wrist last year. The best athlete and fastest player in the system, Span has been timed at 3.8 seconds to first base. He has the potential to be a game-changer on the bases, and in center his speed enables him to outrun mistakes. He does show some prowess for drawing walks, helping him achieve his main goal: to get on base. The Twins believe he'll develop some gap power down the road, though he's been just a slap hitter to this point. Span must prove he can stay healthy after nagging ankle and leg injuries limited his availability in 2003 as well. He has a below-average arm and remains extremely raw. Span was the talk of instructional league, where he began to make significant improvements in nearly every area of his game. He put more balls in play, bunted for base hits and showed a physical and mental maturity that had been missing. Despite his limited experience, he figures to begin 2005 in high Class A.

Year	Club (League)	Class	AVG	G	AB	R	H	2B	3B	HR	RBI	BB	SO	SB	OBP	SLG
2003	Elizabethton (Appy)	R	.271	50	207	34	56	5	1	1	18	23	34	14	.355	.319
2004	Quad Cities (Mid)	A	.267	64	240	29	64	4	3	0	14	34	49	15	.363	.308
MINOR LEAGUE TOTALS			.268	114	447	63	120	9	4	1	32	57	83	29	.359	.313

15 Jay Rainville, rhp

Born: Oct. 16, 1985. **Ht.:** 6-3. **Wt.:** 230. **Bats:** R. **Throws:** R. **School:** Bishop Hendricken HS, Pawtucket, R.I. **Career Transactions:** Selected by Twins in first round (39th overall) of 2004 draft; signed June 24, 2004. **Signed by:** Jay Weitzel.

A product of the same Bishop Hendricken High (Warwick, R.I.) program as Devil Rays outfielder Rocco Baldelli, Rainville came flying out of the gate in his pro debut. After signing for $875,000, he dominated the Rookie-level Gulf Coast League with two plus pitches: a 91-94 mph sinker and a power curve that already ranks among the best in the organization. He was recommended by area scout Jay Weitzel, whose Florida-based brother Brad landed three other high-round arms for the Twins last June: Matt Fox, Anthony Swarzak and Eduardo Morlan. Of all the pitchers Minnesota signed out of the draft, Rainville projects to throw the hardest. He posted a 38-3 strikeout-walk ratio in the GCL and reminded some observers of a young Curt Schilling with his strong thighs and big frame. He still has to sharpen his changeup in order to convince the Twins he should stay in the rotation. He could wind up as a short reliever, a role that might better suit his intensity and aggressiveness, two traits that helped make him a National Hockey League prospect as a defensemen. Rainville's strong summer ended somewhat murkily when an exit physical revealed weakness in his throwing shoulder. However, an MRI was negative and the Twins believe he should be fully healthy in 2005, when he'll pitch in low Class A.

Year	Club (League)	Class	W	L	ERA	G	GS	CG	SV	IP	H	R	ER	HR	BB	SO	AVG
2004	Twins (GCL)	R	3	2	1.83	8	7	0	0	34	39	19	7	1	3	38	.272
MINOR LEAGUE TOTALS			3	2	1.83	8	7	0	0	34	39	19	7	1	3	38	.272

16 Justin Jones, lhp

Born: Sept. 25, 1984. **Ht.:** 6-4. **Wt.:** 195. **Bats:** L. **Throws:** L. **School:** Kellam HS, Virginia Beach. **Career Transactions:** Selected by Cubs in second round of 2002 draft; signed June 25, 2002 . . . Traded by Cubs to Twins as part of four-way trade in which Red Sox received 1B Doug Mientkiewicz from Twins and SS Orlando Cabrera from Expos; Expos received SS Alex S. Gonzalez and 3B Brendan Harris from Cubs, and Cubs received SS Nomar Garciaparra and OF Matt Murton from Red Sox, July 31, 2004. **Signed by:** Billy Swoope (Cubs).

Ranked No. 2 on Baseball America's deep Cubs prospect list a year ago, Jones was acquired in the four-team Nomar Garciaparra/Orlando Cabrera trade that cost Minnesota Doug Mientkiewicz. Jones wasn't very impressive in his limited Twins debut, and he complained of elbow discomfort. Numerous tests turned up nothing definitive, and Jones was sent home from instructional league without having pitched. When he's right, his fastball sits between 89-92 mph and touches 94. He also has shown a plus curve, an advanced changeup and the makings of a splitter. Jones has never had arm surgery, but his durability is a major question after he has been shut down late the past two seasons. Jones was one of the youngest pitchers in the low Class A Midwest League in 2003 and he figures to return there to start 2005. Minnesota still isn't sure what it has in Jones but hopes he stays healthy so it can find out.

Year	Club (League)	Class	W	L	ERA	G	GS	CG	SV	IP	H	R	ER	HR	BB	SO	AVG
2002	Cubs (AZL)	R	3	1	1.80	11	11	0	0	50	31	12	10	0	18	63	.181
	Boise (NWL)	A	1	0	1.80	1	1	0	0	5	4	1	1	0	3	4	.211
2003	Lansing (Mid)	A	3	5	2.28	16	16	0	0	71	56	29	18	1	32	87	.215
2004	Lansing (Mid)	A	3	3	3.78	14	14	0	0	64	62	33	27	6	22	59	.254
	Quad Cities (Mid)	A	0	2	5.31	7	4	0	0	20	20	17	12	2	14	17	.256
MINOR LEAGUE TOTALS			10	11	2.91	49	46	0	0	211	173	92	68	9	89	230	.224

17 Matt Fox, rhp

Born: Dec. 4, 1982. **Ht.:** 6-3. **Wt.:** 192. **Bats:** R. **Throws:** R. **School:** University of Central Florida. **Career Transactions:** Drafted by Twins in first round (35th overall) of 2004 draft; signed June 14, 2004. **Signed by:** Brad Weitzel.

Fox turned down a sixth-round offer from the Diamondbacks in 2001 to play both ways at Central Florida. He had elbow surgery as a freshman and posted a 6.36 ERA in his first two seasons before becoming a full-time pitcher in 2004. That decision paid off, as he became a first-team All-American and a supplemental first-round pick. Recommended by area scout

Brad Weitzel, Fox pitches at 88-92 mph and touches 94 with good location on his fastball, and he also shows touch and feel for both a slider and curveball. He even has the makings of a decent changeup. The Twins were frustrated by Fox' inability to stay healthy after signing for $950,000. He was bothered by shoulder tendinitis and was sent to Minneapolis for tests. Nothing turned up, which heightened the aggravation on all parts. Fox attended instructional league but wasn't able to throw, though he did earn points with an upbeat attitude and willingness to learn. He could start the year in the low Class A rotation.

Year	Club (League)	Class	W	L	ERA	G	GS	CG	SV	IP	H	R	ER	HR	BB	SO	AVG
2004	Elizabethton (Appy)	R	2	1	5.40	8	5	0	0	27	27	18	16	6	8	32	.257
MINOR LEAGUE TOTALS			2	1	5.40	8	5	0	0	27	27	18	16	6	8	32	.257

18 Michael Restovich, of

Born: Jan. 3, 1979. **Ht.:** 6-4. **Wt.:** 251. **Bats:** R. **Throws:** R. **School:** Mayo HS, Rochester, Minn. **Career Transactions:** Selected by Twins in second round of 1997 draft; signed Aug. 15, 1997. **Signed by:** Joel Lepel.

A native Minnesotan, Restovich continues to slip in the eyes of the organization. He ranked in the top five on this list each year from 1999-2003, but has plateaued over the last two seasons while others have blown past him. Restovich still has the best raw power in the system. He drills fastballs with a smooth, sound swing. Quality breaking balls are another story, however. Strikeouts have been a problem along the way, and his walk rate dropped noticeably last year. Restovich is a good athlete for his size. His speed, corner-outfield defense and arm are all fine. He has played sparingly in the majors during the past three seasons, and he's now out of minor league options. The Twins decided to bring Jacque Jones back for 2005, but fellow outfield prospect Jason Kubel's knee injury may enhance Restovich's chances of making the club. He broke his right collarbone when he fell on some ice during Thanksgiving weekend, but should be completely healthy for spring training.

Year	Club (League)	Class	AVG	G	AB	R	H	2B	3B	HR	RBI	BB	SO	SB	OBP	SLG
1998	Elizabethton (Appy)	R	.355	65	242	68	86	20	1	13	64	54	58	5	.489	.607
	Fort Wayne (Mid)	A	.444	11	45	9	20	5	2	0	6	4	12	0	.490	.644
1999	Quad City (Mid)	A	.312	131	493	91	154	30	6	19	107	74	100	7	.412	.513
2000	Fort Myers (FSL)	A	.263	135	475	73	125	27	9	8	64	61	100	19	.350	.408
2001	New Britain (EL)	AA	.269	140	501	69	135	33	4	23	84	54	125	15	.345	.489
2002	Edmonton (PCL)	AAA	.286	138	518	95	148	32	7	29	98	53	151	11	.353	.542
	Minnesota (AL)	MAJ	.308	8	13	3	4	0	0	1	1	1	4	1	.357	.538
2003	Rochester (IL)	AAA	.275	119	454	75	125	34	2	16	72	47	117	10	.346	.465
	Minnesota (AL)	MAJ	.283	24	53	10	15	3	2	0	4	10	12	0	.406	.415
2004	Rochester (IL)	AAA	.247	106	425	65	105	20	3	20	63	25	104	4	.291	.449
	Minnesota (AL)	MAJ	.255	29	47	9	12	3	0	2	6	4	10	0	.314	.447
MAJOR LEAGUE TOTALS			.274	61	113	22	31	6	2	3	11	15	26	1	.364	.442
MINOR LEAGUE TOTALS			.285	845	3153	545	898	201	34	128	558	372	767	71	.366	.492

19 Terry Tiffee, 3b

Born: April 21, 1979. **Ht.:** 6-3. **Wt.:** 215. **Bats:** S. **Throws:** R. **School:** Pratt (Kan.) CC. **Career Transactions:** Selected by Twins in 26th round of 1999 draft; signed Aug. 17, 1999. **Signed by:** Gregg Miller.

A 260-pound load in high school, Tiffee pared down to 230 by the time the Twins drafted him in 1999, when he was MVP of the Kansas Jayhawk Community College Conference. Now at 215, he filled in capably for Minnesota when Corey Koskie was hurt in September. Tiffee had injury problems of his own in 2004, dealing with back and hamstring woes in the minors and dislocating his right shoulder in the majors. He still kept producing runs with a line-drive swing from both sides of the plate. He shows more loft power from the right side. Offensively, his greatest need is to show more patience. Though he's in much better shape than he was as an amateur, Tiffee still lacks the lateral mobility and first-step quickness to make anything more than routine plays. He has worked hard on his defense and has average hands and arm strength. With Koskie leaving for Toronto as a free agent, Tiffee's main competition for the third-base job is Michael Cuddyer. While Cuddyer is the favorite, Tiffee at least should find a big league role as a backup.

Year	Club (League)	Class	AVG	G	AB	R	H	2B	3B	HR	RBI	BB	SO	SB	OBP	SLG
2000	Quad City (Mid)	A	.254	129	493	59	125	25	0	7	60	29	73	2	.292	.347
2001	Quad City (Mid)	A	.309	128	495	65	153	32	1	11	86	32	48	3	.347	.444
2002	Fort Myers (FSL)	A	.281	126	473	47	133	31	0	8	64	25	49	0	.316	.397
2003	New Britain (EL)	AA	.315	139	530	77	167	31	3	14	93	31	49	4	.351	.464
2004	Rochester (IL)	AAA	.307	82	316	42	97	26	3	12	68	21	26	0	.357	.522
	Minnesota (AL)	MAJ	.273	17	44	7	12	4	0	2	8	3	3	0	.333	.500
MAJOR LEAGUE TOTALS			.273	17	44	7	12	4	0	2	8	3	3	0	.333	.500
MINOR LEAGUE TOTALS			.293	604	2307	290	675	145	7	52	371	138	245	9	.331	.429

Alexander Smit, lhp

Born: Oct. 2, 1985. **Ht.:** 6-3. **Wt.:** 215. **Bats:** L. **Throws:** L. **Career Transactions:** Signed out of the Netherlands by Twins, July 14, 2002. **Signed by:** Howard Norsetter.

A rare big-ticket international signing for the Twins, Smit came aboard for $800,000 in July 2002. International scout Howard Norsetter first saw Smit at age 13, when he was playing first base. Rated the top junior pitcher in the Netherlands in 2001-02, Smit has left in the middle of the last two seasons to pitch for the Dutch national team. He pitched in relief at the Sydney Olympics, throwing six strong innings against Canada but getting shelled by Australia. While Smit has pitched very well in pro ball and is still just 19, Minnesota wishes his velocity was more consistent. He pitches at 86-90 mph and tops out at 92. He made strides with his knuckle-curve and the arm action on his changeup, though neither pitch is totally reliable. He projects as a No. 2 or 3 starter if he develops the plus fastball the Twins expect, but he remains fairly raw. Smit has a good frame and durability, and he has gained 17 pounds since signing. He figures to move up to low Class A in 2005, when he once again will be one of the youngest pitchers in his league.

Year	Club (League)	Class	W	L	ERA	G	GS	CG	SV	IP	H	R	ER	HR	BB	SO	AVG
2003	Twins (GCL)	R	3	0	1.18	8	7	0	0	38	19	8	5	0	20	40	.156
2004	Elizabethton (Appy)	R	1	1	2.54	6	5	0	0	28	25	9	8	0	10	43	.243
MINOR LEAGUE TOTALS			4	1	1.76	14	12	0	0	66	44	17	13	0	30	83	.196

Scott Tyler, rhp

Born: Aug. 20, 1982. **Ht.:** 6-5. **Wt.:** 240. **Bats:** R. **Throws:** R. **School:** Downingtown (Pa.) HS. **Career Transactions:** Selected by Twins in second round of 2001 draft; signed July 8, 2001. **Signed by:** John Wilson.

Tyler has ridden a roller coaster as a pro. He led the Appalachian League in strikeouts in 2002, had difficulty finding the plate in 2003, then bounced back when he repeated the Midwest League. Physically imposing with a large, stiff body, he tends to struggle with his delivery and command. However, he got in a little better shape in 2004, showed some mental maturity and improved his approach. He pitched at 92-94 mph and topped out at 95. He shows a hard curve that he throws at 80 mph, as well as a decent changeup. A below-average athlete, he still hasn't proven he should be a starter for the long term. He must improve his durability and strength, and he has to reverse a tendency to fall apart in the middle innings. He runs up high pitch counts quickly, a trait which has slowed his development. Tyler figures to start this year in the high Class A rotation, but a move to the bullpen might not be far away.

Year	Club (League)	Class	W	L	ERA	G	GS	CG	SV	IP	H	R	ER	HR	BB	SO	AVG
2001	Twins (GCL)	R	0	1	6.75	5	3	0	0	11	11	8	8	0	2	14	.256
2002	Elizabethton (Appy)	R	8	1	2.93	14	13	0	0	68	37	23	22	5	46	92	.161
2003	Quad City (Mid)	A	6	12	5.50	30	20	0	0	106	93	70	65	7	82	110	.234
2004	Quad Cities (Mid)	A	7	4	2.60	22	19	0	0	104	73	33	30	3	64	132	.201
MINOR LEAGUE TOTALS			21	18	3.90	71	55	0	0	287	214	134	125	15	194	348	.207

Johnny Woodard, 1b

Born: Sept. 15, 1984. **Ht.:** 6-4. **Wt.:** 220. **Bats:** L. **Throws:** R. **School:** Cosumnes River (Calif.) JC. **Career Transactions:** Selected by Twins in third round of 2003 draft; signed June 4, 2003. **Signed by:** Kevin Bootay.

A surprise third-rounder in 2003, Woodard had a rough pro debut but repaid the Twins' faith in him with a solid 2004. A late bloomer on the diamond, he focused mainly on basketball in high school and didn't play baseball at all as a junior. Minnesota first noticed him as a high school senior, and got good reports on him from Tony Bloomfield, an associate scout who doubles as the head coach at Cosumnes River (Calif.) JC, where Woodward was the 2003 Bay Valley Conference player of the year. Woodard has a short, fluid swing and 30-homer potential. He uses his lower half well at the plate, hits the gaps and sprays line drives to all fields. He runs decently for a big man and has solid makeup. He is an average defender with good hand-eye coordination and footwork around first base. Though he has made 26 errors in 93 pro games, Minnesota isn't concerned. The Twins were hoping he might show enough versatility to play left field, but it looks like he'll stay at first. He's ready for his first taste of full-season ball.

Year	Club (League)	Class	AVG	G	AB	R	H	2B	3B	HR	RBI	BB	SO	SB	OBP	SLG
2003	Twins (GCL)	R	.238	52	172	19	41	6	1	1	15	22	42	1	.330	.302
2004	Elizabethton (Appy)	R	.309	57	194	37	60	8	4	8	35	24	56	5	.386	.515
MINOR LEAGUE TOTALS			.276	109	366	56	101	14	5	9	50	46	98	6	.360	.415

David Winfree, 3b/1b

Born: Aug. 5, 1985. **Ht.:** 6-3. **Wt.:** 225. **Bats:** R. **Throws:** R. **School:** First Colonial HS, Virginia Beach. **Career Transactions:** Selected by Twins in 13th round of 2003 draft; signed July 19, 2003. **Signed by:** John Wilson.

When the Twins were zeroing in on Matt Moses as their 2003 first-rounder, they got a chance to see more of Winfree at a rival high school. Winfree had been a catcher, but the Twins tried him at first base in his pro debut, then moved him over to third base in 2004. Like fellow 2003 draftee Johnny Woodard, Winfree was overmatched in his first summer before making the necessary adjustments and displaying big-time power in year two. He has a big frame and the ability to turn around quality fastballs. His batting-practice sessions are among the most impressive in the system. Also like Woodard, he strikes out too much and doesn't walk enough. But the potential is there for everything to click. Winfree has plus makeup and dedication to his craft. He left home after his junior year of high school to play in an advanced summer league in Ohio. A below-average runner, Winfree has average range and a slightly better arm at third. He still could end up back behind the plate, but figures to start 2005 at the hot corner in low Class A.

Year	Club (League)	Class	AVG	G	AB	R	H	2B	3B	HR	RBI	BB	SO	SB	OBP	SLG
2003	Twins (GCL)	R	.129	23	70	4	9	1	2	0	3	2	16	0	.164	.200
2004	Elizabethton (Appy)	R	.286	59	217	31	62	8	0	8	37	18	51	1	.349	.433
MINOR LEAGUE TOTALS			.247	82	287	35	71	9	2	8	40	20	67	1	.306	.376

Frank Mata, rhp

Born: March 11, 1984. **Ht.:** 6-0. **Wt.:** 168. **Bats:** R. **Throws:** R. **Career Transactions:** Signed out of Venezuela by Twins, May 1, 2002. **Signed by:** Jose Leon.

Signed at 18 out of Venezuela, Mata's combination of a big body and a big-time arm reminds some of a young Bartolo Colon. He has a strong lower half and thick back to go with short arms that produce 94-96 mph fastballs. He also has a hard slider that has a chance to become a plus pitch. His power stuff enabled him to tie for the Appalachian League in saves last year, and he has been unhittable in the lower minors. He has good makeup and toughness, and he shows a keen baseball mind. The Twins forced Mata to use his changeup more in instructional league, and the pitch needs much more work. He received a scare at the end of instructional league when he was shut down with elbow pain. Minnesota initially feared he might require Tommy John surgery, but it turned out to be a strained ligament instead of a tear. Mata spent the winter rehabilitating his elbow in preparation for going to low Class A in 2005.

Year	Club (League)	Class	W	L	ERA	G	GS	CG	SV	IP	H	R	ER	HR	BB	SO	AVG
2002	Cagua (VSL)	R	3	1	3.38	22	0	0	0	40	24	18	15	0	16	37	.171
2003	Cagua (VSL)	R	5	2	3.47	26	0	0	7	36	28	19	14	1	19	51	.201
2004	Elizabethton (Appy)	R	2	2	3.73	26	1	0	13	31	22	15	13	1	6	39	.193
MINOR LEAGUE TOTALS			10	5	3.53	74	1	0	20	107	74	52	42	2	41	127	.187

Boof Bonser, rhp

Born: Oct. 14, 1981. **Ht.:** 6-4. **Wt.:** 250. **Bats:** R. **Throws:** R. **School:** Gibbs HS, St. Petersburg, Fla. **Career Transactions:** Selected by Giants in first round (21st overall) of 2000 draft; signed July 3, 2000 . . . Traded by Giants with RHP Joe Nathan and LHP Francisco Liriano to Twins for C A.J. Pierzynski and a player to be named, Nov. 14, 2003. **Signed by:** Alan Marr (Giants).

Bonser was one of the Giants' top pitching prospects when they included him in the A.J. Pierzynski trade in November 2003. With the Twins, his profile dropped dramatically, and he moped somewhat about that in the early going last year. After giving up far too many home runs in the first half, Bonser turned it on down the stretch and won his final eight decisions. He also earned a late promotion to Triple-A, where he'll likely start out in 2005. Bonser, who legally changed his name from John in high school, pitches at 89-92 mph but no longer hits the mid-90s as he did earlier in his pro career. Part of that is due to his Rick Reuschelesque frame, which usually carries 250-260 pounds. In the latter part of 2004, Bonser did a better job of keeping the ball down and changing speeds to set up his fastball. He has shown a plus curve in the past but still needs work on his changeup. His concentration and location need sharpening as well. He projects as a back-end-of-the-rotation option but could wind up as a long reliever.

Year	Club (League)	Class	W	L	ERA	G	GS	CG	SV	IP	H	R	ER	HR	BB	SO	AVG
2000	Salem-Keizer (NWL)	A	1	4	6.00	10	9	0	0	33	21	23	22	2	29	41	.188
2001	Hagerstown (SAL)	A	16	4	2.49	27	27	0	0	134	91	40	37	7	61	178	.192
2002	San Jose (Cal)	A	8	6	2.88	23	23	0	0	128	89	44	41	9	70	139	.195
	Shreveport (TL)	AA	1	2	5.55	5	5	0	0	24	30	15	15	3	14	23	.316
2003	Norwich (EL)	AA	7	10	4.00	24	24	1	0	135	122	80	60	11	67	103	.245
	Fresno (PCL)	AAA	1	2	3.13	4	4	0	0	23	17	13	8	4	8	28	.195
2004	New Britain (EL)	AA	12	9	4.37	27	27	0	0	154	160	89	75	22	56	146	.266
	Rochester (IL)	AAA	1	0	1.29	1	1	0	0	7	5	1	1	1	1	7	.192
MINOR LEAGUE TOTALS			47	37	3.65	121	120	1	0	639	535	305	259	59	306	665	.228

26 Alex Romero, of

Born: Sept. 9, 1983. **Ht.:** 6-0. **Wt.:** 180. **Bats:** L. **Throws:** R. **Career Transactions:** Signed out of Venezuela by Twins, July 2, 2000. **Signed by:** Rudy Hernandez.

Romero has evolved into a different player than the Twins envisioned when they signed him at age 16 out of Venezuela. He has added strength and thickness, especially in his lower half. He doesn't run well anymore, sacrificing plus speed for more sock at the plate, and no longer has the range to play center field. Romero has continued to hit, however. A switch-hitter, he owns a career .308 average as a pro. He shows good patience at the plate and has walked at least as much as he has struck out in each of his four seasons. Now primarily a right fielder, he does have good instincts and an average arm. Romero still lacks the sort of power production teams look for on the corners, which leaves him as a classic 'tweener. He should move up to Double-A in 2005.

Year	Club (League)	Class	AVG	G	AB	R	H	2B	3B	HR	RBI	BB	SO	SB	OBP	SLG
2001	San Joaquin (VSL)	R	.347	49	167	22	58	9	0	2	30	11	9	10	.388	.437
2002	Twins (GCL)	R	.333	56	186	31	62	13	2	2	42	29	14	16	.423	.457
2003	Quad City (Mid)	A	.296	120	423	50	125	16	3	4	40	43	43	11	.359	.376
2004	Fort Myers (FSL)	A	.292	104	380	59	111	21	2	6	42	54	47	6	.387	.405
MINOR LEAGUE TOTALS			.308	329	1156	162	356	59	7	14	154	137	113	43	.383	.407

27 David Shinskie, rhp

Born: May 4, 1984. **Ht.:** 6-4. **Wt.:** 205. **Bats:** R. **Throws:** R. **School:** Mt. Carmel Area HS, Kulpmont, Pa. **Career Transactions:** Selected by Twins in fourth round of 2003 draft; signed July 11, 2003. **Signed by:** Jay Weitzel.

Shinskie was recruited as a quarterback by several Big Ten Conference football programs out of Mount Carmel Area High, where he passed for 57 touchdowns and led the team to a pair of Pennsylvania 2-A titles. He signed to play football and baseball at Delaware, then gave that up for a $280,000 bonus from the Twins. He's one of several former quarterbacks in the organization, a list that includes righthander T.J. Prunty, a backup at Miami; catchers Joe Mauer (Florida State) and Eli Tintor (Minnesota-Duluth), who turned down college scholarships; and righty Colby Miller, who won an Oklahoma 4-A state championship in 1999. Shinskie has average stuff across the board, pitching at 89-91 mph and topping out at 93. He has a good slider that he locates well and a circle change that he throws in the mid-70s. A strike-thrower, he projects as a third or fourth starter at best. However, his athleticism and football background make him a good bet to tough it out along the way. He has strong makeup and shows good competitiveness. He wasn't dominant in the Appalachian League in his first full pro season, but he should move up to low Class A, where rotation spots will be at a premium.

Year	Club (League)	Class	W	L	ERA	G	GS	CG	SV	IP	H	R	ER	HR	BB	SO	AVG
2003	Twins (GCL)	R	1	4	7.41	5	5	0	0	17	20	18	14	0	10	13	.294
2004	Elizabethton (Appy)	R	7	3	4.19	11	11	0	0	54	59	31	25	6	17	28	.282
MINOR LEAGUE TOTALS			8	7	4.97	16	16	0	0	71	79	49	39	6	27	41	.285

28 Juan Portes, inf

Born: Nov. 26, 1985. **Ht.:** 5-11. **Wt.:** 170. **Bats:** R. **Throws:** R. **School:** Malden (Mass.) HS. **Career Transactions:** Selected by Twins in 15th round of 2004 draft; signed June 12, 2004. **Signed by:** Jay Weitzel.

A native Dominican, Portes played some high school baseball in Massachusetts, then dropped out and spent what would have been his senior year on the showcase circuit. He probably should have gone much earlier in the draft but slipped through the cracks and signed with the Twins as a 15th-rounder, in large part because of the diligence of area scout Jay Weitzel. Portes received a general equivalency degree and speaks fluent English, but baseball is his primary language. His bat is his best tool, as he led the Gulf Coast League lead in homers and slugging percentage. He projects to hit for even more power as he matures, despite his relatively small frame. Finding him a position is another matter. A shortstop as an amateur, Portes also played third and second base after signing. All told, he committed 24 errors in 30 games in the field. He has decent hands and slightly above arm strength, but he needs to improve his footwork and the accuracy of his throws. He'll probably spend most of his time at second in the Appalachian League this year.

Year	Club (League)	Class	AVG	G	AB	R	H	2B	3B	HR	RBI	BB	SO	SB	OBP	SLG
2004	Twins (GCL)	R	.327	44	168	24	55	8	1	8	31	12	28	4	.380	.530
MINOR LEAGUE TOTALS			.327	44	168	24	55	8	1	8	31	12	28	4	.380	.530

29 Eduardo Morlan, rhp

Born: March 1, 1986. **Ht.:** 6-2. **Wt.:** 210. **Bats:** R. **Throws:** R. **School:** Coral Park HS, Miami. **Career Transactions:** Selected by Twins in third round of 2004 draft; signed June 10, 2004. **Signed by:** Brad Weitzel.

Another of area scout Brad Weitzel's finds, Morlan comes from the same Coral Park High (Miami) program that produced Jose Canseco. Just before Morlan signed for $420,000, the Twins diagnosed him with an enlarged heart. He was shut down for a month until the condition was analyzed sufficiently, then he got down to business in the Gulf Coast League. In part because of the layoff, Morlan was the hardest thrower for the Twins at instructional league, regularly pitching at 93 mph and peaking at 95-96. He has a big body, an aggressive approach and a high-intensity, high-torque delivery that leaves some observers nervous. The combination of his hard sinking fastball and power slider have some thinking that his future lies in short relief. Morlan has tried to throw a changeup but hasn't grown comfortable with it yet. He might not ever gain the touch on a changeup because he has a full-effort delivery. He could open 2005 either in extended spring training or in the bullpen in low Class A.

Year	Club (League)	Class	W	L	ERA	G	GS	CG	SV	IP	H	R	ER	HR	BB	SO	AVG
2004	Twins (GCL)	R	1	2	2.84	11	2	0	1	25	25	14	8	1	10	28	.245
MINOR LEAGUE TOTALS			1	2	2.84	11	2	0	1	25	25	14	8	1	10	28	.245

30 Errol Simonitsch, lhp

Born: Aug. 24, 1982. **Ht.:** 6-4. **Wt.:** 225. **Bats:** L. **Throws:** L. **School:** Gonzaga University. **Career Transactions:** Selected by Twins in sixth round of 2003 draft; signed June 28, 2003. **Signed by:** Bill Lohr.

Bothered by shoulder tendinitis in the spring of 2003, Simonitsch made just eight starts in his junior year at Gonzaga. Twins scouting director Mike Radcliff wasn't able to see him in person, but area scout Bill Lohr and scouting supervisor Deron Johnson saw enough of Simonitsch to recommend him. Cleared to pitch upon signing, Simonitsch promptly helped Elizabethton win the Appalachian League title. In his first full pro season, he pitched at 86-88 mph but didn't touch 90 mph as often as he did in his debut. He got good results and used his changeup more often and more effectively. He also has a plus curveball. A classic finesse lefty, he has a clean delivery, loose arm, solid frame and good mound presence. He has a lower ceiling than many other Minnesota pitching prospects but is a safer bet to reach the majors. He reminds some of former Twins pitcher Mark Redman, another soft-tossing lefty with a college background.

Year	Club (League)	Class	W	L	ERA	G	GS	CG	SV	IP	H	R	ER	HR	BB	SO	AVG
2003	Elizabethton (Appy)	R	5	1	1.76	10	8	0	0	46	39	13	9	1	6	57	.220
2004	Quad Cities (Mid)	A	6	2	2.56	20	20	0	0	109	100	41	31	5	36	107	.244
MINOR LEAGUE TOTALS			11	3	2.32	30	28	0	0	155	139	54	40	6	42	164	.237

NEW YORK
METS

BY **J.J. COOPER**

STEVE MOORE

pparently, the worst thing that could have happened to the 2004 Mets was a little success. They began July 30 with a 49-52 record, six games back in the National League East and seven behind in the NL wild-card race. Nevertheless, the Mets decided their future was now. Rather than wait for some of its best prospects—lefthander Scott Kazmir, righty Matt Peterson and catcher Justin Huber—to mature and join **David Wright** and Jose Reyes in the majors, New York dealt them away to make a playoff run.

But even before their widely panned trades for Kris Benson and Victor Zambrano, the Mets were beginning to fade. New York went 22-39 the rest of the way to record its third straight losing season.

Before the season began, owner Fred Wilpon proclaimed he wouldn't trade away the team's future. Four months later, the Mets did exactly that. They gutted their minor league depth for no short-term benefit. They also overpaid Benson (three years, $22.5 million) on the free-agent market rather than face the stigma of dealing away prospects for a rental. As the industry wondered why the Mets would trade Kazmir to get Zambrano, the club offered a variety of excuses. One was that Kazmir wasn't nearly ready to contribute at the major league level. But he looked like a future ace at times after the Devil Rays called him up in August.

Worse, the Mets' front office turned out to be in chaos, with members jockeying to get the ear of Wilpon's son Jeff, the club's chief operating officer, and undermining general manager Jim Duquette. After the season, the Mets hired Expos GM Omar Minaya for the same role in New York, where he previously had been a senior assistant GM.

Duquette now works under Minaya as a senior vice president of baseball operations. Assistant GM Gary LaRocque had the scope of his duties reduced from director of baseball operations to overseeing only scouting. Russ Bove, a national crosschecker with the Expos under Minaya, became the new director of amateur scouting, replacing Jack Bowen, who remains with the club. The scouting department has had its hands tied in recent years as the Mets surrendered their second- and third-round picks in both 2002 and 2003 as free-agent compensation.

As Minaya tried to retool the Mets during the offseason, he realized the farm system wasn't going to provide immediate help. So he re-signed Benson, lavished a four-year, $53 million contract on Pedro Martinez, and topped it all off by signing outfielder Carlos Beltran, the most hotly pursued free agent this offseason, for $119 million.

Maybe New York will be improved in 2005. More certain is that its fans will cringe every time Kazmir takes the mound for Tampa Bay. The Mets' future is playing elsewhere and the present doesn't look too appealing—though the addition of Beltran and Martinez may ease some of the sting.

TOP 30 PROSPECTS

1. Lastings Milledge, of
2. Yusmeiro Petit, rhp
3. Philip Humber, rhp
4. Gaby Hernandez, rhp
5. Ambiorix Concepcion, of
6. Alay Soler, rhp
7. Shawn Bowman, 3b
8. Victor Diaz, of
9. Jesus Flores, c
10. Matt Lindstrom, rhp
11. Jamar Hill, of
12. Jeff Keppinger, 2b
13. Aarom Baldiris, 3b
14. Matt Durkin, rhp
15. Brian Bannister, rhp
16. Carlos Gomez, of
17. Anderson Hernandez, ss
18. Dae-Sung Koo, lhp
19. Bartolome Fortunato, rhp
20. Craig Brazell, 1b/of
21. Alhaji Turay, of
22. Blake McGinley, lhp
23. Angel Pagan, of
24. Brett Harper, 1b
25. Bob Keppel, rhp
26. Wayne Lydon, of
27. Bob Malek, of
28. Tyler Yates, rhp
29. Sean Henry, ss
30. Mike Jacobs, c

ORGANIZATION OVERVIEW

General Manager: Omar Minaya. **Farm director:** Kevin Morgan. **Scouting director:** Russ Bove.

2004 PERFORMANCE

Class	Team	League	W	L	Pct.	Finish*	Manager
Majors	New York	National	71	91	.438	12th (16)	Art Howe
Triple-A	Norfolk Tides	International	72	72	.500	7th (14)	John Stearns
Double-A	Binghamton Mets	Eastern	76	66	.535	4th (12)	Ken Oberkfell
High A	St. Lucie Mets	Florida State	64	65	.496	7th (12)	Tim Teufel
Low A	#Capital City Bombers	South Atlantic	89	47	.654	1st (16)	Jack Lind
Short-season	Brooklyn Cyclones	New York-Penn	43	31	.581	3rd (14)	Tony Tijerina
Rookie	Kingsport Mets	Appalachian	32	36	.471	6th (10)	Mookie Wilson
Rookie	GCL Mets	Gulf Coast	36	24	.600	t-2nd (12)	Brett Butler
OVERALL 2004 MINOR LEAGUE RECORD			412	341	.547	4th (30)	

*Finish in overall standings (No. of teams in league). #Affiliate will be in Hagerstown (South Atlantic) in 2005.

ORGANIZATION LEADERS

BATTING
*Minimum 250 at-bats
*AVG	Ian Bladergroen, Capital City	.342
R	Blake Whealy, Capital City	100
H	Victor Diaz, Norfolk	154
TB	Victor Diaz, Norfolk	259
2B	Prentice Redman, Norfolk/Binghamton	46
3B	Angel Pagan, Norfolk/Binghamton	11
HR	Jamar Hill, Capital City	26
RBI	Victor Diaz, Norfolk	94
BB	Blake Whealy, Capital City	66
SO	Corey Ragsdale, Norfolk/St. Lucie	156
SB	Wayne Lydon, Binghamton	65
*OBP	David Wright, Norfolk/Binghamton	.441
*SLG	David Wright, Norfolk/Binghamton	.605

PITCHING
#Minimum 75 innings
W	Blake McGinley, Norfolk/Binghamton	12
	Yusmeiro Petit, Bing./St. Lucie/Capital City	12
L	Three tied at	10
#ERA	Greg Ramirez, Capital City	2.06
G	P.J. Bevis, Norfolk/Binghamton	49
CG	Bryan Edwards, Binghamton/St. Lucie	2
SV	Heath Bell, Norfolk/Binghamton	16
	Jose Parra, Norfolk/Binghamton	16
IP	Brian Bannister, Binghamton/St. Lucie	155
BB	Jose Diaz, Binghamton	70
SO	Yusmeiro Petit, Bing./St. Lucie/Capital City	200

BEST TOOLS

Best Hitter for Average	Aarom Baldiris
Best Power Hitter	Jamar Hill
Best Strike Zone Discipline	Jeff Keppinger
Fastest Baserunner	Wayne Lydon
Best Athlete	Lastings Milledge
Best Fastball	Matt Lindstrom
Best Curveball	Philip Humber
Best Slider	Dae-Sung Koo
Best Changeup	Blake McGinley
Best Control	Yusmeiro Petit
Best Defensive Catcher	Joe Hietpas
Best Defensive Infielder	Anderson Hernandez
Best Infield Arm	Corey Ragsdale
Best Defensive Outfielder	Lastings Milledge
Best Outfield Arm	Bob Malek

PROJECTED 2008 LINEUP

Catcher	Jesus Flores
First Base	Doug Mientkiewicz
Second Base	Kaz Matsui
Third Base	David Wright
Shortstop	Jose Reyes
Left Field	Lastings Milledge
Center Field	Carlos Beltran
Right Field	Mike Cameron
No. 1 Starter	Pedro Martinez
No. 2 Starter	Kris Benson
No. 3 Starter	Yusmeiro Petit
No. 4 Starter	Philip Humber
No. 5 Starter	Gaby Hernandez
Closer	Braden Looper

LAST YEAR'S TOP 20 PROSPECTS

1. Kazuo Matsui, ss
2. Scott Kazmir, lhp
3. David Wright, 3b
4. Matt Peterson, rhp
5. Lastings Milledge, of
6. Justin Huber, c
7. Bob Keppel, rhp
8. Jeremy Griffiths, rhp
9. Victor Diaz, 2b
10. Craig Brazell, 1b
11. Aaron Baldiris, 3b
12. Tyler Yates, rhp
13. Royce Ring, lhp
14. Kole Strayhorn, rhp
15. Mike Jacobs, c
16. Danny Garcia, 2b
17. Joselo Diaz, rhp
18. Matt Lindstrom, rhp
19. Prentice Redman, of
20. Orber Moreno, rhp

TOP PROSPECTS OF THE DECADE

Year	Player, Pos.	Current Team
1995	Bill Pulsipher, lhp	Long Island (Atlantic)
1996	Paul Wilson, rhp	Reds
1997	Jay Payton, of	Red Sox
1998	Grant Roberts, rhp	Mets
1999	Alex Escobar, of	White Sox
2000	Alex Escobar, of	White Sox
2001	Alex Escobar, of	White Sox
2002	Aaron Heilman, rhp	Mets
2003	Jose Reyes, ss	Mets
2004	Kazuo Matsui, ss	Mets

TOP DRAFT PICKS OF THE DECADE

Year	Player, Pos.	Current Team
1995	Ryan Jaroncyk, ss	Out of baseball
1996	Robert Stratton, of	Reds
1997	Geoff Goetz, lhp	Yankees
1998	Jason Tyner, of	Indians
1999	Neal Musser, lhp (2)	Mets
2000	Billy Traber, lhp	Indians
2001	Aaron Heilman, rhp	Mets
2002	Scott Kazmir, lhp	Devil Rays
2003	Lastings Milledge, of	Mets
2004	Philip Humber, rhp	Mets

ALL-TIME LARGEST BONUSES

Philip Humber, 2004	$3,000,000
Scott Kazmir, 2002	$2,150,000
Lastings Milledge, 2003	$2,075,000
Geoff Goetz, 1997	$1,700,000
Paul Wilson, 1994	$1,550,000

New York METS

Impact Potential: C

Lastings Milledge has five-tool ability and gives the Mets a potential future all-star. Philip Humber has yet to throw a pitch as a pro, and he'll try to buck the poor track record of recent Rice pitchers (Matt Anderson, Mario Ramos, Kenny Baugh) in the pro ranks. Yusmeiro Petit piled up gaudy stats in 2004, but some scouts remain unconvinced that he'll be as effective at higher levels.

Depth: D

The Mets had some, then traded much of it with an eye on winning now. Losing Scott Kazmir was one thing, but New York also used up much of its trade fodder in losing the likes of Matt Peterson, Justin Huber and Ian Bladergroen. The Mets' biggest strength is in the outfield, where they have speed to burn and potential power bats in Jamar Hill and Victor Diaz.

Depth charts prepared by John Manuel and Allan Simpson. Numbers in parentheses indicate prospect rankings.

LF
Victor Diaz (8)
Alhaji Turay (21)
Ryan Harvey
Corey Coles

CF
Lastings Milledge (1)
Angel Pagan (23)
Wayne Lydon (26)
Prentice Redman
Dante Brinkley

RF
Ambiorix Concepcion (5)
Jamar Hill (11)
Carlos Gomez (16)
Bob Malek (27)
Jesus Gamero

3B
Shawn Bowman (7)
Nick Evans

SS
Anderson Hernandez (17)
Corey Ragsdale
Ryan Coultas

2B
Jeff Keppinger (12)
Aarom Baldiris (13)
Sean Henry (29)

1B
Craig Brazell (20)
Brett Harper (24)
Mike Carp
Tyler Davidson
Jim Burt

SOURCE of TALENT

HOMEGROWN		ACQUIRED	
College	5	Trades	5
Junior College	2	Rule 5 draft	0
Draft-and-follow	4	Independent leagues	0
High School	7	Free agents/waivers	0
Nondrafted free agent	0		
Foreign	7		

C
Jesus Flores (9)
Mike Jacobs (30)
Joe Hietpas
Aaron Hathaway
Yunir Garcia

LHP

Starters	Relievers
Neal Musser	Dae-Sung Koo (18)
Evan MacLane	Blake McGinley (22)
	Shane Hawk
	Royce Ring
	Ryan Olson

RHP

Starters	Relievers
Yusmeiro Petit (2)	Matt Lindstrom (10)
Philip Humber (3)	Bartolome Fortunato (19)
Gaby Hernandez (4)	Tyler Yates (28)
Alay Soler (6)	Greg Ramirez
Matt Durkin (14)	Kole Strayhorn
Brian Bannister (15)	Heath Bell
Bob Keppel (25)	Celso Rondon
Kevin Deaton	
Jason Scobie	
Orlando Roman	
Scott Hyde	
Vince Cordova	
Michael Devaney	
Miguel Pinango	

DRAFT ANALYSIS

2004

Best Pro Debut: RHP Gaby Hernandez (3) was named the Rookie-level Gulf Coast League's top pitching prospect and won the ERA title, going 4-3, 1.03 with a 64-12 K-BB ratio in 53 innings. SS Sean Henry (20) made the GCL all-star team after hitting .282-4-30 with 10 steals. RHP Michael Devaney (23) used a three-pitch mix to go 5-0, 1.95 at short-season Brooklyn.

Best Athlete: Henry runs well and has more pop than expected from a 5-foot-10, 155-pounder. He has arm strength as well, though his throws need to be more accurate and he may have to move to another position. OF Brahiam Maldonado (10) has all-around tools and was a top youth basketball player in Puerto Rico.

Best Pure Hitter: 1B Mike Carp (9) has a nice line-drive stroke from the left side of the plate. He batted .267-4-26 in the GCL. Henry also shows promise.

Best Raw Power: OF Caleb Stewart (22) went deep five times in 25 games in low Class A. He played at Kentucky, as did the area scout who signed him, Rod Henderson.

Fastest Runner: OF B.J. Suggs (27) can fly down the line, getting from the left side of the plate to first base in 3.95 seconds. He's still learning how to use his speed.

Best Defensive Player: C Aaron Hathaway (4) is athletic for his position and has the arm to shut down the running game. He led the short-season New York-Penn League by throwing out 39 percent of basestealers.

Best Fastball: RHP Philip Humber (1), the third overall pick, hit 97 mph while at Rice, a tick ahead of RHP Matt Durkin (2). Hernandez has the best command of his fastball, and he touches 94 mph with sink-

RICH ABEL

Hathaway

ing, riding action at age 18.

Best Breaking Ball: New York ranked Humber's 12-to-6 curveball as the best breaking pitch in the entire draft. Among the players who got on the mound last summer, RHP Scott Hyde (7) has a hard slider.

Most Intriguing Background: 1B/DH Jim Burt Jr.'s (19) father was a Pro Bowl defensive lineman who won Super Bowls with the New York Giants and San Francisco 49ers. Hyde was MVP of the NCAA Division III World Series after pitching George Fox (Ore.) to the championship.

Closest To The Majors: Even though he missed his first season, Humber may not need much more than a year before he's ready to help the Mets.

Best Late-Round Pick: The Mets are pleased with Henry, Stewart, Devaney and RHP Mike Swindell (29). Swindell has an average fastball and a plus curveball.

The One Who Got Away: RHP Brad Meyers (14) should become a premium draft pick after three years at Loyola Marymount. He's projectable at 6-foot-6 and already can touch 92-93 mph with his sinker.

Assessment: After trading their two most advanced pitching prospects in ill-advised midseason deals, the Mets at least can take solace in adding Humber, Durkin and Hernandez. The pitchers in this crop are much more impressive than the position players.

2003 OF Lastings Milledge (1) fell to the Mets at No. 12, and early returns are strong. Giving up their second- and third-round picks made it difficult to do much afterward, but RHP Brian Bannister (7) is a sleeper. *GRADE:* B

2002 We don't grade teams for what they do with their picks in trades. So we'll give New York credit for snatching LHP Scott Kazmir (1) and continue to wonder why it used him to deal for . . . Victor Zambrano? The Mets also have traded draft-and-follow 1B Ian Bladergroen

(44) for Doug Mientkiewicz. *GRADE:* B+

2001 New York has signed a lot of exciting young talent recently, none better than 3B David Wright (1). The other first-rounder, RHP Aaron Heilman, didn't work out nearly as well. *GRADE:* A

2000 LHP Billy Traber (1) went to Cleveland and blew out his elbow. RHP Matt Peterson (2) was dealt for Kris Benson last summer. In between, the Mets took RHP Bob Keppel (1), who can't stay healthy. *GRADE:* C

Draft analysis prepared by Jim Callis. Numbers in parentheses indicate draft rounds.

TONY FARLOW

Lastings
MILLEDGE

Born: April 5, 1985.
Ht.: 6-1. **Wt.:** 185.
Bats: R. **Throws:** R.
School: Lakewood Ranch HS, Palmetto, Fla.
Career Transactions: Selected by Mets in first round (12th overall) of 2003 draft; signed Aug. 19, 2003.
Signed by: Joe Salermo.

Baseball is in Milledge's blood. His father Tony Sr. was the Cardinals' third-round pick in the secondary phase of the January 1973 draft and played one year in Rookie ball. Lastings' older brothers Anthony and Tony Jr. also played professionally, though neither made it out of Class A. That won't be a problem for Milledge, who projected as a future first-round pick since he was a high school sophomore. New York was able to get him with the 12th overall pick in 2003 because of his mixed success with wood bats, a rumored high price tag and allegations of improper sexual conduct—none of which was ever substantiated. The Mets say he has been a solid citizen since signing for $2.075 million, the third-highest bonus in club history. Milledge missed the first month of the 2004 season after breaking a finger when he was hit by a pitch during bunting drills in spring training. Once he returned, he quickly showed all of the tools the Mets have been salivating about. Though he struggled after a promotion to high Class A St. Lucie and returned to low Class A Capital City to help the Bombers' playoff run, he showed signs of being able to adjust and his effort never wavered.

Milledge's bat speed is exceptional, giving him the ability to wait on pitches and drive them to all fields. He already has above-average power and should be a No. 3 hitter in the majors. He's most comfortable roping line drives to the gaps, but he can also bounce balls off of light towers on occasion. Since he's an above-average runner (4.1 seconds from the right side of the plate to first base), he also has the ability to serve as a tablesetter. He batted almost exclusively out of the leadoff spot last season. His speed, range and arm strength make him the best defensive outfielder in the system. Milledge's all-around tools compare favorably to those of anyone in the minors, and he has delivered production to go along with his potential.

Milledge covers plenty of ground in center field, but he still needs to improve his jumps. He also had trouble going back on balls in 2004. If he's blocked in center by Carlos Beltran or even Mike Cameron, he could handle a move to right field. While he has plenty of speed and has succeeded on 31 of his 40 pro steal attempts, Milledge needs to take more chances on the bases. On the other hand, he's sometimes too aggressive at the plate. His exceptional bat speed keeps him from being a 100-strikeout guy, but he doesn't work counts particularly well and he doesn't draw a lot of walks.

Milledge's first full season was everything the Mets had hoped for. He'll return to high Class A to start 2005 but should reach Double-A Binghamton before too long. In an organization that promoted one potential all-star (David Wright) and traded another away (Scott Kazmir) in the second half of the 2004 season, Milledge could move quickly. There isn't another player in the system whose ceiling approaches his.

Year	Club (League)	Class	AVG	G	AB	R	H	2B	3B	HR	RBI	BB	SO	SB	OBP	SLG
2003	Kingsport (Appy)	R	.231	7	26	4	6	2	0	0	2	3	4	5	.323	.308
2004	Capital City (SAL)	A	.340	65	262	66	89	22	1	13	58	17	53	23	.399	.580
	St. Lucie (FSL)	A	.235	22	81	6	19	6	2	2	8	9	21	3	.319	.432
MINOR LEAGUE TOTALS			.309	94	369	76	114	30	3	15	68	29	78	31	.376	.528

Yusmeiro Petit, rhp

Born: Nov. 22, 1984. **Ht.:** 6-0. **Wt.:** 180. **Bats:** R. **Throws:** R. **Career Transactions:** Signed out of Venezuela by Mets, Nov. 15, 2001. **Signed by:** Gregorio Machado.

Petit has dominated at every step up the ladder. He has struck out more than a batter an inning in all six minor league stops, finishing second in the minors with 200 whiffs in 2004. He followed up with a strong winter in Venezuela. Petit's fastball leaves batters and scouts scratching their heads. It has solid velocity (89-91 mph, touching 93) and movement, but nothing about it appears to be exceptional—except how hitters never seem to get a good swing against it. His slider is already average and has plus potential. His changeup is more advanced than his slider, but with less room for growth. It's uncertain whether Petit's fastball will play as well against more advanced hitters. However, those questions are diminishing as he continues to have success. Petit carries a little extra weight and will need to make sure he doesn't add too much more. The trade of Scott Kazmir left Petit as the Mets' best pitching prospect, though first-round pick Philip Humber may have something to say about that after signing in January. Petit will likely begin 2005 in Double-A.

Year	Club (League)	Class	W	L	ERA	G	GS	CG	SV	IP	H	R	ER	HR	BB	SO	AVG
2002	Universidad (VSL)	R	3	5	2.43	12	11	0	0	56	53	25	15	1	16	62	.252
2003	Kingsport (Appy)	R	3	3	2.32	12	12	0	0	62	47	19	16	2	8	65	.219
	Brooklyn (NY-P)	A	1	0	2.19	2	2	0	0	12	5	3	3	0	2	20	.119
2004	Capital City (SAL)	A	9	2	2.39	15	15	0	0	83	47	29	22	8	22	122	.159
	St. Lucie (FSL)	A	2	3	1.22	9	9	1	0	44	27	9	6	0	14	62	.175
	Binghamton (EL)	AA	1	1	4.50	2	2	0	0	12	10	6	6	0	5	16	.222
MINOR LEAGUE TOTALS			19	14	2.27	52	51	1	0	269	189	91	68	11	67	34	.196

Philip Humber, rhp

Born: Dec. 21, 1982. **Ht.:** 6-4. **Wt.:** 220. **Bats:** R. **Throws:** R. **School:** Rice University. **Career Transactions:** Selected by Mets in first round of 2004 draft; signed Jan. 11, 2005. **Signed by:** Dave Lottsfeldt.

One of three Rice righthanders to go in the top eight picks of the 2004 draft, Humber was the first selected and the first to sign. He waited until early January to come to terms, inking a five-year major league contract that includes a club-record $3 million bonus and $4.2 million in guaranteed money. Humber didn't have the highest ceiling in the draft, but he could make a case for being the safest choice. He has three potential plus pitches, starting with a 12-to-6 curveball the Mets rated as the best breaking ball in the entire draft. He also has a 90-94 mph fastball that has touched 97, and a splitter he uses as a changeup. He has clean mechanics, a sturdy frame and a resilient arm. Humber also has a long track record of success, going 35-8, 2.80 in three years at Rice and winning the College World Series-clinching game in 2003. His fastball can straighten out at times and there's a little recoil in his delivery, but neither is a major concern. Intense and introverted, Humber likely will begin his pro career in the warm weather of St. Lucie. With his pedigree and ability, he should reach Double-A quickly and may not need much more than a season in the minors before he pushes for a big league job.

Year	Club (League)	Class	W	L	ERA	G	GS	CG	SV	IP	H	R	ER	HR	BB	SO	AVG
2004	Did not play—Signed 2005 contract																

Gaby Hernandez, rhp

Born: May 21, 1986. **Ht.:** 6-3. **Wt.:** 215. **Bats:** R. **Throws:** R. **School:** Belen Jesuit HS, Miami. **Career Transactions:** Selected by the Mets in third round of 2004 draft; signed June 22, 2004. **Signed by:** Joe Salermo.

Hernandez was one of the top high school pitchers in Florida in 2003 and 2004, leading Belen Jesuit to the state 3-A finals as a junior. After signing for $480,000, he won the Rookie-level Gulf Coast League ERA title and pitched the Mets to the league playoffs, where he got shelled. Hernandez features an 89-94 mph sinker that he already commands like a veteran. He baffled GCL hitters by throwing it to both sides of the plate. He also has a sharp curveball with good bite that he throws for strikes. His body is the prototype for a righthander. With all that, the Mets say his poise may be his best attribute. Hernandez is more polished than the average teenager, but he still can improve his mechanics. His changeup is solid but still can improve. More than anything, he just needs experi-

ence. Hernandez aced his first exam. The Mets place an emphasis on winning at short-season Brooklyn, so they could send him there in 2005 even though he probably could handle an assignment to their new low Class A Hagerstown affiliate.

Year	Club (League)	Class	W	L	ERA	G	GS	CG	SV	IP	H	R	ER	HR	BB	SO	AVG
2004	Mets (GCL)	R	3	3	1.09	10	9	2	0	50	25	10	6	1	12	58	.150
	Brooklyn (NY-P)	A	1	0	0.00	1	0	0	0	3	2	0	0	0	0	6	.200
MINOR LEAGUE TOTALS			4	3	1.02	11	9	2	0	53	27	10	6	1	12	64	.153

5 Ambiorix Concepcion, of

Born: Oct. 15, 1983. **Ht.:** 6-2. **Wt.:** 180. **Bats:** R. **Throws:** R. **Career Transactions:** Signed out of Dominican Republic by Mets, July 3, 2000. **Signed by:** Eddy Toledo.

When scouts saw Concepcion earn recognition as the top prospect in the short-season New York-Penn League last summer, they had a reason to wonder where he came from. One of many Dominicans caught in the visa crackdowns, he previously had been known as Robert Solano, though his age remained the same. Concepcion's pitch recognition improved in 2004, which paid off in increased average and vastly improved power. He projects as a near-.300 hitter with 20-25 homers a year. Though he's only an average runner, he has demonstrated basestealing ability. He plays a solid right field with a plus arm. As good as Concepcion's season was, he still has yet to play in a full-season league. He has been around long enough that the Mets had to protect him on their 40-man roster, which started his options clock ticking. Thanks to a long swing, he strikes out too much. He's also prone to errors. Concepcion will be the marquee player at Hagerstown in 2005. With a successful first half, he could earn a promotion to high Class A.

Year	Club (League)	Class	AVG	G	AB	R	H	2B	3B	HR	RBI	BB	SO	SB	OBP	SLG
2001	Mets (DSL)	R	.264	37	129	17	34	6	0	0	16	9	23	5	.317	.310
2002	Kingsport (Appy)	R	.276	57	228	25	63	13	4	4	31	7	51	6	.302	.421
2003	Kingsport (Appy)	R	.214	45	168	22	36	8	3	0	19	9	35	10	.256	.298
2004	Brooklyn (NY-P)	A	.305	66	259	38	79	14	3	8	46	13	54	28	.338	.475
MINOR LEAGUE TOTALS			.270	205	784	102	212	41	10	12	112	38	163	49	.306	.394

6 Alay Soler, rhp

Born: Oct. 9, 1979. **Ht.:** 6-4. **Wt.:** 240. **Bats:** R. **Throws:** R. **Career Transactions:** Signed out of Cuba by Mets, Sept. 1, 2004. **Signed by:** Rafael Bournigal.

Soler helped Cuba win the 2002 World University Games, where he didn't allow a run in two starts, and led the island's major league with a 2.01 ERA in 2003. He defected by boat in November 2003, received asylum in the Dominican Republic and signed a three-year big league contract worth $2.8 million last September. Soler throws a 91-93 mph fastball that can touch 95. It features good armside run when he keeps it down in the zone. His 80-82 mph slider has tight spin with good depth, and his changeup is an average pitch that he can throw for strikes. He has a strong frame and a clean delivery. One scout who saw Soler in the Dominican League this winter said he struggled with his fastball command and his mechanics when he hit 94-95 mph. He sometimes fails to get on top of the ball from his three-quarters delivery. He has a lot of history to overcome, as most Cuban defectors have failed to live up to their hype. Several Cubans were sent straight to the majors, but the Mets will take a more pragmatic approach. Soler will start at high Class A or Double-A.

Year	Club (League)	Class	W	L	ERA	G	GS	CG	SV	IP	H	R	ER	HR	BB	SO	AVG
2004	Did not play—Signed 2005 contract																

7 Shawn Bowman, 3b

Born: Dec. 9, 1984. **Ht.:** 6-2. **Wt.:** 190. **Bats:** R. **Throws:** R. **School:** Dr. Charles Best SS, Coquitlam, B.C. **Career Transactions:** Selected by Mets in 12th round of 2002 draft; signed Aug. 18, 2002. **Signed by:** Claude Pelletier.

When Bowman was hitting .187 in his 2003 pro debut, the Mets remained confident he was a prospect. He repaid that faith with a solid 2004 season. One of the system's hardest workers, he trains during the winter at the club's Dominican academy, where his fluent Spanish comes in handy. Bowman began to hit once he fixed mechanical problems with his swing and got more balanced in his stance. He showed the consistency at the plate the Mets envisioned when he hit .395 with a team-best four homers for

Canada at the 2002 World Junior Championship. He's an above-average third baseman, with a plus arm and good lateral movement. Bowman still strikes out too much, largely because his pitch recognition needs work. He'll gear up for a fastball and get fooled easily by breaking stuff. Bowman is ready for high Class A. David Wright seemingly has third base to himself with the Mets, but there are no immediate plans to play Bowman at a different position because he's above-average at third base.

Year	Club (League)	Class	AVG	G	AB	R	H	2B	3B	HR	RBI	BB	SO	SB	OBP	SLG
2003	Brooklyn (NY-P)	A	.203	42	138	10	28	7	1	0	5	10	49	2	.260	.268
	Kingsport (Appy)	R	.121	10	33	2	4	1	0	0	3	1	13	0	.216	.152
2004	Capital City (SAL)	A	.255	116	396	65	101	17	1	18	66	39	121	5	.336	.439
MINOR LEAGUE TOTALS			.235	168	567	77	133	25	2	18	74	50	183	7	.311	.381

8 Victor Diaz, of

Born: Dec. 10, 1981. **Ht.:** 6-0. **Wt.:** 200. **Bats:** R. **Throws:** R. **School:** Grayson County (Texas) CC. **Career Transactions:** Selected by Dodgers in 37th round of 2000 draft; signed May 19, 2001 . . . Traded by Dodgers with RHP Kole Strayhorn and RHP Joselo Diaz to Mets for OF Jeromy Burnitz, July 14, 2003. **Signed by:** Mike Leuzinger/ Bob Szymkowski (Dodgers).

Diaz won two batting titles in two full seasons in the Dodgers system before joining the Mets as part of the Jeromy Burnitz deal in 2003. He has continued to hit, including three homers in his 15-game big league debut last September. The biggest blast was a three-run shot in the ninth on Sept. 25 against the Cubs, signaling the beginning of their fall. Diaz has a quick bat that sprays line drives. In past years, there was a concern that he never would have more than gap power, but he hit 27 homers in 2004. His arm is average and better suited to the outfield than the infield, where he played until last season. Diaz never will be a selective hitter. His increased power came with a corresponding jump in strikeouts. He doesn't run well and that shows in the outfield, where he makes routine plays but little more. Conditioning never has been his forte. The Mets still don't know if Diaz is a future big league regular or just a useful reserve. The Carlos Beltran signing means he'll have to come off the bench in 2005 once Mike Cameron returns from wrist surgery.

Year	Club (League)	Class	AVG	G	AB	R	H	2B	3B	HR	RBI	BB	SO	SB	OBP	SLG
2001	Dodgers (GCL)	R	.354	53	195	36	69	22	2	3	31	16	23	6	.414	.533
2002	South Georgia (SAL)	A	.350	91	349	64	122	26	2	10	58	27	69	20	.407	.521
	Jacksonville (SL)	AA	.211	42	152	22	32	7	0	4	24	7	42	7	.258	.336
2003	Jacksonville (SL)	AA	.291	85	316	42	92	20	2	10	55	27	60	8	.353	.462
	Binghamton (EL)	AA	.354	45	175	29	62	11	0	6	23	8	32	7	.382	.520
2004	Norfolk (IL)	AAA	.292	141	528	81	154	31	1	24	94	31	133	6	.332	.491
	New York (NL)	MAJ	.294	15	51	8	15	3	0	3	8	1	15	0	.321	.529
MAJOR LEAGUE TOTALS			.294	15	51	8	15	3	0	3	8	1	15	0	.321	.529
MINOR LEAGUE TOTALS			.310	457	1715	274	531	117	7	57	285	116	359	54	.359	.486

9 Jesus Flores, c

Born: Oct. 26, 1984. **Ht.:** 6-1. **Wt.:** 180. **Bats:** R. **Throws:** R. **Career Transactions:** Signed out of Venezuela by Mets, March 12, 2002. **Signed by:** Junior Roman/Gregorio Machado.

Flores' bat came alive in his first season in the United States. After posting a .233 average in two seasons in the Rookie-level Venezuelan Summer League, he batted .320 over here. He also continued to provide stellar defense, leading Gulf Coast League regulars by throwing out 44 percent of basestealers. Though he's just 20, Flores already rivals veteran Joe Hietpas as the organization's best defensive catcher. He handles pitchers well, blocks pitches with aplomb and has solid footwork. His arm may be his best tool, as he consistently shows 1.9-2.0-second pop times from glove to second base. At the plate, he has a solid swing and already uses the entire field with average power. Despite his strong year, Flores' bat isn't nearly as advanced as his defensive skills. He struggles with breaking balls because he doesn't identify them well. He moves well for a catcher, but his speed still grades out as below-average. Flores could be the all-around catcher the Mets have been searching for. He's ticketed for Brooklyn in 2005.

Year	Club (League)	Class	AVG	G	AB	R	H	2B	3B	HR	RBI	BB	SO	SB	OBP	SLG
2002	Universidad (VSL)	R	.203	40	123	10	25	8	0	1	8	10	29	2	.305	.293
2003	Troncoraro (VSL)	R	.255	52	166	26	42	16	0	4	32	21	24	2	.303	.424
2004	Mets (GCL)	R	.319	45	141	16	45	12	3	4	25	8	26	1	.368	.532
	Brooklyn (NY-P)	A	.333	3	6	1	2	0	0	1	3	0	1	0	.333	.833
MINOR LEAGUE TOTALS			.262	140	435	52	114	36	3	10	68	39	80	5	.355	.428

Matt Lindstrom, rhp

10

Born: Feb. 11, 1980. **Ht.:** 6-4. **Wt.:** 205. **Bats:** R. **Throws:** R. **School:** Ricks (Idaho) JC. **Career Transactions:** Selected by Mets in 10th round of 2002 draft; signed June 14, 2002. **Signed by:** Jim Reeves.

Lindstrom is raw for a 25-year-old because he spent two years on a Mormon mission to Sweden. He returned to play a year at Ricks (Idaho) Junior College with his brother Rob. After a solid 2004 season, he attracted the attention of scouts in the Arizona Fall League, so the Mets protected him on the 40-man roster. Lindstrom has the best arm in the Mets system, with a fastball that sits at 94-96 and touched 100 mph during the season. He carries his velocity deep into his starts, and when he's locked in he can dominate hitters. His slider and curveball are average pitches. For a guy that can put triple digits on the radar gun, Lindstrom is passive too often. His fastball lacks movement and hitters get a good look at it coming out of his hand. He needs to pitch to both sides of the plate, tighten his slider and stay on top of his pitches. His changeup is merely usable. At some point Lindstrom has to turn projection into production, but his arm will buy him time. He'll probably return to high Class A to begin 2005. His long-term role could be in relief.

Year	Club (League)	Class	W	L	ERA	G	GS	CG	SV	IP	H	R	ER	HR	BB	SO	AVG
2002	Kingsport (Appy)	R	0	6	4.84	12	11	0	0	48	56	45	26	6	21	39	.280
2003	Capital City (SAL)	A	2	3	2.86	12	11	0	0	57	46	21	18	2	33	50	.228
	Brooklyn (NY-P)	A	7	3	3.44	14	14	0	0	65	61	28	25	2	27	52	.250
2004	Capital City (SAL)	A	3	2	3.21	12	11	0	0	56	47	26	20	3	10	64	.223
	St. Lucie (FSL)	A	5	5	3.73	14	14	1	0	80	83	44	33	5	20	50	.272
MINOR LEAGUE TOTALS			17	19	3.59	64	61	1	0	306	293	164	122	18	111	255	.252

Jamar Hill, of

11

Born: Sept. 20, 1982. **Ht.:** 6-4. **Wt.:** 200. **Bats:** R. **Throws:** R. **School:** Santa Ana (Calif.) JC. **Career Transactions:** Selected by Mets in 48th round of 2001 draft; signed May 27, 2002. **Signed by:** Steve Leavitt.

A native of Alaska, Hill had fewer at-bats than the typical junior-college product when he signed in 2002. He struggled in his adjustment to pro ball because he overanalyzed everything. Hill is intelligent and a hard worker. The game started to click for him in 2004, allowing him to start to take advantage of his multitude of tools. Hill is an average runner with a strong arm (he threw 90-92 mph as a pitcher in junior college), but his calling card is his pop. He has the best raw power in the system, with wiry strength that allows him to whip the bat through the zone. With the power comes plenty of strikeouts. Hill has made some improvement and isn't fooled by pitches as often as he was in the past, but he'll always be somewhat of a feast-or-famine hitter. If he can continue the strides he made in 2004 this year in high Class A, he quickly could become part of the Mets' future plans.

Year	Club (League)	Class	AVG	G	AB	R	H	2B	3B	HR	RBI	BB	SO	SB	OBP	SLG
2002	Kingsport (Appy)	R	.295	56	200	34	59	14	2	8	31	22	48	7	.374	.505
2003	Kingsport (Appy)	R	.241	44	170	22	41	12	0	6	26	10	45	14	.280	.418
	Capital City (SAL)	A	.300	8	20	0	6	1	0	0	1	1	6	0	.364	.350
2004	Capital City (SAL)	A	.271	121	458	83	124	21	1	26	89	37	110	20	.334	.491
MINOR LEAGUE TOTALS			.271	229	848	139	230	48	3	40	147	70	209	41	.334	.476

Jeff Keppinger, 2b

12

Born: April 21, 1980. **Ht.:** 6-0. **Wt.:** 180. **Bats:** R. **Throws:** R. **School:** University of Georgia. **Career Transactions:** Selected by Pirates in fourth round of 2001 draft; signed Aug. 3, 2001 . . . Traded by Pirates with RHP Kris Benson to Mets for 3B Ty Wigginton, RHP Matt Peterson and 3B Jose Bautista, July 30, 2004. **Signed by:** Jack Powell (Pirates).

The younger brother of Billy Keppinger, whom the Royals converted from an outfielder to a pitcher last year, Keppinger has shown the ability to hit for average throughout his pro career. Acquired from the Pirates in the Kris Benson trade, he doesn't blow scouts away with any exceptional tools. But he's able to put the bat on the ball in almost any situation, a skill he continued to show off after his major league promotion. Keppinger's value is almost entirely derived from his batting average, as his contact approach diminishes his power potential and reduces his walks. He homered twice off Mark Prior in a 2001 College World Series game, but has gone deep just seven times in two years after leaving low Class A. He has average speed and defensive ability at second base. He has good body control and decent hands. Keppinger's value to the Mets depends on his ability to add some versatility. He was a shortstop in college, but hasn't played there as a pro. New York wants him to play some shortstop and third base this spring to help him battle for a utility role.

Year	Club (League)	Class	AVG	G	AB	R	H	2B	3B	HR	RBI	BB	SO	SB	OBP	SLG
2002	Hickory (SAL)	A	.276	126	478	75	132	23	4	10	73	47	33	6	.344	.404
2003	Lynchburg (Car)	A	.325	92	342	55	111	21	2	3	51	23	28	3	.365	.424
2004	Altoona (EL)	AA	.338	82	320	45	108	17	2	1	33	27	17	10	.387	.413
	Binghamton (EL)	AA	.362	14	47	14	17	3	1	0	5	6	2	2	.426	.468
	Norfolk (IL)	AAA	.316	6	19	1	6	1	0	0	2	4	2	0	.458	.368
	New York (NL)	MAJ	.284	33	116	9	33	2	0	3	9	6	7	2	.317	.379
MAJOR LEAGUE TOTALS			.284	33	116	9	33	2	0	3	9	6	7	2	.317	.379
MINOR LEAGUE TOTALS			.310	320	1206	190	374	65	9	14	164	107	82	21	.366	.414

13 Aarom Baldiris, 3b

Born: Jan. 5, 1983. **Ht.:** 6-2. **Wt.:** 195. **Bats:** R. **Throws:** R. **Career Transactions:** Signed out of Venezuela by Mets, July 2, 1999. **Signed by:** Gregorio Machado.

Baldiris contended for the high Class A Florida State League batting title, but he failed to show any glimpse of power potential. He has topped .300 in all but two of his eight minor league stops, but he failed to slug .400 with either of his two teams last year. Baldiris has a terrific batting eye and a solid swing that stays inside the ball as he uses the entire field. But he seems unlikely to develop power, struggling whenever he gets more pull-conscious. He gained weight in his lower half, which made him a little slower in the field. Even so, the Mets are considering moving Baldiris to second base in Double-A this year. He tried the position in instructional league, and he would have more value as a top-of-the-order hitter if he can handle the position switch. His arm and soft hands would be an asset at second base, though there are questions about whether he would have enough range, as his foot speed is a tick below-average. If he remains at third base, he doesn't have enough pop to profile for the position—and he'll never dislodge David Wright from the hot corner.

Year	Club (League)	Class	AVG	G	AB	R	H	2B	3B	HR	RBI	BB	SO	SB	OBP	SLG
2000	Universidad (VSL)	R	.353	44	139	24	49	9	1	7	35	37	23	4	.489	.583
	Kingsport (Appy)	R	.219	32	105	14	23	3	1	2	20	7	20	2	.265	.324
2001	Did not play—Injured															
2002	Kingsport (Appy)	R	.327	58	217	31	71	9	1	3	24	14	24	9	.390	.419
	Brooklyn (NY-P)	A	.303	9	33	5	10	1	0	0	2	1	2	2	.343	.333
2003	Capital City (SAL)	A	.313	107	393	55	123	19	4	6	68	51	55	13	.396	.427
	Brooklyn (NY-P)	A	.364	26	88	20	32	5	2	0	18	14	13	2	.451	.466
2004	St. Lucie (FSL)	A	.305	107	406	57	124	15	5	4	45	46	64	6	.384	.397
	Binghamton (EL)	AA	.235	21	81	8	19	3	1	0	8	6	13	0	.284	.296
MINOR LEAGUE TOTALS			.308	404	1462	214	451	64	15	22	220	176	214	38	.389	.418

14 Matt Durkin, rhp

Born: Feb. 22, 1983. **Ht.:** 6-4. **Wt.:** 220. **Bats:** R. **Throws:** R. **School:** San Jose State University. **Career Transactions:** Selected by Mets in second round of 2004 draft; signed Aug. 25, 2004. **Signed by:** Chuck Hensley Jr.

Durkin made a gaudy debut at San Jose State, going 11-3, 2.75 as a freshman, and had a solid sophomore season. He headed into last spring with lofty expectations but his ERA jumped to 4.49. He still became the second-highest draft pick in Spartans history (behind only Mark Langston) when the Mets took him in the second round and signed him for $800,000. Durkin's problems at San Jose State could be traced to his inconsistent command and over-reliance on his fastball. He showed little knack for changing speeds and tried to blow the ball past hitters. The Mets were encouraged that he started to regain the feel on his curveball late in the spring, as he won his last four decisions. Durkin didn't sign until late in the season, so the Mets won't get a good look at him in game action until 2005. They like his live arm, which delivers a 92-94 mph fastball that touches 96. He also has an effective cut fastball and changeup, and he's regaining the plus curveball he had as a freshman. With his loose delivery and sturdy frame, he should be durable. Durkin probably will make his pro debut in low Class A but could get a promotion before his first full season ends.

Year	Club (League)	Class	W	L	ERA	G	GS	CG	SV	IP	H	R	ER	HR	BB	SO	AVG
2004	Did not play—Signed 2005 contract																

15 Brian Bannister, rhp

Born: Feb. 28, 1981. **Ht.:** 6-1. **Wt.:** 205. **Bats:** R. **Throws:** R. **School:** University of Southern California. **Career Transactions:** Selected by Mets in seventh round of 2003 draft; signed June 7, 2003. **Signed by:** Steve Leavitt.

The son of former No. 1 overall pick and major leaguer Floyd Bannister, Bannister has the advanced approach expected of a pitcher's son. He has made a quick ascent up the minor league ladder, holding his own in Double-A in his first full season of pro ball. Bannister throws five different pitches and can locate them all. He works with a 90-92 mph fastball, a

12-to-6 curveball that's inconsistent but can be an out pitch, an average changeup and an average slider. Last year he added an 87-88 mph cut fastball that could be another out pitch. His cutter has good movement and generates a lot of bad swings. Bannister throws strikes, though he's not overpowering and is fairly hittable. He doesn't have a high ceiling, but with good control, a feel for pitching and a solid repertoire, he could develop into a solid back-of-the-rotation starter, maybe as soon as 2006. He's likely to start 2005 at Triple-A Norfolk.

Year	Club (League)	Class	W	L	ERA	G	GS	CG	SV	IP	H	R	ER	HR	BB	SO	AVG
2003	Brooklyn (NY-P)	A	4	1	2.15	12	9	0	1	46	27	12	11	0	18	42	.173
2004	Binghamton (EL)	AA	3	3	4.06	8	8	0	0	44	45	23	20	2	17	28	.276
	St. Lucie (FSL)	A	5	7	4.24	20	20	0	0	110	111	63	52	6	27	106	.263
MINOR LEAGUE TOTALS			12	11	3.72	40	37	0	1	201	183	98	83	8	62	176	.247

16 Carlos Gomez, of

Born: Dec. 4, 1981. **Ht.:** 6-4. **Wt.:** 190. **Bats:** R. **Throws:** R. **Career Transactions:** Signed out of Dominican Republic by Mets, July 27, 2002. **Signed by:** Eddy Toledo.

When the Mets signed Gomez at age 16, he was a rail-thin but speedy outfielder. Now he has grown two inches and started to fill out his 6-foot-4 frame while retaining much of his speed. He's still a long way from Shea Stadium, but Gomez' tools compare favorably with those of any outfielder in the system except Lastings Milledge. He deftly handled the transition from his native Dominican Republic to the United States last year. Gomez projects to have average or better tools across the board. He flashes plus speed and good bat speed while showing a plus arm and plus range in right field. Power is his least developed tool, but he already can drive balls to the gaps. With his bat speed, scouts expect home runs to come. He'll have to tone down his aggressive approach at higher levels. He'll probably move up just one level to Brooklyn this year and make his full-season debut in 2006.

Year	Club (League)	Class	AVG	G	AB	R	H	2B	3B	HR	RBI	BB	SO	SB	OBP	SLG
2003	Mets (DSL)	R	.240	58	208	26	50	7	0	1	10	7	37	13	.283	.288
2004	Kingsport (Appy)	R	.287	38	150	24	43	10	4	1	20	5	29	8	.333	.427
	Mets (GCL)	R	.268	19	71	10	19	7	0	0	11	2	9	9	.303	.366
MINOR LEAGUE TOTALS			.224	115	429	60	112	24	4	2	41	14	75	30	.304	.350

17 Anderson Hernandez, ss

Born: Oct. 30, 1982. **Ht.:** 5-9. **Wt.:** 160. **Bats:** B. **Throws:** R. **Career Transactions:** Signed out of Dominican Republic by Tigers, April 23, 2001 . . . Traded by Tigers to Mets for C Vance Wilson, Jan. 6, 2005. **Signed by:** Ramon Pena (Tigers).

Acquired in a January deal for catcher Vance Wilson, Hernandez immediately became the Mets' best shortstop prospect. Long considered the top defensive shortstop in the Tigers organization, Hernandez bounced back last year after a pair of disappointing seasons to show his bat isn't a lost cause. He still has work to do offensively, however. While added strength has helped him at the plate, he strikes out too much to take advantage of his above-average speed and doesn't drive the ball. He operates with more of a slap-hitting approach, which doesn't complement his free-swinging style. Hernandez' glove is major league-ready. He has fluid shortstop actions, excellent range and a strong arm. He has the athletic ability and body control to make accurate throws from all angles on the run. He toned down his tendency to be too flashy last season and was much more consistent on routine plays. Hernandez probably will open 2005 in Triple-A, but it's hard to imagine him pushing Jose Reyes or Kaz Matsui for a starting job in the Mets' middle infield.

Year	Club (League)	Class	AVG	G	AB	R	H	2B	3B	HR	RBI	BB	SO	SB	OBP	SLG
2001	Tigers (GCL)	R	.264	55	216	37	57	5	11	0	18	13	38	34	.303	.389
	Lakeland (FSL)	A	.190	7	21	2	4	0	1	0	1	0	8	0	.190	.286
2002	Lakeland (FSL)	A	.259	123	410	52	106	13	7	2	42	33	102	16	.310	.339
2003	Lakeland (FSL)	A	.229	106	380	47	87	11	4	2	28	27	69	15	.278	.295
2004	Lakeland (FSL)	A	.289	26	97	14	28	3	3	0	9	6	19	5	.327	.381
	Erie (EL)	AA	.274	101	394	65	108	19	3	5	29	26	89	17	.326	.376
MINOR LEAGUE TOTALS			.257	418	1518	217	390	51	29	9	127	105	325	87	.305	.347

18 Dae-Sung Koo, lhp

Born: Aug. 2, 1968. **Ht.:** 5-11. **Wt.:** 185. **Bats:** L. **Throws:** L. **Career Transactions:** Signed out of Korea by Mets, Jan. 12, 2005. **Signed by:** Isao O'Jimi.

Koo is a hero in his native Korea for his work in the 2000 Olympics, when he outdueled Japan's Daisuke Matsuzaka in the bronze-medal game, notching 10 strikeouts. By then, he already had established himself as one of the best pitchers in the Korean Baseball Organization. He was the league's MVP in 1996, when he went 18-3, 1.88 with 24 saves. He added to his fame by becoming one of the few Korean players to make a successful transition to the Japanese majors. Koo flirted with signing with the Yankees before agreeing to a one-year contract with the Mets. He'll earn $400,000 if he makes the big league team, with the possibility for another $700,000 in incentives. Primarily a starter in Japan, Koo will pitch out of the bullpen for New York. He has a twisting windup that hides the ball, especially from lefthanders. His stuff is solid, as he complements an 86-89 mph fastball with a slider that rates a tick above-average. He can get righthanders out with an average curveball and will occasionally use a below-average changeup, so he could see action as a spot starter.

Year	Club (League)	Class	W	L	ERA	G	GS	CG	SV	IP	H	R	ER	HR	BB	SO	AVG
2001	Orix (PL)	JAP	7	9	4.06	51	8	1	10	126	96	58	57	14	71	143	..211
2002	Orix (PL)	JAP	5	7	2.52	22	21	1	0	146	122	45	41	13	47	144	.226
2003	Orix (PL)	JAP	6	8	4.99	19	19	0	0	114	131	72	63	23	51	118	.289
2004	Orix (PL)	JAP	6	10	4.32	18	15	3	0	117	105	65	56	24	44	99	.240
JAPANESE LEAGUE TOTALS			24	34	3.88	110	63	5	10	503	454	240	217	74	213	504	.241

19 Bartolome Fortunato, rhp

Born: Aug. 24, 1974. **Ht.:** 6-1. **Wt.:** 180. **Bats:** R. **Throws:** R. **Career Transactions:** Signed out of Dominican Republic by Devil Rays, Aug. 15, 1996 . . . Traded by Devil Rays with RHP Victor Zambrano to Mets for LHP Scott Kazmir and RHP Jose Diaz, July 30, 2004. **Signed by:** Rudy Santin (Devil Rays).

The other player the Mets acquired in the Victor Zambrano/Scott Kazmir deal last July, Fortunato took a long and winding road from the Dominican Republic to the majors. The Devil Rays signed him as an outfielder, but quickly found out his arm was more valuable than his bat. They were less thrilled to discover he was actually six years older than originally believed, in the visa crackdowns after the Sept. 11 attacks. Fortunato likely wouldn't have gotten a chance at pro ball if it had been known he was nearly 22 at the time of his signing, but he has made it to the majors despite not making it out of the DSL until he was 25 years old. Equipped with a 93-95 mph fastball, an average slider and a solid changeup, he has the stuff to contribute to the big league bullpen this season. Throwing strikes on a consistent basis is his biggest obstacle. His ceiling is limited, of course, by his age.

Year	Club (League)	Class	AVG	G	AB	R	H	2B	3B	HR	RBI	BB	SO	SB	OBP	SLG
1997	Devil Rays (DSL)	R	.288	37	104	12	30	3	0	0	11	9	13	4	,342	.317
1998	Devil Rays (DSL)	R	.271	40	107	21	29	4	0	1	10	6	21	8	.331	.336
MINOR LEAGUE TOTALS			.280	77	211	33	59	7	0	1	21	15	34	12	.336	.327

Year	Club (League)	Class	W	L	ERA	G	GS	CG	SV	IP	H	R	ER	HR	BB	SO	AVG
1999	Devil Rays (DSL)	R	7	0	2.57	13	5	1	1	49	38	18	14	3	32	44	.215
2000	Princeton (Appy)	R	3	4	4.63	17	5	0	1	47	56	31	24	4	19	51	.284
2001	Hudson Valley (NY-P)	A	2	5	5.13	16	9	0	0	60	70	35	34	3	29	53	.299
2002	Bakersfield (Cal)	A	2	4	4.01	25	5	0	0	61	58	31	27	3	25	85	.251
	Orlando (SL)	AA	3	0	2.10	10	2	0	0	26	16	7	6	2	11	34	.180
	Durham (IL)	AAA	1	0	4.15	2	0	0	0	4	6	3	2	1	2	0	.333
2003	Orlando (SL)	AA	4	2	3.06	35	1	0	0	53	48	25	18	4	20	63	.242
	Durham (INL)	AAA	1	2	3.32	5	4	0	0	22	15	11	8	3	11	20	.192
2004	New York (NL)	MAJ	1	0	3.86	15	0	0	1	19	14	8	8	2	13	20	.203
	Norfolk (IL)	AAA	0	0	3.38	6	0	0	2	5	4	2	2	0	3	5	.211
	Durham (IL)	AAA	4	3	2.42	34	0	0	9	45	28	14	12	4	21	54	.183
	Tampa Bay (AL)	MAJ	0	0	3.68	3	0	0	0	7	10	3	3	1	2	5	.357
MAJOR LEAGUE TOTALS			1	0	3.81	18	0	0	1	26	24	11	11	3	15	25	.247
MINOR LEAGUE TOTALS			27	20	3.57	163	31	1	13	371	339	177	147	27	173	409	.243

20 Craig Brazell, 1b/of

Born: May 10, 1980. **Ht.:** 6-3. **Wt.:** 210. **Bats:** L. **Throws:** R. **School:** Jefferson Davis HS, Montgomery, Ala. **Career Transactions:** Selected by Mets in fifth round of 1998 draft; signed June 4, 1998. **Signed by:** Bob Rossi.

The Mets used to dream of what Brazell might become if he could be more selective, but at this point it's unlikely he'll ever walk much or cut down on his strikeouts. As a result, his performance has steadily dropped as he has faced more experienced pitchers. Brazell, whose father Ted caught and managed in the Tigers system, too often ends up behind in the count because pitchers have figured out that he's almost always looking for something he can drive. His aggressive swings and strength give him plus power when he connects. He has soft hands, but he has below-average speed and limited range and arm strength at both first base and left field. He got his first taste of Shea Stadium with a September callup, but New York's trade for Doug Mientkiewicz relegates Brazell to a big league reserve at best.

Year	Club (League)	Class	AVG	G	AB	R	H	2B	3B	HR	RBI	BB	SO	SB	OBP	SLG
1998	Mets (GCL)	R	.298	13	47	6	14	3	1	6	2	13	0	.340	.468
1999	Kingsport (Appy)	R	.385	59	221	27	85	16	1	6	39	7	34	6	.422	.548
2000	Capital City (SAL)	A	.241	112	406	35	98	28	0	8	57	15	82	3	.279	.369

2001	Capital City (SAL)	A	.308	83	331	51	102	25	5	19	72	15	74	0	.343	.586
2002	St. Lucie (FSL)	A	.266	100	402	38	107	25	3	16	82	13	78	2	.292	.463
	Binghamton (EL)	AA	.308	35	130	14	40	8	0	6	19	1	28	0	.343	.508
2003	Binghamton (EL)	AA	.292	111	432	58	126	23	2	17	76	23	97	2	.331	.472
	Norfolk (IL)	AAA	.261	12	46	4	12	3	0	0	1	1	8	1	.292	.326
2004	New York (NL)	MAJ	.265	24	34	3	9	2	0	1	3	1	7	0	.286	.412
	Norfolk (IL)	AAA	.265	121	475	66	126	22	2	23	67	21	99	1	.300	.465
MAJOR LEAGUE TOTALS			.265	24	34	3	9	2	0	1	3	1	7	0	.286	.412
MINOR LEAGUE TOTALS			.285	646	2490	299	710	153	14	96	419	98	513	15	.320	.473

21 Alhaji Turay, of

Born: Sept. 22, 1982. **Ht.:** 6-1. **Wt.:** 207. **Bats:** R. **Throws:** R. **School:** Auburn (Wash.) HS. **Career Transactions:** Selected by Mets in second round of 2001 draft; signed July 5, 2001. **Signed by:** Jim Reeves.

A year ago, the Mets were wondering if Turay's talent would be smothered by his lack of concentration and disciplinary problems. They sent him home early in 2002 after he alienated people in Brooklyn with run-ins with fans (he professed not to know English and signed autographs as "Tom Hanks"), lackadaisical effort and a tantrum that included bashing a water cooler. A bone bruise in his leg cut short his 2003 season, but he put forth the kind of effort New York had been looking for last year and showed signs of accepting instruction. He took a significant step forward with his power. Turay's pop rates with anyone's in the system. His plus bat speed and short swing allow him to get around on good fastballs. His power-happy approach leaves him vulnerable to offspeed stuff, and he doesn't work counts well. He's a good athlete and an average runner, but he has yet to refine his routes in right field or get good jumps on the basepaths. With a below-average arm, he'll probably move to left field eventually. Turay should get his first action in Double-A this year.

Year	Club (League)	Class	AVG	G	AB	R	H	2B	3B	HR	RBI	BB	SO	SB	OBP	SLG
2001	Kingsport (Appy)	R	.245	43	163	21	40	8	3	2	20	9	46	8	.286	.368
2002	Brooklyn (NY-P)	A	.327	40	153	21	50	10	4	19	11	48	7	.380	.484
2003	Capital City (SAL)	A	.236	85	314	44	74	19	3	6	45	28	94	14	.324	.373
2004	St. Lucie (FSL)	A	.256	86	308	35	79	12	0	16	44	22	81	11	.313	.451
MINOR LEAGUE TOTALS			.259	254	938	121	243	49	7	28	128	70	269	40	.323	.416

22 Blake McGinley, lhp

Born: Aug. 2, 1978. **Ht.:** 6-1. **Wt.:** 175. **Bats:** R. **Throws:** L. **School:** Texas Tech. **Career Transactions:** Selected by Mets in 21st round of 2001 draft; signed June 10, 2001. **Signed by:** Dave Lottsfeld.

He didn't match the 1.02 ERA that left scouts shaking their heads in 2003, but McGinley did enough last year to show he can be a major league reliever. His mix of top-notch command, plus changeups, show-me curveballs and 85-88 mph fastballs continued to pile up strikeouts at Double-A and Triple-A. What jumps out about McGinley is his moxie. He has no fear of throwing an 85 mph fastball right down the pipe, trusting that its sink and his ability to outthink hitters will allow him to get away with pitches that should be pounded. McGinley has a little twist in his delivery that adds deception, but as with Yusmeiro Petit, it's tough to explain how he has 10.2 strikeouts per nine innings as a pro. He's ticketed for Triple-A, and before long he'll get a chance to see if he can get major league hitters out.

Year	Club (League)	Class	W	L	ERA	G	GS	CG	SV	IP	H	R	ER	HR	BB	SO	AVG
2001	Brooklyn (NY-P)	A	5	0	1.94	18	0	0	4	46	30	12	10	3	11	59	.182
2002	Capital City (SAL)	A	1	1	1.80	26	0	0	10	35	19	9	7	3	6	53	.154
	St. Lucie (FSL)	A	1	1	5.97	18	0	0	4	32	40	22	21	2	13	22	.299
2003	St. Lucie (FSL)	A	9	1	1.02	37	0	0	7	79	51	11	9	0	20	86	.183
2004	Binghamton (EL)	AA	9	2	3.72	33	0	0	1	73	61	32	30	9	15	83	.222
	Norfolk (IL)	AAA	3	3	4.05	13	0	0	2	27	30	15	12	1	7	28	.280
MINOR LEAGUE TOTALS			28	8	2.75	145	0	0	28	292	231	101	89	18	72	331	.213

23 Angel Pagan, of

Born: July 2, 1981. **Ht.:** 6-1. **Wt.:** 180. **Bats:** B. **Throws:** R. **School:** Republica de Colombia HS, Rio Piedras, P.R. **Career Transactions:** Selected by Mets in fourth round of 1999 draft; signed June 1, 2000. **Signed by:** Gary LaRocque.

Pagan's climb hasn't gone nearly as quickly as he can get around the bases, but he showed consistency in 2004 after lacking it in previous seasons. He has a nice mix of tools, with above-average speed, an average arm and the ability to hit for average. He has stolen more than 30 bases in each of the past four seasons, and he showed a better feel for getting jumps and picking his spots last year. His 85 percent success rate was the highest of his career. At the plate, Pagan has developed gap power, so he's no longer just a bunt-and-slap hitter. He still doesn't control the strike zone like a top-of-the-order hitter should, however. In the outfield, Pagan has the speed and range to handle center field, and his strong, accurate arm allows him to fill in as a right fielder. His versatility could help him earn a role as a fourth outfielder in the majors, though he'll head to Triple-A this spring to add further polish first.

Year	Club (League)	Class	AVG	G	AB	R	H	2B	3B	HR	RBI	BB	SO	SB	OBP	SLG
2000	Kingsport (Appy)	R	.361	19	72	13	26	5	1	0	8	6	8	6	.410	.458
2001	Capital City (SAL)	A	.298	15	57	4	17	1	1	0	5	6	5	3	.365	.351
	Brooklyn (NY-P)	A	.315	62	238	46	75	10	2	0	15	22	30	30	.388	.374
2002	Capital City (SAL)	A	.279	108	458	79	128	14	5	1	36	32	87	52	.325	.338
	St. Lucie (FSL)	A	.343	16	67	12	23	2	1	1	7	7	9	10	.405	.448
2003	St. Lucie (FSL)	A	.249	113	441	64	110	15	5	1	33	35	80	35	.307	.313
2004	Norfolk (IL)	AAA	.289	12	45	13	13	3	3	0	1	4	8	4	.347	.489
	Binghamton (EL)	AA	.288	112	448	71	129	25	8	4	63	42	96	29	.346	.406
MINOR LEAGUE TOTALS			.285	457	1826	302	521	75	26	7	168	154	323	169	.342	.366

24 Brett Harper, 1b

Born: July 31, 1981. **Ht.:** 6-4. **Wt.:** 180. **Bats:** L. **Throws:** R. **School:** Scottsdale (Ariz.) CC. **Career Transactions:** Selected by Mets in 45th round of 2000 draft; signed May 28, 2001. **Signed by:** Kevin Frady.

Harper's father Brian spent 16 seasons in the majors and his uncle Glenn played in the Mets system in the mid-1970s. Brett attracted little notice during his first three seasons with the Mets, but that changed with a loud three months in the Florida State League last year, when he hit .350 with power. He always had put the bat on the ball, but he showed the ability to pull the ball instead of just serving singles to the opposite field. His improved pitch recognition allowed him to get into hitter's counts and show the raw power the Mets had seen in batting practice. The former third baseman is a little stiff at first base. As good as Harper's high Class A stint was, he will have to prove himself against better pitching. He struggled in Double-A, where his strikeout rate soared, and he looked no better in the Arizona Fall League. He's expected to head back to Double-A this year to regroup.

Year	Club (League)	Class	AVG	G	AB	R	H	2B	3B	HR	RBI	BB	SO	SB	OBP	SLG
2001	Kingsport (Appy)	R	.336	38	146	24	49	9	1	0	19	8	30	3	.386	.411
	Capital City (SAL)	A	.182	10	33	1	6	1	0	0	4	3	14	0	.250	.212
2002	Brooklyn (NY-P)	A	.279	53	183	21	51	6	0	1	20	14	37	2	.333	.328
2003	St. Lucie (FSL)	A	.205	13	44	5	9	2	0	0	4	5	13	1	.308	.250
	Capital City (SAL)	A	.329	23	79	5	26	6	0	1	9	4	20	1	.376	.443
	Kingsport (Appy)	R	.429	11	35	6	15	8	0	2	10	3	9	0	.500	.829
	Brooklyn (NY-P)	A	.299	28	87	5	26	8	0	1	18	5	12	1	.337	.425
2004	St. Lucie (FSL)	A	.350	60	220	32	77	18	1	9	55	35	53	1	.440	.564
	Binghamton (EL)	AA	.247	45	174	24	43	12	0	7	26	14	60	0	.309	.437
MINOR LEAGUE TOTALS			.302	281	1001	123	302	70	2	21	165	91	248	9	.367	.439

25 Bob Keppel, rhp

Born: June 11, 1982. **Ht.:** 6-5. **Wt.:** 205. **Bats:** R. **Throws:** L. **School:** DeSmet HS, Chesterfield, Mo. **Career Transactions:** Selected by Mets in first round (36th overall) of 2000 draft; signed July 7, 2000. **Signed by:** Larry Chase.

Only a year ago, Keppel was considered one of the top pitching prospects in the organization. But injuries continue to bother the former high school basketball star, who could have played hoops at Notre Dame had he not signed for $895,000. He missed time in 2003 with a strained forearm, then had to skip the Arizona Fall League because of a stiff shoulder. Shoulder tendinitis flared up again in spring training last year, forcing Keppel to get off to a late start to the season. He missed further time in August and was shut down a week early. When healthy, he has a 90-91 mph fastball that touches 93, a major league changeup and a curveball and slider that are less advanced. Limited by his shoulder, Keppel had only one month of effectiveness in a rough introduction to Triple-A. He never has missed many bats but was absolutely tattooed in Triple-A, where opponents hit .304 against him. If he's healthy, Keppel's feel for pitching and solid stuff should be enough to allow him to succeed, but he has to prove that his shoulder is sound. He skipped instructional league again and the Mets hope he'll be healthy for spring training.

Year	Club (League)	Class	W	L	ERA	G	GS	CG	SV	IP	H	R	ER	HR	BB	SO	AVG
2000	Kingsport (Appy)	R	1	2	6.83	8	6	0	0	29	31	22	22	1	13	29	.261
2001	Capital City (SAL)	A	6	7	3.11	26	20	1	0	124	118	58	43	6	25	87	.249
2002	St. Lucie (FSL)	A	9	7	4.32	27	26	0	0	152	162	83	73	13	43	109	.277
2003	Binghamton (EL)	AA	7	4	3.04	18	17	2	0	95	92	36	32	6	27	46	.264
	Brooklyn (NY-P)	A	2	0	2.51	3	3	0	0	14	10	5	4	0	2	13	.189
2004	Norfolk (IL)	AAA	3	7	4.71	17	16	1	0	94	111	51	49	8	22	42	.304
	St. Lucie (FSL)	A	1	1	0.90	2	2	0	0	10	7	2	1	0	2	6	.200
MINOR LEAGUE TOTALS			29	28	3.89	101	90	4	0	518	531	257	224	34	134	332	.268

26 Wayne Lydon, of

Born: April 17, 1981. **Ht.:** 6-2. **Wt.:** 190. **Bats:** B. **Throws:** R. **School:** Valley View HS, Archibald, Pa. **Career Transactions:** Selected by Mets in ninth round of 1999 draft; signed June 4, 1999. **Signed by:** Joe Nigro.

He's still not a .300 hitter, and he likely never will be. He strikes out more than a leadoff hitter should, and he probably won't ever develop more than gap power. But as long as Lydon continues to improve and steal 60-plus bases a year—he has won league stolen-base titles in each of his three full seasons—the Mets will continue to believe he can help them in the majors. Lydon has top-of-the-line speed and takes the most aggressive leads in the system, practically daring pitchers to try to pick him off. He has adapted to switch-hitting, something the Mets got him to try in 2003. Despite an athletic frame, Lydon has virtually no power. He draws a decent amount of walks, though not enough to make him a true on-base threat, and still has to find a way to make more consistent contact. His blazing speed allows him to run down balls in the gaps in center field, where his arm is below-average. He'll get his first opportunity in Triple-A this year.

Year	Club (League)	Class	AVG	G	AB	R	H	2B	3B	HR	RBI	BB	SO	SB	OBP	SLG
1999	Mets (GCL)	R	.183	37	60	13	11	3	0	0	5	7	13	0	.279	.233
2000	Kingsport (Appy)	R	.203	55	172	34	35	4	1	3	20	24	47	35	.300	.291
2001	Kingsport (Appy)	R	.184	26	98	14	18	7	0	0	8	11	35	15	.266	.255
	Brooklyn (NY-P)	A	.246	21	57	12	14	1	1	0	1	7	18	10	.348	.298
2002	Capital City (SAL)	A	.294	127	473	93	139	9	5	0	46	54	104	87	.368	.334
2003	St. Lucie (FSL)	A	.264	133	488	83	129	14	7	4	44	52	96	75	.342	.346
2004	Binghamton (EL)	AA	.270	123	507	78	137	18	6	5	43	49	119	65	.339	.359
MINOR LEAGUE TOTALS			.260	522	1855	327	483	56	20	12	167	204	432	287	.338	.332

27 Bob Malek, of

Born: July 6, 1981. **Ht.:** 6-3. **Wt.:** 205. **Bats:** L. **Throws:** R. **School:** Michigan State University. **Career Transactions:** Selected by Mets in fourth round of 2002 draft; signed June 6, 2002. **Signed by:** Terry Tripp.

Malek has an abundance of tools, but the Mets are still waiting for him to put it all together. He runs well for a big man, owns a decent batting eye and has a plus arm. He has bounced back from 2002 Tommy John surgery with few ill effects, but his adjustment to wood bats hasn't gone as well. He won Big 10 Conference batting (.427 as a sophomore) and home run (16 as a junior) titles, but hasn't been able to combine hitting for average and power as a pro. When he repeated high Class A last year, he did show more pop. Malek's swing is a little long, and he's not strong enough to produce power without trying to pull the ball. When he does that, it takes away from his ability to use the entire field. There's still room for projection in his upper body. He has good instincts and a strong arm in right field. New York hopes he'll take a huge step forward this year in Double-A.

Year	Club (League)	Class	AVG	G	AB	R	H	2B	3B	HR	RBI	BB	SO	SB	OBP	SLG
2002	Brooklyn (NY-P)	A	.207	28	111	7	23	3	1	0	10	3	20	4	.235	.252
2003	Capital City (SAL)	A	.262	43	149	20	39	11	0	1	26	26	22	11	.369	.356
	St. Lucie (FSL)	A	.280	79	286	45	80	20	1	2	36	30	50	17	.354	.378
2004	St. Lucie (FSL)	A	.266	111	425	63	113	23	6	13	58	32	82	15	.321	.440
	Binghamton (EL)	AA	.222	14	54	7	12	2	0	1	1	2	13	0	.263	.315
MINOR LEAGUE TOTALS			.260	275	1025	142	267	59	8	17	131	93	187	47	.326	.383

28 Tyler Yates, rhp

Born: Aug. 7, 1977. **Ht.:** 6-4. **Wt.:** 220. **Bats:** R. **Throws:** R. **School:** University of Hawaii-Hilo. **Career Transactions:** Selected by Athletics in 23rd round of 1998 draft; signed June 10, 1998 . . . Traded by Athletics with LHP Mark Guthrie to Mets for OF David Justice and cash, Dec. 14, 2001. **Signed by:** Eric Kubota (Athletics).

Yates started 2004 as the Mets' fifth starter, shutting out the Expos for six innings in his first outing. He was shelled in subsequent starts and eventually sent to Triple-A to see if he could get settled as a reliever. The time in Norfolk paid off, as he worked on using his two-seam fastball, which has nice movement and sink. When he returned to New York for a September callup, he went nine straight outings without allowing a run. The positive end to the season was dashed in February, however, when Yates had arthroscopic shoulder surgery to repair a torn rotator cuff. Yates' stuff had been good enough to get major leaguers out, as he threw a 92-95 mph fastball, an average slider and changeup. Like many hard throwers, he learned that command and the ability to speed or slow down hitters' bats is as important as raw velocity. Yates showed signs that he was beginning to take those lessons in September and was a strong candidate for the big league bullpen, but because of the shoulder surgery he is now expected to miss the entire 2005 season.

Year	Club (League)	Class	W	L	ERA	G	GS	CG	SV	IP	H	R	ER	HR	BB	SO	AVG
1998	Athletics (AZL)	R	0	0	3.91	15	0	0	2	23	28	12	10	0	14	20	.304
	So. Oregon (NWL)	A	0	0	0.00	2	0	0	1	2	2	0	0	0	0	1	.222
1999	Visalia (Cal)	A	2	5	5.47	47	1	0	4	82	98	64	50	12	35	74	.290
2000	Modesto (Cal)	A	4	2	2.86	30	0	0	1	57	50	23	18	2	23	61	.237
	Midland (TL)	AA	1	1	6.15	22	0	0	0	26	28	20	18	2	15	24	.275
2001	Midland (TL)	AA	4	6	4.31	56	0	0	17	63	66	39	30	4	27	61	.261
	Sacramento (PCL)	AAA	1	0	0.00	4	0	0	1	5	3	0	0	0	1	3	.167
2002	Norfolk (IL)	AAA	2	2	1.32	24	0	0	6	34	29	10	5	1	13	34	.227
2003	St. Lucie (FSL)	A	1	2	4.31	14	11	0	0	48	41	28	23	5	24	49	.232
	Binghamton (EL)	AA	1	2	4.35	8	8	0	0	39	33	21	19	4	17	36	.223
	Norfolk (IL)	AAA	1	2	4.05	4	4	0	0	20	22	9	9	1	9	15	.289
2004	New York (NL)	MAJ	2	4	6.36	21	7	0	0	47	61	36	33	6	25	35	.311
	Norfolk (IL)	AAA	6	2	3.18	30	1	0	4	40	28	18	14	2	22	43	.194
MAJOR LEAGUE TOTALS			2	4	6.36	21	7	0	0	47	61	36	33	6	25	35	.311
MINOR LEAGUE TOTALS			23	24	4.01	256	25	0	36	440	428	244	196	33	200	421	.252

29 Sean Henry, ss

Born: Aug. 18, 1985. **Ht.:** 5-10. **Wt.:** 154. **Bats:** R. **Throws:** R. **College:** Diablo Valley (Calif.) JC. **Career Transactions:** Selected by Mets in 20th round of 2004 draft; signed June 15, 2004. **Signed by:** Chuck Hensley.

Henry was one of the highest unsigned draft-and-follows from 2003. The Tigers took him in the 10th round, and he spent that summer with the U.S. junior national team that also included 2004 first-round picks Matt Bush, Billy Butler and Neil Walker. Originially committed to Tony Gwynn's San Diego State program, Henry decided to attend Diablo Valley (Calif.) Junior College. Detroit couldn't get a deal done last spring, so the Mets were able to draft and sign him as a 20th-rounder in June. In his first exposure to pro ball, Henry showed solid gap and opposite-field power despite a smallish frame. He might end up needing to cut down on his swing, which is a little long. It might cut into his home run numbers, but he can be a solid hitter even if his power is reduced to line-drives. In the field, Henry likely will have to move from shortstop. His arm is strong enough and he has a quick release, but his throws are erratic. He's not particularly fluid at shortstop, though he has the quickness to potentially slide over to second base. Henry has average speed, but he knows how to get jumps and takes extra bases with heady aggressiveness. How he performs in extended spring training will determine whether he moves up to Kingsport or Brooklyn in 2005.

Year	Club (League)	Class	AVG	G	AB	R	H	2B	3B	HR	RBI	BB	SO	SB	OBP	SLG
2004	Mets (GCL)	R	.282	56	202	35	57	9	5	4	30	22	43	10	.364	.436
MINOR LEAGUE TOTALS			.282	56	202	35	57	9	5	4	30	22	43	10	.364	.436

30 Mike Jacobs, c

Born: Oct. 30, 1980. **Ht.:** 6-2. **Wt.:** 200. **Bats:** L. **Throws:** R. **School:** Grossmont (Calif.) JC. **Career Transactions:** Selected by Mets in 38th round of 1999 draft; signed June 25, 1999. **Signed by:** Bob Minor.

After winning the Mets' minor league player of the year award with a Double-A breakthrough in 2003, Jacobs barely played last year. A torn labrum and a cyst that had to be removed from his shoulder destroyed his season. If healthy, he's the best-hitting catcher in the system, offering outstanding opposite-field power and a fluid stroke. The labrum actually affected his hitting much more than his work behind the plate, because he had little strength in his swing before he was shut down in late April. His strike-zone discipline never has been as an asset. Before his shoulder problems, Jacobs already faced questions about his catching ability. He has a below-average arm, partly because he gets too tall while coming out of his crouch, slowing his release. He also is a below-average receiver. If he can't make it behind the plate, his bat will have to carry him if he becomes a first baseman. Jacobs wasn't cleared to swing the bat in time for instructional league, but New York hopes he'll be ready for spring training. If he's ready to go, he'll begin the 2005 season in Triple-A.

Year	Club (League)	Class	AVG	G	AB	R	H	2B	3B	HR	RBI	BB	SO	SB	OBP	SLG
1999	Mets (GCL)	R	.333	44	147	18	49	12	0	4	30	14	30	2	.383	.497
2000	Capital City (SAL)	A	.214	18	56	1	12	5	0	0	8	6	19	1	.290	.304
	Kingsport (Appy)	R	.270	59	204	28	55	15	4	7	40	33	62	6	.371	.485
2001	Brooklyn (NY-P)	A	.288	19	66	12	19	5	0	1	15	6	11	1	.364	.409
	Capital City (SAL)	A	.278	46	180	18	50	13	0	2	26	13	46	0	.328	.383
2002	St. Lucie (FSL)	A	.251	118	467	62	117	26	1	11	64	25	95	2	.291	.381
2003	Binghamton (EL)	AA	.329	119	407	56	134	36	1	17	81	28	87	0	.376	.548
2004	Norfolk (IL)	AAA	.177	27	96	8	17	3	0	2	6	9	30	0	.245	.271
MINOR LEAGUE TOTALS			.279	450	1623	203	453	115	6	44	270	134	380	12	.336	.439

NEW YORK
YANKEES

BY **JOHN MANUEL**

The challenge for the Yankees every year is to add World Series championship No. 27. Losing to their most bitter rival in history-making fashion doesn't add to the pressure to win. The Yankees already put enough of that on themselves.

However, blowing a 3-0 lead to the Red Sox in the American League Championship Series did highlight New York's shortcomings. The big league team lacked pitching depth both in its aging rotation and particularly in its bullpen. With a payroll of $188 million in 2004, that's an indictment of both the Yankees' choices of how to spend that money and the farm system's inability to develop low-cost players to fill holes.

Changes were forthcoming whether the Yankees held their lead or not. Albatross contracts such as **Jason Giambi's** (owed $82 million over the next four seasons) and Kevin Brown's ($15 million in 2005) will be next to impossible to move. That left New York with little flexibility, so the only way to improve the club was to take the payroll well past $200 million. The Yankees didn't hesitate to do just that, with the trade for Randy Johnson highlighting another winter of high-priced imports.

The Yankees have to get help from outside the organization because their farm system has little to offer in the upper levels. A series of conservative and essentially fruitless drafts from 1998-2002 are at the root of the upper-level talent gap. That cost scouting director Lin Garrett his job; he was reassigned and put in charge of international

LARRY GOREN

scouting after the 2004 draft.

Yet his last effort might have been Garrett's best, as the organization is excited about a quintet of righthanders, led by high schoolers Philip Hughes and Christian Garcia along with collegians Jeff Marquez, Brett Smith and Jesse Hoover. Add in the development of 2003 draftees Steven White and Tyler Clippard, and the Yankees have started to build up their minor league mound corps.

The Yankees have also reshuffled their minor league operation. Vice president Damon Oppenheimer, who had overseen player development, will focus on scouting. The new farm director and field coordinator is former Astros minor league hitting coordinator Pat Roessler, who was an assistant coach under Newman at Old Dominion.

New York continues to rely on its Latin American department. In addition to Robinson Cano and the departed Dioner Navarro, infielder Marcos Vechionacci and outfielders Melky Cabrera and Rudy Guillen also intrigue the Yankees. They have the resources to be a factor in the pursuit of every major international (and, of course, domestic) free agent.

Just being a player isn't enough for Steinbrenner and the Yankees. It's not good enough when their payroll dwarfs that of every other team. And it hasn't been good enough to win a World Series in the 21st century.

TOP 30 PROSPECTS

1. Eric Duncan, 3b
2. Robinson Cano, 2b
3. Philip Hughes, rhp
4. Steven White, rhp
5. Christian Garcia, rhp
6. Marcos Vechionacci, inf
7. Melky Cabrera, of
8. Bronson Sardinha, 3b/of
9. Chien-Ming Wang, rhp
10. Jeff Marquez, rhp
11. Brett Smith, rhp
12. Rudy Guillen, of
13. Jesse Hoover, rhp
14. Tim Battle, of
15. Matt DeSalvo, rhp
16. Edwardo Sierra, rhp
17. Tyler Clippard, rhp
18. Andy Phillips, 1b/3b
19. Abel Gomez, lhp
20. Jon Poterson, of
21. Sean Henn, lhp
22. Scott Proctor, rhp
23. Ramon Ramirez, rhp
24. Jason Jones, rhp
25. Kevin Thompson, of
26. Ben Julianel, lhp
27. Mario Holmann, 2b
28. Hector Made, ss
29. Omir Santos, c
30. Maximo Nelson, rhp

ORGANIZATION OVERVIEW

General manager: Brian Cashman. **Farm director:** Pat Roessler. **Scouting director:** Damon Oppenheimer.

2004 PERFORMANCE

Class	Team	League	W	L	Pct.	Finish*	Manager(s)
Majors	New York	American	101	61	.623	1st (14)	Joe Torre
Triple-A	Columbus Clippers	International	80	64	.556	3rd (14)	Bucky Dent
Double-A	Trenton Thunder	Eastern	64	78	.451	10th (12)	Stump Merrill
High A	Tampa Yankees	Florida State	75	58	.564	+3rd (12)	Bill Masse
Low A	#Battle Creek Yankees	Midwest	71	68	.511	9th (14)	Mitch Seoane/Bill Mosiello
Short-season	Staten Island Yankees	New York-Penn	28	44	.389	13th (14)	Tommy John
Rookie	GCL Yankees	Gulf Coast	36	23	.610	+1st (12)	Oscar Acosta
OVERALL 2004 MINOR LEAGUE RECORD			354	335	.514	9th (30)	

*Finish in overall standings (No. of teams in league). +League champion. #Affiliate will be in Charleston, S.C. (South Atlantic) in 2005.

ORGANIZATION LEADERS

BATTING
*Minimum 250 At-Bats
*AVG	Andy Phillips, Columbus/Trenton	.319
R	Kevin Reese, Columbus/Trenton	98
H	Kevin Reese, Columbus/Trenton	168
TB	Andy Phillips, Columbus/Trenton	274
	Kevin Reese, Columbus/Trenton	274
2B	Kevin Reese, Columbus/Trenton	50
3B	Robinson Cano, Columbus/Trenton	10
	John Rodriguez, Columbus	10
HR	Mitch Jones, Trenton	39
RBI	Andy Phillips, Columbus/Trenton	100
BB	Eric Duncan, Tampa/Battle Creek	69
SO	Mitch Jones, Trenton	152
SB	Kevin Thompson, Trenton/Tampa	38
*OBP	Craig Wilson, Trenton	.435
*SLG	Andy Phillips, Columbus/Trenton	.576

PITCHING
#Minimum 75 Innings
W	Jon Skaggs, Tampa	13
L	Javier Ortiz, Columbus/Trenton	12
#ERA	Colter Bean, Columbus	2.29
G	Paul Thorp, Battle Creek	55
CG	Three tied at	3
SV	Edwardo Sierra, Tampa	28
IP	Sean Henn, Trenton	163
BB	Abel Gomez, Battle Creek	73
SO	Abel Gomez, Battle Creek	149

BEST TOOLS

Best Hitter for Average	Melky Cabrera
Best Power Hitter	Jon Poterson
Best Strike-Zone Discipline	Jon-Mark Sprowl
Fastest Baserunner	Tim Battle
Best Athlete	Tim Battle
Best Fastball	Edwardo Sierra
Best Curveball	Christian Garcia
Best Slider	Ramon Ramirez
Best Changeup	Matt DeSalvo
Best Control	Tyler Clippard
Best Defensive Catcher	Omir Santos
Best Defensive Infielder	Mario Holmann
Best Infield Arm	Robinson Cano
Best Defensive Outfielder	Melky Cabrera
Best Outfield Arm	Rudy Guillen

PROJECTED 2008 LINEUP

Catcher	Jorge Posada
First Base	Eric Duncan
Second Base	Robinson Cano
Third Base	Alex Rodriguez
Shortstop	Derek Jeter
Left Field	Hideki Matsui
Center Field	Melky Cabrera

Right Field	Rudy Guillen
Designated Hitter	Gary Sheffield
No. 1 Starter	Carl Pavano
No. 2 Starter	Jaret Wright
No. 3 Starter	Philip Hughes
No. 4 Starter	Steven White
No. 5 Starter	Christian Garcia
Closer	Jesse Hoover

LAST YEAR'S TOP 20 PROSPECTS

1. Dioner Navarro, c
2. Eric Duncan, 3b
3. Rudy Guillen, of
4. Joaquin Arias, ss
5. Ramon Ramirez, rhp
6. Robinson Cano, 2b
7. Ferdin Tejeda, ss
8. Jorge DePaula, rhp
9. Estee Harris, of
10. Bronson Sardinha, 3b
11. Edwardo Sierra, rhp
12. Chien-Ming Wang, rhp
13. Scott Proctor, rhp
14. Danny Borrell, lhp
15. Matt DeSalvo, rhp
16. Hector Made, ss
17. Sean Henn, lhp
18. Mark Phillips, lhp
19. Melky Cabrera, of
20. Jose Garcia, rhp

TOP PROSPECTS OF THE DECADE

Year	Player, Pos.	Current Team
1995	Ruben Rivera, of	Campeche (Mexican)
1996	Ruben Rivera, of	Campeche (Mexican)
1997	Ruben Rivera, of	Campeche (Mexican)
1998	Eric Milton, lhp	Reds
1999	Nick Johnson, 1b	Nationals
2000	Nick Johnson, 1b	Nationals
2001	Nick Johnson, 1b	Nationals
2002	Drew Henson, 3b	Out of baseball
2003	Jose Contreras, rhp	White Sox
2004	Dioner Navarro, c	Dodgers

TOP DRAFT PICKS OF THE DECADE

Year	Player, Pos.	Current Team
1995	Shea Morenz, of	Out of baseball
1996	Eric Milton, lhp	Reds
1997	*Tyrell Godwin, of	Nationals
1998	Andy Brown, of	Out of baseball
1999	David Walling, rhp	Out of baseball
2000	David Parrish, c	Yankees
2001	John-Ford Griffin, of	Blue Jays
2002	Brandon Weeden, rhp (2)	Dodgers
2003	Eric Duncan, 3b	Yankees
2004	Philip Hughes, rhp	Yankees

*Did not sign.

ALL-TIME LARGEST BONUSES

Hideki Irabu, 1997	$8,500,000
Jose Contreras, 2002	$6,000,000
Wily Mo Pena, 1999	$2,440,000
Drew Henson, 1998	$2,000,000
Chien-Ming Wang, 2000	$1,900,000

New York YANKEES

RANK: **24**

Impact Potential: D

Eric Duncan and Robinson Cano have solid lefthanded bats, but neither profiles as an all-star. And that makes it unlikely they'll break into the Yankees' $200 million payroll anytime soon. The Yankees with the most upside are almost all teenagers who have yet to pass the full-season test. Similarly, New York has plenty of high-end arms, but none has made a mark above Class A yet.

Depth: C

The Yankees lacked the frontline talent to trade for Randy Johnson during the 2004 season, and when they got the Big Unit in the offseason, it cost them depth in lefthander Brad Halsey and former No. 1 prospect Dioner Navarro, leaving them barren behind the plate. However, the Yankees had a productive 2004 draft, hauling in several power arms—the best currency in July deadline trades.

*Depth charts prepared by **John Manuel** and **Allan Simpson**. Numbers in parentheses indicate prospect rankings.*

LF
Melky Cabrera (7)
Bronson Sardinha (8)
Jon Peterson (20)
Bubba Crosby
Kevin Reese

CF
Tim Battle (14)
Kevin Thompson (25)
Evan Tierce

RF
Rudy Guillen (12)
Michael Vento
Estee Harris

3B
Eric Duncan (1)
Marcos Vechionacci (6)
Willie Vasquez

SS
Hector Made (28)
Andy Cannizaro
Ferdin Tejada

2B
Robinson Cano (2)
Mario Holmann (27)
Nick Walsh
Justin Christian

1B
Andy Phillips (18)
Erold Andrus
Mitch Jones
Jon Urick

SOURCE of TALENT

Homegrown		Acquired	
College	5	Trades	3
Junior college	2	Rule 5 draft	0
Draft-and-follow	2	Independent leagues	0
High School	7	Free agents/waivers	0
Nondrafted free agents	1		
Foreign	10		

C
Omir Santos (29)
Jon-Mark Sprowl
Tommy Rojas
Nathan Phillips

LHP

Starters	Relievers
Abel Gomez (19)	Ben Julianel (26)
Sean Henn (21)	Alex Perez
Alex Graman	
Toni Lara	
Michael Wagner	

RHP

Starters	Relievers
Philip Hughes (3)	Jesse Hoover (13)
Steven White (4)	Edwardo Sierra (16)
Christian Garcia (5)	Scott Proctor (22)
Chien-Ming Wang (9)	Ramon Ramirez (23)
Jeff Marquez (10)	Maximo Nelson (30)
Brett Smith (11)	Jason Anderson
Matt DeSalvo (15)	Sam Marsonek
Tyler Clippard (17)	Colter Bean
Jason Jones (24)	T.J. Beam
Erick Abreu	Brandon Harmsen
Elvys Quezada	Mike Martinez
Jay Stephens	
Jon Skaggs	

DRAFT ANALYSIS

2004

Best Pro Debut: RHP Jesse Hoover (5) led the NAIA with 14.7 strikeouts per nine innings at Indiana Tech, then averaged 14.6 per nine while going 2-1, 1.78 at short-season Staten Island. OF Evan Tierce (17) was too old for Rookie ball at 22, but he did top the Gulf Coast League in batting (.361) and on-base percentage (.420).

Best Athlete: SS Nate Phillips (6) could have been drafted as a pitcher, and the Yankees like his arm and mobility so much that they converted him to catcher in instructional league. RHP Philip Hughes (1) is athletic for a pitcher.

Best Pure Hitter: OF Jon Poterson (1) is a switch-hitter who can center the ball on the bat. After hitting .202 in the GCL, he looked better in instructional league. IF/OF Yosvany Almario-Cabrera (18) hit .481 to win the Florida juco batting title at Miami-Dade CC South, and then hit .346 in the GCL. He's even older than Tierce, though.

Best Raw Power: Poterson, 6-foot-1 and 220 pounds, finished one shy of the GCL lead with seven homers.

Fastest Runner: Speed is Tierce's best tool. He can run 60 yards in 6.6 seconds.

Best Defensive Player: SS Grant Plumley (9) made just four errors in 61 games at Oral Roberts and tied for the short-season New York-Penn League lead with 44 double plays.

Best Fastball: Hoover has an explosive 94-95 mph fastball that peaks at 97. Hughes and RHP Christian Garcia (3), who converted from catching as a high school senior, can reach the mid-90s as well. RHP Jeff Marquez (1) throws 92-94 mph with sink.

Best Breaking Ball: RHP Brett Smith's (2) slider or Garcia's curveball.

Hoover

Most Intriguing Background: LHP Clint Preisendorfer's (32) father Rusty is a noted surfboard shaper and the founder of Rusty Surfboards. RHP Matt Harrington (36), the No. 7 overall pick in 2000, was drafted for the fifth straight year. Cabrera is a Cuban defector whose age is listed at 24 and could be as high as 27. OF Rod Allen Jr.'s (12) father is a TV broadcaster for the Tigers and played in the majors, as did RHP Jeremiah Shepherd's (27) dad Ron. RHP Ryan Rote's (37) grandfather Tobin quarterbacked the Detroit Lions to their last NFL championship in 1957. Cabrera and Allen are the only players from this group to sign.

Closest To The Majors: Smith would have been the favorite if he hadn't held out all summer. Hoover can pass him if he adds a feel for pitching to his sheer arm strength.

Best Late-Round Pick: 1B Ben Jones (14) has intriguing power.

The One Who Got Away: C Alex Garabedian (7), who has defensive skills and power, didn't come close to signing and is attending Miami. 3B Chris Davis (50) could be the best two-way player at Texas since Brooks Kieschnick.

Assessment: New York used three first-round picks to add much-needed depth to its system. But the Yankees continued to be unusually conservative in the draft, which led to scouting director Lin Garrett being reassigned.

2003 3B Eric Duncan (1) is the lone blue-chip prospect in the system. RHP Steven White (4) had a fine pro debut in 2004, but the Yankees blew it by not signing LHP David Purcey (17), a first-rounder in 2004, and RHP Daniel Bard (1), who will be one in 2006. **GRADE:** B

2002 New York gave up its first two picks, then started its draft with since-traded RHP Brandon Weeden (2). The best choice was mediocre LHP Brad Halsey (8), part of the Randy Johnson deal this offseason. **GRADE:** F

2001 Among three first-rounders, only 3B Bronson Sardinha has a chance to amount to anything. OF John-Ford Griffin (1) has stalled since being dealt, while injuries have waylaid RHP Jon Skaggs. **GRADE:** D

2000 The Yankees began by over-drafting C David Parrish (1). Giving $1.701 million to draft-and-follow LHP Sean Henn (26) also hasn't worked. RHP Jason Anderson (10), who played briefly in the majors and was traded, may have the best career of the bunch. **GRADE:** F

*Draft analysis prepared by **Jim Callis**. Numbers in parentheses indicate draft rounds.*

MICHAEL WALBY

Eric
DUNCAN

Born: Dec. 7, 1984.
Ht.: 6-3. **Wt.:** 195.
Bats: L. **Throws:** R.
School: Seton Hall Prep, Florham Park, N.J.
Career Transactions: Selected by Yankees in first round (27th overall) of 2003 draft; signed June 11, 2003.
Signed by: Cesar Presbott.

When his family moved from California to New Jersey when he was in fifth grade, Duncan was on his way to becoming a Yankees fan. Duncan, whose father Hal idolized Mickey Mantle, grew up admiring the stars of the recent New York dynasty such as Derek Jeter and Paul O'Neill, his favorite player. Less than a year after being drafted 27th overall in 2003, he found himself working out next to Jeter at the club's indoor facility in New York. Duncan had committed to Louisiana State, where the coaches considered him the nation's top prep hitter likely to go to college. Once the Yankees selected him in the first round though, it was clear he wasn't going to school. Duncan improved his draft stock by hitting six balls out of the Great American Ball Park during a predraft workout for the Reds, who strongly considered him at No. 14.

An advanced hitter for his age, Duncan has significant power. He doesn't have a perfect swing or one that's exceptionally short, but it's a simple stroke that he repeats easily, and he generates good bat speed. His lefthanded pull power should make him an ideal fit for Yankee Stadium, and he's not afraid to go the other way. He overpowers pitches left over the plate. Duncan impressed the Yankees by showing up to spring training in excellent shape, adding muscle and quickness during the offseason. Low Class A Battle Creek manager Bill Mosiello likened Duncan's work ethic and approach to that of a lefthanded slugger he coached at the University of Tennessee: Todd Helton. Duncan thrived after a promotion to high Class A Tampa, improving both his plate discipline and his defensive consistency at third base.

Duncan's arm is average at best because he short-arms the ball and doesn't always follow through properly, a correctable flaw. His agility and first-step quickness also are a little below hot-corner standards. With repetition and experience, the Yankees say he'll be an average defender at third. He tends to get a little pull-happy as many young sluggers do, and he slumped late in his stint at Battle Creek when pitchers exploited that weakness. New York correctly deduced that Duncan was getting stale facing Midwest League pitching and playing for a mediocre team and challenged him with a promotion. He responded by making more consistent contact against tougher competition.

Duncan was pushed aggressively in part because the Yankees needed to showcase their most talented minor leaguer as trade bait. Alex Rodriguez is entrenched as New York's third baseman and is signed for six more seasons. If the Yankees could somehow unload Jason Giambi, Duncan could give them a powerful, cheap option at first base. He probably needs two more years of minor league at-bats before that could happen. In the interim, he remains New York's most valuable bargaining chip.

Year	Club (League)	Class	AVG	G	AB	R	H	2B	3B	HR	RBI	BB	SO	SB	OBP	SLG
2003	Yankees (GCL)	R	.278	47	180	24	50	12	2	2	28	18	33	0	.348	.400
	Staten Island (NY-P)	A	.373	14	59	11	22	5	4	2	13	2	11	1	.413	.695
2004	Battle Creek (Mid)	A	.260	78	288	52	75	23	2	12	57	38	84	7	.351	.479
	Tampa (FSL)	A	.254	52	177	24	45	20	2	4	26	31	47	0	.364	.458
MINOR LEAGUE TOTALS			.273	191	704	111	192	60	10	20	124	89	175	8	.359	.472

2 Robinson Cano, 2b

Born: Oct. 22, 1982. **Ht.:** 6-0. **Wt.:** 170. **Bats:** L. **Throws:** R. **Career Transactions:** Signed out of Dominican Republic by Yankees, Jan. 5, 2001. **Signed by:** Carlos Rios.

Cano's name was tossed around in trade rumors when the Yankees unsuccessfully tried to acquire Randy Johnson at the July 31 deadline, but he was not part of the deal when New York finally got Johnson over the winter. A confident player, Cano plays as if he belongs in the majors. His father Jose pitched briefly in the big leagues. Cano's arm is his best tool and rates as a 65 on the 20-80 scouting scale. More important, he can hit. He has good bat speed and a fluid swing, allowing him to catch up to good fastballs. His improving plate discipline helped his power numbers increase; he set career highs in walks and slugging in 2004. Cano hasn't handled lefthanders well, with just seven extra-base hits in 130 at-bats against southpaws above Class A. He's a below-average runner for an infielder, and his lower half figures to get thicker as he gets older. He has solid infield actions and the Yankees refute reports that he has below-average range. Cano could be a bench option in New York for 2005, but he'll likely head back to Columbus for a full season in Triple-A after the Yankees signed free agent Tony Womack.

Year	Club (League)	Class	AVG	G	AB	R	H	2B	3B	HR	RBI	BB	SO	SB	OBP	SLG
2001	Yankees (GCL)	R	.230	57	200	37	46	14	2	3	34	28	27	11	.330	.365
	Staten Island (NY-P)	A	.250	2	8	0	2	0	0	0	2	0	2	0	.250	.250
2002	Greensboro (SAL)	A	.276	113	474	67	131	20	9	14	66	29	78	2	.321	.445
	Staten Island (NY-P)	A	.276	22	87	11	24	5	1	1	15	4	8	6	.308	.391
2003	Tampa (FSL)	A	.276	90	366	50	101	16	3	5	50	17	49	1	.313	.377
	Trenton (EL)	AA	.280	46	164	21	46	9	1	1	13	9	16	0	.341	.366
2004	Trenton (EL)	AA	.301	74	292	43	88	20	8	7	44	24	40	2	.356	.497
	Columbus (IL)	AAA	.259	61	216	22	56	9	2	6	30	18	27	0	.316	.403
MINOR LEAGUE TOTALS			.273	465	1807	251	494	93	26	37	254	129	247	22	.327	.415

3 Philip Hughes, rhp

Born: June 24, 1986. **Ht.:** 6-5. **Wt.:** 220. **Bats:** R. **Throws:** R. **School:** Foothill HS, Santa Ana, Calif. **Career Transactions:** Selected by Yankees in first round (23rd overall) of 2004 draft; signed June 9, 2004. **Signed by:** Jeff Patterson.

The Yankees had Hughes ranked higher on their 2004 draft board than 23rd overall, but that's where they got him. After getting drafted, Hughes joked that he had been raised a Red Sox fan but was pleased to be with the Yankees. His stuff, size and control have the organization comparing Hughes with Roger Clemens. He has similar velocity, with a fastball that touches 95 mph and sits at 90-94, and he generates it with an easy, fluid motion. His fastball also has late life up in the strike zone. Hughes changes a hitter's sight-line with a slider that at times has good bite and depth. He's also shown good arm action on his changeup. Hughes was shut down more than a month after his pro debut with a sore elbow that turned out to be nothing more than tendinitis. He returned with two excellent outings in August before breaking his toe after kicking a door. He also threw well in the Yankees' fall minicamp, dampening concerns about his health. The Yankees consider Hughes a high school power arm with the polish of a college pitcher. So if he's healthy, he'll move quickly. He'll start 2005 at their new low Class A Charleston affiliate.

Year	Club (League)	Class	W	L	ERA	G	GS	CG	SV	IP	H	R	ER	HR	BB	SO	AVG
2004	Yankees (GCL)	R	0	0	0.00	3	3	0	0	5	4	0	0	0	0	8	.222
MINOR LEAGUE TOTALS			0	0	0.00	3	3	0	0	5	4	0	0	0	0	8	.222

4 Steven White, rhp

Born: June 15, 1981. **Ht.:** 6-5. **Wt.:** 205. **Bats:** R. **Throws:** R. **School:** Baylor University. **Career Transactions:** Selected by Yankees in fourth round of 2003 draft; signed April 7, 2004. **Signed by:** Steve Boros/Mark Newman.

White set a Baylor record with 28 career wins. As a senior, he led the Bears to within one victory of the College World Series. He didn't turn pro until April 2004, and tragedy struck during his holdout when he discovered the body of his mother Brenda, who had died at home. White's fastball, which had reached the mid-90s early in his college career, bounced back to touch 95-96 mph late in the 2004 season, though he pitched more at 92-93. He showed better control of the pitch the more he threw it. He showed more power and command with his curveball, which had been inconsistent at

Baylor. He rarely gets rattled. White pitches off his fastball nearly 80 percent of the time, and he lost some of the feel for his changeup in the process. He needs to refine it to combat left-handers at higher levels. White's development was an important step for the Yankees, who could use an innings-eater as soon as possible. He fits that profile, but he'll need at least a year to hone his secondary stuff. He'll start 2005 in Double-A.

Year	Club (League)	Class	W	L	ERA	G	GS	CG	SV	IP	H	R	ER	HR	BB	SO	AVG
2004	Battle Creek (Mid)	A	5	2	2.65	9	9	2	0	58	36	19	17	4	26	56	.183
	Tampa (FSL)	A	6	2	2.56	12	12	1	0	60	51	26	17	4	19	44	.226
MINOR LEAGUE TOTALS			11	4	2.61	21	21	3	0	117	87	45	34	8	45	100	.206

5 Christian Garcia, rhp

RICK BATTLE

Born: August 24, 1985. **Ht.:** 6-4. **Wt.:** 175. **Bats:** R. **Throws:** R. **School:** Gulliver Prep, Miami. **Career Transactions:** Selected by Yankees in third round of 2004 draft; signed June 9, 2004. **Signed by:** Dan Radison.

The strong-armed Garcia committed to South Carolina as a catcher prior to his senior season at Gulliver Prep. Then his new high school coach, former University of Miami pitching coach Lazaro Collazo, put Garcia on the mound with electric results. Garcia helped Gulliver Prep win the Florida 3-A championship in a game played at the Yankees' Legends Field in Tampa, then signed for $390,000. His combination of size, projection and pure arm strength gives Garcia a high ceiling. He has easy velocity on his fastball, working at 93-94 mph and topping out at 96. With more experience and refinement, he should throw even harder. His curveball, at times a true power hammer, could be a better pitch. Garcia is still raw on the mound. His changeup needs work and he must learn how to set up hitters and hold runners. He sometimes falls in love with his curve and doesn't throw his live fastball enough. Garcia could start 2005 in extended spring training before a June assignment to short-season Staten Island. A good spring would land him in low Class A.

Year	Club (League)	Class	W	L	ERA	G	GS	CG	SV	IP	H	R	ER	HR	BB	SO	AVG
2004	Yankees (GCL)	R	3	4	2.84	13	6	0	0	38	26	13	12	1	17	47	.188
MINOR LEAGUE TOTALS			3	4	2.84	13	6	0	0	38	26	13	12	1	17	47	.188

6 Marcos Vechionacci, inf

SPORTS ON FILM

Born: Aug. 7, 1986. **Ht.:** 6-2. **Wt.:** 170. **Bats:** B. **Throws:** R. **Career Transactions:** Signed out of Venezuela by Yankees, Aug. 26, 2002. **Signed by:** Ricardo Finol.

Vechionacci has grown four inches since signing out of Venezuela as a 16-year-old. He's so mature at the plate that the Yankees promoted him from extended spring camp to Tampa as an emergency fill-in in May. Later, he starred in the Rookie-level Gulf Coast League. Vechionacci can hit. His advanced approach includes plate discipline, smooth swing mechanics and the ability to use the whole field. He shows developing power as well. His greatest improvement in 2004 was his willingness to stay back on breaking balls. Defensively, he has excellent tools with a plus arm, body control and natural infield actions. The Yankees need to determine Vechionacci's best position. He has played more at third base while also seeing time at shortstop and second base. How he fills out and whether he can maintain his average speed will determine if he can play at short. Vechionacci seems primed to move quickly through the system. He's likely to start 2005 in low Class A as a shortstop.

Year	Club (League)	Class	AVG	G	AB	R	H	2B	3B	HR	RBI	BB	SO	SB	OBP	SLG
2003	Yankees (DSL)	R	.300	62	200	28	60	10	4	2	30	37	22	4	.410	.420
2004	Tampa (FSL)	A	.250	1	4	1	1	0	0	0	0	0	0	0	.250	.250
	Staten Island (NY-P)	A	.292	19	72	13	21	5	0	0	8	11	13	0	.393	.361
	Yankees (GCL)	R	.336	36	131	24	44	9	1	4	22	12	19	5	.392	.511
MINOR LEAGUE TOTALS			.310	118	407	66	126	24	5	6	60	60	54	9	.401	.437

Melky Cabrera, of

Born: Aug. 11, 1984. **Ht.:** 5-11. **Wt.:** 170. **Bats:** B. **Throws:** L. **Career Transactions:** Signed out of Dominican Republic by Yankees, Nov. 13, 2001. **Signed by:** Victor Mata/Carlos Rios.

Cabrera signed for $175,000 in 2001 and has quickly developed into one of the organization's better hitters. He was slated to appear in the Midwest League's all-star game before getting a promotion to high Class A, where he showed the best power of his career. Cabrera's swing and hand-eye coordination make him the best hitter for average in the system. One club official compared his offensive game to Jose Vidro's. Cabrera has a quick stroke from both sides of the plate, with quick hands that allow him to catch up to quality fastballs. He punishes breaking balls and lashes line drives from gap to gap. He has an above-average throwing arm. An average runner, Cabrera projects as no more than an average defender in center field. There's some thought that as he matures physically and slows down, he'll have to move to an outfield corner. His approach and swing are geared more toward line drives and contact, so he doesn't profile as well on a corner. The Yankees have time to figure out where Cabrera fits. His advanced approach will enable him to begin 2005 in Double-A.

Year	Club (League)	Class	AVG	G	AB	R	H	2B	3B	HR	RBI	BB	SO	SB	OBP	SLG
2002	Yankees (DSL)	R	.335	60	218	37	73	19	3	3	29	18	23	7	.388	.491
2003	Staten Island (NY-P)	A	.283	67	279	34	79	10	2	2	31	23	36	13	.345	.355
2004	Battle Creek (Mid)	A	.333	42	171	35	57	16	3	6	31	16	15	23	7	.383	.462
	Tampa (FSL)	A	.288	85	333	48	96	20	3	8	51	23	59	3	.341	.438
MINOR LEAGUE TOTALS			.305	254	1001	154	305	65	11	13	127	79	141	30	.360	.431

Bronson Sardinha, 3b/of

Born: April 6, 1983. **Ht.:** 6-1. **Wt.:** 195. **Bats:** L. **Throws:** R. **School:** Kamehameha HS, Honolulu. **Career Transactions:** Selected by Yankees in first round (34th overall) of 2001 draft; signed June 13, 2001. **Signed by:** Gus Quattlebaum.

Sardinha is the youngest of three brothers in the minors (Dane plays for the Reds, Duke with the Rockies). He has yet to find a home defensively, having played shortstop as well as left and center field before trying third base in 2004. There, he ranked third in the minors with 43 errors. Sardinha is a polished offensive player who uses a textbook swing to handle both lefthanded and righthanded pitchers. He shows the ability to make adjustments within at-bats and isn't afraid to work deep counts. He's an efficient basestealer and average runner. The Yankees blame Sardinha's high error totals on lapses in concentration. With Eric Duncan behind him and Alex Rodriguez ahead of him at third base, Sardinha likely will return to the outfield in 2005. He has never shown much power at the plate, and he tries to cheat on good fastballs in an attempt to hit homers. Sardinha's development hit a speed bump in the Arizona Fall League when he broke a finger on his glove hand just before the season started. He'll return to Double-A in 2005.

Year	Club (League)	Class	AVG	G	AB	R	H	2B	3B	HR	RBI	BB	SO	SB	OBP	SLG
2001	Yankees (GCL)	R	.303	55	188	42	57	14	3	4	27	28	51	11	.398	.473
2002	Greensboro (SAL)	A	.263	93	342	49	90	13	0	12	44	34	78	15	.334	.406
	Staten Island (NY-P)	A	.323	36	124	25	40	0	0	4	16	24	36	4	.433	.484
2003	Tampa (FSL)	A	.193	59	212	23	41	8	2	1	17	24	57	8	.279	.264
	Battle Creek (Mid)	A	.275	71	269	54	74	16	0	8	41	40	40	5	.374	.424
2004	Tampa (FSL)	A	.315	63	248	37	78	12	2	2	33	29	39	9	.389	.403
	Trenton (EL)	AA	.267	72	266	37	71	11	1	6	29	37	65	4	.356	.383
MINOR LEAGUE TOTALS			.273	449	1649	267	451	82	8	37	207	216	366	56	.361	.400

Chien-Ming Wang, rhp

Born: March 31, 1980. **Ht.:** 6-3. **Wt.:** 200. **Bats:** R. **Throws:** R. **Career Transactions:** Signed out of Taiwan by Yankees, May 5, 2000. **Signed by:** John Cox/Gordon Blakeley.

Wang signed for $1.9 million out of Taiwan in 2000, and he's close to paying dividends after being deterred by shoulder surgery in 2001 and a shoulder strain in 2003. He shined for Taiwan in the 2004 Olympics, going 1-0, 1.98 in two starts. Wang has one of the best fastballs in the organization. His fastball velocity returned to its pre-injury level late in 2004, as he worked at 92-95 mph and touched 97. He showed durability by logging a career-high 149 innings. His splitter and slider are solid-average pitches. While

Wang's fastball has excellent velocity, it tends to get straight. He needs to use his changeup and splitter better against lefthanders, who tattooed him for a .307 average in 2004. Wang's medical history isn't encouraging, and he pulled a hamstring in the Triple-A International League playoffs, knocking him out of the organization's fall minicamp. Wang was the Yankees' best option for a low-cost starter, but the addition of Randy Johnson, Carl Pavano and Jaret Wright means he'll only be in the big leagues in case of emergency in 2005.

Year	Club (League)	Class	W	L	ERA	G	GS	CG	SV	IP	H	R	ER	HR	BB	SO	AVG
2000	Staten Island (NY-P)	A	4	4	2.48	14	14	2	0	87	77	34	24	2	21	75	.233
2001	Did not play—Injured																
2002	Staten Island (NY-P)	A	6	1	1.72	13	13	0	0	78	63	23	15	2	14	64	.219
2003	Trenton (EL)	AA	7	6	4.65	21	21	2	0	122	143	71	63	7	32	84	.294
	Yankees (GCL)	R	0	0	0.00	1	1	0	0	3	2	0	0	0	0	2	.182
2004	Trenton (EL)	AA	6	5	4.05	18	18	0	0	109	112	53	49	6	26	90	.266
	Columbus (IL)	AAA	5	1	2.01	6	5	2	0	40	31	9	9	3	8	35	.215
MINOR LEAGUE TOTALS			28	17	3.28	73	72	6	0	440	428	190	160	20	101	350	.254

10 Jeff Marquez, rhp

Born: Aug. 10, 1984. **Ht.:** 6-2. **Wt.:** 175. **Bats:** R. **Throws:** R. **School:** Sacramento CC. **Career Transactions:** Selected by Yankees in first round (41st overall) of 2004 draft; signed June 9, 2004. **Signed by:** Jeff Patterson.

Originally a walk-on at Sacramento City College, Marquez emerged as the ace of the perennial juco power in 2004. He quickly graduated from relief to the rotation thanks to a leap in velocity. After throwing in the low 80s in 2003, Marquez jumped to the low 90s during the spring. A supplemental first-round pick who signed for $790,000, he peaked at 94 mph with the Yankees. He throws a heavy sinker with excellent movement that one club official compared to vintage Ramiro Mendoza. Marquez' hard curveball is just spotty—accounting in part for his relatively low strikeout totals in his debut—but he shows the ability to spin the ball. New York is confident he'll have at least an average breaking pitch to go with a changeup he has shown some feel for. At times his changeup is better than the curve, and he'll be able to make it as a starter once he gains more consistency with his secondary pitches and his fastball command. Marquez has limited experience as a starter, and his competitiveness and heavy sinker could tempt the Yankees to move him quickly as a middle reliever. He'll open 2005 in the rotation at low Class A.

Year	Club (League)	Class	W	L	ERA	G	GS	CG	SV	IP	H	R	ER	HR	BB	SO	AVG
2004	Yankees (GCL)	R	3	1	3.51	4	2	0	0	14	10	1	1	0	4	18	.188
	Staten Island (NY-P)	A	2	4	2.96	11	11	0	0	52	51	26	17	2	20	37	.254
MINOR LEAGUE TOTALS			5	5	2.96	15	13	0	0	66	61	27	18	2	20	37	.240

11 Brett Smith, rhp

Born: Aug. 12, 1983. **Ht.:** 6-5. **Wt.:** 225. **Bats:** R. **Throws:** R. **School:** UC Irvine. **Career Transactions:** Selected by Yankees in second round of 2004 draft; signed Aug. 27, 2004. **Signed by:** Jeff Patterson.

Taken by the Diamondbacks in the 21st round of the 2001 draft coming out of high school, he became the highest-drafted player in UC Irvine history three years later and has the inside track to becoming the first Anteater to reach the major leagues since Brady Anderson. When the program was resuscitated for the 2002 season, Smith was one of the keys to the first recruiting class of then-coach John Savage. He took most of last summer before signing for $800,000 as the top pick in the second round. Smith has good size at 6-foot-4, and he uses it to keep his power repertoire down in the strike zone. In the spring, he worked consistently at 90-92 mph with his fastball. He was at his best when he threw his slider at 86-88 mph, and at times it has sharp, late bite. Smith also throws a curveball and changeup, though the change is in need of work. His delivery, which includes a mid-stride hesitation, could use refinement. When he's off, he gets mechanical and leaves his stuff up in the zone. He figures to join fellow 2004 draft picks Philip Hughes, Jeff Marquez, Christian Garcia, Jason Jones and Jesse Hoover on a prospect-laden low Class A staff.

Year	Club (League)	Class	W	L	ERA	G	GS	CG	SV	IP	H	R	ER	HR	BB	SO	AVG
2004	Did not play—Signed 2005 contract																

12 Rudy Guillen, of

Born: Nov. 23, 1983. **Ht.:** 6-3. **Wt.:** 185. **Bats:** R. **Throws:** R. **Career Transactions:** Signed out of Dominican Republic by Yankees, July 2, 2000. **Signed by:** Victor Mata.

The best news the Yankees got from Guillen in 2004 came in their fall minicamp, when he gave hints that his lost season was an aberration. He was coming off an impressive low Class A performance and appeared to be developing into a prototype right fielder, with power in his bat and arm. But in his encore, he missed nearly two months with a high ankle sprain and never showed the same pop or approach that had led one club official to compare him to Manny Ramirez. Guillen has great hands and kills offspeed pitches, but pitchers pound him inside with hard fastballs and he hasn't yet shown the ability to adjust. He has to learn how to pull the ball, rather than trying to serve most everything to the opposite field. Showing more patience at the plate also would help. The Yankees want Guillen to be less analytical and let his natural ability—which includes solid-average speed—take over. They may send him back to high Class A to open 2005 so he can get off to a good start.

Year	Club (League)	Class	AVG	G	AB	R	H	2B	3B	HR	RBI	BB	SO	SB	OBP	SLG
2001	Yankees (DSL)	R	.281	62	231	38	65	13	2	11	41	15	50	11	.337	.498
2002	Yankees (GCL)	R	.306	59	219	38	67	7	2	3	35	14	39	7	.351	.397
2003	Battle Creek (Mid)	A	.260	133	493	64	128	29	4	13	79	32	87	13	.311	.414
2004	Tampa (FSL)	A	.264	79	307	40	81	16	2	1	42	22	59	1	.313	.339
MINOR LEAGUE TOTALS			.273	333	1250	180	341	65	10	28	197	83	235	32	.324	.408

13 Jesse Hoover, rhp

Born: Jan. 8, 1982. **Ht.:** 6-3. **Wt.:** 210. **Bats:** R. **Throws:** R. **School:** Indiana Tech. **Career Transactions:** Selected in fifth round of 2004 draft by Yankees; signed June 14, 2004. **Signed by:** Mike Gibbons.

The Yankees had a potentially impressive haul of arms from the 2004 draft, and none made an immediate impact like Hoover, who was a junior-varsity pitcher/outfielder as a freshman at Indiana Tech and worked just 57 innings in his first three seasons. He emerged as the team's ace in 2004, leading NAIA pitchers with 14.7 strikeouts per nine innings. His velocity increased from the high 80s to 93-95 mph during the spring, and he touched 96-97 out of the bullpen after signing for $90,000. He ranked second in the short-season New York-Penn League with 90 strikeouts in just 55 innings, relying mostly on his fastball and a hard curveball. Hoover's curve can be a plus pitch, but he needs better command of it. He has toyed with a changeup and a splitter, focusing more on the latter with some success late in the summer. The development of the splitter could be the key to whether Hoover is relegated to the bullpen or is given a chance to start. Some in the organization want to see him smooth out his delivery, which has some deception in the way he brings the ball out of his glove. He attended the organization's fall minicamp and impressed the Yankees with his work ethic. Ticketed for low Class A, he could advance quickly as a power reliever.

Year	Club (League)	Class	W	L	ERA	G	GS	CG	SV	IP	H	R	ER	HR	BB	SO	AVG
2004	Staten Island (NY-P)	A	2	1	1.78	16	9	0	0	56	28	14	11	0	26	90	.151
MINOR LEAGUE TOTALS			2	1	1.78	16	9	0	0	56	28	14	11	0	26	90	.151

14 Tim Battle, of

Born: Sept. 10, 1985. **Ht.:** 6-2. **Wt.:** 185. **Bats:** R. **Throws:** R. **School:** McIntosh HS, Peachtree City, Ga. **Career Transactions:** Selected by Yankees in third round of 2003 draft; signed June 9, 2003. **Signed by:** Steve Swail.

A few weeks after the Yankees made him a third-round pick in 2003, Battle felt weak. Doctors diagnosed a form of bone cancer in Battle, and he had to go through multiple chemotherapy treatments. New York owner George Steinbrenner paid Battle's medical bills and brought him to the 2003 World Series as a guest of the team. When Battle returned in 2004, he showed the best five-tool ability in the system. His speed rates an 80 on the 20-80 scouting scale, and his light-tower power and arm are both well-above-average. He has had great difficulty in translating his physical gifts into production on the diamond, however. Battle struggles to recognize breaking balls and is a dead-pull hitter who is struggling to learn that he doesn't have to yank the ball to get it out of the park. Yankees hitting coaches have gone to extremes with him, ending batting-practice sessions whenever he pulls the ball. He's also raw on the basepaths and has done his best work on defense in center field. While he's still young and has plenty of time, the Yankees were displeased by Battle's constant tardiness and overall lack of professionalism last year. So hard as it may be to believe, the makeup of a player coming back from cancer was a problem. He showed better dedication during minicamp, but he still may not be ready for full-season ball.

Year	Club (League)	Class	AVG	G	AB	R	H	2B	3B	HR	RBI	BB	SO	SB	OBP	SLG
2003	Yankees (GCL)	R	.208	27	106	14	22	5	0	0	5	7	33	5	.270	.255
2004	Staten Island (NY-P)	A	.246	53	199	28	49	8	2	1	20	14	74	13	.302	.322
	Yankees (GCL)	R	.320	12	50	11	16	3	3	1	4	4	15	5	.364	.560
MINOR LEAGUE TOTALS			.245	92	355	53	87	16	5	2	29	25	122	23	.295	.335

15 Matt DeSalvo, rhp

Born: Sept. 11, 1980. **Ht.:** 6-0. **Wt.:** 170. **Bats:** R. **Throws:** R. **School:** Marietta (Ohio) College. **Career Transactions:** Signed as nondrafted free agent by Yankees, May 15, 2003. **Signed by:** Mike Gibbons.

In the first half of the season, DeSalvo treated the Florida State League as if it were the Ohio Athletic Conference, which he dominated for four seasons and part of a fifth. At Division III Marietta (Ohio), DeSalvo set NCAA all-division records for wins (53) and strikeouts (603). The Yankees signed him as a fifth-year senior before the 2003 draft, after his slight build and a knee injury kept him from being picked the previous year. He relies heavily on his 88-90 mph fastball and gets away with it because of his command and movement on the pitch. His quick arm and high, overhand arm angle give his fastball good life down in the zone. DeSalvo has fringy secondary pitches, with his changeup grading out a bit better than his loopy curveball. His best attribute is his competitiveness. His overall combination wasn't good enough in his first try at Double-A, and he missed much of the second half of the season with back pain. A healthy DeSalvo will get another shot at Double-A in 2005.

Year	Club (League)	Class	W	L	ERA	G	GS	CG	SV	IP	H	R	ER	HR	BB	SO	AVG
2003	Staten Island (NY-P)	A	3	3	1.84	10	10	1	0	49	42	18	10	2	19	52	.232
	Battle Creek (Mid)	A	2	0	0.82	3	3	0	0	22	15	5	2	0	5	21	.195
2004	Trenton (EL)	AA	2	2	6.59	5	5	0	0	27	27	20	20	3	10	24	.260
	Tampa (FSL)	A	6	3	1.43	13	13	0	0	75	48	20	12	1	30	80	.176
MINOR LEAGUE TOTALS			13	8	2.28	31	31	1	0	174	132	63	44	6	64	177	.208

16 Edwardo Sierra, rhp

Born: April 15, 1982. **Ht.:** 6-3. **Wt.:** 185. **Bats:** R. **Throws:** R. **Career Transactions:** Signed out of Dominican Republic by Athletics, Feb. 15, 1999 . . . Traded by Athletics with SS J.T. Stotts to Yankees for LHP Chris Hammond and cash, Dec. 18, 2003. **Signed by:** Bernardino Rosario (Athletics).

The Athletics have a history of giving up young, hard-throwing Dominicans in trades, such as Jesus Colome (to Tampa Bay) and Franklyn German (to Detroit in a three-team deal that netted them Ted Lilly and minor leaguers Jason Arnold and John-Ford Griffin from the Yankees). Neither has had the kind of success that makes Oakland regret the moves. Sierra will try to buck the trend after coming to New York for Chris Hammond following the 2003 season. He led the high Class A Florida State League in saves last year, showing a lively 95 mph fastball that's the best in the system. When he's on, he complements it with an upper-80s splitter and a hard slider that he added late in the year. However, Sierra doesn't throw strikes consistently enough with the fastball. He tends to fly open in his delivery, which leads him to leave his fastball up and out of the strike zone. He also gets too satisfied after he makes a great pitch, lacking the focus he needs. The Yankees will find out much more about Sierra and whether he can help their bullpen in the near future after his first foray into Double-A.

Year	Club (League)	Class	W	L	ERA	G	GS	CG	SV	IP	H	R	ER	HR	BB	SO	AVG
1999	Athletics East (DSL)	R	1	3	5.02	6	5	0	0	29	32	24	16	1	19	27	.288
	Athletics West (DSL)	R	1	1	3.18	8	1	0	1	28	26	18	10	1	13	27	.248
2000	Athletics West (DSL)	R	4	2	2.22	10	9	1	0	65	56	27	16	1	24	50	.230
	Athletics East (DSL)	R	1	2	3.57	4	4	0	0	23	21	9	9	0	9	19	.263
2001	Athletics (AZL)	R	2	1	3.02	12	6	0	1	45	45	19	15	1	9	41	.262
2002	Vancouver (NWL)	A	0	2	6.11	9	7	0	0	28	42	24	19	0	17	23	.336
	Athletics (AZL)	R	2	1	4.64	6	6	0	0	33	29	19	17	2	10	35	.240
2003	Kane County (Mid)	A	3	5	2.09	51	0	0	17	60	46	23	14	2	24	52	.204
2004	Tampa (FSL)	A	2	3	3.33	45	0	0	28	49	44	22	18	2	45	57	.246
MINOR LEAGUE TOTALS			16	20	3.36	151	38	1	47	359	341	185	134	10	170	331	.250

17 Tyler Clippard, rhp

Born: Feb. 14, 1985. **Ht.:** 6-4. **Wt.:** 170. **Bats:** R. **Throws:** R. **School:** J.W. Mitchell HS, Trinity, Fla. **Career Transactions:** Selected by Yankees in ninth round of 2003 draft; signed June 6, 2003. **Signed by:** Scott Pleis.

Kicked off his high school baseball team as a senior for drinking alcohol and driving under the influence, Clippard signed as ninth-round pick for $75,000. The Yankees watched him closely in low Class A last year to see how he'd respond to his first full pro season. He passed the test by taking the ball every turn and developing into Battle Creek's most consistent pitcher. Clippard has savvy and control but not overwhelming stuff. At times his curveball is an above-average pitch. He sets it up by spotting his 87-91 mph fastball, which he throws for strikes and works inside. He also throws a changeup and slider. The changeup potentially could be an average big league pitch as well, and it has allowed him to keep lefthanders in check. Clippard still has a gangly physique, and the best-case scenario is that he'll gain velocity on his fastball as he matures physically while retaining his control. He's ready for high Class A.

Year	Club (League)	Class	W	L	ERA	G	GS	CG	SV	IP	H	R	ER	HR	BB	SO	AVG
2003	Yankees (GCL)	R	3	3	2.89	11	5	0	0	44	33	16	14	3	5	56	.212
2004	Battle Creek (Mid)	A	10	10	3.44	26	25	1	0	149	153	71	57	12	32	145	.261
MINOR LEAGUE TOTALS			13	13	3.32	37	30	1	0	193	186	87	71	15	37	201	.251

18 Andy Phillips, 1b/3b

Born: April 6, 1977. **Ht.:** 6-0. **Wt.:** 205. **Bats:** R. **Throws:** R. **School:** University of Alabama. **Career Transactions:** Selected by Yankees in seventh round of 1999 draft; signed June 25, 1999. **Signed by:** Leon Wurth.

Phillips doesn't fit the profile of a typical Yankees prospect, and he'll be 28 when the 2005 season starts. But he has something many other New York farmhands lack: a proven ability to hit, which he has done throughout the minors. He wasn't fazed when he made his major league debut in September, homering off Terry Adams in his first at-bat. Phillips, who holds the Southeastern Conference record with a 36-game hitting streak, drilled 30 homers in 2004 to rank second in the system. His approach and performance draw comparisons to those of Kevin Millar, who didn't become a big league regular until he was 27. Like Millar, Phillips is limited defensively, and an ankle injury that essentially eliminated his 2003 season moved him off second base permanently. He'll have to prove he can play third base in addition to first to earn a spot with the Yankees, but he's on the 40-man roster and has enough bat to be an effective reserve or platoon player.

Year	Club (League)	Class	AVG	G	AB	R	H	2B	3B	HR	RBI	BB	SO	SB	OBP	SLG
1999	Staten Island (NY-P)	A	.322	64	233	35	75	11	7	7	48	37	40	3	.417	.519
2000	Tampa (FSL)	A	.287	127	478	66	137	33	2	13	58	46	98	2	.346	.446
	Norwich (EL)	AA	.250	7	28	5	7	2	1	0	3	3	11	1	.323	.393
2001	Norwich (EL)	AA	.268	51	183	23	49	9	2	6	25	21	54	1	.340	.437
	Tampa (FSL)	A	.302	75	288	43	87	17	4	11	50	25	55	3	.353	.503
2002	Norwich (EL)	AA	.305	73	272	58	83	24	2	19	51	33	56	4	.381	.618
	Columbus (IL)	AAA	.263	51	205	32	54	11	1	9	36	10	46	0	.296	.459
2003	Columbus (IL)	AAA	.209	17	67	7	14	4	0	2	5	5	17	0	.264	.358
2004	Trenton (EL)	AA	.357	10	42	8	15	2	1	4	16	3	1	3	.383	.738
	Columbus (IL)	AAA	.316	115	434	82	137	19	6	25	84	51	61	2	.386	.560
	New York (AL)	MAJ	.250	5	8	1	2	0	0	1	2	0	1	0	.250	.625
MAJOR LEAGUE TOTALS			.250	5	8	1	2	0	0	1	2	0	1	0	.250	.625
MINOR LEAGUE TOTALS			.295	590	2230	359	658	132	26	96	376	234	439	19	.360	.507

19 Abel Gomez, lhp

Born: Nov. 24, 1984. **Ht.:** 6-0. **Wt.:** 170. **Bats:** L. **Throws:** L. **Career Transactions:** Signed out of Dominican Republic by Yankees, Feb. 28, 2002. **Signed by:** Carlos Rios.

Gomez doesn't even weigh as much as his listed 170 pounds, but that doesn't keep him from having one of the organization's liveliest arms. He teamed with Tyler Clippard to form an effective one-two punch at Battle Creek in 2004, with a different approach. While Clippard controls four average pitches, Gomez brings heat, throwing his fastball consistently at 91-93 mph and touching 95. He remains immature physically, so he could throw even harder as he gets stronger. Gomez generates excellent arm speed with textbook actions. He doesn't have feel for commanding his fastball, though, and led the system in walks. While his fastball could be a plus-plus pitch in the future, he lacks a quality secondary offering. His curveball and changeup are fringy pitches but do have potential. Gomez might take awhile but he has significant upside, so the Yankees will be patient. He'll move up one step to high Class A this year.

Year	Club (League)	Class	W	L	ERA	G	GS	CG	SV	IP	H	R	ER	HR	BB	SO	AVG
2002	Yankees (DSL)	R	2	1	2.04	12	6	0	0	40	15	15	9	0	18	55	.110
2003	Yankees (GCL)	R	2	2	2.63	11	7	1	0	38	19	14	11	1	26	43	.157
2004	Battle Creek (Mid)	A	9	10	3.66	29	25	0	0	143	115	73	58	7	73	149	.222
MINOR LEAGUE TOTALS			13	13	3.19	52	38	1	0	220	149	102	78	8	117	247	.192

20 Jon Poterson, of

Born: Feb. 10, 1986. **Ht.:** 6-1. **Wt.:** 215. **Bats:** B. **Throws:** R. **School:** Chandler (Ariz.) HS. **Career Transactions:** Selected by Yankees in first round (37th overall) of 2004 draft; signed June 15, 2004. **Signed by:** Mike Baker.

Six of the Yankees' first seven picks in the 2004 draft were pitchers. The lone exception was Poterson, a supplemental first-rounder taken with a pick they received as compensation for the loss of Andy Pettitte. Poterson, who grew up a Yankees fan and lived in New York until he was 10, won over the club during a predraft workout when he launched several balls into the upper deck in right field at Yankee Stadium. He signed for $925,000. A switch-hitter who's slightly better from the left side, he has light-tower raw power that ranks at the top of the system, which is curiously absent of sluggers, and was just one off the Gulf Coast League home run lead. He has a balanced approach and a knack for staying inside the ball. Poterson was a catcher in high school, but the Yankees moved him to the outfield after drafting him because of his below-average receiving skills. Poterson got off to a horrible start to his pro career, but came around in August and performed well in instructional league, offsetting any doubts the Yankees might have had. He's slated to begin 2005 in low Class A.

Year	Club (League)	Class	AVG	G	AB	R	H	2B	3B	HR	RBI	BB	SO	SB	OBP	SLG
2004	Yankees (GCL)	R	.202	56	198	24	40	7	1	7	30	22	60	1	.280	.354
MINOR LEAGUE TOTALS			.202	56	198	24	40	7	1	7	30	22	60	1	.280	.354

21 Sean Henn, lhp

Born: April 23, 1981. **Ht.:** 6-5. **Wt.:** 200. **Bats:** R. **Throws:** L. **School:** McLennan (Texas) JC. **Career Transactions:** Selected by Yankees in 26th round of 2000 draft; signed May 25, 2001. **Signed by:** Mark Batchko.

Henn has struggled to live up to the hype he garnered when New York signed him in 2001 for $1.701 million, then a record for a draft-and-follow. He consistently threw in the upper 90s in junior college, but he has settled into the 91-93 mph range as a pro since recovering from Tommy John surgery, which hit after just 42 professional innings and cost him the 2002 season. Henn led Yankees minor leaguers in innings last year, proving his durability, and he looked good in a fall minicamp, hitting 96 mph in shorter outings and showing a sharper power slider. Despite its power, the slider is just an average pitch at this point because he lacks feel for it. That and his relatively straight heater account for a power lefty missing so few bats. Henn also lacks a decent changeup, which hurts him against righthanders. The Yankees need lefthanded relief help, so they'll probably move Henn to the bullpen in spring training before sending him to Double-A or Triple-A.

Year	Club (League)	Class	W	L	ERA	G	GS	CG	SV	IP	H	R	ER	HR	BB	SO	AVG
2001	Staten Island (NY-P)	A	3	1	3.00	9	8	0	1	42	26	15	14	3	15	49	.178
2002	Did not play—Injured																
2003	Tampa (FSL)	A	4	3	3.61	16	16	0	0	72	69	31	29	3	37	52	.259
	Yankees (GCL)	R	1	1	2.25	2	1	0	0	8	5	3	2	1	3	10	.167
2004	Trenton (EL)	AA	6	8	4.41	27	27	0	0	163	173	94	80	11	63	118	.273
MINOR LEAGUE TOTALS			14	13	3.94	54	52	0	1	286	273	143	125	18	118	229	.254

22 Scott Proctor, rhp

Born: Jan. 2, 1977. **Ht.:** 6-1. **Wt.:** 198. **Bats:** R. **Throws:** R. **School:** Florida State University. **Career Transactions:** Selected by Dodgers in fifth round of 1998 draft; signed June 6, 1998 . . . Traded by Dodgers with OF Bubba Crosby to Yankees for 3B Robin Ventura, July 31, 2003. **Signed by:** Bill Pleis.

The Yankees needed bullpen help during the 2004 regular season, and they were glad to have Proctor around after acquiring him from the Dodgers the previous summer. Proctor's velocity started to blossom before the trade, and he touched 100 mph after switching organizations. He pitched at 94-96 mph last year in the majors, but his performance wasn't good enough to merit a spot on the playoff roster. Though he throws hard, his fastball lacks deception and he didn't command it well enough to earn manager Joe Torre's trust. Proctor tends to elevate his fastball, and he can't get away with that against major league hitters. His slider and changeup are serviceable. However, that kind of velocity is hard to ignore, and New York protected Proctor on the 40-man roster after the season. Following the Yankees' trade for Felix Rodriguez, Proctor will have to compete with Jason Anderson, Colter Bean and Sam Marsonek (all also on the 40-man roster) for a big league job in spring training.

Year	Club (League)	Class	W	L	ERA	G	GS	CG	SV	IP	H	R	ER	HR	BB	SO	AVG
1998	Yakima (NWL)	A	0	1	10.80	3	1	0	2	5	9	8	6	1	1	4	.391
1999	Yakima (NWL)	A	4	2	7.20	16	6	0	0	50	57	45	40	4	26	41	.286
2000	Vero Beach (FSL)	A	3	7	5.16	35	5	0	1	89	93	65	51	13	54	70	.268
2001	Vero Beach (FSL)	A	6	4	2.48	15	15	0	0	91	73	30	25	8	30	79	.226
	Jacksonville (SL)	AA	4	3	4.17	10	9	0	0	50	39	26	23	6	31	48	.220
2002	Jacksonville (SL)	AA	7	9	3.51	26	25	0	0	133	111	63	52	10	85	131	.227
2003	Jacksonville (SL)	AA	1	2	1.00	17	0	0	0	27	20	6	3	0	7	24	.208
	Las Vegas (PCL)	AAA	4	2	3.66	24	0	0	1	39	35	17	16	2	13	35	.246
	Columbus (IL)	AAA	2	0	1.42	10	0	0	0	19	13	3	3	2	3	26	.197
2004	Columbus (IL)	AAA	2	3	2.86	35	0	0	4	44	37	15	14	4	18	42	.222
	New York (AL)	MAJ	2	1	5.40	26	0	0	0	25	29	18	15	5	14	21	.284
MAJOR LEAGUE TOTALS			2	1	5.40	26	0	0	0	25	29	18	15	5	14	21	.284
MINOR LEAGUE TOTALS			33	33	3.83	191	61	0	8	547	487	278	233	50	268	500	.240

23 Ramon Ramirez, rhp

Born: Aug. 31, 1981. **Ht.:** 5-11. **Wt.:** 170. **Bats:** R. **Throws:** R. **Career Transactions:** Signed out of Dominican Republic by Rangers, Dec. 27, 1996 . . . Released by Rangers, June 4, 1998 . . . Signed by Hiroshima (Japan), 2002 . . . Signed by Yankees, March 5, 2003. **Signed by:** Cornelio Pena (Rangers).

Ramirez' career has taken plenty of turns, and it appears ready to take another one—to the bullpen. A former Rangers minor league outfielder, he spent four years out of baseball before resurfacing as a pitcher in Japan in 2002. The Yankees outbid the Phillies for his rights, sending $350,000 to the Hiroshima Carp and signing him for $175,000. After initially struggling in 2003, his power stuff and adjusted mechanics helped him to a short-but-tantalizing stretch in the upper minors. He began 2004 in Triple-A but struggled and was demoted to Double-A. Ramirez pitched better than his misleading ERA would indicate. He goes right after hitters with a 92-94 mph fastball and a hard curveball, and he throws a splitter he picked up in Japan. His curve is his best pitch, but he throws it too much. As with many short righthanders, his fastball tends to stay up in the strike zone. He doesn't change speeds well and is susceptible to home runs. The Yankees have decided to try moving him into middle relief in Triple-A this year, a role that seems better suited to his repertoire.

Year	Club (League)	Class	AVG	G	AB	R	H	2B	3B	HR	RBI	BB	SO	SB	OBP	SLG
1997	Rangers (DSL)	R	.245	39	94	12	23	4	0	2	9	16	21	2	.355	.351
MINOR LEAGUE TOTALS			.245	39	94	12	23	4	0	2	9	16	21	2	.355	.351

Year	Club (League)	Class	W	L	ERA	G	GS	CG	SV	IP	H	R	ER	HR	BB	SO	AVG
2002	Hiroshima (CL)	JPN	0	0	3.00	2	0	0	0	3	3	1	1	0	2	3	—
2003	Tampa (FSL)	A	2	8	5.21	14	14	0	0	74	88	47	43	7	20	70	.291
	Trenton (EL)	AA	1	1	1.69	4	3	0	0	21	18	8	4	3	8	21	.231
	Columbus (IL)	AAA	0	1	4.50	2	1	0	0	6	5	5	3	1	1	5	.208
2004	Columbus (IL)	AAA	0	3	8.50	4	4	0	0	18	25	19	17	3	8	17	.329
	Trenton (EL)	AA	4	6	4.66	18	18	1	0	114	115	60	59	11	32	128	.260
MINOR LEAGUE TOTALS			7	19	4.85	42	40	1	0	234	251	139	126	25	69	241	.272

24 Jason Jones, rhp

Born: Nov. 20, 1982. **Ht.:** 6-5. **Wt.:** 225. **Bats:** R. **Throws:** R. **School:** Liberty University. **Career Transactions:** Selected by Yankees in fourth round of 2004 draft; signed June 11, 2004. **Signed by:** Brian Barber.

Jones doesn't have the arm strength of the other pitcher the Yankees took early in the 2004 draft, but he's no soft-tosser. He missed the 2003 season at Liberty with a knee injury but rebounded to become the first player drafted out of the Big South Conference last year. He came back throwing 90-92 mph. He's a big guy who pounds the strike zone with his fastball, which has some sink. Jones also has a solid-average slider, and works in a curveball and changeup. Nothing in his repertoire induces swings and misses, but he can throw all four pitches for strikes. He walked just six batters in 79 innings during his debut. The Yankees also like his aptitude and intelligence, which could prompt them to let him begin his first full year in high Class A. His ceiling is limited to a back-of-the-rotation starter, however.

Year	Club (League)	Class	W	L	ERA	G	GS	CG	SV	IP	H	R	ER	HR	BB	SO	AVG
2004	Battle Creek (Mid)	A	3	1	2.87	6	6	0	0	31	38	11	10	2	3	19	.309
	Staten Island (NY-P)	A	2	3	2.44	8	8	1	0	48	42	15	13	3	3	27	.239
MINOR LEAGUE TOTALS			5	4	2.61	14	14	1	0	79	80	26	23	5	6	46	.268

25 Kevin Thompson, of

Born: Sept. 18, 1979. **Ht.:** 5-10. **Wt.:** 185. **Bats:** R. **Throws:** R. **School:** Grayson County (Texas) JC. **Career Transactions:** Selected by Yankees in 31st round of 1999 draft; signed June 7, 2000. **Signed by:** Mark Batchko.

The Yankees have been patient with Thompson, who finally experienced his first success above Class A last season and was sent to the Arizona Fall League. He hit a grand slam in his first game in Arizona, and few players in the system can match his power-speed combination. Thompson has plenty of tools, with his 70 speed (on the 20-80 scouting scale) being his best. He also has a plus arm and average hitting ability and power. Most of his home runs come to the pull side and he doesn't generate much opposite-field pop. Thompson never seems to put everything together. He doesn't carry adjustments from batting practice to games, and he's not fundamentally sound. He has the tools to play center field, though he lacks the instincts and savvy to man the position full-time. He does show good baserunning instincts, and the Yankees believe he may be starting to get it. Offseason elbow surgery kept him out of the lineup until June, but when he returned, he hit much better in Double-A than he had in 2003. He profiles best an energetic, explosive fourth outfielder.

Year	Club (League)	Class	AVG	G	AB	R	H	2B	3B	HR	RBI	BB	SO	SB	OBP	SLG
2000	Yankees (GCL)	R	.267	20	75	13	20	7	1	2	9	10	14	2	.356	.467
2001	Staten Island (NY-P)	A	.262	68	260	46	68	11	4	6	33	36	48	11	.360	.404
2002	Greensboro (SAL)	A	.283	62	226	44	64	24	3	3	31	37	42	14	.396	.456
	Tampa (FSL)	A	.184	25	87	10	16	5	0	0	7	13	15	11	.298	.241
	Staten Island (NY-P)	A	.302	36	139	25	42	5	2	4	14	17	24	6	.376	.453
2003	Tampa (FSL)	A	.331	44	163	42	54	13	4	5	25	32	27	16	.433	.552
	Trenton (EL)	AA	.226	86	328	48	74	16	2	5	20	37	57	47	.310	.332
2004	Tampa (FSL)	A	.356	11	45	12	16	4	0	2	6	4	7	9	.420	.578
	Trenton (EL)	AA	.281	69	270	43	76	17	0	9	17	30	40	29	.362	.444
MINOR LEAGUE TOTALS			.270	421	1593	283	430	102	16	36	162	216	274	145	.363	.422

26 Ben Julianel, lhp

Born: Sept. 4, 1979. **Ht.:** 6-2. **Wt.:** 180. **Bats:** B. **Throws:** L. **School:** San Diego State University. **Career Transactions:** Selected by Cardinals in 12th round of 2001 draft; signed June 8, 2001 . . . Traded by Cardinals with RHP Justin Pope to Yankees for LHP Sterling Hitchcock, Aug. 22, 2003. **Signed by:** Dan Ontiveros (Cardinals).

Since arriving from the Cardinals in a trade for lefthander Sterling Hitchcock, Julianel has emerged as the best in-house option the Yankees have for filling the lefty specialist role in the bullpen. He dominated lefthanders last year, holding them to a .184 average, one homer and 35 strikeouts in 96 plate appearances. And Julianel may have enough stuff to be more than a specialist. After previously using a three-quarters delivery, he raised his arm angle a bit in 2004 and his slider improved to where it's now a plus pitch. He also throws an 88-89 mph fastball and an average changeup. He has the makeup to pitch in crucial situations and has been compared with Steve Kline for his stuff and his guts. Julianel probably will return to Double-A to begin 2005 but could contribute in New York by the end of the season.

Year	Club (League)	Class	W	L	ERA	G	GS	CG	SV	IP	H	R	ER	HR	BB	SO	AVG
2001	New Jersey (NY-P)	A	6	6	3.48	15	15	0	0	85	88	38	33	1	26	86	.270
2002	Peoria (Mid)	A	8	3	3.50	38	8	0	1	100	106	49	39	9	32	96	.270
2003	Peoria (Mid)	A	4	2	1.05	51	0	0	9	52	41	11	6	1	25	78	.215
	Battle Creek (Mid)	A	0	0	1.69	4	0	0	0	5	6	1	1	0	2	10	.273
2004	Trenton (EL)	AA	1	2	5.68	6	0	0	0	6	6	4	4	0	3	5	.250
	Tampa (FSL)	A	5	5	2.49	44	0	0	10	61	53	23	17	2	24	72	.235
MINOR LEAGUE TOTALS			24	18	2.90	158	23	0	20	310	300	126	100	13	112	347	.254

27 Mario Holmann, 2b

Born: May 21, 1984. **Ht.:** 6-0. **Wt.:** 160. **Bats:** B. **Throws:** R. **Career Transactions:** Signed out of Nicaragua by Yankees, Dec. 31, 2002. **Signed by:** Carlos Rios/Edgar Rodriguez.

Holmann earned a promotion to the Florida State League after opening his first season in the United States in the Gulf Coast League, but that stint ended after four games because he broke his left thumb when he was hit by a pitch trying to bunt. Though he has just 63 games of pro experience, Holmann already has endeared himself to the Yankees with his tools, skills and intelligence. He's one of the fastest runners in the organization, covering 60 yards in 6.4 seconds. He has pure natural explosion and speed, giving him excellent range at second base and making him a good basestealer. At the plate, he lacks power but has good bat control and a sound swing that he repeats easily. Holmann doesn't quite have the arm strength for shortstop, so the Yankees have put his natural infield actions and soft hands to work at second base. He figures to team with Marcos Vechionacci to form Charleston's double-play combination in 2005.

Year	Club (League)	Class	AVG	G	AB	R	H	2B	3B	HR	RBI	BB	SO	SB	OBP	SLG
2003	Yankees (DSL)	R	.311	39	106	33	33	6	1	0	10	34	33	16	.493	.387
2004	Yankees (GCL)	R	.258	20	66	12	17	1	1	1	7	13	17	10	.370	.348
	Tampa (FSL)	A	.286	4	7	1	2	1	0	0	1	0	3	0	.286	.429
MINOR LEAGUE TOTALS			.291	63	179	46	52	8	2	1	18	47	53	26	.444	.374

28 Hector Made, ss

Born: Dec. 18, 1984. **Ht.:** 6-1. **Wt.:** 155. **Bats:** R. **Throws:** R. **Career Transactions:** Signed out of Dominican Republic by Yankees, July 17, 2001. **Signed by:** Carlos Rios.

The Yankees once had high hopes for a number of their Dominican shortstop prospects, but those hopes have dimmed significantly. They sent Joaquin Arias to the Rangers in the Alex Rodriguez trade and released Erick Almonte in the past year. They still have Made and Ferdin Tejada (who was lost to the Padres on waivers, then reclaimed), but neither profiles as a big league regular. Made played every day in low Class A at age 19, showing plus range and arm strength at shortstop, but he plays with too much flash. He led Midwest League shortstop with 32 errors, and New York wants him to make the routine play more frequently. He is nothing special offensively, flashing gap power but not displaying much discipline. He doesn't do anything exeptionally well, and his best value in the big leagues might be as a utility player. He'll try to show he's capable of more than that in high Class A.

Year	Club (League)	Class	AVG	G	AB	R	H	2B	3B	HR	RBI	BB	SO	SB	OBP	SLG
2002	Yankees (DSL)	R	.283	61	191	34	54	8	0	0	10	30	31	13	.389	.325
2003	Yankees (GCL)	R	.236	52	178	28	42	6	2	5	18	20	19	8	.314	.376
	Staten Island (NY-P)	A	.259	7	27	4	7	1	0	1	1	0	5	3	.259	.407
2004	Battle Creek (Mid)	A	.289	128	515	68	149	30	1	5	52	33	76	12	.336	.381
MINOR LEAGUE TOTALS			.277	248	911	134	252	45	3	11	81	83	131	36	.342	.369

29 Omir Santos, c

Born: April 29, 1981. **Ht.:** 6-1. **Wt.:** 200. **Bats:** R. **Throws:** R. **School:** East Central (Mo.) JC. **Career Transactions:** Selected by Yankees in 21st round of 2001 draft; signed June 11, 2001. **Signed by:** Dave Jorn.

While Dioner Navarro was struggling with his receiving and his hitting last year, Santos quietly established himself as the system's best defensive catcher. Santos, who often goes by the nickname Pito, also showed signs that he might hit enough to be at least a backup in the big leagues. His defense always has been his strong suit, and now it's better than ever. He's a quiet receiver with excellent footwork, which makes him a standout at blocking balls in the dirt. The quick glove-to-hand transfer on his throws and his slightly above-average arm allow him to consistently post 1.89-1.95 pop times to second base. Santos will have to keep hitting like he did in his second-half callup to high Class A to be a legitimate prospect. His swing is mechanical, though with more playing time he got into a groove and showed more offensive potential than the Yankees expected. They like how he leads a pitching staff, so if he hits enough he'll move up to Double-A. That also would give Navarro more motivation to avoid a repeat of 2004.

Year	Club (League)	Class	AVG	G	AB	R	H	2B	3B	HR	RBI	BB	SO	SB	OBP	SLG
2001	Staten Island (NY-P)	A	.274	44	117	11	32	5	1	0	8	6	25	0	.310	.333
2002	Greensboro (SAL)	A	.233	23	73	7	17	2	1	1	8	2	15	0	.275	.329
	Staten Island (NY-P)	A	.289	61	232	22	67	10	0	7	44	12	32	2	.331	.422
2003	Battle Creek (Mid)	A	.235	82	277	35	65	11	0	2	30	25	36	0	.297	.296
	Yankees (GCL)	R	.000	1	0	0	0	0	0	0	0	0	0	0	.000	.000
2004	Battle Creek (Mid)	A	.240	56	171	21	41	7	0	2	16	7	27	4	.277	.316
	Tampa (FSL)	A	.286	37	119	18	34	6	1	2	13	6	17	1	.341	.403
MINOR LEAGUE TOTALS			.259	304	989	114	256	41	3	14	119	58	152	7	.307	.349

30 Maximo Nelson, rhp

Born: April 21, 1982. **Ht.:** 6-5. **Wt.:** 160. **Bats:** R. **Throws:** R. **Career Transactions:** Signed out of Dominican Republic by Yankees, Oct. 31, 2000. **Signed by:** Carlos Rios/Victor Mata/Rudy Jabalera.

Known as Willy Pie when he signed, Nelson's age was revised 22 months upward after he was forced to use his proper visa prior to the 2003 season. Despite his jump in age, the Yankees have been patient with Nelson, keeping him in the Rookie-level Dominican Summer League for three seasons before bringing him to the Gulf Coast League in 2004. He started and won the championship clincher against the Red Sox in the GCL playoffs. Tall and gangly, Nelson is starting to harness a power arm that pumps fastballs up to 96 mph. He could improve his fastball, which he relies on about 90 percent of the time, by staying tall in his delivery. He showed improvement with his nascent curveball, but it doesn't project as more than an average pitch at this point. Nelson won't be more than a reliever without better secondary stuff, but he has a live arm. He'll move up to low Class A in 2005.

Year	Club (League)	Class	W	L	ERA	G	GS	CG	SV	IP	H	R	ER	HR	BB	SO	AVG
2001	Yankees (DSL)	R	0	0	2.13	6	0	0	1	13	9	5	3	2	4	7	.214
2002	Yankees (DSL)	R	1	3	6.32	9	0	0	0	47	65	47	33	1	24	35	.316
2003	Yankees (DSL)	R	3	0	1.66	11	7	0	1	38	26	15	7	0	1	35	.167
2004	Yankees (GCL)	R	6	3	2.63	12	9	0	0	55	48	16	16	6	12	54	.235
MINOR LEAGUE TOTALS			10	6	3.49	38	16	0	2	152	148	83	59	9	41	131	.243

OAKLAND
ATHLETICS
BY **KEVIN GOLDSTEIN**

H e's the most well-known and talked-about general manager in baseball. And now Billy Beane is about to spend more time under the microscope. For the first time in five years, the Athletics failed to make the postseason. After they fell one game short of the Angels in the American League West, Beane's reaction was dramatic. Fearing the loss of Tim Hudson to free agency following the 2005 season and Mark Mulder after 2006, Beane made a pre-emptive strike. He sent Hudson to Atlanta and Mulder to St. Louis in December trades two days apart. The gambit is a risk, but Beane received plenty of young talent in return. Lefty Dan Meyer and righty Dan Haren are expected to step into the rotation, while pure hitter Daric Barton could be the real prize.

While the A's officially are rebuilding, they should remain competitive. Acquiring Meyer and Haren was important to a team that has had a problem developing starting pitchers since the Big Three of Hudson, Mulder and Barry Zito arrived in 1999-2000. Rich Harden has proven capable of filling a rotation slot, but Joe Blanton is the only other minor league starter close to being ready. The bullpen picture is prettier, as reinforcements are on the way to shore up one of the club's biggest weaknesses in 2004. Huston Street and Jairo Garcia are both closer-worthy and ready to contribute in 2005. They should provide the A's with a quality 1-2 punch for some time.

Though they've scored less than the aver-age AL club in each of the last two years, Oakland has fewer questions on offense. **Bobby Crosby** stepped in at shortstop last year, and Nick Swisher is a lock for a corner-outfield job this year and should match the production of Jermaine Dye, who left as a free agent. First baseman Dan Johnson has hit at every level, and he could take the place of Scott Hatteberg or Erubiel Durazo. The A's addressed an organizational weakness by drafting two of the top college catchers available in 2004, Landon Powell and Kurt Suzuki, then trading for Jason Kendall in the offseason.

The A's drafting philosophy has remained consistent for nearly two decades, as they focus almost exclusively on college players. In many ways, the 2004 draft was a sequel to the "Moneyball" class of 2002, as Oakland owned six of the first 67 picks. While the A's did select six collegians, they didn't make any signability choices and their overall effort received high grades.

While Oakland still isn't drafting many high schoolers—2004 fourth-rounder Ryan Webb was their highest prep pick since 2001 first-rounder Jeremy Bonderman—the club has renewed its efforts in Latin America. Garcia, a Dominican, made a meteoric rise in 2004. Two of the system's highest-ceiling position players are Venezuelan outfielder Javier Herrera and Dominican outfielder Alexi Ogando.

TOP 30 PROSPECTS

1. Nick Swisher, of
2. Daric Barton, 1b/c
3. Javier Herrera, of
4. Dan Meyer, lhp
5. Joe Blanton, rhp
6. Dan Johnson, 1b
7. Huston Street, rhp
8. Jairo Garcia, rhp
9. Richie Robnett, of
10. Omar Quintanilla, ss
11. Kurt Suzuki, c
12. Landon Powell, c
13. Danny Putnam, of
14. John Baker, c/1b
15. Brian Snyder, 3b
16. Andre Ethier, of
17. Jason Windsor, rhp
18. Brad Knox, rhp
19. Tyler Johnson, lhp
20. Alexi Ogando, of
21. John Rheinecker, lhp
22. Keiichi Yabu, rhp
23. Kevin Melillo, 2b
24. Brad Sullivan, rhp
25. Freddie Bynum, util
26. Jason Perry, of
27. Gregorio Petit, ss
28. Brant Colamarino, 1b
29. Mike Rouse, ss/2b
30. Ryan Webb, rhp

General manager: Billy Beane. **Farm director:** Keith Lieppman. **Scouting director:** Eric Kubota.

2004 PERFORMANCE

Class	Team	League	W	L	Pct.	Finish*	Manager
Majors	Oakland	American	91	71	.562	5th (14)	Ken Macha
Triple-A	Sacramento RiverCats	Pacific Coast	79	65	.549	5th (16)	Tony DeFrancesco
Double-A	Midland RockHounds	Texas	72	68	.514	4th (8)	Webster Garrison
High A	#Modesto A's	California	90	50	.643	1st (10)	Von Hayes
Low A	Kane County Cougars	Midwest	83	56	.597	1st (14)	Dave Joppie
Short-season	Vancouver Canadians	Northwest	42	34	.553	t-1st (8)	Dennis Rogers
Rookie	AZL Athletics	Arizona	34	22	.607	2nd (9)	Ruben Escalera
OVERALL 2004 MINOR LEAGUE RECORD			400	295	.576	1st (30)	

*Finish in overall standings (No. of teams in league). #Affiliate will be in Stockton (California) in 2005.

ORGANIZATION LEADERS

BATTING *Minimum 250 At-Bats
*AVG	Brian Stavisky, Modesto	.343
R	Nelson Cruz, Sacramento/Midland/Modesto	109
	Nick Swisher, Sacramento	109
H	Brian Stavisky, Modesto	176
TB	Nelson Cruz, Sacramento/Midland/Modesto	301
2B	Jason Perry, Midland/Modesto	44
3B	Freddie Bynum, Sacramento/Midland	7
HR	Dan Johnson, Sacramento	29
	Nick Swisher, Sacramento	29
RBI	Dan Johnson, Sacramento	111
BB	Nick Swisher, Sacramento	103
SO	Nelson Cruz, Sacramento/Midland/Modesto	149
SB	Freddie Bynum, Sacramento/Midland	39
*OBP	Brian Snyder, Kane County	.421
*SLG	Jason Perry, Midland/Modesto	.613

PITCHING #Minimum 75 Innings
W	Steven Bondurant, Midland/Kane County	16
L	Brad Weis, Midland	12
#ERA	Mike McGirr, Kane County/Vancouver	2.37
G	Daniel Fyvie, Kane County	59
CG	Steven Bondurant, Midland/Kane County	2
	Drew Dickinson, Midland	2
SV	Jeff Coleman, Midland/Modesto	23
IP	Joe Blanton, Sacramento	176
BB	Brad Weis, Midland	69
SO	Brad Knox, Kane County	174

BEST TOOLS

Best Hitter for Average	Omar Quintanilla
Best Power Hitter	Dan Johnson
Best Strike-Zone Discipline	Nick Swisher
Fastest Baserunner	Freddie Bynum
Best Athlete	Javier Herrera
Best Fastball	Jairo Garcia
Best Curveball	Brad Knox
Best Slider	Huston Street
Best Changeup	Jason Windsor
Best Control	Joe Blanton
Best Defensive Catcher	Kurt Suzuki
Best Defensive Infielder	Gregorio Petit
Best Infield Arm	Francis Gomez
Best Defensive Outfielder	Marcus McBeth
Best Outfield Arm	Alexi Ogando

PROJECTED 2008 LINEUP

Catcher	Landon Powell
First Base	Dan Johnson
Second Base	Omar Quintanilla
Third Base	Eric Chavez
Shortstop	Bobby Crosby
Left Field	Nick Swisher
Center Field	Mark Kotsay
Right Field	Eric Byrnes
Designated Hitter	Daric Barton
No. 1 Starter	Rich Harden
No. 2 Starter	Barry Zito
No. 3 Starter	Dan Haren
No. 4 Starter	Dan Meyer
No. 5 Starter	Joe Blanton
Closer	Huston Street

LAST YEAR'S TOP 20 PROSPECTS

1. Bobby Crosby, ss
2. Joe Blanton, rhp
3. Dan Johnson, 1b
4. Brad Sullivan, rhp
5. Graham Koonce, 1b
6. Nick Swisher, of
7. Omar Quintanilla, ss
8. Mike Rouse, ss
9. Andre Ethier, of
10. Justin Duchscherer, rhp
11. Chad Harville, rhp
12. Mike Wood, rhp
13. John Rheinecker, lhp
14. Jeremy Brown, c
15. Mark Teahen, 3b
16. Freddie Bynum, 2b
17. Ben Fritz, rhp
18. John Baker, c
19. John McCurdy, ss
20. Justin Lehr, rhp

TOP PROSPECTS OF THE DECADE

Year	Player, Pos.	Current Team
1995	Ben Grieve, of	Pirates
1996	Ben Grieve, of	Pirates
1997	Miguel Tejada, ss	Orioles
1998	Ben Grieve, of	Pirates
1999	Eric Chavez, 3b	Athletics
2000	Mark Mulder, lhp	Cardinals
2001	Jose Ortiz, 2b	Out of baseball
2002	Carlos Pena, 1b	Tigers
2003	Rich Harden, rhp	Athletics
2004	Bobby Crosby, ss	Athletics

TOP DRAFT PICKS OF THE DECADE

Year	Player, Pos.	Current Team
1995	Ariel Prieto, rhp	Tigers
1996	Eric Chavez, 3b	Athletics
1997	Chris Enochs, rhp	Astros
1998	Mark Mulder, lhp	Cardinals
1999	Barry Zito, lhp	Athletics
2000	Freddie Bynum, ss (2)	Athletics
2001	Bobby Crosby, ss	Athletics
2002	Nick Swisher, of	Athletics
2003	Brad Sullivan, rhp	Athletics
2004	Landon Powell, c	Athletics

ALL-TIME LARGEST BONUSES

Mark Mulder, 1998	$3,200,000
Nick Swisher, 2002	$1,780,000
Barry Zito, 1999	$1,625,000
Joe Blanton, 2002	$1,400,000
John McCurdy, 2002	$1,375,000

MINOR LEAGUE DEPTH CHART

Oakland ATHLETICS

Impact Talent: C

The ballyhooed "Moneyball" draft of 2002 should bear fruit in 2005, when Nick Swisher and Joe Blanton settle into big league roles. The rest of the class, aside from third baseman Mark Teahen (traded to the Royals), has proved less than revolutionary, and the poor performance of those pitchers forced GM Billy Beane to make trades to secure his future pitching staff, rather than rely on his farm system.

Depth: A

The A's took two of the top college catchers in the 2004 draft, and only an injury to John Suomi keeps them from having offensively capable catchers at every level. The addition of Daric Barton deepens Oakland's enviable group of left-handed hitters with power, which includes Dan Johnson, Danny Putnam and switch-hitters Landon Powell and Swisher. Acquiring Dan Meyer addressed their biggest weakness, lefthanded pitching.

*Depth charts prepared by **John Manuel** and **Allan Simpson**. Numbers in parentheses indicate prospect rankings.*

LF
Nick Swisher (1)
Daric Barton (2)
Danny Putnam (13)
Andre Ethier (16)
Jason Perry (26)
Matt Watson
Brian Stavisky

CF
Javier Herrera (2)
Freddie Bynum (25)
Dustin Majewski
Steve Stanley

RF
Richie Robnett (9)
Alexi Ogando (20)
Matt Allegra
Marcus McBeth

3B
Brian Snyder (15)
Vasili Spanos
Wilber Perez
Adam Morrissey
John McCurdy

SS
Omar Quintanilla (10)
Gregorio Petit (27)
Mike Rouse (29)
Frank Martinez

2B
Kevin Melillo (23)
Mark Kiger
Francis Gomez

1B
Dan Johnson (6)
Brant Colamarino (28)
Don Sutton
Tommy Everidge

SOURCE of TALENT

Homegrown		Acquired	
College	17	Trades	4
Junior College	2	Rule 5 draft	1
Draft-and-follow	0	Independent leagues	0
High school	1	Free agents/waivers	0
Nondrafted free agents	0		
Foreign	5		

C
Kurt Suzuki (11)
Landon Powell (12)
John Baker (14)
Jeremy Brown
Raul Padron
David Castillo

LHP

Starters	Relievers
Dan Meyer (4)	Tyler Johnson (19)
John Rheinicker (21)	Steven Bondurant
Dallas Braden	Trent Peterson
	Matt Lynch

RHP

Starters	Relievers
Joe Blanton (5)	Huston Street (7)
Jason Windsor (17)	Jairo Garcia (8)
Brad Knox (18)	Jose Corchado
Keiichi Yabu (22)	Marc Gwyn
Brad Sullivan (24)	Connor Robertson
Ryan Webb (30)	Steve Obenchain
Michael Rogers	Shawn Kohn
Danielin Acevedo	Chris Mabeus

DRAFT ANALYSIS
2004

Best Pro Debut: RHP Huston Street (1), a major part of Texas' College World Series title in 2002, won another title at Triple-A Sacramento. He made five scoreless appearances in the Pacific Coast League playoffs, after a 1-1, 1.38 regular season. They were too old for the Rookie-level Arizona League, but 3B Wes Long (29) and RHP Connor Robertson (31) made the all-star team.

Best Athlete: OF Richie Robnett (1) has above-average offensive potential and average speed. Street filled in at third base for the Longhorns in 2003. Robertson set Birmingham-Southern's career home run record with 60 and pitched just six innings for the Panthers before 2004.

Best Pure Hitter: OF Danny Putnam (1) is the most advanced, though he batted just .237-9-30 mostly in low Class A. Robnett isn't as developed but has tremendous hand-eye coordination. C Kurt Suzuki (2), who drove in the CWS-winning run for Cal State Fullerton, has the best approach.

Best Raw Power: Robnett's bat speed should give him the most power in time. The biggest threat at the moment is C Landon Powell (1).

Fastest Runner: OF Andre Piper-Jordan (28) has plus speed. He entered college as a wide receiver at Eastern Washington but transferred to Everett (Wash.) CC so he'd be eligible for the 2004 draft.

Best Defensive Player: Either Powell or Suzuki could be Oakland's answer behind the plate. Powell has better catch-and-throw skills, while Suzuki has more agility.

Best Fastball: Street pitched at 88-92 mph last spring while battling a groin injury, but touched 93-94 mph all summer.

Powell

His sink and command make his fastball play better than its velocity.

Best Breaking Ball: Street's slider is his out pitch. LHP Dallas Braden's (24) screwball enabled him to strike out 63 batters in 42 pro innings.

Most Intriguing Background: RHP Jason Windsor (3) was the MVP of the 2004 CWS. Robertson was MVP of the 2001 NAIA World Series—because of his bat. Unsigned LHP Drew Saberhagen's (38) father Bret won two Cy Young Awards. RHP Ryan Webb's (4) dad Hank also pitched in the majors. Unsigned RHP Matt Cassel (36) was a tight end on Southern California's 2003 football national champion. Street's father James quarterbacked Texas to the 1969 national football title and starred in baseball.

Closest To The Majors: Street could open 2005 in Oakland's bullpen.

Best Late-Round Pick: Braden, whose fastball jumped from 85-87 mph at Texas Tech to 88-90 in his pro debut.

The One Who Got Away: OF Jeremy Slayden (18), the A's highest unsigned pick, might have been a first-round pick had a torn rotator cuff not ruined his junior season at Georgia Tech.

Assessment: Oakland's interest in Putnam and Street was well known, but the A's were able to wait until the supplemental first round to get them. That freed them to spend earlier choices on Powell and Robnett, who were more coveted by other clubs.

2003 Getting RHP Brad Sullivan (1) at No. 25 seemed like a coup, but he hasn't pitched well as a pro. The other first-rounders, SS Omar Quintanilla and 3B Brian Snyder, have fared better, but they may all be role players. *Grade:* C

2002 The "Moneyball" draft was solid but not revolutionary. Oakland hit on three of seven first-rounders, and the two best—OF Nick Swisher (1) and RHP Joe Blanton (1)—were projected first-rounders by many teams. The third, 3B Mark Teahen (1), was traded in the Octavio Dotel deal last year. *Grade:* B+

2001 SS Bobby Crosby (1) and RHP Jeremy Bonderman (1) should have long careers, and 1B Dan Johnson (7) could push for a starting job in Oakland in 2005. *Grade:* A

2000 Giving up a first-round pick to sign Mike Magnante was a curious decision, as was using their top choice on INF/OF Freddie Bynum (2). But the A's made up for both with draft-and-follow RHP Rich Harden (17). *Grade:* B+

Draft analysis prepared by Jim Callis. Numbers in parentheses indicate draft rounds.

Nick
SWISHER

Born: Nov. 25, 1980.
Ht.: 6-0. **Wt.:** 190.
Bats: B. **Throws:** L.
School: Ohio State University
Career Transactions: Selected by Athletics in first round (16th overall) of 2002 draft; signed June 14, 2002.
Signed by: Rich Sparks.

Despite setting a West Virginia state record with 17 home runs as a senior at Parkersburg High, Swisher wasn't drafted in 1999. The son of former first-round pick and all-star catcher Steve Swisher, Nick starred at Ohio State, becoming the Big 10 Conference freshman of the year in 2000 and an all-conference pick the next two seasons. The highest June regular phase draft pick in Buckeyes history, Swisher was Oakland's No. 1 target and went 16th overall in the club's much publicized "Moneyball" draft in 2002. He made slow and steady progress in his first two years before breaking out at Triple-A Sacramento in 2004, leading the minor leagues in walks and tying Dan Johnson for the organizational lead in home runs. He spent September playing a significant role in Oakland's playoff push, performing admirably in his big league debut. The accomplishments were made all the more impressive by the postseason discovery that he played the entire season with a fracture and a torn tendon in his left thumb.

Swisher is a prime example of what Oakland looks for in a batting prospect. He has a quick, quiet swing that generates plus power from both sides of the plate, and he projects to hit 25-30 home runs annually. His uncanny plate discipline should make him a productive middle-of-the-order hitter, with the ability to both score and drive in 100 runs annually. The A's believe his .269 average at Sacramento represents the low end of his capabilities. Swisher brings a major league swagger to the field and backs it up with an outstanding work ethic. He's a true baseball rat who spent many summers traveling with his father during the elder Swisher's career as a minor league coach and manager. Swisher is sound defensively with good instincts and an average arm. While he has played just six games at first base as a pro, he's a potential Gold Glove candidate at that position, though Oakland currently has no plans of moving him from the outfield.

Swisher tends to chase outside pitches, especially from the left side of the plate. At times, he can be too patient, shown by a remarkable 43 walks in 28 June games. He changed his approach in the final two months at Sacramento, hitting 15 home runs in the season's final 50 games by focusing more on working himself into hitter's counts, as opposed to simply trying to draw walks. Primarily a center fielder in the minors, he has no better than average speed and will have to play on a corner in the majors. He's still learning to channel his intensity and can be too hard on himself, leading to extended slumps.

The A's saved $14 million by declining Jermaine Dye's option, all but handing Swisher a starting job in 2005. He had thumb surgery in October and should be 100 percent for spring training. The A's think Swisher can match Dye's production immediately. He should be the first of the "Moneyball" picks to contribute at the big league level and is a prime candidate for 2005 Rookie of the Year honors.

Year	Club (League)	Class	AVG	G	AB	R	H	2B	3B	HR	RBI	BB	SO	SB	OBP	SLG
2002	Vancouver (NWL)	A	.250	13	44	10	11	3	0	2	12	13	11	3	.433	.455
	Visalia (Cal)	A	.240	49	183	22	44	13	2	4	23	26	48	3	.340	.399
2003	Modesto (Cal)	A	.296	51	189	38	56	14	2	10	43	41	49	0	.418	.550
	Midland (TL)	AA	.230	76	287	36	66	24	2	5	43	37	76	0	.324	.380
2004	Sacramento (PCL)	AAA	.269	125	443	109	119	28	2	29	92	103	109	3	.406	.537
	Oakland (AL)	MAJ	.250	20	60	11	15	4	0	2	8	8	11	0	.352	.417
MAJOR LEAGUE TOTALS			.250	20	60	11	15	4	0	2	8	8	11	0	.352	.417
MINOR LEAGUE TOTALS			.258	314	1146	215	296	82	8	50	213	220	293	9	.380	.475

Daric Barton, 1b/c

DAVID STONER

Born: Aug. 16, 1985. **Ht.** 6-0. **Wt.:** 205. **Bats:** L. **Throws:** R. **School:** Marina HS, Huntington Beach, Calif. **Career Transactions:** Selected by Cardinals in first round (28th overall) of 2003 draft; signed June 10, 2003 . . . Traded by Cardinals with RHP Kiko Calero and RHP Dan Haren to Athletics for LHP Mark Mulder, Dec. 18, 2004. **Signed by:** Dan Ontiveros (Cardinals).

Barton was considered one of the best high school hitters in the 2003 draft, but concerns about his defense dropped him into the lower half of the first round. He proved to be one of the better offensive prospects in baseball in his first full season, leading the low Class A Midwest League in on-base percentage while finishing fourth in slugging. While Dan Haren and even Kiko Calero will pay more immediate dividends, many consider Barton to be the real prize Oakland received in the Mark Mulder trade with St. Louis. General manager Billy Beane called him the best pure hitter in the minors after dealing for him. Barton has a fast bat, uses all fields and already shows plus game power. He has an advanced understanding of the strike zone, and his offensive approach fits in perfectly with the A's philosophies. While few doubt Barton's ability to reach the majors on his bat alone, his defensive future is a question mark. Behind the plate he has a below-average arm and receiving skills. He threw out 25 percent of basestealers last year. His lack of athleticism and quickness were going to make catching a stretch, and Oakland has decided it's more important to develop his bat. He'll move to first base at Oakland's new high Class A Stockton affiliate this year.

Year	Club (League)	Class	AVG	G	AB	R	H	2B	3B	HR	RBI	BB	SO	SB	OBP	SLG
2003	Johnson City (Appy)	R	.294	54	170	29	50	10	0	4	29	37	48	0	.420	.424
2004	Peoria (Mid)	A	.313	90	313	63	98	23	0	13	77	69	44	4	.445	.511
MINOR LEAGUE TOTALS			.306	144	483	92	148	33	0	17	106	106	92	4	.436	.480

Javier Herrera, of

JOHN SPEAR

Born: April 9, 1985. **Ht.:** 5-10. **Wt.:** 160. **Bats:** R. **Throws:** R. **Career Transactions:** Signed out of Venezuela by Athletics, July 27, 2001. **Signed by:** Julio Franco.

In 2003, his first season in the United States, Herrera crashed into the wall during a Rookie-level Arizona League game and temporarily lost all feeling in his legs. Fully recovered in 2004, he was named MVP of the short-season Northwest League, where he was the lone player to reach double figures in both home runs and stolen bases. On pure tools and athletic ability, Herrera has more upside than any player in the system. He grades out at average or above in all five tools. He already has translated his power to game situations and was successful on 23 of 24 steal attempts in the NWL. Defensively, he has the speed to play center field and the arm for right. Herrera's aggressive approach at the plate could use refinement, and he has trouble with good breaking balls. In the outfield, he often must use his plus speed to offset bad jumps. He's understandably still a little tentative going back on balls toward the wall. Javier is ready to showcase his skills at the full-season level. He should spend most or all of 2005 at low Class A Kane County.

Year	Club (League)	Class	AVG	G	AB	R	H	2B	3B	HR	RBI	BB	SO	SB	OBP	SLG
2002	Oakland East (DSL)	R	.286	65	227	40	65	14	5	5	47	23	56	21	.359	.458
2003	Athletics (AZL)	R	.230	17	61	12	14	3	1	2	13	7	19	3	.329	.410
2004	Vancouver (NWL)	A	.331	65	263	50	87	15	4	12	47	24	59	23	.392	.555
MINOR LEAGUE TOTALS			.301	147	551	102	166	32	10	19	107	54	134	47	.372	.499

Dan Meyer, lhp

RODGER WOOD

Born: July 3, 1981. **Ht.** 6-3. **Wt.:** 190. **Bats:** R. **Throws:** L. **School:** James Madison University. **Career Transactions:** Selected by Braves in first round (34th overall) of 2002 draft; signed June 7, 2002 . . . Traded by Braves with RHP Juan Cruz and OF Charles Thomas to Athletics for RHP Tim Hudson, Dec. 16, 2004. **Signed by:** J.J. Picollo (Braves).

When the A's traded Tim Hudson to the Braves, general manager Billy Beane insisted on getting Meyer, the top lefthanded pitching prospect in Triple-A last season. A supplemental first-round pick in 2002, he was the highest-drafted college player by the Braves since they took Mike Kelly second overall in 1991. Meyer does a fine job of throwing strikes and keeping the ball down in the zone, and though he's usually around the plate he's not easy to hit. He has two plus pitches in his 91-93 mph fastball and his tight slider, and his changeup is also effective. After using it mainly for show in the past, Meyer began relying on his changeup more often in

2004. He still could use some more depth on his changeup and more consistency with his slider. He made his major league debut with two scoreless innings in September, and Oakland will give him every opportunity to win a rotation job in spring training. If he doesn't make the cut, he shouldn't need too much more time in Triple-A.

Year	Club (League)	Class	W	L	ERA	G	GS	CG	SV	IP	H	R	ER	HR	BB	SO	AVG
2002	Danville (Appy)	R	3	3	2.74	13	13	1	0	66	47	22	20	4	18	77	.198
2003	Rome (SAL)	A	4	4	2.87	15	15	0	0	82	76	35	26	6	15	95	.248
	Myrtle Beach (Car)	A	3	6	2.87	13	13	0	0	78	69	29	25	7	17	63	.236
2004	Greenville (SL)	AA	6	3	2.22	14	13	0	0	65	50	17	16	1	12	86	.209
	Richmond (IL)	AAA	3	3	2.79	12	11	0	0	61	62	23	19	6	25	60	.264
	Atlanta (NL)	MAJ	0	0	0.00	2	0	0	0	2	2	0	0	0	1	1	.286
MAJOR LEAGUE TOTALS			0	0	0.00	2	0	0	0	2	2	0	0	0	1	1	.286
MINOR LEAGUE TOTALS			19	19	2.71	67	65	1	0	352	304	126	106	24	87	381	.232

5 Joe Blanton, rhp

Born: Dec. 11, 1980. **Ht.:** 6-3. **Wt.:** 225. **Bats:** R. **Throws:** R. **School:** University of Kentucky. **Career Transactions:** Selected by Athletics in first round (24th overall) of 2002 draft; signed July 20, 2002. **Signed by:** Rich Sparks.

Blanton took the system by storm in 2003, leading the Midwest League in strikeouts despite leaving for Double-A by the end of July. Bumped to Triple-A for 2004, Blanton proved to be more hittable, but he impressed the A's in a brief major league look in September. Blanton has solid stuff and impeccable control. His lively fastball sat at 89-91 mph for much of the year, but he threw 92-94 coming out of the bullpen in Oakland. He throws strikes with his slider and curveball. He has a durable frame and should eat up innings in the major leagues. Blanton's changeup is still developing. He doesn't have a true out pitch, and Pacific Coast League observers liked his command and tenacity more than his stuff. He's still learning to change speeds and outthink hitters, as he can't simply overmatch them as he did at the lower levels. With his September showing, he convinced the A's he was ready to pitch in the majors in 2005. They traded Tim Hudson, Mark Mulder and Mark Redman with the idea that Blanton would fill one of the rotation vacancies.

Year	Club (League)	Class	W	L	ERA	G	GS	CG	SV	IP	H	R	ER	HR	BB	SO	AVG
2002	Vancouver (NWL)	A	1	1	3.14	4	2	0	0	14	11	5	5	0	2	15	.216
	Modesto (Cal)	A	0	1	7.50	2	1	0	0	6	8	6	5	1	6	6	.296
2003	Kane County (Mid)	A	8	7	2.57	21	21	2	0	133	110	47	38	6	19	144	.219
	Midland (TL)	AA	3	1	1.26	7	5	1	1	36	21	6	5	1	7	30	.174
2004	Sacramento (PCL)	AAA	11	8	4.19	28	26	1	0	176	199	101	82	13	34	143	.284
	Oakland (AL)	MAJ	0	0	5.63	3	0	0	0	8	6	5	5	1	2	6	.214
MAJOR LEAGUE TOTALS			0	0	5.63	3	0	0	0	8	6	5	5	1	2	6	.214
MINOR LEAGUE TOTALS			23	18	3.33	62	55	4	1	365	349	165	135	21	68	338	.249

6 Dan Johnson, 1b

Born: Aug. 10, 1979. **Ht.:** 6-2. **Wt.:** 220. **Bats:** L. **Throws:** R. **School:** University of Nebraska. **Career Transactions:** Selected by Athletics in seventh round of 2001 draft; signed June 18, 2001. **Signed by:** Jim Pransky.

A late bloomer at Nebraska, Johnson has produced consistently as a pro. His 225 RBIs in 2003-04 top all minor leaguers, and he tied for the system lead in homers while winning the regular-season and playoff MVP awards in the Pacific Coast League. He hit .468 in seven postseason games as Sacramento won its second straight championship. Oakland called him up afterward, but Johnson came down with a case of vertigo that kept him from making his big league debut. He recovered in time to have a productive winter in the Mexican Pacific League. Johnson has power to all fields and a solid understanding of the strike zone. He makes consistent contact for a power hitter and mashes mistakes. He has worked hard to improve at first, and even put in time in left field late in the year, but he'll never be more than an adequate first baseman. He's lumbering on the basepaths. Oakland decided to bring back both Scott Hatteberg and Erubiel Durazo back for 2005, so Johnson will have to be content with a reserve role at the start of the season.

Year	Club (League)	Class	AVG	G	AB	R	H	2B	3B	HR	RBI	BB	SO	SB	OBP	SLG
2001	Vancouver (NWL)	A	.283	69	247	36	70	15	2	11	41	27	63	0	.354	.494
2002	Modesto (Cal)	A	.293	126	426	56	125	23	1	21	85	57	87	4	.371	.500
2003	Midland (TL)	AA	.290	139	538	90	156	26	4	27	114	68	82	7	.365	.504
	Sacramento (PCL)	AAA	.250	1	4	0	1	1	0	0	0	0	0	0	.250	.500
2004	Sacramento (PCL)	AAA	.299	142	535	95	160	29	5	29	111	89	93	0	.403	.535
MINOR LEAGUE TOTALS			.293	477	1750	277	512	94	12	88	351	241	325	11	.377	.511

Huston Street, rhp

Born: August. 2, 1983. **Ht.:** 6-0. **Wt.:** 190. **Bats:** R. **Throws:** R. **School:** University of Texas. **Career Transactions:** Selected by Athletics in first round (40th overall) of 2004 draft; signed July 15, 2004. **Signed by:** Blake Davis.

Street holds the career saves records for Texas, Team USA and the College World Series. After signing for $800,000 on July 15, he was closing games in the Pacific Coast League playoffs by September. One scout who saw him in the Arizona Fall League opined that the A's would have made the playoffs had they promoted him in September. Street pitches mostly at 89-92 mph, but his fastball has heavy sink and he can dial it up to 94 mph when needed. His slider is more notable for its break than its velocity, but it's a major league out pitch. The ultimate competitor, Street has off-the-charts makeup. He won't beat himself with walks. Street doesn't have a classic closer repertoire, leaving some scouts to project him more as a set-up man. He still needs to find a consistent way to retire lefthanders, so the A's had him working on his changeup in the Arizona Fall League. Street could start his first full season as a big league set-up man and could become Oakland's closer in the very near future.

Year	Club (League)	Class	W	L	ERA	G	GS	CG	SV	IP	H	R	ER	HR	BB	SO	AVG
2004	Kane County (Mid)	A	0	1	1.69	9	0	0	4	11	9	2	2	0	5	14	.225
	Midland (TL)	AA	1	0	1.35	10	0	0	3	13	10	2	2	0	3	14	.217
	Sacramento (PCL)	AAA	0	0	0.00	2	0	0	1	2	2	0	0	0	0	2	.250
MINOR LEAGUE TOTALS			1	1	1.39	21	0	0	8	26	21	4	4	0	8	30	.223

Jairo Garcia, rhp

Born: March 7, 1983. **Ht.:** 6-0. **Wt.:** 165. **Bats:** R. **Throws:** R. **Career Transactions:** Signed out of Dominican Republic by Athletics, Jan. 31, 2000. **Signed by:** Bernardino Rosario/Raymond Abreu.

The Athletics always had faith in Garcia's stuff, but nagging arm troubles limited his innings and hindered his development. Moved full-time to the bullpen in 2004, he flourished. He shot from low Class A to the majors and led all minor league relievers with 14.9 strikeouts per nine innings. Garcia's pitches have drawn comparisons to Eric Gagne's. His fastball sits in the 93-95 mph range with good movement, and he consistently touches 97. His sharp-breaking slider is another plus pitch, and he has a strong changeup. Garcia's control fell apart after he left the Midwest League, as he failed to react well to getting hit and began aiming the ball. He needs to trust his stuff better while also learning that he can get hitters out with more than just his fastball. Like Street, Garcia is in a position to contribute in the majors in 2005. He does need a little more refinement, so he's more likely than Street to begin the year in Triple-A.

Year	Club (League)	Class	W	L	ERA	G	GS	CG	SV	IP	H	R	ER	HR	BB	SO	AVG
2000	Oakland (DSL)	R	6	2	3.26	11	10	0	0	47	33	24	17	2	29	56	.189
2001	Athletics (AZL)	R	4	2	2.85	12	7	0	0	47	37	19	15	2	6	50	.214
2002	Athletics (AZL)	R	2	1	2.44	13	8	0	1	59	56	24	16	5	17	66	.258
	Vancouver (NWL)	A	0	3	7.30	3	3	0	0	12	15	11	10	1	7	16	.300
2003	Kane County (Mid)	A	1	2	2.55	14	9	0	0	42	40	14	12	0	19	28	.250
2004	Kane County (Mid)	A	1	0	0.30	25	0	0	16	30	16	2	1	0	6	49	.154
	Midland (TL)	AA	2	0	1.50	13	0	0	2	18	10	3	3	0	15	32	.161
	Sacramento (PCL)	AAA	1	2	3.95	11	0	0	1	14	10	6	6	1	9	21	.208
	Oakland (AL)	MAJ	0	0	12.71	4	0	0	0	6	5	8	8	3	9	5	.227
MAJOR LEAGUE TOTALS			0	0	12.71	4	0	0	0	6	5	8	8	3	9	5	.227
MINOR LEAGUE TOTALS			16	11	2.67	102	37	0	20	270	217	103	80	11	108	318	.219

Richie Robnett, of

Born: Sept. 17, 1983. **Ht.:** 5-10. **Wt.:** 195. **Bats:** L. **Throws:** L. **School:** Fresno State University. **Career Transactions:** Selected by Athletics in first round (26th overall) of 2004 draft; signed July 19, 2004. **Signed by:** Scott Kidd.

Robnett's draft stock rose more than most last spring, as he opened scouts' eyes with a 6-for-11 weekend against Rice's trio of first-round pitchers. After sitting out 2003 in junior college, he led the Western Athletic Conference in batting (.384), slugging (.699) and stolen bases (21). He received the top bonus ($1.325 million) in Oakland's draft class, and capped a strong pro debut by batting .321 in the Midwest League playoffs. Robnett offers a tantalizing combination of power and speed. He puts on a show in batting practice, and the ball makes that special sound coming off his bat. Despite his inexperience, he shows a solid understanding of the strike zone. He has a strong build and the speed to play center field. Robnett has a tendency to club at the ball, making his swing long and hindering his ability to catch up to good fastballs. He needs to improve his jumps in center, and may profile better in right field, where his arm plays well. The A's were excited about Robnett's summer and think he could move quickly through the system. He'll start 2005 at one of their Class A affiliates.

Year	Club (League)	Class	AVG	G	AB	R	H	2B	3B	HR	RBI	BB	SO	SB	OBP	SLG
2004	Vancouver (NWL)	A	.299	43	164	26	49	14	1	4	36	28	43	1	.395	.470
MINOR LEAGUE TOTALS			.299	43	164	26	49	14	1	4	36	28	43	1	.395	.470

10 Omar Quintanilla, ss

Born: Oct. 24, 1981. **Ht.:** 5-9. **Wt.:** 190. **Bats:** L. **Throws:** R. **School:** University of Texas. **Career Transactions:** Selected by Athletics in first round (33rd overall) of 2003 draft; signed July 13, 2003. **Signed by:** Tim Holt.

After a successful college career at Texas, Quintanilla has continued to do nothing but hit as a pro. He owns a career .330 average in 171 pro games, and registered a hit in all but two games after an August promotion to Double-A Midland. Quintanilla's line-drive stroke leads to consistent contact and surprising gap power for his size. He has soft hands and excellent fundamentals in the field, making plays on any ball he can reach. He's a better baserunner than his average speed might indicate. His instincts accentuate his tools. His aggressive hitting style leads to few walks, and Quintanilla has resisted a more patient approach because of the success he's achieved so far. He may lack the athleticism and arm strength to stay at shortstop, but would profile as a solid second baseman. With Bobby Crosby entrenched at shortstop, Quintanilla is Oakland's second baseman of the future. He'll stay on the left side of the infield for now and return to Double-A.

Year	Club (League)	Class	AVG	G	AB	R	H	2B	3B	HR	RBI	BB	SO	SB	OBP	SLG
2003	Vancouver (NWL)	A	.341	32	129	22	44	5	4	0	14	12	20	7	.401	.442
	Modesto (Cal)	A	.417	8	36	9	15	3	0	2	6	3	6	0	.462	.667
2004	Modesto (Cal)	A	.315	108	451	75	142	32	5	11	72	37	54	1	.370	.481
	Midland (TL)	AA	.351	23	94	20	33	10	0	2	20	10	9	2	.419	.521
MINOR LEAGUE TOTALS			.330	171	710	126	234	50	9	15	112	62	89	10	.387	.489

11 Kurt Suzuki, c

Born: Oct. 4, 1983. **Ht.:** 6-1. **Wt.:** 200. **Bats:** R. **Throws:** R. **School:** Cal State Fullerton. **Career Transactions:** Selected by Athletics in second round of 2004 draft; signed July 15, 2004. **Signed by:** Randy Johnson.

Suzuki turned down a scholarship to stay home at Hawaii in order to walk on at Cal State Fullerton so he could face top competition. He capped an All-America .413-16-87 season in 2004 with the game-winning hit in the College World Series. He signed for $550,000 and had a solid pro debut, marred only by an 0-for-13 showing in the Northwest League championship series. Suzuki has a mature approach at the plate, consistently working himself into hitter's counts and demonstrating gap power. He's a natural leader on the field and is exceptionally good at blocking balls and framing pitches. Suzuki needs to use all fields with his line-drive stroke. He has average power at best, but is still pull-conscious from swinging metal bats. His arm graded as above-average in college but regressed during the summer, which might be due to fatigue. Suzuki shared catching duties with Landon Powell at short-season Vancouver, but they'll be separated in 2005 to give them both plenty of time behind the plate. Two years younger than Powell, Suzuki will begin the year one step below him in low Class A.

Year	Club (League)	Class	AVG	G	AB	R	H	2B	3B	HR	RBI	BB	SO	SB	OBP	SLG
2004	Vancouver (NWL)	A	.297	46	175	27	52	10	3	3	31	18	26	0	.394	.440
MINOR LEAGUE TOTALS			.297	46	175	27	52	10	3	3	31	18	26	0	.394	.440

12 Landon Powell, c

Born: March 19, 1982. **Ht.:** 6-3. **Wt.:** 235. **Bats:** B. **Throws:** R. **School:** University of South Carolina. **Career Transactions:** Selected by Athletics in first round (24th overall) of 2004 draft; signed July 19, 2004. **Signed by:** Michael Holmes.

The third time was a charm for Powell, whose first two attempted forays into pro ball ended in disappointment. He tried an unprecedented gambit as a high school junior, entering the draft after getting his GED diploma and becoming a free agent when he went unpicked. When no club met his price, he went on to a successful career at South Carolina but lasted until the Cubs took him in the 25th round of the 2003 draft because of concerns about his physique and signability. He hired a personal trainer and put up career-best .330-19-66 numbers as a senior. After Oakland took him 24th overall in 2004 and signed him for $1 million, an American League executive said, "Landon Powell is what Billy Beane thought Jeremy Brown was," referring to the 2002 supplemental first-round pick and darling of "Moneyball." Powell is a rare commodity, a switch-hitting catcher with power, plate discipline and defensive chops. He's surprisingly agile for his size and has a strong, accurate arm. Powell's body always will be a concern. He weighed as much as 260 pounds as a college junior, and he'll have to work hard to avoid getting too soft. He's slow but not a baseclogger. Two years older than 2004 supplemental first-round catcher Kurt Suzuki, Powell will be pushed a little harder, but his 2005 season will start late. He tore cartilage in his left knee while working out in January and was scheduled to have surgery, which will keep him out of spring training. When he is healthy, Powell will likely head to high Class A.

Year	Club (League)	Class	AVG	G	AB	R	H	2B	3B	HR	RBI	BB	SO	SB	OBP	SLG
2004	Vancouver (NWL)	A	.244	38	135	24	33	6	1	3	19	26	22	0	.368	.370
MINOR LEAGUE TOTALS			.244	38	135	24	33	6	1	3	19	26	22	0	.368	.370

13 Danny Putnam, of

Born: Sept. 17, 1982. **Ht.:** 5-10. **Wt.:** 200. **Bats:** L. **Throws:** L. **School:** Stanford University. **Career Transactions:** Drafted by Athletics in first round (36th overall) of 2004 draft; signed June 22, 2004. **Signed by:** Scott Kidd.

Putnam set career records for homers (33) and RBIs (118) at San Diego's famed Rancho Bernardo High program, which also has produced Hank Blalock and first-round picks Cole Hamels, Scott Heard, Jaime Jones and Matt Wheatland. Rancho Bernardo head coach Sam Blalock also coached Billy Beane at San Diego's Mount Carmel High. After high school, Putnam went to Stanford, where he blossomed into an All-American and a supplemental first-rounder who signed for $950,000. The A's had their sights on him all year and were pleasantly surprised when he was still available with the 36th overall pick. He had a disappointing debut but finished strong by leading all Midwest Leaguers with a .375 average in the postseason. Putnam was one of the best pure hitters in the 2004 draft. He has above-average bat speed and surprising power. Like most Oakland draft picks, he has an advanced understanding of the strike zone. His bat will be his ticket to the majors, as his weak arm and lack of speed limit him to left field. He can press when in slumps, and needs to learn to trust his tools and not tinker with his swing mechanics too much. The A's think Putnam is ready for a challenge and most will assign him to high Class A.

Year	Club (League)	Class	AVG	G	AB	R	H	2B	3B	HR	RBI	BB	SO	SB	OBP	SLG
2004	Vancouver (NWL)	A	.289	11	38	10	11	2	0	2	3	14	8	1	.481	.500
	Kane County (Mid)	A	.220	50	164	30	36	5	2	7	28	30	42	0	.348	.402
MINOR LEAGUE TOTALS			.233	61	202	40	47	7	2	9	31	44	50	1	.376	.421

14 John Baker, c/1b

Born: Jan. 20, 1981. **Ht.:** 6-1. **Wt.:** 215. **Bats:** L. **Throws:** R. **School:** University of California. **Career Transactions:** Selected by Athletics in fourth round of 2002 draft; signed June 28, 2002. **Signed by:** Will Schock.

Baker is a poor man's version of Daric Barton, with a similar profile but four years older and with a lower ceiling. Both are offensive-minded catchers whose fringy defensive skills likely will force them to move. Baker continued to hit in 2004 and added power to his game, drilling 15 homers after totaling just eight in his first two seasons. He was impressive after a final-month promotion to Triple-A. Baker crowds the plate and uses a short stroke from the left side of the plate. He needs to improve his ability to go the other way with outside pitches, and his strike-zone judgment has deteriorated as he has risen through the minors. Baker has put in extra work to improve his defense, but he'll go only as far as his bat will take him. His arm is below average, and a labrum tear prior to the 2004 season only made things worse. He threw out just 17 percent of basestealers last year. His other defensive skills are also adequate at best, leaving first base as his only other logical position. Baker will begin 2005 in Triple-A and should make his major league debut at some point.

Year	Club (League)	Class	AVG	G	AB	R	H	2B	3B	HR	RBI	BB	SO	SB	OBP	SLG
2002	Vancouver (NWL)	A	.235	39	115	15	27	5	0	1	13	22	37	2	.389	.304
2003	Kane County (Mid)	A	.309	82	304	42	94	23	2	6	49	47	77	1	.414	.457
	Midland (TL)	AA	.240	43	150	16	36	3	0	1	21	14	46	0	.316	.280
2004	Midland (TL)	AA	.280	117	439	67	123	32	5	15	78	37	94	0	.355	.478
	Sacramento (PCL)	AAA	.347	14	49	11	17	3	0	0	10	6	23	0	.429	.408
MINOR LEAGUE TOTALS			.281	295	1057	151	297	66	7	23	171	126	277	3	.374	.422

15 Brian Snyder, 3b

Born: March 17, 1982. **Ht.:** 6-0. **Wt.:** 195. **Bats:** R. **Throws:** R. **School:** Stetson University. **Career Transactions:** Selected by Athletics in first round (26th overall) of 2003 draft; signed July 1, 2003. **Signed by:** Kelly Heath

The A's zeroed in on Conor Jackson in the 2003 draft, but they doubted he'd fall to them in the late first round and were proven correct when the Diamondbacks selected him 19th overall. Oakland was happy to land its second-favorite hitter, Brian Snyder, who already had proven his ability to hit with wood bats during a solid Cape Cod League showing in 2002. After a lackluster pro debut, he had a successful first full season, finishing second in the Midwest League in on-base percentage despite missing time with shoulder and hip injuries. Snyder is a natural hitter and the A's expect him to gain power with experience. Other than Nick Swisher and Daric Barton, he has the best plate discipline in the system. Snyder sets up very far off the plate, leaving him susceptible to pitches on the outer half. He gained upwards of 20 pounds during the season, and his lack of physical conditioning may have contributed to his health problems. The weight gain also led to questions about his work ethic and his ability to stay at third base. Whether he'll have enough pop for the hot corner also is uncertain. Snyder's offensive skills are obvious, but his other tools regressed in 2004. The A's hope he'll have learned from the season, allowing him to jump to Double-A this year.

Year	Club (League)	Class	AVG	G	AB	R	H	2B	3B	HR	RBI	BB	SO	SB	OBP	SLG
2003	Vancouver (NWL)	A	.253	44	146	14	37	6	0	1	17	39	36	9	.409	.315
2004	Kane County (Mid)	A	.311	101	366	54	114	18	3	13	61	67	82	3	.421	.484
MINOR LEAGUE TOTALS			.295	145	512	68	151	24	3	14	78	106	118	12	.417	.436

16 Andre Ethier, of

Born: April 10, 1982. **Ht.:** 6-3. **Wt.:** 195. **Bats:** L. **Throws:** L. **School:** Arizona State University. **Career Transactions:** Selected by Athletics in second round of 2003 draft; signed July 1, 2003. **Signed by:** John Kuehl.

Until a stress fracture in his back shut him down at the end of July, Ethier ranked among the California League leaders in batting and hits during his first full pro season. The A's drafted him twice for his batting prowess, in the 37th round out of Chandler-Gilbert (Ariz.) CC in 2001 and in the second round out of Arizona State two years later. Ethier uses the entire field and should continue to hit for average. He has yet to show much power in games, but club officials and most scouts still see him hitting 20-plus homers annually once he learns how to drive the ball. While he drew 52 walks in 68 games in his final year at Arizona State, he has yet to show that kind of discipline as a pro. Ethier has average speed and fine outfield instincts, but he's not quick enough to play center field in the majors and his arm is a tick below average. He takes well to coaching, works hard and is driven to succeed. Ethier's back injury is not expected to have any long-term effects, and he'll advance to Double-A to begin 2005.

Year	Club (League)	Class	AVG	G	AB	R	H	2B	3B	HR	RBI	BB	SO	SB	OBP	SLG
2003	Vancouver (NWL)	A	.390	10	41	7	16	4	1	1	7	3	3	2	.444	.610
	Kane County (Mid)	A	.272	40	162	23	44	10	0	0	11	19	25	2	.355	.333
2004	Modesto (Cal)	A	.313	99	419	72	131	23	5	7	53	45	64	2	.383	.442
MINOR LEAGUE TOTALS			.307	149	622	102	191	37	6	8	71	67	92	6	.380	.424

17 Jason Windsor, rhp

Born: July 7, 1982. **Ht.:** 6-2. **Wt.:** 220. **Bats:** R. **Throws:** R. **School:** Cal State Fullerton. **Career Transactions:** Selected by Athletics in third round of 2004 draft; signed July 19, 2004. **Signed by:** Rick Magnante.

Windsor had an incredible two-year run at Cal State Fullerton, going 26-4, 1.82 and finishing his career as the Most Outstanding Player at the 2004 College World Series, where he capped a 5-0, 0.61 postseason with a complete-game victory in the title-clincher against Texas. Because they thought he had been worked hard in college, the A's used him sparingly out of the bullpen after signing him as a third-round pick for $270,000. He continued to shine, pitching seven hitless innings with 13 strikeouts during the Midwest League playoffs. Windsor is a classic overachiever, pitching beyond his ordinary stuff with excellent command and a strong competitive drive. His fastball regularly sits at 86-89 mph, though he hit 92 out of the bullpen when he didn't have to worry about conserving his energy. His circle change is his best pitch, featuring plenty of deception and a late break that makes hitters look foolish at times. He also throws a curveball and a slider, with his curve having more potential. He seems to pitch better in clutch situations. Though he lacks projection, the A's think Windsor could move as fast as anyone other than Huston Street from their 2004 draft class. He most likely will begin the year in high Class A but could get bumped to Double-A with a strong spring.

Year	Club (League)	Class	W	L	ERA	G	GS	CG	SV	IP	H	R	ER	HR	BB	SO	AVG
2004	Vancouver (NWL)	A	0	0	0.00	4	0	0	1	5	4	0	0	0	0	5	.222
	Kane County (Mid)	A	1	0	2.77	9	0	0	3	13	11	4	4	0	5	13	.216
MINOR LEAGUE TOTALS			1	0	2.00	13	0	0	4	18	15	4	4	0	5	18	.217

18 Brad Knox, rhp

Born: May 27, 1982. **Ht.:** 6-3. **Wt.:** 210. **Bats:** R. **Throws:** R. **School:** Central Arizona JC. **Career Transactions:** Selected by Athletics in 14th round of 2002 draft; signed June 6, 2002. **Signed by:** John Kuehl.

The A's signed Knox out of Central Arizona Junior College—the same place they found Rich Harden—where he was an integral part of a 2002 National Junior College World Series championship club. Oakland has brought Knox along slowly, but in his first taste of full-season ball last year he led the Midwest League in strikeouts, tied for top honors in victories and finished second to teammate Steven Bondurant in ERA. At 22 he was old for low Class A, but his stuff took a major step forward in 2004. He uses an average 89-91 mph fastball to set up his plus pitch, a knee-buckling curveball that he can break into the strike zone. His changeup is usable but needs improvement. Knox succeeds primarily on excellent command and the ability to change speeds, and there's some doubt as to whether that will be enough at higher levels. The A's still aren't sure what they have in him, but they like what they see so far. He'll be challenged in 2005 with a likely assignment to Double-A.

Year	Club (League)	Class	W	L	ERA	G	GS	CG	SV	IP	H	R	ER	HR	BB	SO	AVG
2002	Athletics (AZL)	R	2	3	4.17	10	7	0	0	41	44	28	19	2	9	42	.268
2003	Vancouver (NWL)	A	6	3	2.06	15	12	0	0	70	55	21	16	2	18	63	.208
2004	Kane County (Mid)	A	14	5	2.59	26	25	0	0	156	141	53	45	11	24	174	.235
MINOR LEAGUE TOTALS			22	11	2.69	51	44	0	0	267	240	102	80	15	51	279	.234

19 Tyler Johnson, lhp

Born: June 7, 1981. **Ht.:** 6-2. **Wt.:** 180. **Bats:** B. **Throws:** L. **School:** Moorpark (Calif.) JC. **Career Transactions:** Selected by Cardinals in 34th round of 2000 draft; signed May 15, 2001 . . . Selected by Athletics from Cardinals in major league Rule 5 draft, Dec. 13, 2004. **Signed by:** Chuck Fick (Cardinals).

The Cardinals are thin on lefthanders, especially after including Chris Narveson in the Larry Walker trade, yet they gambled by not protecting Johnson on their 40-man roster this offseason. The A's pounced on him in the major league Rule 5 draft because they think he has a good chance to stick on their big league club—if he doesn't, they'll have to put him on waivers and offer him back to St. Louis for half his $50,000 draft price—and he immediately becomes the top lefty reliever in a system bereft of southpaws. Johnson led Cardinals minor leaguers with 15 wins in 2002, his first full season, before moving to the bullpen in 2003. His 4.79 ERA last year was deceiving, because he struggled with shoulder soreness early before posting a 2.04 ERA over the final three months following a short stint on the disabled list. Johnson thrives with a sharp-breaking curve, which grades as a plus-plus pitch. He sets the curve up with his 88-91 mph fastball, and rarely uses his mediocre changeup as a reliever. He needs to do a better job with his conditioning. Unless he bombs this spring, Johnson should break camp with Oakland.

Year	Club (League)	Class	W	L	ERA	G	GS	CG	SV	IP	H	R	ER	HR	BB	SO	AVG
2001	Johnson City (Appy)	R	1	1	2.66	9	9	0	0	41	26	17	12	1	21	58	.181
	Peoria (Mid)	A	0	1	3.95	3	3	0	0	14	14	9	6	1	10	15	.255
2002	Peoria (Mid)	A	15	3	2.00	22	18	0	0	121	96	35	27	7	42	132	.218
2003	Palm Beach (FSL)	A	5	5	3.08	22	10	0	0	79	79	29	27	2	38	81	.262
	Tennessee (SL)	AA	1	0	1.65	20	0	0	0	27	16	7	5	1	15	39	.168
2004	Tennessee (SL)	AA	2	2	4.79	53	0	0	4	56	48	32	30	4	37	77	.230
MINOR LEAGUE TOTALS			24	12	2.85	129	40	0	4	338	279	129	107	16	163	402	.224

20 Alexi Ogando, of

Born: Oct. 5, 1983. **Ht.:** 6-4. **Wt.:** 160. **Bats:** R. **Throws:** R. **Career Transactions:** Signed out of Dominican Republic by Athletics, March 26, 2002. **Signed by:** Raymond Abreu/Juan Martinez.

Ogando represents another toolsy, high-upside player from the A's renewed focus in Latin America, which they see as another source of low-cost talent. While his numbers declined as he repeated the Arizona League, club officials were excited about the progress he made in his all-around game. More than one refers to him as "the kind of player you can dream about." With a skinny 6-foot-5 frame, he physically resembles a young Vladimir Guerrero. While Oakland wants him to fill out his frame, Ogando already displays plus power to all fields and can unleash tape-measure shots when he gets his arms extended. He runs well and his arm is the strongest in the system, rating close to an 80 on the 20-80 scouting scale. Ogando's approach at the plate is still raw, leading to too many swings and misses, though he was making progress in instructional league. He shortened his stride to quicken his bat, and also improved at recognizing breaking balls. With Javier Herrera and Ogando, Kane County should have one of the most exciting outfields in the Midwest League this year.

Year	Club (League)	Class	AVG	G	AB	R	H	2B	3B	HR	RBI	BB	SO	SB	OBP	SLG
2002	Athletics (DSL)	R	.189	54	164	17	31	5	0	3	17	16	59	2	.270	.274
2003	Athletics (AZL)	R	.342	48	190	33	65	13	1	7	36	7	42	5	.379	.532
2004	Vancouver (NWL)	A	.150	7	20	3	3	0	0	1	6	4	9	1	.320	.300
	Athletics (AZL)	R	.267	47	180	26	48	13	1	6	24	14	57	3	.340	.450
MINOR LEAGUE TOTALS			.265	156	554	79	147	31	2	17	83	41	167	11	.331	.421

21 John Rheinecker, lhp

Born: May 29, 1979. **Ht.:** 6-2. **Wt.:** 215. **Bats:** L. **Throws:** L. **School:** Southwest Missouri State University. **Career Transactions:** Selected by Athletics in first round (37th overall) of 2001 draft; signed June 30, 2001. **Signed by:** Jim Pransky.

Rheinecker's prospect status has dimmed considerably since he ranked No. 2 on this list entering 2003. He has yet to find consistent success at the higher levels, as hitters have lit him up for a .298 average and 36 homers over the last two seasons. His control also regressed in 2004. Rheinecker has good stuff for a lefty, with an 87-90 mph fastball, a plus slider and a decent changeup. He added a cutter last year and showed good progress with it as the season wore on. He can be maddening to watch, as Rheinecker will look ready for the big leagues one inning and deserving of a demotion the next. The A's don't see converting him into a reliever because of his lack of a dominating lefty-on-lefty pitch, as well as the organizational shortage of southpaws. Rheinecker will return to Triple-A to begin the season.

Year	Club (League)	Class	W	L	ERA	G	GS	CG	SV	IP	H	R	ER	HR	BB	SO	AVG
2001	Vancouver (NWL)	A	0	1	1.59	6	5	0	0	23	13	5	4	0	4	17	.161
	Modesto (Cal)	A	0	1	6.30	2	2	0	0	10	10	7	7	1	5	5	.256
2002	Visalia (Cal)	A	3	0	2.31	9	9	0	0	51	41	16	13	2	10	62	.216
	Midland (TL)	AA	7	7	3.38	20	20	1	0	128	137	63	48	7	24	100	.274
2003	Midland (TL)	AA	9	6	4.74	23	23	1	0	142	186	90	75	13	32	89	.313
	Sacramento (PCL)	AAA	2	0	3.79	6	6	0	0	38	47	19	16	1	12	26	.303
2004	Sacramento (PCL)	AAA	11	9	4.44	28	27	0	0	172	194	102	85	22	51	129	.283
MINOR LEAGUE TOTALS			32	24	3.96	94	92	2	0	564	628	302	248	46	138	428	.280

22 Keiichi Yabu, rhp

Born: Sept. 28, 1968. **Ht.:** 6-0. **Wt.:** 200. **Bats:** R. **Throws:** R. **Career Transactions:** Signed out of Japan by Athletics, Jan. 12, 2005. **Signed by:** Erik Kubota.

Looking for some veteran pitching depth at the major league level after trading Tim Hudson and Mark Mulder, the A's dipped into the Asian market to sign Yabu in January. General manager Billy Beane first took note of Yabu when he pitched well against the Yankees in exhibition games before the 2004 season. An 11-year veteran of Japan's Hanshin Tigers, Yabu was the 1994 Central League rookie of the year. He signed a one-year contract with a $750,000 salary for 2005, plus either a $250,000 buyout or $1.5 million for 2006. A classic Japanese pitcher who has no single eye-popping pitch, Yabu throws strikes with a rich variety of offerings. His fastball sits at 88-90 mph, and he can dial it up to 92 on occasion. He also uses a cutter, splitter, slider and changeup. Oakland anticipates Yabu will have little difficulty adjusting to the U.S. majors and, at 36, won't require any minor league seasoning. He'll compete with youngsters Joe Blanton, Dan Haren and Dan Meyer for the open rotation spots behind Rich Harden and Barry Zito. The A's think Yabu also could succeed in a swing role if necessary.

Year	Club (League)	Class	W	L	ERA	G	GS	CG	SV	IP	H	R	ER	HR	BB	SO	AVG
1994	Hanshin (CL)	JAP	9	9	3.18	26	17	8	0	181	174	67	64	12	42	110	—
1995	Hanshin (CL)	JAP	7	13	2.98	27	20	7	0	196	185	73	65	19	50	118	—
1996	Hanshin (CL)	JAP	11	14	4.01	30	24	6	0	195	204	97	87	14	51	145	—
1997	Hanshin (CL)	JAP	10	12	3.59	29	22	4	0	184	172	79	73	23	62	111	—
1998	Hanshin (CL)	JAP	11	10	3.51	24	21	3	0	165	159	74	64	11	51	90	—
1999	Hanshin (CL)	JAP	6	16	3.95	28	23	4	0	173	175	80	76	16	57	95	—
2000	Hanshin (CL)	JAP	6	10	4.17	25	23	1	0	152	162	76	70	19	30	95	—
2001	Hanshin (CL)	JAP	0	4	4.09	17	8	0	0	56	55	32	25	2	33	26	—
2002	Hanshin (CL)	JAP	10	6	3.14	20	15	5	0	132	118	48	46	14	30	97	—
2003	Hanshin (CL)	JAP	8	3	3.96	23	15	0	0	98	97	50	43	13	27	67	.264
2004	Hanshin (CL)	JAP	6	9	3.02	19	18	1	0	116	108	44	39	8	36	75	.252

23 Kevin Melillo, 2b

Born: May 14, 1982. **Ht.:** 6-0. **Wt.:** 190. **Bats:** L. **Throws:** R. **School:** University of South Carolina. **Career Transactions:** Selected by Athletics in fifth round of 2004 draft; signed July 15, 2004. **Signed by:** Michael Holmes.

Melillo played with Brewers top prospect Rickie Weeks at Lake Brantley High (Altamonte Springs, Fla.) before playing in three College World Series in four years at South Carolina. The A's had their eye on Melillo for years while also scouting Gamecocks catcher Landon Powell, and they took Melillo four rounds after Powell last June, signing him for $200,000 in the fifth round. Melillo projects as an offensive second baseman. Hitting comes easy to him, as he owns a short, line-drive stroke, developing power and a solid understanding of the strike zone. He lacks defensive instincts but has soft hands. He never has put any priority on his glovework, but the A's feel he can become adequate at second base if he puts the time in. Melillo's makeup is strong. He worked in instructional league shadowing Mark Ellis to learn what it takes to be a second baseman at the major league level, while also working on specific exercises to improve his speed. The A's feel he can skip a level and begin the year in high Class A.

Year	Club (League)	Class	AVG	G	AB	R	H	2B	3B	HR	RBI	BB	SO	SB	OBP	SLG
2004	Vancouver (NWL)	A	.340	22	94	22	32	11	2	2	21	11	16	2	.422	.564
MINOR LEAGUE TOTALS			.340	22	94	22	32	11	2	2	21	11	16	2	.422	.564

24 Brad Sullivan, rhp

Born: Sep. 12, 1981. **Ht.:** 6-0. **Wt.:** 195. **Bats:** R. **Throws:** R. **School:** University of Houston. **Career Transactions:** Selected by Athletics in first round (25th overall) of 2003 draft; signed July 21, 2003. **Signed by:** Steve Bowden.

Sullivan was the system's biggest disappointment in 2004, delivering just nine quality starts in 27 tries and getting battered around for a .303 average. He has yet to show the stuff he had as a Houston sophomore, when he projected as a possible top pick in the 2003 draft. He tailed off as a junior, allowing the A's to get him with the 25th overall pick. After throwing 91-93 mph in college, Sullivan has dipped to the high 80s and rarely has touched 90 as a pro. His slider, which is his best pitch, also decreased from the mid-80s to the high 70s. His mechanics fell apart in high Class A, as he consistently flew open with his front side. That gave batters a long look at his pitches, and led not only to the drop in velocity but also a disturbing loss of movement on all of his pitches. He also throws a curveball and change-up. Sullivan showed a strong work ethic throughout his troubles, but the lack of results frustrated him and led to a loss in confidence. He had trouble with breathing and with sinus headaches during 2004, attributed to a serious car accident he was in at age 10. Offseason surgery to remove a plate from his head and rebuild the bridge of his nose should correct those problems. Sullivan is ticketed to return to the high Class A California League this year.

Year	Club (League)	Class	W	L	ERA	G	GS	CG	SV	IP	H	R	ER	HR	BB	SO	AVG
2003	Kane County (Mid)	A	1	0	3.18	6	0	0	0	11	9	4	4	1	7	9	.225
2004	Modesto (Cal)	A	8	11	4.65	27	27	0	0	147	180	89	76	13	48	99	.303
MINOR LEAGUE TOTALS			9	11	4.55	33	27	0	0	158	189	93	80	14	55	108	.298

25 Freddie Bynum, util

Born: Feb. 15, 1980. **Ht.:** 6-1. **Wt.:** 180. **Bats:** L. **Throws:** R. **School:** Pitt (N.C.) CC. **Career Transactions:** Selected by Athletics in second round of 2000 draft; signed June 19, 2000. **Signed by:** Billy Owens.

The A's surprising top pick (second round) in 2000, Bynum has become a bit of a test-tube player. Drafted as a shortstop, he played every position but catcher and first base in 2004 as Oakland attempts to groom him as a supersub in the mold of Anaheim's Chone Figgins. Bynum is one of the top athletes in the system, with his plus-plus speed giving him above-average range at any position. He lacks power but has a solid line-drive stroke and the ability to leg out infield hits. His instincts and routes in the outfield were pleasant surprises. While Bynum has held his own offensively, he has yet to take the step forward to prove he can be productive against major league pitching on an everyday basis. He needs to focus more on playing the little man's game, improving his bunting and on-base skills. He still can be sloppy in the infield, relying solely on his athleticism to make plays. Bynum will return to Triple-A in 2004, but his ability to eventually free up extra roster spots provides value to the budget-minded A's.

Year	Club (League)	Class	AVG	G	AB	R	H	2B	3B	HR	RBI	BB	SO	SB	OBP	SLG
2000	Vancouver (NWL)	A	.256	72	281	52	72	10	1	1	26	31	58	22	.341	.310
2001	Modesto (Cal)	A	.261	120	440	59	115	19	7	2	46	41	95	28	.325	.350

2002	Visalia (Cal)	A	.306	135	539	83	165	26	5	3	56	64	116	41	.385	.390
2003	Midland (TL)	AA	.263	132	510	84	134	18	9	5	58	56	135	22	.344	.363
2004	Midland (TL)	AA	.268	65	265	38	71	13	4	1	22	24	56	18	.332	.358
	Sacramento (PCL)	AAA	.287	66	258	42	74	11	3	2	26	19	61	21	.343	.376
MINOR LEAGUE TOTALS			.275	590	2293	358	631	97	29	14	234	235	521	152	.348	.361

26 Jason Perry, of

Born: Aug. 18, 1980. **Ht.:** 6-0. **Wt.:** 200. **Bats:** L. **Throws:** R. **School:** Georgia Tech. **Career Transactions:** Selected by Blue Jays in sixth round of 2002 draft; signed June 22, 2002 . . . Traded by Blue Jays to Athletics, June 23, 2003, completing trade in which Athletics sent OF John-Ford Griffin to Blue Jays for a player to be named. **Signed by:** Charles Aliano (Blue Jays).

In the first draft where they adopted a "Moneyball" approach, the Blue Jays made Perry their sixth-round pick in 2002. A proven wood-bat performer who led the Cape Cod League with eight homers in 2002, he joined the A's in a mid-2003 trade for former Yankees first-round pick John-Ford Griffin. Perry opened his first full season in the Oakland system in Double-A, but was dogged by back problems that affected him at the plate and eventually landed him on the disabled list. Once he returned, there was no room for him on the Midland roster, so he was demoted to high Class A. He dominated at that level, leading the California League in on-base percentage, slugging percentage and extra-base hits (64) despite playing in just 83 games. Perry has a track record of hitting for average and finally began to show the plus power that long had been projected for him. At 23 he was old for the Cal League, and he'll have his share of naysayers until he performs at the upper levels. He struggles versus good lefties and still struck out more than once per game even while he was mashing in 2004. He's not very athletic, limiting him to left field or first base, where he's just adequate. Perry held his own in the Arizona Fall League and will begin 2005 with a return engagement in Double-A.

Year	Club (League)	Class	AVG	G	AB	R	H	2B	3B	HR	RBI	BB	SO	SB	OBP	SLG
2002	Medicine Hat (Pio)	R	.425	30	106	25	45	6	2	10	36	12	19	0	.508	.802
	Dunedin (FSL)	A	.289	13	45	7	13	3	0	1	5	5	11	0	.389	.422
2003	Dunedin (FSL)	A	.304	39	135	17	41	11	1	1	17	10	32	1	.356	.422
	Modesto (Cal)	A	.305	50	190	28	58	9	1	4	26	21	46	0	.393	.426
2004	Midland (TL)	AA	.198	28	81	11	16	5	1	1	11	4	23	3	.275	.321
	Modesto (Cal)	A	.338	83	325	81	110	39	1	24	80	34	87	4	.431	.686
MINOR LEAGUE TOTALS			.321	243	882	169	283	73	6	41	175	86	218	8	.405	.557

27 Gregorio Petit, ss

Born: Dec. 10, 1984. **Ht.:** 5-10. **Wt.:** 186. **Bats:** R. **Throws:** R. **Career Transactions:** Signed out of Venezuela by Athletics, July 17, 2001. **Signed by:** Julio Franco.

Petit is another in a long line of Venezuelan shortstops known more for their glovework than their bat. He has Gold Glove potential with good range and instincts, soft hands and a strong, accurate arm. Unlike many young shortstops, he also takes pride in making the routine play and isn't susceptible to errors. As advanced as Petit is in the field, he still has a long ways to go offensively. He carried a .292 average a month into the Northwest League season last year, but hit just .234 the rest of the way. He has a decent understanding of the strike zone, but he can lose his concentration from at-bat to at-bat and is prone to strike-outs. He's a gap-to-gap hitter who probably won't ever hit for much power. With average speed, he's not much of a basestealing threat either. After putting on weight during the summer, he'll need to watch his conditioning. The A's think Petit has the potential to be a special defensive player with just enough bat to make it. He'll get his first taste of full-season ball in 2005 in low Class A.

Year	Club (League)	Class	AVG	G	AB	R	H	2B	3B	HR	RBI	BB	SO	SB	OBP	SLG
2002	Athletics (DSL)	R	.280	63	218	44	61	11	5	1	21	39	44	5	.392	.390
2003	Athletics (AZL)	R	.265	32	117	13	31	6	0	0	12	10	22	3	.323	.316
2004	Vancouver (NWL)	A	.256	68	254	34	65	9	2	4	35	20	67	3	.315	.354
MINOR LEAGUE TOTALS			.267	163	589	91	157	26	7	5	68	69	133	11	.347	.360

28 Brant Colamarino, 1b

Born: Dec. 4, 1980. **Ht.:** 5-11. **Wt.:** 205. **Bats:** L. **Throws:** L. **School:** University of Pittsburgh. **Career Transactions:** Selected by Athletics in seventh round of 2002 draft; signed June 15, 2002. **Signed by:** Tom Clark.

Colamarino went to Pittsburgh's Central Catholic High and then played collegiately at Pitt, the same route that NFL Hall of Fame quarterback Dan Marino took. Colamarino tied a Panthers record with 19 homers in 2002, when the A's made him a seventh-round pick. In the bestseller "Moneyball," then-Oakland assistant general manager Paul DePodesta said,

"No one else in baseball will agree, but Colamarino might be the best hitter in the country." No one would come close to agreeing two years later, though he did get his bat going in high Class A last season. After hitting .259 in each of his first two seasons, he reported to spring training in the best shape of his life, dropping 20 pounds. He was among the California League leaders in all three triple-crown categories—though old for high Class A at age 23—before a promotion to Double-A. Colamarino has a quick, short swing that generates good contact and power. While solid across the board offensively, he lacks one plus tool to profile as an everyday player. Colamarino is a surprising good athlete and the best defensive first baseman in the system. He's also ambidextrous, and is known to take fielding practice at third base and throw with his right arm. He's a below-average runner but not a clogger, and he has good instincts on the basepaths. He's headed back to Double-A.

Year	Club (League)	Class	AVG	G	AB	R	H	2B	3B	HR	RBI	BB	SO	SB	OBP	SLG
2002	Vancouver (NWL)	A	.259	67	228	30	59	6	2	6	41	27	54	3	.348	.382
2003	Kane County (Mid)	A	.259	133	498	68	129	26	0	19	80	59	101	1	.350	.426
2004	Modesto (Cal)	A	.355	50	183	41	65	8	2	11	41	28	23	1	.450	.601
2004	Midland (TL)	AA	.272	78	309	40	84	22	2	8	50	27	60	0	.331	.434
MINOR LEAGUE TOTALS			.277	328	1218	179	337	62	6	44	212	141	238	5	.361	.446

29 Mike Rouse, ss/2b

Born: April 25, 1980. **Ht.:** 5-11. **Wt.:** 190. **Bats:** L. **Throws:** R. **School:** Cal State Fullerton. **Career Transactions:** Selected by Blue Jays in fifth round of 2001 draft; signed July 2, 2001 . . . Traded by Blue Jays with RHP Chris Mowday to Athletics for RHP Cory Lidle, Nov. 16, 2002. **Signed by:** Demerius Pittman (Blue Jays).

Not only did Rouse watch Bobby Crosby cement himself as Oakland's shortstop in 2004, but he also was unable to fill-in for an injured Crosby in late April. Rouse missed the entire first month after spraining his right ankle during fielding drills in big league camp. Once he returned, he put up his usual solid numbers. Rouse understands his role offensively, hitting for a decent average, getting on base and showing occasional pop and OK speed. He's susceptible to breaking balls and after having no previous trouble with lefties, batted just .209 against them last year. Rouse doesn't cover a lot of ground at shortstop and his arm is average at best, but he's fundamentally sound and makes all the plays he gets to. He looked good in a handful of games at second base in 2004. Rouse got down about being blocked by Crosby, and scouts saw a lack of effort at time. He projects as no more than a utilityman with Oakland at this point and might be best served by a change in scenery. He'll return to Triple-A to begin 2005.

Year	Club (League)	Class	AVG	G	AB	R	H	2B	3B	HR	RBI	BB	SO	SB	OBP	SLG
2001	Dunedin (FSL)	A	.272	48	180	27	49	17	2	5	24	13	45	3	.327	.472
2002	Tennessee (SL)	AA	.260	71	231	35	60	11	0	9	43	29	47	7	.342	.424
2003	Midland (TL)	AA	.300	129	457	75	137	33	3	3	53	63	83	7	.392	.405
	Sacramento (PCL)	AAA	.429	2	7	2	3	0	0	0	1	0	0	0	.429	.429
2004	Sacramento (PCL)	AAA	.276	99	323	53	89	11	2	10	40	50	68	0	.379	.415
MINOR LEAGUE TOTALS			.282	349	1198	192	338	72	7	27	161	155	243	17	.370	.422

30 Ryan Webb, rhp

Born: Feb. 5, 1986. **Ht.:** 6-6. **Wt.:** 190. **Bats:** R. **Throws:** R. **School:** Clearwater Central Catholic HS, Palm Harbor, Fla. **Career Transactions:** Selected by Athletics in fourth round of 2004 draft; signed June 15, 2004. **Signed by:** Steve Barningham.

The son of former major league pitcher Hank Webb, Ryan became a story when Oakland took him in the fourth round last June. He became just the second high schooler the A's have taken in the first five rounds this decade, joining 2001 first-rounder Jeremy Bonderman. In another departure from most Oakland draft picks, Webb is all about projection. His fastball is in the 86-88 mph range but could increase considerably as he adds bulk to his long, skinny frame. For a teenager who is all arms and legs, he has a consistent release point and an uncanny knack for throwing strikes, as evidenced by just one walk in his pro debut. He shows a good feel for a changeup but still is trying to find a breaking ball he can trust. His slider is flat and slurvy. Webb isn't especially athletic, so he struggles to hold runners and field his position. The A's have no real roadmap for projectable teenage pitchers, so they'll take it slow with him. His performance in spring training will determine whether he begins the year at Kane County or Vancouver.

Year	Club (League)	Class	W	L	ERA	G	GS	CG	SV	IP	H	R	ER	HR	BB	SO	AVG
2004	Athletics (AZL)	R	1	1	4.87	8	7	0	0	20	18	11	11	2	1	23	.227
MINOR LEAGUE TOTALS			1	1	4.87	8	7	0	0	20	18	11	11	2	1	23	.227

PHILADELPHIA
PHILLIES

BY **WILL KIMMEY**

The Phillies finished 86-76 in 2004, posting consecutive winning seasons for the first time since 1982-83, as they opened Citizens Bank Ballpark. That would be seen as a positive year for many franchises, but because of the club's expectations, it was deemed a failure.

Philadelphia had raised its Opening Day payroll from $57 million in 2002 to $93 million in 2004, and pundits figured the reinforcements would enable the hillies to overcome the Braves in the National League East. Bad call. Two days before Atlanta won its 13th straight division title, the Phillies fired manager Larry Bowa after four tumultuous years. It was the only move they could make. They have given out too many long-term, big-money contracts to meaningfully shake up their nucleus.

General manager Ed Wade rightly predicted the new park would play like a bandbox and that the pitching staff might be thin. Since the end of the 2003 season, he dealt nine pitchers ranked on Baseball America's Phillies top 30 prospects list to add Billy Wagner, Eric Milton, Cory Lidle, Felix Rodriguez and Todd Jones. He also signed free agents Kevin Millwood, Tim Worrell and Roberto Hernandez. All those deals, plus the loss since 2000 of five draft picks in the top three rounds as free-agent compensation, have rendered the farm system thin at the upper levels.

That doesn't mean, however, that Philadelphia's player-development system has been unproductive. It has produced four of the club's eight starting position players, including second baseman **Chase Utley**.

To increase the flow of talent into the organization, the Phillies renewed their efforts in Latin America after letting them lapse for years. They're one of the few teams with academies in both the Dominican Republic and Venezuela. Instructors travel back and forth from the academies to the club's Clearwater, Fla., training complex to develop a rapport with the players. That creates an early support system that helps them adjust to American culture as well as baseball once they come to the United States.

"This is all part of a master plan that's paying dividends," Latin American operations director Sal Artiaga said, crediting international scouting surpervisor Sal Agostinelli's aggressive approach for securing nine of the members of the organization's top 30 list. Agostinelli and the Phillies have continued to expand the breadth of the scouting operation, pushing into Nicaragua and creating a strong focus in Australia.

The Phillies' international efforts haven't been as costly or as flashy as those of other clubs, but team officials say they've been just as successful. It's part of their plan of continuing to improve the club through a productive farm system. But if they're to dethrone the Braves in 2005, they'll probably have to look outside the organization for help.

TOP 30 PROSPECTS

1. Ryan Howard, 1b
2. Gavin Floyd, rhp
3. Cole Hamels, lhp
4. Greg Golson, of
5. Michael Bourn, of
6. Scott Mathieson, rhp
7. Jake Blalock, of
8. Carlos Carrasco, rhp
9. Edgar Garcia, rhp
10. Scott Mitchinson, rhp
11. Carlos Ruiz, c
12. Chris Roberson, of
13. Jason Jaramillo, c
14. Zach Segovia, rhp
15. Keith Bucktrot, rhp
16. J.A. Happ, lhp
17. Andy Baldwin, rhp
18. Eude Brito, lhp
19. Shane Victorino, of
20. Juan Richardson, 3b
21. Sean Gamble, of
22. Welinson Baez, 3b
23. Kiel Fisher, 3b
24. Carlos Rodriguez, ss
25. Robinson Tejeda, rhp
26. Maximino de la Cruz, rhp
27. Louis Marson, c
28. Terry Jones, 3b
29. Kyle Kendrick, rhp
30. Curt Miaso, of

ORGANIZATION OVERVIEW

General manager: Ed Wade. **Farm director:** Steve Noworyta. **Scouting director:** Marti Wolever.

2004 PERFORMANCE

Class	Team	League	W	L	Pct.	Finish*	Manager(s)
Majors	Philadelphia	National	86	76	.531	8th (16)	L. Bowa/G. Varsho
Triple-A	Scranton/W-B Red Barons	International	69	73	.486	8th (14)	Marc Bombard
Double-A	Reading Phillies	Eastern	64	77	.454	9th (12)	Greg Legg
High A	Clearwater Threshers	Florida State	55	82	.401	11th (12)	Mike Schmidt
Low A	Lakewood Blue Claws	South Atlantic	70	66	.515	6th (16)	P.J. Forbes
Short-season	Batavia Muckdogs	New York-Penn	28	46	.378	14th (14)	Luis Melendez
Rookie	GCL Phillies	Gulf Coast	36	24	.600	t-2nd (12)	Roly deArmas
OVERALL 2004 MINOR LEAGUE RECORD			322	368	.467	24th (30)	

*Finish in overall standings (No. of teams in league).

ORGANIZATION LEADERS

BATTING
*Minimum 250 At-Bats
*AVG	Lou Collier, Scranton	.326
R	Ryan Howard, Scranton/Reading	94
H	John Castellano, Scranton/Reading/Clearwater	152
TB	Ryan Howard, Scranton/Reading	309
2B	Jake Blalock, Lakewood	40
3B	Mark Budzinski, Scranton	15
HR	Ryan Howard, Scranton/Reading	46
RBI	Ryan Howard, Scranton/Reading	131
BB	Michael Bourn, Lakewood	85
SO	Ryan Howard, Scranton/Reading	166
SB	Michael Bourn, Lakewood	58
*OBP	Michael Bourn, Lakewood	.431
*SLG	Ryan Howard, Scranton/Reading	.637

PITCHING
#Minimum 75 Innings
W	Dan Giese, Scranton	12
	C.J. Woodrow, Clearwater/Lakewood	12
L	Kyle Kendrick, Lakewood/Batavia	16
#ERA	Cory Schultz, Clearwater/Lakewood	2.24
G	Spike Lundberg, Scranton/Reading	56
CG	Alfredo Simon, Clearwater	4
SV	Jim Crowell, Scranton	16
IP	Erick Arteaga, Lakewood	159
BB	Nick Bourgeois, Clearwater	68
SO	Robinson Tejeda, Reading	133

BEST TOOLS

Best Hitter for Average	Michael Bourn
Best Power Hitter	Ryan Howard
Best Strike-Zone Discipline	Michael Bourn
Fastest Baserunner	Michael Bourn
Best Athlete	Greg Golson
Best Fastball	Eude Brito
Best Curveball	Gavin Floyd
Best Slider	Zach Segovia
Best Changeup	Cole Hamels
Best Control	Cole Hamels
Best Defensive Catcher	Jason Jaramillo
Best Defensive Infielder	Brad Harman
Best Infield Arm	Welinson Baez
Best Defensive Outfielder	Michael Bourn
Best Outfield Arm	Greg Golson

PROJECTED 2008 LINEUP

Catcher	Carlos Ruiz
First Base	Ryan Howard
Second Base	Placido Polanco
Third Base	Chase Utley
Shortstop	Jimmy Rollins
Left Field	Pat Burrell
Center Field	Michael Bourn

Right Field	Bob Abreu
No. 1 Starter	Vicente Padilla
No. 2 Starter	Gavin Floyd
No. 3 Starter	Randy Wolf
No. 4 Starter	Brett Myers
No. 5 Starter	Cole Hamels
Closer	Scott Mathieson

LAST YEAR'S TOP 20 PROSPECTS

1. Cole Hamels, lhp
2. Gavin Floyd, rhp
3. Ryan Howard, 1b
4. Ryan Madson, rhp
5. Keith Bucktrot, rhp
6. Alfredo Simon, rhp
7. Michael Bourn, of
8. Elizardo Ramirez, rhp
9. Juan Richardson, 3b
10. Terry Jones, 3b
11. Anderson Machado, ss
12. Kiel Fisher, 3b
13. Kyle Kendrick, rhp
14. Scott Mathieson, rhp
15. Javon Moran, of
16. Francisco Butto, rhp
17. Chris Roberson, of
18. Josh Hancock, rhp
19. Danny Gonzalez, ss
20. Jake Blalock, of

TOP PROSPECTS OF THE DECADE

Year	Player, Pos.	Current Team
1995	Scott Rolen, 3b	Cardinals
1996	Scott Rolen, 3b	Cardinals
1997	Scott Rolen, 3b	Cardinals
1998	Ryan Brannan, rhp	Out of baseball
1999	Pat Burrell, 1b	Phillies
2000	Pat Burrell, 1b/of	Phillies
2001	Jimmy Rollins, ss	Phillies
2002	Marlon Byrd, of	Phillies
2003	Gavin Floyd, rhp	Phillies
2004	Cole Hamels, lhp	Phillies

TOP DRAFT PICKS OF THE DECADE

Year	Player, Pos.	Current Team
1995	Reggie Taylor, of	White Sox
1996	Adam Eaton, rhp	Padres
1997	*J.D. Drew, of	Dodgers
1998	Pat Burrell, 1b	Phillies
1999	Brett Myers, rhp	Phillies
2000	Chase Utley, 2b	Phillies
2001	Gavin Floyd, rhp	Phillies
2002	Cole Hamels, lhp	Phillies
2003	Tim Moss, 2b (3)	Phillies
2004	Greg Golson, of	Phillies

*Did not sign.

ALL-TIME LARGEST BONUSES

Gavin Floyd, 2001	$4,200,000
Pat Burrell, 1998	$3,150,000
Brett Myers, 1999	$2,050,000
Cole Hamels, 2002	$2,000,000
Chase Utley, 2000	$1,780,000

MINOR LEAGUE DEPTH CHART

Philadelphia PHILLIES

Impact Potential: B

No one in pro baseball in 2004 hit more than Ryan Howard's 48 homers (46 in the minors, two in Philadelphia), turning him from solid prospect to potential all-star, but he's blocked in Philadelphia by perennial all-star Jim Thome. Gavin Floyd seems ready for prime time, and Cole Hamels has ace potential if he stays healthy and matures. Speedy outfielders Michael Bourn and Greg Golson could end the Phillies'

center field drought soon.

Depth: D

The Phillies' refrain remains the same: three to five prospects who look like sure big leaguers (or have very high ceilings), spackled together by raw athletes, hard-throwing pitchers yet to throw above Class A and organizational players. Several trades (Billy Wagner, Cory Lidle) that gave up prospects for big league help also taxed the system's depth. The 2004 draft addressed a key need, bringing in a pair of intriguing catchers.

*Depth charts prepared by **John Manuel** and **Allan Simpson**. Numbers in parentheses indicate prospect rankings.*

LF
Jake Blalock (7)
Sean Gamble (21)
Richard Plumsky

CF
Greg Golson (4)
Michael Bourn (5)
Chris Roberson (12)
Shane Victorino (19)

RF
Curt Miaso (30)
Jorge Padilla
Chris Klemm

3B
Juan Richardson (20)
Welinson Baez (22)
Kiel Fisher (23)
Terry Jones (28)

SS
Carlos Rodriguez (24)
John Hardy
Brad Harman
Danny Gonzalez

2B
Tim Moss
Mitch Graham

1B
Ryan Howard (1)
Buck Shaw
Ryan Barthelemy

SOURCE of TALENT

HOMEGROWN		ACQUIRED	
College	6	Trades	0
Junior College	1	Rule 5 draft	1
Draft-and-follow	0	Independent leagues	0
High School	12	Free agents/waivers	0
Nondrafted free agent	0		
Foreign	10		

C
Carlos Ruiz (11)
Jason Jaramillo (13)
Louis Marson (27)
Charles Cresswell
Tim Gradoville

RHP

Starters	Relievers
Gavin Floyd (2)	Pedro Liriano
Scott Mathieson (6)	Francisco Butto
Carlos Carrasco (8)	Lee Gwaltney
Edgar Garcia (9)	Martire Franco
Scott Mitchinson (10)	Andrew Barb
Zach Segovia (14)	Yoel Hernandez
Keith Bucktrot (15)	Clemente Doble
Andy Baldwin (17)	
Robinson Tejeda (25)	
Maximino De la Cruz (26)	
Kyle Kendrick (29)	
Nate Cabrera	
Franklin Perez	
Kelvin Pichardo	
Lenin Gazo	
Joe Bisenius	
Erick Arteaga	

LHP

Starters	Relievers
Cole Hamels (3)	Eude Brito (18)
J.A. Happ (16)	Daniel Hodges
	Kevin Shepard
	Zac Cline

DRAFT ANALYSIS

2004

Best Pro Debut: 1B Buck Shaw (21) tied for the Rookie-level Gulf Coast League home run title with eight. Scouts thought OF Greg Golson (1) would have to make adjustments, but the Phillies left him alone and he batted .295 with 12 steals in the GCL.

Best Athlete: Golson is the best athlete in the system. His speed is his most obvious tool, but he doesn't have a weakness. He has the bat speed, hand-eye coordination and strength to hit for power and average, the range for center field and the arm for right.

Best Pure Hitter: OF Sean Gamble (6) hit better with wood at short-season Batavia (.304) and in the Cape Cod League (.319) than he did with aluminum in three years at Auburn (.290). His short stroke is conducive to contact but doesn't generate power.

Best Raw Power: OF Curt Miaso (42) doesn't show it in games yet, but his home run potential has been compared to that of fellow Chaparral High (Scottsdale, Ariz.) product Paul Konerko. 1B Carl Galloway (11) holds the career home run record at Biola (Calif.) with 45, two more than SS/3B Sam Orr (8), who holds the season mark with 24. Shaw also deserves mention.

Fastest Runner: The quickest player in the draft, Golson gets to first from the right side in 3.83 seconds.

Best Defensive Player: Not only does Golson have tremendous speed, but he also makes good reads and takes direct routes in center . C Jason Jaramillo (2), who addressed the organization's thin catching, is solid behind the plate.

Best Fastball: RHP Andy Baldwin (5) pitches at 91-92 mph and can touch 94. RHP Joe Bisenius (12) can get his fastball to 93.

RICH ABEL

Happ

Best Breaking Ball: Baldwin's slider is better than LHP J.A. Happ's (3) curveball.

Most Intriguing Background: The Phillies drafted 1B Matt Johnson (50) as a tribute to his perseverance. After getting cancer and having his left leg amputated below the knee as a sophomore, he made it back to play football and baseball at his Omaha high school. Baldwin's uncle John Hiller, Gamble's father Oscar, unsigned RHP Alex McAnaney's (34) dad Will and SS Andrew Romine's (36) dad Kevin all played in the majors. SS John Hardy's (7) cousin J.J. is a shortstop prospect in the Brewers system.

Closest To The Majors: Jaramillo's all-around skills give him the edge over Happ's deceptive arsenal.

Best Late-Round Pick: Miaso plummeted in the draft because of his commitment to Arizona State. Besides his bat, his right-field play and makeup are also assets.

The One Who Got Away: LHP James Adkins (13, now at Tennessee), Romine (Arizona State), 3B Steve Marquardt (37, Washington State) and RHP Aaron Brown (46, Houston) all would have been much higher picks had they been signable. Marquardt already transferred to junior college, but the Phillies still lost his rights.

Assessment: With their system short on athletes and catchers, the Phillies took Golson and Jaramillo. Happ and Baldwin give Philadelphia a pair of interesting lefties.

2003 The Phillies didn't sign their best choice, projected 2006 first-rounder and RHP Blair Erickson (28), and only OF Michael Bourn (4) offers much promise. They gave up their first two picks for free agents and spent their top choice on 2B Tim Moss (3). *GRADE:* D

2002 If LHP Cole Hamels (1) can stay healthy and out of fights, he's a potential ace. RHP Scott Mathieson (17) and OF Jake Blalock (5), Hank's little brother, are two of Philadelphia's better prospects. *GRADE:* B

2001 1B Ryan Howard (3) led the minor leagues with 46 home runs in 2004. He and RHP Gavin Floyd (2) are the best the Phillies system has to offer right now. *GRADE:* B+

2000 Believe it or not, 2B Chase Utley is the second-best player from 2000's first round, taking a back seat to only Tampa Bay's Rocco Baldelli. RHP Taylor Buchholz (6) slumped in 2004, but he was the key player in the deal with the Astros that brought Billy Wagner to the Phillies. *GRADE:* C+

Draft analysis prepared by Jim Callis. Numbers in parentheses indicate draft rounds.

Ryan
HOWARD

Born: Nov. 19, 1979.
Ht.: 6-4. **Wt.:** 230.
Bats: L. **Throws:** L.
School: Southwest Missouri State University.
Career Transactions: Selected by Phillies in fifth round of 2001 draft; signed July 2, 2001.
Signed by: Jerry Lafferty.

Howard enjoyed a standout sophomore season at Southwest Missouri State and looked poised to be a 2001 first-round pick. But he slumped with a wood bat while with Team USA, and the struggles continued into his junior year. On the verge of setting several school records, he wound up breaking only the record for strikeouts in a season with 74. Teams backed off until the Phillies took a chance on him in the fifth round. They were rewarded when he regained his power stroke. Howard fell seven RBIs shy of winning the high Class A Florida State League triple crown in 2003, then crushed 46 homers to lead the minors last season. He went on a couple of homer binges, launching 10 in a nine-game span at Double-A Reading and eight over 11 days in Triple-A Scranton/Wilkes-Barre. He was leading the minors with 131 RBIs when he left to make his big league debut and finished second in that category, as well as fourth in total bases (309) and fifth in slugging (.637). Howard continued to make an impression in the majors, drilling homers off Bartolome Fortunato and T.J. Tucker, and then led the Arizona Fall League with 14 doubles.

Howard's prodigious power rivals that of any prospect. He can hit home runs from foul pole to foul pole, and when he gets his pitch—especially one low and inside—he rarely misses it. Howard used to be vulnerable to inside fastballs, but he made that adjustment and can jerk those pitches over the wall now as well. He also made strides in laying off bad breaking balls on the outer half. He's willing to take walks when pitchers refuse to challenge him. Howard plays better defense than most give him credit for. He's surprisingly nimble for such a big man and possesses average hands and average range.

Howard strikes out a lot, including 179 times in 524 at-bats in 2004. He has tried unsuccessfully to put more balls in play, but the Phillies won't mind lofty strikeout totals as long as he brings that lefthanded power to the plate. There's still concern about how he'll handle quality fastballs in on his hands. Jim Thome's presence prompted the organization to send big league coach Milt Thompson to the AFL to work with Howard on a possible position change. Howard showed just enough range and a solid arm to be able to play left field occasionally, but he's not going to be able to move there full-time. He doesn't run well, but he has decent instincts and isn't a baseclogger. For all his success, Howard is 25 and always has been a bit old for the leagues he has played in.

Realistically, Philadelphia knows it must trade Howard because Thome is signed through 2008. Even if he could handle left field regularly, Pat Burrell would block him. The Phillies won't give away one of the game's best power prospects, so if they can't find a good trade he'll have to settle for a major league reserve job or a return to Triple-A in 2005.

Year	Club (League)	Class	AVG	G	AB	R	H	2B	3B	HR	RBI	BB	SO	SB	OBP	SLG
2001	Batavia (NYP)	A	.272	48	169	26	46	7	3	6	35	30	55	0	.384	.456
2002	Lakewood (SAL)	A	.280	135	493	56	138	20	6	19	87	66	145	5	.367	.460
2003	Clearwater (FSL)	A	.304	130	490	67	149	32	1	23	82	50	151	0	.374	.514
2004	Reading (EL)	AA	.297	102	374	73	111	18	1	37	102	46	129	1	.386	.647
	Scranton/WB (IL)	AAA	.270	29	111	21	30	10	0	9	29	14	37	0	.362	.604
	Philadelphia (NL)	MAJ	.282	19	39	5	11	5	0	2	5	2	13	0	.333	.564
MAJOR LEAGUE TOTALS			.282	19	39	5	11	5	0	2	5	2	13	0	.333	.564
MINOR LEAGUE TOTALS			.290	444	1637	243	474	87	11	94	335	206	517	6	.375	.528

2 Gavin Floyd, rhp

Born: Jan. 27, 1983. **Ht.:** 6-5. **Wt.:** 210. **Bats:** R. **Throws:** R. **School:** Mount St. Joseph HS, Baltimore. **Career Transactions:** Selected by Phillies in first round (fourth overall) of 2001 draft; signed Aug. 24, 2001. **Signed by:** Ken Hultzapple.

Floyd was the first of three Mount St. Joseph High products selected in the 2001 draft, going fourth overall, one pick before Mark Teixeira and 21 rounds before his brother Mike. Gavin and Mike Floyd both signed days before they were to attend classes at South Carolina, with Gavin getting a club-record $4.2 million signing bonus. Though he was out of gas in September, he pitched well in his major league debut. Floyd's 12-to-6 hammer curveball rates as one of the best in the minors and proved effective against major leaguers. His fastball sits at 89-90 mph, topping out at 94. His changeup has improved to a consistent solid-average pitch that's a plus offering at times. Floyd's velocity tailed off and his delivery was less consistent at the end of 2004. He must improve his stamina and lower-half strength. Floyd also needs to command his fastball better. Floyd could make the 2005 rotation, but will return to Triple-A if he's not ready. He projects as a No. 2 or 3 starter.

Year	Club (League)	Class	W	L	ERA	G	GS	CG	SV	IP	H	R	ER	HR	BB	SO	AVG
2002	Lakewood (SAL)	A	11	10	2.77	27	27	3	0	166	119	59	51	13	64	140	.200
2003	Clearwater (FSL)	A	7	8	3.00	24	20	1	0	138	128	61	46	9	45	115	.247
2004	Scranton/WB (IL)	AAA	1	3	4.99	5	5	0	0	31	39	20	17	4	9	18	.312
	Philadelphia (NL)	MAJ	2	0	3.49	6	4	0	0	28	25	11	11	1	16	24	.312
	Reading (EL)	AA	6	6	2.57	20	20	2	0	119	93	39	34	5	46	94	.212
MAJOR LEAGUE TOTALS			2	0	3.49	6	4	0	0	28	25	11	11	1	16	24	.312
MINOR LEAGUE TOTALS			25	27	2.94	76	72	6	0	454	379	179	148	31	164	367	.226

3 Cole Hamels, lhp

Born: Dec. 27, 1983. **Ht.:** 6-3. **Wt.:** 170. **Bats:** L. **Throws:** L. **School:** Rancho Bernardo HS, San Diego. **Career Transactions:** Selected by Phillies in first round (17th overall) of 2002 draft; signed Aug. 28, 2002. **Signed by:** Darrell Conner.

The organization's top prospect after posting a 1.34 ERA in his 2003 pro debut, Hamels looked just as good in big league camp last spring. But he tried to throw too hard too early, pulling his left triceps muscle. He never felt right and made just four appearances all year. Hamels will throw his plus-plus changeup in any count, sinking and fading it away from righthanders. He pitches at 88-91 mph and can reach 93-94. His poise and feel for pitching are advanced. Hamels' curveball shows the makings of a third plus pitch, but he needs to locate it more consistently. Though the Phillies have no long-term concerns about his health, he has a checkered medical history. He broke the humerus bone in his left arm in high school, scaring some teams off in the 2002 draft. He also pulled a muscle behind his right shoulder in 2003, costing him a spot on the U.S. Olympic qualifying team. He got back on the mound in instructional league, where his arm and stuff were fine, but then broke his left hand in Clearwater, Fla., in January, in what the Phillies described only as an altercation. He could miss as much as three months, and when he returns he'll go to Double-A.

Year	Club (League)	Class	W	L	ERA	G	GS	CG	SV	IP	H	R	ER	HR	BB	SO	AVG
2003	Lakewood (SAL)	A	6	1	0.84	13	13	1	0	75	32	8	7	0	25	115	.136
	Clearwater (FSL)	A	0	2	2.73	5	5	0	0	26	29	9	8	0	14	32	.299
2004	Clearwater (FSL)	A	1	0	1.13	4	4	0	0	16	10	2	2	0	4	24	.182
MINOR LEAGUE TOTALS			7	3	1.31	22	22	1	0	117	71	19	17	0	43	171	.183

4 Greg Golson, of

Born: Sept. 17, 1985. **Ht.:** 6-0. **Wt.:** 190. **Bats:** R. **Throws:** R. **School:** John Connally HS, Austin. **Career Transactions:** Selected by Phillies in first round (21st overall) of 2004 draft; signed June 20, 2003. **Signed by:** Steve Cohen.

The best athlete in the 2004 draft, Golson turned down the University of Texas to sign for $1.475 million as the 21st overall pick. There were some questions about his swing, but he made adjustments and finished eighth in the Rookie-level Gulf Coast League batting race. Golson displays excellent baseball instincts along with blazing speed that gets him from home to first base in 3.8 seconds. Those feet, along with an above-average arm that would play in right field, make him a top-flight center fielder capable of stealing doubles from hitters and bases off pitchers. He also has the strength to become a 20-homer threat. Golson's older brother Justin is a Naval Academy graduate, and he shows similar makeup and work ethic. Though he fared well in the GCL, Golson needs to see more professional-quality breaking balls to get better at hitting them. He struck out too frequently in his debut, which cut down on his chances to use his speed. With the similar Michael Bourn two steps ahead of him, the Phillies have no need to rush Golson. If he has a good spring he'll open the season at low Class A Lakewood.

Year	Club (League)	Class	AVG	G	AB	R	H	2B	3B	HR	RBI	BB	SO	SB	OBP	SLG
2004	Phillies (GCL)	R	.295	47	183	34	54	8	5	1	22	10	54	12	.345	.410
MINOR LEAGUE TOTALS			295	47	183	34	54	8	5	1	22	10	54	12	.345	.410

5 Michael Bourn, of

Born: Dec. 27, 1982. **Ht.:** 5-11. **Wt.:** 180. **Bats:** L. **Throws:** R. **School:** University of Houston. **Career Transactions:** Selected by Phillies in fourth round of 2003 draft; signed July 24, 2003. **Signed by:** Dave Owen.

The Astros chose Bourn in the 19th round out of high school, but he opted to attend Houston, where he stole 90 bases in three years. He picked up two hits, two walks and three steals in his first game of 2004 and never looked back. He tied for third in the minors in triples while leading the South Atlantic League in walks, on-base percentage and steals. Bourn knows his role as a leadoff hitter. He works counts, hits the ball on the ground and then makes use of his excellent speed. He beat Greg Golson by a step in a 60-yard dash in instructional league. He's also an above-average defender with good instincts. His arm is average. Hitting instructor Donnie Long reminds Bourn not to always beat the ball into the ground because he has enough strength to drive low, inside pitches for extra-base hits. Bourn's a solid bunter but the Phillies want him to get better. Bourn's first two pro seasons impressed the Phillies enough that they now consider him their long-term center fielder. He'll move to high Class A Clearwater and could reach Double-A by the end of 2005.

Year	Club (League)	Class	AVG	G	AB	R	H	2B	3B	HR	RBI	BB	SO	SB	OBP	SLG
2003	Batavia (NY-P)	A	.280	35	125	12	35	0	1	0	4	23	28	23	.404	.296
2004	Lakewood (SAL)	A	.315	109	413	92	130	20	14	5	53	85	88	58	.431	.467
MINOR LEAGUE TOTALS			.307	144	538	104	165	20	15	5	57	108	116	81	.424	.428

6 Scott Mathieson, rhp

Born: Feb. 27, 1984. **Ht.:** 6-3. **Wt.:** 190. **Bats:** R. **Throws:** R. **School:** Aldergrove (B.C.) SS. **Career Transactions:** Selected by Phillies in 17th round of 2002 draft; signed July 3, 2002. **Signed by:** Tim Kissner.

Mathieson played with fellow British Columbia natives Adam Loewen and Jeff Francis on Canadian national teams, and he went 16 rounds after them in the 2002 draft. His grandfather Doug tried out for the Athletics during the Connie Mack era and played first base for the Air Force at Pearl Harbor. After going 2-9, 5.09 in his first two seasons, Mathieson made considerable progress in 2004. Mathieson threw 84 mph as a high school senior, but the Phillies gambled on his projectability because he had a lanky frame, loose arm and smooth mechanics. It's paying off as he hit 96 mph last season while consistently pitching in the low 90s with average life. His changeup has improved to an average pitch. Mathieson is finally done growing into his body, so now is the time for him to fine-tune his command across the board. His curveball breaks straight down but not consistently enough. It's still a below-average pitch. If Mathieson masters his curve, he could emerge as a No. 2 or 3 starter. Otherwise, he shows the makings of a power reliever. He's ready for high Class A Clearwater.

Year	Club (League)	Class	W	L	ERA	G	GS	CG	SV	IP	H	R	ER	HR	BB	SO	AVG
2002	Phillies (GCL)	R	0	2	5.40	7	2	0	0	17	24	11	10	0	6	14	.338
2003	Phillies (GCL)	R	2	7	5.52	11	11	0	0	59	59	42	36	5	13	51	.247
	Batavia (NY-P)	A	0	0	0.00	2	0	0	1	6	0	0	0	0	0	7	.000
2004	Lakewood (SAL)	A	8	9	4.32	25	25	1	0	131	130	73	63	7	50	112	.254
MINOR LEAGUE TOTALS			10	18	4.61	45	38	1	1	213	213	126	109	12	69	184	.254

Jake Blalock, of

RODGER WOOD

Born: Aug. 6, 1983. **Ht.:** 6-4. **Wt.:** 210. **Bats:** R. **Throws:** R. **School:** Rancho Bernardo HS, San Diego. **Career Transactions:** Selected by Phillies in fifth round of 2002 draft; signed July 25, 2002. **Signed by:** Darrell Conner.

Blalock played with Cole Hamels at San Diego's Rancho Bernardo High. He's more associated with his all-star brother Hank, but Jake couldn't be more different as he possesses more raw power but not the same ability to hit for average. A high school shortstop, Blalock moved to third base and then the outfield as a pro. Blalock worked hard on his defense, playing an average left field and showing solid arm strength in 2004. Relaxing on defense helped him do the same at the plate, where he boosted his average by making more contact. He also learned to keep his front side closed longer against breaking balls, allowing him to show plus power to the opposite field. He led the South Atlantic League in doubles. Blalock is still a streaky hitter. He didn't homer until May and ran hot and cold all season long. Though he cut down on his strikeouts, he still whiffed 126 times and may be exploited by more advanced pitchers. The Phillies will continue to show patience with Blalock. He'll go to Clearwater, where the spacious Florida State League parks should test his power output and hitting skill.

Year	Club (League)	Class	AVG	G	AB	R	H	2B	3B	HR	RBI	BB	SO	SB	OBP	SLG
2002	Phillies (GCL)	R	.250	25	88	13	22	6	0	1	13	10	15	3	.317	.352
2003	Batavia (NY-P)	A	.245	72	261	36	64	23	7	5	31	30	81	9	.323	.444
2004	Lakewood (SAL)	A	.271	131	517	81	140	40	2	16	90	61	126	4	.350	.449
MINOR LEAGUE TOTALS			.261	228	866	130	226	69	9	22	134	101	222	16	.338	.438

Carlos Carrasco, rhp

Born: March 21, 1987. **Ht.:** 6-3. **Wt.:** 178. **Bats:** R. **Throws:** R. **Career Transactions:** Signed out of Venezuela by Phillies, Nov. 25, 2003. **Signed by:** Sal Agostinelli.

Carrasco signed for $300,000 out of a Venezuelan tryout camp and did nothing but improve during his first year with the organization. He added 20 pounds and really turned a corner from extended spring training through instructional league. Carrasco works at 92-93 mph now and should add velocity over the next few years. He throws his fastball on a downhill plane with average life. He showed consistent improvement with his curveball, which should develop into a plus power pitch. His smooth delivery and good changeup are reminiscent of a much older pitcher. He's an excellent athlete, which enables him to repeat his delivery. Carrasco needs to relax on the mound. Early in the season when things didn't go well, he tended to get amped up rather than thinking about what adjustments he needed to make to throw quality strikes. His breaking ball needs more consistency and depth. Carrasco should be ready for a full-season league, but an organizational logjam of starting pitchers probably will keep him at short-season Batavia. Considering his age, there's no rush.

Year	Club (League)	Class	W	L	ERA	G	GS	CG	SV	IP	H	R	ER	HR	BB	SO	AVG
2004	Phillies (GCL)	R	5	4	3.56	11	8	0	0	48	53	23	19	2	15	34	.276
MINOR LEAGUE TOTALS			5	4	3.56	11	8	0	0	48	53	23	19	2	15	34	.276

Edgar Garcia, rhp

RICK BATTLE

Born: Nov. 22, 1987. **Ht.:** 6-2. **Wt.:** 190. **Bats:** R. **Throws:** R. **Career Transactions:** Signed out of Dominican Republic by Phillies, Oct. 26, 2004. **Signed by:** Sal Agostinelli/Wil Tejada.

Sal Agostinelli and Wil Tejada doggedly tracked Garcia's progress for a year before he headed to the Perfect Game/Baseball America World Wood Bat Championship last fall. Garcia made a quick pit stop to pitch at the Phillies' training complex in nearby Clearwater, and the staff regarded him as the equivalent of a second- or third-round pick. They signed him for $500,000. In his Clearwater workout, Garcia showed off a plus fastball that reached 94 mph and flashed a power 12-to-6 curveball at 80 mph. His delivery and arm action are clean, especially for a 17-year-old pitcher with limited experience. His big, strong frame should lend itself to durability and more velocity down the road. The Phillies also like his tenacity on the mound. Garcia's changeup still has a ways to go before it's considered average. His biggest need now is more experience to learn how to make in-game adjustments. His arm slot is a little high, but that should be easily correctable. Garcia will make his pro debut in the Gulf Coast League in 2005. He should emerge as a No. 2 or 3 starter.

Year	Club (League)	Class	W	L	ERA	G	GS	CG	SV	IP	H	R	ER	HR	BB	SO	AVG
2004	Did not play—Signed 2005 contract																

10 Scott Mitchinson, rhp

Born: Dec. 28, 1984. **Ht.:** 6-3. **Wt.:** 185. **Bats:** R. **Throws:** R. **Career Transactions:** Signed out of Australia by Phillies, Feb. 10, 2003. **Signed by:** Kevin Hooker.

The Phillies signed Mitchinson on the first of what has become an annual scouting trip to Australia for youth tournaments. He was one of four Aussies to debut in the U.S. in 2004, with four more coming in '05. Mitchinson received a $10,000 bonus and spent a year at Major League Baseball's academy in Australia before tying for the Gulf Coast League lead in wins in his U.S. debut. Mitchinson's fastball has improved from 85 mph to the low 90s in two years and there's room for more velocity. But his heater takes a backseat to his command, and he posted a jaw-dropping 60-1 strikeout-walk ratio in the GCL. He throws his curveball and changeup for strikes. Mitchinson succeeds more because of his feel for pitching than raw stuff. That was enough to dominate young hitters, but he'll need to improve the quality of his pitches to succeed as he rises up the ladder. He appears ready for the challenge of low Class A. But as with Carlos Carrasco, a backlog of starters could lead to Mitchinson spending 2005 at short-season Batavia.

Year	Club (League)	Class	W	L	ERA	G	GS	CG	SV	IP	H	R	ER	HR	BB	SO	AVG
2004	Phillies (GCL)	R	7	0	1.75	10	10	0	0	62	40	12	12	2	1	60	.181
MINOR LEAGUE TOTALS			7	0	1.75	10	10	0	0	62	40	12	12	2	1	60	.181

11 Carlos Ruiz, c

Born: Jan. 22, 1979. **Ht.:** 5-10. **Wt.:** 180. **Bats:** R. **Throws:** R. **Career Transactions:** Signed out of Panama by Phillies, Dec. 4, 1998. **Signed by:** Allan Lewis.

Sal Agostinelli watched a young Ruiz playing second base in Panama, noticing both his lack of agility and impressive arm strength. Agostinelli put Ruiz behind the plate, liked what he saw and signed him for $8,000. The Phillies profiled Ruiz as a backup catcher with solid defense and a little pop in his bat, but he had struggled to get in an entire season between platoon duties and minor injuries. He opened 2004 in a platoon, but an injury to Russ Jacobson opened the door to a more regular role that his bat and improved maturity meant he wouldn't relinquish. Ruiz set career highs in nine offensive categories, none more eye-opening than his home run total. His raw power emerged as everyday at-bats allowed him to make adjustments and cut down his swing. He capped his year by hitting .297/.409/.622 in the Arizona Fall League and getting added to the 40-man roster. Now, Ruiz projects as a .250 hitter capable of delivering 20 home runs in a season. Defensively, Ruiz shows an above-average arm, quick feet and a strong lower half. He ranked sixth in the Double-A Eastern League by throwing out 29 percent of basestealers. At Triple-A in 2005, Ruiz will be just a step away from backing up Mike Lieberthal, or possibly replacing him in 2006 if the Phillies buy out his $7.5 million option for $1.25 million.

Year	Club (League)	Class	AVG	G	AB	R	H	2B	3B	HR	RBI	BB	SO	SB	OBP	SLG
1999	Phillies (DSL)	R	.305	60	226	39	69	15	5	4	35	9	11	3	.351	.469
2000	Phillies (GCL)	R	.277	38	130	11	36	7	1	1	22	9	9	3	.329	.369
2001	Lakewood (SAL)	A	.261	73	249	21	65	14	3	4	32	10	27	5	.290	.390
2002	Clearwater (FSL)	A	.213	92	342	35	73	18	3	5	32	18	30	3	.264	.327
2003	Clearwater (FSL)	A	.315	15	54	5	17	0	0	2	9	2	5	2	.339	.426
	Reading (EL)	AA	.266	52	169	22	45	6	0	2	16	12	15	1	.321	.337
2004	Reading (EL)	AA	.284	101	349	45	99	15	2	17	50	22	37	8	.338	.484
MINOR LEAGUE TOTALS			.266	431	1519	178	404	75	14	35	196	82	134	25	.313	.403

12 Chris Roberson, of

Born: Aug. 23, 1979. **Ht.:** 6-2. **Wt.:** 180. **Bats:** R. **Throws:** R. **School:** Feather River (Calif.) JC. **Career Transactions:** Selected by Phillies in ninth round of 2001 draft; signed June 7, 2001. **Signed by:** Scott Ramsey.

Roberson's athleticism has never been a question. It comes from his father Rick, who played seven seasons in the NBA. He finally turned those skills into production in 2004, a year after the Phillies lauded his potential following a low Class A campaign in which he hit just .234 with a .309 slugging percentage and 108 strikeouts in 132 games. Roberson made as much improvement as any Phillies prospect by cutting down on his swing and making adjustments to better handle breaking balls. He not only trimmed his strikeouts but also ramped up his power while moving into the less forgiving ballparks of the Florida State League, where he was voted an all-star. Once Roberson got going, the confidence boost helped him carry the success through the season—which ended in mid-July following a stress fracture in his right leg. He's more physical than the organization's other center fielders (Greg Golson and Michael Bourn), but doesn't possess their baseball instincts or do things as easily. Still, Roberson's above-average speed and arm strength make him a strong outfielder, but he trimmed his basestealing attempts. He's slated for Double-A this year.

Year	Club (League)	Class	AVG	G	AB	R	H	2B	3B	HR	RBI	BB	SO	SB	OBP	SLG
2001	Phillies (GCL)	R	.248	38	133	17	33	8	1	0	13	16	30	6	.336	.323
2002	Batavia (NY-P)	A	.276	62	214	29	59	8	3	2	24	26	51	17	.377	.369
2003	Lakewood (SAL)	A	.234	132	470	64	110	19	5	2	32	57	108	59	.331	.309
2004	Clearwater (FSL)	A	.307	83	313	52	96	13	6	9	38	27	71	16	.371	.473
MINOR LEAGUE TOTALS			.264	315	1130	162	298	48	15	13	107	126	260	98	.351	.367

13 Jason Jaramillo, c

Born: Oct. 9, 1982. **Ht.:** 6-0. **Wt.:** 200. **Bats:** B. **Throws:** R. **School:** Oklahoma State University. **Career Transactions:** Selected by Phillies in second round of 2004 draft; signed July 21, 2004. **Signed by:** Paul Scott.

Jaramillo's older brothers both played in the minors, with Frankie playing shortstop for the Rangers and Lee a catcher for the Brewers. The Phillies drafted Jaramillo in the 39th round out of high school in Franksville, Wis., in 2001 but he instead went to college, as each of his brothers had. His college career included a championship summer with Orleans of the Cape Cod League, where he teamed with fellow 2004 Phillies pick Anthony Buffone (22nd round). Jaramillo's catch-and-throw skills combined with above-average arm strength allow him to rate as the best defensive catcher in the organization, though he managed to gun down just two of 15 basestealers at Batavia. He moves well behind the plate to block balls and does a good job calling games since gaining practice with that type of autonomy as a junior at Oklahoma State. Pitchers like throwing to him. Jaramillo won't be a power hitter; he's more likely to make solid contact and shoot doubles alley to alley. The natural righthanded hitter began to switch-hit in high school and now swings the bat just as well from either side. He profiles as a solid major league catcher who bats in the lower portion of the order. He'll begin 2005 working with a talented staff in low Class A.

Year	Club (League)	Class	AVG	G	AB	R	H	2B	3B	HR	RBI	BB	SO	SB	OBP	SLG
2004	Phillies (GCL)	R	.667	1	3	1	2	0	0	0	1	0	0	0	.667	.667
	Batavia (NY-P)	A	.232	31	112	11	26	5	0	1	14	12	27	0	.307	.304
MINOR LEAGUE TOTALS			.243	32	115	12	28	5	0	1	15	12	27	0	.323	.313

14 Zach Segovia, rhp

Born: April 11, 1983. **Ht.:** 6-2. **Wt.:** 220. **Bats:** R. **Throws:** R. **School:** Forney (Texas) HS. **Career Transactions:** Selected by Phillies in second round of 2002 draft; signed July 2, 2002. **Signed by:** Paul Scott.

Segovia debuted at No. 10 on this list in 2002, but struggled in 2003 when he tried to pitch with a tender arm by not telling the organization. He ended up having Tommy John surgery that fall, missed all of 2004 before returning for four instructional league outings 11 months after the operation. The Phillies wonder if a 150-pitch outing during the Texas high school playoffs contributed to the arm trouble, but credit Segovia's work ethic and his speedy return from surgery. His arm worked—and he said felt—fine in instructs, and his velocity was just under the 92-93 mph he showed prior to surgery. Segovia's fastball also features heavy sinking action, while his hard, biting slider rates as the organization's best. A full year of experience should help his changeup progress to average as he gains a better feel for it. Segovia will start his comeback at high Class A, and could ultimately develop into a No. 2-3 starter, though his mindset and fastball-slider combination could also yield a closer.

Year	Club (League)	Class	W	L	ERA	G	GS	CG	SV	IP	H	R	ER	HR	BB	SO	AVG
2002	Phillies (GCL)	R	3	2	2.10	8	8	0	0	34	21	11	8	0	3	30	.174
2003	Lakewood (SAL)	A	1	5	3.99	11	10	0	0	50	63	25	22	2	14	27	.307
	Phillies (GCL)	R	0	1	4.00	5	4	0	0	9	8	5	4	0	0	6	.235
2004	Did not play—Injured																
MINOR LEAGUE TOTALS			4	8	3.29	24	22	0	0	93	92	41	34	2	17	63	.256

15 Keith Bucktrot, rhp

Born: Nov. 27, 1980. **Ht.:** 6-2. **Wt.:** 180. **Bats:** L. **Throws:** R. **School:** Claremore (Okla.) HS. **Career Transactions:** Selected by Phillies in third round of 2000 draft; signed June 26, 2000. **Signed by:** Paul Scott.

Bucktrot's raw stuff has always tantalized the Phillies. He can fire his fastball up to 95 mph, and it regularly reaches 90-93 with sinking action. After switching from a curveball, his slider bites so hard it also can be considered a plus pitch. His changeup is also solid. But command and poor mechanics have always spoiled the package—so much so that some teams liked him better as a hitter out of high school. Bucktrot has worked to hone his command, trimming his walk totals the past two seasons, but it has come at the expense of his ability to strike out hitters. He missed last June with tendinitis, then followed it with an ordinary summer. Then, in a move that surprised the same official, Bucktrot seemed to translate his pro experience into a newfound maturity in the Arizona Fall League, showing better command while finally seeming to take what his coaches taught him and putting it to work. He issued 11 walks in 31 AFL innings, but with 31 hits allowed and 22 strikeouts. He'll move to Triple-A, with the Phillies hoping that being just a step from the majors will give him a sense of urgency to maintain his work ethic and continue improving.

Year	Club (League)	Class	W	L	ERA	G	GS	CG	SV	IP	H	R	ER	HR	BB	SO	AVG
2000	Phillies (GCL)	R	3	2	4.78	11	7	0	0	38	39	21	20	5	19	40	.267
2001	Lakewood (SAL)	A	6	11	5.28	24	24	3	0	135	139	93	79	16	58	97	.269
2002	Clearwater (FSL)	A	8	9	4.88	27	24	2	0	160	167	101	87	10	78	84	.276
2003	Clearwater (FSL)	A	7	7	3.33	19	17	0	0	111	104	50	41	8	29	68	.250
	Reading (EL)	AA	3	1	2.56	7	7	0	0	46	34	17	13	3	15	30	.217
2004	Reading (EL)	AA	4	7	4.87	20	20	0	0	105	140	65	57	16	39	60	.321
MINOR LEAGUE TOTALS			31	37	4.50	108	99	5	0	594	623	347	297	58	238	379	.274

16 J.A. Happ, lhp

Born: Oct. 19, 1982. **Ht.:** 6-5. **Wt.:** 202. **Bats:** L. **Throws:** L. **School:** Northwestern University. **Career Transactions:** Selected by Phillies in third round of 2004 draft; signed June 11, 2004. **Signed by:** Bob Szymkowski.

Happ is a good athlete—he's the all-time leading scorer for his high school basketball program—who became the first Northwestern baseball player to be named first-team all-Big 10 Conference three times. He shows a great feel for pitching and a deceptive delivery. Hitters rarely get a good look at his offerings, and righthanders often swing late on his upper-80s fastball, which can touch 90. Happ can locate that pitch and his slider to either side of the plate, and features an average changeup. Those attributes helped Happ register better than a strikeout per inning during his college career, a trend that carried over to his pro debut. His polish should allow him to quickly reach his eventual future as a back-of-the-rotation starter, beginning this year in low Class A.

Year	Club (League)	Class	W	L	ERA	G	GS	CG	SV	IP	H	R	ER	HR	BB	SO	AVG
2004	Batavia (NY-P)	A	1	2	2.02	11	11	0	0	36	22	8	8	1	18	37	.180
MINOR LEAGUE TOTALS			1	2	2.02	11	11	0	0	36	22	8	8	1	18	37	.180

17 Andy Baldwin, rhp

Born: Oct. 20, 1982. **Ht.:** 6-5. **Wt.:** 215. **Bats:** R. **Throws:** R. **School:** Oregon State University. **Career Transactions:** Selected by Phillies in fifth round of 2004 draft; signed June 11, 2004. **Signed by:** Tim Kissner.

Baldwin rates as an intriguing pick on several levels, the first being that the Phillies brought in solid fifth-rounders the previous three years in Javon Moran, Jake Blalock and Ryan Howard. Baldwin's uncle John Hiller was a Tigers reliever who missed 1971 after a heart attack, but returned to set a major league record with 38 saves in 1973. Baldwin went 5-5, 5.10 as a draft-eligible sophomore at Oregon State (where he also sat on a student-athlete advisory committee), and impressed Phillies scouts with a lively 91-94 mph fastball and plus slider in a February appearance before losing his confidence and command late in the season. The Phillies still liked his potential for two plus pitches, and they say his athleticism and inexperience work in his favor because his arm is fresh and there's room for projection. His changeup and breaking ball are inconsistent. Baldwin could emerge as a No. 3 or 4 starter at the major league level, but he'll need to miss more bats after leading the New York-Penn League in hits allowed. He'll begin this year in the low Class A rotation.

Year	Club (League)	Class	W	L	ERA	G	GS	CG	SV	IP	H	R	ER	HR	BB	SO	AVG
2004	Batavia (NY-P)	A	4	6	5.17	15	15	0	0	71	96	50	41	2	14	54	.323
MINOR LEAGUE TOTALS			4	6	5.17	15	15	0	0	71	96	50	41	2	14	54	.323

18 Eude Brito, lhp

Born: Aug. 19, 1978. **Ht.:** 5-11. **Wt.:** 160. **Bats:** L. **Throws:** L. **Career Transactions:** Signed out of Dominican Republic by Phillies, July 3, 1998. **Signed by:** Wil Tejada.

Brito's fastball jumped from the low 90s to consistently hitting 95 and 96 mph out of the bullpen in 2004. It allowed the organization to project a much brighter future for him. Brito made a few spot starts in 2004, but was much more effective out of the bullpen. He posted a 61-28 strikeout-walk ratio in 69 relief innings, working predominantly off his fastball and slurvy slider. Lefties hit .276 in 105 at-bats against Brito, but the Phillies don't necessarily see lefty specialist as his long-term role anyway. The sinking, tailing action on his fastball should give righthanders fits as well, and he can show a changeup when needed. Once he hones his command—no reliever should walk a batter every other inning—Brito could be used as a two- or three-inning arm out of the bullpen. He could work out of the Triple-A rotation to get more innings in 2005, but he could also have a shot at making the Phillies bullpen out of spring training if he shows improved command.

Year	Club (League)	Class	W	L	ERA	G	GS	CG	SV	IP	H	R	ER	HR	BB	SO	AVG
1999	Phillies (GCL)	R	0	1	5.02	12	3	0	0	29	39	22	16	0	19	23	.336
2000	Phillies (GCL)	R	3	5	2.54	9	7	0	0	50	38	20	14	1	19	42	.210
	Batavia (NY-P)	A	1	1	5.40	4	3	0	0	18	16	14	11	0	3	11	.225
2001	Lakewood (SAL)	A	4	3	2.73	44	0	0	6	69	53	28	21	7	14	58	.210
2002	Lakewood (SAL)	A	1	1	2.55	11	0	0	1	18	14	5	5	1	6	11	.226
	Clearwater (FSL)	A	3	3	5.71	20	0	0	0	35	40	22	22	5	14	27	.292
2003	Clearwater (FSL)	A	4	3	3.09	36	0	0	6	58	50	21	20	3	27	54	.231
2004	Reading (EL)	AA	8	6	4.42	43	7	1	4	98	95	56	48	10	41	84	.255
MINOR LEAGUE TOTALS			24	23	3.78	179	20	1	17	374	345	188	157	27	143	310	.245

19 Shane Victorino, of

Born: Nov. 30, 1980. **Ht.:** 5-9. **Wt.:** 160. **Bats:** B. **Throws:** R. **School:** St. Anthony HS, Wailuku, Hawaii. **Career Transactions:** Selected by Dodgers in sixth round of 1999 draft; signed June 8, 1999 . . . Selected by Padres from Dodgers in major league Rule 5 draft, Dec. 16, 2002; returned to Dodgers, May 28, 2003 . . . Selected by Phillies from Dodgers in major league Rule 5 draft, Dec. 13, 2004. **Signed by:** Hank Jones (Dodgers).

Victorino knows the major league Rule 5 draft well, with the Padres selecting him in the 2002 edition and the Phillies plucking him this offseason. He hit .151 in 73 at-bats for San Diego before being returned in 2003, but could stick in Philadelphia as a fifth outfielder and pinch-runner. If he doesn't, he'll have to clear waivers and then be offered back to Los Angeles for half the $50,000 draft price before he can be sent to the minors. Victorino signed out of high school as a second baseman but moved to center field, where his plus-plus speed and plus arm make him an above-average defender. His offensive game is built around making consistent contact and using his speed, but Victorino has shown a shift in his approach over the last year. He reached double-figures in home runs for the first time during 2004, then continued to show improved power in Venezuela over the winter. The extra pop also comes with a decline in plate discipline, however, with Victorino's strikeout-walk ratio changing for the worse. He continued to hit lefties (.366) noticeably better than righties (.258).

Year	Club (League)	Class	AVG	G	AB	R	H	2B	3B	HR	RBI	BB	SO	SB	OBP	SLG
1999	Great Falls (Pio)	R	.280	55	225	53	63	7	6	2	25	20	31	20	.335	.391
2000	Yakima (NWL)	A	.246	61	236	32	58	7	2	2	20	20	44	21	.310	.318
2001	Wilmington (SAL)	A	.283	112	435	71	123	21	9	4	32	36	61	47	.344	.400
	Vero Beach (FSL)	A	.167	2	6	2	1	0	0	0	0	3	1	0	.444	.167
2002	Jacksonville (SL)	AA	.258	122	481	61	124	15	1	4	34	47	49	45	.328	.318
2003	San Diego (NL)	MAJ	.151	36	73	8	11	2	0	0	4	7	17	7	.232	.178
	Jacksonville (SL)	AA	.282	66	266	37	75	9	4	2	15	21	41	16	.340	.368
	Las Vegas (PCL)	AAA	.390	11	41	6	16	1	2	1	9	1	5	0	.395	.585
2004	Las Vegas (PCL)	AAA	.235	55	200	28	47	9	1	3	20	11	37	7	.278	.335
	Jacksonville (SL)	AA	.327	75	294	70	96	13	7	16	43	20	65	9	.373	.582
MAJOR LEAGUE TOTALS			.151	36	73	8	11	2	0	0	4	7	17	7	.232	.178
MINOR LEAGUE TOTALS			.276	559	2184	360	603	82	32	34	198	179	334	165	.335	.390

20 Juan Richardson, 3b

Born: Jan. 27, 1979. **Ht.:** 6-1. **Wt.:** 175. **Bats:** R. **Throws:** R. **Career Transactions:** Signed out of Dominican Republic by Phillies, July 1, 1998. **Signed by:** Wil Tejada.

Richardson, who had two years added to his age after the visa crackdowns in 2002, was leading the Eastern League in home runs in 2003 when he slipped on the stairs at his home, spraining his ankle and ending his season. He tore the labrum in his throwing shoulder that offseason and didn't get on the field in 2004 until the end of June, when he was sent down to high Class A to regain his stroke as a DH. Richardson returned to form once he returned to Double-A in August. He started cranking home runs with his ferociously aggressive approach—one that also helps him pile up strikeouts. The Phillies hoped Richardson might correct that flaw, but now are willing to accept his high strikeout totals because of his 30-home run power potential. He spent the winter in the Dominican Republic trying to get his arm strength back. When healthy, it's average, just like his overall defensive play. Richardson will move to Triple-A in 2005 and could see Philadelphia before the end of the year.

Year	Club (League)	Class	AVG	G	AB	R	H	2B	3B	HR	RBI	BB	SO	SB	OBP	SLG
1999	Phillies (GCL)	R	.226	46	164	27	37	14	0	5	23	11	46	7	.290	.402
	Piedmont (SAL)	A	.167	4	12	0	2	1	0	0	2	1	5	0	.231	.250
	Batavia (NY-P)	A	.125	7	24	1	3	0	0	1	2	2	8	0	.222	.250
2000	Piedmont (SAL)	A	.242	43	149	19	36	11	0	2	15	17	43	0	.327	.356
	Batavia (NY-P)	A	.154	10	39	0	6	2	0	0	2	3	15	0	.214	.205
2001	Lakewood (SAL)	A	.240	137	505	68	121	31	2	22	83	51	147	7	.325	.440
2002	Clearwater (FSL)	A	.257	122	456	52	117	21	2	18	83	44	122	0	.339	.430
2003	Reading (EL)	AA	.270	65	248	37	67	9	0	15	34	17	69	2	.327	.488
2004	Clearwater (FSL)	A	.220	42	159	9	35	7	0	4	12	5	44	0	.248	.340
	Reading (EL)	AA	.282	18	71	10	20	1	0	5	13	1	16	0	.297	.507
MINOR LEAGUE TOTALS			.243	494	1827	223	444	97	4	72	269	152	515	16	.314	.419

21 Sean Gamble, of

Born: June 23, 1983. **Ht.:** 6-0. **Wt.:** 195. **Bats:** L. **Throws:** L. **School:** Auburn University. **Career Transactions:** Selected in sixth round of 2004 draft by Phillies; signed June 8, 2004. **Signed by:** Mike Stauffer.

The Phillies see a lot of 17-year major league veteran Oscar Gamble in his son Sean. The Blue Jays did as well in 2001, drafting him in the 11th round out of high school. He played in the same outfield with Phillies 2003 fifth-round pick Javon Moran at Auburn. Gamble's success with a wood bat in the Cape Cod League in 2003—his .319 average ranked sixth in the league—offset a college career when he hit .300 as a sophomore, but never better. Gamble was more successful with wood again after he signed, finishing eighth in the short-season New York-Penn League batting race in his pro debut. Phillies officials cite Gamble's feel for hitting—he trusts his hands and uses them well—as the reason. His power rates below-average, partly because his short stroke is designed more for making contact than for driving the ball, but there's hope because his father also developed power late. Despite above-average speed, Gamble will be relegated to left field because his arm also is below-average. He could play center in a pinch, and for that reason profiles best as a fourth out-fielder with doubles power. He'll likely begin 2005 in low Class A.

Year	Club (League)	Class	AVG	G	AB	R	H	2B	3B	HR	RBI	BB	SO	SB	OBP	SLG
2004	Batavia (NY-P)	A	.304	64	247	36	75	15	6	1	19	31	49	7	.383	.425
MINOR LEAGUE TOTALS			.304	64	247	36	75	15	6	1	19	31	49	7	.383	.425

22 Welinson Baez, 3b

Born: July 7, 1984. **Ht.:** 6-3. **Wt.:** 190. **Bats:** R. **Throws:** R. **Career Transactions:** Signed out of Dominican Republic by Phillies, Aug. 28, 2002. **Signed by:** Wil Tejada.

Baez is still working on translating the immense raw tools that earned him a $250,000 bonus into consistent performance in games. He is an impressive physical specimen with the size and strength to hit for plus power. His athleticism and soft hands should make him a superior defender. He can make backhanded plays at third base that some in the organization call amazing. His plus-plus arm strength moved some in the organization to think about putting Baez on the mound. He would benefit greatly from maturity, as a person and a player. Baez must learn to recognize breaking balls better, though he stopped fishing for the bad ones as much as the season progressed. Making consistent contact is still more of a goal than reality. He puzzled some in the organization by hitting well in extended spring training and instructional league, but not producing during the regular season. That could be because he lacked game experience after being signed out of a tryout camp. Baez remains the type who could be an explosive player if everything clicks, though that process could take a while. The Phillies hope it happens at Batavia following another stint in extended spring training.

Year	Club (League)	Class	AVG	G	AB	R	H	2B	3B	HR	RBI	BB	SO	SB	OBP	SLG
2003	Phillies (GCL)	R	.246	41	142	20	35	6	1	3	17	12	37	3	.319	.366
2004	Phillies (GCL)	R	.234	51	171	24	40	7	2	4	13	10	54	3	.320	.368
MINOR LEAGUE TOTALS			.240	92	313	44	75	13	3	7	30	22	91	6	.320	.367

23 Kiel Fisher, 3b

Born: Sept. 29, 1983. **Ht.:** 6-4. **Wt.:** 200. **Bats:** L. **Throws:** R. **School:** Riverside Poly HS, Riverside, Calif. **Career Transactions:** Selected by Phillies in third round of 2002 draft; signed June 18, 2002. **Signed by:** Darrell Connor.

Fisher was a somewhat surprising third-round pick in 2002, and passed on a scholarship to Cal Poly to sign with the Phillies. He displays a great approach to the game and loves to play, though a stress fracture in a vertebrae in his back kept him out of action for all of 2004. It's the same injury David Bell went through in 2003. Fisher was healthy enough to get on the field in instructional league, where he showed up stronger after bulking up to 200 pounds. His bat speed and natural loft indicate he'll develop power, while his patience at the plate means he could emerge as a solid middle-of-the-order hitter. Fisher's feet and hands make him a solid third baseman with average range, and his arm strength rates average as well. He'll try to make up for lost time in low Class A this year.

Year	Club (League)	Class	AVG	G	AB	R	H	2B	3B	HR	RBI	BB	SO	SB	OBP	SLG
2002	Phillies (GCL)	R	.229	35	105	9	24	4	1	3	20	13	34	1	.322	.371
2003	Phillies (GCL)	R	.323	29	96	16	31	6	3	1	13	18	21	4	.429	.479
	Batavia (NY-P)	A	.340	26	97	12	33	4	2	1	11	13	26	3	.420	.454
2004	Did not play—Injured															
MINOR LEAGUE TOTALS			.295	90	298	37	88	14	6	5	44	44	81	8	.389	.433

24 Carlos Rodriguez, ss

Born: Oct. 4, 1983. **Ht.:** 6-0. **Wt.:** 170. **Bats:** B. **Throws:** R. **Career Transactions:** Signed out of Dominican Republic by Phillies, Oct. 13, 2000. **Signed by:** Sal Agostinelli.

Rodriguez' immaturity and lack of focus forced the Phillies to send him home to the Dominican Republic for a month in 2003. He repeated low Class A in 2004, showing an improved attitude under manager P.J. Forbes, whom the Phillies credit with providing good leadership for Rodriguez. Still, being ready to play every day and every pitch remains a challenge for him, as Rodriguez delivers flashes of greatness followed by subpar play. It led the player with the organization's best defensive tools at shortstop to top the South Atlantic League in errors. His range, hands, arm strength and agility all rate better than average. Rodriguez shows above-average bat speed and hit .307 against lefties versus .257 when facing righthanders. He'll open 2005 in high Class A, and a strong start could mean a push to Double-A by midseason. If he stays focused and produces, Rodriguez is still young enough to end up as an everyday player at the major league level and help the Phillies get something for the $700,000 bonus they paid him to sign after the 2000 Area Code Games.

Year	Club (League)	Class	AVG	G	AB	R	H	2B	3B	HR	RBI	BB	SO	SB	OBP	SLG
2001	Phillies (GCL)	R	.297	35	128	22	38	10	1	3	23	11	25	6	.461	.368
2002	Batavia (NY-P)	A	.290	61	248	29	72	7	3	0	15	19	48	21	.343	.351
2003	Lakewood (SAL)	A	.196	93	322	27	63	10	3	0	24	30	63	18	.245	.270
2004	Lakewood (SAL)	A	.268	112	440	56	118	27	2	6	57	26	68	20	.315	.380
MINOR LEAGUE TOTALS			.256	301	1138	134	291	54	9	9	119	86	204	65	.317	.343

25 Robinson Tejeda, rhp

Born: March 24, 1982. **Ht.:** 6-3. **Wt.:** 180. **Bats:** R. **Throws:** R. **Career Transactions:** Signed out of Dominican Republic by Phillies, Nov. 24, 1998. **Signed by:** Wil Tejada.

Tejeda's 2003 season got sidetracked after a typographical error on his visa application raised a red flag with immigration officials, delaying his return to the United States until May. The lost time meant he had to drop down to low Class A to begin the year. Tejeda kept his place in the Phillies prospect list last year by pitching with more maturity and a better work ethic, two areas where he impressed again in 2004. He struggled to 14 losses and an ugly ERA, but still produced a strong strikeout rate thanks to improved command of his fastball, which frequently touched 94-95 mph. His curveball command varied game to game, and the pitch was flat at times. Command and keeping his average changeup lower in the strike zone remain the keys to his future. Tejeda, who has often been compared to former Phillies righy Carlos Silva in build and repertoire, moves up to Triple-A this season after getting added to the 40-man roster over the winter. If he's to follow Silva's move from relief to the rotation, Tejeda must improve his offspeed pitches.

Year	Club (League)	Class	W	L	ERA	G	GS	CG	SV	IP	H	R	ER	HR	BB	SO	AVG
1999	Phillies (GCL)	R	1	3	4.27	12	9	0	0	46	47	27	22	5	27	39	.273
2000	Phillies (GCL)	R	2	5	5.54	10	6	1	0	39	44	30	24	3	12	22	.273
2001	Lakewood (SAL)	A	8	9	3.40	26	24	1	0	151	128	74	57	10	58	152	.228
2002	Clearwater (FSL)	A	4	8	3.97	17	17	1	0	100	73	48	44	14	48	87	.204
2003	Lakewood (SAL)	A	0	3	5.30	5	4	0	0	19	17	11	11	4	16	20	.246
	Clearwater (FSL)	A	2	4	3.20	11	11	1	0	65	53	25	23	4	23	42	.221
2004	Reading (EL)	AA	8	14	5.15	27	26	0	0	150	148	93	86	29	59	133	.253
MINOR LEAGUE TOTALS			25	46	4.22	108	97	4	0	569	510	308	267	69	243	495	.238

26 Maximino de la Cruz, rhp

Born: Oct. 7, 1980. **Ht.:** 6-1. **Wt.:** 163. **Bats:** R. **Throws:** R. **Career Transactions:** Signed out of Dominican Republic by Phillies, Nov. 7, 2001. **Signed by:** Wil Tejada.

De la Cruz shows a power repertoire with the ability to understand pitching at a young age. He ranked third in the Gulf Coast League in ERA in 2004, flashing a plus fastball and curveball. His fastball works in the 90-91 mph range, topping out at 93-94 with good movement. His skinny build and loose arm allow scouts to project more velocity. De la Cruz has drawn physical comparisons to Pascual Perez and former Phillies farmhand Ezequiel Astacio. His breaking ball could become a power pitch because of its bite. It has improved markedly since the Phillies signed him, but it still lacks consistency. De la Cruz needs to improve his changeup while enhancing his command across the board. He has some effort in his delivery, and he needs to mature, both from a physical and mental perspective. He'll go to Batavia for 2005, with more experience his key to progressing at this point.

Year	Club (League)	Class	W	L	ERA	G	GS	CG	SV	IP	H	R	ER	HR	BB	SO	AVG
2002	Phillies (DSL)	R	4	2	2.48	11	10	0	0	58	43	20	16	3	16	40	.206
	Phillies (GCL)	R	1	0	1.17	2	1	0	0	8	4	1	1	0	2	5	.160
2003	Phillies (DSL)	R	5	3	3.55	18	8	1	2	71	72	32	28	2	14	72	.267
2004	Phillies (GCL)	R	4	3	2.11	12	11	0	0	60	64	25	14	1	13	54	.274
MINOR LEAGUE TOTALS			14	8	2.70	43	30	1	2	196	183	78	59	6	45	171	.248

27 Louis Marson, c

Born: June 26, 1986. **Ht.:** 6-1. **Wt.:** 195. **Bats:** R. **Throws:** R. **School:** Coronado HS, Scottsdale, Ariz. **Career Transactions:** Selected by Phillies in fourth round of 2004 draft; signed June 10, 2004. **Signed by:** Therron Brockish.

Marson rated as a top high school quarterback recruit until he broke his collarbone three games into his senior season. He was healthy enough to play baseball in the spring, and he boosted his stock by homering five times, including once off potential 2005 first-rounder Ike Davis of Chaparral High, a team that included fellow Phillies prospect Curt Miaso. Marson's impressive pro debut and subsequent instructional league play led the Phillies to call him the surprise of their draft. His athleticism, strength, makeup and tools give him the ability to develop into a frontline catcher. Marson shows a plus arm with good hands and feet. His blocking and game-calling should improve with experience. His plus power potential offers the chance for 20-plus home runs if he can learn to use his lower half better, and his approach could lead to a solid average in the .270 area. He's ticketed for Batavia in 2005.

Year	Club (League)	Class	AVG	G	AB	R	H	2B	3B	HR	RBI	BB	SO	SB	OBP	SLG
2004	Phillies (GCL)	R	.257	38	113	18	29	3	0	4	8	13	18	4	.333	.389
MINOR LEAGUE TOTALS			.257	38	113	18	29	3	0	4	8	13	18	4	.333	.389

28 Terry Jones, 3b

Born: March 20, 1983. **Ht.:** 6-2. **Wt.:** 190. **Bats:** R. **Throws:** R. **School:** Upland (Calif.) HS. **Career Transactions:** Selected by Phillies in fourth round of 2001 draft; signed July 26, 2001. **Signed by:** Matt Lundine.

Jones, NFL quarterback Rodney Peete's second cousin, drew Chipper Jones comparisons in high school, and the Phillies liked the athleticism enough to pay $500,000 to keep him from a scholarship to California. Like Juan Richardson, Jones' professional career has been held back by injury. A stress fracture in his foot sidelined him until July of last season, and he showed plenty of rust when he returned. His bat was slow—he hit just .164 in July—as were his defensive actions. Jones rated as the best defensive third baseman in the system entering the season because of his athleticism and average to above-average arm. He finally caught up in instructional league before stopping early due to plantar fasciitis. Jones did show improvement during his brief season, trimming his strikeout rate from earlier in his career. He didn't drive balls as well as he had previously, however. Jones will need to trim down his lower half before taking another crack at high Class A in 2005. The Phillies want to see if he can stay healthy long enough to emerge as the .280 hitter with 20-25 home run power they predicted a year ago.

Year	Club (League)	Class	AVG	G	AB	R	H	2B	3B	HR	RBI	BB	SO	SB	OBP	SLG
2001	Phillies (GCL)	R	.194	9	36	3	7	0	0	0	4	2	5	0	.237	.194
2002	Batavia (NY-P)	A	.223	43	157	13	35	8	4	1	16	12	40	5	.297	.344
2003	Lakewood (SAL)	A	.240	129	454	57	109	27	4	11	66	43	111	11	.306	.390
2004	Clearwater (FSL)	A	.204	44	147	14	30	7	0	4	21	18	30	3	.300	.333
MINOR LEAGUE TOTALS			.228	225	794	87	181	42	8	16	107	75	186	19	.300	.361

29 Kyle Kendrick, rhp

Born: Aug. 26, 1984. **Ht.:** 6-3. **Wt.:** 190. **Bats:** R. **Throws:** R. **School:** Mount Vernon (Wash.) HS. **Career Transactions:** Selected by Phillies in seventh round of 2003 draft; signed June 25, 2003. **Signed by:** Tim Kissner.

Kendrick and Scott Mathieson produced similar 2003 seasons in the Gulf Coast League, but they went in different directions in their full-season debuts. The Phillies aggressively moved both to low Class A to start 2004, but Kendrick struggled with his command and ended up at Batavia, where he led the New York-Penn League in losses. Still, his body type, stuff and command issues remind the Phillies of a young Jason Schmidt, right down to Kendrick's also hailing from Washington, where he was a three-sport high school athlete. Kendrick's 11-strikeout, no-walk, one-hit perfromance against Oneonta provided a strong reason to keep the faith, something Kendrick needs to do himself. He often panicked at the first sign of trouble, working backward and letting bad pitches and at-bats snowball. His fastball shows good movement in the low-90s, his curveball is a potential hammer and his changeup is developing. All the ingredients for a power pitcher are there, but Kendrick must sharpen his command while regaining his confidence. His situation reminds some in the organization of Keith Bucktrot. Kendrick will start this year back in low Class A.

Year	Club (League)	Class	W	L	ERA	G	GS	CG	SV	IP	H	R	ER	HR	BB	SO	AVG
2003	Phillies (GCL)	R	0	4	5.46	9	5	0	0	31	40	24	19	3	12	26	.305
2004	Lakewood (SAL)	A	3	8	6.08	15	15	0	0	67	85	56	45	9	33	36	.313
	Batavia (NY-P)	A	2	8	5.48	13	12	0	0	71	94	52	43	6	18	53	.326
MINOR LEAGUE TOTALS			5	20	5.71	37	32	0	0	169	219	132	107	18	63	115	.317

30 Curt Miaso, of

Born: Sept. 28, 1985. **Ht.:** 6-3. **Wt.:** 205. **Bats:** R. **Throws:** R. **School:** Chaparral HS, Scottsdale, Ariz. **Career Transactions:** Selected by Phillies in 42nd round of 2004 draft; signed Aug. 17, 2004. **Signed by:** Therron Brockish.

Miaso tied Paul Konerko's career runs record at Chaparral High, thanks to hitting in a lineup that featured a pair of intriguing prospects for the 2005 draft in Ike Davis and Austin Yount, the nephew of Robin Yount. He projected as an eighth- to 10th-round pick in the 2004 draft based on talent, but a strong commitment to Arizona State caused him to slide all the way to the 42nd round. He decided to sign just before fall classes began, and debuted in instructional league. Once there, Miaso impressed the Phillies staff with his confidence and aggressiveness at the plate. He shows interesting power potential—even drawing comparisons to Konerko—but also swings and misses frequently. He runs well and possesses a strong right-field arm. Miaso's limited experience could land him in the Gulf Coast League for his debut, with Batavia a longshot.

Year	Club (League)	Class	AVG	G	AB	R	H	2B	3B	HR	RBI	BB	SO	SB	OBP	SLG
2004	Did not play—Signed 2005 contract															

PITTSBURGH
PIRATES

BY **JOHN PERROTTO**

The Pirates have talked for years about turning their fortunes around by producing players from within. While Pittsburgh went 72-89 in 2004, its 12th consecutive losing season, the good news was that it did have an influx of young players after relying on veteran fill-ins in recent years. The Pirates began 2004 with seven rookies. By the end of a season that included flameouts by such veterans as Raul Mondesi, Randall Simon and Chris Stynes, they had 13 rookies on the roster.

Leading the rookie brigade was outfielder **Jason Bay**, named National League rookie of the year after being acquired from the Padres in 2003 as part of a three-player package for Brian Giles. Bay hit .282-26-82 as Pittsburgh became the last pre-expansion era franchise to have a rookie of the year.

Lefthander Sean Burnett turned in five consecutive quality starts before fading and then injuring his elbow, requiring Tommy John surgery. Jose Castillo showed promise as the starting second baseman, while lefthanders Mike Gonzalez and John Grabow were mainstays in the bullpen.

In the minors, the Pirates weren't able to repeat their 2003 success, when all six of their farm clubs qualified for the playoffs. However, their affiliates combined to go 354-339 for a third straight winning year, a significant achievement after Pittsburgh farm clubs had finished above .500 just once in the previous 33 seasons.

The Pirates also had two of the top performers in the minor leagues in lefthander Zach Duke and first baseman Brad Eldred, who split the season between high Class A Lynchburg and Altoona. Duke topped the minor leagues in ERA by going a combined 15-6, 1.46 with 142 strikeouts in 148 innings. Eldred was the overall RBI leader as he hit .301-38-137.

The Pirates system continues to be tilted toward pitching, as six of the top seven prospects and 16 of the top 30 are pitchers. That's less pronounced than a year ago, when 10 of the top 15 and 20 of the top 30 were pitchers.

Pittsburgh looked for hitters in the draft after taking pitchers with their previous six first-round picks. They went for switch-hitting catcher Neil Walker in the first round, then selected Eastern Michigan shortstop Brian Bixler in the second and Atlanta-area third baseman Eddie Prasch in the third.

"We're looking for better balance and we brought some interesting bats into the organization," scouting director Ed Creech said.

While general manager Dave Littlefield, farm director Brian Graham and Creech continue to do their best to resurrect the team, the Pirates and Brewers still have gone longer than any two franchises in major professional sports without reaching .500. Pittsburgh's streak doesn't look like it will end in 2005, but at least there's more hope for the future than in recent years.

TOP 30 PROSPECTS

1. Zach Duke, lhp	16. Chris Duffy, of
2. Neil Walker, c	17. Eddie Prasch, 3b
3. John Van Benschoten, rhp	18. Blair Johnson, rhp
4. Ian Snell, rhp	19. Cory Stewart, lhp
5. Tom Gorzelanny, lhp	20. Brian Bixler, ss
6. Bryan Bullington, rhp	21. Javier Guzman, ss
7. Paul Maholm, lhp	22. Bobby Bradley, rhp
8. Brad Eldred, 1b	23. Mike Johnston, lhp
9. Matt Peterson, rhp	24. Wardell Starling, rhp
10. Nate McLouth, of	25. Joe Bauserman, rhp
11. Rajai Davis, of	26. Craig Stansberry, 2b
12. Jose Bautista, 3b	27. Russell Johnson, rhp
13. Freddy Sanchez, 2b/ss	28. Jason Quarles, rhp
14. Ryan Doumit, c	29. J.R. House, c/1b
15. Steve Lerud, c	30. Jeff Miller, rhp

LARRY GOREN

ORGANIZATION OVERVIEW

General manager: David Littlefield. **Farm director:** Brian Graham. **Scouting director:** Ed Creech.

2004 PERFORMANCE

Class	Team	League	W	L	Pct.	Finish*	Manager(s)
Majors	Pittsburgh	National	72	89	.447	11th (16)	Lloyd McClendon
Triple-A	#Nashville Sounds	Pacific Coast	63	79	.444	14th (16)	Trent Jewett
Double-A	Altoona Curve	Eastern	85	56	.603	1st (12)	Tony Beasley
High A	Lynchburg Hillcats	Carolina	57	81	.413	7th (8)	Jay Loviglio/Tom Prince
Low A	Hickory Crawdads	South Atlantic	85	55	.607	+2nd (16)	Dave Clark
Short-season	Williamsport Crosscutters	New York-Penn	34	40	.459	9th (14)	Jeff Branson
Rookie	GCL Pirates	Gulf Coast	30	28	.517	6th (12)	Woody Huyke
OVERALL 2004 MINOR LEAGUE RECORD			354	339	.511	11th (30)	

*Finish in overall standings (No. of teams in league). +League champion. #Affiliate will be in Indianapolis (International) in 2005.

ORGANIZATION LEADERS

BATTING   *Minimum 205 at-bats
*AVG	Jeff Keppinger, Altoona	.337
R	Chris Truby, Nashville	96
H	Nate McLouth, Altoona	166
TB	Brad Eldred, Altoona/Lynchburg	292
2B	Chris Truby, Nashville	41
3B	Rich Thompson, Nashville	13
HR	Brad Eldred, Altoona/Lynchburg	38
RBI	Brad Eldred, Altoona/Lynchburg	137
BB	Adam Boeve, Hickory	61
SO	Brad Eldred, Altoona/Lynchburg	148
SB	Rajai Davis, Lynchburg	57
*OBP	Jon Benick, Hickory	.396
*SLG	Brad Eldred, Altoona/Lynchburg	.606

PITCHING   #Minimum 75 innings
W	Zach Duke, Altoona/Lynchburg	15
L	John Van Benschoten, Nashville	11
#ERA	Zach Duke, Altoona/Lynchburg	1.46
G	Jeff Miller, Altoona	52
CG	Nelson Figueroa, Nashville	4
SV	Chris Hernandez, Hickory	24
IP	Nelson Figueroa, Nashville	152
BB	Josh Sharpless, Hickory	55
SO	Tom Gorzelanny, Lynchburg/Hickory	167

BEST TOOLS

Best Hitter for Average	Nate McLouth
Best Power Hitter	Brad Eldred
Best Strike-Zone Discipline	Rajai Davis
Fastest Baserunner	Rajai Davis
Best Athlete	Neil Walker
Best Fastball	Jeremy Harts
Best Curveball	Bobby Bradley
Best Slider	Tom Gorzelanny
Best Changeup	Zach Duke
Best Control	Zach Duke
Best Defensive Catcher	Ronny Paulino
Best Defensive Infielder	Craig Stansberry
Best Infield Arm	Javier Guzman
Best Defensive Outfielder	Chris Duffy
Best Outfield Arm	A.J. Johnson

PROJECTED 2008 LINEUP

Catcher	Neil Walker
First Base	Brad Eldred
Second Base	Jose Castillo
Third Base	Ty Wigginton
Shortstop	Jack Wilson
Left Field	Jason Bay
Center Field	Nate McLouth

Right Field	Craig Wilson
No. 1 Starter	Oliver Perez
No. 2 Starter	Kip Wells
No. 3 Starter	Zach Duke
No. 4 Starter	John Van Benschoten
No. 5 Starter	Ian Snell
Closer	Tom Gorzelanny

LAST YEAR'S TOP 20 PROSPECTS

1. John VanBenschoten, rhp
2. Sean Burnett, lhp
3. Jason Bay, of
4. Bryan Bullington, rhp
5. Blair Johnson, rhp
6. Ian Snell, rhp
7. Freddy Sanchez, ss/2b
8. Paul Maholm, lhp
9. Cory Stewart, lhp
10. Ryan Doumit, c
11. Mike Johnston, lhp
12. Jose Castillo, 2b/ss
13. J.J. Davis, of
14. Matt Capps, rhp
15. Zach Duke, lhp
16. Nyjer Morgan, of
17. Jorge Cortes, of
18. Nate McLouth, of
19. Tom Gorzelanny, lhp
20. Mike Gonzalez, lhp

TOP PROSPECTS OF THE DECADE

Year	Player, Pos.	Current Team
1995	Trey Beamon, of	Gary (Northern)
1996	Jason Kendall, c	Athletics
1997	Kris Benson, rhp	Mets
1998	Kris Benson, rhp	Mets
1999	Chad Hermansen, of	Blue Jays
2000	Chad Hermansen, of	Blue Jays
2001	J.R. House, c	Pirates
2002	J.R. House, c	Pirates
2003	John Van Benschoten, rhp	Pirates
2004	John Van Benschoten, rhp	Pirates

TOP DRAFT PICKS OF THE DECADE

Year	Player, Pos.	Current Team
1995	Chad Hermansen, ss	Blue Jays
1996	Kris Benson, rhp	Mets
1997	J.J. Davis, of	Nationals
1998	Clint Johnston, lhp/of	Blue Jays
1999	Bobby Bradley, rhp	Pirates
2000	Sean Burnett, lhp	Pirates
2001	John Van Benschoten, rhp/of	Pirates
2002	Bryan Bullington, rhp	Pirates
2003	Paul Maholm, lhp	Pirates
2004	Neil Walker, c	Pirates

ALL-TIME LARGEST BONUSES

Bryan Bullington, 2002	$4,000,000
John Van Benschoten, 2001	$2,400,000
Bobby Bradley, 1999	$2,225,000
Paul Maholm, 2003	$2,200,000
Kris Benson, 1996	$2,000,000

MINOR LEAGUE DEPTH CHART

Pittsburgh PIRATES

Impact Potential: C
Two of the Pirates' top four prospects were drafted in the 20th round or later, and both rank ahead of Bryan Bullington, the 2002 No. 1 overall pick. While Bullington searches for the velocity he showed in college, B.J. Upton—selected one pick later—has reached the big leagues. Four former No. 1 prospects—John Van Benschoten, Sean Burnett, Bobby Bradley and J.R. House—have had injury issues, with Van

Benschoten having shoulder surgery in January.
Depth: B
Despite the injuries to top prospects, the Pirates have found strength in numbers. For every Burnett, they have come up with a Zach Duke. For every Bradley, there's Ian Snell. And while House no longer profiles as an everyday catcher, the Pirates are flush with prospects behind the plate, starting with 2004 first-round pick Neil Walker. The organization could use more power bats behind first baseman Brad Eldred.

*Depth charts prepared by **John Manuel** and **Allan Simpson**. Numbers in parentheses indicate prospect rankings.*

LF
Ray Sadler

CF
Rajai Davis (11)
Chris Duffy (16)
Nyjer Morgan
Rich Thompson

3B
Jose Bautista (12)
Eddie Prasch (17)
John Santiago

SS
Brian Bixler (20)
Javier Guzman (21)
Brandon Chaves
Taber Lee
David Munoz

RF
Nate McLouth (10)
Jorge Cortes
Antonio Sucre
Adam Boeve
A.J. Johnson

2B
Freddy Sanchez (13)
Craig Stansberry (26)
Alexander Peraltz

SOURCE of TALENT

HOMEGROWN		ACQUIRED	
College	9	Trades	3
Junior College	4	Rule 5 draft	0
Draft-and-follow	1	Independent leagues	0
High School	12	Free agents/waivers	0
Nondrafted free agent	0		
Foreign	1		

1B
Brad Eldred (8)
Carlos Rivera

C
Neil Walker (2)
Ryan Doumit (14)
Steve Lerud (15)
J.R. House (29)
Ronny Paulino
Humberto Cota
Mike McCuiston

RHP

Starters	Relievers
John Van Benschoten (3)	Jason Quarles (28)
Ian Snell (4)	Jeff Miller (30)
Bryan Bullington (6)	Basilio Alvarez
Matt Peterson (9)	Josh Sharpless
Blair Johnson (18)	Justin Reid
Bobby Bradley (22)	Henry Owens
Wardell Starling (24)	Josh DeMaria
Joe Bauserman (25)	Christopher Hernandez
Russell Johnson (27)	Dustin Craig
Kyle Pearson	Derek Drage
Luis Valdez	Matt Bishop
Matt Capps	Eric Ridener
Derek Hankins	Kendy Ramos
Landon Jacobsen	Kelly Arias
Jonathan Albaladejo	
Matt Guillory	
Sergio Silva	

LHP

Starters	Relievers
Zach Duke (1)	Mike Johnston (23)
Tom Gorzelanny (5)	Frank Brooks
Paul Maholm (7)	Jeremy Harts
Cory Stewart (19)	Shane Youman
Kyle Bloom	
Brian Holliday	
Mike Connolly	

DRAFT ANALYSIS

2004

Best Pro Debut: 2B/OF Jermel Lomack (14) hit .283 and led the short-season New York-Penn League with 29 steals. RHP Eric Ridener (8) used his sinker/slider combination to post a 1.53 ERA and 33 strikeouts in 35 innings in the Rookie-level Gulf Coast League, where he held hitters to a .134 average. C Neil Walker (1) got his career off to a good start, batting a combined .276-4-27 between the GCL and NY-P.

Best Athlete: A star wide receiver and defensive back in high school, Walker is a good athlete for a catcher. OF A.J. Johnson (6) has raw power, arm strength and speed. RHP Joe Bauserman (4) was a top quarterback recruit of Ohio State.

Best Pure Hitter: 3B Eddie Prasch (3) has an effortless lefthanded swing, though he batted just .220 in the GCL. SS Brian Bixler (2) rebounded from a disastrous .120 Cape Cod League performance in 2003 to finish second in the NCAA Division I batting race with a .453 average for Eastern Michigan. He hit .276 in the NY-P.

Best Raw Power: Walker has a strong 6-foot-2, 205-pound build and a fluid uppercut swing from both sides of the plate.

Fastest Runner: Lomack's 6.4-second speed in the 60-yard dash allowed him to succeed on 88 percent of his steal attempts.

Best Defensive Player: Pittsburgh drafted INF Dan Schwartzbauer (41) for his hands and accurate arm. They were pleasantly surprised when he hit .366 in the GCL, though he was old for Rookie ball at 22.

Best Fastball: RHP Jason Quarles (7) batted .397 at Glen Oaks (Mich.) CC in 2003 but couldn't crack Southern's outfield after transferring. Coaches noted his arm

Bixler

strength and moved him to the mound, and he soon was putting 98s on radar guns. He threw 94-96 mph for most of the summer.

Best Breaking Ball: Because he's 6-foot-1 and has a devastating curveball, Quarles is compared to Tom Gordon, and the Pirates say his curve is the pitch that will get him to the majors.

Most Intriguing Background: Walker's father Tom and uncle Chip Lang played in the majors. Johnson was named national junior college player of the year after batting .388-18-88 at Tallahassee (Fla.) CC.

Closest To The Majors: Bixler, who lacks only home run power, or LHP Kyle Bloom (5). Bloom shows three average or better pitches at times.

Best Late-Round Pick: INF Brett Grandstrand (13) and Schwartzbauer both stand out for their defensive versatility. Grandstrand, who hit .268 in the NY-P, has more offensive potential.

The One Who Got Away: Louisiana State-bound 3B J.P. Padron (12) has tremendous raw power, but a sore shoulder contributed to a disappointing spring so he dropped in the draft. Miami (Ohio) C John Slone (15) stood out with his bat and athleticism in the Cape Cod League last summer.

Assessment: Walker, Bixler and Prasch give the Pirates balance in a system known more for its pitching. Quarles is raw but could prove to be a steal.

2003 The Pirates landed a solid pair of lefthanders in Paul Maholm (1) and Tom Gorzelanny (2). **GRADE:** C+

2002 Pittsburgh's decision to spend the No. 1 overall pick on Bryan Bullington rather than B.J. Upton looks more regrettable by the day. 1B Brad Eldred (6) topped the minors with 137 RBIs last season. **GRADE:** C

2001 The Pirates let SS Stephen Drew (11) get away, and he became a first-rounder in 2004. But they did land their top two pitching prospects, LHP Zach Duke (20) and RHP John Van Benschoten (1). 2B Jeff Keppinger (4/traded), 1B/C Chris Shelton (33/lost in Rule 5 draft) and OFs Rajai Davis (38) and Chris Duffy (8) also show promise. **GRADE:** B

2000 LHP Sean Burnett (1) needed Tommy John surgery shortly after reaching the majors, and RHP Chris Young (3) was traded away. Pittsburgh did tremendous work late to find RHP Ian Snell (26), OF Nate McLouth (25) and draft-and-follow 3B Jose Bautista (20). **GRADE:** B

Draft analysis prepared by Jim Callis. Numbers in parentheses indicate draft rounds.

Zach
DUKE

Born: April 19, 1983.
Ht.: 6-2. **Wt.:** 207.
Bats: L. **Throws:** L.
School: Midway HS, Clifton, Texas.
Career Transactions: Selected by Pirates in 20th round of 2001 draft; signed July 31, 2001.
Signed by: Grant Brittain.

While the Pirates don't regret drafting John Van Benschoten with their first-round pick in 2001, it now looks like they may have found an even better prospect 19 rounds later. Duke, who grew up in Waco, Texas, idolizing fellow Midway High product Casey Fossum, signed too late to debut that season but immediately opened eyes with his performance in instructional league. He hasn't done anything to tarnish that initial impression, going 31-14, 2.21 in three minor league seasons while rapidly moving up the organization ladder. He had his best year in 2004, leading the minors with a 1.46 ERA. He allowed two earned runs or fewer in 25 of his 26 starts, including his first 22, and surrendered three in his other outing. Duke was the high Class A Carolina League pitcher of the year and finished the season with two quality starts in the Eastern League playoffs for Double-A Altoona. A year ago, he looked like he'd continue to move a level a year, but now he's definitely on the fast track.

Duke gets his highest marks for his mound presence and poise. Quiet by nature, he never gets rattled and has a precise plan of what he wants to do with each pitch. He has the best command of any pitcher in the system. Duke's best offering is a curveball that he can throw for strikes at any point in the count. The curve has a big, sweeping movement and left-handed batters find it unhittable. They batted just .192 with one homer in 156 at-bats against Duke last season. His fastball topped out at 88 mph when he was drafted but now reaches 93 as his body has matured. It usually sits in the 89-91 range. After fading down the stretch in 2003, Duke maintained his strength throughout the 2004 season. His performance didn't slip at all, even after his promotion to Double-A. Duke is a good athlete who fields his position and holds runners well.

Duke doesn't have the ability to overpower hitters, so he can't reach back for something extra when he needs a big out. His body continues to fill out, however, so he possibly could add velocity to his heater. Duke's changeup is an average pitch at best, and he needs to refine it because he will need a third offering against major league hitters, especially righthanders, as a starter. His changeup has improved each year, however, and could develop into a plus pitch down the road.

Duke got his first look at PNC Park last September, when the Pirates honored him as their minor league pitcher of the year in a pregame ceremony. There's a good chance he could call Pittsburgh home by the end of this season. Duke will begin 2005 at the Pirates' new Triple-A Indianapolis affiliate, and he'll get the call to the major leagues if he comes remotely close to duplicating last year's performance. He doesn't have the pure stuff of a No. 1 starter, but his curveball and smarts give him the look of a solid No. 2.

Year	Club (League)	Class	W	L	ERA	G	GS	CG	SV	IP	H	R	ER	HR	BB	SO	AVG
2002	Pirates (GCL)	R	8	1	1.95	11	11	1	0	60	38	15	13	2	18	48	.185
2003	Hickory (SAL)	A	8	7	3.11	26	26	1	0	142	124	66	49	7	46	113	.237
2004	Lynchburg (Car)	A	10	5	1.39	17	17	1	0	97	73	24	15	3	20	106	.207
	Altoona (EL)	AA	5	1	1.58	9	9	0	0	51	41	11	9	2	10	36	.227
MINOR LEAGUE TOTALS			31	14	2.21	63	63	3	0	350	276	116	86	14	94	303	.219

Neil Walker, c

RICH ABEL

Born: Sept. 10, 1985. **Ht.:** 6-3. **Wt.:** 205. **Bats:** S. **Throws:** R. **School:** Pine Richland HS, Gibsonia, Pa. **Career Transactions:** Selected by Pirates in first round (11th overall) of 2004 draft; signed June 17, 2004. **Signed by:** Jon Mercurio.

Walker became the first Pittsburgh-area player ever drafted by the Pirates in the first round when they used the 11th overall pick on him last year. Also a star wide receiver and defensive back in high school, he signed for $1.95 million and instantly became the best athlete in the organization. He has good bloodlines, as his father Tom and uncle Chip Lang pitched in the majors. Walker is a switch-hitter with power and the ability to hit for average from both sides of the plate. He could develop into a .300 hitter capable of 30 homers a season. His power is particularly good from the left side. He has good feet and hands behind the plate, and he throws well. A better athlete than most catchers, he's a solid-average runner. Walker's righthanded swing needs to be smoothed out a little bit. Some in the organization worry that catching may take too much of a toll on his bat. If a change of positions is in order, he easily could shift to a corner infield or outfield position. Walker will begin the year at low Class A Hickory. The Pirates won't rush him, but his raw talent could push him to Pittsburgh quickly.

Year	Club (League)	Class	AVG	G	AB	R	H	2B	3B	HR	RBI	BB	SO	SB	OBP	SLG
2004	Pirates (GCL)	R	.271	52	192	28	52	12	3	4	20	10	33	3	.313	.427
	Williamsport (NY-P)	A	.313	8	32	2	10	3	0	0	7	2	1	1	.343	.406
MINOR LEAGUE TOTALS			.277	60	224	30	62	15	3	4	27	12	34	4	.316	.424

John Van Benschoten, rhp

Born: April 14, 1980. **Ht.:** 6-4. **Wt.:** 217. **Bats:** R. **Throws:** R. **School:** Kent State University. **Career Transactions:** Selected by Pirates in first round (eighth overall) of 2001 draft; signed July 3, 2001. **Signed by:** Duane Gustavson.

Van Benschoten hit 31 home runs to lead NCAA Division I in 2001, but the Pirates drafted him as a pitcher. He made his big league debut last season, but was shut down in September. He had surgery to repair his non-throwing shoulder, and then the Pirates discovered in January that he had a cyst and slightly torn labrum in his right shoulder. He had surgery to repair the damage. Van Benschoten has four pitches that could be average or better. He has a 90-92 mph fastball with good movement and a curveball that can be outstanding at times. His slider and changeup aren't quite as advanced. He's a tough competitor who won 26 straight starts without losing from 2002-03. He nibbled too much in the majors and needs better command of his pitches. That should come with experience, as Van Benschoten pitched only in relief at Kent State. His delivery tends to get out of whack at times, which affects his location. Though the operation on his right shoulder went better than expected, Van Benschoten still will be out until instructional league, costing him a crucial season of development as he tries to gain experience as a pitcher.

Year	Club (League)	Class	W	L	ERA	G	GS	CG	SV	IP	H	R	ER	HR	BB	SO	AVG
2001	Williamsport (NY-P)	A	0	2	3.51	9	9	0	0	26	23	11	10	0	10	19	.247
2002	Hickory (SAL)	A	11	4	2.80	27	27	0	0	148	119	57	46	6	62	145	.219
2003	Lynchburg (Car)	A	6	0	2.22	9	9	0	0	49	33	14	12	1	18	49	.192
	Altoona (EL)	AA	7	6	3.69	17	17	1	0	90	95	46	37	5	34	78	.268
2004	Nashville (PCL)	AAA	4	11	4.72	23	23	0	0	132	135	75	69	16	49	101	.261
	Pittsburgh (NL)	MAJ	1	3	6.91	6	5	0	0	29	33	27	22	3	19	18	.300
MAJOR LEAGUE TOTALS			1	3	6.91	6	5	0	0	29	33	27	22	3	19	18	.300
MINOR LEAGUE TOTALS			28	23	3.52	85	85	1	0	444	405	203	174	28	173	392	.241

Ian Snell, rhp

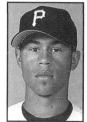

Born: Oct. 30, 1981. **Ht.:** 5-11. **Wt.:** 170. **Bats:** R. **Throws:** R. **School:** Caesar Rodney HS, Camden, Del. **Career Transactions:** Selected by Pirates in 26th round of 2000 draft; signed June 21, 2000. **Signed by:** Dana Brown.

Snell has been known as Ian Oquendo at various points in his career, but went back to his birth name prior to last season and intends to stick with it. He finished second in the Eastern League in strikeouts and might have won the title had he not been promoted to Pittsburgh in August. Snell has a lively fastball that sits around 93 mph and touches 95-96. He also throws a sharp curveball with such a late break that some opposing hitters and scouts call it a slider. He doesn't back down from anyone. Snell needs to stay on top of his fastball, which tends to flatten out and become hittable. His changeup is improving, but he needs better command of it before he's ready for major league hitters. His small stature leads to questions about his durability. He also could use a dose of maturity. Snell will pitch in the rotation this season at Triple-A and likely will receive a promotion to the majors at some point. If he doesn't prove strong enough to remain a starter, he has the arm to be a fine set-up man.

Year	Club (League)	Class	W	L	ERA	G	GS	CG	SV	IP	H	R	ER	HR	BB	SO	AVG
2000	Pirates (GCL)	R	1	0	2.35	4	0	0	0	8	5	2	2	1	1	8	.200
2001	Pirates (GCL)	R	3	0	0.47	3	3	0	0	19	12	2	1	0	5	13	.185
	Williamsport (NY-P)	A	7	0	1.39	10	9	1	0	65	55	16	10	2	10	56	.230
2002	Hickory (SAL)	A	11	6	2.71	24	22	0	0	140	127	49	42	8	45	149	.243
2003	Lynchburg (Car)	A	10	3	3.33	20	20	1	0	116	105	46	43	3	33	122	.244
	Altoona (EL)	AA	4	0	1.96	6	6	0	0	37	36	13	8	2	10	23	.252
2004	Altoona (EL)	AA	11	7	3.16	26	26	3	0	151	147	54	53	16	40	142	.259
	Pittsburgh (NL)	MAJ	0	1	7.50	3	1	0	0	12	14	10	10	2	9	9	.298
MAJOR LEAGUE TOTALS			0	1	7.50	3	1	0	0	12	14	10	10	2	9	9	.298
MINOR LEAGUE TOTALS			47	16	2.68	93	86	5	0	533	487	182	159	32	144	513	.244

5 Tom Gorzelanny, lhp

RICH ABEL

Born: July 12, 1982. **Ht.:** 6-2. **Wt.:** 202. **Bats:** L. **Throws:** L. **School:** Triton (Ill.) JC. **Career Transactions:** Selected by Pirates in second round of 2003 draft; signed July 1, 2003. **Signed by:** Mark Germann.

Gorzelanny began his college career at Kansas before academic difficulties led him to transfer to Triton, the alma mater of Hall of Famer Kirby Puckett. He moved quickly in his first full pro season, allowing two earned runs or fewer in 15 of his 16 starts in low Class A. He spent the second half at high Class A Lynchburg, then turned in two strong relief outings in the Double-A Eastern League playoffs. Gorzelanny throws hard for a lefthander, reaching 94-95 mph and sitting at 91-92 with his fastball. He also has an above-average slider that's tough on lefthanders. Like Pittsburgh's other top pitching prospects, he's a battler who refuses to give in to hitters. Gorzelanny doesn't maintain a consistent delivery, dropping his arm slot and losing command of his slider. His changeup lags behind his other two pitches. He sometimes has a hard time shaking off adversity and needs to have a shorter memory. Gorzelanny will begin the season in Double-A. If he polishes up his mechanics, he could see the major leagues by 2006 and become a solid middle-of-the-rotation starter.

Year	Club (League)	Class	W	L	ERA	G	GS	CG	SV	IP	H	R	ER	HR	BB	SO	AVG
2003	Williamsport (NY-P)	A	1	2	1.78	8	8	0	0	30	23	6	6	1	10	22	.215
2004	Hickory (SAL)	A	7	2	2.23	16	15	1	0	93	63	30	23	9	34	106	.193
	Lynchburg (Car)	A	3	5	4.85	10	10	0	0	56	54	31	30	6	19	61	.255
MINOR LEAGUE TOTALS			11	9	2.97	34	33	1	0	179	140	67	59	16	63	189	.217

6 Bryan Bullington, rhp

RICH ABEL

Born: Sept. 30, 1980. **Ht.:** 6-5. **Wt.:** 220. **Bats:** R. **Throws:** R. **School:** Ball State University. **Career Transactions:** Selected by Pirates in first round (first overall) of 2002 draft; signed Oct. 30, 2002. **Signed by:** Duane Gustavson.

Bullington was the No. 1 overall pick in the 2002 draft, getting a $4 million signing bonus after holding out for nearly five months. The player picked after him, high school shortstop B.J. Upton, looks like a future star and made his big league debut in Tampa Bay last year, while Bullington hasn't gotten past Double-A. The Pirates took Bullington for his two dominant pitches, a lively fastball and sharp slider. His velocity has dropped from 94-95 mph at Ball State to 90-93 in the pros, however, and his slider hasn't had the same bite. He has compensated by showing a knack for making pitches in tight situations, and the Pirates still hope he'll regain his zip. Bullington's biggest need is to get back the stuff he showed in college. He also must refine his changeup to give him a third pitch to make it as a big league starter. Bullington has good control but could use better command—he's hittable because he's around the plate so much with his pitches. Bullington will go to Triple-A with hopes of finding his fastball. This year figures to go a long way in telling whether he's a top-of-the-rotation pitcher, a No. 5 starter or a set-up man.

Year	Club (League)	Class	W	L	ERA	G	GS	CG	SV	IP	H	R	ER	HR	BB	SO	AVG
2003	Hickory (SAL)	A	5	1	1.39	8	7	0	0	45	25	10	7	3	11	46	.155
	Lynchburg (Car)	A	8	4	3.05	17	17	2	0	97	101	39	33	5	27	67	.270
2004	Altoona (EL)	AA	12	7	4.10	26	26	0	0	145	160	77	66	18	47	100	.283
MINOR LEAGUE TOTALS			25	12	3.32	51	50	2	0	288	286	126	106	26	85	213	.260

Paul Maholm, lhp

Born: June 25, 1982. **Ht.:** 6-2. **Wt.:** 215. **Bats:** L. **Throws:** L. **School:** Mississippi State University. **Career Transactions:** Selected by Pirates in first round (eighth overall) of 2003 draft; signed July 9, 2003. **Signed by:** Everett Russell.

Maholm signed for $2.2 million as the eighth pick in the 2003 draft. His first full season was ruined May 15, when a line drive hit him in the face, breaking his nose and the orbital bone around his left eye. He returned in August but needed more surgery to remove scar tissue, knocking him out of instructional league and the Arizona Fall League. Maholm has a good feel for pitching and a strong mound presence. He also has good control of four pitches: an 88 mph fastball, curveball, slider and changeup. The curveball and changeup are his best pitches at this point. He doesn't have an overpowering pitch, so Maholm won't have much margin for error against advanced hitters. It's uncertain whether he'll have any long-term effects from getting hit in the face, but the Pirates are confident he will put the incident behind him. Maholm will start the season in high Class A but will move quickly to Double-A Altoona if he pitches well. He has a chance to get to Pittsburgh by late 2006 and should be a No. 3-5 starter.

Year	Club (League)	Class	W	L	ERA	G	GS	CG	SV	IP	H	R	ER	HR	BB	SO	AVG
2003	Williamsport (NY-P)	A	2	1	1.83	8	8	0	0	34	25	11	7	1	10	32	.197
2004	Hickory (SAL)	A	0	2	9.49	3	3	0	0	12	17	14	13	2	10	12	.354
	Lynchburg (Car)	A	1	3	1.84	8	8	0	0	44	39	11	9	2	15	28	.236
MINOR LEAGUE TOTALS			3	6	2.88	19	19	0	0	91	81	36	29	5	35	72	.238

Brad Eldred, 1b

Born: July 12, 1980. **Ht.:** 6-5. **Wt.:** 274. **Bats:** R. **Throws:** R. **School:** Florida International University. **Career Transactions:** Selected by Pirates in sixth round of 2002 draft; signed June 5, 2002. **Signed by:** Delvy Santiago.

After ranking second in NCAA Division I with 29 homers in 2002, Eldred has continued to hit the longball as a pro. He has led the Pirates system in homers in each of his two full years, and he topped the minors with 137 RBIs last year. He was Carolina League MVP and Pittsburgh's minor league player of the year. Eldred has big-time power and dropped plenty of jaws last season with tape-measure homers. He has greatly improved his balance, swing and pitch recognition. He's also a good fielder and decent runner for a big man. Eldred strikes out a ton and doesn't walk much, a tradeoff the Pirates will live with in exchange for his home runs. Already large, he must keep an eye on his weight. Though he drove in 60 runs in 39 games at Altoona, Eldred is ticketed to return to Double-A to start 2005. A midseason promotion to Triple-A is likely and his big league debut is a possibility. Starved for power, the Pirates hope he develops into their cleanup hitter.

Year	Club (League)	Class	AVG	G	AB	R	H	2B	3B	HR	RBI	BB	SO	SB	OBP	SLG
2002	Williamsport (NY-P)	A	.283	72	276	43	78	22	3	10	48	18	74	10	.338	.493
2003	Hickory (SAL)	A	.250	115	420	62	105	22	0	28	80	38	142	7	.326	.502
2004	Lynchburg (Car)	A	.310	91	335	54	104	22	1	21	77	35	97	5	.397	.570
	Altoona (EL)	AA	.279	39	147	24	41	9	0	17	60	6	51	0	.329	.687
MINOR LEAGUE TOTALS			.278	317	1178	183	328	75	4	76	265	97	364	22	.350	.542

Matt Peterson, rhp

Born: Feb. 11, 1982. **Ht.:** 6-5. **Wt.:** 210. **Bats:** R. **Throws:** R. **School:** Rapides HS, Alexandria, La. **Career Transactions:** Selected by Mets in second round of 2000 draft; signed Aug. 9, 2000 . . . Traded by Mets with 3B Ty Wigginton and IF Jose Bautista to Pirates for RHP Kris Benson and 2B Jeff Keppinger, July 30, 2004. **Signed by:** Bob Rossi (Mets).

Peterson came to the Pirates in the three-team deal that sent Kris Benson to the Mets last July. He missed two starts before the trade with a strained side muscle, and that affected his control. He uncharacteristically walked 19 batters and threw six wild pitches in his last five starts of the season. Though Peterson has the frame to throw hard, he has better offspeed pitches at this stage of his career. His changeup is outstanding, particularly against lefthanded hitters, and he possesses a true 12-6 curveball. His fastball is no slouch, as it sits at 90-92 mph and runs up to 94. Peterson could stand to add muscle to his lanky frame. He also needs to gain better command of all his pitches. His inability to locate consistently led to 18 homers in 2004. How Peterson performs in spring training will determine whether he starts this season back in Double-A or gets moved up to Triple-A. He's still somewhat raw and won't see the majors until 2006, but he has a chance to develop into a first-rate starter.

Year	Club (League)	Class	W	L	ERA	G	GS	CG	SV	IP	H	R	ER	HR	BB	SO	AVG
2001	Capital City (SAL)	A	2	6	4.99	18	14	0	0	79	87	46	44	9	29	72	.275
	Brooklyn (NY-P)	A	2	2	1.62	6	6	0	0	33	26	7	6	0	14	19	.217
2002	Capital City (SAL)	A	8	10	3.86	26	26	1	0	138	109	67	59	13	61	153	.221
	St. Lucie (FSL)	A	1	0	1.50	1	1	0	0	6	5	2	1	0	2	5	.217
2003	St. Lucie (FSL)	A	9	2	1.71	15	15	1	0	84	65	24	16	2	24	73	.212
	Binghamton (EL)	AA	1	2	3.45	6	6	0	0	31	29	18	12	2	20	23	.248
2004	Binghamton (EL)	AA	6	4	3.27	19	18	0	0	105	97	44	38	11	45	90	.253
	Altoona (EL)	AA	3	2	6.25	7	7	0	0	36	36	25	25	7	22	29	.269
MINOR LEAGUE TOTALS			32	28	3.53	98	93	2	0	512	454	233	201	44	217	464	.240

10 Nate McLouth, of

Born: Oct. 28, 1981. **Ht.:** 5-11. **Wt.:** 186. **Bats:** L. **Throws:** R. **School:** Whitehall (Mich.) HS. **Career Transactions:** Selected by Pirates in 25th round of 2000 draft; signed Aug. 29, 2000. **Signed by:** Duane Gustavson.

MIKE JANES

McLouth was the Michigan high school player of the year in 2000 but lasted until the 25th round because of his commitment to the University of Michigan. The Pirates signed him for $500,000. After repeating high Class A in 2003, he had the best year of his career in 2004, leading the Eastern League in runs, hits and doubles. McLouth always seems to get the sweet spot of the bat on the ball. He is a contact hitter with the strength to reach the gaps. He's getting better at working counts. He has above-average speed and is a good basestealer, with an 83 percent success rate as a pro. McLouth saw extended duty in center field during 2003, but his range is a step short to play there in the majors. He saw more time last year in right field, where his arm is adequate. To play there in the majors, he'll have to develop more home run power. The hard-nosed McLouth will begin this season at Indianapolis and will be a legitimate candidate to start on a corner for the Pirates in 2006 if his homers increase. At worst, he'll be a fourth outfielder in the majors.

Year	Club (League)	Class	AVG	G	AB	R	H	2B	3B	HR	RBI	BB	SO	SB	OBP	SLG
2001	Hickory (SAL)	A	.285	96	351	59	100	17	5	12	54	43	54	21	.371	.464
2002	Lynchburg (Car)	A	.244	114	393	58	96	23	4	9	46	41	48	20	.324	.392
2003	Lynchburg (Car)	A	.300	117	440	85	132	27	2	6	33	55	68	40	.386	.411
2004	Altoona (EL)	AA	.322	133	515	93	166	40	4	8	73	48	62	31	.384	.462
MINOR LEAGUE TOTALS			.291	460	1699	295	494	107	15	35	206	187	232	112	.368	.433

11 Rajai Davis, of

Born: Oct. 19, 1980. **Ht.:** 5-11. **Wt.:** 188. **Bats:** B. **Throws:** R. **School:** Connecticut-Avery Point JC. **Career Transactions:** Selected by Pirates in 38th round of 2001 draft; signed June 26, 2001. **Signed by:** Charlie Sullivan.

Davis was a late-round draft pick who did not have much baseball experience. He has steadily improved and had a breakthrough season last year, winning the Carolina League batting title and leading the league in runs, hits and stolen bases. Davis has outstanding speed and has learned how to use it by bunting, working deep counts and becoming a good basestealer. He has good bat speed and makes consistent contact, showing more power from the left side and better contact from the right. He also plays a solid center field and has a decent arm. He doesn't have a lot of power, but his hand strength should help him find the gaps more often. Davis' routes can get sloppy in center field. He was older than most of the competition in high Class A and will get a good test this season in Double-A. If he continues to develop, he could settle in as the center fielder and leadoff hitter in Pittsburgh in 2007.

Year	Club (League)	Class	AVG	G	AB	R	H	2B	3B	HR	RBI	BB	SO	SB	OBP	SLG
2001	Williamsprt (NY-P)	A	.083	6	12	1	1	0	0	0	0	2	4	0	.214	.083
	Pirates (GCL)	R	.262	26	84	19	22	1	0	0	4	13	26	11	.364	.274
2002	Pirates (GCL)	R	.384	58	224	38	86	16	5	4	35	20	25	24	.436	.554
	Williamsprt (NY-P)	A	.000	1	4	0	0	0	0	0	0	0	1	0	.000	.000
	Hickory (SAL)	A	.429	6	14	4	6	0	0	0	3	6	2	2	.619	.429
2003	Hickory (SAL)	A	.305	125	478	84	146	21	7	6	54	55	65	40	.383	.416
2004	Lynchburg (Car)	A	.314	127	509	91	160	27	7	5	38	59	60	57	.388	.424
MINOR LEAGUE TOTALS			.318	349	1325	237	421	65	19	15	134	155	183	134	.393	.429

12 Jose Bautista, 3b

Born: Oct. 19, 1980. **Ht.:** 6-0. **Wt.:** 190. **Bats:** R. **Throws:** R. **School:** Chipola (Fla.) JC. **Career Transactions:** Selected in 20th round of 2000 draft by Pirates; signed May 19, 2001 . . . Selected by Orioles from Pirates in major league Rule 5 draft, Dec. 15, 2003 . . . Designated for assignment by Orioles May 25, 2004 . . . Claimed on waivers by Devil Rays, June 3, 2004 . . . Sold to Royals, June 28, 2004 . . . Traded by

Royals to Mets for C Justin Huber, July 30, 2004 . . . Traded by Mets with 3B Ty Wigginton and RHP Matt Peterson to Pirates for RHP Kris Benson and 2B Jeff Keppinger, July 30, 2004. **Signed by:** Jack Powell.

Bautista had an interesting 2004 season that ended with him back in his original organization after the three-team Kris Benson deadline deal. Bautista hit a combined .205-0-2 in 88 big league at-bats last year, but he has a quick bat with the potential to hit for both power and average. He is a good athlete and could become an above-average defender at either third base or center field with his plus range and strong arm. He hasn't played much the last two seasons, held back by a broken hand in 2003 and seeing limited action as a major league Rule 5 draft pick last year. Bautista also needs to stay under control, as he broke his right hand while punching a garbage can. He will likely start this season at Double-A and get much-needed at-bats. Bautista figures to get back to the major leagues in 2006 or 2007.

Year	Club (League)	Class	AVG	G	AB	R	H	2B	3B	HR	RBI	BB	SO	SB	OBP	SLG
2001	Williamsprt (NY-P)	A	.286	62	220	43	63	10	3	5	30	21	41	8	.364	.427
2002	Hickory (SAL)	A	.301	129	438	72	132	26	3	14	57	67	104	3	.402	.470
2003	Lynchburg (Car)	A	.242	51	165	28	40	14	2	4	20	27	48	1	.359	.424
	Pirates (GCL)	R	.348	7	23	5	8	1	0	1	3	4	7	0	.429	.522
2004	Baltimore (AL)	MAJ	.273	16	11	3	3	0	0	0	0	1	3	0	.333	.273
	Tampa Bay (AL)	MAJ	.167	12	12	1	2	0	0	0	0	3	7	0	.333	.167
	Kansas City (AL)	MAJ	.200	13	25	1	5	1	0	0	1	1	12	0	.231	.240
	Pittsburgh (NL)	MAJ	.200	23	40	1	8	2	0	0	0	2	18	0	.238	.250
MAJOR LEAGUE TOTALS			.205	64	88	6	18	3	0	0	2	7	40	0	.263	.239
MINOR LEAGUE TOTALS			.287	249	846	148	243	51	8	24	110	119	200	12	.385	.452

13 Freddy Sanchez, 2b/ss

Born: Dec. 21, 1977. **Ht.:** 5-11. **Wt.:** 180. **Bats:** R. **Throws:** R. **School:** Oklahoma City University. **Career Transactions:** Selected by Red Sox in 11th round of 2000 draft; signed June 14, 2000 . . . Traded by Red Sox with LHP Mike Gonzalez and cash to Pirates for RHP Jeff Suppan, RHP Brandon Lyon and RHP Anastacio Martinez, July 31, 2003. **Signed by:** Ernie Jacobs (Red Sox).

Sanchez was considered one of the Red Sox' best prospects when Boston sent him to the Pirates at the trade deadline in 2003. However, he played just one game with Triple-A Nashville before having a bone spur removed from his right ankle in November 2003, which also caused him to miss the first 2½ months of last season. Sanchez makes consistent contact and has hit for average at just about every stop of his career. He is an excellent bat handler who excels at the hit-and-run. He's also an intelligent player who makes up for a lack of pure athletic ability with smarts. He has little power, and his range and arm at the two middle-infield spots is only adequate, though he is surehanded. Sanchez was born with a clubfoot on his right leg, and though he has overcome it, it is cause for long-range concern. He will likely be the Pirates' utility infielder this season with his ability to play second, third and shortstop. Sanchez was considered the second baseman of the future at the time of the trade, but Jose Castillo now stands in his way after a decent rookie season in 2004.

Year	Club (League)	Class	AVG	G	AB	R	H	2B	3B	HR	RBI	BB	SO	SB	OBP	SLG
2000	Lowell (NY-P)	A	.288	34	132	24	38	13	2	1	14	9	16	2	.347	.439
	Augusta (SAL)	A	.303	30	109	17	33	7	0	0	15	11	19	4	.372	.367
2001	Sarasota (FSL)	A	.339	69	280	40	95	19	4	1	24	22	30	5	.388	.446
	Trenton (EL)	AA	.326	44	178	25	58	20	0	2	19	9	21	3	.363	.472
2002	Trenton (EL)	AA	.328	80	311	60	102	23	1	3	38	37	45	19	.403	.437
	Pawtucket (IL)	AAA	.301	45	183	25	55	10	1	4	28	12	21	5	.350	.432
	Boston (AL)	MAJ	.188	12	16	3	3	0	0	0	2	2	3	0	.278	.188
2003	Pawtucket (IL)	AAA	.341	58	211	46	72	17	0	5	25	31	36	8	.430	.493
	Boston (AL)	MAJ	.235	20	34	6	8	2	0	0	2	0	8	0	.235	.294
	Nashville (PCL)	AAA	.400	1	5	1	2	1	0	0	0	0	1	0	.400	.600
2004	Nashville (PCL)	AAA	.264	44	125	10	33	7	1	1	11	11	17	4	.326	.360
	Pittsburgh (NL)	MAJ	.158	9	19	2	3	0	0	0	2	0	3	0	.158	.158
MAJOR LEAGUE TOTALS			.203	41	69	11	14	2	0	0	6	2	14	0	.225	.232
MINOR LEAGUE TOTALS			.318	405	1534	248	488	117	9	17	174	142	206	50	.380	.439

14 Ryan Doumit, c

Born: April 3, 1981. **Ht.:** 6-0. **Wt.:** 190. **Bats:** B. **Throws:** R. **School:** Moses Lake (Wash.) HS. **Career Transactions:** Selected by Pirates in second round of 1999 draft; signed June 16, 1999. **Signed by:** James House.

Injuries have dogged Doumit throughout his professional career, as he has played 100 games in a season only once in six years. A sore elbow limited him to DH after June 2 last season, and he did not play at all after July 24. Doumit has outstanding gap power and is beginning to hit balls over the fence. He has improved defensively over the years, both with his throwing and footwork behind the plate. Staying healthy has been a major problem, but the Pirates were encouraged that he did not need elbow surgery last season. While Doumit has a good bat, almost all of his power comes from the left side. He has hit 28 of his 30 professional home runs off righthanders, suggesting that he might want to abandon switch-hitting. He will begin this season in Triple-A despite having his season cut short last year. More than anything, Doumit needs to play a full season. If he makes strides this year, he would be in line to win at least a backup job in the major leagues in 2006.

Year	Club (League)	Class	AVG	G	AB	R	H	2B	3B	HR	RBI	BB	SO	SB	OBP	SLG
1999	Pirates (GCL)	R	.282	29	85	17	24	5	0	1	7	15	14	4	.410	.376
2000	Williamsprt (NY-P)	A	.313	66	246	25	77	15	5	2	40	23	33	2	.371	.439
2001	Hickory (SAL)	A	.270	39	148	14	40	6	0	2	14	10	32	2	.333	.351
	Pirates (GCL)	R	.235	7	17	2	4	2	0	0	3	2	0	0	.316	.353
	Altoona (EL)	AA	.250	2	4	0	1	0	0	0	2	1	1	0	.400	.250
2002	Hickory (SAL)	A	.322	68	258	46	83	14	1	6	47	18	40	3	.377	.453
2003	Lynchburg (Car)	A	.275	127	458	75	126	38	1	11	77	45	79	4	.351	.434
2004	Altoona (EL)	AA	.262	67	221	31	58	20	0	10	34	21	49	0	.343	.489
MINOR LEAGUE TOTALS			.287	405	1437	210	413	100	7	32	224	135	248	15	.360	.434

15 Steve Lerud, c

Born: Oct. 13, 1984. **Ht.:** 6-1. **Wt.:** 205. **Bats:** L. **Throws:** R. **School:** Galena HS, Reno, Nev. **Career Transactions:** Selected by Pirates in fourth round of 2003 draft; Signed June 29, 2003. **Signed by:** Jaron Madison.

Lerud hit 60 home runs in his high school career to set the Nevada state prep record. He wasn't able to start his professional career after signing in 2003 because of a broken foot, and he stayed behind in extended spring training last season in an attempt to help him make up for lost time on the field. He has a good lefthanded power stroke and could be capable of hitting 20 home runs a season. Lerud is solid behind the plate, moves well and shows a good arm. He is also a willing learner and has a good work ethic. At the plate, he is prone to striking out with his big swing, though he is likely to cut down on the whiffs with more experience. He is also a slow runner. Lerud will spend this season in low Class A and share catching and DH duties with Neil Walker, the Pirates' first-round draft pick last year. While Walker is a candidate to change positions, Lerud's ticket to the major leagues will be at catcher.

Year	Club (League)	Class	AVG	G	AB	R	H	2B	3B	HR	RBI	BB	SO	SB	OBP	SLG
2004	Pirates (GCL)	R	.246	48	175	22	43	12	1	5	20	11	38	0	.297	.411
	Williamsport (NY-P)	A	.241	8	29	2	7	0	0	0	2	4	6	0	.353	.241
MINOR LEAGUE TOTALS			.245	56	204	24	50	12	1	5	22	15	44	0	.305	.387

16 Chris Duffy, of

Born: April 20, 1980. **Ht.:** 5-10. **Wt.:** 183. **Bats:** S. **Throws:** L. **School:** Arizona State University. **Career Transactions:** Selected by Pirates in eighth round of 2001 draft; signed June 8, 2001. **Signed by:** Ted Williams.

Duffy was an all-Pacific-10 Conference selection at Arizona State and hit .300 in each of his first two professional seasons. After slipping to .274 in Double-A in 2003, he repeated the level last year and finished among the Eastern League leaders in batting, runs, hits and stolen bases. He is an outstanding defensive center fielder who covers both gaps and has an above-average arm. Duffy hits for average and battles pitchers. He has good speed and has stolen 117 bases in his four pro seasons, but he strikes out far too much and walks far too little for a leadoff hitter, though he improved last season. He also needs to work on bunting and keeping the ball on the ground. A sprained wrist kept Duffy from playing in the Arizona Fall League, but the injury wasn't considered serious and he should be the leadoff hitter and center fielder in Triple-A this year. He's on the doorstep of the major leagues, and plate discipline will likely decide whether he becomes a starter or fourth outfielder.

Year	Club (League)	Class	AVG	G	AB	R	H	2B	3B	HR	RBI	BB	SO	SB	OBP	SLG
2001	Williamsport (NY-P)	A	.321	64	218	47	70	12	4	1	23	32	33	29	.442	.427
2002	Lynchburg (Car)	A	.301	132	539	85	162	27	5	10	52	33	101	22	.353	.425
2003	Altoona (EL)	AA	.273	137	494	84	135	23	6	1	42	44	78	34	.355	.350
2004	Altoona (EL)	AA	.309	113	453	84	140	23	6	8	41	33	77	32	.378	.439
MINOR LEAGUE TOTALS			.298	446	1704	300	507	85	21	20	158	142	289	117	.372	.407

17 Eddie Prasch, 3b

Born: Jan. 25, 1986. **Ht.:** 6-1. **Wt.:** 180. **Bats:** L. **Throws:** R. **School:** Milton HS, Alpharetta, Ga. **Career Transactions:** Selected by Pirates in third round of 2004 draft; signed July 3, 2004. **Signed by:** Jack Powell.

Prasch was an Atlanta-area high school standout and Pirates scouting director Ed Creech, who lives in Georgia, saw him often last spring. Prasch hit 13 homers and drove in 52 runs to lead Alpharetta High to the state 5-A title, but he struggled in his first taste of professional baseball after signing for $500,000. He has one above-average tool, and that's his bat. Scouts rated it behind only that of Rockies first-rounder Chris Nelson among Georgia high schoolers. Prasch is a line-drive hitter who uses the whole field and handles lefthanded pitching well for a young lefthanded hitter. He also has an outstanding feel for the game. Moved from shortstop to third base when he entered pro ball, Prasch has yet to show the power expected from a corner infielder. He should add pop as his body matures. He has made the transition to third smoothly and has good hands and an average arm. He's an average runner. The Pirates will take it slow with him, and he almost certainly will begin 2005 in extended spring training. Prasch is likely to repeat the Rookie-level Gulf Coast League to begin with, and the Pirates are willing to be patient and wait for his bat to develop.

Year	Club (League)	Class	AVG	G	AB	R	H	2B	3B	HR	RBI	BB	SO	SB	OBP	SLG
2004	Pirates (GCL)	R	.220	32	118	11	26	6	2	0	21	12	27	1	.301	.305
MINOR LEAGUE TOTALS			.220	32	118	11	26	6	2	0	21	12	27	1	.301	.305

18 Blair Johnson, rhp

Born: March 25, 1984. **Ht.:** 6-4. **Wt.:** 210. **Bats:** R. **Throws:** R. **School:** Washburn HS, Topeka, Kan. **Career Transactions:** Selected by Pirates in second round of 2002 draft; signed June 24, 2002. **Signed by:** Jim Rough.

The Pirates drafted Johnson as a raw high school pitcher, and he may have been more raw than they thought. He began last season in low Class A but was sent back to extended spring training after allowing four earned runs or more in six of his nine starts. Johnson finished strong at Williamsport, winning his last six decisions in eight starts. He has a big, athletic body and easily throws his sinking fastball at 94-95 mph, and he could add velocity once his body fills out. He showed a good slider in high school, though he hasn't used it as a pro because the Pirates have wanted him to develop his fastball and curveball. Johnson doesn't strike out as many hitters as he should with his lively fastball, which is cause for concern. He struggles to command his curveball and needs to develop better poise and presence on the mound. He'll get another shot at full-season ball at Hickory this season, and how he handles it will be telling. He remains a project whose raw ability makes him intriguing.

Year	Club (League)	Class	W	L	ERA	G	GS	CG	SV	IP	H	R	ER	HR	BB	SO	AVG
2002	Pirates (GCL)	R	0	1	8.10	2	1	0	0	3	4	6	3	0	3	4	.286
2003	Pirates (GCL)	R	4	1	1.34	9	9	0	0	47	32	9	7	2	11	42	.188
	Hickory (SAL)	A	1	1	8.71	2	2	0	0	10	11	10	10	0	3	7	.282
2004	Hickory (SAL)	A	1	4	7.83	9	8	0	0	44	59	40	38	7	14	22	.331
	Williamsport (NY-P)	A	6	1	2.44	14	14	2	0	89	62	34	24	2	12	40	.197
MINOR LEAGUE TOTALS			12	8	3.82	36	34	2	0	193	168	99	82	11	43	115	.235

19 Cory Stewart, lhp

Born: Nov. 14, 1979. **Ht.:** 6-4. **Wt.:** 200. **Bats:** L. **Throws:** L. **School:** Boerne (Texas) HS. **Career Transactions:** Selected by Reds in 27th round of 1998 draft; signed Aug. 17, 1998 . . . Released by Reds, March 24, 2001 . . . Signed by independent Amarillo (Texas-Louisiana), May 2001 . . . Signed by Padres, Oct. 15, 2001 . . . Traded by Padres to Pirates, Oct. 2, 2003, completing trade in which Pirates sent OF Brian Giles to Padres for LHP Oliver Perez, OF Jason Bay and a player to be named (Aug. 26, 2003). **Signed by:** Johnny Almaraz (Reds).

Stewart was the player to be named in the late-season 2003 trade that shipped Brian Giles to San Diego. While Jason Bay won the National League rookie of the year last season and Oliver Perez developed into a promising big league starter, Stewart struggled in Triple-A as he was hindered by a strained muscle in his side that sidelined him for six weeks at midseason. When healthy, he can be overpowering, with a fastball that reaches 94 mph and sits at 88-92 with good movement. Stewart has a big-breaking curveball that can be tough on lefthanded hitters. He lost velocity and the snap on his curve last season because of his injury, and he has a tendency to hang the curveball at times, which leads to home runs. He also needs to improve his changeup to give him a third pitch to keep hitters honest. Stewart will go back to Triple-A after his frustrating 2004 season and pitch in the rotation. If he stays healthy, there is a good chance he will make his major league debut sometime in 2005.

Year	Club (League)	Class	W	L	ERA	G	GS	CG	SV	IP	H	R	ER	HR	BB	SO	AVG
1999	Billings (Pio)	R	2	0	3.14	10	10	0	0	49	50	25	17	2	21	37	.263
2000	Did not play—Injured																
2001	Amarillo (T-L)	IND	6	6	5.39	22	20	3	0	120	132	87	72	9	67	107	.276
2002	Fort Wayne (Mid)	A	6	3	2.39	17	11	0	0	64	46	21	17	4	18	86	.198
	Lake Elsinore (Cal)	A	5	3	3.20	12	12	0	0	65	60	29	23	3	29	69	.251
2003	Mobile (SL)	AA	12	7	3.72	24	24	0	0	126	104	60	52	10	50	133	.222
2004	Nashville (PCL)	AAA	7	6	5.13	18	18	0	0	93	112	59	53	11	47	53	.302
MINOR LEAGUE TOTALS			32	19	3.68	81	75	0	0	396	372	194	162	30	165	378	.248

20 Brian Bixler, ss

Born: Oct. 22, 1982. **Ht.:** 6-1. **Wt.:** 188. **Bats:** R. **Throws:** R. **School:** Eastern Michigan University. **Career Transactions:** Selected by Pirates in second round of 2004 draft; signed June 25, 2004. **Signed by:** Duane Gustavson.

Bixler finished second in NCAA Division I with a .453 average last season for Eastern Michigan, and he put up a .520 on-base percentage. That enabled him to erase the doubts that cropped up after he hit just .120 in the Cape Cod League the previous summer. Bixler has plus speed and uses it well as a baserunner and basestealer. He's athletic and shows good quickness in the field, particularly with his feet. He plays hard all the time and exhibits great hustle and desire, the sign of an overachiever. Despite his gaudy college average, Bixler's bat is still a question in professional baseball. He strikes out too much for a player who relies on speed and needs to sharpen his eye at the plate. He has minimal power. Bixler could get to the major leagues quickly, and his bat will ultimately determine whether he is a starter or utility infielder. He will be the starting shortstop in low Class A to begin this season.

Year	Club (League)	Class	AVG	G	AB	R	H	2B	3B	HR	RBI	BB	SO	SB	OBP	SLG
2004	Williamsport (NY-P)	A	.276	59	228	40	63	7	4	0	21	15	51	14	.321	.342
MINOR LEAGUE TOTALS			.276	59	228	40	63	7	4	0	21	15	51	14	.321	.342

21 Javier Guzman, ss

Born: May 4, 1984. **Ht.:** 5-11. **Wt.:** 160. **Bats:** B. **Throws:** R. **Career Transactions:** Signed out of Dominican Republic by Pirates, Aug. 19, 2000. **Signed by:** Jose Luna.

Guzman has been considered one of the top shortstops in his league every season since making his debut in the United States in 2002. Hickory manager Dave Clark compared him to fellow Dominican shortstop Tony Fernandez last year. Guzman is an athletic player with good speed. He has the tools to be a good defensive shortstop, with the best infield arm in the system as well as good hands and range. But he is inconsistent in the field and often botches routine plays because of a lack of concentration. Guzman took up switch-hitting last season after being exclusively a righthanded hitter, and had a .312 average from the left side. He needs to hone his eye at the plate and read pitchers' moves better in order to take advantage of his speed. He has not handled adversity well so far in his career. Guzman will be the shortstop in high Class A this season. He is still raw and will need a fair amount of seasoning before reaching the major leagues, which probably won't be until at least 2007.

Year	Club (League)	Class	AVG	G	AB	R	H	2B	3B	HR	RBI	BB	SO	SB	OBP	SLG
2001	Pirates (DSL)	R	.209	57	206	30	43	4	3	0	15	27	49	23	.311	.257
2002	Pirates (GCL)	R	.307	50	199	42	61	6	6	5	20	12	25	13	.347	.472
2003	Williamsprt (NY-P)	A	.243	47	173	19	42	9	2	2	24	10	26	4	.283	.353
2004	Hickory (SAL)	A	.306	124	470	75	144	20	12	2	63	20	78	31	.334	.413
MINOR LEAGUE TOTALS			.277	278	1048	166	290	39	23	9	122	69	178	71	.323	.384

22 Bobby Bradley, rhp

Born: Dec. 15, 1980. **Ht.:** 6-1. **Wt.:** 180. **Bats:** R. **Throws:** R. **School:** Wellington (Fla.) Community HS. **Career Transactions:** Selected by Pirates in first round (eighth overall) of 1999 draft; signed July 7, 1999. **Signed by:** Rob Sidwell.

Bradley has had plenty of bad luck since being taken in the first round in 1999. He has gone through two elbow surgeries, including Tommy John in 2001, as well as a shoulder operation. Bradley was slowed by strained muscles in his shoulder and neck last season and has thrown just 317 minor league innings over five years. His best offering has always been his big-breaking curveball, and the pitch still has outstanding bite despite all of his physical woes. Bradley has improved his fastball over the years, and it now reaches 90-91 mph and has outstanding sinking action. He has problems getting his changeup over for strikes but is getting more consistent with it. Bradley is hesitant to pitch to contact at times and needs to have more faith in his stuff. He'll begin the season in the Triple-A rotation and should make his major league debut later in the year. He still has a chance to be a No. 3 or 4 starter, though his injury history suggests he may be better suited for middle relief in the long run.

Year	Club (League)	Class	W	L	ERA	G	GS	CG	SV	IP	H	R	ER	HR	BB	SO	AVG
1999	Pirates (GCL)	R	1	1	2.90	6	6	0	0	31	31	13	10	2	4	31	.258
2000	Hickory (SAL)	A	8	2	2.29	14	14	3	0	83	62	31	21	3	21	118	.203
2001	Lynchburg (Car)	A	1	2	3.12	9	9	0	0	49	44	23	17	3	20	46	.238
2002	Did not play—Injured																
2003	Lynchburg (Car)	A	3	2	3.40	12	12	0	0	50	43	21	19	1	28	36	.232
	Pirates (GCL)	R	0	0	0.00	1	1	0	0	3	1	0	0	0	1	4	.111
2004	Altoona (EL)	AA	5	4	3.11	19	19	0	0	101	85	42	35	8	41	78	.229
MINOR LEAGUE TOTALS			18	11	2.89	61	61	3	0	317	266	130	102	17	115	313	.226

23 Mike Johnston, lhp

Born: March 30, 1979. **Ht.:** 6-3. **Wt.:** 200. **Bats:** L. **Throws:** L. **School:** Garrett (Md.) CC. **Career Transactions:** Selected by Pirates in 20th round of 1998 draft; signed June 4, 1998. **Signed by:** Craig Kornfeld.

Johnston, along with Jim Eisenreich, are the only known players with Tourette's Syndrome to reach the major leagues. Johnston made the Pirates out of spring training last season after six years in the minor leagues. He did not allow a run in his first nine appearances, but then struggled and did not pitch in the majors after June 21 because of a sore elbow. Johnston went on an injury rehabilitation assignment to Triple-A on July 15 and spent the rest of the season there. He can be overpowering when healthy, with a fastball that tops out at 96 mph and routinely sits at 93-94. Johnston also has a hard, slurvy breaking ball that can be particularly tough on lefthanded hitters. He tends to be too slow in his delivery, which causes him to lose velocity and movement on his pitches. Johnston also needs to tighten up his breaking ball. He will compete for a major league bullpen job in spring training, and at worst begin the season at Triple-A. Johnston proved he can get major league hitters out last season, and now he needs to prove he can do it on a consistent basis.

Year	Club (League)	Class	W	L	ERA	G	GS	CG	SV	IP	H	R	ER	HR	BB	SO	AVG
1998	Pirates (GCL)	R	1	2	3.34	13	3	0	0	30	28	17	11	1	10	17	.248
	Erie (NY-P)	A	0	0	4.50	2	0	0	0	2	4	4	1	0	1	2	.364
1999	Williamsport (NY-P)	A	3	2	4.25	14	2	0	2	42	46	26	20	5	18	30	.267
2000	Hickory (SAL)	A	4	2	6.22	26	0	0	2	51	66	42	35	2	30	52	.320
2001	Lynchburg (Car)	A	4	4	3.34	11	10	1	0	62	66	27	23	2	24	44	.272
	Hickory (SAL)	A	4	5	3.38	16	16	0	0	93	88	47	35	5	42	80	.249
2002	Lynchburg (Car)	A	4	2	3.63	15	10	0	0	57	50	29	23	2	26	50	.230
2003	Altoona (EL)	AA	6	2	2.12	46	0	0	7	72	49	17	17	4	27	65	.199
2004	Pittsburgh (NL)	MAJ	0	3	4.37	24	0	0	0	23	29	16	11	2	15	18	.315
	Nashville (PCL)	AAA	0	0	8.40	19	0	0	0	15	19	14	14	3	13	6	.306
MAJOR LEAGUE TOTALS			0	3	4.37	24	0	0	0	23	29	16	11	2	15	18	.315
MINOR LEAGUE TOTALS			26	19	3.80	162	41	1	11	424	416	223	179	24	191	346	.256

24 Wardell Starling, rhp

Born: March 14, 1983. **Ht.:** 6-4. **Wt.:** 200. **Bats:** R. **Throws:** R. **School:** Odessa (Texas) CC. **Career Transactions:** Selected by Pirates in fourth round of 2002 draft; signed May 25, 2003. **Signed by:** Tom Barnard.

Starling was an outstanding two-way player in leading Elkins High in suburban Houston to a No. 1 final national ranking in 2002. He accepted a scholarship from San Diego State but decided to go the junior-college route instead, signing with the Pirates as a draft-and-follow in 2003. Starling finished second in the low Class A South Atlantic League in wins last season, winning seven straight decisions after starting the year 4-7. He has a big, strong body that is perfect for a pitcher. He also has good velocity, throwing his fastball consistently at 88-92 mph and occasionally touching 94. He has an advanced changeup for a young pitcher. Starling throws a curveball and slider but needs to become much more consistent with both pitches. He tends to lose concentration from time to time and needs to develop better mound presence. He also needs to brush up on the finer points of pitching such as holding runners and fielding his position. He has plenty of upside as a starter and the Pirates won't rush him. He'll move up to high Class A and probably won't see the major leagues until 2007 or 2008.

Year	Club (League)	Class	W	L	ERA	G	GS	CG	SV	IP	H	R	ER	HR	BB	SO	AVG
2003	Pirates (GCL)	R	4	1	3.94	11	11	0	0	48	47	23	21	5	13	52	.247
2004	Hickory (SAL)	A	11	8	4.11	26	26	1	0	140	133	84	64	10	51	114	.249
MINOR LEAGUE TOTALS			15	9	4.07	37	37	1	0	188	180	107	85	15	64	166	.249

25 Joe Bauserman, rhp

Born: Oct. 4, 1985. **Ht.:** 6-2. **Wt.:** 220. **Bats:** R. **Throws:** R. **School:** Lincoln HS, Tallahassee, Fla. **Career Transactions:** Selected by Pirates in fourth round of 2004 draft; signed June 17, 2004. **Signed by:** Rob Sidwell.

Like fellow Pirates prospect J.R. House, Bauserman was a two-sport star in high school who played in different states to maximize his exposure. Bauserman moved from Winchester, Va., to Tallahassee, Fla., in order to face better competition, and it paid off with a football scholarship to play quarterback at Ohio State. He passed up the chance to play for the Buckeyes and signed for a $300,000 bonus as a fourth-round pick last June. Befitting a big-time quarterback recruit, Bauserman has a strong arm. His fastball was clocked as high as 97 mph during his senior season of high school but was mainly 89-91 mph during his first taste of professional baseball as he wore down. He also has a good change of pace with an above-average curveball and a potentially outstanding changeup. He has a somewhat soft body and needs to build strength in order to maintain the velocity on his fastball. Bauserman's curveball has a sharp downward break but it won't become a plus pitch unless he commands it more consistently. He will either begin this season in low Class A or extended spring training, depending on how he fares this spring. Bauserman is a talented but raw prospect and likely won't reach the major leagues until at least 2008.

Year	Club (League)	Class	W	L	ERA	G	GS	CG	SV	IP	H	R	ER	HR	BB	SO	AVG
2004	Pirates (GCL)	R	2	2	2.79	9	8	0	0	39	26	13	12	4	10	35	.187
MINOR LEAGUE TOTALS			2	2	2.79	9	8	0	0	39	26	13	12	4	10	35	.187

26 Craig Stansberry, 2b

Born: March 8, 1982. **Ht.:** 6-0. **Wt.:** 182. **Bats:** R. **Throws:** R. **School:** Rice University. **Career Transactions:** Selected by Pirates in fifth round of 2003 draft; signed July 1, 2003. **Signed by:** Tom Barnard.

Stansberry has done nothing but win the last two years. He was part of Rice's College World Series championship team in 2003, then won a short-season New York-Penn League championship later that year after turning pro. He played a key role in Hickory's South Atlantic League title run last season. Stansberry does not have great tools, but his instincts are superb. He hits for average and decent power and has a knack for delivering in the clutch, hitting .362 with runners in scoring position last season. His speed is just a tick above-average, yet he gets his fair share of stolen bases. Stansberry also made a smooth transition from third base to second base last season. He has sure hands and a strong arm, and the Pirates consider him the system's best defensive infielder. He'll need to hit with more pop if he is to continue to move up the organizational ladder. He missed a month with a jammed left wrist last season and that bears watching. Stansberry could get to the major leagues quickly, perhaps by late 2006. Even if Stanberry doesn't become a regular in the major leagues, he would figure to have a career as a utility player.

Year	Club (League)	Class	AVG	G	AB	R	H	2B	3B	HR	RBI	BB	SO	SB	OBP	SLG
2003	Williamsport (NY-P)	A	.307	45	166	19	51	9	3	2	21	13	25	5	.370	.434
2004	Hickory (SAL)	A	.286	106	391	57	112	14	5	9	67	52	88	20	.377	.417
MINOR LEAGUE TOTALS			.293	151	557	76	163	23	8	11	88	65	113	25	.375	.422

27 Russell Johnson, rhp

Born: Jan. 6, 1985. **Ht.:** 6-2. **Wt.:** 200. **Bats:** L. **Throws:** R. **School:** Benjamin Russell HS, Alexander City, Ala. **Career Transactions:** Selected by Pirates in seventh round of 2003 draft; signed June 4, 2003. **Signed by:** Everett Russell.

Johnson's career got off to a slow start, as he pitched just once in Rookie ball in 2003 before having surgery to remove his gall bladder. He stayed back in extended spring training last year but wound up getting a taste of full-season ball at high Class A late in the season, when Lynchburg had injury problems. Johnson has good pure stuff, most notably a fastball with good late life that reaches 95 mph and he routinely throws at 92-93. He also has an outstanding curveball with a sharp downward bite. Johnson has a sturdy body, giving him the look of a durable, innings-eating starter. He needs to refine his changeup quite a bit, to give him something to keep hitters off his fastball and curve. Johnson also needs to pile up innings after missing so much time because of his gall bladder operation. He likely won't be on the fast track since he has his share of rough spots to smooth out. He'll begin this season in low Class A and doesn't figure to reach the major leagues until late 2008.

Year	Club (League)	Class	W	L	ERA	G	GS	CG	SV	IP	H	R	ER	HR	BB	SO	AVG
2003	Pirates (GCL)	R	0	0	0.00	1	1	0	0	3	0	0	0	0	0	4	.000
2004	Pirates (GCL)	R	1	2	4.53	13	9	0	0	46	42	24	23	3	15	50	.253
	Lynchburg (Car)	A	0	1	10.32	3	3	0	0	11	18	14	13	2	3	11	.367
MINOR LEAGUE TOTALS			1	3	5.40	17	13	0	0	60	60	38	36	5	18	65	.268

28 Jason Quarles, rhp

Born: April 20, 1983. **Ht.:** 6-1. **Wt.:** 190. **Bats:** R. **Throws:** R. **School:** Southern University. **Career Transactions:** Selected by Pirates in seventh round of 2004 draft; signed June 11, 2004. **Signed by:** Everett Russell.

Quarles completed an improbable rise last year by getting drafted, and now he'll try to complete the story by reaching the major leagues. Southern recruited him as an outfielder from Glen Oaks (Mich.) Community College, but he failed to crack the lineup in the seventh round. He was then converted to a pitcher and wound up being drafted in the seventh round. He has a sizzling fastball that was routinely clocked at 98 mph last spring in college and 96 in his first taste of professional ball, though he controls it better when he throws at 91-93. Quarles also has a devastating curveball with a 12-to-6 break that he throws with maximum effort. His curve and his size have drawn him frequent Tom Gordon comparisons. He has little pitching experience and needs to smooth out his mechanics. He has almost no experience pitching out of the windup or throwing a changeup, though that doesn't come into play much as a reliever. Quarles will begin this season in low Class A and still has a lot of work to do. Though his future is in the bullpen, the Pirates may use him as a starter to give him more innings. If he adapts well, his live arm could get him to the major leagues quickly.

Year	Club (League)	Class	W	L	ERA	G	GS	CG	SV	IP	H	R	ER	HR	BB	SO	AVG
2004	Williamsport (NY-P)	A	0	4	3.47	23	0	0	0	23	30	15	9	1	18	30	.294
MINOR LEAGUE TOTALS			0	4	3.47	23	0	0	0	23	30	15	9	1	18	30	.294

29 J.R. House, c/1b

Born: Nov. 11, 1979. **Ht.:** 5-10. **Wt.:** 202. **Bats:** R. **Throws:** R. **School:** Seabreeze HS, Daytona Beach, Fla. **Career Transactions:** Selected by Pirates in fifth round of 1999 draft; signed June 12, 1999. **Signed by:** Rob Sidwell.

House was ranked as the Pirates' top prospect in 2001 and 2002 before his career was derailed by reconstructive elbow surgery and two sports hernia operations. He was healthy for the first time in three years last season, except for a stint on the disabled list at Triple-A after he sprained his ankle in a collision at home plate. House's best attribute is his ability to hit for average and power. He has improved his defense as a catcher in recent years and became more adept at calling pitches. He has an outstanding work ethic and positive attitude, which has kept him going through adversity. Despite improvement, his throwing and receiving skills behind the plate may prevent him from being a full-time catcher in the major leagues, so he began playing some first base and left field last season. He is also a very slow runner. House is out of minor league options, so the Pirates must make a decision on him during spring training. With a good spring, he should be a reserve in the major leagues this season, playing primarily against lefthanders after hitting .360 against them at Nashville last season.

Year	Club (League)	Class	AVG	G	AB	R	H	2B	3B	HR	RBI	BB	SO	SB	OBP	SLG
1999	Pirates (GCL)	R	.327	33	113	13	37	9	3	5	23	11	23	1	.394	.593
	Williamsport (NY-P)	A	.300	26	100	11	30	6	0	1	13	9	21	0	.358	.390
	Hickory (SAL)	A	.273	4	11	1	3	0	0	0	0	0	3	0	.273	.273
2000	Hickory (SAL)	A	.348	110	420	78	146	29	1	23	90	46	91	1	.414	.586
2001	Altoona (EL)	AA	.258	112	426	51	110	25	1	11	56	37	103	1	.323	.399
2002	Altoona (EL)	AA	.264	30	91	9	24	6	0	2	11	13	21	0	.349	.396
	Pirates (GCL)	R	.313	5	16	3	5	2	0	1	2	3	1	0	.421	.625
2003	Pirates (GCL)	R	.400	20	65	16	26	9	0	4	23	12	5	0	.476	.723
	Altoona (EL)	AA	.333	20	63	12	21	6	0	2	11	5	11	0	.382	.524
	Pittsburgh (NL)	MAJ	.000	1	1	0	1	0	0	0	0	0	0	0	1.000	1.000
2004	Nashville (PCL)	AAA	.288	92	309	38	89	21	1	15	49	23	72	1	.344	.508
	Pittsburgh (NL)	MAJ	.111	5	9	1	1	1	0	0	0	0	2	0	.111	.222
MAJOR LEAGUE TOTALS			.200	6	10	1	2	1	0	0	0	0	2	0	.200	.300
MINOR LEAGUE TOTALS			.304	452	1614	232	491	113	6	64	278	159	351	4	.370	.501

30 Jeff Miller, rhp

Born: Feb. 1, 1980. **Ht.:** 6-4. **Wt.:** 220. **Bats:** R. **Throws:** R. **School:** University of New Orleans. **Career Transactions:** Selected by Pirates in 15th round of 2001 draft; signed June 13, 2001. **Signed by:** Dana Brown.

Miller was primarily an outfielder in college, first at Rutgers, then New Orleans. The Pirates drafted him as a pitcher and immediately converted him into a short reliever. Miller's greatest attribute as a reliever is his aggressiveness. He has no fear of any situation and attacks hitters. His fastball is in the 90-92 mph range, but he consistently throws it for strikes and works both sides of the plate with it. He also has a good slider with a quick, late break. Miller lacks the experience of most pitchers his age because of his college background and because he was used in relief in pro ball. He doesn't have a good feel for a changeup, though that is not a major factor with him working out of the bullpen. Miller had a fine Arizona Fall League after spending the second half of last season as a closer in Double-A. He will likely share closing duties with veteran Mark Corey in Triple-A this season and has a good chance of making his major league debut later in the year.

Year	Club (League)	Class	W	L	ERA	G	GS	CG	SV	IP	H	R	ER	HR	BB	SO	AVG
2001	Williamsport (NY-P)	A	0	0	1.13	21	0	0	15	24	17	3	3	1	5	28	.198
2002	Hickory (SAL)	A	13	5	3.75	31	15	0	4	103	100	44	43	11	28	75	.253
2003	Lynchburg (Car)	A	5	6	4.88	27	7	1	0	76	89	51	41	4	25	59	.302
2004	Altoona (EL)	AA	5	4	2.91	52	0	0	18	68	48	25	22	8	28	79	.198
MINOR LEAGUE TOTALS			23	15	3.62	131	22	1	37	271	254	123	109	24	86	241	.249

ST. LOUIS
CARDINALS

BY **WILL LINGO**

U ntil they ran into a team of destiny in the World Series and got swept by the Red Sox, the Cardinals had a dream season in 2004.

The offense was the most potent in the National League, leading the league in both average and runs. And a pitching staff that was considered a question mark when the season began finished behind only the Braves in the NL with a 3.75 ERA. The result was 105 wins and a runaway in the NL Central, as well as the team's first trip to the World Series since 1987.

Aside from Albert Pujols, St. Louis had few significant contributors who were produced by the farm system. Pujols and So Taguchi—a veteran player signed after playing several years in Japan—were the only everyday players originally signed by the organization, though **Yadier Molina** stepped in as backup catcher and should take over the starting job in 2005. On the pitching staff, Dan Haren and Matt Morris were the only players with at least 45 innings who started their careers with the Cardinals.

While St. Louis hasn't incorporated homegrown talent into its major league roster, it has skillfully used prospects in deals to bolster the big league club. Key 2004 contributors such as Jim Edmonds, Edgar Renteria, Scott Rolen and Woody Williams came over in trades. General manager Walt Jocketty made another blockbuster last summer, sending three minor leaguers to the Rockies for Larry Walker. He followed it up with an even bigger deal after the season, recognizing that the pitching staff, while solid, lacked an ace. So he sent the organization's best hitting prospect, catcher Daric Barton, along with Haren and Kiko Calero to the Athletics for Mark Mulder. Mulder clearly strengthens the pitching staff, but the trade took away another premium prospect from a system with precious few of them. The organization has also been hurt by injuries to its prospects over the years, particularly pitchers.

Trades and injuries aren't the only reason the system is thin, however. The Cardinals haven't been satisfied with their production from the draft, so they overhauled the scouting department for 2004. Assistant GM John Mozeliak took leadership of the department, and St. Louis hired Jeff Luhnow as vice president of baseball development to assist their scouting efforts with improved technology. The new approach was said to mimic the Athletics, but in truth the Cardinals have always leaned toward college players in the draft. The lean became even more pronounced in 2004, however, with St. Louis drafting just four high school players out of 47 picks and signing none of them.

Mozeliak said the Cardinals didn't exclude high school players from their scouting, but wanted advanced players who could add immediate depth. Early returns indicate they did get players who will patch holes in the minors, but few who could be significant big leaguers.

TOP 30 PROSPECTS

1. Anthony Reyes, rhp	16. Mark Michael, rhp
2. Adam Wainwright, rhp	17. Mike Parisi, rhp
3. Blake Hawksworth, rhp	18. Travis Hanson, 2b/3b
4. Chris Lambert, rhp	19. John Gall, of/1b
5. Stuart Pomeranz, rhp	20. Skip Schumaker, of
6. Brad Thompson, rhp	21. Eric Haberer, lhp
7. Brendan Ryan, ss	22. John Nelson, ss
8. Chris Duncan, 1b	23. Rhett Parrott, rhp
9. Cody Haerther, of	24. Mark Worrell, rhp
10. Carmen Cali, lhp	25. Calvin Hayes, 2b
11. Reid Gorecki, of	26. Gabe Johnson, 3b/c
12. Mike Ferris, 1b	27. Jose Delgado, 2b
13. Brandon Yarbrough, c	28. Brandon DeJaynes, rhp
14. Donnie Smith, rhp	29. Jimmy Journell, rhp
15. Juan Lucena, ss	30. Andy Schutzenhofer, 1b

ORGANIZATION OVERVIEW

General manager: Walt Jocketty. **Farm director:** Bruce Manno. **Scouting director:** John Mozeliak.

2004 PERFORMANCE

Class	Team	League	W	L	Pct.	Finish*	Manager
Majors	St. Louis	National	105	57	.648	1st (16)	Tony La Russa
Triple-A	Memphis Redbirds	Pacific Coast	73	71	.507	8th (16)	Danny Sheaffer
Double-A	#Tennessee Smokies	Southern	69	71	.493	6th (10)	Mark DeJohn
High A	Palm Beach Cardinals	Florida State	73	61	.545	6th (12)	Tom Nieto
Low A	@Peoria Chiefs	Midwest	75	64	.540	t-4th (14)	Joe Cunningham
Short-Season	New Jersey Cardinals	New York-Penn	41	34	.547	5th (14)	Tommy Shields
Rookie	Johnson City Cardinals	Appalachian	33	35	.485	5th (10)	Tom Kidwell
OVERALL 2004 MINOR LEAGUE RECORD			364	336	.520	8th (30)	

*Finish in overall standings (No. of teams in league). #Affiliate will be in Springfield (Texas) in 2005. @Affiliate will be in Quad Cities (Midwest) in 2005.

ORGANIZATION LEADERS

BATTING
*Minimum 250 at-bats

*AVG	Brendan Ryan, Peoria	.322
R	Anthony Monegan, Peoria	97
H	Skip Schumaker, Tennessee	163
TB	Kevin Witt, Memphis	286
2B	John Gall, Memphis	34
3B	Anthony Monegan, Peoria	9
HR	Kevin Witt, Memphis	36
RBI	Kevin Witt, Memphis	107
BB	Daric Barton, Peoria	69
SO	Terry Evans, Palm Beach/Peoria	121
SB	Papo Bolivar, Tennessee	51
*OBP	Daric Barton, Peoria	.445
*SLG	Kevin Witt, Memphis	.600

PITCHING
#Minimum 75 innings

W	Stuart Pomeranz, Peoria	12
L	Luis Martinez, Memphis/Tennessee	12
	Kyle McClellan, Peoria	12
#ERA	Anthony Rawson, Memphis/Palm Beach	2.08
G	Josh Kinney, Tennessee/Palm Beach	57
CG	Tyler Adamczyk, Palm Beach	3
	Jordan Pals, Palm Beach/Peoria	3
SV	Al Reyes, Memphis	23
IP	Buddy Blair, Tennessee/Palm Beach	171
BB	Alan Benes, Memphis	79
SO	Dan Haren, Memphis	150

BEST TOOLS

Best Hitter for Average	Cody Haerther
Best Power Hitter	Chris Duncan
Best Strike-Zone Discipline	John Gall
Fastest Baserunner	Matt Lemanczyk
Best Athlete	Brendan Ryan
Best Fastball	Anthony Reyes
Best Curveball	Adam Wainwright
Best Slider	Justin Garza
Best Changeup	Blake Hawksworth
Best Control	Brad Thompson
Best Defensive Catcher	Jason Motte
Best Defensive Infielder	Travis Hanson
Best Infield Arm	John Nelson
Best Defensive Outfielder	Reid Gorecki
Best Outfield Arm	Skip Schumaker

PROJECTED 2008 LINEUP

Catcher	Yadier Molina
First Base	Albert Pujols
Second Base	Brendan Ryan
Third Base	Scott Rolen
Shortstop	Hector Luna
Left Field	Jim Edmonds
Center Field	Reid Gorecki

Right Field	Cody Haerther
No. 1 Starter	Anthony Reyes
No. 2 Starter	Chris Carpenter
No. 3 Starter	Jason Marquis
No. 4 Starter	Matt Morris
No. 5 Starter	Adam Wainwright
Closer	Chris Lambert

LAST YEAR'S TOP 20 PROSPECTS

1. Blake Hawksworth, rhp
2. Adam Wainwright, rhp
3. Chris Narveson, rhp
4. Yadier Molina, c
5. Jimmy Journell, rhp
6. Travis Hanson, 3b
7. John Gall, 1b/of
8. Rhett Parrott, rhp
9. Hector Luna, ss
10. Daric Barton, c
11. Tyler Johnson, lhp
12. Shaun Boyd, of/2b
13. John Nelson, ss
14. Mark Michael, rhp
15. Stuart Pomeranz, rhp
16. Cody Haerther, of/3b
17. John Santor, 1b
18. Brendan Ryan, ss
19. Anthony Reyes, rhp
20. Josh Axelson, rhp

TOP PROSPECTS OF THE DECADE

Year	Player, Pos.	Current Team
1995	Alan Benes, rhp	Out of baseball
1996	Alan Benes, rhp	Out of baseball
1997	Matt Morris, rhp	Cardinals
1998	Rick Ankiel, lhp	Cardinals
1999	J.D. Drew, of	Dodgers
2000	Rick Ankiel, lhp	Cardinals
2001	Bud Smith, lhp	Phillies
2002	Jimmy Journell, rhp	Cardinals
2003	Dan Haren, rhp	Athletics
2004	Blake Hawksworth, rhp	Cardinals

TOP DRAFT PICKS OF THE DECADE

Year	Player, Pos.	Current Team
1995	Matt Morris, rhp	Cardinals
1996	Braden Looper, rhp	Mets
1997	Adam Kennedy, ss	Cardinals
1998	J.D. Drew, of	Dodgers
1999	Chance Caple, rhp	Cardinals
2000	Shaun Boyd, of	Cardinals
2001	Justin Pope, rhp	Yankees
2002	Calvin Hayes, ss (3)	Cardinals
2003	Daric Barton, c	Athletics
2004	Chris Lambert, rhp	Cardinals

ALL-TIME LARGEST BONUSES

J.D. Drew, 1998	$3,000,000
Rick Ankiel, 1997	$2,500,000
Chad Hutchinson, 1998	$2,300,000
Shaun Boyd, 2000	$1,750,000
Braden Looper, 1996	$1,675,000

MINOR LEAGUE DEPTH CHART

St. Louis CARDINALS

Impact Potential: D

The Cardinals have no potential impact bats in the minors. Of course, given their big league offense, they don't have much need for help. Anthony Reyes has frontline starter stuff, and Southern California pitchers have a good track record of success in pro ball, but Reyes has to prove he can stay healthy over an entire season. The Cardinals' pitching-heavy top 10 has been hit by injuries throughout the list.

Depth: F

The biggest reason the Cardinals sit last in our talent rankings, St. Louis' system has few players who even profile as big league reserves, not to mention regulars on a championship club. Few of the top position players have much power to speak of, and most of those who do have not played above Class A. The college-heavy 2004 draft appeared to be geared toward just filling holes in the farm system, as St. Louis signed 41 of its 47 selections.

*Depth charts prepared by **John Manuel** and **Allan Simpson**. Numbers in parentheses indicate prospect rankings.*

LF
Cody Haerther (9)
John Gall (19)
Shaun Boyd
Dee Haynes

CF
Reid Gorecki (11)
Skip Schumaker (20)

RF
Wes Swackhamer

3B
Gabe Johnson (26)
Jake Mullinax
Tony Granadillo

SS
Brendan Ryan (7)
Juan Lucena (15)
John Nelson (22)
Matt Shepherd

2B
Travis Hanson (18)
Calvin Hayes (25)
Jose Delgado (27)
Kevin Estrada
Jarrett Hoffpauir

1B
Chris Duncan (8)
Mike Ferris (12)
Andy Schutzenhofer (30)
John Santor
Billy Becher

SOURCE of TALENT

HOMEGROWN		ACQUIRED	
College	18	Trades	1
Junior College	1	Rule 5 draft	0
Draft-and-follow	1	Independent leagues	0
High School	6	Free agents/waivers	0
Nondrafted free agent	2		
Foreign	1		

C
Brandon Yarbrough (13)
Jason Motte

LHP

Starters	Relievers
Eric Haberer (21)	Carmen Cali (10)
Buddy Blair	Josh Brey
	Brantley Jordan
	Joey Siak

RHP

Starters	Relievers
Anthony Reyes (1)	Brad Thompson (6)
Adam Wainwright (2)	Brandon DeJaynes (28)
Blake Hawksworth (3)	Jimmy Journell (29)
Chris Lambert (4)	Evan Rust
Stuart Pomeranz (5)	Jeremy Cummings
Donnie Smith (14)	Justin Garza
Mark Michael (16)	Jason Burch
Mike Parisi (17)	Dennis Dove
Rhett Parrott (23)	Jeremy Zick
Mark Worrell (24)	
Jordan Pals	
Tyler Adamczyk	
Josh Teekel	
Kyle McClellan	
Chris Bova	
Quinton Robertson	

DRAFT ANALYSIS

2004

Best Pro Debut: RHP Chris Lambert (1) didn't have his best stuff last summer, but he still went 1-1, 2.58 with 46 strikeouts in 38 innings in low Class A. 2B Chris Patrick (37) made the short-season New York-Penn League all-star team after hitting .319-2-28. Sidearming RHP Mike Sillman (21) had a 1.55 ERA and 41-10 K-BB ratio in 29 innings, mostly in the NY-P.

Best Athlete: OF Chad Gabriel (20) is more well-rounded than OF Simon Williams (11). 3B Jake Mullinax (14), like Sillman an unheralded pick out of Nebraska, showed surprising tools while hitting .290-3-36 in the NY-P. Lambert was more of a prospect as a hockey defenseman in high school.

Best Pure Hitter: 1B Mike Ferris (2), despite his .199 average in the NY-P. He knows how to work counts, and scouts likened him to Sean Casey and Rafael Palmeiro. Mullinax has more pure hitting ability than the Cardinals realized.

Best Raw Power: Ferris set a Miami (Ohio) record with 21 homers during the spring. He's not pull-conscious and can drive balls out to the opposite field. 1B Billy Becher topped NCAA Division I in homers and RBIs per game in each of the last two seasons. While he was helped by the altitude at New Mexico State, the 6-foot-5, 240-pounder has legitimate bat speed and pop. 1B Brett Cooley (34) tied for the Cape Cod League lead with seven homers in 2002, but a torn left hamstring ruined his final two seasons at Houston.

Fastest Runner: Williams and SS Daniel Nelson (13) are above-average runners but not blazers.

Best Defensive Player: SS Matt

MIKE JANES

Hoffpauir

Shepherd's (8) hands stand out in this class.

Best Fastball: Lambert pitched at 90-96 mph at Boston College before dipping to 88-93 as a pro. RHPs Donnie Smith (4), Mike Parisi (9) and Mark Worrell (12) all can hit 93 and ranked among Division I leaders in strikeouts per nine innings.

Best Breaking Ball: Parisi has a hard curve to go with his fastball. Smith has the best slider.

Most Intriguing Background: 2B Jarrett Hoffpauir (6) starred at Southern Mississippi, and his older brother Josh played there as well and finished the season in independent ball after four years in the affiliated minors.

Closest To The Majors: Lambert has a higher ceiling than any of St. Louis' current big league starters except Mark Mulder.

Best Late-Round Pick: The Cardinals like Worrell, Mullinax, three-pitch RHP Phillip Andersen (23) and scrappy 2B Jose Delgado (24).

The One Who Got Away: St. Louis signed 42 of its 47 picks but couldn't get LHP Buck Cody (7) to leave Texas. SS Cameron Blair (18) decided to return to Texas Tech, then earned recognition as the Alaska League's most valuable player.

Assessment: With an ownership enamored of "Moneyball," the Cardinals drastically switched draft approaches. No team signed more players or drafted fewer high schoolers: four, with the first not coming until the 27th round.

2003 C/1B Daric Barton (1) was the Cardinals' top prospect until they included him in the Mark Mulder trade with the Athletics. Now that honor belongs to RHP Anthony Reyes (15). RHP Stuart Pomeranz (2) also has some potential. *GRADE:* B+

2002 After sitting out the first two rounds, St. Louis reached for 2B Calvin Hayes (3), who has played sparingly so far in his career. OF Cody Haerther (6) looks like he might be the best of a very weak bunch. *GRADE:* D

2001 RHP Dan Haren (2) looked like the future ace of the Cardinals until he left in the Mulder deal. Now that role could fall to draft-and-follow RHP Blake Hawksworth (28), if he can stay healthy. Since-traded RHP Justin Pope (1) has faded quickly. *GRADE:* B+

2000 OF Shaun Boyd and RHP Blake Williams were disappointments as first-round picks. C Yadier Molina (4) will start for St. Louis this year, and LHP Chris Narveson (2) was used in the Larry Walker trade last summer. *GRADE:* C+

Draft analysis prepared by Jim Callis. Numbers in parentheses indicate draft rounds.

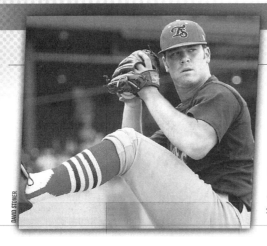

DAVID STONER

Anthony
REYES

Born: Oct. 16, 1981.
Ht.: 6-2. **Wt.:** 215.
Bats: R. **Throws:** R.
School: University of Southern California.
Career Transactions: Selected by Cardinals in 15th round of 2003 draft; signed Aug. 29, 2003.
Signed by: Nakia Hill.

Back in 2000, Reyes was a freshman at Southern California and looked every bit as dominant as teammate Mark Prior as the Trojans advanced to the College World Series. But while Prior got on the fast track to Chicago with the Cubs, Reyes faltered in his sophomore and junior seasons, thanks to a series of nagging elbow injuries. Once regarded as a cinch first-rounder, he fell to the 13th round of the 2002 draft and turned down the Tigers to return for his senior season. Elbow tendinitis limited him again and he slipped even further to the Cardinals in the 15th round in 2003. Now Reyes looks like he could be the steal of that draft. He missed six weeks early last season with shoulder inflammation, but after that he made every start and had no arm problems. More significant, he showed the same dominant stuff that once made him a premium prospect in college. After just six starts at high Class A Palm Beach he was promoted to Double-A Tennessee, where scouts and managers regarded him as the second-best pitching prospect in the Southern League, behind only Jose Capellan. The Cardinals didn't send Reyes anywhere to pitch over the winter, instead putting him on a workout program in an effort to make sure his arm remains sound.

Reyes has everything teams look for in a front-of-the-rotation starter, from his body to his stuff. His fastball was up to 94-96 mph by the end of the 2004 season—after dipping into the high 80s during the worst stretches of his college career—and he generally worked anywhere from 90-95 with running life. His breaking ball and changeup also made significant progress. His 81-83 mph slider shows good, tight spin at times, and his changeup bottoms out late. Command may be Reyes' biggest strength, however. He works hitters effectively to all four quadrants and attacks their weaknesses. Even when he was battling arm problems, Reyes maintained his easy delivery. He also has a great work ethic and does the little things well. One manager said Reyes' inside pickoff move to second base was as good as any he'd seen.

Until he gets a full, healthy season under his belt, Reyes' durability will continue to be a question. The Cardinals are handling him carefully, and he threw more than 100 pitches just once last year—108 in a start after he had an extra day of rest. His secondary pitches still need work. His slider can get slurvy at times, and he has limited experience throwing his changeup. Some scouts have questioned his arm action, but others who saw him last year said it wasn't a problem and St. Louis agrees.

Though he has made just 18 pro starts, Reyes is an experienced pitcher who could move quickly provided he can keep taking the mound every fifth day. The Cardinals have no obvious pitching prospects ahead of him, so he could get to St. Louis as soon as the second half of the 2005 season. He'll be expected to win a spot in the Triple-A Memphis rotation out of spring training.

Year	Club (League)	Class	W	L	ERA	G	GS	CG	SV	IP	H	R	ER	HR	BB	SO	AVG
2004	Tennessee (SL)	AA	6	2	3.03	12	12	0	0	74	62	27	25	3	13	102	.225
	Palm Beach (FSL)	A	2	0	4.40	6	6	0	0	31	32	17	15	3	7	36	.276
MINOR LEAGUE TOTALS			8	2	3.43	18	18	0	0	105	94	44	40	6	20	138	.240

Adam Wainwright, rhp

Born: Aug. 30, 1981. **Ht.:** 6-8. **Wt.:** 205. **Bats:** R. **Throws:** R. **School:** Glynn Academy, St. Simon's Island, Ga. **Career Transactions:** Selected by Braves in first round (29th overall) of 2000 draft; signed June 12, 2000 . . . Traded by Braves with RHP Jason Marquis and LHP Ray King to Cardinals for OF J.D. Drew and OF Eli Marrero, Dec. 13, 2003. **Signed by:** Rob English (Braves).

Wainwright was the Braves' best pitching prospect when they sent him to the Cardinals in the J.D. Drew deal in December 2003. He jumped to Triple-A but never showed his best stuff, trying to pitch through an elbow strain before getting shut down. He came back healthy, pitching 10 innings in the Arizona Fall League, and is expected to be at full strength for spring training. The Cardinals were impressed with Wainwright in spring training last year, the only time he really showed his full arsenal: a 92-93 mph fastball, a curveball with good rotation and a solid changeup. The curve may be his best pitch. He has a long, loose arm and great makeup, which may have worked against him as he tried to grind through his pain. Wainwright went on a strengthening program when he was hurt in an effort to make both his body and his arm stronger. In spite of his above-average stuff, he never has dominated hitters for long stretches. He needs to trust his stuff more. Wainwright's upside is nearly the equal of Anthony Reyes'. They should both be in the Triple-A rotation to start the season.

Year	Club (League)	Class	W	L	ERA	G	GS	CG	SV	IP	H	R	ER	HR	BB	SO	AVG
2000	Braves (GCL)	R	4	0	1.13	7	5	0	0	32	15	5	4	1	10	42	.136
	Danville (Appy)	R	2	2	3.68	6	6	0	0	29	28	13	12	3	2	39	.252
2001	Macon (SAL)	A	10	1	3.77	28	28	1	0	165	144	89	69	9	48	184	.230
2002	Myrtle Beach (Car)	A	9	6	3.31	28	28	1	0	163	149	67	60	7	66	167	.240
2003	Greenville (SL)	AA	10	8	3.37	27	27	1	0	150	133	59	56	9	37	128	.242
2004	Memphis (PCL)	AAA	4	4	5.37	12	12	0	0	64	68	47	38	12	28	64	.267
MINOR LEAGUE TOTALS			39	21	3.57	108	106	3	0	603	537	280	239	41	191	624	.236

Blake Hawksworth, rhp

Born: March 1, 1983. **Ht.:** 6-3. **Wt.:** 195. **Bats:** R. **Throws:** R. **School:** Bellevue (Wash.) CC. **Career Transactions:** Selected by Cardinals in 28th round of 2001 draft; signed May 30, 2002. **Signed by:** Dane Walker.

The Cardinals gave Hawksworth a $1.475 million bonus as a draft-and-follow right before the 2002 draft, making up for their lack of a first- or second-round pick that year. He missed time in 2003 because of bone spurs in his ankle, then pitched just 11 innings last year because of a shoulder injury that required surgery. Hawksworth offers a complete package if he's healthy. His best pitch is probably his changeup, but he also works with a fastball that sits in the low 90s and can touch 96 mph, as well as a good curveball. Injuries have kept Hawksworth from getting on the fast track as St. Louis had hoped. He had surgery to clean up his shoulder last May, though doctors found no structural damage. In addition to proving he's healthy, he needs to polish his breaking ball and improve his command. A year ago Hawksworth was the organization's top prospect. Now he's its most significant question mark. The Cardinals expect him to be at 100 percent in spring training and will send him back to high Class A.

Year	Club (League)	Class	W	L	ERA	G	GS	CG	SV	IP	H	R	ER	HR	BB	SO	AVG
2002	Johnson City (Appy)	R	2	4	3.14	13	12	0	0	66	58	31	23	8	18	61	.232
	New Jersey (NY-P)	A	1	0	0.00	2	2	0	0	10	6	0	0	0	2	8	.171
2003	Peoria (Mid)	A	5	1	2.30	10	10	0	0	55	37	16	14	0	12	57	.187
	Palm Beach (FSL)	A	1	3	3.94	6	6	0	0	32	28	14	14	2	11	32	.235
2004	Palm Beach (FSL)	A	1	0	5.91	2	2	0	0	11	10	7	7	2	3	11	.250
MINOR LEAGUE TOTALS			10	8	3.02	33	32	0	0	173	139	68	58	12	46	169	.217

Chris Lambert, rhp

Born: March 8, 1983. **Ht.:** 6-1. **Wt.:** 205. **Bats:** R. **Throws:** R. **School:** Boston College. **Career Transactions:** Selected by Cardinals in first round (19th overall) of 2004 draft; signed June 28, 2004. **Signed by:** Joe Rigoli.

Lambert looked like a better hockey prospect coming out of high school in New Hampshire, but he showed a low-90s fastball at a Perfect Game showcase the summer after he graduated and earned a scholarship to Boston College. He was the Big East Conference pitcher and rookie of the year in 2002, but an inconsistent junior season had some wondering if he would go in the first round until the Cardinals took him 19th overall. He signed for $1.525 million. Lambert has a strong frame and quick arm that produce fastballs in the 90-96 mph range with explosive life. He also throws a promising changeup and a slider that can freeze righthanders when he throws it for strikes. Lambert's command was an issue during college and remains one because there's a lot of effort in his delivery. He'll have to smooth out his mechanics, and he needs to add sharpness and depth to his slider. He looked tired in his pro debut, pitching at 88-93 mph. Lambert has limited baseball experience and might not move as quickly as the average first-round college pitcher. He'll begin his first full season in high Class A.

Year	Club (League)	Class	W	L	ERA	G	GS	CG	SV	IP	H	R	ER	HR	BB	SO	AVG
2004	Peoria (Mid)	A	1	1	2.58	9	9	0	0	38	31	15	11	2	24	46	.218
MINOR LEAGUE TOTALS			1	1	2.58	9	9	0	0	38	31	15	11	2	24	46	.218

5 Stuart Pomeranz, rhp

Born: Dec. 17, 1984. **Ht.:** 6-7. **Wt.:** 220. **Bats:** R. **Throws:** R. **School:** Houston HS, Collierville, Tenn. **Career Transactions:** Selected by Cardinals in second round of 2003 draft; signed July 23, 2003. **Signed by:** Marty Denton.

Pomeranz was a High School All-American in 2003, after a 13-1, 0.52 season his high school coach said was the most dominant he had ever seen. The Cardinals kept him in extended spring training to open the 2004 season, but he still led the system in wins despite making just 17 starts. Pomeranz throws an 88-92 mph fastball that showed good sink and more life last year than it had in 2003. He throws a knuckle-curve that's becoming more consistent, as well as an average changeup. He has a loose arm and a nice feel for pitching. His command is good for his stage of development. The Cardinals will take it slow with Pomeranz, as he's still learning how to handle a pro workload and needs to improve his conditioning. His offspeed pitches also need refinement and consistency. It's too early to know exactly what Pomeranz' ceiling might be, but his big frame and mound presence suggest he could pitch in the middle of a big league rotation someday. He'll move up to high Class A to start 2005.

Year	Club (League)	Class	W	L	ERA	G	GS	CG	SV	IP	H	R	ER	HR	BB	SO	AVG
2003	Johnson City (Appy)	R	1	1	6.14	4	3	0	0	15	13	10	10	2	4	14	.236
2004	Peoria (Mid)	A	12	4	3.55	17	17	0	0	101	95	59	40	10	25	88	.244
MINOR LEAGUE TOTALS			13	5	3.88	21	20	0	0	116	108	69	50	12	29	102	.243

6 Brad Thompson, rhp

Born: Jan. 31, 1982. **Ht.:** 6-1. **Wt.:** 190. **Bats:** R. **Throws:** R. **School:** Dixie State (Utah) JC. **Career Transactions:** Selected by Cardinals in 16th round of 2002 draft; signed Aug. 3, 2002. **Signed by:** Manny Guerra.

Thompson drew national notice at Tennessee, opening with 49 straight scoreless innings to set a Southern League record. The streak seemed to take a toll on him, however, as he lost strength in his shoulder and had to be shut down for two months. He came back at the end of the season and pitched well in limited Arizona Fall League duty. Command and approach are Thompson's best attributes. He works hitters inside and outside, and changes speeds and elevations. His best pitch is an 89-91 mph sinker, and he complements it with a sharp slider. Thompson doesn't overpower hitters, so he has to be sharp. His changeup needs more work if he's to get big league lefthanders out. His shoulder problems raised questions about whether he can handle a starter's workload. While Thompson's performance means he'll get the opportunity to pitch in the Triple-A rotation, he might be more useful as a middle reliever down the road. In that role, he could move quickly, as St. Louis pitching coach Dave Duncan loves groundball pitchers.

Year	Club (League)	Class	W	L	ERA	G	GS	CG	SV	IP	H	R	ER	HR	BB	SO	AVG
2003	Peoria (Mid)	A	5	3	2.91	30	4	0	0	65	70	23	21	2	10	43	.273
	Palm Beach (FSL)	A	1	0	0.00	2	1	0	0	6	3	0	0	0	0	4	.158
2004	Memphis (PCL)	AAA	1	0	5.52	3	3	0	0	15	20	10	9	3	3	10	.323
	Tennessee (SL)	AA	8	2	2.36	13	12	2	0	72	56	19	19	6	11	57	.212
MINOR LEAGUE TOTALS			15	5	2.79	48	20	2	0	158	149	52	49	11	24	114	.248

Brendan Ryan, ss

Born: March 26, 1982. **Ht.:** 6-2. **Wt.:** 195. **Bats:** R. **Throws:** R. **School:** Lewis-Clark State (Idaho) College. **Career Transactions:** Selected by Cardinals in seventh round of 2003 draft; signed June 14, 2003. **Signed by:** Dane Walker.

Ryan won a national championship with NAIA power Lewis-Clark State and the National Baseball Congress World Series with the Alaska Goldpanners in 2002, but he was dismissed from the Warriors program before they repeated in 2003. His first full season started late after he sprained his wrist in spring training, but he came back to lead the low Class A Midwest League in batting. None of Ryan's tools is overwhelming, but he's the best all-around athlete in the system, swings the bat well and plays a premium position. He plays with energy and a good understanding of the game. He should be an above-average hitter who uses the whole park, and also a plus runner. The Cardinals say Ryan should have enough arm and quickness to stay at shortstop, but he committed 31 errors in 2004. He should get stronger as he matures, but he'll never be a power hitter. Ryan will be the starting shortstop in high Class A this year, and he's athletic enough to play other positions. His bat will determine if he's an everyday player or a utilityman.

Year	Club (League)	Class	AVG	G	AB	R	H	2B	3B	HR	RBI	BB	SO	SB	OBP	SLG
2003	New Jersey (NY-P)	A	.311	53	193	20	60	14	4	0	13	14	25	11	.363	.425
2004	Peoria (Mid)	A	.322	105	426	72	137	21	4	2	59	24	42	30	.356	.404
MINOR LEAGUE TOTALS			.318	158	619	92	197	35	8	2	72	38	67	41	.359	.410

Chris Duncan, 1b

Born: May 5, 1981. **Ht.:** 6-5. **Wt.:** 210. **Bats:** L. **Throws:** R. **School:** Canyon Del Oro HS, Tucson.. **Career Transactions:** Selected by Cardinals in first round (46th overall) of 1999 draft; signed June 23, 1999. **Signed by:** Manny Guerra.

Duncan, whose father Dave is the Cardinals' pitching coach, was a supplemental first-round pick in 1999 but had just 25 at-bats above Class A by the end of 2003. He broke out last year in a pivotal season in Double-A, showing power, plate discipline and improved defense. Duncan entered 2004 with a .255 career average but finally made some adjustments at the plate, harnessing his power and hitting to all fields. He got shorter and quicker with the bat, hitting balls harder and more consistently. His speed and quickness drills also paid off with improved defense at first base. While Duncan has worked hard on quickening his feet and improving his hands, he'll be an average defender at best. He'll still have to show more over-the-fence power at higher levels to be an everyday first baseman in the majors. Though Duncan will be entering his seventh season in the organization, he'll still open the season at 23 in Triple-A. With Albert Pujols around, there's no obvious opening in St. Louis, so Duncan could become trade bait.

Year	Club (League)	Class	AVG	G	AB	R	H	2B	3B	HR	RBI	BB	SO	SB	OBP	SLG
1999	Johnson City (Appy)	R	.214	55	201	23	43	8	1	6	34	25	62	3	.300	.353
2000	Peoria (Mid)	A	.256	122	450	52	115	34	0	8	57	36	111	1	.318	.384
2001	Potomac (Car)	A	.179	49	168	12	30	6	0	3	16	10	47	4	.229	.268
	Peoria (Mid)	A	.306	80	297	44	91	23	2	13	59	36	55	13	.386	.529
2002	Peoria (Mid)	A	.271	129	487	58	132	25	4	16	75	44	118	5	.337	.437
2003	Palm Beach (FSL)	A	.254	121	425	26	108	20	0	7	47	44	115	4	.322	.315
	Tennessee (SL)	AA	.200	10	25	1	5	1	0	1	3	0	6	0	.200	.360
2004	Tennessee (SL)	AA	.289	120	387	57	112	23	0	16	65	64	94	8	.393	.473
MINOR LEAGUE TOTALS			.261	686	2440	273	636	140	7	65	351	259	608	38	.335	.404

Cody Haerther, of

Born: July 14, 1983. **Ht.:** 6-0. **Wt.:** 190. **Bats:** L. **Throws:** R. **Career Transactions:** Selected by Cardinals in sixth round of 2002 draft; signed July 31, 2002. **Signed by:** Steve Gossett.

The Cardinals gave Haerther $250,000, the largest bonus in the sixth round in 2002, to sway him from a commitment to UC Irvine. He followed up a strong debut in 2003 with a good performance in low Class A, but his season ended early because of a hairline fracture of the tibia in his left leg. Haerther is one of the best young hitters in the organization. He has a smooth, short stroke and makes good contact. He has an advanced approach at the plate, showing good patience for a young hitter and not swinging at many bad pitches. He doesn't have a lot of raw power but gets the most out of what he does have. He's an average runner. St. Louis drafted Haerther as a third baseman but has played him in left field because he's more comfortable there and has a better chance of helping the big league club there down the road. His arm is playable but he needs to work on his left-field defense. Despite his injury, Haerther showed St. Louis he's ready to move up to high Class A. He could progress quickly if he continues hitting because there are few legitimate prospects in his way.

Year	Club (League)	Class	AVG	G	AB	R	H	2B	3B	HR	RBI	BB	SO	SB	OBP	SLG
2003	Johnson City (Appy)	R	.332	63	226	31	75	12	6	3	39	22	30	2	.390	.478
2004	Peoria (Mid)	A	.316	86	326	48	103	20	2	5	45	32	59	7	.383	.436
MINOR LEAGUE TOTALS			.322	149	552	79	178	32	8	8	84	54	89	9	.386	.453

10 Carmen Cali, lhp

BILL MITCHELL

Born: Nov. 4, 1978. **Ht.:** 5-10. **Wt.:** 185. **Bats:** L. **Throws:** L. **School:** Florida Atlantic University. **Career Transactions:** Selected by Cardinals in 10th round of 2000 draft; signed June 12, 2000. **Signed by:** Steve Turco.

Cali established himself as a durable but erratic reliever in his first four years in the organization, and he hadn't made it past Class A. He came to spring training in great shape in 2004, however, and after opening the season at Tennessee made his big league debut in September. He always had arm strength, but conditioning and a lack of focus held Cali back until the end of the 2003 season, when he started to put it together and throw the ball over the plate. Now he consistently shows his good fastball, which sits at 90-91 mph and peaks at 94-95, as well as a slider and curveball. His arm is resilient and well suited for the bullpen. Cali made a breakthrough last year, but he's still learning how to pitch. He needs to repeat his delivery and show consistent command of all his pitches. He has a tendency to overthrow. With the departure of Steve Kline, the Cardinals could have an opening for a lefthander in their bullpen. Cali will compete for a job and head back to Triple-A to hone his pitches if he doesn't win it.

Year	Club (League)	Class	W	L	ERA	G	GS	CG	SV	IP	H	R	ER	HR	BB	SO	AVG
2000	New Jersey (NY-P)	A	2	7	4.89	14	14	0	0	70	68	45	38	3	30	55	.261
2001	Peoria (Mid)	A	7	3	6.00	39	0	0	1	48	53	40	32	4	29	47	.275
	Potomac (Car)	A	1	0	2.19	12	0	0	0	12	12	4	3	1	6	9	.279
2002	Potomac (Car)	A	2	2	4.11	29	0	0	0	35	31	18	16	1	21	24	.248
	Peoria (Mid)	A	1	1	1.78	24	0	0	2	35	36	17	7	0	14	27	.259
2003	Palm Beach (FSL)	A	2	1	4.99	62	0	0	3	70	72	49	39	2	32	70	.265
2004	Memphis (PCL)	AAA	1	1	2.70	17	0	0	3	20	17	6	6	4	4	20	.227
	St. Louis (NL)	MAJ	0	0	8.59	10	0	0	0	7	13	7	7	1	6	8	.394
	Tennessee (SL)	AA	1	2	2.91	38	0	0	14	46	43	19	15	3	19	47	.246
MAJOR LEAGUE TOTALS			0	0	8.59	10	0	0	0	7	13	7	7	1	6	8	.394
MINOR LEAGUE TOTALS			17	17	4.16	235	14	0	23	337	332	198	156	18	155	299	.259

11 Reid Gorecki, of

Born: Dec. 22, 1980. **Ht.:** 6-1. **Wt.:** 180. **Bats:** R. **Throws:** R. **School:** University of Delaware. **Career Transactions:** Selected by Cardinals in 13th round of 2002 draft; signed June 10, 2002. **Signed by:** Tom Shields.

Gorecki, an unheralded 13th-round pick after an all-Colonial Athletic Association junior season at Delaware, has put up consistently solid numbers since signing, earning a spot in the Arizona Fall League after the 2004 season. He batted .363 with a .449 on-base percentage in the AFL and was added to the 40-man roster. Gorecki is the best outfielder in the organization, a legitimate major league center fielder with speed and instincts as well as a good arm. He's a line-drive hitter with quick hands and the willingness to take a walk. He has a great work ethic. While he's a good athlete, Gorecki needs to get stronger to give him more pop. He strikes out too much for his offensive profile, and he needs to improve his baserunning. The Cardinals sent Gorecki to Double-A at the end of last season, and he'll return there to continue his steady progression through the organization. If his bat develops, he will be an everyday center fielder in the big leagues.

Year	Club (League)	Class	AVG	G	AB	R	H	2B	3B	HR	RBI	BB	SO	SB	OBP	SLG
2002	New Jersey (NY-P)	A	.281	73	274	55	77	8	13	8	52	20	57	22	.327	.493
2003	Peoria (Mid)	A	.267	128	480	77	128	19	8	15	61	51	90	23	.338	.433
2004	Palm Beach (FSL)	A	.277	118	440	74	122	23	3	8	47	46	80	23	.343	.398
	Tennessee (SL)	AA	.320	7	25	1	8	3	0	0	1	2	3	1	.370	.440
MINOR LEAGUE TOTALS			.275	326	1219	207	335	53	24	31	161	119	230	69	.338	.434

12 Mike Ferris, 1b

Born: Dec. 31, 1982. **Ht.:** 6-2. **Wt.:** 225. **Bats:** L. **Throws:** L. **School:** Miami (Ohio) University. **Career Transactions:** Selected by Cardinals in second round of 2004 draft; signed July 5, 2004. **Signed by:** Tom Shields.

Ferris wasn't drafted coming out of high school in Cincinnati, and he hit .226 at Kentucky as a freshman before transferring to Miami (Ohio). He hit .360 with five homers as a sophomore, then added 20 pounds of muscle and batted .361-21-62 to earn first-team All-America honors as a junior last spring. Like several other clubs, the Cardinals considered him a possible first-round talent, but they got him in the second and landed him for $600,000. Ferris signed about a month after the draft, and the rust was evident in his swing during his lackluster pro debut. In college, he consistently drove the ball to all fields with a quick, powerful stroke that drew him comparisons to Sean Casey and Rafael Palmeiro. Ferris also showed a good eye in college, laying off pitches until he found one he could handle. He's a below-average runner, but his defense at first base was better than St. Louis expected. Ferris has as much raw power as anyone in the organization, and he'll start with a clean slate in low Class A this spring.

Year	Club (League)	Class	AVG	G	AB	R	H	2B	3B	HR	RBI	BB	SO	SB	OBP	SLG
2004	New Jersey (NY-P)	A	.199	41	146	18	29	5	0	3	14	19	44	2	.295	.295
MINOR LEAGUE TOTALS			.199	41	146	18	29	5	0	3	14	19	44	2	.295	.295

13 Brandon Yarbrough, c

Born: Nov. 9, 1984. **Ht.:** 6-2. **Wt.:** 180. **Bats:** L. **Throws:** R. **School:** Richmond HS, Ellerbe, N.C. **Career Transactions:** Selected by Cardinals in fifth round of 2003 draft; signed July 11, 2003. **Signed by:** Randy Benson.

Yarbrough barely played after signing late in 2003, so he returned to the Appalachian League in 2004 and finished two hits shy of wresting the batting title from Johnson City teammate Juan Lucena. The Cardinals love Yarbrough's lefthanded bat and think he'll be an above-average hitter who could add power as he gets stronger. He has a short, quick and balanced swing. Yarbrough uses the whole field and has a willingness to take the ball back up the middle. While he draws walks, he'll need to make more consistent contact. Though he threw out 32 percent of basestealers last summer, it's not clear yet that he'll be able to stay behind the plate. Yarbrough has an average arm but his footwork and blocking must get better. As a high school catcher he'll require patience, and some think he would be better off moving to left field or first base. That way he wouldn't have to worry as much about defense and his bat could flourish. For now, though, the Cardinals see Yarbrough as a catcher, and they'll send him to low Class A to open 2005.

Year	Club (League)	Class	AVG	G	AB	R	H	2B	3B	HR	RBI	BB	SO	SB	OBP	SLG
2003	Johnson City (Appy)	R	.238	13	42	1	10	2	1	0	10	2	17	0	.273	.333
2004	Johnson City (Appy)	R	.326	48	175	37	57	10	1	6	33	25	55	3	.411	.497
	New Jersey (NY-P)	A	.143	5	14	1	2	0	0	0	1	1	5	0	.200	.143
MINOR LEAGUE TOTALS			.299	66	231	39	69	12	2	6	44	28	77	3	.375	.446

14 Donnie Smith, rhp

Born: Jan. 14, 1983. **Ht.:** 6-2. **Wt.:** 195. **Bats:** R. **Throws:** R. **School:** Old Dominion University. **Career Transactions:** Selected by Cardinals in fourth round of 2004 draft; signed June 21, 2004. **Signed by:** Tom Shields.

It's hard to believe a college staff with two arms the quality of Justin Verlander (the No. 2 overall pick by Detroit last year) and Smith could have a losing record, but that's what happened to 26-28 Old Dominion in 2004. Smith led the Colonial Athletic Association with a 2.29 ERA and had been the top prospect in the Atlantic Collegiate League the previous summer, but he really got scouts' attention when he started hitting 93 mph and showing a nasty slider. It was tough to get a good read on him, though, because he alternated between starting and relieving with little rhyme or reason. Smith had a tired arm after signing for $235,000, so the Cardinals used him on long rest and in short outings until the end of the summer. While his numbers weren't great, he got into a rotation and routine, which was important because he's raw. His fastball could be a plus pitch but needs more movement. He also throws a changeup with room for improvement. He's a strike-throwing bulldog with strong makeup. How he looks in the spring will determine which Class A stop Smith will begin his first full season at.

Year	Club (League)	Class	W	L	ERA	G	GS	CG	SV	IP	H	R	ER	HR	BB	SO	AVG
2004	New Jersey (NY-P)	A	3	3	3.88	11	11	1	0	46	52	23	20	4	5	41	.283
MINOR LEAGUE TOTALS			3	3	3.88	11	11	1	0	46	52	23	20	4	5	41	.283

15 Juan Lucena, ss

Born: Jan. 20, 1984. **Ht.:** 5-10. **Wt.:** 155. **Bats:** R. **Throws:** R. **Career Transactions:** Signed out of Venezuela by Cardinals, June 6, 2002. **Signed by:** Enrique Brito.

St. Louis hasn't gotten much production from Latin America, but Lucena could prove to be an exception. After spending a season each in the Rookie-level Venezuelan and Dominican Summer leagues, he led the Appalachian League in batting in his U.S. debut last year. He topped that off by getting significant time at shortstop for the Aragua Tigers in his native Venezuela over the winter, hitting .346 as a 20-year-old facing older veterans. Lucena is a line-drive hitter who has a knack for making contact, though he could stand to draw more walks. He led Appy shortstops with a .965 fielding percentage and has an average arm. His speed is a tick below average, but it hasn't held him back at shortstop yet because he has good instincts. While he doesn't need to be a power hitter, he'll need to get stronger to maintain his offensive production at higher levels. After his promising winter performance, Lucena should be the starting shortstop at St. Louis' new low Class A Quad Cities affiliate.

Year	Club (League)	Class	AVG	G	AB	R	H	2B	3B	HR	RBI	BB	SO	SB	OBP	SLG
2002	Carora (VSL)	R	.191	16	47	4	9	1	0	0	3	1	2	0	.208	.213
2003	Cardinals (DSL)	R	.234	64	248	44	58	11	6	0	18	14	9	6	.287	.327
2004	Johnson City (Appy)	R	.332	56	205	35	68	8	1	4	30	11	16	7	.365	.439
MINOR LEAGUE TOTALS			.270	136	500	83	135	20	7	4	51	26	27	13	.312	.362

16 Mark Michael, rhp

Born: Aug. 25, 1982. **Ht.:** 6-4. **Wt.:** 215. **Bats:** R. **Throws:** R. **School:** University of Delaware. **Career Transactions:** Selected by Cardinals in fourth round of 2003 draft; signed June 5, 2003. **Signed by:** Tom Shields.

Michael was a two-way player both in high school—at Gloucester (N.J.) Catholic High, which won the national high school championship in 2000—and college, playing his freshman year at Old Dominion before transferring to Delaware for two seasons. The Cardinals selected him in the fourth round solely for his mound prowess even though he went 3-4, 6.96 in his draft year of 2003. The early returns were promising—until Michael came down with shoulder problems in his first full season. Doctors initially thought he had tendinitis, but he had surgery after an MRI revealed a frayed rotator cuff and a small ligament tear. He would have been ready for instructional league had the Cardinals' camp not been canceled because of hurricane damage. When healthy, Michael shows an 89-93 mph fastball that's a plus pitch because of its movement. His curveball and changeup should become average. He likes to work inside and tied for the Midwest League lead by hitting 19 batters last year. He's still learning how to pitch and needs to show better control (he also led the MWL with 23 wild pitches) as well as the confidence to make quality pitches when he's behind in the count. He sometimes rushes his delivery, which causes his arm to drop from its usual three-quarters slot. Michael showed enough before his injury that the Cardinals will move him up to high Class A if he's healthy in spring training.

Year	Club (League)	Class	W	L	ERA	G	GS	CG	SV	IP	H	R	ER	HR	BB	SO	AVG
2003	New Jersey (NY-P)	A	1	2	3.17	11	10	0	0	54	50	23	19	0	20	56	.249
2004	Peoria (Mid)	A	6	6	3.36	20	20	1	0	121	117	59	45	9	39	95	.260
MINOR LEAGUE TOTALS			7	8	3.30	31	30	1	0	175	167	82	64	9	59	151	.257

17 Mike Parisi, rhp

Born: April 18, 1983. **Ht.:** 6-3. **Wt.:** 215. **Bats:** R. **Throws:** R. **School:** Manhattan College. **Career Transactions:** Selected by Cardinals in ninth round of 2004 draft; signed June 17, 2004. **Signed by:** Joe Rigoli.

Parisi was a strikeout machine at Manhattan, setting the school record for strikeouts in a season as a sophomore (87 in 77 innings) before breaking it as a junior (104 in 81 innings) and adding the career standard (272 in 244 innings) for good measure. He moved quickly after signing for $60,000, reaching low Class A after seven starts and taking a no-hitter into the seventh inning of his first start there. Parisi shows a good feel for pitching along with three quality pitches: a fastball that sits in the low 90s, peaks at 94 mph and shows good life; a downer curveball; and a developing changeup. He's a competitor who works hard and is focused on the mound. He has to refine his command as well as his delivery, which has some effort to it. But he has upside and should open 2005 in the high Class A rotation.

Year	Club (League)	Class	W	L	ERA	G	GS	CG	SV	IP	H	R	ER	HR	BB	SO	AVG
2004	New Jersey (NY-P)	A	4	2	4.42	7	7	0	0	37	40	18	18	3	6	26	.280
	Peoria (Mid)	A	1	1	3.28	6	6	0	0	36	30	16	13	1	15	36	.229
MINOR LEAGUE TOTALS			5	3	3.86	13	13	0	0	72	70	34	31	4	21	62	.255

18 Travis Hanson, 2b/3b

Born: Jan. 24, 1981. **Ht.:** 6-2. **Wt.:** 195. **Bats:** L. **Throws:** R. **School:** University of Portland. **Career Transactions:** Selected by Cardinals in ninth round of 2002 draft; signed June 9, 2002. **Signed by:** Dane Walker.

On June 3, Cardinals farm director Bruce Manno got a call early in the evening to inform him that Double-A shortstop John Nelson had torn ligaments in his ankle. Shortly after he hung up, Manno's telephone rang again with the news that Hanson had broken his ankle in two places sliding into second base. St. Louis tried to find him a new defensive home in 2004. He played shortstop in college before moving to third base as a pro, but Scott Rolen is entrenched at the hot corner for the Cardinals. Hanson's offensive profile fits second base better anyway, so he moved there in spring training last year. With his arm, hands and work ethic, Hanson immediately took to the change and was improving rapidly when he got hurt. He has a good approach at the plate and is able to make adjustments, but he hasn't delivered much offense as a pro. He lacks home run power and doesn't draw many walks. The best defensive infielder in the system, he might not be more than a line-drive hitting utilityman. St. Louis will give Hanson time to ease back into action at its new Double-A Springfield affiliate, probably putting him at third base to start the season before moving him back to second.

Year	Club (League)	Class	AVG	G	AB	R	H	2B	3B	HR	RBI	BB	SO	SB	OBP	SLG
2002	New Jersey (NY-P)	A	.294	75	272	31	80	17	5	4	40	12	55	1	.326	.438
2003	Peoria (Mid)	A	.277	136	527	70	146	31	5	9	78	35	104	3	.325	.406
2004	Palm Beach (FSL)	A	.259	57	224	26	58	11	0	2	35	19	38	2	.321	.335
MINOR LEAGUE TOTALS			.278	268	1023	127	284	59	10	15	153	66	197	6	.324	.399

19 John Gall, of/1b

Born: April 2, 1978. **Ht.:** 6-0. **Wt.:** 195. **Bats:** R. **Throws:** R. **School:** Stanford University. **Career Transactions:** Selected by Cardinals in 11th round of 2000 draft; signed June 22, 2000. **Signed by:** Jay North.

Gall keeps hitting but still hasn't made it up to the big leagues yet. After a record-setting college career at Stanford, Gall batted .300 in his first three full pro seasons before falling just short last year. He battled a shoulder problem in the second half of the season, which led to him hitting .252 with two homers over the final two months. Because he wasn't swinging the bat well and was unlikely to get much playing time in St. Louis, he didn't get called up. Gall is the system's most polished hitter but he has been held back by his lack of power and athleticism. He did show more pop than ever in 2004, with 22 homers and a system-high 34 doubles in Triple-A. Limited on the bases and in the field, he's adequate at best in left field and has a below-average arm. He has an outside chance of winning a bench job in St. Louis, but more likely will spend a third season in Memphis.

Year	Club (League)	Class	AVG	G	AB	R	H	2B	3B	HR	RBI	BB	SO	SB	OBP	SLG
2000	New Jersey (NY-P)	A	.239	71	259	28	62	10	0	2	27	25	37	16	.304	.301
2001	Peoria (Mid)	A	.302	57	205	27	62	23	0	4	44	16	18	0	.353	.473
	Potomac (Car)	A	.317	84	319	44	101	25	0	4	33	24	40	5	.369	.433
2002	New Haven (EL)	AA	.316	135	526	82	166	45	3	20	81	38	75	4	.362	.527
2003	Memphis (PCL)	AAA	.312	123	461	62	144	24	1	16	73	39	56	5	.368	.473
	Tennessee (SL)	AA	.327	12	52	6	17	1	0	3	12	3	4	0	.357	.519
2004	Memphis (PCL)	AAA	.292	135	506	77	148	34	0	22	84	48	68	1	.350	.490
MINOR LEAGUE TOTALS			.301	617	2328	326	700	162	4	71	354	193	298	31	.354	.465

20 Skip Schumaker, of

Born: Feb. 3, 1980. **Ht.:** 5-10. **Wt.:** 175. **Bats:** L. **Throws:** R. **School:** UC Santa Barbara. **Career Transactions:** Selected by Cardinals in fifth round of 2001 draft; signed June 26, 2001. **Signed by:** Steve Gossett.

After three mediocre seasons, Schumaker finally began to show why the Cardinals made him an outfielder rather than a pitcher after he played both ways at UC Santa Barbara, where he flashed a 92-mph fastball. In 2004, he led the Southern League in hits, finished fourth in the batting race and made the postseason all-star team. He worked with a personal trainer to get into better shape and avoid injuries—a stress fracture in his right leg and a hand ailment cost him playing tim in 2003—and Tennessee hitting coach Steve Balboni helped him change his hands and his whole approach to hitting. Schumaker carried his momentum into a strong winter in Venezuela, where he batted .350 in 103 at-bats before sustaining a minor knee injury. While he can hit for average and draw his share of walks, he offers very little power at the plate. He runs well but isn't a good basestealer. Yet one Southern League scout graded Schumaker as a potential big leaguer based solely on his defense in center field. He has the best outfield arm in the organization. If he can repeat his

2004 production in Triple-A, he'll get an opportunity in the major leagues, albeit as a reserve.

Year	Club (League)	Class	AVG	G	AB	R	H	2B	3B	HR	RBI	BB	SO	SB	OBP	SLG
2001	New Jersey (NY-P)	A	.253	49	162	22	41	10	1	0	14	29	33	11	.368	.327
2002	Potomac (Car)	A	.287	136	551	71	158	22	4	2	44	45	84	26	.342	.352
2003	Tennessee (SL)	AA	.251	91	342	43	86	20	3	2	22	37	54	6	.330	.345
2004	Tennessee (SL)	AA	.316	138	516	78	163	29	6	4	43	60	61	19	.389	.419
MINOR LEAGUE TOTALS			.285	414	1571	214	448	81	14	8	123	171	232	62	.357	.370

21 Eric Haberer, lhp

Born: Sept. 14, 1982. **Ht.:** 6-5. **Wt.:** 220. **Bats:** L. **Throws:** L. **School:** Southern Illinois University. **Career Transactions:** Selected by Cardinals in third round of 2004 draft; signed June 17, 2004. **Signed by:** Scott Melvin.

Haberer was slated to be a closer at Southern Illinois in 2004, but he moved into the rotation after the Salukis lost their first nine games and quickly established himself as the best draft prospect in the state. He didn't put up great numbers after signing for $422,500, but his arm strength impressed the Cardinals and earned him a promotion to short-season New Jersey so he could face more advanced hitters. He threw consistently at 92 mph with good life on his fastball and good command. He uses both a slider and curveball at this point, and St. Louis will try to get him to settle on one breaking ball this season. He shows feel for a changeup, leading the Cardinals to believe he can make it as a starter. Haberer earned comparisons to Mike Stanton in college, but he'll get every opportunity to stay in the rotation. He'll open his first full season in low Class A but could move quickly.

Year	Club (League)	Class	W	L	ERA	G	GS	CG	SV	IP	H	R	ER	HR	BB	SO	AVG
2004	Johnson City (Appy)	R	2	2	4.69	9	9	0	0	40	47	30	21	3	13	37	.283
	New Jersey (NY-P)	A	0	0	2.37	3	3	0	0	19	14	7	5	1	9	12	.219
MINOR LEAGUE TOTALS			2	2	3.94	12	12	0	0	59	61	37	26	4	22	49	.265

22 John Nelson, ss

Born: March 3, 1979. **Ht.:** 6-1. **Wt.:** 190. **Bats:** R. **Throws:** R. **School:** University of Kansas. **Career Transactions:** Selected by Cardinals in eighth round of 2001 draft; signed June 17, 2001. **Signed by:** Dave Karaff.

Nelson never has been able to return to the heights he reached in 2002, when he moved from outfield to shortstop and showed promise with the glove and bat. He has battled poor performance and injuries since then, and his 2004 season got derailed by torn ligaments in his ankle. Nelson was showing more of his old form while repeating Double-A and would have been promoted to Triple-A at midseason if he hadn't gotten hurt. He tried to return too quickly and was ineffective late in the season. Nelson's only truly plus tool is his arm, which is so strong that one Southern League scout suggested he might have more promise as a pitcher. He's a tease with the bat. When Nelson is on pitches, he can drive them out of the park. But he's not on pitches enough, and he hasn't made adjustments to shorten his swing and make better contact. At 26, he's starting to run out of time to do so. He runs well but isn't a big basestealing threat. Nelson began his pro career as a center fielder, and his best future role might be as a utilityman who can offer occasional righthanded pop. He'll try to win the Triple-A shortstop job this year.

Year	Club (League)	Class	AVG	G	AB	R	H	2B	3B	HR	RBI	BB	SO	SB	OBP	SLG
2001	New Jersey (NY-P)	A	.238	66	252	43	60	16	3	8	26	35	76	14	.332	.421
2002	Peoria (Mid)	A	.274	132	481	85	132	28	5	16	63	54	123	16	.349	.453
2003	Tennessee (SL)	AA	.237	136	506	60	120	22	1	5	42	44	117	10	.301	.314
2004	Tennessee (SL)	AA	.301	63	206	41	62	16	3	8	29	31	56	6	.396	.524
MINOR LEAGUE TOTALS			.259	397	1445	229	374	82	12	37	160	164	372	46	.337	.409

23 Rhett Parrott, rhp

Born: Nov. 12, 1979. **Ht.:** 6-2. **Wt.:** 190. **Bats:** R. **Throws:** R. **School:** Georgia Tech. **Career Transactions:** Selected by Cardinals in ninth round of 2001 draft; signed July 11, 2001. **Signed by:** Roger Smith.

Add Parrott to the Cardinals' long list of pitching wounded in 2004. His shoulder bothered him almost from the outset of the season, and he made just seven Triple-A starts before he was shut down. He had arthroscopic surgery to clean out the shoulder and is expected to be ready for spring training. Parrott usually features an 89-91 mph fastball and an average changeup, but he didn't show his good stuff at all last year. He still hasn't settled on a breaking pitch, throwing both a slider and curveball that are consistent. The best part of Parrott's package is his approach and mental toughness, and St. Louis believes that will allow him to come back from his injury relatively quickly. He'll need to refine his command, and will probably open the season in the Triple-A rotation to prove he's healthy. He's almost ready for a spot on the big league staff.

Year	Club (League)	Class	W	L	ERA	G	GS	CG	SV	IP	H	R	ER	HR	BB	SO	AVG
2001	New Jersey (NY-P)	A	1	3	4.93	11	11	0	0	46	45	27	25	3	28	58	.262
2002	Potomac (Car)	A	8	5	2.71	19	19	2	1	113	91	42	34	6	41	82	.221
	New Haven (EL)	AA	4	1	2.86	9	9	3	1	66	53	24	21	3	13	38	.223
2003	Tennessee (SL)	AA	8	9	3.27	21	21	1	0	124	122	52	45	11	40	112	.259
	Memphis (PCL)	AAA	2	3	3.54	7	7	0	0	41	39	16	16	2	19	25	.257
2004	Memphis (PCL)	AAA	2	2	5.29	7	7	1	1	34	44	21	20	7	15	15	.338
MINOR LEAGUE TOTALS			25	23	3.42	74	74	7	3	423	394	182	161	32	156	330	.250

24 Mark Worrell, rhp

Born: March 18, 1982. **Ht.:** 6-1. **Wt.:** 200. **Bats:** R. **Throws:** R. **School:** Florida International University. **Career Transactions:** Selected by Cardinals in 12th round of 2004 draft; signed June 19, 2004. **Signed by:** Steve Turco.

Worrell pitched for the U.S. junior team and showed a 92-94 mph fastball as a high schooler, but concerns about his size and unorthodox delivery dropped him to the 11th round of the 2001 draft. After declining to sign with the Devil Rays, he spent one season each at Indian River (Fla.) CC, Arizona and Florida International before the Cardinals took him in the 12th round last June. Worrell still has a heavy fastball and he backs it up with a tight 12-6 curveball. He'll even show a decent changeup on occasion, but he won't need it much because St. Louis plans on channeling his aggressiveness by making him a reliever. His mechanics still aren't pretty, as he uses no windup, has a short arm action and works from a high three-quarters slot. While there's some effort in his delivery, Worrell somehow is able to repeat it and throws consistent strikes. After blowing through two minor league stops with ease in his pro debut, Worrell is ready for high Class A.

Year	Club (League)	Class	W	L	ERA	G	GS	CG	SV	IP	H	R	ER	HR	BB	SO	AVG
2004	Johnson City (Appy)	R	1	0	1.16	18	0	0	7	23	12	3	3	1	7	37	.156
	Peoria (Mid)	A	0	2	4.30	12	0	0	6	15	9	10	7	2	6	20	.176
MINOR LEAGUE TOTALS			1	2	2.37	30	0	0	13	38	21	13	10	3	13	57	.164

25 Calvin Hayes, 2b

Born: March 21, 1984. **Ht.:** 5-9. **Wt.:** 190. **Bats:** R. **Throws:** R. **School:** East Rowan HS, Salisbury, N.C. **Career Transactions:** Selected by Cardinals in third round of 2002 draft; signed Aug. 20, 2002. **Signed by:** Randy Benson.

The Cardinals gave up their first two picks in the 2002 draft as free-compensation for Tino Martinez and Jason Isringhausen, and many clubs felt they reached when they spent their top choice on Hayes in the third round. He has struggled to get on the field since signing for $400,000, missing time in 2003 with a strained wrist and spending most of 2004 bothered by a hamstring injury. The Cardinals have moved Hayes to second base after giving him a chance to play shortstop in his first season, and they envision him as an offensive second baseman in the mold of Ray Durham. Hayes will need a lot of work to approach that comparison, though, because his approach at the plate is rough. He's too aggressive and needs to play more like a tablesetter. He's a dynamic athlete with above-average speed and the ability to put a charge in the ball. But from basestealing to defense, he needs to refine his game. More than anything else, he needs to stay healthy and pile up at-bats, because he has just 283 so far in his pro career. He'll probably go back to low Class A to start the year.

Year	Club (League)	Class	AVG	G	AB	R	H	2B	3B	HR	RBI	BB	SO	SB	OBP	SLG
2003	Johnson Cty (Appy)	R	.304	35	125	25	38	5	0	2	11	14	20	16	.387	.392
2004	Peoria (Mid)	A	.304	41	158	28	48	2	0	2	12	16	25	6	.368	.354
MINOR LEAGUE TOTALS			.304	76	283	53	86	7	0	4	23	30	45	22	.377	.371

26 Gabe Johnson, 3b/c

Born: Sept. 21, 1979. **Ht.:** 6-1. **Wt.:** 195. **Bats:** R. **Throws:** R. **School:** Atlantic HS, Delray Beach, Fla. **Career Transactions:** Selected by Cardinals in third round of 1998 draft; signed June 7, 1998. **Signed by:** Doug Carpenter.

While people may have been ready to write off Johnson, he decided he was ready to get his career going. Johnson hadn't made it past Class A and had a .217 average to show for six years of pro ball before 2004. He finally got to Double-A last year and had his best offensive season by far, another reclamation project credited to Tennessee hitting coach Steve Balboni. Johnson's swing didn't change much, but his approach improved significantly and he started using the whole field. He stopped focusing on power, concentrating instead on making quality contact and pulling balls only when he was pitched inside. He's adequate on defense, but he's so slow that one scout said, "He couldn't catch a dead man in a funeral home." Johnson played 16 games at catcher last year, showing enough arm and aptitude for the position that the Cardinals think he could be a big league utility player if he keeps hitting. He'll try to continue his progress in Triple-A.

Year	Club (League)	Class	AVG	G	AB	R	H	2B	3B	HR	RBI	BB	SO	SB	OBP	SLG
1998	Johnson City (Appy)	R	.251	57	187	30	47	11	3	9	32	20	71	3	.335	.487
1999	New Jersey (NY-P)	A	.194	35	124	12	24	5	2	5	14	9	49	1	.252	.387
2000	Peoria (Mid)	A	.157	58	197	20	31	8	0	4	22	13	91	1	.223	.259
2001	Potomac (Car)	A	.189	86	281	24	53	14	0	4	22	21	113	2	.250	.281
	Peoria (Mid)	A	.224	36	134	17	30	10	4	2	17	16	49	1	.312	.403
2002	Peoria (Mid)	A	.248	134	516	76	128	32	0	26	93	57	153	6	.324	.461
2003	Palm Beach (FSL)	A	.213	107	385	50	82	12	3	8	40	52	104	5	.308	.322
2004	Tennessee (SL)	AA	.267	127	450	64	120	27	0	18	66	43	118	7	.334	.447
MINOR LEAGUE TOTALS			.226	640	2274	293	515	119	12	76	306	231	748	26	.302	.390

27 Jose Delgado, 2b

Born: Sept. 10, 1983. **Ht.:** 5-9. **Wt.:** 180. **Bats:** B. **Throws:** R. **School:** Texas Tech. **Career Transactions:** Selected by Cardinals in 24th round of 2004 draft; signed June 14, 2004. **Signed by:** Joel Ronda.

The Cardinals drafted Texas Tech's double-play combination in 2004, failing to land shortstop Cameron Blair as an 18th-rounder but signing Delgado as a 24th-rounder. He led the Appalachian League in on-base percentage during his debut, and he projects as a top-of-the-order hitter if he refines his game. Delgado needs to make better contact. He chases too many balls off the plate now, has a long swing and must learn the nuances of situational hitting. He's a plus runner but needs to get better leads. Delgado is an average defender whose arm is slightly below average, but he makes up for it with accuracy and a quick release. He's perfectly suited for second base. The Cardinals will give him a chance to win a job in low Class A, and because he's a college player the organization would like to see him move on a fast track.

Year	Club (League)	Class	AVG	G	AB	R	H	2B	3B	HR	RBI	BB	SO	SB	OBP	SLG
2004	Johnson City (Appy)	R	.278	63	216	47	60	9	5	3	28	53	65	17	.431	.407
	New Jersey (NY-P)	A	.158	6	19	1	3	1	0	0	3	2	10	0	.227	.211
MAJOR LEAGUE TOTALS			.268	69	235	48	63	10	5	3	31	55	75	17	.415	.391

28 Brandon DeJaynes, rhp

Born: Sept. 10, 1980. **Ht.:** 6-2. **Wt.:** 190. **Bats:** R. **Throws:** R. **School:** Quincy (Ill.) University. **Career Transactions:** Signed as nondrafted free agent by Cardinals, May 26, 2003. **Signed by:** Scott Melvin.

DeJaynes hurt his arm early in his career at Quincy (Ill.) University and spent two years as a full-time outfielder before returning to the mound. He was the NCAA Division II pitcher of the year in 2003, when he led that level in ERA (10-1, 0.71) and finished second in strikeouts per nine innings (12.8). Because he was a fifth-year senior, the Cardinals were able to sign him as a free agent before the draft. DeJaynes' combination of a nasty curveball and deceptive arm action has made him nearly impossible to hit at the lower levels of the minors. In 2004, he ranked third among minor league relievers in opponent batting average (.156) and fourth in strikeouts per nine (13.4). DeJaynes doesn't have a whole lot else going for him, as his fastball sits in the high 80s and his control is shaky. At 23, he was much older than most of the low Class A hitters he dominated last year. But with his curve, he'll keep getting chances until he stops getting outs. Because of his age, St. Louis will try to get him to Double-A at some point this year.

Year	Club (League)	Class	W	L	ERA	G	GS	CG	SV	IP	H	R	ER	HR	BB	SO	AVG
2003	Johnson City (Appy)	R	5	1	1.10	25	0	0	1	33	24	9	4	0	13	27	.202
	Peoria (Mid)	A	0	0	0.00	2	0	0	0	3	3	0	0	0	0	2	.300
2004	Peoria (Mid)	A	5	3	4.29	49	1	0	2	71	38	39	34	6	57	106	.156
MINOR LEAGUE TOTALS			10	4	3.19	76	1	0	3	107	65	48	38	6	70	135	.171

29 Jimmy Journell, rhp

Born: Dec. 29, 1977. **Ht.:** 6-4. **Wt.:** 205. **Bats:** R. **Throws:** R. **School:** University of Illinois. **Career Transactions:** Selected by Cardinals in fourth round of 1999 draft; signed Aug. 12, 1999. **Signed by:** Scott Melvin.

Just when it looked like Journell had found a role that suited him mentally and physically, he encountered another major setback. He pitched just three innings in Triple-A last year before getting shut down with a sore shoulder that required season-ending surgery to repair a torn labrum. He ranked No. 1 on this list three years ago as a starter but showed better stuff when he moved back to the bullpen in 2003. He pitched in relief in college at Illinois and likes that role. When he's healthy, Journell can show electric stuff—a mid-90s fastball and a sharp slider. His mechanics are inconsistent, however, affecting his control and limiting his durability as a starter. The Cardinals hoped he would be in their big league bullpen last year, but his shoulder short-circuited that plan. He's supposed to be at 100 percent in spring training and should open the season in Triple-A. He needs to show he's sound because time is running out for him at age 27.

Year	Club (League)	Class	W	L	ERA	G	GS	CG	SV	IP	H	R	ER	HR	BB	SO	AVG
2000	New Jersey (NY-P)	A	1	0	1.97	13	1	0	0	32	12	12	7	0	24	39	.111
2001	Potomac (Car)	A	14	6	2.50	26	26	0	0	151	121	54	42	8	42	156	.220
	New Haven (EL)	AA	1	0	0.00	1	1	1	0	7	0	0	0	0	3	6	.000
2002	New Haven (EL)	AA	3	3	2.70	10	10	2	0	67	50	22	20	3	18	66	.206
	Memphis (PCL)	AAA	2	4	3.68	7	7	0	0	37	38	16	15	3	18	32	.264
2003	Memphis (PCL)	AAA	6	6	3.92	40	7	0	5	78	80	38	34	3	32	70	.268
	St. Louis (NL)	MAJ	0	0	6.00	7	0	0	0	9	10	7	6	0	11	8	.278
2004	Memphis (PCL)	AAA	0	0	0.00	4	0	0	1	3	4	0	0	0	0	5	.333
MAJOR LEAGUE TOTALS			0	0	6.00	7	0	0	0	9	10	7	6	0	11	8	.278
MINOR LEAGUE TOTALS			27	19	2.84	101	52	3	6	374	305	142	118	17	138	374	.222

30 Andy Schutzenhofer, 1b

Born: Jan. 24, 1981. **Ht.:** 6-0. **Wt.:** 195. **Bats:** L. **Throws:** L. **School:** University of Illinois. **Career Transactions:** Signed as nondrafted free agent by Cardinals, June 12, 2003. **Signed by:** John Vuch.

Schutzenhofer grew up as a Cardinals fan, which is natural because his father Dennis pitches batting practice for the team, in addition to coaching baseball at suburban Belleville East High across the Illinois border. Andy went to the University of Illinois out of high school, playing in all 225 games of his four-year college career and starting the last 224. A four-time all-Big Ten Conference selection, Schutzenhofer didn't get drafted because he offers limited power at first base. Since St. Louis signed him as a nondrafted free agent, he has batted .301, albeit still with little pop. He has a knack for putting the bat on the ball and controls the strike zone well. He makes good adjustments at the plate, too. Though he's a below-average runner, Schutzenhofer should be at least an average defender. But if he doesn't show more power this season in Double-A, he'll be hard-pressed to continue moving up in the organization.

Year	Club (League)	Class	AVG	G	AB	R	H	2B	3B	HR	RBI	BB	SO	SB	OBP	SLG
2003	Johnson City (Appy)	R	.316	41	136	28	43	11	1	2	19	15	12	1	.396	.456
	Palm Beach (FSL)	A	.326	13	46	11	15	3	1	0	10	11	5	0	.456	.435
2004	Palm Beach (FSL)	A	.292	121	373	65	109	15	2	3	56	51	36	3	.386	.367
MINOR LEAGUE TOTALS			.301	175	555	104	167	29	4	5	85	77	53	4	.394	.395

SAN DIEGO
PADRES

BY **KEVIN GOLDSTEIN**

CARL KLINE

The Padres promised their fans they would put a winning team on the field when Petco Park opened . . . in 2002. While the opening of the new stadium was delayed by two years, the team made good on its word. San Diego stayed in the National League West race until the final weeks of the 2004 season and went 87-75, its first winning season since reaching the World Series in 1998. Much of the success centered around homegrown players. **Khalil Greene**, a 2002 first-round pick, won Baseball America's Rookie of the Year award and quickly established himself as one of the NL's top shortstops. Sean Burroughs still hasn't provided typical third-base power, but he solidified the leadoff spot and set career highs in batting (.298) and runs (76). Brian Lawrence and Jake Peavy tied for the team lead with 15 wins, with Peavy also topping the NL with a 2.22 ERA.

Is there more help on the way? Yes and no. The Padres have several upper-level players on the verge of contributing in the big leagues. But with the exception of second baseman Josh Barfield and possibly center fielder Freddy Guzman, few project as regulars on a first-division club. The lower levels aren't exactly teeming with impact talent either, because San Diego has one of the thinnest systems in the game.

The Padres had a chance to add blue-chip prospects with the fourth overall pick in 2003 and the No. 1 choice in 2004, but both of their selections have had dubious beginnings. After San Diego took Tim Stauffer in 2003, an MRI revealed weakness in his shoulder, and the club cut its bonus offer from $2.6 million to $750,000. Stauffer didn't require surgery and reached Triple-A in his pro debut last June, but he lacks the ceiling expected of such an early pick.

Last June, the Padres had no second-round pick, so they limited their scouting to a handful of players for the top choice. They zeroed in on Florida State shortstop Stephen Drew, but three days before the draft upper management decided the cost of signing Drew would far exceed his worth. San Diego had to scramble before settling on local prep shortstop Matt Bush, who accepted a a below-market $3.15 million. The pick already was being criticized when Bush was arrested outside an Arizona nightclub before playing in his first pro game. The Padres since have acknowledged that Bush, who had a rough debut, wasn't the top player in the draft.

San Diego should be able to sustain its major league success, at least for the short term, because the NL West is one of baseball's least treacherous divisions. To remain a contender beyond that, the Padres will have to develop more homegrown talent. They won't pick near the top of the draft in 2004, as they start 18th overall. But that may not be a bad thing, as the club's best recent choice was a mid-first-rounder: Greene, who went 13th in 2002.

TOP 30 PROSPECTS

1. Josh Barfield, 2b	16. Ben Johnson, of
2. Freddy Guzman, of	17. Chris Oxspring, rhp
3. George Kottaras, c	18. Daryl Jones, 1b
4. Travis Chick, rhp	19. Fabian Jimenez, lhp
5. Tim Stauffer, rhp	20. Rusty Tucker, rhp
6. Matt Bush, ss	21. J.J. Furmaniak, ss
7. Justin Germano, rhp	22. Wilmer Villatoro, rhp
8. Sean Thompson, lhp	23. Yordany Ramirez, of
9. Brad Baker, rhp	24. Natanael Mateo, rhp
10. Paul McAnulty, of/1b	25. Ryan Bukvich, rhp
11. Jon Knott, of	26. Michael Johnson, 1b
12. Tagg Bozied, 1b	27. Luis Cruz, ss
13. Humberto Quintero, c	28. Javier Martinez, rhp
14. Billy Killian, c	29. Dale Thayer, rhp
15. Jared Wells, rhp	30. Randy Williams, lhp

ORGANIZATION OVERVIEW

General manager: Kevin Towers. **Farm director:** Tye Waller. **Scouting director:** Bill Gayton.

2004 PERFORMANCE

Class	Team	League	W	L	Pct.	Finish*	Manager
Majors	San Diego	National	87	75	.537	7th (16)	Bruce Bochy
Triple-A	Portland Beavers	Pacific Coast	84	60	.583	1st (16)	Craig Colbert
Double-A	Mobile BayBears	Southern	73	67	.521	+4th (10)	Gary Jones
High A	Lake Elsinore Storm	California	68	72	.486	7th (10)	Rick Renteria
Low A	Fort Wayne Wizards	Midwest	72	68	.514	t-7th (14)	Randy Ready
Short-season	Eugene Emeralds	Northwest	26	50	.342	8th (8)	Roy Howell
Rookie	AZL Padres	Arizona	26	30	.464	7th (9)	Carlos Lezcano
OVERALL MINOR LEAGUE RECORD			349	347	.501	17th (30)	

*Finish in overall standings (No. of teams in league). +League Champion.

ORGANIZATION LEADERS

BATTING
*Minimum 250 at-bats
*AVG	Xavier Nady, Portland	.333
R	Paul McAnulty, Lake Elsinore	98
H	Fernando Valenzuela, Fort Wayne	148
TB	Paul McAnulty, Lake Elsinore	258
2B	Paul McAnulty, Lake Elsinore	36
3B	Brian Wahlbrink, Fort Wayne	8
HR	Greg Sain, Mobile	28
RBI	Josh Barfield, Mobile	90
BB	Paul McAnulty, Lake Elsinore	88
SO	Kervin Jacobo, Lake Elsinore	171
SB	Freddy Guzman, Portland/Mobile	65
*OBP	George Kottaras, Fort Wayne	.415
*SLG	Xavier Nady, Portland	.632

PITCHING
#Minimum 75 innings
W	Four tied at	11
L	Three tied at	12
#ERA	Roger Deago, Portland/Mobile/L. Elsinore	2.01
G	Brad Baker, Portland/Mobile	63
CG	Three tied at	2
SV	Brad Baker, Portland/Mobile	34
IP	Brian Whitaker, Mobile/Lake Elsinore	169
BB	David Pauley, Lake Elsinore	60
SO	Sean Thompson, Fort Wayne	157

BEST TOOLS

Best Hitter for Average	Josh Barfield
Best Power Hitter	Jon Knott
Best Strike-Zone Discipline	Paul McAnulty
Fastest Baserunner	Freddy Guzman
Best Athlete	Ben Johnson
Best Fastball	Travis Chick
Best Curveball	Sean Thompson
Best Slider	Chris Oxspring
Best Changeup	Brad Baker
Best Control	Tim Stauffer
Best Defensive Catcher	Humberto Quintero
Best Defensive Infielder	Luis Cruz
Best Infield Arm	Matt Bush
Best Defensive Outfielder	Freddy Guzman
Best Outfield Arm	Yordany Ramirez

PROJECTED 2008 LINEUP

Catcher	George Kottaras
First Base	Ramon Hernandez
Second Base	Josh Barfield
Third Base	Sean Burroughs
Shortstop	Khalil Greene
Left Field	Brian Giles
Center Field	Freddy Guzman
Right Field	Xavier Nady

No. 1 Starter	Jake Peavy
No. 2 Starter	Adam Eaton
No. 3 Starter	Travis Chick
No. 4 Starter	Tim Stauffer
No. 5 Starter	Brian Lawrence
Closer	Scott Linebrink

LAST YEAR'S TOP 20 PROSPECTS

1. Josh Barfield, 2b	11. Chris Oxspring, rhp
2. Khalil Greene, ss	12. Rusty Tucker, lhp
3. Freddy Guzman, of	13. Jared Wells, rhp
4. Tim Stauffer, rhp	14. Sean Thompson, lhp
5. Akinori Otsuka, rhp	15. Justin Germano, rhp
6. Ben Howard, rhp	16. Javier Martinez, rhp
7. Jon Knott, of/1b	17. Edgar Huerta, lhp
8. David Pauley, rhp	18. Michael Johnson, 1b
9. Kennard Jones, of	19. Humberto Quintero, c
10. Tagg Bozied, 1b	20. Wilmer Villatoro, rhp

TOP PROSPECTS OF THE DECADE

Year	Player, Pos.	Current Team
1995	Dustin Hermanson, rhp	White Sox
1996	Ben Davis, c	White Sox
1997	Derrek Lee, 1b	Cubs
1998	Matt Clement, rhp	Red Sox
1999	Matt Clement, rhp	Red Sox
2000	Sean Burroughs, 3b	Padres
2001	Sean Burroughs, 3b	Padres
2002	Sean Burroughs, 3b	Padres
2003	Xavier Nady, of	Padres
2004	Josh Barfield, 2b	Padres

TOP DRAFT PICKS OF THE DECADE

Year	Player, Pos.	Current Team
1995	Ben Davis, c	White Sox
1996	Matt Halloran, ss	Out of baseball
1997	Kevin Nicholson, ss	Pirates
1998	Sean Burroughs, 3b	Padres
1999	Vince Faison, of	Mariners
2000	Mark Phillips, lhp	Royals
2001	Jake Gautreau, 3b	Indians
2002	Khalil Greene, ss	Padres
2003	Tim Stauffer, rhp	Padres
2004	Matt Bush, ss	Padres

LARGEST BONUSES IN CLUB HISTORY

Matt Bush, 2004	$3,150,000
Mark Phillips, 2000	$2,200,000
Sean Burroughs, 1998	$2,100,000
Jake Gautreau, 2001	$1,875,000
Khalil Greene, 2002	$1,500,000

MINOR LEAGUE DEPTH CHART

San Diego PADRES

Impact Potential: D
Top prospect Josh Barfield hit just .248 in Double-A but remains the organization's top talent. His bat up the middle of the diamond would make him a possible all-star— if he can stay at second. Matt Bush has big tools, including a well-above-average throwing arm, but clearly wasn't the nation's No. 1 talent in 2004, and just as clearly has a lot of maturing to do to reach his potential.

Depth: D
Fortunately for the Padres, they picked up hard-throwing Travis Chick from the Marlins, because otherwise the organization has a serious lack of power arms who also throw strikes. In fact, trades account for nearly a quarter of the players on the top 30. The various options at first base all come with modest power. San Diego has depth behind the plate, where draft-and-follow George Kottaras has emerged as one of the system's top hitters.

*Depth charts prepared by **John Manuel** and **Allan Simpson**. Numbers in parentheses indicate prospect rankings.*

LF
Jon Knott (11)
Corey Smith
Jordan Pickens
Matt Thayer

CF
Freddy Guzman (2)
Yordany Ramirez (23)
Kennard Jones
Drew Macias

RF
Ben Johnson (16)
Josh Carter

3B
Julio Cruceta

SS
Matt Bush (6)
Luis Cruz (27)
Sean Kazmar
Juan Ciriaco

2B
Josh Barfield (1)
J.J. Furmaniak (21)
Trino Aguilar

1B
Paul McAnulty (10)
Tagg Bozied (12)
Daryl Jones (18)
Michael Johnson (26)
Fernando Valenzeula
Greg Sain
Lachlan Dale

SOURCE of TALENT

HOMEGROWN		ACQUIRED	
College	6	Trades	7
Junior College	0	Rule 5 draft	0
Draft-and-follow	2	Independent leagues	1
High School	6	Free agents/waivers	1
Nondrafted free agent	2		
Foreign	5		

C
George Kottaras (3)
Humberto Quintero (13)
Billy Killian (14)
Colt Morton
Nick Trzesniak

RHP

Starters	Relievers
Travis Chick (4)	Brad Baker (9)
Tim Stauffer (5)	Wilmer Villatoro (22)
Justin Germano (7)	Natanael Mateo (24)
Jared Wells (15)	Ryan Bukvich (25)
Chris Oxspring (17)	Dale Thayer (29)
Javier Martinez (28)	Aaron Coonrod
Clark Girardeau	Alfredo Fernandez
Joel Santo	Leo Rosales
Brian Whitaker	R.D. Spiehs
Vern Sterry	
Ben Krosschell	
Jonathan Ellis	
Greg Condon	
Dirk Hayhurst	
Eddie Bonine	
Michael Ekstrom	
Clayton Hamilton	
Clay Hensley	
Mike Thompson	

LHP

Starters	Relievers
Sean Thompson (8)	Rusty Tucker (20)
Fabian Jimenez (19)	Randy Williams (30)
Daniel Moore	Edgar Huerta
Roger Deago	

DRAFT ANALYSIS

2004

Best Pro Debut: RHP Vern Sterry (8) went 4-3, 3.38 with a 78-16 K-BB ratio in 80 pro innings, and he posted a 2.40 ERA in five starts after a promotion to low Class A. Gritty OF Chris Kolkhorst (10) hit .337 with a .476 on-base percentage at three stops.

Best Athlete: SS Matt Bush (1) has an 80 arm on the 20-80 scouting scale and was clocked as high as 96 mph when he pitched in high school. A stellar defender with average speed, he's surprisingly strong for a 5-foot-10, 170-pounder.

Best Pure Hitter: C Billy Killian (3) will improve on his .225 average in the Rookie-level Arizona League because he makes consistent hard contact.

Best Raw Power: 1B Daryl Jones (4) has opposite-field power now and will be even more dangerous once he learns to pull balls with more consistency.

Fastest Runner: SS Sean Kazmar (5), Kolkhorst and OF Matt Thayer (31) are plus runners.

Best Defensive Player: Bush has the tools and instincts to be a Gold Glove shortstop. Though he made 17 errors in 28 pro games, that's not a long-term concern. His arm is so strong that he sometimes sits back on grounders, which should be correctable.

Best Fastball: Bush is the hardest thrower the Padres signed but among pitchers, RHPs David O'Hagan (9), Mike Ekstrom (12) and Ben Krosschell (16) can reach 93 mph. Krosschell is three years younger and has a more projectable frame, so he should pass them in time.

Best Breaking Ball: O'Hagan's slider. He worked just seven innings in his pro debut after coming down with a tired arm.

BILL MITCHELL

Killian

Most Intriguing Background: Killian's father Bill is a part-time scout for the Padres, but nepotism was not at work in his selection. Bush became the first No. 1 overall choice taken by his hometown team since the Twins' Joe Mauer in 2001.

Closest To The Majors: Sterry is the front-runner because he has an effective changeup and locates his high-80s fastball.

Best Late-Round Pick: Krosschell. He has an average slider to go with his fastball.

The One Who Got Away: The Padres almost ran the table. They signed or control the rights to all but two of their 49 picks. 3B Michael Moon (18) opted not to play pro ball. 3B Robert Spain (39), a lefty power hitter, is at Oklahoma City.

Assessment: Upper management put the scouting department in a bind when it decided three days before the draft the Padres weren't going to spend the money to sign Stephen Drew. Because San Diego didn't pick again until the third round, it had targeted just two other players, Jeff Niemann and Jered Weaver, who also were deemed too expensive. The feel-good aspect of taking a local product soured when Bush was arrested following a bar scuffle, earning him a monthlong suspension. He was the first of three high school picks at the top of the Padres' draft after they took just three prepsters in the first 10 rounds of the previous three drafts.

2003 RHP Tim Stauffer (1) had shoulder weakness diagnosed after the Padres took him. He has pitched but hasn't regained his previous velocity. And that's the good news: LHP Daniel Moore (2) got hurt; C Colt Morton (3) can't make contact; 2B Peter Stonard (4) retired; and OF Billy Hogan (5) turned off San Diego before being traded. **GRADE:** D

2002 SS Khalil Greene (1) was Baseball America's 2004 Rookie of the Year. Draft-and-follow C George Kottaras (20) and OF/1B Paul

McAnulty (12) have blossomed after going in the late rounds. **GRADE:** B+

2001 2B Josh Barfield (4) has been a consistent run producer in the minors. SS Jason Bartlett (13) is ready for big league action—but he was traded to the Twins for Brian Buchanan. **GRADE:** B+

2000 OF Xavier Nady (2) has hit in Triple-A but not the majors. LHP Mark Phillips' (1) was traded and faded quickly. RHP Justin Germano (13) could surpass them both. **GRADE:** C

Draft analysis prepared by Jim Callis. Numbers in parentheses indicate draft rounds.

Josh
BARFIELD

Born: Dec. 17, 1982.
Ht.: 6-0. **Wt.:** 185.
Bats: R. **Throws:** R.
School: Klein HS, Spring, Texas.
Career Transactions: Selected by Padres in fourth round of 2001 draft; signed June 15, 2001.
Signed by: Jimmy Dreyer.

Though he had obvious bloodlines as the son of former American League home run king Jesse Barfield, Barfield didn't get a ton of play as a high school prospect. The Padres did a good job of scouting him, however, and signed him away from a Baylor scholarship by giving him $400,000 as a fourth-round pick in 2001. After leading the minors in hits (185), doubles (46), RBIs (128) and extra-base hits (68) while bothered by a sore wrist in 2003, he entered last season as San Diego's top prospect, just ahead of eventual Baseball America Rookie of the Year Khalil Greene. Barfield injured a hamstring in spring training and it never fully healed, hurting his offensive game. He batted just .248—68 points below his previous career average—but missed just two games, set a career high with 18 homers and led the Double-A Southern League with 90 RBIs. Even with his off year, he's still easily the top hitter in the system.

Barfield has a quick swing and uses the whole field, with no discernible weakness when it comes to pitch location. His power continues to develop and he projects to hit 20-25 home runs annually in the big leagues. Barfield provides an argument to those who believe that there's no such thing as clutch hitting. He seems to take pressure situations as a personal challenge. Over the last three years, he has hit an average of 52 points higher with runners in scoring position, including a .331 mark in 2004. He's an average baserunner, making up for speed that's a tick below-average with excellent instincts. Once thought to be destined for left field, Barfield has put considerable effort into his second-base defense. He should be able to stay at second and provide average glovework with a plus arm. His make-up is another positive.

Barfield became frustrated by his inability to find a groove in 2004 and pressed at times. That led to a long swing and a pull-happy approach. He's guilty of guessing on pitches too often. He has a bit of a late trigger in his swing, so he can be neutralized with good fastballs when he's looking for something else. Barfield has problems with righthanders—he hit .196 against them last year—particularly with diving and breaking pitches that finish outside of the plate. Defensively, he still needs to work on his lateral movement and his double-play pivot. He has played all but seven games the last two years, but he rarely has been completely healthy during that time.

San Diego sees Barfield's batting average as the only real bump in the road from his Double-A performance, and has no worries about him. With Mark Loretta coming off a career year and locked up through 2006, the Padres have no reason to rush Barfield. He's expected to be 100 percent physically in spring training and should spend most of the season at Triple-A Portland. He'll likely make his major league debut in September.

Year	Club (League)	Class	AVG	G	AB	R	H	2B	3B	HR	RBI	BB	SO	SB	OBP	SLG
2001	Idaho Falls (Pio)	R	.310	66	277	51	86	15	4	4	53	16	54	12	.350	.437
2002	Fort Wayne (Mid)	A	.306	129	536	73	164	22	3	8	57	26	105	26	.340	.403
	Lake Elsinore (Cal)	A	.087	6	23	2	2	0	0	0	4	1	4	0	.120	.087
2003	Lake Elsinore (Cal)	A	.337	135	549	99	185	46	6	16	128	50	122	16	.389	.530
2004	Mobile (SL)	AA	.248	138	521	79	129	28	3	18	90	48	119	4	.313	.417
MINOR LEAGUE TOTALS			.297	474	1906	304	566	111	16	46	332	141	404	58	.346	.444

Freddy Guzman, of

Born: Jan. 20, 1981. **Ht.:** 5-10. **Wt.:** 165. **Bats:** B. **Throws:** R. **Career Transactions:** Signed out of Dominican Republic by Padres, March 21, 2000. **Signed by:** Bill Clark/Modesto Ulloa.

Guzman's prospect status took a hit after the 2002 season when his age was revised upward by 2½ years. Still, he led the minors with 90 steals in 2003 and had another solid season last year, surfacing as San Diego's starting center fielder for two weeks in August. The Padres called him up for his defense, but his bat wasn't ready. Guzman has game-changing speed, with 253 stolen bases in 369 minor league games and an 83 percent success rate. Unlike many minor league burners, he has a solid understanding of the strike zone. Defensively, he accentuates his speed with good jumps, allowing him to effortlessly run down balls from gap to gap. Guzman has little power and tries to do too much at the plate instead of concentrating on reaching base. He can get out of control at times and expand his strike zone, a weakness that was exploited in the majors. He has a below-average arm. The Padres believe Guzman needs another half-season in Triple-A, so they acquired Dave Roberts as a stopgap in center field. Guzman could push Roberts to a bench role by July.

Year	Club (League)	Class	AVG	G	AB	R	H	2B	3B	HR	RBI	BB	SO	SB	OBP	SLG
2000	Padres (DSL)	R	.210	49	167	38	35	6	1	1	10	46	38	24	.386	.275
2001	Idaho Falls (Pio)	R	.348	12	46	11	16	4	1	0	5	2	10	5	.388	.478
2002	Lake Elsinore (Cal)	A	.259	21	81	13	21	3	0	1	6	8	12	14	.326	.333
	Fort Wayne (Mid)	A	.279	47	190	35	53	7	5	0	18	18	37	39	.341	.368
	Eugene (NWL)	A	.225	21	80	14	18	2	1	0	8	7	15	16	.293	.275
2003	Lake Elsinore (Cal)	A	.285	70	281	64	80	12	3	2	22	40	60	49	.375	.370
	Mobile (SL)	AA	.271	46	177	30	48	5	2	1	11	26	34	38	.368	.339
	Portland (PCL)	AAA	.300	2	10	1	3	0	0	0	0	0	1	3	.300	.300
2004	Mobile (SL)	AA	.283	35	138	21	39	5	2	1	7	16	28	17	.359	.370
	Portland (PCL)	AAA	.292	66	264	48	77	12	4	1	19	30	46	48	.365	.379
	San Diego (NL)	MAJ	.211	20	76	8	16	3	0	0	5	3	13	5	.250	.250
MAJOR LEAGUE TOTALS			.211	20	76	8	16	3	0	0	5	3	13	5	.250	.250
MINOR LEAGUE TOTALS			.272	369	1434	275	390	56	19	7	106	193	281	253	.361	.352

George Kottaras, c

Born: May 16, 1983. **Ht.:** 6-0. **Wt.:** 190. **Bats:** B. **Throws:** L. **School:** Connors State (Okla.) JC. **Career Transactions:** Selected by Padres in 20th round of 2002 draft, signed May 26, 2003. **Signed by:** Lane Decker.

Signed for fourth-round money ($375,000) as a draft-and-follow, Kottaras played just 78 games last year because he spent a month with the Greek Olympic team, for which he went 3-for-12 as a backup in Athens. A native Canadian, he played more fast-pitch softball than baseball as a youth. Kottaras has a natural swing with plenty of power, and he projects as a 20-homer hitter. His understanding of the strike zone is advanced for a player with such little experience. He's a hard worker and takes well to instruction. He is mobile behind the plate and is good at blocking balls in the dirt. Despite a solid arm, Kottaras is easy to run on because he has a long release. He also needs refinement in the other nuances of catching. He can get overly patient at the plate. Like most catchers, he's a slow runner, but he's not a baseclogger. Kottaras boosted his stock more than any player in the system last year. The Padres see him as similar to Jason Kendall but with more power and less speed. His progress will continue at high Class A Lake Elsinore in 2005.

Year	Club (League)	Class	AVG	G	AB	R	H	2B	3B	HR	RBI	BB	SO	SB	OBP	SLG
2003	Idaho Falls (Pio)	R	.259	42	143	27	37	8	1	7	24	19	36	1	.348	.476
2004	Fort Wayne (Mid)	A	.310	78	271	40	84	18	1	7	46	51	41	0	.415	.461
MINOR LEAGUE TOTALS			.292	120	414	67	121	26	2	14	70	70	77	1	.393	.466

Travis Chick, rhp

Born: June 10, 1984. **Ht.:** 6-3. **Wt.:** 220. **Bats:** R. **Throws:** R. **School:** Whitehouse (Texas) HS. **Career Transactions:** Selected by Marlins in 14th round of 2002 draft; signed June 7, 2002 . . . Traded by Marlins to Padres for RHP Ismael Valdes, July 31, 2004. **Signed by:** Dennis Cardoza (Marlins).

The Padres got away with larceny when they acquired Chick from the Marlins for veteran Ismael Valdez in July. After starting the year in the bullpen, Chick found a groove after moving into the rotation at low Class A Greensboro and built upon that success after switching organizations. Chick's size, aggressiveness, velocity and ability to throw strikes remind some scouts of a young Curt Schilling. He consistently gets ahead in the count with a fastball that sits in the low 90s and touches 94-95. He has a hard slider and an advanced changeup for his age. Chick can depend on his fastball too much, and his changeup will improve more quickly if he uses it more often. He overthrows his slider, causing it to lose its horizontal break. He also works too high in the strike zone at times. Chick continued to impress in the offseason, as San Diego named him the MVP of its instructional league program. He'll likely begin the year in high Class A and could reach Double-A Mobile by mid-season.

Year	Club (League)	Class	W	L	ERA	G	GS	CG	SV	IP	H	R	ER	HR	BB	SO	AVG
2002	Marlins (GCL)	R	3	2	2.76	12	8	0	1	46	40	16	14	1	19	39	.227
2003	Jamestown (NY-P)	A	1	2	5.71	13	10	0	0	52	63	41	33	3	26	48	.301
2004	Greensboro (SAL)	A	6	4	4.04	28	11	0	0	91	79	51	41	11	27	112	.228
	Fort Wayne (Mid)	A	5	0	2.13	7	7	0	0	42	32	12	10	4	9	55	.206
MINOR LEAGUE TOTALS			15	8	3.81	60	36	0	1	231	214	120	98	19	81	254	.241

5 Tim Stauffer, rhp

Born: June 2, 1982. **Ht.:** 6-2. **Wt.:** 205. **Bats:** R. **Throws:** R. **School:** University of Richmond. **Career Transactions:** Selected by Padres in first round (fourth overall) of 2003 draft; signed Aug. 11, 2003. **Signed by:** Tripp Keister.

Originally offered $2.6 million as the fourth overall pick in 2003, Stauffer settled for $750,000 after an MRI revealed weakness in his shoulder that hadn't been detected before the draft. He didn't require surgery but wasn't able to make his pro debut until 2004. He tied for the system lead with 11 victories while progressing from high Class A to Triple-A. Stauffer's best pitch is a plus changeup. He also throws an 89-92 mph fastball, a cutter and a developing curveball. His pitches work better than their grades because he can throw all of them for strikes at any point in the count. Managers and coaches at every level praised his grit and determination. Stauffer lacks a true major league out pitch, and he was hittable last year. He's close to his ceiling, leaving little room for projecting him beyond a No. 3 or 4 starter, not the typical expectation for a No. 4 overall choice. His curve can flatten out at times. The signings of Woody Williams and Darrell May lessen Stauffer's chances of making the big league club. He'll probably spend the year in Triple-A and won't have to be added to the 40-man roster until after the 2006 season.

Year	Club (League)	Class	W	L	ERA	G	GS	CG	SV	IP	H	R	ER	HR	BB	SO	AVG
2004	Mobile (SL)	AA	3	2	2.63	8	8	1	0	51	56	17	15	3	13	33	.286
	Portland (PCL)	AAA	6	3	3.54	14	14	0	0	81	83	46	32	15	26	50	.261
	Lake Elsinore (Cal)	A	2	0	1.78	6	6	0	0	35	28	10	7	0	9	30	.215
MINOR LEAGUE TOTALS			11	5	2.89	28	28	1	0	168	167	73	54	18	48	113	.259

6 Matt Bush, ss

Born: Feb. 8, 1986. **Ht.:** 5-10. **Wt.:** 170. **Bats:** R. **Throws:** R. **School:** Mission Bay HS, San Diego. **Career Transactions:** Selected by Padres in first round (first overall) of 2004 draft; signed June 7, 2004. **Signed by:** Tim McWilliam/Bill Gayton.

A local two-way star who went No. 1 overall in the 2004 draft when San Diego looked to save money, Bush had a rough introduction to pro ball. After signing for a club-record $3.15 million, he was suspended before playing a game for his part in a fight outside of an Arizona nightclub. After taking the field in July, he never found a rhythm at the plate or in the field as he dealt with a hamstring injury. Taking Bush with the first pick was a reach, but Bush was a consensus top 10 talent. The best defensive player in the draft, he has a cannon for an arm and plus range to both sides. Some scouts have concerns about his offensive ability, but the Padres believe he'll hit. They say he understands the strike zone and has surprising strength for his size. He's an average runner out of the box, and above-average once he gets going. Bush's performance at the plate in his debut didn't quiet his critics. He needs to focus on making contact and not worry about trying to be a power hitter. He can get out of control at times trying to make flashy plays, the main reason he committed 17 errors in 28 games. San Diego hopes Bush can see 2005 as a fresh start after he showed marked improvement both on and off the field during instructional league. He'll begin his first full season in low Class A.

Year	Club (League)	Class	AVG	G	AB	R	H	2B	3B	HR	RBI	BB	SO	SB	OBP	SLG
2004	Padres (AZL)	R	.181	21	72	12	13	2	1	0	10	11	17	4	.302	.236
	Eugene (NWL)	A	.222	8	27	1	6	2	0	0	3	2	9	0	.276	.296
MINOR LEAGUE TOTALS			.192	29	99	13	19	4	1	0	13	13	26	4	.296	.253

Justin Germano, rhp

Born: Aug. 6, 1982. **Ht.:** 6-2. **Wt.:** 190. **Bats:** R. **Throws:** R. **School:** Claremont (Calif.) HS. **Career Transactions:** Selected by Padres in 13th round of 2000 draft; signed June 13, 2000. **Signed by:** Jim Woodward.

Germano continued his history of overachieving and rapid development in 2004, forcing his way to Triple-A after just five starts and making his major league debut on May 22, earning the win with five solid innings against the Phillies. Germano is a strike-thrower with an advanced feel for pitching. His fastball features good movement, and he can ratchet it up into the low 90s at times. His out pitch is his curveball, an overhand bender that he can break into or out of the zone. His changeup is average now and could become a plus pitch. His fastball velocity is a tick below-average at 87-89 mph. For the first time in his career, Germano didn't trust his stuff when he got to San Diego. He tried to nibble, leaving him behind in the count and hittable. Germano is currently a step ahead of Stauffer because of his experience, and he'll be first in line if an opening develops in San Diego's rotation. He should join Stauffer in the Triple-A rotation to start the season.

Year	Club (League)	Class	W	L	ERA	G	GS	CG	SV	IP	H	R	ER	HR	BB	SO	AVG
2000	Padres (AZL)	R	5	5	4.59	17	8	0	1	67	65	36	34	4	9	67	.249
2001	Fort Wayne (Mid)	A	2	6	4.98	13	13	0	0	65	80	47	36	7	16	55	.302
	Eugene (NWL)	A	6	5	3.49	13	13	2	0	80	77	35	31	5	11	74	.246
2002	Fort Wayne (Mid)	A	12	5	3.18	24	24	1	0	156	166	63	55	14	19	119	.269
	Lake Elsinore (Cal)	A	2	0	0.95	3	3	0	0	19	12	3	2	1	5	18	.174
2003	Lake Elsinore (Cal)	A	9	5	4.23	19	19	1	0	111	127	61	52	4	25	78	.287
	Mobile (SL)	AA	2	5	4.34	9	9	1	0	58	60	34	28	6	13	44	.268
2004	Mobile (SL)	AA	2	1	2.51	5	5	0	0	32	31	11	9	3	7	20	.258
	Portland (PCL)	AAA	9	5	3.38	20	20	2	0	123	113	48	46	12	25	98	.241
	San Diego (NL)	MAJ	1	2	8.86	7	5	0	0	21	31	24	21	2	14	16	.341
MAJOR LEAGUE TOTALS			1	2	8.86	7	5	0	1	21	31	24	21	2	14	16	.341
MINOR LEAGUE TOTALS			49	37	3.71	123	114	7	2	710	731	338	293	56	130	573	.263

Sean Thompson, lhp

Born: Oct. 13, 1982. **Ht.:** 5-11. **Wt.:** 160. **Bats:** L. **Throws:** L. **School:** Thunder Ridge HS, Denver. **Career Transactions:** Selected by Padres in fifth round of 2002 draft; signed June 24, 2002. **Signed by:** Darryl Milne.

Off-the-field problems led to Thompson changing high schools and living with a foster family as a senior. His full-season debut in 2004 was a huge success, as he allowed two or fewer earned runs in 21 of 27 starts. Thompson has a plus-plus curveball, a true knee-buckler that's the best in the system. He's aggressive on the mound and thrives on competition, tossing seven shutout innings against Lansing in Mark Prior's highly publicized first rehab start last May. He has an excellent pickoff move. His fastball has below-average velocity at 86-89 mph, but it has just enough juice and movement for Thompson to set up his curve. He's still prone to bouts of wildness, and when he misses he's vulnerable because he misses up in the zone. He's a slow starter, often not finding his groove until the third or fourth inning. Logically, Thompson's next assignment would be to high Class A. However, because of his success and his flyball tendencies (which wouldn't be a good fit in the California League), he may be pushed to Double-A.

Year	Club (League)	Class	W	L	ERA	G	GS	CG	SV	IP	H	R	ER	HR	BB	SO	AVG
2002	Idaho Falls (Pio)	R	4	3	3.83	13	11	0	0	56	51	34	24	4	38	69	.249
2003	Eugene (NWL)	A	7	1	2.48	15	15	0	0	80	58	28	22	5	39	97	.204
2004	Fort Wayne (Mid)	A	9	6	3.10	27	27	0	0	148	125	60	51	15	57	157	.234
MINOR LEAGUE TOTALS			20	10	3.07	55	53	0	0	284	234	122	97	24	134	323	.228

Brad Baker, rhp

Born: Nov. 6, 1980. **Ht.:** 6-2. **Wt.:** 180. **Bats:** R. **Throws:** R. **School:** Pioneer Valley Regional HS, Northfield, Mass. **Career Transactions:** Selected by Red Sox in first round (40th overall) of 1999 draft; signed July 26, 1999 . . . Traded by Red Sox with RHP Dan Giese to Padres for LHP Alan Embree and RHP Andy Shibilo, June 23, 2002. **Signed by:** Ray Fagnant (Red Sox).

Baker looked like a local kid made good when the Red Sox made him a supplemental first-round pick in 1999, and he rated as their top pitching prospect following his first full season. Inconsistency afterward led to his inclusion in a trade for Alan Embree in 2002. Baker's struggles continued until he became a closer in mid-2003, and his turnaround included being named the

Southern League pitcher of the year in 2004. Often described as a trick pitcher, Baker has one of the best changeups in the minors. It draws comparisons to Trevor Hoffman's, and he sets it up by commanding an 88-91 mph fastball. His fearless nature allows him to thrive in pressure situations. Baker has yet to develop a breaking ball of note, which is why he didn't develop as a starter. His fastball is average at best, and he'll have little margin for error, even as a set-up man. Baker will compete for a role in a crowded Padres bullpen this spring. He'll probably have to spend extended time in Triple-A before getting his first big league rotation.

Year	Club (League)	Class	W	L	ERA	G	GS	CG	SV	IP	H	R	ER	HR	BB	SO	AVG
1999	Red Sox (GCL)	R	1	0	0.79	4	3	0	0	11	10	3	1	0	2	10	.227
2000	Augusta (SAL)	A	12	7	3.07	27	27	0	0	138	125	58	47	3	55	126	.245
2001	Sarasota (FSL)	A	7	9	4.73	24	23	0	0	120	132	77	63	8	64	103	.272
2002	Sarasota (FSL)	A	7	1	2.79	12	12	1	0	61	53	22	19	4	25	65	.233
	Mobile (SL)	AA	4	4	4.48	12	12	1	0	64	47	33	32	5	45	57	.208
2003	Mobile (SL)	AA	1	6	5.68	17	9	0	0	51	50	34	32	3	36	53	.263
	Lake Elsinore (Cal)	A	3	0	2.01	27	4	0	12	45	31	13	10	2	14	69	.187
2004	Mobile (SL)	AA	2	1	1.57	55	0	0	30	57	37	11	10	2	24	68	.179
	Portland (PCL)	AAA	1	0	0.93	8	0	0	4	10	5	2	1	0	4	17	.143
MINOR LEAGUE TOTALS			38	28	3.47	186	90	2	46	557	490	253	215	27	269	568	.234

10 Paul McAnulty, of/1b

CARL KLINE

Born: Feb. 24, 1981. **Ht.:** 5-10. **Wt.:** 220. **Bats:** L. **Throws:** R. **School:** Long Beach State University. **Career Transactions:** Selected by Padres in 12th round of 2002 draft; signed June 8, 2002. **Signed by:** Jason McLeod.

McAnulty led the Rookie-level Pioneer League in batting (.379) in his 2002 pro debut, but followed that up with a mediocre showing in low Class A as his weight ballooned to 260 pounds. He showed up to camp last spring in the best shape of his career and responded with a breakout season. He went 8-for-17 with a homer as Mobile shared the championship in the Southern League playoffs. McAnulty's hitting ability is obvious. He has quick hands, developing power and an excellent feel for the strike zone. He projects to hit for average with 20-25 homers a year. He has great instincts at the plate and makes savvy adjustments from at-bat to at-bat. Other than the bat, McAnulty offers little else in terms of tools. Both his range and arm are lacking in left field, so he'll probably have to play first base in the majors. He's slow, though he runs the bases intelligently. His build and offensive package have drawn comparisons to Matt Stairs, who has created a lengthy career for himself as a grinder who can swing the bat. McAnulty will begin 2005 at Double-A.

Year	Club (League)	Class	AVG	G	AB	R	H	2B	3B	HR	RBI	BB	SO	SB	OBP	SLG
2002	Idaho Falls (Pio)	R	.379	67	235	56	89	29	0	8	51	49	43	7	.488	.604
2003	Fort Wayne (Mid)	A	.273	133	455	48	124	27	0	7	73	62	72	5	.370	.378
2004	Lake Elsinore (Cal)	A	.297	133	495	98	147	36	3	23	87	88	106	3	.404	.521
MINOR LEAGUE TOTALS			.304	333	1185	202	360	92	3	38	211	204	231	15	.409	.483

11 Jon Knott, of

Born: Aug. 4, 1978. **Ht.:** 6-3. **Wt.:** 220. **Bats:** R. **Throws:** R. **School:** Mississippi State University. **Career Transactions:** Signed as nondrafted free agent by Padres, Sept. 28, 2001. **Signed by:** Mal Fichman.

The Padres have as many prospects who were signed out of indy ball or tryout camps as any organization, and Knott remains the poster boy for the team's success outside the draft, after he went undrafted out of Mississippi State due to a leg injury. Knott's pure power ranks with any other Padres farmhand in the upper levels of the system. An imposing presence at the plate, Knott takes a long swing, but makes enough contact to prevent it from becoming an issue. He has a good feel for the strike zone, though his plate discipline took a dip in 2004 against stronger pitching. He's an average runner but a below-average fielder, often getting bad jumps on balls and taking poor routes. Some feel Knott's game is better suited to the American League, where he can serve in a first base/DH role. Still blocked in San Diego, he's slated for a retrun to Triple-A , but could be one of the Padres' stronger trading chips.

Year	Club (League)	Class	AVG	G	AB	R	H	2B	3B	HR	RBI	BB	SO	SB	OBP	SLG
2002	Fort Wayne (Mid)	A	.333	37	126	19	42	12	3	3	18	17	33	2	.411	.548
	Lake Elsinore (Cal)	A	.341	93	367	55	125	33	8	8	73	46	68	5	.414	.540
2003	Mobile (SL)	AA	.252	127	432	83	109	32	0	27	82	82	117	5	.387	.514
	Portland (PCL)	AAA	.346	7	26	5	9	1	0	1	5	4	3	0	.433	.500
2004	Portland (PCL)	AAA	.290	113	435	79	126	22	3	26	85	58	110	5	.376	.533
	San Diego (NL)	MAJ	.214	9	14	1	3	2	0	0	1	1	5	0	.267	.357
MAJOR LEAGUE TOTALS			.214	9	14	1	3	2	0	0	1	1	5	0	.267	.357
MINOR LEAGUE TOTALS			.297	377	1386	241	411	100	14	65	263	207	331	17	.394	.530

Tagg Bozied, 1b

Born: July 24, 1979. **Ht.:** 6-3. **Wt.:** 210. **Bats:** R. **Throws:** R. **School:** University of San Francisco. **Career Transactions:** Signed by independent Sioux Falls (Northern), June 2001 . . . Selected by Padres in third round of 2001 draft; signed Nov. 9, 2001. **Signed by:** Bill Gayton.

Bozied's second go-around at Triple-A was off to a strong start in 2004, as he matched his previous year's home run total in just 46 games. His season ended in freakish fashion less than two weeks later, as he ruptured his left patella tendon when he jumped on home plate to celebrate hitting a game-winning grand slam. Bozied has the ability to clear the fence from pole-to-pole, while making excellent contact for a power hitter. He could draw more walks, but coaches don't want to tinker with the success he had in 2004. He has worked hard to become an adequate defender, but he won't ever be more than that. Bozied still has holes in his swing and a tendency to chase breaking balls on the outer half. His power against left-handers is limited, reducing his value as a potential platoon player. Bozied is expected to be healthy for spring training, but the presence of Ryan Klesko and Phil Nevin mean he'll return to Triple-A, where he'll look to pick up where he left off.

Year	Club (League)	Class	AVG	G	AB	R	H	2B	3B	HR	RBI	BB	SO	SB	OBP	SLG
2001	Sioux Falls (Nor)	IND	.307	58	228	35	70	17	0	6	31	13	34	3	.359	.461
2002	Lake Elsinore (Cal)	A	.298	71	282	45	84	23	1	15	60	35	60	3	.377	.546
	Mobile (SL)	AA	.214	60	234	35	50	14	0	9	32	16	43	1	.268	.389
2003	Portland (PCL)	AAA	.273	119	450	59	123	25	2	14	59	38	80	1	.331	.431
2004	Portland (PCL)	AAA	.315	57	213	41	67	17	1	16	58	18	29	0	.374	.629
MINOR LEAGUE TOTALS			.280	365	1407	215	394	96	4	60	240	120	246	8	.341	.482

Humberto Quintero, c

Born: Aug. 2, 1979. **Ht.:** 6-1. **Wt.:** 190. **Bats:** R. **Throws:** R. **Career Transactions:** Signed out of Venezuela by White Sox, Jan. 16, 1997 . . . Traded by White Sox with OF Alex Fernandez to Padres for 3B D'Angelo Jimenez, July 12, 2002. **Signed by:** Hector Rincones (White Sox).

Quintero has hit .305 over the past two seasons in the minors to establish himself as more than just a defensive specialist. Quintero's contact-focused approach allows him to hit for a high average, though he offers little in the way of power, plate discipline or speed. Quintero's glovework alone should guarantee him a major league career. He has the ability to shut down the running game with a plus-plus arm and excels at blocking pitches in the dirt. Quintero needs to add an element to his offensive game to project as more than a back-up. Bulking up would not only possibly give him more power, but it would also allow him to better withstand the grind of a full season behind the plate. Quintero will enter 2005 as the favorite to earn the backup job behind Ramon Hernandez in San Diego.

Year	Club (League)	Class	AVG	G	AB	R	H	2B	3B	HR	RBI	BB	SO	SB	OBP	SLG
1997	Guacara 1 (VSL)	R	.262	24	42	4	11	2	0	0	0	5	9	1	.333	.310
1998	Miranda (VSL)	R	.205	30	73	6	15	1	0	0	1	3	12	0	.266	.219
1999	Bristol (Appy)	R	.277	48	155	30	43	5	2	0	15	9	19	11	.341	.335
2000	White Sox (AZL)	R	.393	15	56	13	22	2	2	0	8	0	3	1	.414	.500
	Burlington (Mid)	A	.238	75	248	23	59	12	2	0	24	15	31	10	.287	.302
2001	Kannapolis (SAL)	A	.269	60	197	32	53	7	1	1	20	8	20	7	.321	.330
	Winston-Salem (Car)	A	.240	43	154	15	37	6	0	0	12	5	19	9	.268	.279
	Birmingham (SL)	AA	.211	5	19	0	4	0	0	0	2	0	2	0	.250	.211
2002	Winston-Salem (Car)	A	.194	52	160	15	31	1	1	0	12	8	23	2	.247	.213
	Birmingham (SL)	AA	.500	4	12	1	6	0	0	0	3	0	1	1	.538	.500
	Charlotte (IL)	AAA	.220	15	41	2	9	1	0	0	5	3	8	0	.273	.244
	Mobile (SL)	AA	.240	37	125	11	30	8	0	1	14	5	12	0	.286	.328
2003	Mobile (SL)	AA	.298	110	386	37	115	26	0	3	52	19	41	0	.343	.389
	San Diego (NL)	MAJ	.217	12	23	1	5	0	0	0	2	1	6	0	.250	.217
2004	Portland (PCL)	AAA	.317	68	259	36	82	25	0	5	30	8	18	0	.348	.471
	San Diego (NL)	MAJ	.250	23	72	7	18	3	0	2	10	5	16	0	.295	.375
MAJOR LEAGUE TOTALS			.242	35	95	8	23	3	0	2	12	6	22	0	.284	.337
MINOR LEAGUE TOTALS			.268	586	1927	225	517	96	8	10	198	88	218	42	.314	.342

Billy Killian, c

Born: June 12, 1986. **Ht.:** 6-1. **Wt.:** 190. **Bats:** L. **Throws:** R. **School:** Chippewa Hills HS, Stanwood, Mich. **Career Transactions:** Selected by Padres in third round of 2004 draft: signed June 8, 2004. **Signed by:** Jeff Stewart.

Killian is the son of Padres part-time scout Bill Killian, but he earned his $450,000 bonus as a third round pick on talent. While he did little in his pro debut outside of playing three games at Triple-A Portland as an emergency backup, the Padres attributed his struggles to the expected adjustment period after he played lower-level competition in northwest Michigan. A fresher Killian looked much better in instructional league, and displayed all the skills scouts look for in a catcher. He's a switch-hitter with quick wrists and a mature approach, already showing power from both sides of the plate in batting practice. Defensively, he has a strong, accurate arm, but needs to work on nuances of catching like blocking balls and working with pitchers. He's surprisingly fast for his position, but the Padres would like to see him bulk up to withstand the rigors of catching. Killian is a baseball rat with great instincts and an excellent work ethic. Killian's ceiling is higher that any other Padres catching prospect, but his development will require patience. He'll likely begin the year in extended spring training before reporting to short-season Eugene.

Year	Club (League)	Class	AVG	G	AB	R	H	2B	3B	HR	RBI	BB	SO	SB	OBP	SLG
2004	Padres (AZL)	R	.230	40	135	17	31	7	2	0	13	11	21	3	.293	.311
	Portland (PCL)	AAA	.143	3	7	0	1	0	0	0	0	1	0	0	.250	.143
MINOR LEAGUE TOTALS			.225	43	142	17	32	7	2	0	13	12	21	3	.291	.303

15 Jared Wells, rhp

Born: Oct. 31, 1981. **Ht.:** 6-4. **Wt.:** 200. **Bats:** R. **Throws:** R. **School:** San Jacinto (Texas) JC. **Career Transactions:** Selected by Padres in 31st round of 2002 draft; signed May 31, 2003. **Signed by:** Paul Fletcher.

A high-profile draft-and-follow, Wells' production continued to fall short of his stuff in his full-season debut. Wells has a prototypical pitcher's body and can light up radar guns with a mid-90s fastball, while also delivering a sharp-breaking slider. His changeup is still in the developmental stage, but should become a usable pitch. Wells is raw and illustrates the difference between control and command. While his walk rates are low, he often leaves his pitches too hittable and needs to work the count and get batters to chase his breaking ball. A star high school quarterback, Wells brings a gridiron mentality to the mound, and at times his attitude borders on arrogance. His work ethic and conditioning have come into question as well. One of the few pitchers in the Padres system who features a power arsenal, Wells will return to high Class A in 2005, and some say he's a few refinements from taking off.

Year	Club (League)	Class	W	L	ERA	G	GS	CG	SV	IP	H	R	ER	HR	BB	SO	AVG
2003	Eugene (NWL)	A	4	6	2.75	14	14	0	0	79	77	34	24	6	32	53	.256
2004	Fort Wayne (Mid)	A	4	6	4.09	14	14	1	0	81	91	42	37	6	19	72	.278
	Lake Elsinore (Cal)	A	4	6	4.52	13	12	0	0	72	81	44	36	5	30	38	.289
MINOR LEAGUE TOTALS			12	18	3.77	41	40	1	0	232	249	120	97	17	81	163	.274

16 Ben Johnson, of

Born: Jan. 18, 1981. **Ht.:** 6-1. **Wt.:** 200. **Bats:** R. **Throws:** R. **School:** Germantown (Tenn.) HS. **Career Transactions:** Selected by Cardinals in fourth round of 1999 draft; signed June 24, 1999 . . . Traded by Cardinals with RHP Heathcliff Slocumb to Padres for C Carlos Hernandez and SS Nate Tebbs, July 31, 2000. **Signed by:** Randy Benson (Cardinals).

While Johnson's tools compare with those of anyone in the organization, the Padres may have rushed him after acquiring him from the Cardinals at the 2000 trade deadline. Johnson began to translate many of his tools to in-game situations last year in his third Double-A season. Much of his success was credited to extensive sessions with roving hitting instructor Rob Deer. He continued to impress people with a strong showing in the Arizona Fall League. Johnson grades out at least average in all five tools. He's an excellent athlete with plus power and a plus arm. He's no longer the burner he once was, but he's still an above-average runner who can hold his own in center field, though he's better suited to right. Johnson has a good feel for the strike zone, but still has an all-or-nothing swing. Johnson's 2004 season did wonders for his confidence, and that may be all he needed to reach his potential. He'll begin the season at Triple-A, looking to prove his breakout campaign was no fluke.

Year	Club (League)	Class	AVG	G	AB	R	H	2B	3B	HR	RBI	BB	SO	SB	OBP	SLG
1999	Johnson City (Appy)	R	.330	57	203	38	67	9	1	10	51	29	57	14	.423	.532
2000	Fort Wayne (Mid)	A	.193	29	109	11	21	6	2	3	13	7	25	0	.261	.367
	Peoria (Mid)	A	.242	93	330	58	80	22	1	13	46	53	78	17	.353	.433
2001	Lake Elsinore (Cal)	A	.276	136	503	79	139	35	6	12	63	54	141	22	.358	.441
2002	Mobile (SL)	AA	.241	131	456	58	110	23	4	10	55	65	127	11	.337	.375
2003	Mobile (SL)	AA	.181	44	127	8	23	5	0	1	7	10	36	0	.252	.244
	Lake Elsinore (Cal)	A	.266	52	184	30	49	9	0	8	29	20	49	6	.354	.446
2004	Mobile (SL)	AA	.251	136	475	80	119	28	6	23	85	55	136	5	.335	.480
MINOR LEAGUE TOTALS			.255	678	2387	362	608	137	20	80	349	293	649	75	.344	.429

17 Chris Oxspring, rhp

Born: May 13, 1977. **Ht.:** 6-1. **Wt.:** 180. **Bats:** L. **Throws:** R. **Career Transactions:** Signed out of Australia by independent Cook County (Frontier), June 2000 . . . Signed by Padres, Oct. 31, 2000. **Signed by:** Bill Bryk/Bill Clark/Mal Fichman.

Oxspring is a testament to the tenacity of Padres scouts, who decided to look at a few independent Frontier League pitchers when the game they attended in order to scout batters was rained out. Oxspring became a national hero in his native Austrailia in 2004 when he pitched 15 scoreless innings in a pair of victories to guide his squad to the silver medal in the Athens Olympics. Oxspring has solid stuff, with a low-90s fastball, plus slider and improved changeup. His control is erratic, and at times he can get frustrated and overthrow, which leads to greater troubles. His inability to trust his stuff has been a concern, but he returned from Athens a much more confident pitcher. Oxspring is 27, so there's little projection left in him, but his stuff is good enough to be a fifth starter. He'll go into spring training with a chance to earn a bullpen role, but he'll likely return to Triple-A.

Year	Club (League)	Class	W	L	ERA	G	GS	CG	SV	IP	H	R	ER	HR	BB	SO	AVG
2000	Cook County (Fron)	IND	1	0	3.10	13	2	0	1	29	29	18	10	1	15	29	—
2001	Fort Wayne (Mid)	A	4	1	4.15	41	2	0	0	56	66	29	26	5	25	54	.297
2001	Lake Elsinore (Cal)	A	0	0	0.64	7	0	0	0	14	10	2	1	1	6	17	.200
2002	Lake Elsinore (Cal)	A	0	1	4.78	15	1	0	0	26	24	16	14	2	8	30	.238
	Mobile (SL)	AA	0	0	1.26	6	1	0	0	14	13	3	2	0	8	21	.245
2003	Mobile (SL)	AA	10	6	2.92	40	18	1	0	136	106	47	44	6	62	129	.211
2004	Portland (PCL)	AAA	6	4	3.99	17	17	0	0	86	82	45	38	7	44	81	.247
MINOR LEAGUE TOTALS			20	12	3.38	126	39	1	0	332	301	142	125	21	153	332	.239

18 Daryl Jones, 1b

Born: Sept. 1, 1986. **Ht.:** 6-3. **Wt.:** 200. **Bats:** R. **Throws:** R. **School:** Westchester HS, Gardena, Calif. **Career Transactions:** Selected by Padres in fourth round of 2004 draft; signed June 8, 2004. **Signed by:** Anup Sinha.

The Padres selected college players with their first 25 picks in 2003, but they reversed that trend by taking high school players with their first three picks in 2004. The last of the group was Jones, who participated in Major League Baseball's RBI (Reviving Baseball in Inner Cities) program as a youth player. He reached base in all but five games before his season was cut short by a sprained ankle. Jones' raw power ranked among the best of prep players available in the draft. Just 17 when drafted, Jones' long, muscular frame generates plus power to all fields. He's a surprisingly adept defender, with soft hands and a solid arm. Padres officials were impressed with his desire and work ethic. Jones' swing has a bit of a hitch, and coaches are working with him to get his bat into the zone quicker. He is learning how to pick his pitch, and needs to develop a better understanding of the strike zone. Yet the Padres were surprised by the overall polish in Jones' game. His performance in the spring will dictate whether he reports to low Class A or extended spring training.

Year	Club (League)	Class	AVG	G	AB	R	H	2B	3B	HR	RBI	BB	SO	SB	OBP	SLG
2004	Padres (AZL)	R	.295	36	149	19	44	11	0	1	25	7	38	1	.327	.389
MINOR LEAGUE TOTALS			.295	36	149	19	44	11	0	1	25	7	38	1	.327	.389

19 Fabian Jimenez, lhp

Born: Aug. 27, 1986. **Ht.:** 6-3. **Wt.:** 170. **Bats:** L. **Throws:** L. **Career Transactions:** Signed out of Colombia by Padres, Aug. 27, 2002. **Signed by:** Robert Rowley.

Pitching in Venezuela as a 16-year old, Jimenez's raw arm attracted the interest of other teams, who have already inquired about him in trade talks. He has the highest upside of any lefthander in the system. Tall and lanky, Jimenez delivers fastballs in the 90-92 mph range, and the Padres believe he could reach the mid-90s as he matures. He generates considerable tilt on his breaking ball, has a good feel for pitching and knows how to set up hitters. Jimenez is still young and raw, and has problems with keeping his mechanics consistent, leading to control problems. He needs to learn how to throw his breaking ball out of the strike zone and get hitters to chase the pitch. His changeup is still far from being a usable offering. With youth on his side, there's no need to rush Jimenez. The co-winner of most improved pitcher honors during instructional league, he'll likely play at Eugene in 2005, but could see time in low Class A if he progresses more quickly.

Year	Club (League)	Class	W	L	ERA	G	GS	CG	SV	IP	H	R	ER	HR	BB	SO	AVG
2003	Tronconerol (VSL)	R	2	2	3.30	16	8	0	0	60	48	30	22	3	23	48	.221
2004	Padres (AZL)	R	2	6	6.95	12	9	0	0	45	60	40	35	0	28	28	.330
MINOR LEAGUE TOTALS			4	8	4.87	28	17	0	0	105	108	70	57	3	51	76	.271

20 Rusty Tucker, rhp

Born: July 15, 1980. **Ht.:** 6-1. **Wt.:** 190. **Bats:** R. **Throws:** L. **School:** University of Maine. **Career Transactions:** Selected by Padres in 21st round of 2001 draft; signed June 11, 2001. **Signed by:** Rene Mons.

Tucker is one of the better stories in the Padres system. Drafted in 2001, he touched the low 90s in his pro debut, but began the 2002 season sitting in the mid-90s and touching 99.

He shot through the Padres system and looked like the team's closer of the future before he had Tommy John surgery in August 2003. Tucker's rehab went as scheduled, and he returned to the mound for late-season work in high Class A last year. When healthy, Tucker's velocity was the best in the system, and he was back to throwing consistently in the low 90s during instructional league. He needs to find the velocity he once had, as his heater offers little in the way of movement. His breaking ball has always been slurvy, and his command spotty. The Padres hope the injury will be a blessing in disguise, forcing Tucker to become more of a pitcher than a thrower. He'll begin anew in 2005, most likely in Double-A.

Year	Club (League)	Class	W	L	ERA	G	GS	CG	SV	IP	H	R	ER	HR	BB	SO	AVG
2001	Idaho Falls (Pio)	R	0	2	7.13	30	0	0	0	35	41	41	28	4	50	43	.297
2002	Fort Wayne (Mid)	A	5	1	1.01	31	0	0	13	36	19	8	4	2	10	50	.150
	Lake Elsinore (Cal)	A	2	3	2.43	26	0	0	14	30	26	10	8	1	18	33	.226
2003	Mobile (SL)	AA	2	6	3.74	51	0	0	28	53	49	26	22	4	31	63	.240
2004	Lake Elsinore (Cal)	A	0	0	7.71	8	0	0	0	7	9	8	6	1	5	6	.300
MINOR LEAGUE TOTALS			9	12	3.81	146	0	0	55	161	144	93	68	12	114	195	.235

21 J.J. Furmaniak, ss

Born: July 31, 1979. **Ht.:** 6-0. **Wt.:** 190. **Bats:** R. **Throws:** R. **School:** Lewis (Ill.) University. **Career Transactions:** Selected by Padres in 22nd round of 2000 draft; signed June 21, 2000. **Signed by:** Bob Cummings.

Furmaniak was seen as an organizational player before finding his stroke in high Class A in 2003. Promoted to Triple-A early in 2004 to replace an injured Jose Nieves, Furmaniak took over at shortstop and never relinquished the position. He has a tremendous work ethic and baseball instincts that allow him to consistently play better than his raw tools would lead you to expect. He doesn't have the prettiest swing, but he gets the job done while showing surprising pop for a middle infielder. Defensively, Furmaniak has a solid arm, but lacks the soft hands required for an everyday shortstop. He would make an excellent utility player, and the Padres sent him to play winter ball in Mexico, where he got time in at second and third base for the first time since 2002. He has an outside chance of earning a utility role in spring training, but at the least should make his major league debut in 2005.

Year	Club (League)	Class	AVG	G	AB	R	H	2B	3B	HR	RBI	BB	SO	SB	OBP	SLG
2000	Idaho Falls (Pio)	R	.343	62	245	72	84	18	2	5	38	44	48	10	.446	.494
2001	Fort Wayne (Mid)	A	.220	123	436	57	96	24	3	5	35	55	117	11	.309	.323
2002	Lake Elsinore (Cal)	A	.257	106	381	50	98	16	6	7	43	26	100	11	.311	.386
2003	Lake Elsinore (Cal)	A	.314	78	309	65	97	22	8	9	54	36	55	10	.397	.524
	Mobile (SL)	AA	.262	31	103	10	27	4	1	3	11	8	27	0	.336	.408
2004	Mobile (SL)	AA	.196	14	51	10	10	4	0	1	8	7	15	1	.305	.333
	Portland (PCL)	AAA	.292	120	425	71	124	24	4	17	73	33	86	8	.346	.487
MINOR LEAGUE TOTALS			.275	534	1950	335	536	112	24	47	262	209	448	51	.351	.429

22 Wilmer Villatoro, rhp

Born: June 27, 1983. **Ht.:** 6-0. **Wt.:** 150. **Bats:** R. **Throws:** R. **Career Transactions:** Signed out of El Salvador by Padres, June 13, 2000. **Signed by:** Bill Clark.

Villatoro continued in his quest to become the first player of El Salvadorian descent to reach the majors with a solid showing in high Class A in 2004. He missed the first month of the season with visa problems and got off to a slow start, but was lights-out in the second half of the year, holding his opponents hitless in 11 of his last 16 outings. Villatoro effortlessly throws a lively fastball that sits at 90-92 mph and can touch 94, a velocity reading that could become more common as he fills out his skinny frame. His slider has a strong break across the plate, but lacks sink and is left up in the zone too often. He has long arms, and his whip-like motion makes his pitches difficult to pick up. He can overthrow at times, sacrificing both command and movement. His slight stature and lack of an offspeed pitch relegate him to the bullpen. He'll get his first big test in 2005 in Double-A.

Year	Club (League)	Class	W	L	ERA	G	GS	CG	SV	IP	H	R	ER	HR	BB	SO	AVG
2000	Padres (AZL)	R	0	0	5.43	2	0	0	0	2	3	4	4	0	2	5	.375
2001	Idaho Falls (Pio)	R	0	3	5.26	30	0	0	3	38	39	24	22	7	21	35	.267
2002	Eugene (NWL)	A	3	7	5.13	22	7	0	2	53	50	36	30	8	19	69	.245
2003	Fort Wayne (Mid)	A	3	2	2.62	39	0	0	2	55	31	20	16	7	28	77	.164
2004	Lake Elsinore (Cal)	A	6	2	2.84	47	0	0	0	67	50	29	21	4	35	67	.218
MINOR LEAGUE TOTALS			12	14	3.90	140	7	0	7	214	173	113	93	26	105	253	.223

23 Yordany Ramirez, of

Born: July 31, 1984. **Ht.:** 6-1. **Wt.:** 160. **Bats:** R. **Throws:** R. **Career Transactions:** Signed out of Dominican Republic by Padres, April 23, 2001. **Signed by:** Felix Francisco/Modesto Ulloa.

A series of minor, nagging injuries have limited Ramirez to just 88 games in his three years, frustrating team officials who see him as possessing possibly the best all-around package of tools in the organization. He flashed them all in Arizona, while also still showing how raw he is. Ramirez has a smooth swing and gap power that should increase as he learns to incorporate his lower half into his swing. He's a flashy center fielder with plus speed and the best outfield arm in the organization. He's too aggressive at the plate and needs to get on base more to take advantage of his excellent baserunning skills. Health is the key for Ramirez, and the Padres would like to see him get a full season in. He made progress in instructional league, choking up on the bat in order to make more contact, and spent the winter on a conditioning program. He'll spend 2005 patrolling center field in low Class A.

Year	Club (League)	Class	AVG	G	AB	R	H	2B	3B	HR	RBI	BB	SO	SB	OBP	SLG
2002	Idaho Falls (Pio)	R	.179	23	78	8	14	1	0	0	5	3	24	0	.244	.192
2003	Idaho Falls (Pio)	R	.266	22	79	7	21	3	0	0	5	3	17	7	.301	.304
2004	Padres (AZL)	R	.264	39	159	23	42	7	5	1	21	4	26	16	.300	.390
	Eugene (NWL)	A	.200	4	15	1	3	0	0	1	3	1	5	0	.250	.400
MINOR LEAGUE TOTALS			.242	88	331	39	80	11	5	2	34	11	72	23	.285	.323

24 Natanael Mateo, rhp

Born: Dec. 24, 1980. **Ht.:** 6-1. **Wt.:** 160. **Bats:** R. **Throws:** R. **Career Transactions:** Signed out of Dominican Republic by Phillies, Nov. 7, 1998 . . . Released by Phillies, June 1, 2000 . . . Signed by Padres, Aug. 13, 2003. **Signed by:** Wil Tejada (Phillies).

Mateo had pitched for five seasons before making his stateside debut. Both the Phillies (for whom he pitched in the Dominican Summer League) and the Hiroshima Carp (for whom he pitched in the Japanese minor leagues) gave up on Mateo, who was signed by the Padres after the 2003 season on the recommendation of one of San Diego's Dominican scouts. Mateo has a live arm, sitting at 90-93 and often touching the mid-90s. He has excellent command of the pitch, not just throwing strikes, but also consistently painting the corners with it. That pitch alone was enough to succeed in A-ball, but he'll need to expand his repertoire to succeed at the higher levels. His slider is flat and slurvy and his changeup is well-below-average. Mateo's delivery is somewhat violent, and he has problems getting into fielding position after release. He will continue to struggle against lefthanded batters, who hit .293 against him last year, unless he can find a secondary offering to combat them. The Padres hope he finds a second pitch quickly as he begins the year in Double-A.

Year	Club (League)	Class	W	L	ERA	G	GS	CG	SV	IP	H	R	ER	HR	BB	SO	AVG
1999	Phillies (DSL)	R	0	0	3.48	6	1	0	0	10	13	12	4	1	2	7	.277
2004	Lake Elsinore (Cal)	A	6	3	2.79	39	0	0	2	52	46	20	16	2	11	59	.228
MINOR LEAGUE TOTALS			6	3	2.90	45	1	0	2	62	59	32	20	3	13	66	.237

25 Ryan Bukvich, rhp

Born: May 13, 1978. **Ht.:** 6-2. **Wt.:** 250. **Bats:** R. **Throws:** R. **School:** University of Mississippi. **Career Transactions:** Selected by Royals in 11th round of 2000 draft; signed June 9, 2000 . . . Traded by Royals with LHP Darrell May to Padres for RHP Dennis Tankersley, OF Terrence Long and cash, Nov. 8, 2004. **Signed by:** Mark Willoughby (Royals).

Inneffectiveness and ineligibility (as a senior) pushed Bukvich down in the draft coming out of college, but Royals scout Mark Willoughby persuaded Kansas City to take him based on the arm strength he showed at Division II Delta State (Miss.) as a freshman. He looked like the Royals' closer of the future after shooting through the system, but problems with command and finding a secondary pitch kept him bouncing between Triple-A Omaha and the majors last season, and the Royals included him with Darrell May in a trade that netted Terrence Long and a Triple-A pitcher the Padres were frustrated with, Dennis Tankersley. Bukvich still has a plus fastball, a power pitch that sits in the mid-90s and generates plenty of swings and misses. But his slider is too slurvy and his changeup lacks movement. He hasn't been able to develop either into an effective offering, and his command has regressed. The Padres still believe in his upside, and hope a change of scenery will be just the ticket for him to put things together at Triple-A and finally break through to the big leagues.

Year	Club (League)	Class	W	L	ERA	G	GS	CG	SV	IP	H	R	ER	HR	BB	SO	AVG
2000	Spokane (NWL)	A	2	0	0.64	10	0	0	2	14	5	1	1	0	9	15	.111
	Charleston WV (SAL)	A	0	0	1.88	11	0	0	4	14	6	3	3	0	7	17	.128
	Wilmington (Car)	A	0	1	8.00	2	0	0	0	2	3	4	4	0	5	3	.375
2001	Wilmington (Car)	A	0	1	1.72	37	0	0	13	58	41	16	11	1	31	80	.194
	Wichita (TL)	AA	0	0	3.75	7	0	0	0	12	9	6	5	2	2	14	.200
2002	Wichita (TL)	AA	1	1	1.31	23	0	0	8	34	17	8	5	0	15	47	.145
	Omaha (PCL)	AAA	1	0	0.00	12	0	0	8	14	4	0	0	0	7	17	.093
	Kansas City (AL)	MAJ	1	0	6.12	26	0	0	0	25	26	19	17	2	19	20	.277
2003	Kansas City (AL)	MAJ	1	0	9.58	9	0	0	0	10	12	11	11	2	9	8	.293

			W	L	ERA	G	CG	SV		IP	H	R	ER	HR	BB	SO	AVG
	Omaha (PCL)	AAA	1	2	4.91	34	0	0	5	37	39	21	20	2	25	44	.273
2004	Omaha (PCL)	AAA	3	4	4.37	38	0	0	7	47	33	25	23	4	30	60	.193
	Kansas City (AL)	MAJ	0	0	3.68	9	0	0	1	7	4	3	3	0	7	7	.182
MAJOR LEAGUE TOTALS			2	0	6.54	44	0	0	1	43	42	33	31	4	35	35	.268
MINOR LEAGUE TOTALS			8	9	2.79	174	0	0	47	232	157	84	72	9	131	297	.189

26 Michael Johnson, 1b

Born: June 25, 1980. **Ht.:** 6-3. **Wt.:** 215. **Bats:** L. **Throws:** R. **School:** Clemson University. **Career Transactions:** Selected by Padres in second round of 2002 draft; signed June 2, 2003. **Signed by:** Mike Rikard.

Johnson was one of the biggest disappointments in the organization in 2004. Drafted in 2002 one round after his Clemson teammate, Khalil Greene, Johnson returned to Clemson when negotiations broke down but was able to sign a week before the 2003 draft for $500,000 because he was a fifth-year senior. The Padres planned for Johnson to open his first full season in high Class A with a midseason promotion to Double-A, but a slew of injuries, including a dislocated kneecap that cost him a month, limited his playing time. When he was healthy, he was far from an offensive force. Johnson does have skills. He has plus raw power and draws plenty of walks, and he's a solid defender. Johnson can get too pull-conscious, leaving him susceptible on the outer half of the plate. His confidence took a hit during the year, causing him to get what one scout called "passive aggressive," as he'd wait too long for the perfect pitch and then overswing, trying to hit the ball a mile. He's a below-average runner. Johnson will turn 25 during the 2005 season and needs to start moving. He was impressive in instructional league, so the Padres hope he'll carry that success into 2005 in Double-A.

Year	Club (League)	Class	AVG	G	AB	R	H	2B	3B	HR	RBI	BB	SO	SB	OBP	SLG
2003	Lake Elsinore (Cal)	A	.275	46	178	22	49	17	1	5	24	17	48	0	.343	.466
2004	Lake Elsinore (Cal)	A	.254	90	331	55	84	23	2	15	64	52	106	0	.353	.471
MINOR LEAGUE TOTALS			.261	136	509	77	133	40	3	20	88	69	154	0	.350	.470

27 Luis Cruz, ss

Born: Feb. 10, 1984. **Ht.:** 6-1. **Wt.:** 180. **Bats:** R. **Throws:** R. **Career Transactions:** Signed out of Mexico by Red Sox, Aug. 29, 2000 . . . Traded by Red Sox to Padres for 2B Cesar Crespo, Dec. 16, 2002. **Signed by:** Ray Poitevint/Lee Sigman (Red Sox).

Originally signed by the Red Sox, Cruz was one of the youngest everyday players in high Class A last year, and he showed marked improvement in his all-around game. Cruz is a defensive whiz, with plus range, a solid arm and remarkably quick hands and feet. He takes an aggressive, contact-oriented approach to the plate, and while he rarely strikes out, he does have gap power. He offers little in the way of projection offensively, however, and too often chases balls out of the zone. Already an average runner at best, he has a thick lower half, leaving a concern that he'll lose quickness as his body matures. Cruz has seen limited time at second base and third in the past two seasons and looked good at both positions, so he projects as a defense-first utilityman in the majors. He'll spend the 2005 season at Mobile, a far different hitter's environment from Lake Elsinore, which should present a significant challenge to his offensive game.

Year	Club (League)	Class	AVG	G	AB	R	H	2B	3B	HR	RBI	BB	SO	SB	OBP	SLG
2001	Red Sox (GCL)	R	.259	53	197	18	51	9	0	3	18	7	17	1	.285	.350
2002	Augusta (SAL)	A	.188	58	202	16	38	7	1	3	15	9	30	0	.221	.277
	Red Sox (GCL)	R	.292	21	72	10	21	4	0	0	9	3	6	2	.329	.347
2003	Fort Wayne (Mid)	A	.231	129	481	55	111	24	1	8	53	30	55	2	.279	.335
2004	Lake Elsinore(Cal)	A	.277	124	512	75	142	35	3	8	72	24	56	3	.310	.404
MINOR LEAGUE TOTALS			.248	385	1464	174	363	79	5	22	167	73	164	8	.285	.354

28 Javier Martinez, rhp

Born: Dec. 9, 1982. **Ht.:** 6-3. **Wt.:** 170. **Bats:** B. **Throws:** R. **Career Transactions:** Signed out of Mexico by Padres, March 26, 2000. **Signed by:** Jack Pierce.

With their major league team just 15 miles from the Mexican border, Padres scouts have worked hard in Mexico, and they still believe they found a gem in Martinez, who has been sidetracked by injuries over the last two years. He was plagued by elbow soreness in 2003, while arthroscopic shoulder surgery cost him the entire 2004 season. When healthy, Martinez' total package still reminds scouts of former Padres farmhand Oliver Perez, another find from Mexico whom the Padres traded to the Pirates in the Brian Giles deal. Martinez has four solid pitches. His fastball sits in the low 90s, and his splitter gives batters a different look and has good movement. Both his curveball and changeup have the potential to be plus offerings. Adjusting his mechanics to catch up with his physical maturity led to injuries, but the Padres say he could be on the verge of a breakthrough if he can stay healthy. Martinez made up for lost time by pitching in the Mexican Pacific League over the winter, and will begin the year in high Class A, with a midseason promotion to Double-A in the plans.

Year	Club (League)	Class	W	L	ERA	G	GS	CG	SV	IP	H	R	ER	HR	BB	SO	AVG
2000	Padres (AZL)	R	0	0	0.00	3	0	0	1	3	0	0	0	0	3	2	.000
2001	Idaho Falls (Pio)	R	1	4	6.43	10	8	0	0	42	42	35	30	6	26	38	.261
2002	Eugene (NWL)	A	0	0	4.50	2	2	0	0	10	4	5	5	2	5	6	.121
	Fort Wayne (Mid)	A	6	4	3.38	12	12	0	0	69	55	28	26	5	19	69	.211
2003	Lake Elsinore (Cal)	A	6	3	3.23	16	16	0	0	84	76	35	30	7	23	70	.234
2004	Did not play—Injured																
MINOR LEAGUE TOTALS			13	11	3.93	43	38	0	1	208	177	103	91	20	76	185	.224

29 Dale Thayer, rhp

Born: Dec. 17, 1980. **Ht.:** 6-0. **Wt.:** 190. **Bats:** R. **Throws:** R. **School:** Chico State (Calif.) University. **Career Transactions:** Signed as nondrafted free agent by Padres, Sept. 25, 2002. **Signed by:** Mal Fichman.

Thayer is yet another free agent find for the Padres, as he went undrafted despite leading the Orange Empire Conference in saves at Santa Ana (Calif.) Junior College in 2001, and earning Division II all-America honors at Chico State in 2002. In his first pro season, managers named him the low Class A Midwest League's best relief prospect. Thayer gave up seven runs in his first outing of 2004, but then just five runs in his next 49 games, settling into the closer role at Lake Elsinore and earning a late promotion to Mobile. Thayer's hard slider is a true out pitch, breaking sharply across the plate. His fastball sits at 89-92 mph, leaving scouts to wonder if his velocity is enough to set up the slider at the higher levels. Short and stocky, Thayer doesn't get much of a downward plane on any of his pitches, so location is a key. The Padres are excited about the trio of relievers who pitched at Lake Elsinore in 2004, and Thayer will join Wilmer Villatoro and Natanael Mateo in the Mobile bullpen to open 2005.

Year	Club (League)	Class	W	L	ERA	G	GS	CG	SV	IP	H	R	ER	HR	BB	SO	AVG
2003	Fort Wayne (Mid)	A	1	3	2.06	45	0	0	25	48	31	15	11	2	15	72	.182
2004	Mobile (SL)	AA	1	1	3.68	8	0	0	0	7	8	3	3	1	1	7	.267
	Lake Elsinore (Cal)	A	2	1	1.63	50	0	0	23	55	36	12	10	1	11	54	.181
MINOR LEAGUE TOTALS			4	5	1.95	103	0	0	48	111	75	30	24	4	27	133	.188

30 Randy Williams, lhp

Born: Sept. 18, 1975. **Ht.:** 6-3. **Wt.:** 190. **Bats:** L. **Throws:** L. **School:** Lamar University. **Career Transactions:** Selected by Cubs in 12th round of 1997 draft; signed June 6, 1997 . . . Released by Cubs, March 24, 2001 . . . Signed by Mariners, Sept. 30, 2002 . . . Traded by Mariners to Padres for OF Billy Hogan, Nov. 19, 2004. **Signed by:** Buzzy Keller (Cubs).

Looking to shore up an organizational weakness in lefty relievers, the Padres made an off-season deal with the Mariners to acquire Williams for 2003 fifth-round pick Billy Hogan, whose play and makeup had been a disappointment. Williams was drafted by the Cubs in 1997, but pitched in just 16 games over four years, sidelined by a variety of injuries including Tommy John surgery in 2000. He gave baseball another shot in 2002, when he dominated in the independent Central League and caught the eyes of Mariners scouts, who like the Padres watch the indy leagues closely. Williams was the pitcher of the year at Triple-A Tacoma in 2004, and earned an emergency callup to the big leagues in September, holding lefthanded batters hitless in seven at-bats. Williams has average velocity and a good slider, which give him a chance to have success as a lefty specialist. At 29, he is what he is, and he'll enter spring training as a favorite to win a bullpen job.

Year	Club (League)	Class	W	L	ERA	G	GS	CG	SV	IP	H	R	ER	HR	BB	SO	AVG
1997	Did not play—Injured																
1998	Cubs (AZL)	R	1	0	.00	2	1	0	0	3	0	0	0	0	2	6	.000
1999	Daytona (FSL)	A	3	4	4.75	14	9	0	1	53	55	36	28	5	30	47	.266
2000	Did not play—Injured																
2001	Did not play																
2002	Edinburg (Cent)	IND	5	2	1.20	42	0	0	10	53	36	8	7	1	12	77	.193
2003	San Antonio (TL)	AA	4	1	1.73	29	0	0	2	42	33	9	8	2	7	38	.213
2003	Tacoma (PCL)	AAA	2	2	5.26	18	0	0	1	26	25	17	15	3	11	19	.253
2004	Tacoma (PCL)	AAA	7	2	3.63	50	0	0	8	79	68	37	32	6	46	64	.230
	Seattle (AL)	MAJ	0	0	5.79	6	0	0	0	5	3	3	3	0	6	4	.188
MAJOR LEAGUE TOTALS			0	0	5.79	6	0	0	0	5	3	3	3	0	6	4	.188
MINOR LEAGUE TOTALS			17	9	3.67	113	10	0	22	204	181	99	83	16	96	174	.236

SAN FRANCISCO
GIANTS
BY **JOHN MANUEL**

The Giants don't want a book written about how they run their baseball operation. They have no desire to be Organization of the Year. They just want to win the World Series. That hasn't happened since 1954, when the franchise was still based in New York.

With Barry Bonds still hitting like few humans ever have, San Francisco has chosen to go all out to maximize their opportunity. As one club official said, "Very few clubs can afford to spend at both the top end and the bottom end of the organization," so the Giants have chosen to spend at the top. Bonds can best be helped by major league free agents, not amateurs signed through the draft who might take years to reach San Francisco. After closer Robb Nen got hurt and missed the last two seasons, for example, the Giants replaced him with free-agent closer Armando Benitez.

San Francisco has focused so much on pitching that it hasn't developed an everyday player since drafting Bill Mueller and Chris Singleton in 1993. So to fill out the lineup around Bonds, the Giants have added free agents Moises Alou (39, son of manager Felipe), catcher Mike Matheny (34) and shortstop Omar Vizquel (37).

Vice president of player personnel Dick Tidrow's scouting and player-development staffs are proficient at finding and cultivating pitching, and San Francisco remains flush in minor league arms even after trading or graduating several. Behind imported ace Jason Schmidt, four homegrown starters

STEVE MOORE

will compete for innings in 2005: Jerome Williams, Brad Hennessey, **Noah Lowry** and Jesse Foppert. The farm system has more pitching available, starting with right-hander Matt Cain, who spent half the 2004 season in Double-A at 19. Power right-handers Merkin Valdez and David Aardsma are ready to help the big league bullpen after appearing briefly with the Giants last year.

San Francisco is making an attempt to address its shortcoming in developing hitters—which becomes all the more evident now that the big league lineup's youngest player is 31-year-old Edgardo Alfonzo. New minor league hitting instructor Bob Mariano has some interesting bats to work with. Tidrow used his first three picks last June on outfielders. Eddy Martinez-Esteve (second round) and Clay Timpner (fourth) finished the summer with San Jose in the high Class A California League playoffs, while John Bowker (third) hit .371 in the lower minors. San Jose's postseason lineup included most of the organization's top hitters, including outfielders Freddy Lewis and Nate Schierholtz and corner infielders Travis Ishikawa and Brian Buscher.

This offseason's free-agent signings have left San Francisco without choices in the first three rounds of the 2005 draft. That doesn't mean the Giants have given up on their farm system. They'd just rather spend their money on the present than on the future.

TOP 30 PROSPECTS

1. Matt Cain, rhp	16. Justin Knoedler, c
2. Merkin Valdez, rhp	17. Marcus Sanders, 2b
3. Fred Lewis, of	18. Clay Timpner, of
4. Eddy Martinez-Esteve, of	19. Jeremy Accardo, rhp
5. Nate Schierholtz, of/3b	20. Billy Sadler, rhp
6. Alfredo Simon, rhp	21. Lance Niekro, 1b/3b
7. Brad Hennessey, rhp	22. Brian Burres, lhp
8. Craig Whitaker, rhp	23. Jonathan Sanchez, lhp
9. David Aardsma, rhp	24. Garrett Broshuis, rhp
10. Travis Ishikawa, 1b	25. Scott Munter, rhp
11. Pat Misch, lhp	26. Todd Jennings, c
12. Dan Ortmeier, of	27. Pablo Sandoval, c
13. John Bowker, of	28. Mike Mooney, of
14. Brian Buscher, 3b	29. Chris Begg, rhp
15. Todd Linden, of	30. Erick Threets, lhp

ORGANIZATION OVERVIEW

General manager: Brian Sabean. **Farm and scouting director:** Dick Tidrow.

2004 PERFORMANCE

Class	Farm Team	League	W	L	Pct.	Finish*	Manager
Majors	San Francisco	National	91	71	.562	5th (16)	Felipe Alou
Triple-A	Fresno Grizzlies	Pacific Coast	62	82	.431	15th (16)	Fred Stanley
Double-A	Norwich Navigators	Eastern	69	73	.486	t-7th (12)	Shane Turner
High A	San Jose Giants	California	74	66	.529	4th (10)	Lenn Sakata
Low A	#Hagerstown Suns	South Atlantic	49	88	.358	16th (16)	Mike Ramsey
Short-season	Salem-Keizer Volcanoes	Northwest	37	39	.487	6th (8)	Joe Strain
Rookie	AZL Giants	Arizona	36	19	.655	+1st (9)	Bert Hunter
OVERALL 2004 MINOR LEAGUE RECORD			327	367	.471	22nd (30)	

*Finish in overall standings (No. of teams in league). +League champion. #Affiliate will be in Augusta (South Atlantic) in 2005.

ORGANIZATION LEADERS

BATTING
*Minimum 250 at-bats

*AVG	Brian Horwitz, Salem-Keizer	.347
R	Todd Linden, Fresno	93
H	Jason Ellison, Fresno	159
TB	Mike Cervenak, Fresno/Norwich	266
2B	Nate Schierholtz, San Jose/Hagerstown	40
3B	Doug Clark, Norwich	13
HR	Mike Cervenak, Fresno/Norwich	26
RBI	Mike Cervenak, Fresno/Norwich	98
BB	Fred Lewis, Fresno/San Jose	89
SO	Todd Linden, Fresno	149
SB	Fred Lewis, Fresno/San Jose	34
*OBP	Fred Lewis, Fresno/San Jose	.424
*SLG	Mike Cervenak, Fresno/Norwich	.586

PITCHING
#Minimum 75 innings

W	Matt Cain, Norwich/San Jose	13
L	Josh Habel, Norwich	10
	Brian Stirm, San Jose	10
#ERA	Joe Bateman, Norwich/Hagerstown	2.30
G	Jeremy Accardo, Norwich/San Jose	57
	Lee Gardner, Fresno	57
CG	Pat Misch, Norwich	4
SV	Jeremy Accardo, Norwich/San Jose	28
IP	Ryan Jensen, Fresno	170
BB	Ryan Jensen, Fresno	81
SO	Matt Cain, Norwich/San Jose	161

BEST TOOLS

Best Hitter for Average	Eddy Martinez-Esteve
Best Power Hitter	Nate Schierholtz
Best Strike-Zone Discipline	Fred Lewis
Fastest Baserunner	Marcus Sanders
Best Athlete	Fred Lewis
Best Fastball	Merkin Valdez
Best Curveball	Matt Cain
Best Slider	Brad Hennessey
Best Changeup	Pat Misch
Best Control	Pat Misch
Best Defensive Catcher	Justin Knoedler
Best Defensive Infielder	Derin McMains
Best Infield Arm	Jeremiah Luster
Best Defensive Outfielder	Clay Timpner
Best Outfield Arm	Mike Mooney

PROJECTED 2008 LINEUP

Catcher	Justin Knoedler
First Base	Travis Ishikawa
Second Base	Marcus Sanders
Third Base	Edgardo Alfonzo
Shortstop	Jeremiah Luster
Left Field	Eddy Martinez-Esteve
Center Field	Fred Lewis
Right Field	Nate Schierholtz

No. 1 Starter	Jason Schmidt
No. 2 Starter	Jesse Foppert
No. 3 Starter	Matt Cain
No. 4 Starter	Jerome Williams
No. 5 Starter	Noah Lowry
Closer	Merkin Valdez

LAST YEAR'S TOP 20 PROSPECTS

1. Merkin Valdez, rhp	11. Todd Jennings, c
2. Matt Cain, rhp	12. Nate Schierholtz, 3b
3. David Aardsma, rhp	13. Erick Threets, lhp
4. Dan Ortmeier, of	14. Lance Niekro, 1b
5. Todd Linden, of	15. Noah Lowry, lhp
6. Kevin Correia, rhp	16. Brooks McNiven, rhp
7. Travis Ishikawa, 1b	17. Justin Knoedler, c
8. Craig Whitaker, rhp	18. Jon Armitage, of
9. Fred Lewis, of	19. Jamie Athas, 2b/ss
10. Brian Buscher, 3b	20. Glenn Woolard, rhp

TOP PROSPECTS OF THE DECADE

Year	Player, Pos.	Current Team
1995	J.R. Phillips, 1b	Out of baseball
1996	Shawn Estes, lhp	Diamondbacks
1997	Joe Fontenot, rhp	Out of baseball
1998	Jason Grilli, rhp	White Sox
1999	Jason Grilli, rhp	White Sox
2000	Kurt Ainsworth, rhp	Orioles
2001	Jerome Williams, rhp	Giants
2002	Jerome Williams, rhp	Giants
2003	Jesse Foppert, rhp	Giants
2004	Merkin Valdez, rhp	Giants

TOP DRAFT PICKS OF THE DECADE

Year	Player, Pos.	Current Team
1995	Joe Fontenot, rhp	Out of baseball
1996	*Matt White, rhp	Devil Rays
1997	Jason Grilli, rhp	White Sox
1998	Tony Torcato, 3b	Giants
1999	Kurt Ainsworth, rhp	Giants
2000	Boof Bonser, rhp	Twins
2001	Brad Hennessey, rhp	Giants
2002	Matt Cain, rhp	Giants
2003	David Aardsma, rhp	Giants
2004	Eddy Martinez-Esteve, of (2)	Giants

*Did not sign.

ALL-TIME LARGEST BONUSES

Jason Grilli, 1997	$1,875,000
David Aardsma, 2003	$1,425,000
Brad Hennessey, 2001	$1,380,000
Matt Cain, 2002	$1,375,000
Osvaldo Fernandez, 1996	$1,300,000
Kurt Ainsworth, 2000	$1,300,000

MINOR LEAGUE DEPTH CHART

San Francisco GIANTS

Impact Potential: B

In Matt Cain, the Giants have one of the game's elite prospects, a power righthander who succeeded in Double-A as a teenager. Merkin Valdez, David Aardsma and Brad Hennessey all have already reached the majors, and all could fill roles in San Francisco in 2005. Fred Lewis is on the older side, but his 20-20 power-speed potential is tantalizing.

Depth: C

It would be hard for any organization to maintain pitching depth while graduating (Jerome Williams, Jesse Foppert, Noah Lowry) or trading (Boof Bonser, Francisco Liriano, Josh Habel, Glenn Woolard) so many pitchers. And the Giants' depth has taken a hit. But the organization has more position players with potential than it has had in at least a decade.

*Depth charts prepared by **John Manuel** and **Allan Simpson**. Numbers in parentheses indicate prospect rankings.*

LF
Eddy Martinez-Esteve (4)
John Bowker (13)
Todd Linden (15)
Adam Shabala
Tony Torcato
Mike Wagner

CF
Fred Lewis (3)
Clay Timpner (18)
Jason Ellison
Emanuel Cividanes

RF
Nate Schierholtz (5)
Dan Ortmeier (12)
Mike Mooney (28)
Jon Armitage
Carlos Sosa

3B
Brian Buscher (14)
Mike Cervenak
Lisandro Disla

SS
Jeremiah Luster
Tim Hutting

2B
Marcus Sanders (17)
Kevin Frandsen
Aaron Sobieraj
Derin McMains

1B
Travis Ishikawa (10)
Lance Niekro (21)
Brad Vericker
Will Thompson

SOURCE of TALENT

HOMEGROWN		ACQUIRED	
College	16	Trades	2
Junior College	4	Rule 5 draft	0
Draft-and-follow	2	Independent leagues	1
High School	3	Free agents/waivers	0
Nondrafted free agent	1		
Foreign	1		

C
Justin Knoedler (16)
Todd Jennings (26)
Pablo Sandoval (27)
Trey Lunsford

RHP

Starters	Relievers
Matt Cain (1)	David Aardsma (9)
Merkin Valdez (2)	Jeremy Accardo (19)
Alfredo Simon (6)	Billy Sadler (20)
Brad Hennessey (7)	Scott Munter (25)
Craig Whitaker (8)	Joe Bateman
Garrett Broshuis (24)	Sean Martin
Chris Begg (29)	Hairo Solis
Kelvyn Acosta	
Kellen Ludwig	
Justin Hedrick	
Brooks McNiven	
Ben Thurmond	
Brian Wilson	
Osiris Matos	
Benny Cepeda	

LHP

Starters	Relievers
Pat Misch (11)	Erick Threets (30)
Brian Burres (22)	Tim Alvarez
Jonathan Sanchez (23)	Travis Nesmith
Jesus Reina	Eugene Espinelli

DRAFT ANALYSIS

2004

Best Pro Debut: OF Eddy Martinez-Esteve (2) hit .329 between four clubs, including .420 at high Class A. OF John Bowker (3) opened 22-for-43 in the Rookie-level Arizona League and hit .371-6-27 overall.

Best Athlete: OF Emanuel Cividanes (16) and SS Jeremiah Luster (18), though both are raw. Cividanes was ineligible at Broward (Fla.) CC during the spring and didn't get much exposure. Luster drew interest from college football and basketball recruiters. OF Clay Timpner (4) is an excellent center fielder with solid tools and more polish.

Best Pure Hitter: Martinez-Esteve or Bowker. Martinez-Esteve just missed the Atlantic Coast Conference triple crown by two RBIs at Florida State by hitting .385-19-81.

Best Raw Power: Again, it's Martinez-Esteve or Bowker. Bowker can pound fastballs and breaking balls alike, and he has more present power. Martinez-Esteve is just scratching the surface of his potential because he's content to use the whole field.

Fastest Runner: Draft-and-follow 2B Marcus Sanders (17 in 2003) has top-of-the-line speed. He gets from the right side to first base in under 4.0 seconds, and he led the AZL with 28 steals. Among this year's crop, Timpner is fastest. His speed rates a 60 on the 20-80 scouting scale, and his first-step quickness is better.

Best Defensive Player: Timpner is an excellent center fielder. His speed, jumps and routes are all assets. 2B Kevin Frandsen (12) has quick hands and actions.

Best Fastball: RHP Jonathan Sanchez' (27) explosive 89-94 mph fastball allowed him to strike out 61 in 48 pro innings. RHP Justin Hedrick (6) pitches at 88-92 but hit-

BILL MITCHELL

Martinez-Esteve

ters don't see his fastball well. He led the Cape Cod League in strikeouts in 2003 and fanned 48 in 36 pro innings.

Best Breaking Ball: RHP Garrett Broshuis' (5) best pitch is his slider. Hedrick's splitter was much more effective last summer than it was at Northeastern.

Most Intriguing Background: Luster is a distant cousin of Devil Rays phenom B.J. Upton.

Closest To The Majors: The three outfielders at the top of the draft are logical candidates, but the Giants always seem to expedite the development of a pitcher. Broshuis, who also throws a plus changeup and an 88-89 mph fastball, could be the guy.

Best Late-Round Pick: Area scout Sean O'Connor not only sold San Francisco on Ohio Dominican teammates Sanchez and RHP Benny Cepeda (48), but he also told the Giants they could be drafted late. Cepeda has a 92-93 mph fastball. Though they need to refine their secondary pitches, there's no questioning that they have live arms.

The One Who Got Away: LHP Jamie Arnesen (9) is 6-foot-5 and flashes a 90-91 mph fastball. An honors student in high school, he's attending Fresno State.

Assessment: The Giants haven't developed an everyday big leaguer since drafting Bill Mueller and Chris Singleton in 1993. Between Martinez-Esteve, Bowker and Timpner, they hope they've ended that drought.

2003 The Giants didn't find any stars, but they got several players off to promising starts: RHPs David Aardsma (1) and Craig Whitaker (1), OF/3B Nate Schierholtz (2), 3B Brian Buscher (7), LHP Pat Misch (7) and draft-and-follow 2B Marcus Sanders (17). **GRADE:** B

2002 RHP Matt Cain (1) is one of the game's top pitching prospects. OFs Fred Lewis (2) and Dan Ortmeier (3), RHP Kevin Correia (4) and 1B Travis Ishikawa (21) should provide help as well. **GRADE:** B+

2001 RHP Brad Hennessey (1) and LHP Noah Lowry (1) contributed in the rotation down the stretch last year, but the other first-rounder, OF Todd Linden, hasn't been able to establish himself in the majors. RHP Jesse Foppert (2) was far ahead of all three of them before requiring Tommy John surgery. **GRADE:** B

2000 RHP Boof Bonser (1) was overdrafted, but at least he was used to get A.J. Pierzynski. 1B/3B Lance Niekro (2) and LHP Erick Threets (7) have done nothing more than tease. **GRADE:** D

Draft analysis prepared by Jim Callis. Numbers in parentheses indicate draft rounds.

rhp

Matt
CAIN

Born: Oct. 1, 1984.
Ht.: 6-3. **Wt.:** 180.
Bats: R. **Throws:** R.
School: Houston HS, Germantown, Tenn.
Career Transactions: Selected by Giants in first round (25th overall) of 2002 draft; signed June 26, 2002.
Signed by: Lee Elder.

C ain came up through suburban Memphis' competitive amateur system, which in recent years has produced such pitchers as early 2003 draft picks Paul Maholm (Pirates, first round) and Stuart Pomeranz (Cardinals, second) and college prospects Mark Holliman (Mississippi), Conor Lalor (South Carolina) and John Lalor (Mississippi State). After playing for the Dulin's Dodgers, a national amateur power, and starring for Houston High (also the alma mater of Pomeranz and the Lalor brothers), Cain committed to play college ball at Memphis. The Giants changed his plans when they drafted him 25th overall in 2002 and gave him a $1.375 million bonus. He pitched briefly that summer, then had his first full season truncated by a stress fracture in his right elbow. Cain was healthy in 2004 and didn't miss a start. He had a string of 19 straight outings without allowing more than two earned runs, including his first seven after a promotion to Double-A Norwich at age 19. He tired in late August, in part because he worked 159 innings after totaling 93 in his first two seasons, but that couldn't take the edge off his tremendous performance.

Cain matches a mature approach to pitching with electric stuff. His fastball consistently sits at 92-95 mph while touching 97, and he's learning to change speeds with it. His power breaking ball, more of a curveball than a slider, is a second plus pitch, a 77-80 mph downer with the potential to be better as he tightens its rotation and learns how to set it up. He has made great strides with his straight changeup, and scouts say it has a chance to be an average or even above-average pitch thanks to his simple delivery and clean arm action. For all his stuff, the Giants say Cain's best traits are his maturity and strong desire to be great. He's a student of the game who takes his side work seriously. He asks intelligent questions of his coaches, then shows the aptitude to take what he has learned to the mound.

Cain dispelled doubts about his health by holding up for the entire 2004 season, but the toll it took on him was evident at the end. His velocity tailed off and he got hammered in his last three starts. The Giants are confident that as he continues to mature physically and becomes more accustomed to the rigors of pro ball, he'll be strong enough to handle the full-season grind. His control wasn't nearly as sharp in Double-A as it had been at high Class A San Jose, though that probably was the result of fatigue.

The Giants have enough young arms competing for innings in San Francisco that they can afford to be patient with Cain—who has a higher ceiling than any of them. He's not yet on the 40-man roster, but he's accelerating his timetable and the Giants haven't been shy about promoting their top arms. Though he may begin 2005 back in Double-A, he could finish the season in the majors.

Year	Club (League)	Class	W	L	ERA	G	GS	CG	SV	IP	H	R	ER	HR	BB	SO	AVG
2002	Giants (AZL)	R	0	1	3.72	8	7	0	0	19	13	10	8	1	11	20	.197
2003	Hagerstown (SAL)	A	4	4	2.55	14	14	0	0	74	57	24	21	5	24	90	.209
2004	Norwich (EL)	AA	6	4	3.35	15	15	0	0	86	73	44	32	7	40	72	.227
	San Jose (Cal)	A	7	1	1.86	13	13	0	0	73	58	25	15	5	17	89	.216
MINOR LEAGUE TOTALS			17	10	2.71	50	49	0	0	252	201	103	76	18	92	271	.217

Merkin Valdez, rhp

Born: Nov. 5, 1981. **Ht.:** 6-3. **Wt.:** 170. **Bats:** R. **Throws:** R. **Career Transactions:** Signed out of Dominican Republic by Braves, Nov. 18, 1999 . . . Traded by Braves with LHP Damian Moss to Giants for RHP Russ Ortiz, Dec. 17, 2002. **Signed by:** Felix Francisco (Braves).

He hadn't pitched above Rookie ball when the Giants got him from the Braves in the Russ Ortiz trade in December 2002, but Valdez quickly burst onto the prospect scene with a dominant 2003 season at low Class A Hagerstown. He never found a consistent rhythm in 2004, because he came down with shoulder tendinitis and shuttled between four teams. Valdez has two pitches that can make hitters look bad. His fastball sits in the mid-90s when he starts and touches 99 mph when he relieves. His mid-80s power slider, which touches 87 mph, has excellent bite when he stays on top of it. His compact delivery helps him harness his power. His feel for pitching improved in 2004, as he learned when to take a little off his fastball and how to move it to different quadrants of the strike zone. Because he sometimes wraps his hand around his slider and gets under it, Valdez can lose the feel for his second pitch. He doesn't trust his developing changeup, which he'll need to remain a starter. The Giants have yet to decide if Valdez, who has closer's stuff, is better suited for relief. That's their more immediate need, and he worked in that role in winter ball. He could win a big league job this spring as a set-up man for Armando Benitez.

Year	Club (League)	Class	W	L	ERA	G	GS	CG	SV	IP	H	R	ER	HR	BB	SO	AVG
2000	Braves (DSL)	R	1	5	1.57	14	7	0	0	57	52	27	10	2	14	32	.234
2001	Braves (DSL)	R	6	7	2.93	15	14	1	0	92	93	41	30	0	18	48	.258
2002	Braves (GCL)	R	7	3	1.98	12	8	1	0	68	47	18	15	0	12	76	.193
2003	Hagerstown (SAL)	A	9	5	2.25	26	26	2	0	156	119	42	39	11	49	166	.213
2004	Fresno (PCL)	AAA	0	0	7.20	1	1	0	0	5	6	4	4	0	4	5	.333
	San Jose (Cal)	A	3	1	2.52	7	7	0	0	36	30	12	10	4	5	44	.219
	San Francisco (NL)	MAJ	0	0	27.00	2	0	0	0	2	4	5	5	1	3	2	.444
	Norwich (EL)	AA	1	4	4.32	10	7	0	1	42	35	21	20	3	15	31	.224
MAJOR LEAGUE TOTALS			0	0	27.00	2	0	0	1	2	4	5	5	1	3	2	.444
MINOR LEAGUE TOTALS			27	25	2.53	85	70	4	0	456	382	165	128	20	117	402	.225

Fred Lewis, of

Born: Dec. 9, 1980. **Ht.:** 6-2. **Wt.:** 190. **Bats:** L. **Throws:** R. **School:** Southern University. **Career Transactions:** Selected by Giants in second round of 2002 draft; signed June 20, 2002. **Signed by:** Tom Korenek.

A two-sport athlete who played football at Mississippi Gulf Coast Junior College and Southern, Lewis was raw when he was drafted but added significant polish in 2004. He fought off nagging leg injuries early in the season to lead the system in on-base percentage, walks and steals, making it an easy decision for the Giants to protect him on the 40-man roster. No one in the system can match Lewis' all-around offensive tools, and his skills are starting to catch up. His bat speed and plate discipline are the best among Giants farmhands. As he grows into his pull power, he should start to hit 20-25 homers annually. He runs well and has good range in center field, where his jumps and routes have improved. Lewis doesn't play with consistent intensity and can be moody, and he needs experience to improve his instincts and learn nuances of the game such as pitch recognition and situational hitting. He's most raw on the basepaths, where he needs to learn to take more aggressive leads and get better jumps. Though he struggled in the Arizona Fall League, Lewis' combination of tools and hitting ability have him close to breaking the Giants' drought of developing an everyday player. He'll start 2005 in Double-A and isn't far from supplanting veteran Marquis Grissom in center field for San Francisco.

Year	Club (League)	Class	AVG	G	AB	R	H	2B	3B	HR	RBI	BB	SO	SB	OBP	SLG
2002	Salem-Keizer (NWL)	A	.322	58	239	43	77	9	3	1	23	26	58	9	.396	.397
2003	Hagerstown (SAL)	A	.250	114	420	61	105	17	8	1	27	68	112	30	.361	.336
2004	San Jose (Cal)	A	.301	115	439	88	132	20	11	8	57	84	109	33	.424	.451
	Fresno (PCL)	AAA	.304	6	23	3	7	1	0	1	2	5	5	1	.429	.478
MINOR LEAGUE TOTALS			.286	293	1121	195	321	47	22	11	109	183	284	73	.395	.397

Eddy Martinez-Esteve, of

Born: July 14, 1983. **Ht.:** 6-3. **Wt.:** 193. **Bats:** R. **Throws:** R. **School:** Florida State University. **Career Transactions:** Selected by Giants in second round of 2004 draft; signed July 8, 2004. **Signed by:** Paul Turco Jr.

An unsigned third-round pick of the Mariners in 2002, Martinez-Esteve was plagued by hamstring problems as a freshman at Florida State. He moved from third base to the outfield last spring and missed winning the Atlantic Coast Conference triple crown by two RBIs. Signed for $537,500 as a draft-eligible sophomore, he just kept hitting as a pro, batting .455 in the California League playoffs. It's all about the bat for Martinez-Esteve. He's adept at making adjustments at the plate because he has a low-maintenance swing that he repeats easily. He has solid bat speed and excellent raw strength, overpowering balls to all fields. Martinez-Esteve had average arm strength before he had offseason shoulder surgery to repair a torn right labrum. It's unclear how his arm will come back. He already had earned a reputation as an indifferent defender in college. His routes and instincts will have to improve to make him a passable left fielder. The Giants aren't in a hurry to replace their current left fielder, so Martinez-Esteve will have time to learn the position. His bat could expedite his route to San Francisco. He'll start 2005 down the road at San Jose.

Year	Club (League)	Class	AVG	G	AB	R	H	2B	3B	HR	RBI	BB	SO	SB	OBP	SLG
2004	Giants (AZL)	R	.357	4	14	2	5	2	0	0	4	0	2	2	.375	.500
	Salem-Keizer (NWL)	A	.286	10	35	5	10	4	0	0	2	6	7	0	.405	.400
	Hagerstown (SAL)	A	.217	13	46	4	10	1	1	1	11	8	8	1	.339	.348
	San Jose (Cal)	A	.420	17	69	11	29	7	2	0	14	4	9	0	.446	.580
MINOR LEAGUE TOTALS			.329	44	164	22	54	14	3	1	31	18	26	3	.399	.470

Nate Schierholtz, of/3b

Born: Feb. 15, 1984. **Ht.:** 6-2. **Wt.:** 215. **Bats:** L. **Throws:** R. **School:** Chabot (Calif.) JC. **Career Transactions:** Selected by Giants in second round of 2003 draft; signed June 25, 2003. **Signed by:** Matt Nerland.

After starring at Chabot Junior College—vice president of player personnel Dick Tidrow's alma mater—Schierholtz won over the Giants with an impressive workout at their ballpark prior to the 2003 draft. Schierholtz was easily the system's top power prospect before Eddy Martinez-Esteve's arrival, and he still rates a slight edge. He has above-average bat speed, thanks to strong hands that produce a balanced, short swing. He drives the ball from pole to pole, and the Giants view his aggressiveness as a positive. He's an average runner. Drafted as a third baseman, Schierholtz had trouble with his footwork on his throws, so San Francisco moved him to the outfield last August. His inexperience showed, but he has enough arm and athletic ability for right field. Offensively, Schierholtz could walk more and has to trust his hands against breaking balls from lefties. The Giants' outfield picture suddenly looks crowded, but Schierholtz' lefthanded power should help him stand out. He'll need to show defensive aptitude to keep moving quickly, and should return to high Class A to start 2005.

Year	Club (League)	Class	AVG	G	AB	R	H	2B	3B	HR	RBI	BB	SO	SB	OBP	SLG
2003	Giants (AZL)	R	.400	11	45	5	18	0	2	0	5	3	8	4	.449	.489
	Salem-Keizer (NWL)	A	.306	35	124	23	38	6	2	3	29	12	15	0	.382	.460
2004	Hagerstown (SAL)	A	.298	59	235	41	70	22	0	15	54	19	52	1	.356	.583
	San Jose (Cal)	A	.295	62	258	39	76	18	9	3	31	15	41	3	.338	.469
MINOR LEAGUE TOTALS			.305	167	662	108	202	46	13	21	119	49	116	8	.361	.509

Alfredo Simon, rhp

Born: May 8, 1981. **Ht.:** 6-4. **Wt.:** 215. **Bats:** R. **Throws:** R. **Career Transactions:** Signed out of Dominican Republic by Phillies, July 2, 1999 . . . Traded by Phillies with OF Ricky Ledee to Giants for RHP Felix Rodriguez, July 30, 2004. **Signed by:** Wil Tejada/Sal Agostinelli (Phillies).

Formerly known as Carlos Cabrera, Simon's true age (21 months older than originally believed) and name were discovered in June 2003. He was establishing himself as one of the Phillies' top prospects when the Giants got him in the Felix Rodriguez trade last July. Simon tied for the minor league lead with four complete games and three shutouts in 2004. Big and physical, Simon is a power pitcher who worked off his 90-95 mph fastball more than 80 percent of the time with the Phillies. His fastball touched 97 with the Giants, and he has improved at throwing it to both sides of the plate. He has a smooth delivery. San Francisco has overhauled Simon's offspeed stuff, particularly his changeup. One club official likened his old change to an eephus pitch. The Giants like his feel for a curveball and slider, though neither will be a plus pitch. He lacks deception, so hitters see his pitches well. San Francisco believes Simon's upside ranks just a notch below that of Matt Cain and Merkin Valdez. He's a potential innings-eater who should start 2005 in Double-A.

Year	Club (League)	Class	W	L	ERA	G	GS	CG	SV	IP	H	R	ER	HR	BB	SO	AVG
2000	Phillies (DSL)	R	0	0	1.46	4	4	0	0	12	6	3	2	0	9	10	.136
2001	Phillies (GCL)	R	2	2	2.91	10	8	0	0	43	35	23	14	2	23	40	.220
2002	Batavia (NYP)	A	9	2	3.59	15	14	0	0	90	79	44	36	5	46	77	.237
2003	Lakewood (SAL)	A	5	0	3.79	14	7	0	2	71	59	32	30	4	25	66	.224
2004	Clearwater (FSL)	A	7	9	3.27	22	21	4	0	135	121	58	49	13	38	107	.240
	San Jose (Cal)	A	1	2	5.68	6	6	0	0	32	44	24	20	7	12	21	.328
MINOR LEAGUE TOTALS			24	15	3.54	71	60	4	2	384	344	184	151	31	153	321	.239

⟇ Brad Hennessey, rhp

Born: Feb. 7, 1980. **Ht.:** 6-2. **Wt.:** 185. **Bats:** R. **Throws:** R. **School:** Youngstown State University. **Career Transactions:** Selected by Giants in first round (21st overall) of 2001 draft; signed June 30, 2001. **Signed by:** Steve Arnieri.

One of baseball's best stories last year, Hennessey missed all of 2002 and half of 2003 after having two operations to remove benign tumors from his back. The Giants weren't sure they'd get a return on the third-largest signing bonus in club history ($1.38 million), but Hennessey reached the majors in his first full season back. Hennessey's slider is an above-average strikeout pitch with sharp two-plane bite. His fastball touches 93 mph, but it's more effective when he keeps it at 89-91. At that reduced velocity, he commands it better and throws it with more life down in the zone. He's athletic, has a clean delivery and his makeup is as good as it gets. Hennessey has a tendency to push his fastball and his changeup. When he does, both pitches flatten out and he becomes him hittable. He could stand to get stronger, as would be expected after his layoff and surgeries. Hennessey's stuff fits the profile of a setup man if the Giants need him in that role, but they like his upside as a starter, particularly if he can get his fastball and changeup to sink consistently. Unless he has a huge spring, he'll probably open 2005 at Triple-A Fresno.

Year	Club (League)	Class	W	L	ERA	G	GS	CG	SV	IP	H	R	ER	HR	BB	SO	AVG
2001	Salem-Keizer (NWL)	A	1	0	2.38	9	9	0	0	34	28	9	9	1	11	22	.224
2002	Did not play—Injured																
2003	Hagerstown (SAL)	A	3	9	4.20	15	15	1	0	79	81	49	37	6	27	44	.265
2004	Norwich	AA	5	5	3.56	18	18	0	0	101	106	42	40	8	34	55	.272
	Fresno	AAA	4	1	2.02	5	5	0	0	36	26	8	8	2	15	16	.202
	San Francisco		2	2	4.98	7	7	0	0	34	42	24	19	2	15	25	.294
MAJOR LEAGUE TOTALS			2	2	4.98	7	7	0	0	34	42	24	19	2	15	25	.294
MINOR LEAGUE TOTALS			13	15	3.38	47	47	1	0	250	241	108	94	17	87	137	.254

⟇ Craig Whitaker, rhp

Born: Nov. 19, 1984. **Ht.:** 6-4. **Wt.:** 170. **Bats:** R. **Throws:** R. **School:** Lufkin (Texas) HS. **Career Transactions:** Selected by Giants in first round (34th overall) of 2003 draft; signed June 19, 2003. **Signed by:** Tom Korenek.

A supplemental first-round pick and the fourth high school righthander drafted in 2003, Whitaker turned down Texas A&M for a $975,000 bonus. Because his mechanics are raw and his body is still developing, the Giants kept him in extended spring training last year until the short-season Northwest League started. A fierce competitor, Whitaker's a lanky build that reminds San Francisco of former farmhand Joe Nathan. Whitaker's fastball is 90-95 mph now with more velocity to come as he fills out. His curveball isn't as nasty as Matt Cain's, but it has similar 12-to-6 break at times. He has feel for an average changeup. Maturity and experience should cure what ails Whitaker, which is inconsistency with his curveball and his command. His fastball and curve are sometimes too lively for his own good, as he led the NWL in walks and wild pitches (14). A more even-keeled approach would serve him well. The Giants are confident that as Whitaker matures physically and emotionally, he'll harness his stuff and become a No. 2 or 3 starter. He's ticketed for the organization's new low Class A Savannah affiliate.

Year	Club (League)	Class	W	L	ERA	G	GS	CG	SV	IP	H	R	ER	HR	BB	SO	AVG
2003	Giants (AZL)	R	0	1	1.69	3	1	0	0	5	2	2	1	0	4	8	.105
2004	Salem-Keizer (NWL)	A	4	2	3.44	15	15	0	0	71	58	33	27	4	43	77	.234
MINOR LEAGUE TOTALS			4	3	3.32	18	16	0	0	76	60	35	28	4	47	85	.225

David Aardsma, rhp

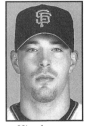

Born: Dec. 27, 1981. **Ht.:** 6-5. **Wt.:** 200. **Bats:** R. **Throws:** R. **School:** Rice University. **Career Transactions:** Selected by Giants in first round of 2003 draft; signed June 29, 2003. **Signed by:** Tom Korenek.

The closer on Rice's 2003 national championship team, Aardsma made his major league debut 10 months after signing for $1.425 million. He won the game in Houston in front of family and friends, though it proved to be the highlight of his season. He spent most of his time in Triple-A. When Aardsma is mechanically sound, he pitches at 93-95 mph and reaches 97 with late life and carry on his explosive fastball. He can sink a two-seamer or throw a four-seamer by hitters up in the strike zone. His changeup, which has become average, was his second-best pitch in 2004. Aardsma's elbow gets floppy in his delivery, and it hurt his velocity and his slider last year. He mostly pitched in the low 90s with his fastball, and he lost both the movement and command of his slider. The Giants were encouraged that his slider came around in the fall, when he kept his delivery more compact. San Francisco had few other options in its depleted bullpen to open the 2004 season, so Aardsma was rushed. The return of his slider would make him a candidate to set up Armando Benitez in San Francisco this season.

Year	Club (League)	Class	W	L	ERA	G	GS	CG	SV	IP	H	R	ER	HR	BB	SO	AVG
2003	San Jose (Cal)	A	1	1	1.96	18	0	0	8	18	14	4	4	2	7	28	.212
2004	Fresno (PCL)	AAA	6	4	3.09	44	0	0	11	55	46	21	19	2	30	53	.217
	San Francisco (NL)	MAJ	1	0	6.75	11	0	0	0	11	20	8	8	1	10	5	.417
MAJOR LEAGUE TOTALS			1	0	6.75	11	0	0	0	11	20	8	8	1	10	5	.417
MINOR LEAGUE TOTALS			7	5	2.81	62	0	0	19	74	60	25	23	4	36	81	.216

Travis Ishikawa, 1b

Born: Sept. 24, 1983. **Ht.:** 6-3. **Wt.:** 190. **Bats:** L. **Throws:** L. **School:** Federal Way (Wash.) HS. **Career Transactions:** Selected by Giants in 21st round of 2002 draft; signed July 11, 2002. **Signed by:** Todd Woodward.

The Giants have been patient with Ishikawa, a former high school football player whose swing and defense at first base drew John Olerud comparisons. His power started to blossom in 2004, when his 16 homers doubled his previous career total. His $955,000 signing bonus—as a 21st-rounder, no less—remains the second-largest San Francisco ever has given a hitter out of the draft. Ishikawa's consistent swing and good bat speed give him above-average power potential. He crushes balls in the lower half of the strike zone. He knows the value of a walk and isn't afraid to hit behind in the count. He's a fine defender at first base with soft hands, and he's athletic enough to play left field as well. Ishikawa hit .188 with 66 strikeouts in his first 47 games last year because he was patient to the point of being passive and wasn't offering at pitches he could drive. As he got more aggressive, his power and average picked up. The Giants say his pitch recognition is improving, and that with more experience he'll find the right blend of patience and aggression. Lefthanded power is hard to find, and San Francisco thinks Ishikawa is turning the corner. He'll return to high Class A to start 2005.

Year	Club (League)	Class	AVG	G	AB	R	H	2B	3B	HR	RBI	BB	SO	SB	OBP	SLG
2002	Giants (AZL)	R	.279	19	68	10	19	4	2	1	10	7	20	7	.364	.441
	Salem-Keizer (NWL)	A	.307	23	88	14	27	2	1	1	17	5	22	1	.347	.386
2003	Hagerstown (SAL)	A	.206	57	194	20	40	5	0	3	22	33	69	3	.329	.278
	Salem-Keizer (NWL)	A	.254	66	248	53	63	17	4	3	31	44	77	0	.376	.391
2004	Hagerstown (SAL)	A	.257	98	358	59	92	19	2	15	54	45	110	10	.357	.447
	San Jose (Cal)	A	.232	16	56	10	13	7	0	1	10	10	16	0	.353	.411
MINOR LEAGUE TOTALS			.251	279	1012	166	254	54	9	24	144	144	314	21	.356	.393

Pat Misch, lhp

Born: Aug. 18, 1981. **Ht.:** 6-2. **Wt.:** 170. **Bats:** R. **Throws:** L. **School:** Western Michigan University. **Career Transactions:** Selected by Giants in seventh round of 2003 draft; signed June 8, 2003. **Signed by:** Steve Arnieri.

The Giants pushed Misch aggressively in 2004, and he responded better than anyone could have expected. Signed as a senior in the seventh round the year before—after failing to come to terms with the Astros as a fifth-rounder in 2002—Misch skipped two levels and pitched in Double-A. San Francisco counted on his maturity and savvy command of a four-pitch mix to help him survive the jump. Misch was Norwich's most consistent pitcher, only twice failing to reach the fifth inning, and he tied fellow Giant Alfredo Simon for the minor league lead with four complete games and three shutouts. At times, all four of Misch's offerings are average big league pitches. His curveball and changeup are usually his best offerings, and he commands them as well as his 86-89 mph fastball and his slider to all four quadrants of the strike zone. Though he set Western Michigan records for whiffs in a game (19), season (99) and career (265), Misch won't be a big strikeout pitcher as a pro. He's similar to Giants mainstay Kirk Rueter. Misch will begin this year in Triple-A and should be among the first pitchers promoted when San Francisco needs reinforcements.

Year	Club (League)	Class	W	L	ERA	G	GS	CG	SV	IP	H	R	ER	HR	BB	SO	AVG
2003	Salem Keizer (NWL)	A	7	5	2.18	14	14	0	0	87	78	33	21	3	20	61	.247
2004	Norwich (EL)	AA	7	6	3.00	26	26	4	0	159	138	61	53	13	35	123	.235
MINOR LEAGUE TOTALS			14	11	2.71	40	40	4	0	246	216	94	74	16	55	184	.239

12 Dan Ortmeier, of

Born: May 11, 1981. **Ht.:** 6-4. **Wt.:** 220. **Bats:** B. **Throws:** L. **School:** University of Texas-Arlington. **Career Transactions:** Selected by Giants in third round of 2002 draft; signed June 23, 2002. **Signed by:** Todd Thomas.

Coming into 2004, the Giants considered Ortmeier their top position-player prospect because of his combination of usable skills, hustle and tools. They still regard him highly, but want to see him have a healthy season to know what kind of big leaguer he'll be. His all-out style already had led to shoulder problems in the past, and three separate injuries hampered him for most of last year. He put Reading catcher Carlos Ruiz in the hospital after a home-plate collision May 5 that injured his shoulder. He missed a week and he wasn't the same player when he returned, as his average dropped 36 points in a month. Ortmeier missed more time in July with a left wrist injury, though an MRI revealed no significant damage. His season came to an early end Aug. 16 when he collided with Norwich second baseman Jay Pecci while chasing a popup, giving him a concussion. The injuries sapped Ortmeier of his game power, and his ability to translate his above-average raw pop into production will determine whether he becomes an everyday right fielder in the majors. He runs well for his size and has an average right-field arm when at full strength. Ortmeier had more trouble making contact in 2004 than he had in the past, though that may be attributable to his physical problems. He'll probably return to Double-A at the outset of the season.

Year	Club (League)	Class	AVG	G	AB	R	H	2B	3B	HR	RBI	BB	SO	SB	OBP	SLG
2002	Salem-Keizer (NWL)	A	.292	49	195	32	57	9	1	5	31	18	37	3	.352	.426
2003	San Jose (Cal)	A	.304	115	408	62	124	32	6	8	56	39	89	13	.378	.471
2004	Norwich (EL)	AA	.252	106	377	55	95	23	6	10	48	47	110	18	.353	.424
MINOR LEAGUE TOTALS			.282	270	980	149	276	64	13	23	135	104	236	34	.363	.444

13 John Bowker, of

Born: July 8, 1983. **Ht.:** 6-2. **Wt.:** 190. **Bats:** L. **Throws:** L. **School:** Long Beach State University. **Career Transactions:** Selected by Giants in third round of 2004 draft; signed July 13, 2004. **Signed by:** Lee Carballo.

Bowker missed all of 2002 with a broken right wrist before leading Long Beach State in homers each of the next two seasons. Offensive numbers are often misleading at the 49ers' Blair Field, a pitcher's paradise, but scouts didn't need stats to tell them the ball makes a different sound coming off Bowker's bat. He ranks among the Giants' best pure hitters thanks to above-average bat speed and excellent hand-eye coordination. He hit safely in 33 of 41 games during his pro debut. If he continues to fill out his athletic body, Bowker has the potential to hit for power and average. He trusts his quick hands, allowing him to wait on pitches and drive them the other way when needed. He isn't a great runner and is limited to an outfield corner, probably left field because his arm is fringe-average. Bowker's left-handed bat is a nice complement to fellow 2004 draftee Eddy Martinez-Esteve's mashing from the right side. The duo should man the outfield corners in high Class A this year.

Year	Club (League)	Class	AVG	G	AB	R	H	2B	3B	HR	RBI	BB	SO	SB	OBP	SLG
2004	Salem-Keizer (NWL)	A	.323	31	127	23	41	9	2	4	16	8	25	1	.390	.520
MINOR LEAGUE TOTALS			.323	31	127	23	41	9	2	4	16	8	25	1	.390	.520

14 Brian Buscher, 3b

Born: April 18, 1981. **Ht.:** 6-0. **Wt.:** 201. **Bats:** L. **Throws:** R. **School:** University of South Carolina. **Career Transactions:** Selected by Giants in third round of 2003 draft; signed June 29, 2003. **Signed by:** Lee Elder.

Buscher began 2004 late after offseason surgery to remove bone chips from his right elbow. When he returned, he spent most of his time at DH before getting in a few games at third base late in the year. Buscher's only above-average tool is his ability to hit for average, but his game also lacks any glaring weaknesses. He has hit at every level, and he led the Southeastern Conference with a .393 average in 2003. He has a mature approach and a solid line-drive swing. He uses the whole field and has enough bat speed to catch up to good inside fastballs. Buscher's power is fringe-average, as his swing lacks natural loft. He's fundamentally sound at third base, with nice footwork and the ability to handle bunts well. His arm came back strong toward the end of 2004. Buscher's grinder mentality and quiet confidence make him a classic overachiever. His successful return to third base helped push Nate Schierholtz to the outfield, where his lefthanded bat can move quicker. A healthy Buscher could move fast as well. He'll report to Double-A for 2005.

Year	Club (League)	Class	AVG	G	AB	R	H	2B	3B	HR	RBI	BB	SO	SB	OBP	SLG
2003	Hagerstown (SAL)	A	.275	54	200	19	55	7	1	0	26	10	25	0	.318	.320
2004	San Jose (Cal)	A	.292	88	343	50	100	14	7	4	56	33	61	5	.359	.408
MINOR LEAGUE TOTALS			.285	142	543	69	155	21	8	4	82	43	86	5	.344	.376

15 Todd Linden, of

Born: June 30, 1980. **Ht.:** 6-3. **Wt.:** 210. **Bats:** S. **Throws:** R. **School:** Louisiana State University. **Career Transactions:** Selected by Giants in first round (41st overall) of 2001 draft; signed Sept. 4, 2001. **Signed by:** Tom Korenek.

No position player has been better positioned to break into the Giants' lineup the last two years, but Linden has failed to prove he can contribute in San Francisco. After bursting on the scene in 2002, he finished his first pro season in Triple-A—and has been mostly stuck at Fresno ever since. A .186 hitter in his cups of coffee with the Giants, Linden has been unable to make adjustments, forcing the club to go with stopgap corner outfielders such as Michael Tucker. He has yet to temper his all-or-nothing approach, as he sells out for home runs and makes it easy for pitchers to exploit the holes in his swing. He led the system with 149 strikeouts last year and continued to have difficulty making contact in Venezuela in winter ball. Linden does have above-average power from both sides of the plate, and enough athleticism and arm strength to play solid defense at either corner-outfield spot. He'll be waiting in Triple-A if 39-year-old Moises Alou or 40-year-old Barry Bonds breaks down in San Francisco.

Year	Club (League)	Class	AVG	G	AB	R	H	2B	3B	HR	RBI	BB	SO	SB	OBP	SLG
2002	Shreveport (TL)	AA	.314	111	392	64	123	26	2	12	52	61	101	9	.419	.482
	Fresno (PCL)	AAA	.250	29	100	18	25	2	1	3	10	20	35	2	.380	.380
2003	Fresno (PCL)	AAA	.278	125	471	75	131	24	3	11	56	40	105	14	.356	.412
	San Francisco (NL)	MAJ	.211	18	38	2	8	1	0	1	6	1	8	0	.231	.316
2004	San Francisco (NL)	MAJ	.156	16	32	6	5	1	0	0	1	5	7	0	.289	.188
	Fresno (PCL)	AAA	.260	130	489	93	127	28	2	23	75	63	149	8	.349	.466
MAJOR LEAGUE TOTALS			.186	34	70	8	13	2	0	1	7	6	15	0	.260	.257
MINOR LEAGUE TOTALS			.280	395	1452	250	406	80	8	49	193	184	390	33	.373	.447

16 Justin Knoedler, c

Born: July 17, 1980. **Ht.:** 6-2. **Wt.:** 210. **Bats:** R. **Throws:** R. **School:** Miami (Ohio) University. **Career Transactions:** Selected by Giants in fifth round of 2001 draft; signed June 20, 2001. **Signed by:** Steve Arnieri.

While Knoedler caught in college until a broken left hand sidelined him in 2001, Giants scouts loved his power arm and were afraid his funky, high-maintenance swing wouldn't allow him to hit with wood. They moved him to the mound after he signed, but their catching shortage led them to put him back behind the plate in 2002, and two years later Knoedler reached the majors. It's quite an accomplishment for the organization's ultimate overachiever and hardest worker. Knoedler is also one of the Giants' strongest players, spending his offseasons in workouts with his twin brother Jason, a minor league outfielder for the Tigers, and the Dodgers' Jayson Werth. Knoedler's strength allows him to handle the demands of his position, and he led the Double-A Eastern League with 102 games caught in 2004. He has well above-average arm strength, and does a capable job of receiving and blocking pitches. He progressed with the bat last year, showing average power and hitting a career-best .274 while working from a simpler, more upright stance. He was more consistent with his swing and tinkered less, though he still has holes. San Francisco's signing of Mike Matheny blocks Knoedler for the short term, and he'll head to Triple-A in 2005.

Year	Club (League)	Class	W	L	ERA	G	GS	CG	SV	IP	H	R	ER	HR	BB	SO	AVG
2001	Salem-Keizer (NWL)	A	1	1	1.26	13	0	0	1	29	22	4	4	0	9	38	.211
MINOR LEAGUE TOTALS			1	1	1.26	13	0	0	1	29	22	4	4	0	9	38	.211

Year	Club (League)	Class	AVG	G	AB	R	H	2B	3B	HR	RBI	BB	SO	SB	OBP	SLG
2002	Hagerstown (SAL)	A	.257	86	280	32	72	16	2	5	33	37	56	6	.349	.382
2003	San Jose (Cal)	A	.257	101	354	48	91	25	2	10	43	35	78	13	.326	.424

2004	Norwich (EL)	AA	.274	115	409	64	112	28	3	9	47	32	98	5	.335	.423
	San Francisco (NL)	MAJ	.000	1	1	0	0	0	0	0	0	0	0	0	.000	.000
MAJOR LEAGUE TOTALS			.000	1	1	0	0	0	0	0	0	0	0	0	.000	.000
MINOR LEAGUE TOTALS			.264	302	1043	144	275	69	7	24	123	104	232	24	.336	.412

17 Marcus Sanders, 2b

Born: Aug. 25, 1985. **Ht.:** 6-0. **Wt.:** 160. **Bats:** R. **Throws:** R. **School:** South Florida CC. **Career Transactions:** Selected by Giants in 17th round of 2003 draft; signed May 29, 2004. **Signed by:** Paul Turco Jr.

The Giants haven't had a middle-infield prospect of note since trading Mike Caruso to the White Sox in 1997. They have high hopes for Sanders, whose athletic ability and offensive potential make him a different animal from the likes of Cody Ransom, Jamie Athas and Angel Chavez, failed San Francisco infield prospects of the recent past. Sanders was a short-stop until he injured his right shoulder playing wide receiver at Sarasota (Fla.) High. Though he had shoulder surgery, San Francisco drafted him in the 17th round in 2003. He signed as a draft-and-follow after leading Florida juco players with 44 steals at South Florida Community College last spring. In his pro debut, Sanders was the igniter and best prospect on the Giants' Rookie-level affiliate that won the Arizona League title. He led the AZL in runs and steals and is the fastest runner in the organization, with 80 speed on the 20-80 scouting scale. More than just a speedster, Sanders has enough bat speed and strength in his wiry frame to make him a dangerous line-drive hitter with enough power to keep pitchers honest. He's a patient hitter who also knows when to be aggressive. He has some smoothness to his infield actions as well, though his hands could be softer. He'll head to low Class A for his first full season.

Year	Club (League)	Class	AVG	G	AB	R	H	2B	3B	HR	RBI	BB	SO	SB	OBP	SLG
2004	Giants (AZL)	R	.292	55	209	54	61	12	4	3	21	35	45	28	.415	.431
MINOR LEAGUE TOTALS			.292	55	209	54	61	12	4	3	21	35	45	28	.415	.431

18 Clay Timpner, of

Born: May 13, 1983. **Ht.:** 6-2. **Wt.:** 197. **Bats:** L. **Throws:** L. **School:** University of Central Florida. **Career Transactions:** Selected by Giants in fourth round of 2004 draft; signed June 15, 2004. **Signed by:** Paul Turco Jr.

A three-year starter at Central Florida, Timpner batted .371 and led the Atlantic Sun Conference in hits (96), doubles (20), triples (six) and steals (43) last spring. His track record and solid all-around tools prompted the Giants to draft him in the fourth round. He finished a strong pro debut by joining Fred Lewis and Eddy Martinez-Esteve in San Jose's outfield for the California League playoffs. He instantly became the best defensive outfielder in the system, as he's more accomplished than Lewis in center field. Timpner has above-average speed and maximizes his range by getting great jumps and taking good routes. His arm is average. He's an efficient basestealer who reads pitchers well, and he already is one of the better baserunners in the organization. San Francisco doesn't expect him to hit for power at the big league level, but still isn't sure how much he'll drive the ball or if he'll be a slap hitter. Timpner doesn't try to muscle up for home runs and was tired at season's end, but he had enough left to hit .367 in the playoffs. His bat will determine whether he can be an everyday center fielder or just a useful extra outfielder. He figures to return to high Class A to start 2005.

Year	Club (League)	Class	AVG	G	AB	R	H	2B	3B	HR	RBI	BB	SO	SB	OBP	SLG
2004	Salem-Keizer (NWL)	A	.293	68	294	37	86	7	2	5	28	20	35	16	.339	.381
	San Jose (Cal)	A	.280	6	25	4	7	2	0	0	2	1	2	1	.296	.360
MINOR LEAGUE TOTALS			.292	74	319	41	93	9	2	5	30	21	37	17	.335	.379

19 Jeremy Accardo, rhp

Born: Dec. 8, 1981. **Ht.:** 6-2. **Wt.:** 180. **Bats:** R. **Throws:** R. **School:** Illinois State University. **Career Transactions:** Signed as nondrafted free agent by Giants, Aug. 12, 2003. **Signed by:** Doug Mapson.

The Giants' knack for finding power arms in unlikely places led them to sign Accardo in the summer of 2003. Accardo had served as Illinois State's closer and earned a school-record 12 career saves, but he was better known as a shortstop and wasn't drafted. His velocity increased during a summer stint in the Alaska League, where San Francisco clocked his fastball at 92-93 mph. The Giants signed him before he returned to Illinois State for his senior year. Accardo settled into the 90-93 range in high Class A last year and touched 95. The Giants were impressed with how he held up under the workload of being a full-time closer, and he led the California League in saves despite a brief callup to Double-A. Accardo still can get better, as he worked off his fastball for most of 2004. He should get better at commanding it as he learns to keep his front shoulder closed and tries not to overthrow. His slider showed flashes and can be a plus pitch, but he didn't throw it for strikes consistently and was left without a strikeout pitch. He tinkered with a cutter and splitter. As he moves up, he'll need one of his secondary pitches to at least be average. His athletic ability, durability and potential fastball command project Accardo as a set-up man who could help the Giants soon.

Year	Club (League)	Class	W	L	ERA	G	GS	CG	SV	IP	H	R	ER	HR	BB	SO	AVG
2004	Norwich (EL)	AA	2	1	5.40	7	0	0	1	8	9	5	5	1	2	5	.290
	San Jose (Cal)	A	1	2	4.25	50	0	0	27	55	57	28	26	3	15	43	.268
MINOR LEAGUE TOTALS			3	3	4.40	57	0	0	28	63	66	33	31	4	17	48	.270

20 Billy Sadler, rhp

Born: Sept. 21, 1981. **Ht.:** 6-0. **Wt.:** 190. **Bats:** R. **Throws:** R. **School:** Louisiana State University. **Career Transactions:** Selected by Giants in sixth round of 2003 draft; signed June 28, 2003. **Signed by:** Tom Korenek.

The Giants have gone to the Louisiana State well repeatedly in recent years, drafting such Tigers stalwarts as Jake Esteves, Todd Linden, Brian Wilson and Sadler. Sadler spent time as LSU's closer, but profiles as a set-up man because he lacks command of his power pitches. A smallish, aggressive competitor, he has a big arm. He pitches at 92-94 mph and touches 96 with his fastball, though the pitch can arrive on a flat plane because he's just six feet tall. Sadler's curveball can be a plus pitch at times and he has a resilient arm, leading the system with 60 appearances last year. Fiery and emotional, Sadler tends to get himself into trouble when he gets too amped up and loses his mechanics. He overthrows his fastball at times, leaving it up in the zone, and tends to lose his arm slot, causing him to get underneath his curve. Sadler has swing-and-miss stuff, though, and big league managers covet power set-up men. Sadler should team with closer Jeremy Accardo again in 2005, this time in Double-A.

Year	Club (League)	Class	W	L	ERA	G	GS	CG	SV	IP	H	R	ER	HR	BB	SO	AVG
2003	Hagerstown (SAL)	A	0	0	4.80	12	0	0	1	15	15	8	8	4	13	10	.263
2004	Norwich (EL)	AA	0	3	3.86	17	0	0	0	30	22	16	13	3	18	24	.208
	San Jose (Cal)	A	2	2	2.38	30	3	0	0	57	29	17	15	1	40	66	.154
MINOR LEAGUE TOTALS			2	5	3.18	59	3	0	1	102	66	41	36	8	71	100	.188

21 Lance Niekro, 1b/3b

Born: Jan. 29, 1979. **Ht.:** 6-3. **Wt.:** 210. **Bats:** R. **Throws:** R. **School:** Florida Southern College. **Career Transactions:** Selected by Giants in second round of 2000 draft; signed July 3, 2000. **Signed by:** Alan Marr.

The son of Joe and nephew of Hall of Famer Phil, Niekro once seemed destined for a long major league career of his own. Like Todd Linden, he starred in the Cape Cod League prior to signing and has been on the verge of earning a job in San Francisco for a couple of years. But Niekro has been waylaid by injuries, including right shoulder surgery (2001), a broken left hand (2002) and hamstring woes (2003) that pushed him to first base after he played third as an amateur. He has seen time at the hot corner the last two seasons, and he was consistent enough making routine plays that the Giants consider him capable of backing up at third in the majors. Niekro's bat was supposed to carry him to San Francisco by now, but he showed an alarming lack of power before 2004. He added a high right ankle sprain to his medical chart in spring training, but he got hot once he returned to the field, slugging a career-high .554. He has bat speed and leverage in his swing, and he unlocked his power once he became more selective. If Pedro Feliz falters, Niekro could enter the picture in a similar role as a reserve at first, third and left field. He'll return to Triple-A to start the season.

Year	Club (League)	Class	AVG	G	AB	R	H	2B	3B	HR	RBI	BB	SO	SB	OBP	SLG
2000	Salem-Keizer (NWL)	A	.362	49	196	27	71	14	4	5	44	11	25	2	.404	.551
2001	San Jose (Cal)	A	.288	42	163	18	47	11	0	3	34	4	14	4	.298	.411
2002	Shreveport (TL)	AA	.310	79	297	33	92	20	1	4	34	7	32	0	.327	.424
2003	Fresno (PCL)	AAA	.302	98	381	43	115	15	2	4	41	19	39	3	.334	.383
	San Francisco (NL)	MAJ	.200	5	5	2	1	1	0	0	2	0	1	0	.200	.400
2004	San Jose (Cal)	A	.311	15	61	13	19	7	1	1	14	2	5	0	.328	.508
	Fresno (PCL)	AAA	.298	67	242	42	72	21	4	12	47	14	32	1	.337	.566
MAJOR LEAGUE TOTALS			.200	5	5	2	1	1	0	0	2	0	1	0	.200	.400
MINOR LEAGUE TOTALS			.310	350	1340	176	416	88	12	29	214	57	147	10	.339	.459

22 Brian Burres, lhp

Born: April 8, 1981. **Ht.:** 6-1. **Wt.:** 171. **Bats:** L. **Throws:** L. **School:** Mount Hood (Ore.) CC. **Career Transactions:** Selected by Giants in 31st round of 2000 draft; signed May 26, 2001. **Signed by:** John Shafer.

Nicknamed "the Blade" for his slender build, Burres emerged in his second high Class A season and could help the Giants address their lack of lefthanded pitching. He was on track to be a situational lefty, but struggled at the beginning of 2004. His curveball got too loopy, and his 84-89 mph fastball and decent changeup weren't enough for him to be effective. But once he got a chance to start in mid-June after Matt Cain's promotion to Double-A, Burres took to a new cut fastball he learned from San Jose pitching coach Trevor Wilson and suddenly became the team's ace. He won nine of his last 10 starts, including the last seven in a row, and went 12-0, 1.87 as a member of the rotation. His stunning success was the product of painting the outer half of the strike zone with his fastball and pounding hitters inside with his cutter. He ran out of gas in the California League playoffs, but he'll report to Double-A as a starter in 2005 and see if he can repeat his late-season magic.

Year	Club (League)	Class	W	L	ERA	G	GS	CG	SV	IP	H	R	ER	HR	BB	SO	AVG
2001	Salem-Keizer (NWL)	A	3	1	3.10	14	6	0	1	41	43	20	14	2	11	38	.274
2002	Hagerstown (SAL)	A	5	10	4.75	32	16	0	1	119	114	78	63	15	53	119	.252
2003	San Jose (Cal)	A	3	3	3.86	39	0	0	1	61	55	33	26	4	36	64	.239
2004	San Jose (Cal)	A	12	1	2.84	36	15	0	0	124	115	49	39	10	30	114	.249
MINOR LEAGUE TOTALS			23	15	3.71	121	37	0	3	344	327	180	142	31	130	335	.251

23 Jonathan Sanchez, lhp

Born: Nov. 19, 1982. **Ht.:** 6-2. **Wt.:** 165. **Bats:** L. **Throws:** L. **School:** Ohio Dominican College. **Career Transactions:** Selected by Giants in 27th round of 2004 draft; signed June 11, 2004. **Signed by:** Sean O'Connor.

On the second day of the 2004 draft, San Francisco looked to NAIA power Ohio Dominican for a pair of picks, taking Sanchez in the 27th round and righthander Benny Cepeda in the 48th. Sanchez, who holds school records for strikeouts in a game (16), season (105) and career (311), helped pitch the Panthers to three straight NAIA World Series from 2001-03. He impressed the Giants with his aptitude in instructional league, then drew the attention of scouts in winter ball by having one of the best fastballs in a down year in his native Puerto Rico. Sanchez has a loose, quick arm that generates 92-94 mph heat despite his slight frame. His fastball is a swing-and-miss pitch when he commands it. He has to iron out his mechanics and hone his curveball. Sanchez also will have to work on his changeup to remain a starter in pro ball. He'll pitch in the low Class A rotation in 2005.

Year	Club (League)	Class	W	L	ERA	G	GS	CG	SV	IP	H	R	ER	HR	BB	SO	AVG
2004	Giants (AZL)	R	5	0	2.77	9	3	0	1	26	22	9	8	0	9	27	.229
	Salem-Keizer (NWL)	A	2	1	4.84	6	6	0	0	22	16	13	12	3	19	34	.203
MINOR LEAGUE TOTALS			7	1	3.72	15	9	0	1	48	38	22	20	3	28	61	.217

24 Garrett Broshuis, rhp

Born: Dec. 18, 1981. **Ht.:** 6-3. **Wt.:** 170. **Bats:** R. **Throws:** R. **School:** University of Missouri. **Career Transactions:** Selected by Giants in fifth round of 2004 draft; signed June 18, 2004. **Signed by:** Todd Thomas.

Broshuis endeared himself to Giants minor league pitching coordinator Bert Bradley because he shares Bradley's idea of pitching: throw quality strikes early in the count, no matter what your velocity. Broshuis doesn't have overpowering stuff, but his advanced feel for pitching helped him go from the fifth round last June to high Class A in a month. He didn't stick around for the playoffs or instructional league, returning to Missouri to finish his psychology degree. Broshuis went 11-0, 2.61 for the Tigers last spring after lowering his arm slot from overhand to three-quarters. He sacrificed velocity and ended up throwing in the 87-89 mph range, but he gained good movement on his sinker. The new arm slot also prompted him to switch from a curveball to a slider. He already has good feel for the slider, an average pitch, adding and subtracting velocity as needed. His changeup is solid, and Broshuis moves all three pitches around the strike zone. He's a good athlete who fields his position well and has a good pickoff move. He'll return to San Jose for 2005, where he'll need to show a little less respect for hitters and return to his attacking style.

Year	Club (League)	Class	W	L	ERA	G	GS	CG	SV	IP	H	R	ER	HR	BB	SO	AVG
2004	Salem-Keizer (NWL)	A	3	0	1.37	5	2	0	0	20	15	4	3	0	4	23	.203
	San Jose (Cal)	A	4	3	5.19	10	8	0	0	52	60	32	30	4	16	47	.287
MINOR LEAGUE TOTALS			7	3	4.14	15	10	0	0	72	75	36	33	4	20	70	.265

25 Scott Munter, rhp

Born: March 7, 1980. **Ht.:** 6-6. **Wt.:** 235. **Bats:** R. **Throws:** R. **School:** Butler County (Kan.) CC. **Career Transactions:** Selected by Giants in 47th round of 2001 draft; signed June 7, 2001. **Signed by:** Todd Thomas.

No pitcher in the system came as far last year as Munter, who zoomed from low Class A in 2003 to Triple-A and a spot on the 40-man roster. He has battled his weight, which at one point reached 270 pounds. As he's gotten in better shape, he has improved his mechanics, which in turn helped him start to command his heavy sinker. One Giants official compared Munter's sinker to a bowling ball thrown out of a helicopter. He throws it in the low 90s and reaches 95 mph, using his 6-foot-6 frame to deliver it at a steep downward angle. Munter had an impressive 147-41 groundball-flyball ratio in 2004, allowing just five homers. He also has a hard slider that's an average pitch. He went to the Arizona Fall League to work on his changeup, and made enough progress for the Giants to protect him from the Rule 5 draft. Munter has a shot at a big league bullpen job in spring training.

Year	Club (League)	Class	W	L	ERA	G	GS	CG	SV	IP	H	R	ER	HR	BB	SO	AVG
2001	San Jose (Cal)	A	0	0	0.38	3	0	0	0	4	12	5	5	0	4	2	.571
	Salem Keizer (NWL)	A	1	2	5.91	15	0	0	0	35	42	26	23	3	12	28	.296
	Hagerstown (SAL)	A	1	0	3.38	1	1	0	0	5	5	3	2	0	1	2	.278
2002	Salem Keizer (NWL)	A	1	1	6.98	10	4	0	0	30	33	24	23	0	20	20	.287
2003	Hagerstown (SAL)	A	3	5	2.36	40	0	0	5	69	61	28	18	3	28	47	.230
2004	Norwich (EL)	AA	2	4	2.35	42	0	0	3	65	63	19	17	4	22	30	.265
	Fresno (PCL)	AAA	1	1	3.45	13	0	0	1	16	20	8	6	1	4	5	.303
MINOR LEAGUE TOTALS			9	13	3.78	124	5	0	9	224	236	113	94	11	91	134	.273

26 Todd Jennings, c

Born: Dec. 10, 1981. **Ht.:** 6-0. **Wt.:** 190. **Bats:** R. **Throws:** R. **School:** Long Beach State University. **Career Transactions:** Selected by Giants in second round of 2003 draft; signed June 20, 2003. **Signed by:** Lee Carballo.

The Giants had no depth at catcher two years ago and hoped Jennings would fill the void. They're not giving up on him by any means, but they consider 2004 a wasted year. Sent to high Class A to start the season, he hurt his right shoulder, which sapped his arm strength, eroded his confidence and eventually robbed him of his ability to drive the ball. Jennings became his own worst critic and didn't show his past form until he went to short-season Salem-Keizer. Wiry strong, he has more pop than he has shown as a pro. More athletic than most catchers, he also played second and third base and the outfield at Long Beach State. He has a solid arm, getting the ball to second base in roughly 2.0 seconds. Jennings has to prove he's healthy and can handle the daily grind of catching in Class A this year, and he may see some time at other positions as well. Adding strength and regaining his confidence are his biggest needs.

Year	Club (League)	Class	AVG	G	AB	R	H	2B	3B	HR	RBI	BB	SO	SB	OBP	SLG
2003	Salem-Keizer (NWL)	A	.296	59	233	27	69	9	2	3	32	15	36	5	.346	.391
2004	San Jose (Cal)	A	.186	45	177	20	33	6	0	1	12	10	36	5	.246	.237
	Salem-Keizer (NWL)	A	.329	17	70	7	23	3	0	3	11	3	12	0	.356	.500
MINOR LEAGUE TOTALS			.260	121	480	54	125	18	2	7	55	28	84	10	.311	.350

27 Pablo Sandoval, c

Born: Aug. 11, 1986. **Ht.:** 5-11. **Wt.:** 180. **Bats:** B. **Throws:** R. **Career Transactions:** Signed out of Venezuela by Giants, May 8, 2003. **Signed by:** Ciro Villalobos.

Signed in a rare Giants venture into Venezuela, Sandoval is a catch-and-throw specialist who shows the ability to receive and block well. He impressed Arizona League managers last summer with how well he handled the oldest pitching staff in the league. San Francisco believes he can play an important role in the future if he can keep his pudgy body in check. He's believed to weigh as much as 40 pounds more than his listed weight of 180, which hinders his bat speed and offensive potential. Sandoval has athletic ability and hand-eye coordination, but his size isn't translating to power, and he has to become more patient as well. A switch-hitter, he also can throw with either arm. His (right) arm isn't overly strong, but it's accurate and he threw out 30 percent of basestealers last year. If Sandoval comes to spring training in shape, he could share the catching duties in low Class A.

Year	Club (League)	Class	AVG	G	AB	R	H	2B	3B	HR	RBI	BB	SO	SB	OBP	SLG
2004	Giants (AZL)	R	.266	46	177	21	47	9	5	0	26	5	17	4	.287	.373
MINOR LEAGUE TOTALS			266	46	177	21	47	9	5	0	26	5	17	4	.287	.373

28 Mike Mooney, of

Born: June 8, 1983. **Ht.:** 6-1. **Wt.:** 205. **Bats:** R. **Throws:** R. **School:** JC of San Mateo (Calif.). **Career Transactions:** Selected by Giants in 16th round of 2003 draft, June 9, 2003. **Signed by:** Matt Nerland.

Mooney's stock is on the rise after he hit .375 in a banner instructional league performance. The Giants took him in the 16th round after he won Northern California juco player of the year honors in 2003, when he hit .436 with 22 homers at the College of San Mateo. He was an all-star in the Arizona League last summer, but he was much too old for Rookie ball at age 21. He was placed there because of the shortage of visas for minor league players last year, which made it difficult for the Giants to fill out rosters with lower-level players. Mooney has a strong body and average bat speed, and if he learns the strike zone he should hit for above-average power. He's an average runner and can become an asset in right field with more experience. His plus arm is the best among the system's outfielders. Mooney plays the game hard but his youth shows through at times, and he needs to handle both success and failure better. He should be the everyday right fielder this year in low Class A.

Year	Club (League)	Class	AVG	G	AB	R	H	2B	3B	HR	RBI	BB	SO	SB	OBP	SLG
2003	Giants (AZL)	R	.290	56	221	30	64	15	6	1	39	18	55	9	.346	.425
2004	Giants (AZL)	R	.312	55	215	43	67	11	7	6	57	25	45	7	.394	.512
	Salem-Keizer (NWL)	A	.100	3	10	0	1	1	0	0	3	0	2	0	.100	.200
MINOR LEAGUE TOTALS			.296	114	446	73	132	27	13	7	99	43	102	16	.365	.462

29 Chris Begg, rhp

Born: Sept. 12, 1979. **Ht.:** 6-3. **Wt.:** 195. **Bats:** R. **Throws:** R. **School:** Niagara University. **Career Transactions:** Signed by independent Johnstown (Frontier), June 2001 . . . Signed by independent Albany-Colonie (Northeast), June 2002 . . . Signed by independent St. Paul (Northern), June 2003 . . . Contract purchased by Giants from St. Paul, July 9, 2003. **Signed by:** Tom Sullivan.

The Giants haven't made many forays into independent ball, but Begg might encourage them to scout the indy ranks for pitching in the future. He spent three years in the Frontier, Northeast and Northern leagues before San Francisco brought him into Organized Ball in July 2003. He has breezed through high Class A and Double-A with a combined 15-3, 2.34 record, but he struggled mightily in Triple-A. Begg took some time off last summer to pitch in the Olympics, where he took the defeat in Canada's semifinal loss to Cuba. He doesn't have big stuff, working in the high 80s and only touching 90 with his two-seam fastball, but he has excellent command. He's a sinker-slider pitcher, and his changeup can be average at times. Begg gave Triple-A hitters too much credit, and got pounded when he uncharacteristically fell behind in the count. He can't be afraid to pitch inside but must do so judiciously. He has a chance to become a No. 5 starter in the majors, but middle relief is a more realistic aspiration.

Year	Club (League)	Class	W	L	ERA	G	GS	CG	SV	IP	H	R	ER	HR	BB	SO	AVG
2001	Johnstown (Fron)	IND	0	0	7.36	1	0	0	0	4	5	3	3	1	1	2	.333
2002	Albany-Colonie (NE)	IND	3	2	2.53	21	4	0	1	53	42	20	15	0	15	39	.209
2003	St. Paul (Nor)	IND	7	0	1.50	10	8	0	0	66	52	15	11	2	15	63	.219
	San Jose (Cal)	A	4	1	1.15	7	5	1	0	39	30	5	5	3	4	21	.213
	Norwich (EL)	AA	2	1	4.38	4	4	0	0	25	31	14	12	2	13	13	.323
2004	Norwich (EL)	AA	9	1	2.30	16	14	0	0	94	87	27	24	3	11	61	.249
	Fresno (PCL)	AAA	2	5	6.97	9	9	0	0	41	55	32	32	10	18	17	.337
MINOR LEAGUE TOTALS			17	8	3.30	36	32	1	0	199	180	78	73	18	46	112	.249

30 Erick Threets, lhp

Born: Nov. 4, 1981. **Ht.:** 6-5. **Wt.:** 240. **Bats:** L. **Throws:** L. **School:** Modesto (Calif.) JC. **Career Transactions:** Selected by Giants in seventh round of 2000 draft; signed Aug. 1, 2000. **Signed by:** Matt Nerland.

Giants fans have been teased by rare Threets sightings since he reportedly reached 103 mph in instructional league following the 2001 season. Command and injury problems have limited him to 89 innings over the last three years, and he missed all of 2004 after May surgery to repair a small labrum tear in his shoulder. Threets was able to throw in the bullpen last fall, and his fastball was back in the mid- to upper 90s. That was enough for San Francisco to protect him on the 40-man roster for a second straight year. With his fastball and a power slider, Threets has the raw stuff to become a premier reliever. But the emphasis is on the word "raw." He has walked nearly a batter per inning as a pro and has little feel for the strike zone. He also throws across his body, which doesn't bode well for his health. The Giants have tinkered with his delivery to try to smooth him out, but Threets hasn't stayed on the mound enough to put his new mechanics to use.

Year	Club (League)	Class	W	L	ERA	G	GS	CG	SV	IP	H	R	ER	HR	BB	SO	AVG
2001	San Jose (Cal)	A	0	10	4.25	14	14	0	0	59	49	34	28	2	40	60	.224
	Hagerstown (SAL)	A	2	0	0.75	12	0	0	1	24	13	3	2	1	9	32	.155
2002	San Jose (Cal)	A	0	1	6.67	26	0	0	0	28	23	24	21	2	28	43	.225
2003	Norwich (EL)	AA	0	0	15.88	11	0	0	0	11	15	20	20	1	21	16	.306
	Hagerstown (SAL)	A	2	3	3.26	22	0	0	0	50	26	20	18	2	42	47	.159
2004	Did not play—Injured																
MINOR LEAGUE TOTALS			4	14	4.64	85	14	0	1	173	126	101	89	8	140	198	.204

SEATTLE
MARINERS

BY **JIM CALLIS**

ill Bavasi's first year as Seattle general manager couldn't have gone much worse. Succeeding Pat Gillick, whose clubs averaged 98 wins and reached two American League Championship Series in four years, Bavasi presided over the Mariners' plummeting to 63-99 and finishing last for the first time since 1992.

Most of Bavasi's offseason acquisitions didn't work out. Eddie Guardado got hurt, while Rich Aurilia and Scott Spiezio were disasters. Making matters worse, the addition of Aurilia led to the trade of Carlos Guillen, who became an all-star in Detroit. Bavasi's best move came in June, when he traded pending free agent Freddy Garcia for young catcher Miguel Olivo and two of the White Sox' top prospects, outfielder Jeremy Reed and shortstop Michael Morse.

By that point, there was little to cheer for outside of Ichiro's successful pursuit of the single-season hits record. The Mariners soon gave up on the season and began taking a look at their young talent, as a club-record 16 players made their major league debuts. Lefthander Bobby Madritsch turned in the best performance among the rookies, using a deceptive changeup to go 6-3, 3.27. Cult hero **Bucky Jacobsen** whacked nine homers in 42 games before having knee surgery.

Seattle's biggest phenom didn't make it to Safeco, though righthander Felix Hernandez might have acquitted himself well had he been given his chance. He conquered every other challenge thrown his way, dominating high Class A and Double-A and establishing himself as the game's best pitching prospect—all at the age of 18.

Hernandez sits atop a prospect list that once again has a heavy international flavor. Six of the players were signed on the international market, coming from Australia, Cuba, Curacao, Korea and Venezuela. Seattle may have the most diverse organization in baseball, with players from Aruba, Canada, China, Colombia, Dominican Republic, Ecuador, Japan, Netherlands, Nicaragua, Panama, South Africa and Taiwan.

The foreign players stand out, in part, because the Mariners haven't drafted well. They were without a first-round pick for the fourth time in five years in 2004, but scouting director Bob Fontaine Jr. found an equivalent talent in third-rounder Matt Tuiasosopo. A heralded quarterback recruit, Tuiasosopo signed for $2.29 million.

The Mariners will move on with several new faces in 2004. Roger Jongewaard, who became Seattle's scouting director in 1985 and was in charge of both scouting and player development from 1989-2003, took a job with the Devil Rays. Manager Bob Melvin was fired and replaced with Mike Hargrove. Seven-time all-star Edgar Martinez retired. The biggest on-field changes are the addition of free agents Adrian Beltre (five years, $64 million) and Richie Sexson (four years, $50 million), to beef up a lineup that scored fewer runs than any AL team last year.

TOP 30 PROSPECTS

1. Felix Hernandez, rhp	16. Cha Seung Baek, rhp
2. Jeremy Reed, of	17. Ryan Feierabend, lhp
3. Shin-Soo Choo, of	18. Cesar Jimenez, lhp
4. Clint Nageotte, rhp	19. Mike Morse, ss
5. Matt Tuiasosopo, ss	20. Rich Dorman, rhp
6. Travis Blackley, of	21. Rene Rivera, c
7. Chris Snelling, of	22. Bobby Livingston, lhp
8. Adam Jones, ss	23. Yung-Chi Chen, 2b/3b
9. Yuniesky Betancourt, ss/2b	24. Oswaldo Navarro, 2b/ss
10. Wladimir Balentien, of	25. Chai-An Huang, rhp
11. Asdrubal Cabrera, ss/2b	26. Matt Thornton, lhp
12. Jamal Strong, of	27. Rob Johnson, c
13. George Sherrill, lhp	28. Shawn Nottingham, lhp
14. Greg Dobbs, 3b	29. Mark Lowe, rhp
15. Justin Leone, inf/of	30. Aaron Jensen, rhp

ORGANIZATION OVERVIEW

General manager: Bill Bavasi. **Farm director:** Frank Mattox. **Scouting director:** Bob Fontaine.

2004 PERFORMANCE

Class	Team	League	W	L	Pct.	Finish*	Manager
Majors	Seattle	American	63	99	.389	13th (14)	Bob Melvin
Triple-A	Tacoma Rainiers	Pacific Coast	79	63	.556	3rd (16)	Dan Rohn
Double-A	San Antonio Missions	Texas	66	72	.478	6th (8)	Dave Brundage
High A	Inland Empire 66ers	California	77	63	.550	3rd (10)	Daren Brown
Low A	Wisconsin Timber Rattlers	Midwest	57	82	.410	12th (14)	Steve Roadcap
Short-season	Everett AquaSox	Northwest	41	35	.539	t-3rd (8)	Pedro Grifol
Rookie	AZL Mariners	Arizona	31	25	.554	4th (9)	Scott Steinmann
OVERALL 2004 MINOR LEAGUE RECORD			351	340	.507	12th (30)	

*Finish in overall standings (No. of teams in league).

ORGANIZATION LEADERS

BATTING
*Minimum 250 At-Bats
*AVG	Carlos Arroyo, Inland Empire	.323
R	Gary Harris, Inland Empire	92
H	Shin-Soo Choo, San Antonio	163
TB	A.J. Zapp, Tacoma	266
2B	Jesus Guzman, Inland Empire	35
3B	Gary Harris, Inland Empire	18
HR	A.J. Zapp, Tacoma	29
RBI	A.J. Zapp, Tacoma	101
BB	Dustin Delucchi, San Antonio	71
SO	A.J. Zapp, Tacoma	184
SB	Shin-Soo Choo, San Antonio	40
*OBP	Bucky Jacobsen, Tacoma	.422
*SLG	Bucky Jacobsen, Tacoma	.661

PITCHING
#Minimum 75 Innings
W	Felix Hernandez, San Antonio/Inland Empire	14
L	Nibaldo Acosta, Wisconsin	14
#ERA	Cesar Jimenez, Inland Empire	2.32
G	Tim Rall, San Antonio	56
CG	Travis Blackley, Tacoma	2
SV	Rick Guttormson, San Antonio	25
IP	Bobby Livingston, Inland Empire	187
BB	Gustavo Martinez, Tacoma/San Antonio	82
SO	Thomas Oldham, Inland Empire/Wisconsin	188

BEST TOOLS

Best Hitter for Average	Jeremy Reed
Best Power Hitter	Wladimir Balentien
Best Strike-Zone Discipline	Jeremy Reed
Fastest Baserunner	Jamal Strong
Best Athlete	Matt Tuiasosopo
Best Fastball	Felix Hernandez
Best Curveball	Felix Hernandez
Best Slider	Clint Nageotte
Best Changeup	Cesar Jimenez
Best Control	Bobby Livingston
Best Defensive Catcher	Rene Rivera
Best Defensive Infielder	Oswaldo Navarro
Best Infield Arm	Adam Jones
Best Defensive Outfielder	Jamal Strong
Best Outfield Arm	Shin-Soo Choo

PROJECTED 2008 LINEUP

Catcher	Miguel Olivo
First Base	Richie Sexson
Second Base	Jose Lopez
Third Base	Adrian Beltre
Shortstop	Yuniesky Betancourt
Left Field	Shin-Soo Choo
Center Field	Jeremy Reed
Right Field	Ichiro Suzuki
Designated Hitter	Matt Tuiasosopo

No. 1 Starter	Felix Hernandez
No. 2 Starter	Joel Piniero
No. 3 Starter	Gil Meche
No. 4 Starter	Bobby Madritsch
No. 5 Starter	Travis Blackley
Closer	Clint Nageotte

LAST YEAR'S TOP 20 PROSPECTS

1. Felix Hernandez, rhp	11. Justin Leone, 3b
2. Clint Nageotte, rhp	12. Bobby Madritsch, lhp
3. Travis Blackley, lhp	13. Greg Dobbs, 3b
4. Jose Lopez, ss/2b	14. Ryan Feierabend, lhp
5. Shin-Soo Choo, of	15. Aaron Taylor, rhp
6. Chris Snelling, of	16. Wladimir Balentien, of
7. Rett Johnson, rhp	17. J.J. Putz, rhp
8. Cha Baek, rhp	18. Ryan Ketchner, lhp
9. Adam Jones, ss	19. Matt Thornton, lhp
10. Jamal Strong, of	20. Rene Rivera, c

TOP PROSPECTS OF THE DECADE

Year	Player, Pos.	Current Team
1995	Alex Rodriguez, ss	Yankees
1996	Jose Cruz Jr., of	Diamondbacks
1997	Jose Cruz Jr., of	Diamondbacks
1998	Ryan Anderson, lhp	Mariners
1999	Ryan Anderson, lhp	Mariners
2000	Ryan Anderson, lhp	Mariners
2001	Ryan Anderson, lhp	Mariners
2002	Ryan Anderson, lhp	Mariners
2003	Rafael Soriano, rhp	Mariners
2004	Felix Hernandez, rhp	Mariners

TOP DRAFT PICKS OF THE DECADE

Year	Player, Pos.	Current Team
1995	Jose Cruz Jr., of	Diamondbacks
1996	Gil Meche, rhp	Mariners
1997	Ryan Anderson, lhp	Mariners
1998	Matt Thornton, lhp	Mariners
1999	Ryan Christianson, c	Mariners
2000	Sam Hays, lhp (4)	Mariners
2001	Michael Garciaparra, ss	Mariners
2002	*John Mayberry Jr., of	Stanford U.
2003	Adam Jones, ss/rhp	Mariners
2004	Matt Tuiasosopo, ss (3)	Mariners

*Did not sign.

ALL-TIME LARGEST BONUSES

Ichiro Suzuki, 2000	$5,000,000
Matt Tuiasosopo, 2004	$2,290,000
Ryan Anderson, 1997	$2,175,000
Ryan Christianson, 1999	$2,100,000
Kazuhiro Sasaki, 2000	$2,000,000
Michael Garciaparra, 2001	$2,000,000

MINOR LEAGUE DEPTH CHART

Seattle MARINERS

Impact Talent: C
The Mariners earn an average grade mainly because of one extremely above-average player: Felix Hernandez. The best pitching prospect in the minor leagues could become one of the majors' best when he's still a teenager. Elsewhere, the Mariners' high-ceiling players all carry high risks, such as Chris Snelling's injury history, Matt Tuiasosopo's inexperience and Wladimir Balentien's lack of plate discipline.

Depth: C
Seattle's repeated forays into international signings have helped it supplement weak drafts. For example, in 2000 Seattle didn't pick until the fourth round, and Jamal Strong is likely to be the best player from that class. That August, though, the Mariners scouted the World Junior Championship heavily and ended up with three stars from the tournament: Korea's Shin-Soo Choo, Australia's Travis Blackley and the January 2005 signee Yuniesky Betancourt of Cuba.

Depth charts prepared by John Manuel and Allan Simpson. Numbers in parentheses indicate prospect rankings.

LF
Chris Snelling (7)
Greg Dobbs (13)
Jon Nelson
Greg Jacobs
Casey Craig
Billy Hogan

CF
Jeremy Reed (2)
Jamal Strong (12)
Josh Womack
Michael Wilson
Gary Harris
Jairo Hernandez
Josh Ellison

RF
Shin-Soo Choo (3)
Wladimir Balentien (10)
T.J. Bohn

3B
Matt Tuiasosopo (5)
Justin Leone (15)
Mike Morse (19)
Jesus Guzman
Hunter Brown

SS
Adam Jones (8)
Yuniesky Betancourt (9)
Asdrubal Cabrera (11)
Oswaldo Navarro (24)
Juan Gonzalez

2B
Yung-Chi Chen (23)
Ismael Castro
Luis Valbuena

1B
Jeff Flaig
Daniel Santin
Luis Soto
Greg Holman

SOURCE of TALENT

Homegrown		Acquired	
College	7	Trades	2
Junior College	0	Rule 5 draft	0
Draft-and-follow	0	Independent leagues	1
High school	8	Free agents/waivers	0
Nondrafted free agents	0		
Foreign	12		

C
Rene Rivera (21)
Rob Johnson (27)
Ryan Christianson

LHP

Starters	Relievers
Travis Blackley (6)	George Sherrill (13)
Ryan Feierabend (17)	Cesar Jimenez (18)
Bobby Livingston (22)	Matt Thornton (26)
Shawn Nottingham (28)	Jared Thomas
Tom Oldham	
Steve Uhlmansiek	
Jason Mackintosh	
Casey Abrams	
Jose Escalona	

RHP

Starters	Relievers
Felix Hernandez (1)	Mark Lowe (29)
Clint Nageotte (4)	Scott Atchison
Cha Baek (16)	Rick Guttormson
Rich Dorman (20)	Aaron Looper
Chai-An Huang (25)	Mumba Rivera
Aaron Jensen (30)	Mike Hyrnio
Jon Huber	Sean Green
Brandon Moorhead	
Brett Evert	
Sterling Soto	

DRAFT ANALYSIS

2004

Best Pro Debut: Did SS Matt Tuiasosopo (3) let the pressure of a $2.29 million bonus—a record for his round—get to him? Absolutely not. He started his summer by hitting .412/.528/.721 with four homers and 12 RBIs in 20 games in the Rookie-level Arizona League, where he was rated the No. 1 prospect. Then he moved up to the short-season Northwest League and held his own against much older competition.

Best Athlete: Tuiasosopo surpassed the old third-round bonus mark of $2 million held by Drew Henson and Grady Sizemore. All three were big-time quarterback recruits, and Tuiasosopo was headed to Washington had he not signed. His bat, power and arm are all plus tools, and his makeup is also well above average. The only real question is whether he can stick at shortstop.

Best Pure Hitter: Tuiasosopo.

Best Raw Power: Tuiasosopo. OF/1B Marshall Hubbard (8) also has pop.

Fastest Runner: OFs Jermaine Brock (6) and Sebastien Boucher (7) both have speed that rates 70 on the 20-80 scouting scale.

Best Defensive Player: C Rob Johnson (4) is an athletic backstop with solid catch-and-throw skills. Brock chases balls down easily in center field. SS/2B Jeff Dominguez has good actions but needs more polish.

Best Fastball: RHP Mark Lowe (5) took the 2003 season off at Texas-San Antonio to focus on his mechanics. His work paid off, as he pitched in the low 90s during the spring and peaked at 97 mph after signing. RHP Mumbo Rivera (21) surprised the Mariners with his stuff after signing. His fastball sat in the low 90s and touched 94 mph.

Best Breaking Ball: Rivera's curveball

BILL MITCHELL

Brock

also stands out. Another late-round choice, RHP Aaron Trolia (27) has a good slider.

Most Intriguing Background: Tuiasosopo is just the latest member of his family to leave his mark on the Seattle sporting scene. His father Manu (with the NFL's Seahawks) and older brothers Marques and Zach (at Washington) all played football in the city. His sister Leslie starred in volleyball for the Huskies and serves as an assistant volleyball coach for them. 2B Jack Arroyo's (18) father Rudy and unsigned LHP James Russell's (37) dad Jeff played in the majors.

Closest To The Majors: Lowe or Johnson.

Best Late-Round Pick: LHP Steve Uhlmansiek (12) and Rivera. Uhlmansiek was the top prospect in Kansas until he blew out his elbow and needed Tommy John surgery. Area scout Mark Lummus did a good job monitoring Uhlmansiek's signability, and he should be able to regain his 88-92 mph sinker and plus changeup.

The One Who Got Away: Seattle would have loved to add another strong defensive catcher in J.P. Arencibia (17), but he decided to go to Tennessee.

Assessment: The Mariners surrendered their top two picks to sign free agents Eddie Guardado and Raul Ibanez, but they compensated with the bold signing of Tuiasosopo. Once he's healthy, Uhlmansiek could be another steal.

2003 Several teams preferred SS Adam Jones (1) as a pitcher, but the Mariners are pleased with how he's developing. LHP Ryan Feierabend (3) could turn into something. **GRADE:** C

2002 Seattle didn't get 1B/OF John Mayberry Jr. (1), a projected first-round pick for 2005, or OF Eddy Martinez-Esteve (3), a Giants second-round pick last year. OF Josh Womack (2), the highest-drafted player who signed, isn't in their class. No member of this draft cracked the top 30 prospects list. **GRADE:** F

2001 SS Michael Garciaparra was one of the more shocking first-round picks in recent years. C Rene Rivera (2) and LHP Bobby Livingston (4) are lower-tier prospects. **GRADE:** C

2000 The Mariners didn't pick until the fourth round, when they invested $1.2 million in Sam Hays—who has had shoulder problems and delivered three wins as a pro. OF Jamal Strong (6) is their best hope for a contribution from this group, but he's had injury troubles of his own. **GRADE:** C

Draft analysis prepared by Jim Callis. Numbers in parentheses indicate draft rounds.

ANDREW WOOLLEY

Felix
HERNANDEZ

Born: April 8, 1986.
Ht.: 6-3. **Wt.:** 170
Bats: R. **Throws:** R.
Career Transactions: Signed out of Venezuela by Mariners, July 4, 2002.
Signed by: Emilio Carresquel.

Celebrating his 18th birthday the day before his first outing in 2004, Hernandez turned in the most dominating season for a player that age since Dwight Gooden was BA's Minor League Player of the Year in 1983. He allowed more than three earned runs in just four of his 25 starts, and he was named the top prospect in both the high Class A California and Double-A Texas leagues, just as he had been in the short-season Northwest League in 2003. He was the youngest player in both circuits, just as he had been in the NWL. Hernandez also worked a perfect inning at the Futures Game, highlighted by an effortless strikeout of the Mets' David Wright. His $710,000 bonus now looks like a huge bargain, as he has become unquestionably the best pitching prospect in baseball.

It's difficult to project Hernandez' ceiling because his ability seems limitless. All three of his pitches are above average, and the Mariners won't even let him use his best offering. His fastball and curveball are the best in the system, each rating a 70 on the 20-80 scouting scale, and some club officials give his 60 changeup top billing as well. Hernandez has true power stuff, as his fastball sits in the mid-90s and touches 97 mph while his curveball arrives in the mid-80s. He has yet to completely fill out, so his radar-gun readings could climb. His changeup was inconsistent early in the season, but he has refined it into a pitch that repeatedly throws hitters off balance. Word is that Hernandez' 88-90 mph slider puts his other pitches to shame, but Seattle is keeping it under wraps in the interest of his health. Considering his age, his command and savvy are as extraordinary as his stuff. He can blow the ball by hitters up in the strike zone but excels at keeping it down, as evidenced by his 2.3-1 groundball-flyball ratio in 2004. His mechanics are sound and his arm action is electric. Hernandez also takes care of the little things, such as holding baserunners and fielding his position. Despite all the hype swirling around him, he hasn't let it get to him.

At times Hernandez will overthrow when he's in a jam, forgetting that each of his pitches is good enough to get outs. He needs to locate his fastball a little better to help set up his curveball and changeup. He may have to watch his weight as he gets older, though his work ethic isn't a concern.

An injury is all that could derail Hernandez from stardom, and the Mariners are going to great lengths to keep him healthy. Besides taking away his slider, they've held him to strict pitch and inning counts and persuaded him to skip winter ball in his native Venezuela this offseason. They plan on him beginning 2005 in Triple-A, though he could force the issue of a big league promotion in spring training. Regardless of where he starts the year, Hernandez will get to Seattle and become the No. 1 starter soon enough.

Year	Club (League)	Class	W	L	ERA	G	GS	CG	SV	IP	H	R	ER	HR	BB	SO	AVG
2003	Everett (NWL)	A	7	2	2.29	11	7	0	0	55	43	17	14	2	24	73	.218
	Wisconsin (Mid)	A	0	0	1.93	2	2	0	0	14	9	4	3	1	3	18	.176
2004	San Antonio (TL)	AA	5	1	3.30	10	10	1	0	57	47	23	21	3	21	58	.220
	Inland Empire (Cal)	A	9	3	2.74	16	15	0	0	92	85	31	28	5	26	114	.245
MINOR LEAGUE TOTALS			21	6	2.72	39	34	1	0	218	184	75	66	11	74	263	.227

Jeremy Reed, of

LARRY GOREN

Born: June 15, 1981. **Ht.:** 6-0. **Wt.:** 185. **Bats:** L. **Throws:** L. **School:** Long Beach State University. **Career Transactions:** Selected by White Sox in second round of 2002 draft; signed June 25, 2002 . . . Traded by White Sox with C Miguel Olivo and SS Mike Morse to Mariners for RHP Freddy Garcia, Ben Davis and cash, June 27, 2004. **Signed by:** Joe Butler/Matt Hattabaugh (White Sox).

Reed ranked as the White Sox' top prospect after leading the minors with a .373 average and .453 on-base percentage in 2003. When they traded Freddy Garcia, the Mariners insisted on Reed in a package that included Miguel Olivo and Mike Morse. He batted .397 in his big league debut. A natural line-drive hitter, Reed controls the strike zone and makes consistent sweet-spot contact. He runs well; his instincts make him a stolen-base threat. His September performance convinced Seattle he can handle center field. His arm is average. Scouts from other clubs aren't as sure he can stay in center—particularly in spacious Safeco Field. He needs to improve his jumps and routes on fly balls. Reed may max out at 15 homers a season, which would be below-average power if he has to move to left. Already having proven he's more qualified than Randy Winn, Reed should open 2005 as Seattle's center fielder. He should fit nicely behind Ichiro Suzuki in the No. 2 slot in the order.

Yr	Club (League)	Class	AVG	G	AB	R	H	2B	3B	HR	RBI	BB	SO	SB	OBP	SLG
2002	Kannapolis (SAL)	A	.319	57	210	37	67	15	0	4	32	11	24	17	.377	.448
2003	Winston-Salem (Car)	A	.333	65	222	37	74	18	1	4	52	41	17	27	.431	.477
	Birmingham (SL)	AA	.409	66	242	51	99	17	3	7	43	29	19	18	.474	.591
2004	Charlotte (IL)	AAA	.275	73	276	44	76	14	1	8	37	36	34	12	.357	.420
	Tacoma (PCL)	AAA	.305	61	233	40	71	10	5	5	36	23	22	14	.366	.455
	Seattle (AL)	MAJ	.397	18	58	11	23	4	0	0	5	7	4	3	.470	.466
MAJOR LEAGUE TOTALS			.397	18	58	11	23	4	0	0	5	7	4	3	.470	.466
MINOR LEAGUE TOTALS			.327	322	1183	209	387	74	10	28	200	140	116	88	.401	.478

Shin-Soo Choo, of

Born: July 13, 1982. **Ht.:** 5-11. **Wt.:** 170. **Bats:** L. **Throws:** L. **Career Transactions:** Signed out of Korea by Mariners, Aug. 14, 2000. **Signed by:** Jae Lee/Jim Colborn.

Choo dominated the 2000 World Junior Championship as a pitcher, winning MVP honors. The Mariners signed him afterward for $1.335 million and made the two-way star a full-time outfielder. The organization's 2004 minor league player of the year, Choo played in his second Futures Game and set personal bests in average, homers and steals. Choo keeps his hands back and stays inside the ball, slashing liners to the opposite field. An above-average runner, he improved his aggressiveness and basestealing success in 2004. His plus-plus arm rated as the best among Texas League outfielders. He has the strength to hit 25 homers, but Choo's approach isn't conducive to power. He'll need to close his swing and do a better job of recognizing inside pitches. His outfield instincts are lacking and limit him to the corners. His throws could use more accuracy. Choo has moved one level at a time and should spend most of 2005 at Triple-A Tacoma. He has right-field tools, but figures to be Seattle's left fielder of the future unless Ichiro moves to center.

Year	Club (League)	Class	AVG	AB	R	H	2B	3B	HR	RBI	BB	SO	SB	OBP	SLG
2001	Mariners (AZL)	R	.302	51	199	51	60	10	10	4	35	34	49	12	.420	.513
	Wisconsin (Mid)	A	.462	3	13	1	6	0	0	0	3	1	3	2	.533	.462
2002	Wisconsin (Mid)	A	.302	119	420	69	127	24	8	6	48	70	98	34	.417	.440
	Inland Empire (Cal)	A	.308	11	39	14	12	5	1	1	9	9	9	3	.460	.564
2003	Inland Empire (Cal)	A	.286	110	412	62	118	18	13	9	55	44	84	18	.365	.459
2004	San Antonio (TL)	AA	.315	132	517	89	163	17	7	15	84	56	97	40	.382	.462
MINOR LEAGUE TOTALS			.304	426	1600	286	486	74	39	35	234	214	340	109	.395	.464

Clint Nageotte, rhp

Born: Oct. 25, 1980. **Ht.:** 6-3. **Wt.:** 200. **Bats:** R. **Throws:** R. **School:** Brooklyn (Ohio) HS. **Career Transactions:** Selected by Mariners in fifth round of 1999 draft; signed Aug. 18, 1999. **Signed by:** Ken Madeja.

Nageotte cruised through the minors, leading the minors in strikeouts in 2002 and topping the Texas League in whiffs in 2003. But when he got to the majors last season, his stuff declined and he got throttled. He threw six shutout innings against the Astros for his lone victory. Nageotte has one of the nastiest sliders in baseball, as it has violent break and tops out at 87 mph. He also owns a power fastball, working from 92-

97 mph. That dynamic combination has led several scouts to project him as a closer. In order to remain a starter, Nageotte will have to refine his changeup and throw it more often. He'll also have to throw more strikes with his fastball. He tried to be so fine with his pitches in Seattle that his heater dropped to 88-93 mph and his slider regressed to a slurve. He uses his slider too much, leading to concerns about his durability that weren't eased by elbow tendinitis in 2003 and a lower-back strain in 2004. Nageotte needs some time in Triple-A to straighten himself out. The Mariners will leave him in the rotation for now.

Year	Club (League)	Class	W	L	ERA	G	GS	CG	SV	IP	H	R	ER	HR	BB	SO	AVG
2000	Mariners (AZL)	R	4	1	2.16	12	7	0	1	50	29	15	12	0	28	59	.167
2001	Wisconsin (Mid)	A	11	8	3.13	28	26	0	0	152	141	65	53	10	50	187	.246
2002	Inland Empire (Cal)	A	9	6	4.54	29	29	1	0	165	153	101	83	10	68	214	.241
2003	San Antonio (TL)	AA	11	7	3.10	27	27	2	0	154	127	60	53	6	67	157	.224
2004	Tacoma (PCL)	AAA	6	6	4.46	14	14	0	0	81	78	42	40	9	35	63	.256
	Seattle (AL)	MAJ	1	6	7.36	12	5	0	0	37	48	31	30	3	27	24	.324
MAJOR LEAGUE TOTALS			1	6	7.36	12	5	0	0	37	48	31	30	3	27	24	.324
MINOR LEAGUE TOTALS			41	28	3.60	110	103	3	1	602	528	283	241	35	248	680	.234

5 Matt Tuiasosopo, ss

Born: May 10, 1986. **Ht.:** 6-2. **Wt.:** 210. **Bats:** R. **Throws:** R. **School:** Woodinville (Wash.) HS. **Career Transactions:** Selected by Mariners in third round of 2004 draft; signed July 2, 2004. **Signed by:** Phil Geisler.

His father Manu and brother Marques played in the NFL, and Tuiasosopo seemed destined for football as a University of Washington quarterback recruit. The Mariners changed that by giving him a third-round record $2.29 million bonus. He homered in his first pro at-bat and was the top prospect in the Rookie-level Arizona League. Tuiasosopo has the swing and strength to be a middle-of-the-order run producer. Advanced for his age, he forced a promotion to short-season Everett and held his own. The best all-around athlete in the system, he has a strong arm and good speed. Seattle raves about his makeup as much as his tools. Though he made progress with his footwork and release, Tuiasosopo likely won't be able to stay at shortstop because his actions are too long. He'll have to tighten holes in his swing that older Northwest League pitchers were able to exploit. Tuiasosopo should be able to handle an assignment to low Class A Wisconsin, where he'd share shortstop with Oswaldo Navarro and see time at third base. His bat should play anywhere.

Year	Club (League)	Class	AVG	G	AB	R	H	2B	3B	HR	RBI	BB	SO	SB	OBP	SLG
2004	Mariners (AZL)	R	.412	20	68	18	28	5	2	4	12	13	14	1	.528	.721
	Everett (NWL)	A	.255	30	106	20	27	6	1	3	17	11	38	4	.350	.415
MINOR LEAGUE TOTALS			.316	50	174	38	55	11	3	7	29	24	52	5	.420	.534

6 Travis Blackley, lhp

Born: Nov. 4, 1982. **Ht.:** 6-3. **Wt.:** 190. **Bats:** L. **Throws:** L. **Career Transactions:** Signed out of Australia by Mariners, Oct. 29, 2000. **Signed by:** Jim Colborn.

While the Mariners were zeroing in on Shin-Soo Choo at the 2000 World Junior Championship, they also discovered Blackley. He tied for the minor league lead with 17 wins in 2003, but like Nageotte had a difficult time handling his first big league trial in 2004. His brother Adam pitches in the Red Sox system. At his best, Blackley confuses hitters by mixing four pitches and draws comparisons to Mark Buehrle. His changeup is his best pitch, the key to his consistent success against righthanders. He also uses an 87-92 mph fastball with natural cutting action, a curveball and a slider. Blackley tried to pitch away from contact in the majors, with disastrous results. He lost his command and his fastball dropped to 82-85 mph, losing separation from his changeup. He needs to find a consistent breaking ball to get lefties out. He does get good spin on his curve, and it was the one pitch he got major league hitters to miss. He'll return to Tacoma to begin 2005. The Mariners believe he'll learn from his adversity.

Year	Club (League)	Class	W	L	ERA	G	GS	CG	SV	IP	H	R	ER	HR	BB	SO	AVG
2001	Everett (NWL)	A	6	1	3.32	14	14	0	0	79	60	34	29	7	29	90	.211
2002	Inland Empire (Cal)	A	5	9	3.49	21	20	1	0	121	102	52	47	11	44	152	.227
2003	San Antonio (TL)	AA	17	3	2.61	27	27	0	0	162	125	55	47	11	62	144	.215
2004	Seattle (AL)	MAJ	1	3	10.04	6	6	0	0	26	35	31	29	9	22	16	.321
	Tacoma (PCL)	AAA	8	6	3.83	19	18	2	0	110	100	49	47	14	47	80	.249
MAJOR LEAGUE TOTALS			1	3	10.04	6	6	0	0	26	35	31	29	9	22	16	.321
MINOR LEAGUE TOTALS			36	19	3.24	81	79	3	0	473	387	190	170	43	182	466	.225

Chris Snelling, of

Born: Dec. 3, 1981. **Ht.:** 5-10. **Wt.:** 160. **Bats:** L. **Throws:** L. **Career Transactions:** Signed out of Australia by Mariners, March 2, 1999. **Signed by:** Barry Holland.

Snelling never has hit less than .305 in six pro seasons, but he never has stayed healthy for a full season, playing just 96 games in 2002-03 because of left knee problems that required multiple surgeries. A deep bone bruise in his right wrist cost him all but 10 games in 2004. Snelling's explosive hands generate hard line drives to all fields. His instincts and drive allow him to maximize his tools. He has average arm strength and can handle either outfield corner. Given his injury history—which also includes breaks in his left hand, right thumb and right ankle, plus a strained left wrist—Snelling needs to tone down his aggressiveness. He hurt his right wrist because he was so eager to come back that he took too many swings. The knee operations have left him with slightly below-average speed. His power ceiling may be 15 homers, subpar for a corner outfielder. Snelling had a setback late in 2004, so the Mariners had him take the winter off. The goal is for him to be 100 percent for spring training and help the big league club after a tuneup in Triple-A.

Year	Club (League)	Class	AVG	G	AB	R	H	2B	3B	HR	RBI	BB	SO	SB	OBP	SLG
1999	Everett (NWL)	A	.306	69	265	46	81	15	3	10	50	33	24	8	.388	.498
2000	Wisconsin (Mid)	A	.305	72	259	44	79	9	5	9	56	34	34	7	.386	.483
2001	San Bernardino (Cal)	A	.336	114	450	90	151	29	10	7	73	45	63	12	.418	.491
2002	San Antonio (TL)	AA	.326	23	89	10	29	9	2	1	12	12	11	5	.429	.506
	Seattle (AL)	MAJ	.148	8	27	2	4	0	0	1	3	2	4	0	.207	.259
2003	San Antonio (TL)	AA	.333	47	186	24	62	12	2	3	25	8	30	1	.371	.468
	Tacoma (PCL)	AAA	.269	18	67	11	18	2	0	3	10	5	12	1	.333	.433
2004	Mariners (AZL)	R	.313	10	32	8	10	4	1	0	9	7	3	1	.476	.500
MAJOR LEAGUE TOTALS			.148	8	27	2	4	0	0	1	3	2	4	0	.207	.259
MINOR LEAGUE TOTALS			.320	351	1343	233	430	80	23	33	229	139	178	34	.398	.488

Adam Jones, ss

Born: Aug. 1, 1985. **Ht.:** 6-2. **Wt.:** 180. **Bats:** R. **Throws:** R. **School:** Morse HS, San Diego. **Career Transactions:** Selected by Mariners in first round (37th overall) of 2003 draft; signed July 18, 2003. **Signed by:** Joe Bohringer.

Jones lit up radar guns with some 96s as a high school senior, leading many clubs to target him as a pitcher. The Mariners liked him both ways and granted his wish to play shortstop after signing him for $925,000 as their top pick in 2003. A premium athlete, Jones continues to draw gasps with his arm, rated the best among Midwest League infielders. He hit 11 homers as a teenager in low Class A, and there's more power coming. He has a sound swing and has been compared to Reggie Sanders, who also began his career as a shortstop. Jones runs well once under way and has solid range at shortstop. Jones needs to improve his grasp of the strike zone and his ability to work counts. He did show aptitude for making adjustments, overswinging less and using the whole field more later in the season. Though he could outgrow shortstop, he should retain his athleticism and at worst would become a center fielder. The Mariners like to work their shortstops at multiple positions, and Jones will get a taste of that in 2005. He's ready for high Class A.

Year	Club (League)	Class	AVG	G	AB	R	H	2B	3B	HR	RBI	BB	SO	SB	OBP	SLG
2003	Mariners (AZL)	R	.284	28	109	18	31	5	1	0	8	5	19	5	.368	.349
	Everett (NWL)	A	.462	3	13	2	6	1	0	0	4	1	3	0	.467	.538
2004	Wisconsin (Mid)	A	.267	130	510	76	136	23	7	11	72	33	124	8	.314	.404
MINOR LEAGUE TOTALS			.274	161	632	96	173	29	8	11	84	39	146	13	.327	.397

Yuniesky Betancourt, ss/2b

Born: Jan. 31, 1982. **Ht.:** 5-10. **Wt.:** 190. **Bats:** R. **Throws:** R. **Career Transactions:** Signed out of Cuba by Mariners, Jan. 26, 2005. **Signed by:** Bob Engle.

As if they weren't loaded with shortstop prospects already, Seattle added to the strongest position in its system by signing Betancourt, a Cuban defector, in January. He received a four-year major league contract worth $3.65 million as general manager Bill Bavasi called him the equivalent of a first- or second-round pick. He starred at the 2000 World Junior Championship, where the Mariners first spotted Shin-Soo Choo and Travis Blackley, hitting .429 as Cuba won the bronze medal. He fled Cuba on a raft in 2003, eventually landing in Mexico, and didn't play in 2004. Agent Jaime Torres showcased Betancourt's skills by bringing him to several big league training sites last spring. He's a live-bodied athlete with all-around skills. Betancourt makes consistent hard contact, and while he doesn't have loft power, he's strong enough to drive his share of balls into the gaps. He has well above-average speed. Where Betancourt will wind up defensively is uncertain. He has the actions, feet and hands to play shortstop, as well as enough arm strength. But he spent his last three seasons in Cuba at second base because he was on the same Villa Clara club with longtime Cuban national team shortstop Eduardo Paret. The organization's logjam at the position makes it possible that Betancourt will move off shortstop anyway, and third base and the outfield also are possibilities. The Mariners will give him a long look at spring training and have no definite starter at shortstop, but they plan on sending Betancourt to Double-A San Antonio to begin his U.S. career.

Year	Club (League)	Class	AVG	G	AB	R	H	2B	3B	HR	RBI	BB	SO	SB	OBP	SLG
2004	Did not play—Signed 2005 contract															

10 Wladimir Balentien, of

RICH ABEL

Born: July 2, 1984. **Ht.:** 6-2. **Wt.:** 160. **Bats:** R. **Throws:** R. **Career Transactions:** Signed out of Curacao by Mariners, July 9, 2000 **Signed by:** Karel Williams.

After winning home run crowns in the Rookie-level Venezuelan and Arizona leagues the previous two years, Balentien continued to mash in 2004. Counting the California League playoffs and Olympics (he played for the Netherlands), he hit 20 home runs in 98 games. Balentien has extraordinary power to all fields and has the tools to be more than just a slugger. His speed and arm strength are average. His primary 2004 position was center field, though he's destined for right. Balentien tries to pull every pitch, so he has poor discipline, makes infrequent contact and struggles against breaking balls. He worries solely about his hitting, leading to poor jumps and lapses in the outfield. He needs to prepare to play hard every day, and he'll have to watch that his big build doesn't lose its flexibility. The Mariners have a number of outfielders established in the big leagues or ahead of Balentien on the system's depth chart, but none of them can approach his power. They hope he'll mature in all phases of the game at high Class A Inland Empire in 2005.

Year	Club (League)	Class	AVG	G	AB	R	H	2B	3B	HR	RBI	BB	SO	SB	OBP	SLG
2001	Aguirre (VSL)	R	.206	53	131	27	27	2	1	0	9	25	48	7	.333	.237
2002	Aguirre (VSL)	R	.279	59	197	41	55	13	4	10	39	34	52	6	.390	.538
2003	Mariners (AZL)	R	.283	50	187	42	53	12	5	16	52	22	55	4	.363	.658
2004	Wisconsin (Mid)	A	.277	76	260	39	72	12	3	15	46	12	77	10	.315	.519
	Inland Empire (Cal)	A	.289	10	38	5	11	1	0	2	5	4	10	1	.357	.474
MINOR LEAGUE TOTALS			.268	248	813	154	218	40	13	43	151	97	242	28	.350	.508

11 Asdrubal Cabrera, ss/2b

Born: Nov. 13, 1985. **Ht.:** 6-0. **Wt.:** 170. **Bats:** B. **Throws:** R. **Career Transactions:** Signed out of Venezuela by Mariners, Aug. 26, 2002. **Signed by:** Emilio Carrasquel.

Cabrera was the Rookie-level Venezuelan Summer League's all-star shortstop in his pro debut, so the Mariners skipped him past the Arizona League in 2004. He repeated as an all-star in the Northwest League, where at 18 he was the youngest regular in the league. Polished for his age, Cabrera's all-around game is similar to that of Orlando Cabrera (no relation). A switch-hitter with some gap power, he may have the most pure bat among the system's shortstop prospects. He's also one of its better athletes. An acrobatic defender, Cabrera covers plenty of ground and has reliable hands. He has average arm strength and better accuracy. Cabrera's lower half looks like it could get too thick for shortstop, but he's so smooth that Seattle doesn't foresee that he'll have to move to another position. He'll need to show more patience to fit into his projected No. 2 spot in the batting order. The Mariners are ready to jump Cabrera a level again, deeming him ready for high Class A in 2005. He'll split time at shortstop with Adam Jones after doing so with Oswaldo Navarro in 2004.

Year	Club (League)	Class	AVG	G	AB	R	H	2B	3B	HR	RBI	BB	SO	SB	OBP	SLG
2003	Aguirre (VSL)	R	.283	55	198	31	56	12	4	0	29	16	31	5	.367	.384
2004	Everett (NWL)	A	.272	63	239	44	65	16	3	5	41	21	43	7	.330	.427
MINOR LEAGUE TOTALS			.277	118	437	75	121	28	7	5	70	37	74	12	.347	.407

12 Jamal Strong, of

Born: Aug. 5, 1978. **Ht.:** 5-10. **Wt.:** 180. **Bats:** R. **Throws:** R. **School:** University of Nebraska. **Career Transactions:** Selected by Mariners in sixth round of 2000 draft; signed June 14, 2000. **Signed by:** Mark Lummus.

Strong is a better center fielder than Jeremy Reed or Randy Winn, but injuries have prevented him from showing what he can do the last two years. He tore his labrum and dislocated his left shoulder on a headfirst slide during spring training in 2003, then missed most of the final two months last season after sustaining a bone bruise on his right knee when he ran into an outfield wall. After minor surgery, he spent the winter at the Mariners' Arizona complex trying to strengthen the muscles around his knee. He should regain the speed that made him one of the fastest players in the minors. Strong understands his role is to get on base, and he plays it to the hilt, focusing on drawing walks and keeping the ball on the ground. Though he's never going to have much pop, he didn't get beat up by fastballs in on his hands as much in 2004 as he did in the past. Seattle considers him the best outfield defender in the system, but he still has room for improvement. While Strong's speed gives him tremendous range, he's much better going back on balls than making plays in front of him. His arm is below-average. The Mariners would prefer Strong to play regularly than sit on the big league bench, so he's probably headed back to Triple-A.

Year	Club (League)	Class	AVG	G	AB	R	H	2B	3B	HR	RBI	BB	SO	SB	OBP	SLG
2000	Everett (NWL)	A	.314	75	296	63	93	7	3	1	28	52	29	60	.422	.368
2001	Wisconsin (Mid)	A	.353	51	184	41	65	12	1	0	19	40	27	35	.478	.429
	San Berndno (Cal)	A	.311	81	331	74	103	11	2	0	32	51	60	47	.411	.356
2002	San Antonio (TL)	AA	.278	127	503	63	140	16	5	1	31	62	87	46	.366	.336
2003	Mariners (AZL)	R	.714	2	7	5	5	0	1	0	4	3	1	3	.692	1.000
	Tacoma (PCL)	AAA	.305	56	210	38	64	6	1	2	19	25	38	26	.390	.371
	Seattle (AL)	MAJ	.000	12	2	2	0	0	0	0	0	0	0	0	.000	.000
2004	Tacoma (PCL)	AAA	.324	64	238	46	77	11	2	3	24	38	29	19	.421	.424
MAJOR LEAGUE TOTALS			.000	12	2	2	0	0	0	0	0	0	0	0	.000	.000
MINOR LEAGUE TOTALS			.309	456	1769	330	547	63	15	7	157	271	271	236	.408	.374

13 George Sherrill, lhp

Born: April 19, 1977. **Ht.:** 6-0. **Wt.:** 225. **Bats:** L. **Throws:** L. **School:** Austin Peay State University. **Career Transactions:** Signed by independent Evansville (Frontier), May 1999 . . . Signed by independent Sioux Falls (Northern), May 2001 . . . Signed by independent Winnipeg (Northern), May 2003 . . . Contract purchased by Mariners from Winnipeg, July 2, 2003. **Signed by:** Charley Kerfeld.

Former scout Charley Kerfeld, who resigned from the Mariners after the season, had been the club's point man in scouring independent leagues for talent. Sherrill spent five seasons in independent ball, mainly because his weight ballooned to as much as 300 pounds and scared big league clubs off, before Kerfeld signed him in July 2003. He was in Seattle nearly a year later and pitched well for the Mariners before wearing down in mid-September. Sherrill is in better shape but his body still isn't pretty, and his deliberate, stiff delivery isn't either. But he has uncanny command for someone with his build and mechanics, and he throws the ball from behind his ear, making it difficult for batters to pick up his pitches. When he's fresh, Sherrill is nasty on lefthanders with his low-90s fastball and good slider. He's OK but not nearly as effective against righthanders, and needs to improve his changeup to fare better against them. Counting winter ball, Sherrill had pitched nearly nonstop since signing with Seattle, and he just needed some time off. The Mariners are counting on him to be one of their primary lefty relievers in 2005.

Year	Club (League)	Class	W	L	ERA	G	GS	CG	SV	IP	H	R	ER	HR	BB	SO	AVG
1999	Evansville (Fron)	IND	2	4	3.15	22	4	1	2	40	40	20	14	3	18	33	.268
2000	Evansville (Fron)	IND	3	5	4.66	13	13	1	0	75	71	45	39	5	35	61	.250
2001	Sioux City (NorC)	IND	4	4	2.45	48	2	0	0	59	53	20	16	3	14	45	.249
2002	Winnipeg (NorC)	IND	3	5	3.07	38	0	0	2	41	35	16	14	6	13	61	.227
2003	Winnipeg (Nor)	IND	1	0	1.13	16	0	0	1	16	8	2	2	0	4	30	.151
	San Antonio (TL)	AA	3	0	0.33	16	0	0	0	27	19	2	1	1	12	31	.198
2004	Seattle (AL)	MAJ	2	1	3.80	21	0	0	0	24	24	12	10	3	9	16	.258
	Tacoma (PCL)	AAA	4	2	2.32	36	0	0	13	50	42	13	13	4	9	62	.223
MAJOR LEAGUE TOTALS			2	1	3.803	21	0	0	0	24	24	12	10	3	9	16	.258
MINOR LEAGUE TOTALS			7	2	1.622	52	0	0	13	78	61	15	14	5	21	93	.215

14 Greg Dobbs, 3b

Born: July 2, 1978. **Ht.:** 6-1. **Wt.:** 200. **Bats:** L. **Throws:** R. **School:** University of Oklahoma. **Career Transactions:** Signed as nondrafted free agent by Mariners, May 28, 2001. **Signed by:** Mark Lummus.

Dobbs completed a successful comeback from a ruptured left Achilles tendon that ended his 2003 season after two games, becoming the first Mariner to homer in his initial big league at-bat. Seattle initially drafted him in the 53rd round out of high school in 1996 but didn't land him until he signed as a fifth-year senior before the 2001 draft. He has hit everywhere he has played. His mechanics, swing and plate coverage have made him a consistent .300 hitter, and he has enough power to hit 15-20 homers on an annual basis. He doesn't walk a lot, in part because he makes contact so easily. Dobbs looked better defensively in the majors than he had in the minors, but it's still unlikely that he can handle third base on an everyday basis. Though he has worked hard on playing the hot corner, his range is very fringy and his arm and hands are only adequate. He doesn't profile to have enough power to play first base, but his ability to play either infield corner is moot after Seattle signed free agents Richie Sexson and Adrian Beltre in the offseason. Dobbs' best bet for regular playing time appears to be left field, though the Mariners also have a crowded outfield picture. Because he has spent just 2½ months in Triple-A and has no opening in the majors, he's ticketed to return to Tacoma at the start of 2005.

Year	Club (League)	Class	AVG	G	AB	R	H	2B	3B	HR	RBI	BB	SO	SB	OBP	SLG
2001	Everett (NWL)	A	.321	65	249	37	80	17	2	6	41	30	39	5	.396	.478
	San Bernardino (Cal)	A	.385	3	13	2	5	1	0	1	3	0	4	0	.357	.692
2002	Wisconsin (Mid)	A	.275	86	320	43	88	16	2	10	48	31	50	13	.338	.431
	San Antonio (TL)	AA	.365	27	96	13	35	2	0	5	15	9	17	1	.425	.542
2003	San Antonio (TL)	AA	.333	2	6	0	2	2	0	0	0	0	1	0	.333	.667
2004	San Antonio (LX)	AA	.325	51	203	25	66	14	4	5	34	11	23	5	.373	.507
	Tacoma (PCL)	AAA	.271	67	255	28	69	9	2	8	31	5	36	4	.286	.416
	Seattle (AL)	MAJ	.226	18	53	4	12	1	0	1	9	1	14	0	.250	.302
MAJOR LEAGUE TOTALS			.226	18	53	4	12	1	0	1	9	1	14	0	.250	.302
MINOR LEAGUE TOTALS			.302	301	1142	148	345	61	10	35	172	86	170	28	.354	.465

15 Justin Leone, inf/of

Born: March 9, 1977. **Ht.:** 6-1. **Wt.:** 210. **Bats:** R. **Throws:** R. **School:** St. Martin's (Wash.) College. **Career Transactions:** Selected by Mariners in 13th round of 1999 draft; signed June 8, 1999. **Signed by:** Phil Geisler.

Leone followed up a breakthrough 2003 season by scalding the ball for three months in Triple-A, which earned him Seattle's third-base job. He continued to hit for power in the majors until Matt Kinney broke two fingers on his left hand with a pitch in mid-August. Leone won't regain his starting role now that the Mariners have signed Adrian Beltre, but he still could help the club with his versatility. His hands, arm and actions have allowed him to play all four infield positions and both outfield corners in the minors. He has Gold Glove potential at third base, though he made erratic throws and lost confidence in his first taste of the majors. Believing in himself is a key for Leone, who struggled with self-doubt for much of his first four seasons. He's one of the better power hitters in the system, though he's a streaky hitter who doesn't always make consistent contact. His selectivity regressed last year, perhaps because he was trying to make an impression by hitting homers. Willie Bloomquist is an organization favorite, but Leone could offer Seattle more as a utilityman.

Year	Club (League)	Class	AVG	G	AB	R	H	2B	3B	HR	RBI	BB	SO	SB	OBP	SLG
1999	Everett (NWL)	A	.263	62	205	34	54	14	2	6	35	32	49	5	.361	.439
2000	Wisconsin (Mid)	A	.267	115	374	77	100	32	3	18	63	79	107	9	.407	.513
2001	San Bernardino (Cal)	A	.233	130	485	70	113	27	4	22	69	57	158	4	.318	.441
2002	San Bernardino (Cal)	A	.249	98	358	64	89	20	5	18	58	57	98	6	.358	.483
2003	San Antonio (TL)	AA	.288	135	455	103	131	38	7	21	92	92	104	20	.405	.541
2004	Tacoma (PCL)	AAA	.269	68	253	56	68	10	5	21	51	26	82	5	.344	.597
	Seattle (AL)	MAJ	.216	31	102	15	22	5	0	6	13	9	32	1	.298	.441
MAJOR LEAGUE TOTALS			.216	31	102	15	22	5	0	6	13	9	32	1	.298	.441
MINOR LEAGUE TOTALS			.261	608	2130	404	555	141	26	106	368	343	598	49	.367	.500

16 Cha Seung Baek, rhp

Born: May 29, 1980. **Ht.:** 6-4. **Wt.:** 190. **Bats:** R. **Throws:** R. **Career Transactions:** Signed out of Korea by Mariners, Sept. 25, 1998. **Signed by:** Jim Colborn.

Seattle kicked off its aggressive pursuit of international talent by signing Baek, who played with Shin-Soo Choo at Pusan High in Korea, for $1.3 million in 1998. He missed most of 2001 and all of 2002 after Tommy John surgery. He hasn't totally regained the low-90s velocity he had before his injury, but he's never been about blowing hitters away. Baek succeed by locating his full repertoire, which includes an 88-92 mph two-seam fastball, a four-seamer, a curveball, a slider and a changeup. His best pitches are his changuep and his curveball. Though he has no difficulty throwing strikes, Baek must work more aggressively to get the ball in on hitters. Big leaguers quickly learned to lean out over the plate and look for pitches on the outer half against him, though he did spin eight shutout innings against the Rangers in his final outing of the season. He's not going to strike out a lot of batters, so he'll need his defense to make plays for him. Baek could crack the Opening Day rotation, though his chances are tied to Joel Pineiro's health and Ron Villone's role.

Year	Club (League)	Class	W	L	ERA	G	GS	CG	SV	IP	H	R	ER	HR	BB	SO	AVG
1999	Mariners (AZL)	R	3	0	3.67	8	4	0	0	27	30	13	11	2	6	25	.283
2000	Wisconsin (Mid)	A	8	5	3.95	24	24	0	0	128	137	71	56	13	36	99	.275

Year	Club (League)	Class	W	L	ERA	G	GS	CG	SV	IP	H	R	ER	HR	BB	SO	AVG
2001	Inland Empire (Cal)	A	1	0	3.43	5	4	0	0	21	17	10	8	2	2	16	.224
2002	Did not play—Injured																
2003	Inland Empire (Cal)	A	5	1	3.65	13	10	0	1	57	55	27	23	3	9	50	.249
	San Antonio (TL)	AA	3	3	2.57	9	9	0	0	56	49	18	16	2	17	46	.238
2004	Seattle (AL)	MAJ	2	4	5.52	7	5	0	0	31	35	23	19	5	11	20	.278
	Tacoma (PCL)	AAA	5	4	4.21	14	14	0	0	73	85	41	34	7	24	56	.290
	San Antonio (TL)	AA	0	0	0.00	1	1	0	0	5	2	0	0	0	0	5	.125
MAJOR LEAGUE TOTALS			2	4	5.52	7	5	0	0	31	35	23	19	5	11	20	.278
MINOR LEAGUE TOTALS			25	13	3.64	74	66	0	1	366	375	180	148	29	94	297	.265

17 Ryan Feierabend, lhp

Born: August 22, 1985. **Ht.:** 6-3. **Wt.:** 190. **Bats:** L. **Throws:** L. **School:** Midview HS, Grafton, Ohio. **Career Transactions:** Selected by Mariners in third round of 2003 draft; signed July 13, 2003. **Signed by:** Ken Madeja.

The Mariners like to collect lefthanders with a feel for pitching, and after Travis Blackley, Feierabend is their best. Seattle has compared him to a younger version of Blackley, and Feierabend already has more velocity. His fastball ranges from 86-92 mph, and he should have at least consistent average velocity once his lanky frame matures. His circle changeup and curveball are average pitches, but his stuff plays up because he's willing to throw any pitch in any count and has the command to locate them where he wants. Feierabend's feel and poise may be his most impressive attributes. Easily the Midwest League's youngest starting pitcher in 2004, he turned in 18 quality starts in 26 outings, including in each of his last six. He also shared Wisconsin's pitcher-of-the-year award with Oldham. Feierabend has a sharp pickoff move, leading the MWL with 16 basestealers caught. He didn't miss a lot of bats last season, though that can be attributed partly to his age. If his stuff develops like Seattle thinks it will, that won't be an issue. He'll pitch in high Class A this year.

Year	Club (League)	Class	W	L	ERA	G	GS	CG	SV	IP	H	R	ER	HR	BB	SO	AVG
2003	Mariners (AZL)	R	2	3	2.61	6	5	0	1	21	23	11	6	0	6	12	.288
2004	Wisconsin (Mid)	A	9	7	3.63	26	26	1	0	161	158	78	65	17	44	106	.259
MINOR LEAGUE TOTALS			11	10	3.52	32	31	1	1	182	181	89	71	17	50	118	.262

18 Cesar Jimenez, lhp

Born: Nov. 12, 1984. **Ht.:** 5-11. **Wt.:** 180. **Bats:** L. **Throws:** L. **Career Transactions:** Signed out of Venezuela by Mariners, July 2, 2001. **Signed by:** Emilio Carrasquel.

Though he made the Midwest League midseason all-star team as an 18-year-old starter in 2003, Jimenez appeared tentative and faded badly down the stretch, losing seven of his final nine starts. The Mariners moved him to the bullpen last year and he seemed much more comfortable, having no trouble handling a high Class A hitter's league despite being its third-youngest regular pitcher. Jimenez owns the best changeup in the system, though he still needs to find a way to keep righthanders in check. His 87-91 mph fastball and his curveball are both solid pitches for him, and he pitches above his stuff because he's so driven. Because he owns three effective pitches, Seattle is debating on whether to return him to the rotation in 2005. Regardless of his role, he'll pitch in Double-A San Antonio.

Year	Club (League)	Class	W	L	ERA	G	GS	CG	SV	IP	H	R	ER	HR	BB	SO	AVG
2002	Aguirre (VSL)	R	7	1	0.83	11	11	2	0	65	37	6	6	0	12	67	.167
	Mariners (AZL)	R	0	0	3.38	1	0	0	0	3	3	2	1	0	0	3	.300
	Everett (NWL)	A	2	1	2.70	8	0	0	1	20	12	7	6	2	5	25	.174
2003	Wisconsin (Mid)	A	8	11	2.94	28	20	0	0	126	134	61	41	7	46	76	.273
2004	Inland Empire (Cal)	A	6	7	2.32	43	2	0	6	85	80	28	22	3	18	80	.250
MINOR LEAGUE TOTALS			23	20	2.29	91	33	2	7	299	266	104	76	12	81	251	.237

19 Mike Morse, ss

Born: March 22, 1982. **Ht.:** 6-4. **Wt.:** 180. **Bats:** R. **Throws:** R. **School:** Nova HS, Ft. Lauderdale, Fla. **Career Transactions:** Selected by White Sox in third round of 2000 draft; signed June 19, 2000 . . . Traded by White Sox with C Miguel Olivo and OF Jeremy Reed to Mariners for RHP Freddy Garcia, C Ben Davis and cash, June 27, 2004. **Signed by:** Jose Ortega (White Sox).

The third player in the Freddy Garcia trade with the White Sox, Morse drilled 17 homers in 95 games last year after hitting 18 in his first four seasons combined. That breakthrough would be cause for more excitement if Morse had much of a chance to stay at shortstop and hadn't been suspended twice in 2004. Chicago suspended him shortly before the trade and Seattle suspended him again for the final three weeks of the season, reportedly for the use of over-the-counter banned substances. Morse has plenty of power, though his aggressiveness and lack of strike-zone discipline make it unlikely he'll ever hit for much of an average. He also has a strong arm and his hands are OK, but his lack of first-step quickness and range will limit his defensive options at the major league level. Third base and first base might be his only possibilities, and newcomers Adrian Beltre and Richie Sexson are imposing road-blocks there. Morse likely will get more exposure at new positions in Triple-A this season.

Year	Club (League)	Class	AVG	G	AB	R	H	2B	3B	HR	RBI	BB	SO	SB	OBP	SLG
2000	White Sox (AZL)	R	.256	45	180	32	46	6	1	2	24	15	29	5	.308	.333
2001	Bristol (Appy)	R	.227	57	181	23	41	7	3	4	27	17	57	6	.324	.365
2002	Kannapolis (SAL)	A	.257	113	417	43	107	30	4	2	56	25	73	7	.310	.362
2003	Winston-Sal (Car)	A	.245	122	432	45	106	30	2	10	55	25	91	4	.296	.394
2004	Birmingham (SL)	AA	.287	54	209	30	60	9	5	11	38	15	46	0	.336	.536
	San Antonio (TL)	AA	.274	41	157	18	43	10	1	6	33	9	27	0	.326	.465
MINOR LEAGUE TOTALS			.256	432	1576	191	403	92	16	35	233	106	323	22	.313	.401

20 Rich Dorman, rhp

Born: Sept. 30, 1978. **Ht.:** 6-2. **Wt.:** 210. **Bats:** R. **Throws:** R. **School:** Western Baptist (Ore.) College. **Career Transactions:** Selected by Devil Rays in 13th round of 2000 draft; signed June 9, 2000 . . . Released by Devil Rays, Jan 8, 2002 . . . Signed by Mariners, Feb 8, 2002. **Signed by:** Paul Kirsch (Devil Rays).

The Devil Rays made Dorman the first player ever drafted from Western Baptist College, only to release him in January 2002. A former catcher who didn't become a full-time pitch-er until 2000, he made decent progress in his first two years in the Seattle system before shooting forward last season. After pitching primarily in relief in 2003, he moved to the rotation in 2004 and quickly earned a promotion to Double-A, where he was San Antonio's pitcher of the year. If he hadn't fallen 3⅓ innings shy of qualifying, he would have ranked second in the Texas League in strikeouts per nine innings (11.3) and opponent batting aver-age (.231). The biggest reasons for Dorman's advancement last year were that his plus curve-ball and his mechanics became more consistent. He located his 87-93 mph fastball better as well. He still pitches up in the strike zone too often, which could be his undoing at higher levels. He's making progress with his slider and changeup, and he could be a No. 3 or 4 starter if they continue to develop. If not, he could be an effective reliever relying on his fastball and curve. For now, he'll remain in the rotation and move up to Triple-A.

Year	Club (League)	Class	W	L	ERA	G	GS	CG	SV	IP	H	R	ER	HR	BB	SO	AVG
2000	Hudson Valley (NY-P)	A	2	6	3.47	14	14	0	0	70	71	47	27	0	40	46	.253
2001	Charleston, SC (SAL)	A	1	5	6.51	17	9	0	0	57	61	47	41	3	41	41	.282
	Hudson Valley (NY-P)	A	3	0	2.58	17	3	0	0	45	37	14	13	2	20	34	.226
2002	Everett (NWL)	A	5	6	4.30	15	15	0	0	75	85	53	36	2	33	68	.281
2003	Wisconsin (Mid)	A	1	2	2.80	25	1	0	4	45	36	19	14	1	24	62	.222
	Inland Empire (Cal)	A	5	0	2.65	13	5	0	1	37	29	11	11	1	21	40	.218
2004	San Antonio (TL)	AA	8	4	3.48	20	20	1	0	109	93	44	42	8	64	137	.231
	Inland Empire (Cal)	A	3	2	2.68	7	7	0	0	37	35	13	11	0	12	36	.248
MINOR LEAGUE TOTALS			28	25	3.692	128	74	1	5	475	447	248	195	17	255	464	.248

21 Rene Rivera, c

Born: July 31, 1983. **Ht.:** 5-10. **Wt.:** 190. **Bats:** R. **Throws:** R. **School:** Papa Juan XXIII HS, Bayamon, P.R. **Career Transactions:** Selected by Mariners in second round of 2001 draft; signed June 14, 2001. **Signed by:** Pedro Grifol.

Rivera received a couple of surprise promotions from high Class A at the end of last sea-son. When the Mariners traded Triple-A catcher Pat Borders to the Twins in late August, they replaced Borders with Rivera for the final week of the Pacific Coast League season. Rivera returned to Inland Empire for the California League playoffs, then got summoned to Seattle in September. Rivera already could survive in the big leagues with his defensive prowess. Managers rated him the best defensive catcher in the Cal League, which he led by throwing out 41 percent of basestealers. Though he has a chunky body, he moves well behind the plate and has receiving skills to match his strong, accurate arm. How much Rivera will hit remains in question. His swing is long, he's too aggressive and he's still learning to deal with breaking balls and understand the strike zone. He's still young, though, so if he can make some adjustments he could hit .260 with gap power. He already shows raw power to all fields but hasn't tapped into it yet. He's a well below-average runner, not a shock for a catch-er. After his roller-coaster ride to finish 2004, Rivera will catch in Double-A this year.

Year	Club (League)	Class	AVG	G	AB	R	H	2B	3B	HR	RBI	BB	SO	SB	OBP	SLG
2001	Everett (NWL)	A	.089	15	45	3	4	1	0	2	3	1	19	0	.106	.244
	Mariners (AZL)	R	.338	21	71	13	24	4	0	2	12	2	11	0	.360	.479
2002	Everett (NWL)	A	.242	62	227	29	55	18	1	1	26	16	38	5	.314	.344
2003	Wisconsin (Mid)	A	.275	116	407	39	112	19	0	9	54	38	81	2	.344	.388
2004	Inland Empire (Cal)	A	.235	107	379	41	89	22	1	6	53	28	70	0	.300	.346
	Tacoma (PCL)	AAA	.400	4	15	3	6	1	0	1	1	0	3	0	.400	.667
	Seattle (AL)	MAJ	.000	2	3	0	0	0	0	0	0	0	1	0	.000	.000
MAJOR LEAGUE TOTALS			.000	2	3	0	0	0	0	0	0	0	1	0	.000	.000
MINOR LEAGUE TOTALS			.253	325	1144	128	290	65	2	21	149	85	222	7	.316	.369

22 Bobby Livingston, lhp

Born: Sept. 3, 1982. **Ht.:** 6-3. **Wt.:** 190. **Bats:** L. **Throws:** L. **School:** Trinity Christian HS, Lubbock, Texas. **Career Transactions:** Selected by Mariners in fourth round of 2001 draft; signed Aug. 18, 2001. **Signed by:** Kyle Van Hook.

Livingston is an enigma, but a successful one at that. He had a low-90s fastball as a high school senior in 2001, but his velocity dropped to 86-87 mph before the draft and never has come back. Though he now pitches at 86-87 mph and rarely cracks 90 mph, Livingston nevertheless has been successful. He has been his team's pitcher of the year the last two years, setting a Wisconsin record with 15 victories in 2003 and leading the California League in innings pitched in 2004. He has the best command and might be the most competitive pitcher in the farm system, allowing him to win with marginal stuff. Livingston has good sink on his fastball, throws his curveball and changeup for strikes and has developed a cutter to use against righthanders. His willingness to use any pitch in any count helps him keep batters off balance. Livingston doesn't have much margin for error and whether he has enough stuff to succeed at upper levels remains to be seen, but he's an organization favorite and the Mariners want to find out. His next challenge will come in Double-A.

Year	Club (League)	Class	W	L	ERA	G	GS	CG	SV	IP	H	R	ER	HR	BB	SO	AVG
2002	Everett (NWL)	A	6	5	3.02	15	14	0	0	80	80	33	27	2	14	76	.255
2003	Wisconsin (Mid)	A	15	7	2.73	26	26	1	0	178	176	72	54	10	28	105	.259
2004	Inland Empire (Cal)	A	12	6	3.57	28	27	1	0	187	187	90	74	15	30	141	.261
MINOR LEAGUE TOTALS			33	18	3.13	69	67	2	0	445	443	195	155	27	72	322	.259

23 Yung-Chi Chen, 2b/3b

Born: July 13, 1983. **Ht.:** 5-11. **Wt.:** 172. **Bats:** R. **Throws:** R. **Career Transactions:** Signed out of Taiwan by Mariners, July 13, 1983. **Signed by:** Jamey Storvick.

Chen's profiles best at second base, but he saw more time at third base last year, both with Everett and as the youngest player on the Taiwanese Olympic team. He started every game at the hot corner for fifth-place Taiwan at the Athens Games, and split time between second and third for Everett in deference to Asdrubal Cabrera and Oswaldo Navarro, who shuttled between shortstop and second. Chen won't have enough power to play third base in the majors, but he shows some offensive promise. He has strong wrists and a knack for centering the ball on the bat, and he can drill line drives to both gaps. He could use some more patience at the plate, however. Chen owns just average speed, but he has good instincts on the bases and had 25 steals in 28 attempts during his pro debut. He's a dependable defender who makes the routine play well, though he looked overmatched at shortstop, where he made four errors in 11 chances. Chen likely faces another year moving between second and third base, as he'll likely be on the same team with shortstop prospects Matt Tuiasosopo and Oswaldo Navarro in low Class A.

Year	Club (League)	Class	AVG	G	AB	R	H	2B	3B	HR	RBI	BB	SO	SB	OBP	SLG
2004	Everett (NWL)	A	.300	49	200	37	60	13	1	3	34	16	36	25	.353	.420
MINOR LEAGUE TOTALS			.300	49	200	37	60	13	1	3	34	16	36	25	.353	.420

24 Oswaldo Navarro, 2b/ss

Born: Oct. 2, 1984. **Ht.:** 6-0. **Wt.:** 155. **Bats:** B. **Throws:** R. **Career Transactions:** Signed out of Venezuela by Mariners, Aug. 12, 2001. **Signed by:** Emilio Carrasquel.

Of all the Mariners' middle-infield prospects, Navarro is the best defender. He played more second base than shortstop last year because he was teammates with Adam Jones at Wisconsin and Asdrubal Cabrera at Everett. Seattle likes to enhance the versatility of its infielders by using them at a variety of positions—Navarro also saw brief action at first and third base—but he definitely can play shortstop. He has the surest hands in the system, can make all the throws and covers a solid amount of ground. Though he led the Northwest League in doubles after a midseason demotion from low Class A, Navarro will have to get much stronger to succeed at the plate. He'll also need to tighten his strike zone and focus more on getting on base. He's an above-average runner, but not as quick as his stolen-base totals (21 in 26 attempts last year) might indicate. Navarro likely will have to share shortstop again in 2005, as both he and Matt Tuiasosopo are headed to low Class A.

Year	Club (League)	Class	AVG	G	AB	R	H	2B	3B	HR	RBI	BB	SO	SB	OBP	SLG
2002	Aguirre (VSL)	R	.261	37	119	13	31	4	1	0	9	12	21	3	.338	.311
2003	Everett (NWL)	A	.258	61	233	42	60	12	1	0	23	10	39	16	.302	.318
2004	Wisconsin (Mid)	A	.211	40	109	13	23	4	0	0	7	11	19	4	.295	.248
	Everett (NWL)	A	.273	68	267	38	73	27	1	1	30	21	59	17	.331	.393
MINOR LEAGUE TOTALS			.257	206	728	106	187	47	3	1	69	42	138	40	.318	.334

25 Chai-An Huang, rhp

Born: Nov. 11, 1985. **Ht.:** 6-2. **Wt.:** 204. **Bats:** R. **Throws:** R. **Career Transactions:** Signed out of Taiwan by Mariners, March 30, 2004. **Signed by:** Jamey Storvick.

The Mariners were excited to sign Huang to a six-figure bonus last April, even if he wasn't able to make his U.S. debut in 2004. He graduated in high school in June, but Seattle couldn't immediately get him a visa because the quota for foreign players for 2004 had been exceeded several weeks earlier. He failed to make the Taiwanese Olympic team, though he did begin college in order to get a deferment from mandatory military service. Huang has a strong frame and a quick, smooth arm action, allowing him to deliver low-90s fastballs and top out at 94 mph. He backs up his heater with a hard three-quarters breaking ball. He also throws a forkball and changeup, though those pitches are less polished. Huang should be able to come to the States in 2005, though the Mariners are cautious about where he'll start his career. As a teenager who'll have to adapt to an entirely new culture, it's likely he'll begin the season in extended spring training.

Year	Club (League)	Class	W	L	ERA	G	GS	CG	SV	IP	H	R	ER	HR	BB	SO	AVG
2004	Did not play																

26 Matt Thornton, lhp

Born: Sept. 15, 1976. **Ht.:** 6-6. **Wt.:** 220. **Bats:** L. **Throws:** L. **School:** Grand Valley State (Mich.) College. **Career Transactions:** Selected by Mariners in first round (22nd overall) of 1998 draft; signed July 3, 1998. **Signed by:** Ken Madeja.

Thornton completed an arduous climb when he shut out the Padres for four innings in his big league debut. The biggest surprise in 1998's first round—Thornton had more success as a basketball player in college—he didn't win a game in college or as a pro until 2000. He had a breakout year in 2001, when he was the California League pitcher of the year and strikeout leader, only to succumb to Tommy John surgery in 2002. Thornton has regained the 94-96 mph fastball he had before his elbow injury, but his slider hasn't been as sharp. He never has trusted his changeup or had much command, so he'll probably settle in as a reliever in the majors. To make the Mariners this spring, he'll need to throw more strikes and make progress with his slider. He did well on both counts in Venezuela over the winter.

Year	Club (League)	Class	W	L	ERA	G	GS	CG	SV	IP	H	R	ER	HR	BB	SO	AVG
1998	Everett (NWL)	A	0	0	7.00	2	0	0	0	1	1	4	4	0	3	0	.200
1999	Wisconsin (Mid)	A	0	0	4.91	25	1	0	1	29	39	19	16	1	25	34	.320
2000	Wisconsin (Mid)	A	6	9	4.01	26	17	0	0	103	94	59	46	2	72	88	.245
2001	Inland Empire (Cal)	A	14	7	2.52	27	27	0	0	157	126	56	44	9	60	192	.220
2002	San Antonio (TL)	AA	1	5	3.63	12	12	0	0	62	52	31	25	3	29	44	.237
2003	Inland Empire (Cal)	A	0	0	4.00	2	2	0	0	9	9	4	4	2	4	14	.265
	San Antonio (TL)	AA	3	0	.36	4	4	0	0	25	8	3	1	0	9	18	.104
	Tacoma (PCL)	AAA	0	2	8.00	2	2	0	0	9	14	11	8	2	3	5	.359
2004	Seattle (AL)	MAJ	1	2	4.13	19	1	0	0	33	30	15	15	2	25	30	.250
	Tacoma (PCL)	AAA	7	5	5.42	16	15	1	0	83	86	58	50	4	63	74	.273
MAJOR LEAGUE TOTALS			1	2	4.13	19	1	0	0	33	30	15	15	2	25	30	.250
MINOR LEAGUE TOTALS			31	28	3.72	116	80	1	1	479	429	245	198	23	268	469	.243

27 Rob Johnson, c

Born: July 22, 1983. **Ht.:** 6-1. **Wt.:** 200. **Bats:** R. **Throws:** R. **School:** University of Houston. **Career Transactions:** Selected by Mariners in fourth round of 2004 draft; signed June 23, 2004. **Signed by:** Kyle Van Hook.

After leading Saddleback to a second-place finish in the 2003 California Community College playoffs, Johnson had options. The Phillies drafted him in the 18th round and offered him $275,000 to sign, and several top college programs wanted him as well. Johnson decided to attend Houston, where he disappointed scouts when he hit just seven homers. Thin on catchers, the Mariners focused on Johnson's hitting ability and catch-and-throw skills and signed him for $260,000. Because he strained his elbow, Johnson wasn't able to showcase his defense until instructional league. More athletic than most catchers, he moves well behind the plate, where his main need is to improve his throwing accuracy. Johnson will show plus power in batting practice, though he uses more of a line-drive, gap approach during games. Roving hitting instructor Glenn Adams helped him smooth out his swing, which was long and had a slow trigger. Johnson will begin 2005 in low Class A.

Year	Club (League)	Class	AVG	G	AB	R	H	2B	3B	HR	RBI	BB	SO	SB	OBP	SLG
2004	Everett (NWL)	A	.234	20	77	17	18	3	1	1	7	4	10	6	.286	.338
	Mariners (AZL)	R	.222	8	27	4	6	1	0	0	1	3	7	1	.323	.259
MINOR LEAGUE TOTALS			.231	28	104	21	24	4	1	1	8	7	17	7	.296	.317

28 Shawn Nottingham, lhp

Born: Jan. 22, 1985. **Ht.:** 6-1. **Wt.:** 190. **Bats:** L. **Throws:** L. **School:** Jackson HS, Canton, Ohio. **Career Transactions:** Selected by Mariners in 13th round of 2003 draft; signed June 23, 2003. **Signed by:** Ken Madeja.

Part of a Kent State 2003 recruiting class that also included Ryan Feierabend, Nottingham ranked right with him as a prospect as a high school senior. But when Nottingham was dismissed from his team following his arrest for underage drinking and didn't pitch at all that spring, his draft stock plummeted. Seattle took Feierabend in the third round, Nottingham in the 13th. The biggest difference between Nottingham and the other finesse lefties on this list is that he's shorter and less projectable. He does have similar stuff, as his best pitch is his changeup and he can throw both a below-average fastball (85-89 mph) and a curveball for strikes. The Mariners showed what they thought of Nottingham's poise when they promoted him at age 19 from extended spring training to fill a bullpen emergency in Triple-A last June. He went from there to the Northwest League, which he led in wins, innings and strikeouts. He's ready for low Class A and with his moxie, he could push for a midseason promotion.

Year	Club (League)	Class	W	L	ERA	G	GS	CG	SV	IP	H	R	ER	HR	BB	SO	AVG
2003	Mariners (AZL)	R	1	0	3.72	12	0	0	0	19	17	10	8	2	8	17	.227
2004	Everett (NWL)	A	9	3	3.15	15	14	0	0	89	74	34	31	8	29	87	.223
	Tacoma (PCL)	AAA	0	0	13.50	3	0	0	0	2	4	3	3	0	3	2	.444
MINOR LEAGUE TOTALS			10	3	3.44	30	14	0	0	110	95	47	42	10	40	106	.228

29 Mark Lowe, rhp

Born: June 7, 1983. **Ht.:** 6-4. **Wt.:** 180. **Bats:** R. **Throws:** R. **School:** University of Texas-Arlington. **Career Transactions:** Selected by Mariners in fifth round of 2004 draft; signed June 15, 2004. **Signed by:** Mark Lummus.

Lowe barely pitched in his first two years at Texas-Arlington, redshirting in 2003 to focus on his mechanics. He unveiled a low-90s sinker in the Northwoods League that summer, and that's the pitch that got him drafted in the fifth round and earned him a $170,000 bonus last June. Lowe can hit the mid-90s on occasion, but he's still primarily a work in progress. He never filled a more challenging role than setup man as an amateur, and had more success as a closer than as a starter in his pro debut. That's because he's still rounding out his repertoire. His hard slider is still inconsistent and takes a back seat to his changeup, which also needs refinement. He's also working on improving the location of his pitches because he doesn't always throw quality strikes. Lowe may project better as a reliever, but he does have the arm and stamina to handle starting. The Mariners will keep him in the rotation this year in low Class A.

Year	Club (League)	Class	W	L	ERA	G	GS	CG	SV	IP	H	R	ER	HR	BB	SO	AVG
2004	Everett (NWL)	A	1	2	4.93	18	3	0	7	38	42	22	21	4	14	38	.280
MINOR LEAGUE TOTALS			1	2	4.93	18	3	0	7	38	42	22	21	4	14	38	.280

30 Aaron Jensen, rhp

Born: June 11, 1984. **Ht.:** 6-2. **Wt.:** 180. **Bats:** R. **Throws:** R. **School:** Springville (Utah) HS. **Career Transactions:** Selected by Mariners in 19th round of 2003 draft; signed Aug. 25, 2003. **Signed by:** Steve Peck.

Utah's top prospect for the 2003 draft, Jensen led Springville High to the state 4-A title and figured to go in the second to fourth round on talent alone. But his commitment to Brigham Young scared off clubs until the Mariners took him in the 19th round, and they were able to sign him late in the summer for third-round money. He didn't make his pro debut until 2004, when health issues unrelated to baseball partially sapped his stuff. He had shown a 90-94 mph fastball and a hard 12-6 curveball, but neither pitch was as crisp last summer. To Jensen's credit, he didn't miss a start and even when he got tired at the end of the summer, he never used his health as an excuse. He's fully recovered now and should be at full strength again in 2005. He has an athletic frame and throws with little effort. He's still young and raw, so he still has a ways to go with his changeup, command and consistency. How Jensen looks in spring training will determine whether he begins the year in low Class A or extended spring.

Year	Club (League)	Class	W	L	ERA	G	GS	CG	SV	IP	H	R	ER	HR	BB	SO	AVG
2004	Everett (NWL)	A	7	4	5.29	16	16	0	0	80	90	53	47	12	36	56	.280
MINOR LEAGUE TOTALS			7	4	5.29	16	16	0	0	80	90	53	47	12	36	56	.280

TAMPA BAY
DEVIL RAYS

BY **BILL BALLEW**

History was made in Tampa Bay in 2004, and it involved something other than adding to the franchise's wretched past. The Devil Rays became the first team since the 1899 Louisville Colonels to reach the .500 level after being 18 or more games under the break-even mark, going from 10-28 on May 19 to 36-35 on June 27.

 Tampa Bay also ran off a franchise-best 12-game winning streak, reached the 70-win mark and avoided last place in the American League East for the first time, thanks in part to the supply of talent developed in the farm system.

Top prospect **B.J. Upton** made the jump to the majors in August. While his defense and his ability to remain at shortstop remain uncertain, his talent is obvious. Upton became the first teenager to homer in the majors since July 1998. Infielder Jorge Cantu and outfielder Joey Gathright also got their first taste of the majors and should be lineup mainstays along with Upton and young veterans Rocco Baldelli, Carl Crawford and Aubrey Huff.

Tampa Bay further bolstered its youth movement when it robbed the Mets of left-hander Scott Kazmir in a July trade for Victor Zambrano, whose command and pending price tag weren't to the Rays' liking. Kazmir shut out the Mariners for five innings in his big league debut and later beat the eventual champion Red Sox with six scoreless innings and nine strikeouts.

More help is on the way. The Devil Rays had another solid draft, signing first-rounder Jeff Niemann in January. It shouldn't be long before he teams with Kazmir to give Tampa Bay two formidable starters at the front of the rotation. Shortstop Reid Brignac (second round) is yet another promising young position player, while righthanders Wade Davis (third), Matt Walker (10th) and Andy Sonnanstine (13th) and lefty Jacob McGee (fifth) add some pitching depth.

The strength of the organization remains its outfielders, both at the major and minor league levels. Delmon Young, the No. 1 over-all pick in the 2003 draft, had an impressive pro debut and should be on the same fast track to Tampa Bay that Baldelli, Crawford and Upton rode. The Rays have so many outfield options that they've had to move some of their prospects to other positions, most notably Wes Bankston from right field to first base. The logjam makes the continuing disappointment of Josh Hamilton easier to take. The top pick in the 1999 draft, Hamilton was suspended for all of 2004 after violating Major League Baseball's drug policy, then had the suspension extended for repeated violations.

The Devil Rays continued to make baby steps in 2004. Larger leaps are a distinct possibility if the ongoing influx of young players can live up to high expectations. Tampa Bay still is a long ways from doing battle with the likes of the Red Sox and Yankees, whose nine-figure payrolls dwarf the Rays', but at long last there's reason for optimism.

TOP 30 PROSPECTS

1. Delmon Young, of	16. Chris Seddon, lhp
2. Scott Kazmir, lhp	17. Jonny Gomes, of
3. Jeff Niemann, rhp	18. Angel Garcia, rhp
4. Joey Gathright, of	19. Gabby Martinez, 1b/3b
5. Jason Hammel, rhp	20. Matt Diaz, of
6. Reid Brignac, ss	21. Jonathan Barratt, lhp
7. James Houser, lhp	22. Matt Walker, rhp
8. Elijah Dukes, of	23. Jacob McGee, lhp
9. Chad Orvella, rhp	24. Fernando Cortez, 2b
10. Seth McClung, rhp	25. Shawn Riggans, c
11. Wes Bankston, 1b/of	26. Franklin Nunez, rhp
12. Elliot Johnson, 2b	27. Jose de la Cruz, rhp
13. Jason Pridie, of	28. Jino Gonzalez, lhp
14. Wade Davis, rhp	29. Jose Diaz, rhp
15. Travis Schlichting, 3b	30. John Jaso, c/1b

ORGANIZATION OVERVIEW

General manager: Chuck LaMar. **Farm and scouting director:** Cam Bonifay.

2004 PERFORMANCE

Class	Team	League	W	L	Pct.	Finish*	Manager
Majors	Tampa Bay	American	70	91	.435	11th (14)	Lou Piniella
Triple-A	Durham Bulls	International	77	67	.535	4th (14)	Bill Evers
Double-A	Montgomery Biscuits	Southern	57	83	.407	10th (10)	Charlie Montoyo
High A	#Bakersfield Blaze	California	59	81	.421	8th (10)	Mako Oliveras
Low A	@Charleston RiverDogs	South Atlantic	76	63	.547	4th (16)	Steve Livesey
Short-season	Hudson Valley Renegades	New York-Penn	39	33	.542	6th (14)	Dave Howard
Rookie	Princeton Devil Rays	Appalachian	23	44	.343	10th (10)	Jamie Nelson
OVERALL 2004 MINOR LEAGUE RECORD			331	371	.472	21st (30)	

*Finish in overall standings (No. of teams in league)
#Affiliate will be in Visalia (California) in 2005. @Affiliate will be in Southwest Michigan (Midwest) in 2005.

ORGANIZATION LEADERS

BATTING   *Minimum 250 At-Bats
*AVG   Matt Diaz, Durham .... .332
R   Jason Pridie, Charleston 103
H   Matt Diaz, Durham 167
TB   Matt Diaz, Durham 287
2B   Matt Diaz, Durham 47
3B   Jason Pridie, Charleston 11
HR   Midre Cummings, Durham 27
RBI   Delmon Young, Charleston 116
BB   Midre Cummings, Durham 86
SO   Jared Sandberg, Durham 138
SB   Joey Gathright, Durham/Montgomery 43
      Elliot Johnson, Charleston 43
*OBP   B.J. Upton, Durham/Montgomery .... .410
*SLG   Jorge Cantu, Durham .... .576

PITCHING   #Minimum 75 Innings
W   Chris Seddon, Montgomery/Bakersfield 14
L   Mark Comolli, Bakersfield 15
#ERA   Jason Hammel, Bakersfield/Charleston 2.66
G   Joe Yarbrough, Bakersfield 60
CG   Jim Magrane, Durham/Montgomery 3
SV   Scott Vandermeer, Charleston 22
IP   Jason Hammel, Bakersfield/Charleston 166
BB   Mark Comolli, Bakersfield 131
SO   Jason Hammel, Bakersfield/Charleston 153

BEST TOOLS

Best Hitter for Average .... Delmon Young
Best Power Hitter .... Delmon Young
Best Strike-Zone Discipline .... Elliot Johnson
Fastest Baserunner .... Joey Gathright
Best Athlete .... Elijah Dukes
Best Fastball .... Jeff Niemann
Best Curveball .... Jason Hammel
Best Slider .... Scott Kazmir
Best Changeup .... Chad Orvella
Best Control .... Chad Orvella
Best Defensive Catcher .... Shawn Riggans
Best Defensive Infielder .... Fernando Cortez
Best Infield Arm .... Travis Schlichting
Best Defensive Outfielder .... Jason Pridie
Best Outfield Arm .... Delmon Young

PROJECTED 2008 LINEUP

Catcher.. Toby Hall
First Base .... Aubrey Huff
Second Base .... Jorge Cantu
Third Base .... Reid Brignac
Shortstop .... B.J. Upton
Left Field .... Carl Crawford

Center Field .... Joey Gathright
Right Field .... Rocco Baldelli
Designated Hitter....................................... Delmon Young
No. 1 Starter .... Scott Kazmir
No. 2 Starter... Jeff Niemann
No. 3 Starter... Jason Hammel
No. 4 Starter .... Dewon Brazelton
No. 5 Starter .... Doug Waechter
Closer .... Chad Orvella

LAST YEAR'S TOP 20 PROSPECTS

1. B.J. Upton, ss
2. Delmon Young, of
3. Doug Waechter, rhp
4. James Houser, lhp
5. Joey Gathright, of
6. Chad Gaudin, rhp
7. Wes Bankston, of
8. Seth McClung, rhp
9. Antonio Perez, 2b
10. Jonny Gomes, of
11. Pete LaForest, c
12. Elijah Dukes, of
13. Jason Pridie, of
14. Jon Switzer, lhp
15. Scott Autrey, rhp
16. Josh Hamilton, of
17. Chris Seddon, lhp
18. Jon Barratt, lhp
19. Shawn Riggans, c
20. Travis Schlichting, 3b

TOP PROSPECTS OF THE DECADE

Year	Player, Pos.	Current Team
1997	Matt White, rhp	Devil Rays
1998	Matt White, rhp	Devil Rays
1999	Matt White, rhp	Devil Rays
2000	Josh Hamilton, of	Devil Rays
2001	Josh Hamilton, of	Devil Rays
2002	Josh Hamilton, of	Devil Rays
2003	Rocco Baldelli, of	Devil Rays
2004	B.J. Upton, ss	Devil Rays

TOP DRAFT PICKS OF THE DECADE

Year	Player, Pos.	Current Team
1996	Paul Wilder, of	Out of baseball
1997	Jason Standridge, rhp	Devil Rays
1998	Josh Pressley, 1b (4)	Mets
1999	Josh Hamilton, of	Devil Rays
2000	Rocco Baldelli, of	Devil Rays
2001	Dewon Brazelton, rhp	Devil Rays
2002	B.J. Upton, ss	Devil Rays
2003	Delmon Young, of	Devil Rays
2004	Jeff Niemann, rhp	Devil Rays

ALL-TIME LARGEST BONUSES

Matt White, 1996 .... $10,200,000
Rolando Arrojo, 1997 .... $7,000,000
B.J. Upton, 2002 .... $4,600,000
Dewon Brazelton, 2001 .... $4,200,000
Josh Hamilton, 1999 .... $3,960,000

MINOR LEAGUE DEPTH CHART

Tampa Bay DEVIL RAYS

Impact Potential: A
The Devil Rays aim high, and they draft high. The combination gives them potential future stars such as Delmon Young, Reid Brignac and big league rookie B.J. Upton; players with 80 tools such as Joey Gathright; and a future ace in Jeff Niemann. They also traded for the minors' top lefthander, Scott Kazmir. They almost all have to come through for the Rays to break through in the division, though.

Depth: C
The Rays have plenty of outfielders who could help soon, which helps mitigate Rocco Baldelli's injury, and they have options behind the plate. Niemann and Kazmir, though, head a thin group of pitchers, and the Rays must get better at producing their own power arms to go with their impact bats.

*Depth charts prepared by **John Manuel** and **Allan Simpson**. Numbers in parentheses indicate prospect rankings.*

LF
Elijah Dukes (8)
Jonny Gomes (17)
Matt Diaz (20)
Shaun Cumberland
Brian Martin

CF
Joey Gathright (4)
Jason Pridie (13)
Luis Mateo

RF
Delmon Young (1)
Matt Rico
Josh Hamilton

3B
Travis Schlichting (15)
Gabriel Martinez (19)

SS
Reid Brignac (6)

2B
Elliot Johnson (12)
Fernando Cortez (24)
Luis DePaula

1B
Wes Bankston (11)

SOURCE of TALENT

Homegrown		Acquired	
College	3	Trades	2
Junior college	3	Rule 5 draft	1
Draft-and-follow	2	Independent leagues	0
High School	15	Free agents/waivers	1
Nondrafted free agent	1		
Foreign	2		

C
Shawn Riggans (25)
Pete LaForest (30)
John Jaso
Colt Simmons
Matt Spring
Josh Arhart

LHP

Starters	Relievers
Scott Kazmir (2)	Sam Walton
James Houser (7)	Bobby Seay
Chris Seddon (16)	Brian Henderson
Jonathan Barratt (21)	Mike Prochaska
Jacob McGee (23)	Jason Cromer
Jino Gonzalez (28)	
Jon Switzer	

RHP

Starters	Relievers
Jeff Niemann (3)	Chad Orvella (9)
Jason Hammel (5)	Franklin Nunez (26)
Seth McClung (10)	Jose de la Cruz (27)
Wade Davis (14)	Jose Diaz (29)
Angel Garcia (18)	Carlos Hines
Matt Walker (22)	Juan Salas
Brian Stokes	Josh Parker
John Webb	Tim Corcoran
Tony Peguero	Austin Coose
Andy Sonnanstine	
Nick DeBarr	
Jamie Shields	
Scott Autrey	
Brain Bulger	
Chris Flinn	
Jarrod Matthews	

DRAFT ANALYSIS

2004

Best Pro Debut: SS Reid Brignac (2) hit .361-1-25 in the Rookie-level Appalachian League, then went 7-for-14 with five RBIs in a three-game cameo in low Class A. RHP Andrew Sonnanstine (13) went 5-1, 0.78 with a 66-10 K-BB ratio in 58 innings between the short-season New York-Penn League and low Class A. He has a sharp slider, an average fastball and an affinity for altering his arm angle.

Best Athlete: OF Fernando Perez' (7) speed made him the highest-drafted player ever from Columbia University. Brignac's all-around tools are impressive.

Best Pure Hitter: Brignac drilled 17 hits in his first seven pro games and kept hitting all summer. 1B Rhyne Hughes (8) batted .401 at Pearl River (Miss.) CC in the spring.

Best Raw Power: OF Ryan Royster (5) hit a 470-foot blast as an Oregon high schooler last spring.

Fastest Runner: Perez is a sub-4.0 runner to first base from the right side. He stole 24 bases in 28 attempts in the NY-P.

Best Defensive Player: Steady, instinctive 2B/SS Josh Asanovich (11). Tampa Bay also drafted him in the 21st round out of high school in 2001.

Best Fastball: RHP Jeff Niemann (1) not only throws 92-97 mph, but at 6-foot-9 he also delivers his heat on a nasty downward plane. RHP Wade Davis (3) touched 94 during the summer, while RHP Matt Walker (10) did so during the spring.

Best Breaking Ball: Niemann's slider reaches 87 mph and can be flat-out unhittable. Before Niemann signed, LHP Jacob McGee's (5) slider is the best.

Most Intriguing Background: SS Cale

Davis

Iorg's (16) father Garth and uncle Dane are ex-big leaguers. His brother Eli was the Cubs' 14th-round pick in June, and another brother, Issac, plays in the Braves system. The Devil Rays signed the sons of two Triple-A managers: RHP Billy Evers Jr. (35), whose dad skippers Durham in their own system; and RHP Chris Kelly (46), whose father Pat pilots Richmond for the Braves. Offensive-minded C Matt Spring (4) was MVP of the Junior College World Series as Dixie State (Utah) won the championship.

Closest To The Majors: Niemann likely will begin his pro career in high Class A.

Best Late-Round Pick: Better known as a potential NCAA Division I quarterback last spring, Walker looked like a possible supplemental first-rounder before tiring late in the spring. He signed for $600,000.

The One Who Got Away: Iorg, who is attending Alabama, can play in the middle infield and has enough power in case he moves to third base. He's more polished than Santa Clara-bound SS Ryan Conan, who's more physical. LHP Matt Goyen (27) was the Cape Cod League pitcher of the year and strikeout leader, but he returned to Georgia College & State.

Assessment: Had he not been slowed by arthroscopic elbow surgery and a nagging groin injury, Niemann could have been the No. 1 overall pick in the draft. Getting Brignac in the second round also could be a coup.

2003 OF Delmon Young (1) has justified his No. 1 overall selection, and unsigned LHP Andrew Miller (3) could achieve the same status in 2006. The Devil Rays also expect good things from LHP James Houser (2) and RHP Chad Orvella (13). *GRADE:* A

2002 SS B.J. Upton (2) looks like a steal—as the No. 2 overall pick. RHP Jason Hammel (10), OF Elijah Dukes (3), 1B/OF Wes Bankston (4) and OF Jason Pridie (2) can be part of the franchise's future. *GRADE:* A

2001 RHP Dewon Brazelton (1) is the lone player among the first five picks who doesn't look like a star. The Rays did score in the late rounds with OFs Joey Gathright (32) and Jonny Gomes (18) and RHP Chad Gaudin (34). Unsigned RHP Thomas Diamond (38) blossomed into a 2004 first-rounder. *GRADE:* C+

2000 As it turns out, there was one quality first-rounder among the 30 picks. Tampa Bay got him at No. 6 with OF Rocco Baldelli, then didn't choose again until the fifth round. *GRADE:* B+

Draft analysis prepared by Jim Callis. Numbers in parentheses indicate draft rounds.

CARL KLINE

Delmon
YOUNG

Born: Sept. 14, 1985.
Ht.: 6-3. **Wt.:** 205.
Bats: R. **Throws:** R.
School: Camarillo (Calif.) HS.
Career Transactions: Selected by Devil Rays in first round (first overall) of 2003 draft; signed Sept. 8, 2003.
Signed by: Rich Aude.

Tampa Bay narrowed its options for the No. 1 overall pick in 2003 to two players, Young and second baseman Rickie Weeks. Though their greatest strength was their outfield depth, the Devil Rays couldn't resist taking Young. He may not have reached the majors during his first pro season after predicting he would shortly after signing a big league deal with a $5.8 million guarantee, but he was anything but a disappointment. The right fielder overcame a modest start to display outstanding maturity and consistency for a teenager making his pro debut. Young fanned 19 times in 84 at-bats during April before warming with the weather. He led the low Class A South Atlantic League in hits and RBIs, earning recognition as the league's top prospect as well as a spot in the Futures Game. His older brother Dmitri was the fourth overall pick in 1991, making them the highest-drafted siblings in history. They might be displaced in 2005, however, as B.J. Upton's younger brother Justin could go as high as No. 1 three years after the Devil Rays took B.J. with the No. 2 choice.

An intimidating presence from the right side of the plate who elicits Albert Belle comparisons, Young has a powerful, consistent stroke. He's selective at the plate and has outstanding baseball instincts, thanks in part to his close relationship with Dmitri. His quick bat and plus power enable him to hit the ball out of any part of any ballpark. Unlike many young sluggers, Young doesn't try to pull every pitch, mainly because his opposite-field power is outstanding. His ability to hit for power and average also stems from the fact that the head of his bat stays in the strike zone a long time. His plus arm has plenty of strength for him to play right field in the majors.

SAL pitchers retired Young early in the season by busting him with inside fastballs. While he was able to adjust, some scouts believe he still has a minor hitch in his swing that leaves him vulnerable to heat on the inner half. He showed some patience at the plate in 2004 but his strikeout-walk ratio still has room for improvement that the Rays believe will come with experience. Though he has a cannon arm, his throws could be more accurate. His routes on fly balls also need to get better. Scouts have noted that his body continues to look more like his brother's, which isn't among the game's most impressive physiques. Young currently has average speed but will slow down as he gets older and heavier.

Though he spent his first full season entirely in low Class A, it wouldn't be a surprise if Young reached the big leagues in 2005. He progressed at a rapid rate and showed the ability to make adjustments, and Tampa Bay probably has to jump him to Double-A Montgomery in order to give him a bit of a challenge. Young is a special hitter with more offensive upside than any of the organization's rising stars: Rocco Baldelli, Carl Crawford and Upton.

Year	Club (League)	Class	AVG	G	AB	R	H	2B	3B	HR	RBI	BB	SO	SB	OBP	SLG
2004	Charleston, S.C. (SAL)	A	.322	131	513	95	165	26	5	25	116	53	120	21	.388	.538
MINOR LEAGUE TOTALS			.322	131	513	95	165	26	5	25	116	53	120	21	.388	.538

Scott Kazmir, lhp

Born: Jan. 24, 1984. **Ht.:** 6-0. **Wt.:** 170. **Bats:** L. **Throws:** L. **School:** Cypress Falls HS, Houston. **Career Transactions:** Selected by Mets in first round (15th overall) of 2002 draft; signed Aug. 2, 2002 . . . Traded by Mets with RHP Jose Diaz to Devil Rays for RHP Victor Zambrano and RHP Bartolome Fortunato, July 30, 2004. **Signed by:** Dave Lottsfeld (Mets).

The Devil Rays were able to swipe Kazmir from the Mets at the trade deadline last year. He struggled early in 2004 with his mechanics and an abdominal strain. Once healthy, he breezed through the minors. Kazmir has an overpowering 93-97 mph fastball that he complements with a nasty slider with outstanding bite, giving him better pure stuff than any young lefty in the game. His changeup has good fade and depth, showing the makings of becoming a third plus pitch. A good athlete with a clean delivery, he has a steady mound demeanor. After dealing Kazmir, Mets officials anonymously questioned whether his size would allow him to remain healthy and in the rotation, and they also knocked his makeup. Kazmir still needs to refine his command and his changeup. He will compete for a job in Tampa Bay's rotation and could develop into either a No. 1 starter or the next Billy Wagner.

Year	Club (League)	Class	W	L	ERA	G	GS	CG	SV	IP	H	R	ER	HR	BB	SO	AVG
2002	Brooklyn (NY-P)	A	0	1	.50	5	5	0	0	18	5	2	1	0	7	34	.089
2003	Capital City (SAL)	A	4	4	2.36	18	18	0	0	76	50	26	20	6	28	105	.185
	St. Lucie (FSL)	A	1	2	3.27	7	7	0	0	33	29	15	12	0	16	40	.240
2004	St. Lucie (FSL)	A	1	2	3.42	11	11	0	0	50	49	20	19	3	22	51	.257
	Binghamton (EL)	AA	2	1	1.73	4	4	0	0	26	16	6	5	0	9	29	.188
	Montgomery (SL)	AA	1	2	1.44	4	4	0	0	25	14	7	4	0	11	24	.171
	Tampa Bay (AL)	MAJ	2	3	5.67	8	7	0	0	33	33	22	21	4	21	41	.256
MAJOR LEAGUE TOTALS			2	3	5.67	8	7	0	0	33	33	22	21	4	21	41	.256
MINOR LEAGUE TOTALS			9	12	2.40	49	49	0	0	228	163	76	61	9	93	283	.202

Jeff Niemann, rhp

Born: Feb. 28, 1983. **Ht.:** 6-9. **Wt.:** 260. **Bats:** R. **Throws:** R. **School:** Rice University. **Career Transactions:** Selected by Devil Rays in first round (fourth overall) of 2004 draft; signed Jan. 20, 2005. **Signed by:** Jonathan Bonifay.

Niemann made history in 2003, tying an NCAA Division I record by going 17-0 and leading Rice to the College World Series championship, setting himself up as a premium pick in the 2004 draft. Though the Padres considered him with the first choice, they passed because he rarely was 100 percent as a junior. He had arthroscopic surgery in the fall of 2003 to clean out inflamed tissue in his elbow, then strained his groin in mid-April. Neither is a long-term concern, but the setbacks allowed the Devil Rays to get him with the fourth overall pick. It took them seven months to sign Niemann, who received a five-year major league contract worth a guaranteed $5.2 million, including a $3.2 million bonus. Tampa Bay has had little luck developing pitchers, so Niemann won't have to do much to become the best homegrown arm in club history. He's equipped with the stuff to be a No. 1 starter, starting with a 92-97 mph fastball and a slider that ranked as the best breaking pitch in the 2004 draft. He's intimidating at 6-foot-9 and 260 pounds, and he uses his large frame to drive the ball deep down in the strike zone. He has exceptional body control and feel for pitching for his size. Niemann also throws a spike curveball and a change-up, but didn't have to go to them often in college. Now that he's healthy again, he should rush through the minors. He'll probably begin his pro career in high Class A or Double-A.

Year	Club (League)	Class	W	L	ERA	G	GS	CG	SV	IP	H	R	ER	HR	BB	SO	AVG
2004	Did not play—Signed 2005 contract																

Joey Gathright, of

Born: April 22, 1982. **Ht.:** 5-10. **Wt.:** 170. **Bats:** L. **Throws:** R. **School:** Bonnabal HS, Metairie, La. **Career Transactions:** Selected by Devil Rays in 32nd round of 2001 draft; signed Aug. 29, 2001. **Signed by:** Benny Latino.

Gathright's progression through the system has been as rapid as his world-class speed. He reached the big leagues less than one year after earning rookie-of-the-year honors in the high Class A California League. Perhaps the fastest runner in baseball, Gathright ranked third in the Triple-A International League in steals despite playing just 60 games there. He is beginning to master the art of slapping the ball on the ground and using his legs to get on base. He also has outstanding range in center field. To become an effective leadoff hitter, Gathright must work counts better and draw more walks. He has trouble getting around on inside fastballs. He'll be a better basestealer once he learns how to read pitchers better. His arm strength and accuracy are below-average. Shortly after Gathright got to Triple-A, the Rays opened discussions on a long-term contract with him. He's likely to break camp with the big league team after Rocco Baldelli tore his ACL playing backyard baseball with his brother during the offseason, which could keep him out until July.

Year	Club (League)	Class	AVG	G	AB	R	H	2B	3B	HR	RBI	BB	SO	SB	OBP	SLG
2002	Charleston, S.C. (SAL)	A	.264	59	208	30	55	1	0	0	14	21	36	22	.360	.269
2003	Bakersfield (Cal)	A	.324	89	340	65	110	6	3	0	23	41	54	57	.406	.359
	Orlando (SL)	AA	.376	22	85	12	32	1	0	0	5	5	15	12	.419	.388
2004	Montgomery (SL)	AA	.341	32	126	23	43	5	1	0	8	11	30	10	.399	.397
	Durham (IL)	AAA	.326	60	236	34	77	9	1	0	8	19	46	33	.384	.373
	Tampa Bay (AL)	MAJ	.250	19	52	11	13	0	0	0	1	2	14	6	.316	.250
MAJOR LEAGUE TOTALS			.250	19	52	11	13	0	0	0	1	2	14	6	.316	.250
MINOR LEAGUE TOTALS			.319	262	995	164	317	22	5	0	58	97	181	134	.391	.351

5 Jason Hammel, rhp

Born: Sept. 2, 1982. **Ht.:** 6-6. **Wt.:** 200. **Bats:** R. **Throws:** R. **School:** Treasure Valley (Ore.) CC. **Career Transactions:** Selected by Devil Rays in 10th round of 2002 draft; signed June 6, 2002. **Signed by:** Paul Kirsch.

Hammel's 2003 season was cut short when he fell during pregame warmups and injured his right wrist in July. He emerged as one of the system's top pitching prospects during the second half of 2004, posting a 0.25 ERA and 42 strikeouts in his final 36 innings at high Class A Bakersfield. Hammel projects well with his long and lean frame. Possessing a quick arm with outstanding extension out front, he has a plus fastball that jumped from 89-91 to 92-94 mph in 2004. He also throws a sometimes-nasty 12-6 curveball at 76-78 mph. His command is a positive. His changeup is an average pitch at times, but Hammel needs to show more consistency with it as well as his curveball. While he has good coordination and body control for his size, he must maintain his mechanics in order to reach his potential. Hammel made as much progress as anyone in the organization in 2004. His lanky body produces easy heat that continues to improve. A promotion to Double-A is in Hammel's immediate future, and the Rays envision him as a middle-of-the-rotation starter.

Year	Club (League)	Class	W	L	ERA	G	GS	CG	SV	IP	H	R	ER	HR	BB	SO	AVG
2002	Princeton (Appy)	R	0	0	0.00	2	0	0	1	5	7	0	0	0	0	5	.318
	Hudson Valley (NY-P)	A	1	5	5.23	13	10	0	1	52	71	41	30	0	14	38	.314
2003	Charleston, S.C. (SAL)	A	6	2	3.40	14	12	1	0	77	70	32	29	2	27	50	.246
2004	Charleston, S.C. (SAL)	A	4	7	3.23	18	18	0	0	95	94	54	34	7	27	88	.253
	Bakersfield (Cal)	A	6	2	1.89	11	11	0	0	71	52	18	15	4	20	65	.207
MINOR LEAGUE TOTALS			17	16	3.24	58	51	1	2	300	294	145	108	13	88	246	.254

6 Reid Brignac, ss

Born: Jan. 16, 1986. **Ht.:** 6-1. **Wt.:** 185. **Bats:** L. **Throws:** R. **School:** St. Amant (La.) HS. **Career Transactions:** Selected by Devil Rays in second round of 2004 draft; signed July 30, 2004. **Signed by:** Benny Latino.

After Brignac led St. Amant High to the Louisiana state 5-A championship, the Devil Rays signed him away from Louisiana State for $795,000. He homered and drove in five runs in his first pro game, and went on to rank as the fourth-best prospect in the Rookie-level Appalachian League. Brignac is an aggressive hitter with outstanding hand-eye coordination and good strike-zone judgment. His exceptional bat speed should produce plus power down the road. His above-average arm strength, good defensive actions and athleticism should enable him to play anywhere on the field. Though scouts project Brignac to eventually outgrow shortstop and move to third base, the Rays believe he can stick at short. He shortened his arm action during instructional league. At the plate, he tends to become pull-conscious. Brignac has an advanced approach at the plate for a player fresh out of high school. The Rays will send the natural line-drive hitter to low Class A Southwest Michigan for his first full season.

Year	Club (League)	Class	AVG	G	AB	R	H	2B	3B	HR	RBI	BB	SO	SB	OBP	SLG
2004	Princeton (Appy)	R	.361	25	97	16	35	4	2	1	25	9	10	2	.413	.474
	Charleston, S.C. (SAL)	A	.500	3	14	3	7	1	0	0	5	1	2	0	.533	.571
MINOR LEAGUE TOTALS			.378	28	111	19	42	5	2	1	30	10	12	2	.427	.486

James Houser, lhp

Born: Dec. 15, 1984. **Ht.:** 6-4. **Wt.:** 185. **Bats:** L. **Throws:** L. **School:** Sarasota (Fla.) HS. **Career Transactions:** Selected by Devil Rays in second round of 2003 draft; signed June 17, 2003. **Signed by:** Kevin Elfering.

Houser was coming off consecutive scoreless outings in May when his elbow began to bother him. Though he didn't require surgery, the Devil Rays decided to play it safe and shut him down for the rest of the season. They were encouraged with the way he bounced back during instructional league. Houser is a polished lefty with a lean, projectable body and the potential for three plus pitches. He employs a three-quarters delivery to throw a low- to mid-90s fastball with good movement. He also has an above-average changeup and two versions of a curveball, including one that back-doors righthanders. Health remains the biggest concern regarding Houser. A heart murmur scared some teams and caused him to fall out of the first round in 2003. He has made progress with the depth of his changeup and the consistency of his curves, but all of his pitches could use some refinement and more consistency. Provided he remains healthy, Houser could move quickly through the system. If he looks strong in spring training, he could begin 2005 at high Class A Visalia.

Year	Club (League)	Class	W	L	ERA	G	GS	CG	SV	IP	H	R	ER	HR	BB	SO	AVG
2003	Princeton (Appy)	R	0	4	3.73	10	10	0	0	41	43	23	17	1	13	44	.262
2004	Charleston, S.C. (SAL)	A	3	1	2.20	7	7	0	0	33	27	9	8	1	13	27	.225
MINOR LEAGUE TOTALS			3	5	3.05	17	17	0	0	74	70	32	25	2	26	71	.246

Elijah Dukes, of

Born: June 26, 1984. **Ht.:** 6-2. **Wt.:** 225. **Bats:** B. **Throws:** R. **School:** Hillsborough HS, Tampa. **Career Transactions:** Selected by Devil Rays in third round of 2002 draft; signed Aug. 21, 2002. **Signed by:** Kevin Elfering.

A top linebacker prospect in high school, Dukes is one of the best natural athletes in the minors. He spent a month in a team-mandated anger-management seminar following a run-in with a South Atlantic League umpire but controlled his emotions and performed well in high Class A. In January, however, Dukes was charged with first-degree misdemeanor battery (domestic violence)—his third arrest in 13 months—after an argument with his sister. Dukes has five-tool ability and above-average instincts despite his limited experience. He has the power and speed to be a 30-30 player in the majors. Though he played mainly left field in 2004, Dukes also has seen time in center field and is a capable defender who takes good routes on flyballs. Dukes' makeup has been questioned since his high school days in Tampa. He has difficulty with authority, and his overall discipline is lacking. His defense and patience at the plate are both inconsistent. Dukes has the talent to become the Rays' first major homegrown, hometown standout and he'll move up to Double-A in 2005. His maturity will determine the pace of his progress.

Year	Club (League)	Class	AVG	G	AB	R	H	2B	3B	HR	RBI	BB	SO	SB	OBP	SLG
2003	Charleston, S.C. (SAL)	A	.245	117	383	51	94	17	4	7	53	45	130	33	.338	.366
2004	Charleston, S.C. (SAL)	A	.288	43	163	26	47	12	2	2	15	18	47	14	.368	.423
	Bakersfield (Cal)	A	.332	58	211	44	70	16	2	8	34	26	50	16	.416	.540
MINOR LEAGUE TOTALS			.279	218	757	121	211	45	8	17	102	89	227	63	.366	.427

Chad Orvella, rhp

Born: Oct. 1, 1980. **Ht.:** 5-11. **Wt.:** 190. **Bats:** R. **Throws:** R. **School:** North Carolina State University. **Career Transactions:** Selected by Devil Rays in 13th round of 2003 draft; signed June 9, 2003. **Signed by:** Hank King.

Primarily a shortstop in college, Orvella took a shipment of bats with him to short-season Hudson Valley after signing. The Devil Rays had no intention of having him do anything other than pitch. The initial results have been amazing, with a 132-11 strikeout-walk ratio and .158 opponent average in 86 pro innings. Orvella works off a late-moving 92-94 mph fastball that touches 97. He also has a plus changeup with fade and depth, as well as a slider that can be unhittable. His command and aggressiveness make his stuff even better. Orvella's slurvy breaking ball needs more consistency, and he doesn't have prototype size, though that hasn't held him back. A full-time pitcher for less than two years, he's still learning his craft. The Rays will give Orvella a long look during spring training. Though he could return to Triple-A Durham to open 2005, he's on track to become the first homegrown closer in franchise history.

Year	Club (League)	Class	W	L	ERA	G	GS	CG	SV	IP	H	R	ER	HR	BB	SO	AVG
2003	Hudson Valley (NY-P)	A	0	0	0.00	10	0	0	0	12	6	0	0	0	1	15	.140
2004	Charleston, S.C. (SAL)	A	1	0	1.33	22	0	0	4	47	28	9	7	4	5	76	.168
	Bakersfield (Cal)	A	0	1	3.06	15	0	0	4	18	13	7	6	2	4	24	.203
	Montgomery (SL)	AA	0	0	0.00	6	0	0	4	7	0	0	0	0	0	15	.000
	Durham (IL)	AAA	0	0	5.40	2	0	0	0	2	1	1	1	1	1	2	.143
MINOR LEAGUE TOTALS			1	1	1.46	55	0	0	12	86	48	17	14	7	11	132	.158

10 Seth McClung, rhp

Born: Feb. 7, 1981. **Ht.:** 6-6. **Wt.:** 235. **Bats:** R. **Throws:** R. **School:** Greenbrier East HS, Lewisburg, W.Va.. **Career Transactions:** Selected by Devil Rays in fifth round of 1999 draft; signed June 21, 1999. **Signed by:** Doug Witt.

McClung opened 2003 in Tampa Bay's bullpen and moved into the rotation before succumbing to Tommy John surgery in June. He returned to the mound last July and showed that he's on track to fully regain his power stuff. McClung has lost little if anything from his mid-90s fastball, and he should be back to full strength by mid-2005. His hard curveball has tight spin and sharp movement. Manager Lou Piniella loves his aggressive approach, as McClung isn't afraid to challenge hitters or back them off the plate. McClung never has shown the consistent changeup and reliable control to remain a starter in the major leagues. If he doesn't develop those attributes, he'll return to the bullpen, possibly as a closer. Contrary to his nature, McClung was determined not to rush back from surgery and every indication shows that his patience was prudent. He regained noticeable strength during the 2004 season and should return to the majors before mid-2005.

Year	Club (League)	Class	W	L	ERA	G	GS	CG	SV	IP	H	R	ER	HR	BB	SO	AVG
1999	Princeton (Appy)	R	2	4	7.69	13	10	0	0	46	53	47	39	3	48	46	.285
2000	Hudson Valley (NY-P)	A	2	2	1.85	8	8	0	0	44	37	18	9	0	17	38	.227
	Charleston, S.C. (SAL)	A	2	1	3.19	6	6	0	0	31	30	14	11	0	19	26	.246
2001	Charleston, S.C. (SAL)	A	10	11	2.79	28	28	2	0	164	142	72	51	6	53	165	.231
2002	Bakersfield (Cal)	A	3	2	2.92	7	7	0	0	37	35	16	12	1	11	48	.243
	Montgomery (SL)	AA	5	7	5.37	20	19	0	0	114	138	74	68	12	53	64	.299
2003	Tampa Bay (AL)	MAJ	4	1	5.35	12	5	0	0	39	33	23	23	6	25	25	.241
2004	Charleston, S.C. (SAL)	A	0	0	0.00	3	3	0	0	9	5	0	0	0	4	10	.152
	Montgomery (SL)	AA	1	1	4.73	3	3	0	0	13	10	7	7	3	4	8	.217
	Durham (IL)	AAA	2	1	3.29	11	0	0	0	14	10	5	5	0	7	12	.208
MAJOR LEAGUE TOTALS			4	1	5.35	12	5	0	0	39	33	23	23	6	25	25	.241
MINOR LEAGUE TOTALS			27	29	3.85	99	84	2	0	472	460	253	202	25	216	417	.253

11 Wes Bankston, 1b/of

Born: Nov. 23, 1983. **Ht.:** 6-4. **Wt.:** 210. **Bats:** R. **Throws:** R. **School:** Plano East HS, Plano, Texas. **Career Transactions:** Selected by Devil Rays in fourth round of 2002 draft; signed June 17, 2002. **Signed by:** Milt Hill.

After leading the Appalachian League with 18 homers and 57 RBIs in his pro debut, Bankston was sidetracked by a wrist injury in 2003. He returned to low Class A in 2004 and showed significant progress in all phases of his game. He ranked among South Atlantic League leaders in homers, RBIs, extra-base hits and on-base percentage. A former high school quarterback, Bankston has good all-around tools. His above-average raw power stands out the most, and he has good speed and mobility for a big man. His strong arm is suitable for right field; he moved to first base because of the organization's outfield depth. His improved numbers were due in part to better pitch selection. Bankston's swing remains a little too long for his own good. He goes through stretches where he doesn't make consistent contact. As his lower half has thickened, he has lost some athleticism. The Rays can afford to be patient with Bankston, though he should move quicker as a first baseman than he would have as a right fielder. He could reach Double-A at some point in 2005 and the majors by the end of 2006.

Year	Club (League)	Class	AVG	G	AB	R	H	2B	3B	HR	RBI	BB	SO	SB	OBP	SLG
2002	Princeton (Appy)	R	.301	62	246	48	74	10	1	18	57	18	46	2	.346	.569
	Hudson Valley (NY-P)	A	.303	8	33	2	10	1	0	0	1	0	6	1	.294	.333
2003	Charleston, S.C. (SAL)	A	.256	103	375	46	96	18	1	12	60	53	94	2	.346	.405
2004	Charleston, S.C. (SAL)	A	.289	127	470	82	136	30	3	23	101	73	104	9	.390	.513
MINOR LEAGUE TOTALS			.281	300	1124	178	316	59	5	53	219	144	250	14	.364	.484

12 Elliot Johnson, 2b

Born: March 9, 1984. **Ht.:** 6-0. **Wt.:** 171. **Bats:** B. **Throws:** R. **School:** Thatcher (Ariz.) HS. **Career Transactions:** Signed as nondrafted free agent by Devil Rays, June 29, 2002. **Signed by:** Craig Weissmann.

On May 28, 2004, Johnson became the second player in professional baseball history to hit three homers in the first three innings of a game, joining Carl Reynolds of the 1930 White Sox. Power isn't Johnson's game, however. A nondrafted free agent from a high school in a remote part of Arizona, he's a speedy scrapper with a knack for getting on base. He hit just three more homers the rest of 2004, but ranked fourth in the South Atlantic League in steals and tied for fifth in runs. A switch-hitter, he has fine strike-zone judgment and usually tries to hit everything on the ground in order to best use his wheels. However, he may have lost a bit of focus after his three-homer game as he hit just .243 the rest of the way while his strikeout-walk ratio deteriorated. Scouts believe Johnson will be able to drive more pitches once he matures physically. Johnson's body remains underdeveloped and lacks both strength and stamina. Despite his overall athleticism, his defensive skills are limited to the right side of the diamond. He also can learn to read pitchers better on steal attempts. The Rays believe that with continued improvement, Johnson could emerge as their starting second baseman. He has an outside chance of winning a job in Double-A, but he most likely will start 2005 in high Class A.

Year	Club (League)	Class	AVG	G	AB	R	H	2B	3B	HR	RBI	BB	SO	SB	OBP	SLG
2002	Princeton (Appy)	R	.263	42	152	21	40	10	1	1	13	18	48	14	.345	.362
2003	Charleston, S.C. (SAL)	A	.212	54	151	22	32	4	0	0	15	38	32	8	.370	.238
2004	Charleston, S.C. (SAL)	A	.262	126	503	92	132	22	7	6	41	54	91	43	.339	.370
MINOR LEAGUE TOTALS			.253	222	806	135	204	36	8	7	69	110	171	65	.346	.344

13 Jason Pridie, of

Born: Oct. 9, 1983. **Ht.:** 6-1. **Wt.:** 180. **Bats:** L. **Throws:** R. **School:** Prescott (Ariz.) HS. **Career Transactions:** Selected by Devil Rays in second round of 2002 draft; signed June 12, 2002. **Signed by:** Craig Weissmann.

After Pridie wore down markedly during the second half of 2003, his first full pro season, the Devil Rays sent him back to low Class A Charleston. He showed improved stamina and power while leading the South Atlantic League in runs. The younger brother of Twins minor league righty Jon Pridie, he possesses one of the best pure strokes in the organization, combining balance at the plate and the ability to use his hands. His biggest weakness is that he tries to pull too many pitches instead of hitting to the opposite field, though he has shown the ability to do so in the past. He's an above-average runner, which serves him well on the basepaths and in center field. He could use his speed more often if he'd learn to draw more walks. His instincts and aggressiveness are assets on defense, and the former high school pitcher's arm ranks among the best in the system. Part of the Rays' tremendous outfield depth, he's ready for high Class A in 2005.

Year	Club (League)	Class	AVG	G	AB	R	H	2B	3B	HR	RBI	BB	SO	SB	OBP	SLG
2002	Princeton (Appy)	R	.368	67	285	60	105	12	9	7	33	19	35	13	.410	.547
	Hudson Valley (NY-P)	A	.344	8	32	4	11	1	1	1	1	3	6	0	.400	.531
2003	Charleston, S.C. (SAL)	A	.260	128	530	75	138	28	10	7	48	30	113	26	.302	.391
2004	Charleston, S.C. (SAL)	A	.276	128	515	103	142	27	11	17	86	37	114	17	.327	.470
MINOR LEAGUE TOTALS			.291	331	1362	242	396	68	31	32	168	89	268	56	.336	.457

14 Wade Davis, rhp

Born: Sept. 7, 1985. **Ht.:** 6-5. **Wt.:** 220. **Bats:** R. **Throws:** R. **School:** Lake Wales (Fla.) HS. **Career Transactions:** Selected by Devil Rays in third round of 2004 draft; signed June 15, 2004. **Signed by:** Kevin Elfering.

The Rays did their homework on Davis, deemed a difficult sign because he was committed to attending the University of Florida. They landed him for $475,000 after drafting him in the third round last June. He put together a solid pro debut before wearing down in August, when he had a 10.90 ERA in five starts. Inconsistency also hindered him throughout the spring, but he has promising stuff with a picturesque, easy delivery and a good body. Davis has the potential to be a power pitcher and workhorse at the major league level. His fastball features plus movement, sits at 90-91 right now and should develop into a consistent 93-94 mph pitch. His slider has hard, late bite and could become a plus pitch. Davis also has command and poise. He's very coachable and has a good idea of what he's doing for a young player. His immediate goals are achieving tighter spin on his curveball and developing a changeup. He also needs to keep the ball down in the zone to avoid giving up homers. Davis will address those shortcomings in low Class A this year.

Year	Club (League)	Class	W	L	ERA	G	GS	CG	SV	IP	H	R	ER	HR	BB	SO	AVG
2004	Princeton (Appy)	R	3	5	5.93	13	13	0	0	58	71	46	38	8	19	38	.302
MINOR LEAGUE TOTALS			3	5	5.93	13	13	0	0	58	71	46	38	8	19	38	.302

15 Travis Schlichting, 3b

Born: Oct. 19, 1984. **Ht.:** 6-4. **Wt.:** 188. **Bats:** R. **Throws:** R. **School:** Round Rock (Texas) HS. **Career Transactions:** Selected by Devil Rays in fourth round of 2003 draft; signed June 21, 2003. **Signed by:** Jonathan Bonifay.

Several members of Tampa Bay's front office believe that Schlichting is on the verge of a breakthrough season in 2005.They think he's further along in his development than Elliot Johnson was at the same point in his career. A pure tools performer who moved from shortstop in high school to third base in pro ball, Schlichting overcame a tough start last year to salvage a respectable season at the plate. He has made the adjustments from swinging an aluminum bat as an amateur. He has a quick and potentially powerful bat from the right side, and he hits lefties and righties equally well. Once he fills out his lanky frame, he should be much more of a threat at the plate. Schlichting possesses solid speed and very good baserunning instincts. His reactions, soft hands and strong arm make him a natural at third base. Slowed at times by a strained oblique muscle in 2004, Schlichting may return to low Class A at the beginning of this year, allowing him to build some confidence. They Rays had positive results when they did the same thing with Wes Bankston, Johnson and Jason Pridie last season.

Year	Club (League)	Class	AVG	G	AB	R	H	2B	3B	HR	RBI	BB	SO	SB	OBP	SLG
2003	Princeton (Appy)	R	.226	46	146	18	33	2	2	0	9	14	38	6	.298	.267
2004	Charleston, S.C. (SAL)	A	.260	94	331	50	86	19	1	2	34	36	71	6	.341	.341
MINOR LEAGUE TOTALS			.249	140	477	68	119	21	3	2	43	50	109	12	.328	.319

16 Chris Seddon, lhp

Born: Oct. 13, 1983. **Ht.:** 6-3. **Wt.:** 170. **Bats:** L. **Throws:** L. **School:** Canyon HS, Santa Clarita, Calif. **Career Transactions:** Selected by Devil Rays in fifth round of 2001 draft; signed July 31, 2001. **Signed by:** Fred Repke.

Seddon continued to make steady if unspectacular progress in 2004, maintaining his status as one of the top lefthanders in the system. He dominated the California League for seven starts, then settled in at the Double-A level. Seddon isn't overpowering, but his mix of pitches works well together and has drawn him comparisons to San Francisco's Kirk Rueter. He has more velocity than Rueter, working with a 90-91 mph fastball with movement. He keeps righthanders honest by pitching inside with his slider and by using his average changeup. Seddon doesn't have much margin for error, so he has to keep his pitches down in the strike zone. The 19 homers he allowed in 21 Double-A starts were the second-most in the Southern League. He needs at least another year in the minors, but the Devil Rays believe he'll be pushing for a job at the end of their rotation sometime in 2006.

Year	Club (League)	Class	W	L	ERA	G	GS	CG	SV	IP	H	R	ER	HR	BB	SO	AVG
2001	Princeton (Appy)	R	1	2	5.11	4	2	0	0	12	15	7	7	2	6	18	.300
2002	Charleston, S.C. (SAL)	A	6	8	3.62	26	20	0	1	117	93	63	47	7	68	88	.218
2003	Bakersfield (Cal)	A	9	11	5.00	26	26	0	0	133	147	93	74	12	54	95	.279
2004	Bakersfield (Cal)	A	5	0	0.65	7	7	0	0	41	30	4	3	0	8	41	.201
	Montgomery (SL)	AA	9	10	4.39	21	21	1	0	119	129	67	58	19	44	102	.281
MINOR LEAGUE TOTALS			30	31	4.02	84	76	1	1	423	414	234	189	40	180	344	.257

17 Jonny Gomes, of

Born: Nov. 22, 1980. **Ht.:** 6-1. **Wt.:** 205. **Bats:** R. **Throws:** R. **School:** Santa Rosa (Calif.) JC. **Career Transactions:** Selected by Devil Rays in 18th round of 2001 draft; signed June 13, 2001. **Signed by:** Hank King.

After making tremendous strides with his approach at the plate and earning big league manager Lou Piniella's seal of approval in 2003, Gomes reverted to his pull-conscious ways last year in Triple-A. The Devil Rays were encouraged by his willingness to hit the ball to the opposite field two years ago, but the temptation offered by the left-field wall at Durham Bulls Athletic Park was too much for him to avoid. Getting him to use the entire field again may be difficult because he was much more productive in 2004 than '03. Though he has the strength and bat speed to knock the ball out of any part of any park, the Rays may have to accept that he's not going to change his approach. Gomes swings mightily with every cut and may never hit for average. He plays hard, but he's a subpar fielder. He lacks range and arm strength, and he needs to get better jumps and take more direct routes on flyballs. He's a below-average runner as well. Tampa Bay could give him a look as a DH in 2005.

Year	Club (League)	Class	AVG	G	AB	R	H	2B	3B	HR	RBI	BB	SO	SB	OBP	SLG
2001	Princeton (Appy)	R	.291	62	206	58	60	11	2	16	44	33	73	15	.442	.597
2002	Bakersfield (Cal)	A	.278	134	446	2	124	24	9	30	72	91	173	15	.432	.574
2003	Orlando (SL)	AA	.249	120	442	68	110	28	3	17	56	53	148	23	.348	.441
	Durham (IL)	AAA	.316	5	19	2	6	2	1	0	1	2	5	0	.435	.526
	Tampa Bay (AL)	MAJ	.133	8	15	1	2	1	0	0	0	0	6	0	.188	.200
2004	Durham (IL)	AAA	.257	114	389	73	100	27	1	26	78	51	136	8	.368	.532
	Tampa Bay (AL)	MAJ	.071	5	14	0	1	0	0	0	1	1	6	0	.133	.071
MAJOR LEAGUE TOTALS			.103	13	29	1	3	1	0	0	1	1	12	0	.161	.138
MINOR LEAGUE TOTALS			.266	435	1502	203	400	92	16	89	251	230	535	61	.394	.527

18 Angel Garcia, rhp

Born: Oct. 28, 1983. **Ht.:** 6-7. **Wt.:** 210. **Bats:** R. **Throws:** R. **School:** Nicolas Sevilla HS, Dorado, P.R. **Career Transactions:** Selected by Twins in fourth round of 2001 draft; signed June 19, 2001 . . . Selected by Devil Rays from Twins in major league Rule 5 draft, Dec. 13, 2004. **Signed by:** Hector Otero (Twins).

The Twins have so much minor league talent that they couldn't protect all of their prospects on their 40-man roster during the offseason. Their loss was the Devil Rays' gain, as the Diamondbacks took Garcia with the first pick in the major league Rule 5 draft, then sold him to Tampa Bay for $100,000 on top of the $50,000 draft price. Garcia has pitched just 132 innings since Minnesota drafted him in the fourth round in 2001, missing most of 2003 with elbow problems that required Tommy John surgery. Like many pitchers coming back from that operation, Garcia has regained his velocity before his command. He was pitching at 90-93 mph and touching 94-95 in winter ball in his native Puerto Rico. His changeup rates as major league average but his curveball needs considerable improvement. With his limited repertoire, Garcia would fit best in Tampa Bay this season as a reliever. If he can't stick with the big league club, the Rays would have to place him on waivers and offer him back to the Twins for $25,000 before they could send him to the minors. His long-term promise is considerable enough that Tampa Bay will do what it can to hold onto him.

Year	Club (League)	Class	W	L	ERA	G	GS	CG	SV	IP	H	R	ER	HR	BB	SO	AVG
2001	Twins (GCL)	R	0	3	5.60	9	6	0	0	18	20	15	11	0	12	22	.286
2002	Twins (GCL)	R	4	4	3.40	13	7	0	0	53	41	24	20	0	31	63	.217
2003	Elizabethton (Appy)	R	2	1	2.89	9	9	0	0	37	37	18	12	5	18	44	.257
2004	Twins (GCL)	R	0	0	0.00	6	1	0	0	8	6	2	0	0	3	9	.181
	Quad Cities (Mid)	A	2	1	4.50	7	2	0	0	16	13	8	8	2	5	16	.220
MINOR LEAGUE TOTALS			8	9	3.48	44	25	0	0	132	117	67	51	7	69	154	.240

19 Gabby Martinez, 1b/3b

Born: May 17, 1983. **Ht.:** 6-2. **Wt.:** 180. **Bats:** L. **Throws:** R. **School:** Blanca Malaret HS, Sabana Grande, P.R. **Career Transactions:** Selected by Devil Rays in 27th round of 2001 draft; signed Sept. 11, 2001. **Signed by:** Edwin Rodriguez.

Martinez made as much progress as any player in the organization last year. Drafted out of Puerto Rico in 2001, he blossomed offensively in high Class A. He owns one of the purest swings in the organization, a smooth lefthanded stroke capable of raking doubles from gap to gap. Martinez even hits southpaws well, batting .301 against them in 2004. He has gained 25 pounds since signing, but his athletic frame is still maturing. As he gets stronger and improves his plate discipline, Rays officials expect some of his doubles to become home runs. They project him to develop at least average power, capable of hitting 20 or more homers per season. Martinez started games at first, second and third base in 2004, as well as at all three outfield spots. He may get more time in Double-A this year at the hot corner, where he has good hands and enough arm. He'll need to upgrade his footwork. In any case, Martinez' bat will be his calling card.

Year	Club (League)	Class	AVG	G	AB	R	H	2B	3B	HR	RBI	BB	SO	SB	OBP	SLG
2002	Princeton (Appy)	R	.323	60	217	28	70	17	1	5	26	27	38	1	.400	.479
2003	Hudson Valley (NY-P)	A	.292	70	243	27	71	21	2	2	43	22	52	0	.354	.420
2004	Bakersfield (Cal)	A	.323	116	436	54	141	39	3	4	47	30	90	4	.371	.454
MINOR LEAGUE TOTALS			.315	246	896	109	282	77	6	11	116	79	180	5	.374	.451

20 Matt Diaz, of

Born: March 3, 1978. **Ht.:** 6-1. **Wt.:** 206. **Bats:** R. **Throws:** R. **School:** Florida State University. **Career Transactions:** Selected by Devil Rays in 17th round of 1999 draft; signed June 24, 1999. **Signed by:** Mark McKnight.

A late-blooming prospect, Diaz has mashed his way into prospect status the last two seasons. After ranking second in the minors with a .354 average in 2003, he did nothing but rake again last season. He finished second in the minors with 47 doubles, and second in the International League in batting, hits, extra-base hits and slugging percentage. He also put together a 22-game hitting streak and drilled his first big league homer in September. However, Diaz faces a significant challenge because of Tampa Bay's crowded outfield picture. He's an adequate runner and right fielder with a solid arm, and his hustle and instincts help him on the bases and in the field. The Devil Rays toyed with the idea of making him a catcher but ultimately decided the conversion wouldn't work. Rocco Baldelli's knee injury has created an opening on the big league roster. While Diaz likely won't be an Opening Day starter, his chances of making the big league club have increased.

Year	Club (League)	Class	AVG	G	AB	R	H	2B	3B	HR	RBI	BB	SO	SB	OBP	SLG
1999	Hudson Valley (NY-P)	A	.245	54	208	22	51	15	2	1	20	6	43	6	.284	.351
2000	St. Petersburg (FSL)	A	.270	106	392	37	106	21	3	6	53	11	54	2	.305	.385
2001	Bakersfield (Cal)	A	.328	131	524	79	172	40	2	17	81	24	73	11	.370	.510
2002	Orlando (SL)	AA	.274	122	449	71	123	28	1	10	50	34	72	31	.337	.408
2003	Orlando (SL)	AA	.383	60	227	32	87	21	0	5	41	19	24	9	.444	.542
	Durham (IL)	AAA	.328	67	253	35	83	18	3	8	45	16	45	6	.382	.518
	Tampa Bay (AL)	MAJ	.111	4	9	2	1	0	0	0	0	1	3	0	.200	.111
2004	Durham (IL)	AAA	.332	134	503	81	167	47	5	21	93	26	96	15	.377	.571
	Tampa Bay (AL)	MAJ	.190	10	21	3	4	1	1	1	3	1	6	0	.292	.476
MAJOR LEAGUE TOTALS			.167	14	30	5	5	1	1	1	3	2	9	0	.265	.367
MINOR LEAGUE TOTALS			.309	674	2556	357	789	190	16	68	383	136	407	80	.357	.475

21 Jonathan Barratt, lhp

Born: March 19, 1985. **Ht.:** 5-9. **Wt.:** 165. **Bats:** R. **Throws:** L. **School:** Hillcrest HS, Springfield, Mo. **Career Transactions:** Selected by Devil Rays in fifth round of 2003 draft; signed Aug. 25, 2003. **Signed by:** Ricky Drexler.

It took nearly a year, but the Rays were enthused when Barratt finally made his pro debut. A fifth-round pick in 2003, he didn't sign for $300,000 until that August. He spent that summer serving as the ace of the U.S. junior national team that won a silver medal at the Pan American Cup in Curacao. Limited by a sore arm in extended spring training, he saw his first official game action last June. Though tight pitch counts contributed, he didn't allow more than two earned runs in any of his 10 starts against more experienced hitters in the short-season New-York Penn League. Barratt has an amazingly quick arm and exceptional mechanics that produce stunning stuff considering his size, which is listed generously at 5-foot-9. With little effort, he throws low-90s fastballs with good movement. His changeup has good depth and can be a plus pitch, while his hard curveball shows considerable promise despite its occasional inconsistency. Barratt also has little trouble throwing strikes. The biggest concern is his slight build, which leads to questions about his durability. In addition to his setback in extended spring training, he strained his back in August. That ended the possibility of a late-season promotion to low Class A, where he'll pitch in 2005.

Year	Club (League)	Class	W	L	ERA	G	GS	CG	SV	IP	H	R	ER	HR	BB	SO	AVG
2004	Hudson Valley (NY-P)	A	2	3	2.74	10	10	1	0	43	38	21	13	2	11	50	.230
MINOR LEAGUE TOTALS			2	3	2.74	10	10	1	0	43	38	21	13	2	11	50	.230

22 Matt Walker, rhp

Born: Aug. 16, 1986. **Ht.:** 6-3. **Wt.:** 193. **Bats:** R. **Throws:** R. **School:** Central HS, Baton Rouge, La. **Career Transactions:** Selected by Devil Rays in 10th round of 2004 draft; signed Aug. 21, 2004. **Signed by:** Benny Latino.

Entering last spring, Walker's future appeared to be in football. A quarterback, he drew interest from NCAA Division I-A programs. But when he started throwing 92-94 mph and flashed a plus curveball, his destiny became baseball. By the time crosscheckers came in to see him, Walker was tired and his stuff was down, ending any possibility that he might go in the first round. In fact, he fell all the way to the 10th but Walker signed at the end of the summer for $600,000, easily the highest bonus in his round and the equivalent of mid-second-round money. He's extremely athletic and projectable, and there's no reason he shouldn't regain his low-90s fastball and it's possible he could add more velocity. At its best, his curve is a hard breaker that arrives at 77-80 mph. He's still raw, and his command and his changeup will need work. He could start on the same path as Jonathan Barratt, waiting to make his pro debut until June.

Year	Club (League)	Class	W	L	ERA	G	GS	CG	SV	IP	H	R	ER	HR	BB	SO	AVG
2004	Did not play—Signed 2005 contract																

23 Jacob McGee, lhp

Born: Aug. 6, 1986. **Ht.:** 6-2. **Wt.:** 185. **Bats:** L. **Throws:** L. **School:** Edward Reed HS, Sparks, Nev. **Career Transactions:** Selected by Devil Rays in fifth round of 2004 draft; signed June 9, 2004. **Signed by:** Fred Repke.

After nabbing McGee in the fifth round last June, the Rays believe the projectable lefty may be one of the biggest steals from the first 10 rounds. In a dozen starts in the Appalachian League and during instructional league, he opened eyes with his overall package. Despite his slender build, McGee held his 88-91 mph velocity throughout the year. His fastball also has plus movement, but his best pitch currently is a sharp curveball with tight spin. He has made significant strides with his changeup, with the pitch displaying nice fade and needing only consistency. McGee is a good athlete with plenty of arm speed and a clean arm action, and he repeats his delivery well. He'll jump up to low Class A in 2005.

Year	Club (League)	Class	W	L	ERA	G	GS	CG	SV	IP	H	R	ER	HR	BB	SO	AVG
2004	Princeton (Appy)	R	5	1	3.97	12	12	0	0	57	49	30	25	5	25	53	.231
MINOR LEAGUE TOTALS			5	1	3.97	12	12	0	0	57	49	30	25	5	25	53	.231

24 Fernando Cortez, 2b

Born: Aug. 10, 1981. **Ht.:** 6-1. **Wt.:** 175. **Bats:** L. **Throws:** R. **School:** Grossmont (Calif.) JC. **Career Transactions:** Selected by Devil Rays in ninth round of 2001 draft; signed June 12, 2001. **Signed by:** Craig Weissmann.

Cortez is a classic example of a player whose sum is greater than his individual tools. A product of the talent-rich San Diego area, he combines baseball savvy and instincts with impressive makeup and work ethic. He was the Pacific Coast Conference player of the year in 2001 at Grossmont JC, where Marcus Giles won the same award in 1997. Cortez has a compact stroke and the ability to drive the ball. He needs to improve his strike-zone judgment and patience. His speed is just fringe average, though he runs very aggressively. A good defensive second baseman, Cortez has sure hands and turns the double play well. His season ended in July when he hurt his left knee, but the Devil Rays still honored him as their Double-A player of the year. They like the way Cortez plays under control and never appears to be overwhelmed by the speed of the game, which has helped him with adjustments to higher levels. Not far from contributing in the majors, he'll begin the 2005 season in Triple-A.

Year	Club (League)	Class	AVG	G	AB	R	H	2B	3B	HR	RBI	BB	SO	SB	OBP	SLG
2001	Hudson Valley (NY-P)	A	.278	55	234	36	65	14	3	1	25	15	26	6	.327	.376
2002	Charleston, S.C. (SAL)	A	.267	127	475	60	127	14	5	2	49	41	59	37	.327	.331
2003	Bakersfield (Cal)	A	.281	102	384	53	108	19	0	1	53	41	61	32	.346	.339
	Orlando (SL)	AA	.316	30	114	15	36	3	1	1	6	3	22	1	.333	.386
2004	Montgomery (SL)	AA	.287	94	359	51	103	20	5	3	30	32	60	8	.345	.396
MINOR LEAGUE TOTALS			.280	408	1566	215	439	70	14	8	163	132	228	84	.336	.358

25 Shawn Riggans, c

Born: July 25, 1980. **Ht.:** 6-2. **Wt.:** 190. **Bats:** R. **Throws:** R. **School:** Indian River (Fla.) CC. **Career Transactions:** Selected by Devil Rays in 24th round of 2000 draft; signed May 7, 2001. **Signed by:** Kevin Elfering.

Riggans' development has been delayed by a string of injuries. He needed Tommy John surgery shortly after signing as a draft-and-follow in 2001, and got only a half-season as a DH in 2002. He was off to a great start with the bat last year before elbow problems cropped up again in mid-May, sidelining him for two months. When healthy, Riggans is the best defensive catcher in the organization. His arm strength and accuracy are solid, though his elbow woes enabled him to throw out just 24 percent of basestealers last year. He calls a good game and works well with pitchers, though he needs to upgrade his footwork and agility. Riggans has gotten barely more than a full season's worth of at-bats as a pro, but he has shown the promise to hit for average and gap power. He has strong wrists and a quick swing. The Rays envision him driving in runs from the lower half of the lineup, and hope he can stay healthy this year in Double-A.

Year	Club (League)	Class	AVG	G	AB	R	H	2B	3B	HR	RBI	BB	SO	SB	OBP	SLG
2001	Princeton (Appy)	R	.345	15	58	15	20	4	0	8	17	9	18	1	.433	.828
2002	Hudson Valley (NY-P)	A	.263	73	266	34	70	13	0	9	48	32	72	2	.343	.414
2003	Charleston, S.C. (SAL)	A	.280	68	232	33	65	17	0	3	34	19	35	3	.340	.392
	Orlando (SL)	AA	.274	22	62	7	17	6	0	1	11	4	14	0	.319	.419
2004	Bakersfield (Cal)	A	.346	34	127	20	44	11	0	5	22	15	23	0	.417	.551
	Montgomery (SL)	AA	.222	10	36	3	8	1	0	2	7	2	14	0	.282	.417
MINOR LEAGUE TOTALS			.287	222	781	112	224	52	0	28	139	81	176	6	.356	.461

26 Franklin Nunez, rhp

Born: Jan. 18, 1977. **Ht.:** 6-0. **Wt.:** 175. **Bats:** R. **Throws:** R. **Career Transactions:** Signed out of Dominican Republic by Dodgers, Sept. 1, 1994 . . . Released by Dodgers, Jan. 12, 1996 . . . Signed by Phillies, June 20, 1998 . . . Claimed on waivers by Mets from Phillies, Oct. 10, 2002 . . . Signed by Mets, March 31, 2003 . . . Granted free agency, Oct. 15, 2003 . . . Signed by Devil Rays, Feb. 4, 2004. **Signed by:** Rafael Gonzalez (Dodgers).

After getting released by the Dodgers, waived by the Phillies and pitching sparingly in the Mets system in 2003, Nunez put it all together last year. The Devils named him their Triple-A pitcher of the year, and he capped the season with eight appearances in Tampa Bay. His success centers on an explosive fastball that has been clocked as high as 100 mph, proving he's all the way back from shoulder surgery in July 2002. Nunez never has shown a reliable second pitch or command, and his ability to do so will determine whether he can reach his ceiling as a setup man. His first stint in the majors was up and down. He blew hitters away at times, highlighted by four strikeouts in a perfect two-inning outing against Oakland, but fell behind in the count too often and became hittable. Nunez will have to be more consistent to grab a bullpen job in spring training.

Year	Club (League)	Class	W	L	ERA	G	GS	CG	SV	IP	H	R	ER	HR	BB	SO	AVG
1995	Dodgers (DSL)	R	1	0	7.36	12	1	0	0	22	27	25	18	0	20	17	.290
1996	Did not play																
1997	Did not play																
1998	Phillies (DSL)	R	0	2	2.18	5	5	1	0	33	23	14	8	1	14	37	.198
	Greeneville (Appy)	R	2	2	2.49	6	4	0	0	25	23	10	7	0	8	19	.232
1999	Piedmont (SAL)	A	4	8	3.39	13	13	1	0	77	69	39	29	4	25	88	.238
2000	Clearwater (FSL)	A	10	4	3.62	23	14	1	2	112	112	54	45	4	57	81	.264
2001	Reading (EL)	AA	8	7	4.42	39	14	0	3	110	107	68	54	9	51	112	.252
2002	Scranton/WB (IL)	AAA	2	1	3.18	4	4	0	0	17	9	6	6	2	12	16	.158
	Phillies (GCL)	R	0	0	0.00	1	1	0	0	2	2	0	0	0	1	4	.250
2003	Brooklyn (NY-P)	A	0	0	5.06	7	0	0	0	5	5	4	3	0	4	8	.250
2004	Montgomery (SL)	AA	0	1	0.84	6	0	0	0	11	4	3	1	0	3	19	.114
	Durham (IL)	AAA	4	2	2.81	40	0	0	9	51	36	21	16	1	34	70	.193
	Tampa Bay (AL)	MAJ	0	3	5.91	8	0	0	0	11	11	8	7	1	7	14	.268
MAJOR LEAGUE TOTALS			0	3	5.91	8	0	0	0	11	11	8	7	1	7	14	.268
MINOR LEAGUE TOTALS			31	27	3.61	156	56	3	14	466	417	244	187	21	229	471	.238

27 Jose de la Cruz, rhp

Born: Sept. 23, 1983. **Ht.:** 6-6. **Wt.:** 206. **Bats:** R. **Throws:** R. **Career Transactions:** Signed out of Dominican Republic by Devil Rays, Nov. 20, 2002. **Signed by:** Junior Ramirez.

One glance at the imposing de la Cruz is all it takes before images of Armando Benitez and Jose Mesa emerge. A massive 6-foot-6, he fires his fastball at 90-94 mph and one day could reach triple digits. While he throws strikes with his heater, he has problems maintaining consistent mechanics and body control, partly because of his huge frame. As a result, he has made slow progress with his breaking ball. The positive side is that with his arms and legs appearing to fly in every direction during his delivery, de la Cruz makes it tough for hitters to pick up his pitches. He has allowed just one homer in 81 pro innings. He'll need plenty of time to round out his game but could develop into a closer if everything clicks. The next step for him will be low Class A this year.

Year	Club (League)	Class	W	L	ERA	G	GS	CG	SV	IP	H	R	ER	HR	BB	SO	AVG
2003	Princeton (Appy)	R	0	2	1.33	15	1	0	1	27	25	8	4	1	9	15	.248
2004	Hudson Valley (NY-P)	A	2	0	1.02	18	0	0	8	44	30	8	5	0	13	46	.184
MINOR LEAGUE TOTALS			2	2	1.14	33	1	0	9	71	55	16	9	1	22	61	.208

28 Jino Gonzalez, lhp

Born: Sept. 5, 1982. **Ht.:** 6-2. **Wt.:** 210. **Bats:** L. **Throws:** L. **School:** CC of Southern Nevada. **Career Transactions:** Selected by Devil Rays in 46th round of 2002 draft; signed June 2, 2003. **Signed by:** Fred Repke.

Though he missed all of 2002 with a shoulder injury, the Devil Rays took Gonzalez in the 42nd round anyway. He came back the next year to pitch Southern Nevada to the Junior College World Series championship, then signed for $200,000 as a draft-and-follow. Hit hard during his first couple of months at low Class A last year, he adjusted by coming up with a hard sinker. It generated plenty of groundball outs and proved a nice complement to his 89-92 four-seam fastball, decent changeup and developing slider. It's inconsistent, but when it's on, his slider is his most devastating pitch. His straight change and his command also could use some polish. Gonzalez was suspended for 15 days toward the end of the season after testing positive for a banned substance. He'll open 2005 in high Class A with a shot of reaching Double-A later in the season.

Year	Club (League)	Class	W	L	ERA	G	GS	CG	SV	IP	H	R	ER	HR	BB	SO	AVG
2003	Princeton (Appy)	R	2	1	2.00	3	1	0	0	9	5	6	2	0	1	10	.143
	Hudson Valley (NY-P)	A	0	1	4.50	3	3	0	0	12	11	7	6	0	6	11	.244
2004	Charleston, S.C. (SAL)	A	9	5	4.56	24	23	0	0	120	128	74	61	11	53	98	.279
MINOR LEAGUE TOTALS			11	7	4.39	30	27	0	0	141	144	87	69	11	60	119	.268

29 Jose Diaz, rhp

Born: April 13, 1980. **Ht.:** 6-0. **Wt.:** 225. **Bats:** R. **Throws:** R. **Career Transactions:** Signed out of Dominican Republic by Dodgers, Aug. 24, 1996 . . . Traded by Dodgers with 2B Victor Diaz and RHP Kole Strayhorn to Mets for OF Jeromy Burnitz and cash, July 14, 2003 . . . . Traded by Mets with LHP Scott Kazmir to Devil Rays for RHP Victor Zambrano and RHP Bartolome Fortunato, July 30, 2004. **Signed by:** Pablo Peguero (Dodgers).

Scott Kazmir wasn't the only flamethrower the Mets included in their widely panned trade for Victor Zambrano. Though Diaz was unspectacular in seven Double-A outings after the deal and ranked second in the minors in walks, he has a potentially lethal arsenal. He has an explosive mid-90s fastball, as well as a promising changeup that could make his heater all but unhittable. However, he's still very much a work in progress. Originally signed as a catcher by the Dodgers, Diaz batted .195 in four seasons before moving to the mound. His command isn't much better than his hitting ability, and he's still learning the nuances of pitching. His mechanics need refinement, particularly in terms of keeping his head still and repeating his delivery, which would improve his ability to locate his pitches. He needs to trust his changeup more often, and his hard breaking ball is far from reliable. The Devil Rays will try to be patient, and they'll send him back to Double-A this year.

Year	Club (League)	Class	AVG	G	AB	R	H	2B	3B	HR	RBI	BB	SO	SB	OBP	SLG
1997	Dodgers (DSL)	R	.147	30	95	12	14	1	0	1	5	6	30	3	.189	.212
1998	Dodgers (DSL)	R	.209	51	163	24	34	6	0	1	27	15	34	4	.264	.299
1999	Did not play—Injured															
2000	Great Falls (Pio)	R	.219	57	210	29	46	9	1	7	31	18	52	2	.371	.292
2001	Wilmington (SAL)	A	.175	23	80	7	14	4	0	2	5	4	31	1	.300	.214
	Great Falls (Pio)	R	.189	48	159	18	30	8	0	3	17	15	38	2	.296	.284
MINOR LEAGUE TOTALS			.195	212	717	93	140	28	1	15	88	59	188	12	.273	.298

Year	Club (League)	Class	W	L	ERA	G	GS	CG	SV	IP	H	R	ER	HR	BB	SO	AVG
2001	Great Falls (Pio)	R	0	0	0.00	1	0	0	0	1	0	0	0	0	0	2	.000
2002	South Georgia (SAL)	A	3	1	4.21	19	0	0	1	26	14	12	12	1	25	33	.163
2003	Vero Beach (FSL)	A	5	2	3.50	15	11	0	1	62	39	25	24	2	48	69	.181
	Jacksonville (SL)	AA	1	0	0.00	5	0	0	0	8	5	1	0	0	3	7	.185
	St. Lucie (FSL)	A	2	2	2.97	11	2	0	1	30	16	12	10	0	25	41	.162
2004	Binghamton (EL)	AA	4	7	5.18	21	19	1	0	83	59	53	48	3	70	90	.203
MINOR LEAGUE TOTALS			15	12	4.03	72	32	1	3	210	153	103	94	6	171	242	.184

30 John Jaso, c/1b

Born: Sept. 19, 1983. **Ht.:** 6-2. **Wt.:** 205. **Bats:** R. **Throws:** R. **School:** Southwestern (Calif.) JC. **Career Transactions:** Selected by Devil Rays in 12th round of 2003 draft; signed June 9, 2003. **Signed by:** Craig Weissmann.

Drafted out of the Pacific Coast Conference, the same juco circuit that produced Fernando Cortez, Jaso could emerge as the top catching prospect in the organization in a hurry. He returned to Hudson Valley for his second pro season and displayed steady improvement in all phases of his game. Jaso raised his batting average 75 points and also drove balls with more frequency. The Devil Rays believe he'll develop into an above-average hitter and produce more power as his body fills out. He's an excellent low-ball hitter and uses the whole field. Jaso's catch-and-throw skills also got noticeably better, as did his ability to work with pitchers. He's an excellent athlete for a catcher, and he also saw time at first base as well as one game at shortstop. Jaso could have a breakout year in low Class A in 2005.

Year	Club (League)	Class	AVG	G	AB	R	H	2B	3B	HR	RBI	BB	SO	SB	OBP	SLG
2003	Hudson Valley (NY-P)	A	.227	47	154	20	35	7	0	2	20	25	26	2	.344	.312
2004	Hudson Valley (NY-P)	A	.302	57	199	34	60	17	2	2	35	22	32	1	.378	.437
MINOR LEAGUE TOTALS			.269	104	353	54	95	24	2	4	55	47	58	3	.363	.382

TEXAS
RANGERS

BY **JOHN MANUEL**

Some things went just the way the Rangers planned in 2004. Powered by an all-star shortstop, they mashed their way into the American League playoff race until the final week of the regular season. The farm system, handed over nearly three years ago to former Athletics scouting director Grady Fuson, started producing dividends. The system provided enough depth to help prop up an injury-riddled pitching staff with fill-ins such as 2002 draftees Kameron Loe and Sam Narron, and trade acquisitions Frankie Francisco and Chris Young. Shortstop Ian Kinsler, a 17th-round pick in 2003, had one of the best seasons in the minors and helped Double-A Frisco win the Texas League championship. Every minor league club had a winning record.

Some things, though, didn't follow the plan. The shortstop in question was Michael Young, as the Rangers changed the face of the organization by dealing Alex Rodriguez to the Yankees in February. And Fuson, once virtually handed the keys to the organization as assistant general manager and John Hart's designated successor as GM, was forced out when Hart decided to return for 2005 after all.

It's not just Hart's show. Manager Buck Showalter also played a major role in convincing owner Tom Hicks that Hart should stay and Fuson should be squeezed out. Together, Hart and Showalter are in charge of the direction of the organization and split Fuson's duties three ways. They elevated 26-year-old Jon Daniels to assistant GM, pro-moted savvy veteran Dom Chiti to farm director and installed Fuson's chief lieutenant, Ron Hopkins, as scouting director.

The changes were subtle but immediate. The tandem-starter system Fuson installed at the lower levels of the organization was halted. Players were pushed more aggressively, and the Rangers signaled a renewed commitment to Latin America.

Fuson's legacy in Texas will be the vastly improved pitching depth he leaves behind. Hart prefers power arms, while Fuson liked power arms only if they also throw strikes. The Rangers likely don't have a future No. 1 starter, but they've acquired a number of quality arms in first-round picks John Danks, Thomas Diamond and Eric Hurley; hard-throwing Dominican Edison Volquez; and 2003 draftees John Hudgins, Wes Littleton and Matt Lorenzo. Such is their depth that the 40-man roster wasn't big enough to include Colby Lewis and Ben Kozlowski, considered the organization's top arms as recently as two years ago. Both were lost on waiver claims.

If the pitching prospects develop sooner rather than later, or if Hart can trade them for big league pitching, Texas should be able to contend for the foreseeable future. The big league infield of **Mark Teixeira**, Alfonso Soriano, Hank Blalock and Young is the American League's best, with Soriano the oldest member at 27.

TOP 30 PROSPECTS

1. Thomas Diamond, rhp	16. Matt Lorenzo, rhp
2. John Danks, lhp	17. Nick Masset, rhp
3. Joaquin Arias, ss	18. Kameron Loe, rhp
4. Ian Kinsler, ss	19. Wes Littleton, rhp
5. Chris Young, rhp	20. K.C. Herren, of
6. John Hudgins, rhp	21. Anthony Webster, of
7. Juan Dominguez, rhp	22. Ramon Nivar, of/2b
8. Adrian Gonzalez, 1b	23. Jason Bourgeois, 2b
9. Josh Rupe, rhp	24. Mike Nickeas, c
10. Vincent Sinisi, of	25. Drew Meyer, ss
11. Jason Botts, 1b/of	26. Erik Thompson, rhp
12. Edison Volquez, rhp	27. John Bannister, rhp
13. Eric Hurley, rhp	28. Nick Regilio, rhp
14. Juan Senreiso, of	29. Jeremy Cleveland, of
15. Michael Schlact, rhp	30. Ryan Wing, lhp

ORGANIZATION OVERVIEW

General manager: John Hart. **Farm director:** Dom Chiti. **Scouting director:** Ron Hopkins.

2004 PERFORMANCE

Class	Team	League	W	L	Pct.	Finish*	Manager
Majors	Texas	American	89	73	.549	6th (14)	Buck Showalter
Triple-A	Oklahoma RedHawks	Pacific Coast	81	63	.563	2nd (16)	Bobby Jones
Double-A	Frisco RoughRiders	Texas	81	59	.579	2nd (8)	Tim Ireland
High A	#Stockton Ports	California	72	68	.514	5th (10)	Arnie Beyeler
Low A	Clinton LumberKings	Midwest	74	64	.536	6th (14)	Carlos Subero
Short-season	Spokane Indians	Northwest	41	35	.539	t-3rd (8)	Darryl Kennedy
Rookie	AZL Rangers	Arizona	32	24	.571	3rd (9)	Pedro Lopez
OVERALL 2004 MINOR LEAGUE RECORD			381	313	.549	3rd (30)	

*Finish in overall standings (No. of teams in league). #Affiliate will be in Bakersfield (California) in 2005.

ORGANIZATION LEADERS

BATTING
*Minimum 250 At-Bats

*AVG	Chad Allen, Oklahoma	.358
R	Ian Kinsler, Frisco/Clinton	103
H	Ian Kinsler, Frisco/Clinton	174
TB	Ian Kinsler, Frisco/Clinton	289
2B	Ian Kinsler, Frisco/Clinton	51
3B	Joaquin Arias, Stockton	8
	Rick Asadoorian, Frisco	8
HR	Jason Botts, Frisco	24
RBI	Ian Kinsler, Frisco/Clinton	99
BB	Jason Botts, Frisco	77
SO	Nate Gold, Stockton	140
	Santiago Perez, Oklahoma/Frisco	140
SB	Cameron Coughlan, Stockton	35
*OBP	Ian Kinsler, Frisco/Clinton	.429
*SLG	Ian Kinsler, Frisco/Clinton	.573

PITCHING
#Minimum 75 Innings

W	Sam Narron, Oklahoma/Frisco	14
L	Three tied at	10
#ERA	Jason Andrew, Oklahoma/Frisco/Stockton	2.59
G	Brad Clontz, Oklahoma	59
CG	John Wasdin, Oklahoma	2
SV	Brad Clontz, Oklahoma	18
IP	Kameron Loe, Oklahoma/Frisco	166
BB	Kelvin Jimenez, Frisco	67
SO	John Hudgins, Oklahoma/Frisco/Stockton	145

BEST TOOLS

Best Hitter for Average	Ian Kinsler
Best Power Hitter	Jason Botts
Best Strike-Zone Discipline	Vincent Sinisi
Fastest Baserunner	Ramon Nivar
Best Athlete	Joaquin Arias
Best Fastball	Thomas Diamond
Best Curveball	John Danks
Best Slider	Travis Hughes
Best Changeup	Juan Dominguez
Best Control	Erik Thompson
Best Defensive Catcher	Mike Nickeas
Best Defensive Infielder	Joaquin Arias
Best Infield Arm	Joaquin Arias
Best Defensive Outfielder	Rick Asadoorian
Best Outfield Arm	Juan Senreiso

PROJECTED 2008 LINEUP

Catcher	Gerald Laird
First Base	Mark Teixeira
Second Base	Michael Young
Third Base	Hank Blalock
Shortstop	Joaquin Arias
Left Field	Richard Hidalgo
Center Field	Laynce Nix

Right Field	Alfonso Soriano
Designated Hitter	Kevin Mench
No. 1 Starter	Ryan Drese
No. 2 Starter	Thomas Diamond
No. 3 Starter	John Danks
No. 4 Starter	Chris Young
No. 5 Starter	Josh Rupe
Closer	Francisco Cordero

LAST YEAR'S TOP 20 PROSPECTS

1. Adrian Gonzalez, 1b	11. Kelvin Jimenez, rhp
2. John Danks, lhp	12. Anthony Webster, of
3. Ramon Nivar, of	13. Ben Kozlowski, lhp
4. Juan Dominguez, rhp	14. Edwin Moreno, rhp
5. Vince Sinisi, of	15. Erik Thompson, rhp
6. Gerald Laird, c	16. C.J. Wilson, lhp
7. Wes Littleton, rhp	17. Kameron Loe, rhp
8. Jason Bourgeois, 2b	18. Will Smith, of
9. Drew Meyer, ss/of	19. Jason Botts, of
10. Josh Rupe, rhp	20. Ryan Snare, lhp

TOP PROSPECTS OF THE DECADE

Year	Player, Pos.	Current Team
1995	Julio Santana, rhp	Out of baseball
1996	Andrew Vessel, of	Out of baseball
1997	Danny Kolb, rhp	Braves
1998	Ruben Mateo, of	Royals
1999	Ruben Mateo, of	Royals
2000	Ruben Mateo, of	Royals
2001	Carlos Pena, 1b	Tigers
2002	Hank Blalock, 3b	Rangers
2003	Mark Teixeira, 3b	Rangers
2004	Adrian Gonzalez, 1b	Rangers

TOP DRAFT PICKS OF THE DECADE

Year	Player, Pos.	Current Team
1995	Jonathan Johnson, rhp	Out of baseball
1996	R.A. Dickey, rhp	Rangers
1997	Jason Romano, 3b	Reds
1998	Carlos Pena, 1b	Tigers
1999	Colby Lewis, rhp	Tigers
2000	Scott Heard, c	Out of baseball
2001	Mark Teixeira, 3b	Rangers
2002	Drew Meyer, ss	Rangers
2003	John Danks, lhp	Rangers
2004	Thomas Diamond, rhp	Rangers

ALL-TIME LARGEST BONUSES

Mark Teixeira, 2001	$4,500,000
John Danks, 2003	$2,100,000
Vincent Sinisi, 2003	$2,070,000
Thomas Diamond, 2004	$2,025,000
Drew Meyer, 2002	$1,875,000

MINOR LEAGUE DEPTH CHART

Texas RANGERS

Impact Potential: C

By their own admission, the Rangers don't have a future ace in their deepened stable of pitchers. However, Thomas Diamond and John Danks both have the stuff to pitch toward the front of a rotation, and both should move fairly quickly. Several Rangers with big upside, such as Latin players Joaquin Arias, Juan Senreiso and Edison Volquez, remain rather raw and less likely to reach their significant potential.

Depth: B

Here's where Grady Fuson, forced out after 2½ years as assistant general manager and leader of the organization's scouting and player-development departments, did the most good. Texas has multiple options at nearly every position but catcher and third, where the big league team is set with Hank Blalock. And the Rangers, perennially pitching-poor, have much greater numbers on the mound—and more quality—though attrition has thinned their ranks of lefthanders.

*Depth charts prepared by **John Manuel** and **Allan Simpson**. Numbers in parentheses indicate prospect rankings.*

LF
Vince Sinisi (10)
Jason Botts (11)
Jeremy Cleveland (29)
Will Smith

CF
K.C. Herren (20)
Anthony Webster (21)
Ramon Nivar (22)
Adam Bourassa

RF
Juan Senreiso (14)
Ben Harrison
Andrew Wishy
Brandon Boggs

3B
Marshall McDougall
Travis Metcalf

SS
Joaquin Arias (3)
Ian Kinsler (4)
Drew Meyer (25)

2B
Jason Bourgeois (23)
Ruddy Yan
Tug Hulett

1B
Adrian Gonzalez (8)
Nate Gold
Jim Fasano
Freddy Thon

SOURCE of TALENT

Homegrown		Acquired	
College	11	Trades	5
Junior College	1	Rule 5 draft	0
Draft-and-follow	2	Independent leagues	0
High school	5	Free agents/waivers	1
Nondrafted free agents	1		
Foreign	4		

C
Mike Nickeas (24)

RHP

Starters	Relievers
Thomas Diamond (1)	Kameron Loe (18)
Chris Young (5)	Erik Thompson (26)
John Hudgins (6)	Travis Hughes
Juan Dominguez (7)	Agustin Montero
Josh Rupe (9)	Edwin Moreno
Edison Volquez (12)	Omar Beltre
Eric Hurley (13)	Chris Jaile
Michael Schlact (15)	
Matt Lorenzo (16)	
Nick Masset (17)	
Wes Littleton (19)	
John Bannister (27)	
Nick Regilio (28)	
Kelvin Jimenez	
Mark Roberts	
Matt Farnum	

LHP

Starters	Relievers
John Danks (2)	Clint Brannon
Ryan Wing (30)	Joel Kirsten
Ryan Snare	Craig Frydendall
Brian Mattoon	
C.J. Wilson	
A.J. Murray	

DRAFT ANALYSIS
2004

Best Pro Debut: LHP Clint Brannon (34) set a short-season Northwest League ERA record (0.59) and had a 58-14 K-BB ratio in 61 innings. RHP Thomas Diamond (1) was more overpowering, with a 2.15 ERA and a 68-13 K-BB ratio in 46 innings, mostly in low Class A. OF K.C. Herren (2) was a Rookie-level Arizona League all-star after batting .297-0-21, while C Mike Nickeas (5) earned recognition in the NWL for hitting .288-10-55. 3B Travis Metcalf (11) led the NWL with 37 extra-base hits, and 2B Tug Hulett (14) led the league with a .444 on-base percentage.

Best Athlete: Washington recruited Herren for baseball and invited him to try out for football as a running back/defensive back. OF Brandon Boggs (4) is a switch-hitter with similarities to Jay Payton, who preceded him at Georgia Tech.

Best Pure Hitter: Herren.

Best Raw Power: OF Ben Harrison (7), 1B Jim Fasano (9) and Metcalf all have plus power. Metcalf hit 15 NWL homers after setting a Kansas record with 18 in the spring.

Fastest Runner: SS Luis Rodriguez (33) has above-average raw speed but it hasn't translated on the bases yet.

Best Defensive Player: Nickeas has an average arm, good hands and decent game-calling skills.

Best Fastball: Diamond never wavered from the mid-90s all year. RHP Eric Hurley (1) threw 92-95 in high school but was tired and not as overpowering as a pro. RHP Jarrad Burcie (16) has a max-effort delivery that allows him to reach 95 out of the pen.

Best Breaking Ball: Hurley's slider is a potential out pitch. Diamond flashes a plus slider at times.

PAUL JASIENSKI

Diamond

Most Intriguing Background: Wolfson High (Jacksonville, Fla.) products Hurley and Royals 3B Billy Butler became the fifth prep teammates to go in the first round of the same draft. INF Wally Backman Jr.'s (30) father was a 1977 Mets first-round pick. Two other draftees are also relatives of former big league infielders: Hulett, son of Tim; and 1B Freddy Thon (18), nephew of Dickie.

Closest To The Majors: Diamond already has proven that low Class A hitters are no match for him, and Texas obviously needs pitching reinforcements.

Best Late-Round Pick: RHP Marc Cornell (19) was mentioned as a possible No. 1 overall pick in 2003, then got side-tracked by shoulder problems that ruined his 2004 season as well. If he returns to health, the Rangers will have a pitcher capable of throwing 93-97 mph.

The One Who Got Away: OF Justin Maxwell (10) went back to Maryland after a snakebitten 2004. He broke his right forearm in preseason drills and never got into a game. Then he went to the Cape Cod League, but a pitch broke his right hand.

Assessment: The Rangers hope to plug pitching holes with Diamond, Hurley and 6-foot-7 RHP Michael Schlact (3). Grady Fuson won't direct future Rangers drafts after losing out in a front-office power play, but new scouting director Ron Hopkins should have a similar approach.

2003 LHP John Danks (1) is just the type of pitching help the Rangers crave. If SS Ian Kinsler's (17) 2004 breakthrough was no fluke, he could be a classic draft steal. RHP John Hudgins (3) and OF Vincent Sinisi (2) also could play key roles in Texas. *GRADE:* B+

2002 SS Drew Meyer (1) was a huge reach, and the Rangers didn't have another pick before the sixth round. This draft rests on the arms of RHP Erik Thompson (12) and LHP Sam Narron (15), lost on waivers to the Brewers. *GRADE:* D

2001 Texas benefited when signability caused 1B Mark Teixeira (1) to last until the fifth pick. The Rangers didn't get anyone else of note, but Teixeira alone earns a top grade. *GRADE:* A

2000 All three first-rounders—C Scott Heard, OF Tyrell Godwin, RHP Chad Hawkins—did little as pros, with Godwin underachieving elsewhere after spurning the Rangers. They regrettably included 3B Edwin Encarnacion (9) in a deal for Rob Bell, leaving them with just OF Laynce Nix (4). *GRADE:* C+

Draft analysis prepared by Jim Callis. Numbers in parentheses indicate draft rounds.

Thomas
DIAMOND

Born: April 6, 1983.
Ht.: 6-3. **Wt.:** 230.
Bats: R. **Throws:** R.
School: University of New Orleans.
Career Transactions: Selected by Rangers in first round (10th overall) of 2004 draft; signed June 29, 2004.
Signed by: Randy Taylor.

Diamond entered 2004 with the goal of being drafted in the first 10 picks. He just squeezed his way in, completing his rise from a little-known 38th-round pick out of high school whose only significant scholarship offer came from New Orleans. With the Privateers, Diamond developed first into a dominant reliever and then into one of college baseball's top starters. Diamond honed his stuff in two summers in the Northwoods League, surpassing Jeff Weaver as the highest-drafted alumnus of that summer league. Diamond was the Northwoods League's No. 1 prospect in 2003, striking out 103 in 72 innings while hitting 97 mph and throwing a no-hitter. He exhibited similar dominance in 2004 for New Orleans and then after signing with the Rangers. Going into the draft, the Rangers' top scouts, Grady Fuson and Ron Hopkins, considered Diamond on the same level as the more-heralded Rice trio of Philip Humber, Jeff Niemann and Wade Townsend, all taken in the first eight picks. And while Diamond got his pro career off to a fine start after agreeing to a $2.025 million bonus, the Rice pitchers either didn't sign at all (Townsend) or signed during the offseason and won't start their careers until the 2005 season.

Diamond can command a fastball with above-average velocity and also shows feel for a changeup, a rare combination for a young pitcher. His fastball sat at 90-94 mph after he signed, and the Rangers like the ease with which he throws and his aggressive use of the pitch. Diamond has smoothed out his mechanics since high school, when he topped out at 92, and now has good deception on both his fastball and changeup. He readily repeats his delivery and has a smooth arm action. His changeup is an above-average pitch, with occasional plus life down in the zone. His strong, physical frame should enable him to be an innings-eating workhorse in the rotation. His ceiling is as a No. 2 or 3 starter.

Diamond's breaking ball is clearly his third pitch. It's not that he doesn't know how to spin the ball, but he hasn't thrown his curveball or slider consistently enough to trust either one. The Rangers are split on which breaking pitch he should use. Some like his curveball better and want him to focus on throwing it harder. He usually throws it out of the zone, hoping hitters will chase. His arm slot has other scouts preferring his slider, which at times has good bite. He threw more curves after signing and apparently prefers that pitch.

He needs experience, but Diamond has the stuff to move quickly. He ate up lower levels because of his fastball command and changeup, and the Rangers are eager to see how that combination plays at higher levels. His mission in spring training will be to pick a breaking ball and stick with it for a year. How well that pitch works will determine whether he spends all year at Texas' new high Class A Bakersfield affiliate or moves up to Double-A Frisco.

Year	Club (League)	Class	W	L	ERA	G	GS	CG	SV	IP	H	R	ER	HR	BB	SO	AVG
2004	Spokane (NWL)	A	0	2	2.35	5	3	0	1	15	13	5	4	0	5	26	.228
	Clinton (Mid)	A	1	0	2.05	7	7	0	0	31	18	8	7	1	8	42	.167
MINOR LEAGUE TOTALS			1	2	2.15	12	10	0	1	46	31	13	11	1	13	68	.188

2 John Danks, lhp

Born: April 15, 1985. **Ht.:** 6-2. **Wt.:** 190. **Bats:** L. **Throws:** L. **School:** Round Rock (Texas) HS. **Career Transactions:** Selected by Rangers in first round (ninth overall) of 2003 draft; signed June 29, 2003. **Signed by:** Randy Taylor.

Danks wasn't good enough to make the roster for scout Randy Taylor's Area Code Games team as a high school junior in 2002. A year later, Taylor and the Rangers drafted him with the ninth overall pick. His younger brother Jordan, an outfielder, is a top prospect for the 2005 draft. Danks has excellent athletic ability and has grown much stronger since Taylor cut him. He throws his fastball at 87-92 mph and projects to throw as hard as 90-95 in the future. His hammer curveball has excellent bite and is the best in the system. The Rangers took away Danks' curveball in spring training to make him work on his changeup, and while it made significant progress, it's still his third pitch. He showed good stuff after a promotion to high Class A Stockton, but he left too many pitches over the plate. He needs to handle in-game adversity better. Danks' spring will determine whether he's pushed to Double-A or returns to the California League.

Year	Club (League)	Class	W	L	ERA	G	GS	CG	SV	IP	H	R	ER	HR	BB	SO	AVG
2003	Rangers (AZL)	R	1	0	0.69	5	3	0	0	13	6	3	1	0	4	22	.136
	Spokane (NWL)	A	0	2	8.53	5	5	0	0	13	12	12	12	0	7	13	.267
2004	Stockton (Cal)	A	1	4	5.24	13	13	0	0	55	62	38	32	5	26	48	.290
	Clinton (Mid)	A	3	2	2.17	14	8	0	0	50	38	17	12	4	14	64	.202
MINOR LEAGUE TOTALS			5	8	3.94	37	29	0	0	130	118	70	57	9	51	147	.240

3 Joaquin Arias, ss

Born: Sept. 21, 1984. **Ht.:** 6-0. **Wt.:** 155. **Bats:** R. **Throws:** R. **Career Transactions:** Signed out of Dominican Republic by Yankees, July 12, 2001 . . . Traded by Yankees to Rangers, April 6, 2004, completing trade in which Yankees received SS Alex Rodriguez from Rangers for 2B Alfonso Soriano and a player to be named (Feb. 14, 2004). **Signed by:** Victor Mata/Carlos Rios/Freddy Tiburcio (Yankees).

Arias will forever be known as part of the Alex Rodriguez trade. He reluctantly left the Yankees organization but settled in after a modest April to bat .300 or better in every month the rest of the way. Arias has superior athletic ability and premium tools in his long, wiry frame. He grades out as average or better across the board, with well-above-average speed and arm strength. While he made 40 errors in high Class A, the Rangers consider him a premium defender with good hands who can make the play in the hole. Arias won't be a weak hitter, but he also won't be an animal. While he has some raw power, he's more of a gap-to-gap hitter. His game needs refinement, from making routine plays to having more quality at-bats and fewer giveaways at the plate due to poor discipline. The Rangers liked Stephen Drew, the top-rated position player in the 2004 draft, but say Arias has better tools, is two years younger and has a better chance to play shortstop in the majors. He'll start 2005 in Double-A.

Year	Club (League)	Class	AVG	G	AB	R	H	2B	3B	HR	RBI	BB	SO	SB	OBP	SLG
2002	Yankees (GCL)	R	.300	57	203	29	61	7	6	0	21	12	16	2	.338	.394
2003	Battle Creek (Mid)	A	.266	130	481	60	128	12	8	3	48	26	44	12	.306	.343
2004	Stockton (Cal)	A	.300	123	500	77	150	20	8	4	62	31	53	30	.344	.396
MINOR LEAGUE TOTALS			.286	310	1184	166	339	39	22	7	131	69	113	44	.328	.374

4 Ian Kinsler, ss

Born: June 22, 1982. **Ht.:** 6-0. **Wt.:** 175. **Bats:** R. **Throws:** R. **School:** University of Missouri. **Career Transactions:** Selected by Rangers in 17th round of 2003 draft; signed June 24, 2003. **Signed by:** Mike Grouse.

Kinsler played at three colleges in three years before settling at Missouri, where in 2003 he helped the Tigers to their first NCAA playoff berth in seven years. An offseason strength program coupled with his already short swing and instruction from Rangers coaches allowed Kinsler's bat to blossom in 2004. He tied for the minor league lead with 51 doubles and has average major league power for a middle infielder. He swings with gusto but still makes consistent contact and gets his share of walks and hit by pitches (18). Kinsler's hands, arm, speed and instincts are all average. That may not be enough for him to stay at shortstop, and second base is his likely future destination. He lost 15 pounds during the season, and he'll have to work to keep his strength up over a full year. No one predicted Kinsler's outburst, but no scout who saw him in 2004 called it a fluke. Doing it again is the challenge, one he likely will face as Triple-A Oklahoma's shortstop.

Year	Club (League)	Class	AVG	G	AB	R	H	2B	3B	HR	RBI	BB	SO	SB	OBP	SLG
2003	Spokane (NWL)	A	.277	51	188	32	52	10	6	1	15	20	34	11	.352	.410
2004	Clinton (Mid)	A	.401	60	227	52	91	30	1	11	53	26	37	16	.465	.687
	Frisco (TL)	AA	.300	71	277	51	83	21	1	9	46	32	47	7	.400	.480
MINOR LEAGUE TOTALS			.327	182	692	135	226	61	8	21	114	78	118	34	.408	.529

5 Chris Young, rhp

Born: May 25, 1979. **Ht.:** 6-10. **Wt.:** 250. **Bats:** R. **Throws:** R. **School:** Princeton University. **Career Transactions:** Selected by Pirates in third round of 2000 draft; signed Sept. 6, 2000 . . . Traded by Pirates with RHP Jon Searles to Expos for RHP Matt Herges, Dec. 20, 2002 . . . Traded by Expos with C Josh McKinley to Rangers for C Einar Diaz, RHP Justin Echols and cash, April 3, 2004. **Signed by:** Dana Brown (Pirates).

An all-Ivy League center, Young's basketball potential has paid off for him in baseball. He signed with the Pirates for $1.65 million in 2000, then got a three-year, $1.5 million contract extension from the Rangers last fall after the NBA's Sacramento Kings approached him. An athletic giant, Young always has had good command and the ability to repeat his delivery. Minor league pitching coaches Steve Luebber and Glenn Abbott tweaked his mechanics, changing his arm angle so Young could throw on a better downhill plane. The more he worked off his fastball, the harder he threw it, and he regularly hit 95 mph in the majors. Young used to rely more on a solid-average curveball and developing changeup. With his new delivery and approach, his feel for his secondary stuff slipped a bit. As long as Young is healthy and throwing like he did in the second half in 2004, he should earn a spot in Texas' 2005 rotation.

Year	Club (League)	Class	W	L	ERA	G	GS	CG	SV	IP	H	R	ER	HR	BB	SO	AVG
2001	Hickory (SAL)	A	5	3	4.12	12	12	2	0	74	79	39	34	6	20	72	.269
2002	Hickory (SAL)	A	11	9	3.11	26	26	1	0	145	127	57	50	11	34	136	.234
2003	Brevard County (FSL)	A	5	2	1.62	8	8	0	0	50	26	9	9	3	5	39	.150
	Harrisburg (EL)	AA	4	4	4.01	15	15	0	0	83	83	39	37	9	22	64	.259
2004	Frisco (TL)	AA	6	5	4.48	18	18	0	0	88	94	48	44	9	31	75	.269
	Texas (AL)	MAJ	3	2	4.71	7	7	0	0	36	36	21	19	7	10	27	.250
	Oklahoma (PCL)	AAA	3	0	1.48	5	5	1	0	30	20	7	5	2	9	34	.189
MAJOR LEAGUE TOTALS			3	2	4.71	7	7	0	0	36	36	21	19	7	10	27	.250
MINOR LEAGUE TOTALS			34	23	3.42	84	84	4	0	471	429	199	179	40	121	420	.240

6 John Hudgins, rhp

Born: Aug. 31, 1981. **Ht.:** 6-2. **Wt.:** 195. **Bats:** R. **Throws:** R. **School:** Stanford University. **Career Transactions:** Selected by Rangers in third round of 2003 draft; signed July 17, 2003. **Signed by:** Tim Fortugno.

Hudgins earned Most Outstanding Player honors in the 2003 College World Series with three victories in 10 days. He pitched just two innings in his first pro summer because of thoracic outlet syndrome, a circulatory condition he overcame without surgery. Cerebral and competitive, Hudgins knows how to use and command his average stuff. His best pitch is his changeup, which should develop into an above-average pitch due to its movement and deception. He has the confidence to throw it in any count. His solid-average curve also could become a plus pitch. He pounds the strike zone with an 87-91 mph fastball and average slider. Hudgins' fastball can reach 93 mph, but it also can be ordinary. Always searching for an edge, Hudgins toyed with a cutter and a split-finger fastball in the Arizona Fall League. He could arrive in Arlington in the second half of 2005.

Year	Club (League)	Class	W	L	ERA	G	GS	CG	SV	IP	H	R	ER	HR	BB	SO	AVG
2003	Clinton (Mid)	A	0	0	0.00	1	0	0	0	2	1	0	0	0	0	4	.143
2004	Stockton (Cal)	A	3	1	2.35	15	11	0	0	65	49	19	17	4	18	73	.201
	Frisco (TL)	AA	5	3	3.13	12	12	0	0	69	57	29	24	12	18	64	.226
	Oklahoma (PCL)	AAA	0	1	7.50	3	2	0	0	12	19	10	10	1	5	8	.365
MINOR LEAGUE TOTALS			8	5	3.10	31	25	0	0	148	126	58	51	17	41	149	.227

7 Juan Dominguez, rhp

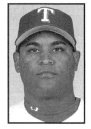

Born: May 18, 1980. **Ht.:** 6-2. **Wt.:** 180. **Bats:** R. **Throws:** R. **Career Transactions:** Signed out of Dominican Republic by Rangers, Dec. 26, 1999. **Signed by:** Rodolfo Rosario.

Dominguez had a roller-coaster season. He earned his first big league victory in late May at Yankee Stadium. After missing almost two months with a strained back, he finished the season on the disabled list with a right knee injury, a stint the Rangers extended as Dominguez struggled to deal with the death of his mother. Dominguez has two above-average big league pitches with a 91-96 mph fastball and a plus-plus changeup with good tumble. Both pitches look the same leaving his hand, and he's tougher on left-handers than righthanders. Dominguez' lack of maturity chafed the big league staff. That's a bigger problem than his fringy slider, which made progress and at times was an average pitch in 2004. It's fair to say Dominguez has nothing left to prove in the minors. The Rangers are counting on him to earn a spot in the big league rotation out of spring training.

Year	Club (League)	Class	W	L	ERA	G	GS	CG	SV	IP	H	R	ER	HR	BB	SO	AVG
2000	Rangers (DSL)	R	1	6	4.52	14	14	0	0	68	69	49	34	2	38	56	.253
2001	Rangers (GCL)	R	4	2	4.01	11	9	1	0	58	56	29	26	4	12	55	.250
	Charlotte (FSL)	A	1	0	3.60	2	0	0	0	5	4	2	2	1	1	5	.235
2002	Rangers (DSL)	R	0	0	0.00	1	1	0	0	1	1	0	0	0	0	0	.250
	Savannah (SAL)	A	1	3	2.16	16	9	0	1	67	50	23	16	4	21	70	.209
2003	Stockton (Cal)	A	4	0	2.84	16	9	0	1	63	55	27	20	3	16	72	.226
	Frisco (TL)	AA	5	0	2.60	9	9	0	0	55	35	17	16	2	21	54	.178
	Oklahoma (PCL)	AAA	1	0	3.50	3	3	0	0	18	15	7	7	1	3	14	.227
	Texas (AL)	MAJ	0	2	7.16	6	3	0	0	16	16	14	13	5	12	13	.271
2004	Frisco (TL)	AA	0	0	1.08	3	2	0	0	8	4	1	1	0	1	11	.143
	Oklahoma (PCL)	AAA	5	1	3.13	9	9	1	0	55	41	20	19	3	19	41	.205
	Texas (AL)	MAJ	1	2	3.91	4	4	0	0	23	25	11	10	2	5	14	.281
MAJOR LEAGUE TOTALS			1	4	5.26	10	7	0	0	39	41	25	23	7	17	27	.277
MINOR LEAGUE TOTALS			22	12	3.19	84	65	2	2	398	330	175	141	20	132	378	.221

8 Adrian Gonzalez, 1b

Born: May 8, 1982. **Ht.:** 6-2. **Wt.:** 190. **Bats:** L. **Throws:** L. **School:** Eastlake HS, Chula Vista, Calif. **Career Transactions:** Selected by Marlins in first round (first overall) of 2000 draft; signed June 6, 2000 . . . Traded by Marlins with OF Will Smith and LHP Ryan Snare to Rangers for RHP Ugueth Urbina, July 11, 2003. **Signed by:** David Finley (Marlins).

Gonzalez was the No. 1 overall pick in 2000, a signability choice that looks better in retrospect as that draft's first round appears to be the worst since 1975's historically poor crop. Texas acquired Gonzalez from the Marlins for Ugueth Urbina in a July 2003 trade. Gonzalez is a natural with the bat. He has a smooth, sweet lefthanded swing that gives him the ability to hit line drives from foul pole to foul pole. He's outstanding defensively at first with soft hands, an accurate arm and good footwork. His total package resembles that of Doug Mientkiewicz. Some scouts have never believed in Gonzalez' power, and his modest slugging numbers against Triple-A and major league pitching didn't allay those fears. Never blessed with a great body, he's a poor runner who remains soft and needs to hit the weight room. With Mark Teixeira ahead of him and powerful Jason Botts behind him, Gonzalez needs to make a move in 2005. He'll probably start the year back in Triple-A.

Year	Club (League)	Class	AVG	G	AB	R	H	2B	3B	HR	RBI	BB	SO	SB	OBP	SLG
2000	Utica (NYP)	A	.310	8	29	7	9	3	0	0	3	7	6	0	.444	.414
	Marlins (GCL)	R	.295	53	193	24	57	10	1	0	30	32	35	0	.397	.358
2001	Kane County (Mid)	A	.312	127	516	86	161	37	1	17	103	57	83	5	.382	.486
2002	Portland (EL)	AA	.266	138	508	70	135	34	1	17	96	54	112	6	.344	.437
2003	Albuquerque (PCL)	AAA	.216	39	139	17	30	5	1	1	18	14	25	1	.286	.288
	Carolina (SL)	AA	.307	36	137	15	42	9	1	1	16	14	25	1	.368	.409
	Frisco (TL)	AA	.283	45	173	16	49	6	2	3	17	11	27	0	.326	.393
2004	Oklahoma (PCL)	AAA	.304	123	457	61	139	28	3	12	88	39	73	1	.364	.457
	Texas (AL)	MAJ	.238	16	42	7	10	3	0	1	7	2	6	0	.273	.381
MAJOR LEAGUE TOTALS			.238	16	42	7	10	3	0	1	7	2	6	0	.273	.381
MINOR LEAGUE TOTALS			.289	569	2152	296	622	132	10	51	371	228	386	14	.360	.431

9 Josh Rupe, rhp

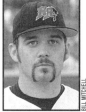

Born: Aug. 18, 1982. **Ht.:** 6-2. **Wt.:** 195. **Bats:** R. **Throws:** R. **School:** Louisburg (N.C.) JC. **Career Transactions:** Selected by White Sox in third round of 2002 draft; signed June 14, 2002 . . . Traded by White Sox with OF Anthony Webster and RHP Franklin Francisco to Rangers, July 24, 2003, completing trade in which Rangers sent OF Carl Everett and cash to White Sox for three players to be named (July 1, 2003). **Signed by:** John Tumminia (White Sox).

Rupe grew up playing with and against some of the game's top young talent, such as B.J. Upton, in Virginia's Tidewater region. He joined the Rangers in the fruitful Carl Everett trade in 2003 that also netted Franklin Francisco and Anthony Webster. Rupe missed two months with a forearm strain in 2004 but had a healthy, productive second half. He has shown four quality pitches. The best is his cut fastball, which he throws at 87-88 mph when it's at its best. His low-90s fastball works well when he keeps it down in the zone. He throws his solid curveball and changeup for strikes. Rupe needs to work off his fastball more and harness his command of the pitch. At times, he flies open with his front shoulder and drags his arm. When Rupe realizes that he can succeed without throwing 95 mph, staying healthy will be his biggest obstacle. Ticketed for Double-A to start 2005, he can become a middle-of-the-rotation starter.

Year	Club (League)	Class	W	L	ERA	G	GS	CG	SV	IP	H	R	ER	HR	BB	SO	AVG
2002	Bristol (Appy)	R	3	3	5.26	17	2	0	0	38	38	23	22	4	22	40	.260
2003	Kannapolis (SAL)	A	5	5	3.02	26	7	2	6	66	50	27	22	0	36	69	.212
	Clinton (Mid)	A	4	1	3.90	6	5	0	0	28	29	14	12	1	7	23	.266
2004	Frisco (TL)	AA	2	2	4.38	7	6	0	0	37	41	23	18	5	16	16	.277
	Spokane (NWL)	A	2	0	1.50	4	3	0	0	18	14	3	3	1	3	19	.209
	Stockton (Cal)	A	2	0	0.98	4	3	0	0	18	12	4	2	0	4	14	.182
MINOR LEAGUE TOTALS			18	11	3.48	64	26	2	6	204	184	94	79	11	88	181	.238

10 Vincent Sinisi, of

STEVE MOORE

Born: Nov. 7, 1981. **Ht.:** 6-0. **Wt.:** 203. **Bats:** L. **Throws:** L. **School:** Rice University. **Career Transactions:** Selected by Rangers in second round of 2003 draft; signed Aug. 11, 2003. **Signed by:** Randy Taylor.

Sinisi was Rice's best hitter for two seasons and helped the Owls win the 2003 national championship. He dropped to the second round that June because of signability concerns and agreed to a $2.07 million bonus, almost double the next-largest bonus in the round. Sinisi's first full season ended in mid-June when he broke his left forearm in a collision with Joaquin Arias, and the arm took longer than normal to heal because the break had to be reset. Before he got hurt, Sinisi showed the hitting ability the Rangers coveted. He has a pure lefthanded swing, a smooth stroke that leaves the bat head in the strike zone for a long time. He's short to the ball, hits the ball on the screws consistently and isn't afraid to take a walk or go the other way. His power doesn't wow anyone yet. While it's often the last tool to come, scouts aren't unanimous in believing Sinisi's will develop. His below-average speed limits him to left field or first base. He wasn't healthy enough to swing the bat in instructional league, so he may start slowly in spring training while shaking off rust. His spring performance will determine when he gets his first taste of Double-A.

Year	Club (League)	Class	AVG	G	AB	R	H	2B	3B	HR	RBI	BB	SO	SB	OBP	SLG
2003	Stockton (Cal)	A	.258	14	62	9	16	1	0	1	5	3	8	1	.288	.323
2004	Stockton (Cal)	A	.310	63	248	39	77	13	3	7	40	33	45	7	.383	.472
MINOR LEAGUE TOTALS			.300	77	310	48	93	14	3	8	45	36	53	8	.365	.442

11 Jason Botts, 1b/of

Born: July 26, 1980. **Ht.:** 6-5. **Wt.:** 253. **Bats:** B. **Throws:** R. **School:** Glendale (Calif.) JC. **Career Transactions:** Selected by Rangers in 46th round of 1999 draft; signed May 15, 2000. **Signed by:** Tim Fortugno.

Previously known more for his size and upside, Botts turned potential into production in 2004. He may not cover 60 yards in 6.6 seconds as he did when he first turned pro, but Texas much prefers that Botts is a better hitter now from both sides of the plate. Particularly powerful as a righthanded hitter, Botts has shortened up his swing. At 6-foot-6 with long arms, he still has holes, however. Always a patient hitter, he's learning when to be more aggressive and pounce in hitter's counts, rather than just working walks. Botts continued his development in the Arizona Fall League, playing left field after spending the entire regular season at first. Botts is just adequate defensively at either spot. While he's athletic and still has slightly above-average speed once he gets going, he's not particularly fluid either at the plate or in the field. His work ethic and aptitude have the Rangers excited that Botts can help as a reserve if needed in 2005. If he's not, he'll be ready at Triple-A.

Year	Club (League)	Class	AVG	G	AB	R	H	2B	3B	HR	RBI	BB	SO	SB	OBP	SLG
2000	Rangers (GCL)	R	.319	48	163	36	52	12	0	6	34	26	29	4	.440	.503
2001	Savannah (SAL)	A	.309	114	392	63	121	24	2	9	50	53	88	13	.416	.449
	Charlotte (FSL)	A	.167	4	12	1	2	1	0	0	0	4	4	0	.375	.250
2002	Charlotte (FSL)	A	.254	116	401	67	102	22	5	9	54	75	99	7	.387	.401
2003	Stockton (Cal)	A	.314	76	283	58	89	14	2	9	61	45	59	12	.409	.473
	Frisco (TL)	AA	.263	55	194	26	51	11	1	4	27	21	45	6	.341	.392
2004	Frisco (TL)	AA	.293	133	481	85	141	25	3	24	92	77	126	7	.399	.507
MINOR LEAGUE TOTALS			.290	546	1926	336	558	109	13	61	318	301	450	49	.399	.455

12 Edison Volquez, rhp

Born: July 3, 1983. **Ht.:** 6-1. **Wt.:** 160. **Bats:** R. **Throws:** R. **Career Transactions:** Signed out of Dominican Republic by Rangers, Oct. 29, 2001. **Signed by:** Rodolfo Rosario.

Volquez earns comparisons to Pedro Martinez because he's Dominican and has long fingers, and he studies his idol on television and in video games. Formerly known as Julio Reyes, his name and birthdate (he was 15½ months older than believed) came to light as part of the crackdown on visas. He's still advanced for his age and has a significant ceiling if he can hold up as a starter. Volquez has realized that even with a 90-93 mph fastball that touches 95, he can't pitch up in the strike zone. Blessed with a quick, loose arm, he always has had good life on his fastball, and he became more consistent in throwing it for strikes. His improved command stemmed from better strength, allowing him to maintain his mechanics in games and over the course of the season. Volquez also has a plus changeup and solid slider. He still gets inconsistent with his arm slot, and the Rangers want to see him maintain his stuff over a full season again. He could move up to Double-A to start 2005 with a big spring.

Year	Club (League)	Class	W	L	ERA	G	GS	CG	SV	IP	H	R	ER	HR	BB	SO	AVG
2002	Rangers (DSL)	R	1	2	2.68	14	8	0	0	47	45	19	14	1	14	58	.254
2003	Rangers (AZL)	R	2	1	4.00	10	4	0	0	27	24	14	12	1	11	28	.245
2004	Clinton (Mid)	A	4	4	4.21	21	15	0	0	88	82	49	41	8	27	74	.245
	Stockton (Cal)	A	4	1	2.95	8	8	0	0	40	31	16	13	6	14	34	.214
MINOR LEAGUE TOTALS			11	8	3.58	53	35	0	0	201	182	98	80	16	66	194	.241

13 Eric Hurley, rhp

Born: Sept. 17, 1985. **Ht.:** 6-4. **Wt.:** 195. **Bats:** R. **Throws:** R. **School:** Wolfson HS, Jacksonville. **Career Transactions:** Selected by Rangers in first round (30th overall) of 2004 draft; signed June 18, 2004. **Signed by:** Guy DeMutis.

Jacksonville's Wolfson High became the fifth high school to produce two first-round picks in the same draft, as Billy Butler (14th overall, Royals) and Hurley (30th) improved their stock last spring. Hurley showed one of the best fastballs in the high school ranks. He regularly touched 96 mph, and in one outing several scouts clocked him at 97 three times in the seventh inning. That kind of velocity endears him to Rangers general manager John Hart, who loves power arms. Hurley didn't show the same velocity after signing for $1.05 million, topping out at 92-93 mph. Texas attributed it to pitching more than he had previously and expects his fastball to bounce back. He has a loose arm and projectable frame that should get stronger down the line. Hurley has a hard slider that can be an above-average power pitch, but he doesn't have much of a changeup. Hurley's detractors in the draft pointed to his delivery—his head jerks to one side—which causes him to drop and drag his arm, adversely affecting his velocity and control. The Rangers pushed Hurley aggressively in his first season and plan to start him out at low Class A Clinton in 2005.

Year	Club (League)	Class	W	L	ERA	G	GS	CG	SV	IP	H	R	ER	HR	BB	SO	AVG
2004	Rangers (AZL)	R	0	1	2.35	6	2	0	0	15	20	8	4	1	4	15	.317
	Spokane (NWL)	A	0	2	5.40	8	6	0	0	28	31	18	17	6	6	21	.279
MINOR LEAGUE TOTALS			0	3	4.33	14	8	0	0	44	51	26	21	7	10	36	.304

14 Juan Senreiso, of

Born: Aug. 4, 1981. **Ht.:** 6-1. **Wt.:** 170. **Bats:** R. **Throws:** R. **Career Transactions:** Signed out of Dominican Republic by Rangers, Jan. 25, 2000. **Signed by:** Danilo Troncoso.

Senreiso has had the best package of tools in the system since coming to the United States in 2001. He's another Dominican whose name (formerly known as Julin Charles) and age (thought to be 10 months younger) changed when he was forced to use his real identity. A career .238 hitter entering 2004, he made immense strides and finished the season in Double-A. Blessed with strong, quick hands that give him excellent bat speed, Senreiso benefited as much as any Rangers farmhand from the organization's emphasis on plate discipline. He still doesn't draw tons of walks, but he improved, made more consistent contact and started to unlock his power. He has good speed, though he needs to be a more efficient baserunner. While he has center-field tools, his routes and instincts aren't good enough for the position. He profiles better in right field, where his above-average arm would play well. Senreiso remains raw, as evidenced by his .181 average and 24 strikeouts in 83 at-bats in the Arizona Fall League, so the Rangers left him off their 40-man roster. No one took him in the Rule 5 draft, so he'll return to Double-A and see if he can build on his momentum.

Year	Club (League)	Class	AVG	G	AB	R	H	2B	3B	HR	RBI	BB	SO	SB	OBP	SLG
2000	Rangers (DSL)	R	.274	66	263	28	72	10	3	2	32	17	44	19	.325	.357
2001	Rangers (GCL)	R	.241	52	187	23	45	15	4	1	22	12	41	17	.287	.380
2002	Savannah (SAL)	A	.161	8	31	4	5	0	0	0	2	2	11	0	.212	.226
	Pulaski (Appy)	R	.253	62	241	40	61	12	2	8	44	20	61	18	.321	.419
2003	Clinton (Mid)	A	.216	121	473	48	102	18	4	5	58	30	117	45	.265	.302
2004	Clinton (Mid)	A	.315	33	127	20	40	10	2	2	23	16	31	12	.390	.472
	Stockton (Cal)	A	.296	56	233	36	69	12	2	6	32	15	47	12	.344	.442
	Frisco (TL)	AA	.348	11	46	7	16	1	1	2	5	2	7	0	.375	.543
MINOR LEAGUE TOTALS			.256	409	1601	206	410	78	19	26	216	114	359	123	.310	.377

15 Michael Schlact, rhp

Born: Dec. 9, 1985. **Ht.:** 6-7. **Wt.:** 205. **Bats:** R. **Throws:** R. **School:** Wheeler HS, Marietta, Ga. **Career Transactions:** Selected by Rangers in third round of 2004 draft; signed June 26, 2004. **Signed by:** John Castleberry.

Schlact went to the same high school that yielded first-rounders Josh Burrus (Braves, 2001) and Jeremy Hermida (Marlins, 2002). Schlact didn't quite make it into the first round, but a $455,000 bonus persuaded him to bypass a scholarship to South Carolina. Long, lean and loose-limbed, Schlact is nowhere near a finished product. His fastball has touched 95 mph at times, but he's more regularly in the 87-92 range, velocity he has shown an ability to maintain for six or seven innings. He's coordinated and athletic for such a tall pitcher and has a good feel for his body, resulting in sound mechanics and good control of his fastball. His next-best offering currently is his changeup. He has to tighten up his slurvy curveball, his third pitch. Schlact got off to a great start in the spring before tiring late and needs to get stronger. He should join first-rounder Eric Hurley in the low Class A rotation this spring.

Year	Club (League)	Class	W	L	ERA	G	GS	CG	SV	IP	H	R	ER	HR	BB	SO	AVG
2004	Rangers (AZL)	R	1	1	3.52	10	5	0	0	31	32	18	12	0	9	22	.264
MINOR LEAGUE TOTALS			1	1	3.52	10	5	0	0	31	32	18	12	0	9	22	.264

16 Matt Lorenzo, rhp

Born: June 21, 1982. **Ht.:** 6-3. **Wt.:** 200. **Bats:** L. **Throws:** R. **School:** Kent State University. **Career Transactions:** Selected by Rangers in fifth round of 2003 draft; signed June 10, 2003. **Signed by:** Mark Giegler.

Lorenzo spent his freshman year at Georgia Tech before transferring to Kent State to get more innings. He finished his first full pro season by dealing in the Arizona Fall League and continues to stick out among Texas' flock of pitching prospects whose calling card is their approach. Though he's big and physical, Lorenzo's fastball usually sits at 82-92 mph. It did jump to 93-95 mph when he worked shorter stints in the AFL. His overhand curveball doesn't have true 12-to-6 break, but it's still a plus pitch. He gets strikeouts with his curve because he throws it in the low to mid-80s with good depth. His bender is at its best when he stays on top of it and throws it from the same arm slot as his fastball. Lorenzo flashes above-average command of both pitches and maintained his velocity better than he had in the past. Now he needs to pick up the feel for a changeup. His change has nice movement, but he has to throw it more consistently for strikes and learn to trust it more often. He's one of several candidates for the Double-A rotation in 2005.

Year	Club (League)	Class	W	L	ERA	G	GS	CG	SV	IP	H	R	ER	HR	BB	SO	AVG
2003	Spokane (NWL)	A	5	1	2.53	16	12	0	0	57	43	19	16	2	22	54	.216
2004	Stockton (Cal)	A	1	3	4.60	9	8	0	0	43	42	27	22	3	11	39	.253
	Clinton (Mid)	A	3	7	4.06	17	13	0	0	71	65	35	32	8	22	90	.239
MINOR LEAGUE TOTALS			9	11	3.68	42	33	0	0	171	150	81	70	13	55	183	.235

17 Nick Masset, rhp

Born: May 17, 1982. **Ht.:** 6-4. **Wt.:** 230. **Bats:** R. **Throws:** R. **School:** St. Petersburg (Fla.) CC. **Career Transactions:** Selected by Rangers in eighth round of 2000 draft; signed May 28, 2001. **Signed by:** Jackson Ray.

Masset was a top prospect for the 2000 draft until he had Tommy John surgery as a high school senior. The Rangers drafted him anyway out of Pinellas Park High in Largo, Fla., and signed him the following May for $225,000 after a year of junior college. He hadn't given the club much of a return on its investment, however, until 2004. After missing two months early last season due to a cyst on his right wrist related to his weight-room work, Masset made strides with his maturity and regained his feel for pitching and his confidence. Texas worked with him to lengthen his stride, which improved his balance and ability to stay tall in his delivery. Masset throws four pitches for strikes now. Both of his fastballs—an 89-91 mph two-seamer and a four-seamer that reaches 93—feature good movement. He uses both a curveball and a hard slider, and his changeup can be an average pitch when he commands it. Masset won't be a frontline starter, but he does have big league stuff. Now it's a matter of proving he can stay healthy and maintain success for a full season. The Rangers praise his tough mound demeanor and think he can be a middle-of-the-rotation workhorse. He was protected on the 40-man roster and should start the year in a crowded Double-A rotation.

Year	Club (League)	Class	W	L	ERA	G	GS	CG	SV	IP	H	R	ER	HR	BB	SO	AVG
2001	Rangers (GCL)	R	0	6	4.35	15	14	0	0	31	34	21	15	2	7	32	.281
2002	Savannah (SAL)	A	5	8	4.56	33	16	0	0	120	129	75	61	11	47	93	.276
2003	Clinton (Mid)	A	7	7	4.08	30	20	0	2	124	144	75	56	7	43	63	.292

2004	Frisco (TL)	AA	1	0	1.80	2	1	0	0	10	8	2	2	0	4	8	.242
	Stockton (Cal)	A	6	5	3.51	16	11	0	0	77	71	38	30	6	19	43	.241
MINOR LEAGUE TOTALS			19	26	4.08	96	62	0	2	362	386	211	164	26	120	239	.274

18 Kameron Loe, rhp

Born: Sept. 10, 1981. **Ht.:** 6-8. **Wt.:** 225. **Bats:** R. **Throws:** R. **School:** Cal State Northridge. **Career Transactions:** Selected by Rangers in 20th round of 2002 draft; signed June 8, 2002. **Signed by:** Todd Guggiana.

The Rangers' 2002 draft, the first under Grady Fuson's leadership, has produced a mixed bag. Just three of the first seven players Fuson picked are still in the system. But after wasting $550,000 on 11th-rounder Kiki Bengochea, Texas found three pitchers with value. Loe (20th round) and Erik Thompson (12th) are on this list, and Sam Narron (15th) reached the big leagues in 2004 before being lost on waivers to the Brewers. Loe arrived in Texas shortly after Narron, finishing the year in the bullpen. While he's been a solid starter, the angular Loe figures to be a reliever in the majors. The Rangers have experimented with raising his arm angle, but Loe's strength is his command of a high-80s sinker. He has a deceptive delivery and the ability to throw his plus slider in any count. Righthanders have trouble elevating the ball against him (six homers in 354 at-bats in the minors last year), but lefties have had more success. The Rangers haven't given up on Loe as a starter, but he fits the profile of a right-on-right middle reliever perfectly and could fill that role in Texas as soon as 2005.

Year	Club (League)	Class	W	L	ERA	G	GS	CG	SV	IP	H	R	ER	HR	BB	SO	AVG
2002	Pulaski (APP)	R	4	4	4.47	14	11	0	1	58	64	34	29	3	17	55	.271
2003	Clinton (Mid)	A	4	3	1.95	23	11	0	2	97	78	34	21	3	19	94	.217
	Stockton (Cal)	A	3	0	0.96	9	4	0	1	38	26	7	4	1	6	31	.183
2004	Frisco (TL)	AA	7	7	3.10	19	19	0	0	113	122	42	39	5	29	97	.280
	Oklahoma (PCL)	AAA	5	2	3.27	8	8	0	0	52	52	20	19	6	13	42	.265
	Texas (AL)	MAJ	0	0	5.40	2	1	0	0	7	6	5	4	0	6	3	.273
MAJOR LEAGUE TOTALS			0	0	5.40	2	1	0	0	7	6	5	4	0	6	3	.273
MINOR LEAGUE TOTALS			23	16	2.81	73	53	0	4	359	342	137	112	18	84	319	.250

19 Wes Littleton, rhp

Born: Sept. 2, 1982. **Ht.:** 6-3. **Wt.:** 205. **Bats:** R. **Throws:** R. **School:** Cal State Fullerton. **Career Transactions:** Selected by Rangers in fourth round of 2003 draft; signed June 29, 2003. **Signed by:** Steve Flores.

Littleton entered 2004 with great expectations, but by his own admission his season didn't go as planned. He had an up-and-down career at Cal State Fullerton, where his junior year was interrupted by a suspension. He made a strong pro debut, dominating the short-season Northwest League, but a jump to high Class A didn't go as well. California League hitters pounced on Littleton's 88-92 fastball, which he left up in the strike zone too frequently. He kept opening up his front shoulder, losing his arm slot and causing his once-lively heater to flatten out. He made adjustments as the year went on, but he didn't get ahead of enough hitters to put them away with his slurvy, sweeping slider and inconsistent changeup (which can be a plus pitch at times). Littleton's low three-quarters arm angle is a big reason for his success because it helps give his fastball life and his slider its bite. But as with Kameron Loe, it also allows lefthanders a good look at his pitches. They hit .316 against him last year, compared to .224 by righthanders. Littleton showed progress in the Arizona Fall League, hitting 94 mph while pitching in relief. That may be his best long-term role.

Year	Club (League)	Class	W	L	ERA	G	GS	CG	SV	IP	H	R	ER	HR	BB	SO	AVG
2003	Spokane (NWL)	A	6	0	1.56	12	8	0	0	52	36	9	9	2	8	47	.198
2004	Stockton (Cal)	A	8	10	4.15	30	23	0	0	141	139	76	65	7	56	72	.263
MINOR LEAGUE TOTALS			14	10	3.45	42	31	0	0	193	175	85	74	9	64	119	.246

20 K.C. Herren, of

Born: Aug. 21, 1985. **Ht.:** 6-0. **Wt.:** 210. **Bats:** L. **Throws:** R. **School:** Auburn (Wash.) HS. **Career Transactions:** Selected by Rangers in second round of 2004 draft; signed June 26, 2004. **Signed by:** Gary McGraw.

Herren was a surprise second-round pick in 2004, but the Rangers had the inside track on him. Area scout Gary McGraw followed him closely when he played in the Seattle-area Taylor Baseball amateur program that has produced three other second-rounders in the last four drafts: Andy Sisco (Cubs) and Alhaji Turay (Mets) in 2001, Jon Lester (Red Sox) in 2002. Herren led Auburn (Wash.) High to an undefeated regular season as a senior last spring, when Rangers scouting director and Seattle native Ron Hopkins began following him closely. Herren's solid tools across the board, most notably his bat, earned him a $675,000 bonus. He turned down a baseball scholarship from Washington, which also was open to him trying out for its football team as a running back/defensive back. Herren sprays line drives all over the field with a short, compact stroke, and his gap power should turn into average home run power when he matures physically. He gets good reads and jumps in center field, making him a plus defender, and he owns an accurate if not overly strong arm. His speed will be key, because he probably won't have enough power to be a corner outfielder. Herren's first full-season test will come in low Class A this year.

Year	Club (League)	Class	AVG	G	AB	R	H	2B	3B	HR	RBI	BB	SO	SB	OBP	SLG
2004	Rangers (AZL)	R	.297	46	185	32	55	13	2	0	21	24	54	7	.381	.389
MINOR LEAGUE TOTALS			.297	46	185	32	55	13	2	0	21	24	54	7	.381	.389

21 Anthony Webster, of

Born: April 10, 1983. **Ht.:** 6-0. **Wt.:** 204. **Bats:** L. **Throws:** R. **School:** Riverside HS, Parsons, Tenn. **Career Transactions:** Selected by White Sox in 15th round of 2001 draft; signed June 16, 2001 . . . Traded by White Sox with RHP Josh Rupe and RHP Franklin Francisco to Rangers, July 24, 2003, completing trade in which Rangers sent OF Carl Everett and cash to White Sox for three players to be named (July 1, 2003). **Signed by:** Larry Grefer (White Sox).

Webster ranked as the third-best prospect in the White Sox system entering 2003, the year he came to the Rangers in a fruitful trade for Carl Everett. Webster remains a work in progress, so raw that Texas left him off its 40-man roster and no club took him in the Rule 5 draft. A Tennessee high school football star as a tailback, he still looks too much like a football player. Webster does have plenty of tools. He's an above-average runner, has good enough bat speed that some scouts project plus power, and he has the range and arm to be a solid center fielder. He still has to put his tools to use. Webster's swing can get long, leaving him vulnerable to fastballs inside, and he's still struggling to work his way into hitter's counts. He doesn't take good routes in center, and his lack of instincts eventually may relegate him to left field (his arm is just average). He missed six weeks of crucial development time last season with a groin injury. The Rangers still lack depth in center field, so they hold out hope that Webster will refine his game in Double-A this year.

Year	Club (League)	Class	AVG	G	AB	R	H	2B	3B	HR	RBI	BB	SO	SB	OBP	SLG
2001	White Sox (AZL)	R	.307	55	225	38	69	9	7	0	30	9	33	18	.332	.409
2002	Bristol (Appy)	R	.352	61	244	58	86	7	3	1	30	38	38	16	.448	.418
2003	Kannapolis (SAL)	A	.289	94	363	68	105	18	1	2	33	31	58	20	.353	.361
	Clinton (Mid)	A	.270	18	74	11	20	7	0	1	9	0	8	4	.286	.405
2004	Stockton (Cal)	A	.287	99	380	66	109	20	7	8	44	39	69	20	.363	.439
MINOR LEAGUE TOTALS			.302	327	1286	241	389	61	18	12	146	117	206	78	.368	.406

22 Ramon Nivar, of/2b

Born: Feb. 22, 1980. **Ht.:** 5-10. **Wt.:** 170. **Bats:** R. **Throws:** R. **Career Transactions:** Signed out of Dominican Republic by Rangers, Jan. 25, 1998. **Signed by:** Hector Acevedo.

Just as suddenly as he had a breakthrough season in 2003, shooting from Double-A to the majors after repeating high Class A the year before, Nivar's rapid rise screeched to a halt last season. After rising through the organization as a middle infielder, Nivar moved to the outfield in 2003 and for a time was thought to be the Rangers' answer in center field. But 2004 saw him fail to make improvements or adjustments to take advantage of his electric tools. He's the fastest runner in the organization, but he has never grasped the nuances of basestealing. Nor does he seem to grasp that improved plate discipline would make him a better tablesetter. Nivar has quickness in his bat, giving him surprising power for his size. But he lacks savvy and has been exposed as he tries to learn his way around center field. He too often follows spectacular plays with boneheaded ones. By late July he was back at second base. With Laynce Nix having established himself as the center fielder in Arlington, Nivar's best bet for playing time appears to be as a utilityman.

Year	Club (League)	Class	AVG	G	AB	R	H	2B	3B	HR	RBI	BB	SO	SB	OBP	SLG
1998	Rangers (DSL)	R	.285	54	179	23	51	13	0	3	21	8	7	2	.328	.408
1999	Rangers (DSL)	R	.359	50	195	43	70	19	2	7	44	9	16	7	.409	.585
2000	Charlotte (FSL)	A	.289	42	152	12	44	7	1	1	20	5	28	8	.310	.368
	Savannah (SAL)	A	.311	39	164	19	51	9	0	1	17	2	29	6	.331	.384
2001	Charlotte (FSL)	A	.241	128	515	69	124	20	1	2	32	28	65	28	.286	.295
2002	Charlotte (FSL)	A	.305	114	472	98	144	21	8	3	41	32	44	39	.353	.403
2003	Frisco (TL)	AA	.347	79	317	53	110	17	4	4	37	20	23	9	.387	.464
	Oklahoma (PCL)	AAA	.337	23	89	11	30	2	2	2	12	5	5	6	.368	.472
	Texas (AL)	MAJ	.211	28	90	9	19	1	2	0	7	4	10	4	.253	.267
2004	Oklahoma (PCL)	AAA	.264	113	462	62	122	21	0	10	52	14	43	15	.290	.374
	Texas (AL)	MAJ	.222	7	18	3	4	0	0	0	4	0	7	1	.211	.222
MAJOR LEAGUE TOTALS			.213	35	108	12	23	1	2	0	11	4	17	5	.246	.259
MINOR LEAGUE TOTALS			.293	642	2545	390	746	129	18	33	276	123	260	120	.332	.397

23 Jason Bourgeois, 2b

Born: Jan. 4, 1982. **Ht.:** 5-9. **Wt.:** 185. **Bats:** R. **Throws:** R. **School:** Forest Brook HS, Houston. **Career Transactions:** Selected by Rangers in second round of 2000 draft; signed June 19, 2000. **Signed by:** Randy Taylor.

Like Ramon Nivar, Bourgeois once looked like a future regular in the middle of the diamond for Texas, only to see his stock take a hit last season. He always had surprising raw power for his size, and he adopted a new stance to try to take advantage of it. Bourgeois incorporated a toe-tap, trying to load up with his hands to hit for more power. Instead, it slowed his bat down and he didn't homer until July. He finally ditched the toe-tap late in the season and finished well, including an 8-for-19 effort in the Texas League playoffs. The Rangers have settled on playing Bourgeois at second base, where he has enough range and arm but lacks the technique and knowledge of positioning to be an above-average defender. He still could be an igniter at the top of a lineup if he takes advantage of his strengths, which are his plus speed, savvy baserunning and ability to slash line drives from gap to gap. He'll need a strong spring to earn the starting second-base job in Triple-A.

Year	Club (League)	Class	AVG	G	AB	R	H	2B	3B	HR	RBI	BB	SO	SB	OBP	SLG
2000	Rangers (GCL)	R	.239	24	88	18	21	4	0	0	6	14	15	9	.356	.284
2001	Pulaski (Appy)	R	.311	62	251	60	78	12	2	7	34	26	47	21	.387	.458
2002	Savannah (SAL)	A	.255	127	522	72	133	21	5	8	49	40	66	22	.318	.360
	Charlotte (FSL)	A	.185	9	27	5	5	1	0	0	4	2	4	1	.233	.222
2003	Stockton (Cal)	A	.329	69	277	75	91	22	3	4	34	36	33	16	.416	.473
	Frisco (TL)	AA	.252	55	202	28	51	5	4	4	21	16	45	3	.308	.376
2004	Frisco (TL)	AA	.255	138	530	73	135	19	7	2	58	44	81	30	.313	.328
MINOR LEAGUE TOTALS			.271	484	1897	331	514	84	21	25	206	178	291	102	.341	.377

24 Mike Nickeas, c

Born: Feb. 13, 1983. **Ht.:** 6-0. **Wt.:** 205. **Bats:** R. **Throws:** R. **School:** Georgia Tech. **Career Transactions:** Selected by Rangers in fifth round of 2004 draft; signed June 14, 2004. **Signed by:** John Castleberry

Nickeas has an athletic background. His father, who is British, was a professional soccer player whose career took him to Canada, where he met Nickeas' mother. He was born in Canada but grew up in California, and he played for U.S. national teams both in high school and college. His makeup and leadership qualities led to his repeat stint with Team USA, as did his sound catch-and-throw skills. The Rangers liked him going into the 2004 season and were able to wait until the fifth round to snare him because he struggled at the plate for Georgia Tech. Scouts thought Nickeas was better with the bat than he showed, yet still he surprised club officials with his production in his pro debut despite running out of gas late in the summer. He has decent power, and he's capable of driving balls to the opposite field and hitting 10-15 homers a year. He knows the strike zone and draws walks, but he doesn't always make consistent contact. He's fairly athletic for his position, cerebral as a catcher should be and handles pitchers well. Nickeas is the best catcher in the system and could move quickly, possibly jumping to high Class A in 2005.

Year	Club (League)	Class	AVG	G	AB	R	H	2B	3B	HR	RBI	BB	SO	SB	OBP	SLG
2004	Spokane (NWL)	A	.288	61	233	42	67	18	0	10	55	33	53	2	.384	.494
MINOR LEAGUE TOTALS			.288	61	233	42	67	18	0	10	55	33	53	2	.384	.494

25 Drew Meyer, ss

Born: Aug. 29, 1981. **Ht.:** 5-9. **Wt.:** 202. **Bats:** L. **Throws:** R. **School:** University of South Carolina. **Career Transactions:** Selected by Rangers in first round (10th overall) of 2002 draft; signed June 26, 2002. **Signed by:** Jim Fairey.

Meyer couldn't wait for 2004 to end. He was left off the 40-man roster after he: missed time with a broken collarbone; got out of shape; fell out of favor with the organization after Grady Fuson, who drafted him and was his biggest backer, was forced out; and moved well down the club's depth chart at shortstop, behind big league all-star Michael Young, Joaquin Arias and Ian Kinsler. Meyer's injury and subsequent weight gain sapped him of speed, one of his best tools. After being dressed down by several club officials, he salvaged his season by working his way back into shape and finishing strong. Based on his bat, Meyer didn't merit being drafted as high as he was. He always has struggled with wood bats, as he flies open with his front shoulder and tries to pull too many pitches. Yet he also remains a playmaker, capable of stealing a base, dragging a bunt for a hit or making a key defensive play. He has plenty of arm and enough athletic ability for any infield or outfield spot. Texas seems to value his versatility more than anything. Meyer will return to Double-A to prepare for a future as a utility player, with the chance to be a regular if his bat ever comes around.

Year	Club (League)	Class	AVG	G	AB	R	H	2B	3B	HR	RBI	BB	SO	SB	OBP	SLG
2002	Savannah (SAL)	A	.243	54	214	15	52	5	4	1	24	10	53	7	.274	.318
	Tulsa (TL)	AA	.214	4	14	0	3	0	0	0	0	1	5	0	.267	.214
2003	Stockton (Cal)	A	.281	94	398	59	112	16	9	5	53	32	92	24	.330	.405
	Frisco (TL)	AA	.316	26	98	14	31	1	1	0	6	11	23	9	.385	.347
2004	Frisco (TL)	AA	.241	59	232	35	56	6	2	2	13	22	43	4	.309	.310
MINOR LEAGUE TOTALS			.266	237	956	123	254	28	16	8	96	76	216	44	.317	.354

26 Erik Thompson, rhp

Born: June 23, 1982. **Ht.:** 5-9. **Wt.:** 180. **Bats:** R. **Throws:** R. **School:** Pensacola (Fla.) JC. **Career Transactions:** Selected by Rangers in 12th round of 2002 draft; signed June 21, 2002. **Signed by:** Rick Schroeder.

Thompson and the Rangers admitted the obvious, as his official height dropped two inches to a more truthful 5-foot-9. Despite his size, he would rank much higher if he could stay healthy. He had Tommy John surgery as a junior-college freshman, and more recently came down with a sore shoulder that allowed him to make just one start after the all-star break last year. Thompson pounds the strike zone with a fastball that reaches the mid-90s with average movement. He also has an average changeup and a fringy slider that lacks depth because of his height and inability to stay on top of it. Thompson doesn't have a knockout pitch, as evidenced by his declining strikeout rate as he has advanced, and clearly durability is another question. However, pitchers with his combination of velocity and control—the best in the organization—are hard to find. Thompson likely is headed to the bullpen if his arm holds up. If he takes to the role, he won't be far from helping the big league club.

Year	Club (League)	Class	W	L	ERA	G	GS	CG	SV	IP	H	R	ER	HR	BB	SO	AVG
2002	Rangers (GCL)	R	2	2	2.04	10	5	0	0	40	38	12	9	2	2	34	.250
	Pulaski (Appy)	R	1	1	3.18	3	3	0	0	17	19	6	6	0	2	16	.297
2003	Clinton (Mid)	A	5	2	2.81	14	7	0	2	58	49	24	18	6	5	52	.225
	Stockton (Cal)	A	8	3	2.91	19	9	0	0	80	74	28	26	6	13	62	.243
2004	Frisco (TL)	AA	6	6	2.98	15	15	1	0	91	78	35	30	10	14	65	.229
	Oklahoma (PCL)	AAA	0	0	9.00	1	1	0	0	5	10	5	5	1	0	2	.435
MINOR LEAGUE TOTALS			22	14	2.91	62	40	1	2	290	268	110	94	25	36	231	.243

27 John Bannister, rhp

Born: Jan. 20, 1984. **Ht.:** 6-4. **Wt.:** 180. **Bats:** R. **Throws:** R. **School:** Sabino HS, Tucson. **Career Transactions:** Signed as nondrafted free agent by Rangers, Aug. 22, 2002. **Signed by:** Dave Birecki.

Bannister starred at Sabino High in Tucson, where he played with Brewers shortstop prospect J.J. Hardy, but he wasn't drafted after his senior season in 2002. He planned on attending Yavapai (Ariz.) Junior College before part-time scout Dave Birecki saw his performance catch up to his potential while pitching for the Arizona Firebirds, a Connie Mack team. Birecki, now an area scout for the Mets, signed him as a nondrafted free agent for $17,500. Bannister has impressed the Rangers ever since. He has a long, projectable frame, a loose arm and a smooth arm action that he repeats well. He fills the strike zone with an 87-91 mph fastball that was touching 94-95 mph in instructional league. His 12-to-6 curveball, with refinement, could end up as one of the best in the system. He also throws a developing changeup. Though much less heralded, Bannister will challenge Eric Hurley and Michael Schlact for the No. 1 spot in the low Class A rotation this year.

Year	Club (League)	Class	W	L	ERA	G	GS	CG	SV	IP	H	R	ER	HR	BB	SO	AVG
2003	Rangers (AZL)	R	2	4	4.22	13	7	0	1	43	47	31	20	2	16	28	.283
2004	Spokane (NWL)	A	2	2	3.51	16	7	0	0	59	49	29	23	3	28	67	.223
	Clinton (Mid)	A	0	0	1.80	1	1	0	0	5	5	1	1	0	1	5	.278
MINOR LEAGUE TOTALS			4	6	3.71	30	15	0	1	107	101	61	44	5	45	100	.250

28 Nick Regilio, rhp

Born: Sept. 4, 1978. **Ht.:** 6-2. **Wt.:** 180. **Bats:** R. **Throws:** R. **School:** Jacksonville University. **Career Transactions:** Selected by Rangers in second round of 1999 draft; signed June 11, 1999. **Signed by:** Bobby Heck.

Most pitchers with Regilio's age and medical history don't make prospect lists, but his resilience has impressed the Rangers. They believe his combination of velocity and movement can help their major league staff in 2005. Regilio has overcome injuries each of the last three years and capped his comeback with a brief, unsuccessful big league stint last season. He had biceps tendinitis in 2002 and rotator-cuff surgery in 2003, then had another operation to remove scar tissue that was irritating a nerve in his right shoulder last August. Texas was pleased that he returned and looked strong in the Arizona Fall League. Regilio's top pitch is a sinker that he threw at 88-93 mph in Triple-A and pushed to the mid-90s while working shorter stints in the AFL. There's not a whole lot of finesse to him, as his secondary pitches are both relatively hard: an average slider and a changeup with fade. All of his stuff moves, often too much for him to handle, and he regularly fell behind experienced Triple-A and big league hitters last year. He also has yet to show he has the durability needed from a starter—his career high is 116 innings in a season—particularly in the Texas heat.

Year	Club (League)	Class	W	L	ERA	G	GS	CG	SV	IP	H	R	ER	HR	BB	SO	AVG
1999	Pulaski (Appy)	R	4	2	1.63	11	8	1	0	50	30	12	9	2	16	58	.172
2000	Charlotte (FSL)	A	4	3	4.52	20	20	0	0	86	94	54	43	8	29	63	.286
2001	Charlotte (FSL)	A	6	2	1.55	11	11	1	0	64	47	16	11	5	16	60	.200
	Tulsa (TL)	AA	1	3	5.54	10	10	0	0	52	62	34	32	2	20	40	.297
2002	Tulsa (TL)	AA	6	8	3.44	19	19	2	0	105	97	46	40	8	47	59	.245
	Oklahoma (PCL)	AAA	1	0	10.80	1	1	0	0	5	9	6	6	1	2	4	.391
2003	Rangers (AZL)	R	0	0	0.00	2	2	0	0	5	4	2	0	0	1	7	.235
	Frisco (TL)	AA	0	1	21.60	1	0	0	0	2	5	4	4	0	1	2	.556
2004	Oklahoma (PCL)	AAA	6	5	4.71	17	17	0	0	92	98	49	48	6	46	72	.282
	Texas (AL)	MAJ	0	4	6.05	6	4	0	0	19	20	16	13	3	15	12	.278
MAJOR LEAGUE TOTALS			0	4	6.05	6	4	0	0	19	20	16	13	3	15	12	.278
MINOR LEAGUE TOTALS			28	24	3.78	92	88	4	0	459	446	223	193	32	181	365	.256

29 Jeremy Cleveland, of

Born: Sept. 10, 1981. **Ht.:** 6-2. **Wt.:** 185. **Bats:** R. **Throws:** R. **School:** University of North Carolina. **Career Transactions:** Selected by Rangers in eighth round of 2003 draft; signed June 16, 2003. **Signed by:** John Castleberry.

Cleveland had a huge 2003, winning the Atlantic Coast Conference batting title (.410) and finishing second in the Northwest League race (.322). He lost momentum last year, struggling after an aggressive jump to high Class A. Cleveland has what it takes to be a major league hitter: good pitch recognition, average raw power, confidence in his ability and the work ethic to get better. Cleveland needs that work ethic to adjust his stance, which leaves him drifting into the ball and doesn't allow his hands to generate a load, short-circuiting his power. He wore down as the season progressed, hitting .194 with no homers in the final month as he lost control of the strike zone and couldn't catch up to good fastballs. Though he's just a left fielder, Cleveland has improved defensively, particularly in lengthening out his now-average arm. He now throws well enough for right field, though he's still better suited for left. The Rangers have a crowded outfield picture but believe Cleveland will hit enough to remain in it. He'll have to have a strong spring, however, to earn a promotion to Double-A.

Year	Club (League)	Class	AVG	G	AB	R	H	2B	3B	HR	RBI	BB	SO	SB	OBP	SLG
2003	Spokane (NWL)	A	.322	64	245	64	79	20	3	7	53	40	50	5	.514	.432
2004	Stockton (Cal)	A	.277	129	487	72	135	32	5	8	70	53	110	11	.354	.413
MINOR LEAGUE TOTALS			.292	193	732	136	214	52	8	15	123	93	160	16	.382	.447

30 Ryan Wing, lhp

Born: Feb. 1, 1982. **Ht.:** 6-2. **Wt.:** 170. **Bats:** L. **Throws:** L. **School:** Riverside (Calif.) CC. **Career Transactions:** Selected by White Sox in second round of 2001 draft; signed July 23, 2001 . . . Claimed on waivers by Rangers from White Sox, Oct. 24, 2004. **Signed by:** Joseph Butler (White Sox).

The White Sox have provided a lot of talent to the Rangers the last couple of years. Texas traded Carl Everett for Frank Francisco, Josh Rupe and Anthony Webster in 2003, then claimed Wing and speedy infielder Ruddy Yan off waivers from Chicago after the 2004 season. The White Sox were trying to create room on the 40-man roster by designating Wing for assignment in October when the Rangers scooped him up. They essentially traded lefty Ben Kozlowski to get Wing, losing Kozlowski to the Reds when they took him off their roster to accommodate Wing. Wing didn't pitch in 2004 because of a shoulder injury originally diagnosed as tendinitis. He didn't improve with rest and rehabilitation, so he had surgery in July. Texas already had him on a throwing program by the winter, and he was expected to be ready to return to the mound by the end of spring training. Wing probably will begin his Rangers career in extended spring, as the club looks to see if he regains his low-90s velocity on his sinker. His slider was considered the best in the White Sox system prior to his injury. He does a fine job of controlling the running game, while his changeup and control need improvement.

Year	Club (League)	Class	W	L	ERA	G	GS	CG	SV	IP	H	R	ER	HR	BB	SO	AVG
2001	Bristol (Appy)	R	1	0	9.00	1	0	0	0	1	1	1	1	0	0	2	.200
2002	Kannapolis (SAL)	A	12	7	3.78	25	21	0	0	124	111	64	52	6	60	109	.240
2003	Winston-Salem (Car)	A	9	7	2.98	26	26	0	0	145	116	62	48	9	67	107	.227
2004	Did not play Injured																
MINOR LEAGUE TOTALS			22	14	3.37	52	47	0	0	270	228	127	101	15	127	218	.233

TORONTO
BLUE JAYS

BY **JOHN MANUEL**

I t has been more than a decade since the Blue Jays won back-to-back World Series. Since then, Toronto has seen a change in ownership and management, changed itself from a big spender to a middle-of-the-road franchise, and completely overhauled its organizational philosophy.

After an 86-win, third-place finish in 2003, the Blue Jays took a step in the wrong direction in the third year of general manager J.P. Ricciardi's tenure. With their three stars—Carlos Delgado, Roy Halladay and Vernon Wells—missing significant time with injuries, they lost 94 games and finished in last place in the American League East for the first time since 1981.

"We don't have the resources yet in the minor leagues that can come up and replace a Carlos Delgado if he's out for 30 games," Ricciardi said. "I think we're getting there, but we're not to that point."

The openings at the major league level forced the Jays to promote several prospects who figure into their long-term plans. Right fielder **Alexis Rios** arrived in May and showed promise by hitting .286. Right-hander David Bush joined the rotation shortly before the all-star break and posted a 3.69 ERA in 16 starts. Outfielder Gabe Gross, who came within one at-bat of losing his rookie status, looked overmatched at times. Shortstop Russ Adams, righty Brandon League and catcher Guillermo Quiroz were more impressive in shorter September stints. Another youngster who earned consideration for a spot on the 2005 major league ros-

ter is lefthander Gustavo Chacin. After going 18-2, 2.82 between Double-A and Triple-A, he was sharp in two big league starts.

"At the end of the day, our best baseball is ahead of us. It's just going to take time," Ricciardi said. "That's just the reality of the division and where we're at. Look at teams like Minnesota and Oakland. Those teams lost a lot of games for a lot of years in a row. I don't think we're going to be like that, but I do think it's going to take more time. Maybe even more time than I thought."

Ricciardi and his staff hope to make up ground on AL East powers Boston and New York through player development. Toronto's modified "Moneyball" approach has loaded the system with advanced college players, many of whom have progressed rapidly. However, the Jays lack the impact prospects who once flourished in the system.

Farm director Dick Scott has been able to restore a winning attitude throughout the minor leagues, as the Jays' minor league affiliates combined for a .572 winning percentage in 2004, the second-best in baseball. In its first year as a franchise, New Hampshire won the Eastern League championship, while high Class A Dunedin, low Class A Charleston and short-season Auburn all made the playoffs. In his first year as scouting director, Canadian Jon Lalonde continued Toronto's recent trend of drafting polished college prospects early and often.

TOP 30 PROSPECTS

1. Brandon League, rhp	16. Ismael Ramirez, rhp
2. Aaron Hill, ss	17. Adam Lind, of
3. Guillermo Quiroz, c	18. Robinzon Diaz, c
4. Francisco Rosario, rhp	19. Chi-Hung Cheng, lhp
5. David Purcey, lhp	20. Raul Tablado, ss/3b
6. Russ Adams, ss	21. Jamie Vermilyea, rhp
7. Dustin McGowan, rhp	22. Kurt Isenberg, lhp
8. Zach Jackson, lhp	23. Miguel Negron, of
9. Josh Banks, rhp	24. Justin James, rhp
10. Gustavo Chacin, lhp	25. John-Ford Griffin, of/1b
11. Gabe Gross, of	26. Eric Crozier, 1b/of
12. Yuber Rodriguez, of	27. Ron Davenport, of/1b
13. Vince Perkins, rhp	28. John Hattig, 3b
14. Shawn Marcum, rhp	29. Jason Alfaro, inf/of
15. Curtis Thigpen, c	30. Casey Janssen, rhp

ORGANIZATION OVERVIEW

General manager: J.P. Ricciardi. **Farm director:** Dick Scott. **Scouting director:** Jon Lalonde.

2004 PERFORMANCE

Class	Team	League	W	L	Pct.	Finish*	Manager(s)
Majors	Toronto	American	67	94	.416	12th (14)	Carlos Tosca/John Gibbons
Triple-A	Syracuse SkyChiefs	International	66	78	.458	t-11th (14)	Marty Pevey
Double-A	New Hampshire Fisher Cats	Eastern	84	57	.596	2nd (12)	Mike Basso
High A	Dunedin Blue Jays	Florida State	76	57	.571	2nd (12)	Omar Malave
Low A	#Charleston Alley Cats	South Atlantic	84	56	.600	3rd (16)	Ken Joyce
Short-season	Auburn Doubledays	New York-Penn	50	24	.676	1st (14)	Dennis Holmberg
Rookie	Pulaski Blue Jays	Appalachian	40	27	.597	3rd (10)	Gary Cathcart
OVERALL 2004 MINOR LEAGUE RECORD			400	299	.576	2nd (30)	

*Finish in overall standings (No. of teams in league). #Affiliate will be in Lansing (Midwest) in 2005.

ORGANIZATION LEADERS

BATTING   *Minimum 250 At-Bats
- *AVG Anton French, Syracuse/New Hampshire .... .319
- R   Clint Johnston, Charleston 87
- H   Dominic Rich, New Hampshire 143
- TB   Ron Davenport, Dunedin 219
- 2B   Ron Davenport, Dunedin 40
- 3B   Justin Singleton, New Hampshire 11
- HR   Glenn Williams, Syracuse 23
- RBI Ron Davenport, Dunedin 92
- BB   Ryan Roberts, Dunedin/Charleston 91
- SO   Justin Singleton, New Hampshire 152
- SB   Tyrell Godwin, New Hampshire 42
- *OBP Howie Clark, Syracuse .... .407
- *SLG Raul Tablado, Dunedin .... .585

PITCHING   #Minimum 75 Innings
- W   Gustavo Chacin, Syracuse/New Hampshire 18
- L   Chris Baker, Syracuse/New Hampshire 12
- #ERA Mike MacDonald, Charleston/Auburn 1.71
- G   Jordan DeJong, New Hampshire 57
- CG   David Bush, Syracuse 2
- SV   Bubbie Buzachero, Dunedin 24
- IP   Ismael Ramirez, Dunedin 165
- BB   Josue Matos, Syracuse 56
- SO   Shaun Marcum, Dunedin/Charleston 155

BEST TOOLS

- Best Hitter for Average .... Aaron Hill
- Best Power Hitter .... Guillermo Quiroz
- Best Strike-Zone Discipline .... Russ Adams
- Fastest Baserunner .... Miguel Negron
- Best Athlete .... Miguel Negron
- Best Fastball .... Brandon League
- Best Curveball .... David Purcey
- Best Slider .... Vince Perkins
- Best Changeup .... Shaun Marcum
- Best Control .... Shaun Marcum
- Best Defensive Catcher .... Guillermo Quiroz
- Best Defensive Infielder .... Juan Peralta
- Best Infield Arm .... Jason Alfaro
- Best Defensive Outfielder .... Miguel Negron
- Best Outfield Arm .... Miguel Negron

PROJECTED 2008 LINEUP

- Catcher .... Guillermo Quiroz
- First Base .... Eric Hinske
- Second Base .... Russ Adams
- Third Base .... Corey Koskie
- Shortstop .... Aaron Hill
- Left Field .... Gabe Gross
- Center Field .... Vernon Wells
- Right Field .... Alexis Rios

- Designated Hitter .... Frank Catalanotto
- No. 1 Starter .... Roy Halladay
- No. 2 Starter .... Ted Lilly
- No. 3 Starter .... David Bush
- No. 4 Starter .... Francisco Rosario
- No. 5 Starter .... Dustin McGowan
- Closer .... Brandon League

LAST YEAR'S TOP 20 PROSPECTS

1. Alexis Rios, of
2. Dustin McGowan, rhp
3. Guillermo Quiroz, c
4. Gabe Gross, of
5. Francisco Rosario, rhp
6. Aaron Hill, ss
7. David Bush, rhp
8. Vince Perkins, rhp
9. Russ Adams, ss
10. Brandon League, rhp
11. Josh Banks, rhp
12. Adam Peterson, rhp
13. Kevin Cash, c
14. D.J. Hanson, rhp
15. John-Ford Griffin, of
16. Jason Arnold, rhp
17. Jayson Werth, of
18. Jesse Harper, rhp
19. Tyrell Godwin, of
20. Kurt Isenberg, lhp

TOP PROSPECTS OF THE DECADE

Year	Player, Pos.	Current Team
1995	Shawn Green, of	Diamondbacks
1996	Shannon Stewart, of	Twins
1997	Roy Halladay, rhp	Blue Jays
1998	Roy Halladay, rhp	Blue Jays
1999	Roy Halladay, rhp	Blue Jays
2000	Vernon Wells, of	Blue Jays
2001	Vernon Wells, of	Blue Jays
2002	Josh Phelps, c	Indians
2003	Dustin McGowan, rhp	Blue Jays
2004	Alexis Rios, of	Blue Jays

TOP DRAFT PICKS OF THE DECADE

Year	Player, Pos.	Current Team
1995	Roy Halladay, rhp	Blue Jays
1996	Billy Koch, rhp	Blue Jays
1997	Vernon Wells, of	Blue Jays
1998	Felipe Lopez, ss	Reds
1999	Alexis Rios, of	Blue Jays
2000	Miguel Negron, of	Blue Jays
2001	Gabe Gross, of	Blue Jays
2002	Russ Adams, ss	Blue Jays
2003	Aaron Hill, ss	Blue Jays
2004	David Purcey, lhp	Blue Jays

ALL-TIME LARGEST BONUSES

Felipe Lopez, 1998	$2,000,000
Gabe Gross, 2001	$1,865,000
Russ Adams, 2002	$1,785,000
Aaron Hill, 2003	$1,675,000
Vernon Wells, 1997	$1,600,000
David Purcey, 2004	$1,600,000

MINOR LEAGUE DEPTH CHART

Toronto BLUE JAYS

Impact Potential: C
The Jays' top prospect is a reliever, albeit one of the hardest throwers in the minor leagues. Aaron Hill was the Futures Game MVP, but he said he felt out of place in batting practice, and he lacks a dominant tool. The same can be said for most of the Jays farmhands, most of whom profile as no more than average big leaguers at best.

Depth: B
On the other hand, Toronto has plenty of potential bats, power from the left side, and strength in numbers on the mound. Once an organizational liability, lefthanded starting pitching is now a Jays strength, thanks in part to a pair of first-round picks spent on college southpaws in 2004.

*Depth charts prepared by **John Manuel** and **Allan Simpson**. Numbers in parentheses indicate prospect rankings.*

LF
Adam Lind (17)
John-Ford Griffin (25)
Christian Snavely
Eric Nielson
Aaron Mathews

CF
Yuber Rodriquez (12)
Miguel Negron (23)

RF
Gabe Gross (11)
Ron Davenport (27)
Cory Patton

3B
Raul Tablado (20)
John Hattig (28)
Jason Alfaro (29)
Jesus Gonzalez

SS
Aaron Hill (2)
Russ Adams (6)
Juan Peralta
Ryan Klosterman

2B
Ryan Roberts
Jorge Sequea
Brian Hall
Carlo Cota

1B
Eric Crozier (26)
Vito Chiaravalloti
Joey Metropoulos
Clint Johnston

SOURCE of TALENT

Homegrown		Acquired	
College	5	Trades	3
Junior college	2	Rule 5 draft	0
Draft-and-follow	2	Independent leagues	0
High School	7	Free agents/waivers	0
Nondrafted free agents	1		
Foreign	10		

C
Guillermo Quiroz (3)
Curtis Thigpen (15)
Robinzon Diaz (18)

LHP

Starters	Relievers
David Purcey (5)	Davis Romero
Zach Jackson (8)	Brad Mumma
Gustavo Chacin (10)	Justin Maureau
Chi Hung Cheng (19)	
Kurt Isenberg (22)	
Chris Leonard	

RHP

Starters	Relievers
Brandon League (1)	Jamie Vermilyea (21)
Francisco Rosario (4)	Stephen Andrade
Dustin McGowan (7)	Kevin Frederick
Josh Banks (9)	Danny Hill
Vince Perkins (13)	Jordan DeJong
Shaun Marcum (14)	Jason Arnold
Ismael Ramirez (16)	Felix Romero
Justin James (24)	Bubbie Buzachero
Casey Janssen (30)	Kristian Bell
Edward Rodriguez	Tracey Thorpe
Wilfreddy Aguirre	Chad Pleiness
	D.J. Hanson

DRAFT ANALYSIS

2004

Best Pro Debut: C Curtis Thigpen (2) and OF Adam Lind (3) were short-season New York-Penn League all-stars. Thigpen batted .301-7-29, while Lind hit .312-7-50. LHP Derek Tate (34) overmatched Rookie-level Appalachian League and NY-P hitters with his changeup. He went 6-1, 1.47 with a 65-10 K-BB ratio in 49 innings.

Best Athlete: SS Ryan Klosterman (5) and OF Aaron Mathews (19) are solid if not spectacular athletes.

Best Pure Hitter: Lind has a fluid left-handed swing, bat speed and a knowledgeable approach. Thigpen also should continue to hit as he moves up the ladder.

Best Raw Power: 1B Joey Metropoulos (9) is a 6-foot-1, 230-pound masher. He led the Cape Cod League with 11 homers in 2003. OF Cory Patton (6) was the national junior college player of the year in 2002, when he topped that level with 31 homers and 119 RBIs at Seward County (Kan.) CC. He sustained a stress fracture in his left foot right before the draft and couldn't play before instructional league.

Fastest Runner: Klosterman has 55 speed on the 20-80 scouting scale and his instincts make him dangerous on the bases. He stole 16 bases in 18 tries in the NY-P.

Best Defensive Player: Klosterman has sure hands and makes plays at shortstop despite a slightly below-average arm. Patton has a plus arm and moves better in right field than his 5-foot-10, 210-pound frame might indicate.

Best Fastball: LHP David Purcey (1) pitches at 90-95 mph. LHP Zach Jackson (1) doesn't throw quite as hard, working at 88-93, but he maintains his velocity through-

RICH ABEL

Thigpen

out a game and commands his fastball well. RHP Kristian Bell (11) has touched 95, though there's a fair amount of effort in his delivery.

Best Breaking Ball: RHP Danny Hill's (3) slider made him one of the most attractive senior signs in the draft. Bell and RHP Kyle Yates (12) both have 12-to-6 curveballs. Yates' is more reliable, and he owns an 88-92 mph fastball.

Most Intriguing Background: RHP Joey McLaughlin Jr.'s (18) father pitched for Toronto, and his brother Jeff pitched alongside him at Oklahoma City. LHP Daryl Harang's (23) brother Aaron won 10 games for the Reds in 2004.

Closest To The Majors: Purcey and Jackson are too close to call. Purcey has better pure stuff, but Jackson has more control and consistency.

Best Late-Round Pick: The Blue Jays like what they've seen from Bell, OF Eric Nielsen (12), Yates and Mathews. Nielsen should hit and has a possible right-field arm.

The One Who Got Away: Sophomore-eligible RHP Derek Feldkamp (41) could go much higher in 2005 if he continues to touch 95 mph and show a feel for three pitches. He's back at Michigan.

Assessment: The first round couldn't have worked out any better for the Blue Jays. After deliberating between Purcey and Jackson for the No. 16 pick, they found Jackson still on the board when they picked again at No. 32.

2003 SS Aaron Hill (1) and RHPs Josh Banks (2) and Jamie Vermilyea (8) all could contribute in the majors within two years of being drafted by the Blue Jays. **GRADE:** B

2002 RHP David Bush (2) already has carved out a spot for himself in the Toronto rotation, while SS Russ Adams (1) figures to be the Jays' leadoff hitter this year. RHP Adam Peterson (4) was traded for Shea Hillenbrand. **GRADE:** B

2001 RHP Brandon League (2) is the organization's top prospect, but his future role is unclear. OF Gabe Gross (1) has been mildly disappointing so far. **GRADE:** C+

2000 RHP Dustin McGowan (1) was the class of Toronto's pitching prospects until he needed Tommy John surgery last year. OF Miguel Negron (1) was a signability pick and hasn't progressed much. **GRADE:** C

Draft analysis prepared by Jim Callis. Numbers in parentheses indicate draft rounds.

DAVID SCHOFIELD

Brandon
LEAGUE

Born: March 16, 1983.
Ht.: 6-2. **Wt.:** 180.
Bats: R. **Throws:** R.
School: St. Louis HS, Honolulu.
Career Transactions: Selected by Blue Jays in second round of 2001 draft; signed July 3, 2001.
Signed by: David Blume.

Though the Blue Jays now shy away from spending early picks on high school righthanders, League is the third in recent years to top this list, joining Roy Halladay (1997-99) and Dustin McGowan (2003). Coming out of high school, League was committed to Pepperdine before the Blue Jays persuaded him to sign for $600,000. Toronto initially took a slow-track approach as it did with McGowan and didn't let League make his full-season debut until his third year as a pro. Yet he still managed to reach the majors at 21 and didn't look intimidated in his debut. He entered his first game at Yankee Stadium with two outs, the bases loaded and Gary Sheffield at the plate. He overpowered Sheffield, getting a harmless grounder, and worked 1⅓ scoreless innings. After working almost exclusively as a starter before 2004, League responded to a move to the bullpen. The Jays hoped to accelerate his timetable by shifting him to relief, and he highlighted his breakthrough campaign by hitting 102 mph on the stadium radar gun at the Eastern League all-star game.

League is one of the hardest throwers in the minors, and he has the potential to become either a frontline starter or dominant closer, depending on what Toronto wants. He features a heavy fastball that sits at 95-97 mph. The lively sink and running action on his heater make the pitch difficult for hitters to center. He generates his velocity and life with a lightning-quick arm and throws from a whip-like, lower three-quarters arm slot. Former Blue Jays pitching coach Gil Patterson says the movement on League's fastball reminds him of Halladay's. League works down in the zone and generated a 2.7 groundball/flyball ratio in Double-A. His 87-89 mph slider is also a plus pitch. He has developed an effective third pitch in his changeup, so scouts say he won't have to be limited to short-relief work.

League's work with pitching instructors Dane Johnson and Rick Adair contributed to his rise, but he has further adjustments to make. He needs to maintain his arm slot. He tends to over-rotate in his delivery and drag his arm, which keeps him from staying on top of his slider. Scouts did note that League's delivery was much improved in 2004, as he looked cleaner and used less effort. For a guy with such an electric arm, he doesn't blow away as many hitters as might be expected.

After earning MVP honors in the Eastern League playoffs, League continued to open eyes with his performance in Toronto. He'll go to spring training with a good chance to make the big league club and figures to get his feet wet in the Jays bullpen in 2005. With no established closer in Toronto, League's power repertoire could land him that role. But he also has enough stuff to project as a quality starter and could be more valuable in that role.

Year	Club (League)	Class	W	L	ERA	G	GS	CG	SV	IP	H	R	ER	HR	BB	SO	AVG
2001	Medicine Hat (Pio)	R	2	2	4.66	9	9	0	0	39	36	23	20	3	11	38	.245
2002	Auburn (NY-P)	A	7	2	3.15	16	16	0	0	86	80	42	30	2	23	72	.248
2003	Charleston, WV (SAL)	A	2	3	1.91	12	12	0	0	71	58	15	15	1	18	61	.230
	Dunedin (FSL)	A	4	3	4.75	13	12	0	0	66	76	40	35	3	20	34	.288
2004	New Hampshire (EL)	AA	6	4	3.38	41	10	0	2	104	92	44	39	3	41	90	.240
	Toronto (AL)	MAJ	1	0	0.00	3	0	0	0	5	3	0	0	0	1	2	.176
MAJOR LEAGUE TOTALS			1	0	0.00	3	0	0	0	5	3	0	0	0	1	2	.176
MINOR LEAGUE TOTALS			21	14	3.42	91	59	0	2	365	342	164	139	12	113	295	.250

Aaron Hill, ss

RICH ABEL

Born: March 21, 1982. **Ht.:** 5-11. **Wt.:** 195. **Bats:** R. **Throws:** R. **School:** Louisiana State University. **Career Transactions:** Selected by Blue Jays in first round (13th overall) of 2003 draft; signed June 17, 2003. **Signed by:** Jayme Bane.

Hill was the Southeastern Conference player of the year in 2003, and the Jays drafted him with the idea he'd move quickly. He finished his first season at high Class A Dunedin and spent his first full year in Double-A. When Russ Adams bowed out of the Futures Game with a ribcage injury, Hill replaced him on the U.S. roster and claimed the game's MVP award. Hill offers average to above-average tools across the board, but what sets him apart is his ability to optimize them. He's short to the ball with an easy, compact swing, makes adjustments and uses the entire field. Hill should have at least average power as he learns how to incorporate his lower half for more leverage. He has a tremendous arm and shows good speed and instincts on the basepaths. While there's little doubt Hill profiles as an everyday big leaguer, some scouts question his quickness and footwork at shortstop. He compensates for a lack of range by making good reads on balls. Hill should start 2005 at Triple-A Syracuse, with his major league debut on the horizon. Whether he or Russ Adams sticks at shortstop and forces the other to move has yet to be determined.

Year	Club (League)	Class	AVG	G	AB	R	H	2B	3B	HR	RBI	BB	SO	SB	OBP	SLG
2003	Auburn (NY-P)	A	.361	33	122	22	44	4	0	4	34	16	20	1	.446	.492
	Dunedin (FSL)	A	.286	32	119	26	34	7	0	0	11	11	10	1	.343	.345
2004	New Hampshire (EL)	AA	.280	135	479	78	134	26	2	11	80	63	61	3	.369	.411
MINOR LEAGUE TOTALS			.294	200	720	126	212	37	2	15	125	90	91	5	.376	.414

Guillermo Quiroz, c

RICH ABEL

Born: Nov. 29, 1981. **Ht.:** 6-1. **Wt.:** 200. **Bats:** R. **Throws:** R. **Career Transactions:** Signed out of Venezuela by Blue Jays, Sept. 25, 1998. **Signed by:** Emilio Carrasquel.

Signed for $1.2 million, Quiroz missed time late in 2003 with a partially collapsed lung, and missed most of May and June in 2004 after he broke his left hand. He returned to make his big league debut in September. Quiroz has above-average catch-and-throw skills, with plus arm strength and a quick release. At the plate he makes contact, does a good job of working the count and displays plus raw power. In 2003, Jays coaches used videotape of Quiroz taking batting practice as an example to hold up for other players because he exemplified the organization's approach to hitting. Even before he was hurt last year, Quiroz showed up for spring training out of shape, affecting his performance. His swing can get long, and he may never hit for much of an average. A year after catching 44 percent of basestealers, he nailed just 22 percent in 2004. Quiroz could use more time in Triple-A, but the Jays need help behind the plate and he's not far from sticking in Toronto.

Year	Club (League)	Class	AVG	G	AB	R	H	2B	3B	HR	RBI	BB	SO	SB	OBP	SLG
1999	Medicine Hat (Pio)	R	.221	63	208	25	46	7	0	9	28	18	55	0	.296	.385
2000	Hagerstown (SAL)	A	.162	43	136	14	22	4	0	1	12	16	44	0	.269	.213
	Queens (NY-P)	A	.224	55	196	27	44	9	0	5	29	27	48	1	.329	.347
2001	Charleston, WV (SAL)	A	.199	82	261	25	52	12	0	7	25	29	67	5	.294	.326
2002	Dunedin (FSL)	A	.260	111	411	50	107	28	1	12	68	35	91	1	.330	.421
	Syracuse (IL)	AAA	.222	13	45	7	10	4	0	1	6	3	14	0	.271	.378
2003	New Haven (EL)	AA	.282	108	369	63	104	27	0	20	79	45	83	0	.372	.518
2004	Syracuse (IL)	AAA	.227	76	255	32	58	19	1	8	32	28	54	0	.309	.404
	Toronto (AL)	MAJ	.212	17	52	2	11	2	0	0	6	2	8	1	.263	.250
MAJOR LEAGUE TOTALS			.212	17	52	2	11	2	0	0	6	2	8	1	.263	.250
MINOR LEAGUE TOTALS			.236	551	1881	243	443	110	2	63	279	201	456	7	.321	.397

Francisco Rosario, rhp

RICH BATTLE

Born: Sept. 28, 1980. **Ht.:** 6-0. **Wt.:** 160. **Bats:** R. **Throws:** R. **Career Transactions:** Signed out of Dominican Republic by Blue Jays, Jan. 11, 1999. **Signed by:** Tony Arias.

Rosario emerged as one of the Blue Jays' top pitching prospects with a dominant showing in 2002, but his ascent stalled when he blew out his elbow in the Arizona Fall League that offseason. Tommy John surgery cost him all of 2003, and he returned last May before missing six weeks with an upper-arm injury unrelated to his elbow. Rosario has a loose, easy arm action that helps him fire explosive fastballs in the mid-90s while maintaining solid command. The ball jumps out of his hand from a three-quarters slot, and he creates good sinking life on both his fastball and above-average changeup. Rosario rushes his delivery, causing his arm to drag and his pitches to flatten out. He needs to do a better job of staying on top of his slider for more of a downward tilt through the strike zone. Headed for Triple-A, Rosario has the power stuff to be a top-of-the-rotation starter. He still hasn't quite regained his overpowering form and pinpoint control from 2002.

Year	Club (League)	Class	W	L	ERA	G	GS	CG	SV	IP	H	R	ER	HR	BB	SO	AVG
1999	Blue Jays (DSL)	R	1	0	3.06	18	0	0	3	32	26	16	11	0	11	38	.208
2000	Blue Jays (DSL)	R	2	0	1.21	26	0	0	16	37	21	5	5	0	7	51	.160
2001	Medicine Hat (Pio)	R	3	7	5.59	16	15	0	0	76	79	61	47	8	38	55	.271
2002	Charleston, WV (SAL)	A	6	1	2.57	13	13	1	0	67	50	22	19	5	14	78	.206
	Dunedin (FSL)	A	3	3	1.29	13	12	0	0	63	33	10	9	3	25	65	.151
2003	Did not play—Injured																
2004	Dunedin (FSL)	A	1	1	4.67	6	6	0	0	17	16	12	9	2	11	16	.229
	New Hampshire (EL)	AA	2	4	4.31	12	12	0	0	48	48	25	23	6	16	45	.268
MINOR LEAGUE TOTALS			18	16	3.25	104	58	1	19	340	273	151	123	24	122	348	.217

5 David Purcey, lhp

RICH ABEL

Born: April 22, 1982. **Ht.:** 6-5. **Wt.:** 240. **Bats:** L. **Throws:** L. **School:** University of Oklahoma. **Career Transactions:** Selected by Blue Jays in first round (16th overall) of 2004 draft; signed July 23, 2004. **Signed by:** Ty Nichols.

Purcey was selected in the 20th round by the Mariners out of high school, but declined their $1 million offer and headed to Oklahoma. He also turned down the Yankees as a draft-eligible sophomore in 2003, after going in the 17th round and starring in the Cape Cod League. It all paid off when he signed for $1.6 million as the 16th overall selection last June. Purcey has a loose, fluid arm to go with an imposing frame. He shows the makings of three average to plus pitches, and his primary weapon is a lively 90-95 mph fastball. He also throws two variations of a 75-79 mph curveball that's becoming an above-average pitch. One is a 12-to-6 hammer, while the other is more of a slurve. His changeup grades as solid-average. Purcey's inconsistent mechanics need to be cleaned up to improve his pitch quality and command. He tends to get under his fastball and get on the side of his curveball, costing him movement on both pitches. He didn't pitch well in his two previous draft years, causing some scouts to question his mental toughness. The Jays hope to push Purcey quickly through the system. He'll begin 2005 in high Class A.

Year	Club (League)	Class	W	L	ERA	G	GS	CG	SV	IP	H	R	ER	HR	BB	SO	AVG
2004	Auburn (NY-P)	A	1	0	1.50	3	2	0	0	12	6	2	2	0	1	13	.150
MINOR LEAGUE TOTALS			1	0	1.50	3	2	0	0	12	6	2	2	0	1	13	.150

6 Russ Adams, ss

RICH ABEL

Born: Aug. 30, 1980. **Ht.:** 6-1. **Wt.:** 180. **Bats:** L. **Throws:** R. **School:** University of North Carolina. **Career Transactions:** Selected by Blue Jays in first round (14th overall) of 2002 draft; signed June 7, 2002. **Signed by:** Charles Aliano.

Adams blazed through the Jays system, reaching Double-A in his first full season and the majors by the end of his second. He was selected for the 2004 Futures Game but missed it because of a ribcage injury. The day after he returned, he began a 16-game hitting streak. Adams employs a compact, line-drive stroke with quick hands. He profiles as a No. 2 hitter with gap power, and he has the ability to command the strike zone and make consistent contact. He has plus speed and keen baserunning ability. Defensively, he has soft hands, quick feet and improved range. Adams has below-average arm strength, but compensates with his positioning, reactions and release. He won't ever become a home run threat, though he finds the gaps with regularity. Playing shortstop on artificial turf will be a challenge for Adams, but Toronto likes the progress he has made in the field. He's similar offensively to the Orioles' Brian Roberts and is primed to take shortstop and the leadoff role in Toronto this spring. Aaron Hill could push Adams to second base in the future.

Year	Club (League)	Class	AVG	G	AB	R	H	2B	3B	HR	RBI	BB	SO	SB	OBP	SLG
2002	Auburn (NY-P)	A	.354	30	113	25	40	7	3	0	16	24	11	13	.464	.469
	Dunedin (FSL)	A	.231	37	147	23	34	4	2	1	12	18	17	5	.321	.306
2003	Dunedin (FSL)	A	.279	68	258	50	72	9	5	3	16	38	27	9	.380	.388
	New Haven (EL)	AA	.277	65	271	42	75	10	4	4	26	30	37	8	.349	.387
2004	Syracuse (IL)	AAA	.288	122	483	58	139	37	3	5	54	45	62	6	.351	.408
	Toronto (AL)	MAJ	.306	22	72	10	22	2	1	4	10	5	5	1	.359	.528
MAJOR LEAGUE TOTALS			.306	22	72	10	22	2	1	4	10	5	5	1	.359	.528
MINOR LEAGUE TOTALS			.283	322	1272	198	360	67	17	13	124	155	154	41	.364	.393

7 Dustin McGowan, rhp

Born: March 24, 1982. **Ht.:** 6-3. **Wt.:** 190. **Bats:** R. **Throws:** R. **School:** Long County HS, Ludowici, Ga. **Career Transactions:** Selected by Blue Jays in first round (33rd overall) of 2000 draft; signed June 20, 2000. **Signed by:** Chris Buckley/Joe Siers.

McGowan looked like he was headed for the Toronto rotation after a hot start that had him on the verge of a promotion to Syracuse in early May. But before he reached Triple-A, he learned he needed Tommy John surgery. Elbow troubles coming out of high school nearly caused the Blue Jays to void his $950,000 bonus, and they proceeded with caution by limiting his workload and pitch counts early in his career. When healthy, McGowan brings legitimate frontline starter stuff to the mound. His fastball sits at 94-95 mph and tops out at 97 with above-average life. He has a plus curveball with tight spin and bite, along with a sharp mid-80s slider. He maintains his fastball arm speed when he throws his changeup. The elbow injury clearly affected McGowan's command after he made significant progress the year before. He'll need to re-establish his control as well as the touch on his changeup once he returns. McGowan's rehabilitation has gone well, and Blue Jays officials say they're optimistic he can regain his overpowering stuff and are targeting a May return. He probably won't be at full strength until 2006.

Year	Club (League)	Class	W	L	ERA	G	GS	CG	SV	IP	H	R	ER	HR	BB	SO	AVG
2000	Medicine Hat (Pio)	R	0	3	6.48	8	8	0	0	25	26	21	18	2	25	19	.274
2001	Auburn (NY-P)	A	3	6	3.76	15	14	0	0	67	57	33	28	1	49	80	.234
2002	Charleston, WV (SAL)	A	11	10	4.19	28	28	1	0	148	143	77	69	10	59	163	.251
2003	Dunedin (FSL)	A	5	6	2.85	14	14	1	0	76	62	29	24	1	25	66	.223
	New Haven (EL)	AA	7	0	3.17	14	14	1	0	77	78	28	27	1	19	72	.261
2004	New Hampshire (EL)	AA	2	0	4.06	6	6	0	0	31	24	14	14	4	15	29	.207
MINOR LEAGUE TOTALS			28	25	3.82	85	84	3	0	424	390	202	180	19	192	429	.243

8 Zach Jackson, lhp

Born: May 13, 1983. **Ht.:** 6-5. **Wt.:** 220. **Bats:** L. **Throws:** L. **School:** Texas A&M University. **Career Transactions:** Selected by Blue Jays in first round (32nd overall) of 2004 draft; signed July 21, 2004. **Signed by:** Andy Beene.

After emerging in the Cape Cod League in 2003, Jackson transferred from Louisville to Texas A&M and spun a seven-inning no-hitter in his first start for the Aggies. The Blue Jays targeted both David Purcey and Jackson with the No. 16 overall pick, and were thrilled Jackson was still on the board for them at No. 32. He signed for $1.0175 million. Jackson has more polish than Purcey. His mechanics and easy arm action allow him to command three effective pitches. He hides his tailing 89-93 mph fastball well, and he'll cut it on occasion. He also throws a deceptive circle changeup and an improved slider with late depth. Jackson does a good job of pitching inside and locating his fastball. Jackson doesn't have a true swing-and-miss pitch. He relies more on setting hitters up, making them hit his pitch and depending on his defense to make plays. The Blue Jays limited Jackson to 50 pitches in each of his four pro starts after he worked a staff-high 121 innings at Texas A&M during the spring. He should be a workhorse in the long run, however, and he'll join Purcey in the Dunedin rotation in 2005.

Year	Club (League)	Class	W	L	ERA	G	GS	CG	SV	IP	H	R	ER	HR	BB	SO	AVG
2004	Auburn (NY-P)	A	0	0	5.40	4	4	0	0	15	20	9	9	1	6	11	.308
MINOR LEAGUE TOTALS			0	0	5.40	4	4	0	0	15	20	9	9	1	6	11	.308

9 Josh Banks, rhp

Born: July 18, 1982. **Ht.:** 6-3. **Wt.:** 195. **Bats:** R. **Throws:** R. **School:** Florida International University. **Career Transactions:** Selected by Blue Jays in second round of 2003 draft; signed June 4, 2003. **Signed by:** Tony Arias.

Banks' first-round aspirations were dashed when he came down with blister problems shortly before the 2003 draft. He also missed time as a Florida International sophomore with a strained elbow ligament, but neither injury has kept him from pitching like a first-round talent since signing for $650,000. A reliever in college before his junior season, Banks projects as a No. 3 or 4 starter. He keeps hitters off balance with a five-pitch repertoire, including a 90-94 mph fastball. His 83-85 mph splitter is an out pitch, and he mixes in an 80-82 mph slider, a curveball and a changeup. After getting promoted to Double-A, Banks initially struggled because he left the ball up in the strike zone too much. He made adjustments and finished his first full season with a four-game win streak. He still has work to do with his fastball command, and his slider can become slurvy at times. Banks will head back to Double-A to start 2005. He's on a path similar to that of David Bush, which could put him in Toronto around midseason.

Year	Club (League)	Class	W	L	ERA	G	GS	CG	SV	IP	H	R	ER	HR	BB	SO	AVG
2003	Auburn (NY-P)	A	7	2	2.43	15	15	0	0	67	58	21	18	1	10	81	.233
2004	Dunedin (FSL)	A	7	1	1.80	11	11	0	0	60	49	17	12	4	8	60	.220
	New Hampshire (EL)	AA	6	6	5.03	18	17	1	0	91	89	54	51	15	28	76	.251
MINOR LEAGUE TOTALS			20	9	3.34	44	43	1	0	218	196	92	81	20	46	217	.237

10 Gustavo Chacin, lhp

RICH ABEL

Born: Dec. 4, 1980. **Ht.:** 5-11. **Wt.:** 190. **Bats:** L. **Throws:** L. **Career Transactions:** Signed out of Venezuela by Blue Jays, July 3, 1998. **Signed by:** Luis Feunmayo.

Chacin signed out of the Jays' Venezuela academy for $50,000 and reached Double-A by age 19, but disappeared from the prospect radar when he scuffled and was demoted to the bullpen. He rebounded in 2004, leading the minors with 18 wins and being named Eastern League pitcher of the year before beating the Yankees in his major league debut. Chacin had been a fastball/changeup pitcher with a show-me curveball, and his success can be attributed to the addition of a cut fastball, which helped him get righthanders out. He changes speeds with his 83-89 mph cutter by varying his grip and pressure points. He also gives hitters a difficult look with a slight stutter in his delivery. His two-seam fastball ranges from 87-92 mph, and his changeup is average with good movement. Chacin's curve is still a below-average pitch, and he needs to improve it or find a pitch he can fight lefthanders with. Chacin has pitched his way into the Jays' plans and will vie for a spot at the back of the rotation in spring training.

Year	Club (League)	Class	W	L	ERA	G	GS	CG	SV	IP	H	R	ER	HR	BB	SO	AVG
1998	Blue Jays (DSL)	R	3	2	2.70	9	6	0	0	37	28	12	11	0	15	56	.212
1999	Medicine Hat (Pio)	R	4	3	3.09	15	9	0	1	64	68	33	22	6	23	50	.281
2000	Dunedin (FSL)	A	9	5	4.02	25	21	0	0	128	138	69	57	14	64	77	.269
	Tennessee (SL)	AA	0	2	2.60	2	2	0	0	5	10	7	7	1	6	5	.417
2001	Tennessee (SL)	AA	11	8	3.98	25	23	1	0	140	138	66	62	17	39	86	.257
2002	Tennessee (SL)	AA	6	5	4.66	35	13	1	1	120	131	73	62	12	59	68	.282
2003	New Haven (EL)	AA	3	4	4.15	46	2	0	2	69	78	39	32	1	29	55	.283
2004	New Hampshire (EL)	AA	16	2	2.92	25	25	0	0	142	113	53	46	15	49	109	.215
	Syracuse (IL)	AAA	2	0	2.31	2	2	0	0	12	16	4	3	0	3	14	.327
	Toronto (AL)	MAJ	1	1	2.57	2	2	0	0	14	8	4	4	0	3	6	.167
MAJOR LEAGUE TOTALS			1	1	2.57	2	2	0	0	14	8	4	4	0	3	6	.167
MINOR LEAGUE TOTALS			54	31	3.80	184	103	2	4	716	720	356	302	66	287	520	.261

11 Gabe Gross, of

Born: Oct. 21, 1979. **Ht.:** 6-3. **Wt.:** 200. **Bats:** L. **Throws:** R. **School:** Auburn University. **Career Transactions:** Selected by Blue Jays in first round (15th overall) of 2001 draft; signed July 1, 2001. **Signed by:** Ellis Dungan.

Gross was a two-sport star at Auburn, where he started at quarterback as a true freshman. His father Lee was an offensive lineman in the NFL during the 1970s. Gross hurt his right elbow in mid-April last year, and while he didn't require surgery he was limited to DH duties for six weeks. He's a big, physical athlete with solid tools across the board and employs an advanced approach at the plate, uncommon in most former two-sport athletes. He has made strides driving the ball to the opposite field with his long, lofting swing. He has an average arm and gets down the line in 4.4 seconds, slightly below-average from the left side. Gross has yet to show the above-average power the Jays projected when they drafted him 15th overall in 2001, though the new scouting regime still believes it's only a matter of time. Gross needs to be more aggressive, as he'll get passive after working counts into his favor. Gross also has a bad habit of opening up his front side too quickly on his swing, costing him bat speed and allowing lefthanders to exploit him on the inner half. He managed just one hit in 11 at-bats against southpaws in the majors after hitting .233 with one homer against them in Triple-A. He was overmatched at times with Toronto, but his tools are hard to ignore. The Jays will give him the chance to win the left-field job in spring training.

Year	Club (League)	Class	AVG	G	AB	R	H	2B	3B	HR	RBI	BB	SO	SB	OBP	SLG
2001	Dunedin (FSL)	A	.302	35	126	23	38	9	2	4	15	26	29	4	.426	.500
	Tennessee (SL)	AA	.244	11	41	8	10	1	0	3	11	6	12	0	.373	.488
2002	Tennessee (SL)	AA	.238	112	403	57	96	17	5	10	54	53	71	8	.333	.380
2003	New Haven (EL)	AA	.319	84	310	52	99	23	3	7	51	52	53	3	.423	.481
	Syracuse (IL)	AAA	.264	53	182	22	48	16	2	5	23	31	56	1	.380	.456

2004	Syracuse (IL)	AAA	.294	103	377	52	111	29	2	9	54	53	81	4	.381	.454
	Toronto (AL)	MAJ	.209	44	129	18	27	4	0	3	16	19	31	2	.311	.310
MAJOR LEAGUE TOTALS			.209	44	129	18	27	4	0	3	16	19	31	2	.311	.310
MINOR LEAGUE TOTALS			.279	398	1439	214	402	95	14	38	208	221	302	20	.381	.444

12 Yuber Rodriguez, of

Born: Nov. 17, 1983. **Ht.:** 6-1. **Wt.:** 170. **Bats:** B. **Throws:** R. **Career Transactions:** Signed out of Venezuela by Blue Jays, Nov. 7, 2000. **Signed by:** Raphael Moncada.

Rodriguez may have the highest upside of any position player in the Jays system. He earned all-star honors during his second stint in the Rookie-level Appalachian League, ranking among the leaders in several offensive categories. Managers considered him the top athlete in the league. Rodriguez has a projectable body with plenty of room for added strength. He displays plus raw power, speed and arm strength, and he's a sound center fielder. He has enough bat speed to catch up to quality fastballs and has a chance to develop into a middle-of-the-order threat. Rodriguez' pitch selection has improved, but he still needs to cut down on chasing pitches out of the zone. He'll get his first dose of full-season ball in 2005, as he heads to Toronto's new low Class A Lansing affiliate.

Year	Club (League)	Class	AVG	G	AB	R	H	2B	3B	HR	RBI	BB	SO	SB	OBP	SLG
2001	Toronto (DSL)	R	.182	44	159	21	29	7	0	4	21	13	49	12	.250	.302
2002	Carora (VSL)	R	.272	56	206	33	56	17	2	1	22	7	59	19	.320	.388
2003	Pulaski (Appy)	R	.282	41	131	18	37	11	0	2	15	5	41	1	.333	.412
2004	Pulaski (Appy)	R	.309	63	249	49	77	15	6	7	53	28	71	9	.396	.502
MINOR LEAGUE TOTALS			.267	204	745	121	199	50	8	14	111	53	220	41	.334	.412

13 Vince Perkins, rhp

Born: Sept. 27, 1981. **Ht.:** 6-5. **Wt.:** 220. **Bats:** L. **Throws:** R. **School:** Lake City (Fla.) CC. **Career Transactions:** Selected by Blue Jays in 18th round of 2000 draft; signed May 24, 2001. **Signed by:** Chris Buckley/Joe Siers.

After vaulting to No. 8 on this list a year ago on the heels of his breakthrough 2003 season, Perkins was slowed by injuries in 2004. A back injury forced him to miss most of May and June, and he hurt his elbow six starts after he returned, costing him another six weeks. When he's right, Perkins' stuff is second only to Dustin McGowan's in the system. He can run his fastball up to 94-97 mph with good movement, but he needs to improve his command. He complements his plus velocity with a good changeup and improving power slider in the upper 80s. The slider has nice tilt and has potential as a strikeout pitch. Perkins' arm appears to be sound, as he topped out at 95 mph in instructional league. As long as he doesn't have another setback, he'll start 2005 in the Double-A rotation. He has the repertoire to be a quality starter in the majors, though some scouts say his aggressive delivery and workhorse build are better suited for late-inning relief.

Year	Club (League)	Class	W	L	ERA	G	GS	CG	SV	IP	H	R	ER	HR	BB	SO	AVG
2001	Auburn (NY-P)	A	1	4	3.27	14	14	0	0	52	41	23	19	1	37	67	.220
2002	Auburn (NY-P)	A	5	5	3.34	15	15	0	0	73	51	32	27	3	44	85	.198
2003	Charleston, WV (SAL)	A	3	1	1.83	8	8	0	0	44	19	9	9	1	22	60	.136
	Dunedin (FSL)	A	7	6	2.45	18	17	0	0	84	58	32	23	1	53	69	.201
2004	Dunedin (FSL)	A	1	4	3.95	13	9	0	0	55	53	28	24	2	24	47	.250
MINOR LEAGUE TOTALS			17	20	2.98	68	63	0	0	308	222	124	102	8	180	328	.205

14 Shawn Marcum, rhp

Born: Dec. 14, 1981. **Ht.:** 6-0. **Wt.:** 180. **Bats:** R. **Throws:** R. **School:** Southwest Missouri State University. **Career Transactions:** Selected by Blue Jays in third round of 2003 draft; signed June 23, 2003. **Signed by:** Ty Nichols.

A two-way player at Southwest Missouri State, Marcum was the starting shortstop and closer on the Bears' 2003 College World Series team. His bat wasn't as impressive as his arm, however, so it was a given that he'd move full-time to the mound once he signed. Like David Bush, another star closer in college, Marcum worked in the rotation in his first full pro season. Toronto didn't make the change just to give him more innings, however. He has a four-pitch arsenal that could allow him to start in the majors. His best pitch is a sharp slider, and he throws an 87-92 mph fastball, an average curveball and an improved changeup. Though Marcum didn't need his changeup much in college, he maintains his arm speed and achieves late movement on the pitch. His control has been exemplary thus far, as he has averaged just 1.3 walks per nine innings as a pro. Marcum's defense was his strong suit as a shortstop, and he continues to field his position well. He'll head to Double-A to start 2005, and the Blue Jays expect him to move fast.

Year	Club (League)	Class	W	L	ERA	G	GS	CG	SV	IP	H	R	ER	HR	BB	SO	AVG
2003	Auburn (NY-P)	A	1	0	1.32	21	0	0	8	34	15	6	5	1	7	47	.129
2004	Charleston, WV (SAL)	A	7	4	3.19	13	13	1	0	79	64	32	28	7	16	83	.218
	Dunedin (FSL)	A	3	2	3.12	12	12	0	0	69	74	30	24	6	4	72	.272
MINOR LEAGUE TOTALS			11	6	2.81	46	25	1	8	182	153	68	57	14	27	202	.225

15 Curtis Thigpen, c/1b

Born: April 19, 1983. **Ht.:** 6-0. **Wt.:** 188. **Bats:** R. **Throws:** R. **School:** University of Texas. **Career Transactions:** Selected by Blue Jays in second round of 2004 draft; signed July 9, 2004. **Signed by:** Andy Beene.

Thigpen was a member of three College World Series teams in three years at Texas, where he caught sparingly. Taylor Teagarden, a potential 2005 first-round pick, handled most of the catching duties, while Thigpen played first base. But the Blue Jays saw enough of him behind the plate to take him in the second round as a catcher last June. His offense is ahead of his defense at this point. Thigpen starts from a balanced stance, and he has quick hands and a line-drive stroke. He uses the whole field and has a solid approach, but he doesn't have a lot of lift in his swing. Though he showed good pop in his pro debut, he could have a harder time hitting for power against better pitching. He's agile behind the plate, though his catch-and-throw skills are ordinary. He threw out 29 percent of basestealers in the short-season New York-Penn League. He can play anywhere on the diamond except for shortstop and center field, so even if he doesn't become a big league regular he could become a versatile utilityman. He could handle a jump to high Class A, but Robinzon Diaz is one rung ahead of him in the system, which may mean Thigpen will begin 2005 in low Class A.

Year	Club (League)	Class	AVG	G	AB	R	H	2B	3B	HR	RBI	BB	SO	SB	OBP	SLG
2004	Auburn (NY-P)	A	.301	45	166	34	50	11	2	7	29	23	32	1	.388	.518
MINOR LEAGUE TOTALS			.301	45	166	34	50	11	2	7	29	23	32	1	.388	.518

16 Ismael Ramirez, rhp

Born: March 3, 1981. **Ht.:** 6-3. **Wt.:** 200. **Bats:** R. **Throws:** R. **Career Transactions:** Signed out of Venezuela by Blue Jays, July 30, 1998. **Signed by:** Emilio Carrasquel.

Ramirez had never won more than six games in any of his previous five pro seasons before leading the high Class A Florida State League with 15 victories in 2004. The FSL's most valuable pitcher was a bit old for his level, but he has a nice fastball that should get outs against more advanced hitters. He uses a quick arm action and over-the-top slot to achieve a downward plane on his 90-93 mph heater. The Jays worked with Ramirez to slow down his delivery and keep him more in line to the plate, eliminating his tendency to fly open and elevate pitches. He has a slight hesitation that throws off batters' timing. He throws strikes with all three of his pitches, and his changeup and slider can be plus pitches at times. Ramirez has a good feel for pitching and great competitive makeup. He's finally ready for Double-A.

Year	Club (League)	Class	W	L	ERA	G	GS	CG	SV	IP	H	R	ER	HR	BB	SO	AVG
1999	Chico Canonico (VSL)	R	1	0	4.20	3	3	0	0	15	16	10	7	0	1	8	.281
2000	Chico Canonico (VSL)	R	2	0	3.15	4	4	0	0	20	20	7	7	4	2	13	.253
	Blue Jays (DSL)	R	3	1	3.72	11	7	0	2	46	51	24	19	1	6	26	.276
2001	Medicine Hat (Pio)	R	5	6	5.35	14	14	0	0	74	77	48	44	12	21	35	.267
2002	Medicine Hat (Pio)	R	4	2	2.98	11	10	0	0	54	51	23	18	4	14	51	.249
	Auburn (NY-P)	A	0	2	7.15	3	3	0	0	11	17	10	9	2	2	7	.354
	Charleston, WV (SAL)	A	0	1	4.86	6	1	0	0	17	20	10	9	2	7	14	.290
2003	Charleston, WV (SAL)	A	6	5	3.02	24	22	1	0	119	110	51	40	6	31	70	.243
2004	Dunedin (FSL)	A	15	6	2.72	28	27	0	0	165	151	57	50	5	25	131	.242
MINOR LEAGUE TOTALS			36	23	3.50	104	91	1	2	522	513	240	203	36	109	355	.255

17 Adam Lind, of/1b

Born: July 17, 1983. **Ht.:** 6-2. **Wt.:** 190. **Bats:** L. **Throws:** L. **School:** University of South Alabama. **Career Transactions:** Selected by Blue Jays in third round in 2004 draft; signed June 21, 2004. **Signed by:** Joel Grampietro.

Some Blue Jays scouts say Lind is the best hitter they've selected in the three drafts under general manager J.P. Ricciardi's watch. An eighth-round pick of the Twins out of high school in Indiana in 2002, he batted .372 in two seasons at South Alabama, including a Sun Belt Conference-best .392 average in 2004. Toronto took him as a draft-eligible sophomore with the second of two draft picks it received for the loss of free agent Kelvim Escobar. Lind kept hitting in his pro debut, making the New York-Penn League all-star team, topping the league in doubles and ranking among the leaders in several categories. He has a fluid lefthanded stroke, bat speed and raw power that presently shows up mainly as doubles. His strike-zone judgment and pitch recognition can improve. Lind's bat will have to carry him because his speed and defense are below-average. He played first base as a freshman and right field as a sophomore, then mostly left field as a pro. He was just adequate there and may face a return to first base in the future. The Jays could challenge him by moving him to high Class A to begin his first full season.

Year	Club (League)	Class	AVG	G	AB	R	H	2B	3B	HR	RBI	BB	SO	SB	OBP	SLG
2004	Auburn (NY-P)	A	.308	70	266	43	82	23	0	7	50	24	36	1	.367	.474
MINOR LEAGUE TOTALS			.308	70	266	43	82	23	0	7	50	24	36	1	.367	.474

18 Robinzon Diaz, c

Born: Sept. 19, 1983. **Ht.:** 5-11. **Wt.:** 180. **Bats:** R. **Throws:** R. **Career Transactions:** Signed out of Dominican Republic by Blue Jays, Nov. 19, 2000. **Signed by:** Hilario Soriano.

Diaz won the Appalachian League batting title in 2003 and earned a trip to the Futures Game last summer. While he has a free-swinging approach, he displays tremendous bat control and has established himself as one of the most difficult hitters in the minors to strike out. He has an inside-out stroke and sprays the ball to all fields, though he needs to do a better job of controling the strike zone and getting on base, especially if he wants to get the attention of the Blue Jays brass. Diaz also has shown little power at the plate. Behind the plate, his biggest assets are his leadership skills and ability to block pitches. He has an average arm and release, regularly getting the ball down to second in about 2.0 seconds on steals. He erased 28 percent of basestealers in 2004. Diaz has made progress in calling games. With Guillermo Quiroz and Curtis Thigpen ahead of him on the catching depth chart, Diaz' athletic ability enabled him to work out at second and third base during instructional league to enhance his versatility. He'll move up one level to high Class A this year. If Thigpen is there as well, Diaz could split time between catching and playing the infield.

Year	Club (League)	Class	AVG	G	AB	R	H	2B	3B	HR	RBI	BB	SO	SB	OBP	SLG
2001	Blue Jays (DSL)	R	.312	65	253	49	79	17	2	2	45	20	19	4	.374	.419
2002	Medicine Hat (Pio)	R	.297	58	192	29	57	9	0	0	20	13	19	7	.345	.344
	Dunedin (FSL)	A	.120	10	25	3	3	0	0	0	1	1	4	0	.148	.120
2003	Pulaski (Appy)	R	.374	48	182	33	68	20	2	1	44	10	14	1	.407	.522
2004	Charleston, WV (SAL)	A	.287	106	407	62	117	20	2	2	42	27	31	10	.342	.361
MINOR LEAGUE TOTALS			.306	287	1059	176	324	66	6	5	152	71	87	22	.357	.394

19 Chi-Hung Cheng, lhp

Born: June 20, 1985. **Ht.:** 6-0. **Wt.:** 190. **Bats:** L. **Throws:** L. **Career Transactions:** Signed out of Taiwan by Blue Jays, Nov. 26, 2003. **Signed by:** J.P. Ricciardi.

A member of Taiwan's 1996 Little League World Series championship club, Cheng continued to pitch for national teams in Taiwan as he got older. His heavy amateur workload scared off clubs that scout Asia extensively, but the Jays were undaunted. They signed him for $400,000 after he went 0-1, 5.40 in four appearances at the 2003 World Cup in Cuba. They also agreed to let him pitch in the 2004 Olympics if Taiwan wanted him, but he didn't make the cut. Cheng's health wasn't an issue in his pro debut, as he led the Appalachian League in strikeouts. His advanced feel for pitching was one of the main attributes that attracted the Jays' interest, and it allowed him to carve up Rookie-level hitters. He has a clean delivery, throws strikes and projects to add velocity as he matures physically. He currently operates with an 86-90 mph fastball, a hard-biting curveball and a developing changeup. He'll pitch in low Class A this year.

Year	Club (League)	Class	W	L	ERA	G	GS	CG	SV	IP	H	R	ER	HR	BB	SO	AVG
2004	Pulaski (Appy)	R	4	1	2.82	14	14	0	0	61	47	27	19	4	35	74	.214
	Auburn (NY-P)	A	0	0	4.50	1	0	0	0	2	1	1	1	1	0	3	.143
MINOR LEAGUE TOTALS			4	1	2.87	15	14	0	0	63	48	28	20	5	35	77	.211

20 Raul Tablado, ss/3b

Born: March 3, 1982. **Ht.:** 6-2. **Wt.:** 190. **Bats:** R. **Throws:** R. **School:** Southridge HS, Miami. **Career Transactions:** Selected by Blue Jays in fourth round of 2000 draft; signed July 4, 2000. **Signed by:** Tony Arias.

Tablado has added 30 pounds since signing as a fourth-round pick out of high school in 2000, and his power also grew last year. But he missed six weeks early in the year with a pulled quadriceps muscle, then was suspended at the end of the season when he tested positive for a banned substance (reportedly from an over-the-counter supplement). After hitting 25 homers in his first four pro seasons, he broke out with 21 in just 84 games in high Class A in 2004. The ball carries well off his bat and he now shows above-average raw power. Tablado also matured mentally and impressed the Blue Jays with his renewed focus. He did a better job of staying on pitches rather than pulling off of them, as he had in the past.

Tablado still doesn't have the plate discipline that Toronto preaches, however, and his walk rate dipped in 2004. Though he has a strong arm and reliable hands, he doesn't run well enough or have enough range to play shortstop in the majors. He profiles better as a third baseman. Tablado is destined for a full year in Double-A as he seeks to make up for time lost last season.

Year	Club (League)	Class	AVG	G	AB	R	H	2B	3B	HR	RBI	BB	SO	SB	OBP	SLG
2000	Queens (NY-P)	A	.212	52	198	27	42	8	2	3	29	31	76	1	.318	.318
2001	Charleston, WV (SAL)	A	.253	122	388	49	98	23	2	9	44	45	127	5	.336	.392
2002	Charleston, WV (SAL)	A	.222	103	361	38	80	23	0	2	29	21	98	2	.268	.302
2003	Charleston, WV (SAL)	A	.190	61	226	29	43	10	1	6	26	25	69	2	.272	.323
	Dunedin (FSL)	A	.258	54	182	27	47	9	3	5	19	17	47	1	.328	.423
2004	Dunedin (FSL)	A	.303	84	323	62	98	28	0	21	76	24	91	0	.354	.585
MINOR LEAGUE TOTALS			.243	476	1678	232	408	101	8	46	223	163	508	11	.313	.395

21 Jamie Vermilyea, rhp

Born: Feb. 10, 1982. **Ht.:** 6-4. **Wt.:** 195. **Bats:** R. **Throws:** R. **School:** University of New Mexico. **Career Transactions:** Selected by Blue Jays in ninth round of 2003 draft; signed June 5, 2003. **Signed by:** Tim Huff.

Vermilyea fits perfectly in an organization that relishes drawing walks and abhors giving them up. He owns a 154-32 strikeout-walk ratio in 165 pro innings, and he showed off his fine command by spinning a seven-inning perfect game in his third outing in Double-A. The Blue Jays shuttled Vermilyea between the rotation and bullpen all year to get him extra work, and he'll likely be a reliever in the majors. He has a more diverse repertoire than most relievers, starting with an 89-91 mph fastball with plus run and sink. His 79-82 mph slider features sharp, late break. He changes speeds and planes with his 80-83 mph splitter, his curveball and his fading changeup. He even added a cutter late in the season to attack left-handers. Vermilyea struggles with his delivery from the stretch because he lacks balance, but he generates average arm speed with a three-quarters arm slot and gets good extension out front. He could open 2005 in Triple-A and make his major league debut later in the year.

Year	Club (League)	Class	W	L	ERA	G	GS	CG	SV	IP	H	R	ER	HR	BB	SO	AVG
2003	Auburn (NY-P)	A	5	1	2.37	9	2	0	0	30	22	10	8	0	5	53	.204
	Dunedin (FSL)	A	0	2	2.49	9	0	0	2	22	21	6	6	1	2	25	.253
2004	Dunedin (FSL)	A	5	1	3.09	18	6	0	0	55	54	22	19	4	13	37	.261
	New Hampshire (EL)	AA	3	2	2.47	21	6	1	5	58	43	20	16	2	12	39	.204
MINOR LEAGUE TOTALS			13	6	2.66	57	14	1	7	166	140	58	49	7	32	154	.230

22 Kurt Isenberg, lhp

Born: Jan. 15, 1982. **Ht.:** 6-0. **Wt.:** 190. **Bats:** R. **Throws:** L. **School:** James Madison University. **Career Transactions:** Selected by Blue Jays in fourth round of 2003 draft; signed June 8, 2003. **Signed by:** John Ceprini.

Isenberg's 8-8, 5.95 junior season at James Madison didn't scare off the performance-oriented Blue Jays. They knew he pitched in a hitter-friendly home ballpark, and they liked his athleticism (he also played the outfield for the Dukes) and fluid arm action. He quickly repaid their faith, as his 1.63 ERA in his pro debut easily would have led the New York-Penn League had he worked another one-third of an inning to qualify. Isenberg found the going rougher in his first full pro season, getting demoted from high Class A at midseason and missing a month with soreness in his biceps. He still has interesting stuff, however. He throws strikes with a 90-91 mph fastball, an average changeup and an effective curveball. He had trouble maintaining his release point, causing him to leave hittable pitches up in the strike zone. He also added a slider, which is still a work in progress. Isenberg, who profiles as a back-of-the-rotation starter, will get another opportunity at Dunedin in 2005.

Year	Club (League)	Class	W	L	ERA	G	GS	CG	SV	IP	H	R	ER	HR	BB	SO	AVG
2003	Auburn (NY-P)	A	7	2	1.63	13	13	0	0	61	40	17	11	1	19	57	.183
2004	Charleston, WV (SAL)	A	3	4	3.88	11	10	0	0	51	48	25	22	5	15	34	.242
	Dunedin (FSL)	A	2	4	5.61	14	14	0	0	61	73	46	38	6	20	40	.299
MINOR LEAGUE TOTALS			12	10	3.70	38	37	0	0	173	161	88	71	12	54	131	.244

23 Miguel Negron, of

Born: Aug. 22, 1982. **Ht.:** 6-2. **Wt.:** 170. **Bats:** L. **Throws:** L. **School:** Manuela Toro HS, Caguas, P.R. **Career Transactions:** Selected by Blue Jays in first round (18th overall) of 2000 draft; signed June 12, 2000. **Signed by:** Jorge Rivera.

Of the Blue Jays' top picks in each draft from 1987-2002, Negron (first round, 2000) is the only player who hasn't reached the majors. While he's progressing slowly, though, he's still likely to extend that remarkable streak of success. Negron might have the best raw tools of any Toronto prospect. His defensive ability in center field, complete with plus arm strength and the best speed in the system, is enough by itself to carry him to the big leagues as a reserve outfielder. The question is his bat. He spent parts of three seasons in low Class A before rising to Dunedin last season. Nagging hamstring and elbow injuries have hindered his progress, but he's equipped with good bat speed and average raw power. The Blue Jays are encouraged by his improved knowledge of the strike zone, but he'll need to work counts more and strike out less to be more than a defensive replacement. He will make his Double-A debut in 2005, when the Jays hope he can get 500 at-bats for the first time in his career.

Year	Club (League)	Class	AVG	G	AB	R	H	2B	3B	HR	RBI	BB	SO	SB	OBP	SLG
2000	Medicine Hat (Pio)	R	.232	53	190	26	44	5	0	0	13	23	39	5	.324	.258
2001	Auburn (NY-P)	A	.253	50	186	27	47	6	1	1	13	15	22	7	.314	.312
	Charleston, WV (SAL)	A	.192	25	99	11	19	1	0	0	2	6	21	5	.238	.202
2002	Charleston, WV (SAL)	A	.255	118	420	56	107	15	2	5	41	35	77	20	.312	.336
2003	Charleston, WV (SAL)	A	.303	30	109	13	33	8	1	1	11	2	16	6	.330	.422
2004	Dunedin (FSL)	A	.269	99	372	46	100	16	5	9	48	38	81	3	.341	.411
MINOR LEAGUE TOTALS			.254	375	1376	179	350	51	9	16	128	119	256	46	.318	.339

24 Justin James, rhp

Born: Sept. 13, 1981. **Ht.:** 6-3. **Wt.:** 212. **Bats:** R. **Throws:** R. **School:** University of Missouri. **Career Transactions:** Selected by Blue Jays in fifth round of 2003 draft; signed June 18, 2003. **Signed by:** Ty Nichols.

A sixth-round pick out of an Oklahoma high school by the Red Sox in 2001, James went one round better as a sophomore-eligible coming out of Missouri. He was the highest-drafted Tigers alum since the Astros picked Dave Silvestri in 1988's second round. James cruised through his first two pro stops before stalling in high Class A in the second half of 2004. In order to adjust, he'll need to slow down his mechanics and improve the consistency of his slider, which could become an above-average pitch. James runs his fastball into the low 90s with a maximum-effort delivery that lacks deception. Coming into last season, his changeup was his best pitch. But he didn't fool lefthanders with it as he had previously, and they hit .337 against him. Like many of Toronto's recent picks, he keeps the ball in the yard and throws strikes. He's also aggressive about pitching inside. James could return to high A to open 2005, though he could wind up in Double-A if he has a good spring. He may move to the bullpen in the future.

Year	Club (League)	Class	W	L	ERA	G	GS	CG	SV	IP	H	R	ER	HR	BB	SO	AVG
2003	Auburn (NY-P)	A	2	1	3.20	13	8	0	0	39	34	14	14	2	11	42	.238
2004	Charleston, WV (SAL)	A	5	4	3.00	14	14	0	0	78	67	31	26	2	24	83	.233
	Dunedin (FSL)	A	3	6	5.40	11	11	0	0	50	60	32	30	2	19	41	.299
MINOR LEAGUE TOTALS			10	11	3.77	38	33	0	0	167	161	77	70	6	54	166	.255

25 John-Ford Griffin, of/1b

Born: Nov. 19, 1979. **Ht.:** 6-2. **Wt.:** 215. **Bats:** L. **Throws:** L. **School:** Florida State University. **Career Transactions:** Selected by Yankees in first round (23rd overall) of 2001 draft; signed June 14, 2001 . . . Traded by Yankees with LHP Ted Lilly and RHP Jason Arnold to Athletics as part of three-way trade in which Yankees received RHP Jeff Weaver from Tigers and Tigers received 1B Carlos Pena, RHP Franklyn German and a player to be named from Athletics, July 6, 2002; Tigers acquired RHP Jeremy Bonderman from Athletics to complete trade (Aug. 22, 2002) . . . Traded by Athletics to Blue Jays for a player to be named, Jan. 27, 2003; Athletics acquired OF Jason Perry to complete trade (June 23, 2003). **Signed by:** Scott Pleis (Yankees).

Griffin topped the .400 mark in all three of his seasons at Florida State, where he set a school record with a .427 career average and Seminoles coach Mike Martin called him the best pure hitter in the program's storied history. The Yankees made him a first-round pick in 2001, and two trades later he has yet to make it past Double-A. Griffin has been disappointing for the Blue Jays, who thought they were getting a nearly major league-ready hitting machine. He repeated Double-A last year and didn't make the expected adjustments. He launched a personal-best 22 homers, but at the expense of his ability to hit for average (a career-low .248) and his strike-zone judgment (a career-worst 128 whiffs). He has a smooth, quick swing from the left side and needs to get back to his natural hitting instincts. He fell into the bad habit of working deep counts only to strike out looking on good pitches to hit. Griffin's defense is a significant concern as well. He had surgery on his throwing shoulder after his sophomore year at Florida State, and his arm has been below-average ever since. He injured his wrist in spring training and had to spend most of 2004 as a DH. He's limited to left field or first base, and he's going to have to produce a lot more offense to cut it at either position. Griffin will get an opportunity to turn things around in Triple-A, but his time is running out.

Year	Club (League)	Class	AVG	G	AB	R	H	2B	3B	HR	RBI	BB	SO	SB	OBP	SLG
2001	Staten Island (NY-P)	A	.311	66	238	46	74	17	1	5	43	40	41	10	.413	.454
2002	Tampa (FSL)	A	.267	65	255	32	68	16	1	3	31	29	45	1	.344	.373
	Norwich (EL)	AA	.328	18	67	17	22	3	0	5	10	8	13	0	.400	.597
	Midland (TL)	AA	.143	2	7	0	1	0	0	0	0	0	3	0	.250	.143
2003	New Haven (EL)	AA	.279	104	373	48	104	23	3	13	75	49	85	2	.361	.461
2004	New Hampshire (EL)	AA	.248	129	467	66	116	28	1	22	81	56	128	1	.330	.454
MINOR LEAGUE TOTALS			.274	384	1407	209	385	87	6	48	240	182	315	14	.358	.446

26 Eric Crozier, 1b/of

Born: Aug. 11, 1978. **Ht.:** 6-4. **Wt.:** 200. **Bats:** L. **Throws:** L. **School:** Norfolk State University. **Career Transactions:** Selected by Indians in 41st round of 2000 draft; signed June 15, 2000 . . . Traded by Indians to Blue Jays for 1B/DH Josh Phelps, Aug. 6, 2004. **Signed by:** Dave Miller (Indians).

Josh Phelps was leading the Blue Jays in RBIs in early August, but they were frustrated by his inconsistency at the plate and not thrilled about the prospect of going to arbitration with him. They tried to slip him through waivers, only to have the Indians claim him. When Cleveland offered Crozier to the Jays, they decided not to pull Phelps back. When he got called up in September, Crozier joined former Cardinals outfielder Terry Bradshaw as the only Norfolk State products to reach the majors. His lefthanded power is his best tool. He hit 40 homers in the minors over the last two seasons and went deep twice after his promotion. Crozier doesn't load his hands well, so his swing gets long, hampering his ability to hit for average. He's a decent athlete who moves and throws OK. Though he has mostly played first base, he can help on either outfield corner. Crozier has a chance to make the Blue Jays as a reserve in 2005, and could get consideration to replace Carlos Delgado at first base.

Year	Club (League)	Class	AVG	G	AB	R	H	2B	3B	HR	RBI	BB	SO	SB	OBP	SLG
2000	Mahoning Valley (NY-P)	A	.212	52	179	31	38	9	0	4	24	30	61	4	.324	.330
2001	Columbus (SAL)	A	.235	67	221	41	52	9	2	4	19	37	84	5	.346	.348
2002	Kinston (Car)	A	.326	72	258	40	84	16	2	9	55	42	57	4	.423	.508
	Akron (EL)	AA	.296	43	142	19	42	8	1	1	13	21	50	1	.398	.387
2003	Akron (EL)	AA	.245	108	347	52	85	10	3	19	52	51	92	5	.344	.455
2004	Buffalo (IL)	AAA	.297	84	296	55	88	21	0	20	53	36	67	5	.375	.571
	Syracuse (IL)	AAA	.277	25	94	12	26	8	0	1	16	16	27	3	.393	.394
	Toronto (AL)	MAJ	.152	14	33	5	5	2	0	2	4	6	19	0	.282	.394
MAJOR LEAGUE TOTALS			.152	14	33	5	5	2	0	2	4	6	19	0	.282	.394
MINOR LEAGUE TOTALS			.270	451	1537	250	415	81	8	58	232	233	438	27	.369	.446

27 Ron Davenport, of/1b

Born: Oct. 16, 1981. **Ht.:** 6-2. **Wt.:** 190. **Bats:** L. **Throws:** R. **School:** Leesville Road HS, Raleigh, N.C. **Career Transactions:** Selected by Blue Jays in 22nd round of 2000 draft; signed June 14, 2000. **Signed by:** Charles Aliano.

Davenport got his career off to a fast start when he hit .345 in the Rookie-level Pioneer League in 2000, but he hit a wall when he reached the Florida State League in 2002. It wasn't until 2004, his third FSL season, that he began to show more offensive potential. He recovered from a .200 April to bat .296 the rest of the way, setting a Dunedin record with 40 doubles in the process. He has a pretty lefthanded stroke, makes hard contact and does a good job of using the whole field. Toronto would like him to see more pitches, as he has a tendency to attack early in the count. His speed and arm strength are average, and he improved his defense in right field last year. He also has taken well to spot duty at first base. Davenport will arrive in Double-A in 2005, and his bat will determine whether he can make it as a big league reserve.

Year	Club (League)	Class	AVG	G	AB	R	H	2B	3B	HR	RBI	BB	SO	SB	OBP	SLG
2000	Medicine Hat (Pio)	R	.345	59	229	37	79	16	2	4	46	21	28	5	.404	.485
2001	Charleston, WV (SAL)	A	.289	79	298	37	86	18	2	4	54	20	53	11	.328	.403
2002	Dunedin (FSL)	A	.227	79	264	26	60	15	3	2	21	18	42	5	.282	.330
2003	Dunedin (FSL)	A	.276	119	421	39	116	27	2	5	57	32	74	6	.330	.385
2004	Dunedin (FSL)	A	.278	113	442	63	123	40	4	16	92	47	68	0	.345	.495
MINOR LEAGUE TOTALS			.281	449	1654	202	464	116	13	31	270	138	265	27	.337	.423

28 John Hattig, 3b/1b

Born: Feb. 27, 1980. **Ht.:** 6-2. **Wt.:** 210. **Bats:** B. **Throws:** R. **School:** Southern HS, Santa Rita, Guam. **Career Transactions:** Selected by Red Sox in 25th round of 1998 draft; signed Aug. 24, 1998 . . . Traded by Red Sox to Blue Jays for RHP Terry Adams, July 24, 2004. **Signed by:** Wally Komatsubara (Red Sox).

The first player ever drafted out of Guam, Hattig also is trying to become the first from the island territory to reach the majors. His chances appeared remote after he made little progress in his first four pro seasons, but he turned a corner after deciding to take his conditioning seriously. When the Red Sox were looking for bullpen help in July, they sent him to Toronto for Terry Adams. Hattig's 22 homers last year were six more than he had totaled in his five previous seasons. He works counts to get himself in a position where he can take advantage of his plus raw power. High fastballs give him trouble, however, and he swings and misses a lot. Hattig's arm is playable at third base, but his lack of first-step quickness eventually will force him to move to first base. Back spasms cost him most of June, and his weight will be an ongoing concern. But he has earned a trip to Triple-A and could get a call to Toronto in 2005.

Year	Club (League)	Class	AVG	G	AB	R	H	2B	3B	HR	RBI	BB	SO	SB	OBP	SLG
1999	Red Sox (GCL)	R	.270	50	163	28	44	7	3	1	17	16	20	1	.333	.368
2000	Lowell (NY-P)	A	.289	61	242	30	70	8	1	0	28	20	43	1	.342	.331
2001	Lowell (NY-P)	A	.111	11	45	4	5	0	1	1	5	3	7	1	.184	.222
	Augusta (SAL)	A	.285	50	179	25	51	9	1	1	23	22	42	4	.371	.363
2002	Augusta (SAL)	A	.282	93	347	46	98	20	0	7	56	52	73	1	.377	.401
	Sarasota (FSL)	A	.247	24	85	6	21	6	0	0	6	7	16	0	.301	.318
2003	Sarasota (FSL)	A	.295	114	400	51	118	29	2	6	70	59	70	9	.385	.423
	Portland (EL)	AA	.219	8	32	3	7	2	0	0	1	2	11	0	.265	.281
2004	Portland (EL)	AA	.295	75	264	53	78	21	1	12	35	47	68	3	.411	.519
	New Hampshire (EL)	AA	.296	40	142	24	42	7	0	10	30	12	41	0	.352	.556
MINOR LEAGUE TOTALS			.281	526	1899	270	534	109	9	38	271	240	391	20	.364	.408

29 Jason Alfaro, util

Born: Nov. 29, 1977. **Ht.:** 5-10. **Wt.:** 185. **Bats:** R. **Throws:** R. **School:** Hill (Texas) JC. **Career Transactions:** Selected by Astros in 22nd round of 1997 draft; signed June 30, 1997 . . . Granted free agency, Oct. 15, 2003; re-signed by Astros, Nov. 10, 2003 . . . Granted free agency, Oct. 15, 2004; signed with Blue Jays, Nov. 17, 2004. **Signed by:** Ralph Bratton (Astros).

Drafted as a two-way player out of junior college, Alfaro nearly made the Astros out of spring training last year. A late cut, he settled for making his major league debut in September after his eighth full season in the minors. Despite his limited major league experience, Alfaro will challenge for a utility role in Toronto after signing as a minor league free agent. Alfaro has solid all-around skills. He can swing the bat, owns gap power and is versatile defensively. He played six positions in 2004: shortstop, third base, second base and all three spots in the outfield. His best tool by far is his strong arm, and he also has average speed. Alfaro employs a narrow, straight-up stance, and he incorporates a toe tap as a trigger mechanism. He has a compact stroke, and though he takes aggressive hacks he doesn't strike out excessively. He does lack the home run power and patience to project as an everyday player.

Year	Club (League)	Class	AVG	G	AB	R	H	2B	3B	HR	RBI	BB	SO	SB	OBP	SLG
1997	Astros (GCL)	R	.265	34	102	8	27	5	0	2	13	8	14	6	.324	.373
1998	Astros (GCL)	R	.242	47	178	20	43	8	0	1	18	11	24	5	.286	.303
1999	Michigan (Mid)	A	.271	118	473	74	128	25	4	5	50	23	62	5	.302	.372
2000	Kissimmee (FSL)	A	.250	117	460	58	115	20	1	7	41	25	63	5	.287	.343
2001	Round Rock (TL)	AA	.243	87	284	26	69	16	2	2	29	7	40	2	.264	.335
2002	Round Rock (TL)	AA	.314	124	455	71	143	36	2	16	74	50	75	11	.393	.508
2003	Round Rock (TL)	AA	.148	22	81	6	12	3	0	0	9	5	20	0	.198	.185
	New Orleans (PCL)	AAA	.296	105	361	45	107	20	4	9	49	30	53	2	.354	.449
2004	New Orleans (PCL)	AAA	.325	126	465	62	151	32	0	13	67	26	58	3	.363	.477
	Houston	MAJ	.182	7	11	1	2	0	0	0	0	0	5	0	.182	.182
MINOR LEAGUE TOTALS			.278	780	2859	370	795	165	13	55	350	185	409	36	.325	.403

30 Casey Janssen, rhp

Born: Sept. 17, 1981. **Ht.:** 6-4. **Wt.:** 210. **Bats:** R. **Throws:** R. **School:** UCLA. **Career Transactions:** Selected by Blue Jays in fourth round of 2004 draft; signed June 13, 2004. **Signed by:** Billy Gasparino.

Janssen spent his first three years at UCLA as a two-way player, homering in his first college at-bat and seeing time at both first base and on the mound. He became a full-time pitcher in 2004, with promising results, going 10-4, 3.16 as a senior. He also improved his draft stock, going from a 49th-round pick by the Orioles in 2003 to a fourth-rounder who signed for $150,000 last June. Janssen has a lean, athletic body with room for added weight and strength. He has a no-windup delivery with a high leg kick, and easy arm action from a high three-quarters slot. His best pitch is an 89-92 mph two-seam fastball with good command and sinking action. Janssen also throws a changeup with fastball arm speed, a curveball and slider that have good rotation and spin, and a cutter. He commands and mixes all his pitches well. He figures to start 2005 in Class A.

Year	Club (League)	Class	W	L	ERA	G	GS	CG	SV	IP	H	R	ER	HR	BB	SO	AVG
2004	Auburn (NY-P)	A	3	1	3.60	10	10	0	0	50	46	21	20	2	10	43	.241
MINOR LEAGUE TOTALS			3	1	3.60	10	10	0	0	50	46	21	20	2	10	43	.241

WASHINGTON
NATIONALS

BY **AARON FITT**

For the first time since Major League Baseball assumed ownership of the Expos in 2002, the franchise appeared to have some certainty about its future. After years of dragging its feet, MLB announced in September that it was moving the team to Washington, D.C., for the 2005 season. The renamed Nationals finally had a home after two years of splitting home games between Montreal and San Juan, Puerto Rico.

Not so fast. The deal between MLB and Washington, which called for a publicly funded stadium, began to unravel in December. The D.C. council reneged on that agreement, amending the financing plan to call for at least half the money to come from a private source. MLB abruptly shut down the Nationals' business and promotional operations. But hold on again. A week later the council, the mayor's office and MLB reached a compromise, and a divided council narrowly approved it. The new deal allows the city to pay for the ballpark with tax money while searching for private financing, and splits the liability for cost overruns and missed deadlines evenly between the city and MLB.

While the team will at least be playing in D.C. in 2005, true stability won't arrive until the Nationals get a real owner. The team has operated under tight financial restrictions for years, and the Expos were held to a strict draft budget and had a skeleton staff, with 11 full-time scouts in 2004.

Considering those handicaps, scouting director Dana Brown has done an admirable

MORRIS FOSTOFF

job. His first draft in 2002 netted three of the franchise's Top 10 Prospects. **Chad Cordero** zoomed to the majors after being taken in the first round of the 2003 draft, which also produced righthander Daryl Thompson, third baseman Kory Casto and outfielder Jerry Owens. It's too early to tell how the 2004 draft crop will stack up, but lefthander Bill Bray looks like another first-rounder on the fast track.

Though the club's draft efforts are encouraging, the reality remains that its farm system is one of the worst in the game. Every affiliate had a losing record in 2004, and former general manager Omar Minaya, who bolted for the Mets in October, strip-mined the franchise of most of its top prospects—including Jason Bay, Cliff Lee and Grady Sizemore—in a failed 2002 playoff run. Minaya swung a couple of nice trades in 2004 to get Francis Beltran, Ryan Church and Brendan Harris, but the system remains depleted.

Until a real owner buys the team, MLB has appointed former Reds GM Jim Bowden as Minaya's replacement. Bowden quickly made several aggressive moves, signing free agents Vinny Castilla and Cristian Guzman to contracts totaling $23 million and trading with the Angels for outfielder Jose Guillen. There is enthusiam in Washington, but with the franchise's long-term future still up in the air, its short-term direction is uncertain as well.

TOP 30 PROSPECTS

1. Mike Hinckley, lhp	16. Shawn Hill, rhp
2. Larry Broadway, 1b	17. Josh Karp, rhp
3. Ryan Church, of	18. Tony Blanco, of/1b
4. Clint Everts, rhp	19. Ian Desmond, ss
5. Brendan Harris, 3b/2b	20. Gary Majewski, rhp
6. Bill Bray, lhp	21. Alejandro Machado, 2b/ss
7. Daryl Thompson, rhp	22. Jason Bergmann, rhp
8. Darrell Rasner, rhp	23. Erick San Pedro, c
9. Kory Casto, 3b	24. Tyrell Godwin, of
10. Collin Balester, rhp	25. Greg Bunn, rhp
11. Jerry Owens, of	26. Brandon Watson, of
12. Danny Rueckel, rhp	27. Shawn Norris, inf
13. Rogearvin Bernadina, of	28. Josh Labandeira, ss
14. Edgardo Baez, of	29. Josh Whitesell, 1b
15. J.J. Davis, of	30. Chris Lugo, rhp

ORGANIZATION OVERVIEW

General manager: Jim Bowden. **Farm director:** Adam Wogan. **Scouting director:** Dana Brown.

2004 PERFORMANCE

Class	Team	League	W	L	Pct.	Finish*	Manager
Majors	Montreal	National	67	95	.414	15th (16)	Frank Robinson
Triple-A	#Edmonton Trappers	Pacific Coast	69	74	.483	10th (16)	Dave Huppert
Double-A	Harrisburg Senators	Eastern	52	90	.366	12th (12)	Dave Machemer
High A	@Brevard County Manatees	Florida State	53	72	.424	10th (12)	Tim Raines
Low A	Savannah Sand Gnats	South Atlantic	58	80	.420	14th (16)	Bob Henley
Short-season	Vermont Expos	New York-Penn	34	38	.472	7th (14)	Jose Alguacil
Rookie	GCL Expos	Gulf Coast	22	38	.367	11th (12)	Arturo DeFreites
OVERALL 2004 MINOR LEAGUE STANDINDS			288	392	.424	30th (30)	

*Finish in overall standings (No. of teams in league).
#Affiliate will be in New Orleans (Pacific Coast) in 2005. @Affiliate will be in Potomac (Carolina) in 2005.

ORGANIZATION LEADERS

BATTING
*Minimum 250 At-Bats
*AVG	Ryan Church, Edmonton	.346
R	Alejandro Machado, Harrisburg/B.C.	88
H	Alejandro Machado, Harrisburg/B.C.	163
TB	Kory Casto, Savannah	229
2B	Kory Casto, Savannah	35
3B	Shawn Norris, Harrisburg/Brevard County	10
HR	Val Pascucci, Edmonton	25
RBI	Val Pascucci, Edmonton	92
BB	Shawn Norris, Harrisburg/Brevard County	84
SO	Shawn Norris, Harrisburg/Brevard County	117
SB	Alejandro Machado, Harrisburg/B.C.	30
	Jerry Owens, Savannah	30
*OBP	Ryan Church, Edmonton	.430
*SLG	Ryan Church, Edmonton	.622

PITCHING
#Minimum 75 Innings
W	Mike Hinckley, Harrisburg/Brevard County	11
L	Luke Lockwood, Harrisburg	17
#ERA	Danny Rueckel, Edmonton/Harrisburg	2.11
G	Three tied at	49
CG	Wilton Chavez, Edmonton	3
SV	Gus Hlebovy, Vermont	16
IP	Wilton Chavez, Edmonton	164
BB	Devin Perrin, Savannah	62
SO	Mike Hinckley, Harrisburg/Brevard County	131

BEST TOOLS

Best Hitter for Average	Brendan Harris
Best Power Hitter	Larry Broadway
Best Strike-Zone Discipline	Ryan Church
Fastest Baserunner	Jerry Owens
Best Athlete	Jerry Owens
Best Fastball	Collin Balester
Best Curveball	Danny Rueckel
Best Slider	Bill Bray
Best Changeup	Clint Everts
Best Control	Mike Hinckley
Best Defensive Catcher	Erick San Pedro
Best Defensive Infielder	Shawn Norris
Best Infield Arm	Josh Labandeira
Best Defensive Outfielder	Ryan Church
Best Outfield Arm	Edgardo Baez

PROJECTED 2008 LINEUP

Catcher	Brian Schneider
First Base	Larry Broadway
Second Base	Jose Vidro
Third Base	Brendan Harris
Shortstop	Cristian Guzman
Left Field	Brad Wilkerson
Center Field	Jose Guillen
Right Field	Ryan Church

No. 1 Starter	Livan Hernandez
No. 2 Starter	Mike Hinckley
No. 3 Starter	Zach Day
No. 4 Starter	Tomo Okha
No. 5 Starter	Clint Everts
Closer	Chad Cordero

LAST YEAR'S TOP 20 PROSPECTS

1. Clint Everts, rhp	11. Rogearvin Bernadina, of
2. Mike Hinckley, lhp	12. Jason Bergmann, rhp
3. Larry Broadway, 1b	13. Scott Hodges, 3b
4. Josh Karp, rhp	14. Brandon Watson, of
5. Chad Cordero, rhp	15. Rich Rundles, lhp
6. Shawn Hill, rhp	16. Val Pascucci, of/1b
7. Darrell Rasner, rhp	17. Jerry Owens, of
8. Seung Song, rhp	18. Daryl Thompson, rhp
9. Terrmel Sledge, of	19. Chris Young, rhp
10. Ryan Church, of	20. Antonio Sucre, of

TOP PROSPECTS OF THE DECADE

Year	Player, Pos.	Current Team
1995	Ugueth Urbina, rhp	Tigers
1996	Vladimir Guerrero, of	Angels
1997	Vladimir Guerrero, of	Angels
1998	Brad Fullmer, 1b	Rangers
1999	Michael Barrett, 3b/c	Cubs
2000	Tony Armas, rhp	Nationals
2001	Donnie Bridges, rhp	Nationals
2002	Brandon Phillips, ss	Indians
2003	Clint Everts, rhp	Nationals
2004	Clint Everts, rhp	Nationals

TOP DRAFT PICKS OF THE DECADE

Year	Player, Pos.	Current Team
1995	Michael Barrett, ss	Cubs
1996	*John Patterson, rhp	Nationals
1997	Donnie Bridges, rhp	Nationals
1998	Josh McKinley, ss	Nationals
1999	Josh Girdley, lhp	Nationals
2000	Justin Wayne, rhp	Marlins
2001	Josh Karp, rhp	Nationals
2002	Clint Everts, rhp	Nationals
2003	Chad Cordero, rhp	Nationals
2004	Bill Bray, lhp	Nationals

*Did not sign.

ALL-TIME LARGEST BONUSES

Justin Wayne, 2000	$2,950,000
Josh Karp, 2001	$2,650,000
Clint Everts, 2002	$2,500,000
Grady Sizemore, 2000	$2,000,000
Bill Bray, 2004	$1,750,000

MINOR LEAGUE DEPTH CHART

Washington NATIONALS

Impact Potential: D

Mike Hinckley is one of the minors' best lefties and has had success at Double-A. He's not far from helping in Washington. Clint Everts will likely miss the 2005 season, but if his fastball velocity and big-breaking curveball return after Tommy John surgery, he'll join Hinckley in a future Nats rotation. Ryan Church and Larry Broadway are the best bets among hitters to be everyday players.

Depth: F

Despite the best efforts of scouting director Dana Brown, the franchise has not overcome a bare-bones scouting staff for three years. Throw in some of the deals by Omar Minaya in three years as general manager, and it's a wonder the Nationals will have enough players to fill out minor league rosters. Sign of the times: The Expos' once plentiful Latin American pipeline has dried up, with only one international signee—Netherlands native Rogearvin Bernadina—in the top 30.

*Depth charts prepared by **John Manuel** and **Allan Simpson**. Numbers in parentheses indicate prospect rankings.*

LF
J.J. Davis (15)
Marvin Lowrance
Rich Lane
Doug Vroman

CF
Jerry Owens (11)
Rogearvin Bernadina (13)
Tyrell Godwin (24)
Brandon Watson (26)
Reggie Fitzpatrick

RF
Ryan Church (3)
Edgardo Baez (14)
Frank Diaz

3B
Brendan Harris (5)
Kory Casto (9)
Shawn Norris (27)
Ofilio Castro
Leonard Davis

SS
Ian Desmond (19)
Josh Labandeira (28)
Trey Webb

2B
Alejandro Machado (21)
Seth Bynum

1B
Larry Broadway (2)
Tony Blanco (18)
Josh Whitesell (29)

SOURCE of TALENT

HOMEGROWN		ACQUIRED	
College	13	Trades	5
Junior College	0	Rule 5 draft	2
Draft-and-follow	0	Independent leagues	0
High School	9	Free agents/waivers	0
Nondrafted free agent	0		
Foreign	1		

C
Erick San Pedro (23)
Devin Ivany
Luke Montz

LHP

Starters	Relievers
Mike Hinckley (1)	Bill Bray (6)
Jon Felfoldi	Joe Horgan
Gabriel Sosa	Jason Norderum
Rich Rundles	Jeremy Plexico
Aaron Wideman	
Ricardo Morales	

RHP

Starters	Relievers
Clint Everts (4)	Danny Rueckel (12)
Daryl Thompson (7)	Gary Majewski (20)
Darrell Rasner (8)	Jason Bergmann (22)
Colin Balester (10)	Anthony Pearson
Shawn Hill (16)	Alex Morales
Josh Karp (17)	Chris Schroder
Greg Bunn (25)	Ben Cox
Chris Lugo (30)	David Trahan
Devin Perrin	Brett Reid
Armando Galarraga	Gus Hlebovy
Wilton Chavez	
Gustavo Mata	

DRAFT ANALYSIS

2004

Best Pro Debut: RHPs David Trahan (11) and Ben Cox (19), setup men at short-season Vermont. Trahan used his solid fastball-slider combination to go 3-2, 2.59 with 47 strikeouts in 49 innings. Cox, who has more power to his fastball (up to 95 mph) and slider (up to 83), went 2-0, 2.97 with 38 whiffs in 33 innings.

Best Athlete: SS Ian Desmond (3), whose best tool is his plus-plus arm. OF Duron Legrande (10) was a wide receiver at Division III Averett (Va.) before transferring to North Carolina A&T. Unsigned RHP Andy Gale (43) had NHL potential as a physical 6-foot-6, 220-pound hockey defenseman.

Best Pure Hitter: OF Marvin Lowrance (7) batted .289-3-20 at Vermont. He was the only Expos draftee to hit better than .228 in his pro debut.

Best Raw Power: Lowrance has a lot of pop, but it currently shows up more in batting practice than it does in games. 3B Leonard Davis (8) also has good power.

Fastest Runner: Legrande needs just 4.05 seconds to get to first base from the left side of the plate.

Best Defensive Player: C Erick San Pedro (2) can do it all behind the plate. He has a strong arm, receives and blocks balls well, and has the leadership to run a pitching staff. Desmond and C Devin Ivany (6) are athletic defenders.

Best Fastball: LHP Bill Bray (1), RHP Collin Balester (4) and Cox all top out at 95 mph. Balester has the most projection, because he's 6-foot-6 and 180 pounds and is the lone high schooler in that group.

Best Breaking Ball: Bray has a hard 82-85 mph slider that rates as a 70 pitch on the

RICH ABEL

Bunn

20-80 scouting scale at times. The Expos also like RHP Greg Bunn's (5) true 12-6 curveball.

Most Intriguing Background: Gale's father Rich pitched in the majors. Unsigned SS Steven Hornostaj's (24) brother Aaron is an infielder in the Giants system.

Closest To The Majors: Bray, the second straight college reliever drafted in the first round by Montreal. Unlike Chad Cordero, who quickly made the big league pen, Bray will get the chance to advance as a starter.

Best Late-Round Pick: Cox didn't go higher because his command was erratic at Lamar. RHP Chris Lugo (28) pitched all summer at age 17, showing an 87-91 mph fastball and an intriguing curveball.

The One Who Got Away: LHP Mike Wlodarczyk (15) couldn't crack Boston College's rotation during the spring, but he broke out in the Cape Cod League during the summer. He kept the ball down and threw four pitches for strikes, including an 88-90 mph fastball with running action. The Expos made a run at him but couldn't sign him.

Assessment: Like many things with the Expos, this draft suffered because of Major League Baseball's neglectful ownership of the franchise. With just 11 full-time scouts and a limited budget, Montreal was at a disadvantage. Scouting director Dana Brown did an admirable job holding his department together during the last three years.

2003 RHP Chad Cordero (1) served as a big league closer in his first full pro season. RHP Daryl Thompson (8), 3B Kory Casto (3) and OFs Jerry Owens (2) and Edgardo Baez (4) also made positive first impressions. *GRADE:* B

2002 Despite assembling a skeleton scouting staff three months before the draft, the Expos did just fine. RHP Clint Everts' (1) Tommy John surgery was a blow, but 1B Larry Broadway (3) and RHPs Darrell Rasner (2) and Danny Rueckel (12) add depth to a thin system. *GRADE:* B

2001 LHP Mike Hinckley's (3) development into a frontline pitching prospect has softened the blow of RHP Josh Karp (1) underachieving. *GRADE:* B

2000 RHP Justin Wayne (1) turned out to be worth far less than his club-record $2.95 million bonus, but the Expos found three keepers in OFs Grady Sizemore (3) and Jason Bay (22) and LHP Cliff Lee (4). The bad news is that former GM Omar Minaya traded all three and the franchise has nothing to show for it after releasing Rocky Biddle. *GRADE:* A

Draft analysis prepared by Jim Callis. Numbers in parentheses indicate draft rounds.

lhp

Mike
HINCKLEY

Born: Oct. 5, 1982.
Ht.: 6-3. **Wt.:** 170.
Bats: R. **Throws:** L.
School: Moore (Okla.) HS.
Career Transactions: Selected by Expos in third round of 2001 draft; signed July 5, 2001.
Signed by: Darrell Brown.

Hinckley quickly and quietly has established himself as one of the top lefthanded pitching prospects in the minors. His talent has been evident for some time—he ranked No. 2 in the organization behind Clint Everts in each of the previous two years—and his ascent accelerated rapidly in 2004. The Expos initially brought Hinckley along slowly, pitching him in the Rookie-level Gulf Coast League in his pro debut, then kept him in extended spring training before sending him to short-season Vermont in his second year. He finished strong at high Class A Brevard County in 2003, then handled that level with ease again last season before moving on to Double-A Harrisburg. Hinckley allowed two earned runs or fewer in 19 of his 26 starts while leading the system in victories (11) and strikeouts (131 in 156 innings). He now owns a 32-13, 2.80 career record in the minors and has won 20 of his last 26 decisions.

Hinckley has a lot going for him. He has outstanding command of his fastball, which sits at 89-92 mph and touches 94, and he holds that velocity deep into games. His 76-78 mph curveball has good bite and depth. His changeup already is average. What really puts Hinckley ahead of most 22-year-olds is his makeup, which might be the best in the organization. He knows the game, he studies it and prepares well for every start. He demonstrates an advanced feel and tremendous poise on the mound. His athletic frame is durable and projectable, and his delivery is free and easy. He uses his lower half well, pitching on a downward plane that makes it difficult for hitters to take him deep. Hinckley has been equally effective against lefthanders and righthanders. Lefties hit .288 with five homers off him in Double-A but that likely was just an aberration, as they batted .182 against him in high Class A.

While he does have a long, lean body, Hinckley still needs to fill out. Once he does, his fastball velocity should stay in the 91-94 range more often. How fast he realizes his potential also depends on his ability to refine his secondary pitches. Both his curveball and changeup are effective, but neither is as good as Everts'. If Hinckley can make them more consistent, his curve could be a strikeout pitch and his change could be above-average.

Now that Hinckley has started to move, he should continue to fly through the system. He'll get a look in big league camp after being added to the 40-man roster this offseason, but he's a longshot to make the club. More realistically, he'll start 2005 in the minors and could return to Double-A for the first couple of months, but figures to see Triple-A New Orleans and the majors before the season is out. Few in the organization see Hinckley as a No. 1 starter in the majors, but he has a high probability of reaching the big leagues and becoming a successful No. 2 or 3 starter on a quality team.

Year	Club (League)	Class	W	L	ERA	G	GS	CG	SV	IP	H	R	ER	HR	BB	SO	AVG
2001	Expos (GCL)	R	2	2	5.24	8	5	0	0	34	46	23	20	1	12	28	.329
2002	Vermont (NY-P)	A	6	2	1.37	16	16	0	0	92	60	19	14	4	30	66	.188
2003	Savannah (SAL)	A	9	5	3.64	23	23	2	0	121	124	54	49	4	41	111	.271
	Brevard County (FSL)	A	4	0	0.72	4	4	1	0	25	14	2	2	1	1	23	.159
2004	Harrisburg (EL)	AA	5	2	2.87	16	16	0	0	94	83	34	30	5	23	80	.242
	Brevard County (FSL)	A	6	2	2.61	10	10	0	0	62	47	23	18	6	18	51	.206
MINOR LEAGUE TOTALS			32	13	2.80	77	74	3	0	428	374	155	133	21	125	359	.237

Larry Broadway, 1b

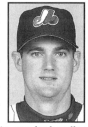

Born: Dec. 17, 1980. **Ht.:** 6-4. **Wt.:** 230. **Bats:** L. **Throws:** L. **School:** Duke University. **Career Transactions:** Selected by Expos in third round of 2002 draft; signed June 13, 2002. **Signed by:** Dana Brown.

The No. 3 starter on a Wellington (Fla.) High staff that included Pirates first-rounders Bobby Bradley and Sean Burnett, Broadway pitched his freshman year at Duke before a nerve problem in his elbow relegated him to first base. He struggled early last season while dealing with back problems, then recovered and hit like he had in his first two years. Broadway is the best power prospect in an organization desperate for power tools. He has the ability to hit for average and hit deep in the count. For a big guy, he handles himself well around the bag, and managers voted him the best defensive first baseman in the Double-A Eastern League. Broadway still has holes in his swing. When pitchers pound him inside, he tends to get jammed, and his stroke can get long. He's a well-below-average runner. Broadway will start 2005 in Triple-A, but he's not farm from the big leagues. He just needs to polish his approach a bit to become a 30-homer-a-year first baseman.

Year	Club (League)	Class	AVG	G	AB	R	H	2B	3B	HR	RBI	BB	SO	SB	OBP	SLG
2002	Vermont (NY-P)	A	.315	35	127	13	40	3	0	4	23	13	33	0	.379	.433
	Expos (GCL)	R	.250	4	8	1	2	0	0	0	0	4	4	0	.500	.250
2003	Savannah (SAL)	A	.307	83	290	56	89	25	4	14	51	44	70	3	.400	.566
	Brevard County (FSL)	A	.224	25	76	8	17	7	1	1	7	18	20	0	.367	.382
	Harrisburg (EL)	AA	.321	21	78	13	25	3	0	5	18	7	15	0	.371	.551
2004	Harrisburg (EL)	AA	.270	131	477	70	129	20	0	22	72	68	102	2	.362	.451
MINOR LEAGUE TOTALS			.286	299	1056	161	302	58	5	46	171	154	244	5	.377	.481

Ryan Church, of

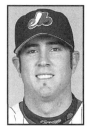

Born: Oct. 14, 1978. **Ht.:** 6-1. **Wt.:** 190. **Bats:** L. **Throws:** L. **School:** University of Nevada. **Career Transactions:** Selected by Indians in 14th round of 2000 draft; signed June 7, 2000 . . . Traded by Indians with IF Maicer Izturis to Expos for LHP Scott Stewart, Jan. 5, 2004. **Signed by:** Paul Cogan (Indians).

Former Expos general manager Omar Minaya made one of his best trades when he acquired Church and infielder Maicer Izturis from Cleveland for lefthander Scott Stewart. Like Larry Broadway, Church began his college career as a pitcher before hurting his arm. By learning to use the entire field and work counts better, he turned in his best offensive season in 2004. In many ways, Church is similar to Brad Wilkerson. He has a quick, classic swing and makes consistent hard contact. Strong and athletic, he's an average runner with a good arm. He could fill in as a center fielder in the majors but fits better in right. He might not have enough power to hit in the middle of the order in the majors. At 26 he's not young for a prospect, and he didn't exactly seize a big league job with his late-season performance. The Nationals' offseason trade for Jose Guillen decreases Church's chances of winning a starting role. In time, he could develop into a .300 hitter with 20-25 homers a year.

Year	Club (League)	Class	AVG	G	AB	R	H	2B	3B	HR	RBI	BB	SO	SB	OBP	SLG
2000	Mahoning Valley (NY-P)	A	.298	73	272	51	81	16	5	10	65	38	49	11	.396	.504
2001	Columbus (SAL)	A	.287	101	363	64	104	23	3	17	76	54	79	4	.385	.507
	Kinston (Car)	A	.241	24	83	16	20	7	0	5	15	18	23	1	.379	.506
2002	Kinston (Car)	A	.326	53	181	30	59	12	1	10	30	31	51	4	.433	.569
	Akron (EL)	AA	.296	71	291	39	86	17	4	12	51	12	58	1	.325	.505
2003	Akron (EL)	AA	.261	99	371	47	97	17	3	13	52	32	64	4	.325	.429
2004	Edmonton (PCL)	AAA	.346	98	347	74	120	29	8	17	79	51	62	0	.430	.622
	Montreal (NL)	MAJ	.175	30	63	6	11	1	0	1	6	7	16	0	.257	.238
MAJOR LEAGUE TOTALS			.175	30	63	6	11	1	0	1	6	7	16	0	.257	.238
MINOR LEAGUE TOTALS			.297	519	1908	321	567	121	24	84	368	236	386	25	.380	.518

Clint Everts, rhp

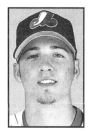

Born: Aug. 10, 1984. **Ht.:** 6-2. **Wt.:** 170. **Bats:** R. **Throws:** R. **School:** Cypress Falls HS, Houston. **Career Transactions:** Selected by Expos in first round (fifth overall) of 2002 draft; signed Aug. 24, 2002. **Signed by:** Ray Corbett.

The No. 1 prospect in the system in 2003 and 2004, Everts still has the highest ceiling of any player in the organization. But his velocity dropped to 84-88 mph last season before it turned out he blew out his elbow and needed Tommy John surgery. He'll miss all of 2005. Without a good fastball, Everts still posted excellent numbers and earned a berth in the Futures Game, played in his hometown of Houston, by relying heavily upon his curveball and changeup, which are both plus-plus pitches. He worked at 88-92 mph and touched 94 with his fastball before his elbow problems. His command and feel for pitching make his stuff that much tougher. Everts looked like a sure thing before he got hurt. Though the track record for comebacks from Tommy John surgery is good, he still has a long road ahead. He can focus on adding strength to his lean upper body during his rehabilitation. If he can regain his health, Everts still can develop into a frontline starter. The plan is for him to be throwing by the end of 2005 and to take the mound again in 2006.

Year	Club (League)	Class	W	L	ERA	G	GS	CG	SV	IP	H	R	ER	HR	BB	SO	AVG
2003	Vermont (NY-P)	A	2	4	4.17	10	10	0	0	54	49	26	25	4	35	50	.247
	Savannah (SAL)	A	0	3	3.46	5	5	0	0	26	23	13	10	1	10	21	.230
2004	Savannah (SAL)	A	7	3	2.49	17	17	1	1	90	67	29	25	3	21	103	.206
	Brevard County (FSL)	A	2	2	2.25	4	4	0	0	20	16	5	5	2	10	19	.222
MINOR LEAGUE TOTALS			11	12	3.07	36	36	1	1	190	155	73	65	10	76	193	.223

5 Brendan Harris, 3b/2b

Born: Aug. 26, 1980. **Ht.:** 6-1. **Wt.:** 190. **Bats:** R. **Throws:** R. **School:** College of William & Mary. **Career Transactions:** Selected by Cubs in fifth round of 2001 draft; signed July 21, 2001 . . . Traded by Cubs with SS Alex Gonzalez and RHP Francis Beltran to Expos as part of four-team trade in which Cubs received SS Nomar Garciaparra and OF Matt Murton from Red Sox, Red Sox received SS Orlando Cabrera from Expos and 1B Doug Mientkiewicz from Twins, and Twins received LHP Justin Jones from Cubs, July 31, 2004. **Signed by:** Billy Swoope (Cubs).

STEVE MOORE

Acquired along with Francis Beltran from the Cubs in the four-team trade highlighted by Orlando Cabrera and Nomar Garciaparra last July, Harris appeared to be the franchise's third baseman of the future. That changed when the Nationals signed Vinny Castilla. Harris is a consistent line-drive hitter with good power to the gaps. Former GM Omar Minaya envisioned Harris as a 20-homer, 80-RBI threat. He has a plus infield arm and displays good athleticism at both second and third. He also has played some shortstop. Harris tends to start his hands a little late in his swing, cutting his reaction time. He's somewhat of a tweener because his bat fits better at second base—where he's blocked by Jose Vidro—but he's a better defender at third. Harris will vie for a big league utility job this spring but might end up back in Triple-A to get more at-bats. He profiles best as a No. 2 hitter, and perhaps as a No. 5 hitter if his power develops.

Year	Club (League)	Class	AVG	G	AB	R	H	2B	3B	HR	RBI	BB	SO	SB	OBP	SLG
2001	Lansing (Mid)	A	.274	32	113	25	31	5	1	4	22	17	26	5	.370	.442
2002	Daytona (FSL)	A	.329	110	425	82	140	35	6	13	54	43	57	16	.395	.532
	West Tenn (SL)	AA	.321	13	53	8	17	4	1	2	11	2	5	1	.345	.547
2003	West Tenn (SL)	AA	.280	120	435	56	122	34	7	5	52	51	72	6	.364	.425
2004	Iowa (PCL)	AAA	.311	69	254	48	79	21	1	11	35	16	40	0	.353	.531
	Edmonton (PCL)	AAA	.269	35	130	20	35	6	0	6	24	10	21	0	.317	.454
	Montreal (NL)	MAJ	.169	23	59	4	10	3	0	1	3	3	12	0	.222	.271
MAJOR LEAGUE TOTALS			.169	23	59	4	10	3	0	1	3	3	12	0	.222	.271
MINOR LEAGUE TOTALS			.301	379	1410	239	424	105	16	41	198	139	221	28	.367	.485

6 Bill Bray, lhp

Born: June 5, 1983. **Ht.:** 6-3. **Wt.:** 215. **Bats:** L. **Throws:** L. **School:** College of William & Mary. **Career Transactions:** Selected by Expos in first round (13th overall) of 2004 draft; signed July 26, 2004. **Signed by:** Alex Smith.

Like Brendan Harris, Bray was a standout at William & Mary. He left with a bit more fanfare, as the Tribe's highest draft pick ever. He worked just seven innings after signing for $1.75 million, so he headed to the Arizona Fall League, where he fanned 16 in 16 innings. Bray has good command of two power pitches, an 89-95 mph fastball and a late-breaking 82-85 mph slider. He is polished and aggressive, and he can put hitters away with both pitches. He provides a deceptive look from a three-quarters slot. Though Bray's changeup shows enough promise for the Nationals to consider him as a long-term starter, it still has a long way to go because he rarely used it in college. If he can't master it, the club will settle for using him in relief. A closer in college, Bray will pitch in the rotation at Washington's new high Class A Potomac affiliate in 2005. Even if he has to return to the bullpen, the innings he'll get as a starter will help his development and arm strength. He'd advance quicker in relief, where he would have a shot at becoming a closer someday.

Year	Club (League)	Class	W	L	ERA	G	GS	CG	SV	IP	H	R	ER	HR	BB	SO	AVG
2004	Brevard County (FSL)	A	0	2	4.91	6	0	0	0	7	9	5	4	0	1	6	.290
MINOR LEAGUE TOTALS			0	2	4.91	6	0	0	0	7	9	5	4	0	1	6	.290

Daryl Thompson, rhp

Born: Nov. 2, 1985. **Ht.:** 6-1. **Wt.:** 170. **Bats:** R. **Throws:** R. **School:** La Plata HS, Mechanicsville, Md. **Career Transactions:** Selected by Expos in eighth round of 2003 draft; signed June 8, 2003. **Signed by:** Alex Smith.

An eighth-round pick in 2003, Thompson is looking more and more like a steal. After shining in his pro debut in the Gulf Coast League, he skipped a level and went to low Class A Savannah at age 18. His numbers weren't outstanding, but he was the youngest pitcher in the South Atlantic League, demonstrating amazing poise for his age and occasional dominance. Thompson works primarily with his 89-94 mph fastball, which features good life and could get even better as he adds strength. He has a wiry, athletic frame, a quick arm and a loose, easy delivery. He resembles a young Oil Can Boyd. Thompson's feel for pitching and makeup are remarkable for such a young pitcher. Like most teenagers, Thompson still is developing his secondary pitches. His curveball has 11-to-5 rotation and average depth, and it could become a plus pitch. He has good feel for a changeup but it isn't reliable yet. Thompson has considerable upside and his best days are ahead. The Nationals believe he can handle a move to high Class A in 2005.

Year	Club (League)	Class	W	L	ERA	G	GS	CG	SV	IP	H	R	ER	HR	BB	SO	AVG
2003	Expos (GCL)	R	1	2	2.15	12	10	0	0	46	49	16	11	1	11	18	.288
2004	Savannah (SAL)	A	4	9	5.08	25	21	0	0	103	117	66	58	13	30	79	.290
MINOR LEAGUE TOTALS			5	11	4.18	37	31	0	0	149	166	82	69	14	41	97	.289

Darrell Rasner, rhp

STEVE MOORE

Born: Jan. 13, 1981. **Ht.:** 6-3. **Wt.:** 210. **Bats:** R. **Throws:** R. **School:** University of Nevada. **Career Transactions:** Selected by Expos in second round of 2002 draft; signed July 2, 2002. **Signed by:** Keith Snider.

As did Ryan Church, Rasner starred at Nevada, where he set records for career wins, strikeouts and innings. Minor shoulder tendinitis slowed him in 2003, his first full pro season, but he remained healthy in 2004 and turned a corner down the stretch. He allowed more than one earned run just once in his final 11 starts and did his best pitching yet in Double-A. Rasner has good control and induces plenty of grounders with his heavy 91-94 mph sinker. He commanded his solid-average curveball much better in 2004 than he had in the past. Rasner's circle changeup still needs plenty of work, and his curve could use more refinement. He lacks a true strikeout pitch and though he's around the plate with his pitches, he has been too hittable. Now that he's healthy, Rasner should advance rapidly through the system. He should return to Double-A to start 2005 and is line for a big league callup toward the end of the year. He doesn't offer a high ceiling but could become a solid fourth starter.

Year	Club (League)	Class	W	L	ERA	G	GS	CG	SV	IP	H	R	ER	HR	BB	SO	AVG
2002	Vermont (NY-P)	A	2	5	4.33	10	10	0	0	44	44	27	21	1	18	49	.262
2003	Savannah (SAL)	A	7	7	4.19	22	22	2	0	105	106	53	49	8	36	90	.268
2004	Harrisburg (EL)	AA	1	1	1.21	5	5	0	0	30	21	4	4	1	9	15	.214
	Brevard County (FSL)	A	6	5	3.17	22	21	0	0	119	133	55	42	6	31	88	.284
MINOR LEAGUE TOTALS			16	18	3.50	59	58	2	0	298	304	139	116	16	94	242	.269

Kory Casto, 3b

Born: Dec. 8, 1981. **Ht.:** 6-1. **Wt.:** 200. **Bats:** L. **Throws:** R. **School:** University of Portland. **Career Transactions:** Selected by Expos in third round of 2003 draft; signed June 8, 2003. **Signed by:** Doug McMillan.

Drafted as an outfielder, Casto made his lackluster pro debut at that position. The Expos moved him to third base in 2004 and in his third game there, he took a grounder off his left eye. He missed two weeks and lost his confidence after he returned. His bat eventually came around, but he made 35 errors in 112 games. If Casto reaches the big leagues, it will be on the strength of his bat. He's a good gap hitter with blossoming home run power. Early in the year, he struggled against breaking balls, particularly from left-handers, but he made adjustments and began driving the ball consistently. He shows a strong arm at third base. Coaches and scouts rave about his work ethic and desire. There are scouts who question whether Casto can become even an average defensive third baseman. His hands are stiff, his feet are heavy and he lacks instincts. He needs to shorten his arm action to make quicker throws across the diamond. Offensively, he needs to learn to work counts better. If Casto doesn't figure out third base, he may have enough bat for left or right field. He likely will begin 2005 at Potomac.

Year	Club (League)	Class	AVG	G	AB	R	H	2B	3B	HR	RBI	BB	SO	SB	OBP	SLG
2003	Vermont (NY-P)	A	.239	71	259	26	62	14	2	4	28	30	47	1	.322	.355
2004	Savannah (SAL)	A	.286	124	483	67	138	35	4	16	88	31	70	1	.337	.474
MINOR LEAGUE TOTALS			.270	195	742	93	200	49	6	20	116	61	117	2	.332	.433

10 Collin Balester, rhp

Born: June 6, 1986. **Ht.:** 6-5. **Wt.:** 190. **Bats:** R. **Throws:** R. **School:** Huntington Beach (Calif.) HS. **Career Transactions:** Selected by Expos in fourth round of 2004 draft; signed July 14, 2004. **Signed by:** Anthony Arango.

Balester wasn't a hot commodity entering his senior season in high school, but he pitched himself into the fourth round with a strong spring. Though he wasn't in peak condition after signing late, he still showed fine command during his pro debut. Tall and thin with a loose, easy arm action, Balester is projectable. His fastball already reaches 91-92 mph and touches 94-95. He's polished for his age and does an excellent job controlling the strike zone. His late-biting curveball is already an average pitch and could become a plus offering. Balester needs a third pitch if he's to succeed as a starter at higher levels. His changeup shows potential, but it's still a long way from being trustworthy. He also needs to strengthen his upper body and build up his durability. Washington views Balester as a combination of power and command who could become a front-of-the-rotation starter if everything clicks. He could begin 2005 in low Class A, but the Nationals may take it slow and start him in extended spring training before sending him to Vermont.

Year	Club (League)	Class	W	L	ERA	G	GS	CG	SV	IP	R	ER	H	HR	BB	SO	AVG
2004	Expos (GCL)	R	1	2	2.19	5	4	0	0	25	8	6	20	0	5	21	.215
MINOR LEAGUE TOTALS			1	2	2.19	5	4	0	0	25	8	6	20	0	5	21	.215

11 Jerry Owens, of

Born: Feb. 16, 1981. **Ht.:** 6-3. **Wt.:** 195. **Bats:** L. **Throws:** L. **School:** The Masters (Calif.) College. **Career Transactions:** Selected by Expos in second round of 2003 draft; signed June 11, 2003. **Signed by:** Anthony Arango.

After catching one pass for nine yards in two injury-plagued seasons as a wide receiver at UCLA, Owens transferred to The Masters College and focused on baseball, which he hadn't played since his sophomore year in high school. He made a name for himself with his blazing speed and won the Golden State Athletic Conference player of the year award in 2003. Owens ran into an outfield wall in his second pro game, injuring his throwing shoulder. He required surgery to repair the shoulder and a pre-existing hernia, ending his debut. He played mostly left field last season to allow his shoulder to heal, but he still profiles as a center fielder. Owens surprised club officials with how advanced he was despite his lack of baseball experience. He knows his game well, making good contact and hitting the ball on the ground to take advantage of his tremendous speed. He needs to improve his bunting and his ability to draw walks, but he's already decent at both skills. Owens never will be a power hitter, though he's strong enough to drive the ball a little more than he has a pro. As fast as he is, he shouldn't have been caught in 13 of his 43 steal attempts last season. He has a below-average arm, but it's playable in center. The Nationals will push Owens because he's already 24, and he could spend the bulk of 2005 in Double-A.

Year	Club (League)	Class	AVG	G	AB	R	H	2B	3B	HR	RBI	BB	SO	SB	OBP	SLG
2003	Vermont (NY-P)	A	.125	2	8	0	1	0	0	0	0	0	2	1	.125	.125
2004	Savannah (SAL)	A	.292	108	418	69	122	17	2	1	37	46	59	30	.365	.349
MINOR LEAGUE TOTALS			.289	110	426	69	123	17	2	1	37	46	61	31	.361	.345

12 Danny Rueckel, rhp

Born: Sept. 25, 1979. **Ht.:** 6-0. **Wt.:** 170. **Bats:** R. **Throws:** R. **School:** Furman University. **Career Transactions:** Selected by Expos in 12th round of 2002 draft; signed June 14, 2002. **Signed by:** Ty Brown.

A four-year starter at shortstop at Furman, Rueckel logged bullpen innings after then-Paladins pitching coach Tommy John noticed his devastating curveball. John coached in the Expos system in 2002 and recommended they draft Rueckel as a pitcher. He really gained command of his curve, a 78-82 mph bender with sharp 12-to-6 bite, down the stretch in 2003, which allowed him to skip a level to Double-A last year. He blossomed there, getting hitters out by varying his grips and arm slots to throw a variety of curves. He also mixes in an 89-92 mph fastball, which he commands well. Athletic and durable, Rueckel can work multiple-inning stints out of the bullpen. He's not too far from being ready for a middle-relief or set-up role in the big leagues, but he will begin 2005 in Triple-A. He probably could pitch in the majors right now just with his curveball, which grades as a 70 on the 20-80 scouting scale, but he'll be more effective when he learns to keep his fastball down in the zone. He's working on a two-seam fastball for just that reason.

Year	Club (League)	Class	W	L	ERA	G	GS	CG	SV	IP	H	R	ER	HR	BB	SO	AVG
2002	Vermont (NY-P)	A	1	1	1.53	10	0	0	3	18	12	8	3	0	3	23	.188
	Clinton (Mid)	A	3	1	4.15	14	0	0	0	26	23	12	12	1	10	25	.232
2003	Savannah (SAL)	A	1	3	4.06	40	1	0	14	69	68	38	31	4	16	64	.260
2004	Edmonton (PCL)	AAA	1	0	2.89	7	0	0	1	9	14	3	3	0	7	10	.359
	Harrisburg (EL)	AA	6	5	2.08	42	0	0	8	78	72	29	18	3	17	56	.247
MINOR LEAGUE TOTALS			12	10	3.02	113	1	0	26	200	189	90	67	8	53	178	.250

13 Rogearvin Bernadina, of

Born: June 12, 1984. **Ht.:** 6-0. **Wt.:** 170. **Bats:** L. **Throws:** L. **Career Transactions:** Signed out of Netherlands by Expos, Nov. 3, 2001. **Signed by:** Fred Ferreira.

Bernadina has continually been touted as the highest-ceiling player in the system, with a caveat—he's raw and young. With three pro seasons under his belt, he still has better tools than any other player in the organization, and he's still raw and young. He repeated low Class A in 2004, increasing his power, walks and stolen bases. But he once again struck out far too often, a problem he'll have to solve before he can become a true threat at the plate. Bernadina has the ability to do it all. His above-average speed and strong arm make him an exciting, natural center fielder. His thin frame is projectable, and he has good baserunning instincts that will only get better. If all goes well, Bernadina can be a five-tool center fielder or right fielder hitting in the middle of a lineup. But he just as easily could flame out in Double-A if he doesn't make the necessary adjustments. He'll move up to high Class A this year.

Year	Club (League)	Class	AVG	G	AB	R	H	2B	3B	HR	RBI	BB	SO	SB	OBP	SLG
2002	Expos (GCL)	R	.276	57	196	22	54	7	0	3	18	19	25	1	.348	.357
2003	Savannah (SAL)	A	.237	77	278	36	66	12	3	4	39	19	53	11	.292	.345
2004	Savannah (SAL)	A	.238	129	450	67	107	24	7	7	66	60	113	24	.338	.369
MINOR LEAGUE TOTALS			.246	263	924	125	227	43	10	14	123	98	191	36	.327	.359

14 Edgardo Baez, of

Born: July 12, 1985. **Ht.:** 6-2. **Wt.:** 190. **Bats:** R. **Throws:** R. **School:** Jose Alegria HS, Dorado, P.R. **Career Transactions:** Selected by Expos in fourth round of 2003 draft; signed July 1, 2003. **Signed by:** Delvy Santiago.

Baez projected to go in the top two rounds in 2003 before an underwhelming performance at a predraft showcase allowed the Expos to get him in the fourth. He was overmatched at low Class A in his first full season, but flashed his plus power potential and strong right-field arm following a demotion to Vermont. It wasn't a phenomenal year, but Baez demonstrated improved selectivity at the plate and a mature approach for a teenager. He has a big, athletic frame and a fluid stroke, and his tools are average or better across the board. He even has enough speed to give the Nationals confidence to put him in center field if necessary. Baez still has a hitch in his swing to work out, and he has difficulty recognizing and hitting breaking pitches. But he's a smart hitter who just needs at-bats, and he will get them as the everyday right fielder in low Class A this year. He's considered a long term project, but Baez profiles as a prototypical right fielder if he reaches his ceiling.

Year	Club (League)	Class	AVG	G	AB	R	H	2B	3B	HR	RBI	BB	SO	SB	OBP	SLG
2003	Expos (GCL)	R	.274	34	117	12	32	7	1	3	15	9	31	1	.323	.427
2004	Savannah (SAL)	A	.173	50	191	16	33	10	0	5	29	19	56	1	.259	.304
	Vermont (NY-P)	A	.248	46	165	18	41	6	1	7	27	20	34	2	.332	.424
MINOR LEAGUE TOTALS			.224	130	473	46	106	23	2	15	71	48	121	4	.300	.376

15 J.J. Davis, of

Born: Oct. 25, 1978. **Ht.:** 6-5. **Wt.:** 240. **Bats:** R. **Throws:** R. **School:** Baldwin Park (Calif.) HS. **Career Transactions:** Selected by Pirates in first round (eighth overall) of 1997 draft; signed June 3, 1997 . . . Traded by Pirates to Nationals for OF Antonio Sucre, Nov. 24, 2004. **Signed by:** Doug Takaragawa (Pirates).

The Nationals were familiar with Davis before new general manager Jim Bowden traded for him. Manager Frank Robinson skippered him on Team USA in the fall of 2003 (before Davis bowed out with a right hamstring injury), and scouting director Dana Brown was a Pirates area scout when Pittsburgh drafted him in 1997. Davis never could crack the Pittsburgh lineup, totaling 80 big league at-bats over the last three seasons and missing almost all of 2004 with injuries to his right pinky and right hip flexor. His tools are obvious, starting with plus power, speed and arm strength. But he's an undisciplined hacker who struggles against breaking balls, and he can look awkward in right field. Davis had a strong winter in the Mexican Pacific League, and he'll compete for a reserve role in Washington this year.

Year	Club (League)	Class	AVG	G	AB	R	H	2B	3B	HR	RBI	BB	SO	SB	OBP	SLG
1997	Erie (NY-P)	A	.077	4	13	1	1	0	0	0	0	0	4	0	.077	.077
	Pirates (GCL)	R	.255	45	165	19	42	10	2	1	18	14	44	0	.315	.358
1998	Erie (NY-P)	A	.270	52	196	25	53	12	2	8	39	20	54	4	.341	.474
	Augusta (SAL)	A	.198	30	106	11	21	6	0	4	11	3	24	1	.220	.368
1999	Hickory (SAL)	A	.265	86	317	58	84	26	1	19	65	44	99	2	.360	.533
2000	Lynchburg (Car)	A	.243	130	485	77	118	36	1	20	80	52	171	9	.319	.445
2001	Altoona (EL)	AA	.250	67	228	21	57	13	3	4	26	21	79	2	.317	.386
	Pirates (GCL)	R	.471	4	17	3	8	1	0	2	6	1	2	0	.500	.882
2002	Altoona (EL)	AA	.287	101	348	51	100	17	3	20	62	33	101	7	.351	.526
	Pittsburgh (NL)	MAJ	.100	9	10	1	1	0	0	0	0	0	4	0	.182	.100
2003	Nashville (PCL)	AAA	.284	122	426	68	121	29	4	26	67	35	85	23	.342	.554
	Pittsburgh (NL)	MAJ	.200	19	35	1	7	0	0	1	4	3	13	0	.263	.286
2004	Pittsburgh (NL)	MAJ	.143	25	35	4	5	1	0	0	3	4	10	2	.225	.171
	Nashville (PCL)	AAA	.250	27	84	11	21	6	1	8	17	3	28	3	.270	.631
MAJOR LEAGUE TOTALS			.163	53	80	6	13	1	0	1	7	7	27	2	.236	.213
MINOR LEAGUE TOTALS			.262	668	2385	345	626	156	17	112	391	226	691	51	.329	.483

16 Shawn Hill, rhp

Born: April 28, 1981. **Ht.:** 6-2. **Wt.:** 180. **Bats:** R. **Throws:** R. **School:** Bishop Reding HS, Georgetown, Ontario. **Career Transactions:** Selected by Expos in sixth round of 2000 draft; signed June 16, 2000. **Signed by:** Alex Agostino.

Hill pitched for Canada at the 2003 Olympic qualifying tournament, but he was in the big leagues when the team set its roster for the Athens Games last year and was left off initially. When the Rockies promoted Jeff Francis to the majors, however, Canada needed a pitcher and turned back to Hill, who was back in Double-A. He pitched well in Athens, beating the Netherlands in the round-robin and holding a 3-2 lead over eventual champion Cuba in the semifinals before Canada's bullpen collapsed. When he returned to the United States, the elbow discomfort Hill had battled for years finally stopped him in his tracks, and he had Tommy John surgery. When he returns to the mound, possibly late in the 2005 season, Hill's velocity could improve. Even with a sore elbow, he threw a heavy 89-92 mph sinker that made him a groundball machine. He also has an improving curveball and changeup to go with a good feel for pitching. Over the past two seasons, he has matured physically and mentally, understanding that he won't blow most hitters away. Still just 22, Hill could vie for a big league job in 2006.

Year	Club (League)	Class	W	L	ERA	G	GS	CG	SV	IP	H	R	ER	HR	BB	SO	AVG
2000	Expos (GCL)	R	1	3	4.81	7	7	0	0	24	25	17	13	0	10	20	.250
2001	Vermont (NY-P)	A	2	2	2.27	7	7	0	0	36	22	12	9	0	8	23	.172
2002	Clinton (Mid)	A	12	7	3.44	25	25	0	0	147	149	75	56	7	35	99	.261
2003	Brevard County (FSL)	A	9	4	2.56	22	21	2	1	127	118	47	36	3	26	66	.248
	Harrisburg (EL)	AA	3	1	3.54	4	4	0	0	20	23	12	8	0	11	12	.280
2004	Harrisburg (EL)	AA	5	7	3.39	17	17	2	0	88	90	39	33	4	20	53	.272
	Montreal (NL)	MAJ	1	2	16.00	3	3	0	0	9.0	17	16	16	1	7	10	.415
MAJOR LEAGUE TOTALS			1	2	16.00	3	3	0	0	9	17	16	16	1	7	10	.415
MINOR LEAGUE TOTALS			32	24	3.16	82	81	4	1	441	427	202	155	14	110	273	.253

17 Josh Karp, rhp

Born: Sept. 21, 1979. **Ht.:** 6-5. **Wt.:** 210. **Bats:** R. **Throws:** R. **School:** UCLA. **Career Transactions:** Selected by Expos in first round (sixth overall) of 2001 draft; signed Sept. 27, 2001. **Signed by:** Pat Puccinelli.

The talented Karp underachived at UCLA and has performed far below expectations since being picked sixth overall in the 2001 draft. The organization expected him to bounce back in 2004 after a rough season in Double-A, but instead he regressed. Making matters worse, he walked away from Triple-A Edmonton in mid-August after allowing 10 runs in a start, exacerbating the already serious doubts about his makeup. Karp has the stuff to be an elite pitcher—a 92-93 mph fastball that reaches 96, an 83 mph curveball and an even better changeup—but never has reached that level. Some club officials say he wants to succeed so much that he's too hard on himself when he struggles, and that he'll be a better pitcher in the majors than he has been in the minors. Others say Karp just lacks mental toughness. Washington isn't giving up on him, of course, and added him to its 40-man roster. Besides competing better, Karp needs to keep the ball down in the zone more often and stop relying on his changeup so much. He will have a chance to make the big league team, but in all likelihood he'll repeat Triple-A.

Year	Club (League)	Class	W	L	ERA	G	GS	CG	SV	IP	H	R	ER	HR	BB	SO	AVG
2002	Brevard County (FSL)	A	4	1	1.59	7	7	0	0	45	31	9	8	1	11	43	.190
	Harrisburg (EL)	AA	7	5	3.84	16	16	0	0	87	83	43	37	6	34	69	.256
2003	Harrisburg (EL)	AA	4	10	4.99	23	23	1	0	123	126	76	68	12	49	77	.266
2004	Edmonton (PCL)	AAA	4	10	5.95	24	24	0	0	127	147	91	84	17	51	102	.295
MINOR LEAGUE TOTALS			19	26	4.65	70	70	1	0	382	387	219	197	36	145	291	.265

18 Tony Blanco, of/1b

Born: Nov. 10, 1981. **Ht.:** 6-1. **Wt.:** 175. **Bats:** R. **Throws:** R. **Career Transactions:** Signed out of Dominican Republic by Red Sox, July 2, 1998 . . . Traded by Red Sox with RHP Josh Thigpen to Reds, Dec. 16, 2002, completing trade in which Reds sent 2B Todd Walker to Red Sox for two players to be named (Dec. 12, 2002) . . . Selected by Nationals from Reds in major league Rule 5 draft, Dec. 13, 2004. **Signed by:** Robinson Garcia (Red Sox).

Washington general manager Jim Bowden acquired Blanco twice in two years. While with the Reds, he got Blanco from the Red Sox in a deal for Todd Walker, and shortly after he took over the Nationals, they selected Blanco from Cincinnati in the major league Rule 5 draft. He needs to stick on the big league roster, or else be exposed to waivers and offered back to the Reds for half his $50,000 draft price. Once Boston's top position-player prospect, Blanco has been waylaid by his inability to manage the strike zone. He led Reds farmhands with a career-high 29 homers and played in the Futures Game in 2004, and his power and bat speed are unquestionable. But he has had difficulty making adjustments. He still tries to pull too many pitches and remains woeful against breaking balls. While he had enough arm strength for third base, his lack of range or soft hands forced him to move to left field and first base. It's hard to see him making the Nationals roster when he should be in Double-A.

Year	Club (League)	Class	AVG	G	AB	R	H	2B	3B	HR	RBI	BB	SO	SB	OBP	SLG
1999	Red Sox (DSL)	R	.277	67	249	36	69	12	5	8	41	29	65	12	.366	.462
2000	Red Sox (GCL)	R	.384	52	190	32	73	13	1	13	50	18	38	6	.442	.668
	Lowell (NY-P)	A	.143	9	28	1	4	1	0	0	0	2	12	1	.226	.179
2001	Augusta (SAL)	A	.265	96	370	44	98	23	2	17	69	17	78	1	.308	.476
2002	Sarasota (FSL)	A	.221	65	244	22	54	13	2	6	32	6	70	2	.250	.365
2003	Potomac (Car)	A	.266	69	241	33	64	17	2	10	49	26	62	0	.338	.477
2004	Potomac (Car)	A	.306	62	216	42	66	10	0	17	47	27	66	2	.403	.588
	Chattanooga (SL)	AA	.245	58	220	25	54	8	1	12	31	15	53	0	.300	.455
MINOR LEAGUE TOTALS			.274	478	1758	235	482	97	13	83	319	140	444	24	.338	.486

19 Ian Desmond, ss

Born: Sept. 20, 1985. **Ht.:** 6-2. **Wt.:** 185. **Bats:** R. **Throws:** R. **School:** Sarasota (Fla.) HS. **Career Transactions:** Selected by Expos in third round of 2004 draft; signed June 11, 2004. **Signed by:** Russ Bove.

The Nationals aren't paying much heed to Desmond's dismal numbers from his pro debut. When it comes to shortstops, his ceiling is easily the highest in the organization, even if at 19 he's far away from the majors. A third-round pick last June who signed for $430,000, he flashes all the tools and has an athletic, live body. He has a plus-plus arm but needs to improve his accuracy after making 25 errors in 51 pro games, many on throws. His actions are smooth in the field, and his confident attitude and high energy level evoke Derek Jeter. Desmond has quite a few adjustments to make at the plate. He needs to establish an approach after striking out four times as often as he walked last summer. He also needs to get a lot stronger in order to hit pro pitching. When he fills out he could become an adequate or maybe even above-average offensive player. He'll probably begin 2005 in extended spring training before going back to short-season Vermont.

Year	Club (League)	Class	AVG	G	AB	R	H	2B	3B	HR	RBI	BB	SO	SB	OBP	SLG
2004	Expos (GCL)	R	.227	55	216	28	49	11	0	1	27	10	40	13	.272	.292
	Vermont (NY-P)	A	.250	4	12	2	3	0	0	1	1	0	2	0	.308	.500
MINOR LEAGUE TOTALS			.228	59	228	30	52	11	0	2	28	10	42	13	.273	.303

20 Gary Majewski, rhp

Born: Feb. 26, 1980. **Ht.:** 6-2. **Wt.:** 200. **Bats:** R. **Throws:** R. **School:** St. Pius X HS, Houston. **Career Transactions:** Selected by White Sox in second round of 1998 draft; signed Sept. 2, 1998 . . . Traded by White Sox with RHP Andre Simpson and LHP Orlando Rodriguez to Dodgers for RHP Antonio Osuna and LHP Carlos Ortega, March 22, 2001 . . . Traded by Dodgers with LHP Onan Masaoka and OF Jeff Barry to White Sox for RHP James Baldwin, July 26, 2001 . . . Selected by Blue Jays from White Sox in major league Rule 5 draft, Dec. 16, 2002; returned to White Sox, March 17, 2003 . . . Traded by White Sox with RHP Jon Rauch to Expos for Carl Everett and cash, July 18, 2004. **Signed by:** Paul Provas (White Sox).

Majewski has become a bit of a journeyman at age 25. He already has been with four organizations, been part of three trades and been selected once in the major league Rule 5 draft. He came to the Expos in the White Sox' second annual deal for Carl Everett last July.

He may finally have found a home in Washington, as he'll probably make the Opening Day roster this year as a middle reliever. Majewski is an aggressive fastball/slider pitcher with a bit of a mean streak. His fastball has good life, sitting at 91-94 mph and maxing out at 96. His hard, 82-86 mph slider can be an out pitch at times. He also has a changeup but doesn't use it often. Majewski held his own in 21 innings with the Expos in 2004, and with a little more confidence he could become a good set-up man in the big leagues.

Year	Club (League)	Class	W	L	ERA	G	GS	CG	SV	IP	H	R	ER	HR	BB	SO	AVG
1999	Bristol (Appy)	R	7	1	3.05	13	13	1	0	77	67	34	26	4	37	91	.243
1999	Burlington (Mid)	A	0	0	7.80	2	0	0	0	3	11	14	14	3	4	1	.524
2000	Burlington (Mid)	A	6	7	3.07	22	22	3	0	135	83	53	46	8	68	137	.182
	Winston-Salem (Car)	A	2	4	5.11	6	6	0	0	37	32	21	21	1	17	24	.239
2001	Vero Beach (FSL)	A	4	5	6.24	23	13	0	1	75	103	57	52	9	36	41	.340
	Winston-Salem (Car)	A	4	2	2.93	9	6	1	0	43	42	15	14	3	10	31	.266
2002	Birmingham (SL)	AA	5	3	2.65	57	1	0	3	75	61	31	22	3	34	75	.221
2003	Charlotte (IL)	AAA	6	4	3.96	42	1	0	4	73	62	33	32	3	29	72	.231
2004	Charlotte (IL)	AAA	3	3	3.19	35	0	0	14	42	30	16	15	2	16	41	.208
	Edmonton (PCL)	AAA	1	2	3.86	15	0	0	1	16	18	8	7	0	8	17	.295
	Montreal (NL)	MAJ	0	1	3.86	16	0	0	1	21	28	15	9	2	5	12	.326
MAJOR LEAGUE TOTALS			0	1	3.86	16	0	0	1	21	28	15	9	2	5	12	.326
MINOR LEAGUE TOTALS			38	31	3.89	224	62	5	23	576	509	282	249	36	259	530	.243

21 Alejandro Machado, 2b/ss

Born: April 26, 1982. **Ht.:** 6-0. **Wt.:** 160. **Bats:** B. **Throws:** R. **Career Transactions:** Signed out of Venezuela by Braves, July 2, 1998 . . . Traded by Braves with RHP Brad Voyles to Royals for SS Rey Sanchez, July 31, 2001 . . . Traded by Royals with RHP Wes Obermueller and cash to Brewers for RHP Curtis Leskanic, July 2, 2003 . . . Traded by Brewers to Expos for a player to be named, March 29, 2004; Brewers received RHP Fernando Rijo to complete deal (April 28, 2004). **Signed by:** Rolando Petit (Braves).

Machado's career was sputtering before the Expos acquired him from Milwaukee last March. The Brewers designated him for assignment after he hit .226 for them in Double-A. Capable of playing either middle-infield position, Machado impressed his latest organization both offensively and defensively. He's fluid and consistent at second base, where he made just four errors in 85 games last year. He has the range to play shortstop, and his arm is adequate there despite his unconventional arm angle. Machado's reactions are terrific both in the field and at the plate, where he's a switch-hitter who makes contact, draws walks, bunts well and sprays the ball to all fields. His speed is average and he enhances it with his intelligence on the bases. But Machado has almost no pop, and he has had a tendency to start hot at the plate and have difficulty sustaining it. At 22, he'll likely begin 2005 in Double-A and could get a September callup. His ceiling is as a second baseman who could bat No. 2 in an order, but a more realistic expectation would be for him to become a utilityman.

Year	Club (League)	Class	AVG	G	AB	R	H	2B	3B	HR	RBI	BB	SO	SB	OBP	SLG
1999	Braves (GCL)	R	.278	56	223	45	62	11	0	0	14	20	22	19	.348	.327
2000	Danville (Appy)	R	.341	61	217	45	74	6	2	0	16	53	29	30	.477	.387
2001	Macon (SAL)	A	.271	82	306	43	83	6	3	1	24	34	56	20	.368	.320
	Burlington (Mid)	A	.239	28	109	17	26	5	0	0	11	10	16	5	.311	.284
2002	Wilmington (Car)	A	.314	101	325	53	102	9	1	2	29	27	43	20	.381	.366
2003	Wichita (TL)	AA	.287	78	289	59	83	13	5	1	31	34	45	19	.368	.377
	Huntsville (SL)	AA	.226	45	155	14	35	4	1	0	13	15	24	11	.302	.265
2004	Brevard County (FSL)	A	.355	46	186	34	66	10	2	1	19	22	27	11	.424	.446
	Harrisburg (EL)	AA	.280	93	346	54	97	5	4	4	26	41	39	19	.365	.353
MINOR LEAGUE TOTALS			.291	590	2156	364	628	69	18	9	183	256	301	154	.377	.353

22 Jason Bergmann, rhp

Born: Sept. 25, 1981. **Ht.:** 6-4. **Wt.:** 190. **Bats:** R. **Throws:** R. **School:** Rutgers University. **Career Transactions:** Selected by Expos in 11th round of 2002 draft; signed June 12, 2002. **Signed by:** Larry Izzo.

Scouting director Dana Brown, a New Jersey native, saw a lot of Bergmann at Rutgers and liked his potential despite an up-and-down college career. A starter his first two pro seasons, he began 2004 in the low Class A rotation but moved to the bullpen when he was promoted in mid-June. He was a little reluctant to become a reliever, but team officials thought his live arm would be most effective in short stints. Bergmann settled into the role as the summer progressed. His fastball is a plus pitch that sits at 90-93 mph and touches 95. He used his slider more as a reliever, and it showed flashes of becoming an above-average pitch. He also added an 88 mph cutter that could be the key to his development. Bergmann's deep repertoire also includes a decent tumbling changeup and an inconsistent curveball. His three-quarters arm angle is tough on righthanders, who hit .160 against him once he moved to the bullpen. At times, however, his arm slot will vary and his delivery gets too long. He still needs to work on his command and learn how to attack hitters as a reliever. Projected as a set-up man, Bergmann will begin 2005 back in Double-A.

Year	Club (League)	Class	W	L	ERA	G	GS	CG	SV	IP	H	R	ER	HR	BB	SO	AVG
2002	Vermont (NY-P)	A	7	4	2.89	14	14	0	0	72	48	27	23	4	33	57	.194
2003	Savannah (SAL)	A	6	11	4.29	23	22	1	0	109	108	57	52	8	53	82	.264
2004	Savannah (SAL)	A	3	7	4.85	13	13	0	0	65	67	43	35	6	34	58	.265
	Harrisburg (EL)	AA	0	2	9.00	2	0	0	0	4	7	5	4	3	2	3	.412
	Brevard County (FSL)	A	3	2	1.14	24	0	0	8	32	20	7	4	0	18	28	.189
MINOR LEAGUE TOTALS			19	26	3.78	76	49	1	8	281	250	139	118	21	140	228	.242

23 Erick San Pedro, c

Born: Oct. 5, 1983. **Ht.:** 6-1. **Wt.:** 210. **Bats:** R. **Throws:** R. **School:** University of Miami. **Career Transactions:** Selected by Expos in second round of 2004 draft; signed July 16, 2004. **Signed by:** Delvy Santiago.

The Expos were thin on catching prior to the 2004 draft, and upgrading the position was one of their top priorities. They drafted six backstops and signed four, starting with San Pedro in the second round and another top college catcher, South Florida's Devin Ivany, in the sixth. San Pedro, who signed for $650,000, does his best work behind the plate. He's agile and does an excellent job blocking balls in the dirt. His plus arm allows him to shut down the running game, he calls a good game and he handles pitchers well. The question with San Pedro is his bat. Though he has some pop, he doesn't have a good approach or strong hitting mechanics at the plate. He makes inconsistent contact and will sometimes lunge at the ball, leaving him vulnerable to offspeed stuff. Still, San Pedro should move quickly in an organization that lacks depth at his position, and he has a good chance to start 2005 in high Class A. If he refines his offensive game, he could develop into an everyday, defensive-minded catcher who could hit in the lower half of a lineup.

Year	Club (League)	Class	AVG	G	AB	R	H	2B	3B	HR	RBI	BB	SO	SB	OBP	SLG
2004	Expos (GCL)	R	.083	4	12	1	1	0	0	0	4	2	4	0	.214	.083
	Savannah (SAL)	A	.200	14	40	3	8	2	0	1	4	9	17	0	.347	.325
MINOR LEAGUE TOTALS			.173	18	52	4	9	2	0	1	8	11	21	0	.317	.269

24 Tyrell Godwin, of

Born: July 10, 1979. **Ht.:** 6-0. **Wt.:** 200. **Bats:** L. **Throws:** R. **School:** University of North Carolina. **Career Transactions:** Selected by Blue Jays in third round of 2001 draft; signed July 2, 2001 . . . Selected by Nationals from Blue Jays in major league Rule 5 draft, Dec. 13, 2004. **Signed by:** Charles Aliano (Blue Jays).

The first of two major league Rule 5 picks by the Nationals in December, Godwin was a first-round pick by the Yankees in 1997 and a supplemental first-rounder by the Rangers in 2000, but he didn't sign until the Blue Jays took him as a third-rounder in 2001. He still has the tools that always have endeared him to scouts, but he has yet to realize his potential and is coming off his worst season as a pro. Godwin has struggled with adjustments from level to level, and he didn't respond well when Toronto tried to tinker with his approach. He has a decent stroke and showed improved mechanics and plate discipline in 2004. But his power never has manifested itself and he struck out at an alarming rate last year. He did make better use of his speed, taking a step forward as a basestealer and continuing to play a solid center field. His arm is average. Godwin wants to improve, and he paid his own way to attend instructional league. His talent makes him a long-term project worth sticking with, but getting chosen by Washington wasn't the best move for his development. Instead of seeing if he could put it all together in Triple-A in 2005, he has to remain with the big league club or be offered back to Toronto for half the $50,000 draft price before being sent to the minors.

Year	Club (League)	Class	AVG	G	AB	R	H	2B	3B	HR	RBI	BB	SO	SB	OBP	SLG
2001	Auburn (NY-P)	A	.368	33	117	26	43	8	2	2	15	19	27	9	.464	.521
2002	Charleston, WV (SAL)	A	.281	48	185	31	52	8	5	0	16	20	23	10	.364	.378
2003	Dunedin (FSL)	A	.273	97	322	52	88	16	0	1	33	29	39	20	.348	.332
	New Haven (EL)	AA	.309	33	123	20	38	6	3	1	13	3	27	6	.328	.431
2004	New Hampshire (EL)	AA	.253	133	521	85	132	21	7	6	40	52	110	42	.326	.355
MINOR LEAGUE TOTALS			.278	344	1268	214	353	59	17	10	117	123	226	87	.351	.375

25 Greg Bunn, rhp

Born: Feb. 3, 1983. **Ht.:** 6-1. **Wt.:** 210. **Bats:** R. **Throws:** R. **School:** East Carolina University. **Career Transactions:** Selected by Expos in fifth round of 2004 draft; signed June 18, 2004. **Signed by:** Fred Wright.

Just minutes after he led East Carolina to an NCAA regional title by striking out 11 UNC Wilmington batters in eight shutout innings, Bunn was drafted in the fifth round by the

Expos. A double major in physics and mathematics who also owned a hot dog stand in college, Bunn signed for $190,000. His out pitch is a plus curveball with good depth. He also has a slightly above-average fastball that tops out at 92 mph. His delivery is sound and his feel for pitching is off the charts. Bunn's makeup is outstanding. He works hard to improve and has great mound presence, drawing rave reviews from everyone in the organization after his pro debut. Bunn will need to develop his changeup and mix speeds better to keep pro hitters off balance, because while he commands his fastball well, it's not overpowering. Bunn logged a staff-high 107 innings for East Carolina last spring, so he didn't get a lot of work after turning pro. He should move quickly, beginning 2005 in Class A, and could crack Washington's rotation at some point in 2007 if he stays on track.

Year	Club (League)	Class	W	L	ERA	G	GS	CG	SV	IP	H	R	ER	HR	BB	SO	AVG
2004	Vermont (NY-P)	A	3	0	3.00	9	5	0	0	24	16	8	8	1	11	27	.186
MINOR LEAGUE TOTALS			3	0	3.00	9	5	0	0	24	16	8	8	1	11	27	.186

26 Brandon Watson, of

Born: Sept. 30, 1981. **Ht.:** 6-1. **Wt.:** 170. **Bats:** L. **Throws:** R. **School:** Westchester HS, Los Angeles. **Career Transactions:** Selected by Expos in ninth round of 1999 draft; signed June 7, 1999. **Signed by:** Mark Baca.

For the second straight year, Watson didn't start hitting until six weeks into the season. He was batting just .232 in mid-May, then hit .299 the rest of the way. In 2003, he shook off a .236 start to bat .349 after mid-May. Though he recovered and was young for Triple-A at age 22, Watson showed no improvement as a leadoff hitter because he doesn't draw enough walks. He has limited power, so setting the table is his ticket. He's a slap hitter who sacrifices his ability to drive the ball for contact. He can bunt fairly well, and his speed is above-average, but he needs to work on his jumps and reads on the basepaths. Watson is a good center fielder with plus range and playable arm strength. For him to be an everyday center fielder in the majors, though, he must become a more patient hitter. Otherwise he'll just be the second coming of Endy Chavez. Watson will repeat Triple-A in 2005.

Year	Club (League)	Class	AVG	G	AB	R	H	2B	3B	HR	RBI	BB	SO	SB	OBP	SLG
1999	Expos (GCL)	R	.303	33	119	15	36	2	0	0	12	11	11	4	.361	.319
2000	Vermont (NY-P)	A	.291	69	278	53	81	9	1	0	30	25	38	26	.354	.331
2001	Clinton (Mid)	A	.327	117	489	74	160	16	9	2	38	29	65	33	.364	.409
2002	Brevard County (FSL)	A	.267	111	424	57	113	16	2	0	24	27	53	22	.314	.314
	Harrisburg (EL)	AA	.333	2	6	2	2	0	0	0	0	1	0	0	.429	.333
2003	Harrisburg (EL)	AA	.319	139	565	86	180	17	6	1	39	38	60	18	.362	.375
2004	Edmonton (PCL)	AAA	.293	139	526	74	154	17	3	2	41	31	68	22	.332	.348
MINOR LEAGUE TOTALS			.302	610	2407	361	726	77	21	5	184	162	295	125	.347	.357

27 Shawn Norris, inf

Born: Aug. 1, 1980. **Ht.:** 6-2. **Wt.:** 170. **Bats:** L. **Throws:** R. **School:** Cal State Fullerton. **Career Transactions:** Selected by Expos in ninth round of 2001 draft; signed June 15, 2001. **Signed by:** Robby Corsaro.

With the acquisition of Brendan Harris and the emergence of Kory Casto, Washington suddenly has depth at third base. That's not good news for Norris, who stands out defensively but lacks the power expected from a corner infielder. As a result, the organization had him play more in the middle infield than at the hot corner in high Class A. While he played exclusively at third base following a promotion to Double-A, he saw time at second, third and shortstop in the Arizona Fall League. Versatility can only help Norris. Outstanding at third base and solid up the middle, he has superb instincts, excellent hands and an accurate arm. At the plate, Norris has a good line-drive stroke and a knack for getting on base. He should hit for average at the higher levels, and Washington hopes his bat speed will allow him to develop a little power as he matures physically. Norris will begin 2005 at Double-A, where the Nationals would like him to settle into one position. They still project him as a third baseman, but his best chance of making the majors is probably as a utilityman.

Year	Club (League)	Class	AVG	G	AB	R	H	2B	3B	HR	RBI	BB	SO	SB	OBP	SLG
2001	Vermont (NY-P)	A	.218	57	197	18	43	4	0	2	21	38	57	0	.347	.269
2002	Clinton (Mid)	A	.269	9	26	2	7	1	0	0	3	6	8	1	.394	.308
	Expos (GCL)	R	.206	9	34	1	7	1	0	0	3	3	3	0	.270	.235
	Vermont (NY-P)	A	.287	42	157	22	45	5	2	4	14	22	23	2	.376	.420
2003	Savannah (SAL)	A	.287	67	223	38	64	19	2	2	35	31	42	4	.375	.417
	Brevard County (FSL)	A	.196	57	194	28	38	9	1	2	14	37	49	1	.331	.284
2004	Brevard County (FSL)	A	.274	97	351	48	96	15	8	2	48	59	80	5	.379	.379
	Harrisburg (EL)	AA	.315	37	124	16	39	10	2	3	33	25	37	1	.429	.500
MINOR LEAGUE TOTALS			.260	375	1306	173	339	64	15	15	171	221	299	14	.368	.366

28 Josh Labandeira, ss

Born: Feb. 25, 1979. **Ht.:** 5-7. **Wt.:** 180. **Bats:** R. **Throws:** R. **School:** Fresno State University.
Career Transactions: Selected by Expos in sixth round of 2001 draft; signed June 13, 2001. **Signed by:** John Hughes.

Labandeira was the Western Athletic Conference player of the year in 2001 at Fresno State and led the WAC with 15 homers and 68 RBIs despite his 5-foot-7 frame. He broke his leg in his first pro game, but since then he has advanced steadily and made his big league debut in 2004. Labandeira is frequently described as gritty and a sparkplug, and that's not a euphemism for a player who lacks talent. He plays the game hard and has tools. He owns the best infield arm in the system, and managers rated him the best defensive shortstop and strongest infield arm in the Eastern League last year. He makes plays in the hole thanks to his smooth footwork and quick release, and his range has improved since he shed extra bulk. Labandeira's tightly wound body generates surprising pop to the gaps. He has average speed and runs the bases well. Labandeira tries to do too much sometimes, hurting him when he's in RBI situations and leading to many of his 32 errors last year. He'll have to prove himself every step along the way, but he'll be the starting shortstop in Triple-A this year.

Year	Club (League)	Class	AVG	G	AB	R	H	2B	3B	HR	RBI	BB	SO	SB	OBP	SLG
2001	Vermont (NY-P)	A	.333	1	3	2	1	0	0	0	0	0	0	0	.333	.333
2002	Clinton (Mid)	A	.286	129	493	60	141	27	3	8	67	45	73	15	.350	.402
2003	Brevard County (FSL)	A	.324	62	238	41	77	13	4	0	25	24	35	6	.386	.412
	Harrisburg (EL)	AA	.239	60	238	25	57	18	2	2	26	20	38	0	.298	.357
2004	Harrisburg (EL)	AA	.270	134	514	72	139	22	4	9	33	53	92	9	.357	.381
	Montreal (NL)	MAJ	.000	7	14	0	0	0	0	0	0	0	4	0	.000	.000
MAJOR LEAGUE TOTALS			.000	7	14	0	0	0	0	0	0	0	4	0	.000	.000
MINOR LEAGUE TOTALS			.279	386	1486	200	415	80	13	19	151	142	238	30	.350	.389

29 Josh Whitesell, 1b

Born: April 14, 1982. **Ht.:** 6-3. **Wt.:** 220. **Bats:** L. **Throws:** L. **School:** Loyola Marymount University. **Career Transactions:** Selected by Expos in sixth round of 2003 draft; signed July 9, 2003. **Signed by:** Anthony Arango.

The Expos were intrigued by Whitesell's huge raw power after seeing him launch balls with wood bats during batting practice at Loyola Marymount. He has hit 21 homers in 162 pro games, but hasn't shown much in other areas of the game. Whitesell is a good fastball hitter with even more strength than Larry Broadway. He had quality at-bats in 2004 and does draw walks, but he still strikes out too often. Whitesell struggles against lefthanders and is streaky. Club officials like Whitesell's high energy level and solid work ethic, which have helped him improve defensively after primarily serving as a DH in college. He won't win any Gold Gloves, but he's fielding grounders more quickly and showing better footwork. He's a below-average runner. Whitesell's enormous power will make him an intriguing middle-of-the-order prospect if he can refine his approach and his defense. He should be the everyday first baseman in high Class A this year.

Year	Club (League)	Class	AVG	G	AB	R	H	2B	3B	HR	RBI	BB	SO	SB	OBP	SLG
2003	Vermont (NY-P)	A	.246	49	167	13	41	10	1	5	19	28	53	0	.365	.407
2004	Savannah (SAL)	A	.250	113	380	56	95	29	0	16	54	58	91	0	.352	.453
MINOR LEAGUE TOTALS			.249	162	547	69	136	39	1	21	73	86	144	0	.356	.439

30 Chris Lugo, rhp

Born: Nov. 10, 1986. **Ht.:** 6-1. **Wt.:** 185. **Bats:** R. **Throws:** R. **School:** Hudson Catholic HS, Hoboken, N.J. **Career Transactions:** Selected by Expos in 28th round of 2004 draft; signed June 14, 2004. **Signed by:** Larry Izzo.

The Expos drafted Lugo last June with the expectation that he would go to junior college and possibly sign as a draft-and-follow if he pitched well in 2005. But when scouting director Dana Brown went home to New Jersey for a postdraft breather, area scout Larry Izzo persuaded him to come watch Lugo pitch firsthand. Brown was so impressed that he decided to sign Lugo rather than risk losing him. Though he was just 17 at the time, Lugo already had a smooth delivery, compact arm action and advanced command. His primary pitches are an 88-91 mph fastball and a promising curveball, and he's also dabbling with a slider and a changeup. As a high school pitcher from the Northeast, Lugo needs innings and is a long-term project. But he's got a lot of potential and the organization is pleased with his initial success. He figures to spend 2005 at short-season Vermont.

Year	Club (League)	Class	W	L	ERA	G	GS	CG	SV	IP	H	R	ER	HR	BB	SO	AVG
2004	Expos (GCL)	R	2	1	1.67	12	2	0	2	43	43	20	8	2	12	34	.260
MINOR LEAGUE TOTALS			2	1	1.67	12	2	0	2	43	43	20	8	2	12	34	.260

SIGNING BONUSES

EVOLUTION of the BONUS RECORD

DOMESTIC PLAYERS ONLY

Pre-Draft Record

Year	Team, Player, Pos., School	Bonus
1964	Angels. Rick Reichart, of, Wisconsin	$205,000

Draft Era Record

Year	Team, Player, Pos., School, Round	Bonus
1965	Athletics. Rick Monday, of, Arizona State (1)	$104,000
1966	Phillies. Steve Arlin, rhp, Ohio State (1/secondary)	105,000
1973	Rangers. David Clyde, lhp, HS—Houston (1)	125,000
1975	Angels. Danny Goodwin, c, Southern (1)	125,000
1978	Braves. Bob Horner, 3b, Arizona State (1)	175,000
	Tigers. Kirk Gibson, of, Michigan State (1)	200,000
1988	Padres. Andy Benes, rhp, Evansville (1)	235,000
1989	Braves. Tyler Houston, c, HS—Las Vegas (1)	241,000
	Orioles. #Ben McDonald, rhp, Louisiana State (1)	350,000
	Blue Jays. John Olerud, 1b, Washington State (3)	575,000
1991	Braves. Mike Kelly, of, Arizona State (1)	575,000
	Yankees. Brien Taylor, lhp, HS—Beaufort, N.C. (1)	1,550,000
1994	Mets. Paul Wilson, rhp, Florida State (1)	1,550,000
	Marlins. Josh Booty, 3b, HS—Shreveport, La. (1)	1,600,000
1996	Pirates. Kris Benson, rhp, Clemson (1)	2,000,000
	*Diamondbacks. Travis Lee, 1b, San Diego State U. (1)	10,000,000
	*Devil Rays. Matt White, rhp, HS—Chambersburg, Pa. (1)	10,200,000

Round indicated in parentheses.

*Declared free agent on contract tendering technicality.

#Signed major league contract (For players signed to major league contracts, the amount is only the stated bonus in the contract. For players signed to standard minor league contracts, the amount is the full compensation to be paid out over the life of the contract.).

LARGEST BONUSES in DRAFT HISTORY

FOR PLAYERS SIGNING WITH THE TEAM THAT DRAFTED THEM

Rank	Club, Year. Player, Pos., School	Bonus
1.	White Sox, 2000. Joe Borchard, of, Stanford	$5,300,000
2.	Twins, 2001. Joe Mauer, c, HS—St. Paul	5,150,000
3.	Devil Rays, 2002. B.J. Upton, ss, HS—Chesapeake, Va.	4,600,000
4.	Rangers, 2001. #Mark Teixeira, 3b, Georgia Tech	4,500,000
5.	Devil Rays, 2001. #Dewon Brazelton, rhp, Middle Tennessee State	4,200,000
	Phillies, 2001. Gavin Floyd, rhp, HS—Severna Park, Md.	4,200,000
7.	Cubs, 2001. #Mark Prior, rhp, Southern California	4,000,000
	Pirates, 2002. Bryan Bullington, rhp, Ball State	4,000,000
9.	Devil Rays, 1999. Josh Hamilton, of, HS—Raleigh, N.C.	3,960,000
10.	Cubs, 1998. Corey Patterson, of, HS—Kennesaw, Ga.	3,700,000
	Devil Rays, 2003. #Delmon Young, of, HS—Camarillo, Calif.	3,700,000
12.	Marlins, 1999. #Josh Beckett, rhp, HS—Spring, Texas	3,625,000
13.	Brewers, 2003. #Rickie Weeks, 2b, Southern	3,600,000
14.	Tigers, 1999. #Eric Munson, c, Southern California	3,500,000
15.	Tigers, 2003. Kyle Sleeth, rhp, Wake Forest	3,350,000
16.	Athletics, 1998. Mark Mulder, lhp, Michigan State	3,200,000
	Devil Rays, 2004. #Jeff Niemann, rhp, Rice	3,200,000
18.	Phillies, 1998. #Pat Burrell, 1b, Miami	3,150,000
	Padres, 2004. Matt Bush, ss, HS—San Diego	3,150,000
	Tigers, 2004. #Justin Verlander, rhp, Old Dominion	3,150,000

Signed major league contract (For players signed to major league contracts, the amount is only the stated bonus in the contract. For players signed to standard minor league contracts, the amount is the full compensation to be paid out over the life of the contract).

SIGNING BONUSES
2004 DRAFT

FIRST ROUND

No. Player, Pos.	Bonus
1. Padres. Matt Bush, ss	$3,150,000
2. Tigers. Justin Verlander, rhp	3,150,000
3. Mets. Philip Humber, rhp	3,000,000
4. Devil Rays. Jeff Niemann, rhp	3,200,000
5. Brewers. Mark Rogers, rhp	2,200,000
6. Indians. Jeremy Sowers, lhp	2,475,000
7. Reds. Homer Bailey, rhp	2,300,000
8. Orioles. Wade Townsend, rhp	Did not sign
9. Rockies. Chris Nelson, ss	2,150,000
10. Rangers. Thomas Diamond, rhp	2,025,000
11. Pirates. Neil Walker, c	1,950,000
12. Angels. Jered Weaver, rhp	Unsigned
13. Expos. Bill Bray, lhp	1,750,000
14. Royals. Billy Butler, 3b	1,400,000
15. Diamondbacks. Stephen Drew, ss	Unsigned
16. Blue Jays. David Purcey, lhp	1,600,000
17. Dodgers. Scott Elbert, lhp	1,575,000
18. White Sox. Josh Fields, 3b	1,550,000
19. Cardinals. Chris Lambert, rhp	1,525,000
20. Twins. Trevor Plouffe, ss	1,500,000
21. Phillies. Greg Golson, of	1,475,000
22. Twins. Glen Perkins, lhp	1,425,000
23. Yankees. Philip Hughes, rhp	1,400,000
24. Athletics. Landon Powell, c	1,000,000
25. Twins. Kyle Waldrop, rhp	1,000,000
26. Athletics. Richie Robnett, of	1,325,000
27. Marlins. Taylor Tankersley, lhp	1,300,000
28. Dodgers. Blake Dewitt, 3b	1,200,000
29. Royals. Matt Campbell, lhp	1,100,000
30. Rangers. Eric Hurley, rhp	1,050,000

SUPPLEMENTAL FIRST-ROUND

No. Player, Pos.	Bonus
31. Royals. J.P. Howell, lhp	1,000,000
32. Blue Jays. Zach Jackson, lhp	1,017,500
33. Dodgers. Justin Orenduff, rhp	1,000,000
34. White Sox. Tyler Lumsden, lhp	975,000
35. Twins. Matt Fox, rhp	950,000
36. Athletics. Danny Putnam, of	950,000
37. Yankees. Jon Poterson, of	925,000
38. White Sox. Gio Gonzalez, lhp	850,000
39. Twins. Jay Rainville, rhp	875,000
40. Athletics. Huston Street, rhp	800,000
41. Yankees. Jeff Marquez, rhp	790,000

SECOND ROUND

No. Player, Pos.	Bonus
42. Yankees. Brett Smith, rhp	800,000
43. Tigers. Eric Beattie, rhp	800,000
44. Mets. Matt Durkin, rhp	800,000
45. Devil Rays. Reid Brignac, ss	795,000
46. Brewers. Yovani Gallardo, rhp	725,000
47. Indians. Justin Hoyman, rhp	725,000
48. Reds. B.J. Szymanski, of	725,000
49. Athletics. Michael Rogers, rhp	700,000

No. Player, Pos.	Bonus
50. Rockies. Seth Smith, of	690,000
51. Rangers. K.C. Herren, of	675,000
52. Pirates. Brian Bixler, ss	670,000
53. White Sox. Wes Whisler, lhp	660,000
54. Expos. Erick San Pedro, c	650,000
55. Royals. Billy Buckner, rhp	635,000
56. Diamondbacks. Jon Zeringue, of	630,000
57. Blue Jays. Curtis Thigpen, c	625,000
58. Dodgers. Blake Johnson, rhp	600,000
59. White Sox. Donny Lucy, c	525,000
60. Cardinals. Mike Ferris, 1b	600,000
61. Twins. Anthony Swarzak, rhp	575,000
62. Phillies. Jason Jaramillo, c	585,000
63. Royals. Eric Cordier, rhp	575,000
64. Astros. Hunter Pence, of	575,000
65. Red Sox. Dustin Pedroia, ss	575,000
66. Cubs. Grant Johnson, rhp	1,260,000
67. Athletics. Kurt Suzuki, c	550,000
68. Marlins. Jason Vargas, lhp	525,000
69. White Sox. Ray Liotta, lhp	499,000
70. Giants. Eddy Martinez-Esteve, of	537,500
71. Braves. Eric Campbell, 3b	500,000

THIRD ROUND

No. Player, Pos.	Bonus
72. Padres. Billy Killian, c	450,000
73. Tigers. Jeff Frazier, of	500,000
74. Mets. Gaby Hernandez, rhp	480,000
75. Devil Rays. Wade Davis, rhp	475,000
76. Brewers. Josh Wahpepah, rhp	400,000
77. Indians. Scott Lewis, lhp	460,000
78. Reds. Craig Tatum, c	450,000
79. Orioles. Jeff Fiorentino, of	450,000
80. Rockies. Steven Register, rhp	450,000
81. Rangers. Michael Schlact, rhp	455,000
82. Pirates. Eddie Prasch, 3b	500,000
83. Blue Jays. Adam Lind, 1b/of	445,000
84. Expos. Ian Desmond, ss	430,000
85. Royals. Josh Johnson, ss	410,000
86. Diamondbacks. Garrett Mock, rhp	440,000
87. Blue Jays. Danny Hill, rhp	275,000
88. Dodgers. Cory Dunlap, 1b	430,000
89. White Sox. Grant Hansen, rhp	430,000
90. Cardinals. Eric Haberer, lhp	422,500
91. Twins. Eduardo Morlan, rhp	420,000
92. Phillies. J.A. Happ, lhp	420,000
93. Mariners. Matt Tuiasosopo, ss	2,290,000
94. Astros. Jordan Parraz, of	400,000
95. Red Sox. Andrew Dobies, lhp	400,000
96. Cubs. Mark Reed, c	650,000
97. Athletics. Jason Windsor, rhp	270,000
98. Marlins. Greg Burns, of	395,000
99. Yankees. Christian Garcia, rhp	390,000
100. Giants. John Bowker, of	405,000

SIGNING BONUSES
2003 DRAFT

FIRST ROUND

No. Player, Pos.	Bonus
1. Devil Rays. Delmon Young, of	$3,700,000
2. Brewers. Rickie Weeks, 2b	3,600,000
3. Tigers. Kyle Sleeth, rhp	3,350,000
4. Padres. Tim Stauffer, rhp	750,000
5. Royals. Chris Lubanski, of	2,100,000
6. Cubs. Ryan Harvey, of	2,400,000
7. Orioles. Nick Markakis, of/lhp	1,850,000
8. Pirates. Paul Maholm, lhp	2,200,000
9. Rangers. John Danks, lhp	2,100,000
10. Rockies. Ian Stewart, 3b	1,950,000
11. Indians. Michael Aubrey, 1b	2,010,000
12. Mets. Lastings Milledge, of	2,075,000
13. Blue Jays. Aaron Hill, ss	1,675,000
14. Reds. Ryan Wagner, rhp	1,400,000
15. White Sox. Brian Anderson, of	1,600,000
16. Marlins. Jeff Allison, rhp	1,850,000
17. Red Sox. David Murphy, of	1,525,000
18. Indians. Brad Snyder, of	1,525,000
19. Diamondbacks. Conor Jackson, 3b	1,500,000
20. Expos. Chad Cordero, rhp	1,350,000
21. Twins. Matt Moses, 3b	1,450,000
22. Giants. David Aardsma, rhp	1,425,000
23. Angels. Brandon Wood, ss	1,300,000
24. Dodgers. Chad Billingsley, rhp	1,375,000
25. Athletics. Brad Sullivan, rhp	1,360,000
26. Athletics. Brian Snyder, 3b	1,325,000
27. Yankees. Eric Duncan, 3b	1,250,000
28. Cardinals. Daric Barton, c	975,000
29. Diamondbacks. Carlos Quentin, of	1,100,000
30. Royals. Mitch Maier, c	900,000

SUPPLEMENTAL FIRST-ROUND

No. Player, Pos.	Bonus
31. Indians. Adam Miller, rhp	1,025,000
32. Red Sox. Matt Murton, of	1,010,000
33. Athletics. Omar Quintanilla, ss	992,500
34. Giants. Craig Whitaker, rhp	975,000
35. Braves. Luis Atilano, rhp	950,000
36. Braves. Jarrod Saltalamacchia, c	950,000
37. Mariners. Adam Jones, ss	925,000

SECOND ROUND

No. Player, Pos.	Bonus
38. Devil Rays. James Houser, lhp	900,000
39. Brewers. Anthony Gwynn, of	875,000
40. Tigers. Jay Sborz, rhp	865,000
41. Padres. Daniel Moore, lhp	800,000
42. Royals. Shane Costa, of	775,000
43. Brewers. Jo Jo Reyes, lhp	800,000
44. Orioles. Brian Finch, rhp	750,000
45. Pirates. Tom Gorzelanny, lhp	775,000
46. Rangers. Vince Sinisi, 1b	2,070,000
47. Rockies. Scott Beerer, rhp	725,000
48. Indians. Javi Herrera, c	710,000
49. Red Sox. Abe Alvarez, lhp	700,000
50. Blue Jays. Josh Banks, rhp	650,000

No. Player, Pos.	Bonus
51. Reds. Thomas Pauly, rhp	660,000
52. White Sox. Ryan Sweeney, of	785,000
53. Marlins. Logan Kensing, rhp	675,000
54. Red Sox. Mickey Hall, of	800,000
55. Giants. Todd Jennings, c	620,000
56. Mariners. Jeff Flaig, 3b	710,000
57. Expos. Jerry Owens, of	600,000
58. Twins. Scott Baker, rhp	600,000
59. Astros. Jason Hirsh, rhp	625,000
60. Angels. Anthony Whittington, lhp	650,000
61. Dodgers. Chuck Tiffany, lhp	1,100,000
62. Athletics. Andre Ethier, of	580,000
63. Giants. Nate Schierholtz, 3b	572,000
64. Yankees. Estee Harris, of	725,000
65. Cardinals. Stuart Pomeranz, rhp	570,000
66. Diamondbacks. Jamie D'Antona, 3b	560,000
67. Braves. Paul Bacot, rhp	550,000

THIRD ROUND

No. Player, Pos.	Bonus
68. Devil Rays. Andrew Miller, lhp	Did not sign
69. Brewers. Lou Palmisano, c	500,000
70. Tigers. Tony Giarratano, ss	500,000
71. Padres. Colt Morton, c	500,000
72. Royals. Brian McFall, 1b	385,000
73. Cubs. Jake Fox, c	500,000
74. Orioles. Chris Ray, rhp	485,000
75. Pirates. Steve Lerud, c	512,500
76. Rangers. John Hudgins, rhp	490,000
77. Rockies. Aaron Marsden, lhp	462,500
78. Indians. Ryan Garko, c	270,000
79. Braves. Jake Stevens, lhp	475,000
80. Blue Jays. Shaun Marcum, rhp	449,000
81. Reds. Jose Ronda, ss	440,000
82. White Sox. Clint King, of	440,000
83. Marlins. Jonathan Fulton, ss	440,000
84. Red Sox. Beau Vaughan, rhp	250,000
85. Phillies. Tim Moss, 2b	440,000
86. Mariners. Ryan Feierabend, lhp	437,500
87. Expos. Kory Casto, of	410,000
88. Twins. John Woodard, 1b	425,000
89. Astros. Drew Stubbs, of	Did not sign
90. Angels. Sean Rodriguez, ss	400,000
91. Dodgers. Cory Van Allen, lhp	Did not sign
92. Athletics. Dustin Majewski, of	220,000
93. Giants. Brian Buscher, 3b	215,000
94. Yankees. Tim Battle, of	425,000
95. Cardinals. Dennis Dove, rhp	400,000
96. Diamondbacks. Matt Chico, lhp	365,000
97. Braves. Matt Harrison, lhp	395,000

FOURTH ROUND

No. Player, Pos.	Bonus
98. Devil Rays. Travis Schlichting, ss	400,000
99. Brewers. Charlie Fermaint, of	295,000
100. Tigers. Josh Rainwater, rhp	300,000

SIGNING BONUSES
2002 DRAFT

FIRST ROUND

No. Player, Pos.	Bonus
1. Pirates. Bryan Bullington, rhp	$4,000,000
2. Devil Rays. B.J. Upton, ss	4,600,000
3. Reds. Chris Gruler, rhp	2,500,000
4. Orioles. Adam Loewen, lhp	*3,200,000
5. Expos. Clint Everts, rhp	2,500,000
6. Royals. Zack Greinke, rhp	2,475,000
7. Brewers. Prince Fielder, 1b	2,400,000
8. Tigers. Scott Moore, ss	2,300,000
9. Rockies. Jeff Francis, lhp	1,850,000
10. Rangers. Drew Meyer, ss	1,875,000
11. Marlins. Jeremy Hermida, of	2,012,500
12. Angels. Joe Saunders, lhp	1,825,000
13. Padres. Khalil Greene, ss	1,500,000
14. Blue Jays. Russ Adams, ss	1,785,000
15. Mets. Scott Kazmir, lhp	2,150,000
16. Athletics. Nick Swisher, of	1,780,000
17. Phillies. Cole Hamels, lhp	2,000,000
18. White Sox. Royce Ring, lhp	1,600,000
19. Dodgers. James Loney, 1b	1,500,000
20. Twins. Denard Span, of	1,700,000
21. Cubs. Bobby Brownlie, rhp	2,500,000
22. Indians. Jeremy Guthrie, rhp	3,000,000
23. Braves. Jeff Francoeur, of	2,200,000
24. Athletics. Joseph Blanton, rhp	1,400,000
25. Giants. Matt Cain, rhp	1,375,000
26. Athletics. John McCurdy, ss	1,375,000
27. Diamondbacks. Sergio Santos, ss	1,400,000
28. Mariners. John Mayberry Jr., of	Did not sign
29. Astros. Derick Grigsby, rhp	1,125,000
30. Athletics. Ben Fritz, rhp	1,200,000

SUPPLEMENTAL FIRST-ROUND

No. Player, Pos.	Bonus
31. Dodgers. Greg Miller, lhp	1,200,000
32. Cubs. Luke Hagerty, lhp	1,150,000
33. Indians. Matt Whitney, 3b	1,125,000
34. Braves. Dan Meyer, lhp	1,000,000
35. Athletics. Jeremy Brown, c	350,000
36. Cubs. Chadd Blasko, rhp	1,050,000
37. Athletics. Steve Obenchain, rhp	750,000
38. Cubs. Matt Clanton, rhp	875,000
39. Athletics. Mark Teahen, 3b	725,000
40. Reds. Mark Schramek, 3b	200,000
41. Indians. Micah Schilling, 2b	915,000

SECOND ROUND

No. Player, Pos.	Bonus
42. Pirates. Blair Johnson, rhp	885,000
43. Devil Rays. Jason Pridie, of	892,500
44. Reds. Joey Votto, c	600,000
45. Orioles. Corey Shafer, of	800,000
46. Expos. Darrell Rasner, rhp	800,000
47. Royals. Adam Donachie, c	800,000
48. Brewers. Josh Murray, ss	825,000
49. Tigers. Brent Clevlen, of	805,000
50. Rockies. Micah Owings, rhp	Did not sign

No. Player, Pos.	Bonus
51. Dodgers. Zach Hammes, rhp	750,000
52. Marlins. Robert Andino, ss	750,000
53. Angels. Kevin Jepsen, rhp	745,000
54. Padres. Michael Johnson, 1b	*500,000
55. Blue Jays. David Bush, rhp	450,000
56. Cubs. Brian Dopirak, 1b	740,000
57. Red Sox. Jon Lester, lhp	1,000,000
58. Phillies. Zach Segovia, rhp	712,500
59. White Sox. Jeremy Reed, of	650,000
60. Dodgers. Jonathan Broxton, rhp	685,000
61. Twins. Jesse Crain, rhp	650,000
62. Cubs. Justin Jones, lhp	625,000
63. Indians. Brian Slocum, rhp	625,000
64. Braves. Brian McCann, c	750,000
65. Braves. Tyler Greene, ss	Did not sign
66. Giants. Fred Lewis, of	595,000
67. Athletics. Steve Stanley, of	200,000
68. Diamondbacks. Chris Snyder, c	567,000
69. Mariners. Josh Womack, of	550,000
70. Astros. Mitch Talbot, rhp	550,000
71. Yankees. Brandon Weeden, rhp	565,000

SUPPLEMENTAL SECOND-ROUND

No. Player, Pos.	Bonus
72. Indians. Pat Osborn, 3b	547,500

THIRD ROUND

No. Player, Pos.	Bonus
73. Pirates. Taber Lee, ss	525,000
74. Devil Rays. Elijah Dukes, of	500,000
75. Reds. Kyle Edens, rhp	300,000
76. Orioles. Val Majewski, of	400,000
77. Expos. Larry Broadway, 1b	450,000
78. Royals. David Jensen, 1b	472,500
79. Brewers. Eric Thomas, rhp	470,000
80. Tigers. Curtis Granderson, of	469,000
81. Rockies. Ben Crockett, rhp	345,000
82. Indians. Jason Cooper, of	472,500
83. Marlins. Trevor Hutchinson, rhp	375,000
84. Angels. Kyle Pawelczyk, rhp	465,000
85. Padres. Kennard Jones, of	465,000
86. Blue Jays. Justin Maureau, lhp	455,000
87. Tigers. Matt Pender, rhp	450,000
88. Red Sox. Scott White, 3b	825,000
89. Phillies. Kiel Fisher, 3b	450,000
90. White Sox. Josh Rupe, rhp	440,000
91. Dodgers. Mike Nixon, c	950,000
92. Twins. Mark Sauls, rhp	Did not sign
93. Cubs. Billy Petrick, rhp	459,500
94. Indians. Daniel Cevette, lhp	400,000
95. Braves. Charlie Morton, rhp	415,000
96. Cubs. Matt Craig, ss	399,000
97. Giants. Dan Ortmeier, of	396,000
98. Athletics. Bill Murphy, lhp	410,000
99. Diamondbacks. Jared Doyle, lhp	390,000
100. Mariners. Eddy Martinez-Esteve, of	Did not sign

Signed in 2003 as draft-and-follow

DRAFT PROSPECTS

COLLEGE TOP 100

CLASS OF 2005

Rank	Player, Pos.	College	Hometown	Class	B-T	HT	WT	Last Drafted
1.	Alex Gordon, 3b	Nebraska	Omaha	Jr.	L-R	6-1	210	Never drafted
2.	Mike Pelfrey, rhp	Wichita State	Wichita	Jr.	R-R	6-7	210	Devil Rays '02 (15)
3.	Luke Hochevar, rhp	Tennessee	Fowler, Colo.	Jr.	R-R	6-4	198	Dodgers '02 (39)
4.	Tyler Greene, ss	Georgia Tech	Plantation, Fla.	Jr.	R-R	6-2	188	Braves '02 (2)
5.	Jeff Clement, c	Southern California	Marshalltown, Iowa	Jr.	L-R	6-1	205	Twins '02 (12)
6.	Wade Townsend, rhp	Rice	Dripping Springs, Texas	Sr.	R-R	6-4	225	Orioles '04 (1)
7.	Troy Tulowitzki, ss	Long Beach State	Sunnyvale, Calif.	Jr.	R-R	6-3	200	Never drafted
8.	Ryan Zimmerman, 3b	Virginia	Virginia Beach, Va.	Jr.	R-R	6-2	210	Never drafted
9.	Stephen Head, 1b/lhp	Mississippi	Raymond, Miss.	Jr.	L-L	6-2	218	Never drafted
10.	John Mayberry, 1b/of	Stanford	Kansas City, Mo.	Jr.	R-R	6-5	210	Mariners '02 (1)
11.	Mark McCormick, rhp	Baylor	Clear Lake Shores, Texas	Jr.	R-R	6-2	190	Orioles '02 (11)
12.	Taylor Teagarden, c	Texas	Carrolton, Texas	Jr.	R-R	6-0	190	Cubs '02 (22)
13.	Craig Hansen, rhp	St. John's	Glen Cove, N.Y.	Jr.	R-R	6-5	193	Never drafted
14.	Travis Buck, of	Arizona State	Richland, Wash.	Jr.	L-R	6-2	190	Mariners '02 (23)
15.	Brian Bogusevic, of/lhp	Tulane	Oak Lawn, Ill.	Jr.	L-L	6-3	200	Never drafted
16.	Daniel Carte, of	Winthrop	Hurricane, W.Va.	Jr.	R-R	6-0	180	Never drafted
17.	Cliff Pennington, ss	Texas A&M	Corpus Christi, Texas	Jr.	B-R	5-11	170	Never drafted
18.	Jed Lowrie, 2b	Stanford	Salem, Ore.	Jr.	B-R	6-0	180	Never drafted
19.	Cesar Ramos, lhp	Long Beach State	Pico Rivera, Calif.	Jr.	L-L	6-1	175	Devil Rays '02 (6)
20.	Stephen Kahn, rhp	Loyola Marymount	Anaheim	Jr.	L-R	6-2	205	Brewers '02 (8)
21.	Ryan Mullins, lhp	Vanderbilt	Nashville, Tenn.	Jr.	L-L	6-6	175	Never drafted
22.	Trevor Crowe, of	Arizona	Portland, Ore.	Jr.	B-R	5-10	185	Athletics '02 (20)
23.	Ricky Romero, lhp	Cal State Fullerton	Los Angeles	Jr.	R-L	6-2	170	Red Sox '02 (37)
24.	Jacoby Ellsbury, of	Oregon State	Madras, Ore.	Jr.	L-L	6-1	175	Devil Rays '02 (23)
25.	Justin Maxwell, of	Maryland	Olney, Md.	Jr.	R-R	6-5	225	Rangers '04 (10)
26.	Matt Liuzza, c	Louisiana State	Metairie, La.	Jr.	R-R	6-0	190	Never drafted
27.	Ryan Braun, ss	Miami (Fla.)	Granada Hills, Calif.	Jr.	R-R	6-2	190	Never drafted
28.	Warner Jones, 2b	Vanderbilt	Nashville, Tenn.	Jr.	R-R	5-10	175	Never drafted
29.	Brad Corley, of	Mississippi State	Louisville	Jr.	R-R	6-2	195	Rockies '02 (16)
30.	J. Brent Cox, rhp	Texas	Bay City, Texas	Jr.	L-R	6-3	200	Blue Jays '02 (50)
31.	Mark Romanczuk, lhp	Stanford	Newark, Del.	Jr.	L-L	6-1	190	Devil Rays '02 (5)
32.	Cesar Carrillo, rhp	Miami (Fla.)	Hammond, Ind.	Jr.	R-R	6-2	160	Royals '02 (33)
33.	Jason Neighborgall, rhp	Georgia Tech	Hillsborough, N.C.	Jr.	R-R	6-5	210	Red Sox '02 (7)
34.	Joey Devine, rhp	North Carolina State	Junction City, Kan.	Jr.	R-R	6-1	198	Never drafted
35.	Tim Lincecum, rhp	Washington	Renton, Wash.	So.	L-R	6-0	160	Cubs '03 (48)
36.	Micah Owings, rhp/1b	Tulane	Gainesville, Ga.	Jr.	R-R	6-4	212	Cubs '04 (19)
37.	Zach Ward, rhp	Gardner-Webb	Kannapolis, N.C.	Jr.	R-R	6-3	225	Never drafted
38.	Brent Lillibridge, ss/of	Washington	Everett, Wash.	Jr.	R-R	5-9	170	Never drafted
39.	Clete Thomas, of	Auburn	Lynn Haven, Fla.	Jr.	L-R	6-0	185	Twins '02 (5)
40.	Jeff Larish, 1b/of	Arizona State	Tempe, Ariz.	Sr.	L-R	6-2	180	Dodgers '04 (13)
41.	Kevin Whelan, rhp	Texas A&M	Kerrville, Texas	Jr.	R-R	6-0	190	Never drafted
42.	Alan Horne, rhp	Florida	Marianna, Fla.	Jr.	R-R	6-4	170	Angels '04 (30)
43.	Mark Holliman, rhp	Mississippi	Germantown, Tenn.	Jr.	R-R	6-1	180	Cubs '02 (41)
44.	Nick Hundley, c	Arizona	Redmond, Wash.	Jr.	R-R	6-1	190	Marlins '02 (5)
45.	Lance Broadway, rhp	Texas Christian	Waxahachie, Texas	Jr.	R-R	6-4	185	Never drafted
46.	Jeremy Slayden, of	Georgia Tech	Murfreesboro, Tenn.	Jr.	L-R	6-0	188	Athletics '04 (18)
47.	Robert Ray, rhp	Texas A&M	Lufkin, Texas	Jr.	R-R	6-3	190	Dodgers '02 (28)
48.	Chris Robinson, c	Illinois	Dorchester, Ontario	Jr.	R-R	6-0	190	Mets '02 (30)
49.	Buck Cody, lhp	Texas	Oklahoma City	Sr.	R-L	6-2	200	Cardinals '04 (7)
50.	Brett Hayes, c	Nevada	Calabasas, Calif.	Jr.	R-R	6-1	170	Never drafted

COLLEGE TOP 100

51.	Sam LeCure, rhp	Texas	Centertown, Mo.	Jr.	R-R	6-0	165	Phillies '02 (45)
52.	Neil Jamison, rhp	Long Beach State	San Diego	Sr.	R-R	6-3	180	Mets '04 (8)
53.	Kris Harvey, rhp/c	Clemson	Catawba, N.C.	Jr.	R-R	6-2	180	Braves '02 (5)
54.	Chris Getz, 2b	Michigan	Gross Pointe, Mich.	Jr.	L-R	6-0	165	White Sox '02 (6)
55.	Chris Leroux, rhp	Winthrop	Mississauga, Ontario	Jr.	L-R	6-5	210	Devil Rays '02 (9)
56.	Lance Pendleton, rhp/of	Rice	Kingwood, Texas	Jr.	L-R	6-3	185	Padres '02 (13)
57.	Matt Green, rhp	Louisiana-Monroe	Monroe, La.	Jr.	R-R	6-4	185	Never drafted
58.	Garrett Olson, lhp	Cal Poly	Clovis, Calif.	Jr.	R-L	6-0	190	Never drafted
59.	Josh Bell, c	Auburn	Jackson, Tenn.	Jr.	R-R	6-0	200	Cardinals '02 (5)
60.	Michael Campbell, of	South Carolina	Winchester, Va.	Jr.	L-L	6-1	172	Never drafted
61.	Brae Wright, lhp	Oklahoma State	Southaven, Miss.	Jr.	L-L	6-4	180	Marlins '02 (26)
62.	Will Startup, lhp	Georgia	Cartersville, Ga.	Jr.	L-L	6-1	185	Never drafted
63.	Dan Dorn, of	Cal State Fullerton	Diamond Bar, Calif.	Jr.	L-L	6-2	180	Never drafted
64.	Steve Pearce, c	South Carolina	Lakeland, Fla.	Sr.	R-R	5-11	187	Red Sox '04 (10)
65.	Chris Rahl, of	William & Mary	Chesapeake, Va.	Jr.	R-R	6-0	185	Never drafted
66.	Joe Ness, rhp	Ball State	Logansport, Ind.	Jr.	R-R	6-5	195	Never drafted
67.	Mike Costanzo, 3b/rhp	Coastal Carolina	Springfield, Pa.	Jr.	L-R	6-3	205	Never drafted
68.	Kevin Roberts, rhp	Houston	Pearland, Texas	Jr.	R-R	6-0	190	Never drafted
69.	Jensen Lewis, rhp	Vanderbilt	Cincinnati	Jr.	R-R	6-3	185	Indians '02 (33)
70.	Matt Goyen, lhp	Georgia College	Athens, Ga.	Sr.	R-L	6-5	220	Devil Rays '04 (27)
71.	Jarrad Page, of	UCLA	San Leandro, Calif.	Jr.	B-R	6-0	200	Brewers '02 (5)
72.	Matt Garza, rhp	Fresno State	Fresno, Calif.	Jr.	R-R	6-4	190	Never drafted
73.	Jason Urquidez, rhp	Arizona State	Simi Valley, Calif.	Sr.	R-R	6-1	165	Reds '04 (11)
74.	Zach Kroenke, lhp	Nebraska	Omaha	Jr.	R-L	6-3	210	Never drafted
75.	Zack Kalter, rhp	Southern California	Pomona, Calif.	Jr.	L-R	6-2	190	Never drafted
76.	Seth Johnston, 2b	Texas	Boerne, Texas	Sr.	R-R	6-3	200	Orioles '04 (7)
77.	Anthony Varvaro, rhp	St. John's	Staten Island, N.Y.	Jr.	R-R	6-0	170	Never drafted
78.	Drew Butera, c	Central Florida	Lake Mary, Fla.	Jr.	R-R	6-1	190	Blue Jays '02 (48)
79.	Justin Tordi, ss	Florida	Orlando, Fla.	Jr.	R-R	6-1	193	Blue Jays '02 (46)
80.	Hector Ambriz, rhp	UCLA	Placentia, Calif.	So.	L-R	6-2	210	White Sox '02 (28)
81.	Paul Phillips, rhp	Oakland	Blissfield, Mich.	So.	R-R	6-2	210	Never drafted
82.	Nic Crosta, of	Santa Clara	Seattle	Sr.	R-R	6-2	205	Rangers '04 (17)
83.	Justin Blaine, lhp	San Diego	Westlake Village, Calif.	Jr.	L-L	6-4	175	Never drafted
84.	John Slone, c	Miami (Ohio)	Cincinnati	Sr.	R-R	6-2	195	Pirates '04 (15)
85.	Erik Lis, 1b	Evansville	Oak Lawn, Ill.	Jr.	L-L	6-1	220	Never drafted
86.	Steven Tolleson, ss	South Carolina	Spartanburg, .C.	Jr.	R-R	5-11	172	Never drafted
87.	Jayson Ruhlman, rhp	Central Michigan	Chesterfield, Mich.	So.	L-R	6-1	170	White Sox '02 (12)
88.	Mike Billek, rhp	Central Florida	Palm Harbor, Fla.	Jr.	R-R	6-4	235	Never drafted
89.	Ron Prettyman, 3b	Cal State Fullerton	Los Alamitos, Calif.	Sr.	L-R	6-2	190	Brewers '04 (28)
90.	John DeFendis, of	Rutgers	Staten Island, N.Y.	Jr.	R-R	6-1	180	Rockies '02 (41)
91.	Tim Grogan, 3b	Western Kentucky	Fort Mitchell, Ky.	Jr.	L-R	6-1	195	White Sox '02 (47)
92.	Cameron Blair, 2b/ss	Texas Tech	Dallas	Sr.	R-R	5-10	175	Cardinals '04 (18)
93.	Matt Avery, rhp	Virginia	McLean, Va.	Jr.	R-R	6-5	230	Never drafted
94.	Neil Wagner, rhp	North Dakota State	Eden Prairie, Minn.	Jr.	R-R	6-0	200	Never drafted
95.	Travis DeBondt, of	Oral Roberts	Bakersfield, Calif.	Jr.	L-L	6-4	180	Tigers '04 (36)
96.	Mark Sauls, rhp	Florida State	Panama City, Fla.	Jr.	R-R	6-3	210	Twins '02 (3)
97.	Chris Dennis, rhp	Auburn	Madison, Ala.	Jr.	L-R	6-1	204	Never drafted
98.	Brad Boyer, 3b	Arizona	Camarillo, Calif.	Jr.	L-R	5-11	180	Never drafted
99.	James Avery, rhp	Niagara	Moose Jaw, Sask.	Jr.	R-R	6-0	200	Twins '02 (29)
100.	Matthew Luca, rhp	Nevada-Las Vegas	Galveston, Texas	Jr.	R-R	6-6	200	Reds '02 (22)

NOTE: List does not include junior college players.

Compiled by Allan Simpson in consultation with major league scouting directors.

DRAFT PROSPECTS

HIGH SCHOOL TOP 100

CLASS OF 2005

Rank	Player, Pos.	B-T	HT	WT	High School	Hometown	Commitment
1.	Justin Upton, ss/of	R-R	6-2	187	Great Bridge	Chesapeake, Va.	North Carolina State
2.	Cameron Maybin, of	B-R	6-3	195	T.C. Roberson	Arden, N.C.	None
3.	Sean O'Sullivan, rhp/of	R-R	6-2	195	Valhalla	El Cajon, Calif.	San Diego State
4.	Justin Bristow, ss/rhp	R-R	6-4	205	Mills Godwin	Richmond, Va.	Auburn
5.	Jordan Danks, of	L-R	6-5	200	Round Rock	Round Rock, Texas	Texas
6.	Zach Putnam, rhp/3b	R-R	6-2	210	Pioneer	Ann Arbor, Mich.	Michigan
7.	Chris Volstad, rhp	R-R	6-7	195	Palm Beach Gardens	Palm Beach Gardens, Fla.	Miami
8.	Andrew McCutchen, of	R-R	5-11	170	Fort Meade	Fort Meade, Fla.	Florida
9.	Brett Jacobson, rhp	R-R	6-6	195	Cactus Shadows	Carefree, Ariz.	Vanderbilt
10.	Austin Jackson, of	R-R	6-2	180	Denton Ryan	Denton, Texas	Georgia Tech
11.	Brandon Snyder, c/ss	R-R	6-2	190	Westfield	Centreville, Va.	Louisiana State
12.	Henry Sanchez, 1b	R-R	6-3	260	Mission Bay	San Diego	San Diego State
13.	David Adams, 3b	R-R	6-1	185	Grandview Prep	Margate, Fla.	Virginia
14.	Jeremy Hellickson, rhp	R-R	6-0	170	Hoover	Des Moines, Iowa	Louisiana State
15.	Ike Davis, 1b/lhp	L-L	6-5	205	Chaparral	Scottsdale, Ariz.	Arizona State
16.	Buster Posey, rhp/ss	R-R	6-1	180	Lee County	Leesburg, Ga.	Florida State
17.	Miers Quigley, lhp	L-L	6-3	190	Roswell	Roswell, Ga.	Alabama
18.	Aaron Thompson, lhp	L-L	6-2	190	Second Baptist	Houston	Texas A&M
19.	Michael Bowden, rhp	R-R	6-3	210	Waubonsie	Aurora, Ill.	Arizona State
20.	Josh Bell, 3b	B-R	6-3	205	Santaluces	Lantana, Fla.	Florida Atlantic
21.	Kyle Hancock, rhp	R-R	6-3	185	Rowlett	Rowlett, Texas	Arkansas
22.	Brad Clark, rhp	R-R	6-6	200	Sickles	Tampa	Okaloosa-Walton CC
23.	Josh Zeid, rhp	R-R	6-4	214	Hamden Hall	New Haven, Conn.	Vanderbilt
24.	Jonathan Egan, c	R-R	6-4	210	Cross Creek	Hephzibah, Ga.	Georgia
25.	P.J. Phillips, ss	R-R	6-3	170	Redan	Stone Mountain, Ga.	Georgia
26.	John Drennen, of	L-L	6-0	180	Rancho Bernardo	San Diego	UCLA
27.	Colby Rasmus, of/lhp	L-L	6-2	183	Russell County	Phenix City, Ala.	Auburn
28.	Craig Italiano, rhp	R-R	6-3	195	Flower Mound	Flower Mound, Texas	Texas Christian
29.	Ryan Tucker, rhp	R-R	6-2	190	Temple City	Temple City, Calif.	Cal State Fullerton
30.	Preston Paramore, c	B-R	6-3	210	Allen	Allen, Texas	Arizona State
31.	Kyle Russell, of	L-L	6-4	180	Tomball	Magnolia, Texas	Texas
32.	Beau Jones, lhp	L-L	6-0	180	Destrehan	Destrehan, La.	Louisiana State
33.	Brandon Erbe, rhp	R-R	6-4	195	McDonough	Baltimore	Miami
34.	Jeff Lyman, rhp	R-R	6-3	215	Monte Vista	Alamo, Calif.	Arizona State
35.	Brent Milleville, c	R-R	6-3	230	Maize	Wichita, Kan.	Stanford
36.	C.J. Henry, ss/of	R-R	6-3	200	Putnam City	Oklahoma City	Georgia Tech
37.	David Duncan, lhp	R-L	6-7	190	New Richmond	New Richmond, Ohio	Georgia Tech
38.	Matthew Olson, rhp	R-R	6-4	185	Western Branch	Chesapeake, Va.	East Carolina
39.	Nick Romero, ss	B-R	6-0	180	Eastlake	Chula Vista, Calif.	San Diego State
40.	Diallo Fon, of	L-L	6-0	190	Las Lomas	Suisan, Calif.	Vanderbilt
41.	Ivan De Jesus, ss	B-R	5-11	175	P.R. Baseball Acad.	Guaynabo, P.R.	None
42.	Jarred Bogany, of	R-R	6-3	199	George Bush	Houston	Louisiana State
43.	Trevor Bell, of/rhp	L-R	6-2	180	La Crescenta	Crescenta Valley, Calif.	None
44.	Jay Bruce, of	L-L	6-2	200	West Brook	Beaumont, Texas	Tulane
45.	Matthew Hall, ss	R-R	6-2	180	Horizon	Scottsdale, Ariz.	Arizona State
46.	Josh Wilson, rhp	R-R	6-0	180	Whitehouse	Whitehouse, Texas	Texas
47.	DeSean Jackson, of	R-R	5-11	175	Long Beach	Long Beach, Calif.	None
48.	David Cooper, of/lhp	L-L	6-0	180	Tokay	Stockton, Calif.	Cal State Fullerton
49.	Iain Sebastian, rhp/1b	L-R	6-4	230	Columbus	Columbus, Ga.	Georgia
50.	Eric Massingham, rhp	R-R	6-2	205	De La Salle	Benicia, Calif.	Cal Poly

HIGH SCHOOL TOP 100

CLASS OF 2005

No.	Name	Bats-Throws	Ht	Wt	School	Hometown	College
51.	Jeremy Bleich, lhp	L-L	6-2	185	Isidore Newman	Metairie, La.	Stanford
52.	Chaz Roe, rhp	R-R	6-5	170	Lafayette	Lexington, Ky.	Kentucky
53.	Mark Pawelek, lhp	L-L	6-2	180	Springville	Springville, Utah	Arizona State
54.	Justin Smoak, 1b	B-L	6-2	175	Stratford	Goose Creek, S.C.	South Carolina
55.	Shooter Hunt, rhp	R-R	6-2	185	Ramapo	Wyckoff, N.J.	Virginia
56.	Chris Dominguez, 1b/3b	R-R	6-5	220	Gulliver Prep	Miami	Louisville
57.	Scott Deal, rhp	R-R	6-3	165	Curtis	University Place, Wash.	Washington State
58.	Justin Sellers, ss	R-R	5-10	160	Marina	Huntington Beach, Calif.	Cal State Fullerton
59.	Jason Ogata, ss	R-R	6-0	170	Westview	Portland, Ore.	Louisiana State
60.	Marcus Jones, of	R-R	6-2	180	Landon School	Washington, D.C.	North Carolina State
61.	Josh Wall, rhp/ss	R-R	6-6	190	Central Private	Walker, La.	Louisiana State
62.	Tim Murphy, lhp	L-L	6-2	195	Rancho Buena Vista	Vista, Calif.	UCLA
63.	Vance Worley, rhp	R-R	6-2	195	McClatchy	Sacramento	Long Beach State
64.	Blair Brejtfus, rhp	R-R	6-3	215	Arcadia	Phoenix	UC Santa Barbara
65.	Shane Funk, rhp	R-R	6-6	225	Arnold	Panama City Beach, Fla.	Alabama
66.	Brett Wallace, 3b/1b	L-R	6-1	205	Justin Siena	Sonoma, Calif.	Arizona State
67.	Ryan DeLaughter, of/rhp	R-R	6-4	215	Denton Ryan	Corinth, Texas	None
68.	Shaun Garceau, rhp	B-R	6-1	185	Royal Palm Beach	Royal Palm Beach, Fla.	Alabama
69.	Charlie Cutler, c	R-R	6-0	180	Lowell	San Fransisco	California
70.	Kieron Pope, of	R-R	6-2	195	East Coweta	Gay, Ga.	Georgia
71.	Tim Dennehy, lhp	L-L	6-1	195	Oak Park	Oak Park, Ill.	Texas
72.	Brad Suttle, 3b/rhp	B-R	6-2	200	Boerne	Boerne, Texas	Texas
73.	Ryan Babineau, c	R-R	6-2	195	Etiwanda	Alta Loma, Calif.	UCLA
74.	Ben Booker, ss	L-R	6-3	180	Lorena	Bruceville, Texas	Baylor
75.	John Matulia, of	L-L	6-0	165	Eustis	Eustis, Fla.	Florida
76.	David Phelps, rhp	R-R	6-2	170	Hazelwood West	Hazelwood, Mo.	Notre Dame
77.	Brian Kirwan, rhp	R-R	6-4	195	Christian	Del Mar, Calif.	UCLA
78.	Matt Lea, rhp	R-R	6-5	215	Houston	Collierville, Tenn.	Mississippi State
79.	Jordan Schafer, lhp	L-L	6-1	200	Winter Haven	Winter Haven, Fla.	Clemson
80.	Jemile Weeks, ss	B-R	5-9	150	Lake Brantley	Altamonte Springs, Fla.	Miami
81.	Josh Lindblom, rhp	R-R	6-2	180	Harrison	West Lafayette, Ind.	Tennessee
82.	Ryan Wood, rhp	R-R	6-4	175	C.D. Hylton	Woodbridge, Va.	East Carolina
83.	Bryan Anderson, c	L-R	5-11	185	Simi Valley	Simi Valley, Calif.	Arizona
84.	Dennis Raben, 1b	L-L	6-3	185	Hollywood Hills	Hollywood, Fla.	Miami
85.	Jeremy Farrell, 3b	R-R	6-3	205	St. Ignatius	Westlake, Ohio	Virginia
86.	Mike Broadway, rhp	R-R	6-5	190	Pope	Golconda, Ill.	None
87.	Kyle Maxie, c	L-R	6-2	192	North Forrest	Hattiesburg, Miss.	Florida State
88.	Carlos Heraud, ss	R-R	6-2	189	Elkins	Missouri City, Texas	Houston
89.	Albert Laboy, of	R-R	5-11	165	Boynton Beach	Boca Raton, Fla.	None
90.	Mike Colla, rhp	R-R	6-2	200	Clovis West	Fresno, Calif.	Arizona
91.	Jonathan Niese, lhp	L-L	6-3	190	Defiance	Defiance, Ohio	Cincinnati
92.	Ralph Henriquez, c	B-R	6-1	190	Key West	Key West, Fla.	None
93.	Matt Nevarez, rhp	R-R	6-4	215	San Fernando	San Fernando, Calif.	None
94.	Reese Havens, ss	L-R	6-1	180	Bishop England	Sullivan's Island, S.C.	South Carolina
95.	Daryl Jones, of	L-L	6-1	175	Spring	Spring, Texas	None
96.	Drew Thompson, ss	L-R	5-11	165	Jupiter	Tequesta, Fla.	Florida
97.	Thomas Mendoza, rhp	R-R	6-2	195	Monsignor Pace	Miami, Fla.	Miami
98.	Travis Wood, lhp	R-L	6-0	170	Bryant	Alexander, Ark.	Arkansas
99.	Scott Van Slyke, of	R-R	6-5	210	John Burroughs	St. Louis	Mississippi
100.	Scott Taylor, rhp	R-R	6-4	220	Glen Allen	Glen Allen, Va.	Va. Commonwealth

Compiled by Allan Simpson in consultation with major league scouting directors.

TOP 20 PROSPECTS
in EVERY MINOR LEAGUE

As a complement to our organization-al prospect rankings, Baseball America also ranks prospects in every minor league right after each season. Like the organizational lists, they place more weight on potential than present per-formance and should not be regarded as minor league all-star teams.

The league lists do differ a little bit from the organizational lists, which are taken more from a scouting perspective. The league lists are based on conversations with league managers. They are not strictly polls, though we do try to talk with every manag-er. Some players on these lists, such as Justin Morneau and B.J. Upton, were not eligible for our organization prospect lists because they are no longer rookie-eligible. Such players are indicated with an asterisk (*). Players who have been traded from the organizations they are listed with are indi-cated with a pound sign (#).

Remember that managers and scouts tend to look at players differently. Managers give more weight to what a player does on the field, while scouts look at what a player might eventually do. We think both per-spectives are useful, so we give you both even though they don't always jibe with each other.

For a player to qualify for a league prospect list, he much have spent about one-third of the season in a league. Position players must have one plate appearance per league game. Pitchers must pitch ⅓ inning per league game. Relievers must make at least 20 appearances in a full-season league or 10 appearances in a short season league.

TRIPLE-A

INTERNATIONAL LEAGUE
1. *B.J. Upton, ss, Durham (Devil Rays)
2. *Justin Morneau, 1b, Rochester (Twins)
3. *Grady Sizemore, of, Buffalo (Indians)
4. Jason Kubel, of, Rochester (Twins)
5. #Jeremy Reed, of, Charlotte (White Sox)
6. *Alexis Rios, of, Syracuse (Blue Jays)
7. Ben Hendrickson, rhp, Indianapolis (Brewers)
8. Dan Meyer, lhp, Richmond (Braves)
9. Guillermo Quiroz, c, Syracuse (Blue Jays)
10. Jason Bartlett, ss, Rochester (Twins)
11. Joey Gathright, of, Durham (Devil Rays)
12. Jesse Crain, rhp, Rochester (Twins)
13. *Jorge Cantu, 3b, Durham (Bulls)
14. Robinson Cano, 2b, Columbus (Yankees)
15. John Maine, rhp, Ottawa (Orioles)
16. Russ Adams, ss, Syracuse (Blue Jays)

17. David Krynzel, of, Indianapolis (Brewers)
18. Kelly Shoppach, c, Pawtucket (Red Sox)
19. Francisco Cruceta, rhp, Buffalo (Indians)
20. *David Bush, rhp, Syracuse (Blue Jays)
#Traded to Mariners.

PACIFIC COAST LEAGUE
1. Casey Kotchman, 1b, Salt Lake (Angels)
2. Dallas McPherson, 3b, Salt Lake (Angels)
3. Edwin Jackson, rhp, Las Vegas (Dodgers)
4. Nick Swisher, of, Sacramento (Athletics)
5. *Jose Lopez, inf, Tacoma (Mariners)
6. Jeremy Reed, of, Tacoma (Mariners)
7. Chris Burke, 2b, New Orleans (Astros)
8. Joe Blanton, rhp, Sacramento (Athletics)
9. Juan Dominguez, rhp, Oklahoma (Rangers)
10. *Yadier Molina, c, Memphis (Cardinals)
11. Clint Nageotte, rhp, Tacoma (Mariners)
12. Ryan Church, of, Edmonton (Expos)
13. Dan Johnson, 1b, Sacramento (Athletics)
14. Freddy Guzman, of, Portland (Padres)
15. Clint Barmes, ss, Colorado Springs (Rockies)
16. *Luis Terrero, of, Tucson (Diamondbacks)
17. Garrett Atkins, 3b, Colorado Springs (Rockies)
18. *Bobby Madritsch, lhp, Tacoma (Mariners)
19. Brendan Harris, inf, Edmonton (Expos)
20. *Noah Lowry, lhp, Fresno (Giants)

DOUBLE-A

EASTERN LEAGUE
1. *David Wright, 3b, Binghamton (Mets)
2. Jason Kubel, of, New Britain (Twins)
3. Matt Cain, rhp, Norwich (Giants)
4. Mike Hinckley, lhp, Harrisburg (Expos)
5. Gavin Floyd, rhp, Reading (Phillies)
6. Zach Duke, lhp, Altoona (Pirates)
7. Curtis Granderson, of, Erie (Tigers)
8. Ryan Howard, 1b, Reading (Phillies)
9. J.D. Durbin, rhp, New Britain (Twins)
10. Franklin Gutierrez, of, Akron (Indians)
11. Val Majewski, of, Bowie (Orioles)
12. Michael Aubrey, 1b, Akron (Indians)
13. Larry Broadway, 1b, Harrisburg (Expos)
14. Aaron Hill, ss, New Hampshire (Blue Jays)
15. Brandon League, rhp, New Hampshire (Blue Jays)
16. Robinson Cano, 2b, Trenton (Yankees)
17. Scott Baker, rhp, New Britain (Twins)
18. #Denny Bautista, rhp, Bowie (Orioles)
19. Ian Snell, rhp, Altoona (Pirates)
20. Francisco Rosario, rhp, New Hampshire (Blue Jays)
#Traded to Royals.

SOUTHERN LEAGUE
1. Andy Marte, 3b, Greenville (Braves)
2. Joel Guzman, ss, Jacksonville (Dodgers)
3. Rickie Weeks, 2b, Huntsville (Brewers)
4. Prince Fielder, 1b, Huntsville (Brewers)
5. Jose Capellan, rhp, Greenville (Braves)
6. Edwin Encarnacion, 3b, Chattanooga (Reds)
7. Anthony Reyes, rhp, Tennessee (Cardinals)
8. Kyle Davies, rhp, Greenville (Braves)
9. James Loney, 1b, Jacksonville (Dodgers)
10. Josh Barfield, 2b, Mobile (Padres)

11. Brian Anderson, of, Birmingham (White Sox)
12. Josh Willingham, c/1b, Carolina (Marlins)
13. Renyel Pinto, lhp, West Tenn (Cubs)
14. Freddy Guzman, of, Mobile (Padres)
15. Dan Meyer, lhp, Greenville (Braves)
16. #Michael Morse, ss, Birmingham (White Sox)
17. William Bergolla, 2b/ss, Chattanooga (Reds)
18. Arnie Munoz, lhp, Birmingham (White Sox)
19. Brad Thompson, rhp, Tennessee (Cardinals)
20. Brad Nelson, of/1b, Huntsville (Brewers)
   #Traded to Mariners.

TEXAS LEAGUE
1. Felix Hernandez, rhp, San Antonio (Mariners)
2. Dallas McPherson, 3b, Arkansas (Angels)
3. Jeff Francis, lhp, Tulsa (Rockies)
4. Shin-Soo Choo, of, San Antonio (Mariners)
5. Denny Bautista, rhp, Wichita (Royals)
6. Sergio Santos, ss, El Paso (Diamondbacks)
7. Carlos Quentin, of, El Paso (Diamondbacks)
8. Ezequiel Astacio, rhp, Round Rock (Astros)
9. Ian Kinsler, ss, Frisco (Rangers)
10. Alberto Callaspo, ss/2b, Arkansas (Angels)
11. Conor Jackson, of, El Paso (Diamondbacks)
12. Chris Snyder, c, El Paso (Diamondbacks)
13. Jeff Mathis, c, Arkansas (Angels)
14. Willy Taveras, of, Round Rock (Astros)
15. Jason Botts, 1b, Frisco (Rangers)
16. #Mark Teahen, 3b, Midland (Athletics)
17. Ryan Shealy, 1b, Tulsa (Rockies)
18. D.J. Houlton, rhp, Round Rock (Astros)
19. John Hudgins, rhp, Frisco (Rangers)
20. Dustin Nippert, rhp, El Paso (Diamondbacks)
   #Traded to Royals.

HIGH CLASS A

CALIFORNIA LEAGUE
1. Felix Hernandez, rhp, Inland Empire (Mariners)
2. Matt Cain, rhp, San Jose (Giants)
3. Erick Aybar, ss, Rancho Cucamonga (Angels)
4. Carlos Quentin, of, Lancaster (Diamondbacks)
5. Conor Jackson, of, Lancaster (Diamondbacks)
6. Elijah Dukes, of, Bakersfield (Devil Rays)
7. Fred Lewis, of, San Jose (Giants)
8. Manny Parra, lhp, High Desert (Brewers)
9. Jon Zeringue, of, Lancaster (Diamondbacks)
10. Jeff Salazar, of, Visalia (Rockies)
11. John Danks, lhp, Stockton (Rangers)
12. Steven Shell, rhp, Rancho Cucamonga (Angels)
13. Jeff Baker, 3b, Visalia (Rockies)
14. Nate Schierholtz, 3b, San Jose (Giants)
15. Joaquin Arias, ss, Stockton (Rangers)
16. Jaime D'Antona, 3b, Lancaster (Diamondbacks)
17. Jason Hammel, rhp, Bakersfield (Devil Rays)
18. John Hudgins, rhp, Stockton (Rangers)
19. Omar Quintanilla, ss, Modesto (Athletics)
20. Enrique Gonzalez, rhp, Lancaster (Diamondbacks)

CAROLINA LEAGUE
1. Jeff Francoeur, of, Myrtle Beach (Braves)
2. Michael Aubrey, 1b, Kinston (Indians)
3. Brian Anderson, of, Winston-Salem (White Sox)
4. Zach Duke, lhp, Lynchburg (Pirates)
5. Kyle Davies, rhp, Myrtle Beach (Braves)
6. Brandon McCarthy, rhp, Winston-Salem (White Sox)
7. Ryan Sweeney, of, Winston-Salem (White Sox)
8. Brian McCann, c, Myrtle Beach (Braves)
9. Richie Gardner, rhp, Potomac (Reds)
10. Fernando Nieve, rhp, Salem (Astros)
11. Tom Gorzelanny, lhp, Lynchburg (Pirates)

12. Josh Fields, 3b, Winston-Salem (White Sox)
13. Ryan Garko, 1b/c, Kinston (Indians)
14. Brad Eldred, 1b, Lynchburg (Pirates)
15. Anthony Lerew, rhp, Myrtle Beach (Braves)
16. Chris Ray, rhp, Frederick (Orioles)
17. Sean Tracey, rhp, Winston-Salem (White Sox)
18. Rajai Davis, of, Lynchburg (Pirates)
19. Hayden Penn, rhp, Frederick (Orioles)
20. Mitch Maier, 3b, Wilmington (Royals)

FLORIDA STATE LEAGUE
1. Joel Guzman, ss, Vero Beach (Dodgers)
2. Chad Billingsley, rhp, Vero Beach (Dodgers)
3. Hanley Ramirez, ss, Sarasota (Red Sox)
4. #Scott Kazmir, lhp, St. Lucie (Mets)
5. Scott Olsen, lhp, Jupiter (Marlins)
6. Felix Pie, of, Daytona (Cubs)
7. Mike Hinckley, lhp, Brevard County (Expos)
8. Jeremy Hermida, of, Jupiter (Marlins)
9. Tony Giarratano, ss, Lakeland (Tigers)
10. Eric Duncan, 3b, Tampa (Yankees)
11. Francisco Liriano, lhp, Fort Myers (Twins)
12. Jonathan Broxton, rhp, Vero Beach (Dodgers)
13. Yusmeiro Petit, rhp, St. Lucie (Mets)
14. Jon Papelbon, rhp, Sarasota (Red Sox)
15. Jon Lester, lhp, Sarasota (Red Sox)
16. Andy LaRoche, 3b, Vero Beach (Dodgers)
17. Ismael Ramirez, rhp, Dunedin (Blue Jays)
18. Delwyn Young, 2b, Vero Beach (Dodgers)
19. Josh Banks, rhp, Dunedin (Blue Jays)
20. Kyle Sleeth, rhp, Lakeland (Tigers)
   #Traded to Devil Rays.

LOW CLASS A

MIDWEST LEAGUE
1. Brian Dopirak, 1b, Lansing (Cubs)
2. Daric Barton, c, Peoria (Cardinals)
3. Eric Duncan, 3b, Battle Creek (Yankees)
4. John Danks, lhp, Clinton (Rangers)
5. Brandon Wood, ss, Cedar Rapids (Angels)
6. Jairo Garcia, rhp, Kane County (Athletics)
7. Joey Votto, 1b, Dayton (Reds)
8. Ian Kinsler, ss, Clinton (Rangers)
9. Sean Marshall, lhp, Lansing (Cubs)
10. Adam Harben, rhp, Quad Cities (Twins)
11. Wladimir Balentien, of, Wisconsin (Mariners)
12. Howie Kendrick, 2b, Cedar Rapids (Angels)
13. Adam Jones, ss, Wisconsin (Mariners)
14. Glen Perkins, lhp, Quad Cities (Twins)
15. Melky Cabrera, of, Battle Creek (Yankees)
16. Kevin Jepsen, rhp, Cedar Rapids (Angels)
17. Ambiorix Burgos, rhp, Burlington (Royals)
18. Billy Petrick, rhp, Lansing (Cubs)
19. Baltazar Lopez, 1b, Cedar Rapids (Angels)
20. Dana Eveland, lhp, Beloit (Brewers)

SOUTH ATLANTIC LEAGUE
1. Delmon Young, of, Charleston, S.C. (Devil Rays)
2. Ian Stewart, 3b, Asheville (Rockies)
3. Lastings Milledge, of, Capital City (Mets)
4. Adam Miller, rhp, Lake County (Indians)
5. Yusmeiro Petit, rhp, Capital City (Mets)
6. Chuck Tiffany, lhp, Columbus (Dodgers)
7. Jarrod Saltalamacchia, c, Rome (Braves)
8. Brandon McCarthy, rhp, Kannapolis (White Sox)
9. Andy LaRoche, 3b, Columbus (Dodgers)
10. Clint Everts, rhp, Savannah (Expos)
11. Michael Bourn, of, Lakewood (Phillies)
12. Jacob Stevens, rhp, Rome (Braves)
13. Tom Gorzelanny, lhp, Hickory (Pirates)
14. Josh Anderson, of, Lexington (Astros)

15. Chris Young, of, Kannapolis (White Sox)
16. Nate Schierholtz, 3b, Hagerstown (Giants)
17. Scott Mathieson, rhp, Lakewood (Phillies)
18. Matt Albers, rhp, Lexington (Astros)
19. Chin-Lung Hu, ss, Columbus (Dodgers)
20. Brandon Moss, of, Augusta (Red Sox)

SHORT-SEASON CLASS A

NEW YORK-PENN LEAGUE
1. Ambiorix Concepcion, of, Brooklyn (Mets)
2. Anibal Sanchez, rhp, Lowell (Red Sox)
3. Jason Vargas, lhp, Jamestown (Marlins)
4. Taylor Tankersley, lhp, Jamestown (Marlins)
5. Ben Zobrist, ss, Tri-City (Astros)
6. Jesse Hoover, rhp, Staten Island (Yankees)
7. David Haehnel, lhp, Aberdeen (Orioles)
8. Tony Sipp, lhp, Mahoning Valley (Indians)
9. Christian Lara, ss, Lowell (Red Sox)
10. Jeff Marquez, rhp, Staten Island (Yankees)
11. Curtis Thigpen, c, Auburn (Blue Jays)
12. Mike Butia, of, Mahoning Valley (Indians)
13. Hunter Pence, of, Tri-City (Astros)
14. Tommy Hottovy, lhp, Lowell (Red Sox)
15. Jon Fulton, ss, Jamestown (Marlins)
16. Argenis Reyes, of, Mahoning Valley (Indians)
17. Blair Johnson, rhp, Williamsport (Pirates)
18. J.A. Happ, lhp, Batavia (Phillies)
19. Jake Mullinax, 3b, New Jersey (Cardinals)
20. Jon Barratt, lhp, Hudson Valley (Devil Rays)

NORTHWEST LEAGUE
1. Javier Herrera, of, Vancouver (Athletics)
2. Ryan Harvey, of, Boise (Cubs)
3. Carlos Gonzalez, of, Yakima (Diamondbacks)
4. Craig Whitaker, rhp, Salem-Keizer (Giants)
5. Matt Tuiasosopo, ss, Everett (Mariners)
6. Juan Morillo, rhp, Tri-City (Rockies)
7. Richie Robnett, of, Vancouver (Athletics)
8. Asdrubal Cabrera, ss, Everett (Mariners)
9. Matt Macri, 3b, Tri-City (Rockies)
10. Chris Carter, of/dh, Yakima (Diamondbacks)
11. Jim Miller, rhp, Tri-City (Rockies)
12. Kurt Suzuki, c, Vancouver (Athletics)
13. Eric Hurley, rhp, Spokane (Rangers)
14. Shawn Nottingham, lhp, Everett (Mariners)
15. A.J. Shappi, rhp, Yakima (Diamondbacks)
16. Landon Powell, c, Vancouver (Athletics)
17. Ross Ohlendorf, rhp, Yakima (Diamondbacks)
18. Orlando Mercado Jr., c, Yakima (Diamondbacks)
19. Mike Nickeas, c, Spokane (Rangers)
20. Tomas Santiago, rhp, Tri-City (Rockies)

ROOKIE ADVANCED

APPALACHIAN LEAGUE
1. Mitch Einertson, of, Greeneville (Astros)
2. Francisco Hernandez, c, Bristol (White Sox)
3. Kyle Waldrop, rhp, Elizabethton (Twins)
4. Reid Brignac, ss, Princeton (Devil Rays)
5. Gio Gonzalez, lhp, Bristol (White Sox)
6. Trevor Plouffe, ss, Elizabethton (Twins)
7. Yuber Rodriguez, of, Pulaski (Blue Jays)
8. Brandon Yarbrough, c, Johnson City (Cardinals)
9. Alexander Smit, lhp, Elizabethton (Twins)
10. Troy Patton, lhp, Greeneville (Astros)
11. Matt Fox, rhp, Elizabethton (Twins)
12. Juan Gutierrez, rhp, Greeneville (Astros)
13. Jordan Parraz, of, Greeneville (Astros)
14. Van Pope, 3b, Danville (Braves)
15. Frank Mata, rhp Elizabethton (Twins)
16. J.C. Holt, 2b, Danville (Braves)

17. Javier Castillo, ss, Bristol (White Sox)
18. Juan Valdes, of, Burlington (Indians)
19. Jose Delgado, 2b, Johnson City (Cardinals)
20. Deacon Burns, of, Elizabethton (Twins)

PIONEER LEAGUE
1. Chris Nelson, ss, Casper (Rockies)
2. Blake DeWitt, 3b, Ogden (Dodgers)
3. Sean Rodriguez, ss, Provo (Angels)
4. Billy Butler, 3b, Idaho Falls (Royals)
5. Ray Liotta, lhp, Great Falls (White Sox)
6. Scott Elbert, lhp, Ogden (Dodgers)
7. Cory Dunlap, 1b, Ogden (Dodgers)
8. Sam Deduno, rhp, Casper (Rockies)
9. Luis Cota, rhp, Idaho Falls (Royals)
10. Seth Smith, of, Casper (Rockies)
11. Josh Wahpepah, rhp, Helena (Brewers)
12. B.J. Szymanski, of, Billings (Reds)
13. Billy Buckner, rhp, Idaho Falls (Royals)
14. Brian McFall, of, Idaho Falls (Royals)
15. Mitchell Arnold, rhp, Provo (Angels)
16. Andrew Toussaint, 3b/dh, Provo (Angels)
17. Blake Johnson, rhp, Ogden (Dodgers)
18. J.P. Howell, lhp, Idaho Falls (Royals)
19. Franklin Morales, lhp, Casper (Rockies)
20. Craig Tatum, c, Billings (Reds)

ROOKIE

ARIZONA LEAGUE
1. Matt Tuiasosopo, ss, Mariners
2. Hernan Iribarren, 2b, Brewers
3. Mark Rogers, rhp, Brewers
4. Miguel Vega, 1b/3b, Royals
5. Matt Bush, ss, Padres
6. Daryl Jones, 1b, Padres
7. K.C. Herren, of, Rangers
8. Daniel Santin, c, Mariners
9. Elvin Puello, 3b/ss, Cubs
10. Marcus Sanders, 2b, Giants
11. Josh Johnson, ss, Royals
12. Erik Cordier, rhp, Royals
13. Yovani Gallardo, rhp, Brewers
14. Pablo Sandoval, c, Giants
15. Freddy Parejo, of, Brewers
16. Irving Falu, 2b, Royals
17. Andy Santana, lhp, Cubs
18. Alexi Ogando, of, Athletics
19. Alexi Casilla, 2b/ss, Angels
20. Connor Robertson, rhp, Athletics

GULF COAST LEAGUE
1. Luis Soto, ss, Red Sox
2. Gaby Hernandez, rhp, Mets
3. Greg Golson, of, Phillies
4. Kyle Waldrop, rhp, Twins
5. Neil Walker, c, Pirates
6. Christian Garcia, rhp, Yankees
7. Marcos Vechionacci, 3b, Yankees
8. Jay Rainville, rhp, Twins
9. Christian Lara, ss, Red Sox
10. Greg Burns, of, Marlins
11. Jose Campusano, ss, Marlins
12. Juan Portes, 3b, Twins
13. Jamie Hoffmann, 3b, Dodgers
14. Carlos Carrasco, rhp, Phillies
15. Anthony Swarzak, rhp, Twins
16. Jesus Flores, c, Mets
17. Johan Silva, of, Braves
18. Carlos Gomez, of, Mets
19. Willy Mota, of, Red Sox
20. Scott Mitchinson, rhp, Phillies

INDEX

DeSalvo, Matt (Yankees) 312
Desmond, Ian (Nationals) 489
DeWitt, Blake (Dodgers) 245
Deza, Fredy (Orioles) 73
Diamond, Thomas (Rangers) 450
Diaz, Felix (White Sox) 122
Diaz, Jose (Devil Rays) 445
Diaz, Matt (Devil Rays) 441
Diaz, Robinzon (Blue Jays) 473
Diaz, Victor (Mets) 293
Dickerson, Chris (Reds) 134
Dittler, Jake (Indians) 150
Dlugach, Brent (Tigers) 189
Dobbs, Greg (Mariners) 423
Dobies, Andrew (Red Sox) 89
Dohmann, Scott (Rockies) 169
Dominguez, Juan (Rangers) 452
Dopirak, Brian (Cubs) 98
Dorman, Rich (Mariners) 426
Doumit, Ryan (Pirates) 359
Dubois, Jason (Cubs) 102
Duffy, Chris (Pirates) 360
Duke, Zach (Pirates) 354
Dukes, Elijah (Devil Rays) 437
Duncan, Chris (Cardinals) 373
Duncan, Eric (Yankees) 306
Dunlap, Cory (Dodgers) 249
Durbin, J.D. (Twins) 275
Durkin, Matt (Mets) 295

E

Einertson, Mitch (Astros) 212
Elbert, Scott (Dodgers) 246
Eldred, Brad (Pirates) 357
Encarnacion, Edwin (Reds) 131
Escobar, Alcides (Brewers) 267
Espinosa, David (Tigers) 187
Esposito, Mike (Rockies) 173
Ethier, Andre (Athletics) 328
Eveland, Dana (Brewers) 263
Everts, Clint (Nationals) 483

F

Feierabend, Ryan (Mariners) 425
Ferris, Mike (Cardinals) 375
Fielder, Prince (Brewers) 259
Fields, Josh (White Sox) 115
Finan, Ryan (Orioles) 77
Finch, Brian (Orioles) 74
Fiorentino, Jeff (Orioles) 68
Fisher, Kiel (Phillies) 346
Flores, Jesus (Mets) 293
Flowers, Bo (Tigers) 184
Floyd, Gavin (Phillies) 339
Fontent, Mike (Cubs) 106
Fortunato, Bartolome (Mets) 297
Forystek, Brian (Orioles) 76
Fowler, Dexter (Rockies) 166
Fox, Matt (Twins) 280
Francia, Juan (Tigers) 188
Francis, Jeff (Rockies) 163
Francoeur, Jeff (Braves) 50
Frazier, Jeff (Tigers) 180
Freeman, Choo (Rockies) 171
Fulton, Jon (Marlins) 202
Furmaniak, J.J. (Padres) 394

G

Gall, John (Cardinals) 377
Gallardo, Yovanni (Brewers) 104

Galvez, Gary (Red Sox) 92
Gamble, Sean (Phillies) 346
Garcia, Angel (Devil Rays) 441
Garcia, Christian (Yankees) 308
Garcia, Edgar (Phillies) 341
Garcio, Jairo (Athletics) 325
Gardner, Richie (Reds) 131
Garko, Ryan (Indians) 149
Gathright, Joey (Devil Rays) 435
Germano, Justin (Padres) 389
Gettis, Byron (Tigers) 186
Giarratano, Tony (Tigers) 180
Gimenez, Hector (Astros) 215
Godwin, Tyrell (Nationals) 491
Goleski, Ryan (Indians) 155
Golson, Greg (Phillies) 339
Gomes, Jonny (Devil Rays) 440
Gomez Carlos (Mets) 296
Gomez, Abel (Yankees) 313
Gomez, Mariano (Indians) 156
Gonzalez, Adrian (Rangers) 453
Gonzalez, Carlos (Diamondbacks) 117
Gonzalez, Enrique (Diamondbacks) 40
Gonzalez, Gio (White Sox) 117
Gonzalez, Jino (Devil Rays) 444
Gonzalez, Rafael (Reds) 138
Gorecki, Reid (Cardinals) 374
Gorneault, Nick (Angels) 26
Gorzelanny, Tom (Pirates) 356
Gosling, Mike (Diamondbacks) 40
Gothreaux, Jared (Astros) 218
Gracesqui, Franklyn (Marlins) 203
Granderson, Curtis (Tigers) 178
Gray, Antoin (White Sox) 121
Griffin, John-Ford (Blue Jays) 475
Griffith, Colt (Royals) 237
Gross, Gabe (Blue Jays) 470
Gruler, Chris (Reds) 139
Guerra, Javy (Dodgers) 252
Guevara, Carlos (Reds) 140
Guillen, Rudy (Yankees) 310
Guthrie, Jeremy (Indians) 155
Gutierrez, Franklin (Indians) 147
Gutierrez, Jesse (Reds) 139
Gutierrez, Juan (Astros) 215
Guzman, Angel (Cubs) 99
Guzman, Freddy (Padres) 387
Guzman, Javier (Pirates) 362
Guzman, Joel (Dodgers) 242
Gwynn, Anthony (Brewers) 267

H

Haberer, Eric (Cardinals) 378
Haehnel, Dave (Orioles) 71
Haerther, Cody (Cardinals) 373
Hagerty, Luke (Marlins) 199
Haigwood, Daniel (White Sox) 121
Hall, Mickey (Red Sox) 87
Halsey, Brad (Diamondbacks) 44
Hamels, Cole (Phillies) 339
Hammel, Jason (Devil Rays) 436
Hanrahan, Joel (Dodgers) 248
Hanson, Travis (Cardinals) 377
Happ, J.A. (Phillies) 344
Harben, Adam (Twins) 278
Hardy, J.J (Brewers) 259
Harper, Brett (Mets) 299
Harris, Brendan (Nationals) 484
Hart, Corey (Brewers) 260
Harvey, Ryan (Cubs) 99
Hattig, John (Blue Jays) 476
Hawksworth, Blake (Cardinals) 371

Hawpe, Brad (Rockies) 169
Hayes, Calvin (Cardinals) 379
Heether, Adam (Brewers) 268
Hendrickson, Ben (Brewers) 261
Henn, Sean (Yankees) 314
Hennessey, Brad (Giants) 405
Henry, Sean (Mets) 301
Hermida, Jeremy (Marlins) 194
Hernandez, Anderson (Mets) 296
Hernandez, Diory (Braves) 61
Hernandez, Felix (Mariners) 418
Hernandez, Francisco (White Sox) 117
Hernandez, Gaby (Mets) 291
Hernandez, Luis (Braves) 53
Herren, K.C. (Rangers) 457
Herrera, Javier (Athletics) 323
Hill, Aaron (Blue Jays) 467
Hill, Jamar (Mets) 294
Hill, Koyie (Diamondbacks) 38
Hill, Rich (Cubs) 107
Hill, Shawn (Nationals) 488
Hinckley, Mike (Nationals) 482
Hirsh, Jason (Astros) 220
Holdzkom, Lincoln (Marlins) 205
Holmann, Mario (Yankees) 316
Holt, J.C. (Braves) 59
Honel, Kris (White Sox) 118
Hoover, Jesse (Yankees) 311
Hottovy, Tommy (Red Sox) 89
House, J.R. (Pirates) 365
Houser, James (Devil Rays) 437
Housman, Jeff (Brewers) 265
Howard, Kevin (Reds) 135
Howard, Ryan (Phillies) 338
Howell, J.P. (Royals) 230
Hoyman, Justin (Indians) 152
Hu, Ching-Lung (Dodgers) 247
Huang, Chai-An (Mariners) 428
Huber, Justin (Royals) 228
Hudgins, John (Rangers) 452
Huggins, Mike (Orioles) 76
Hughes, Dusty (Royals) 234
Hughes, Philip (Yankees) 307
Humer, Philip (Mets) 291
Hurley, Eric (Rangers) 455
Hutchinson, Trevor (Marlins) 198

I

Iannetta, Chris (Rockies) 169
Iguchi, Tadahito (White Sox) 116
Iribarren, Hernan (Brewers) 261
Isenberg, Kurt (Blue Jays) 474
Ishikawa, Travis (Giants) 406
Izturis, Maicer (Angels) 24

J

Jackson, Conor (Diamondbacks) 35
Jackson, Edwin (Dodgers) 243
Jackson, Zach (Blue Jays) 469
Jacobs, Sean (Mets) 301
James, Chuck (Braves) 58
James, Jimmy (Red Sox) 89
James, Justin (Blue Jays) 475
Janish, Paul (Reds) 134
Janssen, Casey (Blue Jays) 477
Jaramillo, Jason (Phillies) 343
Jaso, John (Devil Rays) 445
Jenks, Bobby (White Sox) 122
Jennings, Todd (Giants) 412
Jensen, Aaron (Mariners) 429
Jepsen, Kevin (Angels) 25

Jimenez, Cesar (Mariners) 425
Jimenez, Fabian (Padres) 393
Jimenez, Ubaldo (Rockies) 163
Johnson, Ben (Padres) 392
Johnson, Blair (Pirates) 361
Johnson, Blake (Dodgers) 251
Johnson, Dan (Athletics) 324
Johnson, Elliot (Devil Rays) 439
Johnson, Gabe (Cardinals) 379
Johnson, Grant (Cubs) 101
Johnson, James (Orioles) 73
Johnson, Josh (Marlins) 198
Johnson, Kelly (Braves) 53
Johnson, Michael (Padres) 396
Johnson, Rob (Mariners) 428
Johnson, Russell (Pirates) 364
Johnson, Tripper (Orioles) 69
Johnson, Tyler (Athletics) 329
Johnston, Mike (Pirates) 363
Jones, Adam (Mariners) 421
Jones, Brandon (Braves) 58
Jones, Daryl (Padres) 393
Jones, Jason (Yankees) 315
Jones, Justin (Twins) 280
Jones, Mike (Brewers) 266
Jones, Terry (Phillies) 348
Journell, Jimmy (Cardinals) 380
Julianel, Ben (Yankees) 316
Jurries, James (Braves) 61
Jurrjens, Jair (Tigers) 186

K

Karp, Josh (Nationals) 488
Kazmir, Scott (Devil Rays) 435
Kelly, Steve (Reds) 137
Kelton, David (Cubs) 109
Kemp, Matt (Dodgers) 252
Kendrick, Howie (Angels) 21
Kendrick, Kyle (Phillies) 349
Kensing, Logan (Marlins) 201
Keppel, Bob (Mets) 299
Keppinger, Jeff (Mets) 294
Killian, Billy (Padres) 391
Kinsler, Ian (Rangers) 451
Kirkland, Kody (Tigers) 185
Knoedler, Justin (Giants) 408
Knott, Jon (Padres) 390
Knox, Brad (Athletics) 329
Koo, Dae-Sung (Mets) 296
Kotchman, Casey (Angels) 18
Kottaras, George (Padres) 387
Kouzmanoff, Kevin (Indians) 156
Kown, Andrew (Tigers) 186
Kozlowski, Ben (Reds) 136
Kroeger, Josh (Diamondbacks) 37
Krynzel, David (Brewers) 262
Kubel, Jason (Twins) 275

L

Labandeira, Josh (Nationals) 493
Lambert, Chris (Cardinals) 371
Langerhans, Ryan (Braves) 55
Lara, Christian (Red Sox) 86
LaRoche, Andy (Dodgers) 244
League, Brandon (Blue Jays) 466
Lehr, Justin (Brewers) 266
Leicester, Joon (Cubs) 101
Leone, Justin (Mariners) 424
Lerew, Anthony (Braves) 52
Lerud, Steve (Pirates) 360
Lester, Jon (Red Sox) 83

Lewis, Fred (Giants) 403
Lewis, Richard (Cubs) 103
Lewis, Scott (Indians) 153
Lind, Adam (Blue Jays) 472
Linden, Todd (Giants) 408
Lindstrom, Matt (Mets) 294
Liotta, Ray (White Sox) 119
Liriano, Francisco (Twins) 276
Lisson, Mario (Royals) 236
Littleton, Wes (Rangers) 457
Livingston, Bobby (Mariners) 427
Lo, Ching-Lung (Rockies) 172
Loe, Kameron (Rangers) 457
Loewen, Adam (Orioles) 67
Lofgren Chuck (Indians) 151
Loney, James (Dodgers) 243
Lopez, Baltazar (Angels) 22
Lopez, Gonzalo (Braves) 57
Lopez, Pedro (White Sox) 118
Lorenzo, Matt (Rangers) 456
Lowe, Mark (Mariners) 429
Lowery, Devon (Royals) 235
Lubanski, Chris (Royals) 228
Lucena, Juan (Cardinals) 376
Lugo, Chris (Nationals) 493
Lumsden, Tyler (White Sox) 119
Lydon, Wayne (Mets) 300

M

Machado, Alejando (Nationals) 490
Machado, Anderson (Reds) 139
Macri, Matt (Rockies) 168
Made, Hector (Yankees) 316
Madrigal, Warner (Angels) 26
Maholm, Paul (Pirates) 357
Mahoney, Collin (Tigers) 184
Maier, Mitch (Royals) 230
Maine, John (Orioles) 68
Majewski, Gary (Nationals) 489
Majewski, Val (Orioles) 67
Malek, Bob (Mets) 300
Marcum, Shawn (Blue Jays) 471
Markakis, Nick (Orioles) 66
Marmol, Carlos (Cubs) 106
Marquez, Jeff (Yankees) 310
Marshall, Sean (Cubs) 101
Marson, Louis (Phillies) 348
Marte, Andy (Braves) 51
Martin, J.D. (Indians) 154
Martin, Russell (Dodgers) 244
Martinez, Gabbby (Devil Rays) 441
Martinez, Javier (Padres) 396
Martinez-Esteve, Eddy (Giants) 404
Masset, Nick (Rangers) 456
Mata, Frank (Twins) 283
Mateo, Natanael (Padres) 395
Mathieson, Scott (Phillies) 340
Mathis, Jeff (Angels) 19
Mauer, Joe (Twins) 274
Maysonet, Edwin (Astros) 219
McAnulty, Paul (Padres) 390
McBride, Macay (Braves) 56
McCann, Brian (Braves) 51
McCarthy, Billy (Braves) 58
McCarthy, Brandon (White Sox) 115
McClung, Seth (Devil Rays) 438
McConnell, Chris (Royals) 237
McCrory, Bob (Orioles) 71
McFall, Brian (Royals) 231
McGee, Jacob (Devil Rays) 443
McGinley, Blake (Mets) 298
McGowan, Dustin (Blue Jays) 469

McLemore, Mark (Astros) 219
McLouth, Nate (Pirates) 358
McPherson, Dallas (Angels) 19
Medlock, Calvin (Reds) 140
Megrew, Mike (Dodgers) 250
Melillo, Kevin (Athletics) 331
Meredith, Cla (Red Sox) 90
Merricks, Matt (Rockies) 173
Messenger, Randy (Marlins) 199
Meyer, Dan (Athletics) 323
Meyer, Drew (Rangers) 459
Miaso, Curt (Phillies) 349
Michael, Mark (Cardinals) 376
Milledge, Lastings (Mets) 290
Miller, Adam (Indians) 146
Miller, Greg (Dodgers) 245
Miller, Jai (Marlins) 200
Miller, Jeff (Pirates) 365
Miller, Jim (Rockies) 168
Milons, Jerome (Diamondbacks) 44
Miner, Zach (Braves) 60
Misch, Pat (Giants) 406
Mitchinson, Scott (Phillies) 342
Mock, Garrett (Diamondbacks) 38
Mooney, Mike (Giants) 412
Moore, Scott (Tigers) 185
Morales, Kendry (Angels) 20
Moran, Javon (Reds) 136
Morillo, Juan (Rockies) 164
Morlan, Eduardo (Twins) 285
Morse, Mike (Mariners) 425
Morton, Charlie (Braves) 57
Moseley, Dustin (Angels) 23
Moses, Matt (Twins) 277
Moss, Brandon (Red Sox) 83
Moss, Steve (Brewers) 268
Mota, Willy (Red Sox) 93
Munoz, Arnie (White Sox) 120
Munter, Scott (Giants) 411
Murphy, Bill (Diamondbacks) 41
Murphy, David (Red Sox) 88
Murphy, Donald (Royals) 230
Murton, Matt (Cubs) 102

N

Nagoette, Clint (Mariners) 419
Napoli, Mike (Angels) 29
Narverson, Chris (Rockies) 168
Navarro, Dioner (Dodgers) 247
Navarro, Oswaldo (Mariners) 427
Neal, Tony (Orioles) 77
Negron, Miguel (Blue Jays) 474
Nelson, Brad (Brewers) 261
Nelson, Chris (Rockies) 163
Nelson, John (Cardinals) 378
Nelson, Maximo (Yankees) 317
Nickeas, Mike (Rangers) 459
Niekro, Lance (Giants) 410
Niemann, Jeff (Devil Rays) 435
Nieve, Fernando (Astros) 213
Nippert, Dustin (Diamondbacks) 39
Nivar, Ramon (Rangers) 458
Nix, Jayson (Rockies) 165
Nolasco, Ricky (Cubs) 105
Norris, Shawn (Nationals) 492
Nottingham, Shawn (Mariners) 429
Novoa, Roberto (Tigers) 182
Nunez, Franklin (Devil Rays) 444
Nunez, Leo (Royals) 231

O

Ogando, Alexi (Athletics) 329
Ohlendorf, Ross (Diamondbacks) 41
Ohman, Will (Cubs) 105
Olsen, Scott (Marlins) 195
Orenduff, Justin (Dodgers) 251
Ortmeier, Dan (Giants) 407
Orvella, Chad (Devil Rays) 437
Osoria, Franquelis (Dodgers) 252
Owens, Jerry (Nationals) 486
Oxspring, Chris (Padres) 392

P

Pagan, Angel (Mets) 298
Palmisano, Lou (Brewers) 264
Papelbon, Jon (Red Sox) 83
Parisi, Mike (Cardinals) 376
Parra, Manny (Brewers) 262
Parraz, Jordan (Astros) 217
Parrott, Rhett (Cardinals) 378
Patterson, Eric (Cubs) 107
Patton, Troy (Astros) 212
Paul, Xavier (Dodgers) 248
Pauley, David (Red Sox) 91
Pauly, Thomas (Reds) 132
Pedroia, Dustin (Red Sox) 84
Pelland, Tyler (Reds) 133
Pena, Luis (Brewers) 267
Pena, Ramon (Diamondbacks) 37
Pena, T.J. (Braves) 57
Pence, Hunter (Astros) 214
Penn, Hayden (Orioles) 67
Perez, Kenny (Red Sox) 92
Perez, Miguel (Reds) 136
Perez, Rafael (Indians) 157
Perkins, Glen (Twins) 279
Perkins, Vince (Blue Jays) 471
Perry, Jason (Athletics) 332
Pesco, Nick (Indians) 149
Peterson, Adam (Diamondbacks) 42
Peterson, Matt (Pirates) 357
Petit, Gregorio (Athletics) 332
Petit, Yusmeiro (Mets) 291
Petrick, Billy (Cubs) 100
Phillips, Andy (Yankees) 313
Pie, Felix (Cubs) 99
Pimentel, Julio (Dodgers) 246
Pinto, Renyel (Cubs) 100
Plouffe, Trevor (Twins) 279
Pollok, Dwayne (White Sox) 124
Pomeranz, Stuart (Cardinals) 372
Portes, Juan (Twins) 284
Poterson, Jon (Yankees) 313
Powell, Landon (Athletics) 326
Prado, Martin (Braves) 60
Prasch, Eddie (Pirates) 360
Pridie, Jason (Devil Rays) 439
Proctor, Scott (Yankees) 314
Purcey, David (Blue Jays) 468
Putnam, Danny (Athletics) 327

Q

Qualls, Chad (Astros) 214
Quarles, Jason (Pirates) 364
Quentin, Carlos (Diamondbacks) 34
Quintanilla, Omar (Athletics) 326
Quintero, Humberto (Padres) 391
Quiroz, Guillermo (Blue Jays) 467

R

Raburn, Ryan (Tigers) 181
Rainville, Jay (Twins) 280
Rakers, Adam (Orioles) 73
Ramirez, Elizardo (Reds) 134
Ramirez, Hanley (Red Sox) 82
Ramirez, Ismael (Blue Jays) 472
Ramirez, Ramon (Yankees) 315
Ramirez, Santiago (Royals) 233
Ramirez, Wilkin (Tigers) 182
Ramirez, Yordany (Padres) 394
Rasner, Darrell (Nationals) 485
Ray, Chris (Orioles) 69
Reed, Eric (Marlins) 196
Reed, Jeremy (Mariners) 419
Reed, Mark (Cubs) 106
Regilio, Nick (Rangers) 460
Reineke, Chad (Astros) 218
Repko, Jason (Dodgers) 253
Resop, Chris (Marlins) 201
Restovich, Michael (Twins) 281
Reyes, Anthony (Cardinals) 370
Rheinecker, John (Athletics) 330
Rice, Scott (Orioles) 74
Richardson, Juan (Phillies) 345
Riggans, Shawn (Devil Rays) 443
Rine, Jarod (Orioles) 75
Rivera, Juan (Dodgers) 253
Rivera, Rene (Mariners) 426
Roberson, Chris (Phillies) 342
Robinson, Dennis (Orioles) 72
Robnett, Richie (Athletics) 325
Rodrigues, Eddy (Orioles) 72
Rodriguez, Carlos (Phillies) 347
Rodriguez, Rafael (Angels) 24
Rodriguez, Ryan (White Sox) 124
Rodriguez, Sean (Angels) 23
Rodriguez, Yuber (Blue Jays) 471
Rogers, Mark (Brewers) 260
Rogowski, Casy (White Sox) 119
Romero, Alex (Twins) 284
Rosario, Francisco (Blue Jays) 467
Rosario, Rodrigo (Marlins) 202
Rottino, Vinny (Brewers) 269
Rouse, Mike (Athletics) 333
Rozier, Mike (Red Sox) 87
Rueckel, Danny (Nationals) 486
Ruiz, Carlos (Phillies) 342
Rupe, Josh (Rangers) 453
Ryan, Brendan (Cardinals) 373
Ryu, Jae-Kuk (Cubs) 108

S

Sadler, Billy (Giants) 410
Saenz, Chris (Brewers) 269
Salazar, Jeff (Rockies) 165
Salome, Angel (Brewers) 268
Saltalamacchia, Jarrod (Braves) 53
San Pedro, Erick (Nationals) 491
Sanchez, Anibal (Red Sox) 84
Sanchez, Freddy (Pirates) 359
Sanchez, Humberto (Tigers) 180
Sanchez, Jonathan (Giants) 411
Sanchez, Salvador (White Sox) 122
Sanders, Marcus (Giants) 409
Sandoval, Pablo (Giants) 412
Santana, Ervin (Angels) 20
Santangelo, Lou (Astros) 217
Santos, Omir (Yankees) 317
Santos, Sergio (Diamondbacks) 35
Sardinha, Bronson (Yankees) 309

Sardinha, Dane (Reds) 137
Sarfate, Dennis (Brewers) 265
Saunders, Joe (Angels) 23
Sborz, Jay (Tigers) 188
Schierholtz, Nate (Giants) 404
Schlact, Michael (Rangers) 456
Schlichting, Travis (Devil Rays) 440
Schmoll, Steve (Dodgers) 250
Schnurstein, Micah (White Sox) 121
Schumaker, Skip (Cardinals) 377
Schutzenhofer, Andy (Cardinals) 381
Scott, Lorenzo (Orioles) 75
Scott, Luke (Astros) 217
Seddon, Chris (Devil Rays) 440
Segovia, Zach (Phillies) 343
Seifrig, Cole (Marlins) 204
Self, Todd (Astros) 220
Senreiso, Juan (Rangers) 455
Sequea, Jacobo (Orioles) 71
Shafer, David (Reds) 135
Shappi, A.J. (Diamondbacks) 43
Shealy, Ryan (Rockies) 167
Shell, Steven (Angels) 22
Shelton, Chris (Tigers) 182
Sherrill, George (Mariners) 423
Shinskie, David (Twins) 284
Shoppach, Kelly (Red Sox) 85
Sierra, Edwardo (Yankees) 312
Simon, Alfredo (Giants) 404
Simonitsch, Errol (Twins) 285
Simpson, Allan (Rockies) 171
Sing, Brandon (Cubs) 104
Sinisi, Vincent (Rangers) 454
Sipp, Tony (Indians) 154
Sisco, Andy (Royals) 231
Sleeth, Kyle (Tigers) 179
Smith, Alexander (Twins) 282
Smith, Brett (Yankees) 310
Smith, C.J. (Orioles) 77
Smith, Donnie (Cardinals) 375
Smith, Seth (Rockies) 164
Smitherman, Stephen (Reds) 141
Snell, Ian (Pirates) 355
Snelling, Chris (Mariners) 421
Snyder, Brad (Indians) 147
Snyder, Brian (Athletics) 328
Snyder, Chris (Diamondbacks) 36
Soler, Alay (Mets) 292
Soto, Geovany (Cubs) 103
Soto, Luis (Red Sox) 85
Sowers, Jeremy (Indians) 148
Span, Denard (Twins) 279
Spann, Chad (Red Sox) 88
Spears, Nate (Orioles) 70
Speier, Ryan (Rockies) 170
Spidale, Mike (White Sox) 123
Stahl, Richard (Orioles) 76
Stansberry, Craig (Pirates) 364
Starling, Wardell (Pirates) 363
Stauffer, Tim (Padres) 388
Stern, Adam (Red Sox) 90
Stevens, Jake (Braves) 52
Stewart, Cory (Pirates) 361
Stewart, Ian (Rockies) 162
Stokes, Jason (Marlins) 195
Street, Huston (Athletics) 325
Strong, Jamal (Mariners) 422
Sullivan, Brad (Athletics) 331
Sullivan, Cory (Rockies) 172
Sutil, Wladimir (Astros) 221
Suzuki, Kurt (Athletics) 326
Swarzak, Anthony (Twins) 277
Sweeney, Ryan (White Sox) 115

Swisher, Nick (Athletics)	322	Valdez, Merkin (Giants)	403	Whitney, Matt (Indians)	152
Szymanski, B.J. (Reds)	132	Valdez, Raul (Cubs)	108	Whittington, Anthony (Angels)	26
		Valdez, Wilson (White Sox)	125	Williams, Marland (Diamondbacks)	42
		Valido, Robert (White Sox)	119	Williams, Randy (Padres)	397
T		Van Benschoten, John (Pirates)	355	Willingham, Josh (Marlins)	196
Tablado, Raul (Blue Jays)	473	Van Buren, Jermaine (Cubs)	107	Willits, Reggie (Angels)	27
Talbot, Mitch (Astros)	218	Vandenhurk, Rick (Marlins)	200	Wilson, Josh (Marlins)	198
Tallet, Brian (Indians)	156	Vaquedano, Jose (Red Sox)	92	Windsor, Jason (Athletics)	328
Tankersley, Taylor (Marlins)	197	Vargas, Jason (Marlins)	197	Winfree, David (Twins)	283
Tatum, Craig (Reds)	141	Vasquez, Matt (Tigers)	188	Wing, Ryan (Rangers)	461
Taveras, Willy (Astros)	211	Vaughan, Beau (Red Sox)	91	Wood, Brandon (Angels)	20
Taylor, Aaron (Rockies)	170	Vechionacci, Marcos (Yankees)	308	Woodard, Johnny (Twins)	282
Teahen, Mark (Royals)	227	Vega, Miguel (Royals)	234	Woods, Jake (Angels)	25
Tejeda, Juan (Tigers)	183	Verlander, Justin (Tigers)	179	Woodyard, Mark (Tigers)	187
Tejeda, Robinson (Phillies)	347	Vermilyea, Jamie (Blue Jays)	474	Worrell, Mark (Cardinals)	379
Thayer, Dale (Padres)	397	Victorino, Shane (Phillies)	345	Wuertz, Mike (Cubs)	105
Thigpen, Curtis (Blue Jays)	472	Villatoro, Wilmer (Padres)	394		
Thompson, Brad (Cardinals)	372	Volquez, Edison (Rangers)	454		
Thompson, Daryl (Nationals)	485	Votto, Joey (Reds)	131	**Y**	
Thompson, Erik (Rangers)	460			Yabu, Keiichi (Athletics)	330
Thompson, Kevin (Yankees)	315			Yarbrough, Brandon (Cardinals)	375
Thompson, Sean (Padres)	389	**W**		Yates, Tyler (Mets)	300
Thorman, Scott (Braves)	55	Wahpepah, Josh (Brewers)	266	Young, Chris (Rangers)	452
Thornton, Matt (Mariners)	428	Wainwright, Adam (Cardinals)	371	Young, Chris (White Sox)	117
Threets, Erick (Giants)	413	Waldrop, Kyle (Twins)	276	Young, Delmon (Devil Rays)	434
Tiffany, Chuck (Dodgers)	246	Walker, Matt (Devil Rays)	442	Young, Delwyn (Dodgers)	249
Tiffee, Terry (Twins)	281	Walker, Neil (Pirates)	355	Young, Walter (Orioles)	70
Timpner, Clay (Giants)	409	Walton, Jamar (Marlins)	201		
Torres, Eider (Indians)	157	Wang, Chien-Ming (Yankees)	309		
Toussaint, Andrew (Angels)	28	Watson, Brandon (Nationals)	492	**Z**	
Tracey, Sean (White Sox)	116	Webb, Ryan (Athletics)	333	Zeringue, Joe (Diamondbacks)	35
Trahern, Dallas (Tigers)	183	Webster, Anthony (Rangers)	458	Zimmerman, Bob (Angels)	27
Trumbo, Mark (Angels)	22	Weeks, Rickie (Brewers)	258	Zobrist, Ben (Astros)	216
Tucker, Rusty (Padres)	393	Wells, Jared (Padres)	392	Zumaya, Joel (Tigers)	179
Tuiasosopo, Matt (Mariners)	420	West, Jeremy (Red Sox)	91		
Turay, Alhaji (Mets)	298	Whisler, Wes (White Sox)	120		
Tyler, Scott (Twins)	282	Whitaker, Craig (Giants)	405		
		White, Steven (Yankees)	307		
V		Whiteman, Tommy (Astros)	215		
Valdes, Juan (Indians)	151	Whitesell, Josh (Nationals)	493		
		Whiteside, Eli (Orioles)	69		

ALL THROUGH 2005...

Subscribing is easy and you'll save money off the cover price!

We know the Prospect Handbook has a valuable place on your bookshelf as the quintessential guide to baseball's brightest stars of tomorrow.

But what about all the exciting action—on and off the field—that takes place in the new year? From spring training to the World Series, including the most complete draft coverage anywhere (and don't forget statistics for every minor league team), Baseball America magazine is the best source for baseball information. Since 1981, BA has been finding the prospects and tracking them from the bushes to the big leagues. That means you get comprehensive reporting and commentary every step of the way.

So join the team now to receive Baseball America every other week, and be the first to know about today's rising stars.

It's baseball news you can't get anywhere else.

you need Baseball America

BaseballAmerica.com